Effective Cross-Border Pension Information in the Face of Multi-Level Legal Systems

Effective Cross-Border Pension Information in the Face of Multi-Level Legal Systems

A cross-disciplinary research into the cross-border taxation of pensions

Sander Kramer

eleven

This research was finalized on 10 September 2023. Later developments were not taken into account.

Published, sold and distributed by Eleven
P.O. Box 85576
2508 CG The Hague
The Netherlands
Tel.: +31 70 33 070 33
Fax: +31 70 33 070 30
e-mail: sales@elevenpub.nl
www.elevenpub.com

Sold and distributed in USA and Canada
Independent Publishers Group
814 N. Franklin Street
Chicago, IL 60610, USA
Order Placement: +1 800 888 4741
Fax: +1 312 337 5985
orders@ipgbook.com
www.ipgbook.com

Eleven is an imprint of Boom uitgevers Den Haag.

ISBN 978-90-4730-187-5
ISBN 978-94-0011-361-9 (E-book)

For Joyce, Tijn and …

Table of Contents

Preface and Acknowledgements

> "Des Lebens Mühe lehrt uns allein des Lebens Güter schätzen."
> *Johann Wolfgang von Goethe (1749 - 1832) Torquato Tasso, 1807. 5. Akt, 1. Szene, Antonio zu Alfons*

This quote by Goethe (and probably more familiar thanks to Wim de Bie as O. den Beste (*oud-leraar Duits*) in the sketch *gezellig winkelen*) resonated I my mind over the course of my PhD-trajectory. While during my PhD-process, I considered writing the dissertation a 'Mühe', I may now see it as one of life's 'Güter'.

This book marks the end of a fulfilling and enriching academic journey which has occurred to me as one of the most insightful and self-challenging yet, especially when it comes to conquering one's personal tendencies and aspirations. Moreover, writing this dissertation proved to be rather paradoxical, as once completed I had the feeling of having obtained enough knowledge to actually complete it.

Although writing a PhD dissertation is often surrounded by loneliness while delving deeper and deeper into the intricate world of pensions and tax law, one does certainly not do it on its own. Hence, I would like to express my gratitude to those who supported me, in whatever way, over the course of my 'PhD-journey'. Numerous people helped and supported me during this journey. I owe them gratitude for their help and support, but some of them deserve a special word of thankfulness as their support was – in terms of the underlying research – most 'salient'.

First of all, I want to express my sincere gratitude to my supervisors, Prof. Anouk Bollen-Vandenboorn and Prof. Lisa Brüggen for giving me the opportunity of becoming a Phd-candidate, in the first place, in 2016. I truly appreciate your confidence and unconditional support you have had in me over the course of these PhD-years. You were true mentors to me, embodying expertise, empathy, endless patience (despite your overly full agendas) and integrity. Your support and encouragement have been invaluable. Moreover, I'm thankful to you for giving me the possibilities for further pursuing a career in academia.

I'm also indebted to the members of my assessment committee for their efforts to meticulously read, and assess, my dissertation and helping me to further improve this thesis: Prof. dr. mr. Raymond Luja (chair), Dr. Thomas Post, Prof. mr. dr. Bastiaan Starink, Prof. Yves Stevens, and Prof. dr. Marjon Weerepas. Your positive feedback and constructive comments were an indispensable stepping-stone towards finalizing my thesis. Many thanks!

I am also grateful to all of my colleagues at research institute ITEM (Institute for Transnational and Euregional cross border cooperation and Mobility), as well as the Law Faculty's department of Tax Law. Their support, sincere interest, personal attention, as well as, encouragement was of great value. Something I look back on with pleasure especially, were the ITEM PhD-meetings, that have proven to be indispensable in shaping my dissertation.

Further, (staff) members of the Ius Commune Research School deserve a special word of thanks. Despite me being often the 'pension/tax'-outsider, all sessions organized were truly helpful in shaping my (legal) comparative methodology and methods.

I must also mention several experts who supported me in further improving my thesis, during the organized 'expert meetings': Francesco Briganti, Bastiaan Didden, Carlo Douven, Bart van den Hof, Felix Küppers, Jeroen Lenaers, Titus Sips and Jorik van Zanden. Your comments and insightful conversations proved to be very fruitful!

On an 'office-level', a special word of thanks go out to my (former) roommates: Stefan Bemelmans, Nina Büttgen, Bastiaan Didden, Kilian Heller, Eva van Ooij and Susanne Sivonen. Discussing not only legal/scientific matters, but also your small talk enabled me to clear my mind. Thank you for being such nice colleagues!

In terms of support, I want to further thank Licette Poll and the people at the PhD-office. Your support helped me to finalize my PhD-journey in a formal/practical way, as well as making sure that all formalities were complied with.

On a personal level, I owe indescribable gratefulness to my parents, Ruud and Marleen Kramer, for their love, support and patience throughout my whole life. Your sincere efforts incited me to get the best out of myself. Your love and care has been indispensable up until this very day. What is more, a special word of gratefulness to all of my family members and friends who showed sincere interest in my PhD-work and personal well-being, and kept an eye on me.

Practice also fed into this research through my research stay at *Der Gesamtverband der Deutschen Versicherungswirtschaft* (GDV) in the most exciting city of Berlin in 2017. A special word of thanks go to Michaela Willert, as well as Ilka Houben, for their support and hospitality. This period marked the actual start of writing several chapters of my dissertation and allowed me to get a more profound understanding of the ongoing developments in the domain of pensions, taxation, and pension information in Germany, as well as further pinpointing the challenges that policymakers and pension providers see themselves confronted with when it comes to (effective) pension information. This proved to be a truly fruitful period of my PhD-journey, and I believe "*Ich hab' noch einen Koffer in Berlin*".

Lastly, but above all, love of my life, Joyce. I genuinely realize that these 'Phd-years' have almost been as challenging for you as they were to me. Wholeheartedly, I want to thank you for your love, unconditional support, and patience and empathy throughout this journey. Although we were often in the same boat feeling-wise, you always managed to lift my spirit. I couldn't have done it without you!

Tijn, our lovely son, I'm grateful for all the love and joy you have brought into our lives. Waking up each morning, hearing your little voice, is a driving force. Your inexhaustible energy is a true inspiration to me. And our beautiful son/daughter to come, please know that all the same holds with you; you will fill our lives with even more love and happiness.

Maastricht, 1 October 2023

Sander Kramer

Abbreviations

ABP	Algemeen Burgerlijk Pensioenfonds
ABV	Arbeitsgemeinschaft berufsständischer Versorgungseinrichtungen e.V.
AFM	Autoriteit Financiële Markten
ALG	Gesetz über die Alterssicherung der Landwirte
AltEinkG	Alterseinkünftegesetz
AltZertG	Altersvorsorgeverträge-Zertifizierungsgesetz
Anw	Algemene nabestaandenwet
AOW	Algemene Ouderdomswet
art.	article
AVmG	Altersvermögensgesetz
AWR	Algemene wet inzake rijksbelastingen
BAG	Bundesarbeitsgericht
BB	Betriebsberater (journal)
BBG	Bundesbeamtengesetz
BBZ	Bureau Belgisch zaken (SVB)
BDZ	Bureau Duitse zaken (SVB)
BeamtVG	Beamtenversorgungsgesetz
BetrAVG	Betriebsrentengesetz
BFH	Bundesfinanzhof
BGB	Bürgerliches Gesetzbuch
BGBl	Bundesgesetzblatt
BGH	Bundesgerichtshof
BGHZ	Amtliche Sammlung der Entscheidungen des Bundesgerichtshofes in Zivilsachen
BMAS	Bundesministerium für Arbeit und Soziales
BMF	Bunderminister der Finanzen
BRRG	Beamtenrechtsrahmengesetz
Bstbl.	Bundessteuerblatt
BvdB 2001	Besluit voorkoming dubbele belasting 2001
BVerfG	Bundesverfassungsgericht
BvL	Bundesanzeiger Verlag
BW	Burgerlijk Wetboek
CBS	Centraal Bureau voor de Statistiek
cf.	confer

CJEU	Court of Justice of the European Union
DB	Defined Benefit
DB (in footnotes)	Der Betrieb
DC	Defined Contribution
DGB	Directoraat-Generaal Belastingdienst
DNB	De Nederlandsche Bank
DStR	Deutsches Steuerrecht
e.g.	exempli gratia (for example)
EC	European Commission
ECHR	European Convention on Human Rights
ECLI	European Case Law Identifier
EEA	European Economic Area
EIOPA	European Insurance and Occupational Pensions Authority
ELM	Elaboration Likelihood Model
EStG	Einkommensteuergesetz
ETS	Europen Tracking Service
EU	European Union
EUStVUG	Gesetz zur Umsetzung steuerlicher EU-Vorgaben sowie zur Änderung steuerlicher Vorschriften
ff.	and following
FR	FinanzRundschau
GDP	Gross domestic product
GDV	Gesamtverband der Deutschen Versicherung-swirtschaft
GG	Grundgesetz
GVG	Gesellschaft für Versicherungswissenschaft und – Gestaltung e.v.
HGB	Handelsgesetzbuch
HR	Hoge Raad
i.a.	inter alia
i.e.	id est
IAK	Integraal afwegingskader voor beleid en regelgeving
Ibid.	Ibidem (in the same place)
ILO	International Labour Organization
IORP	Institution for Occupational Retirement Provisions
ISCED	International Standard Classification of Education
ITEM	Institute for Transnational and Euregional cross border cooperation and Mobility

JStG	Jahresseteuergesetz
KStG	Körperschaftsteuergesetz
KWG	Kreditwesengesetz
LStDV	Lohnsteuer-Durchführungsverordnung
M	Mean
MBB	Maandblad belastingbeschouwingen
Nibud	Nationaal Instituut voor Budgetvoorlichting
NTFR	Nederlands Tijdschrift voor Fiscaal Recht
OECD	Organisation for Economic Co-operation and Development
OECD MC	OECD Model Convention
OJ	Official Journal of the European Union
para.	paragraph
PEPP	Personal European Pension Plans
PJ	Pensioenjurisprudentie
PSVaG	Pensions-Sicherungs-Verein Versicherungsverein auf Gegenseitigkeit
PW	Pensioenwet
RCT	Rational Choice Theory
SD	Standard deviation
SGB	Sozialgesetzbuch
SozR	Sozialrecht (journal)
StuW	Steuer und Wirtschaft
SVB	Sociale Verzekeringsbank
SvEV	Sozialversicherungsentgeltverordnung
TEU	Treaty on the European Union
TFEU	Treaty on the Functioning of the European Union
TPV	Tijdschrift voor Pensioenvraagstukken
UBLB	Uitvoeringsbesluit loonbelasting 1965
UN	United Nations
UNESCO	United Nations Educational, Scientific and Cultural Organization
URLB	Uitvoeringsregeling loonbelasting 2011
UStIntG	Gesetz zur Vermeidung von Umsatzsteuerausfällen beim Handel mit Waren im Internet und zur Änderung weiterer steuerlicher Vorschriften
VAG	Versicherungsaufsichtsgesetz
VUT	Vervroegde uittreding
VVG	Versicherungsvertragsgesetz

Wet IB 2001	Wet Inkomstenbelasting 2001
Wet LB 1964	Wet op de loonbelasting 1964
WFR	Weekblad fiscal recht
ZfA	Zentralen Zulagenstelle für Altersvermögen
ZfDR	Zentrale Stelle für die Digitale Rentenübersicht

1 Introductory Chapter

This chapter provides an outline of the underlying research, i.e. it addresses the grounds for this research – the Ist-situation and the Soll-situation –, the objective(s) and research question(s), definitions and concepts harnessed in this research, research methodologies and research designs employed. It will be concluded with a description of how each of the separate chapters contribute to attaining this research's objective and it provides an outline of this dissertation.

1.1 Setting the Research Background

1.1.1 A Europe-wide Socio-Economic Predicament: Effective Cross-border Pension Information as a First Step Towards Financial Resilience in Old-age

An ageing European population[1], financial and economic crises, low economic growth, and low interest rates have posed fundamental challenges to national pension systems, leading to an increasing financial pressure on retirement arrangements, reductions in retirement income, and rigorous shifts of risks.[2] In response to these developments, European Member States' pension systems have been reformed continuously and in a rapid pace, although the pace of these pension reforms has slowed across OECD countries.[3] What is more, pension schemes have been subject to structural changes, such as new intergenerational balances, rising old-age dependency ratios in the developed world, shifts from pay-as-you-go funding to funded pensions, and the transition from defined-benefits pension schemes to defined-contribution pension schemes.[4] Most of these reforms were aimed at enhancing the sustainability and adequacy of pension systems, threatened by

1 Whereas in 2020 the ratio is three workers for each pensioner, in 2050, if nothing changes, it will be two workers for each pensioner. See European Commission, 'Communication from the Commission to the European Parliament, the Council, the European Economic and Social Committee and the Committee of the Regions: a Strong Social Europe for Just Transitions' (2020) [COM/2020/14 final] 11.

2 See for instance OECD, 'OECD Pensions Outlook' (2016) 3.

3 OECD, 'Pensions at a Glance 2017: OECD and G20 Indicators' (2017) <https://read.oecd-ilibrary.org/social-issues-migration-health/pensions-at-a-glance-2017_pension_glance-2017-en#page3> 16.

4 This development also occurred in Germany, see B Rürup and M Myßen, 'Die steuerlich geförderte private Altersvorsorge' in B Rürup and F Ruland (eds.), *Alterssicherung und Besteuerung* (Gabler, Wiesbaden 2008) As regards the latter shift of risks, currently, almost 60 million Europeans accrue their pension through a defined-contribution pension scheme, see W Devroe, *Rechtsvergelijking in een context van europeanisering en globalisering* (Acco, Leuven 2010).

changes in labour markets.[5] Furthermore, retirement benefits stemming from government-run pay-as-you-go social security schemes have fallen relative to average earnings, and a subsequent shift from largely single to multi-tiered systems has occurred. These developments have cast doubts about whether pension systems will be able to deliver pension benefits that people would consider adequate to finance their retirement, i.e. potentially endangering pension's adequacy.[6] More than 18% of EU citizens is currently at risk of poverty or social exclusion in older age, turning pension adequacy into a major policy issue for now and the near future.[7] Inadequacy of pension income may cause substantial costs, both for the individuals, as well as for society as a whole. With respect to individuals, these costs pertain to a possible shortage of (future) retirement income; with respect to society, to an increasing reliance by the aforementioned individuals on social security/assistance benefits. This could mean that many of them may encounter an inadequate retirement income, having detrimental welfare effects in retirement, since inadequate pension incomes, or shortfalls in retirement income, may lead to an increasing need for social support.

Parallel to these developments, Member States' pension systems and financial markets grow more complex, and individuals are confronted with highly complex and often irreversible economic decisions.[8] In an increasingly globalised and risk-bearing financial world, (mobile) individuals must be able to make well-informed financial decisions, in particular when it comes to their pension. What is more, individuals have to embark on

---

5 Cf. European Commission, 'Green paper: towards adequate, sustainable and safe European pension systems' (2010) [COM(2010) 365 final] 5. These changes were mainly aimed on encouraging more people to work more and longer in order to gain similar pension entitlements as before, i.e. increasing pensionable ages and therefore rewarding retiring later, penalizing earlier retirement, moving from benefits based on final salary schemes to entitlements based on working career average schemes and enabling older workers to continue working. See for a more comprehensive exposition: Economic Policy Committee and Social Protection Committee, 'Interim Joint Report on pensions' (2010).

6 Multi-pillar pension saving is more effective in providing security against the economic, demographic, and political risks faced by the pension systems, and eventually more effective in securing an adequate pension income. See World Bank, 'The World Bank Pension Conceptual Framework' (World Bank Pension Reform Primer, 2008) 2.

7 High Level Forum on Capital Markets Union, 'A new Vision for Europe's capital markets: Final Report of the High Level Forum on the Capital Markets Union' (2020) 18.

8 As argued by Mitchell and Lusardi with regard to financial markets: OS Mitchell and A Lusardi, 'The Outlook for Financial Literacy' in OS Mitchell and A Lusardi (eds.), *Financial Literacy: Implications for Retirement Security and the Financial Marketplace* (Oxford University Press, Oxford 2011) 1. See also O Gough and C Niza, 'Retirement saving choices: review of the literature and policy implications' 4 Journal of Population Ageing 97, and cited literature. For instance, the implementation of the *reine Beitragszusage* under which new vesting method the employer merely commits the payment of the employers' contribution for financing lifelong retirement benefits, and, thus, more financial risk is attributed to the employee. See Entwurf eines Gesetzes zur Stärkung der betrieblichen Altersversorgung und zur Änderung anderer Gesetze (Betriebsrentenstärkungsgesetz).

financial/retirement planning, and have to make choices with regard to how much to save on their own, probably assisted by financial advisers they also select on their own. To the extent that individuals hire advisers, they may not need to have the financial information themselves, but may, nevertheless, be confused about where to find it, and whom to trust to provide the information.[9] Besides that not every individual can afford to hire a financial adviser in planning for retirement, people hold reasonable expectations of financial advice and its implementation, and they may hold doubts as to whether the adviser acts in their best interest, affecting the level of trust and confidence.[10] Moreover, although possessing the necessary domain-specific (objective) knowledge, even for financial advisors it may be difficult to stay on top of things, as the fields of pension and tax law are renowned for their complexity and intricacy, especially in cross-border situations. As a bottom line, (mobile) pension participants can no longer simply assume that they will be able to maintain their standard of living once they retire.[11] Added to this that peoples' pension awareness is – generally speaking – low and it seems inevitable that they are at considerable risk to face an inadequate income after retirement.[12]

From what has been outlined so far, it is clear, that it is becoming increasingly important for (mobile) participants to get a grasp of their pension status-quo, and engage in pension

9 See AA Hung, N Clancy and J Dominitz, 'Investor Knowledge and Experience with Investment Advisers and Broker-Dealers' in OS Mitchell and A Lusardi (eds.), *Financial Literacy: Implications for Retirement Security and the Financial Marketplace* (Oxford University Press, Oxford 2011).

10 See, for instance, M Ap, 'The Future of Financial Advice Reforms: Restorting Public Trust and Confidence in Financial Advisers – an Unfinished Puzzle' 10 Canberra Law Review 188, D Halstead and others, 'The Customer Orientation of Financial Advisers' Financial Literacy and the Limits of Financial Decision-Making 246, DG Millhouse, 'Best Interest Duties of Financial Advisers – More Law, More Confusion' Enterprise Governance eJournal: Centre for Commercial Law, Bond University. See also D Johnson and K Grayson, 'Cognitive and affective trust in service relationships' 58 Journal of Business Research 500. Upholding 'customer trust' between financial advisor and their clients is an intricate relationship, see M Ligas, 'Personalizing Services Encounters: The Role of Service Provider Actions in Developing Customer Trust' 25 Services Marketing Quarterly 33, AB Eisingerich and SJ Bell, 'Perceived Service Quality and Customer Trust: Does Enhancing Customers' Service Knowledge Matter?' 10 Journal of Service Research 256.

11 Cf. RH Maatman, 'Pensioenfondsen en zorgplichten: uitdijen of indammen?,' in D Busch and others (eds.), *Zorgplicht in de financiële sector* (Serie Onderneming en Recht, Kluwer, Deventer 2020) 170.

12 See, as regards Dutch employees, Aon, 'Survey Financial Pension Planning and Communication' (2020). This research's findings demonstrate that a majority (52%) of Dutch employees are moderately or not well prepared financially for their pension. Almost a third (32%) have no idea what their pension benefits will be. There are considerable differences in the reported levels of pension awareness of employees in different age and income categories. For example, young workers are even to a large extent not interested in the subject of pensions (more than 50% employees 20-30 years of age, almost 30% employees 30-40 years of age). Income also plays a role: 89% of employees with a gross monthly salary of €2,000 or less feel moderately or insufficiently financially prepared for retirement. Among people with an income above €5,000 gross per month, this is still 32%. Three quarters of the respondents would like to be informed about the pension once or twice a year, via a digital platform or by letter/e-mail. On average, 58% of the employees do not inquire about their pension on their own, although this decreases particularly at a later age.

planning in order to secure an adequate retirement income.[13] However, as a general rule, citizens themselves are not able to calculate the amount of future retirement income on the basis of the prevailing pension agreement. Moreover, research findings demonstrate that pension participants have difficulty with understanding pension information, and need a digital overview clarifying the personal pension situation at a glance, i.e. a 'pension dashboard' providing an amount of future retirement income at a certain (pensionable) age.[14] Pension information showing an amount of (expected) future pension income is thus at the centre of pension communication. Providing individuals with such information on their future pension benefits, and the pension benefits they will need, and how they can reach their desired level of pension benefits will empower them in achieving greater financial resilience in retirement, provided that the information is 'effective'.[15] In this vein, effective cross-border pension information is considered an adequate first step towards financial resilience in old-age. This dissertation takes this as the premise underlying the in-depth analysis of the given regulatory frameworks, while the rationale behind this premise will be discussed in more detail in chapter 2. Yet, given pension and tax system's complexity, providing such projections of future retirement income poses considerable tensions in information provision, potentially affecting the information's effectiveness. This will be dealt with in chapter 2 as well.

1.1.2 *Cross-border Pensions: Insight in Accumulated Pension Dispersed Across Member States*

Besides this trend towards increased individual responsibility and growing financial complexity, the structure of labour markets has altered and the mobility of labour increased, resulting in even more individual responsibility with respect to financial

13 E Eberhardt and others, 'Activating pension plan participants: investment and assurance frames' Design paper 72 Netspar Industry Paper Series 8 and M Knoef and others, 'Measuring retirement savings adequacy: developing a multi-pillar approach in the Netherlands' 15 Journal of Pension Economics and Finance 55. Eberthardt e.a. refer to HSBC, 'The Future of Retirement. A Balancing Act. Published by HSBC Holdings plc. London' (2015) which report shows that around 65% of retirees who had insufficient retirement savings did not discover this until after they retired. Also the German legislator has acknowledged that ensuring one's standard of living after retirement calls for a good basis of information, see Entwurf eines Gesetzes zur Verbesserung der Transparenz in der Alterssicherung und der Rehabilitation sowie zur Modernisierung der Sozialversicherungswahlen (Gesetz Digitale Rentenübersicht) 1.

14 J Visser, M Kloosterboer and P Oosterveld, 'Pensioencommunicatie: behoeften en barrières: geïntegreerd rapport van onderzoek onder deelnemers en gepensioneerden' (TNS Nipo, Amsterdam 2012). This research's findings also showed that people are in need of an overview of the financial consequences of certain changes in the personal situation (i.e. life events such as divorce or dismissal) or certain choices (e.g. working longer or part-time retirement). In addition, people would like to have an overview of their statutory pension (i.e. AOW).

15 Cf. M Dolls and others, 'Do retirement savings increase in response to information about retirement and expected pensions?' (CESifo Working Paper 6842, 2018).

security after retirement.[16] Most recent data shows that mobility in the EU continued to grow in 2021, but at a slower pace than in previous years. In 2021, despite the pandemic, 10.2 million working age-Europeans lived in another EU country, amounting to 3.9% of the total labour force.[17] 1.7 million of these mobile EU citizens are cross-border workers, mostly employed in manufacturing or construction.

The relevance of pension information in terms of planning for retirement, becomes even more evident in cross-border situations. Yet, where already non-mobile pension participants may have difficulty with planning for retirement, mobile workers and citizens may experience even more difficulty with retirement planning. In case of working cross-border, consequently pension entitlements will be accrued across the multiple (former) working, and/or residence states. These pension entitlements will, in principle, be dispersed over these different Member States, and possibly different jobs.[18] What is more, mobile individuals – who avail(ed) themselves of their European freedoms of movement – see themselves confronted with a wide range of diverging pension vehicles, schemes, retirement products of all sorts, arising from statutory, occupational and individual pension systems in each of the different (former) working states, and/or residence states. By being mobile, they enter the field of the intersections between different multi-level legal systems (national, EU and international/bilateral) and the interaction of poorly coordinated legal domains (pension and tax law), which can all be interwoven in a personal mobile work situation. This fragmentation of pensions is further exacerbated by

16 Cf. European Commission, 'Green paper: towards adequate, sustainable and safe European pension systems' 16: "*Shifting choice and responsibility to the individual requires that people understand the information in order to make informed choices, especially as pensions have become more complex.*" This is also acknowledged by GVG: GVG, 'Forderung nach mehr Transparanz in der Altersvorsorge' Pressemitteilung 07/2017 1: "*In einem Alterssicherungssystem, das auf mehreren Säule beruht, brauchen die Menschen verständliche Informationen aus allen Systemen, in denen die Ansprüche erworben haben.*" See also J Banks and Z Oldfield, 'Understanding pensions: Cognitive function, numerical ability and retirement saving' 28 Fiscal Studies 143. See also World Bank, 1.

17 European Commission, 'Annual Report on Intra-EU Labour Mobility 2022' (2023) 23 ff.

18 Unless this fragmentation of pension rights and future benefits is obviated by means of improving the process of international pension capital transfer or otherwise enhancing the comparability and mutual recognition of fiscal regulations regarding pensions – which contribute to the unhampered continuation of pension accrual in cross-border situations. In practice the use of the international transfer of pension capital proves to be highly impractical, primarily as a result of fiscal disparities. Member States are not always keen to facilitate the international pension capital transfer, furthermore due to a lack of alignment between Member States' pension systems as well as the non-alignment of national civil law requirements and tax law requirements. It was due to this impracticability of capital transfer, that fostering acquisition and preservation (through the Directive 2014/50/EU of the European Parliament and of the Council of 16 April 2014 on minimum requirements for enhancing worker mobility between Member States by improving the acquisition and preservation of supplementary pension rights [2014] OJ L 128) was felt to be more welcome. See European Commission, 'White paper: an agenda for Adequate, Safe and Sustainable Pensions,' (Brussels 2012) 21.

the high diversity in the methods of tax treatment of statutory, occupational and individual pensions in each Member State, as each State may have different tax rules in place for each of these arrangements. While the relevance of cross-border pension information appears to be evident, the path towards achieving the provision of this cross-border pension information seems more than intricate.

As regards insight into the personal pension situation, to the extent national pension tracking services are in place, they merely offer an overview of national accrued pension entitlements. Therefore, currently, these mobile individuals have no total overview of their accrued pension rights, covering all his[19] pension schemes stemming from their (former) working states, whilst, commonly, retirement forms part of people's entire financial planning. This lack of overview and information impedes the mobile individuals' decision-making in pensions. They, hence, might face a significant risk of inadequacy of their retirement income at retirement, i.e. their 'pension adequacy', and the financial, and even fiscal consequences.[20] Moreover, this lack of overview might influence people's decision to work cross-border, and seems rather anachronistic in a matured European single market.

Ideally, these mobile workers should be offered an overview of their pension rights, accumulated pension entitlements and future pension payments. This overview should further contribute to providing better access to information, and thereby increase people's ability to make informed decisions which best cater for their interests and, eventually, secure or foster their financial resilience at retirement, i.e. secure their pension adequacy. A European Pension Tracking Service takes an eminent role in this regard.[21] Out of many elements, similar figures and data about other sources of pension income will be required. Since pension systems in Europe are as diverse as the European Member States themselves, finding a common way of communicating about pensions is not an easy task. When it comes to communicating about pensions, it is certainly true that 'one size does not fit all'. What central role the taxation of pensions takes in providing effective cross-border pension information will be dealt with in the next section, and more elaborately in chapter 2 and 3 of this research.

---

19 In the interest of the readability of this research, the combination of he/she and his/her and other conjugations has been avoided and therefore the masculine genus has been used, i.e. he/his/him, although the person to which is referred can just as easily be of the female gender. It is in no case intended to suggest that only males are concerned.

20 'Pension adequacy' refers to the extent in which the expected pension income, based on the current accumulated pension, is sufficient to replace the earned income after retirement to secure and maintain the standard of living and herewith reducing the chance of poverty among the retired.

21 See for instance FindYourPension, 'EU project for the pilot phase of a European Tracking Service on Pensions started' <https://www.findyourpension.eu/en/ets/about_ets/> accessed 5 April 2022 and EIOPA, 'Technical Advice on the Development of Pension Tracking Systems' (2021) [EIOPA-BoS-21-535].

1.1.3 *Taxation as Part of Effective Cross-border Pension Information: a Holistic Approach Neglected so Far*

As has been addressed in the above, by availing themselves of their European freedoms of movement, mobile individuals see themselves confronted with a wide range of diverging pension vehicles, schemes, retirement products of all sorts, arising from statutory, occupational and individual pension systems in each of the different (former) working states, and/or residence states. While incorporating the tax treatment of (cross-border) pensions plays an eminent role in effective cross-border pension information – which will be addressed thoroughly in chapter 3 – this incorporation is highly complex and may induce considerable tensions in pension information provision.

The mobile workers' fragmented pension is for tax purposes treated differently per Member State, while the fiscal treatment, in turn, depends on the qualification of the pension as such. This fiscal treatment depends on a wide variety of factual circumstances, such as his working status during his working period, i.e. for instance, was he a posted worker or a cross-border worker?[22] Furthermore, in these cases the complexity grows due to the vast differences in the national tax treatment of pensions, mainly due to the lack of harmonization or coordination of pension tax law between Member States.[23] In this vein, the national tax systems offer different modalities as regards tax benefits, relief, reductions, exemptions, compensation, deferrals and other fiscal advantages[24]. As will be dealt with more extensively later in this research, national tax systems have developed independently over the course of years, giving rise to deviations and disparities between these systems. However, to some extent, these systems have been 'aligned' and brought in conformity with the European Single Market, as a result of 'negative integration' and 'positive integration'. It should be noted in this regard that this is not akin to harmonisation of these

22 In the interest of the readability of this thesis, the combination of he/she and his/her and other conjugations has been avoided and therefore the masculine genus has been used, i.e. he/his/him, although the person to which is referred can just as easily be of the female gender. It is in no case intended to suggest that only males are concerned.

23 See for the difference between harmonisation and coordination: European Commission, *Coordinating Member States' direct tax systems in the Internal Market*, COM(2006)823 final, 4: whereas harmonisation results in the creation of a common body of Community legislation which supersedes national laws, coordination builds on domestic systems to render them compatible with the Treaty and with each other. The aim of co-ordination is not to replace existing national tax systems by a uniform Community system but to ensure that such national systems can be made to work seamlessly together. See also the Communication from the European Commission 'The elimination of tax obstacles to the cross-border provision of occupational pensions', COM (2001)214 final. In this communication, the EC seeks a coordinated approach adapted to the diversity of Member States' rules rather than attempting to achieve harmonisation and calls for the elimination of unduly restrictive or discriminatory tax rules.

24 The CJEU delineates a 'fiscal advantage' as allowing a taxable person to reduce the amount of taxable income. See, *inter alia*, C-480/17 *Montag* ECLI:EU:C:2018:987 (CJEU) para 23.

tax systems. Moreover, in cross-border situations several systems/levels of legislation are interconnected and interaction has nested, e.g. domestic law, international tax treaties, and a supra-national level of European law. Moreover, in this complex multi-layered system, each of the different layers of legislation have adapted to new and different challenges, for instance on a societal, political or economic level. What is more, provisions of these different fields of legislation may also conflict with each other, and each level may have a particular effect on a personal mobile situation.[25]

However, as follows from the foregoing, little to no attention has been paid neither any research has been conducted on the differentiated tax treatment of the fragmented pension rights in each of the (former) working states, and the effect thereof on the ambition to present effective pension information. This holistic approach has largely been neglected so far, and, hence, constitutes the intrinsic objective of the present research, which will be addressed in the section below. What central role the incorporation of taxation of pensions takes in terms of effective cross-border pension information, will be discussed more thoroughly in chapter 2 and 3 of this research.

1.1.4 The European Initiatives: Putting Cross-border Pension Information Provision and Ensuring Pension Adequacy in Motion

The European Commission underlines the central role of cross-border pension information as well. The European Commission stated, that citizens working in another Member State not only need to preserve pension entitlements accrued across borders[26], but emphasized that mobile workers need a clear overview of their accrued pension entitlements stemming from statutory and occupational pension schemes.[27] The Commission also underlined the role of a pension tracking service in ensuring pension adequacy after retirement.[28] In addition, it would be considered how the provision of the required information for pension tracking could be ensured, and a pilot project on cross-border tracking was supported by the Commission.[29] The Commission was – quite ambitiously in my opinion – convinced that, with a minimal harmonization of key features, tracking services at the

25 P Harris and DL Oliver, *International Commercial Tax* (2nd edn Cambridge Tax Law Series, Cambridge University Press, Cambridge 2020) 2.

26 As safeguarded by Mobility Directive 2014/50.

27 European Commission, 'White paper: an agenda for Adequate, Safe and Sustainable Pensions,' 13. See also para 51 preamble Directive (EU) 2016/2341 of the European Parliament and of the Council of 14 December 2016 on the activities and supervision of institutions for occupational retirement provision (IORPs) [2016] OJ L 354.

28 European Commission, 'White paper: an agenda for Adequate, Safe and Sustainable Pensions,' 13.

29 Ibid. 18.

national level could be connected into a European system of tracking services.[30] The European commission supported a step-by-step approach in the development of a European tracking service for pensions.[31]

An adequate and sustainable retirement income for European citizens now and in the future has been put appointed a priority for the European Union.[32] In turn, sound and adequate pension systems, which enable individuals to maintain, to a reasonable degree, their living standard after retirement, are crucial for citizens. The aforementioned ambition of an adequate retirement income is embedded in one of the principles of the European Pillar of Social Rights.[33] This pillar strives to deliver new and more effective rights for citizens and, moreover, is built upon twenty key principles, comprising three categories: equal opportunities and access to the labour market, fair working conditions and social protection and inclusion.[34] Under the latter, the principle of 'old age income and pensions' is formulated, stipulating that workers and the self-employed in retirement have the right to a pension commensurate to their contributions, and ensuring an adequate income. Lastly, the principle prescribes that everyone in old age has the right to resources that ensure living in dignity.

The Commission followed up the EU Pillar by publishing a Communication, in which it sets out how social policy will help deliver on the challenges and opportunities of today, proposing action at EU level, and seeking feedback on further action at all levels in the area of employment and social rights.[35] This communication builds on the European Pillar of Social Rights, proclaimed by EU institutions and leaders in November 2017, setting out the road towards an action plan to implement the Pillar.[36] In early 2021, the Commission presented an action plan that turns the rights and principles as embedded in the Pillar into

30 Ibid. 13.

31 See FindYourPension, 'Creating the Pilot ETS: Finding and understanding pensions (Findyourpension 2.0)' <https://www.findyourpension.eu/en/news/creating-the-pilot-ets-finding-and-understanding-p_kgkg61uu.html> accessed 22 June 2021.

32 Ensuring an adequate retirement income is the purpose of pension systems. See European Commission, 'Green paper: towards adequate, sustainable and safe European pension systems' 8.

33 This 'pillar' has been issued as a non-legally binding inter-institutional declaration. Both the European Parliament, the Council as well as the European Commission proclaimed this pillar in 2017 at the Gothenburg Summit.

34 European Commission, 'The European Pillar of Social Rights in 20 principles' <https://ec.europa.eu/commission/priorities/deeper-and-fairer-economic-and-monetary-union/european-pillar-social-rights/european-pillar-social-rights-20-principles_en> (last accessed on 22 November 2017).

35 European Commission, 'Communication from the Commission to the European Parliament, the Council, the European Economic and Social Committee and the Committee of the Regions: a Strong Social Europe for Just Transitions'.

36 The Commission asked all EU countries, regions and partners to present their views on the way forward as well as their plans to deliver on the Pillar's objectives. See ibid. 2.

reality.[37] Under pillar 15 (old-age income and pensions) the Netherlands implemented three measures: reform of the second pillar of the pension system through the Law on the future of pensions (*Wet Toekomst Pensioenen*); experimenting second pillar pension for the self-employed; increasement of minimum wage (and as a result, state pensions) by 10% in 2023.[38] What is more, in her action plan for a capital markets union, the European Commission expressed that she will also develop best practices for the set-up of national tracking systems for individual Europeans, which tracking systems will enable European citizens to benefit from more adequate retirement income.[39] Subsequently, the European Insurance and Occupational Pensions Authority (EIOPA) published an advice to the European Commission on the development of a pension tracking system.[40] Since recently, European citizens have access to a European pension overview.[41] Belgium's national pension register is hereby the first to be connected to the European pension register. The intention is to connect at least five countries with their own national pension register within the next three to five years (as of 2023). The Dutch Pension Register plans to also make pension data available through the European Pension Register, expected in 2024. The ultimate goal is that after logging in with their national identifier, citizens will be provided with an overview of their accrued pensions across Europe. It remains to be seen

37 Ibid. 3. See also European Commission, 'The European Pillar of Social Rights: turning principles into actions' 4 March 2021) <https://ec.europa.eu/commission/presscorner/detail/en/ip_21_820> accessed 5 March 2021. This European Pillar of Social Rights Action Plan describes concrete actions to further implement the principles as a joint effort by the Members States and the EU, where social partners and civil society are actively involved, see ibid.

38 Minister van Economische Zaken en Klimaat, *European Pillar of Social Rights Report 2023 Netherlands: Reporting on the Implementation of the European Pillar of Social Rights Description of main Measures and their Estimated Impact* (24 April 2023) 6.

39 European Commission, 'A Capital Markets Union for people and businesses-new action plan' (2020) 11-12.

40 EIOPA, 'EIOPA submits its advice on pensions tools to the European Commission' 1 December 2021) <https://www.eiopa.europa.eu/media/news/eiopa-submits-its-advice-pensions-tools-european-commission> accessed 9 December 2021. See also EIOPA, 'Technical Advice on the Development of Pension Tracking Systems'. The pension tracking system seeks to support citizens to understand what retirement income they can expect and raise their awareness on whether this will be sufficient. Currently, in 20 Member States citizens are unable to obtain an overview of their pension entitlements in an accessible way from all possible pension sources. EIOPA – in its advice – provides a set of principles, good practices and recommendations, aiming to facilitate citizens' digital access to personal pension information. The report aims to support Member States in Europe that do not have a pension tracking system in place. To facilitate this process for Member States, EIOPA has developed a visual roadmap that contains four phases from preparation to launch, including relevant conceptual and practical steps to consider under each phase. EIOPA recommends displaying key information in a simple manner to make a pension tracking system appealing and understandable for consumers. Member States are also encouraged to connect to the European Tracking Service to offer intra-EU mobile workers access to their pension entitlements accrued in the course of their career.

41 See FindYourPension, 'Pension Tracker' 2023) <https://www.findyourpension.eu/pension-tracker-coming-soon> accessed 23 February 2023.

when Germany – in the process of developing the national *Digitale Rentenübersicht* – can connect, since this pension overview first needs implementation at the national level.[42]

In view of the above, one could say that the development of a European pension tracking service has been put in further motion. It has become apparent that living in dignity and ensuring an adequate income – which are mutually complementary – forms a priority for the European Union. Yet, the role of the taxation of (cross-border) pensions in cross-border pension information still remains underexposed.

1.2 Objective of the Research and Research Question

Against the foregoing background, this research focuses on the provision of effective pension information and the role of the tax treatment of cross-border pensions in the Netherlands, and Germany, herein. The selection of these two national legal systems will be further clarified in section 1.4.1.A.III. The essential role of this information provision in being able to ensure the adequacy of pensions for mobile individuals has been elaborated on in the previous sections. It is therefore noteworthy to mention that no research has yet been done on this matter in literature. The objective of this study is therefore as follows, after which it will be explained how this objective will be achieved.

General objective of the research: *explore to what extent the regulatory frameworks on a national level in the Netherlands and Germany, on a European level, and on an international level, governing the taxation of (cross-border) statutory, occupational and personal pensions, are fit for the provision of effective pension information (net amounts of future pension income) and, if not so, what legal/non-legal interventions and measures are needed to ensure, and potentially foster, the effectiveness of the pension information provided.*

This general research objective is actually threefold and the following sub-objectives can be distinguished from it. The first goal is to establish a theoretical and conceptual evaluation framework, focusing on the provision of effective pension information. This will be described in chapter 2 of this study. As part of creating this evaluation framework – allowing for the assessment of the regulatory frameworks' fitness – an experimental (empirical) study has been conducted, which will be addressed in more detail in chapter 3.

42 The *Digitale Rentenübersicht* has started recently in the public test phase. Responsible for the project is a newly created authority at the Deutsche Rentenversicherung Bund, the so-called *Zentrale Stelle für die Digitale Rentenübersicht (ZfDR)*. See GDV, 'Digitale Rentenübersicht startet in öffentliche Testphase' 2023) <https://www.gdv.de/gdv/medien/medieninformationen/digitale-rentenuebersicht-startet-in-oeffentliche-testphase-136924> accessed 10 September 2023.

Based on this evaluation framework, the legislative instruments in the Netherlands and Germany will be assessed for their suitability to provide effective pension information. The second objective is a legal comparative study in which the legal frameworks in the Netherlands and Germany, as well as on a European and international level, are mapped out.[43] This part of the research concerns a mainly descriptive study, which incites to critically assess and value a certain legal phenomenon, i.e. the taxation of pensions in cross-border situations. The comparative study allows for defining differences and similarities in the tax treatment of pensions in cross-border situations (by laying the tax systems of the two Member States on top of each other) that form a potential hurdle for the provision of effective pension information. In doing so, the comparison constitutes an objective, rather a means. The third objective is the evaluation of the legal frameworks on the basis of the mentioned ('normative') framework as mentioned under the first objective. Building on this, the 'fitness' of the legal frameworks at the national, European and international level shall be assessed, focusing in particular on any deficiencies that have a (detrimental) effect on the provision of effective information. This evaluation makes it possible to formulate points for improvement and recommendations. The results of this evaluation play an instrumental role in this research, since the main research question is of a normative nature.[44] It is, however, not this research's objective to formulate new legislation on a supranational level (harmonization or unification), through searching for the 'common core' of the legal systems to be harmonised or unified.[45] The above-mentioned three-fold objective is visualized in Figure 1.1.

43 See HEB Tijssen, *De juridische dissertatie onder de loep: de verantwoording van methodologische keuzes in juridische dissertaties* (Boom Juridische Uitgevers, Den Haag 2009) 58 and R Cryer, T Hervey and B Sokhi-Bully, *Research methodologies in EU and International Law* (Hart Publishing, Oxford 2011).

44 Cf. Tijssen, 59 and S Issacharoff, 'The Difficult path from observation to prescription" 77 New York University Law Review 24.

45 See M Oderkerk, 'The Importance of Context: Selecting Legal Systems in Comparative Legal Research' 48 NILR 293, 314.

Figure 1.1 Three-fold Objective of the Present Research

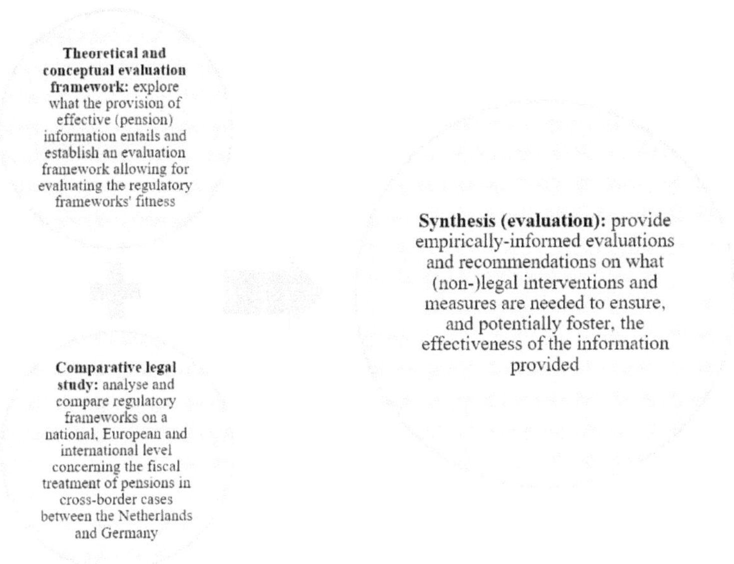

Given this general research objective and the three sub-research objectives depicted in the figure above, the following research question follows from this:

To what extent are the regulatory frameworks on a national level in the Netherlands and Germany, on a European level, and on an international level, governing the taxation of (cross-border) statutory, occupational and personal pensions, fit for the provision of effective information and, if not so, what legal/non-legal interventions and measures are needed to ensure, and potentially foster, the effectiveness of the information provided?

This main research question encompasses the three sub-objectives of this research: effective information (i.e. theoretical and conceptual framework); the regulatory frameworks explored (i.e. comparative legal study), and the evaluation (i.e. synthesis) of the fitness of the regulatory frameworks, and exploring what legal/non-legal interventions and measures are needed.

This main research question can, thus, be divided into three sub-questions:

1. What constitutes a theoretical/conceptual (evaluation) framework for providing effective (pension) information? This is dealt with in chapter 1, 2 and 3.
2. How is (the taxation of) cross-border pensions shaped in Dutch and German domestic law, European law and international tax law? Chapters 4, 5, 6, 7, 8 and 9 revolve around this question.

3. Building on sub-question 1 and 2; to what extent is there room for improvements in terms of legal/non-legal interventions and measures to ensure, and potentially foster, the effectiveness of the pension information provided? This will be addressed in the interim conclusions in each of the chapters, accompanied by a conclusion in chapter 10.

This research's objective, and research question, encompasses the exploration of what legal, and non-legal interventions and measures are needed to ensure, and potentially foster, the effectiveness of pension information provided. What effectiveness of information entails and requires, how this can be ascertained, and how this can be affected will be dealt with elaborately in chapter 2. However, at this point, a brief word concerning necessary legal, and non-legal interventions and measures is considered appropriate. Legal interventions, and measures, concern tools in the sphere of the regulatory frameworks, for instance the adoption of a different approach by the European Commission in her efforts in the field of positive integration, or adapting national legislation. As a rule, it refers to measures that may improve the fitness/aptitude of regulatory frameworks, that may, in turn, ameliorate effective information provision. Non-legal interventions refer to tools in the domain of information provision, for instance, harnessing certain ways of adapting information in order to ensure its effectiveness. As a rule, this concerns tools that improve the provision of information, rather than helping in improving the fitness of the regulatory frameworks as such.

1.3 Terminology, Definitions and Concepts

The terms used and concepts referred to in the main research question leave room for ambiguity. To be clear about how these definitions are harnessed in the present research, these will be addressed in more detail in the section below. While this section primarily serves to provide clarity on terms, it, inevitably, entails certain limitations as regards this research, and delineating perspectives.

1.3.1 Scope Ratione Personae and Materiae

1.3.1.A Scope Ratione Personae: Mobile Citizens

Pension information provision for European mobile citizens seeks to (eventually) provide these citizens with information required to assess their expected retirement income. The term 'European mobile citizens' is, in the context of this research, interpreted as citizens of the EU (all citizens of an EU country are automatically citizens of the EU), exercising (or having exercised) their European freedoms of movement. As an EU citizen, these people have the right to live and move within the EU without being discriminated on the grounds of nationality, and are protected by the citizenship's rights, spelled out in the *Treaty on the Functioning of the European Union* (specifically art. 18) and the *Charter of Fundamental Rights of the European Union*.

These intended users of the information are, through the provision of this information, allowed to assess their 'pension (in)adequacy'. However, as will be dealt with in more detail below, in the cross-border domain, a taxonomy of mobile citizens, irrespective of which capacity in particular, is still lacking. This is partly due to the fact that different fields of legislation (e.g. tax, social security or pensions) apply deviating definitions of the construct. Some fields of law haven't even drawn up a definition.[46] In this regard, it should be stressed that for some fields of regulation a clearly delineated definition is of little, or even no, practical relevance, since they rely on other variables, e.g. sort of income instead of worker's status. For instance, where in social security legislation, more specifically the conflict rules laid down in Regulation 883/2004[47], the worker's status is instrumental in assigning the competent state on the basis of the principle of exclusive effect[48], (bilateral) tax conventions assign taxing rights on the basis of the sort of (elements of) income. From this perspective, it seems straightforward why the exact definition of these terms varies across the different fields of legislation. Moreover, it will become evident in the chapters revolving around the tax treatment of cross-border pensions that each of these different types of mobile workers, is treated differently for fiscal purposes. This has, in turn, a different effect on the provision of effective pension information.

The term 'mobile citizens' thus covers a multitude of different working capacities, or (also) residing, across borders.[49] For instance, in social security law a distinction is drawn between 'civil servant'[50], 'frontier worker'[51] and 'posted worker'[52]. Furthermore, it should be pointed out that the term 'mobile citizens' covers both citizens during their active

46 See for instance Mobility Directive 2014/50. This directive does however define the term in art. 3, under g: "*'outgoing worker' means an active scheme member whose current employment relationship terminates for reasons other than becoming eligible for a supplementary pension and who moves between Member States*".

47 Regulation (EC) No. 883/2004 of the European Parliament and of the Council of 29 April 2004 on the coordination of social security systems [2004] OJ L 166.

48 As laid down in art. 11, para 1 ibid.

49 See also the term 'mobile worker', see European Commission, 'Annual Report on Intra-EU Labour Mobility 2022' 11.

50 Pursuant to art. 1, under d Regulation on the coordination of social security systems 883/2004: "*'civil servant' means a person considered to be such or treated as such by the Member State to which the administration employing him/her is subject;*".

51 Pursuant to art. 1, under f ibid.: "*'frontier worker' means any person pursuing an activity as an employed or self-employed person in a Member State and who resides in another Member State to which he/she returns as a rule daily or at least once a week;*".

52 Pursuant to art. 12 ibid.

(working) period, as well as (retired) citizens during their passive period. It should be noted that the functional distinction drawn between taxable persons in tax law, such as directors[53], entertainers and sportspersons[54], and students[55] is not used in this research, i.e. these types of workers are not addressed in this research.

As will become apparent in chapters 5-9 of this research, from a pension perspective the distinction between these different forms of 'mobile citizens' (migrant, cross-border, posted worker) is of pivotal relevance, in particular in terms of pension accrual. For instance, where a migrant worker resides, works and accrues his pension (either statutory, occupational or personal pension) in one and the same state, a cross-border worker will usually accrue his statutory, and occupational pension in his working state and save for his personal pension in his residence state, while a posted worker will – generally – save for his retirement through statutory, occupational and personal pension schemes in the sending state/residence state. The pivotal role of this personal 'mobility status' should be borne in mind when reading these chapters 5-9.

More specifically, the terms shaping the concept of 'mobile citizens' are interpreted in the present research as follows:

– *Posted worker:* a worker who has an employment contract in his home state, and, for a limited period[56], carries out his work in the territory of a Member State other than the State in which he normally works.[57] Normally, these workers are sent by their employer

53 Art. 16 OECD Model Tax Convention on Income and on Capital.

54 Art. 17 ibid.

55 Art. 20 ibid.

56 Posting is temporary in nature, however, how long this 'limited period' exactly comprises differs per situation. For instance, art. 12, para. 1 Regulation on the coordination of social security systems 883/2004 provides that a posted worker remains insured for social security in the 'sending state', provided that the anticipated duration of such work does not exceed 24 months and that he/she is not sent to replace another posted person. Moreover, this time period can be extended up to 60 months pursuant to article 16 of Regulation 883/2004. For further conditions, see Decision No A2 of 12 June 2009 concerning the interpretation of Article 12 of Regulation (EC) No 883/2004 of the European Parliament and of the Council on the legislation applicable to posted workers and self-employed workers temporarily working outside the competent State [OJ C 106/5] However, Directive (EU) 2018/957 of the European Parliament and of the Council of 28 June 2018 amending Directive 96/71/EC concerning the posting of workers in the framework of the provision of services [2018] OJ L 173 introduced a new rule in the sense that for long-term postings (longer than 12 or 18 months), an extended set of terms and conditions of employment of the receiving Member State applies, see para 9 of the preamble. The reason for this lies in the more prevalent link between the labour market of the host Member State and the workers posted for such long periods.

57 Building on the definitions provided in art. 2 of Directive 96/71/EC of the European Parliament and of the Council of 16 December 1996 concerning the posting of workers in the framework of the provision of services [1996] OJ L 18; Your Europe – European Union, 'National websites on posting' <https://europa.eu/youreurope/citizens/work/work-abroad/posted-workers/index_en.htm#national-websites> accessed 23 January 2020; para. 3 of preamble, art. 4, para 3 Directive 2014/67/EU of the European Parliament and of the Council of 15 May 2014 on the enforcement of Directive 96/71/EC concerning the posting of workers

to work in another EU Member State on a temporary basis, in the context of a contract of services, intra-group hosting or hiring out of labour through a temporary agency. These posted workers differ from other types of mobile workers in that they return, or are expected to resume working in the Member State from which he or she is posted after completion of the work or the provision of services for which he or she was posted.[58] They, thus, do not fully integrate in the labour market of the host state, and will, hence, benefit only partially of the same working conditions and rights as workers in the host state. Their protection as regards mandatory terms and conditions of employment is regulated separately in EU law.[59]

Generally, from a statutory pension point of view these posted workers will not have to deal with pension institutions in different countries when they retire, since the social security institutions in the host state(s) will not be involved.[60] Contrarily, in some circumstances, they will have to deal with pensions funds in the other state, since they will have accrued occupational pension rights. However, this is not the case when they have chosen to continue the pension accrual in their scheme in the sending state.

As regards taxes, the general rule in practice stipulates that if the posted worker works in the host state for less than 183 days (roughly six months), he shall not be liable to

in the framework of the provision of services and amending Regulation (EU) No 1024/2012 on administrative cooperation through the Internal Market Information System [2014] OJ L 159. See also European Commission, 'Annual Report on Intra-EU Labour Mobility 2022' 11.

58 Art. 4, para 3, under d Directive 2014/67/EU of the European Parliament and of the Council of 15 May 2014 on the enforcement of Directive 96/71/EC concerning the posting of workers in the framework of the provision of services and amending Regulation (EU) No 1024/2012 on administrative cooperation through the Internal Market Information System [2014] OJ L 159. See also para 9 preamble Directive 2018/957 amending Directive 96/71.

59 Posted workers are protected by the Posting of Workers Directive 96/71; Enforcement Directive 2014/67 of Posting of Workers Directive 96/71 and Directive 2018/957 amending Directive 96/71. The social security of posted workers is regulated by art. 12 Regulation on the coordination of social security systems 883/2004. The rules of the host state merely apply when these are more advantageous to the posted worker than those of his/hers home country. This set of mandatory rules on EU level, strive to ensure a level-playing field and avoid 'social dumping' (foreign service providers can undermine domestic service providers by lowering their labour standards, and costs). Whilst posted workers are still employed by their sending company, and subject to the legislation of the 'sending state', these rules ensure that they are entitled to a set of core rights, applicable in the host state. These rules relate to minimum rates of pay, maximum work periods and minimum rest periods, minimum paid annual leave, the conditions of hiring out workers through temporary work agencies, health, safety and hygiene at work, and equal treatment between men and women. See Your Europe – European Union. For an overview of the national rules applicable in the receiving Member State, see Staatssecretaris van Financiën, *Besluit Internationaal belastingrecht. Belastingverdragen; uitleg begrip werkgever nr. DGB2010/267M.*

60 Since, under conditions, they will be socially insured in the 'sending state' pursuant to art. 12, para. 1 Regulation on the coordination of social security systems 883/2004.

income tax in the host state.[61] This is not regulated in EU-wide rules but is laid down in domestic legislation and bilateral tax treaties, concluded between countries. What is more, the Dutch State Secretary of Finance introduced the 60-day rule for intra-group posting of workers, stipulating that if the posted worker works in the Netherlands (the host state) for a period of not exceeding 60 (working) days per 12-month period, the worker's income will not be taxed in the Netherlands.[62] Furthermore, with respect to non-contracting States, the *Besluit voorkoming dubbele belasting* (BvdB) 2001 even provides that a short-term secondment does not exceed the threshold of 29 days.[63]

- *Cross-border worker:* (or commonly referred to as 'frontier worker', or 'border commuter') are persons working in one EU Member State but residing in another (neighbouring) state, to which they usually return every day or at least once a week.[64] This type worker can either work temporarily or permanently in another State than his working state. In this respect it should be noted that the precise definition of cross-border worker may vary across different fields of application, and legislation (tax legislation, social security law or welfare entitlements). Contrary to posted workers, cross-border workers, who go to another Member State to seek work and are employed in that state, are entitled to equal treatment with nationals of that working state (i.e. 'equality on the work floor'), as regards working conditions, social security conditions[65], tax conditions etc.

61 Your Europe – European Union, 'Posted workers' <https://europa.eu/youreurope/citizens/work/work-abroad/posted-workers/index_en.htm#national-websites> accessed 23 January 2020. This 183 days-rule has been derived from art. 15 OECD Model Tax Convention on Income and on Capital 2017 (hereinafter: OECD MC). Hereinafter, unless specified otherwise, with 'OECD MC' I refer to the most recent version of the convention, i.e. the version of 21 November 2017. Pursuant to art. 15, para. 2 the posted worker's income shall be taxed only in his home state, provided that the period of posting in the host state does not exceed the threshold of 183 days, assuming that the other conditions, as set out in the second paragraph, are met as well.

62 Staatssecretaris van Financiën, *Besluit Internationaal belastingrecht. Belastingverdragen; uitleg begrip werkgever* (12 January 2010). More specifically, the introduction of this 60 day-rule was introduced in order to interpret the term of material employer (*materieel werkgeversbegrip*) in view art. 15 OECD Model Tax Convention on Income and on Capital.

63 Pursuant to art. 9, para 4 *Besluit voorkoming dubbele belasting* (BvdB).

64 European Commission, 'Cross-border workers' <https://ec.europa.eu/taxation_customs/individuals/personal-taxation/crossborder-workers_en> accessed 29 January 2020. See also art. 2, para 2, under a International Convention on the Protection of the Rights of All Migrant Workers and Members of Their Families. This provision defines a 'frontier worker' as *"a migrant worker who retains his or her habitual residence in a neighbouring State to which he or she normally returns every day or at least once a week;"*. The definition's element of returning, at least, once a week to the state of residence has also been recognized for Dutch tax purposes, see Staatssecretaris van Financiën, *Vraag- en antwoordbesluit CRS/FATCA* (13 March 2018), para 17.

65 Spelled out in para 8 of the preamble Regulation on the coordination of social security systems 883/2004, stipulating: *"The general principle of equal treatment is of particular importance for workers who do not reside in the Member State of their employment, including frontier workers."*

In the context of social security, a cross-border worker is defined as any person pursuing an activity as an employed or self-employed person in a Member State and who resides in another Member State to which he/she returns as a rule daily or at least once a week.[66] Over the years, the protection of cross-border workers has expanded over the different legal domains.[67]

In the field of taxation, no rules at EU level exist with respect to defining the concept of cross-border workers. The most obvious reason for this is that, as mentioned above, the division of taxing rights is governed by bilateral tax conventions, allocating taxing rights based on (elements of) income, rather than (taxable) persons. Double tax conventions' object is to prevent juridical double taxation.[68] It does not lie within the aim of the conventions to ensure that the tax, to which the cross-border worker shall be subject in one State is not higher, compared to the situation where he or she would be subject to tax in the other State.[69] However, taxing rights must nevertheless be exercised consistently with EU law.[70] This will be dealt with thoroughly in chapter 8 of this research. Furthermore, non-resident workers (i.e. cross-border workers) shall enjoy the same (social and) tax advantages as national workers.[71] More particularly, the EU treaty freedoms, and non-discrimination principle, require that the cross-border worker may not be discriminated in his State of residence, because of working in another Member State.[72]

66 Pursuant to art. 1, under f ibid.

67 See for instance the principle of equality of treatment as laid down in art. 7, para 1 Regulation (EU) No 492/2011 of the European Parliament and of the Council of 5 April 2011 on freedom of movement for workers within the Union [2011] OJ L 141. In particular para 2 of the given provision is of specific importance: *"He shall enjoy the same social and tax advantages as national workers."*

68 Juridical double taxation refers to the situation where one person (subject) is subject to tax on one income component or assets in (at least) two states. This falls within the aim of the allocating provisions, laid down in double taxation conventions. Contrarily, economic double taxation occurs when two persons (subject) are both subject to tax in (at least) two states on one income component or assets (object). This does not fall within the scope of double tax conventions. Economic double taxation is as a rule mitigated exclusively through domestic tax regulations.

69 C-336/96 *Gilly* ECLI:EU:C:1998:221 (CJEU), para 46.

70 C-279/93 *Schumacker* ECLI:EU:C:1995:31 (CJEU), para 21.

71 In virtue of art. 7, para 2 Regulation on freedom of movement for workers within the Union 492/2011.

72 However, in respect of tax advantages relating to the personal and family situation, the principle of non-discrimination applies, provided that the situation of a non-resident worker is comparable to the situation of a resident worker. It is settled case-law of the CJEU that, residents and non-residents are, as a rule, not in a comparable situation, and that differences in their tax treatment do not necessarily constitute discrimination. See for instance *C-279/93 Schumacker ECLI: EU: C: 1995: 31 (CJEU), para 31.*A cross-border worker is, virtually, in the same situation as a resident worker if he earns all or almost all of his income (quantified mostly as 90%) in that State. In that case, the non-resident worker may not be subject to a less favourable tax treatment in the State of employment, compared to residents of that State. Furthermore, domestic legislation denying the deduction of costs and expenses (the doctrine of professional

- *Migrant worker:* a person who has ceased his occupational activities in one State, and has/had transferred his residence to another State of which he is not a national, with a view to being engaged in a remunerated activity on the territory of that state, and any person regularly admitted as a migrant worker.[73]

  The definition used in the context of this research, has been drawn from international regulation in the field of protecting the rights of migrant workers, in particular, in respect of conditions of employment, work, and social benefits. This type of mobile citizen is not recognized as a separate group, not in the domain of social security, nor in tax law. The most obvious reason for this is that these citizens entirely integrate in the labour market of their new state of residence, and working state. For social security legislation, as well as pursuant to tax legislation, these workers are considered residents and, therefore, treated accordingly under these fields of legislation. However, the prevalence of distinguishing this group of workers as a separate type, becomes apparent in the tax treatment of their pensions in cross-border situations, for instance, in view of the protective tax assessment (*conserverende aanslag*), imposed pursuant to Dutch domestic tax law.

- *Migrant pensioner:* a migrant pensioner[74] is a person who migrates or has migrated from one country to another, of which he is not a national, after retirement. In that case he has not been an active worker in his new home state.[75] Hence, these individuals are not entitled to invoke the freedom of workers (art. 45 TFEU), but merely the freedom of persons (art. 21 TFEU).[76] This is considered relevant in the light of chapter 8 of this research. This type of former worker, has neither been recognized in the domain of tax law, for the reasons mentioned above, nor in the field of social security law or pension legislation. Nevertheless, this group of (former) workers can be considered one of the stakeholders of cross-border pension information provision.

expenses) is precluded, provided that these costs and expenses are directly linked to the economic activity which generated the taxable income. See, for instance in the domain of pensions *C-480/17 Montag ECLI: EU: C: 2018: 987 (CJEU).*

73 Definition derived from Convention concerning Migrations in Abusive Conditions and the Promotion of Equality of Opportunity and Treatment of Migrant Workers 1975 (No. 143) and art. 2, para 1 International Convention on the Protection of the Rights of All Migrant Workers and Members of Their Families. See also C-275/96 *Kuusijärvi* ECLI:EU:C:1998:279 (CJEU), para 50.

74 A retired person (or 'pensioner') refers to a person who, be it definitively or temporarily, has ceased his occupational activity. See *Kuusijärvi*.

75 See, for instance, C-300/15 *Kohll en Kohll-Schlesser* ECLI:EU:C:2016:361 (CJEU) that illustrates the extent to which active mobile workers may invoke the European freedom of persons.

76 C-520/04 *Turpeinen* ECLI:EU:C:2006:703 (CJEU) para 16.

1.3.1.B Scope Ratione Materiae: Multi-level Regulatory Frameworks

The main research question of this research refers to 'regulatory frameworks' as subject of this research's evaluation. It will be set forth more extensively below, what this term entails. This research covers a multitude of 'government interventions' in the field of law: formal laws, policy decisions (*beleidsbesluiten*), ministerial decrees and memoranda aimed at clarifying the interpretation of given parts of legislation (e.g. *BMF-schreiben*). Yet, all of these fields of law/policy will be referred to as 'legislation' for the purpose of this research, as it potentially affects the tax treatment, and potentially induces tensions in information provision, as will be discussed in more detail in chapter 2. Figure 1.2 depicts these different realms of law, and multi-layered legal systems, incorporated in this research's analysis.[77]

Figure 1.2

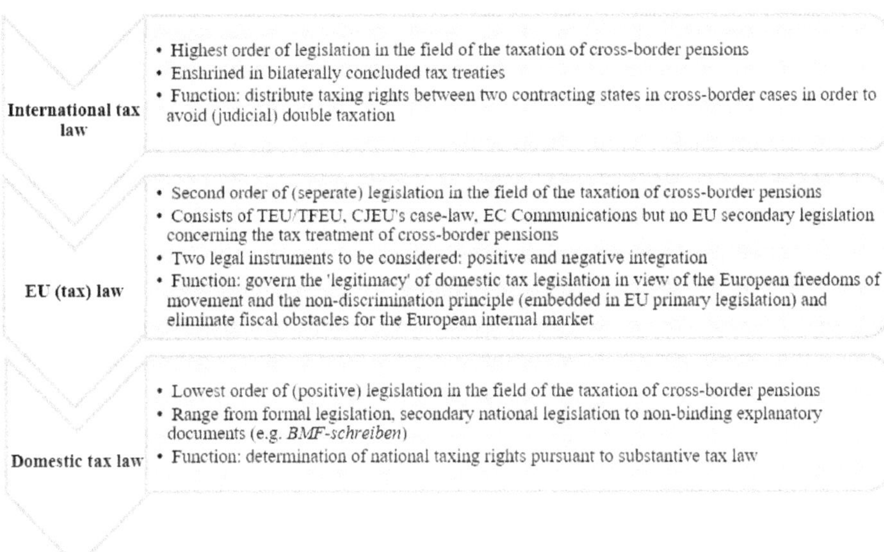

All of the above-mentioned layers of legislation will be included in this research's analysis, as this research focusses on cross-border situations. In such situations these different layers of legislation – national, European, and international – will inevitably intersect. This intersection of these poorly coordinated different layers of multi-level legislation – each having a different function – is then transposed into the context of effective pension information, which is discussed in more detail in chapter 2.

77 For a description of the concept of multi-layered legal systems, see for instance B Pokol, *The concept of law: the multi-layered legal system* (Rejtjel Edition, Budapest 2001).

As far as EU 'legislation' as a regulatory framework is concerned, the following must be pointed out.[78] Article 115 of the TFEU merely points to directives (for the approximation of laws, regulations or administrative provision of the Member States). The directives that have been issued to date, are primarily concerned with the taxation of companies. These directives take effect through the TFEU and have been construed by the CJEU to have direct effect. As will become apparent in the succeeding chapters, no directives have been issued as regards the tax treatment of (cross-border) pensions. Also, the European Convention on Human Rights is yet another treaty that may have an effect on direct taxation. This will merely be discussed where considered appropriate, primarily focussing on treaty provisions that may have implications for direct taxation, e.g. article 1 (protection of property) or article 14 (prohibition of discrimination).

Furthermore, an additional source of law is case-law. In this research, Dutch and German case-law will be incorporated in the analysis, mostly delivered by the Supreme Courts.[79] Also the cases of the Court of Justice of the European Union (hereinafter: CJEU) as regards the cross-border taxation of pensions play a paramount role in the analysis, as a form of negative integration, which will be dealt with in chapter 8. The cases of the European Court of Human Rights (hereinafter: ECHR) will only be touched upon where necessary.

While not constituting a form of legislation, but rather of policy and the interpretation of legislation, documents published by EU institutions, mostly the European Commission will be analysed as well. For instance, in the context of the 'positive integration' of national legal orders, this concerns the EC Communications.[80] Also documents and reports issued by the Organisation for Economic Cooperation and Development (hereinafter: OECD)

78 In a European context, the term 'legislation' refers to either 'regulation' or 'directives', as the only binding legal decisions. A regulation has general application, i.e. being binding in its entirety and directly applicable in all Member States. Contrarily, a directive shall be binding, as to the result to be achieved, upon each Member State to which it is addressed, but shall leave to the national authorities the choice of form and methods. A decision is binding in its entirety upon those to whom it is addressed, and recommendations and opinions shall have no binding force. See art. 249 TEU. For each of these types of 'legislation', different guidelines for drafting these texts have been developed, see European Union, 'Joint Practical Guide of the European Parliament, the Council and the Commission for persons involved in the drafting of European Union legislation' (European Union, 2015) 11 ff.

79 As regards the Netherlands, this refers to the *Hoge Raad*, and with respect to Germany to the *Bundesfinanzhof* and the *Bundesverfassungsgericht*. As has been repeatedly emphasized, a constitutional court does not exist in the Netherlands, due to the prohibition of examining formal laws on the grounds of the constitution, as laid down in art. 120 of the Dutch constitution (*Grondwet*).

80 For instance European Commission, 'The elimination of tax obstacles to the cross-border provision of occupational pensions,' (2001) [COM(2001)214 final].

will be taken into consideration.[81] As regards the OECD, the OECD Model Tax Convention, and its accompanying Commentaries, play a pivotal role in chapter 9.[82]

1.4 Research Design, Methodology and Methods

The section below will discuss what research design, methodology, and methods have been employed in this research in order to answer the main research question. It will both discuss the legal (comparative) analysis, as well as the empirical research. In order to answer the main research question, first the regulatory frameworks governing the taxation of cross-border pensions need to be outlined, i.e. the 'law as it stands'. For a description of what 'the law' embodies in the context of this research, see section 1.3.1.B.

1.4.1 Comparative Legal Analysis

Put simply, a comparative research analysis is aimed at the comparison of legal phenomena, in order to reveal similarities or differences. Through the lens of the evaluation framework outlined in chapter 2, the present research is aimed at revealing impediments in the regulatory frameworks for providing effective pension information. These impediments include, inter alia, differences in the national regulatory frameworks governing the taxation of cross-border pensions. This (externally)[83] comparative research constitutes a preliminary step preceding the evaluative research objective.[84]

1.4.1.A Function and Objective of the Comparison

1.4.1.A.I A Combination of Micro and Macro Comparative Law

The nature of the comparison in the present research can hardly be characterised as either a micro- or macro-comparison. Micro comparative research focuses on specific legal phenomena, problems and solutions in several legal systems.[85] Primarily, the present

81 For instance OECD, 'OECD Pensions at a Glance 2017'.

82 OECD Model Tax Convention on Income and on Capital and; Commentaries on the Articles of the Model Tax Convention.

83 In that two present-day legal systems shall be compared.

84 M Oderkerk, *De preliminaire fase van het rechtsvergelijkend onderzoek* (Ars Aequi Libri, Nijmegen 1999) 16.

85 E Örücü, 'Developing Comparative Law' in E Örücü and D Nelken (eds.), *Comparative Law* (Hart Publishing, Oxford 2007) 32 G Dannemann, 'Comparative Law: Study of Similarities or Differences?' in M Reimann and R Zimmermann (eds.), *Oxford Handbook of Comparative Law* (Oxford University Press, Oxford 2006) 387 and K Zweigert and H Kötz, *Introduction to Comparative Law* (3rd edn Oxford University Press, Oxford 1998) 5. Contrarily, macro comparative law concerns the analysis of legal systems in their

research is focused on the comparison of the regulatory frameworks of the Netherlands and Germany, governing the taxation of cross-border pensions, parallel to the pertinent regulatory frameworks at international, and European level. To a certain extent, however, this entails a mix of both micro and macro comparison, as findings drawing on the macro comparison often explain differences discovered in the micro comparison. For instance, certain characteristics of a legal system (macro) explain differences found on the micro level (taxation of cross-border pensions). Moreover, it can be marked as research into 'non-legal topics', given the assessment framework mapped out in chapter 2, building on findings from the field of behavioural economics, economic psychology and cognitive psychology. In doing so, this research design seeks to be 'original'.[86]

1.4.1.A.II Tertium Comparationis

A *tertium compartionis* (i.e. a common characteristic) is required in each comparison, i.e. in order to compare legal phenomena they need to have something in common.[87] As Zweigert and Kötz articulate it aptly: "*Unvergleichbares kann man nicht sinnvoll vergleichen,...*".[88] For this present research, this *tertium compartionis* lies in legal consequences, i.e. the taxation of cross-border pensions.[89] The two regulatory systems have the same objective – i.e. taxing pensions – but have a different shape, historical development, political background, underlying principles, rationales, modalities, and technicalities.[90]

1.4.1.A.III Auswahlkriterien in Comparative Legal Research: the Netherlands – Germany

The comparative legal part of this research encompasses the regulatory frameworks governing the taxation of cross-border situations in the Netherlands and Germany. It will be elucidated below why these two countries have been selected in the comparative part. These arguments will be touched upon point-by-point. As Zweigert and Kötz argued, it is difficult to speak generally about how the comparatist should choose the legal systems,

---

entirety, focusing on the spirit and style of different legal systems and the respective methods and procedures.

86 See MM Siems, 'Legal Originality' 28 Oxford Journal of Legal Studies 147, 147.

87 J Bell, 'Legal Research and the Distinctiveness of Comparative Law' in M Van Hoecke (ed.), *Methodologies of Legal Research* (Hart Publishing, Oxford 2011) 63 ff. Örücü, 44 and M Van Hoecke, 'Deep Level Comparative Law' in M Van Hoecke (ed.), *Epistemology and Methodology of Comparative Law* (Hart Publishing, Oxford 2004) 48.

88 Zweigert and Kötz, 33.

89 Van Hoecke, 48 and O Sandrock, *Uber Sinn und Methode der zivilistischen Rechtsvergleichung* (Alfred Metzner Verlag, Frankfurt a.M./Berlin 1966) 622.

90 As Danneman argues: "*There is no point in comparing what is identical, and little point in comparing what has nothing in common*". See Dannemann, 384.

since it depends on the precise topic of the research.[91] In principle all legal systems can be compared with every other legal system.[92] As voiced by a wide range of renowned scholars in the field of comparative legal research, as a guiding principle, the choice of legal systems ultimately depends on the main aim and objectives of the particular research.[93] I endorse the position that this should be considered the first criterion.[94] A blueprint for making a selection of legal systems does not exist.[95] The main aim and objectives of this research have been addressed, i.e. explore to what extent the regulatory frameworks on a national level in the Netherlands and Germany, on a European level, and on an international level, governing the taxation of (cross-border) statutory, occupational and personal pensions, are fit for the provision of effective information (net amounts) and, and if not so, what legal/non-legal interventions and measures are needed to ensure, and potentially foster, the effectiveness of the information provided. How this lens of 'effective pension information' is demarcated, and operationalised, shall be elucidated in more detail in chapter 2 of this research. The link between research objective and the selection of the Netherlands and Germany, will be considered in more detail below.

The selection of these two jurisdictions relies (partly) on the second approach, set forth by Oderkerk.[96] This approach restricts the number of eligible legal systems to a pre-selected group of systems, usually based on a number of factors, i.e. *Auswahlkriterium*. Given the fact that the research's objective revolves around the cross-border taxation of pensions, including the Netherlands, it was clear that the jurisdictions to be included, had to concern neighbouring jurisdictions. This narrowed down the range of eligible jurisdictions to either Belgium or Germany. Eventually, Germany was added to the comparison for the following reasons. Firstly, Germany and the Netherlands are neighbouring states, both facing a significant amount of increasing labour mobility, and pension mobility.[97] Besides, both states have several so-called cross-border regions alongside their border, where citizens in particular cope with cross-border issues, e.g. the taxation of pensions in cross-

91 Zweigert and Kötz, 41: *"It is difficult to speak generally of how the comparatist should limit his field of inquiry, since it all depends on the precise topic of his research."*

92 Ibid. 42.

93 See for instance PA de Cruz, *Modern Approach to Comparative Law* (Kluwer, Deventer 1993) 36-37 and JC Reitz, 'How to Do Comparative Law?' 46 American Journal of Comparative Law.

94 Reitz.

95 Oderkerk, 'The Importance of Context: Selecting Legal Systems in Comparative Legal Research' 306.

96 Ibid. 295.

97 Where 'labour mobility' entails mobility of workers during their active working period, 'pension mobility' considers the mobility of pensions after retirement, i.e. during the passive period. It is therefore stressed that 'pension mobility' does not consider the mobility of the pension as such, i.e. due to, for instance, the possibility of international value transfer of the pension between Member States.

border situations.[98] Germany remains one of the main destination countries for EU movers (3.4 million of working age EU movers).[99] What is more, Germany, although also being an important country of origin, still has the largest absolute net incoming mobility, followed by the Netherlands. With respect to cross-border workers, Germany is one of the main countries of destination (378,000).[100] What is more, Germany is one of the most important EU destination country for high-skilled movers (789,000).

Secondly, the development and structure of the pension landscape – and the eventual according tax treatment – raise pertinent questions in the context of this research's subject. Both countries have undergone/are in the process of significant reforms of their pension system – and tax treatment – in recent years, which raise interesting question in the light of this research's objective. With respect to the more 'reflecting' nature of this research's objective[101], i.e. gaining insight into the law from a given perspective, it is expected to find interesting differences in the two legal systems concerned. For instance, the significant role of the third pension pillar in Germany as part of the pension landscape in comparison to the rather minor – yet increasing – role of the third pillar pensions in the Netherlands – and Belgium – is interesting in view of this research's objective. The same – but reverse in terms of importance in both countries – reasoning holds true with respect to the role of second pillar pensions in these states. Furthermore, the interaction between the different forms of pensions in order to secure and maintain the standard of living at retirement especially occurs in Germany due to reforms of the *gesetzliche Rentenversicherung* in the last years. Whilst the German pension system was already considerably more fragmented in terms of *Durchführungswege* compared to the Dutch system, especially

---

98 The number of cross-border employees living in Belgium or Germany but working in the Netherlands in 2018 was considerably higher than the number commuting in the opposite direction. From Germany, almost 43,000 workers cross the border daily to work in the Netherlands, from Belgium almost 41,000. Incidentally, it turns out that inbound cross-border workers often live just across the Dutch border. These cross-border commuters mainly live in relatively small rural municipalities just across the border. The highest concentrations of commuters can be found along the border with Noord-Brabant and Limburg, Twente and Gelderland. In eleven Belgian and German municipalities, more than 10% of the population aged 15 years or older works in the Netherlands. In these municipalities border commuters often have the Dutch nationality. These are often Dutch people who have just crossed the border and continue to work in the Netherlands. From the Netherlands more than 9,000 employees worked in Lower Saxony or North Rhine-Westphalia and 12,000 in Flanders. This is apparent from research by Statistics Netherlands and the statistical offices of North Rhine-Westphalia, Lower Saxony and Belgium, see Grensdata.eu, 'Grenspendel werknemers; nationaliteit, woonland, werkregio (NUTS 3)' <https://opendata.grensdata.eu/portal.html?_la=nl&_catalog=InterReg&tableId=22003NED&_theme=119> accessed 17 December 2020.

99 European Commission, 'Annual Report on Intra-EU Labour Mobility 2022' 11.

100 Ibid. 11.

101 Oderkerk argues that, strictly speaking, it would be better to use the term 'intended applications' of the knowledge obtained, since the only objective of a comparative research project is to obtain knowledge and all other 'objectives' are in fact intended applications. See Oderkerk, 'The Importance of Context: Selecting Legal Systems in Comparative Legal Research' 312.

after the entry into force of the *Altersvermögensgesetz* in 2001 and the *Alterseinkünftegesetz* in 2004, the German pension landscape further diversified. In parallel, this intensified the need of multi-pillar retirement saving in Germany, leading to a more complex retirement saving for pension participants. To a certain extent, the German regulatory system exceeds Belgium in terms of fragmentation, poor coordination, complexity, rigorous developments, and their likely consequences. This is considered most pertinent through the lens of this research's evaluation framework – discussed in chapter 2 – in particular in view of the (translated) non-binding legal principles, which allow for the evaluation of the regulatory frameworks' fitness.

What is more, in the Netherlands a rigorous reform of the occupational pension system is ongoing, pursuant to the *Wet Toekomst Pensioenen*, which will be dealt with elaborately in chapter 6.[102] This reform is extensive and contains fundamental changes to the pension system, and can be considered one of the most significant pension system changes in recent decades throughout Europe. It is, for instance, more ground-breaking than the implementation of the *reine Beitragszusage*, pursuant to the *Betriebsrentenstärkungsgesetz*. Such a development is not that apparent in, for instance, Belgium. All things considered in the above, this renders the comparison of these two legal systems more interesting, and it was expected to lead to a worthwhile comparison, revealing (expected) innovative outcomes.[103]

Thirdly, as regards the stage of development of the regulatory framework governing the taxation of cross-border situations, both jurisdictions have reached the same stage, i.e. they are considered developed in the field of the cross-border taxation of pensions.[104] This ensures a baseline of similarity. Also as regards the pensions systems, both jurisdictions can be considered 'mature'. Fourthly, as regards the argument of 'legal families' supporting this selection, the following can be pointed out.[105] It concerns two pension systems each classified differently, i.e. where the German social security pension system is considered the archetype of Bismarckian retirement systems, the Dutch social security pension system is most often classified as a Beveridge system. This uniqueness of the statutory pension systems in both country render the legal comparison so complex, and, attractive.

102 Kamerstukken II, *Wet toekomst pensioenen* (2019/20).

103 See also Dannemann, 384.

104 Cf. Reitz, 506. De Cruz contends that this does not always needs to be the case because the aim of the research project determines the selection, de Cruz.

105 As regards the use 'legal families', see K Zweigert, 'Zur Methode der Rechtsvergleichung' 13 Studium Generale 193; Zweigert and Kötz.

Importing the legal structure of a pension system from one state to the other is, hence, fairly complex.[106]

Fifth, the discussion on *Säulenübergreifende Altersvorsorgeinformation* has emerged and developed in Germany. Comparing the Netherlands – as a country in which a national pension tracking service already exists – to Germany – a state in the implementation phase of a national pension tracking service – raises questions that are of great importance both from an academic perspective, as well as from a practical perspective.[107] As in the Netherlands, Germany, too, is working on the European ambition to develop a pension register in each European Member State. The first steps towards a German Pension Portal date back ten years. Whereas until recently there were doubts about the political willingness in Germany to develop a German pension portal, such a pension register is now receiving a great deal of attention.[108] This ambition was, eventually, implemented through the *Gesetz Digitale Rentenübersicht.*[109] A digital pension overview will be developed and introduced, enabling citizens to access information about their own entitlements, i.e. projected benefits, arising from statutory, occupational and private pension schemes via a portal.[110] The *Digitale Rentenübersicht* serves to improve citizens' level of knowledge about their respective retirement provision, and contains information in particular about its

106 Cf. Y Stevens, *EU Pension Law* (Elgar European Law, Edward Elgar Publishing, Cheltenham 2022) 9.

107 Herewith, the objective and methodology of the underlying thesis is in accordance with the research objectives of the Faculty of Law of Maastricht University, interfaculty and interdisciplinary research, i.e. research that combines insights from different scientific fields of research and whereby differences between these disciplines are resolved. Secondly, the focus of thesis as well as the research focus of ITEM, i.e. cross-border cooperation and mobility, constitutes one of the research pillars of the Faculty.

108 In addition to the fact that the pension register was included in the election programme of both the FDP and *die Grüne*, the coalition agreement between the new coalition partners CDU, CSU and SPD also expressed the ambition to introduce a pillar-overarching pension information system, allowing German citizens an insight into their individual pension situation, fragmented over all three pension pillars. See Koalitionsvertrag zwischen CDU, CSU und SPD, *Ein neuer Aufbruch für Europa, Eine neue Dynamik für Deutschland, Ein neuer Zusammenhalt für unser Land* (2018) 93. This ambition has been responded to in the *Betriebsrentenstärkungsgesetz.* See Gesetz zur Stärkung der betrieblichen Altersversorgung und zur Änderung anderer Gesetze (Betriebsrentenstärkungsgesetz). In addition to the importance of strengthening the German occupational pension schemes, this law stresses the importance of complete, comprehensible, reliable and comparable cross-pillar pension information for an adequate pension provision. See 29.

109 Gesetz zur Verbesserung der Transparenz in der Alterssicherung und der Rehabilitation sowie zur Modernisierung der Sozialversicherungswahlen und zur Änderung anderer Gesetze (Gesetz Digitale Rentenübersicht).

110 As the overview is designed purely as a means of obtaining information, further offers in the direction of advice or recommendations for action cannot be seriously guaranteed without knowledge of many individual factors of the citizens, such as the individual household context. Entwurf eines Gesetzes zur Verbesserung der Transparenz in der Alterssicherung und der Rehabilitation sowie zur Modernisierung der Sozialversicherungswahlen (Gesetz Digitale Rentenübersicht) 77.

(expected) amount, in order to facilitate them in their retirement planning.[111] For this purpose, the information should be reliable, comprehensible and as comparable as possible.[112] Without the introduction of this Digital Pension Overview, it would remain difficult for citizens to get an overall view of their (German) benefits they can expect from their pension provision.[113] The project is a milestone in the field of old-age provision in Germany's diverse and complex pension landscape, with the central added value being the clear presentation of pension entitlements arising from all three pillars.[114]

Most interesting from this research's perspective, is that the amount of future pension benefits will be depicted as a gross amount.[115] Yet, the majority of benefits will be subject to taxation during the pay-out phase.[116] Against this background, the findings of this study

111 Furthermore, offering a digital pension overview is intended to provide an incentive to deal more intensively with one's own old-age provision, i.e. raising peoples' pension awareness, and strengthening consumer sovereignty.

112 See § 1 Gesetz zur Verbesserung der Transparenz in der Alterssicherung und der Rehabilitation sowie zur Modernisierung der Sozialversicherungswahlen und zur Änderung anderer Gesetze (Gesetz Digitale Rentenübersicht). The Digital Pension Overview will be implemented gradually. The Digital Pension Overview is to be introduced 21 months after the entry into force of this Act in an initial operational phase with selected pension funds.

113 Since the information currently provided by the statutory, occupational and private pension schemes shows significant differences in presentation, is not always easy for citizens to understand and is only suitable to a very limited extent for obtaining an overall view of the pension benefits already achieved or achievable in old age. See Entwurf eines Gesetzes zur Verbesserung der Transparenz in der Alterssicherung und der Rehabilitation sowie zur Modernisierung der Sozialversicherungswahlen (Gesetz Digitale Rentenübersicht) 60, 67 In principle, all pension funds/institutions will be legally obliged to connect to the Central Office for the Digital Pension Overview, and to provide pension status reports at least annually. For pension funds/institutions that are not legally obliged to do so, currently for example providers of *Direktzusagen*, *berufsständische Versorgungswerke* or providers of the pension scheme for civil servants, judges and soldiers, the option of a voluntary connection remains. See ibid. 63. See also § 7 Gesetz Digitale Rentenübersicht.

114 The digital pension overview covers all pension schemes under the statutory old-age provision. As regards occupational pension provisions, reference is made to the *Betriebsrentengesetz* and its legal definition (section 1(1) sentence 1 BetrAVG). In the case of private old-age provision, provision products are covered that clearly serve the purpose of old-age provision, or are typically used by citizens for this purpose. The purpose intended by citizens is to be taken into account, whereby the purpose must be reflected in externally recognisable circumstances in order to avoid a proliferation of the most diverse products that have no direct connection to old-age provision. Private life insurance contracts (*Lebensversicherungsverträge*) are therefore only covered if the contractually agreed start of benefit receipt is close to retirement. Hence, reaching the 60th year of life is set. Thus, *Sparverträge* or, for example, *Fondssparpläne* without a recognisable purpose for old-age provision are generally not covered (except for pension schemes in the form of *Fonds- or Banksparplänen*), since these typically do not provide for an expiry date, and can thus be used for old-age provision in individual cases, but can also be used without restrictions at an earlier point in time and for other purposes due to the product design. This has been stipulated in § 2 Gesetz Digitale Rentenübersicht.

115 Entwurf eines Gesetzes zur Verbesserung der Transparenz in der Alterssicherung und der Rehabilitation sowie zur Modernisierung der Sozialversicherungswahlen (Gesetz Digitale Rentenübersicht) 81.

116 However, no further information on this can be provided in terms of value in the accrual phase, since the household context, tax class, and possible further income are only known to the citizens themselves. In this

have more practical implications, and added value in terms of knowledge valorisation, for Germany, compared to Belgium. When considering the German legislative processes, underlying assumptions and pinpointed challenges in terms of pension information provision were more explicitly spelled out, which increased the relevance for the present research.

Sixth, with regard to the objective of this research, it is not appropriate to speak of *Lösungstypen*, as the starting point of this research is not a 'problem' irrespective of what nature, e.g. legal, social or economic. In that regard, it would have been relevant whether the respective countries have a similar social, political and socio-economic structure. In this sense, the systems are comparable but sufficiently divergent. Lastly, as this research covers all three pension pillars, ranging from the first to the third, in two jurisdictions, including European and international law, it was decided to include no more than two countries, in order to keep the scope of the research proportionate.

1.4.1.A.IV Evaluation Criteria: External

This research incorporates external evaluation criteria to draw conclusions, and recommendations.[117] These external criteria are not derived from the law, or the legal system itself, but, rather, from a non-legal field of research. The use of external criteria in the assessment framework, unequivocally, leads to a multi- or interdisciplinary[118] nature of the legal research. This requires data, methods and insights from other scientific disciplines to test a phenomenon by external criteria. These external criteria will be set forth in chapter 2 shaping the conceptual framework. This enables a scholar, for instance, to determine whether a certain legal rule has a 'deterrent effect' in practice, or is 'fit' to attain a certain objective. The latter forms the main objective of this research, i.e. to explore to what extent the regulatory frameworks are fit for the provision of effective pension information.

---

regard, the pension information's effectiveness can be called into question. At the very least, however, information on whether taxes and/or social security contributions are to be paid shall be provided, see § 5, para 1, nr. 5 Gesetz Digitale Rentenübersicht.

117 It can also be referred to as 'assessment by reference on external standard'. See S Taekema and B Van Klink, 'On the Border. Limits and Possibilities of Interdisciplinary Research' in S Taekema and B Van Klink (eds.), *Law and Method* (Mohr Siebeck, Tübingen 2011) 9-10. Tijssen, 74 G van Dijck, *Kwaliteit van de juridische annotatie: een empirische studie naar kenmerken en kwaliteitsindicatoren* (Boom Juridische Uitgevers, Den Haag 2011) 22 and AR Mackor, 'Legal Doctrine as a Non-Normative Discipline' Recht en Methode 79.

118 Where multidisciplinary refers to the situation where the researcher will use and interpret existing research results or data originating from other scientific domains, interdisciplinary requires the researcher to produce results and data himself by harnessing methods from other scientific disciplines.

1.4.1.A.V Normative Guidance of External (Behavioural) Criteria

However, these external evaluation criteria should be treated with caution as regards their normativity for the law as such, i.e. conclusions offered by the empirical study are to be taken cautiously. Although economic-psychological research is no longer in its infancy, empirical studies often merely provide isolated results, rather than integrative models or theories of people's behaviour.[119] Findings obtained through simulation studies in laboratories can, hence, be criticised as a mere weak proxy for actual behaviour. What is more, research on economic behaviour faces a bulk of methodological issues, vague conceptualisations of phenomena (deviating across different fields of research), heterogeneous operationalisation of assumed determinants of behaviour, heterogeneity of results etc. As has become apparent by the empirical study's results, effects of determinants on people's perceptions were even found to point in the opposite direction to expectations, grounded on the theoretical background. This may either be due to methodological shortcomings in the design of the study, or due to disregarding relevant differentiating variables. These different outcomes may be even be attributed to subjects' cultural or political differences which have been neglected. Furthermore, often the effect of variables is explored in isolation in a laboratory setting, where in many real-life contexts many variables operate jointly.[120] In addition, in general, the effect of cultural differences on certain outcomes are overlooked.

Hence, attention must be paid to 'over-generalisation', i.e. insights gained from empirical research cannot always be copied and applied in other situations without difficulty. Therefore, empirical results should be treated with the appropriate caution when incorporating them into possible 'legal norms', or dictating how 'the law ought to be'. Nevertheless, the accumulated knowledge on people's behaviour as regards economic/financial decisions is of practical relevance for policy-making, in terms of an empirically-informed approach to law- and policy-making. This will be dealt with thoroughly in chapter 2.

This is related to the underlying fundamental question of the normativity of theories: can normative criteria for legal practice be extracted from non-legal theories? For instance, as the scientific domain of behavioural law and economics has not yet developed a normative theory of its own. Empirical findings as such do not readily generate normative conclusions.[121] Furthermore, linking empirical findings too directly to normative

119 Cf. E Kirchler, *The Economic Psychology of Tax Behaviour* (Cambridge University Press, New York 2007) xv.

120 See, for instance, RE Petty and others, 'To Think or Not to Think: Exploring Two Routes to Persuasion' in TC Brock and MC Green (eds.), *Persuasion: Psychological insights and perspectives* (Sage, Thousand Oaks 2005) 100.

121 Cf. A Watson, 36, 39.

conclusions runs the risk of non-valid conclusions. This relates to several facts. The findings of behavioural economics are not necessarily useful for legal researchers, in particular since contextual factors have been shown to exert influence on decision-making.[122] Hence, with respect to the evidence on human behaviour obtained in laboratory settings, the high degree of decontextualization, commonly strived for in laboratory experiments, triggers the question as to whether the examined behavioural patterns will have the same effect in a particularised legal setting.[123] The mere extrapolation of experimental/empirical findings, and neglecting the difficulties of translating sometimes highly context-dependent behavioural patterns into legal settings, and drawing broadly applied prescriptive conclusions can be hazardous, in particular in the absence of more refined theories on the behaviour in question.[124] Nevertheless, these findings can be used for drafting behaviourally informed policy.[125] I endorse Teubner's argument that the way out of this dilemma is to choose a 'distanced approach', whereby the law does not take (social) theories (or insights) at their nominal value, but in a (complex) process of translation, generating 'added value' to legal doctrine.[126] Chapter 2 of this research revolves around this process of translation, rather than extrapolation. Non-legal theories do not necessarily dictate how the law ought to be. These insights, rather, should be used to establish a non-binding framework through which the law shall be evaluated. As will be advocated in chapter 10 of this thesis, policymakers shall have recourse to such a framework in drafting rules and regulations, enabling to incorporate (and weigh) numerous viewpoints and interests related to 'the law', and its corresponding application. It ought to widen the 'paradigm' of law-, and policy-making. In doing so, this research evaluates the law as it stands ('law in the books') through the perspective delineated by the external evaluation criteria ('the law in action').[127] This contextual approach (or 'law in context') – shaped by the external evaluation criteria – helps to explore the operation in

122 J De Coninck, 'Behavioural Economics and Legal Research' in M van Hoecke (ed.), *Methodologies of legal research: which kind of method for what kind of discipline?* (Hart Publishing, Oxford 2011) 265.

123 H Siebert, 'The harmonization issue in Europe: Prior agreement or a competitive process?' in H Siebert (ed.), *The completion of the internal market* (Mohr, Tübingen 1990) 363, 374 and L Kaplow, 'An economic analysis of legal transitions' Harvard Law Review 441, 445 ff.

124 Siebert, 364 who puts it as follows: *"Das Herzstück der Verhaltenswissenschaft sind empirische Befunde. Man muss diese Befunde richtig deuten und ihre Tragweite richtig einschätzen . . . oft fehlen empirische Ergebnisse gerade dort, wo man als Jurist besonders auf sie angewiesen wäre . . . Dann kann man sich nur noch mit Hypothesen helfen. Dafür bräuchte man durchdachte Theorie. Leider fehlt sie oft . . . auch dort, wo man auf empirische Resultate oder theoretische Modelle zurückgreifen kann, sollte man im Auge behalten, dass sie mit einem ganz anderen Erkenntnisinteresse gewonnen worden sind. Deshalb versteht sich die Integration verhaltenswissenschaftlicher Ergebnisse oder Einsichten in das recht nicht von selbst."*

125 See CR Sunstein, 'Empirically Informed Regulation' 78 The university of Chicago Law Review 1349.

126 F Teubner, 'Law and Social Theory: Three Problems' 1 Asian Journal of Law and Society 1.

127 See Örücü, 39.

practice of this particular legal field, which is more revealing than the mere exposition of the legal rules under investigation.

The research question of this thesis will be answered by studying the positive national legislation on the tax treatment of statutory, occupational and individual pensions in the Netherlands and Germany. This part is predominantly of a descriptive nature, and based on positive national pension tax law. The application of this positive law on pensions in cross-border situations may in some cases lead to inconsistency, as will be elaborated on later in this thesis.

At this point, it should be pointed out that a strict legal research framework as such, solely based on legal notions and principles, will not be set up and used. Examples of such principles are tax neutrality, freedom of persons (art. 21 TFEU), freedom of workers (art. 45 TFEU) and simplicity of taxation or equality of taxation. This type of principle-based research framework would not fully fit the purpose of this research, as the research serves multidisciplinary purposes.

1.4.1.B Comparing Regulatory Frameworks: Combining Research Designs

Besides the aforementioned, this research will be conducted from a comparative point of view, regarding the Netherlands and Germany. The national legislation of each of these two Member States will be taken into account to the extent it is relevant for the underlying research, as incongruities in the application of this national legislation can lead to cross-border issues. For this purpose, the comparative research design has been employed, apart from the issue whether there is such a thing as 'the' or 'a' comparative design.[128] I endorse this theorem since the goal of the research determines which method, and the way in which it is conducted, is best suited for carrying out the research. The comparative design can be divided into several steps[129]:

1. A functional question: how are (cross-border) pensions taxed in the Netherlands, and Germany?
2. Describe the legal systems of the Netherlands, and Germany;
3. List similarities and differences in taxing these pensions;
4. Adopt a new point of view from which the differences and similarities should be considered (the effective information provision-perspective);
5. Evaluate findings critically.

128 Cf. FL Leeuw and H Schmeets, *Empirical Legal Research: A Guidance Book for Lawyers, Legislators and Regulators* (Edward Elgar, Cheltenham 2016) 115 and cited literature.

129 See J Husa, 'About the Methodology of Comparative Law – Some Comments Concerning the Wonderland' (Working Paper, Faculty of Law, Maastricht University, 2007) 8-9 and Leeuw and Schmeets, 115.

Since there is no single method or single perspective (or design) exclusive to comparative research, I decided to extract, adapt and apply Husa's approach, while using a slightly different approach.[130] Moreover, this approach reflects the need that comparative law should be set up to serve a new and important role. This (adapted) approach allows to adopt a new point of view from which the explanations of differences and similarities should be considered and, subsequently, to critically evaluate the findings.[131] Findings might suggest that regulatory frameworks do not fit certain needs. For these reasons, I endorse Leeuw's theorem; to combine research designs of experimental empirical research and a comparative research design.[132] As Eberle states, through comparative law we can embark on a new course as we try to figure out what to do in our modern, increasingly globalized world.[133] This research is aimed at comparing the effect of the different fields of multi-level (national) legislation, functioning alongside each other, and evaluating the effect of differences and similarities between the diverging national legal orders from an information provision-perspective.

This research brings together research that has, traditionally, been fragmented into fields of legal and economical-psychological scholarship. Although each of these fields of academia acknowledge the necessity to be aware of each other's findings, yet little research has created a 'coherent framework' that can embody different fields of research. Hence, this research seeks to integrate these two fields of research. By doing so, this research aims to fill the present gap between these two 'camps' of academia by integrating insights from both fields. It seeks to discuss those findings that are both scientifically cutting-edge, and practically applicable, for policy-making.

1.4.1.C Functional Method of Comparative Law

It should be pointed out *a priori* that the present research uses a comparative method *sui generis*, i.e. it is adapted to the specific topic, research question and objective of this research, in order to get a well-founded understanding of 'fitness' of the legal systems in question. The present thesis, although partly, harnesses the functional method of comparative law research, in which the comparison forms a function in evaluating legislation in the concerning legal orders. This method rests on the idea that different societies encounter similar problems/ needs, and in order to cope with these problems/ needs each of these societies provide for different (legal) rules that are, nonetheless,

130 A Orücü, 'Methodology of comparative law' in J Smits (ed.), *Elgar Encyclopedia of Comparative Law* (Edward Elgar, Cheltenham 2012) and Leeuw and Schmeets, 115.

131 Husa, 8-9 and Leeuw and Schmeets, 115.

132 Leeuw and Schmeets, 117.

133 E Eberle, 'The method and role of Comparative law' 8 Washington University Global Studies Law Review 451, 486.

functionally equivalent.[134] In this regard, it can, strictly speaking, not be said that the taxation of pensions is considered a societal problem. It would, rather, concern the functioning of (tax) legislation constituting a potential obstacle from a certain perspective. Therefore, these regulatory frameworks meet the standard of 'functionally equivalence', in that they pursue the same function, i.e. governing the taxation of cross-border pensions. In doing, these systems have developed different (legal) rules. With this underlying premise (*praesumptio similitudinis*), or point of departure, the functional method is used, while exploring the broader legal context.[135]

It follows from using this functional method that many sources (of law) will be analysed, i.e. case law, circulars (*BMF-schreiben*), formal acts, secondary legislation, double tax conventions etc. As the taxation of pensions in cross-border situations is also increasingly regulated through regulatory frameworks on a European and international level, these fields of law will be analysed as well. It should however be noted, that although different fields of legislation (fiscal legislation, civil law etc.) are incorporated, this study does not employ an internal comparative design.[136] As this research is not aimed at disentangling how the different fields of national legislation address or deal with certain phenomena, the internal comparative design is not harnessed.

1.4.2 *Empirical Research*

1.4.2.A Combining Research Designs: Empirical and Comparative

Empirical legal research may serve a variety of purposes, in the light of evaluating legislation.[137] From a legal perspective, the objective of the underlying experiment is to evaluate the legal arrangements, applied to the fiscal treatment of pensions in cross-border pensions, from an information provision-perspective. In fact, this research evaluates *ex-post* the effects of legislation – as it stands – on the provision of effective cross-border

134 See Zweigert and Kötz, 34: "the legal system of every society faces essentially the same problems, and solves these problems by quite different means though often with similar results". 'Functionally' equivalence, refers to 'pursuing the same function, such as solving a specific problem', see M Schmitthoff, 'The science of comparative law' Cambridge Law Journal 22.

135 G Frankenberg, 'Critical Comparisons: Re-thinking Comparative Law' Harvard International Law Journal 170. See also Zweigert and Kötz, 36 G Samuel, *Epistemology and Method in Law* (Ashgate, Alderhot 2003) 167 and H Oost and A Markenhof, *Een onderzoek voorbereiden* (HB-uitgevers, Baarn 2007) 98.

136 See for instance AHH Bollen-Vandenboorn, *De fiscale aspecten van pensioendeling bij echtscheiding* (Fiscaal Wetenschappelijke Reeks, SDU, Den Haag 2004) 15 who used an internal comparative design in order to assess the extent to which civil legislation and fiscal legislation complement each other with regard to the division of a pension provision in cases of divorce.

137 For a delineation of the object of empirical research, i.e. 'laws', 'legislation' and 'regulation' please see Leeuw and Schmeets, 3 ff.

pension information.[138] Therefore, evidence-based regulation would be a more appropriate description of the empirical study, since under this method insights from social sciences, including behavioural economics, are used to help legislators.[139] This is in line with the increasing trend towards evidence-based policy making, as made to a priority by the European Commission.[140] Moreover, these insights will be used to ensure effective information provision regarding cross-border pensions. It remains; however, questionable which goals can be considered as the legislators' goals, apart from the question whether the legislator ought to achieve his objectives through legislation, or other 'interventions' (e.g. providing tailored information or incentives of a different nature). This does not necessarily concern objectives that ought to be pursued by the legislator. However, as Sunstein points out, findings of behavioural economics offer important insights for thinking about regulation, and its likely consequences.[141]

As Orücü rightly states, the possibility of comparison is dependent upon the existence and availability of data.[142] In the light of the empirical research, the data gathered will allow me to compare the national legal orders of Germany and the Netherlands with regard to the tax treatment of pensions in cross-border situations. As set forth above, this enables me to adopt a new point of view from which the explanations of differences and similarities should be considered and, subsequently, to critically evaluate the findings.[143] Furthermore, the most suited means to gather this data is by employing methodologies derived from social sciences.[144] This echoes Leeuw's theorem; to combine research designs of experimental empirical research, and a comparative research design.[145]

1.4.2.B Empirical Study: Experimental Design

This research's empirical study has been conducted through an experimental design, while building on certain behavioural mechanisms explored in the field of 'behavioural

138 Rather than, for instance, ex-ante evaluations or process/implementation (of legal arrangement) evaluations. See ibid. 6.

139 As referred to by ibid. 7.

140 As part of the 'Better regulation' project, see European Commission, 'Better regulation: why and how' 2019) <https://ec.europa.eu/info/law/law-making-process/planning-and-proposing-law/better-regulation-why-and-how_en> accessed 29 May 2019.

141 Sunstein, 8.

142 Orücü, 565.

143 Husa, 8-9 and Leeuw and Schmeets, 115.

144 Leeuw and Schmeets, 117. Orücü considers 'evaluation' one of the key elements of comparative law. For instance, the comparativist could be looking for the most 'efficient' rule or could examine 'user-friendliness', 'speed of procedure'.

145 Ibid. 117.

economics'[146] and pension information provision. These existing concepts of information provision, and the underlying behavioural mechanisms have been subsumed in a different communication setting, i.e. communicating on the tax treatment of cross-border pensions.

The method employed in this research is commonly referred to as RCT[147]: randomized controlled trial. The survey's participants allocated to the treatment group were confronted with the intervention (adjusting the information by showing a net amount of future retirement income, a disclaimer, and additional information on the status of the information in the form of an 'important to know-section'). In contrary, the control group was shown a gross amount of future retirement income. This method of randomized experiment allows to explore whether the 'intervention' has led to any change, i.e. determining the causality between the dependent and independent variable, so that an estimate on the counterfactual can be obtained.[148]

As Leeuw states, most methodologists consider this research design as the most sound choice to address causal questions ('attribution'), such as questions on the impact of interventions.[149] This random allocation to the treatment or control group requires that every person in the target population has the same chance as to be selected for either group, avoiding the 'selection bias'.[150] The randomized controlled trial is considered the most robust design to address the research question analysed in this research. After all, the choice of an adequate, commendable, i.e. a 'fitting' research design is a *condition sine qua non* for the production of valid and reliable evidence.[151] In studying causal relationships, RCT is least prone to threats of internal validity.[152] It, thus, enables to draw unambiguous conclusions as possible, and it enables best to eliminate alternative explanations for

146 For this purpose of this research I endorse the definition of 'behavioural economics' given by De Coninck, i.e. "*Without offering a strict definition, behavioural economics can be described through its concern with improving the explanatory and predictive power of traditional neoclassical economics by providing it with psychologically more realistic assumptions on human judgement and decision making, based on well-documented empirical findings that are obtained through a variety of methods.*" See De Coninck, 258. However, it also aims to create progression in the policy field by focusing on the psychological decision making process.

147 This should not be confounded with the abbreviation 'RCT' referring to 'Rational Choice Theory'.

148 As an alternative to using a control and treatment group, a before-and-after comparison of a treated group, without an untreated control group, could have been used. However, in view of potential (adverse) anchoring effects on the participant's response, this method has not been deployed. Moreover, given the higher degree of external validity of results obtained through a randomized experiment, this is most suited for this study, since the empirical part's results may be embraced in policy-making.

149 Leeuw and Schmeets, 104.

150 See for instance P Rossi, M Lipsey and H Freeman, *Evaluation: A Systematic Approach* (Sage, San Fransisco 2003).

151 Cf. Leeuw and Schmeets, 122.

152 See for threats with regard to validity T Cook and D Campbell, *Quasi-Experimentation: Design and Analysis for Field Settings* (Rand McNally, Chicago 1979).

findings.[153] This is of eminent importance given the 'normativity issues' addressed in section 1.4.1.A.V. Moreover, by employing RCT, external validity is guaranteed as far as possible. This high degree of external validity renders the obtained findings more suitable for normative guidance in legal research.[154] Empirical results devoid of these flaws, may better serve as a foundation for generally applicable legal principles, which legislators should observe. What is more, although it is not entirely clear to what extent respondents reveal what they really think, feel, believe and (would) do, a stronger research design, such as an experiment, is less likely to report desirable effects. Research designs without any control group are poorly equipped to provide evidence to determine whether some intervention was the cause of the outcomes recorded.[155] Moreover, this type of research design is attributed to the highest level in the *Maryland Scientific Methods Scale.*[156]

1.5 CONTRIBUTION OF SEPARATE CHAPTERS AND READER'S GUIDE

The research consists of nine chapters. It begins in chapter 1 by setting the scene with several important preliminary matters, such as the grounds for this research, research question, research design, methodology etc. Chapter 2 conceptualises the notion of 'effective information provision', in the light of which the 'fitness' of the regulatory frameworks will be assessed, i.e. the evaluation framework. In doing so, in terms of empirically-gained non-legal insights, this chapter constitutes the framework *generalis.* Chapter 3 revolves around the empirical study conducted as part of this research. This chapter looks more closely at the notion of 'effective pension information' and, in doing so, serves more as the framework *specialis.* Chapter 4 revolves around the notion of 'pension' in terms of notions, terms and concepts embedded in both the Netherlands, and Germany,

153 See R Gomm, *Social Research Methodology* (Palgrave Macmillan, Houndmills 2008) 12-13 who relates internal validity to Popper's falsificationist epistemology. See also D De Vaus, *Research Design in Social Research* (Sage, London 2001).

154 External validity refers to the extent to which a specific result of a study can be generalized to a wider population; i.e. the approximate truth of conclusions that involve generalization. See, for instance, De Coninck, 261 ff.

155 Gomm, 96.

156 This scale is mainly aimed at communicating to academic scholars, policymakers and practitioners that studies evaluating the effects of criminological interventions differ with regard to methodological quality. Although, primarily aimed at criminological interventions, this scale may be applied to interventions used in other fields of research. Level 5 of the scale refers to methodologies using random assignment and analysis of comparable units to programme and comparison groups. This scale was published as a methodological appendix in the Sherman report: L Sherman and others, 'Preventing crime: what works, what doesn't, what's promising?' Washington DC: Nationale Institute of Justice.The RCT is also ranked as most adequate design in several other publications; see for instance: S Bagshaw and R Bellomo, 'The need to reform our assessment of evidence from clinical trials: a commentary' 3 Philosophy, Ethics, and Humanities in Medicine 1.

as well as several pension classification systems. This will also be evaluated through the lens of 'effective cross-border pension information'. Chapter 5 discusses the relevant fundamentals of the statutory (government-run) pension systems in both countries, as well as their tax treatment (in cross-border situations). It does not address all fundamentals of this system, but merely focuses on those that are of particular importance for the purpose of this research. Along the same lines, chapter 6 looks more closely into occupational pension schemes in both countries. As will become apparent, these pension schemes are fairly different in their form and nature when comparing the Netherlands to Germany. Chapter 7 will proceed by looking into personal pension schemes in the Netherlands and Germany. Chapters 5, 6 and 7 respectively have a similar format in considering the relevant rules in domestic law. These chapters form the central base of the comparison, outlining the background material that is relevant in the evaluations. These chapter are structured under two main headings. The first considers the tax treatment of (cross-border) pensions during the accrual phase (i.e. the pension contributions); where the second part proceeds to consider the tax treatment of pension benefits paid out during the pay-out phase. These headings thus identify a range of tax fundamentals that are important when projected into the evaluation framework.

Chapter 8 will discuss the relevant rules on a European level, considering how the taxation of cross-border pensions is affected by EU law, i.e. exploring how EU law might alter the tax treatment of the relevant cross-border pension. Chapter 9 revolves around the relevant rules on an international level. As regards the latter, this part will broadly follow the structure of the applicable tax treaty, and deals with the different types of relevant treaty provisions separately. Each of the descriptive chapters mapping out the regulatory frameworks, is concluded by an interim conclusion where, along the principles set out in chapter 2 (evaluation framework) the regulatory frameworks will be assessed for their fitness in view of the provision of effective pension information. Chapter 10 looks at the bigger picture, where I will reflect on the research process, evaluated through the lens of the evaluation framework as set forth in chapter 2, answer the main research question, draw conclusions, and put forward recommendations.

2 Evaluation Framework: Assessing Multi-Level Legal Systems through the Lens of Effective Pension Information Provision

As has been set forth in the introductory chapter, this research's first goal is to establish an evaluation framework, building on theory and concepts extracted from the domains of behavioural economics, economic psychology and cognitive psychology focusing on effective (pension) information provision. This chapter deals with the first sub-research question what constitutes a theoretical/conceptual evaluation framework for providing effective (pension) information? The (international) literature is void of an evaluation framework of this kind - focused on this matter - which makes it difficult to expose any shortcomings or inconsistencies in the legal frameworks at issue. This chapter also addresses how these empirically-gained insights can be translated into (more legal applicable) principles along which the multi-level legal systems can be evaluated more aptly. Hence, this chapter establishes such a framework.

This chapter revolves around the insights shaping the foundation of this research's analytical framework. However, solely those empirically-obtained insights are mapped out considered relevant for the purpose of this study. In particular, the objectives of this chapter are to introduce the reader to Rational Choice Theory, the science of behavioural economics, explain the idea of Dual Process Theory, explore the construct of 'social representations' and delineate the notion of 'effectiveness' of information. The lens is also broadened to incorporate tensions arising in information provision, eventually exposing the evaluation framework's boundaries. Through this elaboration, it becomes clear what effective information provision encompasses, and allow for the identification of principles the regulatory frameworks should observe, yielding many fruitful implications for the provision of information. In doing so, this chapter paves the way for the evaluation of the regulatory frameworks, consisting of psychological and sociological variables, and structural characteristics (for instance, the system's complexity). It, thus, adopts a multi-faceted approach. This chapter seeks to discuss those findings that are both scientifically cutting-edge and practically applicable. After assembled with the legal (comparative) research part, it will provide an integrated account of the shortcomings or inconsistencies of the underlying regulatory frameworks, from an information's perspective. What is more, this framework serves as this research's evaluation framework, allowing for the assessment of the regulatory frameworks, i.e. exploring to what extent they are 'fit' as they stand, and from which perspective recommendations will be set forth. It thus relates to this research's main research question, i.e. to explore what legal/non-legal interventions and measures are needed to ensure, and potentially foster, the effectiveness of the information provided.

It is to be noted that the results of the empirical research study, performed as part of this research, will be thoroughly discussed in chapter 3. This empirical study forms – a more particular – part of the notion of what effective pension information should entail. However, the theoretical background discussed in the chapter below, also serves to illustrate this empirical study's theoretical foundations. The value of these empirically-gained insights – in terms of normativity – for legal science have been discussed extensively in chapter 1.

2.1 Rational Choice Theory, Bounded Rationality, and Information Processing

As an underlying mechanism, theories play a foundational role in this research's evaluation framework. Although the theories, presuppositions and mechanisms, underlying the studied regulatory fiscal frameworks, will not be analysed, the role of theories is evident in the empirical part on effective information provision. The theory dealt with in this research, is Rational Choice Theory (RCT). This neoclassical theory of economics portrays people as fully rational, Bayesian, utility maximizing decision makers who have limitless cognitive abilities, motivation, and adhere to the rules of classical statistics.[157] What is more, a key assumption is that if people are provided with sufficient information, they will thoroughly process the information, understand the personal relevance of the information, and choose the option that best caters their personal circumstances, and preferences, accordingly. This assumption of rationality echoes the metaphor of 'homo economicus'. This tends to be a long-serving benchmark for the field of law and policy with respect to (pension) information disclosure. What is more, explanations and predictions of people's choice, in everyday life as well as in social sciences are founded on these fundamental assumptions.[158] In this vein, rational choice theory can be qualified as an 'intervention theory', i.e. the (typically implicit) assumptions of policymakers, legislators, practitioners, lawyers.[159] This increasing tide in this field of research has continued to grow into the present. Although the definition of 'rationality' has not been clearly delineated, there is a

157 Kirchler, 129. See also S Dhami, *The Foundations of Behavioral Economics Analysis* (Oxford University Press, 2016) 1339.

158 Cf. A Tversky and D Kahneman, 'The Framing of Decisions and the Psychology of Choice' 211 Science.

159 Leeuw and Schmeets, 68.

general agreement that rational choices should reflect some elementary requirements of consistency and coherence.[160]

This neoclassical 'rational choice theory', has been refuted by a wide range of findings in the field of behavioural economics, economic psychology and cognitive psychology. These findings showed in the past years that individuals behave systematically – and predictably – different than assumed under RCT. Moreover, these findings prove that people are, particularly in decision-making, myopic, prone to biases, heuristics and inclined to use rules of thumb. For instance, people try to reduce complexity; use heuristics and are prone to biases if they try to understand information and make a decision accordingly. Heuristics are decision rules used by people that are fast (in terms of time required to take the decision) and frugal (in terms of information requirements).[161] Rather than a collection of empirical facts, a growing array of theoretical models on heuristics, and biases, has emerged over the years. For instance, research demonstrates that people are limited information processors, and the more complex a situation is, the more people deviate from what the rational model predicted.[162] Simon conceptualised this as 'bounded rationality' under which people violate, often systematically, the pivots of rationality and lack the ability, and motivation and time, to consider all relevant information in a complex decision-making situation.[163]

Thus, people, in reality, fall victim to numerous heuristics and biases in decision-making, leading to inconsistent judgments and evaluations.[164] These 'cognitive heuristics' are termed as processes to solve problems or take decisions without considering the complexity of all the information, all alternatives, in order to abbreviate the problem-solving or decision-making process, and reach a timely solution.[165] They serve as 'rules of thumb' allowing for 'mental shortcuts' in complex situations, such as retirement planning and tax-

160 Tversky and Kahneman, 453. For instance, depending on whether the outcomes are described as involving gains or involving losses, people's preferences may shift to risk averse or risk taking respectively.

161 Dhami, 1339.

162 Kirchler, 130.

163 HA Simon, 'A behavioral model of rational choice' 69 Quarterly Journal of Economics 99.

164 In the vein of this research's objective, research findings demonstrate that the quantitative frame in which the retirement income prospect is presented, affects individuals' retirement perceptions, i.e. a frame where the future retirement income is represented as a percentage of the current income (percentage frame) seems to result in a better estimate of the degree to which the future (projected) pension is (in)sufficient compared to the euro frame (future retirement income depicted in euros), and a decimal frame (future retirement income presented as decimal of current income). See H Prast and F Teppa, 'Pensioenperceptie: de non-neutraliteit van kwantitatieve communicatie' 21 TPV. See also H Prast and F Teppa, 'The Power of Percentage: Quantitative Framing of Pension Income Communication' 2017 CentER Discussion Paper (Tilburg Center for Economic Research).

165 Kirchler, 131 and cited literature.

related behaviour. This illustrates that the rhetoric of 'rational economic persons' is far from an abstract idea and can become the guide for dealing with everyday life and social problems.[166] In the section below, this idea will be focused on the processing, and perception, of information by individuals, under dual process theory.

2.2 Dual Process Theory: Thinking Fast, Thinking Slow

As has been addressed in the preceding section, the foundational assumptions of Rational Choice Theory have been refuted by a growing body of empirical findings. The cornerstone of most findings in the latter domain for the purpose of this research, is formed by the so-called Dual Process Theory.[167] Numerous well-known scholars in the field of psychology have come to the conclusion that two ways of thinking/ information processing can be distinguished, i.e. dual processing models. This theory provides a generalizable framework for organizing, categorizing, and understanding the basic processes underlying (complex) information processing.[168] This helps in getting a better understanding of what type of information (provision) aids people in making more informed decisions. For the present research, the model allows to infer what effective information provision would entail, and set up an assessment framework for the provision of effective information, building on certain principles. It underlies this research's empirical study – chapter 3 – as well.

Dual Process Theory identifies two distinct routes in which persons come to hold a reasonable attitude or make decisions, and how people are persuaded by information interventions in this regard. Generally, people want to have correct attitudes and beliefs, as this will usually proves to be most helpful in life.[169] These distinct routes of information processing and decision-making have different characteristics: think fast (subconscious), thinking slow (conscious). Where the central (conscious) route entails careful thinking and examining information central to a topic, the peripheral (subconscious) route requires less cognitive effort where people rely on a relatively simple and accessible decision-making process. The latter operates automatically and quickly, with little or no effort and no sense of voluntary control, i.e. people try to come to a reasonable attitude in a rather intuitive way, i.e. the information's source seems to be reliable or information appears to be correct based on a person's first impression. Moreover, under the peripheral

166 Cf. J Cullis and A Lewis, 'Why people pay taxes: From a conventional economic model to a model of social convention' 18 Journal of Economic Psychology 305, 310.

167 A key study in the regard is A Tversky and D Kahneman, 'Judgment under Uncertainty: Heuristics and Biases' 185 Science 1124.

168 RE Petty and JT Cacioppo, 'The Elaboration Likelihood Model of Persuasion' 19 Advances in Experimental Social Psychology 123, 125.

169 Petty and others, 83.

(subconscious) route people tend to tap into heuristics, biases, and other 'mental shortcuts', as these reduce the cognitive load and shorten the decision-making process. These two routes, obviously, constitute the extremes of a realm where people either engage in a comprehensive analysis prior to forming an opinion, or rely on a simple, intuitive way of evaluation. Generally, people find themselves somewhere in between these two extremes. These two extremities ways of think are rarely incited; mostly people rely on a combination of the central and peripheral route. In general, information provision on pensions, and taxes, tends to be geared to the conscious route, assuming that people possess full motivation, ability and time to carefully think over all information provided. However, in the section below it will become apparent that the conscious route of processing information is less often used, compared to the subconscious route. The two systems mapped out in the section above can be summarized as follows:

Figure 2.1 Dual Process Theory

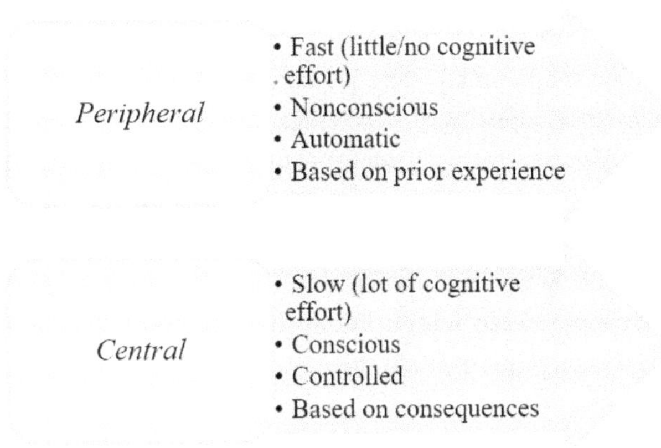

A key finding under Dual Process Theory shows that people neither have the ability nor the motivation to evaluate everything with care.[170] People are busy all day long, have many things to do and live in an (increasingly) complex world. This holds certainly in the context of pensions and taxes. Even persons fond of evaluating and enjoy thinking about most things, probably simply do not have the time, nor the mental energy (i.e. the need for cognition) to carefully scrutinize every decision and every piece of information they

170 See RE Petty and others, 'To think or not to think? Exploring two routes to persuasion' in TC Brock and MC Green (eds.), *Persuasion: Psychological insights and perspectives* (2nd edn Sage Publications, Thousand Oaks 2005) 82 and cited literature.

encounter.[171] In day-to-day situations, people have to make hundreds of small decisions, and cannot deliberate on each of these decisions. For instance, if people go to the supermarket to do some grocery shopping, they do not carefully read each label on all of the products in a certain category, in order to compare products and, eventually, choose the best product. In contrast, people generally spare their mental energy and reserve their effortful thought process for tasks that they perceive as most deserving. If people are, for instance, overwhelmed with arguments why a certain product is 'good', they will put little effort in deliberating whether it actually is, but will choose the 'path of least resistance' and choose for the relatively simple 'cue'. By adding up all these arguments, it requires little mental energy contrary to the situation of thinking over each of these arguments.

In these situations, people (i.e. the recipient) receive communication (i.e. the message) from another person (i.e. the source) in a specific setting (i.e. the context).[172] Each of these modalities have been demonstrated to be of relevance in influencing peoples' attitudes. For the purposes of this research, the 'recipients' are mobile citizens planning for retirement; the 'message' information about their pension, the 'source' is the pension information provider, and the 'context' refers to planning for retirement in cross-border situations. This implies that adjusting the 'message' may have an impact on people's attitudes. For instance, by presenting participants with the essential information, offering information in a way that is meaningful (e.g. net amount per month, or with a reference point), and explicitly and clearly stating what participants can do with the information, the information is more likely to reach participants. In sum, applying this to retirement planning, it seems that people merely want to know when and how much they will receive, and whether this will be enough to maintain their livelihood after retirement.

The foregoing applies to the present research, in that chapter 3 explores the impact of adjusting information along the ways of providing readers net or gross amounts of future retirement income, and including a disclaimer, on the ease of comprehension, informativeness and perceived trustworthiness of the information, next to the persons' expected future financial security, and behavioural expectations. Parallel to this, the study will disentangle the role of financial literacy, perceived fiscal/ pension literacy and self-efficacy in this regard. Moreover, this foundational model allows to set up an evaluation framework that will be set forth in section 2.5.

---

171 See JT Cacioppo and RE Petty, 'The Need for Cognition' 42 Journal of Personality and Social Psychology 116.

172 Petty and others, 83.

2.2.1 *The Central Route: Effortful Deliberation*

This central (or conscious) route of thinking allocates peoples' attention to mental activities that require a lot of cognitive effort. It, thus, entails careful thinking and deliberation about information encountered. Moreover, in order to evaluate information, people have to be both motivated, and able to do so. As regards motivation, it can be argued that a piece of information has to look sufficiently interesting to think about, and with respect to ability, not every situation provides people with sufficient time for effortful elaboration. In cases where people do have the motivation and time, they carefully evaluate the degree to which the information is fundamental to the person, object or issue at hand.[173]

In forming an opinion/attitude towards a certain topic (e.g. pensions and/or taxes) people relate information they have encountered in 'the message' (for instance, "after reaching the applicable retirement age, you will receive a total net pension income of €X per month") to knowledge and information he/she already possess (i.e. the process of 'anchoring'). This knowledge and information that he/she already possesses constitutes the evaluation framework in the process of forming his/her attitude. This allows people to form a new attitude/opinion (e.g. 'I have to take further action in order to ensure an adequate pension at retirement'), not present in the provided information nor in previous knowledge. This elaborate way of thinking is distinctive for the central route, and can be summarized in three steps: pay careful attention to the relevant information in the message ('as of retirement date I will receive €X per month in pension benefits'); relate that information to prior knowledge stored in memory ('how much do I currently receive as earned income per month'); generate new implications of the information ('is the projected amount of pension income enough to maintain my standard of living after retirement?'). This process of elaboration and deliberation generates so-called cognitive responses. These cognitive responses people may have – in response to the message – may be favourable ('the project amount of retirement income is sufficient') or unfavourable ('the projected amount of retirement income is not sufficient').[174] This process of generating cognitive responses can

173 It is to be noted that with regard to the type of information, research findings demonstrate that the type of information that is considered essential, for any particular issue, varies among persons and from situation to situation. This implies that when people are asked to think about the topic of taxes, some people might consider it from a financial point of view, where for others legal arguments may be more prevailing. See D Katz, 'The functional approach to the study of attitudes' 24 Public Opinion Querterly 163. In addition, people might also differ in their judgements in terms of myopia, i.e. some are concerned about immediate consequences of their actions, where other people are most concerned about the future, See A Strathman and others, 'The consideration of future consequences: Weighing immediate and distant outcomes of behavior' 66 Journal of Personality and Social Psychology 742.

174 Petty and others, 84; AG Greenwald, 'Cognitive learning, cognitive responses to persuasion, and attitude change' in AG Greenwald, TC Brock and TM Ostrom (eds.), *Psychological foundations of attitudes*

be considered a private dialogue in which people respond to the information provided.[175] A substantial body of literature demonstrates that within the framework of the central route, the extent to which attitudes may be affected depends on the valence of the cognitive responses generated, the amount of thoughts, and the confidence that people have in their thoughts (i.e. are they valid and informative?).[176] What is more, attitudes formed under the central route are, in general, expected to be relatively easy to call to memory, relatively persistent and stable over time, relatively resistant to challenge, and relatively predictive of the person's attitude-relevant judgments and behaviour.[177]

Moreover, not only people can deviate as regards the dimensions considered pivotal to their attitudes, but also different attitude objects (decisions) may incite common dimensions of evaluation for most people.[178] In addition, next to individual differences or the particular attitude object at issue, people's dimensions to evaluate an object, person, or an issue can also be determined by the information recently activated in memory.[179] It follows from the foregoing that sometimes peoples' attitudes are formed/changed by the central route of thinking, in which people assess the argument against the background of their relevant experiences and knowledge, and evaluate these arguments along the dimensions which they consider central to the objects. However, this process of careful elaboration does not provide certainty that an 'objectively' accurate opinion will be reached.[180] In this regard, social representations play a central role which will be dealt with in section 2.3.[181]

(Academic Press, New York 1968); RM Perloff and TC Brock, 'And thinking makes it so: Cognitive responses to persuasion' in ME Roloff and GR Miller (eds.), *Persuasion: New directions in theory and research* (Sage, Beverly Hills (California) 1980); RE Petty and others, 'Historical foundations of the cognitive response approach to attitudes and persuasion' in RE Petty, TM Ostrom and TC Brock (eds.), *Cognitive responses in persuasion* (Lawrence Erlbaum, Hillsdale 1981).

175 L Festinger and N Maccoby, 'On resistance to persuasive communications' 68 Journal of Abnormal and Social Psychology 359.

176 Petty and others, 84.

177 See also RE Petty, C Haugtvedt and SM Smith, 'Elaboration as a determinant of attitude strength: Creating attitudes that are persistent, resistant and predictive of behavior' in RE Petty and JA Krosnick (eds.), *Attitude strength: Antecendents and consequences* (Lawrence Erlbaum, Mahwah 1995).

178 S Shavitt, 'The role of attitude objects in attitude functions' 26 Journal of Experimental Social Psychology 124, Petty et al provide the example of judging a person's expectation for admission to graduate school where intelligence is considered central, not attractiveness. Contrarily, if this same person is judged for his/her perspective for a modelling career, attractiveness does play a central role. See Petty and others, 85.

179 SJ Sherman, DM Mackie and DM Driscoll, 'Priming and the differential use of dimensions in evaluation' 16 Personality and Social Psychology Bulletin 405.

180 See RE Petty and JT Cacioppo, *Communication and persuasion: Central and peripheral routes to attitude change* (Springer, New York 1986).

181 See for instance S Moscovici, 'The phenomenon of social representations' in S Moscovici and G Duveen (eds.), *Social representations: Explorations in social psychoogy* (New York University Press, New York 2001).

2.2.2 *The Peripheral Route: Tapping into Simple Cues, Shortcuts, and Rules of Thumb*

The peripheral (or subconscious) route, operates almost automatically, and requires little to no cognitive effort. It constitutes a simple and low effort decision strategy since, in forming attitudes and subsequent attitude's change, people rely on simple cues and shortcuts, for instance, of (information) source attractiveness and message length. This route of thinking is, contrary to the central route, void of effortful thinking and elaboration. This peripheral process, for instance, occurs when people retrieve a given rule of decision from their memory usable to evaluate a particular message.[182] This type of processing, distinguishable from the elaboration process under the central route, is commonly referred to as heuristic processing.[183]

The question rises why people even harness this peripheral route of tapping into simple cues, rules of thumb and shortcuts. In order to function in contemporary society, people often are compelled to act as 'cognitive missers'.[184] Ideally, people would hold opinions merely pertaining to topics they have elaborated on effortfully. However, leaving home in the morning, it is simply not very practical, nor possible, for people to put (considerable) mental effort in elaborating in all types of persuasive information they are exposed to during the day, for instance, advertising on their way to work, pop-up messages appearing on their smartphone, attractive-looking soda cans etc. These issues have little direct interest to people, and people have little time to think elaborately about each of these items. Rather than expressing an opinion, people have developed certain types of evaluations for most objects in their environment. These evaluations usually come to their minds once they bump into these objects. This implies that, occasionally, people have recourse to relatively simple instruments in order to evaluate whether something is, in their perception, 'good' or 'bad', i.e. to form an opinion. This may, in a similar manner, apply to information on future retirement benefits. Exposed to the amount of the projection people may have recourse to rules of thumb in order to ascertain whether the amount is 'good' or 'bad', i.e. 'sufficient' or 'insufficient'. Attitudes formed or changed through the peripheral route are demonstrated to be less accessible, persistent, resistant and predictive of behaviour than attitudes formed or changed under the central route.

182 Petty and others, 86.

183 See S Chaiken, 'The heuristic model of persuasion' in M Zanna, J Olson and C Herman (eds.), *Social influence: The Ontario Symposium* (Lawrence Erlbaum, Hillsdale 1987).

184 See SE Taylor, 'The interface of cognitive and social psychology' in JH Harvey (ed.), *Cognition, social behavior, and the environment* (Lawrence Erlbaum, Hillsdale 1981).

Although the two different routes of thinking and information processing have been addressed separately in the section above, they do not operate entirely independent of each other. On the contrary, a certain degree of continuous interaction between the two routes can be observed.[185] Although both systems can be perceived to be continuously activated, the activity of the peripheral/subconscious route is automatic and, hence, people generally do not experience it to be enabled, where the central/conscious route usually operates in a low effort mode, in which its capacity is used only partially. The continuous interaction between the two routes refers to the peripheral/subconscious route generating suggestions for the central/conscious route, which are, generally, adopted by the latter route. This implies that – most of the time – people belief and act upon impressions, and intuition, which usually works fine as most people make good decisions and take appropriate actions accordingly.[186] The interaction between these two routes of think can be illustrated through the so-called Muller-Lyer illusion, in which the conscious system follows the suggestions generated by the subconscious system, reflecting the strength and autonomy of the latter system.[187] This demonstrates that the peripheral/subconscious route is short-term oriented and continuously suggests short-term gratification options to the central/conscious route. As a remedy, the central/conscious route can harness several manners to control people's lack of willpower and repress these suggestions for some time, but this is effortful and the willpower to repress these tempting suggestions is fairly low.

2.2.3 *Steering People in the Direction of Either the Central or Peripheral Route*

Which route people move into – central or peripheral – is dependent on a wide range of variables. Discussing these variables *in extenso* is beyond the scope of this research but I will touch upon the most relevant for the purpose of this research. The diagram drafted by Petty et al depicts how people are steered in a certain direction.[188]

A vast body of literature demonstrates that a wide range of variables (for instance, source credibility) may affect persuasion in different ways along the continuum of elaboration. As regards these variables, a distinction can be drawn that affect motivation to process a message from variables that affect ability to process information (i.e., motivational and ability variables, respectively).[189] These variables can also affect how much thinking a

185 Cf. EIOPA, 'Good practices on information provision for DC schemes: enabling occupational DC scheme members to plan for retirement,' (2013) [EIOPA-BoS-13/010] 17.

186 D Kahneman, *Thinking, fast and slow* (Farrar, Straus and Giroux, New York 2011).

187 Ibid. 29.

188 See Petty and others, 87.

189 Ibid. 88 and cited literature.

person is doing with respect to a message and what kind of thoughts shall be provoked (favourable or unfavourable).

Generally speaking, people steer in the central route if people possess both the motivation as well as the ability (time) to carefully elaborate the arguments. On the contrary, the peripheral route is more likely to arise if people's motivation or ability is low. Thus, the likelihood of elaborating on communication (i.e., elaboration likelihood) – determined by peoples' motivation and ability to think – determines the route to persuasion. If people's level of pension awareness (in general, low) and perception of taxes (in general, overly complex) are taken into account, it seems that people are more likely to tap into the peripheral way of thinking. This seems rather paradoxically as, in particular, these issues should be devoted a considerable amount of attention, given their often-irreversible consequences, and potential implications for the pension's adequacy. This is of particular importance where different legal systems, pension vehicles, rules and regulations intersect, i.e. in cross-border situations.

Some of these motivational/ability variables have been harnessed in this research's chapter 3 to explore the effect of adapting information by exposing people to either a gross, or net amount of future retirement income. Moreover, some of these variables will be used to establish an assessment framework for the effectiveness of information, which will be dealt with in section 2.4. For instance, when people lack the ability to think about a message such as when the message is difficult to understand, or when people have little or no prior information, they tend to be more likely to rely on simple cues and associations, heading towards the peripheral route.[190]

Now that the role of the field of behavioural economics for the present research has been elucidated, while focussing on Dual Process Theory, two routes of thinking, and some situational/motivational variables, in chapter 3 emphasis will be put on a particular bias, i.e. the relativity bias. Moreover, it will be addressed what role this bias takes in retirement planning, and more specifically, in this research.

2.3 SOCIAL REPRESENTATIONS, ATTITUDES AND KNOWLEDGE

The section below revolves around more peculiar modalities, i.e. social representations. This section integrates certain socio-psychological aspects into this research's evaluation framework, which allow to put forward certain recommendations, or draw certain

190 Ibid. 105 and cited literature.

reservations, as they play a potentially pivotal role in establishing effective information provision. Related to Dual Processing Theory discussed in the preceding section, if we want to have a profound understanding of how people – by certain variables – perceive certain pieces of information, a deeper understanding of how these people try to understand, and make sense, of new concepts is pivotal. Social representations, attitudes and knowledge, may affect how people think about information, and behave (in future).[191] For instance, people may base their perception and beliefs with respect to pension information on previous experiences, misconceptions and (false) interpretations of the information they were exposed to.[192] It is hence central that these beliefs and attitudes – which may influence *prima facie* neutral information – are incorporated in pension information provision.[193] In doing so, this section helps to explore what non-legal interventions and measures are needed to ensure, and potentially foster, the effectiveness of the pension information provided.

2.3.1 Social Representations: What You Think You See Is What You Get?

Apart from objective knowledge, people also hold (mental) images about pensions and taxes.[194] Even people who know little, may hold many images, associations, convictions. These images and representations affect – to a large extent – how people perceive information, what is and is not relevant; what they do or don't believe; how terms are interpreted etc. Thus, how people interpret or appraise information does not only arise from the text itself, but is also strongly influenced by their own associations with and beliefs related to concepts. Taking this insufficiently into account may lead to a discrepancy of what readers think they read and the writer has in mind. This might have an effect on the information's effectiveness as it might steer people away from what the information seeks to achieve. For instance, information on taxes (as such) might lead people to think that the information provided is overly complex, and might even provoke emotions of anger. Hence, they might not even read the information, running counter to the information's effectiveness. Moreover, as the underlying research partly builds on people's perception of taxes and tax law it is crucial to get a deeper understanding of (the nature of)

191 See for instance the TNS Beliefs Framework: Visser, Kloosterboer and Oosterveld, 12.

192 See A van Hekken, J Hoofs and EC Bruggen, 'Pension Participants' Attitudes, Beliefs, and Emotional Responses to the New Dutch Pension System' De Economist. The results of this study show that many participants base their comments on previous experiences, misconceptions and (sometimes false) interpretations of the information in the text they were exposed to.

193 Van Hekken, Hoofs and Bruggen point out that a diversified communication strategy, mindful of different beliefs, emotions and attitudes among participants should help to empower citizens to get insight in their financial situation after retirement and to make informed choices, see ibid.

194 See also ibid.

tax law from the perspective of these people, i.e. social constructions. In doing so, this section expands this research evaluation framework, and allows to adopt a holistic approach to taxes and pension information provision.

2.3.2 *Social Representations and Their Role in Subjective Sense-Making: Social Construction*

Cullis and Lewis point out that social constructionism is everywhere in the wind like pollen, i.e. constitute day-to-day topics.[195] For instance, taxpayers have beliefs and notions about taxes, their beliefs and their (expected) behaviour. As Cullis and Lewis rightfully argue, none of these beliefs necessarily have to be 'true' in any 'objective' sense.[196] However, if the abovementioned actors belief that these notions and beliefs are true (and act accordingly) then reality is constructed, i.e. (social) construction. Therefore, the previous section is titled 'what you think you see is what you get'. Building on these notions and beliefs, formed in whatever way, people create their own social construction of pensions, taxes and tax law. Moreover, people's attitudes, judgements, and behavioural expectations are more affected by what they think than what actually is.[197]

When people discuss socially-relevant topics (religion, science, environment, economic issues, taxes) they usually exchange lay knowledge, rather than being an expert in the given field. They try to understand and evaluate the issues or phenomena that are unfamiliar but relevant to them. This, in turn, enables social communication and behaviour.[198] Moscovici termed these concepts in social interaction 'social representations', developing a theory setting forth processes leading from unfamiliar phenomena to familiar concepts.[199] The primary function of these 'social representations' is to create a homogeneous and familiar environment for everyday discourse.[200] Phenomena and contents unknown to people need to be revealed, tried to be understood and be integrated in the field of socially shared and individual knowledge and evaluations. To this end, social representations are made.[201] When confronted with information, people hold these

195 Cullis and Lewis, 310.

196 Ibid. 310.

197 A Lewis, 'Perception of tax rates' 6 British Tax Review 358.

198 See for instance TE Sehity, E Kirchler and S Muehlbacher, 'Rise and Decline of Social Objects: Ten case studies on the social development of meaning structures' Euro-Workshop (IAREP), Vienna, Austria, 2003.

199 S Moscovici, *La Psychanalyse, son image et son public* (Presse Universitaire de France, Paris 1961); Moscovici, 'The phenomenon of social representations'.

200 Kirchler, 29.

201 See J-C Abric, 'A theoretical and experimental approach to the study of social representations in a situation of interaction' in S Moscovici and S Farr (eds.), *Social representations* (Cambridge University Press, Cambridge 1984).

– already gained – social representations which may affect the way they perceive this information.

Social representations are structured by elements referred to as the nucleus and the periphery.[202] Where the nucleus establishes the relevance and particularity of a representation, the periphery (at the border of a representation) functions as links to other concepts. The nucleus constitutes the main content-base in day-to-day conversations; the peripheral elements protect this nucleus of a representation and, simultaneously, serve a mediating role if representations in general change, allowing for adaptation of a given concept to individual's and society's ever-changing knowledge and evaluations. Once day-to-day discourse is confronted with an unfamiliar concept (e.g., newly introduced tax legislation and/or pension reforms), these concepts enter 'the gates' of the already existing compilation of representations.[203] Once entered, these unfamiliar concepts are compared with existing knowledge and, subsequently, integrated. This integration into existing knowledge is obtained by the cognitive processes of anchoring and objectivation. Under the anchoring process, existing representations are memorized, and explored, in order to classify (make sense of) the unfamiliar concept building on already existing categories, and to label these new concepts.[204] In doing so, people try to understand, and make sense, of new concepts. For instance, in cases where a new form of pension scheme is introduced, people tend to compare this new scheme to pensions scheme they are already familiar with, i.e. stored in memory. In these cases, the peripheral elements fulfil their function, i.e. serving as links to other concepts. New concepts are thus compared with already existing – memory-stored – concepts. By contrast, the process of objectivation entails visualisation of a concept. Unfamiliar constructs or contents are, inherently, abstract – i.e. lack an intuitive 'picture' – and, hence, are difficult to understand and communicate.[205] Under the process of objectivation the unknown 'abstract' content is transformed to a 'figurative' object. When putting these two processes together, anchoring established a context in which the unknown content is made sense of, and objectivation transforms an abstract content to a concrete representation. For instance, the relationship between taxable persons and tax authorities may be described figuratively as teacher-pupil.

In the realm of laws and legislation, taxes are the usual suspects for making trouble and achieving little.[206] As tax laws are subject to criticism for being too complex to be fully

202 Kirchler, 29-30.

203 Ibid. 30.

204 As regards anchoring and objectifying see Moscovici, 'The phenomenon of social representations' 28 ff.

205 Kirchler, 30.

206 JD Rosenberg, 'The Psychology of Taxes: Why They Drive Us Crazy, and How We Can Make Them Sane' 16 Virginia Tax Review 162.

understood by ordinary taxpayers, and knowledge on taxes is, in general, limited, representations and evaluations of taxes are primarily a product of myths and misperceptions.[207] These myths – social representations – are to some extent reflected in semantics of tax terminology, terms used by people.[208] When it comes to taxpayers' ideas about taxation, Schmölders asked German citizens what came to their mind when they heard the word 'taxes'.[209] The results revealed that one-third of the associations were related to technical concepts, such tax laws, tax offices etc, and negative associations were found in 29%, primarily related to negative feelings pertaining to too many taxes, high tax burden etc. 23% associated the term taxes with necessary evil. However, numerous of people's negative reactions, attitudes, beliefs and thoughts about taxes are not merely elicited by economic or political shortcomings in tax legislation, but of a combination of perceptual and cognitive distortions.[210] These cognitive distortions cause people to focus unduly on the burdens imposed by tax (law) and its complexity. As regards the shortcomings in tax legislation it can argued, at this point, that the tax systems as such unintentionally maximizes frustration among taxable persons, and minimizes the opportunity for communication.

Contrary to legislative proposals in other fields of law, proposed amendments in tax laws are, as a rule, accompanied – and often driven – by estimates of revenue and charts depicting the project distribution of economic burdens among different categories of incomes and wealth, mainly to progressivity of (most) taxes.[211] This ongoing analysis and

207 Kirchler, 40.

208 Whereas, in German, the word 'Steuer' means 'support' and the Scandinavian 'skat' refers to the common treasure put aside for common purpose, in the Latin world, the word tax means something felt as an 'impostation' upon citizens. Based on such different tax mentalities, closely related to citizens' civic or community-mindedness in general, individual tax-mindedness develops by personal experiences. See G Schmölders, 'Survey research in public finance: A behavioural approach to fiscal theory' 25 Public Finance 300, 301 ff. It can be added that the Dutch term 'belasting' refers to a burden, also meaning 'imposition'.
Against this background, it can be questioned how mobile persons' individual tax-mindedness is shaped as they are subject to different tax systems in each of his (former) working or residence state. This linguistic connotation may manifest itself in people's perceptions. However, it should be emphasized that the explanatory power of such a linguistic analysis is rather limited.

209 G Schmölders, *Das Irrationale in der öffentlichen Finanzwirtschaft* (Suhrkamp, Frankfurt am Main 1960). The author also differentiated between blue-collar workers, white-collar workers, civil servants, self-employed, farmers and retired people. It was also found that low education and lower work status were covarying with negative connotations as regards taxes. See also E Kirchler, 'Differential representations of taxes: Analysis of free associations and judgments of five employment groups' 27 Journal of Socio-Economics 117.

210 Cf. Rosenberg, 160.

211 For instance, during parliamentary scrutiny pertaining to the tax treaty between the Netherlands and Germany it was pointed out that in particular pensioners in Germany receiving a Dutch pension were financially affected by the amendment of the treaty Article on pensions. See Kamerstukken II, *33 615, nr 10*

attention dedicated to the economic burdens imposed by tax legislation, reinforces citizens' perception of taxes being primarily the instrument of 'governmental taking' and the belief that taxes take more and give less compared to other laws.[212] I endorse Rosenberg's argument that people tend to fall victim to such (unexamined) assumptions about tax law, which (vastly) over determine the manner in which they perceive taxes.[213] Thinking differently about taxes and norms is scarce, and most of the time people associate taxes with revenue collection, assess taxes in the light of their economic effect. Hence, tax law seems to lack moral legitimacy.[214]

These considerations of how people perceive, holds attitudes and beliefs, and think about, tax law shapes this research evaluation framework, in terms the of integration of socio-psychological aspects that go beyond mere information provision, and processing (pursuant to Dual Process Theory). What is more, it follows from the above that any informational analysis should assess these social constructions, and it implies that the rhetoric of 'rational economic persons' is far from an abstract idea and can become the guide for dealing with everyday life and social problems.[215] These findings pave the way for putting forward observations, recommendations, and reservations that widen the scope of how we, including law- and policymakers, think about tax law, and how this may potentially affect effective information provision, as social representations may play a pivotal role in the attitudes and beliefs people hold towards certain pieces of information.[216]

2.4 Effectiveness of Information: What Purpose of Information to Be Pursued?

2.4.1 *'Effectiveness' of Information*

This thesis' main research question explores whether, and to what extent, the regulatory frameworks are fit for the provision of effective pension information (net amounts of future pension income) and, if not so, what legal/non-legal interventions and measures are needed to ensure, and potentially foster, the effectiveness of the information provided. Effective (cross-border) pension information remains pivotal and its relevance is growing

(Motie van de leden Nijboer en Kerstens) (2013/14); Kamerstukken I, *33615 nr. B (Voorlopig verslag van de vaste commissie voor Financiën)* (19 November 2014).

212 Rosenberg, 162-164.

213 Ibid. 170.

214 Ibid. 170.

215 Cf. Cullis and Lewis, 310.

216 See for instance Petty and others, 87.

continuously, given developments in the realm of pensions, as set out in chapter 1. In this regard, the question rises what the 'effectiveness of information' entails. This will be discussed below, but apart from this, the term 'effectiveness' will be further defined.

The Oxford Dictionary terms 'effectiveness' as "the quality of being effective (in various senses)".[217] The term 'effective' is, in turn, defined as "powerful in effect; producing a notable effect: effectual". Collins defines 'effective' as "productive of or capable of producing a result".[218] Nevertheless, these definitions have certain elements in common, i.e. being aimed at achieving a particular outcome or result. Given these definitions, for the purpose of this research the term 'effectiveness' is delineated as the degree to which something (i.e. information) is successful in achieving a desired result. Then the question arises what the desired result of information ought to entail. The following section revolves around how the information's objective has been set.

2.4.2 *Setting the Information's Behavioural Purpose: a Functional Analysis*

As indicated in chapter 1, ideally, European mobile workers should have an overview of their pension rights, accumulated pension entitlements and future pension payments. Although the abovementioned 'providing an overview of mobile citizen's pension rights, pension entitlements and pension payments' could be considered a potential behavioural purpose, I find this too vague, in particular in terms of operationalisation for the benefit of this research. The section below will hence revolve around a more specified behavioural purpose, building on a diverse array of research findings. The behavioural purpose is an important guiding principle in information provision.[219]

Prior to starting to develop information provision, an informational purpose should be defined, i.e. what should the reader 'do' with the information; what financial decisions should these persons be able to make after having read the information?[220] By defining such a behavioural purpose the effectiveness of information provision can be evaluated, and ensured. This should be, in information provision, prevailing over thinking about relevant information that should be sent. Policymakers appear to have a tendency to draw

217 Oxford Dictionaries, <www.oxforddictionaries.com>.

218 P Hanks, T Hill Long and L Urdang, *Collins English Dictionary* (Collins London 1979) 467.

219 A Ritchie and others, 'Transforming consumer information' 18 British Actuarial Journal 582 ff. and Sunstein, and Ministerie van Sociale Zaken en Werkgelegenheid, 'Rapport Pensioen in duidelijke taal' (Den Haag juni 2012) <available online: https://www.rijksoverheid.nl/documenten/rapporten/2012/06/26/rapport-pensioen-in-duidelijke-taal>.

220 Cf. EIOPA, 28.

information requirements in view of a legal purpose, i.e. the legal paradigm of information provision.[221] Given these information provisions and with a view to prevent legal claims, information providers tend to provide every (detail of) information that could be relevant, for a variety of reasons, for the recipient. Drawing from RCT, policymakers typically assume that recipients will read, and use, the information in order to make decisions, irrespective of the information's purpose. This assumption has proven to be false in many ways, as has been discussed in further detail in the section above. In this vein, it should be stressed that there is a difference between a mere technical disclosure of information – regardless of form, point in time and related usefulness – and actually sensibly information choices.[222] As Sunstein points out, well-designed disclosure policies shall be preceded by a careful analysis of their likely effects.[223] For instance, since most people are myopic, have limited time, attention and resources for seeking out new information, it is important to make sure that the relevant pension information is salient, easy to find and understandable.[224] What is more, too much information will put off people to read, and use, the information, if they do not see, at a glance, how the information is relevant to them and how they can use the information in financial decision-making.[225] This ties in with the personal relevance of the information. This implies that determining what communication goals ought to be pursued, should be determined from the perspective of the participant, i.e. this entails the 'citizen's perspective'.

Hence, people's behaviour should be incorporated while drawing information provision requirements and, subsequently, providing (pension) information, i.e. adopting an empirically-informed approach in (pension) information provision.[226] The provision of information as such may serve a variety of (behavioural) objectives; increasing pension awareness, pension engagement, increasing the level of pension participants etc. These purposes are reflected in the broad body of literature studying this field of pension information. It is beyond the scope of this research, to discuss all (behavioural) purpose that can be pursued through gearing information.

221 Ibid., 9.

222 Sunstein, 1417.

223 Ibid. 1417. Ritchie et al, distinguishes three types of people's level of engagement and the behaviour it engenders: 'Tell Me', 'Help Me' and 'Enable Me'. See Ritchie and others, 575.

224 Sunstein, 1417.

225 EIOPA, 9.

226 Cf. A Tiffe and others, 'Ausgestaltung eines Produktinformationsblatts für zertifizierte Altersvorsorge- und Basisrentenverträge' (2012) 2.

In this vein, I endorse Lents' statement that it is necessary to think from the perspective of information's goals and not from the point of view of information means/instruments.[227] An analysis of pension communication – more specifically, an analysis of communication goals – involves questions such as what are the goals of pension communication; are those goals desirable and achievable; what means are appropriate for the goals; and what means are most effective for the principal goals? In order to determine what goal is being pursued by certain communications, Lentz and Pander Maat developed the method of 'functional analysis'.[228] This method is also pertinent for determining the purpose of pension information, for the purposes of this research, and will be applied accordingly. According to the functional analysis, the description with regard to the information's objective should explicitly refer to three elements: a specific target group (in this context, mobile individuals); a cognitive effect (i.e. knowing something, in the context of this research how much pension they can expect); the subject matter to which that cognitive effect relates (being able to assess the adequacy of that pension). Putting these three elements together results in the following objective of the cross-border pension information:

> *given their knowledge, attitude and behaviour, mobile individuals – who avail(ed) themselves of their European freedoms of movement – should be informed on an aggregated level about how much pension they can expect, in order to be able to assess the adequacy of their dispersed pension, covering all their forms of pension in each of the (former) working/residence states.*

Herein I refer to cognitive effects; not behavioural effects, e.g. individuals are going to make an effort to ensure adequacy. On the contrary, the cognitive effect relates to knowing, i.e. how much pension they can expect. Obviously, communication can have an effect on people's behaviour and mostly it is (one of) the communication's goal, but this behavioural change is incited by a variation in knowledge, beliefs or attitude.[229] Nevertheless, ensuring that the information provided meets this objective is the first step on the pathway toward an adequate pension for mobile individuals.

This is further supported by recent research findings, since it appears that communication goals can be summarized in three key questions: what will I get? (e.g., participants know how much pension they can expect); is it sufficient? (e.g., participants know if their expected pension will be sufficient); what has been arranged for? (e.g., knowing when

227 L Lentz, 'Pensioencommunicatie: stel niet het middel maar het doel centraal!' 5 Tijdschrift voor Pensioenvraagstukken 1.

228 LR Lentz and HLW Pander Maat, 'Functional analysis for Document Design' 51 Technical Communication 387.

229 Lentz, 1. See also Visser, Kloosterboer and Oosterveld, 12.

action is needed, i.e. providing action perspective).[230] The latter is often referred to as providing people an 'action perspective', enabling them to grasp what measures are needed to ensure an adequate pension income after retirement. In literature, this is commonly referred to as 'actionability' of information.[231] What is more, these key questions address the two most prominent question: how much will I get?; how much pension do I need?[232] Not only policymakers, but also pension participants consider it an important objective of information.[233] But then the question arises as to what extent it is feasible for the pension provider to accurately state an expected amount, since the forecast depends, among other things, on economic developments and life events.[234] The desirability of this goal of pension communication seems little disputable, i.e. what will I get? I will not go further into the question of which actor in the pension domain should provide which information, as this requires a different kind of assessment, i.e. more of a feasibility study.[235]

---

230 LR Lentz, ML Nell and HLW Pander Maat, 'Naar een model voor pensioencommunicatie' Netspar Design Paper 1, They found a set of 433 goals for pension communication in the communication practices of pension organizations and grouped these under six main goals. These main goals were inspired by 'mandatory goals' derived from policy documents. See also Maatman, 143.

231 This is termed as 'when people of diverse backgrounds and varying levels of (financial) literacy can identify what they can do based on the information presented'. Derived and adapted from SJ Shoemaker, MS Wolf and C Brach, 'Development of the Patient Education Materials Assessment Tool (PEMAT): A new measure of understandability and actionability for print and audiovisual patient information' 96 Patient Education and Counseling 395, 3.

232 Hereby the caveat shall be made that this goal can be assigned a different degree of relevance for different age groups. Whereas young participants are too far removed from retirement to be able to answer this question, it is a relevant goal for older age groups as they have little time left to save additionally in case the expected pension turns out to be insufficient. As far as the Netherlands is concerned, the main purpose of pension information has been to enable the individual to check whether there will be sufficient income to uphold his or her standard of living after retirement, distinguished through three levels: overview *(how much will I receive per month?)*; insight *(is that sufficient?)*; action perspective with respect to their total pension income *(should I adjust my retirement planning?)*. However, these three yardsticks have not been clearly demarcated, nor practically operationalised, and remain rather vague as what they should encompass, and potentially provoke. See Minister van Sociale Zaken en Werkgelegenheid, *Aanbiedingsbrief evaluatie Wet pensioencommunicatie* (31 January 2020). Building on Ministerie van Sociale Zaken en Werkgelegenheid, 8. These three levels have also been recognized by the Dutch legislator: Kamerstukken II, *Wijziging van de Pensioenwet en de Wet verplichte beroepspensioenregeling in verband met verbetering van de pensioencommunicatie (Wet pensioencommunicatie)* (2013/14) 10. About a third of Dutch pension participants explicitly stated that they do not know when they will be able to retire and approximately how much they can expect. Furthermore, these participants consider mijnpensioenoverzicht.nl to be the most useful. Research findings suggested that the Dutch Pension Benefits Statement (UPO) contribute to a lesser extent to attaining these policy goals. Pension 1-2-3 makes virtually no contribution to achieving these goals.

233 See Visser, Kloosterboer and Oosterveld, 35. 76% of pension participants consider this the most important question to be answered by the informed provided.

234 Lentz, 2.

235 See ibid.

Nevertheless, those who know what the retirement forecast is, can take the important next step of determining whether that amount is sufficient for the expected standard of living, i.e. assessing the adequacy of the pension. This is tantamount to setting off what he expects to need per year/month (based on the spending pattern) against the expected retirement income (spending limit). On this basis it can be assessed whether the pension is sufficient for the desired expenditure pattern (i.e. adequacy). The pension's 'adequacy', in terms of to what extent the expected retirement income will be sufficient to finance a given standard of living, depends on a variety of country-specific variables. In order to assess the (expected) pension adequacy, people need reference points, or yardsticks. This will be dealt with in more detail in chapter 3 of this research. One of the starting points in assessing adequacy is the readily available income. Taxation of future pension income – in particular in cross-border cases – can have a considerable effect on this spending limits, as it reduces freely disposable income (net income). This supports the hypothesis of incorporating taxes in the information pertaining to the question what will I get? And is this sufficient? However, incorporating the (future) tax treatment of future retirement income, poses a wide range of complex tensions in information provision, which will be discussed in section 2.5. This is tantamount to the overarching objective of this research, i.e. explore what constraints for providing effective pension information lie in the regulatory frameworks, governing the taxation of statutory, occupational and personal pensions in cross-border cases between the Netherlands and Germany.

The ultimate behavioural objective of the information is thus to enable mobile citizens to assess the adequacy of their (future) retirement income. Hitherto, it has not been discussed yet what the term 'adequate pension' or 'pension adequacy' would entail. Hence, to demarcate this construct the following section will go deeper into the meaning of this term, and tries to interpret it for the purpose of this research.

Meeting the abovementioned behavioural purpose, requires, *inter alia*, similar figures and data about other sources of pension income across the (former) working, and/or residence states of the person concerned. Since pension systems in Europe are as diverse as the European Member States themselves, this entails putting a dispersed puzzle together. Obviously, finding a common way of communicating about dispersed pensions is not an easy task. Despite this diversity of national pension systems, the information itself appears generalizable to mobile individuals in terms of what they should be able to do with the information, paradoxically because it is universal for this group to have to contend with a wide variety of pension products, rules, entitlements, rights, etc. This is supported by this research's empirical findings, which will be dealt with in chapter 3.

2.4.3 *Pension Adequacy: What Yardstick?*

As has been discussed in the section above, the eventual goal of providing cross-border pension information is to enable mobile citizens to ensure their pension's adequacy. People, in general, expect a certain standard of living after retirement, and many prefer to retain their pre-retirement standard of living once they have retired. But how much will they actually need after retirement?[236] What is more, the adequacy of retirement income is a central objective of all types of pension system.[237] Hence, a view words on the concept of 'pension adequacy' is considered appropriate.

However, what pension benefit level can be considered adequate remains unclear in literature, as well as in practice. Even in the *Wet Toekomst Pensioenen*, the concept of an adequate pension was not further explained by the Dutch legislator.[238] This leaves the term 'adequate pension' as an open norm where it is precisely one of the tenets of reforming the system. This is reminiscent of the absence of the citizen's perspective in such legislative procedures. In any case, the legislature should consider developing a guideline for the concept of an adequate pension, operationalised by providing certain benchmarks.

Formulating this research's main research question, raised the question how pension adequacy should be measured/ operationalized?[239] In order to determine whether a pension income is, or will be, adequate in future, a yardstick is necessary, i.e. an ambition level. Essentially, this corresponds to the question whether a pension will be sufficient,

---

236 See also M Warnaar and M Visser, 'Een welvaartsrichtlijn voor pensioen. Wat is een adequaat inkomen? (deel 1)' PensioenMagazine. According to Warnaar and Visser, what constitutes an adequate pension is not just about the (testable) question of whether the pension will be sufficient later. They argue that the question of whether you can pay for it now is just as important. In this article, they provide a policy framework for pension adequacy, focusing on post-retirement income. See also M Warnaar and M Visser, 'Een welvaartsrichtlijn voor pensioen. Wat is een adequaat inkomen? (deel 2)' PensioenMagazine.

237 Cf. World Bank, 'Adequacy (1) Pension entitlements, replacement rates and pension wealth' (World Bank Pension Indicators and Database, 2012) 1.

238 Kamerstukken II, *Wet toekomst pensioenen.*

239 For instance, the European Commission has delineated 'adequacy' of pension income by setting three standards. In the EU 2018 Pension Adequacy Report it introduced 'the triangle of adequacy', according to which adequacy should be analysed in terms of effectiveness in poverty reduction, income continuity and average duration of retirement/pension payment. First, the adequacy of pension income is measured by its ability to prevent and mitigate the risk of poverty (i.e. the risk and depth of income poverty and severe material deprivation) among women and men aged 65 and over. Second, adequacy is measured by its capacity to replace earned income before retirement. Using the TRR indicator methodology, the report assesses the adequacy of current pensions for certain cases of career length and income, and compares the findings with similar scenarios four decades later. Lastly, the report addresses the length of retirement to which pensioners are entitled by national pension arrangements. See European Commission, 'Pensioen Adequacy Report 2018: Current and Future Income Adequacy in Old Age in the EU' (Directorate-General for Employement, Social Affairs and Inclusion, 2018) 23.

how much retirement income do I need after retirement? Giving an answer to this question seems quite straightforward but it proves much more difficult to answer it in general. Whether the future retirement income will be 'sufficient' depends on the persons' level of income, expenditure pattern, housing (rental or ownership), physical and mental health after retirement (leading to medical expenses), and other personal and financial facts and circumstances.

Although characterised as a heuristic benchmark, the most recognised and commonly referred to ambition level in international pension literature, is that the retirement income should, at least, constitute 70% of the income received prior to retiring.[240] However, the question remains whether this is an adequate yardstick for formulating what an adequate pension should comprise, since those with lower income may need more that 70% of their current income after retirement to support their basic needs, compared to those having a higher income. For instance, research findings demonstrate that those with a low income often need a retirement income corresponding to a 100% of their income prior to retirement to support their basic needs, while mid-income households need 70-80%, and high-income households just 60%.[241] Moreover, Binswanger and Schunk found that a minimum acceptable income replacement rate, in the Netherlands, range from 75% to 60% across income quintiles.[242]

A more theoretically grounded approach is based on the life-cycle model.[243] Under this model, the formulated pension ambition, i.e. the optimal savings pattern, is based on the

240 R Haveman and others, 'Assessing the Maintenance of Savings Sufficiency over the First Decade of Retirement' 14 International Tax and Public Finance 481. This 70%-ambition is in line with the principle, i.e. ambition level, prescribed by the Dutch legislator's in fiscal legislation until 2014. As of 1 January 2015, the ambition level, delineating the fiscal facilitation of pension accrual, has been set at a pension income 75% of the average income, accrued over 40 years, see Kamerstukken II, (2013/14) 8. In the fragmented German pension system, an explicit ambition level is less sharply defined, see See also C Dudel and J Schmied, 'Pension adequacy standards: An empirical estimation strategy and results for the United States and Germany' (MPIDR Working Paper WP 2019-003, 2019). They found that replacement rates in Germany are too low, and pensioners in the Netherlands seem to be doing well. It is still assumed that ambition is set at a replacement rate of 70% of the net income, despite all reforms in recent years. See S Kluth and M Gasche, 'Ersatzraten in der Gesetzlichen Rentenversicherung' 235 Jahrbücher für Nationalökonomie und Statistik. It is sometimes substantiated by arguing that 70% is the highest value that has ever been provided by the German public pension system.

241 J De Bresser, M Knoef and L Kools, 'Cutting One's Coat According to One's Cloth: How did the Great Recession affect retirement resources and expenditure goals?' 05/2018-029 Netspar Academic Series 1.

242 J Binswanger and D Schunk, 'What is an adequate standard of living during retirement?' Journal of Pension Economics and Finance 203.

243 Introduced by F Modigliani and R Brumberg, 'Utility analysis and the consumption function: An interpretation of cross-section data' in K Kurihara (ed.), *PostKeynesian Economics* (Rutgers University Press, New Brunswick 1954) and M Friedman, *A Theory of the Consumption Function* (Princeton University Press, New Jersey 1957).

personal preferences, such as risk aversion and the propensity to hyperbolic discounting (i.e. how people subjectively value the importance of the present, compared to the future).[244] It proves to be quite laborious to define peoples' preferences in general, mainly due to the huge variety in preferences among people. In order to get a grasp of people's preferences, their actual behaviour could be observed, and documented. Therefore, Knoef suggests to unravel these personal preferences through asking strategic questions.[245] A major drawback of this approach, is that it is proven that people behave irrationally, i.e. people are not full rational human beings, but, rather, prone to biases, rules of thumb etc.[246] Hence, Shefrin and Thaler supplemented this life cycle-model with elements from behavioural economics.[247]

It follows from the above, that several yardsticks can be used in order to measure and determine pension adequacy, depending on the perspective taken. All yardsticks have their pros and cons, but depending on the benchmark used, a different group of persons show inadequacy of their pension. However, it has been found that under all three yardsticks 20-30% of Dutch households accrue insufficiently pension, potentially facing pension inadequacy.[248] This again underscores the relevance of these research findings, since for policy-making it is crucial to find out who faces a (potential) lack of retirement income.

Moreover, replacement rates also vary significantly between countries, i.e. heterogeneity in replacement rates. What is more, the role and proportion of statutory, occupational and personal pension provisions in securing pension adequacy differs across countries. For instance, in Germany pensioners receive a factual net replacement rate of roughly 41.5% from the statutory pension scheme.[249] For many people in Germany, retirement income arising from the statutory pension scheme constitute the primary source of retirement income.[250]

Hence, for the purpose of this research, I refrain from formulating a strict, quantitative norm for pension adequacy and leave the term rather open by adhering to the notion of 'pension adequacy' as referring to the extent to which the expected pension income

---

244 M Knoef, 'Dromen over een goed pensioen: origami en datascience' Inaugural speech 8.

245 Ibid. 8.

246 See for instance D Ariely, *Predictably irrational: the hidden forces that shape our decisions* (HarperCollins, New York 2008).

247 H Shefrin and R Thaler, 'The Behavioral Life-Cycle Hypothesis' 26 Economic Inquiry 609.

248 Knoef, 5.

249 OECD Pensions at a glance 2021, 'Gross replacement rates' 2021) <https://www.oecd.org/publications/oecd-pensions-at-a-glance-19991363.htm> accessed 22 February 2022 141.

250 See Dolls and others.

– based on the current accumulated pension – is sufficient to replace the earned income after retirement to secure and maintain the standard of living after retirement, at a country-specific absolute level. The formulation incorporates, and reflects, the differences in the required replacement rates between low- and high-earners, and across (Member) States, since this definition refers to earned income and standard of living. However, this does not necessarily imply that consumption after retirement should be equal to consumption prior to retirement, as consumption demands are likely to decline when people retire.[251] Moreover, pension adequacy at the date of retirement does not imply that incomes are adequate during the person's remaining lifetime, e.g. pension benefits may be cut or (uncovered) health costs may increase. Lastly, this definition ties in with the objective of the pension information provided, i.e. assess whether the expected retirement income is sufficient to maintain a certain living standard after retirement, regardless of how this is quantified.

2.5 Setting the Boundaries of Effective Information Provision by Building on Dual Process Theory

The behavioural purpose identified in section 2.4.2, indicates what people should be able to do with the pension information provided, i.e. to assess the adequacy of their (accumulated) pension income. While this specifies what information should be provided, it does not yet specify how this information should be provided in terms of effectiveness. How information should be provided remains rather vague in terms of operationalisation, and with respect to what the information should provoke. This renders achieving this research's main objective difficult. For instance, in order for information to achieve its behavioural purpose, it is of eminent importance that people actually read the document, and not be deterred by *prima facie* difficult to understand, not trustworthy or not personally relevant, information, as this would affect the information's effectiveness. As has been thoroughly discussed in section 2.2, ability and motivational factors – under Dual Process Theory – are pivotal in peoples' decision to (whether or not) look closer into particular pieces of information.

Moreover, as has been thoroughly elaborated on in section 2.2, the Dual Process Theory helps in getting a better understanding of what type of information (provision) aids people in making (better) decisions.[252] For the present research, this model allows to set up an

251 Cf. J Scholz, A Seshadri and S Khitatrakun, 'Are Americans saving 'optimally' for retirement?' 114 Journal of Political Economy 607.

252 Petty and Cacioppo, 'The Elaboration Likelihood Model of Persuasion' 125.

assessment framework for the provision of effective information, building on four principles. For instance, since most people are myopic, have limited time, attention and resources for seeking out new information, it is important to make sure that the relevant pension information is understandable, and avoid that people are deterred from reading the information.[253] This can provide valuable insights into, among other things, why information is or is not effective in accomplishing the envisaged behavioural purpose. In doing so, this section gives further substance to the second part of this research's main research question, i.e. what (non-)legal interventions and measures are needed to ensure, and potentially foster, the effectiveness of the information provided. As has been touched upon briefly in chapter 1 of this research, these non-legal interventions refer to tools in the domain of information provision, for instance, harnessing certain ways of adapting information in order to ensure its effectiveness. The section below discusses in more detail the variables – for the purpose of this study – chosen to determine, and delineate, the effectiveness of information (provision): understandability, technical (legal) correctness, accuracy (personal relevance), and trustworthiness.

2.5.1 *Four Principles Enunciating Effectiveness of Information*

In this vein, it can be claimed that providing pension information inevitably leads to tensions. Stevens points out four elements in this regard: the need for transparency, the need for technical correctness, the necessary simplification for the understanding of the average citizen and the legal responsibility for pension communication.[254] He illustrated the tensional relation between these four elements that pension communications entails, by drawing a pension communication plot, serving as a tool in order to evaluate a Members State's pension communication policy. Building on this notion, a typology of pension information's effectiveness has been drawn up, see figure 2.2 A typology of effectiveness of pension information below.

253 Sunstein, 1417.

254 Y Stevens, 'Communication on pension rights in Europe' Report European colloquium and Y Stevens and L Van Assche, 'The right to retirement pension information' discussion paper Peer Review on pension information 8.

Figure 2.2 A Typology of Effectiveness of Pension Information

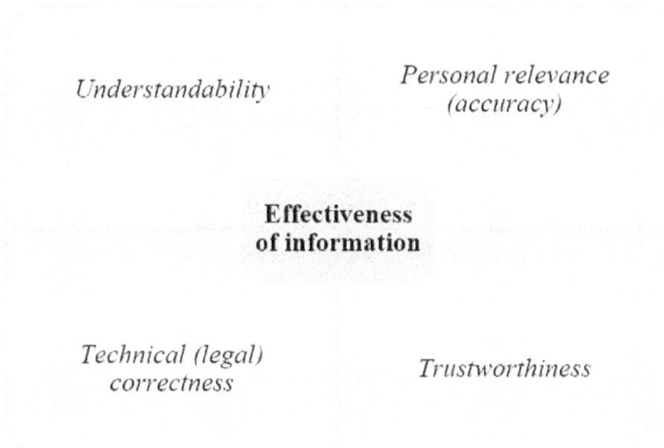

It should be emphasized that the elements across each other do not necessarily constitute each other's opposite, and tensions are not necessarily engendered between each of the four principles. Finding an optimum balance may vary depending a range of circumstances: the content matter, social representations, attitudes and beliefs that people may hold as regard the content matter (e.g. pensions or taxes), the envisaged behavioural purpose, the addressees and their characteristics. What principle of these four should be heeded most, largely depends on the goal of information. For instance, when the mere information's aim is to inform readers, in particular understandability requires adequate attention.

The above-mentioned typology is used in this research to shape the evaluation framework, along the lines of four principles considered pivotal for effective information provision. These principles will be elucidated below. The goal here is not to argue that these principles are the only ones to be taken into account, although I suspect that these four qualities capture most, if not all, of the properties of the effectiveness of information provision, given the considerable body of literature on the Dual Process Theory.[255]

2.5.1.A Understandability

Understandability of information is one of the pivotal qualitative properties, when it comes to the provision of effective cross-border pension information. It should be pointed out at the beginning of this section that the term understandability – in the context of this research – pertains to the information as such, rather than the rules and regulations' level of understandability. This research is not aimed at identifying measures in order to ensure that drafting legislation, as such, is more aligned with this principle, such as drafting

255 See for instance Petty and others.

guidelines for parliamentary draftsmen. Contrarily, it is explored how the regulatory frameworks and/or their modalities, operate in the light of the understandability of the effective pension information provided.

As discussed in section 2.2, under the Dual Process Theory, generally speaking, people are steered in the peripheral route if people's motivation or ability is low. This peripheral involves a simple and low effort decision strategy, and people tap into simple cues and shortcuts, referred to as heuristic processing. A wide range of (motivational and ability) variables may affect persuasion in different ways along the continuum of elaboration. When a message – or piece of information – is hard to understand, especially when people have little or no prior information, they lack the ability to think about a message, and tend to be more likely to rely on simple cues and associations.[256] In terms of ability, generally, financial literacy tends to be low, since most people seem to lack knowledge and appear to be under-informed about even the most basic economic concepts, needed to make financial and retirement decisions.[257] This raises the likelihood of people being steered towards the peripheral route of thinking, generally relying on heuristics and biases. In sum, information's understandability affects people's ability to think about it. This effect can be strengthened when these people hold unfavourable representations when it comes to pensions, and/or taxes.

The conceptualisation – and operationalisation – of the construct of 'understandability' deviates per realm of science.[258] Yet, it is, regardless of what field, universal to present

---

256 Petty and others, 105 and cited literature.

257 M Browning and A Lusardi, 'Household Saving: Micro Theories and Micro Facts' 34 Journal of Economic Literature 1797, 5. For findings on deficient financial literacy I refer to A Lusardi and OS Mitchell, 'Financial Literacy and Retirement Preparedness: Evidence and Implications for Financial Education' Business Economics 35, E Brüggen, 'Tomorrow I will really start with my retirement planning: How to improve retirement decision making' Inaugural speech; ibid., ibid., JR Agnew and LR Szykman, 'Asset Allocation and Information Overload: The Influence of Information Display, Asset Choice, and Investor Experience' 6 Journal of Behavioral Finance 57, D Moore, *Survey of Financial Literacy in Washington State: Knowledge, Behavior, Attitudes, and Experiences* (Social and Economic Sciences Research Center, Washington State University, 2003); A Lusardi, 'Information, Expectations, and Savings for Retirement' in H Aaron (ed.), *In Behavioral Dimensions of Retirement Economics* (Brookings Institution Press, Washington DC 1999); C Logan, *Evaluation research in crime and delinquency: a reappraisal* (Journal of Criminal Law, Criminology and Policy Studies, 1972); G Mastrobuoni, 'Do Better-Informed Workers Make Better Retirement Choice? A Test Based on the Social Security Statement' Mimeo, Collegio Carlo Alberto, and A Lusardi and OS Mitchell, 'Financial Literacy and Planning: Implications for Retirement Wellbeing' Working Paper, Pension Research Council, Wharton School, University of Pennsylvania the latter research measured how workers made saving decisions, how they collected the information for making these decisions, and whether they possessed the financial literacy needed to make informed decisions.

258 For instance, in the field of accountancy it is termed as follows: 'understandable financial accounting information presents data that can be understood by the users of the information and is expressed in a form and with terminology adapted to the users' range of understanding.' See JM Morton, 'Qualitative Objectives

information in a way, readers may access and easily understand the actual content of the information. Understandability is a pivotal factor when assessing relevance (of information) in many domain-specific scenarios, for instance, pension information.[259] Information can be considered 'understandable' as when people of diverse backgrounds and varying levels of (financial) literacy can process, and fully grasp, key messages.[260] 'Understandability' is known to be a multidimensional construct. Albeit it is not easy to operationalize 'understandability' as it is an internal process of humans, understandability may entail numerous topics, for instance, information's content, word choice and style, use of numbers, organization, layout and design, and use of visual aids. In the vast body of literature on the understandability of information – in different domains of research – central elements appear to be the use of terms, and gearing information towards its users.[261] As Sunstein points out, clarity and simplicity of information are often critical.[262] Information should not be too abstract, vague, detailed, complex or overwhelming to be useful.[263] However, understandable information is not a panacea for all complexity people have to contend with. People – even knowledgeable people – may sometimes need to consult a financial expert/advisor in order to understand complex underlying phenomena.

It is to be noted that 'understandability' should not be used interchangeably with information's 'readability'.[264] The latter term refers to the properties of a written piece of information, pertaining to readers' understanding of the information. It depends on the manner in which the information is structured, sentences' structure, and vocabulary used. The use of simple vocabulary fosters the information's understandability which, in turn, lowers the levels of stress and anxiety. The relationship between readability and comprehension of information is obvious: more readable material is typically easier to

---

of Financial Accounting: A Comment on Relevance and Understandability' 12 Journal of Accounting Research 288, 288.

259 See also G Zuccon, 'Understandability Biased Evaluation for Information Retrieval' in N Ferro and others (eds.), *Advances in Information Retrieval: 38th European Conference on IR Research, ECIR 2016* (Springer, Switzerland 2016) 3.

260 Derived and adapted to the scope of the present research: Shoemaker, Wolf and Brach, 3. See also OA Mac and others, 'Web-Based Health Information Following the Renewal of the Cervical Screening Program in Australia: Evaluation of Readability, Understandability, and Credibility' 22 Journal of Medical Internet Research.

261 also A Davidson and RN Kantor, 'On the failure of readability formulas to define readable texts: a case study from adaptations' 17 Reading Research Quarterly 187.

262 Sunstein, 1369.

263 K Ripken, 58 Baylor L Rev 139,160-63 (2006). 'The Dangers and Drawbacks of the Disclosure Antidote: Toward a More Substantive Approach to Securities Regulation' 58 Baylor Law Review.

264 With respect to a text's readability, see Davidson and Kantor; JD Bransford and MK Johnson, 'Contextual prerequisites for understanding: Some investigations of comprehension and recall' 11 Journal of Verbal Learning and Verbal Behavior 717.

understand.[265] Better readability, and hence better understandability, involves the usage of simple and well-known terminology; avoiding jargon and technical terms; using simple sentences or phrase structures.[266] In general, information on taxes (and pensions) is often written in such a manner that understanding is difficult or even impossible. In order to aid (laymen) mobile citizens in decision-making, it is of paramount importance to provide them with understandable information. Although readability does not account for a comprehensive account of understandability, it does constitute one of the aspects affecting information's understanding.[267] Thus, readability serves as a proxy for understandability.[268] The tension between, for instance, understandability, and legal correctness, manifests itself in that the provision of legal correct information requires often difficult terms, elaboration, and contains nuances, exclusions and exceptions, all of which make the text less understandable.

2.5.1.B Technical (Legal) Correctness

That information provided must be (legally) correct seems rather straightforward, but the question rises what 'correct' entails, in the light of the multi-level legal systems, subject of this research. For instance, Dutch government perceives the legal norm of 'correct' in terms of art. 48 Pensioenwet (PW) as an obligation of results.[269] This may have potentially far-reaching consequences.[270]

For the purpose of the present research, the correctness of information entails that the information provided is, in any case, substantively correct, i.e. observing prevailing laws, regulations and policies on a national, European and international level. What the regulatory frameworks encompass, is mapped out in chapter 1. The information must therefore correspond to these complex multi-level legal systems. Furthermore, it requires that the information must be consistent with the pension agreement (between employer and employee) and with the pension regulation (between pension administrator and participant). Providing information on future retirement benefits is herewith marked by an inherent error susceptibility.

---

265 GR Klare, *The Measurement of Readability* (Iowa State University Press, Ames, Iowa 1963) and GR Klare, 'Assessing readability' 10 Reading Research Quarterly 62.

266 C Keinki and others, 'Understandability of Patient Information Booklets for Patients with Cancer' 33 Journal of Cancer Education 517, 518.

267 See YC Xu and Z Chen, 'Relevance judgment: What do information users consider beyond topicality?' 57 Journal of the Association for Information Science and Technology 961.

268 Cf. Zuccon, 8.

269 Kamerstukken II, *Wet pensioencommunicatie* 4.

270 See Maatman, 144 and cited literature.

The notion of technical (legal) correctness does not follow from Dual Process Theory. Yet, it can be assumed that people may rely on the correctness of the information provided.[271] Correctness requires that all case-pertinent rules and regulations – at all levels of the multi-level legal systems – must be observed. It further brings about that information may not contain any contradictions, either within the same content or between different information mediums/sources. Given the complexity of a wide range of diverging pension schemes, and the multi-level legal systems, providing correct information appears to be a considerable challenge, partly in view of the high susceptibility to errors. While entirely upholding legal correctness would lead to too complex and overwhelming information, providing understandable information requires losing nuances, preciseness of particular terms (e.g. 'pension' as dealt with in chapter 4), leaving out exceptions to certain rules, losing particularities for specific situations, and other case-specific details. This implies that understandable information – at the expense of its correctness and personal relevance – is less precise, leaving room for deviating interpretations, potentially engendering ambiguity among readers.

The question then emerges what the risk of providing incorrect information entails from a behavioural point of view, i.e. how may it affect people's attitudes, beliefs, and/or behavioural (expectations), and what tensions (in information provision) may it induce? Against the background of the principles and the framework as set out in this chapter, the most important point is that false information may lead to ambiguity among readers, leading them to call the information's trustworthiness into question. This will be dealt with in more detail in section 2.5.1.D.

In this regard, people's knowledge takes a prominent role, in that in cases where people evaluate the trustworthiness of information, they rely on cognitive authorities, who they regard appropriate sources to do so.[272] In recognizing cognitive authority of information,

---

271 For instance, a citizen may assume that the information on the Tax Administration's website is correct. See Kamerstukken II, *35 586, 6 Verslag over het verzoekschrift van de heer C. te M. Betreffende een verzoek om afgifte van een verklaring niet-afgetrokken lijfrentepremies* (2020/21). This case concerned a balance statement pertaining to deducted annuity premiums. At the time of the request for a balance statement, the Dutch Tax Authorities' website contained incorrect information. A balancing statement is a statement from the tax authorities stating which amount of non-deducted annuity premiums will remain untaxed when the annuity is paid. During the accumulation phase of an annuity the premiums are deductible as far as there is sufficient annual and reserve margin (pension deficit). The periodic payments from this annuity are taxed. The committee's report demonstrates what the legal status of a balance statement is. The Tax Authorities provide a service to the taxpayer, but it has no official status. It constitutes, in legal terms, not a decision. This also means that the taxpayer has no opportunity to lodge an objection or appeal if he disagrees with the balancing statement, or with the Tax Authorities' refusal to issue one.

272 DR Donaldson, 'The Digitized Archival Document Trustworthiness Scale' 11 International Journal of Digital Curation 252, 255.

people rely, *inter alia*, on the intrinsic plausibility of the text.[273] Under this evaluation criterion, people – while relying on their prior knowledge – evaluate the information's content, based on how (plausible) the information looks.[274] This suggests that if people are exposed to a net amount of future retirement income without any disclaimer, they may get the impression that this fairly obvious optimistic estimate may be not entirely correct, while building on their prior knowledge, or social representations, pertaining to taxes. For instance, they may have the knowledge that computing a future amount of retirement income is not as easy as ostensibly depicted, but requires a lot more of personally-relevant facts and circumstances, in particular in cross-border cases (e.g. other relevant income, deductible expenses, their state of mobility, applicable international tax rules etc.)

Moreover, as Sunstein puts it, it must be ensured that information is not merely technically accurate but also understandable, useful and trustworthy.[275] Tensions as regards correctness may arise, when information is simplified for the benefits of its understandability. Simplifying information implies that this may be at the cost of legal correctness, for instance since details or exceptions are left out in order to ensure the information's understandability.

2.5.1.C Personal Relevance

A further principle shaping this research's evaluation framework is information's personal relevance – commonly referred to as accuracy – a motivational variable under Dual Process Theory.[276] As relevance of information increases, people devote more attention to the information.[277] In day-to-day situations, some types of information that people are confronted with have direct personal implications for them (for instance increasing sales tax), whereas others don't (the bilateral tax convention concluded between the Netherlands and Germany will be amended, affecting mobile citizens). Thus, especially where information has direct personal implications, people tend to think it over, since, after all, people can only process a limited amount of information they are exposed to, and it would be most apt to devote most of the time to that information with the most personal consequences. In addition, research findings demonstrate that argument quality is a more important determinant of persuasion when personal relevance is high instead of low.[278]

273 P Wilson, *Second-hand knowledge: An inquiry into cognitive authority* (Greenwood Press, Westport, Connecticut 1983).
274 Donaldson, 255.
275 Cf. Sunstein, 1411.
276 See Petty and others, 87.
277 Ibid. 89 and cited literature.
278 Ibid. 91 and cited literature.

This implies that people are more likely to engage spontaneously in the effortful evaluation process (i.e. central route) as the perceived personal relevance of the message increases.[279]

It is to be noted that although personal relevance is an important determinant of people's motivation to deliberate upon information they are exposed to, it is not the only one. In some cases, tensions may emerge as personal relevant information may be ineffective if the information provided is too detailed, complex, poorly framed or overwhelming to be understandable.[280] It can thus be concluded that personalized information is, in particular, effective in engaging information processing. Tensions may also emerge between personal relevance and understandability; understandability is often achieved at the expense of personal relevance and vice versa. A potential explanation for this lies in the fact that understandability requires that specific personal circumstances and particularities – shaping a taxable person's financial position – are left out, at the expense of the information's personal relevance. Therefore, in practice, a balance must be struck so that the provision is as precise as possible, whilst remaining sufficiently easy to understand.

2.5.1.D Trustworthiness

There is no universal definition of trustworthiness, but it may have different meanings in different contexts. Depending on the context, it may refer to reliability of information, authenticity of information etc. Research demonstrates that people employ systematic and/or heuristic processing when evaluating the trustworthiness of (online) information.[281] Where systematic processing entails the evaluation of content to arrive at trustworthiness judgements, heuristic processing does not entail the evaluation of content, but rather; the reliance on cues related to information objects, in order to come to trustworthiness judgements.[282] Furthermore, people show a higher tendency to employ the heuristic evaluation of trustworthiness, compared to the systematic content evaluation. This is induced by the fact that systematic evaluation requires more cognitive effort, particular for people who are not a domain expert.[283] People believing that they possess domain expertise, and having the motivation to do so, employ a systemic evaluation.[284] What is

279 Ibid. 92. See also RE Burnkrant and HR Unnava, 'Self-referencing: A strategy for increasing processing of message content' 15 Personality and Social Psychology Bulletin 628.

280 See CR Sunstein, 'Empirically informed regulation,' 78 The university of Chicago Law Review 1349, 1370.

281 SS Sundar, 'The MAIN model: A heuristic approach to understanding technology effects on credibility' in MJ Metzger and AJ Flanagin (eds.), *Digital media, youth, and credibility* (MIT Press, Cambridge 2008).

282 Donaldson, 255.

283 Ibid. 255 referring to S Chaiken, 'Heuristic versus systematic information processing and the use of source versus message cues in persuasion' 39 Journal of personality and social psychology 752, and MJ Metzger, 'Making sense of credibility on the Web: Models for evaluating online information and recommendations for future research' 58 Journal of the American Society for Information Science and Technology 2078.

284 Metzger.

more, when evaluating trustworthiness, it appears that in practice, people often tend to rely on heuristic processing, in some cases on systematic processing, and in some cases on a combination of both. Noteworthy at this point is that when people employ systematic content evaluation, or combine systematic and heuristic evaluation, to assess the information's content trustworthiness, the evaluation of trustworthiness may serve as a predictor of the information's understandability.[285] This exemplifies the interrelatedness of the principles demarcating information's effectiveness.

In cases where people evaluate the trustworthiness of information, they rely on cognitive authorities, who they regard appropriate sources to do so.[286] Wilson enumerated four tests in order to recognise cognitive authority of information.[287] First, the cognitive authority of the author (the trustworthiness of an author corresponds to his reputation, i.e. 'we can trust a text if it is the work of an individual or group of individuals whom we can trust'). Second, the publication history (e.g. people trust books published by Oxford University Press because it has earned a reputation of being a publishing house publishing merely high-quality and trustworthy work). The third test is the authority of the text type, for instance, research monographs possess a higher degree of cognitive authority, compared to high school-study books. The most important for the purpose of the present study is the fourth test, i.e. intrinsic plausibility of the text. Under this test, the information's content is evaluated itself, i.e. people trust information because it looks and seems plausible, given what they know.[288] For instance, seemingly too optimistic pension information may cause people to have a too favourable picture of their expected retirement income and, consequently, these people get a wrong impression of their retirement income.[289] Wilson refers to it as 'a text usually has only one chance to capture our attention and interest; reading a few words of it may be enough to discourage us from continuing or may lure us on to reading the whole thing'.[290] With regard to assessing the trustworthiness of online information, people seem to rely on characteristics of information objects, such as content, type of information object, title, structure of the information, and presentation.[291]

In the present research, trustworthiness plays a pivotal role with regard to including a disclaimer in the intervention, given the overly complex multi-level legal systems. From a

285 Donaldson, 257.

286 Ibid. 255.

287 Wilson.

288 Donaldson, 255.

289 Although fairly outdated, see, for instance, Autoriteit Financiële Markten, 'Geef Nederlanders pensioeninzicht: werken aan vertrouwen door dichten van de verwachtingskloof' (2010).

290 Wilson.

291 SY Rieh, 'Judgment of information quality and cognitive authority in the Web' 53 Journal of the American Society for Information Science and Technology 145.

legal perspective, it might seem appropriate to include a disclaimer (pointing out that the depicted amounts may vary in future, due to, for instance, changing legislation), in order to prevent from being held liable for reasons of providing erroneous information.[292] Including a disclaimer may, however, induce ambiguity, causing uncertainty and anxiousness among readers, causing them to question the information's trustworthiness.[293] On the contrary, it could also render the information more realistic and honest(-looking), elevating the information's trustworthiness, in particular as regards net amounts of future retirement income. This will be dealt with in further detail in chapter 3 of this research.

2.6 Translating a Distanced Approach Into an Operationalized Paradigm of 'The Law'

2.6.1 Translation in Lieu of Extrapolation

The previous section outlined the concept of 'effective information'. In outlining this concept, four principles have been set – largely extracted from Dual Process Theory – which shape the subjective (person-centred) perspective of effective information: understandability, technical (legal) correctness, personal relevance, and trustworthiness. In doing so, this research incorporates external evaluation criteria to draw conclusions.[294] This use of external criteria in the assessment framework, unequivocally, leads to an multidisciplinary nature of the legal research.

The mere extrapolation of experimental/empirical findings while neglecting the difficulties of translating these often highly context-dependent empirical patterns into a legal setting, is considered to be hazardous in terms of normativity, and in terms of broadly applicable prescriptive conclusions.[295] One has to bear in mind that where one relies on empirical

292 As done in mijnpensioenregister.nl: 'De bedragen zijn berekend op basis van de huidige wet- en regelgeving en de gegevens van uw pensioenuitvoerder(s).'

293 EIOPA, 46.

294 It can also be referred to as 'assessment by reference on external standard'. See Taekema and Van Klink, 9-10. Tijssen, 74 van Dijck, 22 and Mackor, 79.

295 See C Engel and others, 'Verhaltenswissenschaftliche Analyse: eine Gebrauchsanweisung für Juristen' in C Engel (ed.), *Recht und Verhalten* (Mohr Siebeck, 2007) who puts it as follows: *"Das Herzstück der Verhaltenswissenschaft sind empirische Befunde. Man muss diese Befunde richtig deuten und ihre Tragweite richtig einschätzen . . . oft fehlen empirische Ergebnisse gerade dort, wo man als Jurist besonders auf sie angewiesen wäre . . . Dann kann man sich nur noch mit Hypothesen helfen. Dafür bräuchte man durchdachte Theorie. Leider fehlt sie oft . . . auch dort, wo man auf empirische Resultate oder theoretische Modelle zurückgreifen kann, sollte man im Auge behalten, dass sie mit einem ganz anderen Erkenntnisinteresse gewonnen worden sind. Deshalb versteht sich die Integration verhaltenswissenschaftlicher Ergebnisse oder Einsichten in das recht nicht von selbst."*

results or theoretical models, that they have been obtained with an entirely different interest in knowledge, compared to the legal domain. Hence, the one-on-one integration of empirical results or insights into the realm of law is not self-evident. Nevertheless, these findings can be used for drafting empirically-informed policy.[296] A way out of this predicament is to adopt a 'distanced approach', in which the law does not take these empirically-gained insights at their nominal value, but requires a process of translation, which generates added value to legal doctrine.[297] For the purposes of this research, these empirical insights – extracted from behavioural economics, economic psychology and cognitive psychology – are translated into a paradigm which sees the law as a complex multi-level legal system, (un)fit for the provision of effective pension information. This is more or less tantamount to an empirically-informed approach.[298]

I interpret, and give further effect to, this process of translation by translating/transposing the information's behavioural purpose, and the four principles which delineate the concept of effective pension information – founded on the empirically-shaped Dual Process Theory – into legal (applicable) standards. These legal standards do not necessarily dictate how the law ought to be, but, rather, should be used to establish a non-binding framework through which the law is evaluated. It constitutes the 'paradigm' through which the law is perceived. It is intended to explore the 'fitness' of the regulatory frameworks ('law in action') through the lens of effective information provision, and to see whether legal/non-legal interventions and measures are needed to ensure, and potentially foster, the effectiveness of the information provided. By adopting this distanced/empirically informed approach, however, I believe I see myself much less confronted with the risk of the normativity of empirically-generated insights, as these are not merely extrapolated to the legal domain by forming binding legal standards.

Moreover, this process of translation renders these empirically gained insights far more practically applicable in terms of evaluating 'the law as it stands', as it reflects certain properties of this law better than mere empirical findings. This may be due to the fact that empirical findings have been obtained with an entirely different interest in knowledge, compared to the legal domain. What is more, the process of translation embodies the operationalisation of the insights extracted from behavioural economics, economic psychology and cognitive psychology in terms of legal evaluative research. This allows, for instance, to determine whether a regulatory framework has a 'deterrent effect' in practice, or is 'fit' to attain a certain objective. This is akin to the present research's main objective,

296 See Sunstein.

297 See also Teubner, 1.

298 See Sunstein. See also Teubner, 1.

in short, to explore to what extent the regulatory frameworks on a national level in the Netherlands and Germany, on a European level, and on an international level, governing the taxation of (cross-border) statutory, occupational and personal pensions, are fit for the provision of effective information.

2.6.2 Translating the Two-dimensional Notion of Effectiveness Into Legal Standards

In order to establish a (non-binding) framework on the basis of which the fitness of the regulatory frameworks can be evaluated, it is necessary to fall back on the behavioural purpose and the four principles – based on Dual Process Theory – as cited in sections 2.4 and 2.5. In this way, the empirical insights extracted from the domain of behavioural economics, economic psychology and cognitive psychology are translated (applicably) into the legal domain, rather than extrapolated. This legal lens is better apt for evaluating the fitness of the regulatory frameworks, as it observes certain properties (such as the multi-level property), without accepting it as untestable. While taking the behavioural purpose as the starting point (in terms of effectiveness), combined with the four principles – extracted from Dual Process Theory constitutes the two-dimensionality of the information's effectiveness as visualised in figure 2.3.

Figure 2.3 Typology of the Two Dimensions Of Information's Effectiveness

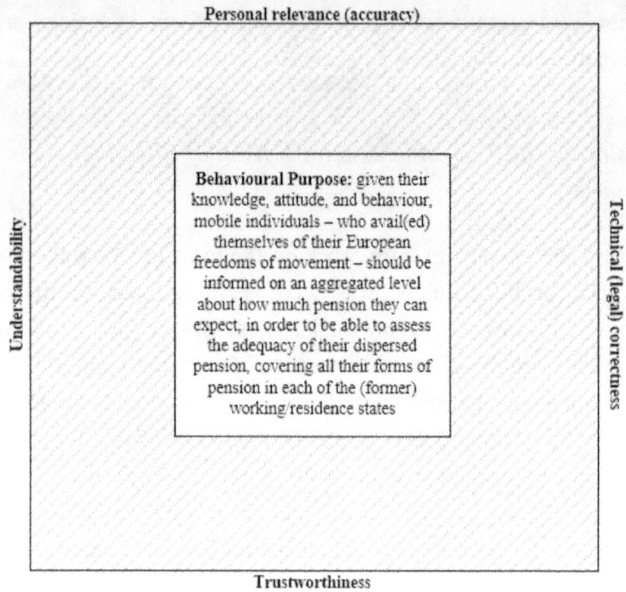

Figure 2.3 represents that effectiveness is determined by the degree to which the behavioural purpose is achieved. In short, if the information provides an answer to these questions – i.e. it contains these information elements – regarding his/her fragmented pension, and the mobile citizen is empowered to assess the pension's adequacy, the information achieves its objective. However, as already indicated in the above, while the information's purpose specifies what information should be provided, it does not yet specify how this information should be provided in terms of effectiveness. Not elaborating on how information should be provided, would deny the comprehensiveness of the construct effectiveness of information. In this vein, it should be stressed that there is a difference between a mere technical disclosure of information – regardless of form, point in time and related usefulness – and actually sensibly information choices.[299] As has been thoroughly discussed in section 2.2, ability and motivational factors are pivotal in peoples' decision to (whether or not) look closer into particular pieces of information. Again, the goal here is not to argue that these principles are the only ones to be taken into account, although I suspect that these four qualities capture most, if not all, of the properties of the effectiveness of information provision, given the considerable body of literature on the Dual Process Theory.

299 Sunstein, 1417.

As illustrated in figure 2.3 above, the information's effectiveness is structured by elements referred to as the nucleus and the periphery. Where the nucleus establishes the information's behavioural purpose, the periphery (at the border) consists of the four principles – extracted from Dual Process Theory – ensuring the information's effectiveness. Once people are exposed to information, they enter 'the gates' of effective information. For instance, in order for information to achieve its behavioural purpose, it is of eminent importance that people actually read the document, and not be deterred by *prima facie* difficult to understand, not trustworthy, not personally relevant, or apparent incorrect information. Once entered, they are closer to the information purpose, where it also remains to be seen whether the information achieves its objective. For a more elaborate discussion on these four principles (understandability, technical (legal) correctness, personal relevance (accuracy), and trustworthiness) I refer to the previous section.

2.6.3 *Effective Information Provision: What it Requires vis-à-vis the Multi-Level Legal Systems*

Providing, on an aggregated level, mobile individuals information about how much pension they can expect – covering all their forms of pension in each of the (former) working/residence states – requires a complex process of incorporating all types of diverging pension vehicles, schemes, products of all sorts, arising from statutory, occupational and individual pension systems in each of the different (former) working states, and/or residence states. This requires a process of converging these deviating systems into standardised/uniform information provision, while upholding the information's effectiveness. Putting this dispersed puzzle together also poses considerable challenges in terms of information provision. This amounts to observing, and 'translating' the intersections between different multi-level legal systems (national, EU and international/bilateral) and the interaction of poorly coordinated legal domains (pension and tax law), which can all be interwoven in a personal mobile situation, into effective pension information. In sum, it must be possible to compile the amounts accrued with different pension providers/schemes so that they can be processed in a standardised manner. It, thus, requires a more holistic approach in terms of information provision.

At this point, it should be noted that not each of these legal principles shall be evaluated to the same extent in each of the chapters that follow. The variety in testing against these principles cannot be reduced to certain standard situations. It is much more of a sliding scale where all variations between fit and unfit can be found. This depends on the pertinence with respect to the domain, properties and modalities, of the regulatory frameworks that will be considered. The intensity of this evaluation is partly determined by the purpose of the particular area of legislation (e.g. EU law), but also by its properties and degree of impact (on e.g. national law). For instance, in chapter 4 – exploring the construct 'pension' – emphasis will be put on the principle of similarity/comparability, since this chapter seeks to delineate, and operationalise the dispersed construct of pension as the subject of this research, and how this relates to the notion of effective pension information. Moreover, the principle of foreseeability plays a role to a lesser extent in this regard. In addition, in chapters 8 and 9, the principle of inter-level coherence is at the centre of the evaluative findings as these chapters explore the taxation of cross-border pensions governed by European law and international tax law, and to what extent there is room for improvement in terms of coherence. It will become apparent that international tax law and EU law – in the field of direct taxes – are inextricably linked in, to some extent, achieving coherence among the different domains of law.

Although the four principles addressed above are foundational in effective pension information, legal content-challenges still persist and potentially hamper this effective information. The challenge remains to offer information based on this complexity of content while upholding the basic principles of effective information. For example, ensuring the legal correctness of information requires systematic monitoring and updating, as laws and policies are constantly changing. What is more, heterogeneity among national legal systems is a universal phenomenon, due to, inter alia, historical developments, adaption to different social developments, economic trends and developments, different political landscapes etc. Hitherto, the consequences of differences in these national systems for the domain of information provision have rarely been addressed. What is required – in terms of information provision – with respect to the legal systems, will be discussed in the section below.

As it is this research's main objective to explore how the regulatory frameworks on a national, European, and an international level operate in the light of effective information provision, it will also be briefly touched upon how these two realms intertwine. For instance, in order to uphold (legal) correctness, combined with understandability, of information, national legal systems need to be aligned in terms of coherence. In addition, to ensure the information's correctness and – in the long run – trustworthiness regulatory frameworks need to adhere to legislation's foreseeability. This elucidates how the realms of empirically-gained insights from behavioural economics, economic psychology and cognitive psychology, and the realm of multi-level legal systems are related. Although portrayed as two separate spheres (effective pension information and multi-level legal systems respectively), it is my belief that these realms should be integrated better, for the benefits of both spheres. The research below seeks to elucidate why this should be done. Moreover, this translation into legal (applicable) concepts, and notions, enables to connect the two abovementioned realms, and enables to address this research's main research objective, and main research question. As the OECD puts it, laws and regulations should be considered as an 'information system' linking (government) administration and citizens.[300] Furthermore, a variety of difficulties may make it difficult for governments to translate new laws and rules into reality. These difficulties relate to complexity, inconsistency, lack of coordination, and lack of information on the effects of laws. Dealing with legal and regulatory burdens of a legal system, may also render legislation non-understandable for citizens.

During the process of law- and policymaking, recourse shall be had to these standards in drafting rules and regulations, enabling to incorporate (and weigh) numerous viewpoints and interests related to 'the law', and its corresponding application. These non-legal insights, and their translation into legal standards ought to widen the 'paradigm' of law- and policy-making. This contextual approach (or 'law in context') – shaped by the external evaluation criteria – helps to explore the operation in practice of this particular legal field, which is more revealing than the mere exposition of the legal rules under investigation.

2.6.3.A Similarity/Comparability

The information's behavioural purpose stipulates that mobile individuals should be informed on an aggregated level about how much pension they can expect, in order to be able to assess the adequacy of their dispersed pension, covering all their forms of pension in each of the (former) working/residence states. This contains the terms 'aggregated' (i.e. assembled at an overall/higher level) and the phrase 'covering all their forms of pension in each of the (former) working/residence states'. This requires putting together dispersed, and deviating, elements of future retirement income, arising in each of these states. In short, it requires to be able to sum up each of these amounts in order to find an answer to the question 'what will I get?'; and 'will this be sufficient?'. Despite the fact that pension systems – and their taxation – in Europe are as diverse as the European Member States themselves, finding a common way of communicating about pensions is not an easy task.

A higher degree of similarity helps to ensure the effectiveness of information in terms of the four principles. For instance, the higher the degree of similarity, the easier it is to uphold the information's correctness, trustworthiness, and personal relevance. After all, with a higher degree of similarity, there is less need to observe any underlying structural

300 OECD, 'Improving the Quality of Laws and Regulations: Economic, Legal, and Managerial Techniques' (1994) [OCDE/GD(94)59] 51. The OECD also points to a variety of serious problems which can arise from incomprehensible legal requirements: low levels of compliance, uncertainty regarding obligations (both for citizens and administrators), problems with enforceability and consistency, and isolation of the law from the general populace and weakening of the commitment to the rule of law.

differences. Moreover, a higher degree of similarity leads to a higher comparability of the different regulatory frameworks/legal constructs, avoiding comparing the incomparable. Similarity/comparability does not only relate to legal constructs but also to the use of terms, definitions, and concepts. What is more, it is revealed that existing categorisation systems (e.g. World Bank Model) are of little use in aiding similarity/comparability, but rather take a role in understanding structural differences, once revealed.

Exploring similarity between systems involves a comparison of certain features. For instance, when it comes to the legal character of 'pensions' it appears that the idea of care and the perception of pension as deferred wage is more or less to be regarded as universal, both in the Netherlands as well as in Germany. The assessment of similarity is described as a feature-matching process, i.e. it measures the degree to which two objects (for instance, the Dutch and German definition of 'pension') – both considered a set of features – match each other.[301] Similarity is tantamount to a measurement of common features, i.e. pensionable age, deductibility of contributions, taxation of benefits etc. It must be pointed out that this measurement of common features cannot be quantified in this comprehensive legal comparison, as this would require adhering a particular weight to each of these features (e.g. accrual method, pensionable age, deductbility of contributions, taxation of benefits). Such a 'quantification' would require a different research methodology, analysing the relative weight of each of these pension features in the overall national pension system. In the present research the evaluation is more of a sliding scale, ranging from 'fit' to 'unfit' along the lines of this research's evaluation framework. The more the systems exhibit common features, the better their comparability. That is, similarity increases with addition of common features and/or deletion of distinctive features.[302] When it comes to the two systems under scrutiny, these two regulatory systems have the same objective – i.e. taxing pensions – but have a different shape, historical development, political background, underlying principles, rationales, modalities, and technicalities.[303] Through the lens of the evaluation framework outlined in chapter 2, the present research is aimed at revealing impediments in the regulatory frameworks for providing effective pension information. These impediments include, inter alia, structural differences in the national regulatory frameworks governing the taxation of cross-border pensions. This (externally)[304] comparative research constitutes a preliminary step preceding the evaluative research objective.[305]

301 A Tversky, 'Features of Similarity' 84 Psychological Review 327, 330.

302 See ibid. 330.

303 As Danneman argues: "*There is no point in comparing what is identical, and little point in comparing what has nothing in common*". See Dannemann, 384.

304 In that two present-day legal systems shall be compared.

305 Oderkerk, *De preliminaire fase van het rechtsvergelijkend onderzoek* 16.

2.6.3.B Inter-level Coherence

In order to prevent discrepancies in information provision, different fields of multi-level law need to be aligned with each other, i.e. national (Netherlands and Germany); European, and international.[306] For the purpose and context of the present research, 'coherence' is termed as 'the situation in which all the levels of the regulatory frameworks are logical and consistent, achieving a harmonious connection of these parts, so that the whole 'hangs together'.[307]

This underlines the relevance of certain properties of regulatory frameworks, and its consequences, for information provision, and corresponding implications. As will become apparent in this research's descriptive chapters, a challenge for the provision of information, along the principles as set forth in section 2.5, is the diversity – and poor coordination – of differentiated pension vehicles, and taxes.[308] From this point of view, in order to uphold the information's effectiveness, it requires a certain degree of coherence among these levels of legislation. At lower levels, this may involve systematic scrutiny of coherence with higher-level regulations and with treaty or other international obligations, which will be dealt with in chapter 8 of this research. A higher degree of coherence also helps to ensure the effectiveness of information in terms of the four principles, in that more coherence between low and higher levels of legislation aids ensuring the information's effectiveness. For instance, in a more coherent (logically and consistent ordered) multi-level legal systems, it is far easier to uphold the information's correctness and trustworthiness, as in such a system, there is less susceptibility to error. It needs to be emphasised that the term 'coherence' should not be confounded with 'cohesion' as used by the CJEU. With the latter term, the CJEU's concept of fiscal cohesion refers to the need to match, within the same tax jurisdiction, tax base reductions and corresponding tax base increases, such as annuity contributions and annuity benefits.[309]

2.6.3.C Inter-system Consistency

In order to prevent discrepancies in information provision, national (Netherlands and Germany) levels of legislation, need to be consistent by themselves. However, legal systems consist of, *inter alia*, a set of rules. In general, legislators would prefer that legislation in a

306 See also OECD, 'Recommendation of the Council of the OECD on Regulatory Policy and Governance' (2012) 14.

307 Oxford Dictionaries.

308 In the same vein: CR Sunstein, 'Informing consumers through smart disclosure' Memorandum for the heads of executive departments and agencies 5.

309 See also PJ Wattel, O Marres and H Vermeulen, *European Tax Law* (Kluwer, Deventer 2018) 680. As a justification ground, the fiscal cohesion-argument first appeared in C-204/90 *Bachmann* ECLI:EU:C:1992:35 (CJEU).

particular legal system were consistent.[310] Not only on a domestic level, but in particular where several national legal systems converge as in this research; on Dutch/German level. This requires a certain form of inter-system consistency. For the purposes of this research 'consistency' is termed as 'the quality, state, or fact of being consistent; agreement, harmony, compatibility'.[311]

Consistency, in this context, refers to – while applying national regulatory frameworks – not leading to incompatible outcomes for a specific case. This construct of consistency of rules is not only of interest for the development of legal systems, but also of practical interest for the provision of information, building on these legal systems. More specifically, in terms of consistency, rules themselves can constitute a constraint relative to which consistency has to be judged.[312] In the context of this study, the consistency of rules is assessed against the background of effective information.

It is not uncommon that rules in two legal systems attach incompatible consequences to a same case. For instance, pursuant to Dutch tax law a similar type of occupational pension is subject to deferred taxation, while Germany tax law denies this preferential treatment of this pension, as it holds a deviating perception on what occupational pension schemes comprise, and, hence, shall be eligible for fiscal facilitation. In such cases, the law contains a *prima facie* cross-border rule conflict. Two or more rules are in actual conflict when they actually apply to one and the same case, and attach incompatible consequences to this case.

The requirement of consistency is not deeply rooted in Dutch, nor German, nor European or international tax legislation. It is even contested that inconsistency is – generally speaking – one of the most frequent manifestations of unfairness that a person may encounter.[313] Where often there are distinctions which justify the difference in treatment, sometimes there is no apparent distinction to be drawn. In this regard, the question rises to what extent – for instance – the CJEU may provide a remedy against the inconsistency of (the application of) legislation. Two distinct types of inconsistency may be discerned: treating a person inconsistently over time, and inconsistency between individuals.[314] Both types will be involved in this research.

310 J Hage, 'Rule consistency' 19 Law and Philosophy 369, 369.
311 Oxford Dictionaries.
312 Hage, 370.
313 K Steyn, 'Consistency – A Principle of Public Law?' 2 Judicial Review 22, 22.
314 Ibid. 22.

2.6.3.D Foreseeability and (Un)predictability

As will set forth in more detail below, no one can, however, simply rely on the maintenance of the law in force.[315] Applicable legislation is designed in view of particular political, economic, societal phenomena. These phenomena tend to change over time, and accordingly, legislation is adapted to the new situation. It is therefore that conveying information on future amounts of retirement income usually involves a certain level of risk as regards continuously changing legislation.

Predictability is a structure, and information lies where unpredictable change occurs.[316] What is more, an aspect that seems inherent to tax law is its complexity.[317] Specific, case and condition-particular, complex rules often lead to uncertainty, especially as regards their application. This uncertainty as regards (the application) of tax law in cross-border cases, originates from various sources, where – as a rule – unpredictability is the outcome of uncertainty. Rules and regulations, surrounded by uncertainty are difficult to predict/ foresee. This means unpredictability of legal systems is intertwined with the ability of these systems to adopt to changes with a different background. First, tax law and regulations are attuned to 'social reality', i.e. it reflects the status quo of society in all its facets. This applies, for example, not only to how citizens relate to each other but particularly how they relate to government. As such, tax law moves with the trends as they are observed in society as a whole, it entails a considerable degree of responsiveness. Second, of a more technical nature, national tax law is responsive to developments in the areas of positive integration, negative integration, and in particular the concept of 'non-discrimination' as interpreted by the CJEU. This will become apparent in chapter 8 of this research. Where national tax legislation is found to be in breach of the non-discrimination principle, Member States are obliged to bring national legislation in line with it, reflecting the concept of the European internal market without internal borders, and ensuring freedom of movement for EU-citizens.

In addition, tax legislation is characterized as the outcome of political decision-making, coalition building and compromise. Choices in the tax domain are of a political-administrative nature, and it is often not for the courts to step in. Although political decision-making can be traced back through parliamentary documents, a certain degree of uncertainty is inherent in the system of coalition building and political compromise. As a rule, the final outcome cannot be foreseen *a priori*. This generally falls short of the

315 P Popelier, 'Beginselen van behoorlijke wetgeving in de rechtspraak' 1995 Tijdschrift voor Privaatrecht (BE) 1049, 1078.
316 See also R Giora, 'On the Informativeness Requirement' 12 Journal of Pragmatics 547, 549.
317 Cf. Kirchler, *The Economic Psychology of Tax Behaviour* 187.

outcome that is seen as theoretically most pure. What is more, long-term decisions incorporate expectations of the future situation (e.g. retirement), as a part of which legal rules and public play an instrumental role.[318]

Also the OECD stressed the relevance of the foreseeability of legislation.[319] Moreover, the OECD stressed that regulations should be clear, consistent, comprehensible and accessible to users.[320] Also the CJEU holds that foreseeability is an imperative requirement which must be strictly complied with, in particular in the case of schemes liable to have financial implications, i.e. the law must be known and its application must be foreseeable.[321]

From a more empirically informed perspective, it can be pointed out that in general tax law is less receptive to embedding morality. Generally, people think of taxes as non-normative – not related to behavioural norms – since we opt to subject economically productive behaviour to tax, instead of immoral behaviour. Hence, tax law seems to lack moral legitimacy.[322] Contrarily, people consider non-tax laws (e.g. civil law or criminal law) to be, in essence, normative, and evaluate them based on moral imperatives. Non-tax laws embody cultural standards, often mirrored in the law as it stands. As these mandates potentially coincide with generally accepted morality, we consider these laws primarily as stimulating, and upholding, morality.[323] People thus tend to focus on the moral content of these non-tax laws, and belief that these domains of legislation are more moral and less economically depriving than tax laws. This bias in our perspective of tax and other realms of law, is not because we have never considered the inevitable impacts of taxes on (changing) behaviour and of non-tax laws on individuals compared to their economic

318 Popelier, 1078; F Lamoreux, 'The retroactivity of Community acts in the case law of the Court of justice' Common Market Law Review 510 and E Fuß, 'Der Schutz des Vertrauens auf Rechtskontinuität im deutschen Verfassungsrecht und europäischen Gemeinschaftsrecht' in W Grewe, H Rupp and H Schneider (eds.), *Europäische Gerichtsbarkeit und nationale Verfassungsgerichtsbarkeit* (Nomos, Baden-Baden 1981) 66.

319 APEC-OECD, 'Integrated Checklist on Regulatory Reform: a Policy Instrument for Regulatory Quality, Competition Policy and Market Openness' (2008) 15. As regards the documents and opinions issued by the OECD, these are non-binding. However, the requirements pertaining to legislation, set by this institution, cannot be easily ignored by affiliated states.

320 OECD, 'Recommendation of the Council on Improving the Quality of Government Regulation' (1995) [C(95)21/FINAL] point 34.

321 See also C-326/85 *Commission vs Netherlands* ECLI:EU:C:1987:547 (CJEU) para 24:„*Moreover, as the Court has repeatedly held, Community legislation must be certain and its application foreseeable by those subject to it. That requirement of legal certainty must be observed all the more strictly in the case of rules liable to entail financial consequences, in order that those concerned may know precisely the extent of the obligations which they impose on them.*" See also C-348/85 *Kingdom of Denmark v Commission* ECLI:EU:C:1987:552 (CJEU); C-30/89 *Commission v French Republic* ECLI:EU:C:1990:114 (CJEU); 92 and 93/87 (joined cases) *Commission vs. French Republic/United Kingdom and Northern-Ireland* ECLI:EU:C:1989:77 (CJEU).

322 Rosenberg, 170.

323 Cf. Ibid. 171.

situation. In endorse Rosenberg's argument that we do not think that way enough and that we tend to fall victim to our (unexamined) assumptions about tax law, which (vastly) over determine the manner in which we both use and perceive taxes/tax law.[324] As moral imperatives alter at a fairly slower pace, and tax law seems to largely lack moral legitimacy, it seems that tax law is less predictable as it lacks a certain 'compass of stability'. In a sense, moral imperatives ensure a degree of foreseeability. Tax law, rather, adapts to the developments as described above. This degree of tax law's volatility engenders uncertainty, and, hence, unforeseeability.

2.7 Interim Conclusion: Where the Realms of Pensions, Taxes and Information Provision Intersect

This chapter has drawn up the boundaries of this research's evaluation framework in order to answer this research's main research question. In sum, the fitness of the regulatory frameworks investigated in this research, are evaluated from the perspective of effective information. Effectiveness is considered a two-dimensional construct where both the information's behavioural purpose, as well as the principle of understandability, technical (legal) correctness, personal relevance, and trustworthiness take an eminent role. These four principles – mainly inferred from the Dual Process Theory – serve as the evaluation framework, after translating them into more legal (applicable) standards: similarity/ comparability, inter-level coherence, inter-system consistency, and foreseeability. Each of the descriptive chapters of this research, is concluded with an interim conclusion pertaining to how the regulatory frameworks stand, and operate in the light of these principles. The chapter above conceptualised the notion of 'effective pension information', in the light of which the 'fitness' of the regulatory frameworks will be assessed, i.e. it established this research's evaluation framework. In doing so, in terms of empirically-gained (non-)legal insights, this chapter constitutes the framework *generalis*. This is tantamount to this research's first goal, i.e. to establish a theoretical and conceptual evaluation framework, focusing on the provision of effective pension information. Building on this, the 'fitness' of the legal frameworks at the national, European and international level shall be assessed, focusing in particular on any deficiencies that have an effect on the provision of effective information. This evaluation allows to formulate points for improvement and recommendations, mainly with regard to what (legal) interventions and measures are needed to ensure, and potentially foster, the effectiveness of the pension information provided (third research objective). Chapter 3 – below – revolves around the empirical study conducted as part of this research. This chapter looks more closely at the

324 Ibid. 170.

notion of 'effective pension information' and, in doing so, serves more as the framework *specialis*. In this vein, recommendations will be put forward – mainly in chapter 10 – pertaining to what (non-)legal interventions and measures are needed to ensure, and potentially foster, the effectiveness of the pension information provided.

3 WHAT WILL I GET? RELATIVITY BIAS DRIVING PEOPLE TOWARDS NET AMOUNTS

This chapter describes the empirical study conducted as part of this research. Where chapter 2 revolved around the theoretical background – serving as this research's general evaluation framework – shaping the notion of 'effective pension information', this chapter narrows down to exploring what effectiveness of information entails when it comes to peoples' question 'what will I get?'. The general purpose of the present empirical study is to explore the impact of adjusting information along the ways of providing readers net or gross amounts of future retirement income, and including a disclaimer, on the ease of comprehension, informativeness, perceived trustworthiness of the information, expected future financial security, and behavioural expectations. In addition, the study examines the potential moderating role of financial literacy, perceived fiscal/ pension literacy and self-efficacy. This chapter addresses the theoretical background, hypotheses, research methodology, various analyses, results, discussion, and managerial and theoretical contributions.

3.1 LITERATURE REVIEW AND THEORETICAL BACKGROUND: RELATIVITY BIAS

Although a certain turnaround can be observed, many economists, as well as policymakers, still tap into assumptions and predictions of people's economic behaviour, founded on full human rationality. In addition, legislation and policies are founded on the assumption that people are full rational human beings, so reading all information, processing it accordingly, and make the best possible decisions, i.e. maximizing utility. This 'rational choice theory', has been disproved by a wide range of findings in the field of 'behavioural economics', proving that people are, particularly in decision-making, myopic, prone to biases, heuristics and inclined to use rules of thumb.

A considerable body of literature in the domain of financial decision-making demonstrates that people are amenable to comparing – i.e. relativity bias – when involved in making a decision. This allows them to make a trade-off and, eventually, make a decision, e.g. whether or not to save more for retirement.[325] It appears that people compare a certain

325 Ariely, chapter 1: The Truth about Relativity referring to Tversky; Tversky and Kahneman, 'The Framing of Decisions and the Psychology of Choice'; J Huber, JW Payne and C Puto, 'Adding Asymmetrically Dominated Alternatives: Violations of Regularity and the Similarity Hypothesis' 9 Journal of Consumer Research 90; I Simonson, 'Choice Based on Reasons: The Case of Attraction and Compromise Effects' 16

variable, serving as the subject of comparison, to the standard, i.e. the referent.[326] This echoes Ariely's argument that most people generally don't know what they want unless they see it in context.[327] He provides the example that people don't know what kind of racing bike they want, until they see a champ in the Tour de France riding a particular model. The latter then serves as a reference point or benchmark in people's decision-making process. When information is void of these reference points, it appears to be less easy for people to evaluate the meaningfulness of the information.[328]

Focusing more on pension planning, findings show that most people appear to stop planning, and take further actions, when they consider the outcome satisfactory.[329] Schwartz et al. point out that if people need to decide for one or another pension product, and information is not making comparisons between products simple, most of them will not seek further to find out which one is best and, thus, choose for a suboptimal product.[330] This suggests that information – whether or not allowing for comparison – may eventually affect pension's adequacy, since a lack of comparison will lead most people to a suboptimal (pension) product. At least, they will not be able to ensure their financial resilience at retirement to their best ability.

Given the prevalence of the heuristic of relativity in decision-making, it can be argued that people need reference points, or benchmarks, when engaged in evaluating the (in) adequacy of their future pension. However, prospect theory – the state-of-the-art model of decision-making – as such does not define what may serve as a reference point in decision-making. What is more, when provided with pension information, exposing people to an indicative projection of future pension income, pension participants may find it difficult to assess whether the projected amount of the future pension income will be sufficient by the time they will retire, i.e. estimating whether the projected retirement income will be adequate (compare 'what will I get?' to 'what will I need?').

---

ibid 158; A Tversky and I Simonson, 'Context-Dependent Preferences' 39 Management Science 1179; D Ariely and TS Wallsten, 'Seeking Subjective Dominance in Multidimensional Space: An Explanation of the Assymetric Dominance Effect' 63 Organizational Behavior and Human Decision Processes 223; C Sedikides, D Ariely and N Olsen, 'Contextual and procedural determinants of partner selection: of assymetric dominance and prominence' 17 Social Cognition.

326 Tversky, 335.

327 Ariely, 3.

328 EIOPA, 20-21.

329 HA Simon, 'Theories of decision-making in economics and behavioural science,' 49 The American Economic Review 253, and B Schwartz and others, 'Maximizing versus satisfying: Happiness is a matter of choice,' 83 Journal of Personality and Social Psychology 1178. See also EIOPA, 16.

330 Schwartz and others.

Considering these research findings, and in line with common practice in the field of pension communication[331], it could, hence, be argued that amounts of future retirement income should be depicted as net amounts of pension. This allows the reader to compare the projected amount of net retirement income to the amount of net (earned) income he/she currently receives on his/her bank account, and harnesses to cover his/her costs of living. This then serves as his reference point.[332] This allows the reader to put the information in 'context', by comparing it to their current (earned) net income, and get a grasp of their pension's adequacy.[333] It could however be argued that the same reasoning holds true with regard to gross income, i.e. the amount of future retirement income could be depicted as a gross amount, allowing people to compare it to their current gross (earned) income. However, esearch findings suggest that people only tend to compare things that are easily comparable and, thus, avoid comparing things that cannot be compared easily.[334] Showing a projection of gross retirement income would render the information not easily comparable, since taxation during retirement is different compared to the taxation of earned income, taxation of pensions in cross-border situation is highly complex, and people generally are not familiar with the applicable tax rates.[335] At this point, it ought to be noted that people will use the comparison between current, and future net income, as a guide to get a grasp of their prospective pension's adequacy[336], while bearing in mind that their situation may change in future, e.g. kids left the house, less groceries, less mortgage payments, less insurance, but more health-related costs. Yet, it is expected that people will use their current situation, and income, as their benchmark, since when making these estimations about whether the projected income will be sufficient[337], people are prone to the so-called availability heuristic.[338] This implies that they are steered by the ease of which they can recall a particular situation from their memory, which holds similarities with the given situation in which they want to make a

331 For instance, the Dutch pension tracking service mijnpensioenoverzicht.nl, and certain personal online environments allow people to check their accumulated pension rights at their specific pension provider (e.g. www.mijnabp.nl).

332 EIOPA, 48.

333 The value of reference points is illustrated by the following experiment, conducted by Kahneman and Tversky: they conducted an experiment with a manipulated wheel of fortune, either stopping at 10 or at 65. During the experiment, students were asked what percentage of the United Nations is an African country, after spinning the wheel. In cases where the wheel stopped at 10, the mean estimate of the students was 25%, when exposed to 65, the mean estimate of the students was 45%. See D Ackley, 'Retirement Benefits Communication Could Use Consumer-Oriented Approach' Pension World.

334 Ariely, 8.

335 See Simonson.

336 Apart from the issue whether people should be informed about the decline in purchasing power, due to inflation, raising tax rates etc.

337 Apart from what 'sufficient' precisely refers to in quantitative terms.

338 A Tversky and D Kahneman, 'Availability: A Heuristic for Judging Frequency and Probability' 5 Cognitive Psychology 207.

decision. This heuristic is part of peoples' peripheral (subconscious) route of thinking – as part of the Elaboration Likelihood Model – to which people are particularly prone when people face limited time and motivation.[339] This has been thoroughly addressed in chapter 2 of this research.

What is more, it can be argued that including a net amount in a comparison renders the information and comparison more meaningful, salient and readily available to people.[340] Another behavioural mechanism, supported by findings in the domain of behavioural economics is that information that people have encountered recently or frequently is better stored in memory, and, hence, easily accessible.[341] In this regard, the salience of the information of events people have encountered are better memorized and, thus, more easily accessible.[342] A net amount seems also a figure that people have encountered recently or frequently, i.e. when involved in financial decision-making (e.g. buying a new car, doing groceries, or deciding whether or not they are financially able to save more for retirement) they would rely on their net (earned) income. It is therefore likely that information on a net amount is better stored in memory, and, hence, more easily accessible. Moreover, research findings suggest that, with regard to pension projections, a recognizable figure in many countries is the monthly net pension income in euros.[343] This is consistent with the assumption that the status quo is a natural referent, and the most likely candidate for the reference point for tax decisions, as this reference point is most salient.[344]

However, these research findings pertain to more salient and more readily available information and comparisons, such as picking a menu, or choosing a product from a wide range of (consumer) products.[345] Besides, as experiences as shopping, partner selection or dining are more pleasant than retirement planning, it needs to be tested whether the same results hold true with regard to a pension context. Furthermore, information on pension

339 EIOPA, 21.

340 Tversky, 337. Some research studies observed a common pattern in the sense that the more salient objects, in comparative tasks, occur more often as a response, compared to the less salient object. Factors contributing to the salience of a stimulus include intensity, frequency, familiarity, good form, and informational content.

341 Ackley, and EIOPA, 21.

342 RG Netemeyer and others, 'How Am I Doing? Perceived Financial Well-Being, Its Potential Antecedents, and Its Relation to Overall Well-Being' 45 Journal of Consumer Research 68.

343 EIOPA, 48 referring to MA Taylor and K Cook, 'Planning and expectations of the retirement experience' 23 Educational Gerontology 273.

344 Kirchler, *The Economic Psychology of Tax Behaviour* 141. See also A Schepanski and T Shearer, 'A prospect theory account of the income tax withholding phenomenon' 63 Organizational Behavior and Human Decision Processes 174; D Kahneman and A Tversky, 'Prospect theory: An analysis of decision under risk' 47 Econometrica 263.

345 Ariely, 18 and cited literature.

accumulation and decumulation is much more complex than information in most other settings, such as picking a brand, so that pension information may also result in more complexity, information overload, and cognitive effort. Research on the effect of providing net amounts of future pension is scarce, and has remained underexposed.

As has been briefly touched upon in the above, tax law is a dynamic field of law where politics, law and economics intersect. The field of tax law is renowned for its complexity and intricacy, in particular the domain of income tax law, requiring a particular level of expertise to understand, and apply it.[346] Furthermore, putting tax law in practice is never pure from a conceptual or theoretical point of view. Hence, due to incorporating (the application of) tax law into pension information provision – by conveying net amounts of future retirement income – information provision may fall prey to errors and inaccuracies. Therefore, from a legal perspective, and the information provider's point of view, it might be considered adequate to include a disclaimer (pointing out that the depicted amounts may vary in future, due to, for instance, changing legislation). This could prevent from being held liable for reasons of providing erroneous information. Including a disclaimer may, however, induce ambiguity and anxiousness among readers, leading them to call the information's trustworthiness into question. Research demonstrates that people mostly employ heuristic processing when evaluating the trustworthiness of (online) information, which requires less cognitive effort than systematic content evaluation.[347] In doing so, they rely on cognitive authorities, who they regard appropriate sources to do so.[348] Wilson identified the intrinsic plausibility of text as a cognitive authority of information.[349] Under this test, the information's content is not evaluated itself, i.e. people trust information because it looks and seems plausible, given what they know.[350] A disclaimer may affect this intrinsic plausibility of information, as it might give people the impression that it leaves room for the unknown when it comes to the information's correctness. In the light of this it is to be expected that the inclusion of a disclaimer – by itself, i.e. not necessarily its content – may have an effect on the information's trustworthiness, from the readers' perspective. In the light of mainly the relativity bias, it is this study's general purpose to explore the impact of adjusting information along the ways of providing readers net or gross amounts of future retirement income, and the use of a disclaimer, on the ease of comprehension, informativeness, perceived trustworthiness of the information, expected

346 E Kades, 'The Laws of Complexity & the Complexity of Laws: The Implications of Computational Complexity Theory for the Law' 49 Rutgers Law Review 403, 408. See on the level of required expertise PH Schuck, 'Legal Complexity: Some Causes, Consequences, and Cures' 42 Duke Law Journal 1, 4.

347 Sundar. See also Donaldson, 255 referring to Chaiken, and Metzger.

348 Donaldson, 255.

349 Wilson.

350 Donaldson, 255.

future financial security, and behavioural expectations. In addition, the study examines the potential moderating role of subjective fiscal/ pension knowledge, objective knowledge (i.e. financial literacy) and self-efficacy.

3.2 Hypotheses

3.2.1 *Ease of Comprehension*

Information's comprehensibility has been recognized as an ability variable under the Elaboration Likelihood Model (ELM). These variables affect people's ability to process the information conveyed, and steer them in the direction of either the central or the peripheral route of thinking.[351] These variables can thus affect how much thinking a person is doing with respect to a message, and what kind of thoughts (favourable or unfavourable) will be provoked. The way in which people think can, thus, be affected by, amongst others, information's comprehensibility. The conceptualisation – and operationalisation – of the construct of 'comprehensibility' and/or 'understandability' deviates per realm of science.[352] For the purpose of this study, this construct has been operationalised as 'ease of comprehension'.

Against this background, it is expected that respondents exposed to a net amount of future retirement income ('net amount-frame' and/or 'net amount accompanied by disclaimer-frame') rate a higher degree of ease of comprehension, compared to respondents which were shown a gross amount of future retirement income ('gross amount-frame'). A potential explanation for this effect lies in the fact that people exposed to a net amount of future retirement income may find it easier to derive meaning from the information, compared to people allocated to the 'gross amount-frame'. What is more, they will harness their net income to finance, and maintain, their standard of living in future. Hence, the net income is easier to recall from their memory. The propensity to compare a net amount of future pension income to the net amount of earned income currently credited to the bank account is expected to account for this effect. This leads to the following hypothesis:

351 Petty and others, 88 and cited literature.

352 For instance, in the field of accountancy it is termed as follows: 'understandable financial accounting information presents data that can be understood by the users of the information and is expressed in a form and with terminology adapted to the users' range of understanding.' See Morton, 288.

H1: *Respondents allocated to the net amount-group, or net amount disclaimer-group, report a higher level of ease of comprehension than respondents allocated to the gross amount-group.*

3.2.2 *Informativeness*

According to classical information theories, a message is conceived informative relative to the number of uncertainties it either reduces or eliminates relative to a question.[353] What is more, informativeness is quantifiable.[354] For instance, Sperber and Wilson measure informative (termed 'relevance' in their research) against the quantity of contextual implications a message has in a certain context.[355]

Against this background, it is expected that respondents exposed to a net amount of future retirement income rate a higher degree of informativeness, compared to respondents which were shown a gross amount of future retirement income. A potential explanation for this effect lies in the fact that people exposed to a net amount of future retirement income may derive more meaning from the information, compared to people allocated to the 'gross amount-frame'. What is more, they will harness their net income to finance, and maintain, their standard of living in future, and hence most 'meaningful' (and hence informative) in this context is expected to be a net amount of future retirement income. Moreover, information on a net amount is expected to reduce the number of uncertainties (e.g. 'what will I get when I retire?') more, compared to showing people a gross amount. The propensity to compare a net amount of future pension income to the net amount of earned income currently credited to the bank account is expected to account for this effect. This leads to the following hypothesis:

H2: *Respondents allocated to the net amount-group, or net amount disclaimer-group, report a higher level of informativeness than respondents allocated to the gross amount-group.*

353 See, inter alia, CE Shannon, 'Prediction and entropy of printed English' 30 Bell System Technical Journal 50, and F Attneave, *Applications of information theory to psychology* (Holt, Rinehart and Winston, New York 1959). Grice distinguishes four properties of information which shape its informativeness: quantity, quality, relation, and manner. See HP Grice, 'Logic and Conversation' in P Cole and J Morgen (eds.), *Syntax and Semantics: Speech Acts* (Academic Press, New York 1957) 45-47.

354 Giora, 550.

355 D Sperber and D Wilson, *Relevance: Communication and Cognition.* (Blackwell's, Oxford 1986). For a different approach see Perry, 1979).

3.2.3 *Trustworthiness*

Generally, people show a tendency of employing heuristic processing when evaluating the trustworthiness of (online) information, rather than systematic processing.[356] This heuristic processing entails the reliance on cues related to information objects – in order to come to trustworthiness judgements – rather than the evaluation of actual information's content.[357] This is, in particular, induced by the fact that systematic evaluation requires more cognitive effort, particular for people (considering themselves) not a domain expert.[358]

In cases where people evaluate the trustworthiness of information, they rely on cognitive authorities, who they regard as appropriate sources to do so.[359] In order to recognise cognitive authority of information, the intrinsic plausibility of the text plays a pivotal role.[360] Under this test, the information's content is evaluated itself, i.e. people trust information because it looks and seems plausible, given what they know.[361] With regard to assessing the trustworthiness of information, people seem to rely on characteristics of information objects, such as content, type of information object, title, structure of the information, and presentation.[362]

In the present study, trustworthiness plays a pivotal role with regard to the treatment condition. As aforementioned, from a legal perspective, it can be considered apt to include a disclaimer (pointing out that the depicted amounts may vary in future, due to, for instance, changing legislation), in order to prevent from being held liable for reasons of providing erroneous information.[363] Including a disclaimer may, however, induce ambiguity, causing uncertainty and anxiousness among readers.[364] This ambiguity might, in turn, cause the reader to call the information's trustworthiness into question, and people might not even use the information in retirement planning. Given this potential effect of including a disclaimer in the text, it is expected that respondents allocated to the 'net

356 Sundar.

357 Donaldson, 255.

358 Ibid. 255 referring to Chaiken, and Metzger. To assess the information's content trustworthiness, the evaluation of trustworthiness may even serve as a predictor of the information's understandability, as it is assumed that readers would first have to understand the content of the information sufficiently, in order to judge information's trustworthiness through systematic evaluation, see Donaldson, 257.

359 Donaldson, 255.

360 Wilson.

361 Donaldson, 255.

362 Rieh.

363 As done in mijnpensioenregister.nl: 'De bedragen zijn berekend op basis van de huidige wet- en regelgeving en de gegevens van uw pensioenuitvoerder(s).'

364 EIOPA, 46.

amount including disclaimer-frame' report a lower degree of trustworthiness, compared to respondents allocated to the 'net amount-frame'. This lower degree of trustworthiness may be caused by the ambiguity, induced by the disclaimer.

Further, as regards the perceived the intrinsic plausibility of the text (amounts shown), it is expected that respondents allocated to the net amount-group report a lower level of trustworthiness than the gross-amount group. The explanation for this may lie in the circumstance that people allocated to the net amount-group may consider the calculation of the net amount – void of a disclaimer – disputable (for instance, what tax rate has been used?). Hence, the following two hypotheses will be tested:

> **H3a:** *Respondents allocated to the net amount-group report a lower level of trustworthiness than respondents allocated to the gross amount-group.*
> **H3b:** *Respondents allocated to the net amount and disclaimer-group report a lower level of trustworthiness than respondents allocated to the net amount-group.*

3.2.4 *Expected Future Financial Security*

When people ask themselves how they are doing in terms of well-being, their personal finances play a prominent role in that assessment.[365] Academic literature on well-being perceives finances as one of many domains of general well-being, mainly using income or money as the sole measure.[366] Research findings demonstrate that perceived financial well-being serves as a key predictor of overall well-being and is comparable in magnitude to the combined effect of other life domains, such as job satisfaction, physical health assessment, and relationship support satisfaction.[367] Netemeyer et al. construed financial well-being as two related, but separate constructs.[368] Firstly, current money management stress, encompassing feelings of being stressed/worried about one's current financial situation and being unable to manage money effectively today to satisfy financial obligations, and to live the life one wants to live. Secondly, expected future financial security, i.e. perceptions of having a financially secure future and meeting future financial goals. The latter, future dimension, is pivotal for the present research and the scale has been employed since it assesses how people feel about the likely future financial state. This

365 Netemeyer and others, 68.
366 P Dolan, T Peasgood and M White, 'Do We Really Know What Makes Us Happy? A Review of the Economic Literature on the Factors Associated with Subjective Well-Being' 29 Journal of Economic Psychology 94.
367 Netemeyer and others, 68.
368 Ibid. 68, 71.

is considered appropriate for the present study as the interventions expose people to amounts of future expected pension, and urge them to think about their financial future. It is expected that expected future financial security increases when people are exposed to a net amount of future retirement income, as it enables them better to have an idea about meeting their future financial goals, and their future financial well-being as they will harness their net income to finance, and maintain, their standard of living in future. What is more, one might expect that by showing gross amounts, some of the (more biased) respondents might misinterpret the gross amounts as rather high and, thus, report a higher level of financial well-being, compared to people exposed to the net amount-text. Nevertheless, although not implausible, I expect the number of such cases/respondents rather low, given the strong prevalence of the relativity-bias when employing heuristic processing – as discussed in section 3.1 – generally steering people towards thinking in net amounts. This is expressed in the hypothesis below.

> **H4:** *Respondents allocated to the net amount-group, or net amount disclaimer-group, report a higher level of expected future financial security than respondents allocated to the gross amount-group.*

3.2.5 *Behavioural Expectations*

Behavioural intention – and the relation to future behaviour – has been explored extensively in literature, most commonly within the framework of Fishbein and Ajzen's 'theory of reasoned action'.[369] Theory of reasoned action models (actual) behaviour as being dependent on behavioural intentions.[370] Behavioural intention has been defined as the degree to which a person has formulated conscious plans to perform, or not perform, some specified future behaviour.[371] Central to this definition are the elements of specified future behaviour, and the conscious planning of these future behaviours.

In some literature the construct of behavioural intention has been considered self-evident[372], although when it is defined, it refers more to behavioural expectation than to

369 Developed by M Fishbein and I Ajzen's, *Belief, attitude, theory and research* (Addison-Wesley, Massachusetts 1975).

370 These behavioural intentions are, in turn, dependent on attitudes towards certain behaviour and people's subjective norms. This will not be discussed any further. See for a more comprehensive discussion Kirchler, 2007 56.

371 PR Warshaw and FD Davis, 'Disentangling Behavioral Intention and Behavioral Expectation' 21 Journal of Experimental Social Psychology 213, 214.

372 See, for instance, Ackley.

behavioural intention.[373] Although behavioural intensions have been evidently used interchangeably with behavioural expectations in literature, on theoretical grounds it can be argued that they are separate constructs, and that behavioural expectations should outperform behavioural intentions in terms of predicting future behaviour.[374] Behavioural expectations is termed as 'the individual's estimation of the likelihood that he or she actually will perform some specified future behaviour'.[375]

For the scope of this study, behavioural expectations is taken as predictor for future behaviour, for which several arguments can be put forward. First, when comparing behavioural intention and behavioural expectations, it is found that behavioural intention involves making behavioural commits to (not) perform a certain behavioural act, whereas behavioural expectation reflects a person's expectation of the likelihood that he will perform the action, whether or not a commitment has been made.[376] This better suits the underlying objective of the question incorporated in the present survey. Furthermore, when people form behavioural expectations, subjects take a variety of factors in consideration that can potentially influence their future behaviour. These factors can relate to the anticipated changes in intention, non-cognitive habits, ability limitations (e.g. self-efficacy which is measured in the present study), and other (external) facilitators or constraints.[377] Since behavioural expectation incorporates, amongst others, these potential behavioural determinants, it should predict future behaviour more accurately, compared to behavioural intention.[378] Moreover, events having a potential effect on the behavioural intention may occur between the measurement of intention and the observation of the actual behaviour, which reduces the predictive accuracy of merely measuring behavioural intention.[379] In rating their expectation that they will engage in certain behaviour, respondents may take into account the possibility of such events. What is more, they may incorporate the possible effect on their behavioural intentions, reflecting the change in intention foreseen in the expectation judgment. In addition to any changes that may occur in the behavioural expectation, it may conceptually incorporate non-intentional behavioural determinants, such as habits, biases, and performance impediments.[380] For instance, in forming behavioural expectations a person may use his present intention as an

373 As pointed out by Warshaw and Davis, referring in this regard to Fishbein and Ajzen's, 288 in which behavioural intention is defined as "a behavioral intention, therefore, refers to a person's subjective probability that he will perform some behavior…".
374 Cf. Warshaw and Davis, 219.
375 Ibid. 215.
376 Ibid. 215.
377 Cf. Ibid. 215.
378 Cf. Ibid. 215.
379 Cf. Ibid. 216 and cited literatureand Fishbein and Ajzen's.
380 Cf. Warshaw and Davis, 215-216.

'anchoring point'[381], making adjustments to reflect the potential impact of factors and changes in their intention.[382] Where behavioural intention is widely considered the major determinant of reasoned behaviour[383], behavioural expectation is considered a cognitive judgment, potentially determining behaviour as well, for unreasoned behaviour.

In the light of the foregoing, it is expected that people who are exposed to a net amount of future retirement income, report a higher level of behavioural expectations compared to the people exposed to a gross amount of future retirement income. It is expected that behavioural expectations increase when people are exposed to a net amount of future retirement income, as it enables them better to have an idea about meeting their future financial goals, and their future financial well-being. In doing so, it provides them with a more concrete action perspective. The propensity to compare a net amount of future pension income to the net amount of earned income currently credited to the bank account, is expected to account for this effect. Given this, the following hypothesis will be tested:

> **H5:** *Respondents allocated to the net amount-group, or net amount disclaimer-group, report a higher level of behavioural expectations than respondents allocated to the gross amount-group.*

3.2.6 Subjective Knowledge

Although conceptual definitions of subjective knowledge in literature are scarce, the concept of (general) subjective knowledge can, for the purposes of the present study, be defined as what the subject thinks he or she knows.[384] Both subjective and objective knowledge are measured in this study, since research findings show that subjective and objective knowledge should both be measured for a comprehensive understanding of the role of knowledge in consumer behavior.[385] However, subjective knowledge should be distinguished from objective knowledge, which will be discussed hereafter, each having a different effect on (information processing and search) behaviour. For instance, it has

381 Ackley.

382 Warshaw and Davis, 216.

383 Ibid. 217 referring to Fishbein and Ajzen's.

384 LR Flynn and RE Goldsmith, 'A Short, Reliable Measure of Subjective Knowledge' 46 Journal of Business Research 57, 57 referring to LF Ackert, BK Church and R Deaves, 'Emotion and financial markets' 88 Federal Reserve Bank of Atlanta Economic Review 33.

385 Ackert, Church and Deaves, and RA Spreng and RW Olshavsky, 'Exploring the Headwaters of the Prior Knowledge – Search Relationship, in Enhancing Knowledge Development in Marketing' American Marketing Association 220.

been demonstrated that subjective knowledge is a stronger motivation of purchase-related behaviour than objective knowledge.[386] Thus, subjective knowledge and objective knowledge are two separate constructs, and have different effects on consumer behaviour.[387]

Moreover, (tax) literature exploring subjective (tax) knowledge is scarce, despite that it can be assumed that people's knowledge and concepts of taxation serve as the basis of their judgements, evaluations, perceptions and subsequent behaviour.[388] What is more, issue-relevant knowledge and prior knowledge have been identified as ability factors affecting elaboration likelihood, i.e. steering people in either the central, or peripheral route of thinking.[389] Furthermore, as a part of social representations, subjective knowledge does not put emphasis on whether knowledge is correct as regards existing laws and regulations, but rather focusses on what knowledge people possess and how this is organized to establish a meaningful representation.[390] Moreover, as part of social representations, it may have an effect on peoples' attitudes towards – or how they perceive – information, and its content.

As a moderator in this study, subjective knowledge may either have an amplifying or weakening effect between the dependent, and independent variable. Against this background, it is expected that people scoring low on subjective knowledge, react even more strongly to the depicted net amounts rather than gross amounts, since they may find it more difficult to derive meaning from gross amounts, compared to people scoring high on subjective knowledge. Moreover, people scoring high on subjective knowledge may react less strongly to net amounts as they may consider themselves knowledgeable enough to appraise the trustworthiness of the depicted net amount, i.e. the net amount is less reliable as it may be inaccurate due to complexity, or constant amendments, of the underlying tax legislation. This is expressed in the hypothesis below:

> **H6:** *The impact of the treatment condition on the ease of comprehension, informativeness, trustworthiness, expected future financial security, and behavioural expectations, is moderated by respondents' pension/fiscal literacy (subjective knowledge), in that a lower level of subjective knowledge strengthens the relationship between treatment condition (net amount-group, and net amount disclaimer-group) and the given dependent variables.*

---

386 Flynn and Goldsmith, 57 referring to F Selnes and SV Troye, 'Buying Expertise, Information Search, and Problem Solving' 10 Journal of Economic Psychology 411.

387 Flynn and Goldsmith, 57 referring to Ackert, Church and Deaves, and Spreng and Olshavsky.

388 Kirchler, *The Economic Psychology of Tax Behaviour* 31.

389 Petty and others, 87 ff.

390 See Moscovici, 'The phenomenon of social representations'.

3.2.7 Objective Knowledge (Financial Literacy)

Objective knowledge (i.e. financial literacy) is defined as an actual knowledge construct as measured by some sort of test.[391] Generally, financial literacy tends to be low, since most people seem to lack knowledge and appear to be under-informed about even the most basic economic concepts, needed to make financial and retirement decisions.[392] In general, people don't know what they are required to contribute to their pension provision, how funds are invested, what eligibility rules apply for minimum guaranteed pensions, and, even, the applicable tax rates.[393] In addition, this study's results revealed that 47% of the respondents did not know what percentage (roughly) of their personal total income they contribute to retirement provisions, see also section 3.5. Furthermore, findings suggest that a lack of planning is tantamount to a lack of saving.[394] This has serious implications for retirement planning, and has potential implications for economic behaviour, since a positive correlation has been found between financial literacy and financial behaviour.[395] What is more, the degree of financial literacy varies widely among people. For instance, the all-correct scores on the questions measuring financial literacy (interest question, inflation question, risk question) was 44.83% in the Netherlands, and 53.2% in Germany.[396]

---

391 Flynn and Goldsmith, 57 referring to Ackert, Church and Deaves.

392 Browning and Lusardi, P Antolín and OM Fuentes Contreras, 'Communicating pension risk to DC scheme members: The Chilean case of a pension risk simulator,' (OECD Working Papers on Finance, Insurance and Private Pensions, no 28, OECD Working party on Private Pensions, 2012) 5. For findings on deficient financial literacy I refer to Lusardi and Mitchell, 'Financial Literacy and Retirement Preparedness: Evidence and Implications for Financial Education', Agnew and Szykman, Moore, Lusardi, Logan, Mastrobuoni and Lusardi and Mitchell, 'Financial Literacy and Planning: Implications for Retirement Wellbeing' the latter research measured how workers made saving decisions, how they collected the information for making these decisions, and whether they possessed the financial literacy needed to make informed decisions.

393 See Simonson.

394 O Mitchell, 'Worker Knowledge of Pensions Provisions' 6 Journal of Labor Economics 21, and Lusardi and Mitchell, 'Financial Literacy and Planning: Implications for Retirement Wellbeing' Mitchell and Lusardi, 2 and Lusardi and Mitchell, 'Financial Literacy and Retirement Preparedness: Evidence and Implications for Financial Education' 35.

395 With regard to the positive correlation between financial literacy and financial behaviour: L Calvert, J Campbell and P Sodini, 'Down or Out: Assessing the Welfare Costs of Household Investment Mistakes' Working Paper, Harvard University; Employee Benefits Research Institute, 'Participant Education: Actions and Outcomes' 169 Issue Brief.

396 Lusardi and Mitchell, 'Financial Literacy and Retirement Preparedness: Evidence and Implications for Financial Education' 43; Simonson. See also MCJ Van Rooij, A Lusardi and RJ Alessie, 'Financial Literacy and Retirement Planning in the Netherlands' 32 Journal of Economic Psychology 593; S Sekita, 'Financial Literacy and Retirement Planning in Japan' 10 Journal of Pension Economics and Finance 637; ibid.; ibid.; A Lusardi and OS Mitchell, 'Financial Literacy around the world: an overview' ibid 497; Sekita, and L Klapper and GA Panos, 'Financial literacy and retirement planning: the Russian case' ibid 599.

It should be pointed out that financial illiteracy may affect achieving the goal of understandable communication.[397] What is more, issue-relevant knowledge and prior knowledge have been identified as ability factors affecting elaboration likelihood, i.e. steering people in either the central, or peripheral route of thinking.[398] Furthermore, research findings show that objective knowledge should be measured for a complete understanding of the role of knowledge in consumer behavior.[399] This suggests that financial literacy serves as a possible moderator, i.e. it may obscure the relationship between the dependent and independent variable. Furthermore, incorporating financial literacy increases the representativeness of the effect of the dependent variable.[400]

Against this background, it is expected that people scoring low on objective knowledge, react even more strongly to the depicted net amounts rather than gross amounts, since they may find it more difficult to derive meaning from gross amounts, compared to people scoring high on objective knowledge. Moreover, people scoring high on objective knowledge may react less strongly to net amounts as they may possess the knowledge to appraise the trustworthiness of the depicted net amount, i.e. the net amount is less reliable as it may be inaccurate due to complexity, or constant amendments, of the underlying tax legislation. This is expressed in the hypothesis below.

> **H7**: *The impact of the treatment condition on the ease of comprehension, informativeness, trustworthiness, expected future financial security, and behavioural expectations, is moderated by respondents' financial literacy (objective knowledge), in that a lower level of financial literacy strengthens the relationship between treatment condition (net amount-group, and net amount disclaimer-group) and the given dependent variables.*

3.2.8 *Self-efficacy*

Financial literacy solely does not necessarily lead to people's 'empowerment' to cope with certain situations, phenomena, developments etc. People also need to have the self-efficacy

397 It must pointed out that understandability is an element ensuring the effectiveness of communication, see C Mihart, 'Impact of Integrated Marketing Communication on Consumer Behaviour: Effects on Consumer Decision – Making Process' 4 International Journal of Marketing Studies 121, 121.

398 Petty and others, 87 ff.

399 Ackert, Church and Deaves, and Spreng and Olshavsky.

400 Further reasons to incorporate moderators in an ANCOVA model are to control for potential confounding, to improve comparison across treatments, to assess model adequacy, and, lastly, to expand the scope of inference. See M Brucks, 'The Effects of Product Class Knowledge on Information Search Behavior' Journal of Consumer Research 1.

to take decisions, and cope with, for instance, fast evolving labour markets and financial (e.g. pension) systems growing more complex, but also – more related to the topic of this research – the growing mobility of workers. What is more, regulatory frameworks, rules and regulations grow more complex in a rapid pace. Over the past two decades, self-efficacy has become one of the most broadly studied variables in psychological sciences.

The construct of self-efficacy is termed as an individual's belief in his or her capacity to muster the cognitive, motivational, and behavioural resources required to perform in a given situation.[401] It is, thus, a situation-specific competence belief. It was found that workers with a higher level of self-efficacy show a higher tendency to plan for retirement in advance, and experience less anxiety about retirement.[402] In addition, some research studies found a positive association between self-efficacy and financial resources, and even adequacy of income.[403] Moreover, research studies on personal adjustment to retirement demonstrate that self-efficacy influences the beliefs of retirees about retirement, negatively associated with anxiety.[404] In this vein, it is expected that people scoring low on self-efficacy, react even more strongly to the depicted net amounts rather than gross amounts, since they may be less confident to interpret, and appraise, gross amounts, compared to people scoring high on self-efficacy. What is more, people scoring high on self-efficacy, may experience less anxiety when confronted with net amounts of future retirement income and, hence, react less strongly compared to people scoring low on self-efficacy. This is expressed in the hypothesis below.

> **H8:** *The impact of the treatment condition on the ease of comprehension, informativeness, trustworthiness, expected future financial security, and behavioural expectations, is moderated by respondents' self-efficacy, in that a lower level of self-efficacy strengthens the relationship between treatment condition (net amount-group, and net amount disclaimer-group) and the given dependent variables.*

The section above outlined what dependent variables and possible moderators will be tested, and why, and which hypotheses will be tested. Now that is has been clarified what

401 A Bandura, *Self-efficacy: The exercise of control* (New York, Freeman & Co 1997).

402 R Schwarzer, *Self-efficacy: Thought control of action* (Hemisphere, Washington DC 1992). See also M Jerusalem and R Schwarzer, 'Self-efficacy as a resource factor in stress appraisal processes.' in R Schwarzer (ed.), *Self-efficacy: Thought control of action* (Hemisphere, Washington DC 1992).

403 R Schwarzer and M Jerusalem, 'Generalized Self-Efficacy scale' in W J., W S. and J M. (eds.), *Measures in health psychology: A user's portfolio Causal and control beliefs* (NFER-NELSON, Windsor 1995).

404 Ibid.

will be evaluated, the following section will discuss how it will be measured/operationalised, i.e. the research methodology.

3.3 Research Methodology

3.3.1 *Experimental Procedure, Sample and Data Collection*

The survey-based experiment was set-up as follows. Participants were first presented a short introductory text. The purpose of the study was explicitly not mentioned in order to avoid biased responses, and desirable responding. The questionnaire started with an open-ended question, asking participants to take a moment to think about their pension, and asked which questions come to their mind, and the most important question for which they would like to get an answer. They were then queried to list the five most pressing questions they may have with respect to their pension, in order of relevance (1= important, 5 = least important).

Respondents were then randomly exposed to one of the three text frames, i.e. the gross frame, net frame without disclaimer, and net frame with disclaimer. In all three frames, subjects were, prior to showing them an amount, asked to imagine that they would receive the following message from their pension fund, and prompted to read it carefully and try to imagine that they were in this situation. The latter (i.e. 'image that you are in this situation'), was mainly aimed at increasing the participants' perceived level of realism of the survey, and to neutralize the possible distorting effect of the amount as such.

In the gross frame the text of the manipulation depicted "After reaching the applicable retirement age, you will receive a total gross pension income of €X per month". In the net frame, the depicted text was similar, but the amount was adapted: "After reaching the applicable retirement age, you will receive a total net pension income of €X per month". Participants assigned to the net, including a disclaimer, frame, were shown the following text: "After reaching the applicable retirement age, you will receive a total net pension income of approximately €X per month". An 'important to know'-section was then added, pointing out that the shown amount may vary in future. The text of the 'important to know-section' as depicted in the survey, is provided below. The text of this section is primarily derived from the text in the Dutch pension register. In the current drafting of the 'important to know-section', the most important and recognisable aspects of the depicted amounts have been incorporated.

The amounts in each of the treatment conditions have been computed by applying an equal amount for all respondents, irrespective of their personal situations, while, of course, a distinction was drawn between net and gross. The amounts have been calculated by multiplying the (net or gross) replacement rates, averaged for Belgium, Germany and the Netherlands, by the average earnings, as established for these three States. Replacement rates were selected for the computation of the future amounts of retirement income, as they are considered the most reliable proxy for an adequate retirement income.[405] Furthermore, to incorporate variable elements as regards the computation of future retirement income, such as purchasing power and related risks, an optimistic, neutral, desirable (70%) and pessimistic replacement rate were used. The amounts have been established by taking an average of a pessimistic, neutral, desirable and optimistic scenario. The average gross pension replacement rate amounted to 63.25%; the net replacement rate 70.75%. Multiplying the gross pension replacement by the average (rounded) annual gross wages of €45,799, covering all three countries, resulted in an annual predicted future retirement income of (rounded) €28,968, i.e. monthly gross (rounded) *€2,414*. Furthermore, after multiplying the average net pension replacement rate by the average (net) annual wages of €33,160, the amount of annual predicted future retirement income is (rounded) €23,461, i.e. (rounded) *€1,955* net per month. To avoid the impression among respondents that the amounts have been calculated precisely, and fully tailored to their personal situation, they have been rounded. Although the amount as such may have had an effect on the participants' response, the survey's main aim was to explore the effect of a gross and net frame. Moreover, the participants were asked to report how realistic they perceived the scenario and, more specifically, the amounts as such. This allowed to control for this effect in the analysis. What is more, the amounts were merely aimed for illustrative purposes, though it was assured that they reflected (the highest possible) level of realism under the participants. For a further detailed description of the calculation of these amounts, and what assumptions, rationales, biases have been incorporated, I refer to Appendix A.

Respondents allocated to the net amount disclaimer-frame were asked whether they would like to see the disclaimer with respect to the amount of future retirement income depicted in the text box. It was recorded which respondents requested to see the additional information. The exact formulation and the underlying (legal) considerations of the additional information are addressed in Appendix B. See the text of this important to know-section below.

405 See OECD, 'OECD Pensions at a Glance 2017'.

Important to know:

- The gross and net amounts of your future pension income are estimates. Your pension income may be higher or lower than the amounts provided above.
- The amounts have been calculated on the basis of current laws and regulations, and the information provided by your pension provider(s).
- If anything changes in your private and/or work situation, your pension often changes as well. Therefore, check this information annually.

After each of the frames, in order to measure the cognitive representations of the text, respondents were asked to respond to an open-ended elaborative stating 'After having read this information, please indicate which questions you still have with regard to your pension, in the text box below'. These responses were then categorized in one of several categories, see section 3.6.5. This was done by manually analysing each respondent's answer to this open-ended question, and then categorizing it into categories that emerged from the data obtained, i.e. through content-analysis. For the purpose of coding these categories a codebook was drafted.

3.3.2 *Experimental Measures*

Directly after respondents were exposed to the text of the manipulation, the effect of the intervention was measured. Five dependent variables were measured in this study: ease of comprehension, informativeness, trustworthiness, expected future financial security, and behavioural expectations. These will be elucidated in more detail below.

In order to measure ease of comprehension, respondents were queried to rate the information on a four item seven-point scale. These statements were extracted and adapted from the scale used by Block and Keller.[406] To measure informativeness, respondents were queried to rate the information on a three item seven-point scale.[407] Trustworthiness of the information was measured by means of the scale developed by Donaldson.[408] Since

406 Drawn, and adapted, from LG Block and PA Keller, 'When to accentuate the negative: the effects of perceived efficacy and message framing on intentions to perform a health-related behavior' Journal of Marketing Research 192.

407 Drawn, and adapted, from ibid.

408 DR Donaldson, *Development of a Scale for Measuring Perceptions of Trustworthiness for Digitized Archival Documents* (2015) and Donaldson, 'The Digitized Archival Document Trustworthiness Scale'. These items, among others, loaded strongly onto the only factor that was retained for further analysis in this research,

this scale was initially aimed at measuring the degree of trustworthiness of digitized archival document, it was slightly adapted to ensure that it fits into the context and purpose of the present study. In addition to these items, two more items were added to the scale in order to ensure a balance between negatively, and positively framed items. These were derived from the 'credibility of information-scale' used by Block and Keller.[409] Employing the scale used by Netemeyer[410], participants were asked to rate their statements reflecting their expected future financial security. Purpose of measuring this variable, is to explore whether showing a net amount of future retirement income has a positive effect on participants' expectations regarding their future financial security. As regards behavioural expectations, the statements referred to twelve behavioural acts that were selected as representing a wide range of activities that subjects may be expected to engage in, in the field of (cross-border) pensions and taxes. The introductory text of the question referred to 'within the next 12 months' in order to make the situations more concrete.[411]

Although the information, and the amounts depicted in the text frames, have been developed with the greatest possible precision and accuracy, both the information and the amounts shown have, to some extent, shortcomings and reservations (in terms of generalisability). In order to control for the potential distorting effect of the (lack of) level of realism of the information, and the amount depicted in the treatment condition, participants were asked to what extent they agreed with four statements.[412]

To measure subjective knowledge, the well-validated five-item, seven-point Likert scale developed by Flynn and Goldsmith was used in this study.[413] However, this scale has been

---

i.e. trustworthiness. As Donaldson claims, items that load strongly onto a factor, represent items as a scale for measurement of that factor. Therefore, these items represent items in a scale for measurement of trustworthiness. Results of one test confirmed the reliability of this scale: α .93.

409 Drawn, and adapted, from Block and Keller.

410 Netemeyer and others.

411 Drawn and adapted from the scale used by E Brüggen, T Post and K Schmitz, 'Interactivity in online pension planners enhances engagement with retirement planning – but not for everyone' 33 Journal of Services Marketing 488. These behavioural acts are: checking the balance of the retirement account of their pension in order to get a total overview of their future pension income; checking the tax treatment of their pension in order to get a total overview of their future pension income; discussing their pension with their friends or family; discussing the tax treatment of their pension with their friends or family; consulting a professional pension advisor; consulting a professional tax advisor; investigating or taking advantage of retirement savings education resources offered; consulting financial or pension related literature or related content from the internet to gain more insights and knowledge about pensions; consulting financial or pension related literature or related content from the internet to gain more insights and knowledge about taxes; spending time working towards identifying or developing additional savings for their retirement (e.g. long-term investment opportunities outside of government and employer-sponsored plans); taking steps to diversify their retirement savings more among a broader set of assets; opening a new retirement account.

412 The reliability of this scale was tested, resulting in a Cronbach alpha coefficient of .86.

413 Flynn and Goldsmith.

slightly adapted for this study, in order to measure participants' subjective knowledge pertaining to pensions and taxes.

For the purpose of this study, objective knowledge is delimited as financial literacy in general, and not necessarily tailored to objective knowledge on pensions.[414] Financial literacy determines how well people make and execute financial decisions, including planning for retirement, and is a phenomenon existing 'naturally' within the participants. In order to measure financial literacy, the widely used and well-validated scale, developed by Lusardi, is relied on. Relying on economic models of saving and portfolio choice, Lusardi identified three economic concepts that individuals should have some understanding of when engaged in financial decisions, if they are to use them.[415] These three concepts are the following: interest compounding, inflation, risk diversification. Building on these three concepts, three questions have been developed by Lusardi and Mitchell, which have become a reliable and valid proxy to measure financial literacy.[416]

Self-efficacy was measured by asking respondents to rate to what extent they agree with ten statements on their capability to cope with certain challenges in certain (often stressful) situations. Participants were asked to react on the statements on a seven-point Likert-scale.

3.3.3 *Lack of Overview, Action Perspective, European Pension Tracking Service*

After measuring the dependent variables, several questions were posed, aimed at exploring the degree of lack of overview, action perspective among (former) mobile workers as regards their retirement income, and to explore the need for a European Pension Tracking Service.[417] It, hence, focused on their mobility and its consequences in terms of planning for retirement. Respondents were asked to what extent they agreed with the following statement on a seven-point Likert-scale:

414 For instance, Banks and Oldfield measured knowledge on pensions, see Banks and Oldfield. They queried respondents whether they knew the pension accrual rate of their pension scheme. They found a correlation between numeracy and financial knowledge. Results indicated that compared to the least numerate group of respondents, the most numerate group were almost 35 percentage points more likely to know their pension accrual rate.

415 Lusardi and Mitchell, 'Financial Literacy around the world: an overview' 499.

416 Ibid. 499.

417 No scales were used to measure these constructs since it was not envisaged to measure a certain underlying (theoretical) construct through several items.

- 'I face a lack of insight into the legal consequences of my mobility for my pension';
- 'I face a lack of insight into the legal consequences of my mobility for the tax treatment of my pension';
- 'A European Pension Tracking Service, providing a total overview of my pension situation, would help me in my retirement planning.'

In addition, depending on respondents' responses to the first two statements (lack of insight legal consequences mobility for pension/tax treatment of my pension), an additional question was posed in order to get a grasp of the implications of this lack of insight. Respondents were exposed to this question only if they reported an answer ranging between 'neither agree nor disagree' and 'strongly agree'. Where respondents did so as regard the statement 'I face a lack of insight into the legal consequences of my mobility for my pension', they were asked to what extent they agree with the statement 'The lack of insight into the legal consequences of my mobility for my pension hinders me in my retirement planning'. In cases where respondents reported that they (to some extent) agreed with the statement 'I face a lack of insight into the legal consequences of my mobility for the tax treatment of my pension', the question was posed to what extent they agree with the following statement: 'The lack of insight into the legal consequences of my mobility for the tax treatment of my pension hinders me in my financial planning'. These questions were raised to explore to what extent mobile persons see themselves faced with a lack of insight in terms of pensions, and taxes, and whether it hinders them in their retirement/financial planning.

3.3.4 *Proxies for Familiarity with Pensions*

Furthermore, participants were asked to report roughly what percentage of their personal total income they contribute to their retirement provisions. Answering options were 0-5%, 5-10%, 10-15%, 15-20%, 20-25%, more than 25% or 'do not know'. Although there is a wide variety of potential question sets on which to draw when studying how familiar participants are with their pension schemes, the survey's question was considered to serve as a general proxy of how well people are informed about their pension in general.[418]

418 See for instance Banks and Oldfield. In this survey, respondents were asked about the type of pension that they had and various details about how the pension plan operates. Results showed that, overall, 58% of the participants knew the answer to this question. Compared to the least numerate group, the most numerate group was almost 35 percentage points more likely to know their pension accrual rate. Furthermore, they were queried about their expectations for future retirement income, and whether they felt that they had had 'enough' information with regard to their pension plan. The research findings showed that around 70% of the respondents indicated they that felt they had received sufficient information about their current

In view of the rising trend among states towards multi-pillar retirement planning, respondents were asked whether they participate(d) in and/or contribute(d) to one of the following pension schemes in their (former) working or (former) residence states:

- a government-run basic mandatory retirement provision (statutory pension scheme);
- as an employee or civil servant to a pension fund/provider through their employer, or as an independent professional (occupational pension scheme);
- a voluntary individual pension product through an insurer or pension provider, outside of their employment relationship (personal pension scheme);
- other arrangements for their retirement apart from the provisions mentioned above, namely: …

Answering options for this question were 'yes', 'no', or 'do not know'. With regard to the 'other arrangements for retirement', respondents were provided the opportunity (through a text entry-field in the questionnaire) to enumerate the arrangements they have arranged for. In particular, this question is interesting in light of the shift from largely single to multi-tiered systems, particularly motivated by the decline in generosity of statutory pensions in securing an income after retirement.

With regard to the question asking respondents their contribution level compared to their income, as well as the latter question, it should be pointed out that, in fact, not knowing the answer is an interesting outcome in itself, as it gives an idea to what degree people are 'aware' of their own retirement arrangements. Therefore, the potential answering option 'do not know' was explicitly included. See table 3.1 for the results. Now that the section above addressed the research methodology, and all its elements, the following section will discuss preliminary results on the effectiveness of the treatment conditions, obtained through the pre-test and manipulation check.

---

pension, and the results indicated that only the most numerate were significantly more likely to feel that they had enough information, compared to the least numerate group. Also, respondents were asked about the changes, that in some point in time, they would not have enough retirement income to meet their needs. Results indicated that less than 40% reported a chance of inadequate retirement income, and that the more numerate group was more likely to be in the group who did not expect to have adequate resources, even conditional on education, as well as financial wealth, both having a positive effect.

Table 3.1 Scale's properties

Scale label	No. of items	Response options	M	SD	Cronbach's alpha
Ease of Comprehension[(a)]	1. The information provided on my pension is easy to comprehend 2. The information provided on my pension is easy to follow 3. It is easy to understand how much pension income I would get 4. The amount of future pension income is easy to understand	7-point Likert-scale (strongly disagree-strongly agree)	4.43	1.52	0.90
Informativeness[(b)]	1. The information provided is helpful when planning for retirement 2. The information provided is useful when planning for retirement 3. The information provided is informative when planning for retirement	7-point Likert-scale (strongly disagree-strongly agree)	4.39	1.54	0.95
Trustworthiness[(c)]	1. The information provided is authentic 2. The information provided is exaggerated 3. The information provided is credible 4. The information provided appears free from error 5. The information provided is what it claims to be 6. The information provided is factual 7. The information provided is unbelievable	7-point Likert-scale (strongly disagree-strongly agree) -> items 2 and 7 reversely scored	4.52	1.05	0.89
Expected Future Financial Security[(d)]	1. I will achieve the financial goals that I have set for myself 2. I am securing my financial future 3. I am becoming financially secure 4. I have saved (or will be able to save) enough money to last me to the end of my life 5. I will be financially secure until the end of my life	7-point Likert-scale (strongly disagree-strongly agree)	4.13	1.29	0.93

Scale label	No. of items	Response options	M	SD	Cronbach's alpha
Behavioural Expectations[(e)]	1. I will check the balance of my retirement account of my pension in order to get a total overview of my future pension income 2. I will check the tax treatment of my pension in order to get a total overview of my future pension income 3. I will discuss my pension with my friends or family 4. I will discuss the tax treatment of my pension with my friends or family 5. I will consult a professional financial advisor 6. I will consult a professional tax advisor 7. I will investigate or take advantage of retirement savings education resources offered 8. I will consult financial or pension related literature or related content from the internet to gain more insights and knowledge about pensions 9. I will consult financial or pension related literature or related content from the internet to gain more insights and knowledge about taxes 10. I will spend time working towards identifying or developing additional savings for my retirement (e.g. long-term investment opportunities outside of government- and employer-sponsored plans) 11. I will take steps to diversify my retirement savings more among a broader set of assets 12. I will upon up a new retirement account	7-point Likert-scale (extremely unlikely – extremely likely)	4.01	1.24	0.91
Subjective Pension Knowledge[(f)]	1. I know pretty much about pensions 2. Among my circle of friends, I'm one of the 'experts' on pensions 3. I do not feel very knowledgeable about pensions 4. Compared to most other people, I know less about pensions 5. When it comes to pensions, I really don't know a lot	7-point Likert-scale (strongly disagree-strongly agree) -> items 3, 4 and 5 reversely scored	3.59	1.66	0.93

Scale label	No. of items	Response options	M	SD	Cronbach's alpha
Subjective Fiscal Knowledge[g]	1. I know pretty much about taxes 2. Among my circle of friends, I'm one of the 'experts' on taxes 3. I do not feel very knowledgeable about taxes 4. Compared to most other people, I know less about taxes 5. When it comes to taxes, I really don't know a lot	7-point Likert-scale (strongly disagree-strongly agree) -> items 3, 4 and 5 reverse scored	4.21	1.58	0.94
Financial Literacy[h]	1. Suppose you had €100 in a savings account and the interest rate was 2% per year. After 5 years, how much do you think you would have in the account if you left the money to grow? 2. Imagine that the interest rate on your savings account was 1% per year and inflation was 2% per year. After 1 year, how much would you be able to buy with the money in this account? 3. Please tell whether this statement is true or false. 'Buying a single company's stock usually provides a safer return than a stock mutual fund'.	More than €102; Exactly €102; Less than €102; Do not know; Refuse to answer. More than today; Exactly the same; Less than today; Do not know; Refuse to answer. True; False; Do not know; Refuse to answer.	2.58 [i]	.667	N/A
Self-efficacy[i]	1. I can always manage to solve difficult problems if I try hard enough 2. If someone opposes me, I can find the means and ways to get what I want 3. It is easy for me to stick to my aims and accomplish my goals 4. I am confident that I could deal efficiently with unexpected events 5. Thanks to my resourcefulness, I know how to handle unforeseen situations	7-point Likert-scale (strongly disagree-strongly agree)	5.28	0.87	0.93

Scale label	No. of items	Response options	M	SD	Cronbach's alpha
	6. I can solve most problems if I invest the necessary effort 7. I can remain calm when facing difficulties because I can rely on my coping abilities 8. When I am confronted with a problem, I can usually find several solutions 9. If I am in trouble, I can usually think of a solution 10. I can usually handle whatever comes my way				

(a)See Block and Keller.

(b)SG Moore, 'Attitude Predictability and Helpfulness in Online Reviews: The Role of Explained Actions and Reactions' 42 Journal of Consumer Research 30. This scale is general in the sense that the items can be used to measure the informativeness of a wide variety of (information) objects.

(c)Building on Donaldson, 'The Digitized Archival Document Trustworthiness Scale'; Donaldson, Development of a Scale for Measuring Perceptions of Trustworthiness for Digitized Archival Documents.

(d)Netemeyer and others.

(e)Derived from, and adapted, from Warshaw and Davis.

(f)Derived, and slightly adapted, from Flynn and Goldsmith.

(g)Derived, and slightly adapted, from Ibid.

(h)Lusardi and Mitchell, 'Financial Literacy around the world: an overview'.

(i)Based on a self-created total dummy variable where scores ranged from min 0 to max 3. For instance, 3 indicates that the respondent answered all three questions – measuring financial literacy – correctly.

(j)This scale has been derived from R Schwarzer and others, 'The assessment of optimistic self-beliefs: Comparison of the German, Spanish, and Chinese versions of the General Self-Efficacy scale' 46 Applied Psychology: An International Review 69, R Schwarzer and A Born, 'Optimistic self-beliefs: Assessment of general perceived self-efficacy in thirteen cultures' 3 World Psychology 177. See also J Bäßler and R Schwarzer, 'Evaluación de la autoeficacia: Adaptación española de la escala de autoeficacia general [Measuring generalized self-beliefs: A Spanish adaptation of the General Self-Efficacy scale]' 2 Ansiedad y Estrés 1, M Knoef and others, 'De toereikendheid van pensioenopbouw na de crisis en pensioenhervormingen' 68 Netspar Industry Paper Series, ibid., The scale has proven to be reliable, but also valid in terms of convergent and discriminant validity.

3.4 Pre-test and Manipulation Check

Prior to sending out the survey, a small pre-test of the survey was conducted among university staff of Maastricht University and Georg-August-Universität Göttingen (n = 33) in order to find out whether wording, and structure, of questions led to any confusion. One of the outcomes of the pre-test, among others, was that the terms 'helpful', 'useful' and 'informative' (items of the dependent variable informativeness) were possibly not clear enough, and suffered from a lack of clear distinction, and could thus be confounded. However, it was decided to not further clarify these terms, nor to adjust the statements, since these items stem from validated scales. In response to the other responses and comments, the survey, and questions, were slightly adapted accordingly to ensure unambiguous wording, and avoid inconsistencies in the survey's structure. Furthermore, it was ensured that the survey was a generalizable instrument for retrieving data from respondents in Germany and the Netherlands (i.e. subjects from these three countries may have a different perception on the notion of first, second and third 'pillar' pension).

Two control questions were included in the survey during the pre-test, in order to explore whether respondents properly understood the information provided on the amount of future pension income, i.e. the intervention.[419] The first control question, queried whether respondents had read a gross amount or net amount of future retirement income. These results allowed checking whether respondents, allocated to either a gross or net amount-condition, correctly understood the message. This is shown in table 3.2 below. The numbers placed in bold indicate an incorrect understanding of the message, e.g. respondents allocated to the net amount, reported to have seen a gross amount. It was therefore decided to better emphasize the amount shown in the survey, being either a gross or net amount, by placing them in a bold format. Pearson Chi-Square was .002 for these differences, indicating that the difference was significant, and in the expected direction.

419 See J Hoewe, 'Manipulation Check' in J Matthes, CS Davis and RF Potter (eds.), *The International Encyclopedia of Communication Research Methods* (Wiley-Blackwell, 2017). However, it should be pointed out that embedding a question in the survey, as part of the manipulation check, may raise some issues, see DJ Hauser, PC Ellwsworth and R Gonzalez, 'Are Manipulation Checks Necessary?' Frontiers in Psychology. The manipulation check, in the form of a question, is a verbal measure (rather than a behavioural) appearing at the same point in the survey (rather than varied in order to assess order effects). Although these checks are considered measures, they may also operate as interventions eliciting results that may otherwise not occur, i.e. unmeasured variables may correlate with the manipulation check and potentially drive the relationship. Hence, the assumption that manipulation checks as such do not have an effect on the experimental conclusions is not unambiguous, since they may amplify, undo or interact with the effects of the manipulation. However, it is believed that the two control questions, and the manner in which they were framed, did not distort the causal relationships and have not led to any unexpected and ambiguous conclusions.

Table 3.2 Results Control Question 1

Control question 1	*Gross amount*	*Net amount*
Group 1 (GA)	14 (correct)	0
Group 2 (NA)	4	7 (correct)
Group 3 (NAD)	5	3 (correct)

The second control question queried respondents whether the information provided on the amount of future retirement income was accompanied by additional important information. This allowed to explore whether respondents, particularly allocated to the net amount and disclaimer-frame, correctly understood that they were provided with this additional information. The results of this question are shown below. The results reveal that respondents reporting that they did see additional important information, while being allocated to the gross amount and net amount-frame, is low. In addition, it can be observed that respondents allocated to the net amount and disclaimer-frame, and reporting that they did not see additional important information is low as well. It can therefore be concluded that the instructions in the survey were sufficiently clear.

Table 3.3 Results Control Question 3

Control question 2	*No*	*Yes*
Group 1 (GA)	12 (correct)	2
Group 2 (NA)	9 (correct)	2
Group 3 (NAD)	1	7 (correct)

The majority of the respondents (roughly 57%), allocated to the gross amount-frame, indicated that they were wondering what they would receive net, i.e. after taxes, endorsing this study's theoretical underpinning. Also, in answering the five open questions at the beginning of the survey, 52% of all respondents indicated that they would like to know what their future (net) amount of pension income would be. Given the small population it was questionable to draw a well-founded conclusion on the effectiveness of the intervention. However, these results, the scales' reliability and the effects sizes, gave the impression that the respondents understood the manipulation correctly. This demonstrated that the manipulation worked as intended on the dependent variables. Hence, it was decided to continue the research, and to disseminate the survey under a (considerable larger) group of (former) mobile workers. Where the section above illustrates that the treatment condition operated as expected – i.e. respondents understood the manipulation – and preliminary results were promising, the next section will provide an overview of the main study's set-up.

Table 3.4 Results Pre-Test

	Group 1 (GA) = M (SD)	Group 2 (NA) = M (SD)	Group 3 (NAD) = M (SD)	p-value	Cronbach's alpha
Ease of Comprehension	4.57 (1.54)	4.66 (1.91)	4.03 (1.76)	.707	.938
Informativeness	3.26 (0.94)	2.94 (0.83)	3.46 (1.21)	.505	.878
Trustworthiness	4.26 (1.0)	3.69 (1.12)	4.05 (.57)	.355	.875
EFFS	3.50 (0.77)	3.09 (0.723)	3.68 (0.34)	.157	.869
Behavioural Expectations	2.68 (0.99)	2.43 (0.67)	2.04 (0.81)	.258	.919

3.5 Main Study

The data for the present study were obtained through an online survey (in English) among (former) mobile workers, i.e. the sample. The survey was sent out in several ways, and sources were recorded. Some respondents were recruited through a newsletter[420], via e-mail to (former) mobile workers, in all capacities of (former) mobility, i.e. migrant worker, cross-border, and posted worker. The group of (possible) respondents was not limited to the bilateral relation Germany-the Netherlands. Moreover, numerous organisations, and institutions, engaged in the field of cross-border (labour) mobility, were approached and asked to disseminate the survey in its network, and among members and interested persons. These respondents were contacted through the 'Grensinformatiepunten', 'Euregions', knowledge institutes, several pension providers etc.

As regards this study's sample, a reservation should be drawn when it comes to the self-selection bias, i.e. those people who volunteered to partake in this study (mobile persons) are usually different from those who don't (non-mobile/domestic persons), in terms of motivation and/or demographics. Generally speaking, I assume that those who have participated (mobile individuals) show a higher motivation and interest in pensions, precisely because of their mobile status, i.e. leading to a higher boundary of effect sizes of this study's results. Differences in characteristics that might play a further role in this regard, relate to level of education, level of income, and level of multi-pillar pension saving. As regards level of education, the majority of the respondents completed bachelor degree-education or higher, resulting from gathering respondent through university networks.[421]

420 For instance, through the ITEM newsletter, or the BBZ/BDZ (SVB) newsletter.

421 In line with the increasing level of (higher) education among EU movers, see European Commission, 'Annual Report on Intra-EU Labour Mobility 2022'. In 2016, 28% of movers completed higher education; in 2021, 32%.

With respect to level of income the majority reported a (net) monthly income between €2,500 and €7,000, i.e. tending to the higher end of the income spectrum. What is more, I expect that mobile persons – given their mobility status – reveal a higher level of multi-pillar pension saving, given their deviating countries of origin, residence, and employment. Each of this states is likely to expose a different compositions for pension income, in terms of pillars, for instance, where in Germany the first pillar plays a more pivotal role supplemented with income in the third pillar, in the Netherlands, the second pillar takes a more pivotal role in this regard. Given these differences in level of education, level of income, and level of multi-pillar pension saving, I expect that this study's results should be interpreted as a higher boundary of effect sizes.

The data were collected over a period of sixteen weeks. Although participation in the survey was voluntary (and anonymous), as an incentive, respondents, who completed the survey, had the chance of winning an iPad. The survey's subjects were randomly, and equally, assigned to one of the three treatment conditions (gross amount (control), net amount, or net amount accompanied with a disclaimer). It is to be stressed that the experiment merely reflected attitudes, perceptions and stated intentions of the participants, rather than actual (savings) behaviour or final decisions at the end of the decision-making funnel, and hence it was expected that the exact status of mobility/employment (migrant/frontier/posted worker) would not have a distorting effect on the study's results. Even if there could be observed such an effect, the random allocation to one of the three groups should ensure that the effects would hold for all three groups equally; the interest of this study is not in absolute effects, but differences between the three groups in terms of the amount depicted in the information.

Eventually, 160 participants opened the survey link, and 135 participants filled out the complete questionnaire. Two respondents were deleted from the initial data set due to unrealistic response times (below 5 min), implying that participation in the survey was not taken seriously. One respondent was removed from the data set as he fell outside the sample group ((former) mobile citizens). The final data set thus comprised N=132 respondents (gross amount-frame: N = 46; net amount-frame: N = 48, net amount and disclaimer-frame, N = 38). Further individual demographics and characteristics are provided in table 3.5.

Table 3.5 Respondents' Characteristics

	N	% of total *N*
Gender		
Male	78	59.1
Female	54	40.9
Age		
18-29	17	12.9
30-39	42	31.8
40-49	25	18.9
50-59	19	14.4
60+	29	22
Have you ever been mobile*?		
Yes	132	100
No	0	0
If the answer to the previous question is yes, please indicate for what reason		
Living	3	2.3
Working	57	43.2
Both	63	47.7
Other: OPEN	4	3
	(5 missing)	(3.8 missing)
Highest level of education completed**		
Primary education	0	0
Pre-vocational education	1	0.8
Pre-university education	1	0.8
Secondary education (high school)	4	3.0
Vocational education	3	2.3
Higher vocational education	6	4.5
Bachelor's degree	19	14.4
Master's degree	41	31.1
Doctor, Ph.D.	56	42.4
No education	1	0.8
Approximate personal monthly net income		
Less than €1,250	5	3.8
At least €1,250 but less than €2,000	11	8.3

	N	% of total *N*
At least €2,000 but less than €2,500	8	21.2
At least €2,500 but less than €3,000	29	22
At least €3,000 but less than €4,000	28	21.2
At least €4,000 but less than €7,000	17	12.9
At least €7,000 but less than €10,000	1	0.8
€10,000 or more	4	3.0
Prefer not to say	8	6.1
	(1 missing)	(0.8 missing)
% personal income pension-contributed		
0-5%	18	13.6
5-10%	27	20.5
10-15%	8	6.1
15-20%	7	5.3
20-25%	1	0.8
More than 25%	8	6.1
Do not know	62	47
	(1 missing)	(0.8 missing)
Current primary mobility status		
Normal (internal) worker	35	26.5
Migrant worker	27	20.5
Cross-border (frontier) worker	51	38.6
Posted worker	1	0.8
Other: OPEN	0	0
Prefer not to say	16	12.1
Do not know	2	1.5
Level of multi-pillar retirement saving		
Statutory pension scheme		
- Yes	102	77.3
- No	14	10.6
- Do not know	16	12.1
Occupational pension scheme		
- Yes	93	70.5
- No	24	18.2
- Do not know	15	11.4

	N	% of total *N*
Personal pension scheme		
- Yes	50	37.9
- No	72	54.5
- Do not know	10	7.6
Other arrangements: OPEN		
- Yes	41	31.1
- No	82	62.1
- Do not know	9	6.8

* The term 'mobile' refers to having worked or having resided in more than one state.

** Since it appears that the more educated people are the more likely they are financially literate, as follows from Lusardi and Mitchell, 'Financial Literacy and Retirement Preparedness: Evidence and Implications for Financial Education'. Furthermore, since countries' education systems vary widely in terms of structure and curricular content, it can be complex to compare these systems and find a general/uniform definition of each of the educational levels, see for instance JHP Hoffmeyer-Zlotnik and U Warner, 'How to Measure Education in Cross-National Comparison: A Matrix of Education as a New Instrument' (European Conference on Quality in Survey Statistics 2006) 1 ff. For the present study, the levels of attained education correspond largely to the UNESCO's International Standard Classification of Education (ISCED) 2011, see UNESCO Institute for Statistics, 'International Standard Classification of Education (ISCED)' (2011). This widely-used comprehensive framework facilitates comparisons of education systems across countries by applying uniform and internationally agreed definitions, serving as a global reference tool for education systems. The UNESCO Institute for Statistics cooperates closely with Member States and its data collection partners, such as OECD and Eurostat.

As the section above clarified the set-up of the study, and provided an overview of the sample, the following section will address the results obtained in the main study. It will *inter alia* touch upon the analysis of the effect of the treatment condition on the dependent variables, the possible moderating effects, the effects of individual characteristics, and participants' responses to the open-ended questions.

3.6 RESULTS

3.6.1 *Analysis of Variance*

A one-way between-groups analysis of variance (ANOVA) was conducted to explore the impact of the three text frames as independent variables (gross amount, net amount and net amount accompanied with disclaimer) on the five dependent variables which will be addressed consecutively below.[422] Table 3.6 presents the mean and p-values for the

422 Results are robust/identical when controlling for the level of realism of the information, and the amounts depicted in the treatment conditions (gross amount; net amount). A one-way between-groups ANCOVA

dependent variables related to H1-H5, and specifies whether the hypotheses were supported.

Table 3.6 Mean and P-values of Dependent Variables, and Indication of Support for Hypotheses

Variables	GA	NA	NAD	*p*-value	H and support
Ease of Comprehension	3.96[a]	4.80[b]	4.52[a, b]	0.022	1 (fully)
Informativeness	4.02[a]	4.54[a]	4.64[a]	0.130	2 (no)
Trustworthiness	4.79[a]	4.11[b]	4.70[a, b]	0.003	3a (fully) 3b (no)
Expected Future Financial Security	3.76[a]	4.19[a, b]	4.49[b]	0.032	4 (partially)
Behavioural Expectations	3.80[a]	4.20[a]	4.03[a]	0.281	5 (partially, item 5)

[abc] *Within a row, means without a common superscript differ significantly ($p < 0.05$).*

The results revealed a significant main effect of the three text frames on the level of ease of comprehension (F (2, 129) = 3.928, p = 0.022) with an effect size, calculated using partial eta squared, of 0.06. The post-hoc comparisons using the Tukey HSD test revealed that the mean score for group 1 (gross amount, M = 3.96, SD = 1.461) was significantly different from group 2 (net amount, M = 4.80, SD = 1.487). Group 3 (net amount accompanied from disclaimer, M = 4.52, SD = 1.503) did not differ significantly from either group 1 or 2. Hence, H1 is supported, as respondents allocated to the net amount-group reported a higher level of ease of comprehension. Secondly, the results revealed no significant statistical difference in informativeness for the three treatment conditions (F (2, 129) = 2.075, p = 0.130), albeit that the net amount-group displayed a higher level of informativeness, compared to the gross amount-group. Hence, H2 is not supported. Although the scale's items all measured the informativeness of the information as such (rather than, for example, the amount displayed), and in the same context ('when planning for retirement'), the scale's items each depicted a different term ('helpful', 'useful', 'informative'). Therefore, a separate analysis for each item of the informativeness scale was conducted. No significant differences were found, although the scale's first item ('the

was performed to control for this potential distorting effect. The results revealed no significant interaction effect for all dependent variables, and the adjusted means (controlling for the effect of the control question as covariate) did not differ considerably from the unadjusted means, i.e. the maximum difference in means amounted to 0.11 as regards trustworthiness in the net amount disclaimer-group (4.59 vs. 4.70 resp.), and behavioural expectations in the gross amount-group (3.91 vs. 3.80 resp.).

information provided is helpful when planning for retirement') was marginally significant at the $p < 0.10$ significance level (F (2, 129) = 2.790, p = 0.065). Furthermore, for H3, the results showed a significant difference in the perceived trustworthiness of the shown information among the three treatment conditions (F (2, 127) = 6.061, p = 0.003). The effect size, calculated using partial eta squared, was high (0.09). The post-hoc comparisons using the Tukey HSD test revealed that the mean score for group 1 (gross amount) was significantly higher than for group 2 (net amount), and, hence, H3a is fully supported. Furthermore, the post-hoc results showed that the mean score for group 2 (net amount) was significantly lower than the mean score for group 3 (net amount accompanied by a disclaimer). Accordingly, H3b is contradicted, as it postulated that respondents allocated to the net amount and disclaimer-group report a lower level of trustworthiness, compared to the net-amount group. Thus, the results revealed, contrarily, that adding a disclaimer to a net amount of future retirement income has a positive effect on the perceived trustworthiness, rather than a detrimental effect. This suggests that including a disclaimer creates a certain feeling that people can rely, and trust, on the information (pertaining to the net amount).

With respect to expected future financial security, the analysis' result showed a significant difference among the three treatment conditions (F (2, 129) = 3.533, p = 0.032), with an effect size, calculated using partial eta squared, of 0.05. The post-hoc comparisons using the Tukey HSD test revealed that the mean score for group 1 (gross amount) was significantly lower than for group 3 (net amount and disclaimer). Group 2 (net amount) did not differ significantly from either group 1 or 3. H4 predicted that respondents allocated to the net amount-group, or net amount disclaimer-group, report a higher level of expected future financial security. This hypothesis has been partially supported, and it appeared that including a disclaimer has had a beneficial effect on peoples' reported expected future financial security.

H5 predicted that respondents allocated to the net amount-groups would report a higher level of behavioural expectations. Yet, the analysis did not yield any significant main effect among the three treatment conditions (F (2, 129) = 1.283, p = 0.281). Respondents in group 2 (net amount) or group 3 (net amount and disclaimer) did report higher levels of behavioural expectations than participants in group 1 (gross amount), but this did not reach statistical significance. Hence, H5 is not supported. However, the twelve items of the behavioural expectations scale concerned a wide range of types of behaviour (ranging from checking the tax treatment of the pension in order to get a total overview of the future pension income to consulting a professional financial advisor). Therefore, a separate analysis for each item was run. Merely the scale's item indicating that he/she will consult a professional financial advisor has been found statistically significant (F (2, 129) = 3.701, p

= 0.027). Group 1 (gross amount, *M* = 3.30, *SD* = 1.533) showed a significantly lower mean compared to group 2 (net amount, *M* = 4.23, *SD* = 1.588); group 3 was not found significant to either group 1 or 2. The effect size of this difference amount to 0.05. Given this result, the question rises why similar results were not found with regard to consulting a professional tax advisor for group 1 (gross amount, *M* = 3.48, *SD* = 1.696) compared to group 2 (net amount, *M* = 4.08, *SD* = 1.674).

In addition, respondents' real behaviour, i.e. the number of clicks, was measured. Interestingly, 35 out of 38 (92.1%) respondents allocated to the net amount and disclaimer-condition actually made use of the additional option to be redirected to the (additional) full-text disclaimer.

3.6.2 *Moderating Effects*

To analyse the effects of the individual moderators – potentially affecting the ANOVA-results – of subjective pension knowledge, subjective fiscal knowledge, and self-efficacy, on the different dependent variables, several standard multiple regressions were performed using the treatment condition and these moderators as independent variables. Moreover, interaction effects were measured. Preliminary analyses displayed no violation of the assumptions of multicollinearity, normality, linearity, homoscedasticity, independence of residuals and no outliers were found.

It was found that for trustworthiness as dependent variable, subjective pension knowledge is a statistically significant predictor at the $p < 0.10$ significance level (beta = 0.399, $p = 0.069$), while the treatment condition (random allocation to group 1, 2 or 3) does not have a statistically significant effect (beta = 0.175, $p = 0.421$). What is more, for behavioural expectations as dependent variable, the treatment condition and self-efficacy (as predictor) explain 6.4% of the variance ($F(3, 128) = 2.915$, $p = 0.037$). Yet, self-efficacy makes a weaker significant unique contribution (beta = 0.708, $p = 0.009$), compared to the treatment condition (beta = 1.524, $p = 0.023$). With regard to objective knowledge (financial literacy) a one-way ANCOVA (inserting financial literacy as a dummy) was performed. This analysis revealed no significant interaction effects for this moderator.

3.6.3 *Lack of Overview, Action Perspective, European Pension Tracking Service: Revealing Results*

To explore the degree of lack of overview, action perspective among (former) mobile workers as regards their retirement income, and to explore the need for a European

Pension Tracking Service, frequencies was run. The results revealed that with respect to the statement 'I face a lack of insight into the legal consequences of my mobility for my pension', 74.2% of respondents either somewhat agreed, agreed or strongly agreed with this statement. As regards the statement 'I face a lack of insight into the legal consequences of my mobility for the tax treatment of my pension', 78.1% of the respondents reported that they either somewhat agree, agree or strongly agree. These results reveal the lack of insight among mobile citizens into the consequences of their mobility in terms of their pensions and its tax treatment, and underlines the growing importance of supporting these mobile citizens in this regard through the provision of cross-border pension information.

Respondents who – to some extent – agreed with the statement 'I face a lack of insight into the legal consequences of my mobility for my pension', were forwarded and asked to respond to the statement 'The lack of insight into the legal consequences of my mobility for my pension hinders me in my retirement planning'. The results show that 64.5% of the respondents exposed to this statement either somewhat agreed, agreed or strongly agreed. With regard to respondent exposed to the statement 'The lack of insight into the legal consequences of my mobility for the tax treatment of my pension hinders me in my financial planning', the results revealed that 62.9% reported that they either somewhat agree or agree. This indicates that the majority of respondents feel in need of a certain instrument to resolve this lack of insight, and to support them in their retirement, and financial planning, while getting a grasp of the legal consequences of their mobility.

In terms of solutions, and interventions needed in the field of cross-border pension information, it was explored to what extent respondents agreed with the statement 'a European Pension Tracking Service, providing a total overview of my pension situation, would help me in my retirement planning.' 87.1% of respondents either somewhat agree, agree or strongly agree with this statement. This indicates the need and importance of developing such a pension tracking service on a European level, incorporating cross-border pensions, and its role in planning for retirement for mobile individuals. The mean and standard deviation of these statements have been depicted in table 3.7.

Table 3.7 Lack of Overview, Action Perspective, European Pension Tracking Service

Item	M	SD
I face a lack of insight into the legal consequences of my mobility for my pension	5.17	1.75
I face a lack of insight into the legal consequences of my mobility for the tax treatment of my pension	5.30	1.61
The lack of insight into the legal consequences of my mobility for my pension hinders me in my retirement planning	4.77	1.26
The lack of insight into the legal consequences of my mobility for the tax treatment of my pension hinders me in my financial planning	4.40	1.46
A European Pension Tracking Service, providing a total overview of my pension situation, would help me in my retirement planning	6.01	1.37

3.6.4 *Effect individual characteristics*

Finally, the effect of individual characteristics (gender, age[423], education, income and mobility status[424]) were explored through a two-way between-groups ANOVA, as they may have had a potential influence on the relationship between the independent variable (treatment) and the dependent variables. Only for age, level of education, and level of income results will be briefly addressed, as results for gender and mobility status did not reach statistical significance.

With regard to respondents' behavioural expectations, the results revealed no significant interaction effect between treatment and age. However, the main effect of age did reach statistical significance (F (4, 117) = 2.547, p = .043, partial eta squared = 0.08). The post-hoc test results – using Tukey's HSD – revealed that the age group 18-29 (M = 4.90, SD = .949) reported significantly higher levels of behavioural expectations compared to the age group 40-49 (M = 2.93, SD = 1.525) in the net amount disclaimer-condition.

With respect to level of education, participants were divided into three levels of education: low, medium, high. With respect to trustworthiness, the results revealed a significant interaction effect for level of education (F (4, 121) = 3.649, p = .008, partial eta squared = 0.108). Moreover, the main effect for level of education was statistically significant ((F (2,

423 Participants were divided into five groups according to their age (group 1: 18-29 years; group 2: 30-39 years; group 3: 40-49 years; group 4: 50-59 years; group 5: 60 years and above).

424 Participants were divided into seven categories: normal (internal) worker; migrant worker; cross-border (frontier) worker; posted worker; prefer not to say; do not know; and other.

121) = 3.642, p = .029, partial eta squared = 0.057); as well as the treatment condition (F (2, 121) = 5.152, p = .007, partial eta squared = 0.078). After splitting the data set into the categories of low, medium, and high level of education, a one-way ANOVA was conducted to unravel the significant interaction effect with respect to trustworthiness. The results revealed that for the high level of education-group the main effect for trustworthiness reached statistical significance (F (2, 52) = 13.1, p = .000, partial eta squared: 0.34); the low and medium level of education groups did not show a statistical difference. For the high level of education group, participants in the net amount-group reported significantly lower trustworthiness (M = 4.01, SD = .982) compared to participants in the gross amount group (M = 4.99, SD = .846); while participants in the net amount disclaimer-group reported significantly higher trustworthiness (M = 5.46, SD = .742) compared to participants in the net amount group (M = 4.01, SD = .982).

With respect to the level of income, participants were divided into three income categories: low, medium, and high.[425] As regards behavioural expectations, the results revealed a significant interaction effect for the level of income (F (5, 121) = 3.776, p = .003, partial eta squared = 0.135), as well as a significant main effect for the level of income (3, 121) = 2.956, p = .035, partial eta squared = 0.068). After splitting the data set into the categories of low, medium, high and other levels of income, a one-way ANOVA was conducted to unravel the significant interaction effect with respect to behavioural expectations. The results indicate that for the low level of income-group the main effect for behavioural expectations reached statistical significance (F (2, 41) = 5.2, p = .01), although the actual difference in mean scores between the groups was fairly small, i.e. an effect size of 0.25 (partial eta squared). The other, medium, and high level of income groups did not show a significant difference. For the low level of income group, participants in the net amount-group indicated significantly higher behavioural expectations (M = 4.65, SD = .895) compared to participants in the gross amount group (M = 3.40, SD = 1.345), while the net amount disclaimer-group did not significantly from the other two groups.

3.6.5 *Open-ended Questions*

The questionnaire started with an open-ended question, asking participants to take a moment to think about their pension, and asked which five questions come to their mind, and the most important question for which they would like to get an answer. It seeks to

425 Low: less than €1,250; at least €1,250 but less than €2,000; at least €2,000 but less than €2,500. Medium: at least €2,500 but less than €3,000; at least €3,000 but less than €4,000. High: at least €4,000 but less than €7,000; at least €7,000 but less than €10,000; €10,000 or more. The group of respondents who preferred not to say was categorised as 'other'.

disentangle what cognitive associations/social representations mobile persons hold with respect to their pension. This allowed to study what people consider as most pressing questions when it comes to their pension, i.e. on which topics they would like to receive (more) information on, i.e. what they consider as relevant, interesting and valuable information. The results are presented in table 8 below. It depicts what proportion of respondents (in %) gave what type of answer to the open question. It reveals that the question how much people will receive is most prevalent. Cross-border issues pertaining to pensions, also appear to be a pressing issue among respondents. These results were not analysed per treatment group (gross amount, net amount, net amount-disclaimer) as these questions were raised prior to the treatment, and, hence, it was expected that there was no relationship between the open-ended questions, and the treatment.

Table 3.8 Results Five Open-ended Question (in % of Total Responses)

Categories of response	Number of questions (in order of relevance ranked by respondents: 1 = most important; 5 = least important)				
	1	2	3	4	5
1 = amount of future pension income (how much?)	37.9	16.7	2.3	1.5	0.8
2 = adequacy of future pension income (enough?)	6.1	3.8	2.3	2.3	1.5
3 = (in)security/sustainability of future pension income	7.6	7.6	4.5	0.8	2.3
4 = retirement age	12.1	9.1	6.1	5.3	3.0
5 = paying institution	-	-	-	0.8	-
6 = tax treatment	4.5	11.4	6.8	5.3	5.3
7 = formalities (e.g. eligibility conditions, application for receiving pension benefits, administrative requirements)	4.5	5.3	10.6	8.3	6.1
8 = information provision/overview/ insight	3.8	2.3	-	5.3	3.0
9 = cross-border issues	9.1	10.6	11.4	6.1	3.0
10 = flexibility (early retirement/ part-time working/retired) and choice options	1.5	4.5	2.3	2.3	3.0
11 = (effect of) (future) changes in laws and regulations	-	1.5	0.8	0.8	-
12 = (need of) additional retirement saving	-	3.0	6.8	4.5	3.0
13 = survivors'/partners' benefits	-	3.0	3.8	2.3	3.0

Categories of response	Number of questions (in order of relevance ranked by respondents: 1 = most important; 5 = least important)				
	1	**2**	**3**	**4**	**5**
14 = consolidate fragmented pensions	0.8	2.3	3.0	1.5	-
15 = (health) insurance	-	3.0	1.5	0.8	1.5
16 = pay-out options	-	-	2.3	3.0	1.5
17 = (cross-border) transferability and portability of pension capital	0.8	3.0	3.8	2.3	1.5
18 = indexation (of pension benefits)	0.8	-	2.3	2.3	-
19 = investment of pension capital	-	2.3	1.5	0.8	-
99 = other	7.6	5.3	12.9	6.8	7.6

In addition, after each of the treatment conditions, in order to measure the cognitive representation of the text, respondents were asked to respond to an open-ended elaborative question ('After having read this information, please indicate which questions you still have with regard to your pension, in the text box below'). The results are presented in table 3.9 below. These results were analysed per treatment group (gross amount, net amount, net amount-disclaimer) as these questions were raised after the treatment, and it was hence expected that there was a relationship between the open-ended questions, and the treatment.

Table 3.9 Results Open-ended Question after Each Treatment Condition (in % of Total Responses)

	GA	NA	NAD
1 = net amount?	63.6	-	3.2
2 = status of amount (projection/credibility)	2.3	2.5	38.7
3 = (in)security/sustainability of future pension income	-	10	3.2
4 = retirement age	2.3	2.5	-
5 = indexation	9.1	10	6.5
6 = tax treatment (cross-border)	2.3	17.5	-
7 = formalities (e.g. eligibility conditions, application for receiving pension benefits, administrative requirements)	2.3	2.5	3.2
8 = (effect of) (future) changes in laws and regulations	-	2.5	6.5
9 = calculation/ composition (of projected (net) amount)	-	25	6.5
10 = survivors'/partners' benefits	-	2.5	-

	GA	NA	NAD
11 = social security contributions	-	2.5	-
12 = adequacy of future pension income (enough?)	2.3	7.5	-
99 = other	15.9	15	32.3

Among respondents allocated to the gross-amount text frame, the most common question was what they would receive as a net amount of future retirement. This supports this research's hypothesis, drawing on the relativity bias, that people want to be provided with a net amount of future retirement income, in order to compare this to their net (earned) income they currently receive, and which they employ to finance their current standard of living. This net amount then serves as a reference point, and research findings demonstrate that people only tend to compare things that are easily comparable and, thus, avoid comparing things that cannot be compared easily.[426] However, among respondents allocated to the net-amount text frame, the most common question related to the tax treatment of their (cross-border) pensions, and the calculation of the projected net amount. For instance, which elements of taxation were included in computing the net amount. In line with the hypothesis formulated in section 3.2, the prevalent question among respondents allocated to the net-amount disclaimer-text frame, pertained to the status of amount, the information's credibility. For instance, what is the informative value of the projected net amount if such a disclaimer is included in the information? People, thus, questioned the value of the information, provoked by the disclaimer. As the section above presented the study's results *in extenso*, the following section places the predominant outcomes against the background of this study's theoretical background, and this study's objective. This allows to understand this study's results in context.

3.7 DISCUSSION OF THE ANALYSES' RESULTS

In this study I investigated whether adjusting pension information along the ways of providing readers net, or gross amounts of future retirement income, and including a disclaimer, enhances or works to the detriment of the information's ease of comprehension, informativeness and perceived trustworthiness, next to the persons' expected future financial security, and behavioural expectations. Moreover, the study explored the moderating effect of financial literacy, perceived fiscal/ pension literacy and self-efficacy in this regard.

426 Ariely, 8.

The results revealed that exposing participants to a net amount of projected future retirement income has a significantly positive effect on the ease of comprehension, while including a disclaimer does not alter this. This demonstrates that providing a net amount of future retirement income renders the (pension) information easier to understand, more salient, and readily available since people have encountered a net amount recently or frequently in financial decision-making (e.g. buying a new car, doing groceries). This is further supported by the results of the five open-ended question in the beginning of the survey, where among respondents allocated to the gross-amount text frame, the predominant question pertained to what they would receive as a net amount of future retirement income. This supports this research's hypothesis, drawing on the relativity bias, that people generally want to be provided with a net amount of future retirement income, in order to compare this (easily) to their current net (earned) income, which they employ to finance their current standard of living. Such an easy comparison enables readers to assess the adequacy of their future retirement income, and offers them an action perspective in order to assess whether additional actions, for instance extra pensions savings, are necessary.

With respect to the information's perceived trustworthiness, the results revealed that incorporating a disclaimer in information depicting a net amount of future pension income has a statistically significant positive effect on the information's perceived trustworthiness (compared to information depicting a net amount without any disclaimer). In order to ameliorate people's perceived trustworthiness of the information showing a net amount of future pension income, a disclaimer appears to play a pivotal role in this regard, implying that in these cases a disclaimer is an apt intervention. As regards the effect of a disclaimer on expected future financial security, one might expect that including a disclaimer would have an adverse effect. On the contrary, the results made apparent that incorporating a disclaimer in information actually has a statistically significant positive effect on participants' reported expected future financial security. Respondents allocated to group 1 (gross amount) reported the lowest level of expected future financial security, followed by group 2 (net amount), and group 3 (net amount accompanied by disclaimer) reporting the highest level. Including a disclaimer seems to induce a certain sense of security. What is more, the effect of adjusting pension information on the information's informativeness, as such, did not yield statistical significance, albeit that the scale's first item ('the information provided is helpful when planning for retirement') was found marginally significant at the $p < 0.10$ significance level. Although the analysis on behavioural expectations did not yield any significant main effect among the three treatment conditions, one of the twelve-point scale was found significant, i.e. the item indicating that he/she will consult a professional financial advisor. The results revealed that people allocated to the net amount group reported statistically higher behavioural expectations, compared to the respondents allocated to the gross amount-group. It may even be argued that due to the absence of the disclaimer, people show higher behavioural expectations with regard to consulting a professional financial advisor, as they may call the information's credibility into question, and therefore feel urged to consult a professional. People exposed to a net amount of future retirement income, thus, seem to rely more on a professional advisor, rather than taking action themselves, i.e. consulting financial or pension related literature or related content from the internet to gain more insights and knowledge about pensions. The twelve items of the behavioural expectations scale pointed, on the one hand, in the direction of pension-related actions, and, on the other hand, to fiscal-related actions. It can be contended that pension-related tasks are more 'salient' than tax-related tasks in retirement planning.[427] People might also perceive tax-related behavioural expectations as requiring more effort, and might therefore be more reluctant to do so. In addition, the results revealed that including an additional option to read a full-text disclaimer, at a deeper layer of information, appears to be effective, as 92.1% of the respondents allocated to the net amount and disclaimer-group actually made use of this option by clicking the button redirecting them to the full-text disclaimer. This suggests – under the Elaboration Likelihood Model – that incorporating such a possibility invokes a certain motivation among people to think elaborately about the (credibility of the) information under the central route of thinking.

Furthermore, with regard to heterogeneity among respondents and the potential influence on the relationship between the independent variable (treatment) and the dependent variables, the impact of the treatment condition and gender, age, level of education, level of income and current (primary) mobility status was explored. As regards gender and age, no significant interaction effects were found, except for the effect of respondents' behavioural expectations, where the main effect of age did reach statistical significance, i.e. the age group 18-29 reported significantly higher levels of behavioural expectations compared to the age group 40-49 in the net amount disclaimer-condition. With regard to the level of income, for none of the dependent variables the interaction effect reached statistical significance, except for behavioural expectations where in the low income-group, participants in the net amount-group indicated significantly higher behavioural expectations compared to participants in the gross amount-group. This indicates that the low-level income-group is more amenable to adjusting information by providing a net amount, in terms of behavioural expectations. For the level of education, the interaction

427 Tversky, 337. Some research studies observed a common pattern in the sense that the more salient objects, in comparative tasks, occur more often as a response, compared to the less salient object. Factors contributing to the salience of a stimulus include intensity, frequency, familiarity, good form, and informational content.

effect was not significant for all dependent variables, except for trustworthiness, where the results revealed that for the high level of education group, participants in the net amount-group reported significantly lower trustworthiness compared to participants in the gross amount group, while participants in the net amount disclaimer-group reported significantly higher trustworthiness compared to participants in the net amount group.

With regard to the moderating effect of subjective pension/fiscal knowledge, financial literacy (i.e. objective knowledge), and self-efficacy on the dependent variables, little effects were found. For trustworthiness, subjective pension knowledge was found statistically significant at the $p < 0.10$ significance level. With regard to objective knowledge (financial literacy) no significant interaction effects for this moderator were found.

Lastly, the study explored the degree of lack of overview, and action perspective among (former) mobile workers as regards their retirement income, and explored the need for a European Pension Tracking Service. The results revealed a considerable lack of insight among mobile citizens into the consequences of their mobility in terms of their pension and its tax treatment, and underlines the growing importance of supporting these mobile citizens in this regard through the provision of cross-border pension information. Further, results indicated that the majority of respondents feel in need of a certain instrument to resolve this lack of insight, and to support them in their retirement, and financial planning, while getting a grasp of the legal consequences of their mobility. In terms of solutions, and interventions needed in the field of cross-border pension information, results revealed that almost 90% of respondents perceive a European Pension Tracking Service, providing a total overview of their pension situation, as helpful in their retirement planning. This supports the call for the development of pension information provision on a European level, aimed at (retired) mobile workers.

3.8 Managerial Contributions

This study's results offer practical insights for improving the effectiveness of (cross-border) pension information provision. First, the results revealed that the most pressing question respondents have when it comes to their pension, is how much they will receive. Furthermore, cross-border pension issues also appear to be a predominant issue among mobile workers. Respondents' question how much they will get, is made even more concrete as the results of the open-ended questions showed that among respondents allocated to the gross-amount text frame, the most common question is what they would receive as a net amount of future retirement income. In addition, among respondents allocated to the net-amount text frame, the most common question related to the tax treatment of their (cross-border) pensions, and the calculation of the projected net amount. Lastly, the prevalent question among respondents allocated to the net-amount disclaimer-text frame, pertained to the status of amount, the projection's credibility. These insights may support in tailoring, and shaping the provision of pension information.

As has been mentioned earlier, conveying a future net amount of future retirement income poses considerable challenges, (legal) risks and tensions in the domain of information provision, for instance, the risk of providing incorrect information due to the legislation's complexity and (un)predictability. In order to mitigate these risks, this study's results provide practical guidance. An instrument to avoid being held liable for providing erroneous information, and making people more aware of the (informative) non-binding status of the information, is including a disclaimer. The results have shown that including a net amount with a disclaimer has a positive effect on the perceived trustworthiness of the information. In addition, including an additional option to read a full-text disclaimer, at a deeper layer of information, appears to be effective, as 92.1% of the respondents allocated to the net amount and disclaimer-group actually made use of this option. Moreover, people exposed to a gross amount reported the highest level of perceived trustworthiness. However, in turn, depicting a gross amount has a negative effect on the perceived ease of comprehension, as aforementioned. This illustrates, part of, the tensions that may arise in pension information provision. Also in terms of people's expected future financial security, providing a net amount of future retirement income accompanied by a disclaimer, appears to have a positive effect, potentially enhancing the information's effectiveness.

In terms of heterogeneity, fairly little differences have been found when it comes to gender, age, level of income, level of education, and mobility status. This suggests that a fairly standardised approach in information provision can be taken when it comes to the form of projections of future retirement income. What is more, it deserves to be noted that although the respondents' primary mobility status did not have a significant moderating effect between treatment and the dependent variables, the respondents differed considerably as regards their mobility status as such (migrant worker, cross-border worker, posted worker etc.). This suggest that a standardised cross-country approach can be taken in the provision of information on future (cross-border) retirement income. Although this does not affect information provision as such, it may have more practical implications in terms of legal consequences of this mobility status for ascertaining the tax treatment of cross-border pensions. A person's mobility status plays a pivotal role in ascertaining the applicable rules and regulations in the domain of the tax treatment of (cross-border) pensions. This poses substantial challenges, and tensions, in the domain of information provision, e.g. leading to a high susceptibility in terms of incorrect information. In turn, providing incorrect information may have a potential detrimental effect on the information's (perceived) credibility. Again, including a disclaimer may play a pivotal role in combatting this risk.

3.9 Theoretical Contributions

Literature on comparability, and salience, of information and consumer (financial) decision-making as it stands pertains to more hedonic, and more readily available information and comparisons, such as picking from a menu, or choosing a product from a wide range of (consumer) products. Moreover, it focusses on more habitual consumer decision-making, such as doing groceries.[428] These contexts, and settings, differ considerably from retirement planning, which can be considered a context in which people's involvement, satisfaction and engagement is generally low.[429] As Brüggen et al. point out with regard to retirement planning, people see the relevance of it, yet still procrastinate it and do not engage in it (sufficiently).[430] Besides, as experiences as shopping, partner selection or dining are more pleasant than retirement planning, it needs to be tested whether the same results hold true with regard to a pension context. What is more, information on pension accumulation and prospective retirement benefits is much more complex than information in most other settings so that pension information may also result in more complexity, information overload, and cognitive effort. Literature on these phenomena in the domain of pension information is scarce, and little is known on how they operate in a cross-border context. Moreover, research on the effect of providing net amounts of future pension is scarce, and has remained underexposed. In this study, we explored these phenomena in a low-involvement domain, i.e. retirement decisions, and it appeared that the relativity bias (drawn from the domain of behavioural economics) also holds in this domain. In doing so, it expands the scope of extant literature in the domain of pension information provision and financial decision-making – in particular pertaining to communication on prospective retirement benefits – and makes these insights more practically applicable.

This study's results revealed that the relativity bias also holds in this domain, since exposing participants to a net amount of projected future retirement income has a significantly positive effect, while including a disclaimer does not alter this. Providing a net amount of future retirement income renders the (pension) information more readily

428 Ariely, 18 and cited literature.

429 Brüggen, Post and Schmitz, referring, in this regard, to C Rickwood and L White, 'Pre-purchase decisionmaking for a complex service: retirement planning' 23.

430 Brüggen, Post and Schmitz, referring to JM Krijnen, M Zeelenberg and SM Breugelmans, 'Decision importance as a cue for deferral' 10 Judgment and Decision Making 407. Brüggen et al. point out that interactive, personal online retirement planning tools, besides allowing people to track their accumulated pension rights, potentially foster user attitudes and generate personalized insights.

available, i.e. people have encountered a net amount recently or frequently when involved in financial decision-making (e.g. buying a new car, doing groceries, or deciding whether or not they are financially able to save more for retirement). This, in turn, makes the comparison of current (earned) income, and future retirement income easier. In doing so, this study advances retirement research by offering a more profound insight into how net amounts of future retirement income (with disclaimer) are evaluated compared to gross amounts. Moreover, the results demonstrate that adding a disclaimer – pointing out the risks when communicating on net amounts of future retirement income – may have a positive effect on the perceived trustworthiness, rather than a detrimental effect.

What is more, this research's results expand the extant literature in the domain of tax law by adopting a novel approach, i.e. evaluating the functioning of regulatory frameworks through the lens of effective cross-border pension information. This evaluation framework has been designed by harnessing findings in the field of behavioural economics (the relativity bias in particular). This renewing approach allowed to perceive the 'law in action', providing information on the tax treatment of cross-border pensions while relying on the prevailing laws and regulations. This has led to (empirically-obtained) evidence-based insights pertaining to effective pension information, in particular on the effect of exposing readers to net amounts of future retirement income (compared to gross amounts), and the effect of incorporating a disclaimer (aimed at preventing from being held liable for providing erroneous information) in terms of the tension manifesting itself between information's correctness, understandability, and trustworthiness.

Moreover, this study contributes to the existing body of literature by exploring heterogeneity among respondents, in terms of gender, age, level of income, level of education, and mobility status. Furthermore, this study contributes to literature by studying the moderating effect of respondents' subjective pension knowledge, subjective fiscal knowledge, (objective) financial literacy, and self-efficacy. However, fairly little heterogenic effects have been found. Despite the growing call to include individual characteristics in enhancing information's effectiveness, the results suggest that a fairly standardised approach in information provision can be taken when it comes to the form of projections of future retirement income. Furthermore, it adds to literature by taking a cross-border approach, where the study's population solely consisted of (former) mobile workers. However, no heterogeneity effects have been found as regards people's mobility status.

Drawing on these results, it is argued that the relativity bias in decision-making also holds in the low-involvement, complex and less pleasant domain of (cross-border) pensions. More precisely, a net amount of projected future retirement income in information has a significantly positive effect on the perception of that information among readers. These beneficial effects of these insights can be transferred to the pension domain. This study expands the growing body of literature, made existing insights more practical applicable, and adopted a (yet underexposed) cross-border approach.

3.10 Limitations and Future Research

Several limitations to the present research should be drawn, and avenues for future research should be pointed out. First, the information on the amount of (gross or net) future retirement income, was fictional and, hence, it might not have elicited the envisaged motivation among participants, as – under the Elaboration Likelihood Model – personally relevant information might induce more motivation among people, and steer them in the direction of more elaborate thinking (central route of thinking). Hence, it would be an interesting avenue for future research to incorporate personal data on the projection of future retirement income, and explore whether the effect would be strengthened or weakened. Second, a further limitation of this study lies in the net replacement rates, used to compute the depicted amount of future pension income in the net amount-frame. In order to reach net replacement rates, the gross replacement rates were reduced by taxes and social contributions. These taxes and social contributions were calculated in a purely domestic situation. However, as discussed in the comparative legal part of this dissertation, taxation and the according effective tax burden, may vary significantly in cross-border situations. The effect of this on the net replacement rates is, thus, not reflected in the net amount depicted in the frames in the survey. Further, the data on earnings and replacement rates concerns normal (internal) workers. It would be an interesting avenue for future research to find out whether these figures, and the effects thereof, would differ for (former) mobile workers.

Limitations were also faced with regard to the available data, used to calculate the final amount of future retirement income, depicted in the survey's text frame. The data used to compute the depicted amounts of gross and net future pension income, has been retrieved from OECD Statlink and Eurostat. Retrieving data from these sources reflects the long time-lags characterising data collection across countries. With regard to these sources, it could, as accurately as possible, be unravelled on the basis of which assumptions the data was calculated, compared to other datasets. Hence, it could be ascertained that it was avoided that incomparable variables were used in the calculation. However, the data referred to either 2018 or 2016. This has, however, been adjusted by multiplying these amounts with price inflation, or nominal wage growth. However, it would be interesting to use real-time data to compute the personal projection of future retirement income.

A further limitation lies in the open-ended questions posed in the beginning of the survey. These questions strived to explore what cognitive associations/social representations mobile persons hold with respect to their pension; it provided a general overview of potential topics for information provision. An interesting avenue for future research would be to explore – in more detail – on what aspects mobile persons would like to receive information when it comes to their pension, i.e. pinpointing 'key (cross-border pension) information elements'.

Furthermore, with regard to measuring knowledge on pensions and taxes, this was in this study limited to measuring subjective knowledge, apart from financial literacy (objective knowledge). This leaves an avenue for future research, i.e. measuring objective knowledge in the domains of pensions and taxes specifically.[431] This requires further research to develop validated and reliable questions in order to measure objective pension/tax knowledge. In addition, although this study incorporated a wide variety of potential moderators, the scope of moderators, in particular personal motivational factors under the Elaboration Likelihood Model, could be expanded to, for instance, the need for cognition. In this way, a more profound understanding can be obtained of what (motivational) factors drive people in the direction of the central route of thinking, and elaborate processing of information.

Lastly, this study explored the number of clicks to measure the degree to which participants read the full-text disclaimer, i.e. a proxy for measuring actual behaviour. Nevertheless, it is possible that participants merely clicked the button, while not actually reading the (entire) disclaimer. These people might have left the disclaimer screen immediately after clinking it. Hence, it would be interesting to explore to what extent people actually read the full-text disclaimer (e.g. through time tracking) to get an impression of the extent to which people read the disclaimer, which allows them to value the depicted information's trustworthiness.

3.11 INTERIM CONCLUSION

Building on the relativity bias in (financial) decision-making, this empirical study explored the impact of adjusting information along the ways of providing readers net or gross amounts of future retirement income, and the use of a disclaimer, on the ease of

431 See for instance Schmölders, *Das Irrationale in der öffentlichen Finanzwirtschaft*. Schmölders' study revealed that German citizens had only vague knowledge pertaining to taxes, i.e. the majority of the people had somewhat of an understanding of their income tax, and they only made vague guesses about the overall taxes paid in their household.

comprehension, informativeness, perceived trustworthiness of the information, and peoples' expected future financial security, and behavioural expectations. The results revealed some significant effects on these dependent variables, e.g. exposing readers to a net amount of future retirement income (significantly) elevates the information's ease of comprehension, while including a disclaimer does not affect this. This is further supported by respondents' answer to various open-ended question, revealing that the most prevalent question pertains to 'what will I get (net)'? This reveals that the relativity bias also holds in the domain of planning for retirement.

What is more, the heterogenic effects of gender, age, education, income and mobility status were tested. The analysis revealed little heterogenic differences. In addition, the study examined the moderating role of peoples' financial literacy, perceived fiscal/ pension literacy and self-efficacy. The results revealed virtually no significant effects for these moderators. This suggests that in information provision – in terms of depicting amounts of future retirement income – a generalized approach can be adopted.

4 'Pensions': Notions, Terms and Concepts Projected Through the Lens of Disciplinary Boundaries

4.1 Introduction

Some terms, notions and concepts (e.g. 'pension' or 'pillar') may be considered a universal legal concept present in both legal systems at issue, but nevertheless having a different meaning in both systems. What is more, mobile individuals – who avail(ed) themselves of their European freedoms of movement – see themselves confronted with a wide range of diverging 'pensions', i.e. pension vehicles, schemes, retirement products of all sorts, arising from statutory, occupational and individual pension systems in each of the different (former) working states, and/or residence states. By being mobile, they enter the field of the intersections between different multi-level legal systems and the interaction of poorly coordinated legal domains, which can all be interwoven in a personal mobile work situation. But what entails a pension (in each of the different states)? What do statutory, occupational, personal pensions encompass? Why shall pension entitlements under these pension schemes be granted? Are there any cross-country pension categorising systems fit for fostering effective pension information in this regard?

The relevance of this chapter's exploration lies in conveying a legal notion such as 'pension' and 'pillar' into the realm of effective pension information provision, while upholding this information's effectiveness, as dealt with in chapter 2 of this research. It is essential, in the context of this research, to explore what pension comprises and to identify characteristic elements, when providing effective pension information on (foreign) pensions to (former) mobile workers, since the concept of pensions may exhibit considerable diversity among national pension systems. The use of the term 'pension' and the (legal) context in which the term is used should be clarified first, in particular when comparing pensions in a cross-border context. During this process of conveying such a legal construct, tensions in information provision may emerge, in particular between correctness and understandability. For instance, where upholding the information's correctness requires that readers shall be informed about properties, and particularities, of each (deviating) national perception of the construct pensions, understandability may require omitting the inclusion of these properties at detail level. Obviously, the more the national (German/Dutch) systems hold similarities/are comparable in terms of 'pensions', the easier it is to uphold the pension information's effectiveness. Thus, a certain degree of comparability would mitigate the aforementioned tensional relationship.

In this vein, the chapter below seeks to delineate, and operationalise the construct of pension as the subject of this research. Besides exploring the etymology of the term 'pension', the (legal) interpretation of this term – and statutory, occupational, personal pensions – in both the Netherlands and Germany will be explored. What is more, this chapter addresses to what extent the existing pension classification systems are apt for facilitating a cross-country comparison of pension systems, and to what extent they would foster the regulatory framework's fitness in the light of effective cross-border pension information. In section 4.5, these comparative findings will be evaluated along the (legal) lines of this research evaluation framework. Not each of these legal principles shall be evaluated to the same extent in section 4.5. As this chapter explores the construct 'pension', emphasis will be put on the principle of similarity/comparability, since this chapter seeks to explore to what extent the operationalisation, and legal interpretation, of the dispersed construct of pension is fit for the provision of effective pension information. What is more, instruments to ameliorate the inter-system consistency, inter-level coherence and foreseeability of the construct 'pension' are lacking. This chapter meets this research second (sub)objective of a legal comparative study in which the legal frameworks in the Netherlands and Germany shall be mapped out. In doing so, this chapter reveals the disciplinary boundaries of the (scientific) realm of pensions.

4.1.1 *The Concept 'Pension': Non-Homogeneity Prevails*

The definition of pensions is non-homogeneous among countries, and a taxonomy of pension (systems) is still missing. Comparing pensions is therefore often likely susceptible to controversy, since each pension and pension systems is unique; developed on the basis of country-specific historical, economic, cultural, political and legal developments over time. It is in most cases difficult to determine which of these developments has contributed most to the national pension system at present, i.e. an interactive process is in many cases discernible. This dependency on country specific characteristics implies that a particular pension system cannot be transplanted from one state, and implemented unchanged in another state. What is more, in comparing pension systems, it may lead to comparing the incomparable.

Although there appears to be a certain degree of consensus among States as regards the goal of 'pension' (i.e. replacing earned income after retirement in order to uphold a given standard of living[432]), the role of pensions in attaining this goal[433], deviates fairly among States, which is reflected in the diverging replacement rates across (Member) States.[434] What is more, a common consensus on a clear delineation and demarcation of the concept of 'pension' is even missing. Although it seems *prima facie* quite straightforward what is considered as 'pensions', the relevance of finding a clear legal definition is often underestimated. However, since there is a wide variety of pension vehicles in each of the European Member States, each having their own different specific characteristics, this inhibits finding a common agreed on definition, for instance to what extent is housing considered a form of pension.

4.1.2 *The Term 'Pension': Beyond a Semantical Discussion*

The Oxford Dictionary[435] rightly differentiates between either 'state pension' (i.e. "*a regular payment made by the state to people of or above the official retirement age and to some widows and disabled people*"), or a company pension scheme (i.e. "*a regular payment made during a person's retirement from an investment fund to which that person or their employer has contributed during their working life*"). The term 'pension' is partly a borrowing from

432 Which, in turn, depends on people's preferences as regards their income and expenses after retirement.

433 The relative importance of occupational schemes in providing a retirement income varies significantly across states, depending on the pension system. Statutory funded pensions established by legislation and financed from a general contribution regime are not considered occupational pensions. Occupational pensions can also be constructed as sector-wide pay-as-you-go schemes or 'book reserves', i.e. pension promises backed by own resources of the company, for instance the German *Direktzusage*. For a rough indication of the coverage ratio of occupational and personal pension: European Commission, 'Pensioen Adequacy Report 2018: Current and Future Income Adequacy in Old Age in the EU' 79-80. In 2016, 57% of the German population aged 15-64 was covered by occupational pensions, while 33.8% of that same group was covered by personal pensions. In contract, in the Netherlands 88% was covered by occupational, and 28.3% by personal pensions. Moreover, as a percentage of GDP, assets in retirement savings plan in Netherlands amounted to 212.7%, in Germany only 8.2%, see OECD Pensions at a glance 2021, 'Assets in retirement savings plans and public pension reserve funds' 2021) <https://www.oecd-ilibrary.org/docserver/d3f11cc6-en.pdf?expires=1692642139&id=id&accname=ocid177396&checksum=9A23AA8939958573C0851CF440B18AC7> accessed 21 August 2023.

434 With respect to the coverage of occupational pensions across EU Member States, a clear regional pattern is discernible. Where in Northern and Western Member States, as a general rule, high or medium supplementary pension coverage is found, coverage remains low to non-existent in the South and East of the EU. High or medium rates of pension coverage are characterised by a pivotal role of social partners in pension policies, and mature financial markets. Low coverage ratios may indicate underlying social and institutional factors, such as a preference for non-funded instruments or insufficient capacity of social partners. See European Commission, 'Pensioen Adequacy Report 2018: Current and Future Income Adequacy in Old Age in the EU' 80.

435 Oxford Dictionaries.

French ('*pencione*'), and partly from Latin ('*pēnsiōn-, pēnsiō*'), both translated roughly as 'payment'. Nevertheless, it is worth noting, that most definitions hold some similarities:

- These definitions hold similarities in terms of referring both to pension as a regular payment (i.e. not as a lump sum).
- The paying agent pays out the pension benefits; albeit the state, the employer, or, for instance, the insurance company.
- The beneficiary is entitled to the payment of the benefits as of a certain point, or event in time; reaching the retirement age.
- The benefits payments strive to provide for certain needs, e.g. enabling to subsist without an earned income.

The confusion with regard to the concept of pension and the comparison thereof, is to a certain extent inherent to the interdisciplinary nature of research on pensions, i.e. the 'same' phenomenon can be described in different kinds of terminology, and different descriptions represent different aspects. This confusion may be due to the fact that the usual way in which we study a topic, often gets projected through the lens of our own disciplinary boundaries, i.e. our own paradigm. This can mean that while exploring the concept from a particular perspective (e.g. a civil law-perspective), we may overlook certain elements that are considered paramount from another perspective (e.g. a tax law-perspective, or an economic perspective). Hence, the perspective taken in research, largely determines how pension is framed and what it should comprise. In other words, a concept's definition determines – but also reflects – our perception of that same concept, e.g. pension. These consequences of diverging perspectives on pensions become manifest in cross-border situations.

4.1.3 *Underlying Rationale as Part of the Conception of 'Pension'*

In addition to the above, as a complicating factor, the underlying rationale for conferring pension rights on eligible persons, deviates between Member States' systems.[436] For instance, the labour performed is considered a means/contribution for saving for retirement, in for instance the German *Beambtenversorgung* and *Direktzusage*.[437] These underlying rationales differ per domain in which the term 'pension' is used, e.g. tax law, civil (pension) law, social security law. This also affects the notion (or the projection thereof) of the term 'pension'. As has been pointed out by Stevens, which viewpoint I

436 Cf. Y Stevens, 'Pensioenen als instrument van geïndividualiseerd arbeidsmarktbeleid en armoedebeleid' in J Put and Y Stevens (eds.), *Ontwikkelingen van de sociale zekerheid 2011-2016* (Die Keure Brugge 2016).

437 Cf. F Ruland, 'Überblick über die Alterssicherung in Deutschland' in B Rürup and F Ruland (eds.), *Alterssicherung und Besteuerung* (Gabler, Wiesbaden 2008) 21.

endorse, the conceptions of pension may differ.[438] He enumerates various – not mutually exclusive – conceptions as regards pensions:

- a form of deserved rest;[439]
- compensating the physical inability to work (any longer);
- part of the wage structure (negotiable remuneration; employment condition; personal character);
- deferred wage/postponed wage; (e.g. Dutch and German occupational pensions, see sections 4.3.3 and 4.4.3);
- a reward for services paid to the country (often civil servant pension schemes);
- a form of saving;
- a form of property;
- a form of individual or collective life insurance;
- a form of social insurance (often in Bismarckian-orientated social security systems)
- a form of shared citizenship (often in Beveridge-orientated social security systems, e.g. Dutch *AOW*).

For instance, the rationale underlying the German *Grundrente* is rewarding lifetime achievements of people who have worked for decades, brought up children and cared for relatives.[440] For this reason, they should be guaranteed a regular old-age income ten percent above the basic security requirement (i.e. the *Grundrente*, which will be arranged through the German *Rentenversicherung*).

It shall be noted that various forms of these pension-conceptions may occur – in varying degrees – simultaneously in a certain state, and may even overlap. As Stevens argues this mixture of pension concepts explains the uniqueness of each national pension landscape.[441] Moreover, these pension concepts/notions – and mixtures – may resonate in citizens' minds in terms of mental images and 'representations', as discussed in chapter 2 of this research, and which will be dealt with in more detail in chapter 10. Stevens refers to this as the historically-/ideologically-embedded 'national pension identity', in which people

438 See Stevens, *EU Pension Law* 4 ff. and cited literature. Stevens refers to a wide variety of authors, books, and articles on this subject matter. In particular read worthy in this regard is JM Werbrouck, *Het multidimensionale pensioenbegrip* (Boomjuridisch, Den Haag 2022). Stevens refers to the term 'pension' as a hypernym: Stevens, *EU Pension Law* 5 and Y Stevens, 'The role of the government in creating or enhancing the access to funded or unfunded pensions in the modern welfare state' in N Da Costa Cabral and N Cunha Rodriques (eds.), *The Future of Pensions Plans in the EU Internal Market* (Springer International Publishing Cham 2019).

439 Based on the ILO Conventions 102 and 128 stating that old-age pensions are to be paid in the form of life annuities. See also Stevens, *EU Pension Law* 5.

440 Koalitionsvertrag zwischen CDU, CSU und SPD, 92.

441 Stevens, *EU Pension Law* 9.

recognize their pension systems as their own.[442] This can serve as a possible explanation for why states prefer to keep pension-matters as close as them as possible, and seem reluctant in extending pension systems to cross-border situations, or attribute the EU more competence in the pension domain.

What is more, the above underscores the relevance of being aware of the fact that there is no uniform concept of 'pension'; the design of each provision differs – and continues to differ – considerably across states, as well as the reasons for conferring such rights. In this regard, notions of classifying systems can merely serve as a guiding principle, and they have to be treated with caution in legally comparing pension systems, and providing effective pension information.

4.1.4 Cross-border Pensions

For the purpose of this research, the term 'cross-border pensions' needs to be clearly delineated, inter alia, in view of the applicable legislation under examination. Cross-border pensions refer to either a statutory, occupational or a personal pension scheme in which one of the three elements are of a transnational nature.[443] These (fiscal) elements refer to either (the tax deduction of) the contributions during the accrual phase, the (taxation of) yields on part of the pension institution and the (taxation of) pension benefits paid out during the pay-out phase. As regards the first element, the beneficiary paying the pension premiums/contributions may not be a resident in the state where the scheme is executed. The second element refers to the situation where the pension fund or institution, insurance company or funding company (for instance as regards the German *Direktzusage*) is established in a different state from that in which the beneficiary is resident. Lastly, the third element amounts to situations where the beneficiary of the pension benefits resides in a different state than the state from which the payment stems from, or where the pension benefits from tax benefits. Therefore, cross-border pensions involve, at least, one of these cross-border elements, which prevent as a case from being considered purely domestic. It should be noted, that a situation may involve more than one transnational element, i.e. more than two states are involved (for instance triangular situations).

As regards different graduations of transnationality in cross-border situations I endorse the distinction made by Prats.[444] These graduations reflect the different tax consequences

442 Ibid. 9.

443 Cf. FAG Prats, 'The Tax Treatment of Cross-Border Pensions from an EC Law Perspective' 41 European Taxation 13.

444 Ibid. 13 ff.

involved and the degree to which Treaty freedoms may apply. It is to be noted that in this research merely cross-border situations between the Netherlands and Germany will be covered. The cross-border situations set forth below indicate the level of 'cross-border' may vary from one situation to another. Consequently, this may provoke different consequences as regards the tax treatment of cross-border pensions on a national, international and European level, see chapters 5, 6, 7, 8 and 9 of this research.

These graduations concern the following:

- Firstly, a person who, while working temporarily in a different state, continues to contribute to a (occupational) pension scheme located in the state of origin. Under certain conditions and within limits, the domestic tax treatment of contributions to the pension scheme, may be extended to contributions to foreign pension schemes, in virtue of the non-discrimination principle. In certain situations, denying this extension impedes the freedom of movement of workers. This situation will be dealt with in this research.
- Secondly, a person who moves to another state after retirement. In this case, the cross-border elements relate to the payment of benefits to a different state than where the pension was accrued. The tax issue relates to the question which state may subject the pension benefits to tax. This has been laid down in the concluded double tax convention.[445] As a general rule, this situation is protected by the free movement of persons.[446] This will be dealt with more thoroughly in chapter 8 and 9.
- Thirdly, the option to participate in a foreign pension scheme in order to accrue an (occupational) pension scheme. In these cases, both migrant workers as well as foreign pension schemes providing the scheme for all domestic employers and employees, are involved.[447] This situation will be dealt with in this research.
- Lastly, the situation where foreign investments are made by pension schemes in order to optimize the results and income of the pension scheme. These situations are protected by the freedom of movement of capital, precluding any unjustified tax

445 Which in most cases adopts the principles as laid down in art. 18 OECD Model Tax Convention on Income and on Capital.

446 See C-406/04 *De Cuyper* ECLI:EU:C:2006:491 (CJEU) para 39-40. In the *Cuyper* case the court refers to C-224/98 *D'Hoop* ECLI:EU:C:2002:432 (CJEU) para 31 and C-224/02 *Pusa* ECLI:EU:C:2004:273 (CJEU) para 19. See also PJG Kapteyn and P VerLoren van Themaat, *Introduction to the Law of the European Communities* (3rd33 edn Kluwer Law International, The Hague 1998) 692.

447 These situations may even give rise to triangular situations where several tax regimes coincide, leading to more technical complexity. From a tax perspective this may concern three elements: the tax treatment of contributions (in the state of residence or activity of the worker), the tax treatment of pension income (in the state of residence of the pensioner), and the tax treatment of contributions paid to the pension scheme (in the state where the pension scheme is located).

mechanisms that may be discriminatory or restrictive. This situation will not be dealt with in this research.

4.2 Models, Typologies, Taxonomies, Classifications: Facilitating Comparison of National Pension Systems?

As has been addressed earlier in this research, European pension systems are as diverse as the member states themselves. In view of the division of competences between the European Union and its Member States, only few aspects can be regulated on a European level when it comes to pensions, since a sufficient ground of competence needs to be provided by the European Treaty (TFEU). What is more, pensions – as an element of social protection – is still mainly considered to constitute a national competence.[448] As a consequence, member states' pension systems still differ widely.

Over the years, many attempts have been made to create a simple, and comprehensive classification system of the multitude of European pension systems, reflecting the predominant characteristics of these plans.[449] A wide range of pension models, categorisations, taxonomies exists. All of these models/taxonomies endeavour to unravel the complexity of pensions.[450] For instance, when analysing different pension systems in the EU, often reference is made to the three pillar structure (statutory pensions, supplementary pensions, personal pensions); a model which has become quasi-archetypical throughout the world. What is more, for instance, the ILO suggests what it calls a four-tier pension system.[451] However, each of these attempts face many obstacles, as

448 Cf. Stevens, *EU Pension Law* 1.

449 In a 2016-study EIOPA revealed that – at that time – 247 occupational pension schemes existed in the European Union, each having a different legal scope. See ibid. 4.

450 Cf. Ibid. 2.

451 See for instance C Gillion, 'The ILO and Pensions' (ILO: Social Security Department, Geneva 1999); ILO, 'The ILO Multi-Pillar pension model: Building equitable and sustainable pension systems' <https://www.social-protection.org/gimi/RessourcePDF.action?id=55234>. Pillar 0 or the pension floor is aimed at establishing a social protection floor for older persons, usually provided through a non-contributory pension scheme and financed from the general budget (often tax-financed). It should guarantee a minimum level of income, with adequate levels of benefit, for a life in decency and dignity. The 1st pillar (social insurance pillar) follows the typical design of social security pension systems, defined-benefit and mandatory, financed through employer and worker contributions. Its objective is to provide higher levels of pension benefits in order to maintain the standard of living after retirement. Thus, pillars 0 and I together represent the fundamental components of the social security pension system. 2nd pillar (complementary pillar) constitutes a complementary contributory component, voluntary or mandatory, employment-based occupational or non-occupational, defined-benefit or defined-contribution, usually financed by employer's contributions and privately managed, aimed at supplementing the pension benefits from the previous two pillars. The 3rd pillar (voluntary personal savings pillar) is also complementary, comprised of a set of voluntary private pension schemes for those with the economic capacity to make additional personal

pension systems deviate significantly across countries, and economic, cultural, legal, and social aspects play a role in how these systems were shaped, and operate. Moreover, as the OECD rightly pointed out, classifying pension systems depends on the perspective taken, e.g. the perspective of the provider or the perspective of the user.[452]

As Stevens rightly argues, whatever model shall be used, two elements are in common.[453] The first element refers to simplification, models try to support in terms of 'understandability'. Although considered desirable in terms of providing transparency, analysing pensions from a legal perspective reveals the intricacy and complexity of this field of law. For average citizens these complex technicalities are very difficult to understand and models support them in getting a grasp of it. Nevertheless, the legal relevance of these models – in studying these systems from a legal perspective – is negligible. A profound analysis of pension schemes' specificities uncovers a high degree of complexity, and demonstrates that an overly simple representation of pensions – e.g. a three-pillar model – is even misleading. The second element is that models present themselves as being neutral in their approach, as if they there were solely grounded on facts and figures.[454] Yet, as has been addressed in section 4.1, perspectives taken play a central role in using these models, based on certain (different) underlying pension ideas, notions, and conceptions, often shaped ideologically (e.g. the idea of the welfare state) and by historical developments.

Nevertheless, pension systems can be categorized rudimentary in view of their common characteristics and their differences. In doing so, one will have to decide which of these characteristics will be decisive for the categorisation, i.e 'the focal point of classification'.[455] It is up to the researcher to determine the 'decisive feature', i.e. to which elements the most weight is ascribed.[456] These decisive features – which depend on the perspective/ discipline – could be related to specific modalities, underlying principles and objectives of a given system. In view of pension systems, these decisive features could concern financing method, underlying reason for the attribution of pension rights (see section 4.1.3), payment of benefits, vesting method, taxation etc. However, it is not this research's purpose to ascertain such a decisive feature of each of the pension systems. Contrarily, this research

savings, generally managed by private pension administrators under full market competition and government regulation.

452 OECD, 'Revised Taxonomy for Pensions Plans, Pension Funds and Pension Entitities' (2002) 19. The OECD suggested five basic criteria for classifying pensions systems: retirement purpose, funding and risk bearing, administration of funded pension plans and funding vehicle, eligibility and participation, and tax treatment.

453 Stevens, *EU Pension Law* 2-3.

454 Ibid. 2-3.

455 Cf. Tijssen, 219.

456 Pintens used the term 'decisive feature' in his book: W Pintens, *Inleiding tot de rechtsvergelijking* (Universitaire Pers Leuven, Leuven 1998).

explores to what extent these classification systems could aid in providing effective pension information. In the light of this, the pension models/taxonomies most used/referred to in practice and/or literature will be elaborated on. Section 4.2.4 revolves around an evaluation of the added value – in terms of this research's evaluation framework – of these classifications/models.

4.2.1 *World Bank Pension Model: Three Pillar-model*

In order to avoid confounding and misinterpretations of the term 'pension', there is a broad consensus to divide pensions into three pillars. However, there is no universally agreed classification; although the use of the term 'pillar' is common, its precise meaning remains obscure.[457] The difference between pillars is rather blurred in many countries. Moreover, some systems distinguish between statutory, occupational and individual pension schemes, while other systems distinguish between mandatory and voluntary pension schemes. Allocating a certain pension vehicle to one of these pillars, is commonly done so on the ground of the claim's basis, as well as its nature (i.e. optional or mandatory participation). The classification of pension vehicles also depends on the allocated functions of old age financial security systems. For instance, the World Bank identified three functions: redistribution, saving, and insurance.[458] In view of these three functions, the World Bank developed a multi-pillar pension system, discussed below. It is to be noted that the World's Bank Model is probably more controversial than the OECD's taxonomy – which will be discussed hereinafter – as it proposes a model rather than serving a taxonomy objective, based on certain criteria. As holds true for the classification discussed in the previous section, it is not always clear to what category an EU Member State's system can be allocated.[459] This is due to the fact that no State entirely follows one of the systems (in its pure form) but, rather, follows the type to a greater or lesser extent.

Under the World Bank Pension Model, the first pension pillar covers the typical mandatory statutory (public) pensions, funded through social security contributions with defined benefits, aimed at replacing some part of (lifetime) pre-retirement income.[460] Contributions under the first pillar are geared to the varying degrees of earnings. They are typically

457 European Commission, 'Green paper: towards adequate, sustainable and safe European pension systems' 22.

458 W Bank, 'Averting the old age crisis: policies to protect the old and promote growth' (1994) xiii.

459 CESifo DICE Report, 'Bismarck versus Beveridge: Social Insurance Systems in Europe' 6 Journal for Institutional Comparisons 70.

460 World Bank, 'The World Bank Pension Conceptual Framework' 3 and R Holzmann and R Hinz, 'Old-Age Income Support in the 21st Century: an International Perspective on Pension Systems and Reform' (The World Bank, Washington D.C. 2005) 81.

financed on a pay-as-you-go basis and, hence, potentially endangering by demographic and political risks. An essential element of this pillar is to provide a minimum level of longevity insurances to retirees, financed through intergenerational transfers.[461] Under this first pillar, a range of risks is addressed, such as, inter alia, risks of individual myopia, low earnings, inappropriate planning horizons due the uncertainty of life expectancies, and the deficiencies or risks of financial markets.[462] Furthermore, in some countries, for instance Germany, the first pillar comprises different retirement schemes for various occupations; the *Gesetzlichen Rentenversicherung* for most private sector employees, *Beambtenversorgung* covering civil servants, and *Alterssicherung der Landwirte* insuring farmers.

The second pillar refers to (mandatory[463]) occupational retirement schemes, typically designed as an individual savings account, offering a wide range of design options, with respect to investment management, and options for the withdrawal phase; for instance, a lump sum payment or annuitization.[464] Historically, these pension schemes were designed as DB-schemes, but a shift towards more DC-schemes is discernible. The latter also applies to the Netherlands (under the *Wet Toekomst Pensioenen*), as well as to Germany (the implementation of the *reine Beitragszusage*). Second pillar schemes may be set up unilaterally by an employer, or as a result of a collective agreement or a contract agreed individually or collectively between the employer(s) and the employee(s) or their respective representatives. However, typically, they should be constructed with specific income-replacement rates. As noted previously, there is clear (ongoing) shift from DB to DC occupational pension schemes. Pertaining to funding of the second pillar, full funding and private asset management are primary elements.

The (voluntary) third pillar comprises many forms of individual retirement savings on a personal level, but commonly relies on private sector institutions.[465] Typically, these are constructed and regulated in order to guarantee a clear retirement objective. This pillar covers a multitude of provisions, e.g. individual savings for retirement, disability or death; employer sponsored; defined benefit or defined contribution.[466] However, these schemes

461 Holzmann and Hinz, 81.

462 Ibid. 42.

463 It should be noted that in the Netherlands, participation in occupational pension schemes, is quasi-mandatory, since a generally applicable participation obligation, pursuant to domestic law, does not exist. These schemes are, however, quasi-mandatory as participation follows from the (collectively binding) Collective Labour Agreements.

464 World Bank, 'The World Bank Pension Conceptual Framework' 3 and Holzmann and Hinz, 81.

465 World Bank, 'The World Bank Pension Conceptual Framework' 3 and Holzmann and Hinz, 83.

466 World Bank, 'The World Bank Pension Conceptual Framework' 3.

are, in nature, flexible and discretionary in nature. Some Member States have personal pension schemes to which both employer and employees contribute.

The World Bank Model distinguishes a zero pillar, and a fourth pillar as well. The former is defined as a non-contributory pillar, for instance in the form of a social pension, or general social assistance typically financed by the local, regional or national government.[467] This 'social safety net-pillar' is explicitly aimed at dealing with poverty alleviation among the elderly, through providing all elderly a minimal level of protection (e.g. the German *Grundrente*). The fourth pillar concerns a non-financial pillar, which includes access to informal support (e.g. family support) or other formal social programs (e.g. health care and/or housing), and other individual financial and non-financial assets (e.g. home ownership, personal savings and reverse mortgages).[468] A considerable part of retirement consumption may be derived from these sources, although not formally 'recognized' as pensions. This designation of five pillars has not been truly replicated, and neither recognized in the Neherlands, nor in Germany.[469] Elements of these five pillars are nevertheless reflected in many countries, including the Netherlands. These two (zero and fourth) pillars are left aside in the present research, since they do not fit in this research's perspective of analysing the fiscal treatment of pensions. For the purpose of this research, the term 'pensions' is considered as covering first, second and third pillar pensions. However, exploring how this zero and fourth pillar contribute to securing an adequate pension income, and whether they should be treated as 'pension' for fiscal purposes, constitutes an interesting avenue for future research.

4.2.2 *OECD Taxonomy of Pension Plans*

In its 2002 report, the OECD developed a taxonomy for pension systems, for the benefit of, *inter alia*, a comparison of pension systems around the world.[470] The OECD rightly pointed out that a classification of pension systems must fulfil two basic critical conditions.[471] First, it must be consistent across the largest possible number of countries, covering as many specific cases as possible; second, it must be based on descriptive criteria, and not on a prescriptive model of pension systems, such as the World Bank model. In this context, reference can be made to the deviating use of the term 'pillar' under the three-pillar model as set out above. The OECD adopted a two-step approach in developing this

467 Ibid. 2 and Holzmann and Hinz, 81.

468 World Bank, 'The World Bank Pension Conceptual Framework' 3.

469 Cf. E Lutjens, *Asser-serie 7-XI – Pensioen (Bijzondere overeenkomsten)* (Asser-serie, Wolters Kluwer, Deventer 2019) nr. 6.

470 OECD, 'Revised Taxonomy for Pensions Plans, Pension Funds and Pension Entitities' 2.

471 Ibid. 2.

taxonomy. First, it identified the various criteria that can be used to classify pension systems; second, it grouped those criteria in order to establish a classification that, as far as possible, meets the two conditions addressed above. The OECD uses several distinctions in this taxonomy: public vs. private, occupational vs. personal, DB vs. DC, funded vs. unfunded. The first two distinctions are the most interesting in the light of the present research.[472]

A public pension plan constitutes a social security, and similar scheme, where the general government (i.e. central, state, and local governments, as well as social security institutions) administer the payment of the pension benefits, and which purpose it is to provide minimum (flat or/and earnings-related) benefits on retirement for the population at large.[473] Where the Dutch *AOW* constitutes such a public pension plan with flat benefits, the German *gesetzlichen Renteversicherung* forms an earnings-related public plan. The OECD further notes that public plans have traditionally been pay-as-you-go-financed (PAYG), although in some OECD countries this has changed. On the contrary, private pension plans concern pension plans where an institution, other than general government, administers the payment of pension benefits.[474] These plans are managed by private agents, i.e. the employer operating as the pension plan sponsor, a pension entity, or a private sector provider. These schemes may be complements, or even substitutes, to social security systems. Generally speaking, private pension plans are capital funded in OECD countries. However, the term 'private' may lead to some controversy as it can refer to different modalities of a pension plan.[475]

From the OECD's perspective, occupational pension plans constitute plans where access to such plans is linked to an employment relationship between the participant, and the pension entity establishing the plan.[476] A pivotal element is that these plans may be established by employers or groups of employers (for instance, industry associations), in some cases in conjunction with labour associations/trade unions. The latter modality often forms a union-corporatist pension system. Under these systems, the plan sponsor is responsible for making contributions to the pension plans, while employees may be also required to contribute to the plan. As regards occupational pension plans, a distinction can be drawn between mandatory, and voluntary occupational pension plans. Under mandatory occupational plans, employers are obliged to participate in a pension plan, by

472 The OECD also sets forth what a 'pension plan' encompasses. This will not be dealt with in any further detail. See ibid. 2-3.
473 Ibid. 3.
474 Ibid. 3.
475 Ibid. 17-18.
476 Ibid. 3.

virtue of law, nation-wide or industry-wide bargaining agreements. Under the obligatory participation, employers are required to establish, and make contributions to occupational pension plans which employees will, usually, have to join. On the contrary, under voluntary occupational plans, establishing these plans is voluntary for employers.

Personal pension plans encompass plans where the access to these plans is not linked to an employment relationship, hence, the term 'personal'.[477] Without any intervention of their employers, individuals choose their pension product/arrangement, although the employer is nonetheless allowed to make contributions into these personal schemes. Under mandatory personal plans, individuals are obliged to join, or these schemes are eligible to be granted mandatory pension contributions and individuals may be required to pay contributions. Contrarily, under voluntary personal plans individuals' participation is voluntary as these individuals are not obliged to participate by law, nor required to make any contributions.

4.2.3 Bismarck, Beveridge (and Soviet)

In addition to the categorisation of all three pension pillars, statutory retirement systems are often classified on the basis of the typology of Bismarck systems, Beveridge systems, and Soviet systems drawing on certain features and characteristics across the range of systems.

The Soviet classification will not be discussed in this research, since none of the systems considered in this research are classified as Soviet systems, nor do they show characteristic elements of this type of system. However, it should be stressed that this qualification merely applies to statutory (social insurance) retirement system. Where the German system is usually considered the archetype of the Bismarck system[478], the Dutch systems is qualified as a Beveridge system.[479] These systems differ with respect to their aim: where the aim of the Bismarck system is to assure a certain standard of living; the Beveridge system

477 Ibid. 3-4.

478 The Bismarck systems are characterised by three points: insured persons are employees or gainfully employed; financing through contributions graduated according to income; and social contributions to be paid are based on wages or salaries. See CESifo DICE Report, 70. This applies to, *grosso modo*, for instance, the German *Gesetzlichen Rentenversicherung.*

479 Characteristics of Beveridge systems are as follows: they include the entire population; is primarily financed from the state budget; and calls for uniform lump-sum contributions. See ibid. and H Berié and U Fink, 'Europas Sozialmodell – Die europäischen Sozialsysteme im Vergleich: Eine volkswirtschaftliche Analyse' (WISO Institut für Wirtschaft und Soziales GmbH, 2000). This applies to, *grosso modo*, for instance, the Dutch *AOW*.

is aimed at securing a subsistence level.[480] Nevertheless, the Bismarck and Beveridge system has two basic goals in common.[481] Firstly, to tackle poverty issues, income inequality, to foster social cohesion and to stimulate the efficiency of the economy as a whole. The second goal is to enhance the individual security, and to lessen unknown social risks.

However, in view of the significant differences in the pension systems across the various (Member) States, it is not always clear to what category an EU Member State's system ought to be allocated.[482] This is due to the fact that no State entirely follows one of the systems (in its pure form) but, rather, follows a type to a greater or lesser extent. For instance, although the Dutch *AOW* is characterised as a Beveridge system, it is only marked partly by this system's characteristics. Moreover, over the past years, there has been a shift, either towards the Beveridge system or the Bismarck model, complicating a clear system allocation.[483]

It has further become apparent over the years that these diverging systems respond differently to certain societal, economic, demographic developments, or phenomena. Since the population pyramid has inverted (due to an ageing population and declining fertility rates), social insurance contributors must uphold an increasing number of non-contributing people, which was not foreseen under the Bismarck systems.[484] Further, demographic development have also put considerable pressure on the Beveridge systems, as, in terms of health care, demographic changes have become a considerable burden on tax revenues. As a consequence, financing the health care system interferes with other fields of policy, in terms of allocating tax revenues. This potentially endangers the financial sustainability of the Beveridge-type social insurance systems.

However, there is a trend discernible in Europe that these two financing systems are converging, for instance, as financing through taxes has increased in countries where financing through contributions used to be prevalent. This is primarily due to the changing, economic and social climate in Europe over the years, for instance, demographic changes (increasing old-age dependency ratios). Yet, given the considerable difference in living standards among European countries, a full convergence of the differing systems is highly unlikely.

480 CESifo DICE Report.
481 Y Stevens, *Pensioenen: cyclusboek 2011-2016* (Die Keure, Brugge 2017).
482 CESifo DICE Report, 70.
483 Cf. H Purton, 'European Welfare States in the 1990's: An Economic Analysis of the Challenges and Efforts at Reform' (CEPS Research Report no. 19, 1996).
484 CESifo DICE Report, 71.

4.2.4 *Models, Typologies, Taxonomies, Classifications: Lack of Consensus and Consistency Hindering a One-Size-Fits-All Approach*

The definition of pensions is non-homogeneous among countries, and a taxonomy of pension (systems) is still missing; do not exist. I endorse Stevens' position that just as pension models do not exist in legal terms; neither do comprehensive taxonomies covering the different pension systems.[485] It is even questionable whether such a categorisation – from a legal point of view – even bears relevance. As has been demonstrated above, it is too complex to develop a coherent European-wide – or cross-country – taxonomy of all retirement schemes available in all (European) Member States. The grounds for this have been set out clearly in the foregoing sections, i.e. the term 'pension' is multidimensional and marked – as a concept – by blurred lines of definition.

In theory, such a taxonomy would constitute a classification system to determine, on the basis of common principles, which scheme is considered 'pension', potentially laid down in secondary legislation. However, this appears to be highly unlikely, partly due to the division of power between the European Union and the Member States; the responsibility for the design of a national pension system lies with the Member States. Moreover, the European Union lacks sufficient competence to intervene in the Member States' pension systems. Over the years, many attempts have been made to create a simple, and comprehensive classification system for pension systems, reflecting the predominant characteristics of these plans.

It has become apparent in the above that even models, typologies, taxonomies, classifications of pension schemes are subject to controversy, and ambiguity. It is disputable whether such a classification should rely on a model, or more on a taxonomy based on certain predefined criteria. As it seems, a taxonomy, building on criteria drawn from a comparative analysis of pension schemes, is most apt for categorising national pension schemes, covering as most national schemes as possible. For instance, the OECD Taxonomy strives to be consistent across the largest possible number of countries, covering as many specific cases as possible; second, it is based on descriptive criteria, and not on a prescriptive model of pension systems, such as the World Bank model. Taking (comparative) descriptive criteria as a guiding principle, renders such a taxonomy more apt for fostering effective pension information, as it incorporates differences between national systems to a greater degree.

485 Cf. Stevens, *EU Pension Law* 4.

Although there is some consensus to divide pensions into three pillars, a universal agreed definition/classification/taxonomy is still missing. The strength of this three-pillar model is that it is an easy way to present different pensions systems; its simplicity is it strength. Almost any state's pension system can be recognized in the three pillar-structure.[486] Nevertheless, as it seems, a disputable classification can hide more than it reveals, at least in legal terms. I endorse Stevens' argument that legally speaking, a three-pillar model cannot be said to exist as the tremendous technical and legal differences – in the domains of civil, fiscal, social rules – between states are just too wide to be covered by such a model.[487] In legal terms, the model over-simplifies matters (which may, in turn, induce anxiety in terms of information provision). Moreover, consensus is missing as on what aspects, elements, modalities of a pension scheme should be prevailing in the classification. Due to this worldwide lack of consensus and consistency, these systems of categorisation merely serve to categorise pension vehicles *grosso modo*, and should be treated with caution when employed in the domain of (cross-border) pension information provision. For instance, when pension vehicles are analysed at a more detailed level, it is often found that the allocation to a certain pillar is subject to controversy. This controversy potentially engenders tensions in information provision, mainly between understandability and correctness of pension information. An explanation can be found in the fact that no State entirely follows one of the systems (in its pure form) but, rather, follows the type to a greater or lesser extent.

4.3 'Pensions' in Germany

In the section below, the German interpretation of the notion of pensions will be discussed. It should be stressed that it concerns the (legal) character of pensions, rather than the qualification of pensions as such. The distinction between 'character' and 'qualification' lies in the method: qualification analyses the underlying determinants that have shaped the national definitions of pension, hereby, i.a. taking into account the historical development of the pension landscape. Since the specific considerations which have led to the present qualification of the concept of pensions is of minor interest for the purpose of this thesis, this chapter will focus on the pension character instead and determine the key features of pensions in Germany, stemming from statutory, occupational and individual pensions. After the analyses of this pension definition, I search for common elements and mismatches in the varying pension definitions of each pillar, taking the viewpoint of pension information, i.e. what are the consequences of these identified mismatches for the

486 Ibid. 1.
487 Ibid. 1 and cited literature.

provision of effective pension information in cross-border cases. This chapter will be complemented with an analysis of the pension definition in the Dutch landscape, ultimately leading to a cross-border analysis of the pension definition, identifying the consequences for effective cross-border pension information provision, through the lens of this research's evaluation framework.

4.3.1 *The Three-pillar Pension System in Germany*

A strict distinction – based on the national characteristics of each pillar in Germany – is difficult.[488] As Scholz notes, the complexity of formulating a strict definition of occupational pensions is illustrated by the unsuccessful attempt of the European Commission to formulate such a European-wide definition.[489] Instead, she adopted a more institutional approach regarding the three-pillar system. Yet, to some extent, each German pension scheme or pension product can be allocated to a particular pillar based on certain characteristics. With this in mind, in Germany two models are harnessed in order to categorise the wide diversity of pension schemes, i.e. the *Dreischichtenmodell* and the *Drei-Säulen-Modell*. These will be considered in the section below.

4.3.1.A Institutional Perspective: Drei-Säulen-Modell

The term *Drei-Säulen-Modell* is used in Germany since the nineteen sixties.[490] The model is still applied unabated.[491] The general principle underlying this model is that the retirement income – ensuring the living standard after retirement – comprises three categories of pensions, thus consisting of a mixed-financed retirement income. It should be stressed that, contrary to the *Dreischichtenmodell*, the *Drei-Säulen-Modell* considers the varying forms of retirement provisions from an institutional perspective, i.e. how the forms of retirement provision should be categorised regarding their respective social political purpose. In this way, the *Drei-Säulen-Modell* seems to fit the World Bank (three pillar) Pension model better than the *Dreischichtenmodell*. As will follow from the next subparagraph, this differentiated categorisation leads to an increasing complexity.

---

488 Also Scholz is critical regarding this demarcation, see S Scholz, *Besteuerung der betrieblichen Altersversorgung in Europa* (Deutscher Universitäts-Verlag, Wiesbaden 2006) 8.

489 Ibid. 8.

490 Rürup and Myßen. See also J Kaempfe, *Die Systemfunktionen privater Altersvorsorge im Gesamtsystem sozialer Alterssicherung* (Nomos, Baden-Baden 2005) 77.

491 This follows from, for instance, Koalitionsvertrag zwischen CDU, CSU und SPD, 93.

Firstly, the *öffentlich-rechtlichen Pflichtsysteme.*[492] This first pillar comprises the pay-as-you-go funded *gesetzliche Rentenversicherung, die Beambtenversorgung*[493], *Alterssicherung der Landwirte* and *berufsständische Versorgungswerke.*[494] The second pillar constitutes the *betriebliche Altersversorgung*, forming in principle a complementing form of pension committed by the employer.[495] Lastly, the third pillar consists of the so-called *private Altersversorgung*. This form of pension may consist of a broad range of provisions, not merely focused on securing an income for retirement. Ensuring an adequate income after retirement is only one of several objectives of this form of retirement saving. This third pillar may therefore include *Banksparpläne, Fondssparpläne, Bausparprodukte*, investment in real estate or even the own personal home.[496] Furthermore, *Kapitallebensversicherungen* play a dominant role in this third pillar. Equally to the second pillar, this third pillar is attributed a more complementing role in ensuring the standard of living after retirement.

4.3.1.B Fiscal Perspective: Dreischichtenmodell

As mentioned in the previous subparagraph, where an institutional perspective underlies the *Drei-Säulen-Modell*, the *Dreischichtenmodell* adopts a sole fiscal perspective. Based on this categorisation – which in turn is based on the decisive characteristics from a fiscal perspective – the fiscal treatment of each form of pension (each *Schicht*) is predominantly determined by means of this model.[497] The key elements of *Säule* either *Schicht* – covering statutory, occupational and individual pensions – have been subject to diffusion over time.[498]

The use of the term 'pillar' in pension pillar is not preferable as a general concept since its translation may refer to *Säule* or *Schicht*, thus both from a different perspective and comprising different consequences. For instance, from the perspective of the *Dreischichtenmodell* the *Riester-Rente* should be categorised under the second pillar. In

492 Commonly referred to as *obligatorischen Alterssicherungssysteme.*

493 Similar to the *Direktzusage*, this form of pension is financed by the employer.

494 This *berufsständische Versorgungswerke* forms a replacement system for the *gesetzliche Rentenversicherung.* Principally, this form of pensions is based on three different funding procedures: *Offene Deckungsplanvefahren, Äquivalenz- Anwartschaftsdeckungsverfahren* and *modifizierte Anwartschaftsdeckungs-Modell.*

495 See also D Birk and R Wernsmann, 'Die Besteuerung der Aufwendungen für die Altersvorsorge und der Alterseinkommen' in B Rürup and F Ruland (eds.), *Alterssicherung und Besteuerung* (Gabler, Wiesbaden 2008).

496 Abschlussbericht der Sachverständigenkommission zur Neuordnung der steuerrechtlichen Behandlung von Altersvorsorgeaufwendungen und Altersbezügen (BMF-Schriftenreihe) 9. The commission considered that a personal home can be converted into cash at any time and does not generate retirement saving in the form of saved rent payments. However, this form of pension is fiscally facilitated generously, pursuant to § 92a EStG.

497 Cf. Ibid. 16 ff: *"Die Kommission schlägt für die Neuordnung der steuerrechtlichen Behandlung von Altersvorsorgeaufwendungen und Altersbezügen ein „Drei-Schichten-Modell" vor."*

498 Cf. Scholz, 62.

contrast, from a '*Säulen*-perspective' it should be regarded as a third pillar pension provision. Another example is the so-called *Rürup-Rente*, from '*Schicht*-perspective' qualified as first pillar, from a '*Säulen*-perspective' qualified as third pillar. The incorrect use of these diffusing terms might therefore lead to an incorrect determination of consequences, including the fiscal consequences.

The in the previous section mentioned subdivision of the German pension system into three forms of pensions was altered in 2002 when the German *Bundesverfassungsgericht*[499] forced the German legislator to redesign the German pension system.[500] The court also found that the differentiating tax treatment of the *Beambtenpensionen* and the *gesetzliche Rentenversicherung* was incompatible with the German constitution and the related tax treatment had to be revised.

Following a combination of increasing life expectancy and decreasing birth numbers, the financial sustainability of the *gesetzliche Rentenversicherung* was significantly jeopardised. In order to maintain this sustainability and secure an adequate retirement income also for future generations, the German legislator was convinced that a pension reform was inevitable.[501] Based hereupon, the – fiscal oriented – *Dreischichtenmodell*[502] was designed: *1. Schicht (Basisversorgung), 2. Schicht (betriebliche Altersversorgung)*[503] and *3. Schicht (private Altersversorgung)*. Attribution to one of these pillars is predominantly based on the extent to which the distributed benefits of the pension provision will be used for the maintenance of the living standard after retirement, rather than the financing method of the provision, the legal compulsory membership or the particular socio-political considerations.[504] The more a pension provision is aimed at securing a retirement income, the likelier it will be allocated to the first pillar. For the purpose of allocating a pension provision to a particular *Schicht*, the level of old-age security of a specific provision is inconclusive.[505]

499 Translated freely as the German Constitutional Court, since in Germany – contrary to the Netherlands – no prohibition exists regarding the constitutional assessment of formal legislation, initiated by parliament.

500 2 BvL 17/99 (BVerfG).

501 Deutscher Bundestag, *Entwurf eines Gesetzes zur Reform der gesetzlichen Rentenversicherung und zur Förderung eines kapitalgedeckten Altersvorsorgevermögens (Altersvermögensgesetz – AVmG)*, (2000) 1.

502 I.e. the three-pillar system.

503 See G Dreher, *Das Alterseinkünftegesetz: Systematische Darstellung und verfassungsrechtliche Zweifelsfragen* (Finanz- und Steuerrecht in Deutschland und Europa, Peter Lang, Frankfurt am Main 2006) who argues that a second pillar in Germany is redundant and leads to an increasing complexity of the pension system.

504 Rürup and Myßen, 190.

505 Ibid. and cited literature.

The German legislator acknowledged that by expanding the pension planning to additional retirement income provisions in the second and third pillar, the living standard during the active working period could be maintained in the passive period after retirement.[506] The first pillar should no longer form the predominant source of securing a retirement income. It is interesting to note that intertemporally a shift occurred in the considerations to what extent retirement income should be ensured by means of social security.[507] The prevalent view is that an adequate retirement income can solely be ensured through a combination of pension forms, stemming from the three different pension pillars.[508] This view is in line with the aforementioned attribution of a pension form to a particular pillar; i.e. the quantitative size is in this perspective negligible. It was also emphasized that saving for retirement should be fostered through fiscal facilitation, i.e. fiscal exemptions and allowances, for instance the so-called *Sonderausgabenabzug*. This would enable individuals to set a larger amount of their wages aside for retirement purposes.

After this reform the statutory pension, *gesetzliche Rentenversicherung*, was considered to form only a basic retirement income *(Basisversorgung)* in the first pillar, supplemented by occupational pensions in the second pillar *(Kapitalgedeckte Zusatzversorgung)* and individual pensions in the third pillar *(Kapitalanlageprodukte)*.[509] As Birk and Wernsmann state, the underlying thought of this reforms was a mixed-financed pension concept in which a balance was sought between a pay-as-you-go financed basic pension form (*i.e. Basisversorgung)* and an additional funded pension form (i.e. *Kapitalgedeckte Zusatzversorgung* respectively *Kapitalanlageprodukte*) in order to maintain the standard of living after retirement.[510] Eventually, the reform of the pension system and the related tax treatment was implemented through the *Altersvermögensgesetz* which entered into force

506 Deutscher Bundestag, *Entwurf eines Gesetzes zur Reform der gesetzlichen Rentenversicherung und zur Förderung eines kapitalgedeckten Altersvorsorgevermögens (Altersvermögensgesetz – AVmG)*, 2.

507 Similarly Rürup and Myßen, 191. Although the data is dated, interesting in this regard is AH Börsch-Supan, F Heiss and J Winter, *Akzeptanzprobleme bei Rentenreformen: Wie die Bevölkerung überzeugt werden kann* (Deutsches Institut für Altersvorsorge, Köln 2004) in which the perspectives under pensioners, pension participants and youngsters (20-) is assessed on the dominance of the first and third pillar in saving for a retirement income. It should be stressed that this assessment was conducted before the reform of the German pension system in 2005.

508 Rürup and Myßen, 191 and Birk and Wernsmann.

509 Abschlussbericht der Sachverständigenkommission zur Neuordnung der steuerrechtlichen Behandlung von Altersvorsorgeaufwendungen und Altersbezügen (BMF-Schriftenreihe). *Sachverständigenkommission* can be translated as expert commission. This degradation of the *gesetzliche Rentenversicherung* to a mere basic pension provision was criticised, see Rürup and Myßen, 188.

510 Birk and Wernsmann, and cited literature. See also Rürup and Myßen, 189.

on 1. of January 2002[511] and the *Alterseinkünftegesetz* respectively, in force as of 1. of January 2005.[512]

Based on the current concepts and insights, the German pension system may be divided into three *Schichten.* Firstly, the so-called *Regelsicherung*[513] in which the *gesetzliche Rentenversicherung* plays a major role. Subsequently, the *Zusatsversicherung*[514] which comprises for instance the *betrieblichen Altersvorsorge* and the fiscally facilitated individual pensions, e.g. the *Riester-Rente.* This *Zusatsversicherung* entails a complementing role in retirement saving, in the sense that it aims to fill possible shortages in pension income – caused by a lack of entitlements from *gesetzlichen Rentenversicherung.*

Contrary to the first pillar which is exclusively aimed at ensuring a lifelong income after retirement, the second pillar comprises the possibility to disburse a certain amount of accrued pension in the form of a lump sum. Especially for the fiscally facilitated *private Altersvorsorge*, a particular amount of accrued pension may be withdrawn prior to retirement for other purposes than retirement saving. However, the granted fiscal facilitation of this amount of pension is then reclaimed accordingly. Therefore, this form is rather treated as third pillar pension. Rürup and Myßen 2008 Rürup and Myßen 2008 Rürup and Myßen 2008 Rürup and Myßen 2008 Regarding their objective, they may or may not comply with the objective of ensuring a retirement income.

The demarcation between the three *Schichten* is not in all cases equally strict and suitable for categorisation purposes. A certain diffusing interaction of the key elements might arise. For instance, the *Beambtenversorgung* or the *knappschaftliche Rentenversicherung* can be considered bifunctional, meaning that they embody features of statutory pension as well as occupational pension-features. Ruland 'Überblick über die Alterssicherung in Deutschland' 2008 Ruland 'Überblick über die Alterssicherung in Deutschland' 2008 Ruland 'Überblick über die Alterssicherung in Deutschland' 2008 Ruland 'Überblick über die Alterssicherung in Deutschland' 2008 The *Rentenversicherung* comprises the possibility of a voluntary insurance that due to its minimal use can be allocated more adequately to the complementing pension products. For the *knappschaftliche Rentenversicherung* this bifunctionality relates to the increase of its benefits as well as its contributions with

511 Gesetz zur Reform der gesetzlichen Rentenversicherung und zur Förderung eines kapitalgedeckten Altersvorsorgevermögens (Altersvermögensgesetz – AVmG).

512 Gesetz zur Neuordnung der einkommensteuerrechtlichen Behandlung von Altersvorsorgeaufwendungen und Altersbezügen (Alterseinkünftegesetz – AltEinkG).

513 Translated freely as 'basic pension'.

514 Translated freely as 'additional pension'.

approximately 33% compared to the basic *Rentenversicherung*, which increase shall be financed by the employer (constituting an occupational pension-feature).

Furthermore, depending on the present characteristics of a particular pension form, a second pillar pension may be allocated to the first pillar, under the condition that it fulfils all the conditions required for the categorisation of first pillar pensions. A particular interesting example in this regard is the categorisation of the *Riester-Rente*.[515] Since this form of pension may be used for the purchase of real estate[516], this pension can under no circumstances be categorised as a *Basisversorgung*. In contrast, the *gesetzliche Rentenversicherung* qualifies as *Basisversorgung*, since it fulfils all requirements. Hereafter, the character of first pillar (statutory), second pillar (occupational) and third pillar (individual) pensions will be discussed more in detail. This comprises the analyses of the key features of the national – in this section German – perception on what these forms of retirement income comprise.

4.3.2 *The Legal Character of German Statutory Pensions*

The general pursued objective of pensions in Germany, is considered the financial insurance of the time span between retiring and decease, insuring the longevity risk.[517] This fundamental idea of pensions, underlies the *Alterseinkünftegesetz* and the *Altersvermögensgesetz*. This conception differs from the view that every capital accumulation should be considered an old-age provision if the pension participant's subjective is aimed thereon accordingly.[518] In my opinion, this may be regarded as a rather 'objective' and technical point of view on what pensions ought to comprise. Besides, it can be questioned what the consequence of such an interpretation of pension is for the legal character of pensions and the related legal consequences, among which the fiscal consequences.[519]

This perception on the concept of retirement provision is, however, not generalisable to all categories of pensions, i.e. first, second and third pillar pensions. The aforementioned perception solely applies to the German first pillar pensions, i.e. *Basisversorgung*. Furthermore, the eligibility criteria for the categorisation under the first pillar as

515 Derived from Rürup and Myßen, 191.

516 Pursuant to § 1, section 1, nr. 10, under c AltZertG (*Altersvorsorgeverträge-Zertifizierungsgesetz*) in conjuction with § 92a EStG (*Einkommensteuergesetz*).

517 Rürup and Myßen, 189.

518 Ibid. 189.

519 In my opinion, the legal character of pensions refers to the key features that constitute pension as a retirement income and the legal conclusions that can be drawn from this, i.a. the fiscal consequences.

Basisversorgung are rather strict and are based on the above-mentioned objective point of view. These criteria among others comprise payment solely as a lifelong annuity and prohibited hereditability, transferability, lendability, realisability, capitalising, capital cover etc.[520]

4.3.3 *The Legal Character of German Occupational Pensions*

Principally, the definition of *betriebliche Altersversorgung* comprises three elements considered predominant: the relationship between employer and employee based on an employment relationship granting a retirement pension, invalidity pension or a surviving relative's pension.[521] Especially, the underlying employment relationship can be regarded of a decisive nature.[522] The pension commitment must form a component of the employment contract and may not be of mere legislative origin.[523] In this regard, a link between the employment relationship and the pension commitment is not sufficient in order to qualify as *betriebliche Altersversorgung*, rather a genuine causal relation must exist.[524] For instance, a retirement provision by reason of marriage does not qualify. To what extent other employees in a comparable position have been attributed an occupational pension may, however, serve as an indication in this respect.[525]

Principally, the *betriebliche Altersversorgung* is characterised by the so-called *Entgeltcharakter*.[526] Over the intervening years, the perception on this element shifted gradually from *Versorgungscharakter*[527] to *Entgeltcharakter*[528], ultimately resulting in a dual nature of pension comprising the two characters but in which the *Entgeltcharakter* prevails.[529] The ultimate retirement benefits are considered a compensation for rendered

520 Abschlussbericht der Sachverständigenkommission zur Neuordnung der steuerrechtlichen Behandlung von Altersvorsorgeaufwendungen und Altersbezügen (BMF-Schriftenreihe) 16.

521 Pursuant to § 1, par. 1, first sentence BetrAVG.

522 Similarly Scholz, 9.

523 Cf. Ibid. 9 and cited literature.

524 W Förster and S Rechtenwald, 'Die betriebliche und private Altersvorsorge' in F Ruland and B Rürup (eds.), *Alterssicherung und Besteuerung* (Gabler, Wiesbaden 2008) 138 and W Blomeyer, K Rolfs and K Otto, *Betriebsrentengesetz: BetrAVG* (C.H. Beck, München 2015). This is confirmed by i.a. BAG, AP 25 January 2000.

525 Förster and Rechtenwald, 138.

526 Cf. BGH, BGHZ 7 July 1998. *Entgeltcharakter* means, freely translated, remuneration character. See also Förster and Rechtenwald, 138.

527 Translated freely as retirement provision character.

528 Translated freely as remuneration character.

529 As can be derived from BAG, NJW 5 July 1979. 1980 and BAG, 29 September 2010. in which the German Federal Labour Court ruled that in exchange for the granting of pension entitlements, the employee renders employee loyalty. The relationship between the pension commitment and the employee loyalty does not qualify as a synallagmatic agreement pursuant to § 320 BGB, see BAG, NZA 26 June 1990. 1991.

work and therefore a particular form of remuneration.[530] In this regard, the *betrieblichen Altersversorgung* fulfils a significant complementary role in saving for retirement.

4.3.4 *The Legal Character of German Individual Pensions*

In contrast to occupational pensions, the interpretation of the concept of German third pillar pension provisions – *private Altersversorgung* – is rather open. Individual pensions are mainly regulated by fiscal legislation, stipulating the criteria regarding their fiscal facilitation. As a rule, each income provision that cannot fulfil the conditions for the qualification of first or second pillar pension, is categorised as third pillar pension. Thus, every form of capital accumulation can be included in the third pillar, if the individual is of the opinion that the capital may serve as a retirement income provision.[531] When it comes to fiscal facilitation of the given personal pension product, the prevailing conditions must be met. In this regard, strict qualification criteria are missing.

Considering the decisive influence of the will of the individual as to whether or not employ the capital accumulation for retirement saving, this standpoint may be considered a 'subjective' interpretation of the concept of third pillar pension. For third pillar pensions, the free disposal of the accumulated capital prevails as a characteristic.[532] Next to *Kapitallebensversicherungen*, also each form of accumulated capital can be considered third pillar pension in Germany, e.g. renting out real estate or even a classic car and saving the revenues primarily with the view of saving for retirement. Rürup and Myßen also point out that the rent-free own home can serve as a provision for retirement, since the saved rents lower the costs of living.[533] Again, the element of free disposal prevails since the individual may decide to sell the own home prior to retirement which is at odds with the qualification as a first pillar *Basisversorgung* as a consequence of the prohibited transferability. It must be recalled that this concerns a national point of view when it comes to the categorisation of pension provisions into three pillars. This is without prejudice to the categorization of the relevant pension provision under e.g. the World Bank pension model or the OECD taxonomy, as discussed earlier.

530 Also confirmed in 1 BvR 2378/10 (BVerfG).
531 Cf. Rürup and Myßen, 192.
532 Cf. Ibid. 192.
533 Birk and Wernsmann, 192.

4.4 'Pensions' in the Netherlands

In the Dutch context, the term 'pension' can be traced back to the term 'pensio', which finds its origin in Roman law and refers to a payment of some kind. The development of the Dutch pension system can be distinguished between the pension for civil servants, the pension for employees in industry and the social security pension.[534] The section below revolves around the three-pillar system in the Netherlands, and the legal character of Dutch statutory, occupational and individual pensions.

4.4.1 The Three-pillar Pension System in the Netherlands

The Dutch pension system can be classified by using the three-pillar system as well: statutory pension, occupational pension and individual pension.[535] To some extent, each pension scheme or pension product can be allocated to a particular pillar based on certain characteristics. A strict distinction – based on the national characteristics of each pillar – is difficult however. Nevertheless, also for the Netherlands the main line of the three-pillar system applies that the first pillar consists of the statutory social security pensions; the second pillar consists of pensions based on the performance of work in the context of an employment relationship or an appointment, or in an occupational profession; the third pillar consists of individual provisions created on the personal initiative of the person concerned. As a planning tool, the Dutch *Pensioenschijf-van-vijf* (pension-five), distinguishes, in addition to the three pillars, other assets (savings, shares, owner-occupied dwelling etc.) and the ability to continue working after retirement as possible additional

534 For instance, the first pension provisions for civil servants date from 1798. The establishment of a voluntary Pension Fund took place in 1802. In 1836, the first manifestation of a General Civilian Pension Fund came into being. As regards employees' pension schemes the following can be pointed out. In the course of the nineteenth century, with the development of large-scale companies, the acknowledgement grew that one's own workers could not be left to fend for themselves in the event of old age or disability. From 1918 onwards, the number of company pension funds rose sharply to 738 in 1938. The granting of a pension was still seen as a gift or the fulfillment of a natural obligation. Only with the rise of collective bargaining in the early twentieth century and the making of pension agreements as part of a collective agreement, the pension developed as a right. The milestone as far as that legislation is concerned is the Pension and Savings Funds Act of 1952, replaced in 2007 by the Pensions Act. See Lutjens, nr. 2/3 and cited literature. The conception that the government had a duty to develop pension provisions providing an income in old age developed later than the pension for government employees and employees in business. The first impetus for the organization of social insurance aimed at old age was given in 1919 with the entry into force of the Old Age Act. Then, in the middle of the twentieth century the modern social insurance concerning pensions developed, with the General Old Age Pensions Act (AOW) in 1956. See ibid. nr 4; A Kuyper, *Proeve van pensioenregeling voor werklieden en huns gelijken* (Wormser, Amsterdam 1905).

535 Cf. Lutjens, nr. 4.

sources of retirement income.[536] Although this tool is helpful in providing people information on the adequacy of their pension savings (expect to have sufficient income to cover all expenses), it must be recalled that other assets and the ability to continue working after retirement are legally not recognized as additional pension 'pillar', nor are they legally embedded in pension legislation and/or fiscal legislation. The *Pensioenschijf-van-vijf* is merely meant as a calculation tool in retirement planning.

The components of Dutch retirement provisions are heterogeneous, and are not mutually comparable concepts. As Dietvorst argues, one can discern several characteristics of retirement provisions in the Netherlands that determine a classification.[537] First, the personal scope of the retirement provision, i.e. for all residents mandatory prescribed or for certain groups only. Further, the direct relationship with performing or having performed work; in other words, whether the retirement provision is inextricably linked to an employment relationship (or self-employment). Lastly, the degree of freedom to participate in a particular pension scheme or to take out a retirement provision. Along the lines of these three properties, *grosso modo*, the first, second and third pillar can be distinguished.

Moreover, the different pillars reflect a difference in the basis for acquiring pension entitlements and a difference in government involvement.[538] The basis for the first pillar is the law, for the second pillar it is labor, and in the case of the third pillar, individual choice. For the first pillar, government involvement consists of creating the legislation from which pension entitlements derive directly.[539] In the case of the second and third pillars, government involvement consists of facilitating the establishment of a provision – by means of (quasi-)compulsory participation and tax relief – and by setting a legal basis to protect pension (entitlements) against loss or impairment.

Contrary to the German pension system, a clear distinction between *Schicht* (fiscal perspective) and *Säul* (institutional perspective) has not been embedded in the Dutch system. In the latter, the different sorts of retirement provisions can be categorised by means of the so-called *pijlers*[540]. This division in *pijlers* applies with regard to civil law, as well as to tax law. As Dietvorst stated, pension is considered an independent legal concept,

536 Developed by MR Visser, 'Verbreding van de digitale snelweg' in B Starink and MR Visser (eds.), *Ondernemend met pensioen: Dietsvorst-bundel* (Wolters Kluwer, Deventer 2015). See also Nibud, 'Pensioenschijf-van-vijf' 2023) <https://www.nibud.nl/tools/pensioenschijf-van-vijf/> accessed 23 February 2023.

537 GJB Dietvorst, *De drie pijlers van toekomstvoorzieningen en belastingen* (Kluwer, Deventer 1994) 54.

538 Cf. Lutjens, nr. 5.

539 Cf. Ibid. nr. 5.

540 Translated freely as 'pillar'.

in which pension should be seen as a specific form of the broader concept of future benefit provisions. The considerations of Dietvorst regarding the subdivision into *pijlers*, although dated, still holds true.[541] Under this division, the first pillar comprises pension of a public law nature, comprising not more than merely a basic provision aimed at securing the minimal livelihood needs, i.e. the Dutch *AOW*. Contrarily, the second pillar comprises pension clearly linked to an employment relationship between an employer and employee.[542] Lastly, the third pillar covers retirement provisions, concluded voluntarily outside an employment relationship, and whether or not in addition to a first or second pillar pension.

4.4.2 *The Legal Character of Dutch Statutory Pension*

The Dutch statutory pension (AOW) seeks to be a government-run 'flat-rate' basic provision to meet minimum living needs, i.e. the *Existenzsicherung*.[543] The basis for the Dutch statutory retirement provision is the law. For statutory pensions, government involvement consists of creating the legislation from which pension entitlements derive directly.[544] The *Algemene Ouderdomswet* (General Old Age Pensions Act) constitutes this legal basis for the Dutch statutory old age pension in the 'first pillar'. This pay-as-you-go financed compulsory old age insurance came into effect on 1 January 1957.

The AOW is part of Dutch social insurance (*volksverzekeringen*), where residency takes a predominant role in determining the obligation to be insured. This is in contrast to employee insurances, such as the Unemployment Insurance Act, where being an employee and working for an employer residing or established in the Netherlands leads to an insurance obligation and, inherently, benefit entitlement. Every resident is considered an insured person, and is therefore entitled to a benefit, regardless of any income received. The rights that one can derive from it are equal for everyone in the same circumstances. When determining the level of pension entitlements to employees (occupational pensions), the first-pillar provisions are taken into account by means of the so-called state pension franchise.

As a rule, insured persons include Dutch residents, as well as non-residents subject to wage tax in respect of employment performed in the Netherlands or on the continental

541 Dietvorst, 54 ff.

542 Cf. Lutjens, *Pensioenvoorziening voor werknemers, juridische beschouwingen voor werknemers* and Dietvorst.

543 Dietvorst, 55.

544 Cf. Lutjens, nr. 5.

shelf.[545] It follows from the latter that people residing abroad, but working in the Netherlands – and hence subject to Dutch wage tax – shall be entitled to AOW benefits. Contrary to Germany, neither the obligation to contribute, nor the entitlement to benefits is directly related to the performance of work or the receipt of income. Compared to Germany, eligibility criteria for categorisation under the first pillar are not strict, see section 4.3.2. However, the personal scope of the Dutch AOW – i.e. all residents – is broader compared to the scope of the German statutory retirement provision.

4.4.3 *The Legal Character of Dutch Occupational Pensions*

The second pillar pension constitutes a supplement to the first-pillar AOW. Hence, the second pillar is marked by a direct link between the performance of work and participation in, and entitlements, to occupational pension schemes.[546] While the performance of work is pivotal in this regard, the form and legal basis of the work is not relevant here. Occupational pension schemes not only cover those who acquire a pension by virtue of their work as an employee on the basis of an employment contract or another employment relationship, but also the person who acquires a pension due to his/her work as a government employee, as a self-employed professional or as a self-employed person on the basis of a contract for work or contract work.[547]

In Dutch literature, there appears to be no consensus with respect to a general, workable and comprehensive definition of occupational pension. In this vein, I endorse Lutjens' perception that the second pillar includes pension plans in which a person participates, and derives entitlements by virtue of the performance of work.[548] From the proposals for a general pension definition put forward in literature, several common elements of pensions may be derived. First, the pension provides for the replacement of an earned income, in cases where a particular risk occurs, e.g. retirement, death or disability, aimed at securing the livelihood.[549] It thus holds a remuneration character.[550] Second, pension comprises a certain degree of objective purpose, i.e. the replacement of an earned income. Alternatively, this means that the purpose of the retirement provision may not be

545 Art. 6, para 1 AOW.
546 Cf. Dietvorst, 57.
547 Lutjens, nr. 11.
548 Ibid. nr. 11.
549 TLJ Bod, LGM Stevens and PHJG van Huizen, *Het pensioenbegrip: enige beschouwingen over het pensioen en zijn rechtskarakter* (Preadvies voor de vergadering van de Vereniging voor Pensioenrecht, W.E.J. Tjeenk Willink, Zwolle 1991) and Lutjens, *De PSW, wetshistorisch overzicht en commentaar*. Bod claims that a pension ought to be defined as an objectively purpose-based annuity. See also Bollen-Vandenboorn, 20.
550 See Lutjens, nr. 73.

determined subjectively, i.e. depending on the will of the taxable person. Third, the pension arises from the employment relationship, i.e. it constitutes an employment condition.[551] Although (occupational) pension holds characteristics of an annuity, it is governed by its own specific legal provisions (*Pensioenwet*) and, hence, must be considered a legal figure on its own.[552] In view of the foregoing, pension can be characterized as a deferred reward with a care-related character.[553] Pension is intended to provide care, and takes shape in the form of deferred wages. The pension may only be used for the provision of living expenses, and is not intended to be a tax-friendly way of forming assets intended for other purposes.

What is more, the relation between fiscal facilitation and saving for retirement shows a strong synergy; the more it is ensured that the capital accumulation will be employed for the use of retirement provision in the form of an annual or temporary lifelong annuity, the more the accumulation of pension capital shall be fiscally facilitated. Furthermore, in the light of the definition of pension, the benefits shall principally be paid out lifelong during the retirement phase. It seems also that pension is characterised by the payment of period payments.[554]

4.4.4 The Legal Character of Dutch Individual Pension Plans

In contrast to Dutch occupational pensions, the interpretation of the concept of third pillar pension provisions is rather open (comparable to Germany), i.e. individual pensions are mainly regulated by fiscal legislation, stipulating the criteria regarding their fiscal

551 Considered from a civil law perspective Lutjens, *Pensioenvoorziening voor werknemers, juridische beschouwingen voor werknemers*; and from a fiscal perspective Dietvorst.

552 Cf. Lutjens, nr. 73.

553 Cf. RMJM de Greef, *Fiscale pensioenbelemmeringen in de gemeenschappelijke markt* (Fiscale Wetenschappelijke Reeks, SDU, Den Haag 2004) 77.

554 Bollen-Vandenboorn, 21 refers in footnote 22 to relevant case-law. In a similar vein, P Clausing, *Oudedagsvoorzieningen – Levensverzekering en Pensioen* (Preadvies voor de Algemene Vergadering van de Broederschap der Candidaat-Notarissen, Nijmegen 1973) 8; 21 and TLJ Bod, *Pensioen en privaatrecht (dissertatie Nijmegen)* (H.D. Tjeenk Willink, Alphen aan den Rijn 1979) 63; 85 and E Lutjens, *Pensioenvoorziening voor werknemers, juridische beschouwingen voor werknemers* (W.E.J. Tjeenk Willink, Zwolle 1989) 40; 88 and Dietvorst, 110. Contrarily, the payment of a pension lump sum is considered at odds with the essence of pension, i.e. maintaining the standard of living after retirement and complying with the purposed-linked nature of pension. However, this position is partially reversed by the Dutch legislator through the introduction of the *Wet bedrag ineens*, which allows up to 10% of the pension to be withdrawn as a lump sum at retirement date. The envisaged date of entry into force of this option is January 1, 2024, see Kamerstukken II, *Wijziging van de Wet bedrag ineens, RVU en verlofsparen in verband met de herziening van de mogelijkheid tot afkoop in de vorm van een bedrag ineens alsmede tot wijziging van de Wet op de loonbelasting 1964 (Wet herziening bedrag ineens) (Nota naar aanleiding van het verslag)* (2022/23) 1.

facilitation. The Dutch third pension pillar embodies individual pension arrangements that a person establishes on his or her own initiative.[555] Life annuities (*lijfrenten*) take a predominant role in the Dutch retirement system, in terms of a supplementary pillar. These are stand-alone individual arrangements, with no basis in a second pillar pension plan. A characteristic of the third pillar pension is that it does not have its basis in the performance of work, as is the case with occupational pensions.[556] However, it does form a supplement to the first, and second pillar Dutch pensions. Annuities in the third pillar are not the purview of pension funds in the Netherlands but of life insurers and banks. As will be dealt with in more detail in chapter 7 of this research, the conditions for annuity premium deduction are quite strict with respect to the allowed annuity products and allowed providers.[557]

As a rule, solely provisions with an insurance element that provide a periodic income in old age (or for the surviving partners) in the event of death are classified (fiscally) under this third pillar.[558] Capital insurance policies do not generate periodic income, and therefore remain excluded from this scope. This approach is not uncommon internationally either. Self-initiative and voluntariness prevail with respect to these pension provisions. Compared to the Dutch first and second pillars, freedom, personal responsibility and flexibility prevail most in the third pillar.

4.5 COMPARATIVE FINDINGS THROUGH THE LENS OF THE EVALUATION FRAMEWORK

Where in the sections above the construct of pension has been delineated and operationalised, in terms of statutory, occupational, personal pensions – in both the Netherlands and Germany – the section below evaluates these findings along the (legal) lines of this research's evaluation framework (similarity/comparability; inter-level coherence; inter-system consistency; foreseeability/unpredictability). It is a sliding scale where all variations between fit and unfit can be observed.

555 Lutjens, *Asser-serie 7-XI – Pensioen (Bijzondere overeenkomsten)* nr 12.

556 Dietvorst, 65.

557 To be eligible for premium deduction, there must be an annuity in terms of the conditions set by art. 1.7 Wet IB 2001: an annuity is a periodic payment; the payments are fixed and regular; the payments must end at the latest at death; the annuity claim may not be taken out as a lump sum, sold, surrendered or formally or actually serve as security other than for the purpose of deferring tax payment. If an annuity agreement does not meet these conditions, the annuity does not qualify for premium deduction and the value of the entire policy shall be taxable as income from assets (BOX 3). See artt. 3.124 Wet IB 2001 ff.

558 GJB Dietvorst, 'Lijfrenten' in AHH Bollen-Vandenboorn (ed.), *Pensioen en de belangrijkste toekomstvoorzieningen* (27 edn Fiscale Geschriften, SDU, Den Haag 2022) section 12.1.

As this chapter explored the construct 'pension', emphasis will be put on the principle of similarity/comparability, since this chapter seeks to explore to what extent the operationalisation, and legal interpretation of the dispersed construct of pension is fit for the provision of effective pension information. As the construct of 'pension' and 'pillar', and the legal characters of statutory, occupational and personal pensions are less subject to amendments, trends, uncertainty and unpredictability – contrary to, for instance, tax law – the legal principle of foreseeability is less pertinent. These constructs are, for instance, less receptive to reflecting social reality or to developments in the areas of EU law, compared to tax legislation. What is more, the construct of 'pension' and 'pillar', and the legal characters, are not marked by a certain degree of coherence between different fields of multi-level law (national, European, international). For instance, due to the division of power between the European Union and the Member States; the responsibility for the design of a national pension system lies with the Member States, and the European Union lacks competence to intervene in the Member States' pension systems. Hence, it does not concern the scrutiny of coherence with higher-level regulations, and with treaty or other international obligations. The principle of inter-level coherence is, hence, left aside. Lastly, as the chapter above did not concern the application of national regulatory (tax) frameworks, leading to potential (in)compatible outcomes for a specific cross-border situation, the principle of inter-system consistency shall be neither evaluated. This chapter meets this research second (sub)objective of a legal comparative study in which the legal frameworks in the Netherlands and Germany, as well as on a European and international level, shall be mapped out. Building on this, the 'fitness' of the legal frameworks at the national, European and international level shall be assessed, focusing in particular on any deficiencies that have an effect on the provision of effective information.

4.5.1 *Similarity/Comparability*

The sections below compare the legal character of German and Dutch statutory, occupational, and personal pensions respectively, and evaluates it in view of the principle of similarity/comparability. Exploring similarity between systems involves a comparison of certain features. The assessment of similarity constitutes a feature-matching process, i.e. it measures the degree to which two objects – the legal character – match each other. Similarity is tantamount to a measurement of common features. A higher degree of similarity helps to ensure the effectiveness of information in terms of the four principles (understandability, correctness, personal relevance and trustworthiness). For instance, the higher the degree of similarity, the easier it is to uphold the information's correctness, trustworthiness, and personal relevance. After all, with a higher degree of similarity, there is less need to observe any underlying structural differences. Moreover, a higher degree of similarity leads to a higher comparability of the different regulatory frameworks/legal constructs, avoiding comparing the incomparable. What is more, it is revealed that existing categorisation systems (e.g. World Bank Model) are of little use in aiding similarity/ comparability, as these insufficiently take account of the existing differences between national pension systems.

With regard to the legal character of pensions the question rises whether there should be a general legal character at all. Provided that the context in which the character shall be used is clearly set in advance, a non-generalised and a context-tailored character should be workable. As Stevens claimed, the legal qualification of pension depends to a high degree on the character and objective of the provision the pension stems from.[559] As demonstrated in this chapter, a general pension character appears to be unrealistic, since pension has a considerable number of modalities, each in which the legal character mainly depends on the scheme or relation the pension stems from.[560] Contrarily, a general definition would seem meaningful, provided that the legal consequences would be equal, irrespective of the character of the pension, or the scheme it arises from.

4.5.1.A Comparing the Legal Character of Dutch and German Statutory Pensions

Comparing the definition, and legal character, of Dutch and German statutory pensions (see sections 4.3.2 and 4.4.2), the following conclusions can be drawn:

- The Dutch statutory pension (AOW) seeks to be a basic provision to meet minimum living needs, i.e. the *Existenzsicherung*. The German *Basisversorgung* is not that explicitly aimed at meeting minimum living needs.

559 LGM Stevens, *Pensioen in de loonsfeer* (FED Fiscale brochures, Deventer 2005) 29. In the same vein, Lutjens, *Pensioenvoorziening voor werknemers, juridische beschouwingen voor werknemers*; Clausing.

560 Cf. E Lutjens, *De PSW, wetshistorisch overzicht en commentaar* (Kluwer, Deventer 1998). In HR, PJ 27 February 1998. 1998b the Dutch Supreme Court ruled that the name of the retirement provision, the amount of the temporary benefit, the paying institution, and the right to non-contributory entitlements might be relevant in the definition of pension. These elements of the pension definition should be seen against the background of the applicable legislation at the moment the *Hoge Raad* ruled in this case. Therefore, these elements do not necessarily hold true in the present state of legislation. Rechtbank Den Haag, ibid 28 August 2002. 2002 considered the name of the provision relevant as well as obtaining benefit entitlements vested in proportion to the period of participation when the active participation in the pension fund is terminated. See also Hoge Raad, ibid 16 September 2005. 2005 in which the The Hague Court of Appeal ruled that the following features might be relevant: the retirement benefit is related to the last-earned salary instead of the number of years of service, the benefits are financed pay-as-you-go, the provision had a temporary nature capped at a term of five years but including the possibility to extend it, the name of the provision, the paying institution and non-contributory entitlements in cases where the participation is terminated prematurely. Noteworthy is that the Court of Appeal found that the link with the loss of an earned income was not decisive.

- The German first pillar consists of a wide range of statutory pension schemes, i.e. *gesetzliche Rentenversicherung, die Beambtenversorgung, Alterssicherung der Landwirte* and *berufsständische Versorgungswerke*, each holding a different ratio in terms of conferring statutory pension rights. In the Netherlands, old age provision in the first pillar is formed by only one pension provision, i.e. the state pension AOW, for which all resident are eligible.
- The AOW is part of Dutch social insurance (*volksverzekeringen*), where residency takes a predominant role in determining the obligation to be insured. Contrary to Germany, neither the obligation to contribute, nor the entitlement to benefits is directly related to the performance of work or the receipt of income. The AOW thus as a much broader personal scope.
- Contrary to the Netherlands, the eligibility criteria for the categorisation under the German first pillar as *Basisversorgung* are rather strict, compared to the Netherlands. These criteria among others comprise payment solely as a lifelong annuity and prohibited hereditability, transferability, lendability, realisability, capitalising, capital cover etc.
- In both countries, the basis for statutory pensions and government involvement is comparable, i.e. the basis for the first pillar is the law, and government involvement consists of creating the legislation from which pension entitlements derive directly.

As addressed in the beginning of this section, exploring similarity between systems involves a comparison of certain features, where similarity is tantamount to a measurement of common features. As follows from the above enumeration, the legal comparison revealed more differences than similarities between the legal characters of Dutch and German statutory pensions. In terms of 'fitness' it can thus be concluded that these structural differences hamper the provision of effective information provision, in terms of similarity/comparability.

4.5.1.B Comparing the Legal Character of Dutch and German Occupational Pensions

Comparing the definition, and legal character, of Dutch and German occupational pensions (see sections 4.3.3 and 4.4.3), the following conclusion can be drawn:

- In both countries an objective perspective is adopted, i.e. not every capital accumulation should be considered a retirement provision if the pension participant's perspective is aimed thereon accordingly, i.e. assets merely held as investment. Rather, this capital accumulation must meet certain conditions as embedded in civil pension legislation.
- In both countries, the second pillar is marked by a direct link between the performance of work, and participation in and entitlements to occupational pension schemes. The

employment relationship takes a pivotal role, also to delineate the other pension pillars of statutory, and personal pension plans.

- Yet, it appears that the idea of care and the perception of pension as deferred wage is more or less to be regarded as universal, both in the Netherlands as well as in Germany. The ultimate retirement benefits are considered a compensation for rendered work, and therefore a particular form of remuneration. In Germany, the perception has shifted gradually from *Versorgungscharakter*[561] to *Entgeltcharakter*[562], ultimately resulting in a dual nature of pension comprising the two characters but in which the *Entgeltcharakter* prevails. Also in the Netherlands, occupational pension is characterized as a deferred reward with a care-related character. These two characteristics can be considered universal, and thus can serve as a basis for coordinating the pension concept bilaterally between the Netherlands and Germany.
- In both countries the concept of pension is framed fiscally; the purpose and actual use of the retirement provision is guaranteed through fiscal measures. What is more, the relation between fiscal facilitation and saving for retirement shows a strong synergy; the more it is ensured that the capital accumulation will be employed for the use of retirement provision in the form of an annual or temporary lifelong annuity, the more the accumulation of pension capital shall be fiscally facilitated. Furthermore, in the light of the definition of pension, the benefits shall principally be paid out lifelong during the retirement phase.
- In both countries, government involvement consists of facilitating the establishment of an occupational pension provision - by means of (compulsory) participation and tax relief - and by setting a legal basis to protect pension (entitlements) against loss or impairment.

As follows from the above enumeration, the legal comparison revealed more similarities than differences when it comes to the legal characters of Dutch and German occupational pensions. In terms of 'fitness' it can thus be concluded that these similarities aid the provision of effective information provision, in terms of similarity/comparability.

4.5.1.C Comparing the Legal Character of Dutch and German Personal Pensions

- As follows from sections 4.3.4 and 4.4.4, in both Germany, as well as the Netherlands, the interpretation of the concept of third pillar pension provisions is left rather open, i.e. strict qualitative criteria are missing. Moreover, individual pensions are mainly

561 Translated freely as retirement provision character.

562 Translated freely as remuneration character.

regulated by fiscal legislation, stipulating the criteria regarding their fiscal facilitation, i.e. the deduction of premiums.

- In both countries, personal pensions are stand-alone individual arrangements, with no basis in a second pillar pension plan, i.e. it does not have its basis in the performance of work, as holds true for occupational pensions.
- As regards personal pensions, both in the Netherlands, as well as in Germany, self-initiative and voluntariness, and flexibility prevail as a characteristic of the third pillar, distinguishing them clearly from statutory and occupational pensions.
- In both countries, government involvement consists of facilitating the establishment of a personal pension provision – by means of tax relief – and by setting a legal basis to protect pension (entitlements) against loss or impairment.
- As has been addressed in section 4.4.4, Germany holds a more subjective interpretation of the concept of personal pensions, contrary to the Netherlands. From this perspective every capital accumulation should be considered an old-age provision if the pension participant's subjective is aimed thereon accordingly. For instance, the rent-free own home can serve as a provision for retirement, since the saved rents lower the costs of living.
- In the Netherlands, as well as in Germany, the most adequate distinctive element between occupational and individual pensions may be considered the organisational implementation of the pension provision. Where in occupational pensions the employer functions as a sort of intermediary, for individual pensions the beneficiary organises his pension on his own account. The significant element of an employment relationship is missing for individual pension provisions.

As follows from the above enumeration, the legal comparison revealed more similarities than differences when it comes to the legal characters of Dutch and German personal pensions. In terms of 'fitness' it can thus be concluded that these similarities aid the provision of effective information provision, in terms of similarity/comparability.

4.6 Interim Conclusion

As has been addressed thoroughly in chapter 1 of this research, the two-dimensional notion of effective pension information articulates that the information's behavioural purpose seeks to inform mobile individuals on an aggregated level about how much pension they can expect, in order to be able to assess the adequacy of their dispersed pension, covering all their forms of pension in each of the (former) working/residence states. However, mobile individuals – who avail(ed) themselves of their European freedoms of movement – see themselves confronted with a wide range of diverging 'pensions', i.e.

pension vehicles, schemes, retirement products of all sorts, arising from statutory, occupational and individual pension systems in each of the different (former) working states, and/or residence states. This requires a process of converging these deviating systems into standardised/uniform information provision, while upholding the information's effectiveness. The relevance of this chapter's exploration lies in conveying a legal notion such as 'pension' and 'pillar' into the realm of effective pension information provision.

However, as has been pointed out in section 4.1, some terms, notions and concepts may be considered a universal legal concept present in both legal systems at issue, but nevertheless having a different meaning in both systems. While taking this as a guiding principle, this chapter reflected on the notions of 'pension' and 'pillar', and explored the legal character of statutory, occupational, and personal pensions in the Netherlands, as well as Germany. These comparative findings were presented in section 4.5, along the lines of the principle of similarity/comparability. This comparison revealed a considerable number of similarities when it comes to the legal character of Dutch and German statutory, occupational, and personal pensions. Moreover, it revealed a range of differences that should be observed when providing effective cross-border pension information. What is more, it was found that although there is some consensus to divide pensions into three pillars, a universal agreed definition/classification/taxonomy is still missing. Moreover, consensus is missing as on what aspects, elements, modalities of a pension scheme should be prevailing in the classification. Due to this worldwide lack of consensus and consistency, these systems of categorisation merely serve to categorise pension vehicles *grosso modo*, and should be treated with caution when employed in the domain of (cross-border) pension information provision. With regard to the German system, it appeared that the diverging use of the terms *Säul*, and *Schicht* works to the detriment of effective pension information, in terms of the construct 'pillar'.

5 Statutory Pensions Systems and Taxation Through the Lens of Effective Pension Information

5.1 Introduction

Mobile individuals – who avail(ed) themselves of their European freedoms of movement – see themselves confronted with a wide range of diverging 'pensions', i.e. pension vehicles, schemes, retirement products of all sorts, arising from statutory pension systems in each of the different (former) working states, and/or residence states. This fragmentation of pensions is further exacerbated by the high diversity in the methods of tax treatment of statutory pensions in each Member State, as each State applies different tax rules to these pension arrangements. Providing, on an aggregated level, mobile individuals information about how much pension they can expect – covering all their forms of pension in each of the (former) working/residence states – requires a complex process of incorporating all types of diverging pension vehicles, schemes, products of all sorts in each of the different (former) working states, and/or residence states. Putting this dispersed puzzle together also poses considerable challenges in terms of information provision. This amounts to observing, and 'translating' the intersections between different multi-level legal systems (national, EU and international/bilateral) and the interaction of poorly coordinated legal domains (pension and tax law) – which can all be interwoven in a personal mobile situation – into effective pension information. For example, ensuring the legal correctness of information requires systematic monitoring and updating, as laws and policies tend to constantly change. What is more, heterogeneity among national legal systems is a universal phenomenon, due to, inter alia, historical developments, adaption to different social developments, economic trends and developments, different political landscapes etc. Hitherto, little to no attention has been paid, neither any research has been conducted on the differentiated tax treatment of the fragmented pension rights in each of the (former) working states, and the effect thereof on the ambition to present effective pension information.

Taking this as a given, this chapter maps out the statutory pension systems in both the Netherlands, as well as Germany. Moreover, it revolves around the tax treatment of these statutory schemes in both the accrual and pay-out phase. It, inter alia, explores to what extent tax relief is granted for statutory pensions in the form of tax base advantages (e.g.

tax exemptions, allowances, deduction from the taxable base, deduction from the tax liability) or tax rate advantages (e.g. flat tax rate). The allocation of company pension expenses at employer level is left aside. The description of this tax treatment is based on national (Dutch and German respectively) tax legislation, while taking account of the applicable tax treaty concluded between the Netherlands and Germany.

What is more, the increase in the mobility of workers implies that the taxation of pensions must not solely be considered from a purely national perspective, but also account must be taken of cross-border aspects. Hence, in sections 5.2.2 and 5.3.3 the tax treatment of Dutch/German statutory pensions in cross-border situations will be discussed, both during the accrual phase as well as in the pay-out phase. As regards the accrual phase, the analysis focuses on whether tax advantages are granted, while, as regards the pay-out phase it is considered how, and to what extent, (foreign and domestic) pension benefits are subjected to tax. It is to be noted at this point, that the allocation of the taxing rights pursuant to a tax treaty, is taken into account as a proviso/prerequisite for the exercise of taxing rights pursuant to domestic (Dutch) tax legislation. These distribution rules will be discussed in chapter 9. The normative framework pertaining to the tax treatment of cross-border pensions, enshrined in EU law, will be discussed in chapter 8.

In section 4.5, these comparative findings will be evaluated along the (legal) lines of this research's evaluation framework: similarity/comparability, inter-level coherence, inter-system consistency, and foreseeability. For instance, the more the national legal systems are aligned in terms of coherence, the fitter they are in terms of upholding the pension information's (legal) correctness, combined with understandability. In addition, to ensure the information's correctness and – in the long run – trustworthiness regulatory frameworks need to adhere to legislation's foreseeability. Not each of these legal principles shall be evaluated to the same extent in section 4.5, as this chapter explores the statutory pension systems, and the tax treatment. This chapter meets this research second (sub) objective of a legal comparative study in which the legal frameworks in the Netherlands and Germany shall be mapped out.

5.2 The Dutch Statutory Retirement System: AOW

As has been addressed in chapter 4, the Dutch statutory pension (AOW) seeks to be a government-run 'flat-rate' basic provision to meet minimum living needs, i.e. the *Existenzsicherung*. The *Algemene Ouderdomswet* (General Old Age Pensions Act) constitutes this legal basis for the Dutch statutory old age pension in the 'first pillar'. This pay-as-you-go financed compulsory old age insurance came into effect on 1 January 1957.

The AOW is part of Dutch social insurance (*volksverzekeringen*), where residency takes a predominant role in determining the obligation to be insured. For 2023 the AOW contribution rate amounts to 17.9%. Contributions are only made by employees. What is more, no minimum insurance period applies.

The AOW provides for a (minimum) old age pension once the retirement age has been reached by the entitled person. In principle, each year of residence in the Netherlands yields 2% of the eventual AOW-benefits. The level of AOW-benefits is related to the Dutch minimum income. Every resident, provided that he is or has been insured, is entitled to an old-age pension if he has reached the pensionable age and has been insured pursuant to the law during the period from the day the insured person reaches the entitlement age to the day the insured person reaches the state pension age. This applies to residents, and persons working in the Netherlands who are subject to wage taxes for this purpose.[563] Inherent in this is the chance of an incomplete state pension, as in the case of emigration. Anyone who has been insured for the maximum insurance period from the starting age, is entitled to an entire AOW benefits.[564] The maximum insurance period amounts to 50 years. The amount of AOW benefits is fixed and independent of previous income and also independent of current income or assets, i.e. 'flat rate' benefits. For unmarried people, the net AOW is equal to 70% of the net minimum wage, for a married pensioner it is 50% of the net minimum wage.

For decades, the state pension age was set at 65. However, the financial sustainability of the pay-as-you-go funded state pension as a retirement provision had come under increasing pressure due to demographic developments (i.e. aging, dejuvenation and increasing average life expectancy). Consequently, raising the state pension age was necessary to safeguard solidarity between those in work and those not in work, as well as between younger and older generations. In the light of these developments, the introduction of the *Wet verhoging AOW- en pensioenrichtleeftijd (Wet VAP)* in 2012 meant that the fixed state pension age of 65 had to be abandoned, and a switch was made to a phased increase and subsequent linkage to the average remaining life expectancy.[565] Subsequently, in 2015, through the introduction of the *Wet versnelling stapsgewijze verhoging AOW-leeftijd*, this phased increase was accelerated.[566] The above two laws were enacted at the time of the

563 Art. 6, para. 1 AOW. For further rules on the circle of insured persons, see *Besluit uitbreiding en beperking kring verzekerden volksverzekeringen 1999*.

564 As regards the starting age see art. 7a AOW.

565 Kamerstukken II, (2011/12).

566 Kamerstukken II, *Wet tot wijziging van de Algemene Ouderdomswet, de Wet op de loonbelasting 1964, de Wet verhoging AOW- en pensioenrichtleeftijd, de Pensioenwet, de Wet verplichte beroepspensioenregeling en Overige fiscale maatregelen 2013 in verband met de versnelling van de stapsgewijze verhoging van de AOW-leeftijd (Wet versnelling stapsgewijze verhoging AOW-leeftijd)* (2014/15).

economic crisis, which put pressure on government finances. As the financial-economic situation has improved since 2012 and the effects of the increase in the state pension age were becoming more tangible, it was decided to mitigate the gradual increase in the state pension age. Hence, the *Wet verandering koppeling AOW-leeftijd* entered into force on 10 December 2020.[567] This legal act is part of the implementation of the reform of the Dutch system of occupational pension schemes, i.e. the 'pension agreement' (*Pensioenakkoord*).[568] The underlying reason for this mitigated short-term increase is that many older workers indicated that they felt overwhelmed by the increase in the state pension age, and that they had serious concerns about whether they would be able to keep up the work, partly because they had not always been able to prepare well for the increase in the state pension age.[569] Pursuant to this act, from 2025 onwards, two thirds of the development of the statutory pension age will be linked to the development of the remaining life expectancy at the age of 65. Hence, each year of life expectancy will result in eight months longer working and four months longer receiving statutory pension benefits. This two-thirds link will also apply to the occupational retirement age. Hence, the state pension age will be set at 66 years and 10 months in 2023, resulting in a retirement age of 67 in 2024. After 2024, the state pension age will not rise by one year for each year of longer life expectancy, but only by eight months. This means that each year of life expectancy gain results in an average – across the population – of eight months longer employment and four months longer state pension.[570] As before, the state pension age will therefore remain linked to life expectancy, but to a lesser extent. For that matter, reaching the state pension age earlier may lead to a loss of income for particular groups of employees. In addition, a proposal to make the state pension age flexible has been rejected in the past.[571] This is a major omission now that the state pension age and the occupational pension age deviate. In addition, this can be a solution for frontier workers who are faced

567 Kamerstukken II, (2019/20).

568 See Minister van Sociale Zaken en Werkgelegenheid, 'Hoofdlijnennotitie uitwerking pensioenakkoord' (22 June 2020).

569 Kamerstukken II, *Wet van 2 december 2020, houdende wijziging van de Algemene Ouderdomswet en de Wet op de loonbelasting 1964 in verband met de verandering van de koppeling van de AOW- en pensioenrichtleeftijd aan de stijging van de levensverwachting (Wet verandering koppeling AOW-leeftijd), nr. 3 (MvT)* (2019/20) 2.

570 Estimates of macro average remaining life expectancy are conducted and published by Statistics Netherlands (Centraal Bureau voor de Statistiek; CBS). See art. 7a, para 4 AOW.

571 See Kamerstukken II, *34 414, nr. 6-9 (Voorstel van wet van het lid Klein tot wijziging van de Algemene Ouderdomswet en de Participatiewet in verband met de introductie van de mogelijkheid het AOW-ouderdomspensioen geheel of gedeeltelijk eerder of later te laten ingaan (Wet flexibilisering ingangsdatum AOW))* (2015/16) and Kamerstukken II, *34 414, nr. 55* (2016/17).

with different pension ages in different European member states.[572] Recently, the statutory pension age for 2027 has been set at 67, as it was for 2026.[573]

Its merits attention from a (legal) information provision perspective, that the Dutch Central Appeal Council (*Centrale Raad van Beroep*) has consistently held that the statement of the future pensionable age for Dutch statutory pensions, provided in a pension benefit statement, constitutes a communication of informative nature, which, in the context of such a statement, is not aimed at attaining a legal effect.[574] Hence, for this part, this does not constitute a decision against which an action before court may be brought.

5.2.1 *The Tax Treatment of the Dutch Algemene Ouderdomswet: the Deductibility of Contributions and the Taxation of Benefits*

The description of the tax treatment of premiums and benefits with respect to the Dutch statutory AOW pension is quite concise. Since the introduction of the Oort-legislation, the tax deduction of AOW contributions is no longer allowed as of January 1, 1990.[575] For the same reason, premiums for equivalent foreign statutory pension schemes, at that time, were excluded from deduction as well.[576] As regards the deduction of contributions paid into (equivalent) foreign statutory pension schemes, see section 5.2.2.B.I. However, tax relief is obtained via the general tax reduction, i.e. via a tax credit, where AOW contributions are incorporated as part of this relief.[577]

Benefits from all forms of Dutch pension schemes are fully included in BOX 1 income (*Inkomen uit werk en woning*) and are subject to a progressive income tax rate. With

572 M.J.G.A.M. Weerepas, 'AOW en Anw' in AHH Bollen-Vandenboorn (ed.), *Pensioen en de belangrijkste toekomstvoorzieningen* (27 edn Fiscale Geschriften, SDU, Den Haag 2022), section 2.2.

573 Staatssecretaris van Sociale Zaken en Werkgelegenheid, *Mededeling van de Staatssecretaris van Sociale Zaken en Werkgelegenheid van 5 november 2021, 2021-0000168058, tot bekendmaking van de pensioengerechtigde leeftijd en de aanvangsleeftijd in 2027* (5 November 2021).

574 See 15-8518 AOW ECLI:NL:CRVB:2016:2610 (Centrale Raad van Beroep) paragraph 4.1.3. This has been confirmed in, *inter alia*, 18 3845 AOW ECLI:NL:CRVB:2020:1927 (Centrale Raad van Beroep) paragraph 4.1. The Council points out that this does not imply that appellant is denied an effective remedy against the future pensionable age applicable to the Dutch AOW, as the appellant has the possibility to oppose the decision issued in response to her application for an AOW pension. In addition, it clarifies the legal nature (i.e. merely informative) of information provided on the pensionable age.

575 Kamerstukken II, *20 595, 3 (Wet vereenvoudiging tariefstructuur en aftrekposten in de loon- en inkomstenbelasting)* (1989/90). This Oort-operation was based on the report *Zicht op eenvoud* of the Commission for the simplification of wage and income taxes (Oort Commission); the commission was led by Prof. Coen Oort.

576 Ibid. 35.

577 Pursuant to art. 8.4 in conjunction with art. 8.10 Wet IB 2001.

respect to a domestic taxpayer, the statutory AOW pension benefits are fully subjected to tax as wages from former employment.[578] From a systemic point of view, this qualification is not entirely accurate since, in order to receive an AOW pension, residency is decisive, not whether or not the person concerned has been involved in an employment relationship, nor are the AOW benefits based on the (amount of) wage from former employment, see chapter 4 with regard to the AOW's legal character. However, this has been implemented in this way with a view to facilitating the levying of income tax, since in cases where the recipients of the benefits receive no further taxable income, and/or have no fiscal deductions, the wage tax for these taxpayers is final and, hence, they do not have to file an income tax return.

5.2.2 The Tax Treatment of Dutch Statutory Pensions in Cross-border Situations

The section elaborates on the tax treatment of Dutch statutory pensions in cross-border situations, during the accrual phase as well as in the pay-out phase. As regards the accrual phase, the analysis focuses on whether tax advantages are granted, while, as regards the pay-out phase it is considered how, and to what extent, (foreign and domestic) pension benefits shall be subjected to tax. The section below solely considers the situations where the accrual, and/or the pay-out, of the given pension entitlements/benefits accrued entirely in either one of the two states, i.e. residence or (former) working state. If, however, the pension entitlements were partly accrued in Germany (a German pension) and partly in the Netherlands (a Dutch pension), the (cross-border) fiscal consequences need to be identified per pension separately (by source of the retirement income). These situations will not be dealt with in the section below, but this section's content, combined with section 5.3.3, allows for the (fiscal) assessment of such (dispersed) mixed-pension cases.

What is more, it is to be noted at this point, that the allocation of the taxing rights pursuant to the applicable tax treaty, is taken into account as a proviso/prerequisite for the exercise of taxing rights pursuant to domestic (Dutch) tax legislation. These distribution rules will be discussed in chapter 9. Moreover, the taxation of Dutch occupational pensions in cross-border situations shall be discussed in chapter 6 of this research; personal pensions in chapter 7.

578 Pursuant to art. 34, para 1, under a in conjunction with art. 11, para 1, under c in conjunction with para 2 Wet LB 1964.

Commonly in cross-border situations, the mobile worker will, during retirement, not reside in the same state as where he resided during the accrual phase (migration). However, if the mobile citizen only works temporarily in one country and later returns to his home country, he will commonly pay his pension contributions to a pension institution in his home country even though he took up residence abroad (posting). Furthermore, a mobile citizen may work in one State, while residing in another (neighbouring) Member State, to which they usually return every day or at least once a week (or commonly referred to as 'frontier worker', or 'border commuter'). The definitions of these different types of workers, have been extensively set forth in chapter 1 under *scope ratione personae*. In the cross-border cases dealt with in the section below, a distinction is drawn between inbound and outbound cases. In the case of migration, the outbound case means that the employee is resident in the national territory during the accrual period and lives abroad during the pay-out phase. In the case of inbound, the employee moves his or her place of residence from abroad to the national territory at the start of the pay-out phase. As regards posting, in the case of an outbound situation, an employee resident in the national territory works abroad for several years. Similarly, in the case of inbound, a foreign employee works in the national territory for a certain period of time, while he or she resides abroad.

5.2.2.A Migrant Worker

Commonly the migrant worker will, during retirement, not reside in the same state as where he resided during the accrual phase (migration). In the accrual phase, the state of employment and the state of residence coincide, whereas in the pay-out phase the state of residence of the (former) employee differs from the (former) state of employment. Where in an outbound migration situation discussed in this section, the employee is resident in the national territory of the Netherlands during the accrual phase and lives abroad (Germany) during the pay-out phase, in the inbound case, the employee is resident abroad (Germany) during the accrual phase, while being a resident of the Netherlands during the pay-out phase.

5.2.2.A.I Outbound

In an outbound case, the employee is resident in the Netherlands (partly) during the accrual phase. The tax treatment and the granting of tax relief is hence akin to the tax treatment in a domestic situation, i.e. there is no cross-border situation. There is no nexus with German income tax, levied during the accrual phase. I therefore refer to section 5.2.1. In short, contributions to the *AOW* are not deductible for tax purposes, so no tax consequences arise during the accrual phase. In contrast, during the pay-out phase, the person concerned resides abroad. Pension benefits arising from Dutch statutory pension schemes are thus paid out abroad.[579] It depends on the allocation of taxing rights enshrined in the applicable tax treaty where the person is liable to tax for the Dutch AOW pension benefits. If the taxing right is allocated to the other state as a residence state (for instance pursuant to article 17, para 1 treaty Netherlands-Germany), the Dutch AOW pension benefits will be subject to German taxation, pursuant to German national tax legislation. This will be discussed in section, 5.3.3.A.I .

In addition to the question of whether the tax treaty concluded with the country of migration grants the country of departure a right of taxation, it is equally important to explore to what extent the country of departure (the Netherlands) includes cross-border retirement benefits in the limited tax liability. In cases where the taxing right on the AOW benefits is allocated to the Netherlands as a source state (for instance pursuant to article 17, para 2 treaty Netherlands-Germany), the beneficiary residing abroad will be treated as a foreign taxable person (*buitenlands belastingplichtige*) provided that he receives domestic income, as the person concerned neither resides in the Netherlands, nor has his habitual abode in the Netherlands during the pay-out phase.[580] The AOW pension benefits will be fully liable to tax as taxable periodical benefits and benefits in kind under public law, received from or on behalf of a Dutch public law legal entity.[581] The AOW pension benefits received are thus qualified differently for foreign taxpayers than for domestic taxpayers, see for the latter section 5.2.1. What is more, this taxable proportion of the benefits is determined irrespective of whether these benefits are derived from contributions which were subject to tax relief.

5.2.2.A.II Inbound

In an inbound case, the employee is a resident of Germany (partly) during the accrual phase, and takes up residence in the Netherlands at the commencement of the pay-out phase. As the person concerned lives and resides in Germany during the accrual phase, he will be subject to the statutory pension schemes in Germany, i.e. there is no cross-border situation. There is no nexus with Dutch income tax, levied during the accrual phase. The tax treatment and the granting of tax relief is hence akin to the tax treatment in a domestic situation, see section 5.3.2.

However, as the person will relocate his residence to the Netherlands during the pay-out phase, it remains to be seen whether and, if so, to what extent, pension benefits derived from the German statutory pension scheme will be subject to Dutch income tax. In cases

579 See article 7 Regulation 883/2004.

580 See article 2.1, para 1, sub b in conjunction with article 7.1 and 7.2 Wet IB 2001.

581 Pursuant to article 7.2, para 2, under e Wet IB 2001.

where the taxing right on the foreign benefits is allocated to Germany as source state (pursuant to article 17, para 2 treaty Netherlands-Germany), the German pension benefits will be subject to German taxation, pursuant to German national tax legislation. This will not be discussed any further in this section, see section 5.3.2. If, however, the taxing right is allocated to the Netherlands as residence state (for instance pursuant to article 17, para 1 treaty Netherlands-Germany), the German statutory pension benefits will be fully subject to Dutch income tax. The functioning of these allocation rules – embedded in the applicable tax treaty – will be discussed in more detail in chapter 9 of this research. As the person resides in the Netherlands during the pay-out phase, he will be subject to Dutch unlimited tax liability.[582] The payments from the German *Rentenversicherungen* are – according to the Secretary of State – to be considered as income from employment because of the relationship with the (current or past) employment of the taxpayer himself or of someone else.[583] These annuities and social security payments are seen as inherent to the (existence of) the employment relationship. Hence, the German statutory pension payments are, as a rule, taxed as wages.[584] The Secretary of State further emphasizes that this does not alter the fact that in certain cases an independent assessment of the actual situation justifies a different view, which must then be followed. This viewpoint has a detrimental effect on the foreseeability of the (application of) legislation. Incidentally, the communication of November 2020 does not provide any clarity as to how benefits arising from *Beamtenversorgung, Alterssicherung der Landwirte, Berufsständischen Versorgungseinrichtunge* will be taxable under Dutch tax law, as this communication merely focusses on the tax treatment of contributions paid into these German schemes. I assume that the general principles as formulated in the Decree of March 24, 2014 apply here *mutatis mutandis*.[585]

5.2.2.B Cross-border (Frontier) Worker

5.2.2.B.I Outbound

In this situation, where the Netherlands is the residence state, it needs to be determined where the cross-border worker is insured, and thus obliged to pay contributions, to the statutory pension scheme. Pursuant to article 11, para 3, sub a Regulation 883/2004 a person pursuing an activity as an employed or self-employed person in a Member State

582 Pursuant to article 2.1, para 1, sub a Wet IB 2001 in conjunction with article 4, para 1 AWR.

583 See Staatssecretaris van Financiën, *Buitenlandse sociale verzekeringen. Duitse, Belgische en Luxemburgse sociale zekerheid. Aftrek premie en belastbaarheid uitkeringen nr. DGB 2014/144M* (24 March 2014), para 5.1.

584 Pursuant to artt. 3.81 and 3.82 Wet IB 2001.

585 See Staatssecretaris van Financiën, *Buitenlandse sociale verzekeringen. Duitse, Belgische en Luxemburgse sociale zekerheid. Aftrek premie en belastbaarheid uitkeringen nr. DGB 2014/144M* para 2.4.

shall be subject to the legislation of the working State (*lex loci laboris*). The person is thus insured in a German statutory pension scheme, and pays contributions under the German statutory pension scheme. As this person is resident in the Netherlands, he will, commonly, be subject to unlimited tax liability in the Netherlands.[586] The question than rises to what extent these foreign paid contributions are taken into account – in terms of deductibility – in the calculation of Dutch income tax. For taxpayers who are not socially insured in the Netherlands, it must be determined how foreign statutory pension schemes should be qualified, pursuant to Dutch law.

The decision of the Secretary of State of March 24, 2014, expressed his stance on the qualification of certain German statutory pension schemes.[587] The latest published elaborations are incorporated in the communication of November 26, 2020.[588] This document provides an overview of the systems examined, indicating for each country whether or not the employee contribution is deductible, and whether the employer contribution is exempt or taxed. The main rule is that contributions paid by the employer for foreign statutory pension schemes that are 'similar in nature and scope' to the Dutch national insurances are part of the Dutch taxable wages. The contribution paid by the employee himself is, in principle, not deductible for income tax purposes. Payments for voluntary insurances do not constitute a premium in this context.

However, if the predominant character of the foreign scheme is that of an occupational pension scheme and, moreover, the scheme does not exceed – in terms of results – what is allowed under the Dutch system, the given scheme is not qualified as an occupational pension scheme, but the entitlements concerned are not taxable and the contributions are deductible. According to the Secretary of State, it is considered predominantly an occupational pension scheme if the maximum salary- or service-related part of the benefit of the foreign social security pension is more than twice the amount of the minimum pension to be acquired on the basis of that plan.

The decision acknowledges that the German *Rentenversicherung*, like many other foreign social security pensions, contains elements of both a Dutch statutory pension scheme, and

586 Pursuant to art. 2.1, para 1, under a Wet IB 2001.

587 Staatssecretaris van Financiën, *Buitenlandse sociale verzekeringen. Duitse, Belgische en Luxemburgse sociale zekerheid. Aftrek premie en belastbaarheid uitkeringen nr. DGB 2014/144M*. The examination of the tax qualification of the foreign social insurance systems is carried out at the foreign office of the Tax Authorities on the basis of the principles included in this Decree.

588 DG Belastingdienst / Concerndirectie Fiscale en Juridische Zaken, *Internationaal belastingrecht. Fiscale kwalificatie buitenlandse socialezekerheidsstelsels DGBD 178296* (26 November 2020). Compared to the January 5, 2016 April publication, this overview has been supplemented by the qualification of four German social insurance schemes. The already assessed schemes and social insurances have not been reassessed.

an occupational pension scheme. It is noted that the *Rentenversicherung*, for example, provides for a minimum pension benefit that is not related to salary and years of contribution, but also provides for a supplementary or substitute part that does relate to salary or years of service. However, because the predominant character of the plan is that of an occupational pension scheme, and, moreover, the plan does not exceed what is allowed under the Dutch system, entitlements accrued are not taxable and contributions are deductible.[589]

However, the most recent communication added the tax treatment, under Dutch tax law, of four German statutory pension schemes.[590] With respect to the *Beamtenversorgung*, employee contributions shall be deductible and employer contributions exempt. The employee contributions for the *Alterssicherung der Landwirte* are not deductible, and the employer contributions taxed. With respect to the *Berufsständischen Versorgungseinrichtungen*, employee contributions shall be deductible and employer contributions are exempt, only if the person concerned is compulsorily insured. If there is a voluntary continuation, employer contributions are not deductible.

Furthermore, in order to avoid an adverse fiscal treatment of pension contributions paid into a foreign pension scheme, paragraph 37 of the Commentaries on the OECD Model Convention contains a provision which is intended to ensure equal treatment with contributions made domestically.[591] It applies to either statutory, occupational and individual pension schemes.[592] Suchlike provision has been laid down in article 24, para 6 of the tax treaty concluded between the Netherlands and Germany, applying to statutory pension schemes as well. Mobile taxable person concerned may have recourse to this provision enshrined in the applicable tax treaty concluded between the Netherlands and Germany. However, for this purpose the pension scheme must be 'generally equivalent' to a pension scheme recognized by that state for tax purposes.

Once retired in the residence state the Netherlands, during the pay-out phase, it remains to be seen whether and, if so, to what extent, pension benefits arising from the German statutory pension scheme will be subject to Dutch income tax. In cases where the taxing right on the foreign benefits is allocated to Germany as source state (for instance pursuant

589 This has been confirmed in ibid.
590 I will leave the *Soldatenversorgung* out of this, as it will not be discussed any further in this study.
591 See also C Bobbett and JF Avery Jones, 'Treaty Issues related to the Treatment of Cross-Border Pension Contributions and Benefits' 58 Bulletin for International Taxation; W Andreoni, 'Cross-Border Tax Issues of Pensions' 34 Intertax 245; L De Broe and R Neyt, 'European Union – Tax treatment of cross-border pensions under the OECD Model and EU law' 63 Bulletin for International Taxation.
592 See paragraph 61 of the OECD commentary on Article 18 OECD MC.

to article 17, para 2 treaty Netherlands-Germany), the German pension benefits will be subject to German taxation, pursuant to German national tax legislation. If, however, the taxing right is allocated to the Netherlands as residence state (for instance pursuant to article 17, para 1 treaty Netherlands-Germany), the German statutory pension benefits will be subject to Dutch income tax, as the pension benefits arising from German statutory pension schemes are treated as benefits arising from Dutch occupational pension schemes. The functioning of these allocation rules – embedded in the applicable tax treaty – will be discussed in chapter 9 of this research.

As this person is resident in the Netherlands, he will, commonly, be subject to unlimited tax liability in the Netherlands.[593] The payments from the German *Rentenversicherungen* are – according to the Secretary of State – to be considered as income from employment because of the relationship with the (current or past) employment of the taxpayer himself, or of someone else. These annuities and social security payments are seen as inherent to the (existence of) the employment relationship. Hence, the German statutory pension payments are, as a rule, taxed as wages.[594] Incidentally, the communication of November 2020 does not provide any clarity as to how benefits arising from *Beamtenversorgung, Alterssicherung der Landwirte, Berufsständischen Versorgungseinrichtunge* will be taxable under Dutch tax law. I assume that the general principles as formulated in the Decree of March 24, 2014 apply here *mutatis mutandis.*[595]

5.2.2.B.II Inbound

In this situation, where the Netherlands is the working state, the cross-border worker is insured, and thus obliged to pay contributions, to the Dutch statutory pension scheme (AOW).[596] Since AOW contributions are not deductible – both in internal and cross-border situations – the question does not arise to what extent these contributions can be deducted from the Dutch income of the cross-border worker, pursuant to Dutch national tax legislation. Hence, the question whether the cross-border worker in question qualifies as a qualifying foreign taxpayer can be left undiscussed.[597] As he has his residence nor his

593 Pursuant to art. 2.1, para 1, under a Wet IB 2001.

594 Pursuant to artt. 3.81 and 3.82 Wet IB 2001.

595 Staatssecretaris van Financiën, *Buitenlandse sociale verzekeringen. Duitse, Belgische en Luxemburgse sociale zekerheid. Aftrek premie en belastbaarheid uitkeringen nr. DGB 2014/144M.*

596 Pursuant to Article 11, para 3, sub a Regulation 883/2004.

597 Pursuant to article 7.8 Wet IB 2001. Based on this scheme, foreign taxpayers are still eligible for the same fiscal facilitations as domestic taxpayers (such as deductions). The essence of this scheme is to give residents of the EU, EEA, Switzerland or the BES island, 90% or more of whose income is subject to wage tax or income tax in the Netherlands, the right to the same fiscal facilitations, in accordance with EU case law. The equal treatment concerns, among other things, the right to the application of a number of personal allowances. Being a qualifying foreign taxpayer is no longer a choice (since 1 January 2015) but applies *ex officio.*

habitual abode in the Netherlands, he will not be fully liable to tax.[598] To what extent the AOW-contributions are deductible for tax purposes in Germany, is discussed in section 5.3.3.B.I.

Once retired in his residence state Germany, during the pay-out phase, it depends on the allocation of taxing rights enshrined in the applicable tax treaty where the person is liable to tax for the Dutch statutory pension benefits. As a main rule, under for instance article 17, para 1 of the treaty Netherlands-Germany, the residence state is allocated the taxing right on these pension benefits. In such as case, he will be fully liable to tax in Germany.

To what extent Germany subjects Dutch statutory pension benefits to income tax, is not discussed any further here, but I refer to section 5.3.3.B.I. This taxable proportion of the benefits is determined irrespective of whether these benefits are derived from contributions which were subject to tax relief during the pay-out phase, either in Germany or abroad.

On the contrary, if the taxing right is attributed to the Netherlands (as source state pursuant to article 17, para 2 of the treaty Netherlands-Germany), the (former) cross-border worker, residing abroad will be treated as a foreign taxable person (*buitenlands belastingplichtige*) provided that he receives domestic income, as the person concerned nor resides in the Netherlands, nor has his habitual abode in the Netherlands during the pay-out phase.[599] The AOW pension benefits will be fully liable to tax as taxable periodical benefits and benefits in kind under public law, received from or on behalf of a Dutch public law legal entity.[600] What is more, this taxable proportion of the benefits is determined irrespective of whether these benefits are derived from contributions which were subject to tax relief. Furthermore, he may apply to be treated as a qualifying foreign taxpayer.

5.2.2.C Posted Worker

A posted worker is a mobile citizen who has an employment contract in his sending state, and, carries out his work, for a limited period of time[601], in the territory of a Member State

598 Pursuant to art. 2.1, para 1, under a Wet IB 2001.

599 See article 2.1, para 1, under b in conjunction with article 7.1 and 7.2 Wet IB 2001.

600 Pursuant to article 7.2, para 2, under e Wet IB 2001.

601 Posting is temporary in nature, however, how long this 'limited period' exactly comprises differs per situation. For instance, art. 12, para 1 Regulation on the coordination of social security systems 883/2004 provides that a posted worker remains insured for social security in the 'sending state', provided that the anticipated duration of such work does not exceed 24 months and that he is not sent to replace another posted person. Moreover, this time period can be extended up to 60 months pursuant to article 16 of Regulation 883/2004. However, Directive 2018/957 amending Directive 96/71 introduced a new rule in the sense that for long-term postings (longer than 12 or 18 months), an extended set of terms and conditions of employment of the receiving Member State applies, see para 9 of the preamble. The reason for this lies in

other than the State in which he usually works.[602] They differ from other types of mobile workers in that they return, or are expected to resume working in the Member State from which he is posted after completion of the work, or the provision of services for which he was posted.[603] They, thus, do not fully integrate in the labour market of the host state, and will, hence, benefit only partially of the same working conditions and rights as workers in the host state. This is partially reflected in the tax treatment of their statutory, occupational, and personal pension schemes.

From a statutory pension point of view, generally, these posted workers will not have to deal with pension institutions in different countries when they retire, since the social security institutions in the host state(s) will not be involved.[604] As a general rule, they remain insured under the sending state's social security system, provided all conditions have been met.[605]

5.2.2.C.I Outbound

As part of the outbound posting case, a Dutch employee is sent by its Dutch employer abroad during the accrual phase, i.e. either as part of (intercompany) secondment sent to a German subsidiary, or in the framework of hiring-out-of-labour sent to a (external) separate entity.[606] It is assumed, and this is peculiar for the case of posting, that the employee concerned will continue to participate, and contribute, to the Dutch statutory pension scheme as the sending state.[607]

---

the more prevalent link between the labour market of the host Member State and the workers posted for such long periods.

602 Building on the definitions provided in art. 2 of Posting of Workers Directive 96/71; Your Europe – European Union, 'National websites on posting'; para 3 of preamble, art. 4, para 3 Enforcement Directive 2014/67 of Posting of Workers Directive 96/71.

603 Article 4, para 3, under d Directive 2014/67/EU of the European Parliament and of the Council of 15 May 2014 on the enforcement of Directive 96/71/EC concerning the posting of workers in the framework of the provision of services and amending Regulation (EU) No 1024/2012 on administrative cooperation through the Internal Market Information System [2014] OJ L 159. See also para 9 preamble Directive 2018/957 amending Directive 96/71.

604 Since, under conditions, they will be socially insured in the 'sending state' pursuant to art. 12, para 1 Regulation on the coordination of social security systems 883/2004. See also Decision No A2 of 12 June 2009 concerning the interpretation of Article 12 of Regulation (EC) No 883/2004 of the European Parliament and of the Council on the legislation applicable to posted workers and self-employed workers temporarily working outside the competent State [OJ C 106/5].

605 Laid down in art. 12 Regulation 883/2004 and Decision No A2 of 12 June 2009 concerning the interpretation of Article 12 of Regulation (EC) No 883/2004 of the European Parliament and of the Council on the legislation applicable to posted workers and self-employed workers temporarily working outside the competent State [OJ C 106/5].

606 See also paragraph 8.3 ff. of the OECD commentary on article 15 OECD MC.

607 Pursuant to art. 12, para 1 Regulation on the coordination of social security systems 883/2004.

According to the applicable treaty provision (art. 14, para 2 i.e. 183 day-rule), during the brief period of posting, the Netherlands is assigned the taxing rights as regards the remuneration. Therefore, the tax treatment, and the tax relief, of the pension contributions paid into the Dutch statutory pension scheme is a matter for the Netherlands. Contributions paid to the AOW-scheme are not deductible, see section 5.2.1.

After the limited time of posting abroad, the posted worker will return to the Netherlands.

As a main rule, under for instance article 17, para 1 of the treaty Netherlands-Germany, the residence state is allocated the taxing right on these Dutch pension benefits. In such a case, he will be fully liable to tax in the Netherlands.[608] The tax treatment of the pension benefits is then akin to a domestic situation, as the residence state and pension state coincide. For an elaborate explanation of the taxation of benefits arising from the AOW, I refer section 5.2.1. The taxable amount is based on the annual amount of the pension benefits paid out, irrespective of whether the contributions from which the benefits emerge, have been subject to tax relief, either in the Netherlands or abroad. What is more, if article 17, para 2 of the treaty Netherlands-Germany applies, the taxing right is allocated to the Netherlands (as source state) as well, and the situation is akin to the situation described above.

5.2.2.C.II Inbound

As part of the inbound posting case, a German employee is sent by its German employer to the Netherlands during the accrual phase, i.e. either as part of (intercompany) secondment sent to a Dutch subsidiary, or in the framework of hiring-out-of-labour sent to a (external) separate entity. As the posting in the Netherlands will be of limited duration, and the worker will not fully integrate in the labour market of the Netherlands, he will continue to participate, and contribute, to the German statutory pension scheme.[609] According to the applicable treaty provision (art. 14, para 2 i.e. 183 day-rule), during the period of posting, Germany (residence state) is allocated the taxing right as regards the remuneration. Therefore, the tax treatment, and the tax relief, of the pension contributions paid into the German statutory pension scheme is a matter for Germany. Contributions paid to German statutory pensions scheme are deductible, see section 5.3.2.

After the limited time of posting abroad, the posted worker will return to Germany. As a main rule, under for instance article 17, para 1 of the treaty Netherlands-Germany, Germany is allocated the taxing right on these pension benefits. In such a case, he will be

608 Pursuant to article 2.1, para 1, sub a Wet IB 2001 in conjunction with article 4, para 1 AWR.

609 Pursuant to art. 12, para 1 Regulation on the coordination of social security systems 883/2004.

fully liable to tax in Germany.[610] The tax treatment of the statutory pension benefits is then akin to a domestic situation, as the residence state and pension state coincide. For an elaborate explanation of the taxation of these benefits, I refer to section 5.3.2. What is more, if article 17, para 2 of the treaty Netherlands-Germany applies, the taxing right is allocated to Germany (as source state) as well, and the situation is akin to the situation described above.

5.3 THE GERMAN STATUTORY RETIREMENT SYSTEM: ÖFFENTLICH-RECHTLICHEN PFLICHTSYSTEME

5.3.1.A Gesetzliche Rentenversicherung

Subject to a long history of development[611], the *gesetzliche Rentenversicherung* is the primary individual social security system in Germany. The *Rentenversicherung* is for consecutive years subject to an increasing deficit, i.e. the amount of disbursed benefits exceeds the amount of contributions.[612] Up to 80% of the working population is member of the *gesetzliche Rentenversicherung*. Furthermore, the *Rentenversicherung* is covered by federal legislation.[613] Subsequently, the administrative competences are divided between the federal government and the federal states.[614] Competent institutions for the insurance of the *gesetzliche Rentenversicherung* are the regional institutions, the German federation of *Rentenversicherung* and the German *Rentenversicherung Knappschaft-Bahn-See*.[615] The *gesetzliche Rentenversicherung* is a statutory pension scheme in that the (federal) state organises the insurance.

In the past decades the *Rentenversicherung* underwent many reforms, primarily marked by retrenchment. Therefore, the public confidence in the *Rentenversicherung* as a basis pension provision has shrunk. However, in the opinion of many authors, the

610 Pursuant to § 1, para 1, sentence 1 EStG.

611 For a complete overview of the German *Rentenversicherung* from Bismarck until the unification of Germany please see R Wernsmann, 'Die steuerliche Förderung der zusätzlichen kapitalgedeckten Altersvorsorge' in E Eichenhofer, H Rische and W Schmähl (eds.), *Handbuch der gesetzlichen Rentenversicherung SGB VI* (Luchterhand, Köln 2012), chapter 1, 2 and 3.

612 Illustrated graphically: Deutsche Rentenversicherung, 'Jahresbericht' (2016) <http://www.deutsche-rentenversicherung.de/Allgemein/de/Navigation/6_Wir_ueber_uns/02_Fakten_und_Zahlen/04_Jahresbericht/jahresbericht_index_node.html> 6.

613 Art. 74, nr. 12 GG.

614 By virtue of Gesetz zur Organisationsreform in der gesetzlichen Rentenversicherung (RVOrgG). For an elaborate overview of the institutional framework: F Ruland, 'Rentenversicherung' in F Ruland and B Rürup (eds.), *Alterssicherung und Besteuerung* (Gabler, Wiesbaden 2008) 72-73.

615 § 23, para. 2, lit. 1 SGB I.

Rentenversicherung is able to withstand the economical, societal and demographic challenges and adapt to these developments continuously.[616]

The initially funded *Rentenversicherung* is since 1957/69 based on the pay-as-you-go principle.[617] This form of statutory pension has been subject to a wide range of reforms, especially between 1992 and 1999, after advancing insights, cumulating in a significant reform in 1999.[618] The underlying problem of these reforms was similar: a continuous increase of the direct and indirect contributions to the *Rentenversicherung*. This increase of direct as well as indirect contributions led to increasing gross labour costs and potentially affecting Germany's international competitive position in the international labour market.[619]

Most insured persons are insured by virtue of law.[620] This particularly applies to dependent workers or employees and, in addition, for workers similar to depended worker, such as craftsmen and artists.[621] Independent workers have the option to become compulsorily insured on application. Non-compulsorily insured persons may be insured voluntarily. Exempt from insurance are employees who are involved in short-term employment (employment within a calendar year does not exceed three months or 70 working days (2023)).[622] However, employees engaged in marginal employment (the remuneration from such employment does not regularly exceed €520 per month (2023))[623] do qualify for

616 Ruland, and cited literature.

617 See for an elaborate overview of the development of the German *Rentenversicherung*: J Rückert, 'Entstehung und Vorläufer der gesetzlichen Rentenversicherung' in F Ruland (ed.), *Handbuch der gesetzlichen Rentenversicherung: Festschrift aus Anlaß des 100jährigen Bestehens der gesetzlichen Rentenversicherung* (Luchterhand, Neuwied 1990) 1 ff.

618 AH Börsch-Supan, 'Zur deutschen Diskussion eines Übergangs vom Umlage- zum Kapitaldeckungsverfahren in der gesetzlichen Rentenversicherung' 55 FinanzArchiv 400.

619 Interesting in this regard is the discussion what comprises direct contributions either indirect contributions. Börsch-Supan considers the taxes financing the federal subsidies (*Bundeszuschuß*) for the *gesetzliche Rentenversicherung* as indirect contributions. The fiscal element in these contributions is nonetheless not decisive in this regard, since also the direct contributions (by employer and employee) have to a significant extent a fiscal character. See ibid.

620 § 2, para 1 SGB IV: „*Die Sozialversicherung umfasst Personen, die kraft Gesetzes oder Satzung (Versicherungspflicht) oder auf Grund freiwilligen Beitritts oder freiwilliger Fortsetzung der Versicherung (Versicherungsberechtigung) versichert sind.*"

621 § 2, para 2, lit 1 SGB IV. For an elaborate overview of the insured persons under the *Rentenversicherung* I refer to Wernsmann, chapter 10.

622 The so-called *kurzfristigen Beschäftigung* enshrined in § 5, para 2, nr 1 SGB VI in conjunction with § 8, para 1, nr 2 SGB IV.

623 The so-called *geringfügigen Beschäftigung* enshrined in § 8, para 1, nr 1 and para 1a SGB IV. See for the *Geringfügigkeitsgrenze* 2023: Deutsche Rentenversicherung, 'Entgeltgrenze für Minijobs steigt auf 520 Euro monatlich' 2023) <https://www.deutsche-rentenversicherung.de/DRV/DE/Rente/Allgemeine-Informationen/Wissenswertes-zur-Rente/FAQs/Gesetzesaenderungen/gesetz_mindestlohn_geringf_beschaeftigung/mindestlohn_geringf_beschaeftg.html> accessed 28 February 2023.

insurance. The insurance obligation follows the employment relationship, instead of the contractual relationship.[624] Decisive feature of the former is working in subordination.[625] Subject of the insurance is the guarantee of the provision of a retirement income on the ground of aging.[626] Standard benefit comprises (i.e. *Regelaltersrente*) the old age retirement benefit from, in principal, the age of 67.[627]

The *Rentenversicherung* constitutes a risk insurance, financed pay-as-you-go.[628] Inherent to this risk insurance character is the lack of individual savings accrual. Ruland rightly points out, that, nevertheless, the risk insurance establishes a type of asset the individual can be conferred on, for instance in case of equalisation of pension entitlements in the event of divorce, irrespective of whether the benefits already have been disbursed.[629]

The *Rentenversicherung* is primarily financed by means of contributions.[630] For 2023 the contribution rate amounts to 18.6%, of which half is to be paid by the employee (9.30%) and half by the employer.[631] The so-called *Beitragsbemessungsgrenze*[632] – i.e. the maximum level of income up to which social security contributions are due – is for 2023 set on €87,600 (West) and €85,200 (East) annually.[633] The exceeding amount of income is not liable for social security contributions. The employee's contributions are withheld from his wage by the employer.

The calculation of benefits follows primarily the amount of wages and income obtained during the insured person's insurance history.[634] Subsequently, the so-called *Entgeltpunkte*[635]

624 Pursuant to § 7, para 1 SGB IV.

625 For multiple examples please see: Ruland, 33.

626 § 23, para 1, lit b SGB I.

627 Pursuant to § 35 SGB VI. See § 235 SGB VI stipulating a gradual increase of the retirement benefit, depending on the year of birth of the beneficiary.

628 However, as Rulands points out, it can be questioned to what extent the *Rentenversicherung* as such qualifies as an insurance, since some elements can be considered atypical for insurances. Furthermore, in view of these atypical elements the social character of the *Rentenversicherung* may be called into question. See Ruland, 32.

629 Ibid. 32 referring to 53, 257 (BVerfG).

630 For an elaborate overview of the contributions and financing methods under the *Rentenversicherung* I refer to Wernsmann, chapter 11 and 23 respectively.

631 Deutsche Rentenversicherung, 'Maßgebliche Rechengrößen und Werte ab 1.1.2023 in der gesetzlichen Rentenversicherung' (2023) <https://www.deutsche-rentenversicherung.de/SharedDocs/Downloads/DE/Statistiken-und-Berichte/statistikpublikationen/aktuelle_daten.html> 2.

632 Translated freely as 'contribution income threshold'.

633 § 4, para 1 and 2 Verordnung über maßgebende Rechengrößen der Sozialversicherung für 2023 (Sozialversicherungs-Rechengrößenverordnung 2023).

634 § 63, para. 1 SGB VI. For an elaborate overview of the benefit calculation, benefit payment and benefits adjustments under the *Rentenversicherung* I refer to Wernsmann, chapter 15.

635 Translated freely as 'earning points'.

are calculated to four decimal places.[636] Principally, the insured period covers the time lapse between the age of 17 – under the condition they are employed – and the insured event, i.e., in this case, reaching the retirement age.[637] The other basic factor in the calculation formula comprises the current pension point value, i.e. *aktueller Rentenwert*.[638] The value reflects the monthly retirement benefit, in case all contributions will be paid based on the average contribution income. This value factor constitutes a dynamic factor, i.e. incorporating factors such as gross wage increases or inflation.[639] Subsequently, the calculation formula is complemented by the *Rentenartfaktor*[640], which determines the insured objective of the pension provision. It equates to one for full retirement benefits.[641] A further elaboration on the calculation of benefits is out of scope for the underlying thesis.[642] The fact remains that this complex calculation process, including its varying exceptions and particularities, may hamper the provision of effective cross-border pension information.

What is worthy of note in this respect, is the difference in the calculation of contributions and benefits of the *gesetzliche Rentenversicherung* between West and East Germany which remained in place after the unification of Germany. The underlying reason was the significant difference in salary levels between East and West.[643] It is expected that the salary levels and, in turn, the calculation rates will be levelled in future.[644] In 2023 the adjustment rates regarding the calculation between East and West still differed. Using a phased approach, these differences ought to be levelled.[645] For 2023, the current pension value for West amounts to €36.02 and for East €35.52.[646] The current pension value (East) will be 98.6% of the current pension value (West) as of July 2022, and 99.3% of the current pension value as of July 2023.

Within the *gesetzliche Rentenversicherung*, a distinction is drawn between the *allgemeine Rentenversicherung* and the *knappschaftliche Rentenversicherung*.[647] The latter is mainly

636 § 121, para. 1 SGB VI.
637 § 72, para. 2 SGV VI.
638 § 68 SGB VI.
639 § 68, para. 1 SGB VI.
640 Translated freely as 'pension type factor'.
641 § 67, nr. 1 SGB VI.
642 For an elaborate and exhaustive overview see: Ruland.
643 For instance a differentiated pension point value, pursuant to § 255a SGB VI (East).
644 Deutsche Rentenversicherung, 9.
645 See § 255a SGB VI.
646 § 68 SGB VI and § 255a SGB VI and Deutsche Rentenversicherung, 'Maßgebliche Rechengrößen und Werte ab 1.1.2023 in der gesetzlichen Rentenversicherung' 2.
647 For an elaborate overview of the *knappschaftlichen Rentenversicherung* I refer to Wernsmann, chapter 16.

characterised by more and higher benefits and higher contributions.[648] This pension provision is mainly aimed at workers in mining operations. The competent institution for the insurance of the *knappschaftliche Rentenversicherung* is the German *Rentenversicherung Knappschaft-Bahn-See.*[649] In this regard, the *knappschaftliche Rentenversicherung* may be attributed a bifunctional role, meaning that it embodies features of statutory pension as well as occupational pension-features. This bifunctionality comprises the increase of its benefits as well as its contributions out of *gesetzliche Rentenversicherung*, with approximately 33%, which increase shall be financed by the employer (forming an occupational pension-feature). This particular form of pension provision is still in place, due to the significant differences compared to the *Rentenversicherung.*[650]

Furthermore, in Germany, the *Grundsicherung im Alter* is a non-contributory minimum provision.[651] Persons entitled to benefits under this *Grundsicherung* are persons with their usual place of residence in Germany who are unable or not sufficiently able to cover their necessary subsistence from income and assets, and who have reached the age limit.[652] This *Grundsicherung* will not be discussed in more detail hereinafter as it qualifies as social welfare (*Existenzminimum*).

5.3.1.B Beambtenversorgung

This form of statutory pension provision is subject to a long history, going back to 1872 in which Prussian civil servants were granted a retirement income.[653] This particular form of pension provision for civil servants is regulated by virtue of civil service law. Therefore, it does not form part of the domain covered by the SGB.[654] This is mainly based on the principle that the legislation regarding the pension provision for civil servants and other civil service law form a legal and objective unity.[655] Therefore, the legislation regarding the pension provision for civil service may not cover benefits which are covered obligatory by other retirement provisions. Although the *Beambtenversorgung* may, from a legal point of

648 See § 3, para 1 and 2 Verordnung über maßgebende Rechengrößen der Sozialversicherung für 2023 (Sozialversicherungs-Rechengrößenverordnung 2023).

649 § 23, para. 2, lit. 2 SGB I.

650 Cf. Ruland, 72.

651 Enshrined in SGB XII.

652 In virtue of § 41, para 1 and 2 SGB XII. Persons shall be entitled to benefits on account of old age if they have reached the age limit. Persons born before 1 January 1947 shall reach the age of 65 years. For persons born after 31 December 1946, the age limit is raised as has been set out in the table enshrined in para 2 of the provision. For persons born after 1964, the age limit is set on 67.

653 For a concise overview of the historical development of the Beambtenversorgung see: F Ruland, 'Die Beambtenversorgung' in F Ruland and B Rürup (eds.), *Alterssicherung und Besteuerung* (Gabler, Wiesbaden 2008) 92.

654 § 2, para. 1 SGB I.

655 Ruland, 'Die Beambtenversorgung' 90.

view, not form a part of social security, regarding its objective – it ensures the civil servants of social security similar to the *Rentenversicherung* for the benefit of non-civil servants – it can be considered a subsystem of the overarching social security system.[656] The particular social political objective of the *Beambtenversorgung* is also underlined by the principal insurance exemption from *Rentenversicherung* for the civil servants.[657] However, if a civil servant decides to resign from civil service – without any accrued pension entitlements – he may be reinsured under the *Rentenversicherung*[658] or, upon request, under the *berufsständische Versorgungswerk*.[659] Furthermore, the *Beambtenversorgung* may be regarded as social security since the benefits are qualified as social security expenses. As Ruland rightly states, despite the differentiating financing methods – the *Rentenversicherung* is financed by means of contributions and the *Beambtenversorgung* is funded through tax revenues – both systems are based on generational levies, i.e. *Generationenumlagen*, meaning that all social security expenses should be financed by means of the national income emerging in the current period.[660] Despite the similar function and social political objective, the *Beambtenversorgung* may be distinguished from the *Rentenversicherung* in the sense that the prior is characterised by a typical occupational element, i.e. its 'bifunctionality'. The *Beambtenversorgung* combines a statutory pension in the form of social security – in the capacity of (federal) government – with occupational pension – in the capacity of employer of the civil servants. Furthermore, under the *Beambtenversorgung* – contrary to the *Rentenversicherung* – a certain amount of the last earning wage is committed as pension entitlement[661], thus leading to a 'back-service' system, which means that an increase in pensionable earnings also applies to the pensions entitlements over the previous years.

The employer – i.e. *Dienstherr* – is designated as pension provider.[662] This follows from the prevailing doctrine that the employer shall take care of his employees, even after retirement. Hence, the *Beambtenversorgung* can be considered as an internalistic system, i.e. the form of pension provider and employer are embodied within the same institution, i.e. the (federal) government. The term employer comprises the federal government, the federal

656 Ibid. 90.

657 Pursuant to § 5, para. 1, nr. 1 SGB VI.

658 Pursuant to § 8, para. 2, nr. 1 SGB VI, which states: „*Nachversichert werden Personen, die als Beamte oder Richter auf Lebenszeit, auf Zeit oder auf Probe, Berufssoldaten und Soldaten auf Zeit sowie Beamte auf Widerruf im Vorbereitungsdienst, versicherungsfrei waren oder von der Versicherungspflicht befreit worden sind, wenn sie ohne Anspruch oder Anwartschaft auf Versorgung aus der Beschäftigung ausgeschieden sind oder ihren Anspruch auf Versorgung verloren haben und Gründe für einen Aufschub der Beitragszahlung (§ 184 Abs. 2) nicht gegeben sind.*"

659 Pursuant to § 186 VI.

660 Ruland, 'Die Beambtenversorgung' and cited literature.

661 Cf. Ibid. 91.

662 This follows from § 78 BBG.

states, the municipalities, the municipal associations and other entities, institutions or foundations under public law.[663]

The *Beambtenversorgung* insures disability for service, retirement and death (for surviving relatives).[664] However, no definition of retirement has been incorporated in the federal-wide *Beamtenversorgungsgesetz.* For federal civil servants, however, this definition has been laid in the *Bundesbeamtengesetz.*[665] The insured civil servant does not have to pay contributions separately.[666] The civil service as such is considered as earning the civil servant his pension entitlements. However, it is questionable whether or not civil servants pay 'hidden' contributions withheld from their gross earnings.[667]

The general pensionable age (*Regelaltersrente)* is set on 67 years.[668] For civil servants, born prior to 1 January 1947, the pensionable age amounts to 65 years.[669] Regarding civil servants born after 31st of December 1946, the pensionable age is raised gradually since 2012.[670] For some categories of civil servants particular provision regarding the pensionable age have been provided.[671] In contrast, the pensionable age may also be postponed upon request, with in principle up to three years.[672] For professors the pensionable age may even be postponed until 75, where this is considered, by reason of particular academic accomplishments, to be in the interest of the service.[673] An elaborate overview of the eligibility criteria and benefits conditions is out of scope for the underlying thesis.[674]

The pension entitlements shall be granted provided that the civil servants' have fulfilled a period of service of a minimum of five years.[675] The provision of benefits for the benefits of civil servants is organised by virtue of law.[676] The federal legislator has only restricted competence in the area of the *Beambtenversorgung* after the federal reform of 2006.[677] Henceforth, the German constitution attributes exclusive legislative competence regarding

663 § 121 BRRG.
664 § 2, para. 1 BeamtVG.
665 § 1 and § 4 ff. BBG.
666 Cf. Ruland, 'Die Beambtenversorgung' 92.
667 Cf. Ibid. 92 and cited literature.
668 § 51, para 1 Gesetz zur Neuordnung und Modernisierung des Bundesdienstrechts (Dienstrechtsneuordnungsgesetz – DNeuG).
669 § 51, para 2 ibid.
670 § 51, para 2 ibid.
671 § 51, para 3 ibid.
672 § 53, para. 1 BeamtVG.
673 § 132, para. 7 BeamtVG.
674 For this I refer to Ruland, 'Die Beambtenversorgung'.
675 § 4, para. 1 BeamtVG.
676 § 3, para. 1 BeamtVG.
677 By virtue of 52. Gesetz zur Änderung des Grundgesetses vom 28.8.2006.

the legal relationship with persons in the service of the federal government or the federal legal entities under public law.[678] The federal government is conferred a competing legislative competence as well, with regard to the statutory rights and obligations of the civil servants in service of the federal states, municipalities or other legal entities under public law.[679] This division of competences may still lead to potentially confusing situations regarding the applicable legislative competence. Since the status of a civil servant is determined on the basis of his career path and salary grade – for which the federal governance has no legislative competence – it is unclear what the aforementioned competence comprises regarding statutory rights and obligations of the civil servants serving the federal states.[680]

5.3.1.C Berufsständische Versorgung

Similar to the gesetzlichen *Rentenversicherung, Beambtenversorgung* and *Alterssicherung der Landwirte*, this statutory pension is organised under public law as an obligatory retirement scheme. This particular pension provision is based on the legislative competence of the federal states, aiming at ensuring a retirement income for the liberal professions such as doctors, pharmacists, public notaries, attorneys, tax lawyers etc.[681] It is the aim of the underlying pension scheme to secure these liberal professionals in case of retirement, disability and provisions for the benefits of surviving relatives. From a social political perspective, the provision's aim is to secure the retirement provisions of professions which secure community goods, such as public health and the legal system. These professions are attributed the function of securing fundamental rights.[682] Hence, it is considered opportune to secure these liberal professionals' retirement income through a statutory institution. Therefore, besides fostering rejuvenation in this sector, the scheme may be attributed a role in labour market policy.[683] Most pension provisions under the *Berufsständische Versorgung* are founded as independent legal institutions or entities under public law.

The historical development of the *Berufsständische Versorgung* started in 1923 with the establishment of the Bavarian pension scheme for doctors. As Jung points out, the year of

678 By virtue of § 73, para. 1, nr. 8 GG: *„Der Bund hat die ausschließliche Gesetzgebung über die Rechtsverhältnisse der im Dienste des Bundes und der bundesunmittelbaren Körperschaften des öffentlichen Rechtes stehenden Personen."*

679 By virtue of § 74, para. 1, nr. 27 GG: *„Die konkurrierende Gesetzgebung erstreckt sich auf folgende Gebiete: die Statusrechte und -pflichten der Beamten der Länder, Gemeinden und anderen Körperschaften des öffentlichen Rechts sowie der Richter in den Ländern mit Ausnahme der Laufbahnen, Besoldung und Versorgung."*

680 Ruland, 'Die Beambtenversorgung' 98.

681 Cf. M Jung, 'Berufständische Versorgung' ibid 115.

682 Cf. JE Cramer, W Förster and F Ruland, *Handbuch Altersversorgung: gesetzliche, betriebliche und private Vorsorge in Deutschland* (Knapp, Frankfurt am Main 1998) 152.

683 Jung, 116.

establishment illustrates the underlying reasons for establishment, i.e. the period of the Weimarer Republic and the subsequent hyperinflation.[684] Accrued pension capital rapidly decreased in value and hence was no longer sufficient in order to secure a retirement income for the liberal professions. Herewith, the notion grew increasingly that also for the pension provision of these liberal professions a collective pension scheme was indispensable. The *Berufsständische Versorgung* continued to grow after the unification of Germany.[685] By now, the vast majority of all liberal professions is covered by pension provisions under the *Berufsständische Versorgung* in all German federal states.

The provision of a retirement income under the *Berufsständische Versorgung* is based on the insurance principle. Furthermore, the provisions are capital funded by means of contributions, without any federal subsidies.[686] The financing methods are based on settled principles of actuarial mathematics. The two main hybrid[687] methods of funding comprise the commonly employed *offene Deckungsplanverfahren* and the *modifizierte Anwartschaftsdeckung*.[688] The insurance objective of the pension provision under the *Berufsständische Versorgung* comprises the provision of an annuity in case of reaching a particular pensionable age. Obligatory insured persons are the members of the Chambers. They may be exempted from insurance under the *Rentenversicherung*.[689] This obligatory insurance under the *Berufsständische Versorgung* shall be terminated provided that the insured person withdraws from the profession. In such cases the former professional may, under strict conditions, request a repayment of contributions paid. The former liberal professional may also, under conditions, take out a reinsurance.[690]

The contributions may vary among the different pension providers. Most commonly the standard contribution is fixed at the maximum contribution under the *Rentenversicherung*.[691] Under other providers, the contribution has been linked to a certain percentage of the professional revenues. However, for all providers an earnings-related fixing of contributions may be in place which is, in turn, again related to particular factors in the *Rentenversicherung*

684 For an elaborate overview of the historical development I refer to: ibid. 116.

685 By virtue of § 18, para. 3 Vertrag über die Schaffung einer Währungs-, Wirtschafts- und Sozialunion zwischen der Bundesrepublik Deutschland und der Deutschen Demokratischen Republik, which states: *„Für Selbständige und freiberuflich Tätige soll bei Nachweis einer ausreichenden anderweitigen Sicherung eine Befreiung von der Sozialversicherungspflicht vorgesehen werden. In diesem Zusammenhang wird die Errichtung von berufsständischen Versorgungswerken außerhalb der Rentenversicherung ermöglicht.“*

686 Cf. Jung, 120.

687 'Hybrid' in the sense that these methods cannot be qualified as fully capital funded nor as pay-as-you-go.

688 For a further elaboration on these funding methods: Jung, 120 as well as ABV, 'Finanzierung' <http://www.abv.de/finanzierung.html> (last accessed on 16 November 2017).

689 Pursuant to § 6, para. 1, nr. 1 SGB VI.

690 § 186 SGB VI.

691 Jung, 123.

such as a contribution income threshold or the contribution rate. In this respect the *Berufsständische Versorgung* is comparable to the *Rentenversicherung*. Incidentally, contributions may be paid exceeding the obligatory rate of contributions.[692] In all cases, obligatory insured professionals shall – as a minimum – pay the contribution they would have had to pay if they were not exempted from insurance under the *Rentenversicherung*.

The retirement ages – and the related flexibility options – vary among the different pension providers under the *Berufsständische Versorgung* and are laid down in profession-specific regulations. However, over the last years these retirement ages have been raised gradually in order to secure the financial sustainability of the pension schemes. Noticeable in this regard is a strong synergy between the development in the *Rentenversicherung* and the *Berufsständische Versorgung*, i.e. intended developments are often derived from reforms in the *Rentenversicherung*.

5.3.1.D Alterssicherung der Landwirte

The *Alterssicherung der Landwirte* comprises a pension provision scheme related to the profession of agriculturalist, his spouses and the cooperating family members employed and working on the farm. Besides securing an income for retirement, this system is characterised by elements specifically aimed at fostering the agricultural industry.[693] The underlying legislation stipulates as subject of the insurance the guarantee of the provision of a retirement income on the ground of aging due to a reduction in the earning capacity.[694] However, as Deisler states, the provision is neither able nor aimed at maintaining the standard of living of the insured persons after retirement but it should rather be considered a partially insurance concept, since agriculturalist are partial insured for retirement by means of the assets substance of their company, for instance the income of rents.[695] As independent entrepreneurs, agriculturalists are, after all, in principal individually responsible for ensuring a retirement income. From a social political perspective, the *Alterssicherung der Landwirte* aims to rejuvenate the agricultural sector and strives for economically more sustainable corporate structures.[696] The significance of this policy is underlined by the so-called *Hofaufgabe*[697].[698]

692 Ibid. 123.
693 W Rombach and C Wirth, *Alterssicherung der Landwirte* (Haufe, Freiburg im breisgau 1995).
694 § 1, para. 2, lit b SGB I.
695 H Deisler, 'Die Alterssicherung der Landwirte' in B Rürup and F Ruland (eds.), *Alterssicherung und Besteuerung* (Gabler, Wiesbaden 2008) 76.
696 Ibid. 76.
697 Translated freely as 'handing over the company'.
698 Pursuant to § 11, para. 1, lit 3 ALG. This *Hofaufgabe* is compatible with the German constitution: 1 BvR 943/81 SozR (BVerfG).

As stated before, insured persons for *Alterssicherung der Landwirte* are the independent agriculturist and his cooperating family members.[699] The definition of agriculturist is also legally stipulated, mainly characterised by his independence, his agriculturist profession and the minimum size of his company.[700] Besides, this definition is characterised by legal neutrality, i.e. it covers both commercial partnerships, as well as participants of legal persons.[701] The legally stipulated eligibility criteria comprise firstly, reaching the retirement age.[702] Secondly, fulfilling the vesting period of fifteen years.[703] Lastly, the aforementioned handing over of the company, i.e. the *Hofaufgabe*.[704] Next to the obligatory insurance, agriculturists may – in order to complement or extend their entitlements – conclude, under certain conditions, a voluntary insurance, for instance in order to fulfil the condition of the waiting period of fifteen years.[705] Alternatively, an exemption of insurance is also provided for.[706]

The *Alterssicherung der Landwirte* provides a broad range of provisions, i.a. retirement income provisions, medical insurance and provisions regarding nursing care and home help in order to maintain the agricultural company. With regard to retirement provisions the following may be of interest. Firstly, the *Regelaltersrente*[707] – i.e. standard pension – of which the eligibility criteria are mentioned above. The retirement age for this provision is set on reaching the age of 67.[708] This retirement age is implemented gradually for birth cohorts as of 1964.[709] Secondly, the *Vorzeitige Altersrente*, i.e. the premature retirement provision. On the one hand the benefits may be withdrawn ten years prior to reaching the retirement age[710] – provided that the spouse already is or has been entitled to the benefits of the *Regelaltersrente* – and otherwise the benefits may be withdrawn after reaching the age of 65[711], provided that the *Hofaufgabe* is adhered to and the increased vesting period of 35 years is met. The benefits shall be granted upon request if the insured person has

699 Pursuant to § 1, para. 1 ALG.

700 Pursuant to § 1, para. 2 ALG.

701 Pursuant to § 1, para. 2 ALG.

702 § 11, para. 1, under 1 ALG.

703 § 11, para. 1, under 2 ALG.

704 § 11, para. 1, under 3 ALG. This *Hofaufgabe* is regulated in § 21 ALG.

705 Pursuant to § 4 and § 5 ALG. See for examples of cases covered by these provisions: Deisler, 78.

706 § 3 ALG.

707 Pursuant to § 11 ALG.

708 Pursuant to § 11, para. 3 ALG.

709 Pursuant to § 87a ALG.

710 Pursuant to § 12, para. 1 ALG. Also for this provision the retirement age has increased gradually for birth cohorts since 1958 pursuant to § 87b ALG.

711 Pursuant to § 12, para. 2 ALG.

reached the retirement age, the waiting period is fulfilled and the agricultural company has been transferred.[712]

Contributions are independent of the income of the insured persons, hence constituting a standard contribution.[713] However, the insured persons receive upon request an income-related allowance to this contribution, which may be considered – in its legal nature – forming a federal social security benefit.[714]

Competent institutions for the insurance of this pension provision is the German *Sozialversicherung für Landwirtschaft, Forst und Gartenbau* as the agricultural statutory old age insurance.[715] Furthermore, the provisions are financed as pay-as-you-go.[716] The income of the pension providers comprise, next to the contributions, the federal funds.[717] Moreover, the level of the contributions – as a result of an unbalanced growth of beneficiaries in comparison to the amount of contributors – has been disconnected from the development of the paid out benefits.[718] The federal government finances the shortcoming in contributions.[719] For this reason, the *Alterssicherung der Landwirte*, is not in need of fluctuation reserves, contrary to the *gesetzlichen Rentenversicherung*.[720]

5.3.2 *The Tax Treatment of the German Basisversorgung*

As a rule, all taxable persons are eligible for the deduction of contributions paid to the *Basisversorgung*, in order to guarantee that each taxable person, generally, has equal opportunities to build up a retirement provision, stemming from untaxed income.[721] This fiscal facilitation is, however, subject to the condition that the given retirement provision, for which the contributions shall be deductible, ensures that the capital will be used for an old-age provision.[722] In developing the framework of fiscal facilitation of pension contributions, the German legislator took the fiscal treatment of the *gesetzlichen Rentenversicherung* as a model. This is reflected in the fiscal facilitation of other retirement

712 For an elaborate overview of the amount of benefits please see: Deisler, 82.
713 Pursuant to § 68 ALG.
714 Deisler, 85.
715 § 23, para. 2, lit. 3 SGB I.
716 § 66, para. 1 ALG, which states: „*Die Ausgaben eines Kalenderjahres werden durch die Einnahmen des gleichen Kalenderjahres gedeckt.*"
717 § 66, para. 2 ALG.
718 Pursuant to Gesetz zur Reform der agrarsozialen Sicherung (Agrarsozialreformgesetz 1995 – ASRG 1995).
719 Pursuant to § 78 ALG.
720 Cf. Deisler, 85.
721 Pursuant to § 10, para 1, nr 2, under a EStG.
722 Rürup and Myßen, 194.

provisions that is made conditional upon the comparability between the entitlements accrued under the *gesetzlichen Rentenversicherung* and the respective retirement provision to facilitate. For this reason, the German legislator has listed limitatively, which retirement provision shall be fiscally facilitated as *Basisversorgung*: contributions to the *gesetzlichen Rentenversicherung*[723], *landwirtschaftliche Alterskassen*[724] and *berufsständischen Versorgungseinrichtungen* that provide benefits similar to the *gesetzlichen Rentenversicherung*[725]. Furthermore, contributions to other life annuities are fiscally facilitated under the *Sonderausgabenabzug*, which may not be heritable[726], transferable[727], lendable[728], saleable[729] nor capitalisable[730].[731] In addition, the latter provision may merely be paid out as a monthly lifelong annuity, after the taxable person has reached the age of 62.[732] This fiscal treatment of these statutory retirement provisions will be discussed below, after a brief overview of the legal development of the fiscal framework with regard to the statutory pensions.

723 Pursuant to § 10, para 1, nr 2, under a EStG.

724 Pursuant to § 10, para 1, nr 2, under a EStG.

725 Pursuant to § 10, para 1, nr 2, under a EStG.

726 When the beneficiary dies, the benefits nor the pension capital may be paid to the heirs. A supplementary provision for surviving dependants is however allowed. The exclusion of heritability is mandatory, since benefits under the *gesetzlichen Rentenversicherung* are excluded from inheritance as well, and the *gesetzlichen Rentenversicherung* still functions as the model for the fiscal framework for other life annuities. Cf. Rürup and Myßen, 200. Furthermore, the fostering of the earnings capacity of the heirs, as a result of the exemption from tax of particular elements of income of the testator, cannot be considered the objective the legislator had in mind as the objective of fiscally facilitating retirement provisions. Cf. P Kirchhof, H Söhn and R Mellinghof, *Einkommensteuergesetz: Kommentar zum EStG* (C.F. Müller, Heidelberg 2018).

727 The benefits may not be transferred to a person, other than the beneficiary. The transferability in the context of divorce settlements is allowed for fiscal purposes. See Rürup and Myßen, 200.

728 The entitlements may not be assigned voluntarily, nor pledged. Similar to the Dutch provision on misuse of deferred taxation, art. 19b, para 1, under c Wet op de loonbelasting 1964.

729 The entitlements may not be sold to a third party. Similar to the Dutch provision on misuse of deferred taxation, art. 19b, para 1, under c Wet op de loonbelasting 1964.

730 The entitlements may not be paid out in any other form than a life annuity, prior to reaching the retirement age. However, a small proportion of the benefits may be paid out as a lump sum (i.e. *Kleinbetragsrente*), pursuant to § 93, para 3, sentence 1 and 2 EStG. This *Kleinbetragsrente* may be paid out merely after reaching the retirement age of 60 or 62 respectively, since only then there is an annuity. See S Goverts and M Knoll, 'Anforderungen an Basisrentenprodukte ("Rürup-Rente") vor dem Hintergrund des BMF-Schreibens vom 24.2.2005' DStR 946.

731 Pursuant to § 10, para 1, nr 2, under bb and sentence 2 EStG. These conditions were already stipulated by Abschlussbericht der Sachverständigenkommission zur Neuordnung der steuerrechtlichen Behandlung von Altersvorsorgeaufwendungen und Altersbezügen (BMF-Schriftenreihe) 4.

732 For retirement provisions, concluded after 31 December 2011, a pay-out prior to reaching the age of 62 is not allowed. With respect to provisions, concluded prior to 1 January 2012, the age of 60 still applies. See RV-Altersgrenzenanpassungsgesetz.

5.3.2.A Brief Overview of the Legal Development of the Fiscal Framework with Regard to Statutory Pensions

The initial full tax liability of the *Rentenversicherung* complied with the consideration of the German legislator during the implementation of the Prussian EStG in 1891. The implementation of the *Reichseinkommensteuergesetz* was also based on this consideration. The so-called formal perception constituted the prevailing perception at that time, meaning that merely the regular payment of pension benefits increases the payment capability[733] of the beneficiaries.[734] On the contrary, in two fundamental judgements[735], the *Bundesfinanzhof* initially ruled that capital annuities[736] shall only be subject to taxation, to the extent that the income exceeds the value of the capital gains. This turning point in the pension taxation jurisprudence has had a significant impact on the dogmatic regarding the fiscal treatment of life annuities in general.[737] In line with this consideration, the *Bundesfinanzhof* ruled that, a renewed fiscal framework for the tax treatment of pension provisions was considered desirable, in particular with regard to the considerable legal relevance of the aforementioned issue.[738] For this reason, the German legislator initiated the reform of the tax treatment in 1954, and drew a legal distinction between the proportion of the capital repayment[739] and the proportion of the income benefits[740] ensued by the pension rights.[741]

The German *Basisversorgung* is principally accrued tax-free, in order to foster retirement saving by individual pension savers. In turn, the disbursed benefits are fully taxable since these are included in the amount of taxable income.[742] This division has been laid down in the table set out in § 22, para. 1 EStG to determine the taxable *Ertragsanteil*.[743] As Birk and Wernsmann claim correctly, since 1955, the *EStG* subdivides the life annuity in a taxable

733 In German commonly referred to as *Leistungsfähigkeit*.

734 Birk and Wernsmann, 231. This formal perception was confirmed by 578/579 VI A 827/27 (RFZ).

735 BFH, BStBl 18 September 1952. 1952 and BFH, BStBl 5 February 1953.

736 In German commonly referred to as *Veräußerungsrente*.

737 Cf. Birk and Wernsmann, 231.

738 BFH. See also W Schmähl, 'Steuerliche Behandlung von Altersvorsorge und Alterseinkünften' Wirtschaftsdienst 22.

739 In German commonly referred to as *Kapitalrückzahlungsanteil*.

740 In German commonly referred to as *Erträgen aus dem Rentenrecht (Stammrecht)*. *Ertrag des Rentenrechts* comprised the difference between the yearly amount of benefits (*Jahresbetrag)* and the capital repayment proportion *(Kapitalrückzahlunganteil)*. The *Kapitalrückzahlunganteil* consisted of the yearly amount of benefits, provided that the total value of the pension rights was paid out equally over the remaining pay-out periods. Cf. Birk and Wernsmann, 231 and cited literature.

741 Laid down in § 22, para 1, sentence 3 EStG.

742 In German: *Bemessungsgrundlage*. This taxation method shows similarity with the Dutch method of taxing statutory pension benefits (AOW), pursuant to article 34 Wet op de loonbelasting 1964 in conjunction with article 11, paragraph 1, lit c Uitvoeringsbesluit loonbelasting 1965.

743 Translated freely as 'income proportion'. In this, *Ertrag* refers to *Ertrag des Rentenrechts*.

Ertragsanteil and a tax-exempted *Rentenstamm*, comprising the aforementioned capital repayment.[744]

The pension contributions, paid during the active working period of the beneficiary were also deductible for tax purposes in the Prussian *EStG* of 1891, as *Sonderausgabenabzug*. Since then, this tax deductibility of the contributions has been upheld in later codifications of the *EStG*.[745] In contrast, the contributions paid by the employer for the *gesetzlichen Rentenversicherung* have been regarded as non-taxable, since by paying these contributions, the employer fulfils an obligation pursuant to public law and, thus, the pension contribution cannot be considered forming remuneration for work performed by the employee.[746]

The above-described tax treatment led to the question to what extent this tax treatment could be considered in conformity with the constitutional principle of equal treatment.[747] The partial tax-free benefit accrual under the *gesetzlichen Rentenversicherung*, i.e. the *Rentenstammrecht*, led to benefits being paid out partially tax-free. In contrast, benefits under occupational pensions were fully taxed as belated earned income.[748] The German legislator tried to solve these fiscal incongruences between *Renten* and *Pensionen* through the granting of a *Versorgungsfreitbetrag* for the benefits of beneficiaries of *Pensionen*.[749] The judgement of the *Bundesverfassungsgericht* in 2002[750] offered the first opportunity to fundamentally renew the tax treatment of old age provisions in the German pension landscape. Subsequently, the *Sachverständigenkommission*[751] outlined a newly designed fiscal framework for old age provisions, based on the principle of deferred taxation.[752] The

---

744 Birk and Wernsmann, 231.

745 Cf. Ibid. 231 and cited literature.

746 Confirmed in BFH, BStBl II 6 June 2002. 2003. Hence, the tax exemption laid down in § 3, para 62 *EStG* insofar has declaratory effect only. Birk and Wernsmann, 231 and Cramer, Förster and Ruland, 837. § 3, para 62 EStG states: „*Steuerfrei sind Ausgaben des Arbeitgebers für die Zukunftssicherung des Arbeitnehmers, soweit der Arbeitgeber dazu nach sozialversicherungsrechtli-chen oder anderen gesetzlichen Vorschriften oder nach einer auf gesetzlicher Ermächtigung beruhenden Bestimmung verpflichtet ist*". Furthermore, some situations – i.a. in which the employee is not ensured for the gesetzlichen Rentenversicherung – are for fiscal purposes equated with situations under which the employee is ensured for gesetzlichen Rentenversicherung. It seems that this equation of tax deductibility ensures the equal treatment of these different pension provisions for tax purposes.

747 Laid down in §3 GG.

748 Pursuant to § 19, para 1, under 2 EStG.

749 See Birk and Wernsmann, 232 and cited literature regarding the controversiality of this solution. For an exhaustive overview of the historical development of the *EStG* see Kirchhof, Söhn and Mellinghof.

750 Ibid.

751 Translated freely as 'expert commission'.

752 Abschlussbericht der Sachverständigenkommission zur Neuordnung der steuerrechtlichen Behandlung von Altersvorsorgeaufwendungen und Altersbezügen (BMF-Schriftenreihe). For a discussion on the reform options see Schmähl.

newly designed fiscal framework was implemented through the *Alterseinkünftegesetz*[753], and the tax system reform was materialized on 1 January 2005.[754]

5.3.2.B The Deductibility of Contributions

Until 31 December 2004, the legal framework regarding the deductibility of contributions was standardised, irrespective of the form of pension contribution.[755] After the entry into force of the *Alterseinkünftegesetz*, the German legislator abandoned this uniform approach. The eligibility of the deduction of pension contributions then differentiated into, on the one side, the contributions to basic retirement provisions in the first pillar, and on the other side, the other contributions to retirement provisions.

As of 2025, contributions to the so-called *Basisversorgung* (i.e. *gesetzlichen Rentenversicherung, landwirtschaftlichen Alterskassen, berufsständischen Versorgungswerken* and the *Rürup-Rente)* shall be fully deductible as *Sonderausgaben*, under the condition that these contributions are – for tax purposes – not taken into account as operating costs[756] or *Werbungskosten*, nor fiscally treated similarly.[757] As regards the *gesetzlichen Rentenversicherung*, this applies to contributions paid to domestic statutory pension institutions, as well as to foreign statutory pension institutions.[758] Furthermore, the taxable person must incur the deductible contributions. As regards the employer's contributions, these are tax-free on the part of the employee.[759] Under the *Beambtenversorgung*, the insured civil servant does not have to pay contributions

753 Gesetz zur Neuordnung der einkommensteuerrechtlichen Behandlung von Altersvorsorgeaufwendungen und Altersbezügen (Alterseinkünftegesetz – AltEinkG).

754 For a concise overview of the tax treatment of German statutory pensions, under the legislation in force until 31 December 2004, See R Brügelmann and W Fuest, *Besteuerung der Altersvorsorge und Alterseinkünfte: ein Vergleich verschiedener Formen der gesetzlichen und privaten Alterssicherung* (Beiträge zur Ordnungspolitiek Institut der deutschen Wirtschaft Köln, Deutscher Instituts-Verlag GmbH, Köln 2003).

755 Cf. Kirchhof, Söhn and Mellinghof.

756 I.e. *Betriebsausgaben*.

757 Pursuant to § 10, para 1, nr 2, under a EStG, which provision states: „*Sonderausgaben sind die folgenden Aufwendungen, wenn sie weder Betriebsausgaben noch Werbungskosten sind oder wie Betriebsausgaben oder Werbungskosten behandelt werden: Beiträge zu den gesetzlichen Rentenversicherungen oder zur landwirtschaftlichen Alterskasse sowie zu berufsständischen Versorgungseinrichtungen, die den gesetzlichen Rentenversicherungen vergleichbare Leistungen erbringen;*".

758 See also BMF, *Einkommensteuerrechtliche Behandlung von Vorsorgeaufwendungen IV C 3 - S 2221/16/10001:004* (24 May 2017) para 4. See also X R 57/06 BStBl 2009 II S. 1000 (BFH) in which the Bundesfinanzhof ruled that the European fundamental freedoms of a frontier worker are not infringed by the limited deduction of *Sonderausgaben* even if another Member State subjects the corresponding pension income to taxation in their entirety on the basis of the right of taxation allocated to it by the double taxation agreement, concluded with Germany.

759 Pursuant to § 3, nr 62 EStG.

separately.[760] The civil service as such is considered as earning the civil servant his pension entitlements. Hence, the deductibility of contributions is not an issue.

With respect to *landwirtschaftliche Alterskasse*, it should be stressed that merely the person legally obliged to contribute to the retirement provision, is entitled to deduct these contributions, if the contributions will be used for the accrual of his own retirement provision. Besides, if the beneficiary is entitled to certain contribution allowances pursuant to the *Gesetz zur Alterssicherung der Landwirte*, these will be offset against the deductible contributions.[761] Regarding the *berufsständischen Versorgungseinrichtungen*, the contributions are merely deductible when the future provided benefits are similar to the *gesetzlichen Rentenversicherung*.[762] The German tax authorities issued a list of the providers of benefits under the *berufsständischen Versorgungseinrichtungen*, which are considered providing benefits comparable to the benefits arising from the *gesetzlichen Rentenversicherung*.[763] To meet this condition, a comparability of benefits is sufficient, i.e. an equivalence with benefits under *gesetzlichen Rentenversicherung* is not required.[764]

The deductibility of contributions is capped at 8% of the *Beitragsbemessungsgrenze* in the *allgemeinen Rentenversicherung*.[765] The employer's tax-exempt contribution to the statutory pension scheme – pursuant to § 3 nr 62 – and a tax-exempt employer's allowance (*Zuschuss*) equivalent thereto shall be added to these contributions.[766] For spouses, and life partners who file their tax returns jointly, this maximum amount shall be doubled, irrespective of who has paid the facilitated contributions.[767] Moreover, the maximum amount shall be reduced for particular categories of persons.[768] This amount of maximum contributions deduction is based on the consideration that contributions paid to this amount, ought to lead to the accrual of an adequate basic pension provision.[769] Furthermore,

760 Cf. Ruland, 'Die Beambtenversorgung' 92.

761 Kirchhof, Söhn and Mellinghof, and Rürup and Myßen, 196.

762 Pursuant to § 10, para 1, nr 2, under a EStG. Regarding the comparability of the benefits, see H Hügelschäffer and others, *Handbuch Alterssicherung* (C.F. Müller, Heidelberg 2006) and Kirchhof, Söhn and Mellinghof.

763 BMF, *Anwendung des § 10 Abs. 1 Nr. 2 Buchstabe a EStG i.d.F. des AltEinkG bei Beiträgen an berufsständische Versorgungseinrichtungen IV C 8-S 2221 - 128/06* (7 February 2007).

764 Rürup and Myßen, 197.

765 This has been raised from 4 to 8% pursuant to the *Betriebsrentenstärkungsgesetz*, see art. 9, para 2, letter 2, under aa Gesetz zur Stärkung der betrieblichen Altersversorgung und zur Änderung anderer Gesetze (Betriebsrentenstärkungsgesetz).

766 § 10, para 1, nr 2, sentence 6 EStG and BMF, *Einkommensteuerrechtliche Behandlung von Vorsorgeaufwendungen IV C 3 - S 2221/16/10001:004* nr. 60.

767 § 10, para 3, sentence 2 EStG and ibid. nr. 60.

768 § 10, para 3, sentence 3. For instance, civil servants, judges, professional soldiers, temporary soldiers and public officials, see ibid., nr. 65.

769 Birk and Wernsmann, 239 and cited literature.

the contributions paid are deemed to have been used for the accrual of a statutory pension, nor is it differentiated whether the contribution is obligatory or voluntary.[770]

It is arguable whether pension contributions – from a tax-systematical viewpoint – ought to be deductible as *Werbungskosten* or as *Sonderausgaben*, each qualification leading to different fiscal consequences.[771] The German legislator could have qualified the contributions as *Werbungskosten*, in conformity with the advice of the *Rürup-Kommission*. Regarding the legislative systematic laid down in the EStG, the qualification of pension contributions as *Werbungskosten*, in principle, takes precedence over the qualification as *Sonderausgaben*.[772] The reasoning that pension contributions should be considered *Sonderausgaben* even holds true with respect to the fundamental principle underlying the German income tax legislation, i.e. mere asset shifts are irrelevant for tax purposes.[773] Contributions may be considered the reduction of assets. From a fiscal perspective, however, these reductions do not exist if the beneficial gains an equivalent asset.[774] For instance, if the taxable person purchases a plot of ground in order to build a house, which will be let, these purchasing costs are not deductible as *Werbungskosten*. Hence, costs that serve the attainment of income[775] cannot be regarded as *Werbungskosten*, nor as operating costs. Since pension benefits may be regarded as savings accrual, resulting from previous financial success – and not as contributions meant for the attainment of income – and as measures of the application of income[776], they cannot be qualified as *Werbungskosten*, rather as *Sonderausgaben*.[777]

5.3.2.C The Taxation of Retirement Benefits

An immediate transition in 2005 to full deferred taxation of benefits, arising from the *gesetzlichen Rentenversicherung*, was considered ineligible, since this would lead to a significant degree of double taxation of parts of the benefits paid out.[778] These accrued retirement benefits originate from three elements: the employer's part, the employee's part and the federal subsidy[779]. The employer's part of the contributions to *gesetzlichen*

---

770 Cf. Rürup and Myßen, 195.

771 The concrete consequences of each of these qualifications for tax purposes is beyond the scope of this section. For this, See Birk and Wernsmann, 239 and cited literature.

772 § 10, para 1, nr 2, under a EStG states: „*Sonderausgaben sind die folgenden Aufwendungen,* wenn sie weder Betriebsausgaben noch Werbungskosten sind *oder wie Betriebsausgaben oder Werbungskosten behandelt werden*".

773 Cf. BFH, BStBl II 21 December 1982. 1983.

774 Cf. Birk and Wernsmann, 240 and cited literature.

775 I.e. *Einkünfteerzielung*.

776 I.e. *Einkommenserzielung*.

777 Cf. Birk and Wernsmann, 241 and cited literature.

778 Ibid. 243.

779 I.e. *Bundeszuschuss*.

Rentenversicherung is not liable for tax.[780] Hence, the employer's part of the contributions is not regarded taxable *Arbeitslohn* on the side of the employee.[781] Furthermore, the federal subsidy part is exempted from taxation as well.

Principally, statutory pension benefits are – under the principle of deferred taxation – fully taxed in the pay-out phase. Benefits paid out of *gesetzlichen Rentenversicherung, landwirtschaftlichen Alterskasse, berufsständischen Versorgungseinrichtung*[782] shall, as of 2040, be fully subject to taxation.[783] From 2005 until 2040 the benefits shall only partially be liable to tax, in accordance with the *Besteuerungsanteil.* The taxable amount is based on the annual amount of the pension benefits paid out. This annual amount shall be multiplied with the percentage of the taxable proportion.[784] This percentage is determined in the first year of benefits pay-out, and then fixed for the remainder of the pay-out phase. This applies from the year following the year of retirement for the entire duration of the pay-out phase.[785] For instance, if the beneficiary retires in 2023, 83% shall be included in the tax base of the taxable person, and subject to taxation. By way of derogation from this, the tax-free part of the pension shall be adjusted when the annual amount of the pension changes. This adjustment is calculated in proportion to the change in the annual pension amount, to the annual pension amount used to determine the tax-exempt part of the pension.[786] The difference between the annual amount of pension and the taxable proportion of the pension constitutes the tax-free amount of pension.[787]

5.3.2.D Transitional Law Leading to (Intertemporal) Double Taxation

The current design of the transitional regime regarding the fixation of the *Besteuerungsanteil*, and the relating tax-free part of the pension benefit paid out[788], leads in certain years (cohorts) to a double taxation of the contributions and the financial return[789] (i.e. the

780 Pursuant to § 3, nr 62 EStG, which provision states: *„Steuerfrei sind: Ausgaben des Arbeitgebers für die Zukunftssicherung des Arbeitnehmers, soweit der Arbeitgeber dazu nach sozialversicherungsrechtlichen oder anderen gesetzlichen Vorschriften oder nach einer auf gesetzlicher Ermächtigung beruhenden Bestimmung verpflichtet ist, und es sich nicht um Zuwendungen oder Beiträge des Arbeitgebers nach den Nummern 56 und 63 handelt."*

781 Translated freely as 'earned income'.

782 Pursuant to § 10, para 1, nr 2, under b EStG.

783 Pursuant to § 22, nr 1, sentence 3, under a, sub aa EStG.

784 This percentage of taxable proportion can be derived from the table listed in § 22, nr 3, under aa EStG.

785 § 22, under aa, sentence 5 EStG. This is accordance with the so-called *Kohortenprinzip*, i.e. the 'principle of cohorts'.

786 § 22, under aa, sentence 6 EStG. Regular adjustments to the annual amount of pension, however, do not lead to a recalculation, and will be disregarded for the recalculation and, hence, will be fully liable to taxation, see § 22, under aa, sentence 7 EStG.

787 § 22, under aa, sentence 4 EStG.

788 Pursuant to § 22, nr 3, under aa EStG.

789 I.e. *Kapitalrückflusses.*

pension benefits).[790] This claim is valid in cases where the beneficial retires in or after 2040, since in these cases the benefits paid out will be fully subject to tax. These benefits then partially consist of the repayment of pension capital already taxed during the accrual phase.[791]

For these beneficiaries, retiring in 2040 and born after 1975, the retirement age is 65. As a result of the increasing retirement age as regards the *gesetzliche Rentenversicherung*, this fiscal issue is growing steadily. Provided that in 2040 the retirement age of 67 applies, these retirees were born in 1973, in which cases the proportion of already taxed income in the pension benefits will be even higher. This fiscal issue mainly relates to the group of beneficiaries paying contributions since the 1990s. In these cases, the employee contributions were not fully deductible.[792] In particular, employees born in 1975 are affected by this double taxation, although the effect of double taxation arises from the birth year 1955.[793]

The classification of the taxable proportion of pensions for the respective cohorts of pensioners on the basis of the retirement year[794], may, however, not lead to double taxation of similar income components.[795] Regarding the foregoing, this may lead to the conclusion that the aforementioned principle of cohorts – which principle underlies the table of the *Besteuerungsanteil* in § 22, nr 3, letter aa EStG – in some cases can be considered at odds with the principle of no double taxation.[796] The double taxation of the pension seems for employees retiring between 2018 and 2066 rather a rule than an exception.[797]

790 Birk and Wernsmann, 243. See also Wernsmann, 785.

791 For elaborate calculation examples, see C Herrmann, G Heuer and A Raupach, *Einkommensteuer- und Körperschaftsteuergesetz: EStG KStG* (Dr. Otto Schmidt, Köln Aktualisierung 2018), para 337.

792 Due to the maximum amount of deductibility in accordance with § 10, para 3 EStG. Cramer, Förster and Ruland, 833 ff. See also Birk and Wernsmann, 244.

793 Birk and Wernsmann refer to calculations of the VDR on the basis of which they reached this conclusion. These calculations, however, can no longer be retrieved. See Birk and Wernsmann, 244.

794 By virtue of § 22, nr 3, under aa EStG.

795 Birk and Wernsmann, 244.

796 In this regard BVerfG 25 March 2002, 2 BvL 17/99, 105, 73 in which decision the BVerfG ruled that „*in jedem Fall sind die Besteuerung von Vorsorgeaufwendungen für die Alterssicherung und die Besteuerung von Bezügen aus dem Ergebnis der Vorsorgeaufwendungen so aufeinander abzustimmen, dass eine doppelte Besteuerung vermieden wird.*" As Birk and Wernsmann point out, „in jedem Fall" (i.e. in any case) does not necessarily mean that each classification for fiscal purposes shall not be applied. For this see ibid. 244, footnote 91.

797 L Osterloh, K Schmidt and H Weber, *Staat, Wirtschaft, Finanzverfassung.: Festschrift für Peter Selmer zum 70. Geburtstag* (Schriften zum Öffentlichen Recht, Duncker & Humblot, Berlin 2004) 889. Birk and Wernsmann argue that in this respect, and with regard to the number of employees affected by this double taxation, and the significant amount of double tax, that the German legislator has exceeded the limits of the acceptable. As they state, a basic tax allowance (*Grundfreibetrag)* would not offer an adequate solution since this comprises not an specific tax allowance for pension income but, rather, a general tax exemption for

In this respect, constitutional concerns with regard to § 22, nr 3, under aa EStG may exist to the extent that the full taxation of the benefits paid out is achieved too early and, especially for employees retiring after 2018, may lead to considerable double taxation.[798] In comparison to recipients of other retirement benefits, the level of taxation may be considered too high. As the *Bundesverfassungsgericht* and *Bundesfinanzhof* ruled, the avoidance of double taxation can only be criticized at the time it will be realised, i.e. the question of unconstitutionality of § 22, nr 3, under aa EStG will be first raised when the employees of the aforementioned birth cohorts retire, and the double taxation will occur.[799] The court ruled that the principle of avoiding double taxation does not give any entitlement to the deductibility of contributions during the accrual phase, since the German legislator may take this constitutional breach into account during the pay-out phase as well. It may be stated that with regard to this intertemporal taxation, a certain level of (intertemporal) coordination is missing. The pensions should either be taxed during the accrual phase or during the pay-out phase.[800]

5.3.3 *Tax Treatment of German Statutory Pensions in Cross-border Situations*

The globalisation of the economy and the related increase in the mobility of workers implies that the taxation of pensions must not solely be considered from a purely national perspective, but also account must be taken of cross-border aspects. Below the tax treatment of German statutory pensions in cross-border cases will be discussed, both during the accrual phase as well as in the pay-out phase. As regards the accrual phase, the analysis focuses on whether tax advantages are granted, while, as regards the pay-out phase it is considered how, and to what extent, (foreign and domestic) pension benefits are subjected to tax. It will become evident below that provisions of national tax law governing the taxation of retirement income, are applied on the basis of an 'isolated approach', without taking into account any previous or subsequent tax treatment in another (member) state. As there is no German mandatory legal principle of tax law requiring a direct connection between the taxation of benefits and the deductibility of contributions (i.e.

---

which all taxpayers may be eligible, apart from the fact that the *Grundfreibetrag* would not offer an adequate solution from the standpoint of legal doctrine. See Birk and Wernsmann, 245, footnote 96.

798 Birk and Wernsmann, 245.

799 See also BFH, BStBl II 1 February 2006. 2006d. This is considered critically by Herrmann, Heuer and Raupach, par. 337.

800 BVerfG 25 March 2002, 2 BvL 17/99, 105, 73 2002). BVerfG. in which judgement the court ruled: *„Fehlt ein Mindestmaß an gegenseitiger* Abstimmung *zwischen ausgleichsbedürftigen Nachteilen einerseits und begünstigenden Ausgleichswirkungen andererseits, so entfällt zugleich der nachvollziehbare Grund für eine ungleich wirkende steuerliche Vergünstigung.“*

coherence), provisions of foreign law are not mentioned in the EStG nor does it contain a general rule that a tax benefit, provided pursuant to foreign tax law, shall be treated equally to the application of the EStG's provision.[801]

It is to be noted at this point, that the allocation of the taxing rights pursuant to a tax treaty, is taken into account as a proviso/prerequisite for the exercise of taxing rights pursuant to domestic (German) tax legislation. These distribution rules will be discussed in chapter 9. The normative framework pertaining to the tax treatment of cross-border pensions, enshrined in EU law, will be discussed in chapter 8.

Different fiscal measures will be considered in this regard. If the employee's pension contributions have been fiscally facilitated, the state of departure has an interest in taxing the retirement benefits as well. A possible (domestic[802]) measure of safeguarding the fiscal interests of the country of departure in the event that a pension saver moves to a country that has been allocated the right to tax the pension benefits pursuant to a tax treaty is to subject the subsidised retirement provision contributions retroactively to tax. Other countries seek to preserve their fiscal interests in cases where taxpayers move away, by, notwithstanding the applicable tax treaty concluded with the country of immigration, extending the unlimited tax liability or stipulate an extended form of limited tax liability, to the time frame after immigration.[803] These types of fiscal measures will be dealt with in more detail below. Furthermore, in cases where a source state taxation has been enshrined in the applicable bilaterally concluded tax treaty (as in article 17, para 2 of the tax treaty Netherlands-Germany), the question rises how pension benefits, paid to foreign recipients, subject to limited tax liability, are taxed in the source state, pursuant to its domestic tax legislation.

If the German taxable person, for instance a migrant worker who resided and worked in Germany, decides to leave Germany and emigrates to another countries, this leads to fiscal consequences with respect to the retirement provisions accrued during his active period

801 See also R Portner, 'Besteuerung der Auszahlung aus einem U.S.-Altersversorgungsplan – selbst wenn die Beiträge ausschließlich nach U.S.-Steuerrecht gefördert sind und die Summe der eingezahlten Beiträge unter dem Auszahlungsbetrag liegt?' 20 BetriebsBerater 1175, 1177.

802 Contrary to seeking to agree on a (conditional) source state taxation of pension benefits pursuant to a bilaterally concluded tax treaty as discussed in chapter 9 of this research.

803 See for instance article 4, para 4 of the tax treaty concluded between Germany and Switzerland. This treaty provision sets out that in the case of a natural person resident in Switzerland who is not a Swiss national and who has been subject to unlimited tax liability in the Federal Republic of Germany for a total of at least five years, the Federal Republic of Germany may, notwithstanding other provisions of the treaty, tax the income originating in the Federal Republic of Germany and the assets located in the Federal Republic of Germany in the year in which the unlimited tax liability last ceased to exist and in the following five years. The taxation of such income or assets in Switzerland permissible under this treaty shall remain unaffected.

in Germany. In particular, these consequences can be considered significant because of the deferred taxation of pensions in Germany, since the principle of deferred taxation stipulates that the fiscally deductible pension contributions paid out of untaxed income during the accrual phase, give rise to benefits paid out during the pay-out phase, which shall be subject to taxation.[804] This can be referred to as the internal coherence of the national tax system. Since the former German taxable person is no longer unlimitedly subject to taxation in Germany, the German tax authorities would seek to guarantee that the future benefits, paid out during the accrual phase abroad, will be subject to taxation. The tax authorities shall strive to recover the lack of tax revenues as a result of the emigration of the former German taxable person. The fiscal interest of Member States may be guaranteed by several measures, for instance extending the tax liability beyond emigration.[805] However, it can be pointed out at the outset that under none of the statutory pension schemes discussed below, the tax relief provided during the period of residence in Germany, is reclaimed upon migration to another State.

In light of the above, the aim of this section is to analyse the tax treatment of pension schemes at the employee level. It is explored to what extent tax relief is granted for pensions in the form of tax base advantages (e.g. tax exemptions, allowances, deduction from the taxable base, deduction from the tax liability) or tax rate advantages (e.g. flat tax rate). The allocation of company pension expenses at employer level is left aside.

5.3.3.A Migrant Worker

As pointed out above, commonly the mobile worker will, during retirement, not reside in the same state as where he resided during the accrual phase (migration). In the accrual phase, the state of employment and the state of residence coincide, whereas in the pay-out phase the state of residence of the (former) employee differs from the (former) state of employment. Where in an outbound migration situation discussed in this section, the employee is resident in the national territory of Germany during the accrual phase and lives abroad (Netherlands) during the pay-out phase, in the inbound case, the employee is resident in the Netherlands during the accrual phase, while being a resident of Germany during the pay-out phase. It can be pointed out at the outset that under none of the statutory pension schemes discussed below, the tax relief provided during the period of residence in Germany, is reclaimed upon migration to another State.

---

804 Cf. R Wernsmann and A Nippert, 'Altersbesteuerung beim Wegzug und Europäisches Gemeinschaftsrecht' FR 1123. In BVerfG, 25 March 2002. the *Bundesverfassungsgericht* ruled that the taxing right is postponed/deferred.

805 Cf. D Wellisch and others, *Besteuerung der Altersvorsorge: ein international Vergleich* (Schriften des Institutes der Ausländisches und Internationales Finanz- und Steuerwesen der Universität Hamburg, Nomos, Baden-Baden 2008) 48.

5.3.3.A.I Outbound

In the outbound case, the employee is resident in Germany (partly) during the accrual phase. The tax treatment and the granting of tax relief is hence akin to the tax treatment in a domestic situation, i.e. there is no cross-border situation. There is no nexus with Dutch income tax, levied during the accrual phase. I therefore refer to section 5.3.2. In short, contributions to the *Basisversorgung* (i.e. *gesetzliche Renteversicherung, landwirtschaftliche Alterskasse, berufsständische Versorgungswerke* and the *Rürup-Rente)* shall be deductible as *Sonderausgaben*, under the condition that these contributions are – for tax purposes – not taken into account as operating costs[806] or *Werbungskosten*, nor fiscally treated similarly.[807]

However, during the pay-out phase, the person concerned resides in the Netherlands. Pension benefits arising from German statutory pension schemes are thus paid out abroad. It depends on the allocation of taxing rights enshrined in the applicable tax treaty where the person is liable to tax for the German statutory pension benefits. If the taxing rights is allocated to Germany as a source state (for instance pursuant to article 17, para 2 treaty Netherlands-Germany), these benefits constitute *Sonstige Einkünfte*, taxed pursuant to § 22, nr 1, sentence 3, letter a, double letter aa, against the *Besteuerungsanteil*. This taxable proportion of the benefits is determined irrespective of whether these benefits are derived from contributions which were subject to tax relief. In 2023, 83% of the benefits are subject to tax.

In addition to the question of whether the tax treaty concluded with the country of migration grants the country of departure a right of taxation, it is equally important to explore to what extent the country of departure includes foreign retirement benefits in the limited tax liability. As the person concerned nor resides in Germany, nor has his habitual abode in Germany, during the pay-out phase he may be subject to limited tax liability pursuant to § 1, para 4 EStG, provided that he receives domestic income within the meaning of § 49 EStG. The principal condition for including these elements of income in the limited tax liability is a domestic source of income.[808] Certain forms of retirement income are considered domestic income, i.e. income from the domestic providers or the *gesetzliche Rentenversicherung, landwirtschaftliche Alterskasse, berufsständische Versorgungseinrichtungen* or domestic insurance companies.[809] These retirement provisions

806 I.e. *Betriebsausgaben*.

807 Pursuant to § 10, para 1, nr 2, under a EStG.

808 Pursuant to § 49, para 1, nr 7 EStG.

809 § 49, para 1, nr 7, which refers to § 22, nr 1, sentence 3, under aa EStG.

have always been subject to the limited tax liability.[810] A domestic source, underlying these elements of income, is no longer required. If the taxable person concluded a *Rürup-Rente* at a foreign EU insurer, the contributions paid during the accrual phase were deductible as *Sonderausgaben*[811], and the future benefits will be included in the limited tax liability[812], since these benefits will be considered domestic income.[813] As mentioned above, this does not apply when the tax treaty does not allocate the taxing right with respect to the retirement benefits to Germany, despite the fact that the limited tax liability shall apply pursuant to German national legislation, and despite the fact that the elements of income are considered domestic income.[814] If the taxing right is allocated to the Netherlands as a residence state (for instance pursuant to article 17, para 1 treaty Netherlands-Germany), German statutory pension benefits will be subject to Dutch income tax. For this I refer to section 5.2.2.B.I.

5.3.3.A.II Inbound

In the inbound case, the employee is a resident of the Netherlands (partly) during the accrual phase, and takes up residence in Germany at the commencement of the pay-out phase. As the person concerned lives and resides in the Netherlands during the accrual phase, he will be subject to the statutory pension schemes in the Netherlands, i.e. there is no cross-border situation. There is no nexus with German income tax, levied during the accrual phase. The tax treatment and the granting of tax relief is hence akin to the tax treatment in a domestic situation, see section 5.2.1.

However, as the person will relocate his residence to Germany during the pay-out phase, it remains to be seen whether and, if so, to what extent, pension benefits derived from a Dutch statutory pension scheme will be subject to German income tax. In cases where the taxing right on the Dutch benefits is allocated to Germany as residence state (pursuant to article 17, para 1 treaty Netherlands-Germany), the Dutch pension benefits will be subject to German taxation, pursuant to German national tax legislation. As the person resides in Germany during the pay-out phase, he will be subject to unlimited tax liability pursuant to § 1, para 1, sentence 1 EStG. Benefits arising from foreign statutory pension schemes are treated as akin to benefits arising from domestic statutory pension schemes, i.e. taxed

810 § 49, para 1, nr 7 EStG in conjunction with § 22, nr 1, sentence 3, under a EStG. Cf. R Wernsmann, 'Die steuerliche Förderung der zusätzlichen kapitalgedeckten Altersvorsorge' in E Eichenhofer, H Rische and W Schmähl (eds.), *Handbuch der gesetzlichen Rentenversicherung SGB VI* (Luchterhand, Köln 2012) 794.

811 § 10, para 1, nr 2, under b in conjunction with § 10, para 2, nr 2, under a EStG.

812 Pursuant to § 1, para 4 in conjunction with § 49, para 1 EStG.

813 § 49, para 1, nr 7 in conjunction with § 10, para 2, nr 2 EStG.

814 See C Richter, *Die Besteuerung grenzüberschreitender Altersversorgung in der EU* (Rechtsordnung und Steuerwesen, Dr. Otto Schmidt, Köln 2010) 352 ff. for elaborate considerations regarding the theoretical basis of the taxing right of the source state.

against the *Besteuerungsanteil* as laid down in § 22, nr 1, sentence 3, letter a, double letter aa EStG. The proportion actually subject to tax is determined by the year of commencement of the pay-out phase. This taxable proportion of the benefits is determined irrespective of whether these benefits are derived from contributions which were subject to tax relief during the pay-out phase, either in Germany or abroad.

If the taxing rights is allocated to the Netherlands as a source state (for instance pursuant to article 17, para 2 treaty Netherlands-Germany), Dutch AOW pension benefits will be subject to Dutch income tax. The beneficiary residing abroad will be treated as a foreign taxable person (*buitenlands belastingplichtige*) provided that he receives domestic income, as the person concerned nor resides in the Netherlands, nor has his habitual abode in the Netherlands during the pay-out phase.[815] The AOW pension benefits will be fully liable to tax as taxable periodical benefits and benefits in kind under public law, received from or on behalf of a Dutch public law legal entity.[816]

5.3.3.B Cross-border (Frontier) Worker

As stated above, a mobile citizen may work in one State, while residing in another (neighbouring) Member State, to which he usually returns every day, or at least once a week (commonly referred to as 'frontier worker', or 'border commuter'). The working state is thus different from the residence state. However, triangular situations, where the pension institution is established in a third state, is left aside for the present research. Where in the outbound situation, Germany is the residence state and the Netherlands the working state; in the inbound situation, Germany is the working state and the Netherlands is the residence state.

5.3.3.B.I Outbound

In this situation, where Germany is the residence state, it needs to be determined where the cross-border worker is insured, and thus obliged to pay contributions, to the statutory pension scheme. Pursuant to article 11, para 3, sub a Regulation 883/2004 a person pursuing an activity as an employed or self-employed person in a Member State shall be subject to the legislation of the working State, i.e. the Netherlands. The person is thus insured in the Dutch statutory pension scheme and pays contributions abroad.

As this person is resident in Germany, he will, commonly, be subject to unlimited tax liability in Germany pursuant to § 1, para 1 EStG. The question than rises to what extent, these Dutch paid contributions are taken into account in the calculation of the German

815 See article 2.1, para 1, sub b in conjunction with article 7.1 and 7.2 Wet IB 2001.
816 Pursuant to article 7.2, para 2, under e Wet IB 2001.

income tax. In principle, contributions to the *Basisversorgung* (i.e. *gesetzliche Rentenversicherung, landwirtschaftliche Alterskassen, berufsständische Versorgungswerken)* shall be deductible as *Sonderausgaben*, under the condition that these contributions are – for tax purposes – not taken into account as operating costs[817] or *Werbungskosten*, nor fiscally treated similarly.[818] This applies similarly to contributions paid to foreign statutory pension institutions.[819] It is not assessed in this regard to what extent the foreign statutory pension scheme is comparable to the domestic statutory pension scheme.[820] The domestic contributions ceilings (*Beitragsbemessungsgrenzen*), applicable to the *gesetzlichen Rentenversicherungen* shall not be decisive in this regard.

The *Bundesfinanzhof* holds that comparability of retirement pensions can be assumed in cases where the foreign pension benefits correspond in its core content to the common and typical features of the domestic benefit.[821] Moreover, it rules that the characteristic of pensions within the meaning of § 22, nr 1, sentence 3, letter a, double letter aa EStG (i.e. *gesetzlichen Rentenversicherung, landwirtschaftlichen Alterskasse, berufsständischen Versorgungseinrichtungen* and *Rürup-Rente*), is that they serve the so-called *Basisversorgung*, i.e. statutory pension schemes. Essential characteristics of this type of retirement provisions is that they are solely disbursed when a certain age limited is reached, or in the event of incapacity to work, and serve as compensation for living expenses, replacing an earned income.

Furthermore, in order to avoid an adverse fiscal treatment of pension contributions paid into a foreign pension scheme, paragraph 37 of the Commentaries on the OECD Model

817 I.e. *Betriebsausgaben.*

818 Pursuant to § 10, para 1, nr 2, under a EStG.

819 See also BMF, *Einkommensteuerrechtliche Behandlung von Vorsorgeaufwendungen IV C 3 - S 2221/16/10001:004* para 4. See also X R 57/06 BStBl 2009 II S. 1000 (BFH) 2009). BFH. X R 57/06 BStBl 2009 II S. 1000 (BFH) VI R 20/07 Bstbl. II 2010 (845) (BFH) in which the *Bundesfinanzhof* ruled that the European fundamental freedoms of a frontier worker are not infringed by the limited deduction of *Sonderausgaben* even if another Member State subjects the corresponding pension income to taxation in their entirety on the basis of the right of taxation allocated to it by the double taxation agreement, concluded with Germany.

820 However, in contrast to the German statutory social security system, there are some foreign social insurance schemes in which no distinction is made between the various domains of social security in terms of contributions and a uniform social security contribution (global contribution) is levied. The global contribution is used to finance benefits for, *inter alia*, unemployment, sickness, maternity protection, disability, old age and death. How the global contribution paid by the taxpayer is to be divided to determine the pension contributions that can be taken into account for tax purposes (e.g. contributions to a foreign statutory pension insurance institution) is announced for each taxable year in a separate *BMF-Schreiben*. See BMF, *Einkommensteuerrechtliche Behandlung von Vorsorgeaufwendungen IV C 3 - S 2221/16/10001:004* para 205. As regards taxable year 2020, see BMF, *Vorsorgeaufwendungen; Aufteilung eines einheitlichen Sozialversicherungsbeitrags (Globalbeitrag); Anpassung der Aufteilungsmaßstäbe für den Veranlagungszeitraum 2020 IV C 3 - S 2221/09/10013:001* (15 October 2019).

821 X R 37/08 BStBl. II 2011 (628) (BFH).

Convention contains a provision which is intended to ensure equal treatment with contributions made domestically.[822] It applies to either statutory, occupational and individual pension schemes.[823] Suchlike provision has been laid down in article 24, para 6 of the tax treaty concluded between the Netherlands and Germany, applying to statutory pension schemes as well. Mobile taxable person concerned may have recourse to this provision enshrined in the applicable tax treaty concluded between the Netherlands and Germany.

If the taxing right is allocated to Germany as residence state (pursuant to article 17, para 1 treaty Netherlands-Germany), the Dutch statutory pension benefits will be fully subject to German income tax, and the person concerned will be fully liable to tax in Germany, pursuant to § 1, para 1, sentence 1 EStG. The pension benefits arising from the Dutch statutory pension schemes are treated as akin to benefits arising from domestic statutory pension schemes, i.e. taxed against the *Besteuerungsanteil* as laid down in § 22, nr 1, sentence 3, letter a, double letter aa.[824] The proportion actually subject to tax is determined by the year of commencement of the pay-out phase. This taxable proportion of the benefits is determined irrespective of whether these benefits are derived from contributions which were subject to tax relief during the pay-out phase, either in Germany or abroad. If the taxing rights is allocated to the Netherlands as a source state (pursuant to article 17, para 2 treaty Netherlands-Germany), Dutch AOW pension benefits will be subject to Dutch income tax. The beneficiary residing abroad will be treated as a foreign taxable person (*buitenlands belastingplichtige*) provided that he receives domestic income, as the person concerned nor resides in the Netherlands, nor has his habitual abode in the Netherlands during the pay-out phase.[825] The AOW pension benefits will be fully liable to tax as taxable periodical benefits and benefits in kind under public law, received from or on behalf of a Dutch public law legal entity.[826] This taxable proportion of the benefits is determined irrespective of whether these benefits are derived from contributions which were subject to tax relief during the pay-out phase, either in the Netherlands or abroad.

5.3.3.B.II Inbound

In this situation, where the Netherlands is the residence state, and Germany the working state, the cross-border worker is insured, and thus obliged to pay contributions, to the

822 See also Bobbett and Avery Jones; Andreoni; De Broe and Neyt.
823 See paragraph 61 of the OECD commentary on article 18 OECD MC.
824 BMF, *Einkommensteuerrechtliche Behandlung von Vorsorgeaufwendungen und Altersbezügen IV C 3 - S 2221/12/10010:004 - IV C 5 - S 2345/08/0001* (19 August 2013) para 190.
825 See article 2.1, para 1, sub b in conjunction with article 7.1 and 7.2 Wet IB 2001.
826 Article 7.2, para 2, under e Wet IB 2001.

German statutory pension scheme.[827] As regards the deductibility of German contributions, it must be determined to what extent the person is liable to tax in Germany. As he has his residence nor his habitual abode in Germany, he will not be fully liable to tax pursuant to § 1, para 1, sentence 1 EStG. Upon request, he may be treated as fully liable to tax,[828] to the extent that they receive domestic income within the meaning of § 49 EStG. This applies solely if the income, received during the entire calendar year, is subject to German income tax for at least 90%, or the income not being subjected to German income tax, does not exceed the exemption threshold (*Grundfreibetrag; 2023: €10,908*) of § 32a, para 1, sentence 2, nr 1 EStG.[829]

If it is assumed that the cross-border worker receives domestic German income within the meaning of § 49 EStG which is subject to German income tax for at least 90%, the tax treatment of the deductions is akin to a domestic situation. The contributions paid to the *Basisversorgung* (i.e. *gesetzliche Rentenversicherung, landwirtschaftliche Alterskassen, berufsständischen Versorgungswerken)* shall, under certain preconditions, be deductible as *Sonderausgaben*, see section 5.3.[830]

Once retired in his residence state the Netherlands, during the pay-out phase, it depends on the allocation of taxing rights enshrined in the applicable tax treaty where the person is liable to tax for the German statutory pension benefits. As a main rule, under for instance article 17, para 1 of the treaty Netherlands-Germany, the Netherlands (residence state) is allocated the taxing right on these pension benefits. In such a case, he will be fully liable to tax in the Netherlands. To what extent this state subjects German statutory pension benefits to income tax, is a matter for the Netherlands, see section 5.2.2.B.I. However, if the taxing right is attributed to Germany (as source state pursuant to article 17, para 2 of the treaty Netherlands-Germany), the (former) cross-border worker, may be subject to German limited tax liability, pursuant to § 1, para 4 EStG. This applies merely in so far as the taxable person received domestic (German) income within the meaning of § 49 EStG. Benefits arising from the *gesetzlichen Rentenversicherung, landwirtschaftlichen Alterskassen* or *berufsständischen Versorgungswerken* are taxed against the *Besteuerungsanteil* as laid down in § 22, nr 1, sentence 3, letter a, double letter aa.[831] The proportion actually subject to tax is determined by the year of commencement of the pay-out phase. This taxable proportion of the benefits is determined irrespective of whether

827 Article 11, para 3, sub a Regulation 883/2004.

828 § 1, para 3 EStG.

829 § 1, para 3, sentence 2 EStG.

830 § 10, para 1, nr 2, under a EstG.

831 BMF, *Einkommensteuerrechtliche Behandlung von Vorsorgeaufwendungen und Altersbezügen IV C 3 - S 2221/12/10010:004 - IV C 5 - S 2345/08/0001* para 190.

these benefits are derived from contributions which were subject to tax relief during the pay-out phase, either in Germany or abroad. These types of benefits are considered German domestic income, pursuant to § 49, para 7 EStG, which fall under German limited tax liability. The (former) cross-border worker residing abroad, may thus be subject to German limited tax liability.

5.3.3.C Posted Worker

In the case of a posted worker, the mobile citizen – as a rule – has an employment contract in his sending state, and, carries out his work, for a limited period, in the territory of a Member State other than the State in which he normally works.[832] These posted workers differ from other types of mobile workers in that they return, or are expected to resume working in the Member State from which he is posted after completion of the work or the provision of services for which he was posted.[833] They, thus, do not fully integrate in the labour market of the host state, and will, hence, benefit only partially of the same working conditions and rights as workers in the host state.

Generally, from a statutory pension point of view these posted workers will not have to deal with pension institutions in different countries when they retire, since the social security institutions in the host state(s) will not be involved.[834] As a general rule, they remain insured under the sending state's social security system.

5.3.3.C.I Outbound

As part of the outbound posting case, a German employee is sent by its German employer to the Netherlands during the accrual phase, i.e. either as part of (intercompany) secondment sent to a Dutch subsidiary, or in the framework of hiring-out-of-labour sent to a (external) separate entity.[835] It is therefore assumed, and this is peculiar for the case of posting, that the employee concerned will continue to participate, and contribute, to the German statutory pension scheme as the sending state.[836]

---

832 Building on the definitions provided in art. 2 of Posting of Workers Directive 96/71; Your Europe – European Union, 'National websites on posting'; para 3 of preamble, art. 4, para 3 Enforcement Directive 2014/67 of Posting of Workers Directive 96/71.

833 Article 4, para 3, under d Directive 2014/67/EU of the European Parliament and of the Council of 15 May 2014 on the enforcement of Directive 96/71/EC concerning the posting of workers in the framework of the provision of services and amending Regulation (EU) No 1024/2012 on administrative cooperation through the Internal Market Information System [2014] OJ L 159. See also para 9 preamble Directive 2018/957 amending Directive 96/71.

834 Since, under conditions, they will be socially insured in the 'sending state' pursuant to art. 12, para 1 Regulation on the coordination of social security systems 883/2004.

835 See also paragraph 8.3 ff. of the OECD commentary on article 15 OECD MC.

836 Pursuant to art. 12, para 1 Regulation on the coordination of social security systems 883/2004.

According to the applicable treaty provision (art. 14, para 2 i.e. 183 day-rule), during the brief period of posting, Germany (residence state) is assigned the taxing rights as regards the remuneration. Therefore, the tax treatment, and the tax relief, of the pension contributions paid into the German statutory pension scheme is a matter for Germany, see section 5.3.2.

After the limited time of posting abroad, the worker will return to Germany. As a main rule, under for instance article 17, para 1 of the treaty Netherlands-Germany, the residence state is allocated the taxing right on these German pension benefits. In such a case, during retirement, he will be fully liable in Germany.[837] The tax treatment of the pension benefits is then akin to a domestic situation, as the residence state and pension state coincide. For an elaborate explanation of the taxation of benefits arising from the *gesetzliche Rentenversicherung, landwirtschaftliche Alterskassen* and *berufständische Versorgung*, I refer section to 5.3.2.C. Benefits paid out of *gesetzliche Rentenversicherung, landwirtschaftliche Alterskasse, berufsständische Versorgungseinrichtung*[838] shall, as of 2040, be fully subject to taxation, pursuant to § 22, nr 1, sentence 3, letter a, double letter aa EStG. From 2005 until 2040 the benefits shall only partially be liable to tax, in accordance with the *Besteuerungsanteil* (2023: 83%). The taxable amount is based on the annual amount of the pension benefits paid out, irrespective of whether the contributions from which the benefits emerge, have been subject to tax relief, either in Germany or abroad. The difference between the annual amount of pension and the taxable proportion of the pension constitutes the tax-free amount of pension.[839] What is more, if article 17, para 2 of the treaty Netherlands-Germany applies, the taxing right is allocated to the Germany (as source state) as well, and the situation is akin to the situation described above.

5.3.3.C.II Inbound

As part of the inbound posting case, a Dutch employee is sent by its Dutch employer to Germany during the accrual phase, i.e. either as part of (intercompany) secondment sent to a German subsidiary, or in the framework of hiring-out-of-labour sent to a (external) separate entity.[840] As the posting in the host state Germany will be of limited duration and the worker will not fully integrate in the labour market of Germany, he will continue to participate, and contribute, to the Dutch statutory pension scheme as the sending state.[841]

837 Pursuant to § 1, para 1, sentence 1 EStG.

838 Pursuant to § 10, para 1, nr 2, under b EStG.

839 § 22, under aa, sentence 4 EStG.

840 See also paragraph 8.3 ff. of the OECD commentary on article 15 OECD MC.

841 Pursuant to art. 12, para 1 Regulation on the coordination of social security systems 883/2004.

According to the applicable treaty provision (art. 15, i.e. 183 day-rule), during the period of posting, the Netherlands (residence state) is allocated the taxing right as regards the remuneration. Therefore, the tax treatment, and the tax relief, of the pension contributions paid into the Dutch statutory pension scheme is a matter for Netherlands, see section 5.3.2.

After the limited time of posting abroad, the worker will return to the Netherlands. As a main rule, under for instance article 17, para 1 of the treaty Netherlands-Germany, the residence state is allocated the taxing right on these Dutch pension benefits. In such a case, during retirement, he will be fully liable in the Netherlands.[842] The tax treatment of the pension benefits is then akin to a domestic situation, as the residence state and pension state coincide, see section 5.2.1. What is more, if article 17, para 2 of the treaty Netherlands-Germany applies, the taxing right is allocated to the Netherlands (as source state) as well, and the situation is akin to the situation described above.

5.4 COMPARATIVE FINDINGS THROUGH THE LENS OF THE EVALUATION FRAMEWORK

Where in the sections above the (tax treatment of) statutory pensions – in both the Netherlands and Germany – have been mapped out, the section below compares these findings along the (legal) lines of this research's evaluation framework (similarity/comparability; inter-level coherence; inter-system consistency; foreseeability/unpredictability). It is a sliding scale where all variations between fit and unfit can be observed.

As this chapter explored the (tax treatment of) statutory pensions, emphasis will be put on the principle of similarity/comparability, since this chapter seeks to explore to what extent the regulatory framework governing the (tax treatment of) statutory pensions in both countries are fit for the provision of effective pension information. This principle is marked by the division of power between the European Union and the Member States; the responsibility for the design of a national pension system lies primarily with the Member States, and the European Union falls short of competence to intervene in the Member States' pension systems (apart from Regulation 883/2004 and Regulation 987/2009 as regards the coordination of social security systems). What is more, as this chapter did not involve the role of European law on taxation, and international tax law as such (this will be discussed in chapters 8 and 9 of this research) the principle of inter-level coherence is not discussed any further. Hence, it does not concern the scrutiny of coherence with

842 Pursuant to art. 2.1, para 1, under a Wet IB 2001.

higher-level regulations, and with treaty or other international obligations. Lastly, as the earlier sections in this chapter addressed the application of national regulatory (tax) frameworks, leading to potential (in)compatible outcomes for a specific cross-border situation, the principle of inter-system consistency shall be evaluated. This chapter meets this research second (sub)objective of a legal comparative study in which the legal frameworks in the Netherlands and Germany, as well as on a European and international level, shall be mapped out. Building on this, the 'fitness' of the legal frameworks at the national, European and international level shall be assessed, focusing in particular on any deficiencies that have a (distorting) effect on the provision of effective information.

5.4.1 Similarity/Comparability

The sections below compare German and Dutch statutory pensions and their tax treatment (in cross-border situations), and evaluates it in view of the principle of similarity/comparability. Exploring similarity between systems involves a comparison of certain features. The assessment of similarity constitutes a feature-matching process, i.e. it measures the degree to which two objects – the legal character – match each other. Similarity is tantamount to a measurement of common features. A higher degree of similarity helps to ensure the effectiveness of information in terms of the four principles (understandability, technical (legal) correctness, personal relevance, trustworthiness). For instance, the higher the degree of similarity, the easier it is to uphold the information's correctness, trustworthiness, and personal relevance. After all, with a higher degree of similarity, there is less need to observe any underlying structural differences. Moreover, a higher degree of similarity leads to a higher comparability of the different regulatory frameworks/legal constructs, avoiding comparing the incomparable.

Comparing Dutch and German statutory pensions (see sections 5.2 and 5.3), the following conclusions can be drawn:

- The German first pillar consists of a wide range of statutory pension schemes, i.e. *gesetzliche Rentenversicherung, die Beambtenversorgung, Alterssicherung der Landwirte* and *berufsständische Versorgungswerke*, each applying different legal bases, ratios for conferral of pension rights, personal scopes, eligibility criteria, calculation of benefits, retirement ages etc. In the Netherlands, old age provision in the first pillar is formed by merely one pension provision, i.e. the state pension AOW, for which all resident are eligible.
- Contrary to the Dutch AOW, under some of the German statutory pension provision, waiting/vesting periods apply. Under the *Beambtenversorgung*, pension entitlements

shall be granted provided that the civil servants' have fulfilled a period of service of a minimum of five years.

– What is more, where the Dutch AOW is a 'flat-rate' pension provision, the calculation of benefits under the *gesetzlichen Rentenversicherung* is earnings-related in terms of following primarily the amount of wages and income during the insured person's insurance history, incorporating the so-called *Entgeltpunkte, aktueller Rentenwert* and the *Rentenartfaktor*. This value factor constitutes a dynamic factor, i.e. incorporating factors such as gross wage increases or inflation. The fact remains that this complex calculation process, including its varying exceptions and particularities, may hamper the provision of effective cross-border pension information.
– However, statutory retirement ages do not deviate considerably between the Netherlands and Germany. For the Dutch AOW, the retirement age in 2023 is set at 66 and 10 months; and 67 in 2024. For the *gesetzliche Rentenversicherung*, the retirement age is set at 67 (*Regelaltersgrenze*); the *Beambtenversorgung* – as a rule – at 67. For the *Berufsständische Versorgung* the retirement ages are laid down in profession specific regulations. However, over the last years these retirement ages have been raised gradually. Lastly, for the *Alterssicherung der Landwirte* ¬the retirement age is set – as a rule – at 67 as well.
– As regards the deduction of contributions, the following difference can be pointed out. In the Netherlands, AOW-contributions are not eligible for deductibility for tax purposes. As regards the deduction of contributions in Germany, until 31 December 2004, the legal framework regarding the deductibility of contributions was standardised, irrespective of the form of pension contribution. However, after the entry into force of the *Alterseinkünftegesetz*, the German legislator abandoned this uniform approach. The eligibility of the deduction of pension contributions then differentiated into, on the one side, the contributions to basic retirement provisions in the first pillar, and on the other side, the contributions to other retirement provisions. As of 2025, contributions to the so-called *Basisversorgung* (i.e. *gesetzliche Rentenversicherung, landwirtschaftlichen Alterskassen, berufsständischen Versorgungswerken* and the *Rürup-Rente*) shall be fully deductible as *Sonderausgaben*, under the condition that these contributions ar – for tax purposes – not taken into account as operating costs or *Werbungskosten*, nor fiscally treated similarly. The deductibility of contributions is capped at 8% of the *Beitragsbemessungsgrenze* in the *allgemeinen Rentenversicherung*.
– With respect to the taxation of pension benefits, the Dutch statutory AOW pension benefits are fully subjected to tax as wages stemming from former employment. As regards Germany, an immediate transition in 2005 to full deferred taxation of benefits, arising from the *gesetzlichen Rentenversicherung*, was considered ineligible, since this would lead to a significant degree of double taxation of parts of the benefits paid out.

These accrued retirement benefits originate from three elements: the employer's part, the employee's part and the federal subsidy. The employer's part of the contributions to *gesetzlichen Rentenversicherung* is not liable for tax; hence not regarded taxable *Arbeitslohn* on the side of the employee. Furthermore, the federal subsidy part is exempted from taxation as well. Principally, German statutory pension benefits are – under the principle of deferred taxation – fully taxed in the pay-out phase. Benefits paid out of *gesetzlichen Rentenversicherung, landwirtschaftlichen Alterskasse, berufsständischen Versorgungseinrichtung*[843] shall, as of 2040, be fully subject to taxation.[844] From 2005 until 2040 the benefits shall only partially be liable to tax, in accordance with the *Besteuerungsanteil*. For instance, if the beneficiary retires in 2023, 83% shall be included in the tax base of the taxable person, and subject to taxation.

– As regards a Dutch, and German, outbound cross-border worker attention should be drawn to the following. For a Dutch outbound cross-border worker – paying contributions under the German statutory pension scheme – the main rule is that contributions paid by the employer for foreign statutory pension scheme should be 'similar in nature and scope' to the Dutch national insurances.[845] The decision acknowledges that the German *Rentenversicherung*, like many other foreign social security pensions, contains elements of both a Dutch statutory pension scheme, and an occupational pension scheme. With respect to the *Beamtenversorgung*, employee contributions shall be deductible and employer contributions exempt. The employee contributions for the *Alterssicherung der Landwirte* are not deductible, and the employer contributions taxed. With respect to the *Berufsständischen Versorgungseinrichtungen*, employee contributions shall be deductible and employer contributions are exempt, only if the person concerned is compulsorily insured. However, mobile taxable persons concerned may have recourse to article 24, para 6 of the tax treaty concluded between the Netherlands and Germany, intended to ensure equal treatment with contributions made domestically. However, for this purpose the pension scheme must be 'generally equivalent' to a pension scheme recognized by that state for tax purposes. For a German outbound cross-border worker – paying contributions under the Dutch statutory pension scheme – these contributions are deductible as *Sonderausgaben*. It is not assessed in this regard to what extent the

---

843 Pursuant to § 10, para 1, nr 2, under b EStG.

844 Pursuant to § 22, nr 1, sentence 3, under a, sub aa EStG.

845 Staatssecretaris van Financiën, *Buitenlandse sociale verzekeringen. Duitse, Belgische en Luxemburgse sociale zekerheid. Aftrek premie en belastbaarheid uitkeringen nr. DGB 2014/144M*. The examination of the tax qualification of the foreign social insurance systems is carried out at the foreign office of the Tax Authorities on the basis of the principles included in this Decree and DG Belastingdienst / Concerndirectie Fiscale en Juridische Zaken. Compared to the January 5, 2016 April publication, this overview has been supplemented by the qualification of four German social insurance schemes. The already assessed schemes and social insurances have not been reassessed.

foreign statutory pension scheme is comparable to the domestic statutory pension scheme. The domestic contributions ceilings (*Beitragsbemessungsgrenzen*), applicable to the *gesetzlichen Rentenversicherungen* shall not be decisive in this regard.

As has been addressed in the beginning of this section, exploring similarity between systems involves a comparison of certain features, where similarity is tantamount to a measurement of common features. A higher degree of similarity helps to ensure the effectiveness of information in terms of the four principles. For instance, the higher the degree of similarity, the easier it is to uphold the information's correctness, trustworthiness, and personal relevance. After all, with a higher degree of similarity, there is less need to observe any underlying structural differences. However, as follows from the above enumeration, the legal comparison revealed more differences than similarities between the Dutch and German regulatory frameworks. In terms of 'fitness' it can thus be concluded that these structural differences hamper the provision of effective information provision, in terms of similarity/comparability.

5.4.2 *Foreseeability and (Un)predictability*

One cannot simply rely on the maintenance of the law in force.[846] Applicable legislation is designed in view of particular political, economic, societal phenomena. These phenomena tend to change over time, and accordingly, legislation is adapted to the new situation. This also applies to the Dutch and German legislation under scrutiny in this chapter. It is therefore that conveying information on future amounts of retirement income usually involves a certain level of risk as regards continuously changing legislation. Put it differently, predictability is a structure, and information lies where unpredictable change occurs. Along the line of foreseeability, the following conclusions can be drawn:

- As discussed in section 5.2 and 5.3 – driven by ageing populations – in both the Netherlands as well in Germany the statutory retirement age will be raised gradually, building on certain birth cohorts. For instance, with regard to the *Beambtenversorgung*, the general pensionable age (*Regelaltersrente)* is set on 67 years.[847] For civil servants, born prior to 1 January 1947, the pensionable age amounts to 65 years. Regarding civil servants born after 31st of December 1946, the pensionable age is raised gradually since 2012. Moreover, as dealt with in section 5.2, the gradual increase of the AOW retirement age has a highly erratic pattern, marked by incremental increase and mitigation of this increase, part of the implementation of the reform of the Dutch

846 Popelier, 1078.

847 § 51, para 1 Gesetz zur Neuordnung und Modernisierung des Bundesdienstrechts (Dienstrechtsneuordnungsgesetz – DNeuG).

system of occupational pension schemes (*Wet Toekomst Pensioenen*). These step-by-step increases and alterations 'back and forth' affect the legislation's (and its application) foreseeability, and renders it fairly unpredictable.

5.4.3 *Inter-system Consistency*

In order to prevent discrepancies in information provision, national (Netherlands and Germany) levels of legislation, need to be consistent by themselves. Legal systems consist of, *inter alia*, a set of rules. In general, legislators would prefer that legislation in a particular legal system were consistent. Not only on a domestic level, but in particular where several national legal systems converge as in this research; on Dutch/German level. This requires a certain form of inter-system consistency. For the purposes of this research 'consistency' is termed as `the quality, state, or fact of being consistent; agreement, harmony, compatibility'.[848] Consistency, in this context, refers to – while applying national regulatory frameworks – not leading to incompatible outcomes for a specific case. Two distinct types of inconsistency may be discerned: treating a person inconsistently over time, and inconsistency between individuals.[849] It is not uncommon that rules in two legal systems attach incompatible consequences to a same case. Two or more rules are in actual conflict when they actually apply to one and the same case, and attach incompatible consequences to this case. Along the line of inter-system consistency the following conclusions can be drawn:

- In terms of inconsistent treatment over time the following should be stressed. The current design of the transitional regime regarding the fixation of the *Besteuerungsanteil*, and the relating tax-free part of the pension benefit paid out[850], leads in certain years to a double taxation of the contributions and the financial return[851] (i.e. the pension benefits). This fiscal issue mainly relates to the group of beneficiaries paying contributions since the 1990s. In these cases, the employee contributions were not fully deductible. In particular, employees born in 1975 are affected by this double taxation, although the effect of double taxation arises from the birth year 1955. It may be stated that with regard to this intertemporal taxation, a certain level of coordination is missing. The pensions should either be taxed during the accrual phase or during the pay-out phase.[852]

848 Oxford Dictionaries.

849 Steyn, 22.

850 Pursuant to § 22, nr 3, under aa EStG.

851 I.e. *Kapitalrückflusses*.

852 BVerfG 25 March 2002, 2 BvL 17/99, 105, 73 in which judgement the court ruled: *„Fehlt ein Mindestmaß an gegenseitiger* Abstimmung *zwischen ausgleichsbedürftigen Nachteilen einerseits und begünstigenden*

In terms of inconsistency between mobile individuals, regarding the tax treatment of their statutory pension in cross-border situations, the following should be pointed out:

- In the case of an outbound migrant worker, no cross-border discrepancies have been found during the accrual phase, as these situations are akin to a domestic situation. However, as regards the pay-out phase of a Dutch outbound migrant worker, the following can be pointed out. During the pay-out phase, the person concerned resides abroad. Pension benefits arising from Dutch statutory pension schemes are thus paid out abroad. If the taxing rights is allocated to Germany as a source state, these Dutch benefits constitute *Sonstige Einkünfte*, taxed pursuant to § 22, nr 1, sentence 3, letter a, double letter aa, against the *Besteuerungsanteil*. In 2023, 83% of the benefits shall be subject to tax. This taxable proportion of the benefits is determined irrespective of whether these benefits are derived from contributions which were subject to tax relief during the pay-out phase, either in Germany or abroad. This means that Dutch statutory pension benefits are only partially subject to German tax, while if the person concern would have remained his residence in the Netherlands, these benefits would be fully subject to Dutch tax. This also holds with regard to the German outbound cross-border worker, and a Dutch inbound cross-border worker.
- In the case of an inbound migrant worker, no cross-border discrepancies have been found during the accrual phase. However, as regards the pay-out phase of a Dutch inbound migrant worker, the following can be pointed out. If the taxing right is allocated to the Netherlands as residence state, the German statutory pension benefits will be subject to Dutch income tax. The payments from the German *Rentenversicherungen* are – according to the Secretary of State – to be considered as income from employment because of the relationship with the (current or past) employment of the taxpayer himself or of someone else.[853] These annuities and social security payments are seen as inherent to the (existence of) the employment relationship. Hence, the German statutory pension payments are, as a rule, taxed as wages.[854] Incidentally, the communication of November 2020 does not provide any clarity as to how benefits arising from *Beamtenversorgung, Alterssicherung der Landwirte, Berufsständischen Versorgungseinrichtunge* will be taxable under Dutch tax law, as this communication merely focusses on the tax treatment of contributions paid into these German schemes. I assume that the general principles as formulated in the Decree of March 24, 2014 apply *mutatis mutandis* in these cases. In terms of consistency between mobile individuals, this means that a Dutch inbound migrant worker (having

Ausgleichswirkungen andererseits, so entfällt zugleich der nachvollziehbare Grund für eine ungleich wirkende steuerliche Vergünstigung.“

853 See Staatssecretaris van Financiën, *Buitenlandse sociale verzekeringen. Duitse, Belgische en Luxemburgse sociale zekerheid. Aftrek premie en belastbaarheid uitkeringen nr. DGB 2014/144M* para 5.1.

854 Pursuant to artt. 3.81 and 3.82 Wet IB 2001.

accrued a German statutory pension) is treated differently from a Dutch domestic worker having accrued an AOW-pension. However, in fact, both workers are not treated differently as both types of pension income are subject to tax in the Dutch BOX 1. What is more, comparing a Dutch inbound migrant worker to a German domestic worker reveals that a German domestic worker is treated more favourable, due to the *Besteuerungsanteil*, while both have accrued pension rights through the same German pension scheme. In 2023, 83% of the benefits are subject to tax. This also applies to the Dutch outbound cross-border worker, and German inbound cross-border worker.

5.5 Interim Conclusion

As has been addressed thoroughly in chapter 2 of this research, the two-dimensional notion of effective pension information articulates that the information's behavioural purpose seeks to inform mobile individuals on an aggregated level about how much pension they can expect, in order to be able to assess the adequacy of their dispersed pension, covering all their forms of pension in each of the (former) working/residence states. The aforementioned behavioural purpose contains the terms 'aggregated' (i.e. assembled at an overall/higher level) and the phrase 'covering all their forms of pension in each of the (former) working/residence states'. However, mobile individuals – who avail(ed) themselves of their European freedoms of movement – see themselves confronted with a wide range of diverging 'pensions', i.e. pension vehicles, schemes, retirement products of all sorts, arising from statutory pension systems in each of the different (former) working states, and/or residence states. This requires putting together dispersed, and deviating, elements of future retirement income, arising in each of these states. This amounts to observing, and 'translating' the intersections between different multi-level legal systems (national, EU and international/bilateral) and the interaction of poorly coordinated legal domains (pension and tax law) – which can all be interwoven in a personal mobile situation – into effective pension information. This was taken as a given and this chapter mapped out the statutory pension systems in both the Netherlands, as well as Germany. Moreover, it revolved around the tax treatment of these statutory schemes in both the accrual and pay-out phase, in both domestic, but in particular in cross-border situations.

The comparative findings were presented in section 4.5, along the lines of this research's evaluation framework. This comparison revealed a considerable number of similarities when it comes to Dutch and German statutory pensions, and their tax treatment in cross-border situations. Moreover, it revealed a considerable range of differences that should be observed when providing effective cross-border pension information. What is more, it was also found that provisions of national tax laws governing the taxation of retirement income, are applied on the basis of an 'isolated approach', without taking into account any previous or subsequent tax treatment in another (member) state. Moreover, it has been revealed that the gradual increase of the AOW retirement age is marked by a highly erratic pattern, as part of the implementation of the reform of the Dutch system of occupational pension schemes, i.e. the 'pension agreement' (*Pensioenakkoord*). These step-by-step increases and alterations 'back and forth' affect the legislation's (and its application) foreseeability, and renders it fairly unpredictable. With respect to inter-system consistency, the findings revealed a number of situations where applying national regulatory frameworks leads to incompatible outcomes for a specific case, in particular with regard to inconsistency of the tax treatment of pensions of mobile individuals. In this vein, this chapter meets this research second (sub)objective of a legal comparative study in which the legal frameworks in the Netherlands and Germany shall be mapped out, and evaluated along the lines of this research's evaluation framework.

6 Occupational Pensions Systems and Taxation Through the Lens of Effective Pension Information

6.1 Introduction

Where in the preceding chapter the (tax treatment of) statutory pension systems - in the Netherlands and Germany - have been mapped out, the chapter below analyses the occupational pension systems. The main distinction between statutory pensions and occupational pensions lies in the role of each of the pension pillars in saving for old age, the replacement ratio, the (historical) development, the (legal) character, and the corresponding tax treatment. What is more, in cross-border situations mobile individuals - who avail(ed) themselves of their European freedoms of movement - see themselves confronted with a wide range of occupational diverging 'pensions', i.e. pension vehicles, schemes, retirement products of all sorts, arising from occupational pension systems in each of the different (former) working states, and/or residence states. Putting this dispersed puzzle together also poses considerable challenges in terms of information provision. As elaborately discussed in chapter 2 of this research, this requires a process of converging these deviating systems, while upholding the information's effectiveness. This amounts to observing, and 'translating' the intersections between different multi-level legal systems (national, EU and international/bilateral) and the interaction of poorly coordinated legal domains (pension and tax law) - which can all be interwoven in a personal mobile situation - into effective pension information.

Taking this as a given, this chapter maps out the occupational pension systems in both the Netherlands, as well as Germany. Moreover, it revolves around the tax treatment of these occupational schemes in both the accrual and pay-out phase, in both domestic, but in particular in cross-border situations. It is explored to what extent tax relief is granted for occupational pensions in the form of tax base advantages (e.g. tax exemptions, allowances, deduction from the taxable base, deduction from the tax liability) or tax rate advantages (e.g. flat tax rate). The allocation of company pension expenses at employer level is left aside. The description of this tax treatment is based on national (Dutch and German respectively) tax legislation, while taking account of the applicable tax treaty concluded between the Netherlands and Germany. The influence of European and international (tax) law on the tax treatment of cross-border pensions as such will be looked into in chapters 8 and 9 of this research. In section 4.5, these comparative findings will be evaluated along the (legal) lines of this research's evaluation framework: similarity/comparability, inter-level coherence, inter-system consistency, and foreseeability. Not each of these legal principles shall be evaluated to the same extent as this chapter explores the occupational systems, and the tax treatment. This chapter meets this research second (sub)objective of a legal comparative study in which the legal frameworks in the Netherlands and Germany shall be mapped out.

6.2 The Netherlands: Aanvullende pensioenen

As part of this research's comparative legal study, this section considers occupational pensions and their tax treatment (in cross-border situations) in the Netherlands. It should be noted that this section provides an elaborate overview of the design of the pension landscape. Elements of national pension systems – considered relevant through this research's evaluation framework – such as pension arrangements, pensionable age, entitlements conditions, vesting methods, pension schemes and the impending fundamental revision of the Dutch occupational pension system will be addressed.

Since each form of pension is characterized by a different history, development, underlying framework and rationale, the applicable laws and regulations also differ widely. With regard to Dutch occupational pensions, the *Pensioenwet* is the most prominent source of law. This act came into force in phases on 1 January 2007 and replaced the *Pensioen- en Spaarfondsenwet* on that date, which had been in force since 1952 and was in need of modernization and revision. As a result of the entry into force of the *Pensioenwet*, the rules for pension funds and insurers are now to be found in a single law, whereas previously pension funds and insurers each were subject to different legislation. The main purpose of this *Pensioenwet* is to ensure that pension entitlements shall be safeguarded. It is to be noted that not all employees in the Netherlands build up a pension through their employer, as there is no legal obligation to do so. Nevertheless, approximately 90% of employees in the Netherlands participate in an occupational pension plan through their employer (of which 75% in a defined benefit-scheme (*uitkeringsovereenkomst*).[855] Hence, it is a matter of securing of benefits by segregating the financial resources intended for that purpose from the employer's business assets. This results in the so-called *witte vlek*[856], i.e. employees not covered by any Dutch occupational pension scheme. This constitutes an increasing

855 DNB, 'Rechtstreekse pensioenregelingen, typen pensioenovereenkomsten' <https://www.dnb.nl/statistieken/data-zoeken/#/details/rechtstreekse-pensioenregelingen-typen-pensioenovereenkomsten/dataset/52c29730-e6d5-44af-b82d-afe561db9a95> accessed 1 March 2022.

856 Translated freely as 'white spot'.

concern of societal relevance, as these employees face the risk of an inadequate pension income at retirement and, hence, have to rely upon social welfare. There is also a multitude of pension-related legislation and regulations.[857] These forms of legislation will be discussed below to the extent they are deemed relevant for this study.

In the analysis of the Dutch occupational pension system in section 6.2, the impending fundamental reform of the Dutch pension system – pursuant to the *Wet Toekomst Pensioenen* – takes a central role. This pension reform as well as the fiscal reforms, and the consequences for existing pension schemes, will be discussed elaborately in section 6.2.3. The date of entry into force of the Future Pensions Act has been postponed to July 1, 2023.[858] The postponement means that employers wishing to enter into a new pension plan as of January 1, 2023, must still rely on the current legislation. After the Future Pensions Act takes effect, a four-year transition phase will apply (2023 to 2027), during which period social partners must agree on a pension plan that fits within the new legal framework, and pension administrators must implement the new pension scheme. No later than January 1, 2027, the new pension scheme that meets the requirements of the Act on Future Pensions must enter into force. In that regard, until 2027, the current pension legislation – under the *Pensioenwet* and *Wet op de loonbelasting 1964* – retains its validity and relevance to this study.

6.2.1 *Foundations, Agreements and Vesting Methods of Occupational Pensions*

The foundation of today's Dutch occupational pension plans was laid in the nineteenth century when the granting of a pension evolved from charity to a legal right.[859] In the seventeenth century guild support funds emerged, which could be seen as the forerunners of the modern pension funds.[860]

An employer and employee may enter into an agreement about various types of entitlements or benefits. Only where it constitutes a pension, the *Pensioenwet* (Pensions

857 A number of obligations stipulated in the *Pensioenwet* are further detailed in subordinate regulations: *Besluit uitvoering PW en Wet verplichte beroepspensioenregeling, Besluit FTK pensioenfondsen, Regeling PW en Wet verplichte beroepspensioenregeling*. Further, there is a range of occupational pension-related regulations: *Wet verplichte deelneming in een bedrijfstakpensioenfonds 2000, Wet verplichte beroepspensioenregeling, Wet op het financieel toezicht, Wet verevening pensioenrechten bij scheiding, Wet op de loonbelasting 1964*.

858 Minister van Armoedebeleid Participatie en Pensioenen, *Antwoorden op Kamervragen over verlaging van de variabele pensioenuitkeringen* (6 October 2022) 8.

859 Lutjens, *Asser-serie 7-XI – Pensioen (Bijzondere overeenkomsten)* nr. 1.

860 Ibid. nr. 1 and cited literature.

Act) applies to that agreement. The concept of pension has thus a central role in the Pensions Act.[861] Occupational pensions are marked by the direct relationship between participation in the relevant pension scheme, and the acquisition of entitlements, to the performance of work.[862] The occupational pension scheme may be grounded on an employment contract (or other employment relationship with an employer), an appointment as civil servant, working in a particular branch of industry, or practicing a particular profession, whether employed or self-employed.[863] Pension is an employment condition and concerns an agreement made in the context of an employment relationship; a pension agreement cannot come into being without an employment contract.[864]

In the Dutch pension system, the content of the pension agreement is primarily a matter between employer and employee.[865] In principle, this relationship is governed by the freedom of contract, which allows employees and the employer to agree on the employee's pension as they see fit. Therefore, the parties concerned may, in principle, freely determine whether the nature of the pension scheme is determined by the benefits, the capital or the contribution. The tripartite relationship between employee, employer and pension provider is at the centre of the *Pensioenwet*, where there is a clear division of responsibility between the three parties involved.[866] What is more, the pension agreement (*pensioenovereenkomst*) concluded between employer and employee forms the basis. In this triangular relation, the employer must allocate the administration of the pension agreement externally to a pension administrator, with which the employee will have an independent relationship with the pension provider (as a pension participant).[867] As part of this, the employer must ensure that agreements made in the pension agreement lead to the corresponding pension scheme rules (*pensioenreglement*). In this *pensioenreglement*, the pension administrator's rights and obligations and those of the employee/participant shall be laid down, while building on the pension agreement and the administration

861 Cf. Ibid. nr. 72.

862 Ibid. nr. 13.

863 See ibid. nr. 14. For practitioners, there may be mandatory participation in an occupational pension scheme pursuant to the Dutch Compulsory Occupational Pension Schemes Act (*Wet verplichte beroepspensioenregeling*). Among others, there are mandatory occupational pension plans for Pharmacists, Veterinarians, Physiotherapists, General practitioners, medical specialists, Midwives. For the self-employed in general, there is no pension scheme in the second pillar, but self-employed persons can, however, by working in a particular branch of industry or by practicing a particular profession, fall under an obligation to participate in an *bedrijfstakpensioenfonds* or *beroepspensioenregeling*.

864 This follows from the definitions of employer and employee as laid down in art. 1 PW.

865 Kamerstukken II, (2005/06), 31.

866 Cf. BT Broers, 'Driehoeksverhouding in de Pensioenwet' in AHH Bollen-Vandenboorn (ed.), *Pensioen en de belangrijkste toekomstvoorzieningen* (27 edn Fiscale Geschriften, SDU, Den Haag 2022) 148.

867 Pursuant to art. 23 PW.

agreement.[868] The implementation of the pension agreement through a third party takes place by means of an administration agreement (*uitvoeringsovereenkomst*), concluded between the employer and the pension administrator.[869] It must be noted that the pension agreement does not grant the employee any direct entitlements vis-à-vis the pension fund and the pension scheme rules do not bind the employer. This triangular relation is visualised in figure 6.1 Triangular relationship pursuant to Pensioenwet below.

Figure 6.1 Triangular Relationship Pursuant to *Pensioenwet*

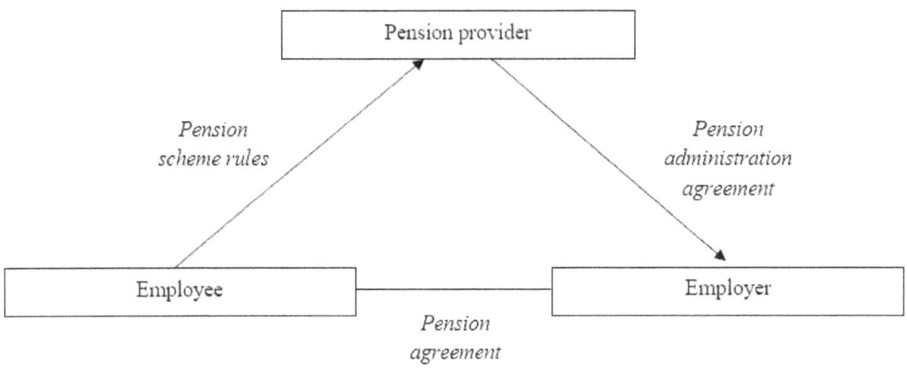

To enable the employee to have an overview of the risks related to his pension provision, several legal provisions with regard to the content of the pension arrangement have been laid down in de *Pensioenwet*.[870] The concept of pension plays a pivotal role. Pursuant to this legal act, the nature of the pension arrangement must be enshrined explicitly by the employer and employee. The legal act stipulates the several types of pension arrangements, falling within the scope of this act, i.e. *uitkeringsovereenkomst, kapitaalovereenkomst* and *premieovereenkomst*.[871] This will be dealt with in more detail in section 6.2.2 below.

6.2.2 *Pension Agreements and Vesting Methods*

When it comes to Dutch occupational pensions, these are collectively organised at the level of either a sector, firm or profession. The content of the Dutch basic pension scheme is usually determined by the social partners – i.e. representatives of employer(s) and

868 Pursuant to art. 35 PW.
869 Pursuant to art. 32 PW.
870 Artt. 10 up to and including 18 Pensioenwet.
871 Pursuant to art. 10 Pensioenwet. Translated freely as defined benefits scheme, capital scheme, and defined contribution scheme.

employees – whereby the agreements made are embedded in pension agreements concluded between the employer(s) and employee.[872] Yet, the *Pensioenwet* provides frameworks and minimum rules for the content of the pension agreement, such as the method of paying out pensions and the character of the pension agreement.[873]

In principle, Dutch occupational pension schemes are not compulsory under (pension) law, i.e. no statutory obligation exists for employers to implement a pension scheme, nor are employees obliged to participate in an occupational pension scheme. However, occupational pensions are often part of collective labour agreements and – at request of the social partners – the *Wet verplichte deelneming in een bedrijfstakpensioenfonds 2000* may assign a pension plan, and its pension provider, as obligatory for an entire sector or industry. This pension scheme is then implemented in an industry pension fund established for that type of industry. Hence, a pension plan may become 'quasi-mandatory'.

The sections below describe the most common pension systems in the Netherlands. A distinction can be drawn between DB and DC plans, whereby the tendency in the Netherlands is also that pension entitlements shall be accrued through a DC plan ever more. These pension vesting methods allow to calculate the future pension benefits, i.e. depending on salary and/or length of service, a certain entitlement to a pension benefit is built up.

The *Pensioenwet* enunciates that a pension agreement should be in the nature of a benefit agreement, a capital agreement or a premium agreement.[874] Other characters are not allowed pursuant to Dutch pension legislation. The *Pensioenwet* uses the word 'character' to clarify the nature of the pension agreement, indicating the characteristic element on which the pension agreement is aimed: the benefit, the capital or the premium.[875] What is more, the three characters are related to the degree to which risks lie with the employee. By choosing a particular vesting method, a choice is also made for certain risks, i.e. longevity risk, investment risk and interest rate risk. By solely allowing the three mentioned characters it is envisaged that it is clear to the employee what he can expect in terms of

872 See also MCD Janse and EHM Janssen, 'Werknemerspensioen in de loonsfeer, beroepspensioen en nettopensioen' in AHH Bollen-Vandenboorn (ed.), *Pensioen en de belangrijkste toekomstvoorzieningen* (27 edn Fiscale Geschriften, SDU, Den Haag 2022) 258.

873 Kamerstukken II, *Wijziging van de Pensioenwet, de Wet inkomstenbelasting 2001 en enige andere wetten in verband met herziening van het pensioenstelsel, standaardisering van het nabestaandenpensioen, aanpassing van de fiscale behandeling van pensioen en enige andere wijzigingen ten aanzien van pensioen (Wet toekomst pensioenen)* (2021/22) 27.

874 Pursuant to art. 10 PW.

875 Lutjens, *Asser-serie 7-XI – Pensioen (Bijzondere overeenkomsten)* nr. 109.

pension entitlements and what risks he faces.[876] However, hybrid pension schemes, or combination of elements of one of these types of agreements also exist. A universal aspect of all of these pension arrangements is that contributions are paid by both the employer and the employee. As a rule, two thirds of the contributions are paid by the employer, while one third is paid by the employee. There is no legal basis for this. These three 'allowed' natures of pension agreements are described in more detail below.

6.2.2.A Uitkeringsovereenkomst (Defined Benefit Agreement)

Firstly, the *uitkeringsovereenkomst* (defined benefit scheme), under which employee and employer enter into an agreement on a payment of a certain amount that is received from a certain age.[877] Under this benefit agreement, the pension accrual is based on either the pensionable salary or the deposited contribution. On the side of the participants, this type of agreement is least risky, i.e. during the accrual phase, as well as during the pay-out phase, the investment risk and longevity risk lies with the pension provider. In the Netherlands, the most common form of a defined benefits agreement is the average pay scheme, which will be elaborated on below. In addition to mixed forms of these accrual methods, the most common methods comprise the final salary scheme (*eindloonregeling*), average salary scheme (*middelloonregeling*) and fixed amount-schemes (*vastebedragenregeling*). The latter can be discussed very briefly at this point.[878] Under a fixed amount scheme, a fixed amount is accrued each year, hence, there is no link to pensionable salary, and the future amount of pension benefit solely depends on the number of working years. The final salary scheme and average salary scheme will be addressed in more detail in the sections below.

6.2.2.A.I Final Pay Scheme (Defined Benefit)

Under the Dutch final pay scheme, the basic principle is that the employer has concluded an agreement with the employee (i.e. pension agreement) on a pension benefit amounting to a certain amount, which benefit is received from a certain age. This therefore qualifies as a DB plan. An entitlement to this benefit is therefore built up whereby this depends on the (pensionable) salary and the pensionable years. Which parts of the salary and the years of service are pensionable, will not be discussed in further detail.[879] In practice, also moderate final pay schemes exist (in addition to the pure final pay scheme). Under these schemes, for example, the increase in salary is not (fully) included in the accrual of pension entitlements or a limitation with respect to the pensionable wage is included.

---

876 Kamerstukken II, (2005/06) 27.

877 See art. 1 PW.

878 The number of *vastebedragenregelingen* in practice is very limited (only 1.6% of all pension arrangements in place), see DNB.

879 See, for this, Janse and Janssen, section 6.5.

The pension is accrued – over the entire period of participation – by using a percentage of the last (prior to retirement) applicable pensionable amount at the age of retiring. However, the maximum accrual of pension entitlements under this scheme is capped for tax purposes. A maximum accrual percentage of 1.657 (% of the pensionable ground) per year (for an accrual period of 40 years) applies to final pay schemes.[880] According to the legislator, this is a reasonable number of years of service that can be required of an employee to build up an acceptable pension according to social standards.[881] These social standards have served as the starting point for the more concrete interpretation of the tax framework.

Under a final pay plan, risks associated with investments, longevity and interest in principle do not lie with the employee, but with the pension administrator. The final pay scheme is marked by the so-called back service-mechanism. Under this mechanism, increases in salary not only have an (beneficial) effect on the future accrual of pension rights (as the pensionable salary increases), but also on already accrued pension entitlements. The latter entitlements are, thus, adapted to the increase in salary, through the kind of retroactive effect of this back service-mechanism. The reason for the increase in pensionable wage does not alter this, it can be either a regular wage indexation or an increase due to a promotion.

These final pay schemes used to be prevailing, but over the years the emphasis has shifted to an average pay plan, which will be elaborated on in the section 6.2.2.A.II below.[882] In terms of pension entitlements for the employee, the final salary scheme is attractive, but it is also particularly expensive because of the allocation of back service.[883]

As of January 1, 2015, an ambition pension level of 75% of the average pensionable income, accrued over 40 years, applies. Following this, the (tax maximum) accrual rates have been drastically reduced and the accrual period extended, in order to ensure the financial sustainability of the pension system.[884] As a supplement to these austerity measures, the capping limit for pensionable wages was introduced on January 1, 2015. This measure stipulates that the tax reversal rule will only be applied for a pensionable income of

880 See art. 18a, para 1, Wet LB 1964.

881 Kamerstukken II.

882 See DNB. The percentage of final pay schemes (in % of total pension schemes) dropped from 64.7% in 1995 to 2.8% in 2019, while the ratio of average pay schemes increased from 12.6% in 1995 to 29.4% in 2019.

883 Lutjens, *Asser-serie 7-XI – Pensioen (Bijzondere overeenkomsten)* 110.

884 Wet van 2 juni 2014 tot wijziging van de Wet inkomstenbelasting 2001, de Wet op de loonbelasting 1964, de Pensioenwet, de Wet verplichte beroepspensioenregeling en de Invoerings- en aanpassingswet Pensioenwet in verband met de aanpassing van het fiscale kader voor oudedagsvoorzieningen (Wet verlaging maximumopbouw- en premiepercentages pensioen en maximering pensioengevend inkomen).

€128,810 (2023)[885]. This maximum is *grosso modo* equal to three times the middle-income. It was the legislator's stance that above a certain income level it is no longer necessary to facilitate pension accrual on a tax-deferred basis.[886] It is assumed that above this income level people themselves are able to provide for a supplement to their retirement income through savings if they wish. For the part of the income above the capping limit a new voluntary savings option was introduced, which will be discussed in section 6.3.4 hereinafter. This capping violates the application of the principle of deferred taxation, and negatively affects the foreseeability and consistency of applying this prominent facility.[887]

6.2.2.A.II Average Pay Scheme (Defined Benefit)

Under the average pay-scheme the basic principle is – similar to the final pay-schemes – that the employer has concluded an agreement with the employee (i.e. pension agreement) on a pension benefit amounting to a certain amount, which benefit is received from a certain age, and, hence, qualifies as a DB plan. This type of agreement is currently the most common variant within the domain of defined benefit agreements.[888]

An entitlement to this benefit is therefore built up whereby this depends on the (pensionable) salary and the pensionable years. The total pension entitlement constitutes an actual reflection of the average salary over the entire period of participation in the pension scheme. Contrary to the final pay-scheme, in an average pay scheme, a pension is granted for each year based on the pensionable earnings of the given year, and not the last applicable pensionable amount at the age of retiring. Hence, the total accrued pension amounts to the sum of all accrued pensions in each year, i.e. the pension to be achieved is related to the average (indexed) pension salary during the entire accrual period. Another difference with the final pay scheme, is that under the average pay schemes, individual salary increases, or decreases, solely have consequences for the years following the change in salary, i.e. no back service is granted. As a result, the pension outcome under an average pay scheme can differ significantly from the outcome under a final salary scheme. However, the maximum accrual of pension entitlements under this scheme is capped for tax purposes. The maximum accrual percentage has been set at 1.875 per year (for an accrual period of 40 years).[889] This should reflect average career development and the

885 See art. 18ga, para 1 Wet LB 1964.

886 Kamerstukken II, (2012/13) 4.

887 In the samen vein Janse and Janssen, 258.

888 DNB.

889 See art. 18a, para 2, Wet LB 1964. In the event where the pension scheme applies a lower accrual percentage that permitted by fiscal legislation, the given participant has the option to save additionally up to the maximum percentage, through a voluntary additional module, under the condition that the employer offers this option in the pension scheme agreed on. In these cases, the additional contributions is deductible for tax purposes as well.

effect it has on pension accrual. The cap on the pension income of €128,810 (2023)[890], applies to average pay schemes as well.

6.2.2.B Kapitaalovereenkomst (Defined Capital Agreement)

Secondly, pension may be accrued through a capital arrangement. Under a capital agreement, solely the amount of capital at the commencement of the retirement phase is determined in the agreement. Although during the accrual phase it is unknown how much the pension benefit to be purchased will be, the capital is already fixed; after all, it is promised. The aim is to build up such a capital that a pension can be purchased equivalent to 75% of the average pensionable income, i.e. the Dutch pension ambition which underlies the tax framework.[891] At commencement of the pay-out phase at the latest, the capital must be converted into a periodic benefit at the rates applicable at that time. During the accrual phase, the investment risk lies with the pension provider. Contrarily, the longevity risk lies, during the pay-out phase, with the employee. Only at the moment of converting the capital into a periodic benefit, the applicable rates will firstly be known. Those calculation rates include, in particular, life expectancy and interest rates. When choosing a defined benefit, these risks shift to the pension administrator in the pay-out phase; in the case of a choice for variable benefits, the risk of financial setbacks – and also financial windfalls – in the pay-out phase lies with the pensioner. Chapter IIB of the Wet LB does not recognise pension schemes with capital agreements, but only benefit agreements such as final pay schemes and average pay schemes on the one hand, and defined contribution schemes on the other. Capital agreements have in common with defined contribution schemes that the pension benefits to be obtained are not fixed in advance. Yet, they do not meet the tax conditions for defined contribution schemes.[892] Hence, in practice, there ambiguity may rise regarding the tax treatment of these capital pension agreements, i.e. how to be treated in fiscal terms. To resolve this lack of clarity, the State Secretary of Finance has designated capital schemes as pension schemes within the meaning of the Wet LB 1964, provided that they comply with the conditions and details set out in Appendix II of the decree, and the conditions set out in Chapter IIB.

6.2.2.C Premieovereenkomst (Defined Contribution Agreement)

Another pension accrual system concerns the defined contribution scheme (DC), in which the pension commitment is merely the provision of a contribution; neither a benefit nor a capital is promised. Under such an agreement, solely the amount of contribution is

890 See art. 18ga, para 1 Wet LB 1964.

891 For further (fiscal) requirements see Appendix II of Staatssecretaris van Financiën, *Besluit Loonheffingen, inkomstenbelasting. Pensioenen; beschikbare-premieregelingen en premie- en kapitaalovereenkomsten en nettopensioenregelingen (Staffelbesluit pensioenen) nr. 2019-21333* (20 December 2019).

892 As laid down in art. 18a, para 3 Wet LB 1964.

set in the agreement. The premium includes both employer and employee premiums. In a premium contract, a capital is formed on the basis of the premium paid, together with – positive or negative – returns on the investment of the premium. Similar to a capital agreement, at commencement of the pay-out phase at the latest, the capital must be converted into a periodic benefit at the rates applicable at that time. This type of agreement is currently the most common pension agreement, also in comparison to defined benefit agreements.[893] Over the years, the number of premium contracts has grown tremendously. This method of pension accrual is comparable to the *reine Beitragszusage*, in which only the payment of a pension contribution is promised as well. Under the Dutch available premium scheme – as well as under the *reine Beitragszusage* – both the longevity risk and the investment risk lie with the pension participant. This accrual method therefore entails the greatest risk for the participant, of all pension accrual systems. The basic tax principle is that a pension based on a defined contribution system is built up on a time-proportional basis, on the understanding that after 40 years of accrual the pension will not exceed 75% of the average pensionable pay at that time.[894] The eventual amount of the pension benefit is partly determined by a number of factors, including the age at which the participant joins the fund, and the future career development.

Moreover, in the light of the distribution of risks, three types of defined contributions arrangements can be distinguished.[895] Firstly, the pure contribution scheme.[896] Under this agreement, the contributions paid are invested until retirement date, leaving the amount of future pension capital – accrued by these contributions – in suspense. Under this pure contribution scheme, both the investment crisis and longevity risk, until the retirement date, lies with the employee. Given this allocation of risks, this form of agreement is the riskiest for the employee. Secondly, the agreement exists whereby the premium paid is

893 DNB.

894 Pursuant to art. 18a, para 3 Wet LB 1964. 75% of the average pensionable salary is the starting point for the further design of the tax framework. In order to determine the (defined) contributions, assumptions are made to determine the long-term rate of change. For defined contribution scheme, contribution scales have been established that are based on three principles: age brackets, career development and actuarial interest rate. These scales are used in the administration of the pension agreement, Staatssecretaris van Financiën, Appendix I.

895 Staatssecretaris van Financiën, *Besluit Loonheffingen, inkomstenbelasting. Pensioenen; beschikbare-premieregelingen en premie- en kapitaalovereenkomsten en nettopensioenregelingen (Staffelbesluit pensioenen) nr. 2019-21333* para 2. See also Broers, 155-156.

896 See Staatssecretaris van Financiën, *Besluit Loonheffingen, inkomstenbelasting. Pensioenen; beschikbare-premieregelingen en premie- en kapitaalovereenkomsten en nettopensioenregelingen (Staffelbesluit pensioenen) nr. 2019-21333* para 3. This scheme is identified as a defined contribution scheme within the meaning of the LB Act, provided that this scheme complies with the conditions and details set out in the annex. The scheme must also otherwise comply with the conditions of Chapter IIB of the LB Act.

immediately converted into an entitlement to capital.[897] A capital insurance is purchased immediately after the contribution is made available by the employee, while, on the retirement date, the insured capital then available shall be converted into an entitlement to a payment of capital. The conversion takes place at the then applicable rates. Under this agreement, the investment risk lies with the pension provider, but the longevity risk lies with the employee. Finally, from the employee's point of view, the least risk-bearing form of contribution agreement. Under this agreement, the premium is converted into a benefit entitlement immediately after it has been made available by the employee, i.e. the premium is immediately used to purchase an insurance for a periodic benefit.[898] However, after the conversion of the premium into an entitlement to benefits, a scheme similar to an average pay scheme emerges. In this premium agreement, both the longevity risk and the investment risk lie with the pension provider. What amount of pension benefit can be expected when the pension date is reached is uncertain for the member at the time of granting, since it is not yet known which total benefit the purchased entitlements will lead to. Premium contracts in which the premium is converted directly into an entitlement to a benefit, reflect elements of both an average-premium system, as well as a defined-premium system.

6.2.2.D Combined Pension Arrangements and Vesting Methods

Besides these differences in pension agreements, these accrual methods can also be implemented side by side in a single agreement. For example, the old-age pension may consist of a combination of a benefit agreement up to a certain income threshold or age, and accrual above this income threshold or age is based on a contribution agreement. The *Pensioenwet* does not recognize these forms as being peculiar to a pension agreement. For the application of the *Pensioenwet*, for such a form of pension agreement it will also have to be indicated which of the three recognized characters this pension agreement holds.[899] Furthermore, not merely different types of pension arrangements[900] may be combined in a pension arrangement, but different types of vesting methods may be implemented in one pension arrangement as well, for instance a final salary system with an average salary system. This combination of different vesting methods may be motivated by taking

897 See ibid. para 3. This scheme is identified as a defined contribution scheme within the meaning of the LB Act, provided that this scheme complies with the conditions and details set out in the annex. The scheme must also otherwise comply with the conditions of Chapter IIB of the LB Act.

898 See ibid. para 5. This scheme is identified as a defined contribution scheme within the meaning of the Wet LB 1964, provided that this scheme complies with the conditions and details set out in the annex III. The scheme must also otherwise comply with the conditions of Chapter IIB of the Wet LB 1964.

899 Cf. Lutjens, *Asser-serie 7-XI – Pensioen (Bijzondere overeenkomsten)* nr. 115.

900 Pension arrangements in terms of art. 10 PW.

different salary components into account during the accrual of the pension entitlements.[901] In practice, the best-known examples of such pension agreements are the target plan and the Collective Defined Contribution (CDC) plan; these forms are discussed briefly below.

6.2.2.E Hybrid Pension Schemes

Besides the aforementioned different pension arrangements as such, vesting methods, and combinations thereof, varieties of these pension systems have been implemented in practice. These pension schemes should be qualified as hybrid pension schemes, since they do not qualify for either of the different systems. One example are the so-called target pension schemes (*streefregelingen*), under which, for example, a capital insurance with a pension clause has been taken out.[902] Under such target schemes, an intended retirement pension, based on salary and period of service, is converted into an insured capital. In turn, this insured capital should, on the basis of a number of principles, be sufficient in order to purchase the intended retirement pension on retirement date. Since an intended retirement pension is set as a target, which shall be financed through the accrual, and ultimately the conversion of capital, these types of schemes are referred to as target schemes. The eventual pension benefits received depend on the pension capital available on the retirement date and the applicable rates; no guarantee is given regarding the final pension benefit. Therefore, this scheme does not qualify as a final pay scheme. The scheme does not qualify as a defined contribution scheme either, since the fiscal conditions are not met.[903] These hybrid schemes may put the participants on the wrong foot in that the pension arrangement constitutes a benefit agreement, even though there are certain risks to be borne by the employee. In order to end this ambiguity for the benefit of the participants, it must be made clear in the pension agreement that it comprises a benefit agreement, a capital agreement or a contribution agreement.[904]

6.2.2.F Collective Defined Contribution-schemes

In addition to the above, reference can be made to the so-called CDC schemes (Collective Defined Contribution). This scheme is also hybrid, in the sense that it encompasses modalities of salary/time-of-service schemes (such as average/ final salary schemes) on the one hand, and defined contribution schemes on the other. The scheme appears to be a defined benefit agreement, but clearly also contains features of a defined contribution

901 Since, pursuant to art. 18g, par. 2, lit. b Wet LB 1964 in conjunction with art. 10b UBLB 1965, wage components not forming part of the regularly earned wage, may not be taken into account under a final salary system, contrary to an average salary system.

902 Kamerstukken II, 33 and Bollen-Vandenboorn, 'Werknemerspensioen in de loonsfeer, beroepspensioen en nettopensioen' 223.

903 As laid down in art. 18a, para 3 Wet LB 1964.

904 Pursuant to art. 10 PW.

agreement, i.e. the element of defined contribution from a contribution agreement and a defined benefit from a defined benefit agreement. In the case of hybrid pension schemes, different pension schemes are combined in one pension vehicle. In those cases, Dutch tax legislation stipulates that all elements together are taken into account and considered in conjunction with each other when determining whether the pension scheme should be regarded as a pension scheme based on a final pay scheme, an average pay scheme or a defined contribution scheme.[905]

These CDC schemes have gained ground in the Netherlands in recent years. The starting point for the scheme is – in most cases – an average pay scheme with conditional post-indexation. The term 'collective' in this context refers to the fact that the contributions are invested collectively, with the actuarial and underfunding risk being borne by the participants. The annual pension accrual under this scheme should correspond to the level laid down in the pension scheme, although it is possible that the pension accrual will need to be adjusted if the pension contribution received is insufficient to cover the promised pension accrual, i.e. the annual pension accrual is variable. This risk lies on the participant's side.

As mentioned above, this scheme is marked by a hybrid character, which manifests itself as follows. Under this scheme, the pension contribution – established on actuarial principles – is expressed as a percentage of the total salary or pensionable pay; this (disposable) pension contribution is then used to purchase benefits directly. The premium is determined in advance – for at least five years – so that the employer cannot be held liable by the pension administrator for any shortfalls in coverage. This means that any financial surplus will remain with the pension administrator.[906]

6.2.3 *Wet Toekomst Pensioenen: Imminent Fundamental Revision*

On June 5, 2019, the Dutch Cabinet and employee and employer organizations revealed the outlines of the new pension agreement.[907] Subsequently, on July 4, 2020, the Cabinet and social partners reached an agreement on reforming the pension system in a comprehensive package of measures, i.e. the so-called Pension Agreement.[908] In 2020, agreement was reached on the further elaboration of this in the Outline Memorandum on

905 See art. 19f Wet LB 1964 in conjunction with art. 4.3 Uitvoeringsregeling loonbelasting 2011.

906 See also Janse and Janssen, 263 and cited literature.

907 Kamerstukken II, *Toekomst pensioenstelsel* (2018/19).

908 Kamerstukken II, *Wet toekomst pensioenen.*

the Elaboration of the Pension Agreement (*Hoofdlijnennotitie uitwerking Pensioenakkoord*).[909]

Since autumn 2020, the agreements about the second-pillar pension have been elaborated in the draft bill on future pensions (*Conceptwetsvoorstel Toekomst Pensioenen*). On March 29, 2022 the bill on the future of pensions was presented to the Dutch parliament (*Wetsvoorstel Toekomst Pensioenen*).[910] This draft bill is extensive and contains fundamental changes to the pension system, and can be considered as one of the most significant system changes in recent decades. It is, for instance, more ground-breaking than the implementation of the *reine Beitragszusage*, pursuant to the *Betriebsrentenstärkungsgesetz*.[911]

The pension agreement contains a comprehensive range of agreements and measures. In addition to agreements on reforming the second-pillar pension, agreements have been made regarding improvements to the old-age provision in the Netherlands in general. Among others, agreements have been made about the rate at which the state pension age will be raised. The bill on the lump sum, RVU and leave savings has also already entered partially into force, implementing three measures from the pension agreement.[912]

Rising life expectancy, increasing labour mobility, and the susceptibility of the current system to shocks in financial markets called for a reform of the pension system.[913] The agreements that have been made purportedly ensure a sustainable pension system that offers better prospects for a pension with purchasing power (which also means that the pension will move more directly in line with developments on the financial markets or investment returns), aimed at making pensions more transparent and more personal, and better aligned with developments in society and the labour market.[914] Yet, the Dutch legislator emphasized that solidarity and collectivity remain fundamental principles and the current mandatory rules will be retained.

909 Minister van Sociale Zaken en Werkgelegenheid, 'Hoofdlijnennotitie uitwerking pensioenakkoord'.

910 Ministerie van Sociale Minister voor Armoedebeleid Participatie en Pensioenen, *Wijziging van de Pensioenwet, de Wet inkomstenbelasting 2001 en enige andere wetten in verband met herziening van het pensioenstelsel, standaardisering van het nabestaandenpensioen, aanpassing van de fiscale behandeling van pensioen en enige andere wijzigingen ten aanzien van pensioen (Wet toekomst pensioenen)* (2022).

911 Gesetz zur Stärkung der betrieblichen Altersversorgung und zur Änderung anderer Gesetze (Betriebsrentenstärkungsgesetz).

912 Minister van Sociale Zaken en Werkgelegenheid, *Besluit van 14 januari 2021 tot vaststelling van het tijdstip van inwerkingtreding van de Wet bedrag ineens, RVU en verlofsparen* (21 January 2021).

913 See Minister van Sociale Zaken en Werkgelegenheid, 'Hoofdlijnennotitie uitwerking pensioenakkoord'.

914 Minister van Sociale Zaken en Werkgelegenheid, *Stand van zaken uitwerking pensioenakkoord* (10 May 2021) 2.

It leads to a radical renewal of the occupational retirement pension. These changes affect the vast majority of participants and pensioners, regardless of the type of pension agreement and regardless of the type of pension provider. At the heart of the bill is the transition to a new pension vesting method, i.e. the 'new pension contract'. Two elements are pivotal in this respect: abolishing the so-called *doorsneepremiesystematiek* (average-contribution system), and the accrual of pension rights is solely possible through a premium agreement (DC-scheme). This reflects the reality that pension outcomes of any funded pension contract are determined by the level of contributions made, investment policy and interest rates, rendering the level of pension benefits not fixed.[915] In particular the latter development (which can be observed Europe-wide) leads to an increasing shift of risks towards the individual pension saver, as a consequence of which they will bear greater responsibility for their own financial well-being. The transfer is far-reaching and cannot be changed. It is therefore important that members understand the importance and consequences of the *Wet Toekomst Pensioenen*. Furthermore, it underlines the importance of sound pension information provision, in order to (eventually) enable these pension savers to ensure their pension's adequacy.

The draft act has set many discussions in motion. The consultation round demonstrated that the revision is very topical: no fewer than 800 reactions were posted, many of which were substantive.[916] This, however, has not yet calmed the turmoil. There is still much to be expected regarding this revision, in turn, affecting the foreseeability of this revision and the underlying legislation. However, the Dutch government recognizes that in addition to legislation and regulation, one of its tasks is to educate citizens about what the change in the pension system means for them.[917]

6.2.3.A Postponed Entry into Force: Out of the Frying Pan into the Fire?

The intended date of entry into force of the Future Pensions Act had been pushed back to January 1, 2023. On October 6th 2022, however, the Minister announced that the intended date of entry into force of the Future Pensions Act was being postponed to July 1, 2023.[918] The reason for the postponement is that consideration in the Parliament had not yet been completed, careful consideration must then take place in the Senate, and the minister considered it unlikely that the bill's passage in the Senate can be completed in 2022. The postponement means that employers wishing to enter into a new pension plan as of January 1, 2023, must still rely on the current legislation.

---

915 Kamerstukken II, *Wet toekomst pensioenen* 15.

916 Minister van Sociale Zaken en Werkgelegenheid, *Stand van zaken uitwerking pensioenakkoord* 2.

917 IAK, *Beantwoording van de 7 vragen uit het Integraal afwegingskader voor beleid en regelgeving (IAK)* (16 December 2020).

918 Minister van Armoedebeleid Participatie en Pensioenen, 8.

Initially, the transition period's deadline was set on January 1, 2027. However, on 14 June 2023, the Dutch Minister Schouten informed the House of Representatives about the transition period of the Future Pensions Act.[919] As promised in the Senate, the transition period will be extended by one year, from 1 January 2027 to 1 January 2028. The purpose of the longer transition period is to give implementation – if necessary – more time to achieve a controlled and careful transition. The interim milestones such as the deadline for submitting the transition plan (1 January 2025) and implementation and communication plan (1 July 2025 for pension funds) do not alter. By including the statutory deadlines in lower regulations, the minister is keeping the door open to possibly extending the transition period further, should this prove necessary at any time based on experience during the transition.

Hence, after the Future Pensions Act takes effect, a five-year transition phase will apply (2023 to 2028), during which social partners must agree on a pension plan that fits within the new legal framework, and pension administrators must implement the new pension scheme. No later than January 1, 2028, the new pension scheme that meets the requirements of the Act on Future Pensions must enter into force. However, parties may choose to make the transition at an earlier date within the transition period.

This flexibility in the transition period – allegedly – allows justice to be done to what is needed in specific situations.[920] However, this tailor-made approach adds to the complexity of the entire transition process and it can be called into question to what extent it is reminiscent of the metaphor 'out of the frying pay into the fire'. Moreover, this poses great challenges as regards pension information provision, in terms of consistency. After the entry into force of the new system, it will be possible to leave already accrued pension entitlements and rights unaltered and premium free in the 'old' pension system. However, the basic principle is that entitlements and rights by means of a collective internal value transfer will be brought into the new pension system ('substitution').[921]

6.2.3.B Types of Pension Schemes under the New System

Of the three contract types that the Pensions Act (*Pensioenwet*) – as it stance – distinguishes, i.e. the benefit scheme, the capital scheme and the premium scheme, only the latter type remains after a transition phase. Pension can then only be accrued in a premium scheme

919 Minister voor Armoedebeleid Participatie en Pensioenen, *Volgen voortgang transitieperiode wet toekomst pensioenen* (14 June 2023).

920 Minister van Sociale Zaken en Werkgelegenheid, *Stand van zaken uitwerking pensioenakkoord.*

921 See proposed art. 150m Pensioenwet and 145l Wet verplichte beroepspensioenregeling.

with an age-independent (flat) premium.[922] The premium constitutes the employment commitment, through which the social partners aim to achieve an agreed pension ambition. In the implementation of the pension agreement, existing rights under a defined benefit agreement or a capital agreement would, as far as possible, be converted to the new pension system following a standard entry route. This (flat) age-independent contribution is also more in line with the Dutch third pillar of retirement provision, as this pillar already applies an age-independent maximum contribution. This also corresponds to the proposal to equalise the tax treatment of the second and third pillars as much as possible.

This bill ensures that the distinction between pension agreements in the *Pensioenwet* is made on the basis of whether or not returns and risks are shared within a contribution agreement and the manner in which these are shared.[923] This bill adapts the existing frameworks to the fact that future accrual of a retirement pension on the basis of a defined benefit agreement and a capital agreement is no longer possible. After the entry into force of this bill, parties can only agree on a pension scheme for retirement pension that falls within the statutory framework for one of the three forms of contribution agreements.

A defined contribution agreement involves a fixed pension contribution for the employee's pension accrual.[924] This contribution is in principle a fixed percentage of the annual salary or the pension base. The starting point of the pension commitment is the amount of the pension contribution, which means that the amount of the eventual pension benefit is not fixed in advance, leading to a considerable shift of risks towards pension participants for the adequacy of their pension. The amount of this eventual pension depends, among other things, on the pension contributions, the returns achieved, interest rates and the development of life expectancy. Premium contracts may differ in the way in which financial upsides and downsides are distributed among (active, former and future) participants and pensioners or in which certain risks are insured. What is more, the degree of freedom of choice and flexibility differs as well. Under the new pension system three premium-based schemes are introduced: the solidarity premium agreement; the flexible premium agreement; the premium-benefit agreement.[925] These three types will be discussed in the sections below.

922 Kamerstukken II, *Wijziging van de Pensioenwet, de Wet inkomstenbelasting 2001 en enige andere wetten in verband met herziening van het pensioenstelsel, standaardisering van het nabestaandenpensioen, aanpassing van de fiscale behandeling van pensioen en enige andere wijzigingen ten aanzien van pensioen (Wet toekomst pensioenen)* 27.

923 Ibid. 27.

924 Ibid. 28.

925 See proposed art. 10 Pensioenwet, Ministerie van Sociale Minister voor Armoedebeleid Participatie en Pensioenen.

The transfer to premium schemes with age-independent contributions may have a negative effect on pension accrual, particularly for individuals in the age group of 45-55 years of age. What is more, under the new pension system pension benefits are less certain, as more risks – investment risks, interest risk – are shifted towards participants. Employees affected by the switch to age-independent premiums, and an appropriate pension accrual, in their expected pension result shall be, purportedly, adequately compensated for this. This can be achieved in various ways, for example because after the transition to a new pension contract, financial results are more likely to lead to an increase in pensions or the assets set aside for the pension. Employees who are already accrue pension under a premium agreement with a progressive premium shall be subject to transitional rules. For them, the transition will only have effect if they switch to another employer, as a result of which the age-independent premium will also apply to them. An exception to this is the transitional law for existing participants in contribution schemes and benefit agreements that have been placed with an insurer.

In short, the main specificities of the solidarity-based contribution agreement are a variable pension benefit and the solidarity reserve, where the pension benefit can vary from year to year due to investment returns after retirement date.[926] The main features of the flexible contribution agreement are the choice between a fixed pension benefit that is the same for life or the aforementioned variable pension benefit, as well as the absence of a mandatory solidarity reserve. The main features of the contributory benefit agreement are that it can only be executed by an insurer or contributory pension institution (*premiepensioeninstelling*; *PPI*) and that a fixed and lifelong equal pension benefit can be purchased starting 15 years prior to reaching the state pension age.

Incidentally, existing pension agreements should be brought into the new system as much as possible (referred to as '*invaren*', which is not a legal term).[927] This means converting – through a collective internal value transfer – a pension accrued in a benefit agreement into the pension capital of a contribution agreement. Although this will become the norm for pension funds, the government has refrained from setting this a legal requirement, leaving social partners leeway to deviate from this norm, with justification. If social partners opt for this, employees are confronted with two pensions that will be administered separately from the entry into force of the Future Pension Act: the pension accrued through a benefit agreement and the pension to be accrued through a contribution agreement. In this regard, employees do not have the right of consent and the same applies to former employees and pensioners.

926 See also B Dieleman, 'Wet toekomst pensioenen aangenomen: een analyse van de fiscale aspecten' MBB.
927 See Kamerstukken II, *Wet toekomst pensioenen* 167, 177 ff., 277.

6.2.3.B.I Solidarity Premium Agreement

The solidarity contract qualifies as a contribution agreement in which the contribution is collectively invested and results are allocated to birth cohorts.[928] The assets intended for benefits are used from the retirement date to fund variable benefits.[929] The investment risk and longevity risk are borne by the (former) participants and pensioners. This type of pension contract has a personal capital reserved for benefits for each participant, rendering it clear how much capital is available for their own pension provision. However, the total assets for all participants together are still invested collectively. Contrary to current benefit agreements, the collective investment results, as well as biometric results, are then specifically allocated per age cohort, on the basis of predetermined allocation rules that match the risk attitude of the participants per age cohort.[930] As of the retirement date onward, a proportion of the reserved personal pension capital is periodically withdrawn on the basis of a prudent projection return. The pension benefits will be paid on this basis. Thus, no fixed pension benefit is purchased on the retirement date for the entire pay-pout phase (after all, this is not a DB scheme), but a pension benefit that may vary. On the basis of this personal pension capital and the aforementioned projection return, it can be determined – using a uniform, objective calculation method and legal-embedded parameters – what pension benefit can be expected in the future. This projection return serves to ensure consistency in such areas as communication about expected pension benefits and setting the fiscal contribution limit.

In addition to these personal pension assets, the solidarity reserve is an important and mandatory part of this contract. This embodies risk-sharing between current and future participants. This reserve also makes it possible to absorb fluctuations in pension outcomes by supplementing pension assets and pension benefits, which should result in more stable and/or higher average pension outcomes. The solidarity reserve is funded partly by contributions and/or part of the excess return. Yet, the solidarity reserve is not a separate investment pot. Within the legal possibilities, the pension administrator may determine the filling and distribution rules and set the desired and maximum size.[931] The fiscal treatment of the solidarity reserve shall be laid down in the *Wet op de loonbelasting 1964*.[932]

---

928 Kamerstukken II, *Wijziging van de Pensioenwet, de Wet inkomstenbelasting 2001 en enige andere wetten in verband met herziening van het pensioenstelsel, standaardisering van het nabestaandenpensioen, aanpassing van de fiscale behandeling van pensioen en enige andere wijzigingen ten aanzien van pensioen (Wet toekomst pensioenen)* 28.

929 Proposed article 1 Pensioenwet, see Ministerie van Sociale Minister voor Armoedebeleid Participatie en Pensioenen.

930 Proposed art. 10a, para 4 and 6 Pensioenwet.

931 Proposed art. 10a and 10c Pensioenwet.

932 Proposed art. 18aa Wet LB 1964.

6.2.3.B.II *The Flexible Premium Agreement*

This contract constitutes an already existing form of a (pure) premium scheme, defined as a premium contract in which the premium is invested (until retirement date) individually, and in which the capital resulting from the premium is harnessed from the retirement date onwards to finance a variable benefit, or to purchase a defined benefit.[933] This type of contract is characterized by a separate accrual and pay-out phase, whereby the accrual phase holds a more personal character compared to the aforementioned solidarity contract.[934] Under this type of contract, an individual pension capital is built up (as well) that is converted into or used for a lifelong pension payment on the retirement date.

The investment policy is designed on the basis of specific investment mixes for each age cohort (life-cycles). Financial windfalls and shortfalls are incorporated directly into the individual pension assets on the basis of returns achieved. Depending on the design, participants may or may not have freedom to choose investment profiles. The investment risk and longevity risk are entirely borne by the (former) participants and pensioners. These risks can be shared collectively in the benefit phase through a collective allocation circle, whereby gradual entry into this circle is possible no later than ten years before retirement date.[935] A risk-sharing reserve can be part of a flexible premium contract.[936]

---

933 See proposed art. 10b Pensioenwet; Kamerstukken II, *Wijziging van de Pensioenwet, de Wet inkomstenbelasting 2001 en enige andere wetten in verband met herziening van het pensioenstelsel, standaardisering van het nabestaandenpensioen, aanpassing van de fiscale behandeling van pensioen en enige andere wijzigingen ten aanzien van pensioen (Wet toekomst pensioenen)* 28.

934 The pension contributions are invested on the basis of so-called life cycles. The participant can also choose from various risk profiles, e.g. offensive, neutral and defensive. In contrast to the solidarity contract, the participant in the flexible contract thus has the possibility to control the way in which his/her premiums are invested, within the possibilities offered by the pension provider. Investment results on the contributions are processed directly into the individual pension assets of the participants.

935 Kamerstukken II, *Wijziging van de Pensioenwet, de Wet inkomstenbelasting 2001 en enige andere wetten in verband met herziening van het pensioenstelsel, standaardisering van het nabestaandenpensioen, aanpassing van de fiscale behandeling van pensioen en enige andere wijzigingen ten aanzien van pensioen (Wet toekomst pensioenen)* 28.

936 See proposed art. 10b, para 2 in conjunction with art. 10e Pensioenwet. By means of the risk-sharing reserve, financial windfalls or setbacks are shared collectively in a way that on average leads to more stable or higher future and already paid pension benefits for all generations, compared to the situation where the risk-sharing reserve is not part of the pension plan. A risk-sharing reserve has a maximum size of 15% of the total assets reserved for pension, including the risk-sharing reserve. If a risk-sharing reserve is filled from premiums, the premium contribution shall not exceed 10% of the premium amount per member per year. A risk-sharing reserve is not funded from return on investments.

In contrast to the solidarity contract, the flexible contract does have the possibility of a fixed benefit in addition to the variable benefit.[937] In the case of a variable payment, the pension capital is invested further to a certain risk-bearing extent in the payment phase.

6.2.3.B.III *Premium Benefit Agreement*

This concerns a pure premium scheme up to 15 years before the statutory pension age (AOW).[938] From 15 years before the state pension age, at the member's request, the accrued capital can be used to purchase guaranteed fixed lifelong pension benefits from the retirement date.[939] The participant can choose to purchase guaranteed fixed lifetime pension benefits based on the pension assets accrued to date but also using only future premiums. This can also be a partially fixed benefit. The premium and/or the accrued pension capital can be used directly to purchase that entitlement to a periodic benefit. Both the (micro and macro) longevity risk and the interest rate and investment risk are taken over by the insurer when purchasing a fixed benefit. Only insurers can offer this defined benefit contract since – unlike pension funds – they can guarantee a nominal pension. In the case of variable benefits, financial windfalls or setbacks resulting from the investment risk or from the development of life expectancy are incorporated by means of individual allocation.[940]

6.2.3.C Tax Treatment under the Wet Toekomst Pensioenen

As has been addressed in the previous section, the Dutch occupational pension system will be amended fundamentally, which abolishes benefit plans (DB) and moves to various forms of a defined contribution plan. The new pension system calls for a new tax framework, regulating the conditions under which the principle of deferred taxation may be applied. The fundamental change of accruing pensions also entails a major change to the tax framework, which will be adapted accordingly. The starting point is that the same fiscal framework applies to all types of pension plans.[941] After the transition to the new pension contacts, the tax framework no longer caps the accrual of pension entitlements, but rather the contributions paid shall be capped. This means that an uniform contribution

937 For an general overview of the differences and similarities between the solidarity contract, and the flexible contract, see Janse and Janssen, 289-290.

938 Kamerstukken II, *Wijziging van de Pensioenwet, de Wet inkomstenbelasting 2001 en enige andere wetten in verband met herziening van het pensioenstelsel, standaardisering van het nabestaandenpensioen, aanpassing van de fiscale behandeling van pensioen en enige andere wijzigingen ten aanzien van pensioen (Wet toekomst pensioenen)* 28.

939 See proposed art. 10c, para 2 Pensioenwet.

940 See proposed art. 10c, para 4 Pensioenwet.

941 Kamerstukken II, *Wet toekomst pensioenen* 57.

limit will apply to everyone, with the amount being such that – in the Dutch government's view – adequate pension accrual will be facilitated.[942]

As all forms of DB-schemes will be abolished and DC-schemes will be the solely-existing type of pension scheme, the tax legislation will be adapted by capping on an age-independent premium for all types of pension schemes, instead of capping both the pension entitlements and the contributions (as under the current system). This means that the tax framework no longer differentiates between different types of pension agreements, except for the transitional law for existing participants in premium schemes and in benefit agreements placed with an insurer. From a complexity-reduction perspective, this transition is to be welcomed, as it will lead to less tensions in information provision. However, as a consequence, the vast majority of employers and employees have to adjust their pension agreement. The above also applies to members under a so-called *beroepspensioenregeling*.

6.2.3.C.I Fiscal Contribution Threshold

Thus, the fiscal facilitation will be capped by a contribution threshold, applying to everyone under the new system. The fiscal framework will be adjusted by moving to an age-independent premium for all pension schemes, subject to transitional law.[943] The required contribution is determined on the basis of a measure with generally accepted parameters for life expectancy, *AOW-franchise*, career pattern, starting salary and type of survivor's pension, largely in line with the current premium scales decree.[944] The most important parameter is the expected return, as this has a major impact on the level of premium required. Currently, an expected real return of 1.5% is incorporated. Future adjustments to the tax-based contribution limit will only take into account changes in the real return.[945] By assuming a real return, no additional premium is required to finance indexation. A retirement age of 68 years will be used for this purpose.

942 Kamerstukken II, *Wijziging van de Pensioenwet, de Wet inkomstenbelasting 2001 en enige andere wetten in verband met herziening van het pensioenstelsel, standaardisering van het nabestaandenpensioen, aanpassing van de fiscale behandeling van pensioen en enige andere wijzigingen ten aanzien van pensioen (Wet toekomst pensioenen)* 138.

943 Kamerstukken II, *Wet toekomst pensioenen* 57.

944 Kamerstukken II, *Wijziging van de Pensioenwet, de Wet inkomstenbelasting 2001 en enige andere wetten in verband met herziening van het pensioenstelsel, standaardisering van het nabestaandenpensioen, aanpassing van de fiscale behandeling van pensioen en enige andere wijzigingen ten aanzien van pensioen (Wet toekomst pensioenen)* 139.

945 For this purpose, the Wet LB 1964 maps out which rate of (real) return corresponds to which contribution limit. The premium rate can be a minimum of 13% and a maximum of 48%, see proposed art. 18a, para 6 Wet LB 1964.

A precondition for determining the fiscal contribution limitation in the new pension system is budget neutrality.[946] Currently, the annual (age-independent) budget-neutral contribution limit is capped at 30% of pensionable salary, excluding cost and risk mark-ups.[947] The pensionable base is set by reducing the pensionable wage (capped pursuant to art. 18ga Wet LB 1964) by the AOW-franchise. This 30% premium limit is above the current premium for approximately 90% of the participants. With the proposed contribution limitation, the (maximum) pension ambition formulated in the Pension Accord of 75% average pay in 40 years of accrual (rounded off 80% at age 42) will also be fiscally facilitated in the new pension system, based on an expected return.[948] This limit is equal to the current ambition (for average pay schemes). The 30% limit covers the retirement pension and the surviving dependants' pension that commences upon death on or after the retirement date.

However, the contribution limit will be generically increased by 3% to 33% of the contribution base from the entry into force of this act until 2037.[949] This offers additional opportunities to use the available leeway for pension compensation, aimed at age groups affected detrimentally by abolishing the *doorsneesystematiek*. If the regular available contribution of 30% is fully utilized, a compensatory contribution of 3% remains on balance. Even if the regular maximum contribution limit is not used in a pension agreement, the unused leeway can be used for a higher compensation contribution. The premium available for compensation cannot be used for purposes other than those made possible by this act. The receipt of compensation is not subject to any fiscal limitation. This offers the possibility of making tailor-made agreements so that compensation can be targeted.

If, however, an employee did not accrue or accrued less than the maximum pension in a given year prior to the enactment of the Future Pensions Act, this cannot be done retroactively after this Act entered into force.[950] This is a limitation compared to the regulations currently in force. Catch-up of pension and repurchase of pensionable years

946 Minister van Sociale Zaken en Werkgelegenheid, 'Hoofdlijnennotitie uitwerking pensioenakkoord' 27.

947 See proposed art. 18a, para 1 Wet LB 1964. See also Kamerstukken II, *Wet toekomst pensioenen* 57. The *Hoofdlijnennotitie* announced a premium limit in a range of at least 30% and up to 33%.

948 Kamerstukken II, *Wijziging van de Pensioenwet, de Wet inkomstenbelasting 2001 en enige andere wetten in verband met herziening van het pensioenstelsel, standaardisering van het nabestaandenpensioen, aanpassing van de fiscale behandeling van pensioen en enige andere wijzigingen ten aanzien van pensioen (Wet toekomst pensioenen)* 138.

949 Ibid. 142-143.

950 Kamerstukken II, *Wijziging van de Pensioenwet, de Wet inkomstenbelasting 2001 en enige andere wetten in verband met herziening van het pensioenstelsel, standaardisering van het nabestaandenpensioen, aanpassing van de fiscale behandeling van pensioen en enige andere wijzigingen ten aanzien van pensioen (Wet toekomst Pensioenen) (Nota naar aanleiding van het verslag) nr. 7* (2021/22) 113.

will still be possible after implementation of the new tax system, however, for years of service, in which that new tax system applies.

As regards the *nettopensioen*-vehicle – introduced in 2015 in capping pensionable wages – it is proposed to bring the net pension in line with the changes proposed for the pension to which the principle of deferred taxation applies (the 'gross' pension).[951] Hence, these schemes will be based on a flat-rate (net) premium as well. For the net retirement pension, the same contribution limit is proposed as for the 'gross' pension but corrected by the net factor.[952] For these proposed adjustment to the net pension, no grandfathering clause applies for existing contribution scales as it does with regard to gross pensions. This is considered not necessary since the net premium limit is approximately equal to the percentage that is usually applied in the highest age cohort in the premium scale for the net pension.[953] In addition, net pensions are not subject to the legal requirement of an age-dependent contribution, as they are all voluntary schemes.

6.2.3.C.II Adjusting Mechanism: Reflecting Reality versus Increasing Ambiguity

In addition, there will be a mechanism for adjusting the fiscal contribution limit, which will strike a balance between not adjusting the contribution limit too often, and not allowing the consequences of changing circumstances to affect too much delay (of its implementation).[954] In this way, the Dutch Cabinet aspires to avoid a situation in which there is either structurally too little tax leeway to realize the ambition or, on the other hand, the tax leeway becomes so wide that this has undesirable consequences for labour participation and government finances. Creating a legal basis for the adjustment mechanism will provide certainty about the method of adjustment. The adjustment mechanism is simply implemented by including in the law a table showing the relationship between return and contribution limit.

Of all parameters, only the expected return and inflation will be subject to (major) change. The other parameters either do not change by definition (such as gender and age difference), change only slightly or have little effect on the contribution limit (such as, for

---

951 Kamerstukken II, *Wijziging van de Pensioenwet, de Wet inkomstenbelasting 2001 en enige andere wetten in verband met herziening van het pensioenstelsel, standaardisering van het nabestaandenpensioen, aanpassing van de fiscale behandeling van pensioen en enige andere wijzigingen ten aanzien van pensioen (Wet toekomst pensioenen)* 143-144.

952 This *nettofactor* is laid down in art. 5.16, paragraph 4 Wet IB 2001.

953 Kamerstukken II, *Wijziging van de Pensioenwet, de Wet inkomstenbelasting 2001 en enige andere wetten in verband met herziening van het pensioenstelsel, standaardisering van het nabestaandenpensioen, aanpassing van de fiscale behandeling van pensioen en enige andere wijzigingen ten aanzien van pensioen (Wet toekomst pensioenen)* 144.

954 Ibid. 141.

example, changes in career development, starting salary or deductible) or remain in balance with each other (life expectancy and retirement age).[955] In this way, the government expects that the contribution limit will move with economic conditions in a similar way as it would have done under the current system with the limitation for contribution under the accrual limit.

The contribution limit will be reviewed once every five years. For the sake of clarity, certainty and stability, the contribution limit will, in principle, not be adjusted until immediately after the compensation period ends.[956] This means that the contribution limit will be fixed until 2037; only in the event of a shock of more than 5 percentage points will the contribution limit be adjusted during the compensation period.[957] Adjustments will be communicated three years in advance so that social partners can include this information in collective bargaining negotiations.[958] It should be noted, that this concerns the adjustment mechanism of the tax-based maximum premium. If a previously agreed premium is below the new fiscal premium limit, application of this mechanism does not necessarily lead to an adjustment of the pension scheme. This adjusting mechanism allows the fiscal contribution threshold to keep pace with economic (constructed) reality, based on these parameters.

It appears to be evident – from a legal perspective – that adjusting the tax-based premium threshold calls for revision on a regular basis. However, from an information provision-perspective it seems inevitable that this adjustment mechanism leads to more ambiguity and unforeseeability, rendering effective pension information provision even more difficult.

6.2.3.C.III Transitional Fiscal Scheme

By January 1, 2027 pension agreements must be adjusted in line with the new tax framework.[959] The consequences of not amending a benefit agreement to one of the contributory agreements introduced through the Future Pensions Act before January 1, 2027, are significant. For example, a pension administrator may no longer administer the pension plan, neither will tax facilitation of pensions be granted. However, in the period

955 Ibid. 141.

956 Ibid. 142.

957 As a result, as of January 1, 2037, the proposed section 18ab Wet LB 1964 will be repealed.

958 Kamerstukken II, *Wijziging van de Pensioenwet, de Wet inkomstenbelasting 2001 en enige andere wetten in verband met herziening van het pensioenstelsel, standaardisering van het nabestaandenpensioen, aanpassing van de fiscale behandeling van pensioen en enige andere wijzigingen ten aanzien van pensioen (Wet toekomst pensioenen)* 142.

959 Ibid. 143.

between 30 June 2023, 2023, and January 1, 2027, a transition period applies, during which it is still possible to accrue pension under the current tax framework on the condition that this pension entitlements shall accrue in a scheme existing on 30 June 2023.[960] In cases where the choice is made to insert ('*invaren*') existing accrued pension entitlements, the new tax legislation will also apply to these inserted entitlements. If, however, insertion is not opted for, the current tax framework will continue to apply to pension entitlements accrued no later than December 31, 2026.

For contribution agreements that existed on June 30, 2023, or for benefit agreements that existed on this date, the current tax framework will continue to apply after 2026.[961] The transition from a progressive premium to an (age-independent) flat premium would not be possible within the preconditions of an adequate and cost-neutral compensation.[962] A fiscal maximum premium scale has been included in the legislative proposal and thus provides clarity on the maximum premium scale for which a grandfathering clause applies.[963] This separate premium scale is close to a premium scale in which a discount rate of 1.5% is applied. An insured benefit agreement (e.g. an average wage plan) must therefore be converted before 2027 into a defined contribution plan with a progressive premium ('old system') or into a pension plan in accordance with the new system with equal age-independent premiums ('new system').[964] People who start participating in a pension plan after December 31, 2026, will fall under the new system using the flat contribution rate.[965]

6.2.3.C.IV *Towards a More Harmonized Tax Treatment of Occupational Pensions and Individual (Personal) Pensions*

The Future Pensions Act also points out that changes in society towards a more flexible labour market call for an employment form-neutral pension framework.[966] Hence, a step forward has been taken towards a more employment-neutral pension framework.

960 See proposed art. 38q Wet LB 1964. Ibid. 143.
961 Ibid. 143.
962 See also G Staats and B Starink, 'De fiscale aspecten van het conceptwetsvoorstel Wet toekomst pensioenen' PensioenMagazine 3.
963 See proposed art. 38q, para 2 Wet LB 1964.
964 Staats and Starink, 3.
965 This means that employers who operate an insured pension plan on December 31, 2021 and opt for the transitional law, have to contend with two different pension plans for their employees if new personnel joins after 2025.
966 Kamerstukken II, *Wijziging van de Pensioenwet, de Wet inkomstenbelasting 2001 en enige andere wetten in verband met herziening van het pensioenstelsel, standaardisering van het nabestaandenpensioen, aanpassing van de fiscale behandeling van pensioen en enige andere wijzigingen ten aanzien van pensioen (Wet toekomst pensioenen)* 144.

Despite the common nature of the second pillar (occupational pensions) and the third pillar (individual personal pensions), i.e. securing provisions for old age, the accrual of these provisions is not subject to the same tax rules.[967] Indeed, current differences between the second and third pillars are considerable and sometimes inexplicable. By eliminating these tax differences where possible, more equal opportunities for tax-facilitated accrual of old-age provisions are created, irrespective of the form of employment of taxable persons.

Hence, the Dutch Cabinet proposed to eliminate the difference in fiscal premium leeway between the second and third pillar with respect to old-age provisions.[968] To this end, the percentage of the maximum contribution margin in the third pillar will be increased to the level that will apply in the second pillar, i.e. 30%. This almost completely unifies the tax treatment of the second and third pillar pension schemes, also constituting a considerable expansion of the fiscal facilitation of third pillar pension schemes.[969] However, if taxpayers already accrue a pension in the second pillar, this accrual will reduce the fiscal leeway for tax purposes in the third pillar. In addition, it is possible, as is the case with second-pillar pension accrual, to make tax-facilitated contributions to a third-pillar product up to five years after reaching the state pension age.[970]

What is to be noted, the differences between the contribution base for annuities and the pension base will remain after the Future Pensions Act comes into effect.[971] Differences also remain between annuities and pensions regarding the retroactive payment of premiums. This is because the *Wet Toekomst Pensioenen* provides for a catch-up period for annuities that is limited to ten years.

It has also been proposed to equalise the state pension threshold amount (*AOW-franchise*, i.e. the amount by which the pension or contribution base in the second and third pillar shall be reduced in connection with the state pension.[972] This difference between the second and third pillar in terms of pension and contribution base has been harmonized.

---

967 Ibid. 144.

968 Ibid. 144.

969 Currently the premium threshold is set on 13.3% of the maximum premium base.

970 See article II Wet inkomenbelasting 2001, under E proposed text *Wet Toekomst Pensioenen.*

971 Kamerstukken II, *Wijziging van de Pensioenwet, de Wet inkomstenbelasting 2001 en enige andere wetten in verband met herziening van het pensioenstelsel, standaardisering van het nabestaandenpensioen, aanpassing van de fiscale behandeling van pensioen en enige andere wijzigingen ten aanzien van pensioen (Wet toekomst Pensioenen) (Nota naar aanleiding van het verslag) nr. 7* 111-112.

972 Kamerstukken II, *Wijziging van de Pensioenwet, de Wet inkomstenbelasting 2001 en enige andere wetten in verband met herziening van het pensioenstelsel, standaardisering van het nabestaandenpensioen, aanpassing van de fiscale behandeling van pensioen en enige andere wijzigingen ten aanzien van pensioen (Wet toekomst pensioenen)* 145.

It concerns the difference in the amount and methodology of the reduction related to AOW (in the second pillar an AOW-franchise and in the third pillar an AOW threshold amount), which is part of the pension and contribution base.[973] Initially, the explanatory memorandum of the *Wet Toekomst Pensioenen* stated – as it turned out later inadvertently – that the level of the deductible applicable in the second pillar shall also be applied in the third pillar.[974] This was later rectified by the minister, since introducing a reduced state pension threshold amount in the third pillar would lead to a large increase in complexity for both taxpayers, and the Tax Administration, in particular in cases where taxable persons build up a second-pillar pension, as well as an third pillar-pension.[975] If reduced state pension threshold amounts were to be introduced into the third pillar, a taxpayer must make multiple calculations to see which combination of deductible and contribution rate results in the highest deduction. Proposed alternative systems were deemed error-prone and leading to an increase in supervisory complexity for the Tax Administration. For these reasons, it was decided not to include reduced state pension threshold amounts in the third pillar and rather use one universal method for determining a reduction in pension bases related to state pension by applying a state pension franchise (*AOW-franchise*) of equal amount in the second and third pension pillar (2023: €14,802).[976]

What is more, the period within which the unused tax allowance in the third pillar can be used to build up an annuity (the so-called reserve tax allowance; *reserveringsruimte*) has been extended from the current seven years to ten years, with a nominal maximum of €38,000.[977] This will allow taxpayers to catch up their unused tax allowance in the third pillar over a longer period than under current law. In the second pillar, there is no maximum period within which the unused tax allowance can be recovered, although there must be years of pensionable service that can be made up.

973 See Kamerstukken II, *Wijziging van de Pensioenwet, de Wet inkomstenbelasting 2001 en enige andere wetten in verband met herziening van het pensioenstelsel, standaardisering van het nabestaandenpensioen, aanpassing van de fiscale behandeling van pensioen en enige andere wijzigingen ten aanzien van pensioen (Wet toekomst Pensioenen) (Nota naar aanleiding van het verslag) nr. 7* 112.

974 Kamerstukken II, *Wijziging van de Pensioenwet, de Wet inkomstenbelasting 2001 en enige andere wetten in verband met herziening van het pensioenstelsel, standaardisering van het nabestaandenpensioen, aanpassing van de fiscale behandeling van pensioen en enige andere wijzigingen ten aanzien van pensioen (Wet toekomst pensioenen)* 119-120.

975 See Kamerstukken II, *Wijziging van de Pensioenwet, de Wet inkomstenbelasting 2001 en enige andere wetten in verband met herziening van het pensioenstelsel, standaardisering van het nabestaandenpensioen, aanpassing van de fiscale behandeling van pensioen en enige andere wijzigingen ten aanzien van pensioen (Wet toekomst Pensioenen) (Nota naar aanleiding van het verslag) nr. 7* 112.

976 See article II Wet inkomenbelasting 2001, under E and article III, under B Wet op de loonbelasting 1964 proposed text *Wet Toekomst Pensioenen.*

977 See article II Wet inkomenbelasting 2001, proposed text *Wet Toekomst Pensioenen.*

Despite the substantive connection with the second pillar and the July 1, 2023 enactment of the Future Pensions Act, the widening of the third pillar fiscal facilitation will take effect retroactively through January 1, 2023.[978]

6.2.3.C.V *Imputation of Pension Entitlements from the Second Pillar into the Third Pillar*

Under the current third pillar system, premiums for annuities can only be deducted for tax purposes to the extent a pension shortfall in the second pillar can be established. In short, this is the case if the tax allowance for pension accrual in the second pillar has not entirely been used. To determine the annual margin in the third pillar, a reduction shall take place based on the accrual of pension entitlements in the second pillar. The annual growth in pensions (factor A) in the second pillar is translated by means of a formula into an amount that is deducted from the annual margin in the third pillar. Since this system no longer fits in with the proposed system for the second pillar (from a time-proportional accrual to a premium limitation that is in principle age-independent), it has been proposed to change the system for the reduction. The reduction in connection with the accrual of pension entitlements will, under the new system, be calculated by deducting the premiums paid in the second pillar from the premium volume in the third pillar.[979] Premiums that relate to compensation do not have to be deducted from the premium space in the third pillar. Transitional rules will be introduced for employees who, in the years after 2023, still accrue a pension through an average pay scheme or based on a progressive premium scale. Moreover, the current method of imputing the annual margin will continue to apply to pension accrual in the period January 1, 2023 to June 30, 2023 (under the 'old' system).[980]

6.3 The Tax Treatment of Aanvullende Pensioenen

Where the preceding sections revolved around *aanvullende pensioenen* in terms of foundations, types of pension agreements, schemes and vesting methods, the section below deals with the tax treatment of these second pillar-pensions in domestic situations. It should be emphasized that the term 'pension' as such is not defined in Dutch fiscal legislation. Contrarily, the criteria with regard to fiscally facilitated pension provisions have been stipulated. Merely when pension provisions fulfil these criteria, they, in

978 Staatssecretaris van Financiën – Fiscaliteit en Belastingdienst, *Schriftelijke beantwoording WGO I – Pakket Belastingplan 2023* (20 October 2022) 9.

979 See article II, under F Wet inkomenbelasting 2001, proposed text *Wet Toekomst Pensioenen.*

980 Kamerstukken II, *Wijziging van de Pensioenwet, de Wet inkomstenbelasting 2001 en enige andere wetten in verband met herziening van het pensioenstelsel, standaardisering van het nabestaandenpensioen, aanpassing van de fiscale behandeling van pensioen en enige andere wijzigingen ten aanzien van pensioen (Wet toekomst pensioenen) (Vierde nota van wijziging) nr. 91* (2022/23) 18-19.

principle, shall be fiscally facilitated for income and wage tax purposes. These fiscal criteria are specified in chapter IIB of the *Wet op de loonbelasting 1964*, commonly referred to as the *Witteveenkader*.[981] In cases where legislation refers to a pension scheme, the pension scheme as stipulated in de *Wet op de loonbelasting 1964* is meant. Since 2015, this fiscal framework also applies to the entrepreneur who is covered by a mandatory occupational or industry-wide pension plan.

Within the meaning of *Wet op de loonbelasting 1964*, an occupational pension scheme refers to a scheme which is exclusively or, with a view to exceptional cases of remaining beneficial entitlements, almost exclusively aimed at providing a lifelong income in old-age for employees, and former employees.[982] Furthermore, the pension scheme must provide that the entitlements stemming from the retirement scheme, may not be paid out as a lump sum, sold, relinquished, nor may it, factually or formally, be become capital collateral, other than in cases as stipulated in or by virtue of the *Pensioenwet*.[983] Lastly, the pension scheme must be vested by a body, as referred to in art. 19a, par. 1 Wet LB 1964, i.e. a recognised insurer.[984] Insofar the pension scheme meets the aforementioned criteria, the scheme will, for fiscal purposes, be qualified and facilitated, insofar as it complies with the

981 Named after the head of the commission (*Dirk Witteveen*) which developed the revised framework of tax treatment of pensions in 1995.

982 Pursuant to art. 18, par. 1, lit. a, nr. 1 Wet LB 1964. As implementation of a part of the pension agreement (*Pensioenakkoord*) concluded between Dutch social partners, as of 1 January 2022 it will be possible, under strict conditions, to withdraw a lump-sum amount out of the occupational pension scheme. It is to be noted at this point that it also applies to retirement provisions in the third pillar or a net annuity (*nettolijfrente*). The intended purpose of this amendment is to give people more opportunities to make the moment of withdrawal of an amount fit better with what is appropriate for their personal situation, as far as they want to make use of it. As everyone has to decide for themselves what a desired outcome is, the Minister rightfully points out that a good provision of information remains very important, see Kamerstukken II, 2. This proposal also requires extra effort in terms of explanation and communication towards participants. This possibility of withdrawing a lump sum will be offered only on the retirement date and, hence, not during the retirement phase. During the parliamentary scrutiny it was pointed out that the tax rate in the first bracket depends on the taxpayer's birthday in the year in which he becomes entitled to state pension (AOW), see Minister van Sociale Zaken en Werkgelegenheid, *Kamervragen van het lid Omtzigt (CDA) over de hoge marginale druk over een pensioenuitkering ineens en het feit dat het van je geboortedatum afhangt of je soms 20% extra belasting moet betalen over een uitkering ineens* (5 November 2020). In order to counteract this unequal tax treatment of participants, they shall be offered two options as regard the date of payout of the lump sum. They can either receive this benefit immediately upon retirement, or in February following the year in which they become entitled to AOW-benefits. Although this option of postponing the pay-out date is considered desirable from a fiscal perspective, it is undesirable from a communication and information point of view, since it renders understandable communication on this topic nearly impossible, see also Kamerstukken I, *35 555, nr. H (Motie van het lid Oomen-Ruijten c.s.)* (2020/21). The intended date of entry into force of this option is January 1, 2023, see Kamerstukken I, *35 555, nr. 18 (Verslag van de vergadering van 12 januari 2021)* (2020/21). See also Minister van Sociale Zaken en Werkgelegenheid.

983 Pursuant to art. 18, par. 1, lit. b Wet LB 1964.

984 Pursuant to art. 18, par. 1, lit. c Wet LB 1964.

established fiscal limits, as stipulated in or by virtue of chapter IIB Wet LB 1964.[985] As mentioned in chapter 4 of this research, these fiscal criteria reflect the Dutch considerations on the concept of pension, i.e. a provision aimed at replacing an earned income with, in principle, lifelong benefits in cases where the risk of old-age manifests itself.

For establishing the tax treatment of a pension plan, the pension system used for pension accrual – as discussed in section 6.2.2 – is pivotal: the pension accrual must take place according to a final pay system, an average pay system or a defined contribution system. In a number of cases, premium contracts contain elements of a final pay or average pay scheme in addition to features of a defined contribution scheme, in which cases there is a concurrence of different pension schemes.[986] For tax purposes, all elements of the pension scheme are considered together and in relation to each other. It must then be determined under which of the three schemes the plan falls.[987] If such a qualification is not possible due to the characteristics of the plan, then the plan can be designated as a pension plan, and fiscal facilitation will be granted.[988]

Pension's tax facilitation does not have to be provided from a level at which pension accrual mainly has the function of fiscally facilitated asset accrual. Hence, the Dutch legislator has abandoned the EET system (back-loaded taxation) for pensionable salary exceeding €128,810 (2023) and switched to the TEE system (front-loaded taxation) for pension accrual derived from pensionable salary exceeding this amount.[989] It could be said that in view of the income-replacement nature of a pension, pension accrual does not have to be higher than the income prior to retirement.[990]

985 Pursuant to art. 18, para 1, under lit. c Wet LB 1964.

986 See also Staatssecretaris van Financiën, *Besluit Loonheffingen, inkomstenbelasting. Pensioenen; beschikbare-premieregelingen en premie- en kapitaalovereenkomsten en nettopensioenregelingen (Staffelbesluit pensioenen) nr. 2019-21333.*

987 Pursuant to art. 4.3 URLB 2011.

988 Pursuant to art. 19d Wet LB 1964.

989 Pursuant to Wet van 2 juni 2014 tot wijziging van de Wet inkomstenbelasting 2001, de Wet op de loonbelasting 1964, de Pensioenwet, de Wet verplichte beroepspensioenregeling en de Invoerings- en aanpassingswet Pensioenwet in verband met de aanpassing van het fiscale kader voor oudedagsvoorzieningen (Wet verlaging maximumopbouw- en premiepercentages pensioen en maximering pensioengevend inkomen).

990 Cf. B Starink, *Belastingheffing over particulierpensioen en overheidspension in grensoverschrijdende situaties* (Fiscale monografieën, Wolters Kluwer, Deventer 2015) 33.

6.3.1 Tax Relief during the Accrual Phase

A universal aspect of all pension arrangements – addressed in section 6.2.2 – is that contributions are paid by both the employer and the employee. Generally, two thirds of the contributions are paid by the employer, while one third is paid by the employee. There is no legal basis for this. Neither the employer's nor the employee's part of the premium is paid directly to the employee, but is paid to the pension administrator. On the contrary, for the employee this constitutes an entitlement to a pension, i.e. the employee acquires a right to future pension payments. The part of the premium at the employer's expense constitutes part of the (taxable) salary, without a specific identifiable work performance in return.[991] Thus, the performance of the work as such gives rise to these pension entitlements.

In principle, under the main rule of the Wet LB 1964, any pension premium paid by the employer – as a rule 66% of the total premium contribution – for the benefit of the employee in order to build up the employee's pension constitutes (part of) the taxable wage.[992] In the Netherlands, this system of taxing the pension entitlement is not considered desirable since tax would have to be due on an entitlement that is not actually paid out until after retirement age, i.e. the income deferral theory (*inkomensuitsteltheorie*). Therefore, the principle of deferred taxation is applied, whereby taxation is effectuated at the moment the pensioner actually receives the pension benefits (after reaching the applicable retirement age). In this vein, the principle of deferred taxation can be seen as an incentive for pension savings.

The first aspect of deferred taxation is that the pension entitlement – based on the contributions paid by the employer – shall be exempt from taxation on the employee's side.[993] The pension entitlement, thus, does not constitute taxable wage. Furthermore, the employee's contributions paid to the facilitated pension scheme shall be fully deductible for tax purposes.[994] Solely in situations where a pension scheme as such meets the fiscal conditions as laid down in chapter IIB of the Wet LB 1964 – and remains within the fiscal demarcation of Chapter IIB – it qualifies as a pure pension scheme (*zuiver pensioen*), as a result of which the principle of deferred taxation applies.[995] If, on the other hand, not all conditions are met, the scheme qualifies as impure and the principle of deferred taxation does not apply. This will be discussed in more detail below.

991 See also Janse and Janssen, 258-259.
992 Pursuant to art. 10, para 2 Wet LB 1964.
993 Pursuant to art. 11, par. 1, lit. c Wet LB 1964.
994 Pursuant to art. 11, par. 1, lit. j, nr. 1 Wet LB 1964.
995 If, on the basis of the conditions laid down in the Wet LB 1964 the pension is considered a pure pension, this also applies for the Wet IB 2001.

Conditions as Regards Zuiver Pensioen

Article 18 Wet LB 1964 enunciates the basic conditions with which a pension plan must comply in order to qualify as pure:

1. the specific pension forms and the corresponding circle of beneficiaries
2. the fiscally permitted pension providers
3. specific elements which emphasise the personal nature of a pension.[996]

Furthermore, the pension scheme must exclusively or, with a view to exceptional cases of almost exclusively have as its objective the provision of a specific income. It also specifically indicates which forms of pension may be part of a pure pension plan, including a retirement pension.[997] Further fiscal conditions for the old-age pension are laid down in art. 18a Wet LB 1964. The first three paragraphs list the pension systems on the basis of which the pension can be built up, which have been dealt with in section 6.2.2. A retirement scheme based on a final pay system does not exceed 1.657% of pensionable pay per year of service;[998] a retirement pension based on an average earnings system shall not exceed 1.875% per year of service;[999] a retirement pension based on a defined contribution plan is accrued on a time-proportional basis and is aimed at a pension that, after 40 years of accrual, does not exceed 75% of the average pensionable pay to that time.[1000]

Pensionable Age

The retirement target age pertaining to occupational pensions is currently set at 68.[1001] However, the guiding principle in the legislation up to and including 2013 was that the pension took effect upon reaching the age of 65, because of the link with the state pension age in AOW.[1002] In the *Wet verhoging AOW- en pensioenrichtleeftijd*, the link between the state pension age and the fiscal retirement age was abandoned.[1003] Contrary to the gradual increase of the AOW pensionable age – as discussed chapter 5 of this research – is the occupational retirement age raised to 67 in one step in 2014. Unlike the AOW-age, where the increase in the retirement age is expressed in three months, an increase of the fiscal

996 For example, art. 18, para 1, under b Wet LB 1964 specifically states that pension entitlements cannot be paid out as a lump sum, alienated or surrendered, or become the subject of formal or constructive security, other than in the cases provided for in or by virtue of the PW.

997 See art. 18, para 1, under a, nr. 1 in conjunction with art. 18a Wet LB 1964.

998 Pursuant to art. 18a, para 1 Wet LB 1964.

999 Pursuant to art. 18a, para 2 Wet LB 1964.

1000 Pursuant to art. 18a, para 3 Wet LB 1964.

1001 Using a formula it is possible to calculate whether the pensionable age needs to be adjusted, see art. 18a, para 8 Wet LB 1964.

1002 Kamerstukken II, (1997/98) 24.

1003 Kamerstukken II.

retirement age takes effect with a full year.[1004] Thus, the increase in the AOW pension age and the increase of the occupational pensionable age do not run in parallel.

Under the *Pensioenakkoord*, an adjustment of the formula for determining the (occupational) pensionable age has been implemented.[1005] In order to achieve a better balance, it was decided to link the future increases in the pensionable age to changes in life expectancy by a factor of 2/3 to the development of the remaining life expectancy at age 65, rather than one-to-one.

AOW-franchise

In the tax treatment of the accrual of the old-age pension, the basic principle applies that a pension of 75% of the average pensionable salary must be accrued in at least 40 years. When accruing the tax-facilitated occupational pension, state pension benefits are incorporated, since a pensioner will receive state pension benefits (AOW) in addition to his occupational pension. In this vein, the state pension-franchise per year of service must be set at at least a proportional part of the state pension benefit for a married person without supplement, converted to an annual amount, plus the holiday allowance.[1006] This means that after a pension accrual of 40 years, at least a full state pension for a married person must be incorporated.[1007]

Approved (Pension) Insurer

In order to qualify as a pure pension plan, the pension must be placed with an insurer approved for tax purposes.[1008] In art. 19a, para 1 Wet LB these (fiscally) approved insurers are enumerated:

- Exempted for the *Wet op de vennootschapsbelasting 1969* pension funds or general pension funds within the meaning of the *Pensioenwet*;
- The pension insurer - pursuant to art. 1:1 Financial Supervision Act (*Wet financieel toezicht*), provided that the pension obligation is considered part of the domestic company assets for the purposes of levying corporate tax;
- A pension fund or body not established in the Netherlands which carries on life insurance business provided that the pension is the continuation of a pension that was

1004 Ibid. 2; 12.

1005 Ibid. 14.

1006 Pursuant to art. 18a, para 7 Wet LB 1964.

1007 Two methods exist for incorporating the state pension component in the accrual of occupational pension: the deductibwage is first reduced by a recalculated AOW-franchise, after which the fiscal leeway for fiscal facilitation of the old-age pension is determined on the basis of the accrual percentage and the number of years of service.

1008 Pursuant to art. 18, para 1, under c in conjunction with art. 19a, para 1 Wet LB 1964.

already insured with that insurer in a period in which the (former) employee did not live or work in the Netherlands;

– A pension fund or body authorized to carry on the business of insurance, and which does not fall under one of the above-mentioned bodies and which has been designated as an approved provider, provided that the conditions imposed are met.[1009] These conditions relate to the obligation of the provision of information on the implementation of the pension scheme, and to provide security for the collection of the tax due by the application of irregular settlements of the pension scheme.[1010]

Irregular Settlement of a Pension Plan

As has been discussed in the above, chapter IIB Wet LB 1964, sets out the conditions that a pure pension scheme must meet. If, however, at any time the conditions are violated, this leads to the loss of the tax facilities and to a settlement with the tax authorities.[1011] As a result of the improper actions, the principle of deferred taxation shall be reclaimed. The following are, inter alia, regarded as improper acts: the surrender, disposing or pawning of the pension entitlement. As a consequence, at the time immediately preceding the improper act, the pension entitlement will be regarded as salary arising from a former employment of the (former) employee or, if he/she has died, of the person entitled to the entitlement.[1012] In these cases, in addition to a levy at a progressive rate on the fair value of the (entire) pension entitlement, the loss suffered due to loss of interest must also be compensated.[1013]

6.3.2 *The Tax Treatment of Occupational Pension Benefits during the Pay-out Phase*

Benefits arising from all forms of Dutch pension schemes are fully included in Box 1 income (*Inkomen uit werk en woning*) and subject to a progressive income tax rate. It is not until during the retirement phase, that the pension benefits will be fully taxed as wage,

1009 These further conditions have been laid down in art. 19a, para 3, Wet LB 1964 in conjunction with art. 10d Uitv.besl. LB 1965.

1010 Currently, 17 pension funds – all located in either Belgium, Luxemburg or Malta – have been designated as approved pension insurer, see Staatssecretaris van Financiën, *Internationaal belastingrecht. Toegelaten buitenlandse aanbieders van pensioenen, lijfrenteverzekeringen, lijfrenterekeningen, lijfrentebeleggingsrechten en arbeidsongeschiktheidsverzekeringen nr. 2022-192641* (21 July 2022).

1011 Pursuant to art. 19b, para 1 Wet LB 1964.

1012 Pursuant to art. 19b, para 1 Wet LB 1964.

1013 Pursuant to art. 30i, paragraph 1, part a, in conjunction with paragraph 2, Algemene Wet inzake Rijksbelastingen, in principle 20% of the fair value of the pension entitlement is charged (revisionary interest). On the basis of Article 44b of the Invorderingswet 1990, the insurer is held liable for the tax due and the revision interest due.

stemming from a former employment relationship.[1014] The pension provider must withhold taxes due from the pension benefits paid out. A retirement pension is defined as a lifelong income provision at old age for employees and former employees.[1015] However, in case of benefits arising from a compulsory pension scheme pursuant to the *Wet verplichte deelneming bedrijfstakpensioenfonds 2000, Wet op het Notarisambt* or the *Wet verplichte beroepspensioenregeling*, these benefits shall – in principle – be taxable as periodic benefits, instead of taxable wage arising from former employment.[1016] However, these types of occupational pension benefits are reclassified as fully subject to tax as wages from former employment.[1017]

6.3.3 Tax Treatment of Professional Occupational Pension Schemes (Beroepspensioenregeling)

These pension schemes cover in particular health care professions, the port sector, and entrepreneurs in certain industries (e.g., self-employed painters). Until January 1, 2015, pension accrual pursuant to a mandatory occupational pension plan was subject to compulsory contributions being charged to the profit, and the related pension entitlements were not taken into account for profit calculation. As of 2015, tax limitations that apply with respect to pension accrual for employees also apply to the pension accrual of entrepreneurs for income tax-purposes, and profit earners who are obliged to participate in professional or industry-wide pension plans (*beroeps- of bedrijfstakpensioenregelingen*).[1018] As of 2015, a pension plan is defined as a pension plan participated in on the basis of the *Wet verplichte deelneming in een bedrijfstakpensioenfonds 2000, de Wet op het notarisambt* or the *Wet verplichte beroepspensioenregeling*, both for the part for which participation is mandatory (basic pension scheme), as well as for the voluntary supplement to it.[1019]

Guiding principle for this tax treatment is pension accrual based on an average pay scheme with an accrual rate of 1.875 % and where the pensionable age is linked to the development of life expectancy. These provisions provide clarity on pensionable earnings, the

1014 Pursuant to art. 2, par. 1 in conjunction with art. 9 and 10, par. 1 Wet LB 1964.

1015 This description is consistent with the old age pension concept in Art. 1 PW. According to this provision an old-age pension is said to exist if it is a monetary benefit, which is fixed or variable, for the employee or the former employee by way of income provision in old age.

1016 Pursuant to art. 3.100, paragraph 1, section d in conjunction with art. 1.7, paragraph 2, section b Wet IB 2001.

1017 Pursuant to art. 34, para 1, under a in conjunction with art. 11, para 1, under j, k and u in conjunction with para 2 Wet LB 1964. Pursuant to art. 3.80 in conjunction with art. 3.81 of the Wet IB 2001, the wage is subject to income tax.

1018 Kamerstukken II, 2.

1019 Pursuant to art. 1.7, para 2, under b Wet IB 2001.

consequences of an excessive pensionable earnings and the tax treatment of voluntary pension contributions.[1020] For self-employed professionals and profit earners who participate in an occupational pension scheme, the profit from the business (with some corrections) must be taken as a starting point in determining the extent of the tax relief for their pension accrual.[1021] Under certain conditions, the premiums for an occupational pension plan – within the meaning of art. 1.7, paragraph 2, part b of the Wet IB 2001 – may be eligible for deduction.[1022] The first condition is that the occupational pension plan remains within the applicable standards and limitations of Chapter IIB Wet LB 1964. Hence, the pension must be built up with due regard for the pensionable age, the maximum accrual percentages that apply as of January 1, 2015 and the capping limit on pensionable earnings. Second, lower regulations specifically geared to these professionals apply.[1023] It follows from these lower regulations that the provisions that relate to the application of a final pay system have been declared inapplicable to these professionals (as in general their income fluctuates excessively). Furthermore, as of January 1, 2015, the voluntary pension accrual will also be eligible for tax facilitation under certain conditions.[1024] The conditions include that the total pension accrual remains within the limits of the Chapter IIB Wet LB 1964, and that the voluntary contributions per year do not exceed one-third of the compulsory contributions.

As regards benefits arising from these profession-related pension schemes, all benefits shall be taxable as periodic payments and benefits in kind.[1025] This applies to the benefits arising from the basic pension scheme, as well as the voluntary supplement. For taxation purposes it is not relevant whether or not pension contributions have been deducted.

The changes with regard to these type of occupational pension schemes under the Future of Pensions Act are *grosso modo* similar in nature to the proposed changes to the *Pensioenwet*. For example, in the new pension system occupational pension schemes can only have the legal character of a premium scheme, and an age-independent premium must be applied.[1026] Because of the provisions in art. 3.18 Wet IB 2001, which refer to the Wet LB 1964, the proposed tax changes in the Wet LB apply *mutatis mutandis* to the *beroepspensioenregeling*.

1020 Kamerstukken II, 3.

1021 See art. 3.18, para 4, under d Wet IB 2001.

1022 Pursuant to art. 3.18, para 1 Wet IB 2001.

1023 Pursuant to art. 3.18, para 5 Wet IB 2001.

1024 Pursuant to art. 3.18, para 3 Wet IB 2001.

1025 Pursuant to art. 3.100, para 1, under d Wet IB 2001.

1026 See proposed artt. 23 and 28 Wet verplichte beroepspensioenregeling, see Ministerie van Sociale Zaken en Werkgelegenheid, *Consultatieversie wetsvoorstel Wet toekomst pensioenen* (2020) 35.

6.3.4 The Nettopensioen Pension Scheme

In 2015, the Dutch legislator decided to cap the level of pensionable salary to a maximum of, at that time, €100,000. As a consequence, the accrual of pension rights arising from pensionable salary exceeding this limit, is not fiscally facilitated under the principle of deferred taxation. Hence, pension contributions will be taxed and benefits in the pay-out phase will remain untaxed. In order to enable those people affected by this limitation of pensionable salary to build up a pension on the basis of salary exceeding this limit, the so-called (occupational) *nettopensioen* scheme, and *nettolijfrente*, had been introduced.[1027] In the third pillar, a similar provision is included under the term *nettolijfrente*. For this, anyone with an income above €128,810 (2023) can make use of the net annuity. This will be discussed in more detail in chapter 7. The net pension is a provision for employees or professionals under a compulsory occupational pension scheme, and qualifies as a premium agreement.[1028]

Furthermore, it is a voluntary pension plan within the meaning of the *Pensioenwet, Wet verplichte deelneming Bedrijfstakpensioenfondsen 2000,* and *Wet verplichte beroepspensioenregeling.*[1029] The net pension constitutes an employment agreement

1027 See also Minister van Sociale Zaken en Werkgelegenheid, *Evaluatie vrijstelling voor nettopensioen en nettolijfrente* (2 September 2020). Research findings demonstrate that of the potential target group of 200 000 people, approximately 35 000 people (approximately 17%) participate in a *nettopensioen* scheme. This mainly concerns *nettopensioen*, while *nettolijfrenten* schemes are hardly used in practice. According to the respondents to the participant survey, the relatively low use of the *nettopensioen* scheme is caused by the fact that the capital is not freely available and because the plan does not meet the (otherwise unspecified) needs of the participants. For those who do participate, this is due to trust in the pension administrator, the tax benefit of the exemption and the benefit and risk coverage for surviving dependants in the event of death before the retirement date. For participation, it appears to be particularly important whether the *nettopensioen* scheme is offered as an opt-in (active choice needed to participate) or as an opt-out (participation is automatically arranged and active choice is needed not to participate). In the latter case (opt-out), the degree of participation appears to be much higher. The majority of schemes through pension funds are designed as opt-outs. Data has shown that the assets invested in 2018 were close to €550 million. The study further demonstrated that the capping of pension accrual to an income limit and the introduction of *nettopensioen* scheme above that limit has led to further complexity in the pension domain. The recommendations made therefore mainly relate to reducing what the report considers to be unnecessary complex. For example, it is pointed out that for net pension schemes, the most fiscally generous contribution scale that can be used is the 3% scale, while for gross pension schemes it is permitted to use broader cost-price scales. It is also proposed to abolish the test for an above-average result for tax purposes, the so-called event test, at the 3% scale. The Cabinet endorses the importance of the possibility of building up an adequate retirement provision, although it is questionable whether the current *nettopensioen* scheme will be able to cope with this, given their relatively limited use and the bottlenecks identified, particularly in terms of implementation costs and complexity.

1028 Within the meaning of art. 10 PW.

1029 Net pensions can and may only be administered by authorized providers, i.e. pension funds, pension insurers, PPIs as well as the general pension fund; banks and investment institutions are excluded. See art. 23 PW.

between an employer and an employee. In principle, the entire *Pensioenwet* applies, unless the conditions relating to voluntariness and fiscal hygiene oppose it. What is more, in order to qualify as a net pension, certain conditions – related to the voluntary nature and 'fiscal hygiene' – must be met, laid down in the *Besluit nettopensioen.*[1030] These conditions aim to ensure that no cross-subsidization between regular (gross) pension schemes, and net pension schemes occur, leading to a loss of tax revenue.

The retirement provision built up as a net pension roughly corresponding to an annual gross pension accrual of 1.875% of the average salary, with use being made of a defined contribution scheme.[1031] In principle, the net pension scheme takes the form of a pure DC scheme whereby no guarantee of return is given (until the moment the accrued pension is converted into an entitlement). With respect to taxation, the legislator has opted to include the net pension in the wage tax regime for defined contribution schemes (with the exception of the principle of deferred taxation) and the net annuity to be included in the annuity regime. A net pension can be built up based on the amount that does not form part of the pensionable salary pursuant to art. 18ga of the Wet LB. The conditions for the net pension scheme are included in Section 5.3B of the Wet IB 2001. Contributions paid into these pension scheme remain tax-free as they are paid out of net income.[1032]

Moreover, in principle, the value of these accrued pension entitlement would be subject to tax as income from savings and investments (*BOX 3*). However, the value of these pension entitlements has been exempt from tax, i.e. the accrued pension entitlements under the net pension scheme are exempt from tax in BOX 3.[1033] For the design and limits of the exemption for net pensions, the rules for defined contribution schemes in Chapter IIB of the Wet LB have been followed as closely as possible.[1034] In fact, this exemption from tax (pursuant to *BOX 3*) constitutes the fiscal facilitation of the *nettopensioen*, and *nettolijfrente*

1030 This decree is based on art. 117a *Pensioenwet* and art. 115a *Wet verplichte beroepspensioenregeling*. The degree is included in chapter 9 of *Besluit uitvoering Pensioenwet* and *Wet verplichte beroepspensioenregeling*. In art. 41 of this decree the conditions of fiscal hygiene are laid down. These conditions enable to separate the financial resources for the net pension, from which untaxed benefits are paid, and the funds for the basic pension plan, on which tax must still be levied.

1031 As reaching an income above the capping limit usually only occurs at an older age, the legislator has opted for an age-dependent premium scale. This allows older employees to contribute more than they would if the premium scale was not age-dependent.

1032 The maximum amount of the available premium for a net pension is regulated in artt. 5.17a, 5.17b and 5.17c Wet IB 2001.

1033 Kamerstukken II; Kamerstukken II, (2014/15). See Artt. 5.16 and 5.17 Wet IB 2001.

1034 See Staatssecretaris van Financiën, *Besluit Loonheffingen, inkomstenbelasting. Pensioenen; beschikbare-premieregelingen en premie- en kapitaalovereenkomsten en nettopensioenregelingen (Staffelbesluit pensioenen) nr. 2019-21333* para 8.

scheme. This fiscal facilitation of both schemes has been capped.[1035] Some fiscally not allowed conduct has been fiscally sanctioned, such as lump sum payment.[1036] In such cases, the granted exemption in *BOX 3* will be reclaimed through a flat-rate approach.

If a participant decides to emigrate to another country, he can choose to terminate the participation in the net pension scheme. In such as case the former participant will receive a non-contributory entitlement. What is more, the withdrawal of the net pension will not be subject to tax, i.e. such a withdrawal is not regarded as an (fiscal) improper act.[1037] This prevents the taxpayer from being faced with double taxation, which would occur if the other country were to include the benefits in the tax, while no deductions were allowed for the premiums paid into the net pension scheme. However, a cross-border worker who participates in a net pension plan does not emigrate, and is therefore possibly confronted with double taxation as of the moment of payment. In that context, a statutory concession for the cross-border worker is therefore highly desirable.[1038]

Under the new Dutch pension system – discussed in section 6.2.3 – both net pensions and net annuities will be retained. In addition, the tax framework for net pension schemes in the new pension system will also be brought back into line with the Wet LB 1964.[1039]

6.4 Tax Treatment of Dutch Occupational Pensions in Cross-border Situations

As has been addressed in chapter 5 of this research, the increase in the mobility of workers implies that the taxation of pensions must not solely be considered from a purely national perspective, but also account must be taken of cross-border aspects. In the light of this, the aim of this section is to analyse the (cross-border) tax treatment of pension schemes at the employee level, pursuant to Dutch national tax legislation.

The section below solely considers the situations where the accrual, and/or the pay-out, of the given pension entitlements/benefits accrued entirely in either one of the two states, i.e. residence or (former) working state. If, however, the pension entitlements were partly accrued in Germany (a German pension) and partly in the Netherlands (a Dutch pension), the (cross-border) fiscal consequences need to identified per pension separately (by source

1035 Pursuant to artt. 5.16b, 5.17a, 5.17b, and 5.17c Wet IB 2001.
1036 Pursuant to artt. 5.16c and 5.17e Wet IB 2001.
1037 Pursuant to art. 5.17e, para 5, under a, Wet IB 2001.
1038 Cf. AHH Bollen-Vandenboorn, 'De vergeten grensarbeider en zijn nettopensioen' 09 MBB.
1039 See Ministerie van Sociale Zaken en Werkgelegenheid.

of the retirement income). These situations will not be dealt with in the section below, but this section's content, combined with section 6.6, allow for the (fiscal) assessment of such (dispersed) mixed-pension cases.

6.4.1.A Migrant Worker

6.4.1.A.I Outbound

In the outbound migration situation, the employee is resident in the national territory of the Netherlands (partly) during the accrual phase and resides abroad (Germany) during the pay-out phase. The tax treatment of contributions and the granting of tax relief, during the accrual phase, is hence akin to the tax treatment of a domestic situation, i.e. there is no cross-border situation. There is no nexus with German income tax, levied during the accrual phase. I therefore refer to the section 6.3.

However, during the pay-out phase, the person concerned resides abroad (Germany). It depends on the allocation of taxing rights enshrined in the applicable tax treaty where the person is liable to tax for the Dutch occupational pension benefits. The functioning of these allocation rules – embedded in the applicable tax treaty – will be discussed in more detail in chapters 8 and 9 of this research. If the taxing right on these Dutch pension benefits is allocated to Germany as the residence state, – pursuant to 17, para 1 of the treaty Netherlands-Germany – the migrant worker concerned will be fully liable to tax in Germany (as a resident), and the Dutch occupational pension benefits will be subject to German income tax. This is not discussed any further here, but I refer to section 6.7.1.B.II. If – on the contrary – the taxing right is allocated to the Netherlands as a source state (for instance pursuant to article 17, para 2 treaty Netherlands-Germany), the pension benefits paid out are subject to Dutch income tax – pursuant to Dutch national tax legislation. In such cases, the beneficiary residing abroad will be treated as a foreign taxable person (*buitenlands belastingplichtige*) provided that he receives domestic income, as the person concerned neither resides in the Netherlands, nor has his habitual abode in the Netherlands during the pay-out phase.[1040] The Dutch occupational pension benefits shall be fully liable to tax as 'taxable wages in respect of work performed or having performed in the Netherlands', and are considered 'domestic income'.[1041] What is more, this taxable proportion of the benefits is determined irrespective of whether these benefits are derived from contributions which were subject to tax relief. Furthermore, he may apply to be

---

1040 See article 2.1, para 1, sub b in conjunction with article 7.1 and 7.2 Wet IB 2001.
1041 Pursuant to article 7.2, para 2, under b Wet IB 2001.

treated as a qualifying foreign taxpayer.[1042] To what extent, and how, the Netherlands subjects these Dutch occupational pension benefits to income tax, is not discussed any further here, but I refer to section 6.3.

What is more, pursuant to Dutch national legislation as it stands, upon emigration, a protective tax assessment shall be issued, pursuant to Dutch national tax legislation.[1043] In addition, revisionary interest (*revisierente*) will be included in the protective tax assessment.[1044] For the amount included in the protective tax assessment imposed, deferral of payment shall be granted for a period of ten years.[1045] The granting of deferral of payment does not require a written request and no guarantee is required.[1046] In the event that no irregularities occur – for example a lump-sum payment – during the period of deferral, the protective tax assessment shall be waived after ten years.[1047] If such an irregularity does occur within these ten years, the pension entitlement shall be regarded as wage arising from a previous employment relationship, and the insurer of that entitlement shall be liable, up to a maximum of the entitlements' fair value, for the tax due (against the highest applicable income tax rate; 49,50% in 2023) in respect thereof by the person entitled thereto, as well as for the corresponding revision interest due.[1048]

These protective tax assessments – imposed upon emigration – have moved many authors to reach for their pen, since the tenability of these assessments under international/European law have been called into question.[1049] This tenability will not be addressed *in extenso*, as the focus of this research concerns the law as its stands (positive law), more than how the law ought to be (normative law). Yet, it will be discussed how this has affected

1042 Pursuant to article 7.8 Wet IB 2001. Based on this scheme, foreign taxpayers shall be eligible for the same fiscal facilitations as domestic taxpayers (such as deductions). The essence of this scheme is to give residents of the EU, EEA, Switzerland or the BES islands, 90% or more of whose income is subject to wage tax or income tax in the Netherlands, the right to the same fiscal facilitations, in accordance with EU case law. The equal treatment concerns, among other things, the right to the application of a number of personal allowances. Being a qualifying foreign taxpayer is no longer a choice (since 1 January 2015) but applies *ex officio*.

1043 Pursuant to article 2.8, para 2 in conjunction with artt. 3.83 and 3.136 Wet IB 2001.

1044 Pursuant to article 30i, para 1, under a in conjunction with para 2 Algemene Wet inzake Rijksbelastingen (AWR).

1045 Pursuant to art. 25, para 5 Invorderingswet 1990 (Tax Collection Act 1990).

1046 Pursuant to art. 1e, para 2 Uitvoeringsregeling Invorderingswet 1990.

1047 Pursuant to art. 26, para 2 Invorderingswet 1990. If such an irregularity does occur recovery interest will be charged pursuant to art. 6, para 1 Uitvoeringsbesluit Invorderingswet 1990.

1048 Pursuant to article 44b, para 1 Invorderingswet 1990.

1049 See, for instance, FPG Pötgens, 'Conserverende aanslag pensioen (niet) akkoord' NTFR-B; FPG Pötgens and HM Kappelle, 'Over conserverende aanslagen, belastingverdragen en reparatiewetgeving: de geschiedenis lijkt zich te herhalen' WFR; P Kavelaars, 'Conserverende aanslagen en verdragen (1)' NTFR-B 7; P Kavelaars, 'Conserverende aanslagen en verdragen (2)' NTFR-B 13; F Pötgens, 'Conserverende aanslag bij emigratie van pensioen- en lijfrentegerechtigde (deels) gesauveerd' 11 NTFR Beschouwingen 19.

the law as it stands, taking the form of amendments issued over the course of the years. Moreover, merely the most recent case-law will be addressed more elaborately; preceding case-law will be touched upon only briefly.

Tenability of the Protective Tax Assessment

The section below revolves around the tenability of the protective tax assessment – imposed pursuant to Dutch national tax legislation – in the light of the principle of good faith, which is to be observed in the interpretation of the treaty's text.[1050] This matter has been considered extensively by the Dutch Supreme Court (*Hoge Raad*) in her rulings over the years, most recently in 2017. Moreover, it will be outlined how these judgments have affected Dutch tax legislation (as it stood over the years), i.e. how legislation has been brought in line with these judgements. After all, these judgments have a direct effect on the taxation of cross-border pensions.

The 2009 Cases: Start of a Complex Journey

The Dutch Supreme Court held in her 2009-rulings that issuing these protective assessments, taking effect upon emigration, is considered contrary to the principle of good faith required to be observed in the interpretation and application of tax treaty provisions. The source of this lies in the fact that the Netherlands taxes a benefit that, according to its true nature, has been attributed for tax purposes – potentially or otherwise – to the immigration State, i.e. the other state.[1051]

However, art. 3.146, para 3 and 4 Wet IB 2001 stipulates that the taxable items are deemed to be received at the point in time directly preceding the termination of being a (domestic) tax resident for tax purposes. This provision aimed to – artificially – isolate these situations from the application of the bilateral tax treaties, and thus not being obliged to adhere to the principle of good faith. This would, in principle, mean that the (former) employee cannot, with regard to a levy on that salary, rely on rights which, on the basis of a tax treaty, accrue to residents of the country to which he has transferred his residence. Nevertheless, the court ruled that the pension entitlement is covered by article 15 of the Treaty (income from employment) only at the time of its acquisition, and hence, the fiction contained in the legislative provisions, cannot have the effect of removing the taxation of events occurring after that acquisition from the scope of article 18 of the Treaty (pensions).[1052] The Supreme Court held that such a fiction on the basis of which the value

1050 The principle of good faith has been laid down in art. 31 of the Vienna Convention on the Law of Treaties of 23 May 1969, stating "*A treaty shall be interpreted in good faith in accordance with the ordinary meaning to be given to the terms of the treaty in their context and in the light of its object and purpose.*"

1051 See 43 978, ECLI:NL:PHR:2009:BC5201 (HR) para 3.3.2.

1052 See ibid. para 3.4.2.

of the accrued pension rights is included in the Dutch tax as salary at an indivisible moment prior to emigration, is under these circumstances considered contrary to the good faith.[1053] Furthermore, the Court found that the fact that the person concerned was still residing in the Netherlands at the time the given legislation simulated the taxable event, did not detract from this. The Court concluded that since the allocation of the taxing rights on the basis of the tax treaty became applicable immediately thereafter (allocating the taxing right on the pension to the residence state), the effect of this allocation is frustrated by the disputed fiction in an unacceptable manner just as much as by a similar fiction that is based on events at a moment at which the taxpayer does not (or no longer) reside in the Netherlands. Hence, in all of its decisions of 19 June 2009, it was the Supreme Court's view that issuing a protective tax assessment pursuant to art. 3.83, para 1 Wet IB 2001 infringed the good faith to be observed in applying and interpreting the pensions article of the relevant tax treaties, and hence, should not be applied.

In response to the implication of the Supreme Court's Rulings, the Dutch legislator enacted reparative legislation, having retroactive effect to 15 July 2009.[1054] The envisaged goal of implementing this reparative legislation was to mitigate the implications of the decision of the Supreme Court of 19 June 2009, and to avoid that the imposition of the protective tax assessment – pursuant to domestic tax legislation – ran counter to the good faith required to be observed in interpreting and applying Treaty's provisions. By virtue of this amendment, the amount that shall be included in the protective tax assessment, is differentiated based on whether the applicable tax treaty allocates the taxing right on (future) pension benefits to either the source state, or the residence state. In cases where the tax treaty assigns exclusive taxing rights to the residence state, the assessment may solely include the reversal of tax-facilitated contributions.[1055] However, if the tax treaty assigns (shared) taxing rights to the source state, the protective assessment is allowed to encapsulate the fair market value of the pension claim and annuity rights, i.e. the amount that may be included in the protective tax assessment may be extended as the Netherlands is granted the taxing right.[1056] In cases of continued emigration to a treaty state in relation with which the Netherlands is entitled to levy more or less tax compared to the former emigration, the protective assessment shall be raised or lowered accordingly.[1057] What is more, from the 2011 case it can be inferred that an exit tax imposed on pensions would

1053 See ibid. para 3.4.3.

1054 Wet van 8 juli 2009 tot wijziging van enkele belastingwetten (reparatie in verband met arresten van de Hoge Raad inzake pensioen- en lijfrenteaanspraken).

1055 Pursuant to art. 3.136, para 3 (pensions), and art. 3.136, para 2 (annuities) Wet IB 2001.

1056 Pursuant to art. 3.83, para 1 (pensions), and art. 3.136, para 1 (annuities) Wet IB 2001. A protective tax assessment is imposed pursuant to art. 2.8, para 2 Wet IB 2001.

1057 Pursuant to art. 3.136, para 4 (source state taxation-cases) and para 5 (residence state taxation-cases).

never be regarded as being in good faith under a tax treaty which allocates the taxing right on pension exclusively to the residence state, irrespective of whether the tax-facilitated contributions are recovered or the fair market value of the pension entitlement at the time of emigration is subjected to tax.[1058]

Compartmentalisation of Protective Assessments: Patchwork of Complexity

In her most recent decision, the Dutch Supreme Court held that she supported the legislator's view pertaining to protective tax assessments, both as regards annuities, as well as for pensions.[1059] I endorse Pötgens' argument that this is striking – and a different approach would have been preferable – since the Netherlands is unilaterally undermining the taxation right granted to the other treaty state.[1060] It should have been held to be contrary to the good faith, regardless of the technical structuring, and artificial modalities, as shaped by the legislator.

In this judgment, as a determining factor for the test of good faith, the Court presented the conditionality of the tax facility granted on either pensions, or annuities. This is remarkable as the applicable legislation (in its current drafting) does not take into consideration the probability that the tax facility (deferred taxation) can potentially be recovered or that it is granted only if certain conditions persist to be complied with.[1061] As regards annuities, the Court held – while referring to the Hungary case[1062] – that application of the relevant provision does not lead to the taxation of part of the value of the annuity rights, but rather a conditionally allowed deduction that is being recovered.[1063]

The Court found that in cases where the applicable tax treaty allocated the taxing right on pension and annuity benefits to the residence state, the application of the protective tax assessment needs to be compartmentalized.[1064] As regards occupational pensions, the Court ruled that the inclusion in the protective assessment of negative expenditure upon emigration with regard to a pension entitlement does not conflict with the good faith, in so far as it concerns entitlements and contributions pursuant to a pension scheme which, after 15 July 2009, have not been treated as taxable salary.[1065] Hence, including entitlements

1058 10/00990, ECLI:NL:HR:2011:BN8728 (HR). Cf. F Pötgens and E Kool, 'The Relationship between Tax Treaties and Protective Tax Assessments Issued in Respect of Pensions and Annuities upon Emigration: Pacta sunt servanda and Compartmentalization' 58 European Taxation 435.

1059 17/01256, ECLI:NL:HR:2017:1324, BNB 2017/186 (HR).

1060 Pötgens and Kool, 436.

1061 In the same vein ibid. 436-437.

1062 35 231 ECLI:NL:HR:2001:AD6774 (Hoge Raad).

1063 Art. 3.136, para 2 Wet IB 2001.

1064 As of 1 January 2019, this has been regulated by art. 10a.19 Wet IB 2001.

1065 Art. 3.136, para 3 Wet IB 2001.

accrued and contributions paid prior to this date, runs counter to good faith. This is fairly remarkable as the reparative legislation (entered into force on 15 July 2009) has not changed anything as regards the (initially) unconditionally granted tax exemption.

6.4.1.A.II Inbound

In the inbound case, the employee is a resident of Germany (partly) during the accrual phase, and takes up residence in the Netherlands at the commencement of the pay-out phase. The tax treatment of contributions and the granting of tax relief, during the accrual phase, is hence akin to the tax treatment of a German domestic situation, i.e. there is not cross-border situation. I therefore refer to the section 6.6. There is no nexus (connection) with Dutch income tax, levied during the accrual phase.

However, during the pay-out phase, the person concerned resides in the Netherlands. It depends on the allocation of taxing rights enshrined in the applicable tax treaty where the person is liable to tax for the foreign (German) occupational pension benefits. If the taxing right is allocated to the Germany as a source state (for instance pursuant to article 17, para 2 treaty Netherlands-Germany), the German pension benefits paid out are subject to German income tax, akin to a domestic situation, see section 6.6. However, as the person concerned nor resides in Germany, neither has his habitual abode in Germany, during the pay-out phase he may be subject to limited tax liability pursuant to § 1, para 4 EStG, provided that he receives domestic income within the meaning of § 49 EStG. The principal condition for including these elements of income in the limited tax liability is a domestic source of income.[1066]

If the taxing rights is allocated to the Netherlands as a residence state (for instance pursuant to article 17, para 1 treaty Netherlands-Germany), the benefits arising from the German occupational pension scheme will – as a resident – be fully subject to Dutch income tax.[1067]

The following is central in this regard. Pursuant to art. 3.82 Wet IB 2001, benefits from a foreign pension plan are, in principle, considered taxable wages, i.e. an exception to the legal system, since if a (foreign) pension entitlement is not exempt, the benefits would not be taxed in BOX 1. The legislature did, however, not find this desirable.[1068] Hence, for the purposes of the Dutch Wet IB 2001, the term pension plan is also considered to cover a foreign (occupational) pension plan that is considered a pension plan under the tax laws

1066 Pursuant to § 49, para 1, under 4 or 10 EStG depending on the *Durchführungsweg*.
1067 Pursuant to art. 2.1, para 1, letter a Wet IB 2001.
1068 Kamerstukken II, *26 727, nr. 18* (1999/2000) 31.

of the given country.[1069] The tax legislation of that country must contain a wage or income tax that, in terms of its nature and scope, corresponds to Dutch wage or income tax. Although this leaves the scope of application rather vague, generally speaking, any foreign pension plan qualifies, even if it – for example by allowing lump sum payment – differs considerable from the Dutch concept of 'pension plan'.[1070]

In this vein, the Dutch Supreme Court rightly held that the difference in tax treatment between lifelong Dutch pension schemes and foreign pension schemes that permit unconditional lump sum-payments is caused by the fact that (Member) States impose different conditions on pension schemes.[1071] For instance, the fact that lump sum payment is unconditionally permitted under Belgian law does not therefore mean that the Netherlands is obliged under EU law to always recognize a Belgian pension scheme with the possibility of lump sum for tax purposes by applying the principal of deferred taxation to the entitlements under that scheme. The difference in treatment constitutes a disparity, and is therefore not a prohibited obstacle to the freedom of movement.

The central role of the foregoing section has to be considered in relation to art. 3.81 and 3.82 Wet IB 2001. The latter provision enunciates (under b) that benefits pursuant to a foreign pension plan as referred to in art. 1.7, second paragraph, letter c, shall be taxed as Dutch wages, unless it is plausible that the entitlements under that pension plan have been subject to income tax which, by its nature and tenor, corresponds to Dutch wage tax or income tax.[1072] Put it differently, unless no tax relief was granted abroad during the accrual phase of the pension.[1073] The system is consistent with the levy of Dutch wage tax on pension benefits under a Dutch pension plan. In cases where pension entitlements have

1069 Pursuant to art. 1.7, para 2, under c Wet IB 2001. The purpose of this article is to include definitions of annuity and pension scheme in the Wet IB 2001 in a central place. Consequently, those definitions apply to the entire act and the provisions based on it.

1070 See for instance ECLI:NL:GHAMS:2015:3978 (Hof Amsterdam) in which Hof Amsterdam ruled that a (UK) 'State Pension' did not constitute a pension plan within the meaning of article 1.7 of the Wet IB 2001, as the premiums were not deductible in the UK. See also 06/00183 ECLI:NL:GHSHE:2007:BB2231 (Gerechtshof's-Hertogenbosch) where the court of appeal ruled that a Belgian *groepsverzekeringsovereenkomst* does fall within the meaning of article 1.7 Wet IB 2001, on the basis of the pension regulations and the Belgian tax laws which – according to the court of appeal – correspond in nature and scope to the Dutch wage and income tax. In a similar vein: ECLI:NL:HR:2021:518 (Hoge Raad) where the court ruled that the circumstance that the Netherlands does not have the same regulation and that the tax treatment in the Netherlands and Belgium differs, does not matter in this respect. As regards *groepsverzekeringen* it is stipulated that it concerns both periodic and non-periodic payments.

1071 See ECLI:NL:HR:2021:518 (Hoge Raad).

1072 These foreign occupational pension benefits shall be subject to tax pursuant to art. 3.80, 3.81 and 3.82 Wet IB 2001 in conjunction with art. 9 and 10 Wet LB 1964. Art. 3.82 extends the concept of wages with respect to what is considered wages for the purposes of the LB 1964 Act.

1073 In such cases, the foreign pension plan will be subject to income tax under BOX 3 as income from savings and investments.

already been subject to tax abroad, these pension entitlements will leave the sphere of Dutch wage tax, and the value of these entitlements will be subject to tax in BOX 3 (income arising from savings and investments).

Art. 3.82 Wet IB 2001 concerns pensions to which entitlement is obtained through employment with an employer not established in the Netherlands. The legislative text is drafted in such a manner that not only periodic benefits arising from that foreign pension plan are included in the tax, but lump sum payments as well. What is more, it is not decisive whether the scheme in question would also qualify as a pension scheme according to Dutch standards and conditions. For the application of Article 3.82 no distinction is drawn between private or public pension schemes; both schemes fall within the scope of this provision.

In the situation of an inbound migrant worker, during the pay-out phase, the person concerned receives German occupational pension benefits while residing in the Netherlands, while in the latter state he will be fully liable to tax as a resident.[1074] Given what will be described in section 6.6 as regards German occupational pensions, it is likely that the benefits arising from the German occupational pension scheme will – as a resident – be fully subject to Dutch income tax, pursuant to art. 3.82 Wet IB 2001, since these pension plans constitute a pension plan under German tax legislation.[1075] Generally speaking, any foreign pension plan qualifies, even if it – for example by allowing lump sum payment – differs considerable from the Dutch concept of 'pension plan'. However, the taxable proportion – under Dutch wage tax – of the foreign benefits is thus differentiated as to whether the entitlements, from which these benefits were derived, were subject to tax relief abroad.

6.4.1.B Cross-border (Frontier) Worker

A mobile citizen may work in one State, while residing in another neighbouring Member State, to which he/she usually returns every day, or at least once a week (commonly referred to as 'frontier worker', or 'border commuter'). The working state, and possibly the pension state, thus deviates from the residence state. Triangular situations, where the pension institution is established in a third state, is left aside for the present research.

1074 Pursuant to article 2.1, para 1, sub a Wet IB 2001.

1075 Pursuant to art. 1.7, para 2, under c Wet IB 2001. The purpose of this article is to include definitions of annuity and pension scheme in the Wet IB 2001 in a central place. Consequently, those definitions apply to the entire act and the provisions based on it.

As no allocation rules exist as regards occupational pensions (similar to Regulation 883/2004 applicable to statutory pension schemes), i.e. rules stipulating where the cross-border worker participates in an occupational pension scheme, it needs to be determined where the person concerned does participate in an occupational scheme. What the applicable situation is depends on the specific facts and circumstances of the case, i.e. the employment law agreements between employee and employer, the pension law application conditions for foreign participants, and also this choice of the frontier worker concerned. The tax consequences of both situations will be mapped out below, while taking account of the effect of the prevailing tax treaty, concluded between the Netherlands and Germany.

Contrary to a migrant worker, a cross-border worker – generally – does not have the intention to leave his country of residence permanently, i.e. working across the border is of a temporary nature. Because of this temporary nature of work, it is as a rule not desirable to transfer the accrued pension capital to a pension administrator in the country where the temporary work is being performed.[1076] However, the cross-border worker may either continue to participate, and thus contribute, to a pension scheme in his state of residence, or may become a participant of the occupational pension scheme in his working state. This entails a number of fiscal consequences. In the former case, it remains to be seen if, and if so to what extent, the contributions paid into the residence state-pension scheme are 'recognized'/taken into account in the working state in the calculation of the tax assessment base, provided that the person concerned is fully liable to tax in that (working) state, and the tax treaty allocates the taxing right on the remuneration to the working state. For instance, a person resident in the Netherlands works for a German employer in Germany, while paying contributions to a Dutch occupational pension scheme. Provided that the person concerned earns all or almost all (90%) of his income through his German employment relationship in Germany, he will be fully liable to tax in Germany. It thus shall be assessed to what extent the Dutch occupational pension contributions may be taken into account in calculating German income tax payable. However, despite efforts to enhance the portability of pension rights[1077] and the transferability of pension capital, remaining in the residence state-pension scheme appears to be more desirable in view of possible costs incurred and a possible loss of pension rights. In the section below, both the outbound, as well as the inbound situation will be discussed. Where in the outbound situation, the Netherlands is the residence state, and Germany the working state; in the inbound situation, the Netherlands is the working state and Germany is the residence state.

1076 B Dieleman, 'Internationale aspecten van pensioen' in AHH Bollen-Vandenboorn and others (eds.), *Pensioen en de belangrijkste toekomstvoorzieningen* (SDU, Den Haag 2022) 503.

1077 For instance through Mobility Directive 2014/50.

6.4.1.B.I Outbound

As stated above, in this situation, where the Netherlands is the residence state, the cross-border worker may remain a participant in a Dutch occupational pension scheme, while working abroad in Germany (for a German employer) or become a participant in a (foreign) German occupational pension. What the applicable situation is depends on the specific facts and circumstances of the case, i.e. the employment law agreements between employee and employer, the pension law application conditions for foreign participants, and also this choice of the frontier worker concerned. The tax consequences of both situations will be mapped out below, while taking account of the effect of the prevailing tax treaty, concluded between the Netherlands and Germany.

Continuance of Participating in Dutch Occupational Pension Scheme

Provided that, pursuant to art. 14, para 1 of the Dutch-German tax treaty, the taxing right pertaining to the remuneration is allocated to Germany as the working state, and if the person is fully liable to tax in that state (i.e. as he receives at least 90% of his taxable income in the other state), it is a matter for Germany to determine to what extent it allows the contributions paid to the (foreign) Dutch occupational pension scheme to be taken into account in the calculation of the domestic tax assessment base.[1078] This will be discussed in section 6.7.1.B.II. If, on the contrary, the prevailing tax treaty allocates the taxing right on the remuneration to the Netherlands, it may subject the person to unlimited tax liability, and the tax treatment of the contributions is akin to a domestic situation, see section 6.3.

As the person resides in the Netherlands during the pay-out phase, the taxation of Dutch occupational pension benefits paid out is akin to a domestic situation, provided that the Netherlands is assigned the taxing right (pursuant to art. 17, para 1 or 2 of the applicable tax treaty) see section 6.3. In such case, the person concerned will be fully subject to tax in the Netherlands.[1079]

Participating in Foreign (German) Occupational Pension Scheme

If the cross-border worker, resident in the Netherlands, participates in the foreign (German) occupational pension scheme, the tax treatment of these foreign pension contributions must be assessed. If the applicable tax treaty (art. 14) allocates the taxing right pertaining to the remuneration to Germany as the working state, it is a matter for that state to decide to what extent it subjects the contributions paid into a domestic occupational pension scheme by a non-resident taxpayer to tax (relief). See section 6.6.

1078 This cross-border worker will be fully liable to tax under the conditions of § 1, para 3 EStG.

1079 Pursuant to art. 2.1, para 1, under a Wet IB 2001.

If, on the contrary, the applicable tax treaty allocates the taxing right pertaining to the remuneration to the Netherlands (pursuant to art. 14, para 1 of the treaty), and the person concerned is fully liable to tax in that state, the outbound cross-border worker may continue to pay their pension contributions into the foreign (German) pension schemes. However, Dutch policy as regards the 'fiscal recognition' of contributions paid into foreign occupational schemes has been laid down in a decree, which will be extensively dealt with in the section below (6.4.1.B.II). This decree will be discussed further in that section since it better suits the situation of an inbound German cross-border worker who continues participation in his foreign (German) pension plan.

What is more, in order to avoid an adverse fiscal treatment of pension contributions paid into a foreign pension scheme, paragraph 37 of the Commentaries on the OECD Model Convention contains a provision which is intended to ensure equal treatment with contributions made domestically.[1080] It applies to either statutory, occupational and individual pension schemes.[1081] Suchlike provision has been laid down in article 24, para 6 of the tax treaty concluded between the Netherlands and Germany, applying to occupational pension schemes as well. The outbound cross-border worker, participating in a German occupational pension scheme, may have recourse to this provision enshrined in the applicable tax treaty concluded between the Netherlands and Germany.

As the person resides in the Netherlands during the pay-out phase, and provided that the Netherlands (as source state) is assigned the taxing right pursuant to art. 17, para 1 of the applicable tax treaty, the German occupational pension benefits will be subject to Dutch income tax, as dealt with in section 6.4.1.A.II. In sum, for the purposes of the Dutch Wet IB 2001, the term pension plan is also considered to cover a foreign (occupational) pension plan that is considered a pension plan under the tax laws of the given country.[1082] Benefits pursuant to a foreign pension plan as referred to in art. 1.7, second paragraph, letter c, shall be taxed as Dutch wages, unless it is plausible that the entitlements under that pension plan have been subject to income tax which, by its nature and tenor, corresponds to Dutch wage tax or income tax.[1083] Given what will be described in section 6.6 as regards German occupational pensions, it is likely that the benefits arising from the German occupational pension scheme will – as a resident – be fully subject to Dutch income tax,

1080 See also Bobbett and Avery Jones; Andreoni; De Broe and Neyt.

1081 See paragraph 61 of the OECD commentary on article 18 OECD MC.

1082 Pursuant to art. 1.7, para 2, under c Wet IB 2001. The purpose of this article is to include definitions of annuity and pension scheme in the Wet IB 2001 in a central place. Consequently, those definitions apply to the entire act and the provisions based on it.

1083 These foreign occupational pension benefits shall be subject to tax pursuant to art. 3.80, 3.81 and 3.82 Wet IB 2001 in conjunction with art. 9 and 10 Wet LB 1964. Art. 3.82 extends the concept of wages with respect to what is considered wages for the purposes of the LB 1964 Act.

pursuant to art. 3.82 Wet IB 2001, since these pension plans constitute a pension plan under German tax legislation.[1084] Generally speaking, any foreign pension plan qualifies, even if it – for example by allowing lump sum payment – differs considerable from the Dutch concept of 'pension plan'.[1085] It is important to stress that the taxable proportion – under Dutch wage tax – of the German benefits is thus differentiated as to whether the entitlements, from which these benefits were derived, were subject to tax relief abroad. As the German pension entitlements, accrued under a German occupational pension scheme, will be relieved for tax purposes under Dutch tax legislation, the German occupational benefits will be fully subject to Dutch income tax. If, on the contrary, the prevailing tax treaty allocates the taxing right on the German occupational pension benefits to Germany (as source state), the German pension benefits will be taxed pursuant to German tax legislation received by a non-resident taxpayer, see section 6.6.

6.4.1.B.II Inbound

In the inbound situation of a cross-border worker, he is a resident of Germany, while he works in the Netherlands, returning to Germany at least once a week. He may remain a participant in the German occupational pension scheme, while working in the Netherlands, or become a participant in a Dutch occupational pension scheme. What the applicable situation is depends on the specific facts and circumstances of the case, i.e. the employment law agreements between employee and employer, the pension law application conditions for foreign participants, and also this choice of the frontier worker concerned. The tax

1084 Pursuant to art. 1.7, para 2, under c Wet IB 2001. The purpose of this article is to include definitions of annuity and pension scheme in the Wet IB 2001 in a central place. Consequently, those definitions apply to the entire act and the provisions based on it.

1085 See for instance ECLI:NL:GHAMS:2015:3978 (Hof Amsterdam) in which Hof Amsterdam ruled that a (UK) 'State Pension' did not constitute a pension plan within the meaning of article 1.7 of the Wet IB 2001, as the premiums were not deductible in the UK. See also 06/00183 ECLI:NL:GHSHE:2007:BB2231 (Gerechtshof 's-Hertogenbosch) where the court of appeal ruled that a Belgian *groepsverzekerings-overeenkomst* does fall within the meaning of article 1.7 Wet IB 2001, on the basis of the pension regulations and the Belgian tax laws which – according to the court of appeal – correspond in nature and scope to the Dutch wage and income tax. In a similar vein ECLI:NL:HR:2021:518 (Hoge Raad) where the court ruled that the circumstance that the Netherlands does not have the same regulation and that the tax treatment in the Netherlands and Belgium differs, does not matter in this respect. As regards *groepsverzekeringen* it is stipulated that it concerns both periodic and non-periodic payments. Accordingly, in ECLI:NL:HR:2021:518 (Hoge Raad), the Dutch Supreme Court rightly held that the difference in tax treatment between lifelong Dutch pension schemes and foreign pension schemes that permit unconditional lumpsum payments is caused by the fact that (Member) States impose different conditions on pension schemes. The fact that lump sum payment is unconditionally permitted under Belgian law does not therefore mean that the Netherlands is obliged under EU law to always recognize a Belgian pension scheme with the possibility of lumpsum for tax purposes by applying the principal of deferred taxation to the entitlements under that scheme. The difference in treatment constitutes a disparity, and is therefore not a prohibited obstacle to the freedom of movement.

consequences of both situations will be mapped out below, while taking account of the effect of the prevailing tax treaty, concluded between the Netherlands and Germany.

Continuance of Participating in Foreign (Germany) Occupational Pension Scheme
If, pursuant to art. 14, para 1 of the applicable tax treaty, the taxing right pertaining to the remuneration is allocated to the Netherlands, this situation is, as regards the tax treatment of contributions and benefits, similar to an outbound cross-border worker participating in a German occupational pension scheme. However, contrary to the outbound situation, an essential difference lies in the fact that in the present inbound situation, the person concerned is not fully liable to tax in the Netherlands as he is a resident of Germany. In such cases, the person residing abroad will be treated as a foreign taxable person (*buitenlands belastingplichtige*) provided that he receives domestic income, as the person concerned nor resides in the Netherlands, nor has his habitual abode in the Netherlands during the pay-out phase.[1086] Furthermore, he may apply to be considered a qualifying foreign taxpayer.[1087] Based on this scheme, foreign taxpayers are eligible for (largely) the same fiscal facilitations as domestic taxpayers (such as deductions).

A foreign pension scheme will generally not comply with the provisions of the Wet LB. In that case, the plan would not fall under the scope of deferred taxation. The Dutch State Secretary of Finance considers this undesirable – due to its possible negative effect on labor mobility – and therefore recognizes foreign pension plans as pension plans, subject to conditions.[1088] The recognition is made pursuant to art. 19d, under c Wet LB. This recognition amounts to fiscal recognition by the Netherlands of all occupational pension schemes in the EU/EEA in the event of employment in the Netherlands.[1089] For the sake of simplicity in implementation, the recognition also applies to employees who are employed

1086 See article 2.1, para 1, sub b in conjunction with article 7.1 and 7.2 Wet IB 2001.

1087 Pursuant to article 7.8 Wet IB 2001. Based on this scheme, foreign taxpayers are still eligible for the same fiscal facilitations as domestic taxpayers (such as deductions). The essence of this scheme is to give residents of the EU, EEA, Switzerland or the BES islands, 90% or more of whose income is subject to wage tax or income tax in the Netherlands, the right to the same fiscal facilitations, in accordance with EU case law. The equal treatment concerns, among other things, the right to the application of a number of personal allowances. Being a qualifying foreign taxpayer is no longer a choice (since 1 January 2015) but applies *ex officio*.

1088 See Staatssecretaris van Financiën, *Loonheffingen. Inkomstenbelasting. Internationale aspecten van pensioenen en stamrechten nr. DGB2015/7010M* (28 October 2015). Subsection 2.2.1 of this Decree deals with pensions of employees who are employed in the Netherlands out of the EU or EEA. Subsection 2.2.2 concerns pensions of employees when employed in the Netherlands out of a non-EU/EEA state. Designation of a foreign pension scheme does not affect the possibility of committing an occupational Dutch pension scheme in respect of the salary as long as the entitlements from both pension schemes together remain within the limits of Chapter IIB of the Wet LB 1964.

1089 The background to the tax recognition is the promotion of as much as possible unaltered accrual of the occupational pension of mobile employees as well as the avoidance of complications in implementation due

from another EU member state or EEA country without a formal posting within the meaning of Regulation (EC) No. 883/2004.[1090]

Although in principle in this case, in relation to Germany, the conditions of annex 1 of the Decree would be applicable (inbound worker from an EU member state), annex 3 of the Decree shall apply (recognition and conditions for employment in the Netherlands of employees from a bilateral treaty country containing a pension contribution provision). The tax treaty between the Netherlands and Germany includes such a pension contribution provision in article 24, paragraph 6. On the basis of this provision, in the event of a temporary assignment to the Netherlands, it is possible under certain conditions to deduct contributions paid for foreign pension schemes for tax purposes in the Netherlands (pension contribution provision).

In short, tax recognition brings about that the Netherlands provides tax relief according to Dutch standards, provided the pension plan is fiscally recognized in the temporary employment state (in this case, Germany).[1091] However, if the foreign facilitation goes beyond the Dutch standards, partial recognition is possible.[1092] What is more, the recognition entails that the foreign pension is considered a pension plan in the Netherlands within the meaning of Chapter IIB of the Wet LB. The main condition, pointed out by the State Secretary, included in these tax treaties, is that the foreign pension plan is comparable to a pension plan recognized for tax purposes in the Netherlands. According to the Secretary of State, this is a comparison based on a general assessment, whereby it is not an impediment, for example, if the pension plan of the treaty country does not include a no-redemption clause. However, the accrual in the foreign pension plan (through contribution deduction in the Netherlands in accordance with Dutch limits and standards) must not be substantially greater than the accrual of a comparable employee with a Dutch pension plan. The provision assumes tax deduction of foreign contributions according to the limits and standards of the host country (equal treatment in the host country of foreign and domestic contributions), in this case the Netherlands. This means that in such a situation, when employed in the Netherlands, the limits and standards of premium deduction in the Netherlands must be followed. If the non-discrimination provision applies, the foreign pension plan is treated the same as a pension plan within the meaning of chapter IIB of the Wet LB or the aforementioned art. 1.7, para 2, sub a Wet IB,

to the imposition of additional conditions and the reduction of administrative burdens for employer and employee. See ibid. 3.

1090 Ibid. 3.

1091 Ibid. 4.

1092 Ibid. 13.

respectively. The recognition applies for the period mentioned in the tax treaty, but not for more than a maximum of 10 years from the date of employment.[1093]

For this fiscal recognition the following (material) conditions shall apply:[1094]
- The Dutch employer and the employee continue the accrual of entitlements under the employee's foreign pension plan;
- the tax laws of the foreign state qualify the foreign plan as a pension plan;
- the plan to be continued is an occupational pension plan or, if under the applicable tax treaty a pension plan includes a pension plan under social legislation, a pension plan under the social legislation of the relevant country;
- the foreign pension is insured with a pension insurer as referred to in art. 19a, para 1 Wet LB;
- it concerns a tax-facilitated scheme that is common in the relevant foreign country. The scheme contains an income provision in case of the employee's old age or an income provision for surviving dependents in case of the employee's death or both;
- the tax facilitation does not exceed the limits set by chapter IIB of the Wet LB.

If the German occupational pension scheme meets these conditions – in particular being comparable to a pension plan recognized for tax purposes in the Netherlands – it will be recognized as a Dutch pension plan within the meaning of chapter IIB of the Wet LB. What is more, the provision assumes tax deduction of German contributions according to the limits and standards of the Netherlands. This means that in such a situation, when employed in the Netherlands, the limits and standards of premium deduction in the Netherlands must be followed.

As regards the taxation of German occupational pension benefits during the pay-out phase, the following must be noted. If the applicable tax treaty appoints the cross-border worker's residence state (Germany) as the competent state to tax (pursuant to art. 17, para 1 or 2), this is a (domestic) matter for that State where he will be fully liable to tax. See section 6.6. In this case, the residence state coincides with the pension's source state.

Participating in Dutch Occupational Pension Scheme

If the cross-border worker, resident in Germany, decides to participate in a Dutch occupational pension scheme, the tax treatment of these Dutch pension schemes must be assessed. If the applicable tax treaty allocates the taxing right pertaining to the remuneration/pension to Germany (pursuant to art. 14, para 1), the tax treatment of the

---

1093 Ibid. 12-13.

1094 See appendix 3 of ibid. 12-13.

Dutch pension contributions and benefits is a matter for that state, where the person concerned shall be subject to unlimited tax liability, see section 6.4.1.B.I. However, if the applicable tax treaty allocates the taxing right pertaining to the remuneration to the Netherlands (pursuant to art. 14, para 1), and the person concerned is treated as fully liable to tax (although in principle he is limitedly liable to tax), these type of workers are subject to a tax treatment akin to a domestic worker, notwithstanding that he resides abroad.

As regards the taxation of Dutch occupational pension benefits during the pay-out phase, the following must be noted. If the applicable tax treaty appoints the cross-border worker's residence state (Germany) as the competent state to tax (pursuant to art. 17 para 1) these Dutch pension benefits will be subject to German income tax. This is not discussed any further here, but I refer to section 6.7.1.B.II. If – on the contrary – the taxing right is allocated to the Netherlands as a source state (pursuant to article 17, para 2 treaty Netherlands-Germany), the pension benefits paid out are subject to Dutch income tax – pursuant to Dutch national tax legislation. In such cases, the beneficiary residing abroad will be treated as a foreign taxable person (*buitenlands belastingplichtige*) provided that he receives domestic income, as the person concerned nor resides in the Netherlands, nor has his habitual abode in the Netherlands during the pay-out phase.[1095] The Dutch occupational pension benefits shall be fully liable to tax as 'taxable wages in respect of work performed or having performed in the Netherlands', and shall be considered 'domestic income'.[1096] Furthermore, he may apply to be considered qualifying foreign taxpayer.[1097] To what extent, and how, the Netherlands subjects these Dutch occupational pension benefits to income tax, is not discussed any further here, but I refer to section 6.3. What is more, this taxable proportion of the benefits is determined irrespective of whether these benefits are derived from contributions which were subject to tax relief.

6.4.1.C Posting

In the case of a posted worker, the mobile citizen – as a rule – has an employment contract in his sending state, and, carries out his work, for a limited period, in the territory of a

1095 See article 2.1, para 1, sub b in conjunction with article 7.1 and 7.2 Wet IB 2001.

1096 Pursuant to article 7.2, para 2, under b Wet IB 2001.

1097 Pursuant to article 7.8 Wet IB 2001. Based on this scheme, foreign taxpayers are still eligible for the same fiscal facilitations as domestic taxpayers (such as deductions). The essence of this scheme is to give residents of the EU, EEA, Switzerland or the BES island, 90% or more of whose income is subject to wage tax or income tax in the Netherlands, the right to the same fiscal facilitations, in accordance with EU case law. The equal treatment concerns, among other things, the right to the application of a number of personal allowances. Being a qualifying foreign taxpayer is no longer a choice (since 1 January 2015) but applies *ex officio*.

Member State other than the State in which he normally works.[1098] These posted workers differ from other types of mobile workers in that they return, or are expected to resume working in the Member State from which he is posted after completion of the work or the provision of services for which he was posted.[1099] They, thus, do not fully integrate in the labour market of the host state, and will, hence, benefit only partially of the same working conditions and rights as workers in the host state.

6.4.1.C.I Outbound

As part of the outbound posting case, a Dutch employee is sent by its Dutch employer to Germany during the accrual phase, i.e. either as part of (intercompany) secondment sent to a German subsidiary, or in the framework of hiring-out-of-labour sent to a (external) separate entity.[1100] As the posting in the host state Germany will be of limited duration and the worker will not fully integrate in the labour market of Germany, he will most likely continue to participate, and contribute, to the Dutch occupational pension scheme as the sending state.[1101] Participation in the Dutch pension scheme will thus usually be continued during the period of posting. It is therefore assumed, and this is characteristic for the case of posting, that the employee concerned will continue to participate, and contribute, to the (foreign) occupational pension scheme in the Netherlands.

According to the applicable treaty provision (pursuant to art. 14, para 2, i.e. 183 day-rule), during the period of posting, the Netherlands (residence state) is assigned the taxing rights as regards the remuneration. In such as case, the tax treatment of the pension contributions is akin to a domestic Dutch situation, see section 6.3.[1102] If the taxing right, pertaining to the remuneration, is allocated to Germany as working state (pursuant to art. 14, para 1) the tax treatment, and the tax relief, of the pension contributions paid into the Dutch occupational pension scheme is a matter for Germany, where the posted worker is limited liable to tax. However, upon request, he may be treated as fully liable to tax,[1103] to the extent that he receives domestic income within the meaning of § 49 EStG. This applies solely if the income, received during the entire calendar year, is subject to German

1098 Building on the definitions provided in art. 2 of Posting of Workers Directive 96/71; Your Europe – European Union, 'National websites on posting'; para 3 of preamble, art. 4, para 3 Enforcement Directive 2014/67 of Posting of Workers Directive 96/71.

1099 Article 4, para 3, under d Directive 2014/67/EU of the European Parliament and of the Council of 15 May 2014 on the enforcement of Directive 96/71/EC concerning the posting of workers in the framework of the provision of services and amending Regulation (EU) No 1024/2012 on administrative cooperation through the Internal Market Information System [2014] OJ L 159. See also para 9 preamble Directive 2018/957 amending Directive 96/71.

1100 See also paragraph 8.3 ff. of the OECD commentary on article 15 OECD MC.

1101 Pursuant to art. 12, para 1 Regulation on the coordination of social security systems 883/2004.

1102 Pursuant to article 2.1, para 1, sub a Wet IB 2001.

1103 Pursuant to § 1, para 3 EStG.

income tax for at least 90%, or the income not being subjected to German income tax, does not exceed the exemption threshold (*Grundfreibetrag; 2023: €10,908*).[1104] This will be thoroughly dealt with in section 6.7, where the German regulatory framework shall be elaborated on. In short, in the case of contributions to foreign occupational pension schemes, it must be determined whether the Dutch pension scheme is comparable to an occupational pension scheme under the *Betriebsrentengesetz* or can be assigned to one of the *Durchführungswege* as comparable.[1105]

As regards the pension benefits in the case of posting, these are to be divided.[1106] Firstly, the taxation of the part of the pension benefits which is paid pro rata for employment in the home state the Netherlands, based on the regulations applicable in that state. Secondly, as regards the proportion of pension benefits attributable pro rata to the period of posting, in which both the state of employment (Germany), as well as the residence state are the same for the accrual period. However, in the pay-out phase these two states differ. I will merely focus on the second point hereinafter.

After the limited time of posting abroad, the worker will return to the Netherlands. If the taxing right is allocated to the Netherlands as residence and/or source state (for instance pursuant to article 17, para 1 or 2 treaty Netherlands-Germany), the Dutch pension benefits paid out are subject to Dutch income tax. During retirement, he will be fully liable in the Netherlands.[1107] The tax treatment of the pension benefits is then akin to a domestic situation as the residence state and pension state are similar, see section 6.3. Hence, the taxing right cannot be assigned to Germany as this is nor the residence, nor the source state. However, it must be noted, that the extent to which the Dutch contributions paid abroad during the posting period were subject to tax relief in Germany, is relevant in the tax treatment of the pension benefits pursuant to Dutch national tax law. If the employee was employed abroad (Germany) during the accrual phase, it remains to be seen to what extent the Dutch occupational pension scheme was fiscally facilitated in Germany. The State Secretary also recognizes that it may occur that employees abroad (continue to) accrue pension in a Dutch pension plan that complies with the Dutch tax rules, but not with the foreign rules.[1108] Thus, economic double taxation may occur in such cases. Hence, Dutch policy stipulates that in such cases, a proportion of the Dutch pension benefits may

1104 Pursuant to § 1, para 3, sentence 2 EStG. See § 32a, para 1, sentence 2, nr 1 EStG.

1105 BMF, *Steuerliche Förderung der betrieblichen Altersversorgung IV C 5 - S 2333/19/10008:017* (21 August 2021) para 36.

1106 Cf. Ibid. 21-22. See also D Wellisch, 'Besteuerung der betrieblichen Altersvorsorge bei grenzüberschreitender Mitarbeiterentsendung – ein Ländervergleich mit Gestaltungsüberlegungen' StuW 154.

1107 Pursuant to § 1, para 1, sentence 1 EStG.

1108 Staatssecretaris van Financiën, *Loonheffingen. Inkomstenbelasting. Internationale aspecten van pensioenen en stamrechten nr. DGB2015/7010M* 5.

remain outside the scope of wage and income tax, based on the so-called balance method (*saldomethode*).[1109] Relevant, in this regard, is the amount of pension contributions paid for and by the employee in respect of the foreign employment. A further condition is that the employee did not receive a tax relief for these contributions abroad.

6.4.1.C.II Inbound

As part of the inbound posting case, a German employee is sent by its German employer to the Netherlands during the accrual phase, i.e. either as part of (intercompany) secondment sent to a Dutch subsidiary, or in the framework of hiring-out-of-labour sent to a (external) separate entity.[1110] As the posting in the host state the Netherlands will be of limited duration and the worker will not fully integrate in the labour market of the Netherlands, he will most likely continue to participate, and contribute, to the German occupational pension scheme as the sending state.[1111] Participation in the German pension scheme will thus usually be continued during the period of posting. It is therefore assumed, and this is characteristic for the case of posting, that the employee concerned will continue to participate, and contribute, to the (foreign) occupational pension scheme in Germany.

According to the applicable treaty provision (pursuant to art. 14, para 2), during the period of posting, Germany (residence state) is assigned the taxing right as regards the remuneration. In such as case, the tax treatment of the pension contributions is akin to a domestic German situation, see section 6.6.[1112] If the taxing right, pertaining to the remuneration, is allocated to the Netherlands as working state (pursuant to art. 14, para 1) the tax treatment, and the tax relief, of the pension contributions paid into the German occupational pension scheme is a matter for the Netherlands, where the posted worker is limited liable to tax. In such cases, the person residing abroad will be treated as a foreign taxable person (*buitenlands belastingplichtige*) provided that he receives domestic income, as the person concerned nor resides in the Netherlands, neither has his habitual abode in the Netherlands during the pay-out phase.[1113] Furthermore, he may apply to be considered a qualifying foreign taxpayer.[1114] Based on this scheme, foreign taxpayers are eligible for

---

1109 Ibid. 5. Furthermore, the Secretary of State makes this approval subject to the condition that the taxpayer proves, if requested, that in connection with the acquisition of the pension rights abroad actual taxation has taken place which, in terms of its nature and scope, corresponds with Dutch wage tax or income tax. An actual levy is also understood to mean that there has been no deduction of contributions on the part of the employee.

1110 See also paragraph 8.3 ff. of the OECD commentary on article 15 OECD MC.

1111 Pursuant to art. 12, para 1 Regulation on the coordination of social security systems 883/2004.

1112 Pursuant to § 1, para 1, sentence 1 EStG.

1113 See article 2.1, para 1, sub b in conjunction with article 7.1 and 7.2 Wet IB 2001.

1114 Pursuant to article 7.8 Wet IB 2001. Based on this scheme, foreign taxpayers are still eligible for the same fiscal facilitations as domestic taxpayers (such as deductions). The essence of this scheme is to give residents of the EU, EEA, Switzerland or the BES islands, 90% or more of whose income is subject to wage tax or (largely) the same fiscal facilitations as domestic taxpayers (such as deductions). As regards the tax relief of employer's and employee's contributions (e.g. tax exemption or tax deduction) paid into the German occupational pension scheme during the posting period, pursuant to the Dutch tax legislation, it must be determined to what extent these foreign paid contributions are eligible for tax relief in the Netherlands. A foreign pension scheme will generally not comply with the provisions of the Wet LB. The Dutch State Secretary of Finance considers this undesirable – due to its possible negative effect on labor mobility – and therefore recognizes foreign pension plans as pension plans, subject to conditions.[1115] This has been extensively addressed in the section 6.4.1.B.II. The main condition, pointed out by the State Secretary, is that the foreign pension plan is comparable to a pension plan recognized for tax purposes in the Netherlands. If the German occupational pension scheme meets these conditions – in particular being comparable to a pension plan recognized for tax purposes in the Netherlands – it will be recognized as a Dutch pension plan within the meaning of Chapter IIB of the Wet LB. What is more, the provision assumes tax deduction of German contributions according to the limits and standards of the Netherlands. This means that in such a situation, when employed in the Netherlands, the limits and standards of premium deduction in the Netherlands must be followed.

After the limited time of posting to the Netherlands, the worker will return to his home country Germany. If the applicable tax treaty appoints the posted worker's resident/source state (Germany) as the competent state to tax (pursuant to art. 17, para 1 or 2), this is a (domestic) matter for that State, see section 6.6. Upon retirement, he will be (most likely) fully liable to tax in that state pursuant to the domestic legislation of that state.[1116] The tax treatment of the pension benefits is then akin to a domestic situation as the residence state and pension state are similar. Hence, the taxing right cannot be assigned to the Netherlands as this is nor the residence, nor the source state. Benefits arising from *Direktzusage* and *Unterstützungskasse* are treated as income from dependent employment, fully liable to tax pursuant to § 19, para 1, nr 2 EStG, irrespective of the tax treatment of the contributions from which these benefits emerge. However, it must be noted, that the extent to which the

---

income tax in the Netherlands, the right to the same fiscal facilitations, in accordance with EU case law. The equal treatment concerns, among other things, the right to the application of a number of personal allowances. Being a qualifying foreign taxpayer is no longer a choice (since 1 January 2015) but applies *ex officio*.

1115 See Staatssecretaris van Financiën, *Loonheffingen. Inkomstenbelasting. Internationale aspecten van pensioenen en stamrechten nr. DGB2015/7010M*. Subsection 2.2.1 of this Decree deals with pensions of employees who are employed in the Netherlands out of the EU or EEA. Subsection 2.2.2 concerns pensions of employees when employed in the Netherlands out of a non-EU/EEA state. Designation of a foreign pension scheme does not affect the possibility of committing an occupational Dutch pension scheme in respect of the salary as long as the entitlements from both pension schemes together remain within the limits of Chapter IIB of the Wet LB 1964.

1116 Pursuant to § 1, para 1, sentence 1 EStG.

contributions paid abroad during the posting period were subject to tax relief in the Netherlands, is relevant in the tax treatment of the pension benefits emerging from *Direktversicherungen, Pensionskassen* or *Pensionsfonds*. These benefits are subject to tax as *Sonstige Einkünfte*, pursuant to § 22, nr 5 EstG. The benefits shall be fully liable to tax, to the extent that the benefits emerge from contributions which were not taxed by virtue of § 3, nr 63, §10a or section XI EStG, or the benefits are based on tax-free employer's contributions in the sense of § 3, nr 66 EStG. Insofar as the benefits are based on non-facilitated contributions, they shall be taxed as other income against the *Ertragsanteil* pursuant to § 22, nr 5, sentence 2, letter a in conjunction with § 22, nr 1, sentence 3, letter a, double letter bb EStG. Whether contributions paid into German occupational pension scheme were facilitated under Dutch tax legislation during the posted period is thus relevant.

6.5 Germany: Betriebliche Altersversorgung

In this section occupational pensions and their tax treatment (in cross-border situations) in Germany will be mapped out. It should be noted that this section merely provides an elaborate overview of the design of the pension landscape. Hence, the entitlement conditions, pensionable age, and benefits granted are discussed only peripherally.

The civil framework for occupational pensions is, since 1974, established through the *Betriebsrentengesetz (BetrAVG)*.[1117] Pursuant to this act, the role of the German *betrieblichen Altersversorgung* as complementary to social security, was made more effective and more assured.[1118] The implementation of this act in 1974 not only meant the definitive recognition of the *betrieblichen Altersversorgung* as second pillar in the German pension system, but moreover meant the codification of the labour law consequences in a field that was prior – apart from tax law – regulated only by the principles of civil contractual freedom.[1119]

1117 Gesetz zur Verbesserung der betrieblichen Altersversorgung (Betriebsrentengesetz – BetrAVG). This formal law only applied to the 'old' federal states of Germany. The 'new' federal states were incorporated in the scope of application of this law on 1 January 1992 through a unification treaty. For an elaborate overview of changes as a result of the implementation of the *Altersvermögensgesetz* see R Höfer, 'Die Neuregelung des Betriebsrentenrechts durch das Altersvermögensgesetz (AVmG)' 21 DB (in footnotes) 1145. For an elaborate overview of changes as a result of the implementation of the *Altersvermögensgesetz* see ibid. For an exhaustive overview of the development of the *betrieblichen Altersversorgung* in the German pension landscape please see W Förster and others, *Betriebsrentengesetz: Gesetz zur Verbesserung der betrieblichen Altersversorgung mit zivil-, arbeits- und steuerrechtlichen Vorschriften und Versorgungsausgleich* (Beck'sche Kompakt-Kommentare, C.H. Beck, München 2014) 1-7.

1118 Förster and others, 8.

1119 Ibid. 8.

Furthermore, this act describes occupational pensions as *Zusage von Leistungen der Alters-, Invaliditäts- oder Hinterbliebenenversorgung vom Arbeitgeber an einen Arbeitnehmer aus Anlass seines Arbeitsverhältnisses.*[1120] Besides the general definition of *betriebliche Altersvorge* and the accepted methods of pension accrual, this act i.a. regulates the accrual of benefits, the funding of this accrual and the consequences from the point of view of labour law. Furthermore, the portability of occupational pensions was enhanced through this act.[1121]

The BetrAVG stipulates that the provision of occupational pensions may be organised either directly by the employer (*intern*) or by an external pension provider (*extern*).[1122] Also in the latter case the employer shall retain full responsibility for the fulfilment of the benefits granted. The external pension providers comprise *Unterstützungskasse, Pensionskasse, Pensionsfonds* and *Direktversicherung*. Under all vesting methods, contributions can be paid either by the employer or by the employee. As regards the latter, contributions can be paid either through *Entgeltumwandlung* or by own contributions.

What is more, given the demographic developments and the steadily widening pension gap, German occupational pension provisions have been gaining importance as the second pillar of retirement provisions parallel to statutory pension insurance and private provision for old age.[1123] An occupational pension scheme exists if the employer confers on the employee benefits or contributions to cover at least one biometric risk (old age, death, disability) on the basis of his employment relationship and claims to these benefits only become due when the biological event occurs.[1124] Hence, the employer's commitment must therefore serve a pension purpose regulated in the *Betriebsrentengesetz*, and the obligation to pay benefits must be induced by a biological event specified in the law, and a biometric risk addressed in the law is partially assumed by the benefit provided for.[1125] The assumption of risk must consist of a provision, while the term provision is to be interpreted broadly.[1126] Benefits encapsulate all benefits intended to improve the standard of living of the employee in the event of reaching the retirement age.

1120 Derived from § 1, para. 1 BetrAVG.

1121 Scholz, 64 and cited literature.

1122 Pursuant to § 1, para. 1 BetrAVG. The external pension providers are stipulated in § 1, para. 2 until 4 BetrAVG.

1123 Cf. W Scheffler and S Kölbl, 'Besteuerung der betrieblichen Altersversorgung auf Ebene des Arbeitnehmers im internationalen Kontext' Internationales Steuerrecht 1 and cited literature.

1124 § 1 BetrAVG. See also BMF, *Steuerliche Förderung der betrieblichen Altersversorgung IV C 5 - S 2333/19/10008:017* para 1. See also BAG, 16 March 2010. 2010 para 23 ff.

1125 BMF, *Steuerliche Förderung der betrieblichen Altersversorgung IV C 5 - S 2333/19/10008:017* para 1.

1126 See also BAG, para 23 ff.

6.5.1.A Pension Arrangements, Vesting Methods and their Legal Character

Grosso modo, four different methods of pension vesting exist under the second pension pillar.[1127] The first method is the so-called *Leistungszusage* (defined benefit) under which the employer is obliged to assure a particular benefit (*Leistung)*, which in turn depends on certain reference values.[1128] This type of vesting method marked the implementation of the *Betriebsrentengesetzes* in 1974. An example of this method is the fixed amount method[1129], where a certain benefit is committed nominally. Furthermore, there are so-called benchmark systems[1130] under which the annual accrual of pension is calculated on the basis of a fixed amount multiplied with a predetermined factor (or 'benchmark'). Furthermore, under last salary-schemes a certain percentage of the employee's last salary is committed as pension accrual.

After the entry into force of the *Gesetzes zur Verbesserung der betrieblichen Altersversorgung* in 1974, methods developed in practice in which the contribution or expense prevailed, so-called *beitragsorientierte Leistungszusagen*. Under this DC-method certain contributions to the pension provision are assured by the employer.[1131] These contributions are then converted into an entitlement to retirement benefits. This is most common among current occupational pension provisions. Under this method, the employer's expenses are decisive. This, in turn simplifies the calculation, contrary to the *Leistungszusage.*[1132] The foregoing does not detract from the employer's obligation – similar to the *Leistungszusage* – to render a pension provision. If a pension gap arises under this vesting method, the employer is obliged to resolve this gap. The accrual of this provision is, however, dependent on the contributions paid by the employer. The realisation of this provision follows after the transfer of the contributions paid to an external pension provider and the subsequent rate calculation.[1133] Apart from that, this provision on the basis of defined contributions, leads to an increasing risk for the final benefits on the side of the employee.

1127 Pursuant to § 1, para. 1 and § 2, para 1 and 2 BetrAVG.

1128 I.e. *Gesamtversorgungszusagen, gehaltsabhängigen Zusagen* and *Fixbetragszusagen.* Under *Gesamtversorgungszusagen* a certain pension level shall be ensured, in order to compensate shortcomings in the *gesetzlichen Rentenversicherung*. The provision of *gehaltsabhängigen Zusagen* guarantee benefits in accordance with the final salary, average earnings or other analog variables. Under the *Fixbetragszusagen* a certain fixed amount is ensured in principle.

1129 I.e. *Festbetragssysteme.*

1130 I.e. *Eckwert-systemen.*

1131 § 1, para. 2, nr. 1 BetrAVG.

1132 Cf. Förster and Rechtenwald, 147.

1133 Cf. Ibid. 147.

In the third method, the employer may also commit a *Beitragszusage mit Mindesleistung*[1134].[1135] The vehicle of *Beitragszusage mit Mindestleistung* was integrated into the *BetrAVG* with the *Altersvermögensgesetz* which entered into force in 2002. Under this provision, the employer is legally obliged to finance the contributions to a *Pensionsfonds, Pensionskasse* or *Direktversicherung.*[1136] There is an ongoing debate in literature, on the exact demarcation between *beitragsorientierter Leistungszusage* and *Beitragszusage mit Mindestleistung.*[1137] This will however not be addressed any further since this is considered beyond the scope of this section. Furthermore, the employer shall provide the accumulated pension capital, financed primarily through the contributions. This capital shall, as a minimum, comprise the contributions paid by the employees. This may be considered as the minimum benefit. Besides guaranteeing the payment of the pension contributions, the employer is liable for making this (minimum) pension capital available. Subsequently, this guarantee of a minimum benefit would underpin the thesis that the *Beitragszusage mit Mindesleistung* may also be qualified as a defined-benefit scheme. The pension provider is legally prohibited from paying contributions, up to a certain level, to an external pension provider.[1138] It is obvious that the *Beitragszusage mit Mindestleistung* is exclusively intended for the insurance-based implementation methods of *Direktversicherung, Pensionskasse* and *Pensionsfonds.*[1139] In these insurance-based *Durchführungswegen*, the same economic result is achieved for the beneficiary in most practical cases, regardless of whether a *beitragsorientierte Leistungszusage* or a *Beitragszusage mit Mindestleistung* forms the basis.[1140] However, if the *Beitragsorientierte Leistungszusage* is already equated economically with the *reine Beitragszusage*, there can no longer be any room for an artificial distinction between a *Beitragsorientierte Leistungszusage* and a *Beitragszusage mit Mindestleistung.*[1141]

Furthermore, an odd one out is the so-called *Eigenbeiträge*, constituting a form of occupational pension.[1142] Under this provision, the employee finances his contributions out of his own net income. This form of provision is restricted to *Pensionsfonds, Pensionskasse* or *Direktversicherung.* The rules and regulations pertaining to *Entgeltumwandlung* shall apply similarly.

1134 I.e. 'Defined contribution commitment with minimum benefit.'

1135 Pursuant to § 1, para. 2, nr. 2 BetrAVG.

1136 Therefore, *Direktzusage* and *Unterstützungskasse* are exempted as pension vesting methods.

1137 K Friedrich, B Kovac and T Werner, 'Beitragsorientierte Leistungszusage und Beitragszusage mit Mindestleistung – strikt getrennt oder doch eng miteinander verwandt?' BetriebsBerater and cited literature.

1138 BAG, 7 September 2004.

1139 Friedrich, Kovac and Werner, and cited literature.

1140 See ibid.

1141 Ibid.

1142 Translated freely as ‚own contributions', pursuant to § 1, para. 2, nr. 4 BetrAVG.

Until 1 January 2018, the *Betriebsrentengesetz* only comprised the three vesting methods addressed in the above, i.e. *Leistungszusage, Beitragsorientierte Leistungszusage* (implemented in 1999) and *Beitragszusage mit Mindestleistung* (implemented in 2002). These three methods are marked by the fact that a benefit or minimum benefit can be derived from them at the time of retirement, and the employer is liable for the fulfilment of the promised benefit (*Einstandspflicht*) or, if the employer becomes insolvent, the *Pensions-Versicherungs-Verein* (PSV) secures these benefits. Thus, until 2018 the German legislator made it clear that the employee should always be offered a minimum of security for the later pension payment. However, the German legislator has gradually moved closer to defined contribution schemes. This turnaround manifested itself on 1 January 2018, since as of the date, that *reine Beitragszusage* has been implemented pursuant to the (modernising) *Betriebsrentenstärkungsgesetz* (BRSG).[1143] In addition to amendments of the wage tax-free funding framework for external pension providers, tax incentives for employer-financed pension commitments, a mandatory employer subsidy for *Entgeltumwandlung* when using external pension providers, and other innovations, the legislator provides in particular for a significant expansion of the social responsibility of the collective bargaining partners in occupational pension provision.[1144] Furthermore, the legislator for the first time allows so-called 'opting out' for *Entgeltumwandlung*, under the condition that these are provided for in collective agreements.[1145]

The *reine Beitragszusage* is the core of the so-called *Sozialpartnermodell* (social partner model) and complements (and replaces) the other three types of commitment. From a historical perspective, this can be considered the conclusion of a metamorphosis of German occupational pension law from 'defined benefit to defined contribution'. This *Betriebsrentenstärkungsgesetz* strives to further increase the coverage rate of occupational pension provisions in Germany, in particular in small and medium-sized enterprises, and among low-wage earners.[1146] However, a compulsory occupational pension has been deemed not an adequate solution, as several studies have demonstrated that there are various obstacles to a greater coverage of occupational pension schemes.[1147] Whether this

1143 Gesetz zur Stärkung der betrieblichen Altersversorgung und zur Änderung anderer Gesetze (Betriebsrentenstärkungsgesetz). See § 1, para. 2, nr. 2a BetrAVG.

1144 Cf. C Von Buddenbrock and HM Kühn, 'Das Sozialpartnermodell – Ablösung bestehender Versorgungssysteme in der bAV durch die reine Beitragszusage' 50 BB 2997, 2997.

1145 § 20, para 2 BetrAVG.

1146 This ambition had been pronounced in Koalitionsvertrag zwischen CDU/CSU/SPD, *Deutschlands Zukunft gestalten* (2013) 72-73. In 2019, almost 54% of the employees subject to social security was covered by some form of *betriebliche Altersvorsorge*, see Portal Sozialpolitik, 'Betriebliche Altersversorung sozialversicherungspflichtig Beschäftigter' <http://www.portal-sozialpolitik.de/index.php?page=betriebsrentenstaerkungsgesetz> accessed 18 June 2021.

1147 F Wallau and others, 'Machbarkeitsstudie für eine empirische Analyse von Hemmnissen für die Verbreitung der betrieblichen Altersversorgung in kleinen und mittleren Unternehmen' (Forschungsbericht /

new type of vesting method will actually lead to a further coverage rate of occupational pensions remains to be seen, given the fact that the impediments are manifold.[1148]

However, the Federal Ministry of Labour and Social Affairs considered the employer's liability as a decisive reason for this reform.[1149] Due to the persistent low-interest, many companies are financially suffering from their existing pension systems. In addition, many companies have built up entire 'patchwork carpets' of pension systems over the past.[1150] The question to what extent the new *reine Beitragszusage* can be harnessed for harmonisation or unification of the existing dispersed pension system, remains to be seen. However, it can be said that the implementation of a pure DC-scheme has a considerable impact on the, thus far, DB-orientated German pension system, and it will bring this system more in line with international developments. With abolishing the employer's obligation to maintain the pension scheme, the legislator moved away from one of the core principles of the previous German occupational pension law. Over the years, it had increasingly been perceived as a clubfoot from which the 'gazelle defined contribution scheme' had to be freed.[1151] Furthermore, it amends some principles of the *Betriebsrentengesetzes* (BetrAVG) that have long been considered immutable, and is accompanied by changes in tax and social security law.[1152]

Under this vesting method the employer is obliged by *Tarifvertrag* (collective agreement) or pursuant to a *Tarifvertrag in einer Betriebs- oder Dienstvereinbarung* (collective agreement in a works or service agreement) to pay contributions to finance occupational pension benefits to a *Pensionsfonds, Pensionskasse* or *Direktversicherung*.[1153] Moreover, the

---

Bundesministerium für Arbeit und Soziales, FB444, 2014) 62-69, 93, 97 ff. and D Kiesewetter and others, *Optimierungsmöglichkeiten bei den bestehenden steuer- und sozialversicherungsrechtlichen Förderregelungen der betrieblichen Altersversorgung* (Würzburg University Press, Würzurg 2016) 82, 83, 95. Obstacles on the employer side range from high complexity / high administrative burden for employers to presumed disadvantageousness of the occupational pension for employees (due to tax and social security law). In particular, information effort, legislative risks, and complexity were mentioned. However, on the employee's side it ranged from peoples' tendency towards immediate consumption instead of old-age provision to full crediting of occupational pension benefits to the *Grundsicherung*.

1148 Cf. M Ulbrich, 'Die Reform der Betriebsrente oder die Befreiung einer Gazelle: Das Betriebsrentenstärkungsgesetz (BRSG) Teil I – Arbeitsrecht' 41 BB 2424.

1149 BMAS, 'Neues Sozialpartnermodell Betriebsrente – Mögliche Änderungen im Betriebsrentengesetz' (2015). This refers to the (subsidiary) obligation of the employer to guarantee the promised pension benefits pursuant to § 1, para 1, sentence 3 BetrAVG, which states: *"Der Arbeitgeber steht für die Erfüllung der von ihm zugesagten Leistungen auch dann ein, wenn die Durchführung nicht unmittelbar über ihn erfolgt."*

1150 Von Buddenbrock and Kühn, 2997.

1151 See Ulbrich, 2424 and cited literature.

1152 Cf. Ibid. 2423.

1153 § 22 BetrAVG. See also L Schobert, *Die reine Beitragszusage: Überlegungen zur Stärkung der arbeitgeberfinanzierten betrieblichen Altersversorgung* (Schriften zum Sozial- und Arbeitsrecht, Duncker &

reine Beitragszusage can merely be implemented through one of these three pension vehicles. The extent to which the precise pension accrual is defined, depends on whether it is obligatory pursuant to either a *Tarifvertrag* or *Betriebs- oder Dienstvereinbarung.* However, these *Betriebs- oder Dienstvereinbarung,* in turn, can only make regulations if a *Tarifvertrag* allows for these forms. This mandatory link to a collective agreement is intended to ensure that the interests of employees are adequately taken into account.[1154] However, employers and employees who are not bound by collective agreements can also agree on the application of the relevant collective agreement regulation and thus introduce the *reine Beitragszusage.*[1155] In either case, the *Betriebsrentengesetz* (BetrAVG) applies, accompanied by the consequences pursuant to the applicable tax legislation. The employer, thus, merely commits to pay contributions into the pension scheme, for the benefit of the employee, and no longer has a (subsidiary) obligation to also provide pension benefits. This form of pension vesting is marked by the so-called *Garantieverbot* (guarantee ban), i.e. the employee may not be promised an investment return but a security contribution by the employer should be agreed in the collective agreement.[1156] This applies to both the accrual phase and the pay-out phase. The guarantee ban was one of the most controversial points of the BRSG, also inducing challenges in the domain of pension communication. For instance, since this legal provision stipulates that the amount of the pension benefits may not be guaranteed, this renders communication on what people will get at retirement date (one of the most prevalent questions among people) fairly difficult.

Furthermore, the employer's obligation of *Insolvenzsicherungspflicht* (insolvency insurance obligation) does not apply, i.e. the employer is not obliged to pay any contributions to the *Pensions-Sicherungs-Verein.* The risk of an unfunded pension commitment is thus largely borne by the employee, rather than the employer. Due to the possible disadvantages for the employee, the *reine Beitragszusage* has been strictly regulated.[1157]

6.5.1.B Regulatory Instruments for Pension Vesting

Occupational pension provisions are mainly regulated through (collective) agreements.[1158] For most occupational pension provisions only, an institutional framework has been provided for in legislation, i.e. *BetrAVG*, contrary to the Netherlands where, although

Humblot, Berlin 2017).

1154 Furthermore, a certain form of compensation in favour of the employee is provided by the new regulation in § 1a para. 1a BetrAVG: the employer must transfer at least 15% of the total converted remuneration (*Entgeltumwandlung*) to the implementing insurance company due to the saved social security contributions.

1155 Pursuant to § 24 BetrAVG.

1156 See § 22, para 1, second sentence BetrAVG and § 244b, para 1, nr. 1 VAG.

1157 See § 21-25 BetrAVG.

1158 Cf. Ruland, 21.

partially, a legal compulsory membership for occupational pensions has been provided.[1159] In principle, it is not mandatory for the German employer to implement an occupational pension provision. A legislative act is, however, needed as a legal ground in order to commit a provision of occupational pension, which may be subdivided in individual and collective regulatory instruments.

In most cases, occupational pensions are namely committed through *Tarifverträge*.[1160] In some exceptional cases, the employee may agree on an individual agreement, a so-called *Einzelversorgungsvorsorge*. These *Tarifverträge* are characterised by the sort of pension commitment (regarding future benefits and contributions), the extent of the securing and the form of pension provision. These *Tarifverträge* are however restricted by minimal standards laid down in the *Betriebsrentegesetz*, for instance with regard to insolvency protection.[1161] Under collective agreements, the commitment of occupational pension may be laid down in a so-called *Tarifvertrag*, i.e. a collective agreement.[1162] In the private sectors these agreements play a minor role, contrary to its role in public service.[1163] On the contrary, a major role in vesting pension provisions may be attributed to so-called *Betriebsvereinbarungen*, i.e. company agreements.

Individual regulatory instruments comprise *Einzelzusage*, *Gesamtzusage* or *betriebliche Übung*. Firstly, the *Einzelzusage* – i.e. an individual commitment – is laid down in a contractual agreement between employer and employee, which contract is subject to contract law.[1164] This individual contract shall form part of the employment contract. Secondly, under the *Gesamtzusage* – i.e. the collective commitment – the employer does not conclude a contract with each of his employees but, instead, offers a uniform contract to a particular group of beneficial employees. Lastly, the pension commitment may arise from the *betriebliche Übung*, i.e. common company practice.[1165] According to settled case-law this comprises the frequent repetition of specific behavioural patterns by the employer, to which he is not obliged but enabling the employee to conclude that he shall be granted

1159 Scholz, 8.

1160 Cf. Ruland, 21.

1161 Cf. Ibid. 22.

1162 A persistent downward trend in sectoral collective agreements can be observed. In 2020, about 45 per cent of West German and about 32 per cent of East German employees worked in a company where a sectoral collective agreement applied. In 2019, this was still the case for 46 and 34 per cent respectively. This is shown by data from the IAB Establishment Panel, an annual survey of around 16,000 companies by the Institute for Employment Research, see Institut für Arbeitsmarkt- und Berufsforschung, 'Tarifbindung nimmt in Deutschland weiter ab' 19 May 2021) <https://www.iab.de/de/informationsservice/presse/presseinformationen/tarifbindungabnahme.aspx> accessed 21 May 2021.

1163 Cf. Förster and Rechtenwald, 151.

1164 Cf. Ibid. 152.

1165 Leading to the commitment of occupational pension by virtue of § 1b, para. 1 BetrAVG.

a benefit or a benefit in the long run.[1166] The following section revolve around the several German *Durchführungswege.*

6.5.1.B.I Direktzusage

The *Direktzusage*[1167] may be considered as one of the most generally used vesting method in German occupational pensions, both regarding the number of participants as well as the amount of funds covered.[1168] This type of pension vehicle is unknown in several other European countries, including the Netherlands. Under this pension vesting method, the employer ensures retirement benefits without involvement of any other pension institution, hence the use of the term *Direkt.*[1169] Employer and pension provider are therefore incorporated in the same legal person. The pension commitment by the employer is financed by so-called *Pensionsrückstellungen*, i.e. pension reserves. Since the vesting of pension is agreed on between employer and employee – and without involvement of any pension institution or insurer – the *Betriebsrentengesetz* does not regulate this form of pension provision, apart from certain framework standards.[1170]

From a civil law perspective, the provision of a *Direktzusage* is not subjected to any conditions or criteria. Therefore, this provision can be vested through individual or collective agreements and even through 'common company practice'[1171]. The pension provision may be provided free of format, moreover full capital funding is not required by the *Betriebsrentengesetz* and supervisory legal provisions are missing. Most commonly, however, defined benefit scheme are vested under *Direktzusage*. However, in order to secure the financial sustainability of the pension commitment, most commonly a so-called *Rückdeckungsversicherung* is concluded by the employer.[1172] This insurance mostly takes the form of a life insurance concluded upon the life of the employee.[1173] This does, however, not change the employer's obligation towards the employee to fulfil the granted pension

1166 BAG, BB 16 September 1998. 1999. For a concise overview see: Cf. Förster and Rechtenwald, 152-153.

1167 Translated freely as 'direct commitment'.

1168 See Portal Sozialpolitik. For a concise overview of the history of occupational pensions in Germany, see B Uebelhack, *Betriebliche Altersversorgung: Grundlagen und Praxis* (C.F. Müller, Heidelberg 2017). See also Scheffler and Kölbl, 33. See also R Klein, 'Die Deckungsmitel der betrieblichen Altersversorgung in 2019' 5 BetrAV 429.

1169 For the consequences of the passivation of the pension commitment for the regular (commercial) balance sheet, see § 246 in conjunction with § 249 HGB. For the consequences of the passivation of the pension commitment for the fiscal balance sheet, see § 6a EStG. See also D Wellisch and others, *Besteuerung der Altersvorsorge: ein international Vergleich* (Schriften des Institutes der Ausländisches und Internationales Finanz- und Steuerwesen der Universität Hamburg, Nomos, Baden-Baden 2008) 163.

1170 Cf. Scholz, 66 and cited literature.

1171 In German commonly referred to as 'betriebliche Übung'. For an elaborative discussion of the *Betriebliche Übung* as vesting method, see Förster and others, 49 ff.

1172 Scholz, 67.

1173 Cf. Förster and Rechtenwald, 144.

commitment. The employee is not entitled to the benefits of the *Rückdeckungsversicherung* since the employer remains policy holder as well as beneficiary. Furthermore, for the provision under *Direktzusage* a legal contribution obligation is in place for the *Pension-Sicherungs-Verein a.G. (PSVaG)*.[1174] This is the statutory determined institution to secure occupational pension provisions in Germany from insolvency of the employer, being a member of this association and, therefore, solely liable for contributions.[1175]

In particular sectors, specific pension schemes are offered to particular groups of employees.[1176] These specific schemes are established by associations[1177] in order to secure a uniform application of the pension scheme to the affiliated employers. The employer's membership does not lead to different benefit entitlements, these entitlements remain in place toward the respective employer, instead of the association as such.

6.5.1.B.II Direktversicherung

Under the provision of a *Direktversicherung*, a *Lebensversicherung*[1178] is concluded – for occupational pension purposes – by the employer on the life of the employee.[1179] Furthermore, the employee or his surviving relatives are fully or partially entitled to the benefits in relation to the insurance institution. The insurance contributions may be fully financed by the employer, by means of *Entgeltumwandlung*, either employee's contributions or pro rata by both the employer as well as the employee.[1180] The insurance may be concluded as an individual insurance (*Einzelversicherung*) or as a group insurance (*Gruppenversicherung*).[1181]

With regard to the *Direktversicherung*, the relationship between employer, employee and insurer consitutes a triangular relationship, with different independent legal relationships between each of the actors.[1182] The employer is legally obliged towards his employee to pay the contributions to the insurance institution and providing retirement benefits, stemming from an insurance contract, respectively. The contract underlying the *Direktversicherung* must be concluded by the employer as the policyholder, in which the employee is appointed

1174 Translated freely as 'pension insurance association'. See PSVaG, 'Allgemeines zur Melde- und Beitragspflicht' <https://www.psvag.de/mitglieder-beitrag/allgemeines-zur-melde-und-beitragspflicht.html> accessed 8 March 2022.

1175 With regard to legal measures aimed at protecting the pension provisions against insolvency of the employer, please see Förster and others, 229 ff.

1176 Cf. Förster and Rechtenwald, 144.

1177 For instance, *Bochumer Verband*.

1178 Translated freely as 'life insurance'.

1179 § 1b, para. 2 BetrAVG.

1180 BAG, DB 26 June 1990. 1990.

1181 Förster and Rechtenwald, 144.

1182 Ibid. 144.

as the beneficiary.[1183] This method of concluding the insurance contract is distinctive for the *Direktversicherung*.

Figure 6.2 Triangular Relationship

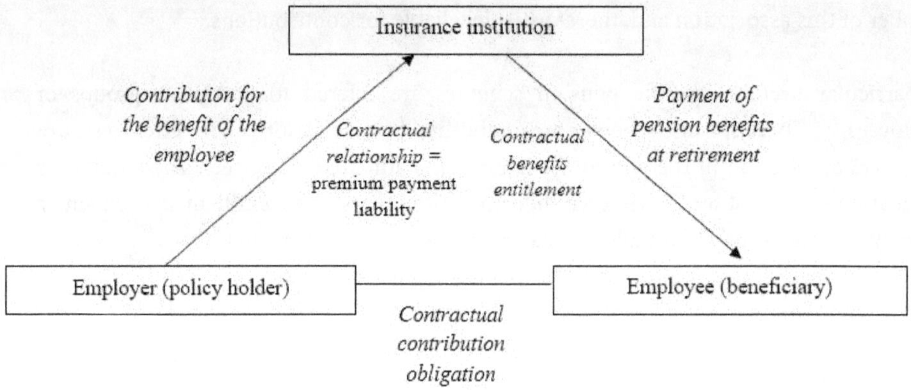

The entitlement to the future benefits under the insurance contract may be either revocable or irrevocable. In case the entitlement to the benefits is revocable, the employer acquires this right to the benefits from the moment of retirement.[1184] If, on the contrary, the entitlement to the future benefits is irrevocable, he acquires this right already from the moment of the contracts' conclusion.[1185]

From the point of view of the employer, the *Direktversicherung* leads to the least administrative hassle.[1186] The main difference to the *Direktzusage* (with *Rückdeckungsversicherung*[1187]) lies in the entitlement to the potential benefits of this insurance, i.e. the employer is solely entitled to these benefits.[1188] On the contrary, under a *Direktversicherung*, the employee has a direct legal claim against the insurer for the pension benefits. Besides the employers' contribution obligations, he carries the risk of a *Subsidiärhaftung*.[1189] For this reason, entitlements of *Direktversicherungen* are in principle exempted from contribution to the *Pension-Sicherungs-Verein a.G. (PSVaG)*.[1190]

1183 The insurance contract is therefore qualified as a *Vertrag zugunsten Dritter* (contract to the benefit of a third party), by virtue of § 328 ff. BGB.

1184 Pursuant to § 159, para. 2 VVG.

1185 Pursuant to § 159, para. 3 VVG.

1186 Cf. Scholz, 74.

1187 Translated freely as 'reinsurance for pension obligations'.

1188 This even holds true if the entitlements to the *Rückdeckungsversicherung* have been pledged to the employee.

1189 Pursuant to § 1, para. 1, third sentence BetrAVG. Translated freely as 'subsidiary liability'.

1190 Unless § 10, para. 3, nr. 2 BetrAVG applies.

6.5.1.B.III Unterstützungskasse

By virtue of the *Betriebsrentengesetz* the *Unterstützungskasse* constitutes a legally shaped retirement benefit scheme on which benefits no legal right is conferred.[1191] The *Kasse* – i.e. the fund – is commonly formed as an association or a limited company which may cover multiple employers or may also cover only one employer.[1192] The *Unterstützungskasse* as such has a separate capital, disengaged from the employer.

As holds true for the *Direktversicherung*, the relationship between employer, employee and *Unterstützungskasse* is triangular. Between employer and *Unterstützungskasse* a commission agreement is concluded.[1193] Pursuant to this agreement, the *Unterstützungskasse* is legally obliged to continue the retirement provision of the employee in accordance with the benefits plan. Furthermore, the relationship between employee and *Unterstützungskasse* is characterised by the fact that no legal right is conferred on the employee as regards the benefits.[1194] What is more, the legal claim exists against the employer. In practice this exclusion of the legal rights has been reduced to an empty shell, since it has been qualified as a revocation right of the employer, based on objective reasons.[1195] As Förster points out, this still leaves the employee de facto with a legal claim.[1196]

The entitled employees formally do not have a legal claim regarding the accrued entitlements, since otherwise the fund ought to be subject to the supervision of the insurance sector. Hence, the asset investment of the accumulated assets retains considerable freedom.

The aforementioned lack of legal claim to the accrued entitlements may, as Scholz rightly claims, be put in perspective since the employer is subject to a so-called *Subsidiärhaftung* (subsidiary liability) in case the *Kasse* cannot comply with her obligation to pay out the accumulated benefits.[1197] Also for pension provisions under *Unterstützungskasse*, a legal contribution obligation is in place for the *Pension-Sicherungs-Verein a.G. (PSVaG)* in order to hedge the risk of insolvency of the employer.

1191 Pursuant to § 1b, para. 4 BetrAVG, which states *‚einer rechtsfähigen Versorgungseinrichtung, die auf ihre Leistungen keinen Rechtsanspruch gewährt'.*

1192 Scholz, 70.

1193 Pursuant to § 662 ff. BGB.

1194 Cf. Förster and Rechtenwald, 146. For this reason the *Unterstützungskasse* had been excluded from the scope of application of Directive 2003/41/EC of the European Parliament and of the Council of 3 June 2003 on the activities and supervision of institutions for occupational retirement provision [2003] OJ L 235. See para 16 of the preamble.

1195 BVerfG, DB 14 Januar 1987. 1987 and BAG, ibid 11 December 2001. 2003.

1196 Cf. Förster and Rechtenwald, 146. This can derived from BverfG, DB 19 October 1983. 1984.

1197 Scholz, 69.

6.5.1.B.IV Pensionskasse

The *Pensionskasse*[1198] comprises a legally shaped retirement benefits scheme which confers a legal right on the employee to occupational pension entitlements.[1199] It represents the most important external vesting scheme, in terms of number of people covered, as well as funds covered.[1200] The *Pensionskasse* is defined as a legally independent assurance institution whose aim is to hedge the lack of earned income as a result of retirement.[1201] Furthermore, the *Pensionskasse* pursues insurance activities by means of the funding principle.[1202] Secondly, benefits may, in principal, only be paid out from the date of the loss of an earned income.[1203] This illustrates the pension bound destination of the retirement funds. When the earned income is lost only partially, the general conditions of insurance may foresee in pro rata benefits. Lastly – at least for this section relevant – the *Pensionskasse* confers a personal right on the insured person to the retirement benefits or, otherwise, renders benefits as *Rückdeckungsversicherung.*[1204] As is also the case for the *Direktversicherung*, the relationship between employer, employee and *Pensionskasse* is triangular.

At least from a civil law perspective, the *Pensionskasse* is considered as a particular form of insurance institution.[1205] This is, for instance, illustrated by the legal regulation of engaging in the *Versicherungsverein auf Gegenseitigkeit* (*VVaG*).[1206] The German *Bundestag* approved a reform of the *Betriebsrentengesetz*, under which *Pensionskassen* also fall under the scope of the *Pension-Sicherungs-Verein a.G. (PSVaG).*[1207] In the event of the employer's insolvency, this association will, under certain conditions, take over the pension liabilities.

The distinction between *Pensionskasse* and *Pensionsfonds* lies not only in the civil law consequences, laid down in the *Betriebsrentengesetz*, but, furthermore, lies in the

1198 Translated freely as 'pension fund'.

1199 Pursuant to § 1b, para. 3 BetrAVG, which states: *„Wird die betriebliche Altersversorgung von einer rechtsfähigen Versorgungseinrichtung durchgeführt, die dem Arbeitnehmer oder seinen Hinterbliebenen auf ihre Leistungen einen Rechtsanspruch gewährt (Pensionskasse und Pensionsfonds), so gilt Absatz 1 entsprechend."*

1200 See Klein, 430.

1201 § 232, para. 1 VAG. Please note that cross-border activities of *Pensionskassen* are regulated in Chapter 3 of the *Versicherungsaufsichtsgesetz (AVG), i.e. 'Grenzüberschreitende Geschäftstätigkeit von Einrichtungen der betrieblichen Altersversorgung'.*

1202 § 232, para. 1, under 1 VAG.

1203 § 232, para. 1, under 2 VAG.

1204 Translated freely as 'reinsurance for pension obligations'.

1205 Cf. Scholz, 71. Also Förster and Rechtenwald, 145.

1206 Pursuant to § 233, para. 1 VAG. Translated freely as 'mutual insurance association'.

1207 Entwurf eines Siebten Gesetzes zur Änderung des Vierten Buches Sozialgesetzbuch und anderer Gesetze (7. SGB IV-ÄndG) 13 March 2020.

prudential regulations pursuant to the *Versicherungsaufsichtsgesetz (VAG).*[1208] This will not be dealt with any further in this research. *Pensionskassen* are subject to a different prudential regulatory framework in comparison to *Pensionsfonds.*[1209] Furthermore, *Pensionskasse* are subject to regulatory insurance supervision by the *Bundesanstalt für Finanzdienstleistungsaufsicht (BaFin)* and must adhere to their regulations regarding asset investment.

The *Pensionskasse* may function as a pension provider for one or more employers.[1210] Employees of one or several employers - grouped within a concern - may be ensured through a so-called *Betriebspensionskasse* or a *Konzernpensionskasse* respectively.[1211] Alternatively, employees of independent employers may be ensured by means of a *Gruppenpensionskasse*[1212], which are in most cases industry-related.

6.5.1.B.V Pensionsfonds

The *Pensionsfonds* has been implemented by the *Altersvermögensgesetz (AVmG)* in 2002 as additional pension vesting method.[1213] A *Pensionsfonds*[1214] constitutes a legally shaped retirement benefits scheme attributing a legal right on the entitlements of an occupational scheme to the employee.[1215] The *Pensionsfonds* is defined as a legally provided retirement provision which renders capital funded retirement benefits as part of an occupational pension scheme for one or more employers for the benefits of their employees.[1216] Secondly, the level of benefits or the level of future contributions to be paid, may not for all benefits be granted by means of insurance-type guarantees.[1217] The retirement provision under the *Pensionsfonds* must grant the employee a personal right to his own benefits against the *Pensionsfonds.*[1218] Lastly, the *Pensionsfonds* is in principle legally obliged to render the

1208 Gesetz über die Beaufsichtigung der Versicherungsunternehmen (Versicherungsaufsichtsgesetz - VAG).

1209 Where the prudential provisions for *Pensionskassen* are laid down in chapter 1 of the VAG, *Pensionsfondsen* are subject to the prudential provisions laid down in chapter 2 VAG.

1210 Cf.Förster and Rechtenwald, 145.

1211 Translated freely as a 'company pension fund' and 'concern pension fund' respectively.

1212 Translated freely as 'group pension fund'.

1213 Gesetz zur Reform der gesetzlichen Rentenversicherung und zur Förderung eines kapitalgedeckten Altersvorsorgevermögens (Altersvermögensgesetz - AVmG).

1214 Translated freely as 'pension fund'.

1215 Pursuant to § 1b, para. 3 BetrAVG, which states: *„Wird die betriebliche Altersversorgung von einer rechtsfähigen Versorgungseinrichtung durchgeführt, die dem Arbeitnehmer oder seinen Hinterbliebenen auf ihre Leistungen einen Rechtsanspruch gewährt (Pensionskasse und Pensionsfonds), so gilt Absatz 1 entsprechend.“*

1216 § 236, para. 1, under 1 VAG. Please note that cross-border activities of *Pensionsfonds* are regulated in Chapter 3 of the *Versicherungsaufsichtsgesetz (AVG), i.e. 'Grenzüberschreitende Geschäftstätigkeit von Einrichtungen der betrieblichen Altersversorgung'.*

1217 § 236, para. 1, under 2 VAG.

1218 § 236, para. 1, under 3 VAG.

retirement benefits as a lifelong payment or as a lump sum.[1219] The aforementioned lifelong payment may be complemented with a partial or full lump-sum option.

At least from a civil law perspective, the *Pensionskasse* is considered as a particular form of insurance institution.[1220] Besides, *Pensionskassen* are subject to a different prudential regulatory framework in comparison to *Pensionsfonds*.[1221] Primarily, the *Pensionsfonds* differentiates from the *Pensionskasse* by more liberal investment regulations. For instance, the pension provisions under the *Pensionsfonds* ought to be capital funded. Since the *Pensionskasse* is characterised more as an insurance scheme - contrary to the *Pensionsfonds* - it is subject to stricter asset investment regulations, supervised by the insurance supervisions institution. For the *Pensionsfonds* suchlike strict asset regulations do not apply. Rather, the asset investment activities of *Pensionsfonds* are liable to more open prudential norms, for instance the pension provision should be capital funded.[1222] Furthermore, for provision under a *Pensionsfonds* a legal contribution obligation applies for the *Pension-Sicherungs-Verein a.G. (PSVaG)*.

6.5.1.B.VI Entgeltumwandlung

In principle, German employers are not subject to a pension vesting obligation[1223], i.e. to implement an occupational pension provision. Until the implementation of the AVmG[1224], the *betrieblichen Altersversorgung* was regarded as a voluntary social benefit provided by the employer. Apart from a - in practice rarely implemented - civil contractual obligation pursuant to a *Tarifvertrag*, the employer was not legally obliged to implement a pension provision.[1225] However, this lack of obligation is to some extent reversed by the so-called *Entgeltumwandlung*[1226]. Principally, this obligation to implement the *Entgeltumwandlung* is at odds with the legal principle of contractual freedom.[1227]

1219 § 236, para. 1, under 4 VAG. Apart from the exception in § 236, para. 2 and para. 2a VAG.

1220 Cf. Scholz, 71.

1221 Where the prudential provisions for *Pensionskassen* are laid down in chapter 1 of the VAG, *Pensionsfondsen* are subject to the prudential provisions laid down in chapter 2 VAG.

1222 For instance, § 239, para. 1 VAG.

1223 Cf. Förster and others, 123.

1224 Gesetz zur Reform der gesetzlichen Rentenversicherung und zur Förderung eines kapitalgedeckten Altersvorsorgevermögens (Altersvermögensgesetz - AVmG).

1225 Förster and others, 123.

1226 Translated freely as 'deferred compensation'.

1227 The from the BetrAVG emerging obligation to implement the *Entgeltumwandlung* as a pension provision is not incompatible with the German constitution: BAG, DB 12 June 2007. 2007, 2722.

This mechanism - which in itself may be considered as a separate form of pension provision[1228] – allows the converting of future salary payment entitlements into entitlements to occupational pension provisions for a similar value.[1229] The employee's entitlement to the *Entgeltumwandlung* shall be precluded to the extent that an occupational pensions provision is in place, funded by means of *Entgeltumwandlung*.[1230] The aforementioned future pension entitlements may not be due, however, the underlying ground for the future payments must exist.

In short, employees invest a percentage of their income into occupational pensions, in a *Direktversicherung, Pensionsfonds* or *Pensionskasse*. Payment to pension provisions in the form of *Direktzusage* or *Unterstützungskasse* is allowed, under the condition of mutual understanding of the employer. The method of vesting the pension (i.e. *Durchführungswege*) is regulated through individual agreement which may not be replaced by a company agreement. The employer has in this regard a right of initiative; if the employer decides to vest pension through a *Pensionsfonds* or *Pensionskasse*, the occupational pension shall be accrued accordingly.[1231] Otherwise, the employee may request the employer to conclude a pension provision by means of *Direktversicherung*.[1232] In accordance with the *Betriebsrentengesetz (BetrAVG)* it may be implemented in two differentiated ways, i.e. by means of the *vertragliche Entgeltumwandlung*[1233] or through *Rechtsanspruch*.[1234] It should be pointed out that through both methods, employees finance their own occupational pension. If contributions are financed out of the net income, the amount of contributions is maximised at €2,100 yearly. However, for these contributions the tax facilities of the *Riester-Förderung*[1235] or *Sonderausgabenabzug*[1236] may be claimed.[1237]

The *Entgeltumwandlung* may be funded from the employee's gross or net income. If he decides to finance it through his gross income, the allowed convertible contribution may

1228 § 1, para. 2, under 3 BetrAVG, which states: „*Betriebliche Altersversorgung liegt auch vor, wenn künftige Entgeltansprüche in eine wertgleiche Anwartschaft auf Versorgungsleistungen umgewandelt werden.*" For the qualification of the *Entgeltumwandlung* from a civil law perspective see: Förster and Rechtenwald, 149 and cited literature.

1229 Similar value is since 2002 required by law pursuant to § 1a BetrAVG. Initiated as a result of BAG. Regarding similar value I refer to: Förster and Rechtenwald, 149 and cited literature.

1230 §1a, para. 2 BetrAVG.

1231 § 1a, para. 1 BetrAVG.

1232 § 1a, para. 1 BetrAVG.

1233 Pursuant to § 1, para. 2, under 3 BetrAVG. Translated freely as 'contractual deferred compensation'.

1234 Pursuant to § 1a BetrAVG. Translated freely as 'legal right'.

1235 Translated freely as '*Riester*-facilitation'.

1236 Translated freely as 'special expenses deduction'.

1237 Using the *Riester-Förderung* for the contributions regarding the *Entgeltumwandlung*, brings the categorisation of *Entgeltumwandlung* as occupational pension at odds, since *Riester-Förderung* in itself is regarded as a fiscally facilitated individual pension provision.

amount up to eight percent of the contribution threshold of the *allgemeinen Rentenversicherung*, under the condition that the pension entitlement is ensured through the permitted pension vesting methods as aforementioned.[1238] In case the employee loses his entitlement to his future benefits, but his employment relationship is continued – for instance, in case of expatriates, he has the right to continue the accrual of the provision by means of his own contributions.[1239] The employer is legally obliged to guarantee these benefits emerging from these contributions as well.[1240]

6.6 The Tax Treatment of German Occupational Pensions (Betrieblichen Altersversorgung)

Occupational pensions existed already during the beginning of the 19th century, prior to the introduction of the *gesetzlichen Rentenversicherung*.[1241] Prior to the commencement of the *Versicherungsaufsichtsgesetz* in 1901, the first *Pensionskassen* were founded. As a result of the fiscal reform of 1934, a clear distinction was introduced regarding the judicable *Unterstützungskassen* – which were exempted from corporate tax[1242] and which allocates no legal claim on their benefits provided – leading to no taxation during the accrual phase.[1243] In contrast, *Pensionskassen* were partially non-judicable employer's savings, granting the employee pension entitlements. Hence, these granted entitlements were considered as leading to enrichment on behalf of the employee, liable for tax purposes.[1244] Furthermore, the *Direktversicherung* – under which the employer concludes a *Lebensversicherung* on behalf of the employee, exists since 1928.[1245] The *Pensionsfonds*, also granting the employee a legal right on the pension entitlement, was introduced under the *Altersvermögensgesetz*[1246], entered into force on 1 January 2002. This highly deviating path of historical development of each form of occupational pension provision has led to a significant amount of deviations, and disparities in the tax treatment of each form of pension. Moreover, each form of occupational pensions has been assigned considerably by

1238 Pursuant to § 3, para. 63 EStG.

1239 § 1a, para. 4 BetrAVG.

1240 § 1a, para. 4 BetrAVG.

1241 Cf. Birk and Wernsmann, 232.

1242 I.e. *Körperschaftsteuer*.

1243 Birk and Wernsmann, 232. For an elaboration on the historical development of the *Unterstützungskasse* Birk and Wernsmann refer to E Heissmann, *Betriebliche Unterstützungskassen* (Schmidt, Köln 1966) 4 ff.

1244 Cf. Birk and Wernsmann, 232 and cited literature.

1245 Ibid. 232 and cited literature in footnote 24. See also P Ahrend, W Förster and N Rößler, *Steuerrecht der betrieblichen Altersversorgung* (Schmidt, Köln 2017).

1246 Gesetz zur Reform der gesetzlichen Rentenversicherung und zur Förderung eines kapitalgedeckten Altersvorsorgevermögens (Altersvermögensgesetz – AVmG).

the fiscal legislation. Therefore, the fiscal legislation regarding the occupational provisions of pension may be regarded as guide of the pension provision under labour law.[1247]

The regulations with respect to the tax treatment of occupational pensions are complex, and are grounded on the principle of intertemporal correspondence.[1248] If the accrual of pension entitlements on the side of the employee is considered his earned income (i.e. *Arbeitslohn*) – and hence allocated to his taxable income – the future pension benefits shall not be subject to taxation, to the extent that no new income has been generated from this accumulated capital.[1249] These newly generated elements of income will then be subject to taxation during the pay-out phase as so-called *Ertragsanteil*[1250]. If the retirement entitlements do not qualify as *Arbeitslohn* or are tax free, the pension benefits, in principle, shall be fully subject to taxation.

The tax treatment of pension contributions paid to, and benefits arising from occupational pensions will be discussed in the sections below.

6.6.1.A Fragmentation of Pension Entitlements and no Uniform Fiscal Concept in the Accrual Phase

It is to be noted at the outset of this section that the fiscal treatment of German (occupational) pensions in the accrual phase is not founded on a uniform established concept.[1251] Birk and Wernsmann typify this by using the following example; the employer's expenses in order to build a retirement provision for the benefit of the employee, are in principle considered taxable *Arbeitslohn*.[1252] This subordinate regulation is inaccurate and in terms of the systematic of the tax regime inconsistent, since the purpose of the employers' expense (i.e. ensuring a pension provision) singly is not decisive.[1253] This does not meet the conditions of *Arbeitslohn*, since this is more aimed on an enrichment of the employee.[1254] The tax treatment of the German occupational pensions is largely different, and in principle depends on the pension vesting methods.

1247 Birk and Wernsmann, 233 and cited literature.

1248 I.e. *intertemporalen Korrrespondenz*. Cf. C Dorenkamp, *Nachgelagerte Besteuerung von Einkommen: Besteuerungsaufschub für investierte Reinvermögensmehrungen* (Duncker & Humblot, Berlin 2004) 46 and G Glaser, *Besteuerungszeitpunkte in der Zusatzversorgung: Verfassungsfragen und einkommenssteuersystematische Einordnung* (Verlag Dr. Kovač, Hamburg 2009) 7 and Birk and Wernsmann, 245.

1249 Birk and Wernsmann, 246.

1250 Translated freely as 'share of income'.

1251 Cf. Birk and Wernsmann, 246.

1252 By virtue of § 2, para 2, nr 3 LStDV, which provision states: "*Zum Arbeitslohn gehören auch: Ausgaben, die ein Arbeitgeber leistet, um einen Arbeitnehmer oder diesem nahestehende Personen für den Fall der Krankheit, des Unfalls, der Invalidität, des Alters oder des Todes abzusichern (Zukunftssicherung).*"

1253 Cf. Birk and Wernsmann, 246.

1254 For this, Birk and Wernsmann refer to § 8, para 1 and § 19, para 1 EStG. See ibid. 246.

6.6.1.B Shift from Pay-As-You-Go to Capital Funded Pension Provisions: Fiscal Consequences

Since the implementation of deferred taxation of occupational pensions, all employers' contributions to *Direktversicherung, Pensionskassen* and *Pensionsfonds* are exempted from taxation, under the condition that the occupational pension provision is built up by means of capital funding.[1255] Consequently, numerous *Pensionskassen* altered their financing method from pay-as-you-go to capital funded.[1256] Since under pay-as-you-go financing the pension entitlements are not covered by invested capital, the shift to capital funding required that these pension coverage loopholes were filled.[1257] These coverage loopholes were then filled by special employer payments[1258]. Then the question arises whether, and to what extent these special employer payments should be considered taxable *Arbeitslohn*. However, these co-called *Sonderzahlungen* do not lead to higher pension entitlements.[1259]

Regarding this qualification of the *Sonderzahlungen* as *Arbeitslohn*, the *Bundesfinanzhof* ruled that the payments should not be considered as leading to an enrichment of the employee, and hence shall not be subject to taxation.[1260] Despite this categorisation of these special payments, the German legislator decided in 2007 to implement a provision stipulating that – contrary to the decision of the *Bundesfinanzhof* – the special payments should be allocated to the taxable *Arbeitslohn*.[1261] Regarding the actual taxation of these special payments, the employer must levy wage taxes at a flat rate of 15% of the *Sonderzahlungen*, i.e. *Pauschalierung der Lohnsteuer*.[1262]

1255 Pursuant to § 3, nr 63 EStG, stipulating: „*Beiträge des Arbeitgebers aus dem ersten Dienstverhältnis an einen Pensionsfonds, eine Pensionskasse oder für eine Direktversicherung zum Aufbau einer kapitalgedeckten betrieblichen Altersversorgung...*"

1256 Birk and Wernsmann, 250.

1257 Cf. Ibid. 250.

1258 I.e. *Sonderzahlungen*.

1259 Birk and Wernsmann, 250.

1260 BFH, BStBl 14 September 2005. 2006c.

1261 Pursuant to § 19, para 1, nr 3, sentence 2 EStG, stating: „*Zu den Einkünften aus nichtselbständiger Arbeit gehören auch Sonderzahlungen, die der Arbeitgeber neben den laufenden Beiträgen und Zuwendungen an eine solche Versorgungseinrichtung leistet*".

1262 Pursuant to § 40b, para 4 EstG. This fixed-rate taxation is by some authors considered unconstitutional, see for instance Birk and Wernsmann, 250and Glaser, 88 ff. An further elaboration on this question is out of scope for this thesis.

6.6.1.C The Tax Treatment of the Internal Pension Vesting Methods: Direktzusage and Unterstützungskasse

6.6.1.C.I Tax Relief during the Accrual Phase

Under both the *Direktzusage*, as well as under the *Unterstützungskasse* an inflow of a monetary advantage[1263] for the employee is missing.[1264] Although the employer builds up a pension capital for the benefits of the employee, the latter has no access nor can derive any legal claims from[1265] the accrued capital, and thus an enrichment of the employee is missing.[1266] This holds true for both the *Direktzusage*, as well as for the *Unterstützungskasse*, since under both provisions the employer is legally the debtor of the pension commitment towards the employee.[1267]

In the case of an occupational pension scheme financed by employer's contributions, the point in time of the inflow of wages is determined by the vesting method of the pension scheme. In the case of a *Direktzusage* or a *Unterstützungskasse*, the *Arbeitslohn* is only paid at the time of payment of the retirement benefits to the employee, i.e. the realisation of the pension entitlement[1268]. This applies to both the employer's contributions, as well as the employee's contributions through *Entgeltumwandlung*.

The *Unterstützungskasse* and *Direktzusage* are fiscally treated similarly, i.e. subject to deferred taxation. However, on the side of the employer, the *Unterstützungskasse* is fiscally treated differently from the *Direktzusage*, but this element of the tax treatment of pensions is out of scope for this research. On the side of the participating employee, the pension as such will be taxed in the pay-out phase, i.e. the pension benefits will be taxed. The disbursed pension benefits are included in the tax assessment basis, as income from dependent personal services.[1269]

1263 Thus leading to taxable income by virtue of § 11, para 1 EStG.

1264 K Heubeck and M Seybold, 'Zur Besteuerung der betrieblichen Altersversorgung nach dem Alterseinkünftegesetz: Übergang vom Drei Säulen- zum Drei-Schichten-Modell nur halbwegs gelungen,' DB 592.

1265 This must be distinguished from the question whether the employee is entitled to the accumulated capital.

1266 Cf. Birk and Wernsmann, 247 and cited literature.

1267 Cf. Ibid. 247.

1268 BMF, *Steuerliche Förderung der betrieblichen Altersversorgung IV C 5 - S 2333/19/10008:017* para 8. Cf. Kirchhof, Söhn and Mellinghof.

1269 Pursuant to § 19 EStG.

6.6.1.C.II *The Tax Treatment of Pension Benefits during the Pay-Out Phase*

Pension benefits paid by the employer on the basis of a *Direktzusage* and pension benefits from a *Unterstützungskasse* constitute income from employment.[1270] These pension benefits arising from the *Direktzusage* or *Unterstützungskasse* are considered belated earned income and, in principle, fully subject to wage taxes withheld from salary.[1271] Tax on these benefits is withheld by the paying institution.[1272]

Regarding the retirement provisions, since 2005, the taxpayer is solely eligible for *Werbungskostenpauschbetrag* of €102 (2023) per tax year, if a higher amount of *Werbungskosten* is not demonstrated.[1273] These *Werbungskosten* lower the taxable person's taxable income. Besides this deductible *Werbungskostenpauschbetrag*, a particular proportion of the retirement benefits shall be exempted from tax under the *Versorgungsfreibetrag*.[1274] In 2023 the percentage of the pension benefits exempted from tax (i.e. the *Versorgungsfreibetrag*) amounts to 13.6%, capped to the amount of €1,020.[1275] In addition, the *Versorgungsfreibetrag* is raised with €326. The ground for this increase of the *Versorgungsfreibetrag* lies in compensating the abolition of the *Arbeitnehmer-Pauschbetrag*. This amount of increase will be reduced to €0 by 2040.[1276] The method of determining the amount of *Versorgungsfreibetrag* depends on the start of the pay-out phase of the pension benefits.[1277] In cases where the pay-out phase started prior to 2005, the amount on the basis of which the exemption is calculated is the twelvefold of the benefits in January 2005. Contrarily, if the pay-out phase started after 2005, it amounts to the twelvefold of the pension benefits for the first full month. An example of the calculation of the *Versorgungsfreibetrag* is provided below.[1278]

1270 Taxed pursuant to § 19 EStG. See also BMF, *Steuerliche Förderung der betrieblichen Altersversorgung IV C 5 - S 2333/19/10008:017* para 146.

1271 By virtue of § 19, para 1, nr 2 EStG in conjunction with § 38, para 1, sentence 1 EStG. See also Kirchhof, Söhn and Mellinghof.

1272 Pursuant to § 38 EStG. The tax withheld is final only if the taxpayer receives, in addition to this income, income of less than €410 and does not apply for a tax assessment. See § 46, para 2 EStG.

1273 By virtue of § 9a, para 1, under b EStG.

1274 Pursuant to § 19, para 2 EStG.

1275 By virtue of § 19, para 2, nr 2, sentence 3 EStG. This *Versorgungsfreibetrag* has been lowered gradually since 2005.

1276 Also by virtue of § 19, para 2, nr 2, sentence 3 EStG.

1277 As laid down in § 19, para 2, nr 2, sentence 4 EStG.

1278 This example is derived from the example provided by Birk and Wernsmann. The example is – for this thesis – adjusted to the figures and percentages applicable for 2012. See Birk and Wernsmann, 252.

Example calculation *Versorgungsfreibetrag*: as of February 2023 individual X receives a monthly pension benefits of €1,000 out of a *Direktzusage*, directly paid by his employer.

Total benefits 2023	€11,000 (11 x €1,000) (as of February)
Minus: Werbungskosten-Pauschbetrag (§9a, nr 1, under b EStG)	- €102
Versorgungsfreibetrag	€1,020 (€12,000 (12 x €1,000) x 13.6% = €1,632, but maximised at €1,020)
Zuschlag zum Versorgungsfreibetrag	€306
Total *Versorgungsfreibetrag*	€1,326
But retirement benefits received as of February 2023 = 11/12	- €1,216 (€1,326 * 11/12)
Taxable benefits 2023	**€9,682**

The total amount of *Versorgungsfreibetrag* and *Zuschlag* are set for the remaining duration of the pay-out phase.[1279] Regular adjustments to the pension benefits do not lead to a recalculation of these amounts.[1280] Further, capital lump sums of *Direktzusage* are subject to a reduced tax treatment.[1281]

An interesting situation arises in cases where the retirement provision from a *Direktzusage* or *Unterstützungskasse* is transferred to a *Pensionsfonds*. The benefits arising from the transferred pension entitlements will be treated for tax purposes as benefits paid out from a *Pensionsfonds*[1282], instead of as earned income arising from prior employment[1283].[1284]

6.6.1.D The Tax Treatment of the External Pension Vesting Methods: Direktversicherung, Pensionskasse and Pensionsfonds

6.6.1.D.I Tax Relief during the Accrual Phase

Eligible Contributions

Only employer's contributions are tax-free.[1285] These are those contributions which are owed by the employer as the policyholder itself and paid to the pension fund. These include, *inter alia*, the employer's contributions, which are paid in addition to the salary

1279 As laid down in § 19, para 2, sentence 8 EStG.
1280 As laid down in § 19, para 2, sentence 9 EStG.
1281 Pursuant to § 34 EStG.
1282 By virtue of § 22, nr 5, sentence 1 EStG.
1283 By virtue of § 19, para 2 EStG.
1284 Birk and Wernsmann, 253.
1285 BMF, *Steuerliche Förderung der betrieblichen Altersversorgung IV C 5 - S 2333/19/10008:017* para 26.

already owed (purely employer-financed contributions or *rein arbeitgeberfinanzierte Beiträge*). Contributions made by the employee, which he is originally obliged to make himself under a separate contractual agreement with the pension fund (so-called employee's own contributions), on the other hand, are excluded from the scope of application of § 3 nr 63 EStG.

The tax relief under § 3 nr 63 EStG can only be claimed if the contribution paid by the employer to finance the promised pension benefits is allocated to the individual employee according to certain individual criteria.[1286] However, the mere distribution of a total contribution paid by the employer according to the number of beneficiary employees is not sufficient. For the application of § 3 nr 63 EStG, it is not a prerequisite that the amount of the promised pension benefit is based on the amount of the employer's paid-in contribution, because according to § 1 BetrAVG, the employer cannot only grant a pure defined contribution plan (*reine Beitragszusage*), a defined contribution plan with minimum benefit (*Beitragszusage mit Mindestleistung*) or a defined contribution plan (*beitragsorientierte Leistungszusage*), but also a defined benefit plan (*Leistungszusage*).

Even if the person is employed in the new federal states or in Berlin (East), the income threshold for the calendar year in question (West) is decisive for limiting the amount of tax exemption to 8% of the income threshold in the *gesetzlichen Rentenversicherung*.[1287] The maximum amount of § 3 nr 63 sentence 1 EStG is an annual amount. A pro rata reduction of the maximum amount is therefore not to be used if the employment relationship does not exist for the entire year or if contributions are not paid for the whole year. The maximum amount can be claimed again if the employee has already exhausted it in a previous employment relationship.

Insofar as the contributions exceed the tax-free maximum amount (8% of the contribution assessment ceiling in the general pension insurance (West) less the contributions actually taxed at a flat rate in accordance with § 40b EStG old version), they are to be taxed individually.[1288] The individually taxed contributions may be eligible for support through the *Sonderausgabenabzug* in accordance with § 10a and an allowance in accordance with Section XI EStG. Where contributions are paid monthly, it is allowed to divide the maximum amount into equal monthly instalments.[1289]

1286 Ibid. para 27.
1287 Ibid. para 28.
1288 Ibid. para 29. For an example of the calculation, see ibid. para 32-33.
1289 Ibid. para 30.

Purely employer-financed contributions (*rein arbeitgeberfinanzierte Beiträge*) are tax-free insofar as they do not exceed the maximum amount.[1290] The tax-free maximum amount is initially filled in by these contributions. To the extent that the tax-free maximum amount has not been exhausted, the remaining employer's contributions based on the employee's various financing shares must be taken into account.

Facilitated Forms of Payment

The prerequisite for tax exemption is that the payment of the promised retirement benefits is provided for in the form of a lifelong pension or a payment plan with subsequent lifelong partial lump-sum annuity.[1291] This also applies to an occupational pension scheme in the form of a pure contribution commitment (*reine Beitragszusage*).[1292] A pension or a pay-out plan is also to be assumed if up to 30% of the capital available at the beginning of the pay-out phase is paid out outside the monthly benefits.[1293] The decision to be made at the beginning of the pay-out phase and the withdrawal of the partial capital amount constitutes *Sonstige Einkünfte* subject to tax accordance with § 22 nr 5 EStG. The mere possibility of choosing a one-off capital payment of 100 % of the capital available at the beginning of the pay-out phase) instead of these forms of pay-out does not yet lead to the denial of tax relief.[1294] If the employee decides in favour of a lump-sum capital payment, the requirements of § 3 nr 63 EStG are no longer fulfilled from this point in time and the contributions paid are taxable. If the option is exercised within the last year before the age-related withdrawal from working life, it is not objectionable for reasons of simplification if the contribution payments continue to be tax-free in accordance with § 3 nr 63 EStG.[1295] The calculation of the one-year period is based on the contractually agreed withdrawal from working life at the time the option is exercised (contractually agreed start of retirement benefits).

Since 1 January 2005 contributions to the *Direktversicherung, Pensionskasse and Pensionsfonds* are fiscally facilitated. As mentioned in paragraph 6.5.1.B.II, these entitlements to retirement benefits constitute a personal legal right to the entitlements of an occupational scheme to the employee.[1296] This legal claim would in principle lead to taxable earned income at the side of the participating employee in the accrual phase, and,

1290 Ibid. para 31.

1291 § 1, para 1, sentence 1, nr 4, letter a AltZertG.

1292 § 21 ff BetrAVG. See BMF, *Steuerliche Förderung der betrieblichen Altersversorgung IV C 5 - S 2333/19/10008:017* para 34.

1293 Ibid. para 34 and 68.

1294 Ibid. para 34. Irrespective of X R 23/15 (BFH).

1295 BMF, *Steuerliche Förderung der betrieblichen Altersversorgung IV C 5 - S 2333/19/10008:017* para 34.

1296 Pursuant to § 1b, para 3 BetrAVG, which states: *„Wird die betriebliche Altersversorgung von einer rechtsfähigen Versorgungseinrichtung durchgeführt, die dem Arbeitnehmer oder seinen Hinterbliebenen auf ihre Leistungen einen Rechtsanspruch gewährt (Pensionskasse und Pensionsfonds), so gilt Absatz 1 entsprechend.“*

thus would constitute *Vorgelagerte Besteuerung.* These contributions would be considered as part of the employee's earned income, earned within his employment relationship, since the employee gains a direct claim against the life insurer.[1297] In this respect, the German *Bundesfinanzhof* refers to this as *abgekürzten Zahlungsweg*[1298] meaning that the employer allocates a certain part of the employee's wage to insure a pension.[1299] It can be argued that the accrual of pay-as-you-go financed pension entitlements does not lead to taxable *Arbeitslohn* since under this financing principle, the actual pensions of the retirees are financed instead of the accrual of future pension entitlements of those who are currently active, although the prevailing opinion, so far, stipulates that it shall lead to a wage inflow.[1300]

In the case of an occupational pension scheme financed by employer's contributions, the point in time of the inflow of wages is determined by the vesting method of the occupational pension scheme. In the case of provision through a *Direktversicherung, Pensionskasse* and *Pensionsfonds*, the point in time of the inflow of wages is the time of payment of the contributions by the employer to the corresponding pension institution.[1301]

Since 2001 the German legislator implemented a gradual and partial transfer to deferred taxation. Contributions paid by the employer – arising from the first employment relationship- to a *Pensionsfonds, Pensionskasse* or *Direktversicherung* for the accrual of a funded occupational pension scheme are exempted from tax.[1302] This exemption therefore constitutes *nachgelagerte Besteuerung.* Until 1 January 2005 the employee had the option to choose for non-application of the exemption in the accrual phase, in according with § 3, nr 63 EStG.[1303] All employees, regardless of whether they are compulsorily insured in the *gesetzlichen Rentenversicherung* or not, belong to the group of persons benefiting from § 3 nr 63 EStG.[1304] The tax exemption only requires an existing first employment relationship.

1297 Cf. Birk and Wernsmann, 248 and Heubeck and Seybold.

1298 Translated freely as 'shortened payment method'.

1299 Birk and Wernsmann refer in this respect to BFH, BFH, ibid 15 February 2006. BFH, BStBl 12 September 2001. 2002, BFH, BFH/NV 30 May 2001. 2001. See Birk and Wernsmann, 248.

1300 Cf. Birk and Wernsmann, 248 und Glaser, 42. As far as it is not tax-free, it may be subject to the fixed-rate taxation of § 40b, para 1 and 2 EStG, stipulating: *„Der Arbeitgeber kann die Lohnsteuer von den Zuwendungen zum Aufbau einer nicht kapitalgedeckten betrieblichen Altersversorgung an eine Pensionskasse mit einem Pauschsteuersatz von 20 Prozent der Zuwendungen erheben. 1Absatz 1 gilt nicht, soweit die zu besteuernden Zuwendungen des Arbeitgebers für den Arbeitnehmer 1 752 Euro im Kalenderjahr übersteigen oder nicht aus seinem ersten Dienstverhältnis bezogen werden."*

1301 BMF, *Steuerliche Förderung der betrieblichen Altersversorgung IV C 5 - S 2333/17/10002* (6 December 2017) para 8. The withholding of wage tax is based on § 38a, paras 1 and 3 EStG.

1302 Pursuant to § 3, nr 63 EStG.

1303 Pursuant to § 52, para 52a EStG which provisions have been deleted.

1304 BMF, *Steuerliche Förderung der betrieblichen Altersversorgung IV C 5 - S 2333/19/10008:017* para 23.

This condition can also be fulfilled if the employment relationship continues without entitlement to a wage (e.g. during parental leave, nursing leave, receipt of sick pay) or if the employment is of a minor nature or a temporary job for which the option of lump-sum taxation according to § 40a EStG is used.[1305] The expenses eligible for tax relief include only contributions to *Pensionsfonds, Pensionskasse* or *Direktversicherung* which are levied for the purpose of building up a company pension scheme using the funded principle.[1306]

This tax exemption of the employer's contributions is maximised on annually 8% (2023) of the *Beitragsbemessungsgrenze*[1307] of the *gesetzlichen Rentenversicherung.* Since the *Beitragsbemessungsgrenze* for the eastern and western federal states deviate, the amount in the West is most commonly leading in this exercise. For 2023, this *Beitragsbemessungsgrenze* amounts to €87,600 (€85,200 for East) on a yearly basis.[1308] Hence, the tax-free amount is €7,008 (2023).

The application of § 3 nr 63 EStG does not require that the amount of the conferred pension benefit shall be based on the amount of the employer's paid-in contribution, since § 1 BetrAVG allows the employer to grant not only a pure defined contribution plan (*reine Beitragszusage*), a defined contribution plan with minimum benefit (*Beitragszusage mit Mindestleistung*) or a defined contribution plan (*beitragsorientierte Leistungszusage*), but also a defined benefit plan (*Leistungszusage*).[1309]

The tax relief mentioned above has been made conditional with regard to future benefits.[1310] The pension provision shall provide monthly benefits in the form of a life annuity or instalments as part of a disbursement plan with a subsequent partial retirement from no later than the age of 85. Furthermore, the benefits must remain the same or increase throughout the pay-out period. The mere option of choosing a capital payment instead of lifelong retirement benefits does not preclude the application of the tax relief of the contributions, since the pension provider and the contractual partner may agree that a maximum of twelve monthly payments may be combined in one payment, i.e. a lump sum.[1311] Up to 30% percent of the initial (at the start of the pay-out phase), available capital

1305 Ibid. para 24.
1306 Ibid. para 25.
1307 Translated freely as 'income threshold'.
1308 § 4, para 1 and 2 Verordnung über maßgebende Rechengrößen der Sozialversicherung für 2023 (Sozialversicherungs-Rechengrößenverordnung 2023).
1309 BMF, *Steuerliche Förderung der betrieblichen Altersversorgung IV C 5 - S 2333/19/10008:017* para 27.
1310 § 3, para 63 EStG refers to § 1, para 1, sub 4, under a AltZertG.
1311 Pursuant to § 1, para 1, sub 4, under a AltZertG.

may be disbursed as a lump sum.[1312] It should be stressed, however, that this is permitted on the ground of civil law.[1313]

What should be pointed out in this respect is that to some extent the employees have the possibility to – within certain limits – stipulate the fiscal facilitation of their occupational pension entitlements. This holds true for employees who are compulsorily insured under the *gesetzlichen Rentenversicherung.*[1314] These employees may waive the tax exemption[1315] in favour of their *Riester* pension regulated in the *Altersvermögensgesetz,* provided that they assert their right to *Entgeltumwandlung*[1316]. This option is limited to the external pension vesting methods, i.e. *Pensionsfonds, Pensionskasse* or *Direktversicherung.* This waive of the fiscal facilitation of the pension contributions[1317] is necessary since the *Sonderausgabenabzug*[1318] or the *Zulage*[1319] require that the contributions arise from already taxed earned income[1320], and thus avoid double tax relief of the contributions.[1321] As Birk and Wernsmann claim rightly, as a result of this option of waiving the tax facilitation, the potential volume of the tax-free contributions does not change; rather the employee may – within the limit of the maximum amount – allocate the tax-free occupational pension provision freely.[1322]

6.6.1.D.II The Tax Treatment of Pension Benefits during the Pay-Out Phase

Pension benefits arising from *Direktversicherungen, Pensionskassen* or *Pensionsfonds* are subject to tax as *Sonstige Einkünfte* (other income).[1323] These benefits will be taxed, to the

1312 § 1, para 4, under a AltZertG.

1313 In this case Gesetz über die Zertifizierung von Altersvorsorgeund Basisrentenverträgen (AltersvorsorgeverträgeZertifizierungsgesetz – AltZertG).

1314 Pursuant to §10a, para 1 EStG stipulating: *„In der inländischen gesetzlichen Rentenversicherung Pflichtversicherte können Altersvorsorgebeiträge (§ 82) zuzüglich der dafür nach Abschnitt XI zustehenden Zulage jährlich bis zu 2 100 Euro als Sonderausgaben abziehen."* Furthermore, § 79 EStG stipulates: *"Die in § 10a Absatz 1 genannten Personen haben Anspruch auf eine Altersvorsorgezulage (Zulage)".*

1315 I.e. the tax facilitation under § 3, nr 63 EStG. This option is set out in sentence 2 of this provision, stipulating: *„Dies gilt nicht, soweit der Arbeitnehmer nach § 1a Absatz 3 des Betriebsrentengesetzes verlangt hat, dass die Voraussetzungen für eine Förderung nach § 10a oder Abschnitt XI erfüllt werden."*

1316 This claim exists by virtue of § 1a para 1 in conjunction with para 3 BetrAVG. The latter article stipulates: *„Soweit der Arbeitnehmer einen Anspruch auf Entgeltumwandlung für betriebliche Altersversorgung nach Abs. 1 hat, kann er verlangen, dass die Voraussetzungen für eine Förderung nach den § 10a, 82 Abs. 2 des Einkommensteuergesetzes erfüllt werden, wenn die betriebliche Altersversorgung über einen Pensionsfonds, eine Pensionskasse oder eine Direktversicherung durchgeführt wird."*

1317 By virtue of § 3, para 63 EStG.

1318 By virtue of § 10a EStG.

1319 Translated freely as 'allowance'. By virtue of § 79 EStG.

1320 This is required by virtue of § 82, para 2 EStG.

1321 Cf. Birk and Wernsmann, 249.

1322 Ibid. 249.

1323 Pursuant to § 22, nr 5 EStG, which states *„Sonstige Einkünfte sind Leistungen aus Altersvorsorgeverträgen, Pensionsfonds, Pensionskassen und Direktversicherungen."*

extent that the benefits emerge from contributions which were not taxed by virtue of § 3, nr 63, §10a or section XI EStG, or the benefits are based on tax-free employer's contributions in the sense of § 3, nr 66 EStG.[1324] The principle of deferred taxation underlies this method of taxation, i.e. the benefits shall only be taxable to the extent they are accrued by means of tax exempted pension contributions. To the extent that no additional expenses have been deducted, an additional *Pauschbetrag* of €102 (2023) may be deducted as well from the tax assessment basis.[1325]

In cases where the pension benefits are based on both facilitated, as well as non-facilitated contributions, the pension benefits must be divided in the pay-out phase.[1326] Insofar as the benefits are based on facilitated contributions, they are fully taxable as other income in accordance with section 22 nr 5 sentence 1 EStG.[1327] Insofar as the benefits are based on non-facilitated contributions, they shall be taxed as other income[1328] against the *Ertragsanteil* pursuant to § 22 nr 5 sentence 2 letter a in conjunction with § 22 nr 1 sentence 3 letter a double letter bb EStG.

To the extent that the pension benefits arise from contributions which were not fiscally facilitated during the accrual phase, but, contrarily, were taxed pursuant to §40b EStG, these benefits will be taxed in accordance with the *Ertragsanteil*.[1329] The correct percentage of the *Ertragsanteil* depends on the year in which the retirement entitlements were committed from which the paid-out benefits arise. In cases where the entitlements were committed prior to 1 January 2005 (so-called *Altzusagen)*, the retirement benefits – arising from non-tax exempted contributions – will be taxed at the *Ertragsanteil*, laid down in § 22, nr 1, sentence 3, under a, letter bb EStG.[1330] Contrarily, if the pension entitlement were committed after 31 December 2004 (so-called *Neuzusagen*), the retirement benefits

1324 BMF, *Steuerliche Förderung der betrieblichen Altersversorgung IV C 5 - S 2333/19/10008:017* para 148.

1325 Pursuant to § 9a, para 3 EStG, which states '*Für Werbungskosten sind bei der Ermittlung der Einkünfte die folgenden Pauschbeträge abzuziehen, wenn nicht höhere Werbungskosten nachgewiesen werden: von den Einnahmen im Sinne des § 22 Nummer 5: ein Pauschbetrag von insgesamt 102 Euro*'.

1326 BMF, *Steuerliche Förderung der betrieblichen Altersversorgung IV C 5 - S 2333/19/10008:017* para 155. BMF, *Steuerliche Förderung der privaten Altersvorsorge und betrieblichen Altersversorgung; Aufteilung von Leistungen bei der nachgelagerten Besteuerung nach § 22 Nr. 5 EStG IV C 3 - S 2257 b - 47/04* (11 November 2004) is to be applied to the issue of the scale of apportionment, taking int account the amendments made by BMF, *Steuerliche Förderung der betrieblichen Altersversorgung; Aufteilung von Leistungen bei der nachgelagerten Besteuerung nach § 22 Nummer 5 EStG IV C 3 - S 2257 b/11/10003* (14 March 2012).

1327 BMF, *Steuerliche Förderung der betrieblichen Altersversorgung IV C 5 - S 2333/19/10008:017* para 156.

1328 In virtue of § 22 nr 5 sentence 2 letter a in conjunction with § 22 nr 1 sentence 3 letter a double letter bb EStG.

1329 By virtue of § 22, nr 5, sentence 2 EStG. See BMF, *Steuerliche Förderung der betrieblichen Altersversorgung IV C 5 - S 2333/17/10002* para 150. See also Wellisch and others, 174-175.

1330 By virtue of § 22, nr 5, sentence 2 in conjunction with § 22, nr 1, sentence 3, under a, letter bb EStG.

– arising from non-tax exempted contributions – will be taxed at the *Besteuerungsanteil*, laid down in § 22, nr 1, sentence 3, under a, letter aa EStG[1331], provided that they meet the criteria as laid down in § 10, para. 1, nr 2, under b EStG[1332]. The latter provision comprises several strict criteria regarding the pension provision: a fully funded retirement provision, the pension agreement merely allows monthly lifelong payments related to the life of the taxpayer and the life annuity may not be paid out prior to reaching the age of 62. If the pension provision deviates from these conditions (for instance annual pay-out of the future retirement benefits), the benefits will be taxed at the *Ertragsanteil* as laid down in § 22, nr 1, sentence 3, under a, letter bb EStG. If the conditions for fiscal facilitation during the accrual phase of the retirement provision are only temporarily met, the benefits paid out during the pay-out phase will have to be divided for tax purposes.[1333] What is more, insofar as pay-as-you-go financed *Pensionskassen* have granted pension entitlements, the paid-out benefits arise from taxed contributions, since the provision granting the fiscal facilitation[1334] requires funded retirement provisions. These benefits will be taxed against the lower *Ertragsanteil.*[1335]

For the so-called old cases, an additional tax deduction applies in the pay-out phase, i.e. the possibility of a *Lohnsteuerpauschalierung.*[1336] This fiscal provision is solely applicable to unfunded occupational pensions in the form of *Pensionskasse.*[1337] Currently, the pension vesting method of *Pensionskasse* is based on the funding principle, this unfunded method is commonly referred to as *Altfälle*, i.e. old cases. On the basis of this provision, the employer may compensate the contributions paid – up to a maximum of €1,752 (2023) annually – for the accrual of the unfunded occupational pension in the form a *Pensionskasse*

1331 § 22, nr 1, sentence 3, under a, letter aa EStG stipulates that the difference between the annual amount of the pension benefits and the taxable portion of the benefits, constitutes the tax-free proportion of the pension benefits. Furthermore, this applies from the year following the year of retirement for the entire duration of the pay-out phase. By way of derogation, where the annual amount of the pension benefit changes, the tax-free portion of the benefit shall be adjusted in proportion to the change in the annual pension amount to the annual pension amount used to determine the tax-exempted part of the pension benefit. However, regular adjustments of the annual amount of the benefit do not lead to a recalculation and will not be taken into account in a recalculation.

1332 § 10, para 1, nr 2, under b EStG stipulates: *„Sonderausgaben sind die folgenden Aufwendungen, wenn sie weder Betriebsausgaben noch Werbungskosten sind oder wie Betriebsausgaben oder Werbungskosten behandelt werden: Beiträge des Steuerpflichtigen zum Aufbau einer eigenen kapitalgedeckten Altersversorgung, wenn der Vertrag nur die Zahlung einer monatlichen, auf das Leben des Steuerpflichtigen bezogenen lebenslangen Leibrente nicht vor Vollendung des 62. Lebensjahres".*

1333 Birk and Wernsmann, 253.

1334 § 3, nr 63 EStG.

1335 § 22, nr 1, sentence 3, under a, letter bb EStG.

1336 Pursuant to § 40b EStG.

1337 For instance, the *Zusatzversorgungskassen für den öffentlichen Dienst.*

with a *Pauschsteuersatz* of 20% of the aforementioned contributions.[1338] Benefits derived from these *Pauschal*-taxed are taxed proportionally.[1339]

6.6.1.E The Tax Treatment of Entgeltumwandlung

Under the *Entgeltumwandlung* the employee can – since 1 January 2001 – demand from his employer that a certain percentage of his future earned income – up to a maximum of 4% (2023) of the contribution income threshold[1340] of the *gesetzlichen Rentenversicherung* – will be used in order to build up an occupational pension provision.[1341] The percentage of his income may be invested into either a *Direktzusage* or an *Unterstützungskasse*, under the condition of mutual understanding of the employer. A distinction must be made between these and the employee's own contributions, which he himself is obliged to make under a separate contractual agreement with the pension institutions.[1342] The employee's own contributions to the occupational pension scheme are made from the remuneration already received and taxed.

When the *Entgeltumwandlung* is employed to finance pension accrual under the *Direktversicherung, Pensionskasse* or *Pensionsfonds*, the employee's contributions constitute an inflow of salary at the time of payment of contributions, and are subject to tax.[1343] In cases where the *Entgeltumwandlung* is implemented under the *Direktzusage*, this leads to a salary waiver in exchange for the pension commitment by the employer. Since this salary waiver comprises future arising entitlements, an inflow of income – relevant for wage taxes – is non-existent.[1344] The same holds true with *Entgeltumwandlung* under the *Unterstützungskasse*, since the salary waiver lowers the future taxable income with the same amount as well. The *Entgeltumwandlung* does not change the tax treatment of the internal pension vesting methods, i.e. the accrual of pension entitlements remains tax-free for the employee.[1345] More specifically, the converted pension entitlement is exempted from taxation and social contribution.[1346] On the contrary, the future disbursed pension

1338 § 40b, para 1 and 2 EStG. This amount will be raised with *Solidaritätszuschlag* and *Kirchensteuer.*

1339 Pursuant to § 22 EStG.

1340 I.e. *Beitragsbemessungsgrenze.*

1341 By virtue of § 1a, para 1, sentence 1 BetrAVG, which provision states: *"Der Arbeitnehmer kann vom Arbeitgeber verlangen, dass von seinen künftigen Entgeltansprüchen bis zu 4 vom Hundert der jeweiligen Beitragsbemessungsgrenze in der allgemeinen Rentenversicherung durch Entgeltumwandlung für seine betriebliche Altersversorgung verwendet werden."* See also BMF, *Steuerliche Förderung der betrieblichen Altersversorgung IV C 5 - S 2333/19/10008:017* para 9.

1342 BMF, *Steuerliche Förderung der betrieblichen Altersversorgung IV C 5 - S 2333/17/10002* para 10.

1343 Ibid. para 8.

1344 Cf. Birk and Wernsmann, 247 and cited literature.

1345 Cf. Ibid. 247.

1346 Pursuant to § 3, para 63 EStG and § 1, para 1, under 4 and 9 SvEV respectively. See also BMF, *Steuerliche Förderung der betrieblichen Altersversorgung IV C 5 - S 2333/19/10008:017* para 26a.

benefits are subject to *Einkommensteuer* and in principle to legal contributions for *Kranken-* and *Pflegeversicherung. Entgeltumwandlung*-contributions to the provisions of *Direktzusage* or *Unterstützungskasse* are tax exempted without any threshold.

6.7 Tax Treatment of German Occupational Pensions in Cross-border Situations

As has been addressed in section 6.4, the globalisation of the economy and the related increase in the mobility of workers implies that the taxation of pensions must not solely be considered from a purely national perspective, but also account must be taken of cross-border aspects. In the section below the tax treatment of German occupational pensions in cross-border cases will be discussed, both during the accrual phase as well as in the pay-out phase. As regards the accrual phase, the analysis focuses on whether tax advantages are granted, while, as regards the pay-out phase it is considered how, and to what extent, (foreign and domestic) pension benefits are subjected to tax. The allocation of the taxing rights pursuant to a tax treaty, is taken into account as a proviso/prerequisite for the exercise of taxing rights pursuant to domestic (German) tax legislation. These distribution rules will be discussed in chapter 9. The normative framework pertaining to the tax treatment of cross-border pensions, enshrined in EU law, will be discussed in chapter 9.

If the German taxable person, for instance a migrant worker who resided and worked in Germany, decides to leave Germany and emigrates to another country, this leads to fiscal consequences with respect to the retirement provisions accrued during his active period in Germany. In particular, these consequences can be considered significant because of the deferred taxation of pensions in Germany, since the principle of deferred taxation stipulates that the fiscally deductible pension contributions paid out of untaxed income during the accrual phase, give rise to benefits paid out during the pay-out phase, which shall be subject to taxation.[1347] This can be referred to as the internal coherence of the national tax system. Since the former German taxable person is no longer unlimitedly subject to taxation in Germany, the German tax authorities would seek to guarantee that the future benefits, paid out during the accrual phase abroad, will be subject to taxation. The tax authorities shall strive to recover the lack of tax revenues as a result of the emigration of the former German taxable person. The fiscal interest of Member States may be guaranteed by several measures, for instance extending the tax liability beyond

1347 Cf. R Wernsmann and A Nippert, 'Altersbesteuerung beim Wegzug und Europäisches Gemeinschaftsrecht' FR 1123, In BVerfG, the *Bundesverfassungsgericht* ruled that the taxing right is postponed/deferred.

emigration.[1348] However, it can be pointed out at the outset that under none of the occupational pension schemes discussed below, the tax relief provided during the period of residence in Germany, is reclaimed upon migration to another State. Most recently, the repayment obligation pursuant to § 93-95 EStG pertaining to *Sonderausgaben*-deduction and allowances granted for the benefit of *Riester-Renten* in the event of relocating the place of residence to another EU Member State has been abolished, in response to the CJEU's ruling.[1349]

As has become apparent in the preceding sections, since different taxation rules are applied to the various occupational pension vesting methods (*Durchführungswege*), a distinction is drawn between the internal vesting methods and the external methods. As regards the tax treatment of employee's contributions, it can be noted at the outset, that under all German pension schemes, these contributions are not subject to taxation during the accrual phase.[1350]

6.7.1.A Migrant Worker

6.7.1.A.I Outbound

In the outbound migration situation, the employee is resident in the national territory of Germany (partly) during the accrual phase and lives in the Netherlands during the pay-out phase. The tax treatment of contributions and the granting of tax relief, during the accrual phase, is hence akin to the tax treatment of a domestic situation in Germany, i.e. there is no cross-border situation. There is no nexus with Dutch income tax, levied during the accrual phase. I therefore refer to the section 6.6.

Internal Vesting Methods: Direktzusage and Unterstützungskasse

Under both the *Direktzusage*, as well as under the *Unterstützungskasse* an inflow of a monetary advantage[1351] for the employee is missing during the accrual phase.[1352] In the case of a *Direktzusage* or a *Unterstützungskasse*, the *Arbeitslohn* is only paid at the time of payment of the retirement benefits to the employee, i.e. the realisation of the pension entitlement.[1353] This applies to both the employer's contributions, as well as the employee's

1348 Cf. D Wellisch and others, *Besteuerung der Altersvorsorge: ein internationaler Vergleich* (Schriften des Institutes der Ausländisches und Internationales Finanz- und Steuerwesen der Universität Hamburg, Nomos, Baden-Baden 2008) 48.

1349 C-269/07 *Commission vs. Germany* ECLI:EU:C:2009:527 (CJEU).

1350 Cf. Wellisch and others, 172.

1351 Thus leading to taxable income by virtue of § 11, para 1 EStG.

1352 Heubeck and Seybold.

1353 BMF, *Steuerliche Förderung der betrieblichen Altersversorgung IV C 5 - S 2333/19/10008:017* para 8.

contributions through *Entgeltumwandlung*. Hence, no tax relief is to be provided during the accrual phase. However, during the pay-out phase, the person concerned resides abroad. It depends on the allocation of taxing rights enshrined in the applicable tax treaty where the person is liable to tax for the German occupational pension benefits. The functioning of these allocation rules – embedded in the applicable tax treaty – will be discussed in more detail in chapter 9 of this research. If the taxing rights is allocated to Germany as a source state (for instance pursuant to article 17, para 2 treaty Netherlands-Germany), the benefits paid by the employer on the basis of a *Direktzusage* and pension benefits from a *Unterstützungskasse* constitute income from employment, taxed pursuant to § 19, para 1, nr 2 EStG.[1354] As the person concerned nor resides in Germany, nor has his habitual abode in Germany, during the pay-out phase he may be subject to limited tax liability pursuant to § 1, para 4 EStG, provided that he receives domestic income within the meaning of § 49 EStG. These pension benefits arising from the *Direktzusage* or *Unterstützungskasse* are considered belated earned income and, in principle, fully subject to wage taxes withheld from salary.[1355] The principal condition for including these elements of income in the limited tax liability is a domestic source of income.[1356] What is more, the taxpayer is eligible for *Werbungskostenpauschbetrag* of €102 per tax year, pursuant to § 9a, para. 1, under b EStG, and the *Versorgungsfreibetrag*, pursuant to § 19, para 2 EStG.

If the taxing right is allocated to the Netherlands as a residence state (for instance pursuant to article 17, para 1 treaty Netherlands-Germany), German occupational pension benefits will be subject to Dutch income tax. For this I refer to section 6.4.1.A.II.

External Vesting Methods: Direktversicherung, Pensionskasse, Pensionsfonds

Since 1 January 2005 contributions to the *Direktversicherung, Pensionskasse and Pensionsfonds* are fiscally facilitated. In the case of provision through a *Direktversicherung, Pensionskasse* and *Pensionsfonds*, the point in time of the inflow of wages is the time of payment of the contributions by the employer to the corresponding pension institution.[1357] Contributions paid by the employer – arising from the first employment relationship- to a *Pensionsfonds, Pensionskasse* or *Direktversicherung* for the accrual of a funded occupational pension scheme are exempted from tax, pursuant to § 3, nr 63 EStG. All employees, regardless of whether they are compulsorily insured in the *gesetzlichen Rentenversicherung* or not, belong to the group of persons benefiting from § 3, nr 63 EStG.[1358] This tax

1354 Ibid. para 146.

1355 By virtue of § 19, para 1, nr 2 EStG in conjuction with § 38, para 1, sentence 1 EStG.

1356 Pursuant to § 49, para 1, nr 4, letter a EStG.

1357 BMF, *Steuerliche Förderung der betrieblichen Altersversorgung IV C 5 - S 2333/19/10008:017* para 8. The withholding of wage tax is based on § 38a, paras 1 and 3 EStG.

1358 Ibid. para 23.

exemption of the employer's contributions is maximised on annually 8% of the *Beitragsbemessungsgrenze*[1359] of the *gesetzlichen Rentenversicherung*.

However, during the pay-out phase, the person concerned resides abroad. It depends on the allocation of taxing rights enshrined in the applicable tax treaty where the person is liable to tax for the German occupational pension benefits. If the taxing right is allocated to Germany as a source state (for instance pursuant to article 17, para 2 treaty Netherlands-Germany), the benefits arising from *Direktversicherungen, Pensionskassen* or *Pensionsfonds* are subject to tax as *Sonstige Einkünfte* (other income).[1360] These benefits will be taxed, to the extent that the benefits emerge from contributions which were not taxed by virtue of § 3, nr 63, §10a or section XI EStG, or the benefits are based on tax-free employer's contributions in the sense of § 3, nr 66 EStG.[1361]

Insofar as the benefits are based on facilitated contributions, they are fully taxable as other income in accordance with section 22, nr 5, sentence 1 EStG.[1362] Insofar as the benefits are based on non-facilitated contributions, they shall be taxed as other income[1363] against the *Ertragsanteil* pursuant to § 22, nr 5, sentence 2, letter a in conjunction with § 22, nr 1, sentence 3, letter a, double letter bb EStG. As the fictional approach of the *Ertragsanteil* corresponds to the interest share encompassed in the pension benefits, they are taxed according to the concept of front-loaded taxation.[1364] In cases where the pension benefits are based on both facilitated, as well as non-facilitated contributions, the pension benefits must be proportioned in the pay-out phase.[1365] It must be pointed out that merely the tax relief granted pursuant to German law is relevant in this regard.

As the person concerned nor resides in Germany, nor has his habitual abode in Germany, during the pay-out phase he may be subject to limited tax liability pursuant to § 1, para 4 EStG, provided that he receives domestic income within the meaning of § 49 EStG. The principal condition for including these elements of income in the limited tax liability is a domestic source of income.[1366] To the extent that no additional expenses have been

1359 Translated freely as 'income threshold'.

1360 Pursuant to § 22, nr 5 EStG, which states *„Sonstige Einkünfte sind Leistungen aus Altersvorsorgeverträgen, Pensionsfonds, Pensionskassen und Direktversicherungen."*

1361 BMF, *Steuerliche Förderung der betrieblichen Altersversorgung IV C 5 - S 2333/19/10008:017* para 148.

1362 Ibid. para 156.

1363 In virtue of § 22, nr 5, sentence 2, letter a in conjunction with § 22, nr 1, sentence 3, letter a, double letter bb EStG.

1364 Scheffler and Kölbl, 18.

1365 BMF, *Steuerliche Förderung der betrieblichen Altersversorgung IV C 5 - S 2333/19/10008:017* para 155.

1366 Pursuant to § 49, para 1, nr 10 EStG.

deducted, an additional *Pauschbetrag* of €102 (2023) may be deducted as well from the tax assessment basis.[1367]

If the taxing right is allocated to the Netherlands as a residence state (for instance pursuant to article 17, para 1 treaty Netherlands-Germany), German occupational pension benefits will be subject to Dutch income tax. For this I refer to section 6.4.1.A.II.

6.7.1.A.II Inbound

In the inbound case, the employee is a resident of the Netherlands (partly) during the accrual phase, and takes up residence in Germany at the commencement of the pay-out phase. The tax treatment of the contributions to the occupational pension scheme is therefore a matter for the Netherlands, where the income of the person concerned will be fully liable to income tax, and contributions may be taken into account in the assessment of income tax, see section 6.3, i.e. there is no cross-border situation. There is no nexus with German income tax, levied during the accrual phase.

However, during the pay-out phase, the person concerned resides in Germany, where he will be fully liable to tax.[1368] It depends on the allocation of taxing rights enshrined in the applicable tax treaty where the person is liable to tax for the foreign (Dutch) occupational pension benefits. If the taxing rights is allocated to Germany as a residence state (for instance pursuant to article 17, para 1 treaty Netherlands-Germany), the benefits arising from the Dutch occupational pension scheme will be subject to German income tax. To what extent these Dutch occupational pension benefits will be subject to German income tax depends on the qualification of the Dutch vesting method (akin to either German internal or external vesting method), see below.

Internal Vesting Methods: Direktzusage and Unterstützungskasse

Akin to benefits from domestic pension schemes, benefits arising from foreign schemes qualified as *Direktzusage and Unterstützungskasse* are treated as income from dependent employment, fully liable to tax pursuant to § 19, para 1, nr 2 EStG.[1369] This is independent of the extent to which the contributions, from which the benefits emerged, have been subject to tax relief, either in Germany or abroad.

1367 Pursuant to § 9a, para 3 EStG, which states *'Für Werbungskosten sind bei der Ermittlung der Einkünfte die folgenden Pauschbeträge abzuziehen, wenn nicht höhere Werbungskosten nachgewiesen werden: von den Einnahmen im Sinne des § 22 Nummer 5: ein Pauschbetrag von insgesamt 102 Euro'.*

1368 Pursuant to § 1, para 1 EStG.

1369 See Wellisch and others, 175. A distinction as regards the taxation of benefits arising from either domestic schemes or foreign schemes is not drawn in BMF, *Steuerliche Förderung der betrieblichen Altersversorgung IV C 5 - S 2333/19/10008:017* para 146.

External Vesting Methods: Direktversicherung, Pensionskasse, Pensionsfonds
Akin to benefits arising from domestic *Direktversicherungen, Pensionskassen* or *Pensionsfonds*, benefits stemming from foreign schemes, similar to these three domestic schemes, are fully subject to tax as *Sonstige Einkünfte* (other income).[1370] What principles, and characteristic elements of the German *Direktversicherung, Pensionskassen* or *Pensionsfonds* are decisive in the qualification of foreign schemes as these types of domestic schemes, will be discussed in section 6.7.1.B.II.

The benefits will be taxed, to the extent that the benefits emerge from contributions which were not taxed by virtue of § 3, nr 63, §10a or section XI EStG, or the benefits are based on tax-free employer's contributions in the sense of § 3, nr 66 EStG.[1371] Insofar as the benefits are based on facilitated contributions, they are fully taxable as other income in accordance with section 22 nr 5 sentence 1 EStG.[1372] Insofar as the benefits are based on non-facilitated contributions, they shall be taxed as other income[1373] against the *Ertragsanteil* pursuant to § 22, nr 5, sentence 2, letter a in conjunction with § 22, nr 1, sentence 3, letter a, double letter bb EStG. In so far as the foreign benefits are thus derived from contributions, not fiscally facilitated in Germany, they shall be taxed as other income[1374] against the *Ertragsanteil*. To the extent the benefits arise from benefits accrued through contributions which have been subject to tax relief in Germany, these shall be fully taxable. The taxable proportion of the foreign benefits is thus not differentiated as to whether the contributions, from which these benefits were derived, were subject to tax relief abroad.[1375]

This reflects that provisions of national tax laws governing the taxation of retirement income, are applied on the basis of an 'isolated approach', without taking into account any previous or subsequent tax treatment in another (member) state. For instance, as there is no German mandatory legal principle of tax law requiring a direct connection between the taxation of benefits and the deductibility of contributions (i.e. coherence), provisions of foreign law are not mentioned in the EStG nor does it contain a general rule that a tax benefit, provided pursuant to foreign tax law, shall be treated equally to the application of the EStG's provision.[1376]

1370 Pursuant to § 22, nr 5 EStG, which states „*Sonstige Einkünfte sind Leistungen aus Altersvorsorgeverträgen, Pensionsfonds, Pensionskassen und Direktversicherungen.*"

1371 BMF, *Steuerliche Förderung der betrieblichen Altersversorgung IV C 5 - S 2333/19/10008:017* para 148.

1372 Ibid. para 156.

1373 In virtue of § 22, nr 5, sentence 2, letter a in conjunction with § 22, nr 1, sentence 3, letter a, double letter bb EStG.

1374 In virtue of § 22 nr 5 sentence 2 letter a in conjunction with § 22 nr 1 sentence 3 letter a double letter bb EStG.

1375 Cf. Wellisch and others, 183.

1376 See also Portner, 1177.

If – on the contrary – the taxing right is allocated to the Netherlands as a source state (for instance pursuant to article 17, para 2 treaty Netherlands-Germany), the pension benefits paid out are subject to Dutch income tax – pursuant to Dutch national tax legislation. In such cases, the beneficiary residing abroad will be treated as a foreign taxable person (*buitenlands belastingplichtige*) provided that he receives domestic income, as the person concerned nor resides in the Netherlands, neither has his habitual abode in the Netherlands during the pay-out phase.[1377] The Dutch occupational pension benefits shall be fully liable to tax as 'taxable wages in respect of work performed or having performed in the Netherlands', and are considered 'domestic income'.[1378] What is more, this taxable proportion of the benefits is determined irrespective of whether these benefits are derived from contributions which were subject to tax relief. Furthermore, he may apply to be considered as a qualifying foreign taxpayer.[1379] To what extent, and how, the Netherlands subjects these Dutch occupational pension benefits to income tax, is not discussed any further here, but I refer to section 6.3.

6.7.1.B Cross-border Worker

As a cross-border worker, the mobile citizen works in one State, while residing in another (neighbouring) Member State, to which they commonly return every day or at least once a week. The working state, and possibly the pension state, is thus different from the residence state. As has been addressed in section 6.4, no allocation rules exist as regards occupational pensions (similar to Regulation 883/2004 applicable to statutory pension schemes), i.e. rules stipulating where the cross-border worker participates in an occupational pension scheme, it needs to be determined where the person concerned does participate in an occupational scheme. What the applicable situation is depends on the specific facts and circumstances of the case, i.e. the employment law agreements between employee and employer, the pension law application conditions for foreign participants, and also this choice of the frontier worker concerned. The tax consequences of both situations will be mapped out below, while taking account of the effect of the prevailing tax treaty, concluded between the Netherlands and Germany.

1377 See article 2.1, para 1, sub b in conjunction with article 7.1 and 7.2 Wet IB 2001.

1378 Pursuant to article 7.2, para 2, under b Wet IB 2001.

1379 Pursuant to article 7.8 Wet IB 2001. Based on this scheme, foreign taxpayers shall be eligible for the same fiscal facilitations as domestic taxpayers (such as deductions). The essence of this scheme is to give residents of the EU, EEA, Switzerland or the BES islands, 90% or more of whose income is subject to wage tax or income tax in the Netherlands, the right to the same fiscal facilitations, in accordance with EU case law. The equal treatment concerns, among other things, the right to the application of a number of personal allowances. Being a qualifying foreign taxpayer is no longer a choice (since 1 January 2015) but applies *ex officio*.

A cross-border worker – generally – does not have the intention to leave his country of residence permanently, i.e. working across the border is temporary.[1380] Hence, the cross-border worker may either continue to participate, and thus contribute, to a pension scheme in his state of residence, or may become a participant of the occupational pension scheme in his working state. This entails a number of fiscal consequences.

6.7.1.B.I Outbound

As stated above, in this situation, where Germany is the residence state, the cross-border worker may remain a participant in a German occupational pension scheme, while working abroad, or become a participant in a (foreign) Dutch occupational pension scheme in the Netherlands. What the applicable situation is depends on the specific facts and circumstances of the case, i.e. the employment law agreements between employee and employer, the pension law application conditions for foreign participants, and also this choice of the frontier worker concerned. The tax consequences of both situations will be mapped out below, while taking account of the effect of the prevailing tax treaty, concluded between the Netherlands and Germany.

Continuance of Participating in German Occupational Pension Scheme

Provided that, pursuant to art. 14, para 1 of the applicable tax treaty, the taxing right pertaining to the remuneration is allocated to the working state (the Netherlands), and if the person is fully liable to tax in that state (for instance, as he receives at least 90% of his taxable income in the other state), it is a matter for the Netherlands to determine to what extent it allows the contributions paid to the German occupational pension scheme to be taken into account in the calculation of the domestic tax assessment base, see section 6.4.1.B.II. If the prevailing tax treaty allocates the taxing right to Germany as residence state (pursuant to art. 14, para 2) it may subject the person to unlimited tax liability, and the tax treatment of the contributions is akin to a domestic situation.[1381] See section 6.6. As the person resides in Germany during the pay-out phase, the taxation of German occupational pension benefits paid out is akin to a domestic situation, provided that Germany is allocated the taxing right pursuant to art. 17, para 1 of the applicable tax treaty, and the person concerned is subject to unlimited tax liability. If the taxing right is assigned (pursuant to art. 17, para 2 of the treaty) to the Netherlands as source state, German occupational pension benefits will be subject to Dutch income tax, see section 6.4.1.B.II.

1380 Dieleman, 'Internationale aspecten van pensioen' 465.

1381 Pursuant to § 1, para 1, sentence 1 EStG.

Participating in Foreign (Dutch) Occupational Pension Scheme

If the cross-border worker, resident in Germany, participates in the Dutch occupational pension scheme, the tax treatment of these foreign pension contributions must be assessed. If the applicable tax treaty allocates the taxing right pertaining to the remuneration to the Netherlands as working state (pursuant to art. 14, para 1), it is a matter for that state to decide to what extent it subjects the contributions paid into a domestic occupational pension scheme by a non-resident taxpayer to tax (relief).

What is more, in order to avoid an adverse fiscal treatment of pension contributions paid into a foreign pension scheme, paragraph 37 of the Commentaries on the OECD Model Convention contains a provision which is intended to ensure equal treatment with contributions made domestically.[1382] It applies to either statutory, occupational and individual pension schemes.[1383] Suchlike provision has been laid down in article 24, para 6 of the tax treaty concluded between the Netherlands and Germany, applying to occupational pension schemes as well. Mobile taxable person concerned may have recourse to this provision enshrined in the applicable tax treaty concluded between the Netherlands and Germany.

Provided that the applicable tax treaty allocates the taxing right pertaining to the remuneration to Germany as residence state (pursuant to art. 14, para 1) and the person concerned is fully liable to tax in Germany, this type of workers may continue to pay their pension contributions into the foreign (recognised) pension schemes.[1384] However, policy as regards contributions paid to foreign occupational schemes has been laid down in a *BMF-schreiben*.

Internal Vesting Methods: Direktzusage and Unterstützungskasse

If the foreign pension scheme is qualified as one of the internal vesting methods, an inflow of a monetary advantage[1385] for the employee is missing during the accrual phase.[1386] In the case of a *Direktzusage* or an *Unterstützungskasse*, the *Arbeitslohn* is only paid at the time of payment of the retirement benefits to the employee, i.e. the realisation of the pension entitlement.[1387] Hence, no tax relief needs to be provided during the accrual phase for the contributions paid into the foreign pension scheme.

1382 See also Bobbett and Avery Jones; Andreoni; De Broe and Neyt.

1383 See paragraph 61 of the OECD commentary on Article 18 OECD MC.

1384 Pursuant to § 1, para 1, sentence 1 EStG.

1385 Thus leading to taxable income by virtue of § 11, para 1 EStG.

1386 Heubeck and Seybold.

1387 BMF, *Steuerliche Förderung der betrieblichen Altersversorgung IV C 5 - S 2333/19/10008:017* para 8.

As the cross-border worker remains resident in Germany during the pay-out phase, he will be fully liable to tax in Germany.[1388] Provided that applicable tax treaty allocated the taxing right to Germany (pursuant to art. 17, para 1), the benefits arising from foreign schemes qualified as *Direktzusage* and *Unterstützungskasse* are treated as income from dependent employment, fully liable to tax pursuant to § 19, para 1, nr 2 EStG. If the taxing right is assigned (pursuant to art. 17, para 2 of the treaty) to the Netherlands as source state, German occupational pension benefits will be subject to Dutch income tax, see section 6.4.1.B.II.

External Vesting Methods: Pensionsfonds, Pensionskasse or Direktversicherung

In the case of contributions to foreign occupational pension schemes, it must be determined whether the foreign pension scheme is comparable to an occupational pension scheme under the *Betriebsrentengesetz* or can be assigned to one of the *Durchführungswege* as comparable.[1389] Corresponding contributions are tax-free in accordance with § 3, nr 63 EStG, if certain conditions are met. Firstly, the foreign occupational pension scheme must be comparable to a *Pensionsfonds, Pensionskasse* or *Direktversicherung*. It is difficult to see that it has not been further elucidated, by instance by setting certain principles or standards of comparability, under what circumstances a foreign occupational pension scheme is considered comparable to one of these pension vesting methods. Secondly, the other essential criteria for the fiscal facilitation of an occupational pension scheme in Germany must also be met (including coverage of at least one biometric risk, narrow definition of survivors, no inheritability, and preferential forms of payment). Lastly, the foreign pension institution must largely comply with the safekeeping, notification and disclosure obligations applicable to domestic pension institutions under the *Einkommensteuergesetz* and *Altersvorsorge-Durchführungsverordnung zur Sicherstellung der Besteuerung der Versorgungsleistungen*. In the 2017 *BMF-schreiben* two additional margins were added. As regards the relation of § 3, nr 63 to double tax conventions, it stipulates that the direct applicability of the EStG-provision may follow from an international agreement.[1390] It is even specified, that in cases of posting, the provision of § 3 nr 63 EStG takes precedence over the provisions of a tax treaty for the employer's contributions to the funded occupational pension scheme.[1391] The tax-exemption of the employer's contributions under the *Pensionsfonds, Pensionskasse* or *Direktversicherung* is thus, in all cases, ensured. If the above conditions are met, the cross-border worker, participating in the occupational

1388 Pursuant to § 1, para 1, sentence 1 EStG.

1389 BMF, *Steuerliche Förderung der betrieblichen Altersversorgung IV C 5 - S 2333/19/10008:017* para 36.

1390 Ibid. para 37 in which reference is made to nr 16 of the Protocol to the USA Double Taxation Convention.

1391 Ibid. para 38.

pension scheme of his (foreign) working state, may deduct the contributions paid to this scheme, from his taxable income in Germany.

Provided that the applicable tax treaty allocates the taxing right to Germany (pursuant to art. 17, para 1), benefits stemming from foreign schemes, comparable to *Direktversicherungen, Pensionskassen* or *Pensionsfonds*, are fully subject to tax as *Sonstige Einkünfte* (other income).[1392] The benefits will be taxed, to the extent that the benefits emerge from contributions which were not taxed by virtue of § 3, nr 63, §10a or section XI EStG, or the benefits are based on tax-free employer's contributions in the sense of § 3, nr 66 EStG.[1393] Insofar as the benefits are based on facilitated contributions, they are fully taxable as other income in accordance with section 22, nr 5, sentence 1 EStG.[1394] Insofar as the benefits are based on non-facilitated contributions, they shall be taxed as other income[1395] against the *Ertragsanteil* pursuant to § 22, nr 5, sentence 2, letter a in conjunction with § 22, nr 1, sentence 3, letter a, double letter bb EStG. The taxable proportion of the foreign benefits is thus not differentiated as to whether the contributions, from which these benefits were derived, were subject to tax relief abroad.[1396] In cases where the pension benefits are based on both facilitated, as well as non-facilitated contributions, the pension benefits must be proportioned in the pay-out phase.[1397] If the applicable tax treaty allocates the taxing right to the Netherlands as source state (pursuant to art. 17, para 2), Dutch pension benefits will be subject to Dutch income taxation. The taxable person concerned will in principle be treated as foreign taxable person as he resides in Germany during the payout phase. For this I refer to section 6.4.1.B.II.

6.7.1.B.II Inbound

In the inbound situation of a cross-border worker, he is a resident of the Netherlands, while he works in Germany, returning to his residence state at least once a week. He may remain a participant in the Dutch occupational pension scheme, while working in Germany, or become a participant in a German occupational pension scheme. What the applicable situation is depends on the specific facts and circumstances of the case, i.e. the employment law agreements between employee and employer, the pension law application conditions for foreign participants, and also this choice of the frontier worker concerned.

1392 Pursuant to § 22, nr 5 EstG.

1393 BMF, *Steuerliche Förderung der betrieblichen Altersversorgung IV C 5 - S 2333/19/10008:017* para 148.

1394 Ibid. para 156.

1395 In virtue of § 22, nr 5, sentence 2, letter a in conjunction with § 22, nr 1, sentence 3, letter a, double letter bb EStG.

1396 Cf. Wellisch and others, 183.

1397 BMF, *Steuerliche Förderung der betrieblichen Altersversorgung IV C 5 - S 2333/19/10008:017* para 155.

The tax consequences of both situations will be mapped out below, while taking account of the effect of the prevailing tax treaty, concluded between the Netherlands and Germany.

Continuance of Participating in Foreign (Dutch) Occupational Pension Scheme
Provided that, pursuant to the applicable tax treaty, the taxing right pertaining to the remuneration is allocated to the Netherlands (pursuant to art. 14, para 1), and if the person is fully liable to tax in that state where he will be a resident for tax purposes, it is a matter for the Netherlands to determine to what extent it allows the contributions paid to its German occupational pension scheme to be taken into account in the calculation of the domestic tax assessment base, see section 6.4.1.B.II. However, if the prevailing tax treaty allocates the taxing right to Germany (pursuant to art. 14, para 1) this situation is, as regards the tax treatment of contributions and benefits, similar to an outbound cross-border worker participating in a foreign occupational pension scheme. However, contrary to the outbound situation, an essential difference lies in the fact that in the present inbound situation, the person concerned is not fully liable to tax in Germany as he is a resident of the other state. However, upon request, he may be treated as fully liable to tax,[1398] to the extent that he receives domestic income within the meaning of § 49 EStG. This applies solely if the income, received during the entire calendar year, is subject to German income tax for at least 90%, or the income not being subjected to German income tax, does not exceed the exemption threshold (*Grundfreibetrag; 2023: €10,908*).[1399] If that proves to be the case, the tax treatment of contributions and benefits is akin to the situation discussed under the preceding (outbound) section, where the cross-border worker contributes to a foreign occupational pension scheme.

As regards the taxation of Dutch occupational pension benefits, the following must be noted. If the applicable tax treaty appoints the cross-border worker's resident state (the Netherlands) as the competent state to tax (pursuant to art. 17, para 1) this is a (domestic) matter for that State. However, if the applicable tax treaty allocates the taxing right on the Dutch occupational pension to Germany (pursuant to art. 17, para 2), the person concerned can merely come within the scope of German income tax as a limited taxable person pursuant to § 1, para 4 EStG, as he nor resides, nor has his habitual abode in German, in so far as he receives domestic income within the meaning of § 49 EStG. The principal condition for including these elements of income in the limited tax liability is a domestic source of income.[1400] Benefits stemming from foreign schemes, comparable to *Direktzusage* and *Unterstützungskasse* are treated as income from dependent employment,

1398 Pursuant to § 1, para 3 EStG.
1399 Pursuant to § 1, para 3, sentence 2 EStG. See § 32a, para 1, sentence 2, nr 1 EStG.
1400 Pursuant to § 49, para 1, under 4 or 10 EStG depending on the *Durchführungsweg*.

fully liable to tax pursuant to § 19, para 1, nr 2 EStG, irrespective of the tax treatment of the contributions from which these benefits emerge. However, it must be noted, that the extent to which the contributions paid abroad during the posting period were subject to tax relief in the Netherlands, is relevant in the tax treatment of the pension benefits stemming from foreign schemes comparable to *Direktversicherungen, Pensionskassen* or *Pensionsfonds*. These benefits are subject to tax as *Sonstige Einkünfte*, pursuant to § 22, nr 5 EstG. The benefits shall be fully liable to tax, to the extent that the benefits emerge from contributions which were not taxed by virtue of § 3, nr 63, §10a or section XI EStG, or the benefits are based on tax-free employer's contributions in the sense of § 3, nr 66 EStG. Insofar as the benefits are based on non-facilitated contributions, they shall be taxed as other income against the *Ertragsanteil* pursuant to § 22, nr 5, sentence 2, letter a in conjunction with § 22, nr 1, sentence 3, letter a, double letter bb EStG. In cases where the pension benefits are based on both facilitated, as well as non-facilitated contributions, the pension benefits must be proportioned in the pay-out phase.[1401] Whether contributions paid into the Dutch occupational pension scheme were facilitated under German tax legislation during the period abroad is thus relevant.

Participating in German Occupational Pension Scheme

If the cross-border worker, resident in the Netherlands, decides to participate in a German occupational pension scheme, the tax treatment of these Dutch pension schemes must be assessed. If the applicable tax treaty allocates the taxing right pertaining to the remuneration/pension to the Netherlands (pursuant to art. 14, para 1) the tax treatment of the German pension contributions and benefits is a matter for that state, where the person concerned shall be subject to unlimited tax liability. See section 6.4.1.B.II. However, if the taxing right pertaining to the remuneration/pension is attributed to Germany (pursuant to art. 14, para 1), and the person concerned is treated as fully liable to tax in Germany, these type of workers are subject to a tax treatment akin to a domestic worker, notwithstanding that he resides abroad. For the tax treatment of the contributions and pension benefits I therefore refer to the relevant sections.

Pension benefits paid by foreign pension institutions – to a German resident – and considered *Pensionskasse, Pensionsfonds* or *Direktversicherung* are merely subject to deferred taxation in Germany under § 22 nr 5 EStG if the contributions made in connection with the occupational pension scheme were fiscally facilitated in Germany under § 3 nr 63 EStG.[1402]

1401 BMF, *Steuerliche Förderung der betrieblichen Altersversorgung IV C 5 - S 2333/19/10008:017* para 155.

1402 Ibid. para 150 ff.

Furthermore, as Scheffler and Kölbl observed, if the employee was employed abroad during the accrual phase, it can be assumed that the occupational pension scheme was not fiscally facilitated in Germany. Therefore, the pension benefits paid out by the foreign pension providers – derived exclusively from non-facilitated contributions – shall be taxed as other income against the *Ertragsanteil*, provided that it is a life-long pension.[1403] It thus constitutes other income within the meaning of § 22, nr 1, sentence 3, letter a, double letter bb EStG.[1404] This means that (full) taxation in accordance with § 22, nr 5 EStG is not applicable.

6.7.1.C Posting

6.7.1.C.I Outbound

As part of the outbound posting case, a German employee is sent by its German employer to the Netherlands during the accrual phase, i.e. either as part of (intercompany) secondment sent to a Dutch subsidiary, or in the framework of hiring-out-of-labour sent to a (external) separate entity.[1405] As the posting in the host state the Netherlands will be of limited duration and the worker will not fully integrate in the labour market of the Netherlands, he will most likely continue to participate, and contribute, to the German occupational pension scheme as the sending state.[1406] Participation in the German pension scheme will thus usually be continued during the period of posting. It is therefore assumed, and this is characteristic for the case of posting, that the employee concerned will continue to participate, and contribute, to the (foreign) occupational pension scheme in Germany.

According to the applicable treaty provision (pursuant to art. 14, para 2), during the period of posting, Germany (residence state) is allocated the taxing rights as regards the remuneration. In such as case, the tax treatment of the pension contributions is akin to a domestic German situation, see section 6.6. Provided that, pursuant to art. 14, para 1 of the applicable tax treaty, the taxing right pertaining to the remuneration is allocated to the working state (the Netherlands), and if the person is fully liable to tax in that state (for instance, as he receives at least 90% of his taxable income in the other state), it is a matter for the Netherlands to determine to what extent it allows the contributions paid to the German occupational pension scheme to be taken into account in the calculation of the domestic tax assessment base, see section 6.4.1.B.II.

1403 In virtue of § 22, nr 5, sentence 2, letter a in conjunction with § 22, nr 1, sentence 3, letter a, double letter bb EStG. See also Scheffler and Kölbl, 17 and W Förster, 'Konsequenzen der steuerlichen Änderungen des Alterseinkünftegesetzes für die betriebliche Altersversorgung' DB 6.

1404 Scheffler and Kölbl, 17. See also Förster.

1405 See also paragraph 8.3 ff. of the OECD commentary on article 15 OECD MC.

1406 Pursuant to art. 12, para 1 Regulation on the coordination of social security systems 883/2004.

As regards the pension benefits in the case of posting, these are to be divided.[1407] Firstly, the taxation of the part of the pension benefits which is paid pro rata for employment in the home state, based on the regulations applicable in that state. Secondly, as regards the proportion of pension benefits attributable pro rate to the period of posting, in which both the state of employment, as well as the residence state are the same for the accrual period. However, in the pay-out phase these two states differ. I will merely focus on the second point hereinafter.

After the limited time of posting abroad, the worker will return to Germany. During retirement, he will be fully liable in Germany.[1408] The tax treatment of the pension benefits is then akin to a domestic situation, as the residence state and pension state are similar. Benefits arising from *Direktzusage* and *Unterstützungskasse* are treated as income from dependent employment, fully liable to tax pursuant to § 19, para 1, nr 2 EStG, irrespective of the tax treatment of the contributions from which these benefits emerge. However, it must be noted, that the extent to which the contributions paid abroad during the posting period were subject to tax relief in Germany, is relevant in the tax treatment of the pension benefits emerging from *Direktversicherungen, Pensionskassen* or *Pensionsfonds.* These benefits are subject to tax as *Sonstige Einkünfte*, pursuant to § 22, nr 5 EstG. The benefits shall be fully liable to tax, to the extent that the benefits emerge from contributions which were not taxed by virtue of § 3, nr 63, §10a or section XI EStG, or the benefits are based on tax-free employer's contributions in the sense of § 3, nr 66 EStG. Insofar as the benefits are based on non-facilitated contributions, they shall be taxed as other income against the *Ertragsanteil* pursuant to § 22, nr 5, sentence 2, letter a in conjunction with § 22, nr 1, sentence 3, letter a, double letter bb EStG. Whether contributions paid into German occupational pension scheme were facilitated under foreign (Dutch) tax legislation during the posted period is thus irrelevant.

6.7.1.C.II Inbound

As part of the inbound posting case, a Dutch employee is sent by its Dutch employer to Germany during the accrual phase, i.e. either as part of (intercompany) secondment sent to a German subsidiary, or in the framework of hiring-out-of-labour sent to a (external) separate entity.[1409] As the posting in the host state Germany will be of limited duration and the worker will not fully integrate in the labour market of Germany, he will most likely continue to participate, and contribute, to the Dutch occupational pension scheme as the

1407 Cf. Ibid. 21-22. See also D Wellisch, 'Besteuerung der betrieblichen Altersvorsorge bei grenzüberschreitender Mitarbeiterentsendung – ein Ländervergleich mit Gestaltungsüberlegungen' StuW 154.

1408 Pursuant to § 1, para 1, sentence 1 EStG.

1409 See also paragraph 8.3 ff. of the OECD commentary on article 15 OECD MC.

sending state.[1410] Participation in the Dutch pension scheme will thus usually be continued during the period of posting. It is therefore assumed, and this is characteristic for the case of posting, that the employee concerned will continue to participate, and contribute, to the (foreign) occupational pension scheme in the Netherlands.

According to the applicable treaty provision (pursuant to art. 14, para 2), during the period of posting, the Netherlands (residence state) is allocated the taxing rights as regards the remuneration. In such as case, the tax treatment of the pension contributions is akin to a domestic Dutch situation, see section 6.3. Provided that, pursuant to art. 14, para 1 of the applicable tax treaty, the taxing right pertaining to the remuneration is allocated to the working state (Germany), and if the person is fully liable to tax in that state (for instance, as he receives at least 90% of his taxable income in the other state), it is a matter for Germany to determine to what extent it allows the contributions paid to the Dutch occupational pension scheme to be taken into account in the calculation of the domestic tax assessment base. As regards the tax relief of employer's and employee's contributions (e.g. tax exemption or tax deduction) paid into the Dutch state's occupational pension scheme during the posting period, pursuant to the Germany's tax legislation, it must be determined through a comparative legal qualification of the Dutch pension scheme, to what extent these foreign paid contributions are eligible for tax relief.[1411] It must be assessed to what extent the Dutch pension scheme is comparable to a German occupational pension scheme. However, this assessment plays also an instrumental role in determining how pension benefits emerging from a foreign scheme are subjected to tax pursuant to German domestic tax legislation.

Internal Vesting Methods: Direktzusage and Unterstützungskasse

If the Dutch pension schemes is qualified as one of the internal vesting methods, an inflow of a monetary advantage[1412] for the employee is missing during the accrual phase.[1413] However, practical guidelines as to when a foreign occupational pension scheme qualifies as either a *Direktzusage* or a *Unterstützungskasse* are not provided by the German legislature, nor the German tax authorities. In this case, the *Arbeitslohn* is only paid at the time of payment of the retirement benefits to the employee, i.e. the realisation of the pension entitlement.[1414] Hence, no tax relief needs to be provided during the accrual phase.

1410 Pursuant to art. 12, para 1 Regulation on the coordination of social security systems 883/2004.
1411 See for instance X R 37/08 BStBl. II 2011 (628) (BFH).
1412 Thus leading to taxable income by virtue of § 11, para 1 EStG.
1413 Heubeck and Seybold.
1414 BMF, *Steuerliche Förderung der betrieblichen Altersversorgung IV C 5 - S 2333/19/10008:017* para 8.

External Vesting Methods: Pensionsfonds, Pensionskasse or Direktversicherung
Accordingly, a foreign pension plan must first be distinguished from the statutory pension schemes in the first *Schicht*, and the private pension schemes in the third *Schicht*. Once the foreign pension scheme has been allocated to the second *Schicht*, it must be ascertained to what extent the scheme fulfils the preconditions under which an occupational pension scheme is qualified as such.[1415] Firstly, the German legislature solely recognizes occupational schemes which fulfil the conditions laid down in § 1 BetrAVG. Secondly, the German tax authorities impose additional requirements on the foreign pension scheme to be eligible for tax relief.[1416] As regards the latter, it must be noted that these additional requirements, required under the *BMF-Schreiben* for the tax recognition of an occupational pension scheme do not arise from the *Betriebsrentengesetz*, the *BMF-Schreiben* is only binding on the tax authorities, but not on courts and taxpayers or the tax advisors of taxpayers. These norm-interpreting tax guidelines are not of a legal norm-quality.

As regards the tax relief provided under § 3, nr 63 EStG, applicable to employer's contributions to *Direktversicherungen, Pensionskasse* and *Pensionsfonds*, German tax authorities have, in the vein of paragraph 37 of the OECD commentary on article 18 OECD MC, explicitly specified to which existing schemes the provision shall apply or to determine how the competent authorities construe the term 'generally corresponding' (how widely interpreted and what tests are imposed).[1417] As regards the latter, Germany elucidated her stance on contributions paid to foreign (occupational) pension schemes.[1418] Germany, very briefly in merely one margin, addressed the issue in a *BMF-Schreiben*. This document points out that in cases where contributions are paid to foreign occupational

---

1415 Cf. R Portner, 'Rechtsvergleichende Qualifizierung ausländischer Altersversorgungspläne/-einrichtungen' 44 BB 2652 2652.

1416 BMF, *Steuerliche Förderung der betrieblichen Altersversorgung IV C 5 - S 2333/19/10008:017* para 1.

1417 See ibid. para 36. Some conditions had already been laid down in BMF, *Steuerliche Förderung der privaten Altersvorsorge und betrieblichen Altersversorgung IV C 3 - S 2222/09/10041* (31 March 2010) para 274. This has been revoked by BMF, *Steuerliche Förderung der privaten Altersvorsorge und betrieblichen Altersversorgung IV C 3 - S 2015/11/10002/ IV C 5 - S 2333/09/10005* (24 July 2013) para 314. The 2010-*schreiben* stipulated that contributions paid into a *Pensionsfonds, Pensionskassen* and – in the case of *Direktversicherungen* – insurance companies established in the EU and third countries, with which a particular type of tax treaty had been concluded (e.g. the treaty Germany-USA) could be facilitated under § 3, nr 63 EStG if the foreign *Pensionsfonds, Pensionskassen* or insurance company was authorised under insurance supervisory law to carry out its activities for the benefit of employees in domestic business premises. These conditions were generally not met by foreign pension institutions as they had no connection to Germany. However, this stance was not supported by the wording of § 3 nr 63 EStG as it does not restrict its scope to contributions paid to domestic pension institutions, nor do additional conditions have to be met in order to leave contributions to foreign pension institutions tax-free, nor does this follow from BMF, *Steuerliche Förderung der betrieblichen Altersversorgung IV C 5 - S 2333/17/10002*.

1418 BMF, *Steuerliche Förderung der privaten Altersvorsorge und betrieblichen Altersversorgung IV C 3 - S 2015/11/10002/ IV C 5 - S 2333/09/10005* para 314 which has been repealed by BMF, *Steuerliche Förderung der betrieblichen Altersversorgung IV C 5 - S 2333/19/10008:017* para 36.

pension schemes, it must be determined whether the foreign pension scheme is comparable to an occupational pension scheme under the Germany *Betriebsrentengesetz* or can be assigned to one of the *Durchführungswege* (vesting methods) as comparable. Corresponding contributions are tax-exempt according to § 3 nr 63 EStG, if (constituting the *essentialia*):

- the foreign occupational pension scheme is comparable to a *Pensionsfonds, Pensionskasse* or *Direktversicherung*;[1419] and
- the other essential criteria for the tax recognition of an occupational pension scheme in Germany are also met (including, *inter alia*[1420], coverage of at least one biometric

1419 The *Direktzusage* and *Unterstützungskasse* are thus out of scope, as there is considered to be no influx of wage under these vesting methods to be exempt.

1420 BMF, *Steuerliche Förderung der betrieblichen Altersversorgung IV C 5 - S 2333/19/10008:017* para 36. stipulates the essential criteria for the tax recognition of an occupational pension scheme, while using 'u.a.' (*unter anderem*). From both a legal certainty and practicability point of view, it is desirable if the German tax authorities would have precisely outlined what are considered 'essential criteria' while avoiding the use of '*inter alia*'. Ambiguity in this regard should be avoided.

risk[1421] (age[1422]), a narrow definition of survivors[1423], no inheritability[1424],

1421 Pursuant to § 1, para 1, sentence 1, BetrAVG, an occupational pension scheme exists if the employer grants the employee old-age, disability or survivors' benefits on the basis of the employment relationship. Through these benefits, the employee is protected (by the employer) against one or more biometric risks that are closely related to the course of life and are associated with fundamental changes in biologically determined living conditions, i.e. biometric risks. This implies that if the (lump-sum) pension benefit can in principle be claimed at any time, this is not considered a pension plan under the given legal provisions. See, for instance, VIII R 39/10 (BFH). This is also the case if the benefit is unlimited and is not only hereditable for certain specifically designated survivors. Until the occurrence of the biometric risk, the employee has a vested right to the pension benefit, see BMF, *Steuerliche Förderung der betrieblichen Altersversorgung IV C 5 - S 2333/19/10008:017* para 1. Pursuant to German civil law, the assertion of the claim by the employee and the fulfilment of the claim by the employer would be deferred until the occurrence of a biometric risk. For instance, pursuant to § 1b BetrAVG, an employee who has been promised benefits from the occupational pension scheme retains the entitlement if the employment relationship ends before the occurrence of the pension event. In foreign plans, on the other hand, the pay-out of benefits before they become due are often permissible, but these payments are regularly subject to additional penalty taxes, aimed at compensating for a previously granted tax advantage. Such foreign pension schemes do not meet the requirements of a German occupational pension scheme. See also 3 AZR 313/02 BB 2004 (269) (BAG); VI R 165/01 BB 2005 (1944) (BFH); I R 11/06 BB 2006 (2240) (BFH) and III 161/54 S BStBl. III 1957 (314) (BFH). The pivotal role of the life risk, i.e. the biometric risk, in the qualification of a life insurance, rather than a savings contract, is also endorsed in Dutch case-law, see, for instance, 19/03758 ECLI:NL:PHR:2020:210 (A-G Niessen).

1422 The biological event in pension provisions is the age-related withdrawal from working life, see BMF, *Steuerliche Förderung der betrieblichen Altersversorgung IV C 5 - S 2333/19/10008:017* para 3. As a rule, the lower limit for occupational pension benefits in the case of age-related retirement is the age of 60. In exceptional cases, occupational pension benefits may be granted before the age of 60 (job-specific peculiarities), for instance as regards aviation pilots, which can be derived from law, collective bargaining agreement or a company agreement. If the employee reaches the age of 60 at the time of payment, but has not yet terminated his or her employment, this is harmless in the case of a *Direktversicherung, Pensionskasse* und *Pensionsfonds*. For pension entitlements granted after 31 December 2011, the age of 62 will regularly replace the age of 60. Several arguments can be put forward supporting the stance that these age limits cannot be decisive in deciding whether contributions to a foreign pension institution remain tax-free under German tax law. Firstly, as a general rule, in foreign pension schemes, the biometric risk of age is generally determined by an age other than the 60th or 62nd year of life (for instance in the Netherlands the age of 68). Secondly, structure-wise, in margin 36, an explicit reference to marginal 3 is lacking. Thirdly, the use of 'inter alia' in marginal 3 suggests that the conditions are not exhaustive. On the contrary, the decisive factor should be whether a foreign pension plan requires that a person has reached an particular age at which, as a rule, old-age benefits can be claimed by virtue of a law, a statutory instrument or a collective agreement. Cf. Portner, 'Rechtsvergleichende Qualifizierung ausländischer Altersversorgungspläne/-einrichtungen' 2655-2656. I endorse Portner's assertion that it would be desirable to clarify that the age of 60 or 62 is not decisive for the tax recognition of foreign pension plans as occupational pensions, but that it is sufficient that a pension benefit cannot be claimed before reaching a given age at which, as a rule, old-age benefits can be claimed on a statutory or similar basis.

1423 See BMF, *Steuerliche Förderung der betrieblichen Altersversorgung IV C 5 - S 2333/19/10008:017* para 4.

1424 See ibid. para 5 and 6. The survivor's pension is essentially limited to benefits for the surviving spouse, partner and children of the employee. As regards children an age limit applies (25 or 27 years depending on the year in which the entitlements were issued). Furthermore, civil partnerships are only recognised if the partners are obliged to support each other. These specific conditions cannot be decisive for the tax recognition of a foreign pension plan as an occupational pension scheme. The concept of surviving dependants is not defined in the EStG nor in the *Betriebsrentengesetz*. It is likely that the German tax authorities will refuse to recognise foreign pension plans for tax purposes if beneficiaries can be assigned

preferential forms of payment);

- the foreign pension institution essentially complies, in a comparable manner, with the safekeeping, notification and certification obligations applicable to domestic pension institutions under the *Einkommensteuergesetz* and the *Altersvorsorge-Durchführungsverordnung* in order to ensure taxation of the pension benefits.[1425]

It must be noted that in the event of posting, the provision of § 3 nr 63 EStG takes precedence over the provisions of a tax treaty for the employer's contributions to the funded occupational pension scheme.[1426] However, it is remarkable to see that more meaningful, or informative, requirements are not provided, although general criteria would have been helpful.[1427] The requirements, although fairly strict, leave ample room for discussion and appear not to be a sufficient solution, and no explanation is provided for the allocation of a foreign pension scheme to one of the three pillars of the domestic

who do not fall within the narrow circle of survivors. Cf. Portner, 'Rechtsvergleichende Qualifizierung ausländischer Altersversorgungspläne/-einrichtungen' 2656. Hereditability means that the benefits may also be paid out to the heirs of the beneficiary who are not entitled to benefits. It thus excludes the biometric risk that is characteristic for occupational pension schemes. The narrow concept of survivorship thus corresponds to the element of the exclusion of hereditability. Furthermore, agreements under which wages are credited and, without covering a biometric risk, paid out at a later date (e.g. when the employment relationship ends), possibly with an increase in value, are also not to be qualified as occupational pension schemes.

1425 The relevance of this requirement can be called into question, parallel to the requirements laid down in § 22a EStG (*Rentenbezugsmitteilungen*). The *BMF-schreiben* is void of explanations as to which information is decisive in the context of the obligations to retain, notify and certify. Pension benefits from a *Pensionsfonds, Pensionskassen and Direktversicherungen* are subject to deferred taxation as other income, provided that the contributions to the pension scheme were facilitated in accordance with one of the provisions set out in § 22, nr 5, sentence 2 EStG. Insofar as the contributions were not facilitated in accordance with one of the provisions of the EStG referred to in § 22, nr 5, sentence 2 EStG, they are taxed against the *Ertragsanteil.* The German legislator thus assumes that contributions were taxed individually, unless they were subject to tax relief under a provision of the EStG. This assumption does not apply if contributions were taxed abroad, as the text of § 22, nr 5 EStG merely refers to tax relief in virtue of provisions enshrined in the EStG. As has become apparent above, foreign pension benefits are then only taxed with the *Ertragsanteil.* Against this background, the retention, notification and certification obligations of a foreign pension institution can only be of relevance for determining the *Ertragsanteil* in the case of a capital payment resulting from the difference between the pension benefit and the total of the contributions made to it. Cf. Portner, 'Rechtsvergleichende Qualifizierung ausländischer Altersversorgungspläne/-einrichtungen' 2657.

1426 BMF, *Steuerliche Förderung der betrieblichen Altersversorgung IV C 5 - S 2333/19/10008:017* para 38.

1427 However, even a tax treaty may stipulate that certain foreign pension plans are recognised as occupational pension schemes for the purpose of applying the treaty, which corresponds to one of the *Durchführungswege* under § 1 BetrAVG, without examining the requirements for an occupational pension scheme. This applies, for example, to the treaty Germany-USA (Article 18A para 3b) in conjunction with Protocol Section 16 letter b, aa. According to this, Germany recognises the US retirement benefit plans listed as such, which correspond to the retirement benefit plans defined in § 1 BetrAVG. Contributions to these pension plans, are subject to tax relief under § 3, nr 63 EStG without further examination.

pension system.[1428] It takes as a given that the foreign occupational pension scheme is allocated to the German second *Schicht* of occupational pension schemes. In the light of legal certainty, general criteria for the allocation of foreign pension schemes to one of the three German pension pillars would be helpful, notably for employers legally obliged to withhold German wage taxes (*Lohnsteuerabzug*).[1429]

Compared to the 2013 version, the 2017, and 2021, versions of the *BMF-schreiben* no longer require that the foreign pension institution is authorized to carry out its business in Germany. Furthermore, as regards third countries, the requirements that a particular type of tax treaty had been concluded, is no longer required neither. What is more, the emphasis of the assessment is no longer put on foreign *Pensionsfonds, Pensionskassen* or insurances, but, rather, on the comparability of the foreign occupational pension institution with a German occupational pension scheme (*Durchführungsweg*) under the *Betriebsrentengesetz* (notably § 1). It is apparent that for the comparability of the foreign pension scheme with the German *Durchführungswege* solely their essential characteristics are relevant, and features considered insignificant are not taken into consideration. The *Bundesfinanzhof*, for instance, holds that comparability of retirement pensions can be assumed in cases where the foreign pension benefits correspond in its core content to the common and typical features of the domestic benefit.[1430] As regards the *Pensionsfonds, Pensionskassen* and *Direktversicherungen* these essential characteristics seem to be[1431]:

- the contributions are paid to a legally independent pension institution, supervised by the supervisory authority;
- to provide occupational pension benefits for one (or more) employer(s) for the benefits of its employees; and
- to confer on employees an own claim on the conferred pension benefits.[1432]

1428 Cf. Portner, 'Rechtsvergleichende Qualifizierung ausländischer Altersversorgungspläne/-einrichtungen' 2653.

1429 Cf. Ibid. 2653. For example, pursuant to German case-law, the Swiss pension fund (*Pensionskasse*) is classified as a first pillar plan (*Basisversorgung*) with respect to its compulsory part, and as a second pillar-supplementary pension plan with respect to its non-compulsory part. The element of compulsory membership thus appears to be a decisive element in this classification as either first pillar or second pillar pension.

1430 X R 37/08 BstBI. II 2011 (628) (BFH). Moreover, it ruled that the characteristic of pensions within the meaning of § 22, nr 1, sentence 3, letter a, double letter aa EStG (i.e. *gesetzlichen Rentenversicherung, landwirtschaftlichen Alterskasse, berufsständischen Versorgungseinrichtungen* and *Rürup-Rente*), is that they serve the so-called *Basisversorgung*, i.e. statutory pension schemes. Essential characteristics of this type of retirement provisions is that they are solely disbursed when a certain age limited is reached, or in the event of incapacity to work, and serve as compensation for living expenses, replacing an earned income.

1431 See Portner, 'Rechtsvergleichende Qualifizierung ausländischer Altersversorgungspläne/-einrichtungen' 2653-2654.

1432 Under § 1, para 2 *Betriebsrentengesetz*, pension entitlements can be granted in the form of a defined benefit plan (*Leistungszusage*), a defined contribution benefit-orientated plan (*leistungsorientierten Beitragszusage*)

Therefore, as discussed in the previous chapter of this research dealing with the *Direktzusage* and *Unterstützungskasse*, these types of pension scheme do not meet these conditions. As regards the *Unterstützungskasse*; although this is an independent legal entity, it is not subject to supervision under insurance law,[1433] nor does it grant the employee a direct personal claim on pension benefits provided by *Unterstützungskasse*. As this concerns an internal vesting method, the employee is solely granted claims towards his employer. With regard to the *Direktzusage*, the employee is granted a pension directly by his employer, without involvement of any legally independent pension institution. Employer and pension provider are therefore incorporated in the same legal person, not subject to any insurance supervision. Concludingly, in regard of the above, by revoking the *2013-BMF-Schreiben*, the *2017-BMF-Schreiben* has missed the opportunity to adopt measures aimed at improving legal certainty, in a domain of taxation highly relevant for cross-border practice, in a maturing European Single Market. If the foreign occupational pension schemes, into which the inbound posted worker continues to pay contributions, meets the criteria set out above, it will be qualified as *Direktversicherungen, Pensionskasse* and *Pensionsfonds*, for German tax purposes. Accordingly, employer's contributions will remain tax-free pursuant to § 3 nr 63 EStG.

After the limited time of posting to Germany, the worker will return to the Netherlands. If the taxing right is allocated to the Netherlands as residence and/or source state (for instance pursuant to article 17, para 1 or 2 treaty Netherlands-Germany), the Dutch pension benefits paid out are subject to Dutch income tax. During retirement, he will be fully liable in the Netherlands.[1434] The tax treatment of the pension benefits is then akin to a domestic situation as the residence state and pension state are similar, see section 6.3. Hence, the taxing right cannot be assigned to Germany as this is nor the residence, nor the source state. However, it must be noted, that the extent to which the Dutch contributions paid abroad during the posting period were subject to tax relief in Germany, is relevant in the tax treatment of the pension benefits pursuant to Dutch national tax law. If the employee was employed abroad (Germany) during the accrual phase, it remains to be seen to what extent the Dutch occupational pension scheme was fiscally facilitated in Germany. The State Secretary also recognizes that it may occur that employees abroad (continue to) accrue pension in a Dutch pension plan that complies with the Dutch tax rules, but not

---

or a defined contribution plan with minimum benefits (*Beitragszusage mit Mindestleistung*), or defined contribution plan (*reine Beitragszusage*). The pension entitlements in the foreign pension scheme must thus be (comparably) vested through one of these pension vesting methods.

1433 More precisely § 1 VAG.

1434 Pursuant to art. 2.1, para 1, under a Wet IB 2001.

with the foreign rules.[1435] Thus, economic double taxation may occur in such cases. Hence, Dutch policy stipulates that in such cases, a proportion of the Dutch pension benefits may remain outside the scope of wage and income tax, based on the so-called balance method (*saldomethode*).[1436] Relevant, in this regard, is the amount of pension contributions paid for and by the employee in respect of the foreign employment. A further condition is that the employee did not receive a tax relief for these contributions abroad (in this case, Germany).

6.8 COMPARATIVE FINDINGS THROUGH THE LENS OF THE EVALUATION FRAMEWORK

Where in the sections above the (tax treatment of) occupational pensions – in both the Netherlands and Germany – have been mapped out, the section below compares these findings along the (legal) lines of this research's evaluation framework (similarity/comparability; inter-level coherence; inter-system consistency; foreseeability/unpredictability). It is a sliding scale where all variations between fit and unfit can be observed.

As this chapter explored the (tax treatment of) occupational pensions, emphasis will be put on the principle of similarity/comparability, since this chapter seeks to explore to what extent the regulatory framework governing the (tax treatment of) occupational pensions in both countries are fit for the provision of effective pension information. This principle is marked by the division of power between the European Union and the Member States; the responsibility for the design of a national pension system lies with the Member States, and the European Union falls short of competence to intervene in the Member States' pension systems. What is more, the principle of foreseeability will be tested. Moreover, as this chapter did involve the allocation of taxing rights pursuant to international tax law as such (this will be discussed in chapter 8 of this research) the principle of inter-level coherence shall also be evaluated. Hence, it does concern the scrutiny of coherence with higher-level regulations, and with treaty or other international obligations. Lastly, as the chapter above addressed the application of national regulatory (tax) frameworks, leading to potential (in)compatible outcomes for a specific cross-border situation, the principle of

1435 Staatssecretaris van Financiën, *Loonheffingen. Inkomstenbelasting. Internationale aspecten van pensioenen en stamrechten nr. DGB2015/7010M* 5.

1436 Ibid. 5. Furthermore, the Secretary of State makes this approval subject to the condition that the taxpayer proves, if requested, that in connection with the acquisition of the pension rights abroad actual taxation has taken place which, in terms of its nature and scope, corresponds with Dutch wage tax or income tax. An actual levy is also understood to mean that there has been no deduction of contributions on part of the employee.

inter-system consistency shall be evaluated. This chapter meets this research second (sub) objective of a legal comparative study in which the legal frameworks in the Netherlands and Germany, as well as on a European and international level, shall be mapped out. Building on this, the 'fitness' of the legal frameworks at the national, European and international level shall be assessed, focusing in particular on any deficiencies that have a (distorting) effect on the provision of effective information.

6.8.1 Similarity/Comparability

The sections below compare the (tax treatment of) occupational pensions in Germany and the Netherlands, and evaluates it in view of the principle of similarity/comparability. Exploring similarity between systems involves a comparison of certain features. The assessment of similarity constitutes a feature-matching process, i.e. it measures the degree to which two objects – the legal character – match each other. Similarity is tantamount to a measurement of common features. A higher degree of similarity helps to ensure the effectiveness of information in terms of the four principles. For instance, the higher the degree of similarity, the easier it is to uphold the information's correctness, trustworthiness, and personal relevance. After all, with a higher degree of similarity, there is less need to observe any underlying structural differences. Moreover, a higher degree of similarity leads to a higher comparability of the different regulatory frameworks/legal constructs, avoiding comparing the incomparable.

6.8.1.A Differences

Comparing (the tax treatment of) Dutch and German occupational pensions, the following differences can be observed:

- Under the German BetrAVG the provision of occupational pensions may be organised either directly by the employer (*intern*) or by an external pension provider (*extern*).[1437] The external pension providers comprise *Pensionskasse, Pensionsfonds* and *Direktversicherung*, the internal *Dutchführungswege* concern *Direktzusage* and *Unterstützungskasse*. Each form of occupational pension provision has developed differently over time. Moreover, each form of occupational pensions has been assigned considerably different by fiscal legislation. This multitude of pension vehicles – and fragmentation – does not exist in the Dutch pension system.
- As has been discussed in section 6.5, the German pension system is marked by the existence of internalised pension schemes, i.e. the (statutory) *Beambtenversorgung*,

1437 Pursuant to § 1, para. 1 BetrAVG. The external pension providers are stipulated in § 1, para. 2 until 4 BetrAVG.

and the (occupational) *Direktzusage*. Under the schemes, the accrual of pension entitlements is not separated from the employer. These types of pension vehicles ('bookresverves') are unknown in several other European countries, including the Netherlands.

- Under the German *Direktzusage* – one of the most used pension schemes in Germany – the employer ensures retirement benefits without involvement of any other pension institution, hence the use of the term *Direkt.*[1438] Hence, employer and pension provider are therefore incorporated in the same legal person, and a triangular relationship cannot be observed. Since the vesting of pension is agreed on without involvement of any pension institution or insurer, the *Betriebsrentengesetz* does not regulate this form of pension provision, apart from certain framework standards. From a fiscal perspective, this also has implications hindering comparability. Under the *Direktzusage* an inflow of a monetary advantage – leading to taxable income by virtue of § 11, para 1 EStG – on the side of the employee is missing, as the employee has no access nor can derive any legal claims from[1439] the accrued capital, and thus an enrichment of the employee is missing. So, under the *Direktzusage*, the *Arbeitslohn* is only paid at the time of payment of the retirement benefits to the employee, i.e. the realisation of the pension entitlement leading to an influx of taxable income. As regards the taxation of pension benefits arising from the type of scheme, they are subject to deferred taxation, i.e. the pension benefits are included in the tax assessment basis, as income from dependent personal services.[1440] These types of pension vehicles – and the according tax treatment – are unknown in several other European countries, including the Netherlands.
- In principle, German employers are not subject to a pension vesting obligation, i.e. to implement an occupational pension provision. Dutch occupational pension schemes are not compulsory under (pension)law either. Yet, it is often part of collective agreements and, thus, becomes quasi-mandatory. In addition, an employee may be entitled to participate in a pension plan because his employer falls under an industry for which compulsory pension accrual applies on the basis of the *Wet verplichte deelneming in een bedrijfstakpensioenfonds 2000*.
- What is more, the pension vesting methods also deviate between the two states, although in both states a distinction between DB- and DC-schemes can be observed. In Germany – see section 6.5.1.A – *grosso modo* four different methods of pension vesting exist under the second pension pillar.[1441] The first method is the so-called

1438 See Portal Sozialpolitik.

1439 This must be distinguished from the question whether the employee is entitled to the accumulated capital.

1440 Pursuant to § 19 EStG.

1441 Pursuant to § 1, para. 1 and § 2, para 1 and 2 BetrAVG.

Leistungszusage (defined benefit) under which the employer is obliged to assure a particular benefit (*Leistung*). Second, the *beitragsorientierte Leistungszusagen* under which DC-method certain contributions to the pension provision are assured by the employer. These contributions are then converted into an entitlement to retirement benefits. This is most common among current occupational pension provisions. Third, the employer may also commit a *Beitragszusage mit Mindesleistung*. Under this provision, the employer is legally obliged to finance the contributions to a *Pensionsfonds, Pensionskasse* or *Direktversicherung*. Furthermore, the employer shall provide the accumulated pension capital, financed primarily through the contributions. This capital shall, as a minimum, comprise the contributions paid by the employees, i.e. the minimum benefit. Fourth, as of 1 January 2018, the *reine Beitragszusage* has been implemented pursuant to the (modernising) *Betriebsrentenstärkungsgesetz* (BRSG).[1442] This form of pension vesting is marked by the so-called *Garantieverbot* (guarantee ban), i.e. the employee may not be promised an investment return but a security contribution by the employer should be agreed in the collective agreement.[1443] With abolishing the employer's obligation to maintain the pension scheme, the legislator moved away from one of the core principles of the previous German occupational pension law. In the Netherlands – see section 6.2.2 – *grosso modo* three different methods of pension vesting exist under the second pension pillar.[1444] Firstly, the *uitkeringsovereenkomst* (defined benefit scheme), under which employee and employer enter into an agreement on a payment of a certain amount that shall be received from a certain age.[1445] The most common methods comprise the final salary scheme (*eindloonregeling*), average salary scheme (*middelloonregeling*) and fixed amount-schemes (*vastebedragenregeling*). Secondly, pension may be accrued through a capital arrangement. Under a capital agreement, solely the amount of capital at the commencement of the retirement phase is determined in the agreement. However, Chapter IIB of the Wet LB does not recognise pension schemes with capital agreements, but only benefit agreements such as final pay schemes and average pay schemes on the one hand, and defined contribution schemes on the other. Another pension accrual system concerns the defined contribution scheme (DC), in which the pension commitment is merely the provision of a contribution; neither a benefit nor a capital is promised. Under such an agreement, solely the amount of contribution is set in the agreement. In the light of the distribution of risks, three types of defined contributions

1442 Gesetz zur Stärkung der betrieblichen Altersversorgung und zur Änderung anderer Gesetze (Betriebsrentenstärkungsgesetz). See § 1, para. 2, nr. 2a BetrAVG.
1443 See § 22, para 1, second sentence BetrAVG and § 244b, para 1, nr. 1 VAG.
1444 See art. 1 PW.
1445 See art. 1 PW.

arrangements are prevailing.[1446] Firstly, the pure contribution scheme.[1447] Under this agreement, the contributions paid are invested until retirement date, inducing uncertainty with regard to the pension capital, accrued by these contributions. Secondly, the agreement exists whereby the premium paid is immediately converted into an entitlement to capital.[1448] A capital insurance is purchased immediately after the contribution is made available by the employee, while, on the retirement date, the insured capital then available shall be converted into an entitlement to a payment of capital. Finally, the least risk-bearing form of contribution agreement. Under this agreement, the premium is converted into a benefit entitlement immediately after it has been made available by the employee, i.e. the premium is immediately used to purchase an insurance for a periodic benefit.[1449]

- Under the Dutch pension system – contrary to Germany – so-called hybrid schemes may exist. The eventual pension benefits received depend on the pension capital available on the retirement date and the applicable rates; no guarantee is given regarding the final pension benefit. Therefore, this scheme does not qualify as a final pay scheme. The scheme does not qualify as a defined contribution scheme either, since the fiscal conditions are not met.[1450] These hybrid schemes may put the participants on the wrong foot in that the pension arrangement constitutes a benefit agreement, even though there are certain risks to be borne by the employee. In order to end this ambiguity for the benefit of the participants, it must be made clear in the pension agreement that it comprises a benefit agreement, a capital agreement or a contribution agreement.[1451]
- In Germany, the fiscal treatment of German (occupational) pensions in the accrual phase is not founded on a uniform established concept.[1452] Moreover, the tax treatment of the external and internal pension vesting methods deviates significantly, see

---

1446 Staatssecretaris van Financiën, *Besluit Loonheffingen, inkomstenbelasting. Pensioenen; beschikbare-premieregelingen en premie- en kapitaalovereenkomsten en nettopensioenregelingen (Staffelbesluit pensioenen) nr. 2019-21333* para 2. See also Broers, 155-156.

1447 See Staatssecretaris van Financiën, *Besluit Loonheffingen, inkomstenbelasting. Pensioenen; beschikbare-premieregelingen en premie- en kapitaalovereenkomsten en nettopensioenregelingen (Staffelbesluit pensioenen) nr. 2019-21333* para 3. This scheme is identified as a defined contribution scheme within the meaning of the LB Act, provided that this scheme complies with the conditions and details set out in the annex. The scheme must also otherwise comply with the conditions of Chapter IIB of the LB Act.

1448 See ibid. para 3. This scheme is identified as a defined contribution scheme within the meaning of the LB Act, provided that this scheme complies with the conditions and details set out in the annex. The scheme must also otherwise comply with the conditions of Chapter IIB of the LB Act.

1449 See ibid. para 5. This scheme is identified as a defined contribution scheme within the meaning of the Wet LB 1964, provided that this scheme complies with the conditions and details set out in the annex III. The scheme must also otherwise comply with the conditions of Chapter IIB of the Wet LB 1964.

1450 As laid down in art. 18a, para 3 Wet LB 1964.

1451 Pursuant to art. 10 PW.

1452 Cf. Birk and Wernsmann, 246.

sections 6.6.1.C and 6.6.1.D. On the contrary, the Dutch fiscal treatment of occupational pensions is grounded on a – more or less – uniform concept (of deferred taxation) laid down in Chapter IIB Wet LB 1964. The legal provisions enuncaite the fiscal treatment along the lines of the allowed pension vesting methods, i.e. *eindloonregeling, middelloonregeling*, and *beschikbarepremieregeling*, see section 6.3. A retirement scheme based on a final pay system does not exceed 1.657 percent of pensionable pay per year of service; a retirement pension based on an average earnings system shall not exceed 1.875% per year of service; a retirement pension based on a defined contribution plan is accrued on a time-proportional basis and is aimed at a pension that, after 40 years of accrual, does not exceed 75% of the average pensionable pay to that time. What is more – as has been dealt with in section 6.3.3 – this also applies to a pension plan participated in on the basis of the *Wet verplichte deelneming in een bedrijfstakpensioenfonds 2000, de Wet op het notarisambt* or the *Wet verplichte beroepspensioenregeling*.[1453] The fiscal treatment of these type of pension schemes is shaped along the lines of Chapter IIB Wet LB 1964 as well. For instance, the guiding principle for this tax treatment is pension accrual based on an average pay scheme with an accrual rate of 1.875 and where the pensionable age is linked to the development of life expectancy. Under certain conditions, the premiums for an occupational pension plan – within the meaning of art. 1.7, paragraph 2, part b of the Wet IB 2001 – may be eligible for deduction.[1454] The first condition is that the occupational pension plan remains within the applicable standards and limitations of Chapter IIB Wet LB 1964. Hence, the pension must be built up with due regard for the pensionable age, the maximum accrual percentages that apply as of January 1, 2015 and the capping limit on pensionable earnings. Second, lower regulations specifically geared to these professionals apply.[1455]

- As regards occupational pensions, non-taxation in the accrual period is achieved in different ways. In the Netherlands, the employer's contributions at the level of the employee are exempt as wages, in Germany an inflow of wages is assumed, but tax liability is avoided by a (partly limited) deduction from the tax base. What is more, in the Dutch fiscal system, the leeway for fiscal facilitation is based on the (pensionable) salary and the pensionable years, where in Germany such a link between these two variables and fiscal facilitation of pension entitlements is not established.
- Under both the German *Direktzusage*, as well as under the *Unterstützungskasse* an inflow of a monetary advantage for the employee is missing. Thus, no pension entitlements have to be exempted for tax purposes. Although the employer builds up

1453 Pursuant to art. 1.7, para 2, under b Wet IB 2001.
1454 Pursuant to art. 3.18, para 1 Wet IB 2001.
1455 Pursuant to art. 3.18, para 5 Wet IB 2001.

a pension capital for the benefits of the employee, the latter has no access nor can derive any legal claims from the accrued capital, and thus an enrichment of the employee is missing. In the case of a *Direktzusage* or an *Unterstützungskasse*, the *Arbeitslohn* is only paid at the time of payment of the retirement benefits to the employee, i.e. the realisation of the pension entitlement. This does not exist in the Netherlands.

- In Germany, civil servants, judges and other receivers of *Pensionen* are no pension premium payments due during their active working phase. To this extent, no application of income emerges, and herewith the question of the tax treatment of possible pension premiums does not arise, since the pension premiums cannot be regarded as *Arbeitslohn*. This does not exist in the Netherlands.
- Only in Germany – contrary to the Netherlands – a tax assessment base advantage (*Bemessungsgrundlagenvorteil*) is granted in the form of a tax deduction or allowance (*Versorgungsfreibetrag* and *Werbungskostenpauschale* for income-related expenses for pension payments or increase in the personal allowance for persons over a certain age). As these relate partly to absolute amounts, partly to a certain percentage of income and in some cases are limited to a maximum amount, the extent of the tax relief depends on the specific individual case. Only in Germany the taxpayer is solely eligible for the exemption of a particular proportion of the retirement benefits under the *Versorgungsfreibetrag*.[1456] In 2023 the percentage of the pension benefits exempted from tax (i.e. the *Versorgungsfreibetrag*) amounts to 13.6 %, capped to the amount of €1,020.[1457] In addition, the *Versorgungsfreibetrag* is raised with €306. What is more, pursuant to Germany tax legislation, an additional *Pauschbetrag* of €102 (2023) may be deducted as well from the tax assessment basis.[1458] In the Netherlands, such a flat-rate deduction does not exist.
- The fiscal framework – laid down in Chapter IIB Wet LB 1964 – builds on the ambition that a pension of 75% of the average pensionable salary must be accrued in at least 40 years. Based on this basic principle the fiscal facilitation of pension accrual through each of the different vesting methods – e.g. *eindloonregeling, middelloonregeling, beschikbare premieregeling* – has been quantified/outlined, see section 6.3.1. The tax treatment of German occupational pensions is void of such a (steering) principal ambition.

1456 Pursuant to § 19, para 2 EStG.

1457 By virtue of § 19, para 2, nr 2, sentence 3 EStG. This *Versorgungsfreibetrag* has been lowered gradually since 2005.

1458 Pursuant to § 9a, para 3 EStG, which states *„Für Werbungskosten sind bei der Ermittlung der Einkünfte die folgenden Pauschbeträge abzuziehen, wenn nicht höhere Werbungskosten nachgewiesen werden: von den Einnahmen im Sinne des § 22 Nummer 5: ein Pauschbetrag von insgesamt 102 Euro"*.

- Contrary to Germany, the Dutch legislator has abandoned the EET system for pensionable salary exceeding €128,810 (2023) and switched to the TEE system for pension accrual derived from pensionable salary exceeding this amount.[1459] It could be said that in view of the income-replacement nature of a pension, pension accrual does not have to be higher than the income prior to retirement.[1460] In Germany, such capping of pensionable earnings does not apply. This reflects that expressing the fiscal treatment of pensions in terms of TEE/EET is limited in terms of generally-applicable use as it insufficiently incorporates cross-border situations and, what is more, insufficiently gives expression to the extent to what fiscal facilitation is granted during the accrual phase, and foreign pension benefits are actually subject to tax in the pay-out phase.
- The retirement target age – for fiscal purposes – in the Netherlands is currently 68; in Germany it is set at 62.
- In the Netherlands, with respect to the tax treatment of the accrual of the old-age pension, the basic principle applies that a pension of 75% of the average pensionable salary must be accrued in at least 40 years. As has been addressed in section 6.3.1, when accruing a tax-facilitated occupational pension, state pension benefits are incorporated, since a pensioner will receive state pension benefits (AOW) in addition to his occupational pension. In this vein, the state pension-franchise per year of service must be set at at least a proportional part of the state pension benefit for a married person without supplement, converted to an annual amount, plus the holiday allowance.[1461] The tax treatment of German occupational pensions is void of such inter-pillar connectedness in terms of incorporating the entitlement to statutory pensions in the (leeway for the) tax facilitation of occupational pensions.
- In Germany, contrary to the Netherlands – *Entgeltumwandlung* – which in itself may be considered as a separate form of pension provision[1462] – allows the converting of future salary payment entitlements into entitlements to occupational pension

1459 Pursuant to Wet van 2 juni 2014 tot wijziging van de Wet inkomstenbelasting 2001, de Wet op de loonbelasting 1964, de Pensioenwet, de Wet verplichte beroepspensioenregeling en de Invoerings- en aanpassingswet Pensioenwet in verband met de aanpassing van het fiscale kader voor oudedagsvoorzieningen (Wet verlaging maximumopbouw- en premiepercentages pensioen en maximering pensioengevend inkomen).

1460 Cf. Starink, 33.

1461 Pursuant to art. 18a, para 7 Wet LB 1964.

1462 § 1, para. 2, under 3 BetrAVG, which states: „*Betriebliche Altersversorgung liegt auch vor, wenn künftige Entgeltansprüche in eine wertgleiche Anwartschaft auf Versorgungsleistungen umgewandelt werden.*" For the qualification of the *Entgeltumwandlung* from a civil law perspective see: Förster and Rechtenwald, 149 and cited literature.

provisions for a similar value.[1463] This type of pension vehicle is unknown in the Netherlands.

– Benefits arising from all forms of Dutch pension schemes are fully included in Box 1 income (*Inkomen uit werk en woning*) and subject to a progressive income tax rate. However, in case of benefits arising from a compulsory pension scheme pursuant to the *Wet verplichte deelneming bedrijfstakpensioenfonds 2000, Wet op het Notarisambt* or the *Wet verplichte beroepspensioenregeling*, these benefits shall – in principle – be taxable as periodic benefits, instead of taxable wage arising from former employment.[1464] In Germany, pension benefits paid by the employer on the basis of a *Direktzusage* and pension benefits from an *Unterstützungskasse* constitute income from employment.[1465] These pension benefits arising from the *Direktzusage* or *Unterstützungskasse* are considered belated earned income and, in principle, fully subject to wage taxes withheld from salary.[1466] Tax on these benefits is withheld by the paying institution.[1467] However, pension benefits arising from the external vesting methods, are differentiated depending on whether they are based on facilitated or non-facilitated contributions. In cases where the pension benefits are based on both facilitated, as well as non-facilitated contributions, the pension benefits must be divided in the pay-out phase.[1468] Insofar as the benefits are based on facilitated contributions, they are fully taxable as other income in accordance with section 22 nr 5 sentence 1 EStG.[1469] Insofar as the benefits are based on non-facilitated contributions, they shall be taxed as other income against the *Ertragsanteil*.[1470] The correct percentage of the *Ertragsanteil* depends on the year in which the retirement entitlements were committed from which the paid out benefits arise. In cases where the entitlements were committed prior to 1 January 2005 (so-called *Altzusagen)*, the retirement benefits – arising from non-tax exempted contributions – will be taxed at the *Ertragsanteil*, laid down in § 22, nr 1, sentence 3, under a, letter bb EStG.[1471] Contrarily, if the pension entitlements were committed after 31 December 2004 (so-called *Neuzusagen*), the retirement benefits – arising from

1463 Similar value is since 2002 required by law pursuant to § 1a BetrAVG. Initiated as a result of BAG. Regarding similar value I refer to: Förster and Rechtenwald, 149 and cited literature.

1464 Pursuant to art. 3.100, paragraph 1, section d in conjunction with art. 1.7, paragraph 2, section b Wet IB 2001.

1465 Taxed pursuant to § 19 EStG. See also BMF, *Steuerliche Förderung der betrieblichen Altersversorgung IV C 5 - S 2333/19/10008:017* para 146.

1466 By virtue of § 19, para 1, nr 2 EStG in conjunction with § 38, para 1, sentence 1 EStG.

1467 Pursuant to § 38 EStG. The tax withheld is final only if the taxpayer receives, in addition to this income, income of less than €410 and does not apply for a tax assessment. See § 46, para 2 EStG.

1468 BMF, *Steuerliche Förderung der betrieblichen Altersversorgung IV C 5 - S 2333/17/10002* para 155.

1469 Ibid. para 156.

1470 In virtue of § 22 nr 5 sentence 2 letter a in conjunction with § 22 nr 1 sentence 3 letter a double letter bb EStG.

1471 By virtue of § 22, nr 5, sentence 2 in conjunction with § 22, nr 1, sentence 3, under a, letter bb EStG.

non-tax exempted contributions – will be taxed at the *Besteuerungsanteil*, laid down in § 22, nr 1, sentence 3, under a, letter aa EStG[1472], provided that they meet the criteria as laid down in § 10, para. 1, nr 2, under b EStG[1473].

– Contrary to Germany, pursuant to Dutch national legislation as it stands, upon emigration, a protective tax assessment shall be issued.[1474] In addition, revisionary interest (*revisierente*) will be included in the protective tax assessment.[1475] For the amount included in the protective tax assessment imposed, deferral of payment shall be granted for a period of ten years.[1476] In the event that no irregularities occur - for example a lump-sum payment - during the period of deferral, the protective tax assessment shall be waived after ten years.[1477] If such an irregularity does occur within these ten years, the pension entitlement shall be regarded as wage arising from a previous employment relationship, and the insurer of that entitlement shall be liable, up to a maximum of the entitlements' fair value, for the tax due in respect thereof by the person entitled thereto, as well as for the corresponding revision interest due.[1478] The tenability of this protective tax assessment has been dealt with in section 6.4.1.A.I. However, in Germany under none of the occupational pension schemes, the tax relief provided during the period of residence in Germany, is reclaimed upon migration to another State. Most recently, the repayment obligation pursuant to § 93-95 EStG pertaining to *Sonderausgaben*-deduction and allowances granted for the benefit of *Riester-Renten* in the event of relocating the place of residence to another EU Member State has been abolished, in response to the CJEU's ruling.[1479] Compared to Germany, the Netherlands, thus, pursues a stricter application with regard to the idea of intertemporal correspondence between the fiscal facilitation of pension contributions

1472 § 22, nr 1, sentence 3, under a, letter aa EStG stipulates that the difference between the annual amount of the pension benefits and the taxable portion of the benefits, constitutes the tax-free proportion of the pension benefits. Furthermore, this applies from the year following the year of retirement for the entire duration of the pay-out phase. By way of derogation, where the annual amount of the pension benefit changes, the tax-free portion of the benefit shall be adjusted in proportion to the change in the annual pension amount to the annual pension amount used to determine the tax-exempted part of the pension benefit. However, regular adjustments of the annual amount of the benefit do not lead to a recalculation and will not be taken into account in a recalculation.

1473 § 10, para 1, nr 2, under b EStG stipulates: *„Sonderausgaben sind die folgenden Aufwendungen, wenn sie weder Betriebsausgaben noch Werbungskosten sind oder wie Betriebsausgaben oder Werbungskosten behandelt werden: Beiträge des Steuerpflichtigen zum Aufbau einer eigenen kapitalgedeckten Altersversorgung, wenn der Vertrag nur die Zahlung einer monatlichen, auf das Leben des Steuerpflichtigen bezogenen lebenslangen Leibrente nicht vor Vollendung des 62. Lebensjahres"*.

1474 Pursuant to article 2.8, para 2 in conjunction with artt. 3.83 and 3.136 Wet IB 2001.

1475 Pursuant to article 30i, para 1, under a in conjunction with para 2 Algemene Wet inzake Rijksbelastingen (AWR).

1476 Pursuant to art. 25, para 5 Invorderingswet 1990 (Tax Collection Act 1990).

1477 Pursuant to art. 26, para 2 Invorderingswet 1990.

1478 Pursuant to article 44b, para 1 Invorderingswet 1990.

1479 *Commission vs. Germany.*

during the accrual phase and the taxation of benefits – based on these facilitated contributions – in the pay-out phase. Where a Dutch outbound migrant worker sees himself confronted with such a protective tax assessment, a German outbound migrant worker does not. Nevertheless, I belief that this amounts to a disparity between the national (pension) tax system, rather than a discrimination on the grounds of EU law, as each (Member) State may impose different (fiscal) conditions on pension schemes.[1480]

– As has been discussed in sections 6.4.1.C.I and 6.7.1.C.II, the extent to which the Dutch contributions paid – by a posted worker – abroad during the posting period were subject to tax relief in Germany, is incorporated in the tax treatment of the pension benefits pursuant to Dutch national tax law. Hence, Dutch policy stipulates that in such cases, a proportion of the Dutch pension benefits may remain outside the scope of wage and income tax, based on the so-called balance method (*saldomethode*).[1481] This proportioning of the taxation of benefits (*saldomethode),* as to whether or not contributions paid abroad during the posting period were subject to tax relief reflects that provisions of national Dutch tax laws governing the taxation of foreign pension benefits, are not applied on the basis of an 'isolated approach'. On the contrary, the taxable proportion – under Dutch wage tax – of the German benefits is differentiated as to whether the entitlements, from which these benefits were derived, were subject to tax relief abroad. On the contrary, as has been elaborated on in sections 6.4.1.C.II and 6.7.1.C.I, this is different in the case of a posted worker returning to Germany. Benefits arising from *Direktzusage* and *Unterstützungskasse* are treated as income from dependent employment, fully liable to tax pursuant to § 19, para 1, nr 2 EStG, irrespective of the tax treatment of the contributions from which these benefits emerge. However, it must be noted, that the extent to which the contributions paid abroad during the posting period were subject to tax relief in Germany, is relevant in the tax treatment of the pension benefits emerging from *Direktversicherungen, Pensionskassen* or *Pensionsfonds*. These benefits are subject to tax as *Sonstige Einkünfte*, pursuant to § 22, nr 5 EstG. The benefits shall be fully liable to tax, to the extent that the benefits emerge from contributions which were not taxed by virtue of § 3, nr 63, §10a or section XI EStG, or the benefits are based on tax-free employer's contributions in the sense of

1480 See, for instance, ECLI:NL:HR:2021:518 (Hoge Raad), in which the Dutch Supreme Court held that the difference in tax treatment between lifelong Dutch pension schemes and foreign pension schemes – that permit unconditional lumpsum payments – is caused by the fact that (Member) States impose different conditions on pension schemes. 2021). Hoge Raad.

1481 Staatssecretaris van Financiën, *Loonheffingen. Inkomstenbelasting. Internationale aspecten van pensioenen en stamrechten nr. DGB2015/7010M* 5. Furthermore, the Secretary of State makes this approval subject to the condition that the taxpayer proves, if requested, that in connection with the acquisition of the pension rights abroad actual taxation has taken place which, in terms of its nature and scope, corresponds with Dutch wage tax or income tax. An actual levy is also understood to mean that there has been no deduction of contributions on the part of the employee.

§ 3, nr 66 EStG. Insofar as the benefits are based on non-facilitated contributions, they shall be taxed as other income against the *Ertragsanteil*.[1482] Whether contributions paid into German occupational pension scheme were facilitated under foreign tax legislation during the posted period is thus irrelevant. This reflects those German provisions of national tax laws governing the taxation of retirement income, are applied on the basis of an 'isolated approach', without taking into account any previous or subsequent tax treatment in another (member) state. Germany does not adhere the principle of intertemporal correspondence (between facilitation during accrual phase and taxation of benefits during pay-out phase) in cross-border situations, as much as it does in domestic situations. Moreover, it reflects that expressing the fiscal treatment of pensions in terms of TEE/EET is limited in terms of generally-applicable use as it insufficiently incorporates cross-border situations and, what is more, insufficiently gives expression to the extent to what fiscal facilitation is granted during the accrual phase, and foreign pension benefits are actually subject to tax in the pay-out phase.

- As addressed in section 6.2.3.C under the *Wet Toekomst Pensioenen*, the Dutch Cabinet proposed to eliminate the difference in fiscal premium leeway between the second and third pillar with respect to old-age provisions.[1483] To this end, the percentage of the maximum contribution margin in the third pillar will be increased to the level that will apply in the second pillar, i.e. 30%. This almost completely unifies the tax treatment of the second and third pillar pension schemes, also constituting a considerable broadening of the fiscal facilitation of third pillar pension schemes.[1484] Such unification of tax treatment between second and third pillar is missing in Germany, and currently not to be expected.

6.8.1.B Similarities

Comparing Dutch and German occupational pensions, the following similarities can be observed:

- As has been revealed in chapter 4 of this research (in terms of the legal character of occupational pensions in both states), in both countries, the second pillar is marked by a direct link between the performance of work, and participation in and entitlements to occupational pension schemes. The employment relationship takes a pivotal role, also to delineate the other pension pillars of statutory, and personal pension plans. This has also become evident in sections 6.2 and 6.5 of the chapter above.
- Practive

1482 Pursuant to § 22, nr 5, sentence 2, letter a in conjunction with § 22, nr 1, sentence 3, letter a, double letter bb EStG.

1483 Kamerstukken II, *Wet toekomst pensioenen* 62.

1484 Currently the premium threshold is set on 13.3% of the maximum premium base.

- As has been dealt with in sections 6.2 and 6.5, the triangular relationship between employee, employer, and pension institution is at the heart of occupational pensions, in both the Netherlands, as well as in Germany. However, how this triangular relationship is given further shape, differs between the two states (in terms of legal rights conferred, vesting methods, pension accrual methods etc.). Under the German BetrAVG the provision of occupational pensions may be organised either directly by the employer (*intern)* or by an external pension provider (*extern*).[1485] The external pension providers comprise *Pensionskasse, Pensionsfonds* and *Direktversicherung*, the internal *Dutchführungswege* concern *Direktzusage* and *Unterstützungskasse*. Under the *Direktzusage* provisions, a triangular relationship does not exist at all since the employer himself provides for a pension provision by means of a book reserve. In the Dutch pension system, the content of the pension agreement is primarily a matter between employer and employee.[1486] In principle, this relationship is governed by the freedom of contract, which allows employees and the employer to agree on the employee's pension as they see fit. The tripartite relationship between employee, employer and pension provider is at the centre of the *Pensioenwet*, where there is a clear division of responsibility between the three parties involved.[1487]
- In terms of uniformity of sources of law pertaining to occupational pensions, the following similarity has been revealed. With regard to Dutch occupational pensions, the *Pensioenwet* is the most prominent source of law. This act came into force in phases on 1 January 2007 and replaced the *Pensioen- en Spaarfondsenwet* on that date, which had been in force since 1952 and was in need of modernization and revision. As a result of the entry into force of the *Pensioenwet*, the rules for pension funds and insurers are now to be found in a single law, whereas previously pension funds and insurers each were subject to different legislation. In Germany, the civil framework for occupational pensions is, since 1974, established through the *Betriebsrentengesetz (BetrAVG)*.[1488] Pursuant to this act, the role of the German *betrieblichen Altersversorgung* as complementary to social security, was made more effective and more assured.[1489] The implementation of this act in 1974 not only meant the definitive recognition of the

1485 Pursuant to § 1, para. 1 BetrAVG. The external pension providers are stipulated in § 1, para. 2 until 4 BetrAVG.

1486 Kamerstukken II, (2005/06), 31.

1487 Cf. Broers, 148.

1488 Gesetz zur Verbesserung der betrieblichen Altersversorgung (Betriebsrentengesetz – BetrAVG). This formal law only applied to the 'old' federal states of Germany. The 'new' federal states were incorporated in the scope of application of this law on 1 January 1992 through a unification treaty. For an elaborate overview of changes as a result of the implementation of the *Altersvermögensgesetz* see Höfer. For an exhaustive overview of the development of the For an elaborate overview of changes as a result of the implementation of the *Altersvermögensgesetz* see ibid.For an exhaustive overview of the development of the *betrieblichen Altersversorgung* in the German pension landscape please see Förster and others, 1-7.

1489 Förster and others, 8.

betrieblichen Altersversorgung as second pillar in the German pension system, but moreover meant the codification of the labour law consequences in a field that was prior - apart from tax law - regulated only by the principles of civil contractual freedom.[1490]

- The occupational pension systems on both states are marked by a shift from predominantly DB to predominantly DC schemes. The latter type of schemes are prevailing more and more. From a historical perspective, this can be considered the conclusion of a metamorphosis of occupational pension law from 'defined benefit to defined contribution'. As has been dealt with in section 6.5.1.A, until 2018 the German legislator made it clear that the employee should always be offered a minimum of security for the later pension payment. This turnaround manifested itself on 1 January 2018, since as of that date, the *reine Beitragszusage* has been implemented pursuant to the (modernising) *Betriebsrentenstärkungsgesetz* (BRSG).[1491] This form of pension vesting is marked by the so-called *Garantieverbot* (guarantee ban), i.e. the employee may not be promised an investment return but a security contribution by the employer should be agreed in the collective agreement.[1492] The implementation of the German *reine Beitragszusage* has a considerable impact on the, thus far, DB-orientated German pension system, and it will bring this system more in line with international developments. As addressed in section 6.2.3, under the Dutch *Wet Toekomst Pensioenen*, all forms of DB-schemes will be abolished and DC-schemes will be the solely-existing type of pension scheme, the tax legislation will be adapted by capping on an age-independent premium for all types of pension schemes, instead of capping both the pension entitlements and the contributions (as under the current system). By introducing age-independent premiums under the *Wet Toekomst Pensioenen*, the Netherlands brings its occupational pension system more in line with common practice in other countries, which is important for companies with employees in different countries. Thus, in both countries a gradual shift towards defined contribution schemes is to be discerned.
- What is more, in terms of vesting methods, similarities have been revealed. In Germany - pursuant to the BetrAVG - under the so-called *Leistungszusage* (defined benefit) the employer is obliged to assure a particular benefit (*Leistung*), for instance, under last salary-schemes a certain percentage of the employee's last salary is committed as pension accrual, see section 6.5.1.A. In the Netherlands such a last salary scheme may be agreed on under an *uitkeringsovereenkomst*, i.e. *eindloonregeling*, see section 6.2.2.A.I.

1490 Ibid. 8.

1491 Gesetz zur Stärkung der betrieblichen Altersversorgung und zur Änderung anderer Gesetze (Betriebsrentenstärkungsgesetz). See § 1, para. 2, nr. 2a BetrAVG.

1492 See § 22, para 1, second sentence BetrAVG and § 244b, para 1, nr. 1 VAG.

- In the Netherlands, in principle, the employee acquires a right to future pension payments. The part of the premium at the employer's expense constitutes part of the (taxable) salary, without a specific identifiable work performance in return.[1493] Thus, the performance of the work as such gives rise to these pension entitlements. In Germany as well, the accrual of pension entitlements on the side of the employee is considered his earned income (i.e. *Arbeitslohn*) - and hence allocated to his taxable income.[1494] Birk and Wernsmann typify this by using the following example; the employer's expenses in order to build a retirement provision for the benefit of the employee, are in principle considered taxable *Arbeitslohn*.[1495]
- In both states - see sections 6.3 and 6.6 - the regulations with respect to the tax treatment of occupational pensions are complex, and grounded on the principle of intertemporal correspondence. If the accrual of pension entitlements on the side of the employee is considered his earned income - and hence allocated to his taxable income - the future pension benefits shall not be subject to taxation. If the retirement entitlements do not qualify as earned income or are tax free, then the pension benefits, in principle, shall be fully subject to taxation. Thus, both states adopted an EET system, although the extent to which this system has been adopted deviates between the two states.
- In both states, the employee may finance his contributions out of his own net income. In Germany under the so-called *Eigenbeiträge*. This form of provision is restricted to *Pensionsfonds, Pensionskasse* or *Direktversicherung*. The rules and regulations regarding *Entgeltumwandlung* shall apply similarly. In the Netherlands contributions may be paid out of the net income under the *nettopensioen* scheme. The net pension is a provision for employees or professionals under a compulsory occupational pension scheme, and qualifies as a premium agreement. The retirement provision built up as a net pension roughly corresponding to an annual gross pension accrual of 1.875% of the average salary, with use being made of a defined contribution scheme.[1496] In principle, the net pension scheme takes the form of a pure DC scheme whereby no guarantee of return is given (until the moment the accrued pension is converted into an entitlement). A net pension can be built up based on the amount that does not form

1493 See also Janse and Janssen, 258-259.

1494 Birk and Wernsmann, 246.

1495 By virtue of § 2, para 2, nr 3 LStDV, which provision states: „*Zum Arbeitslohn gehören auch: Ausgaben, die ein Arbeitgeber leistet, um einen Arbeitnehmer oder diesem nahestehende Personen für den Fall der Krankheit, des Unfalls, der Invalidität, des Alters oder des Todes abzusichern (Zukunftssicherung).*"

1496 As reaching an income above the capping limit usually only occurs at an older age, the legislator has opted for an age-dependent premium scale. This allows older employees to contribute more than they would if the premium scale was not age-dependent.

part of the pensionable salary pursuant to art. 18ga of the Wet LB. Contributions paid into these pension scheme remain tax-free as they are paid out of net income.[1497]

- In both countries, the term 'pension' as such is not defined in fiscal legislation. Yet, the criteria with regard to fiscally facilitated pension provisions have been stipulated. Merely when pension provisions fulfil these criteria, they, in principle, shall be fiscally facilitated for income and wage tax purposes. In the German system, these fiscal criteria are specified in chapter IIB of the *Wet op de loonbelasting 1964*, commonly referred to as the *Witteveenkader*.[1498] Within the meaning of *Wet op de loonbelasting 1964*, an occupational pension scheme refers to a scheme which is exclusively or, with a view to exceptional cases of remaining beneficial entitlements, almost exclusively aimed at providing a lifelong income in old-age for employees, and former employees. Furthermore, the pension scheme must provide that the entitlements stemming from the retirement scheme, may not be paid out as a lump sum, sold, relinquished, nor may it, factually or formally, be become capital collateral, other than in cases as stipulated in or by virtue of the *Pensioenwet*.[1499] Lastly, the pension scheme must be vested by a body, as referred to in art. 19a, par. 1 Wet LB 1964, i.e. a recognised insurer.[1500] Insofar the pension scheme meets the aforementioned criteria, the scheme will, for fiscal purposes, be qualified and facilitated, insofar as it complies with the established fiscal limits, as stipulated in or by virtue of chapter IIB Wet LB 1964.[1501] In the Dutch system, these fiscal criteria are enunciated in § 3, nr. 63, and § 10, para. 1, nr 2, under b EStG[1502]. The latter provision comprises several strict criteria regarding the pension provision: a fully funded retirement provision, the pension agreement merely allows monthly lifelong payments related to the life of the taxpayer and the life annuity may not be paid out prior to reaching the age of 62. What is more, in this vein, Germany elucidated her stance on the comparability of foreign (occupational) pension schemes.[1503] The *essentialia* for the tax recognition of a foreign pension scheme in Germany are, *inter*

1497 The maximum amount of the available premium for a net pension is regulated in artt. 5.17a, 5.17b and 5.17c Wet IB 2001.

1498 Named after the head of the commission (Dirk Witteveen) which developed the revised framework of tax treatment of pensions in 1995.

1499 Pursuant to art. 18, par. 1, lit. b Wet LB 1964.

1500 Pursuant to art. 18, par. 1, lit. c Wet LB 1964.

1501 Pursuant to art. 18, para 1, under lit. c Wet LB 1964.

1502 § 10, para 1, nr 2, under b EStG stipulates: *„Sonderausgaben sind die folgenden Aufwendungen, wenn sie weder Betriebsausgaben noch Werbungskosten sind oder wie Betriebsausgaben oder Werbungskosten behandelt werden: Beiträge des Steuerpflichtigen zum Aufbau einer eigenen kapitalgedeckten Altersversorgung, wenn der Vertrag nur die Zahlung einer monatlichen, auf das Leben des Steuerpflichtigen bezogenen lebenslangen Leibrente nicht vor Vollendung des 62. Lebensjahres"*.

1503 BMF, *Steuerliche Förderung der privaten Altersvorsorge und betrieblichen Altersversorgung IV C 3 - S 2015/11/10002/ IV C 5 - S 2333/09/10005* para 314 which has been repealed by BMF, *Steuerliche Förderung der betrieblichen Altersversorgung IV C 5 - S 2333/19/10008:017* para 36.

alia, coverage of at least one biometric risk (age), a narrow definition of survivors, no inheritability, preferential forms of payment.

As has been addressed in the beginning of this section, exploring similarity between systems involves a comparison of certain features, where similarity is tantamount to a measurement of common features. A higher degree of similarity helps to ensure the effectiveness of information in terms of the four principles. For instance, the higher the degree of similarity, the easier it is to uphold the information's correctness, trustworthiness, and personal relevance. After all, with a higher degree of similarity, there is less need to observe any underlying structural differences. However, as follows from the above enumeration, the legal comparison revealed more differences than similarities between the Dutch and German regulatory frameworks. In terms of 'fitness' it can thus be concluded that these structural differences hamper the provision of effective information provision, in terms of similarity/comparability.

6.8.2 *Foreseeability*

One cannot simply rely on the maintenance of the law in force.[1504] Applicable legislation is designed in view of particular political, economic, societal phenomena. These phenomena tend to change over time, and accordingly, legislation is adapted to the new situation. This also applies to the Dutch and German legislation under scrutiny in this chapter. It is therefore that conveying information on future amounts of retirement income usually involves a certain level of risk as regards continuously changing legislation. Put it differently, predictability is a structure, and information lies where unpredictable change occurs. Along the line of foreseeability, the following conclusions can be drawn:

- As regards the tax relief provided under § 3, nr 63 EStG, applicable to employer's contributions to *Direktversicherungen, Pensionskasse* and *Pensionsfonds*, German tax authorities have, in the vein of paragraph 37 of the OECD commentary on Article 18 OECD MC, explicitly specified to which existing schemes the provision shall apply or to determine how the competent authorities construe the term 'generally corresponding' (how widely interpreted and what tests are imposed).[1505] As regards the latter, Germany

1504 Popelier, 1078.

1505 See BMF, *Steuerliche Förderung der betrieblichen Altersversorgung IV C 5 - S 2333/19/10008:017* para 36. Some conditions had already been laid down in BMF, *Steuerliche Förderung der privaten Altersvorsorge und betrieblichen Altersversorgung IV C 3 - S 2222/09/10041* para 274. This has been revoked by BMF, *Steuerliche Förderung der privaten Altersvorsorge und betrieblichen Altersversorgung IV C 3 - S 2015/11/10002/ IV C 5 - S 2333/09/10005* para 314. The 2010-*schreiben* stipulated that contributions paid into a *Pensionsfonds, Pensionskassen* and – in the case of *Direktversicherungen* – insurance companies established in the EU and third countries, with which a particular type of tax treaty had been concluded (e.g. the treaty Germany-

elucidated her stance on contributions paid to foreign (occupational) pension schemes.[1506] Germany, very briefly in merely one margin, addressed the issue in a *BMF-Schreiben*. This document points out that in cases where contributions are paid to foreign occupational pension schemes, it must be determined whether the foreign pension scheme is comparable to an occupational pension scheme under the Germany *Betriebsrentengesetz* or can be assigned to one of the *Durchführungswege* (vesting methods) as comparable. These conditions have been outlined in, inter alia, section 6.7.1.C.II. However, it is remarkable to see that more meaningful, or informative, requirements are not provided, although general criteria would have been helpful.[1507] The requirements, although fairly strict, leave ample room for discussion, ambiguity and appear not to be a sufficient solution, and no explanation is provided for the allocation of a foreign pension scheme to one of the three pillars of the domestic pension system.[1508] It takes as a given that the foreign pension scheme is allocated to the German second *Schicht* of occupational pension schemes. In the light of foreseeability, general criteria for the allocation of foreign pension schemes to one of the three German pension pillars would be helpful in this regard. This would have ameliorated the foreseeability of (the application of) legislation and government action (i.e. tax authorities). However, even a tax treaty may stipulate that certain foreign pension plans are recognised as occupational pension schemes for the purpose of applying the treaty, which corresponds to one of the *Durchführungswege* under § 1 BetrAVG, without examining the requirements for an occupational pension scheme. For instance, para 16 of the Protocol to the USA Double Taxation Convention, ensures the (fiscal) equal treatment of pension contributions paid to foreign occupational

---

USA) could be facilitated under § 3, nr 63 EStG if the foreign *Pensionsfonds*, *Pensionskassen* or insurance company was authorised under insurance supervisory law to carry out its activities for the benefit of employees in domestic business premises. These conditions were generally not met by foreign pension institutions as they had no connection to Germany. However, this stance was not supported by the wording of § 3 nr 63 EStG as it does not restrict its scope to contributions paid to domestic pension institutions, nor do additional conditions have to be met in order to leave contributions to foreign pension institutions tax-free, nor does this follow from BMF, *Steuerliche Förderung der betrieblichen Altersversorgung IV C 5 - S 2333/17/10002*

1506 BMF, *Steuerliche Förderung der privaten Altersvorsorge und betrieblichen Altersversorgung IV C 3 - S 2015/11/10002/ IV C 5 - S 2333/09/10005* para 314 which has been repealed by BMF, *Steuerliche Förderung der betrieblichen Altersversorgung IV C 5 - S 2333/19/10008:017* para 36.

1507 However, even a tax treaty may stipulate that certain foreign pension plans are recognised as occupational pension schemes for the purpose of applying the treaty, which corresponds to one of the *Durchführungswege* under § 1 BetrAVG, without examining the requirements for an occupational pension scheme. This applies, for example, to the treaty Germany-USA (Article 18A para 3b) in conjunction with Protocol Section 16 letter b, aa. According to this, Germany recognises the US retirement benefit plans listed as such, which correspond to the retirement benefit plans defined in § 1 BetrAVG. Contributions to these pension plans, are subject to tax relief under § 3, nr 63 EStG without further examination.

1508 Cf. Portner, 'Rechtsvergleichende Qualifizierung ausländischer Altersversorgungspläne/-einrichtungen' 2653.

pension schemes, in that it spells out which (US and German) occupational pension schemes are considered qualified for tax relief, for instance, in Germany under § 3, nr 63 EStG. As regards Germany, this concerns pension plans referred to under § 1 of the *Betriebsrentengesetz.*

- The Dutch occupational pension system is subject to a rigorous reform. This draft bill is extensive and contains fundamental changes to the pension system, and can be considered one of the most significant system changes in recent decades. It is, for instance, more ground-breaking than the implementation of the *reine Beitragszusage*, pursuant to the *Betriebsrentenstärkungsgesetz.*[1509] It leads to a radical renewal of the occupational retirement pension. These changes affect the vast majority of participants and pensioners, regardless of the type of pension agreement and regardless of the type of pension provider. At the heart of the bill is the transition to a new pension vesting method, i.e. the 'new pension contract'. Two elements are pivotal in this respect: abolishing the so-called *doorsneepremiesystematiek* (average-contribution system), and the accrual of pension rights is solely possible through a premium agreement (DC-scheme). This flexibility in the transition period – allegedly – allows justice to be done to what is needed in specific situations.[1510] However, this tailor-made approach adds to the complexity of the entire transition process and it can be called into question to what extent it is reminiscent of the metaphor 'out of the frying pay into the fire'. Moreover, this poses great challenges as regards effective pension information provision, in terms of foreseeability of the application of (new) legislation.
- According to well-established case-law of the *Bundesfinanzhof* the decisive factor for the tax treatment of foreign pensions is whether a foreign pension institution is to be assigned to the group of *Durchführungswege* which grant the employee an entitlement to pension benefits (*Direktversicherung, Pensionsfonds, Pensionskasse*) from a pension institution or to the group of *Durchführungswege* in which the employee does not acquire a direct personal entitlement to pension benefits from a pension institution (*Direktzusage* and *Unterstützungskasse*). Where in the former case, pension benefits are taxed pursuant to § 22 EStG as other income, in the latter case, pension benefits, are taxable pursuant to § 19 EStG as income from dependent employment. For the tax treatment of this foreign pension plan it must be determined whether the employee has a direct, personal claim against the foreign pension institution. To this end, foreign legal provisions, such as the articles of association or statutes of a pension institution, must be assessed on the basis of national law and the taxation criteria established by

1509 Gesetz zur Stärkung der betrieblichen Altersversorgung und zur Änderung anderer Gesetze (Betriebsrentenstärkungsgesetz).

1510 Minister van Sociale Zaken en Werkgelegenheid, *Stand van zaken uitwerking pensioenakkoord.*

case-law.[1511] The *Bundesfinanzhof* holds that comparability of retirement pensions can be assumed in cases where the foreign pension benefits correspond in its core content to the common and typical features of the domestic benefit. More meaningful, or informative, requirements are not provided, although general criteria would have been helpful. This approach ('correspond in its core content to common and typical features) leaves ample room for discussion, ambiguity and appear not to be a sufficient solution, and no explanation is provided for the allocation of a foreign pension scheme to one of the three pillars of the domestic pension system.[1512] In the light of foreseeability of the application of tax legislation, generally-applicable, and more meaningful criteria would be helpful in this regard.

- For the purposes of the Dutch Wet IB 2001, the term pension plan is considered to cover a foreign (occupational) pension plan that is considered a pension plan under the tax laws of the given country.[1513] The tax legislation of that country must contain a wage or income tax that, in terms of its nature and scope, correspond to Dutch wage or income tax. Although this leaves the scope of application rather vague, generally speaking, any foreign pension plan qualifies, even if it – for example by allowing lump sum payment – differs considerable from the Dutch concept of 'pension plan'.[1514] In the light of foreseeability, generally-applicable, guiding, and more meaningful criteria would be helpful in this regard.
- As has – inter alia – been elaborated on sections 6.4.1.B.II and 6.7.1.C.II, the fiscal recognition of foreign occupational pensions for tax purposes – pursuant to either

1511 Portner, 'Rechtsvergleichende Qualifizierung ausländischer Altersversorgungspläne/-einrichtungen' 2654.

1512 Cf. Ibid. 2653.

1513 Pursuant to art. 1.7, para 2, under c Wet IB 2001. The purpose of this article is to include definitions of annuity and pension scheme in the Wet IB 2001 in a central place. Consequently, those definitions apply to the entire act and the provisions based on it.

1514 See for instance ECLI:NL:GHAMS:2015:3978 (Hof Amsterdam) in which Hof Amsterdam ruled that a (UK) 'State Pension' did not constitute a pension plan within the meaning of article 1.7 of the Wet IB 2001, as the premiums were not deductible in the UK. See also 06/00183 ECLI:NL:GHSHE:2007:BB2231 (Gerechtshof 's-Hertogenbosch) where the court of appeal ruled that a Belgian *groepsverzekerings-overeenkomst* does fall within the meaning of article 1.7 Wet IB 2001, on the basis of the pension regulations and the Belgian tax laws which – according to the court of appeal – correspond in nature and scope to the Dutch wage and income tax. In a similar vein: ECLI:NL:HR:2021:518 (Hoge Raad) where the court ruled that the circumstance that the Netherlands does not have the same regulation and that the tax treatment in the Netherlands and Belgium differs, does not matter in this respect. As regards *groepsverzekeringen* it is stipulated that it concerns both periodic and non-periodic payments. Accordingly, in ECLI:NL:HR:2021: 518 (Hoge Raad), the Dutch Supreme Court rightly held that the difference in tax treatment between lifelong Dutch pension schemes and foreign pension schemes that permit unconditional lumpsum payments is caused by the fact that (Member) States impose different conditions on pension schemes. The Court held that the fact that lump sum payment is unconditionally permitted under Belgian law does not therefore mean that the Netherlands is obliged under EU law to always recognize a Belgian pension scheme with the possibility of lumpsum for tax purposes by applying the principal of deferred taxation to the entitlements under that scheme. The difference in treatment constitutes a disparity, and is therefore not a prohibited obstacle to the freedom of movement.

Dutch or German fiscal policy – is subject to a range of conditions and requirements. As regards Dutch policy, it is possible under certain conditions to deduct contributions paid to foreign pension schemes for tax purposes in the Netherlands (pension contribution provision). In short, tax recognition brings about that the Netherlands provides tax relief according to Dutch standards, provided the pension plan is fiscally recognized in the temporary employment state (in this case, Germany).[1515] The main condition, pointed out by the State Secretary, included in these tax treaties, is that the foreign pension plan is comparable to a pension plan recognized for tax purposes in the Netherlands. According to the Secretary of State, this is a comparison based on a general assessment, whereby it is not an impediment, for example, if the pension plan of the treaty country does not include a no-redemption clause. This approach (comparison based on a general assessment) leaves ample room for discussion, ambiguity and appears not to be a sufficient solution in terms of foreseeability of the application of legislation.[1516] In the light of foreseeability, generally-applicable, and more meaningful criteria would be helpful in this regard.

- Since 1 January 2005 contributions to the *Direktversicherung, Pensionskasse and Pensionsfonds* are fiscally facilitated. As mentioned in paragraph 6.5.1.B.II, these entitlements to retirement benefits constitute a personal legal right to the entitlements of an occupational scheme to the employee.[1517] This legal claim would in principle lead to taxable earned income at the side of the participating employee in the accrual phase, and, thus would constitute *Vorgelagerte Besteuerung*. In the case of provision through a *Direktversicherung, Pensionskasse* and *Pensionsfonds*, the point in time of the inflow of wages is the time of payment of the contributions by the employer to the corresponding pension institution.[1518] Since 2001 the German legislator implemented a gradual and partial transfer to deferred taxation. Contributions paid by the employer – arising from the first employment relationship – to a *Pensionsfonds, Pensionskasse* or *Direktversicherung* for the accrual of a funded occupational pension scheme are exempted from tax.[1519] In the vein of the applicability of legislation, this gradual transfer from *Vorgelagerte Besteuerung* to *Nachgelagerte Besteuerung* is undesirable.

1515 Staatssecretaris van Financiën, *Loonheffingen. Inkomstenbelasting. Internationale aspecten van pensioenen en stamrechten nr. DGB2015/7010M* 4.

1516 Cf. Portner, 'Rechtsvergleichende Qualifizierung ausländischer Altersversorgungspläne/-einrichtungen' 2653.

1517 Pursuant to § 1b, para 3 BetrAVG, which states: *„Wird die betriebliche Altersversorgung von einer rechtsfähigen Versorgungseinrichtung durchgeführt, die dem Arbeitnehmer oder seinen Hinterbliebenen auf ihre Leistungen einen Rechtsanspruch gewährt (Pensionskasse und Pensionsfonds), so gilt Absatz 1 entsprechend.“*

1518 BMF, *Steuerliche Förderung der betrieblichen Altersversorgung IV C 5 - S 2333/17/10002* para 8.

1519 Pursuant to § 3, nr 63 EStG.

6.8.3 *Inter-system Consistency*

In order to prevent discrepancies in information provision, national (Netherlands and Germany) levels of legislation, need to be consistent by themselves. Legal systems consist of, *inter alia*, a set of rules. In general, legislators would prefer that legislation in a particular legal system were consistent. Not only on a domestic level, but in particular where several national legal systems converge as in this research; on Dutch/German level. This requires a certain form of inter-system consistency. For the purposes of this research 'consistency' is termed as 'the quality, state, or fact of being consistent; agreement, harmony, compatibility'.[1520] Consistency, in this context, refers to – while applying national regulatory frameworks – not leading to incompatible outcomes for a specific case. Two distinct types of inconsistency may be discerned: treating a person inconsistently over time, and inconsistency between individuals.[1521] It is not uncommon that rules in two legal systems attach incompatible consequences to a same case. Two or more rules are in actual conflict when they actually apply to one and the same case, and attach incompatible consequences to this case. In terms of inconsistent treatment over time the following should be stressed.

- The current design of the transitional regime regarding the fixation of the *Besteuerungsanteil*, and the relating tax-free part of the pension benefit paid out[1522], leads in certain years to a double taxation of the contributions and the financial return[1523] (i.e. the pension benefits). This fiscal issue mainly relates to the group of beneficiaries paying contributions since the 1990s. In these cases, the employee contributions were not fully deductible. In particular, employees born in 1975 are affected by this double taxation, although the effect of double taxation arises from the birth year 1955. It may be stated that with regard to this intertemporal taxation, a certain level of coordination is missing. The pensions should either be taxed during the accrual phase or during the pay-out phase.
- As has been discussed in section 6.6, pension benefits stemming from the external *Durchführungswege* are merely taxable in Germany to the extent of the *Ertragsanteil*. As the fictional approach of the *Ertragsanteil* form corresponds to the interest share encompassed in the pension benefits, the external vesting methods in the event of an influx to Germany during the pay-out phase are taxed according to the concept of front-loaded taxation.[1524] The coexistence of front-loaded taxation abroad – during the accrual phase – and back-loaded taxation in Germany – during the pay-out phase –

1520 Oxford Dictionaries.
1521 Steyn, 22.
1522 Pursuant to § 22, nr 3, under aa EStG.
1523 I.e. *Kapitalrückflusses*.
1524 Scheffler and Kölbl, 18.

leads to intertemporal under-taxation.[1525] This affects this system's consistency, as it treats a person inconsistently over time, pursuant to national tax law.

- In terms of treating a person inconsistently over time (as part of inter-system consistency) the following has been observed with regard to the taxation of benefits arising from the external vesting methods (*Direktversicherungen, Pensionskassen* or *Pensionsfonds*). To the extent that the pension benefits arise from contributions which were not fiscally facilitated during the accrual phase, but, contrarily, were taxed pursuant to §40b EStG, these benefits will be taxed in accordance with the *Ertragsanteil*.[1526] The correct percentage of the *Ertragsanteil* depends on the year in which the retirement entitlements were committed from which the paid-out benefits arise. In cases where the entitlements were committed prior to 1 January 2005 (so-called *Altzusagen)*, the retirement benefits – arising from non-tax exempted contributions – will be taxed at the *Ertragsanteil*, laid down in § 22, nr 1, sentence 3, under a, letter bb EStG.[1527] Contrarily, if the pension entitlement were committed after 31 December 2004 (so-called *Neuzusagen*), the retirement benefits – arising from non-tax exempted contributions – will be taxed at the *Besteuerungsanteil*.[1528]

Along the line of inter-system consistency between individuals, the following conclusions can be drawn:

- As has – inter alia – been elaborated on sections 6.4.1.B.II and 6.7.1.C.II, the fiscal recognition of foreign occupational pensions for tax purposes – pursuant to either Dutch or German fiscal policy – is subject to a range of conditions and requirements. As regards Dutch policy, it is possible under certain conditions to deduct contributions paid for foreign pension schemes for tax purposes in the Netherlands (pension contribution provision). In short, tax recognition brings about that the Netherlands provides tax relief according to Dutch standards, provided the pension plan is fiscally recognized in the temporary employment state (in this case, Germany).[1529] The main condition, pointed out by the State Secretary, included in these tax treaties, is that the foreign pension plan is comparable to a pension plan recognized for tax purposes in the Netherlands. According to the Secretary of State, this is a comparison based on a general assessment, whereby it is not an impediment, for example, if the pension plan of the treaty country does not include a no-redemption clause. Although in principle

1525 Cf. Scheffler and Kölbl, 20.

1526 By virtue of § 22, nr 5, sentence 2 EStG. See BMF, *Steuerliche Förderung der betrieblichen Altersversorgung IV C 5 - S 2333/17/10002* para 150. See also Wellisch and others, 174-175.

1527 By virtue of § 22, nr 5, sentence 2 in conjunction with § 22, nr 1, sentence 3, under a, letter bb EStG.

1528 Pursuant to § 22, nr 1, sentence 3, under a, letter aa EStG, provided that they meet the criteria as laid down in § 10, para. 1, nr 2, under b EStG.

1529 Staatssecretaris van Financiën, *Loonheffingen. Inkomstenbelasting. Internationale aspecten van pensioenen en stamrechten nr. DGB2015/7010M* 4.

in this case, in relation to Germany, the conditions of Annex 1 of the Decree would be applicable (inbound worker from an EU member state), Annex 3 of the Decree shall apply (recognition and conditions for employment in the Netherlands of employees from a bilateral treaty country containing a pension contribution provision). The tax treaty between the Netherlands and Germany includes such a pension contribution provision in article 24, paragraph 6. For this fiscal recognition the following (material) conditions shall apply, among which that the tax legislation of the foreign state consider the foreign plan to be a pension plan.[1530] This reflects that provisions of national Dutch tax laws governing the fiscal recognition of foreign pension scheme, are not applied on the basis of an 'isolated approach', without taking into account the tax treatment in the other (member) state. German BMF-policy is void of such an provision reflecting inter-system consistency. For instance, there is no German mandatory legal principle of tax law requiring a direct connection between the taxation of benefits and the deductibility of contributions, provisions of foreign law are not mentioned in the EStG nor does it contain a general rule that a tax benefit, provided pursuant to foreign tax law, shall be treated equally to the application of the EStG's provision.[1531]

- For the purposes of the Dutch Wet IB 2001, the term pension plan is considered to cover a foreign (occupational) pension plan that is considered a pension plan under the tax laws of the given country.[1532] The tax legislation of that country must contain a wage or income tax that, in terms of its nature and scope, correspond to Dutch wage or income tax. Although this leaves the scope of application rather vague, generally speaking, any foreign pension plan qualifies, even if it – for example by allowing lump sum payment – differs considerable from the Dutch concept of 'pension plan'. The reference – and recognition – of a pension plan considered a pension plan under the foreign tax laws reflects that provisions of national Dutch tax laws governing the taxation of foreign pension benefits, are not applied on the basis of an 'isolated approach', without taking into account the tax treatment in the other (member) state. This underlines the inter-system consistency of these Dutch provisions.
- As has been discussed in sections 6.4.1.C.I and 6.7.1.C.II, after the limited time of posting abroad, the posted worker will return to the Netherlands. If the taxing right is allocated to the Netherlands as residence and/or source state (for instance pursuant to article 17, para 1 treaty Netherlands-Germany), the Dutch pension benefits paid out

1530 See appendix 3 of ibid. 12-13.

1531 See also Portner, 'Besteuerung der Auszahlung aus einem U.S.-Altersversorgungsplan – selbst wenn die Beiträge ausschließlich nach U.S.-Steuerrecht gefördert sind und die Summe der eingezahlten Beiträge unter dem Auszahlungsbetrag liegt?' 1177.

1532 Pursuant to art. 1.7, para 2, under c Wet IB 2001. The purpose of this article is to include definitions of annuity and pension scheme in the Wet IB 2001 in a central place. Consequently, those definitions apply to the entire act and the provisions based on it.

are subject to Dutch income tax. During retirement, he will be fully liable in the Netherlands.[1533] The tax treatment of the pension benefits is then akin to a domestic situation as the residence state and pension state coincide, see section 6.3. However, it must be noted, that the extent to which the Dutch contributions paid abroad during the posting period were subject to tax relief in Germany, is incorporated in the tax treatment of the pension benefits pursuant to Dutch national tax law. The State Secretary also recognizes that it may occur that employees abroad (continue to) accrue pension in a Dutch pension plan that complies with the Dutch tax rules, but not with the foreign rules.[1534] Thus, economic double taxation may occur in such cases. Hence, Dutch policy stipulates that in such cases, a proportion of the Dutch pension benefits may remain outside the scope of wage and income tax, based on the so-called balance method (*saldomethode*).[1535] This proportioning of the taxation of benefits (*saldomethode)*, as to whether or not contributions paid abroad during the posting period were subject to tax relief reflects that provisions of national Dutch tax laws governing the taxation of foreign pension benefits, are not applied on the basis of an 'isolated approach'. Moreover, the taxable proportion – under Dutch wage tax – of the German benefits is differentiated as to whether the entitlements, from which these benefits were derived, were subject to tax relief abroad. This demonstrates the inter-system consistency of these Dutch provisions.

- On the contrary, as has been elaborated on in sections 6.4.1.C.II and 6.7.1.C.I, this is different in the case of a posted worker returning to Germany. During retirement, he will be fully liable in Germany.[1536] The tax treatment of the pension benefits is then akin to a domestic situation as the residence state and pension state coincide. Benefits arising from *Direktzusage* and *Unterstützungskasse* are treated as income from dependent employment, fully liable to tax pursuant to § 19, para 1, nr 2 EStG, irrespective of the tax treatment of the contributions from which these benefits emerge. However, it must be noted, that the extent to which the contributions paid abroad during the posting period were subject to tax relief in Germany, is relevant in the tax treatment of the pension benefits emerging from *Direktversicherungen, Pensionskassen* or *Pensionsfonds*. These benefits are subject to tax as *Sonstige Einkünfte*, pursuant to § 22, nr 5 EstG. The benefits shall be fully liable to tax, to the extent that the benefits

1533 Pursuant to § 1, para 1, sentence 1 EStG.

1534 Staatssecretaris van Financiën, *Loonheffingen. Inkomstenbelasting. Internationale aspecten van pensioenen en stamrechten nr. DGB2015/7010M* 5.

1535 Ibid. 5. Furthermore, the Secretary of State makes this approval subject to the condition that the taxpayer proves, if requested, that in connection with the acquisition of the pension rights abroad actual taxation has taken place which, in terms of its nature and scope, corresponds with Dutch wage tax or income tax. An actual levy is also understood to mean that there has been no deduction of contributions on the part of the employee.

1536 Pursuant to § 1, para 1, sentence 1 EStG.

emerge from contributions which were not taxed by virtue of § 3, nr 63, §10a or section XI EStG, or the benefits are based on tax-free employer's contributions in the sense of § 3, nr 66 EStG. Insofar as the benefits are based on non-facilitated contributions, they shall be taxed as other income against the *Ertragsanteil.*[1537] Whether contributions paid into German occupational pension scheme were facilitated under foreign tax legislation during the posted period is thus irrelevant. These foreign pension benefits shall thus be taxed against the *Ertragsanteil.* This reflects that German provisions of national tax laws governing the taxation of retirement income, are applied on the basis of an 'isolated approach', without taking into account any previous or subsequent tax treatment in another (member) state. For instance, as there is no German mandatory legal principle of tax law requiring a direct connection between the taxation of benefits and the deductibility of contributions (i.e. coherence), provisions of foreign law are not mentioned in the EStG nor does it contain a general rule that a tax benefit, provided pursuant to foreign tax law, shall be treated equally to the application of the EStG's provision.[1538] Germany does not adhere the principle of intertemporal correspondence (between facilitation during accrual phase and taxation of benefits during pay-out phase) in cross-border situations, as much as it does in domestic situations. Moreover, it reflects that expressing the fiscal treatment of pensions in terms of TEE/EET is limited in terms of generally-applicable use as it insufficiently incorporates cross-border situations and insufficiently gives expression to the extent to what extent fiscal facilitation is granted during the accrual phase, and foreign pension benefits are actually subject to tax in the pay-out phase.

6.8.4 *Inter-level Coherence*

In order to prevent discrepancies in information provision, different fields of multi-level law need to be aligned with each other, i.e. national (Netherlands and Germany); European, and international.[1539] For the purpose and context of the present research, 'coherence' is termed as 'the situation in which all the levels of the regulatory frameworks are logical and consistent, achieving a harmonious connection of these parts, so that the whole 'hangs together'.[1540] This underlines the relevance of certain properties of regulatory frameworks, and its consequences, for information provision, and corresponding implications. A

1537 Pursuant to § 22, nr 5, sentence 2, letter a in conjunction with § 22, nr 1, sentence 3, letter a, double letter bb EStG.

1538 See also Portner, 'Besteuerung der Auszahlung aus einem U.S.-Altersversorgungsplan – selbst wenn die Beiträge ausschließlich nach U.S.-Steuerrecht gefördert sind und die Summe der eingezahlten Beiträge unter dem Auszahlungsbetrag liegt?' 1177.

1539 See also OECD, 'Recommendation of the Council of the OECD on Regulatory Policy and Governance' 14.

1540 Oxford Dictionaries.

challenge for the provision of effective cross-border pension information is the diversity – and poorly coordination – of differentiates pension vehicles, and taxes.[1541] From this point of view, in order to uphold the information's effectiveness, it requires a certain degree of coherence among these levels of legislation. At lower levels, this may involve systematic scrutiny of coherence with higher-level regulations and with treaty or other international obligations, which will be dealt with in chapters 8 and 9 of this research. A higher degree of coherence also helps to ensure the effectiveness of information in terms of the four principles, in that more coherence between low and higher levels of legislation aids ensuring the information's effectiveness. For instance, in a more coherent (logically and consistent ordered) multi-level legal systems, it is far easier to uphold the information's correctness and trustworthiness, as in such a system, there is less susceptibility to error.

Along the lines of this principle, the chapter above revealed the following findings:

– As has – inter alia – been elaborated on sections 6.4.1.B.II and 6.7.1.C.II, the fiscal recognition of foreign occupational pensions for tax purposes – pursuant to either Dutch or German fiscal policy – is subject to a range of conditions and requirements. As regards Dutch policy, it is possible under certain conditions to deduct contributions paid for foreign pension schemes for tax purposes in the Netherlands (pension contribution provision). In short, tax recognition brings about that the Netherlands provides tax relief according to Dutch standards, provided the pension plan is fiscally recognized in the temporary employment state (in this case, Germany).[1542] The main condition, pointed out by the State Secretary, included in these tax treaties, is that the foreign pension plan is comparable to a pension plan recognized for tax purposes in the Netherlands. According to the Secretary of State, this is a comparison based on a general assessment, whereby it is not an impediment, for example, if the pension plan of the treaty country does not include a no-redemption clause. Although in principle in this case, in relation to Germany, the conditions of Annex 1 of the Decree would be applicable (inbound worker from an EU member state), Annex 3 of the Decree shall apply (recognition and conditions for employment in the Netherlands of employees from a bilateral treaty country containing a pension contribution provision). The tax treaty between the Netherlands and Germany includes such a pension contribution provision in article 24, paragraph 6. On the basis of this provision, in the event of a temporary assignment to the Netherlands, it is possible under certain conditions to deduct contributions paid for foreign pension schemes for tax purposes in the Netherlands (pension contribution provision). In short, tax recognition (under Annex

1541 In the same vein: Sunstein, 'Informing consumers through smart disclosure' 5.

1542 Staatssecretaris van Financiën, *Loonheffingen. Inkomstenbelasting. Internationale aspecten van pensioenen en stamrechten nr. DGB2015/7010M* 4.

3) brings about that the Netherlands provides tax relief according to Dutch standards, provided the pension plan is fiscally recognized in the temporary employment state (in this case, Germany).[1543] However, a recognition under Annex 1 would lead to tax relief corresponding to the foreign (sending state's) standards. As regards the tax relief provided under § 3, nr 63 EStG, applicable to employer's contributions to *Direktversicherungen, Pensionskasse* and *Pensionsfonds*, German tax authorities have, in the vein of paragraph 37 of the OECD commentary on Article 18 OECD MC, explicitly specified to which existing schemes the provision shall apply or to determine how the competent authorities construe the term 'generally corresponding' (how widely interpreted and what tests are imposed).[1544] As regards the latter, Germany elucidated her stance on contributions paid to foreign (occupational) pension schemes.[1545] Germany, very briefly in merely one margin, addressed the issue in a *BMF-Schreiben*. This document points out that in cases where contributions are paid to foreign occupational pension schemes, it must be determined whether the foreign pension scheme is comparable to an occupational pension scheme under the Germany *Betriebsrentengesetz* or can be assigned to one of the *Durchführungswege* (vesting methods) as comparable. Corresponding contributions are tax-exempt according to § 3 nr 63 EStG, i.e. according to German standards (as host country). In the 2017 *BMF-schreiben* two additional margins were added. As regards the relation of § 3, nr 63 to double tax conventions, it stipulated that the direct applicability of the EStG-provision may follow from an international agreement.[1546] It follows from the above that both the Dutch, as well as the German regulatory policy frameworks are fit in terms of inter-level coherence with regard to the fiscal recognition of foreign pension schemes. In the vein of paragraph 37 of the OECD commentary on Article 18 OECD MC, and art. 24, para 6 of the tax treaty concluded between Germany and the Netherlands (intended to ensure equal treatment with contributions made domestically), both states grant fiscal facilitation of foreign occupational pensions according to the fiscal standards of the host state, in cases where a bilateral treaty applies containing a pension contribution provision.

1543 Ibid. 4.

1544 See BMF, *Steuerliche Förderung der betrieblichen Altersversorgung IV C 5 - S 2333/19/10008:017* para 36.

1545 BMF, *Steuerliche Förderung der privaten Altersvorsorge und betrieblichen Altersversorgung IV C 3 - S 2015/11/10002/ IV C 5 - S 2333/09/10005* para 314 which has been repealed by BMF, *Steuerliche Förderung der betrieblichen Altersversorgung IV C 5 - S 2333/19/10008:017* para 36.

1546 BMF, *Steuerliche Förderung der betrieblichen Altersversorgung IV C 5 - S 2333/19/10008:017* para 37 in which reference is made to nr 16 of the Protocol to the USA Double Taxation Convention.

6.9 Interim Conclusion

As has been addressed thoroughly in chapter 1 of this research, the two-dimensional notion of effective pension information articulates that the information's behavioural purpose seeks to inform mobile individuals on an aggregated level about how much pension they can expect, in order to be able to assess the adequacy of their dispersed pension, covering all their forms of pension in each of the (former) working/residence states. The aforementioned behavioural purpose contains the terms 'aggregated' (i.e. assembled at an overall/higher level) and the phrase 'covering all their forms of pension in each of the (former) working/residence states'. However, mobile individuals – who avail(ed) themselves of their European freedoms of movement – see themselves confronted with a wide range of diverging 'pensions', i.e. pension vehicles, schemes, retirement products of all sorts, arising from occupational pension systems in each of the different (former) working states, and/or residence states. This requires putting together dispersed, and deviating, elements of future retirement income, arising in each of these states. This amounts to observing, and 'translating' the intersections between different multi-level legal systems (national, EU and international/bilateral) and the interaction of poorly coordinated legal domains (pension and tax law) – which can all be interwoven in a personal mobile situation – into effective pension information. This was taken as a given and this chapter mapped out the occupational pension systems in both the Netherlands, as well as Germany. Moreover, it revolved around the tax treatment of these occupational schemes in both the accrual and pay-out phase, in both domestic, and in particular in cross-border situations. The comparative findings were presented in section 4.5, along the lines of this research's evaluation framework. This comparison revealed a considerable number of differences when it comes to Dutch and German occupational pensions, and their tax treatment in cross-border situations. These structural differences should be observed when providing effective cross-border pension information. Also, along the principle of foreseeability of (the application of) legislation several findings were revealed. With respect to inter-system consistency, the findings revealed a number of situations where applying national regulatory frameworks leads to incompatible outcomes for a specific case, in particular with regard to inconsistency of the tax treatment of pensions of mobile individuals. What is more, it was also found that provisions of national tax laws governing the taxation of retirement income, are applied on the basis of an 'isolated approach', without taking into account any previous or subsequent tax treatment in another (member) state. Lastly, evaluating the regulatory frameworks through the lens of inter-level coherence revealed findings when it comes to the coherence among these levels of legislation, involving systematic scrutiny of coherence with higher-level regulations and with treaty or other international obligations. In this vein, this chapter meets this research second (sub)objective of a legal comparative study in which the legal frameworks in the

Netherlands and Germany shall be mapped out, and evaluated along the lines of this research's evaluation framework.

7 Personal Pensions Systems and Taxation Through the Lens of Effective Pension Information

7.1 Introduction

Where in the preceding chapter the (tax treatment of) occupational pension systems – in the Netherlands and Germany – has been mapped out, this chapter analyses the personal pension systems. The main distinction between occupational pensions and personal pensions lies in the role of each of the pension pillars in saving for old age, the replacement ratio, the (historical) development, the character, and the corresponding tax treatment. From a cross-border perspective, mobile individuals – who avail(ed) themselves of their European freedoms of movement – see themselves confronted with a wide range of diverging 'pensions', i.e. pension vehicles, schemes, retirement products of all sorts, arising from personal pension systems in each of the different (former) working states, and/or residence states. This fragmentation of pensions – and lack of comparability – is further exacerbated by the high diversity in the methods of tax treatment of personal pensions in each Member State, as each State applies different tax rules to these arrangements. Providing, on an aggregated level, mobile individuals information about how much pension they can expect – covering all their forms of pension in each of the (former) working/residence states – requires a complex process of incorporating all types of diverging pension vehicles, schemes, products of all sorts in each of the different (former) working states, and/or residence states. This requires a process of converging these deviating systems, while upholding the information's effectiveness. Putting this dispersed puzzle together also poses considerable challenges in terms of effective information provision. This amounts to observing, and 'translating' the intersections between different multi-level legal systems (national, EU and international/bilateral) and the interaction of poorly coordinated legal domains (pension and tax law) – which can all be interwoven in a personal mobile situation – into effective pension information. For example, ensuring the legal correctness of information requires systematic monitoring and updating, as laws and policies are constantly changing. What is more, heterogeneity among national legal systems is a universal phenomenon, due to, inter alia, historical developments, adaption to different social developments, economic trends and developments, different political landscapes etc. Hitherto, no attention has been paid neither any research has been conducted on the differentiated tax treatment of the fragmented pension rights in each of the (former) working states, and the effect thereof on the ambition to present effective pension information.

Taking this as a given, this chapter maps out the personal pension systems in both the Netherlands, as well as Germany. Moreover, it revolves around the tax treatment of these personal schemes in both the accrual and pay-out phase, in domestic, but in particular in cross-border situations. It is explored to what extent tax relief is granted for personal pensions in the form of tax base advantages (e.g. tax exemptions, allowances, deduction from the taxable base, deduction from the tax liability) or tax rate advantages (e.g. flat tax rate). The description of this tax treatment is based on national (Dutch and German respectively) tax legislation, while taking account of the applicable tax treaty concluded between the Netherlands and Germany. The influence of European and international (tax) law on the tax treatment of cross-border pensions as such will be looked into in chapters 8 and 9 of this research. In section 4.5, these comparative findings will be evaluated along the (legal) lines of this research's evaluation framework: similarity/comparability, inter-level coherence, inter-system consistency, and foreseeability. In this way, this chapter meets this research second (sub)objective of a legal comparative study in which the legal frameworks in the Netherlands and Germany shall be mapped out.

7.2 The Dutch Pension Tax System in Domestic Situations

As addressed in chapter 4 of this research, the interpretation of the concept of third pillar pension provisions is rather open, similar to the German third pillar. Contrary to statutory and occupational pensions, individual pensions are mainly regulated by fiscal legislation, stipulating the criteria regarding their fiscal facilitation. Hence, the sections below predominantly revolve around fiscal legislation. The Dutch third pension pillar embodies individual pension arrangements that a person establishes on his or her own initiative.[1547] Life annuities (*lijfrenten*) take a predominant role in the Dutch retirement system, in terms of a supplementary pillar. These are stand-alone individual arrangements, with no basis in a second pillar pension plan. A characteristic of the third pillar pension is that it does not have its basis in the performance of work, as is the case with occupational pensions.[1548] However, it does form a supplement to the first, and second pillar Dutch pensions. Annuities in the third pillar are not the purview of pension funds in the

1547 Lutjens, *Asser-serie 7-XI – Pensioen (Bijzondere overeenkomsten)* nr 12.
1548 Dietvorst, *De drie pijlers van toekomstvoorzieningen en belastingen* 65.

Netherlands but of life insurers and banks. The conditions for annuity premium deduction are quite strict with respect to the allowed annuity products and the allowed providers.[1549]

As a rule, solely provisions with an insurance element that provide a periodic income in old age (or for the surviving partners) in the event of death are classified under this third pillar.[1550] Capital insurance policies do not generate periodic income, and therefore remain excluded from this scope. This approach is not uncommon internationally either. Self-initiative and voluntariness prevail with respect to these pension provisions. Compared to the Dutch first and second pillars, freedom, personal responsibility and flexibility prevail most in the third pillar.

With a view to the Dutch third pillar – from a tax and insurance point of view – three types of annuities can be distinguished:[1551]

1. **Pure annuity:** when entering into the contract, the amount of the annuity instalments is fixed and also on whose life the instalments depend, e.g. a retirement pension built up by an employee in a salary/service time arrangement.
2. **Targeted annuity:** it is only determined on whose life the annuity payments will depend in due course. The amount of the instalments will be determined at the time of commencement on the basis of the amount of the available (insured) capital and the interest rate applicable at that time, i.e. a capital insurance with a targeted annuity clause.
3. **Capital insurance with an annuity clause:** at the time of entering into the annuity agreement, it is not clear on whose life the annuity will depend, nor what the amount of the payments will be in due course. The only aspect agreed is that the insured capital will be used to buy an annuity. This form was generally applied until 1992 because it was tax deductible until then.

Also, among life annuities, a distinction can be drawn between the accrual phase on the one hand, and the pay-out phase on the other. While the capital or investment balance is built up in the accumulation phase, this capital must be harnessed for an annuity in the pay-out phase at the end date of the annuity agreement – within a reasonable period of

1549 To be eligible for premium deduction, there must be an annuity in terms of the conditions set by art. 1.7 Wet IB 2001: an annuity is a periodic payment; the payments are fixed and regular; the payments must end at the latest at death; the annuity claim may not be taken out as a lump sum, sold, surrendered or formally or actually serve as security other than for the purpose of deferring tax payment. If an annuity agreement does not meet these conditions, the annuity does not qualify for premium deduction and the value of the entire policy shall be taxable as income from assets (BOX 3).
See artt. 3.124 Wet IB 2001 ff.

1550 Dietvorst, 'Lijfrenten' section 12.1.

1551 Cf. Ibid. 531.

time.[1552] In terms of insurance, the annuity in the accumulation phase is designed as a capital insurance policy that shall be paid out on a pre-agreed date when the insured is alive or in the event of his/her earlier death. Hence, the form of insurance is akin to that of a defined contribution pension scheme. After expiration of the policy, the insured capital will have to be used for one or more permitted annuities. This means that the rates of the insurance company or the bank at that moment are decisive for the amount of the annuity payments.[1553] The allowed forms of annuities are described in art. 3.125 Wet IB 2001.

7.2.1 *Tax Treatment of Third Pillar Contributions: Communicating Vessels*

The tax framework for Dutch life annuities has evolved over several decades, and has become increasingly sophisticated. The Dutch tax treatment of third pillar pensions is marked by a system of communicating vessels.[1554] This is related to the fiscal mechanism, where the first and second pillar pensions shall be taken into account when calculating the fiscal leeway (*jaarruimte*) for the premium deduction. This will be looked further into in the section below.

The tax treatment pertaining to life annuities persists to be subject to amendments. For instance, the *Brede Herwaardering*-scheme, which came into force in 1992. What is more, a further considerable amendment, is the introduction of *banksparen* as of 1st January 2008, which extended the annuity definition and the number of allowed providers, and for which a fiscal framework has been developed that matches as closely as possible the conditions that apply to the traditional annuity.[1555]

7.2.1.A Fiscal Facilitation during the Accrual Phase

In order to be eligible for premium deduction, annuities as such are subject to further conditions.[1556] These conditions are aimed at ensuring that the annuity claim is actually used to provide income to the taxpayer, and/or his partner and children. If during the term of the annuity agreement the set conditions are violated, penalty provisions will take effect. This will be dealt with in more detail below.

1552 The reasonable period ends at the end of the calendar year following the year of expiration in of the second calendar year following the year of expiration or upon death. If no annuity is stipulated after the expiration of the reasonable period, the annuity is considered to be commuted.

1553 Cf. Dietvorst, 'Lijfrenten' 531.

1554 Cf. Ibid. section 12.1.

1555 As Dietvorst points out, this eliminated the insurance element from the annuity, because a bank is not an insurance company and therefore cannot sell products with a mortality risk. See ibid. section 12.3.

1556 See art. 3.124 Wet IB 2001.

The Annuity Definition

In order to be eligible for premium deduction it must constitute an annuity in terms of art. 1.7 Wet IB 2001.[1557] It must constitute a claim under a life insurance contract, a claim to the balance of an annuity savings account (*lijfrentespaarrekening*) or to the value of an annuity investment right (*lijfrentebeleggingsrecht*). The following key elements arise from this definition:[1558]

1. An annuity constitutes a periodic payment: this is not enunciated in the legal provisions, but case-law has clarified this. It should be a payment that is or can be part of a series of payments and that each payment – for itself – is dependent on an uncertain future event.[1559]
2. Benefits must be fixed and equal: the term 'fixed' refers to the amount of the benefit, while evenly refers to the period of time between the dates on which the benefits lapse.[1560]
3. Termination at the latest upon death. The benefits must end at the latest upon death; benefits may also end earlier (i.e. a temporary annuity). The Wet IB 2001 gives the possibility or obligation to use the insured capital for a temporary annuity. When it comes to an old age annuity that is concluded with a life insurer, then the instalments will only end upon the death of the beneficiary. The insured capital can also be used for a temporary retirement annuity.
4. Prohibition of commutation, alienation, surrendered or used as formal or constructive security other than for the purpose of deferring tax payment. If an annuity agreement does not include these the annuity, it does not qualify for deduction. The annuity value will subject to income tax in BOX 3.

1557 Pursuant to art. 1.7, para 1 Wet IB 2001. See also Staatssecretaris van Financiën, *Verzamelbesluit Lijfrenten nr. 2019-115021* (16 May 2019) para 2.1.1. An annuity as referred to in art. 1.7 of the Wet IB 2001 is an entitlement under a life insurance contract as defined in art. 1.6a of the Wet IB 2001. Pursuant to art. 1.6a life insurance means: a life insurance agreement as referred to in Section 1:1 Wet op het financieel toezicht (Wft). The State Secretary hereby enunciates the (fiscal) content of the term life insurance and the further criteria that have been drawn up for this purpose. In summary, this means that a life insurance is only ought to exist if the policyholder/beneficiary has a reasonable chance of the contract yielding a substantially higher return, than the value of the premiums paid plus the return achieved by the insurer (the so-called bonus).

1558 Dietvorst, 'Lijfrenten' 533. The conditions that the Wet IB 2001 impose on annuities are aimed at ensuring that they are actually used to provide income for the taxpayer and/or his/her surviving relatives. If one of the circumstances referred to in article 3.133, 3.135 or 3.136 (irregular settlement, e.g. surrender, alienation, etc) Wet IB 2001 occurs, the premiums and amounts paid for that entitlement and the yield thereon for the policyholder, or if the policyholder is deceased, for the person entitled to that entitlement, are taxable, including revision interest (20%).

1559 JEAM van Dijck, 'Periodieke uitkeringen in de Wet IB' WFR.

1560 See for exception on this criterium Dietvorst, 'Lijfrenten' 533.

What is more, as of 1 January 2008, the definition of annuity in the Wet IB 2001 has been expanded.[1561] The legislator has tried as much as possible to shape the bank annuity in such a way that it resembles an annuity offered by a life insurer.[1562] If one saves at a bank, one speaks of a *lijfrentespaarrekening*. At an investment institution, it is termed *lijfrentebeleggingsrecht*. Both types of annuities are referred to as *banksparen*, i.e. saving for retirement through a bank or investment institution. The yield made can only be added to the savings account or investment right; it cannot be paid out during the accumulation phase. The accumulated capital can only be harnessed to conclude a (permitted) annuity at a bank, investment institution or insurer. Typical differences between the insured annuity and the bank annuity are: in case of death of the insured person, no loss of capital can occur under a bank annuity (the remaining amount is – as a rule – for the benefit of the heirs); lifelong is not actually lifelong but at least 20 years; the bank annuity is not marked by death cover in the form of an extra risk cover for the benefit of the partner.[1563]

Life Annuities Eligible for Fiscal Facilitation

Life annuities eligible for fiscal facilitation are limited to the old age annuity (*oudedagslijfrente*), bridging annuity (*overbruggingslijfrente*), temporary retirement annuity (*tijdelijke oudedagslijfrente*), and survivor's annuity (*nabestaandenlijfrente*).[1564] It follows from this that one can conclude both a temporary, as well as a lifelong annuity. Solely those annuity provisions will be dealt with that cover provision for old age, thus not survivor's annuities. The annuity schemes that will be dealt with are (fiscally) described as follows:

- Old-age annuity: instalments must accrue to the taxpayer. Moreover, terms must be lifelong and start no later than the age that is five years higher than the AOW pension age.[1565] A minimum age as of which the benefits may be paid out does not apply. Under this type of annuity, the policyholder, insured and beneficiary coincide. Moreover, in principle, the amount of the benefits must be fixed.[1566]
- Bridging annuity: an annuity scheme under which benefits shall be terminated in the year in which the taxpayer reaches the (former AOW) age of 65 or in the year in which the taxpayer receives an occupational pension benefit. This type of annuity served as a

1561 Ibid. 536 ff.

1562 Pursuant to art. 1.7, para 1, under b in conjunction with art. 3.126a Wet IB 2001.

1563 See also HPM Van Bijnen and LMP Jacobs, 'Lijfrentesparen versus lijfrenteverzekering' WFR; GJB Dietvorst, 'Geblokkeerd banksparen: evolutie of revolutie?' Ibid; GJB Dietvorst, 'Geblokkeerd banksparen: het vervolg' WFR.

1564 Pursuant to art. 3.125, para 1 Wet IB 2001. The provision does not term these types of annuities as such, but describes them.

1565 Art. 3.125, para 1, sub a Wet IB 2001.

1566 Pursuant to art. 3.125, para 2 Wet IB 2001 permit that the benefit payments shall be lowered at the death of the partner to a maximum of 70% of the amount that was paid until the death of the partner.

bridge until the AOW pensionable age. However, this type of life annuity schemes has been repealed as of 1 January 2006, and is, hence, no longer included in art. 3.125 Wet IB.[1567] As of that date, premium deduction is no longer granted for the bridging annuity.[1568] Hence, this type of annuity scheme will not be discussed any further in this research.

- Temporary retirement annuity[1569]: instalments must accrue to the taxpayer. Also under this type of annuity, the policyholder, insured and beneficiary coincide. Under this type of life annuity scheme the instalments must have a term of at least five years, and must not commence earlier than when the taxpayer has reached the AOW pension age. Furthermore, the instalments may not start later than in the year in which the taxpayer has reached the age that is five years higher than the AOW pensionable age, ensuring that a person cannot stipulate more than a temporary retirement annuity. Moreover, the instalments per year may not exceed an amount of €24,168 (2023).

What is more, a combination of different annuity types is allowed as long as each annuity meets the conditions.[1570] The choice of the type of annuity must be made at the end date of the agreement or within a reasonable period of time.

Permitted Providers

The Wet IB 2001 lists the permitted (domestic and foreign) providers of annuities. Permitted means that annuity contracts can be concluded with these providers eligible for deductibility of annuity premiums. Moreover, the annuity must comply with the applicable legal frameworks. Specific provisions apply to foreign providers. Under the Wet IB 2001, a wide range of annuity providers are permitted:[1571]

- life insurance companies based in the Netherlands, within the meaning of art. 1:1 *Wet op het financieel toezicht*;
- pension funds based in the Netherlands;
- foreign life insurance company or pension fund provided that it is a continuation of an existing scheme;

1567 Since as of that date *Vervroegde uittreding (VUT)* and pre-pension schemes were no longer fiscally allowed. Hence, by way of a accompanying measure, the bridging annuity was abolished.

1568 A transitional provision for existing entitlements has been laid down in art. 10a.1 Wet IB 2001. Pursuant to this provision with regard to premiums paid before January 1, 2006, a bridging annuity can still be stipulated after 2005.

1569 Art. 3.125, para 1, sub c Wet IB 2001.

1570 See also Dietvorst, 'Lijfrenten' 548 ff.

1571 Pursuant to artt. 3.126 and 3.126a Wet IB 2001.

- another foreign life insurance company or foreign provider, provided a number of conditions are met;[1572]
- a natural person or a private limited company, provided that it concerns a business transfer;
- a credit institution;[1573]
- an investment institution.[1574]

Under the *jaarruimte*-system, the amount of the annuity premium deduction depends on the pension accrual in the second pillar. Merely those taxable persons who fall short of pension accrual in the second pillar (*pensioentekort*), are entitled to deduction of annuity premiums in the third pillar. Thus, any alterations change in the first and second pillars will affect the fiscal framework of the third pillar. So, in effect, it is a compensatory third pillar. This type of tax treatment pertaining to annuities is unique in Europe.[1575]

Over the years, the tax framework has evolved from fairly generous to limited and detailed.[1576] This will be addressed briefly below. The premium is – under conditions – deductible from income as an expense for income provisions in BOX 1.[1577] Until the implementation of the *Brede Herwaardering*-scheme in 1992, every taxable person could harness the annuity premium deduction regardless of whether there was a pension deficit.[1578] The fiscal framework in effect before the *Brede Herwaardering*-scheme will not be discussed in more detail in this research since this research focuses on the legislative framework as it stands today. Moreover, it was possible that the annuity payments accrued to someone other than the policyholder. After the introduction of the *Brede Herwaardering*-scheme, the tax framework for annuities became stricter and more detailed.

In the following, only the annuities that serve to compensate a pension deficit (within the meaning of art. 3.124, part a, Wet IB 2001) will be discussed.[1579] Every taxable person is entitled to an annuity premium deduction each year, whereby the amount of deduction is

1572 A life insurer can thus offer life annuity insurance without being established in the Netherlands. In Staatssecretaris van Financiën, *Internationaal belastingrecht. Toegelaten buitenlandse aanbieders van pensioenen, lijfrenteverzekeringen, lijfrenterekeningen, lijfrentebeleggingsrechten en arbeids-ongeschiktheidsverzekeringen nr. 2022-192641* foreign life insurance companies are recognized for tax purposes.

1573 This concerns a so-called bank annuity (*bancaire lijfrente*) included in the Wet IB 2001. Amounts paid into an annuity savings account at a credit institution are equated with premiums for annuities.

1574 The tax regime is similar to that of the bank annuity (*bancaire lijfrente*).

1575 Cf. Dietvorst, 'Lijfrenten' section 12.1.

1576 See for instance Staatssecretaris van Financiën.

1577 Art. 3.124 Wet IB 2001 ff.

1578 Cf. Dietvorst, 'Lijfrenten' section 12.3.

1579 For an extensive discussion of all other types of annuities, see ibid. 538 ff.

determined by the income received in the previous year, and by the increase in value of his pension entitlements in the second pillar in the previous year.[1580] A condition for this is that the taxpayer has not yet reached the AOW retirement age at the start of the calendar year.[1581] Furthermore, there must be a so-called 'pension deficit' in the second pillar pension scheme, in the previous calendar year. This possible pension deficit – calculated by means of the accrual of pension in the second pillar in the previous year – is factored into the calculation of the maximum contribution deduction (*jaarruimte*) in the third pillar.

Provided the strict conditions are met, premiums for annuities may be taken into account up to an aggregate amount not exceeding 13.3% (2023) of the premium base, whereby the premium base is capped at €128,810 (2023), minus an amount of €13,646 (2023), i.e. the so-called *AOW-franchise*.[1582] If the taxpayer has taken less annuity premiums into account in the preceding seven-year period than was possible based on the above mentioned *jaarruimte*, he may, upon request made with his tax return, take into account the unused amount, to the extent that it has not been taken into account in a previous year, starting with the unused amount in the oldest year.[1583] The unused amount to be taken into account shall not exceed 17% (2023) of the contribution base, with a maximum of €8,065 (2023).

7.2.1.B Taxation of Benefits during the Pay-Out Phase

The main rule is that annuity payments, except for the payments arising from the net annuity, shall be fully taxable as periodic payments (against a progressive income tax rate) with the person who receives them, irrespective of whether the benefits arise from contributions which have been deducted.[1584] Until 1 January 2009, the criterion was

1580 This increase in value of the occupational pension entitlements in the previous years is expressed in terms of the factor 'A'. This factor A is the value of the pension entitlements attributable to the preceding year (t-1) in so far as the increase is due to an increase in the pension entitlements. It should be noted that the method of calculating the factor A is no more than a rough approximation. The State Secretary indicated for different types of pension schemes how the factor A should be calculated, see Staatssecretaris van Financiën.

1581 Pursuant to art. 3.127, par. 1 Wet IB 2001.

1582 Pursuant to art. 3.127, par. 1 Wet IB 2001. The premium base consists of the combined amount in the previous calendar year of the profit from business; the taxable wages; the taxable result from other work; the taxable periodic benefits and benefits in kind, see art. 3.127, par. 3 Wet IB 2001. In order to bring the premium deduction for annuities in line with the *Witteveen* framework for occupational pensions, the maximum premium deduction was reduced to 13.3% over a maximum premium base of €128,810 (2023) as of January 1, 2015. See Dietvorst, 'Lijfrenten' section 12.3.

1583 Pursuant to art. 3.127, para 2 Wet IB 2001.

1584 Pursuant to art. 3.100, para 1, sub b Wet IB 2001. Cf. Dietvorst, 'Lijfrenten' 558. The main rule that annuity payments are taxed regardless of whether the premiums have been deducted, led to the issue of box splitting after the introduction of the Wet IB 2001. See ibid. 556 ff. If premiums are not or not fully deducted, the corresponding (part of the) value shall be taxed in box 3. Strictly speaking, the policy will have to be divided into a box 1 and a box 3 part during the accumulation phase. To take into account the non-deducted

whether the premiums had been deducted as expenditure for income provision. Incidentally, there are still many annuity insurances in the Netherlands to which the tax regime of the Wet IB 1964 as it applied before 1992 applies, the so-called *pre-Brede Herwaarderingslijfenten*. The design of these *pre-Brede Herwaarderingslijfrenten* differs strongly from the design of life annuities under the regime of the Wet IB 2001.[1585] These will not be addressed in further detail in this research.

7.2.1.C The Net Annuity (Nettolijfrente)

In addition to the aforementioned forms of (tax-relieved) annuities, since 1 January 2015 it has also been possible to take out a so-called net annuity (*nettolijfrente*). The net annuity is linked to the capping limit for pensions and annuities of €128,810 (2023) – pursuant to art. 18ga Wet LB 1964 – introduced on the same date and seeks to be a voluntary third pillar provision for the income exceeding this limit.[1586] The premium is not deductible and, thus, paid out of the net income. Since the premiums are not deductible, the benefits can be paid out untaxed in due course.[1587] In this regard, the Netherlands deviates from the widely accepted EET system, and applies a TEE-system.

As with gross life annuities, net annuities allow for both the insured and the banked and investment option.[1588] The net annuity enables to build up a provision for old age that roughly corresponds to an annual pension build-up of 1.875% of the average earned income. As with gross annuities, the permitted providers are insurers, banks and investment institutions.[1589] Comparable foreign institutions may – under certain conditions – also offer net annuities. Since a net annuity – in contrast to a net pension – falls under the scope of the *Pensioenwet*, pension funds are not allowed to offer a net annuity.

premiums, a limited balance method was introduced in 2009, see art. 3.107a Wet IB 2001. Insofar as the taxpayer has demonstrated that premiums paid were not deducted in whole or in part, no tax will be due on the benefits. The amount per year of non-deducted premiums that has not been taken into account shall not exceed €2,269 (2023).

1585 See Staatssecretaris van Financiën, section 5.

1586 Wet van 2 juni 2014 tot wijziging van de Wet inkomstenbelasting 2001, de Wet op de loonbelasting 1964, de Pensioenwet, de Wet verplichte beroepspensioenregeling en de Invoerings- en aanpassingswet Pensioenwet in verband met de aanpassing van het fiscale kader voor oudedagsvoorzieningen (Wet verlaging maximumopbouw- en premiepercentages pensioen en maximering pensioengevend inkomen).

1587 See art. 3.100, para 3 Wet IB 2001.

1588 See art. 5.16, para 2 Wet IB 2001.

1589 Pursuant to art. 5.16a, para 1 Wet IB 2001 in conjunction with artt. 3.126, para 1 and art. 3.126a, para 2 Wet IB 2001.

The net life annuity value is exempt in box 3 (income from savings and investments).[1590] The applicable provision enunciate a range of conditions for this: the net annuity must have been taken out voluntarily by the taxpayer; the annuity agreement must reflect that it is a net annuity; the premium must have been charged to the taxpayer and must not have been taken into account as an expense for income provision and must remain within the legal limit; the premium was not paid after the year in which the taxpayer is entitled to AOW pension.[1591] In the event of a non-regular settlement (e.g. surrender, alienation, formal or become a de facto or de jure subject of security), the box 3 exemption will, in principle, lapse in the future.[1592] Settlement upon emigration is explicitly not considered an irregular settlement.[1593]

7.3 TAX TREATMENT OF DUTCH PERSONAL RETIREMENT PROVISIONS IN CROSS-BORDER CASES

As has been addressed earlier in this research, the increase in the mobility of workers implies that the taxation of pensions must not solely be considered from a purely national perspective, but also account must be taken of cross-border aspects. Given this, the aim of this section is to analyse the tax treatment of personal pension schemes (in cross-border situations) at the employee level, pursuant to Dutch national tax legislation. It is explored to what extent tax relief is granted for pensions in the form of tax base advantages (e.g. tax exemptions, allowances, deduction from the taxable base, deduction from the tax liability) or tax rate advantages (e.g. flat tax rate). As regards the pay-out phase it is considered how, and to what extent, (foreign and domestic) pension benefits are subjected to tax. If, however, the pension entitlements were partly accrued in Germany (a German pension) and partly in the Netherlands (a Dutch pension), the (cross-border) fiscal consequences need to be identified per pension separately (by source of the retirement income). These situations will not be dealt with in the section below, but this section's content, combined with section 7.5, allows for the (fiscal) assessment of such (dispersed) mixed-pension cases.

It is to be noted at this point, that the allocation of the taxing rights pursuant to a tax treaty, is taken into account as a proviso/prerequisite for the exercise of taxing rights pursuant to domestic (German) tax legislation. These distribution rules will be discussed in more

1590 Pursuant to art. 5.16 Wet IB 2001.
1591 Pursuant to art. 5.16 Wet IB 2001.
1592 Pursuant to art. 5.16c Wet IB 2001.
1593 Pursuant to art. 5.16c, para 7 Wet IB 2001.

detail in chapter 9. The normative framework pertaining to the tax treatment of cross-border pensions, enshrined in EU law, will be discussed in chapter 8.

Different fiscal measures will be considered in this regard. If the employee's pension contributions have been fiscally facilitated, the state of departure has an interest in taxing the retirement benefits as well. A possible (domestic[1594]) measure of safeguarding the fiscal interests of the country of departure in the event that a pension saver moves to another country is to subject the facilitated retirement provision contributions retroactively to tax. Other countries seek to preserve their fiscal interests in cases where taxpayers move away, by, notwithstanding the applicable tax treaty concluded with the country of immigration, extending the unlimited tax liability or stipulate an extended form of limited tax liability, to the period after immigration.[1595] These types of fiscal measures will be dealt with in more detail below. Furthermore, in cases where a source state taxation has been enshrined in the applicable bilaterally concluded tax treaty (as in art. 17, para 2 of the tax treaty Netherlands-Germany), the question rises how pension benefits, paid to foreign recipients, subject to limited tax liability, are taxed in the source state, pursuant to its domestic tax legislation.

The definitions of the different types of workers that will be considered below have been extensively set forth in chapter 1 under *scope ratione personae*. In the cross-border cases dealt with in the section below, a distinction shall be drawn between inbound and outbound cases.

7.3.1 *Migrant Worker*

7.3.1.A **Outbound**

In the outbound migration situation, the employee is resident in the national territory of the Netherlands (partly) during the accrual phase and lives in Germany during the pay-out phase. The tax treatment of contributions and the granting of tax relief, during the accrual phase, is hence akin to the tax treatment of a domestic situation, i.e. there is no

1594 Contrary to seeking to agree on a (conditional) source state taxation of pension benefits pursuant to a bilaterally concluded tax treaty as discussed in chapter 9 of this research.

1595 See for instance article 4, para 4 of the tax treaty concluded between Germany and Switzerland. This treaty provision sets out that in the case of a natural person resident in Switzerland who is not a Swiss national and who has been subject to unlimited tax liability in the Federal Republic of Germany for a total of at least five years, the Federal Republic of Germany may, notwithstanding other provisions of the treaty, tax the income originating in the Federal Republic of Germany and the assets located in the Federal Republic of Germany in the year in which the unlimited tax liability last ceased to exist and in the following five years. The taxation of such income or assets in Switzerland permissible under this treaty shall remain unaffected.

cross-border situation. There is no nexus with German income tax, levied during the accrual phase. I therefore refer to the section 7.2.

However, during the pay-out phase, the person concerned resides in Germany. It depends on the allocation of taxing rights enshrined in the applicable tax treaty where the person is liable to tax for the Dutch private pension benefits. If the taxing right on these Dutch personal pension benefits is allocated to Germany as the residence state, – pursuant to 17, para 1 of the treaty Netherlands-Germany – the migrant worker concerned will be fully liable to tax in Germany (as a resident), and the Dutch personal pension benefits will be subject to German income tax.[1596] This is not discussed any further here, but I refer to section 7.5.1.B.

If – on the contrary – the taxing right is allocated to the Netherlands as a source state (for instance pursuant to article 17, para 2 treaty Netherlands-Germany), the personal pension benefits paid out are subject to Dutch income tax – pursuant to Dutch national tax legislation. In such cases, the beneficiary residing abroad will be treated as a foreign taxable person (*buitenlands belastingplichtige*) provided that he receives domestic income, as the person concerned nor resides in the Netherlands, nor has his habitual abode in the Netherlands during the pay-out phase.[1597] The Dutch personal pension benefits shall be liable to tax as 'taxable periodical payments and benefits in kind in so far as the premiums paid for them have been taken into account as expenditure for income provisions', and constitute domestic income.[1598] Thus, this taxable proportion of the benefits depends on whether these benefits are derived from contributions which were subject to tax relief in the Netherlands (not abroad). Furthermore, he may apply to be considered as a qualifying foreign taxpayer.[1599]

Moreover, in order to ensure that annuity contracts are settled in a regular manner and to maintain the tax claim, a regulation has been included in the Wet IB 2001, as a result of which a protective assessment shall be imposed upon the emigration of the policyholder.

1596 Fully liable to tax pursuant to § 1, para 1 EStG.

1597 See article 2.1, para 1, sub b in conjunction with article 7.1 and 7.2 Wet IB 2001.

1598 Pursuant to article 7.2, para 2, under d Wet IB 2001. The surrender of periodic income benefits is also covered by this provision.

1599 Pursuant to article 7.8 Wet IB 2001. Based on this scheme, foreign taxpayers shall be eligible for the same fiscal facilitations as domestic taxpayers (such as deductions). The essence of this scheme is to give residents of the EU, EEA, Switzerland or the BES islands, 90% or more of whose income is subject to wage tax or income tax in the Netherlands, the right to the same fiscal facilitations, in accordance with EU case law. The equal treatment concerns, among other things, the right to the application of a number of personal allowances. Being a qualifying foreign taxpayer is no longer a choice (since 1 January 2015) but applies *ex officio*.

Pursuant to Dutch national legislation as it stands, upon emigration, a protective tax assessment shall be issued, pursuant to Dutch national tax legislation.[1600] In addition, revisionary interest (*revisierente*) will be included in the protective tax assessment.[1601] For the amount included in the protective tax assessment imposed, deferral of payment shall be granted for a period of ten years.[1602] In the event that no irregularities occur – for example a lump-sum payment – during the period of deferral, the protective tax assessment shall be waived after ten years.[1603] If such an irregularity does occur within these ten years, the insurer of that entitlement shall be liable, up to a maximum of the entitlements' fair value, for the tax due in respect thereof by the person entitled thereto, as well as for the corresponding revision interest due.[1604]

The tenability of these protective tax assessments – imposed upon emigration – has moved many authors to reach for their pen.[1605] This tenability will not be addressed *in extenso*, as the focus of this research concerns the law as its stands (positive law), more than how the law ought to be (normative law). Yet, it will be discussed how this has affected the law as it stands, taking the form of amendments issued over the course of the years. Moreover, merely the most recent case-law will be addressed more elaborately; preceding case-law will only be touched upon briefly.

The 'Hungary case 2001' played a central role in the drafting of the reparative legislation and the Court's 2017 ruling, as well with regard to the tenability of this legislation under tax treaties, both as regards exit levies on annuities and pensions.[1606] Pursuant to the Dutch income tax legislation applicable at the time the case was decided, amounts previously deducted for tax purposes and paid on annuities surrendered by a non-resident person were fiscally treated as negative personal obligation. With a reference to parliamentary history, the Supreme Court held that, as a starting point, the Dutch legislature considered that the deduction of premiums is granted subject to the condition that the contract in question is actually executed in the agreed manner and is not amended, surrendered, disposed of or pledged, and that, if it is, that deduction is taken into account as negative

1600 Pursuant to article 2.8, para 2 in conjunction with art. 3.136, para 1 and 2 Wet IB 2001.

1601 Pursuant to article 30i, para 1, under a in conjunction with para 2 Algemene Wet inzake Rijksbelastingen (AWR).

1602 Pursuant to art. 25, para 5 Invorderingswet 1990 (Tax Collection Act 1990).

1603 Pursuant to art. 26, para 2 Invorderingswet 1990.

1604 Pursuant to article 44b, para 1 Invorderingswet 1990.

1605 See, for instance, Pötgens; Pötgens and Kappelle; Kavelaars, 'Conserverende aanslagen en verdragen (1)'; Kavelaars, 'Conserverende aanslagen en verdragen (2)'; Pötgens.

1606 35 231 ECLI:NL:HR:2001:AD6774 (2001) (HR) Cf. Pötgens and Kool, 435.

personal obligations.[1607] The consideration that the grant of premium tax relief is conditional also plays a central role in the Supreme Court's considerations in its 2017 judgment, as will also be discussed below. In the Court's view this implies that taxation of the surrender of an annuity on the amount of the premiums paid for the acquisition of that annuity does differ substantially from taxation on (part of) the surrender sum itself. In the latter case, the surrender sum is not taxed and the receipt of that surrender sum has only the meaning that the resolutive condition under which the deduction was granted is fulfilled. As regards the application of the tax treaty provision on other income, the Court held that the negative personal obligations could not be regarded as 'items of income' as they concerned the recapture of contributions deducted in the past. Consequently, the Supreme Court found that the tax treaty did not prevent the Netherlands from including negative personal obligations into account in the event of the surrendering of an annuity on which premiums had been deducted.

In her 2009 rulings, the Supreme Court held that including the fair market value of the accrued annuity rights in the protective tax assessment, at the moment immediately preceding the surrender thereof does not materially deviate from taxation of (part of) the surrender sum itself, and hence is taxable under the tax treaty at hand.[1608] It, thus, not qualified as negative personal obligations, as it did in the Hungary decision, discussed above. A relevant difference, however, was that in this case it also concerned return on these premiums. The Supreme Court concluded that the application of art. 3.136, para 1 Wet IB 2001 in the present case should be abandoned for reasons of infringement of the provisions of the other income article of the Treaty, as the latter provision allocated the taxing right on annuity benefits exclusively to the residence state. It would consequently be contrary to the good faith required to be observed.

In her 'compartmentalisation-case' (of 14 July 2017) the Court found that in cases where the applicable tax treaty allocated the taxing right on pension and annuity benefits to the residence state, the application of the protective tax assessment needs to be compartmentalized.[1609] Hence, not all paid premiums may be taken into account when determining the protective assessment, because, according to the Supreme Court, there is no legal framework for taking negative expenditure into account. With respect to annuities, the inclusion in the protective assessment of negative emigration-related expenditure relating to an annuity claim does not conflict with good faith to be observed in the

1607 35 321 ECLI:NL:HR:2001:AD6774 (2001) (HR)with a reference to *Kamerstukken II*, Brede herwaardering I (1988/89).

1608 44 050, ECLI:NL:PHR:2009:BC4725 (2009) (HR) para 3.3.3.

1609 As of 1 January 2019, this has been regulated by art. 10a.19 Wet IB 2001.

interpretation and application of the Treaty, in so far as the expenditure in question was made in the period from 1 January 1992 to 1 January 2001 or in the period after 15 July 2009.[1610] The court held that annuity premiums paid under the operation of the legislation in force at that time cannot be considered to be of a conditional nature. Consequently, as regards annuities, the following distinction can be drawn:

- Deductible contributions paid prior to 1 January 1992 (contrary to good faith).
- Deductible contributions paid between 1 January 1992 and 1 January 2001 (considered recovery of tax deduction and, hence, not contrary to good faith).
- Deductible contributions paid between 1 January 2001 to 15 July 2009 (contrary to good faith).[1611]
- Deductible contributions paid since 15 July 2009 (not contrary to good faith).[1612]

7.3.1.B Inbound

In the inbound case, the employee is a resident of Germany (partly) during the accrual phase, and takes up residence in the Netherlands at the commencement of the pay-out phase. The tax treatment of contributions and the granting of tax relief, during the accrual phase, is hence akin to the tax treatment of a German domestic situation, i.e. there is no cross-border situation. There is no nexus with Dutch income tax, levied during the accrual phase. I therefore refer to the section 7.4.

However, during the pay-out phase, the person concerned resides in the Netherlands. It depends on the allocation of taxing rights enshrined in the applicable tax treaty where the person is liable to tax for the foreign (German) personal pension benefits. If the taxing right is allocated to the Germany as a source state (for instance pursuant to article 17, para 2 treaty Netherlands-Germany), the German pension benefits paid out are subject to German income akin to a domestic situation, see section 7.4. However, as the person concerned nor resides in Germany, nor has his habitual abode in Germany, during the pay-out phase he may be subject to limited tax liability pursuant to § 1, para 4 EStG, provided that he receives domestic income within the meaning of § 49 EStG. The principal

1610 17/01256, ECLI:NL:HR:2017:1324 (2017) (HR) This concerned the application of art. 3.136, para 2 Wet IB 2001.

1611 In the period between 1 January 2001 and 16 July 2009, the legal regime in force at the time stipulated that when the taxpayer emigrated to any other country, tax was essentially levied on (part of) the value of the annuity entitlement; it had no bearing on the premium paid for the acquisition of the annuity. Therefore, annuity premiums paid under the operation of the then prevailing provisions cannot be said to be of a contingent nature, see Dietvorst, 'Lijfrenten' 565. This also applies to annuity premiums paid before the entry into force of the *Brede Herwaardering I* on 1 January 1992, since at that time the legal provisions did not yet provide for the possibility of withdrawing deducted personal obligations in the event of non-compliance with certain conditions, so that the deduction of the annuity premiums was not conditional either.

1612 This compartmentalization has been laid down in art. 10a.19, para 1 Wet IB 2001.

condition for including these elements of income in the limited tax liability is a domestic source of income, which applies to benefits arising from *Lebensversicherungen, Rürup-Rente,* as well as *Riester-Rente.*[1613] The taxable proportion of these types of benefits depends on whether these benefits are derived from contributions which were subject to tax relief in Germany.[1614]

If – on the contrary – the taxing right on these German personal pension benefits is allocated to the Netherlands as the residence state, – pursuant to 17, para 1 of the treaty Netherlands-Germany – the migrant worker concerned will be fully liable to tax in the Netherlands (as a resident).[1615] Annuity payments arising from a foreign provision of which the object and purport corresponds to a Dutch life annuity – within the meaning of art. 3.124 ff. Wet IB 2001 – shall also be taxable.[1616] However, if and insofar as it can be assumed with regard to this foreign scheme that the premiums paid have not been deducted from the income during the period abroad, this does not constitute a taxable periodical benefit (but to that extent shall be taxable as income arising from saving and investment in BOX 3).[1617] Hence, insofar as the premiums paid abroad have been deducted from taxable income or have otherwise led to a tax reduction, the benefits from the right shall be included in the Dutch income tax. In doing so, a good match is achieved between the actual tax treatment of the personal pension scheme abroad and that in the Netherlands.

It concerns foreign personal pensions provisions that correspond in their scope to annuities that serve to compensate a pension shortfall (within the meaning of art. 3.124, para 1, under a Wet IB 2001). For this to apply, it is not required that a foreign provision corresponds exactly to such a Dutch income provision; it is sufficient that the scope thereof corresponds to an income provision. This implies that the foreign provision must aim to

---

1613 Pursuant to § 49, para 1, under 7 (*Lebensversicherungen* and *Rürup-Rente*) or 10 (*Riester-Rente*) EStG.

1614 As regards this tax relief, § 49, para 1, under 7 (*Lebensversicherungen* and *Rürup-Rente*) or 10 (*Riester-Rente*) EStG refer to § 10, para 1, nr. 2 EStG (*Sonderausgaben*).

1615 Pursuant to art. 2.1, para 1, sub a Wet IB 2001.

1616 Pursuant to art. 3.100, para 1, sub c Wet IB 2001. It should be noted that this provision applies to residents of the Netherlands (domestic taxpayers) where, in accordance with international views, the world income is included in the tax. This world income also includes payments from abroad.

1617 Because foreign provisions can involve widely divergent products, and because it will often be unclear to the Dutch tax authorities how the provision is treated for tax purposes abroad, it was decided to place the burden of proof as to whether or not tax relief has been received on the taxpayer. After all, the taxpayer is in the best position to provide information about his/her actual situation. Possibilities to meet this burden of proof are a reference to foreign tax legislation (for instance if the annuity does not meet the conditions for deduction of premiums applicable there), and the submission of a statement by the foreign tax authorities or the insurer or of relevant tax assessments, see Kamerstukken II, *26 727, nr. 7 (Belastingherziening 2001)* (1999/00) 475.

be a provision for old age.[1618] Which foreign personal pension schemes exactly fall under the scope of article 3.101, first paragraph, section c, will have to be clarified in case law and (possible) policy.

7.3.2 *Cross-border (Frontier) Worker*

A mobile citizen may work in one State (Germany), while residing in another neighbouring Member State (the Netherlands), to which he/she usually returns every day, or at least once a week (commonly referred to as 'frontier worker', or 'border commuter'). The working state, and possibly the pension state, is thus different from the residence state. However, triangular situations, where the pension institution is established in a third state, is left aside for the present research.

As no allocation rules exist as regards personal pensions (similar to Regulation 883/2004 applicable to statutory pension schemes), i.e. rules stipulating where the cross-border worker participates in an personal pension scheme, it needs to be determined where the person concerned does participate in an personal scheme. What is more, such allocation rules would run counter to the voluntary character of third pillar pensions provisions. Contrary to a migrant worker, a cross-border worker - generally - does not have the intention to leave his country of residence permanently, i.e. working across the border is of a temporary nature. Because of this temporary nature of work, it is as a rule not desirable to transfer the accrued pension capital to a pension administrator in the country where the temporary work is being performed.[1619] As addressed in Chapter 4 of this research, when it comes to personal pensions (third pillar), both in the Netherlands as well as in Germany, these pension schemes do not have its basis in the performance of work (like occupational pensions) but characteristics such as freedom, personal responsibility and flexibility prevail prevail. Hence, the cross-border worker may either continue to participate, and thus contribute, to a personal pension scheme in his state of residence, or may become a participant of the personal pension scheme in his working state. This entails a number of fiscal consequences. In the former case, it remains to be seen if, and if so to what extent, the contributions paid into the residence state-pension scheme are 'recognized'/taken into account in the working state in the calculation of the tax assessment base, provided that the person concerned is fully liable to tax in that (working) state, and the tax treaty allocates the taxing right on the remuneration to the working state. For instance, a person resident in the Netherlands works for a German employer in Germany,

1618 Kamerstukken II, *26 727, nr. 3 (Belastingherziening 2001)* (1998/99) 141. In this context, one can think of provisions such as the Individual Retirement Account (IRA).

1619 Dieleman, 'Internationale aspecten van pensioen' 503.

while paying contributions to a Dutch personal pension scheme. Provided that the person concerned earns all or almost all (90%) of his income through his German employment relationship in Germany, he will be fully liable to tax in Germany. It thus shall be assessed to what extent the Dutch personal pension contributions may be taken into account in calculating German income tax payable.

7.3.2.A Outbound

As stated above, in this situation, where the Netherlands is the residence state, the cross-border worker may opt to remain a participant in a Dutch personal pension scheme, while working abroad in Germany, or become a participant in a (foreign) German personal pension. The tax consequences of both situations will be mapped out below, while taking account of the effect of the prevailing tax treaty, concluded between the Netherlands and Germany.

Continuance of Participating in Dutch Personal Pension Scheme

Provided that, pursuant to art. 14, para 1 of the Dutch-German tax treaty, the taxing right pertaining to the remuneration is allocated to Germany as the working state, and if the person is fully liable to tax in that state, it is a matter for Germany to determine to what extent it allows the contributions paid to the (foreign) Dutch personal pension scheme to be taken into account in the calculation of the domestic tax assessment base.[1620] This will be discussed in more detail in section 7.5.2.A. In such cases, it must be determined through a comparative legal qualification of the foreign pension scheme, to what extent these foreign schemes are eligible for tax relief in Germany, but unfortunately, guidelines as to when a foreign private pension scheme qualifies as either a German *Lebensversicherung*, *Rürup-Rente* or *Riester-Rente* are lacking.[1621] If, on the contrary, the prevailing tax treaty allocates the taxing right on the remuneration to the Netherlands, it may subject the person to unlimited tax liability, and the tax treatment of the contributions is akin to a domestic situation, see section 7.2.1.

As the person resides in the Netherlands during the pay-out phase, the taxation of Dutch personal pension benefits paid out is akin to a domestic situation, provided that the Netherlands is assigned the taxing right (pursuant to art. 17, para 1 of the applicable tax treaty), see section 7.2.1. In such case, the person concerned will be fully subject to tax in the Netherlands.[1622] If, on the contrary, the prevailing tax treaty allocates the taxing right on the Dutch personal pension benefits to Germany (pursuant to art. 17, para 2 of the tax

---

1620 This cross-border worker will be fully liable to tax under the conditions of § 1, para 3 EStG.
1621 See X R 37/08 BStBI.II 2011 (628) (BFH).
1622 Pursuant to art. 2.1, para 1, under a Wet IB 2001.

treaty), the Dutch pension benefits will be taxed pursuant to German tax legislation, see section 7.5.2.A. As the person concerned nor resides in Germany, nor has his habitual abode in Germany, during the pay-out phase he may be subject to limited tax liability pursuant to § 1, para 4 EStG, provided that he receives domestic income within the meaning of § 49 EStG. The principal condition for including these elements of income in the limited tax liability is a domestic source of income, which applies to foreign benefits qualified as *Lebensversicherungen, Rürup-Rente*, as well as *Riester-Rente.*[1623] The taxable proportion of these types of benefits depends on whether these benefits are derived from contributions which were subject to tax relief in Germany.[1624]

Participating in Foreign (Dutch) Personal Pension Scheme

If the cross-border worker, resident in the Netherlands, decides to participate in the foreign (German) personal pension scheme, the tax treatment of these foreign pension contributions must be assessed. If the applicable tax treaty allocates the taxing right pertaining to the remuneration to Germany as the working state, it is a matter for that state to decide to what extent it subjects the contributions paid into a domestic personal pension scheme by a non-resident taxpayer to tax (relief), see section 7.4.

If, on the contrary, the applicable tax treaty allocates the taxing right pertaining to the remuneration to the Netherlands (pursuant to art. 14, para 2 of the treaty), and the person concerned is fully liable to tax in that state, the outbound cross-border worker may continue to pay pension contributions into the foreign (German) pension schemes. Dutch policy as regards the 'fiscal recognition' of contributions paid into foreign personal schemes has been laid down in a decree.[1625] The foreign personal pension scheme can – under certain conditions – be continued by means of premium payments. In order to be

1623 Pursuant to § 49, para 1, under 7 (*Lebensversicherungen* and *Rürup-Rente*) or 10 (*Riester-Rente*) EStG.

1624 As regards this tax relief, § 49, para 1, under 7 (*Lebensversicherungen* and *Rürup-Rente*) or 10 (*Riester-Rente*) EStG refer to § 10, para 1, nr. 2 EStG (*Sonderausgaben*).

1625 Staatssecretaris van Financiën, section 4.9. Art. 3.126, para 3 Wet IB 2001 stipulates that further rules may be laid down for the designation of foreign entities as authorised providers of annuities and other income provisions. These further rules are included in art. 14 Uitvoeringsbesluit IB 2001. Pursuant to the seventh paragraph of art. 14 (added with effect from 1 January 2010), both the designation and the withdrawal of a foreign insurer or pension fund by the Minister will be announced in an appropriate manner so that citizens who wish to conclude an annuity insurance with such a provider can be confident that they are purchasing insurance from an authorised provider, i.e. most recently, the announcement Staatssecretaris van Financiën, *Internationaal belastingrecht. Toegelaten buitenlandse aanbieders van pensioenen, lijfrenteverzekeringen, lijfrenterekeningen, lijfrentebeleggingsrechten en arbeidsongeschiktheidsverzekeringen nr. 2022-192641*. Three foreign insurers have been designated as authorised insurers. Publication will take place on the website of the Dutch Tax Authorities. If a taxable person in good faith takes out an annuity insurance policy (or wishes to place an existing annuity entitlement) with a foreign insurer or with a foreign pension fund whose name is mentioned on the published list, he may derive confidence from this that the foreign institution qualifies as an (fiscally) admitted provider.

eligible for the deduction of the premiums paid, the foreign insurance company must meet the conditions set by the Minister of Finance.[1626] The State Secretary sets the following cumulative conditions for this:

- the professional provider or executor must be subject to government supervision that is *comparable* to that under the *Wet op het financieel toezicht*;
- it must be a continuation of an annuity, *the scope of which corresponds* to a Dutch income provision as referred to in Section 3.7 of the Wet IB 2001. This only applies if the time of entering into the foreign agreement was before the domestic tax liability arose. This requires, among other things, that at least one periodic contractual premium payment must have been made before the domestic taxpayer became subject to tax in the Netherlands. It has not been further enunciated which foreign life annuities correspond to an income provision within the meaning of section 3.7 Wet IB 2001, leaving room for ambiguity.

If these conditions are met, the contributions paid into the German foreign personal pension scheme, shall be deductible for Dutch income tax purposes.[1627]

During the pay-out phase, the person concerned resides in the Netherlands. It depends on the allocation of taxing rights enshrined in the applicable tax treaty where the person is liable to tax for the foreign (German) personal pension benefits. If the taxing right is allocated to Germany as a source state (for instance pursuant to article 17, para 2 treaty Netherlands-Germany), the German pension benefits paid out are subject to German income tax, akin to a domestic situation, see section 7.4. However, as the person concerned nor resides in Germany, nor has his habitual abode in Germany, during the pay-out phase he may be subject to limited tax liability pursuant to § 1, para 4 EStG, provided that he receives domestic income within the meaning of § 49 EStG. The principal condition for including these elements of income in the limited tax liability is a domestic source of income, which applies to benefits arising from *Lebensversicherungen, Rürup-Rente*, as well as *Riester-Rente*.[1628] The taxable proportion of these types of benefits depends on whether

1626 Pursuant to art. 3.126, para 1, under c Wet IB 2001.

1627 Furthermore, the State Secretary points out the following. If an immigrant enters into an annuity agreement after the moment of immigration, the domestic income components in the preceding year are missing in the first year of domestic tax liability. In such case, he has no fiscal leeway (*jaarruimte*) for premium deduction in the year of immigration. Proper application of the law means that the immigrant, in the first year of domestic tax liability, may base the calculation of his contribution base for the annuity premium deduction on his corresponding foreign income components in the previous calendar year. Upon request, the immigrant shall provide the inspector with the information relevant for the determination of that foreign income. See Staatssecretaris van Financiën, section 4.9.

1628 Pursuant to § 49, para 1, under 7 (*Lebensversicherungen* and *Rürup-Rente*) or 10 (*Riester-Rente*) EStG.

these benefits are derived from contributions which were subject to tax relief in the Germany.[1629]

If – on the contrary – the taxing right is allocated to the Netherlands as a residence state (for instance pursuant to article 17, para 1 treaty Netherlands-Germany), the German personal pension benefits paid out are subject to Dutch income tax. For this, I refer to section 7.3.1.B.

Annuity payments arising from a foreign provision of which the object and purport corresponds to a Dutch life annuity – within the meaning of art. 3.124 ff. Wet IB 2001 – shall be taxable.[1630] Insofar as the premiums paid abroad have been deducted from taxable income or have otherwise led to a tax reduction, the benefits from the right shall be included in the Dutch income tax. In doing so, a sound level of coherence is achieved between the actual tax treatment of the personal pension scheme abroad and that in the Netherlands. However, in cases where the cross-border worker continued his participance in a German personal pension scheme, tax relief (or deductions) has been granted pursuant to the above-mentioned Dutch decree of, provided that the conditions enunciated have been met.

7.3.2.B Inbound

In the inbound situation of a cross-border worker, he is a resident of Germany, while he works in the Netherlands, returning to Germany at least once a week. He may opt to remain a participant in the German personal pension scheme, while working in the Netherlands, or become a participant in a Dutch personal pension scheme. The tax consequences of both situations will be mapped out below, while taking account of the effect of the prevailing tax treaty, concluded between the Netherlands and Germany.

Continuance of Participating in Germany Personal Pension Scheme

If, pursuant to art. 14, para 1 of the applicable tax treaty, the taxing right pertaining to the remuneration is allocated to the Netherlands, this situation is, as regards the tax treatment of contributions and benefits, similar to an outbound cross-border worker participating in a foreign personal pension scheme. However, contrary to the outbound situation, an essential difference lies in the fact that in the present inbound situation, the person concerned is not fully liable to tax in the Netherlands as he is a resident of Germany. In

1629 As regards this tax relief, § 49, para 1, under 7 (*Lebensversicherungen* and *Rürup-Rente*) or 10 (*Riester-Rente*) EStG refer to § 10, para 1, nr. 2 EStG (*Sonderausgaben*).

1630 Pursuant to art. 3.100, para 1, sub c Wet IB 2001. It should be noted that this provision applies to residents of the Netherlands (domestic taxpayers) where, in accordance with international views, the world income is included in the tax. This world income also includes payments from abroad.

such cases, the person residing abroad will be treated as a foreign taxable person (*buitenlands belastingplichtige*) provided that he receives domestic income, as the person concerned nor resides in the Netherlands, nor has his habitual abode in the Netherlands.[1631] Furthermore, he may apply to be considered a qualifying foreign taxpayer.[1632] Based on this scheme, foreign taxpayers are eligible for (largely) the same fiscal facilitations as domestic taxpayers (such as deductions).

In such case, the inbound cross-border worker may continue to pay pension contributions into the foreign (German) pension schemes. Dutch policy as regards the 'fiscal recognition' of contributions paid into foreign personal schemes has been laid down in a decree.[1633] The foreign personal pension scheme can – under certain conditions – be continued by means of premium payments, see section 6.4.1.B.I. In order to be eligible for the deduction of the premiums paid, the foreign insurance company must meet the conditions set by the Minister of Finance.[1634] If these conditions are met, the contributions paid into the German foreign personal pension scheme, shall be deductible for Dutch income tax purposes.

As regards the taxation of German personal pension benefits during the pay-out phase, the following must be noted. If the applicable tax treaty appoints the cross-border worker's residence state (Germany) as the competent state to tax (pursuant to art. 17, para 1), this is a (domestic) matter for that State where he will be fully liable to tax. See section 7.4. In this case, the residence state coincides with the pension's source state. If the taxing right is assigned (pursuant to art. 17, para 2 of the treaty) to the Netherlands as source state, German personal pension benefits will be subject to Dutch income tax. For this, I refer to section 7.3.1.B. Annuity payments arising from a foreign provision of which the object and purport corresponds to a Dutch life annuity – within the meaning of art. 3.124 ff. Wet IB 2001 – shall be taxable.[1635] Insofar as the premiums paid abroad have been deducted from taxable income or have otherwise led to a tax reduction, the benefits from the right shall be included in the Dutch income tax. In doing so, a sound level of coherence is

1631 See article 2.1, para 1, sub b in conjunction with article 7.1 and 7.2 Wet IB 2001.

1632 Pursuant to article 7.8 Wet IB 2001. Based on this scheme, foreign taxpayers are still eligible for the same fiscal facilitations as domestic taxpayers (such as deductions). The essence of this scheme is to give residents of the EU, EEA, Switzerland or the BES islands, 90% or more of whose income is subject to wage tax or income tax in the Netherlands, the right to the same fiscal facilitations, in accordance with EU case law. The equal treatment concerns, among other things, the right to the application of a number of personal allowances. Being a qualifying foreign taxpayer is no longer a choice (since 1 January 2015) but applies *ex officio*.

1633 Staatssecretaris van Financiën, section 4.9.

1634 Pursuant to art. 3.126, para 1, under c Wet IB 2001.

1635 Pursuant to art. 3.100, para 1, sub c Wet IB 2001. It should be noted that this provision applies to residents of the Netherlands (domestic taxpayers) where, in accordance with international views, the world income is included in the tax. This world income also includes payments from abroad.

achieved between the actual tax treatment of the personal pension scheme abroad and that in the Netherlands. However, in cases where the cross-border worker continued his participance in a German personal pension scheme, tax relief (of deductions) has been granted pursuant to the above-mentioned Dutch decree, provided that the conditions enunciated have been met.

Participating in Dutch Personal Pension Scheme

If the cross-border worker, resident in Germany, decides to participate in a Dutch personal pension scheme, the tax treatment of these Dutch pension schemes must be assessed. If the applicable tax treaty allocates the taxing right pertaining to the remuneration/pension to Germany (pursuant to art. 14, para 1), the tax treatment of the Dutch pension contributions and benefits is a matter for that state, where the person concerned shall be subject to unlimited tax liability. This will be discussed in more detail in section 7.5.2.A. However, if the applicable tax treaty allocates the taxing right pertaining to the remuneration to the Netherlands (pursuant to art. 14, para 1), and the person concerned is treated as fully liable to tax, these type of workers are subject to a tax treatment akin to a domestic worker, notwithstanding that he resides abroad (and hence, in principle, subject to limited tax liability). See section 7.2.1.

As regards the taxation of Dutch personal pension benefits during the pay-out phase, the following must be noted. If the applicable tax treaty appoints the cross-border worker's residence state (Germany) as the competent state to tax (pursuant to art. 17 para 1), these Dutch pension benefits will be subject to German income tax. This is not discussed any further here, but I refer to section 7.5.2.A. If – on the contrary – the taxing right is allocated to the Netherlands as a source state (pursuant to article 17, para 2 treaty Netherlands-Germany), the pension benefits paid out are subject to Dutch income tax – pursuant to Dutch national tax legislation. In such cases, the beneficiary residing abroad will be treated as a foreign taxable person (*buitenlands belastingplichtige*) provided that he receives domestic income, as the person concerned nor resides in the Netherlands, nor has his habitual abode in the Netherlands during the pay-out phase.[1636] Furthermore, he may apply to be considered qualifying foreign taxpayer.[1637] The Dutch personal pension benefits

1636 See article 2.1, para 1, sub b in conjunction with article 7.1 and 7.2 Wet IB 2001.

1637 Pursuant to article 7.8 Wet IB 2001. Based on this scheme, foreign taxpayers are still eligible for the same fiscal facilitations as domestic taxpayers (such as deductions). The essence of this scheme is to give residents of the EU, EEA, Switzerland or the BES island, 90% or more of whose income is subject to wage tax or income tax in the Netherlands, the right to the same fiscal facilitations, in accordance with EU case law. The equal treatment concerns, among other things, the right to the application of a number of personal allowances. Being a qualifying foreign taxpayer is no longer a choice (since 1 January 2015) but applies *ex officio*.

shall be liable to tax as 'taxable periodical payments and benefits in kind in so far as the premiums paid for them have been taken into account as expenditure for income provisions', and constitute domestic income.[1638] Thus, this taxable proportion of the benefits depends on whether these benefits are derived from contributions which were subject to tax relief in the Netherlands (not abroad).

7.3.3 *Posted Worker*

7.3.3.A Outbound

As part of the outbound posting case, a Dutch employee is sent abroad during the accrual phase, i.e. the Dutch parent company posts its Dutch employee to a subsidiary located in Germany. It is therefore assumed, that the employee concerned will continue to participate, and contribute, to the Dutch personal pension scheme in the sending state. The peculiarity of posting is that although the retirement benefits are based on contributions paid and (possibly) fiscally facilitated abroad (pursuant to German tax law), the paying institution is located in the state of residence of the recipient, i.e. a domestic pension institution (the Netherlands).

According to the applicable treaty provision (pursuant to art. 14, para 2), during the period of posting, the Netherlands (residence state) is allocated the taxing rights as regards the remuneration. In such as case, the tax treatment of the pension contributions is akin to a domestic Dutch situation, see section 6.3. Provided that, pursuant to art. 14, para 1 of the applicable tax treaty, the taxing right pertaining to the remuneration is allocated to the working state (Germany), and if the person is fully liable to tax in that state (for instance, as he receives at least 90% of his taxable income in the other state), it is a matter for Germany to determine to what extent it allows the contributions paid to the Dutch personal pension scheme to be taken into account in the calculation of the domestic tax assessment base. This will be discussed in more detail in section 7.5.2.A. In such cases, it must be determined through a comparative legal qualification of the foreign pension scheme, to what extent these foreign schemes are eligible for tax relief in Germany, but unfortunately, guidelines as to when a foreign private pension scheme qualifies as either a German *Lebensversicherung, Rürup-Rente* or *Riester-Rente* are lacking.

After the limited time of posting abroad, the worker will return to the Netherlands. If the taxing right is allocated to the Netherlands as residence and/or source state (for instance pursuant to article 17, para 1 treaty Netherlands-Germany), the Dutch personal pension

1638 Pursuant to article 7.2, para 2, under d Wet IB 2001. The surrender of periodic income benefits is also covered by this provision.

benefits paid out are subject to Dutch income tax. During retirement, he will be fully liable in the Netherlands.[1639] The tax treatment of the pension benefits is then akin to a domestic situation as the residence state and pension state coincide, see section 7.2.1. Hence, the taxing right cannot be assigned to Germany as this is nor the residence, nor the source state.

The main rule is that annuity payments, except for the payments arising from the net annuity, shall be fully taxable as periodic payments (against a progressive income tax rate) with the person who receives them, irrespective of whether the paid contributions have been deducted.[1640] Until 1 January 2009, the criterion was whether the premiums had been deducted as expenditure for income provision. Hence, the extent to which the Dutch contributions paid abroad during the posting period were subject to tax relief in Germany, is irrelevant in the tax treatment of the pension benefits pursuant to Dutch national tax law.

7.3.3.B Inbound

As part of the inbound posting case, a German employee is sent abroad during the accrual phase, i.e. the German parent company posts its German employee to a subsidiary located in the Netherlands. Commonly, the posted worker participates in a personal scheme in his home country Germany, as the posting in the Netherlands will be of limited duration and the worker will not fully integrate in the Dutch labour market, contrary to, for instance, a cross-border worker. Participation in the German pension scheme will thus usually be continued during the period of posting. It is therefore assumed, and this is characteristic for the case of posting, that the employee concerned will continue to participate, and contribute, to the (foreign) personal pension scheme in Germany.

According to the applicable treaty provision (pursuant to art. 14, para 2), during the period of posting, Germany (residence state) is allocated the taxing rights as regards the remuneration. In such as case, the tax treatment of the pension contributions is akin to a domestic German situation, see section 6.6. Provided that, pursuant to art. 14, para 1 of

1639 Pursuant to article 2.1, para 1, sub a Wet IB 2001.

1640 Pursuant to art. 3.100, para 1, sub b Wet IB 2001. Cf. Dietvorst, 'Lijfrenten' 558. The main rule that annuity payments are taxed regardless of whether the premiums have been deducted, led to the issue of box splitting after the introduction of the Wet IB 2001. See ibid. 556 ff. If premiums are not or not fully deducted, the corresponding (part of the) value shall be taxed in box 3. Strictly speaking, the policy will have to be divided into a box 1 and a box 3 part during the accumulation phase. To take into account the non-deducted premiums, a limited balance method was introduced in 2009, see art. 3.107a Wet B 2001. Insofar as the taxpayer has demonstrated that premiums paid were not deducted in whole or in part, no tax will be due on the benefits. The amount per year of non-deducted premiums that has not been taken into account shall not exceed €2,269.

the applicable tax treaty, the taxing right pertaining to the remuneration is allocated to the working state (the Netherlands), and if the person is fully liable to tax in that state (for instance, as he receives at least 90% of his taxable income in the other state), it is a matter for the Netherlands to determine to what extent it allows the contributions paid to the German personal pension scheme to be taken into account in the calculation of the domestic tax assessment base. As regards the tax relief of contributions (e.g. tax exemption or tax deduction) paid into the German personal pension scheme during the posting period, pursuant to the Dutch tax legislation, it must be determined to what extent these foreign paid contributions are eligible for tax relief in the Netherlands, see section 6.4.1.B.I. Dutch policy as regards the 'fiscal recognition' of contributions paid into foreign personal schemes has been laid down in a decree.[1641] The foreign personal pension scheme can – under certain conditions – be continued by means of premium payments. In order to be eligible for the deduction of the premiums paid, the foreign insurance company must meet the conditions set by the Minister of Finance.[1642] If these conditions are met, the contributions paid into the German foreign personal pension scheme, shall be deductible for Dutch income tax purposes.

After the limited time of posting to the Netherlands, the worker will return to his home country Germany. If the applicable tax treaty appoints the posted worker's resident/source state (Germany) as the competent state to tax (pursuant to art. 17, para 1), this is a (domestic) matter for that State, see section 7.5. Upon retirement, he will be (most likely) fully liable to tax in that state pursuant to the domestic legislation of that state.[1643] The tax treatment of the pension benefits is then akin to a domestic situation as the residence state and pension state coincide. Hence, the taxing right cannot be assigned to the Netherlands as this is nor the residence, nor the source state. For this, I refer to section 7.5.3.A. Benefits emerging from *Lebensversicherungen*, concluded after 31 December 2004 – which do not meet the conditions of the *Rürup-Rente* nor the *Riester-Rente* – shall be subject to *Ertragsanteilbesteuerung*, pursuant to § 22, nr 1, sentence 3, letter a, double letter bb EStG, irrespective of the extent to which the benefits emerge from – in Germany – fiscally facilitated contributions. Benefits arising from *Rürup-Rente*, will be taxed against the *Besteuerungsanteil* (2023: 83%)[1644] in so far as these benefits emerge from – in Germany – facilitated contributions, but taxed against the *Ertragsanteil*[1645] in so far as these benefits

1641 Staatssecretaris van Financiën, section 4.9.
1642 Pursuant to art. 3.126, para 1, under c Wet IB 2001.
1643 Pursuant to § 1, para 1, sentence 1 EStG.
1644 Pursuant to § 22, nr 1, sentence 3, letter a, double letter aa EStG.
1645 Pursuant to § 22, nr 1, sentence 3, letter a, double letter bb EStG.

were derived from non-facilitated contributions.[1646] This applies to benefits paid by domestic and foreign pension institutions.[1647] Benefits arising from a *Riester-Rente* will be fully subject to taxation, if the contributions paid to the provision have been fully subject to fiscal facilitation in Germany during the accrual phase, or arise from the provided statutory allowances (i.e. *Zulagen*), to the extent they do not exceed the maximum amount of §10a EStG.[1648] Benefits arising from non-facilitated contributions are taxed against the *Ertragsanteil*.[1649] Whether contributions paid into German personal pension scheme were facilitated under foreign tax legislation during the posted period in the Netherlands is thus relevant. Hence, benefits arising from non-facilitated contributions – paid during the period abroad – shall be taxed against the *Ertragsanteil*, rather than the *Besteuerungsanteil*.

7.4 The German Pension Tax System in Domestic Situations

As dealt with in chapter 4 of this research, the interpretation of the concept of third pillar pension provisions – *private Altersversorgung* – is rather open. On the contrary, individual pensions are mainly regulated by fiscal legislation, stipulating the criteria regarding their fiscal facilitation. Hence, the sections below predominantly revolve around fiscal legislation. Each income provision that cannot fulfil the conditions for the qualification of first or second pillar pension, is categorised as third pillar pension. Thus, every form of capital accumulation can be included in the third pillar, if the individual is of the opinion that the capital may serve as a retirement income provision.[1650] In this regard, strict qualification criteria are missing. Considering the decisive influence of the will of the individual as to whether or not employ the capital accumulation for retirement saving, this standpoint may be considered as a 'subjective' interpretation of the concept of third pillar pension. For third pillar pension, the free disposal of the accumulated capital

1646 Under international tax law, the tax relief, granted during the accrual phase in Germany, is considered a sufficient genuine link which allows Germany to subject the arising benefits to domestic tax. Ibid. 794 and C Richter, *Die Besteuerung grenzüberschreitender Altersversorgung in der EU* (Rechtsordnung und Steuerwesen, Dr. Otto Schmidt, Köln 2010) 352 ff. and 373.

1647 BMF, *Einkommensteuerrechtliche Behandlung von Vorsorgeaufwendungen und Altersbezügen IV C 3 - S 2221/12/10010:004 - IV C 5 - S 2345/08/0001* para 190.

1648 § 22, nr 5, sentence 1 and 2 EStG. Contributions for which the maximum amount of § 10a EStG has been exceeded, shall not be considered facilitated contributions. Neither do contributions for which the taxable person has not received any allowances or did not receive the *Sonderausgabenabzug*, see ibid., nr 134. In addition, income and capital appreciations attributable to unduly paid, and subsequently reclaimed allowances, shall be treated as non-facilitated retirement capital.

1649 § 22, nr 5, sentence, letter a in conjunction with § 22, nr 1, sentence 3, under bb EStG. With respect to *Ertragsanteilbesteuerung*, also see C Herrmann, G Heuer and A Raupach, *Einkommensteuer- und Körperschaftsteuergesetz: EStG KStG* (Dr. Otto Schmidt, Köln Aktualisierung 2018).

1650 Cf. Rürup and Myßen, 192.

prevails as a characteristic.[1651] Next to *Kapitallebensversicherungen*, also each form of accumulated capital can be considered as third pillar pension in Germany, e.g. renting out real estate or even a classic car and saving the revenues primarily with the view of saving for retirement. Rürup and Myßen also point out that the rent-free own home can serve as a provision for retirement, since the saved rents lower the costs of living.[1652] Again, the elements of free disposal prevails since the individual may decide to sell the own home prior to retirement which is at odds with the qualification as a first pillar *Basisversorgung* as a result of the prohibited transferability. Individual pensions, however, are voluntary and not necessarily related to an employment relationship. The insurance under these pension provisions may vary heavily. Many forms of individual pension are fiscally facilitated as *Riester-Rente* or *Rürup-Rente*, to allow also the low-income savers to accrue an adequate pension. To the extent that these individual provisions are fiscally facilitated, legal requirements regarding the composition of these provisions have been issued in order to safeguard that the facilitated provisions will be employed as retirement income provision.[1653] Apart from that, these provisions are subject to supervision by the insurance institutions and the financial institutions. From the above emerges a high degree of fragmentation of legislative basis respectively competence, a result of the lack of coordination between the varying sorts of pension provisions. The domestic coordination of the different pension provisions is, after all, not governed by uniform standards.[1654]

7.4.1 The Tax Treatment of Individual Pensions (Private Altersversorgung)

Prior to the implementation of the *Altersvermögensgesetz (AVmG)* on 1. January 2002, there was no German tax framework particularly tailored to the taxation of the *private Altersvorsorge*.[1655] However, contributions to capital forming life insurances[1656] and to private additional (statutory) pension insurances[1657] could be taken into account as tax-deductible expenses, i.e. *Vorsorgeaufwendungen*.[1658] Life insurance benefits paid out were – and contracts concluded prior to 1 January 2005 are still eligible for this – principally

1651 Cf. Ibid. 192.

1652 Birk and Wernsmann, 192.

1653 Cf. Ruland, 22.

1654 Similarly ibid. 28.

1655 Gesetz zur Reform der gesetzlichen Rentenversicherung und zur Förderung eines kapitalgedeckten Altersvorsorgevermögens (Altersvermögensgesetz – AVmG).

1656 In German commonly referred to as *kapitalbildende Lebensversicherung*. Since then considered as the predominant form of individual pension provision. Cf. Cramer, Förster and Ruland, 249 ff.

1657 In German commonly referred to as *Zusatzrentenversicherung*.

1658 Pursuant to the former § 10, para 3 EStG. Translated freely as 'pension contributions'.

free of tax after a contractual duration of at least twelve years.[1659] Benefits arising from additional pension insurances were taxable merely to the amount of the *Ertragsanteil*, provided that the insurance qualified as a life insurance[1660].[1661]

After the decree of the *Altersvermögensgesetz*, the tax treatment of capital funded pension provisions was revised. Building up a retirement income by means of individual pensions was considered inevitable, in order to secure an adequate income after retirement. Moreover, in order to enable the individual to save more for retirement, the accrual of pension through individual pensions is fiscally facilitated by means of tax allowances and the so-called *Sonderausgabenabzug*.[1662] These measures inflate the net income of the employee, and therefore enable him to potentially save more for retirement. In the context of this objective, new forms of pension products developed, i.e. *Riester-Rente*[1663] and the *Rürup-Rente*[1664], which, typically, are more aimed at the provision of an income after retirement. As a result of these revised tax framework regarding individual pensions, par. 5 was added § 22 EStG, under which provision pension benefits are taxed as other income, in accordance with the principle of deferred taxation.

It may be asked to what extent third pillar pension provisions are likewise considered as retirement income from a fiscal perspective, i.e. to what extent the accrual of these provision is fiscally facilitated. For example, for the purposes of the own home serving as a retirement provision, the fiscal facilitation comprises the so-called *Altersvorsorge-Eigenheimbetrag*.[1665] The relation between fiscal facilitation and saving for retirement

---

1659 Pursuant to § 20, para 1, under 6 EStG.

1660 I.e. *Leibrenten*.

1661 Pursuant to § 22, para 1, sentence 3 EStG. As a result of the entry into force of the *Alterseinkünftegesetz*, the percentages of the *Ertragsanteil* have been lowered considerably. For instance, with respect to a beneficiary who has reached the age of 65 at the beginning of the pay-out phase, the percentage decreased from 27% to 18%. This measure ought to take into account the fact that contributions to *Altverträge* or unqualified contracts are not, or rather limited, facilitated by the *Sonderausgabenabzug*, and, thus, largely paid out of taxed income, as a consequence of the transition to deferred taxation of individual retirement provisions. See T Eckerle, 'Altersvorsorge und Lebensversicherung' in HJ Feyerabend (ed.), *Besteuerung privater Kapitalanlagen* (C.H. Beck, München 2009) 378.

1662 Translated freely as 'deduction of special costs'.

1663 Implemented on 26 June 2001 by Gesetz zur Reform der gesetzlichen Rentenversicherung und zur Förderung eines kapitalgedeckten Altersvorsorgevermögens (Altersvermögensgesetz – AVmG).

1664 Implemented on 5 July 2004 by Gesetz zur Neuordnung der einkommensteuerrechtlichen Behandlung von Altersvorsorgeaufwendungen und Altersbezügen (Alterseinkünftegesetz – AltEinkG).

1665 Pursuant to §92a, para 1, under 1 EStG which states: *Der Zulageberechtigte kann das in einem Altersvorsorgevertrag gebildete und nach § 10a oder nach diesem Abschnitt geförderte Kapital in vollem Umfang oder, wenn das verbleibende geförderte Restkapital mindestens 3 000 Euro beträgt, teilweise wie folgt verwenden (Altersvorsorge-Eigenheimbetrag): bis zum Beginn der Auszahlungsphase unmittelbar für die Anschaffung oder Herstellung einer Wohnung oder zur Tilgung eines zu diesem Zweck aufgenommenen Darlehens, wenn das dafür entnommene Kapital mindestens 3 000 Euro beträgt.*

shows a strong synergy; the more it is ensured that the capital accumulation will be employed for the use of retirement provision, the more the contributions to the accumulation of capital are fiscally facilitated.[1666] In most cases, this fiscal facilitation comprises the exemption of contributions, and subsequently the taxation of disbursed benefits, i.e. deferred taxation,[1667] in order to facilitate the pension saver to save for retirement by increasing his income margin.

The taxation of benefits arising from individual retirement provisions during the pay-out phase, is characterised by the gradual transition to deferred taxation.[1668] If the contributions have been paid from untaxed income, the future benefits shall be fully subject to taxation, i.e. primary condition for the *Sonderausgabenabzug* is that the contributions must be financed out of taxed income taxed on an individual level.[1669] Rürup and Myßen point out that deferred taxation does not automatically lead to an actual taxation of the benefits in the pay-out phase, although the used term may suggest the contrary.[1670] This depends on the decisive facts and circumstances of each case, e.g. is the taxable income lower than the *Grundfreibetrag*[1671]

7.4.1.A *Riester-Rente*

The *Riester-Rente* provides, next to the *Rürup-Rente*, for the second significant possibility of a funded individual retirement provision, as part of supplementary pensions. The *Riester-Rente* was implemented through the *Altersvermögensgesetz (AVmG)*, in force since 1 January 2002, and was revised by the *Alterseinkünftegesetz* in 2005. Due to the latter act, the *Riester-Rente* has been subject to considerable bureaucratic simplifications.[1672] It may

1666 Rürup and Myßen, 193.

1667 In German: *nachgelagerte Besteuerung*.

1668 Cf. Birk and Wernsmann, 262 and Scholz, 76.

1669 § 10, para 2, nr 1 EStG.

1670 Rürup and Myßen, 193.

1671 Translated freely as tax-free allowance.

1672 From the outset, the *Riester-Rente* has repeatedly been subject to considerable criticism, mostly with respect to the complex procedural rules, and related administrative obligations, see A Risthaus, 'Steuerliche Fördermöglichkeiten für eine zusätzliche private Altersvorsorge nach dem Altersvermögensgesetz (AVmG)' 24 DB 1269. In principle, each entitled person is obliged to submit a request, in order to receive the allowances, by the end of the second calendar year following the contribution year, pursuant to § 89, para 1, sentence 1 EStG. This request has even to be submitted in cases where it is proven that the *Sonderausgabenabzug* is more favourable to the taxable person than the allowances. The implementation of the *Alterseinkünftegesetz* intended to simplify the administrative hassle, for instance, through the introduction of the one-off application procedure. Under this procedure, the person entitled to the allowance may mandate his pension provider in writing to apply for the allowance for each contribution year, see § 10a, para 1a, sentence 1 EStG. The entitled person is then still obliged to inform the provider, without delay, of any change in personal circumstances which may lead to a reduction or the withdrawal of the entitlement to the allowance, see § 89, para 1, sentence 5 EStG. The pension provider will transmit the data he received from the entitled person to the *German Rentenversicherung Bund*. This institution shall

be argued that the bureaucratic simplifications have led to a significant increase in the public acceptance of the *Riester-Rente* as a retirement provision.[1673] However, the stunted increase of requested *Zulagen*[1674] indicates that this form of fiscal facilitation has not reached its objective in reaching a wide population. With respect to the complexity of the system of these allowances, it may be claimed that tax relief mechanisms should be simple to understand to reach wide populations.[1675]

Initially, the introduction of the *Riester-Rente* was aimed at putting the retirement provision on a broader financial footing, and, compensating the increasingly diminishing level of care of the *gesetzlichen Rentenversicherung* in the future. Furthermore, the *Riester-Rente* aimed to enable low-income earners to build a fiscally facilitated individual retirement provision.[1676] The fiscal facilitation of this provision comprises allowances granted publicly, and the *Sonderausgabenabzug*, which will be below. This fiscal facilitation seeks to efficiently foster the accrual of supplementary pensions. The most important criteria are laid down in §10a EStG and section XI EStG and AltzertG.

7.4.1.A.I Fiscal facilitation during the accrual phase

Eligible Persons

The circle of beneficiary persons comprises all taxable persons affected by the entry into force of the *Altersvermögensgesetz, Altersvermögensergänzungsgesetz* or *Versorgungsänderungsgesetz.* This comprises all persons affected by the reduction of the

---

determine, on the basis of the data collected or transmitted to it, whether, and to what extent an entitlement to the allowances exists, see § 90, para 1, sentence 1 EStG. In addition, the institution arranges the payment of the allowance to the pension provider in favour of the entitled person, after which the provider shall credit the received allowances immediately to the retirement arrangement of the entitled person, see § 90, para 2, sentence 1 and 3 EStG. In order to ensure the fiscal facilitation of the contributions, the taxable persons must prove the amount of paid pension contributions per contribution year, by means of a certificate, issued by the provider according to an official form, see § 10a, para 5, sentence 1 EStG. Under the *Betriebsrentenstärkungsgesetz* – in force as of 1 January 2018 – the administrative hassle is further reduced, i.e. for certain groups of insured persons, the payroll office shall submit their payroll data to the *Zentralen Zulagenstelle für Altersvermögen*, in order to calculate the allowance.

1673 For instance, the number of concluded *Riester*-provisions almost doubled between 2005 and 2007. See Bundesministerium für Arbeit und Soziales, *Statistik zur privaten Altersvorsorge (Riester-Rente)* (2018).

1674 Bundesministerium der Finanzen, 'Statistische Auswertungen zur Riester-Förderung' 2018) <https://www.bundesfinanzministerium.de/Content/DE/Standardartikel/Themen/Steuern/Weitere_Steuerthemen/Altersvorsorge/2018-02-07-Statistische-Auswertungen-Riester-Foerderung-2018.html?pk_campaign=Newsletter-02.2018&pk_kwd=07.02.2018_Statistische+Auswertungen+zur+Riester-F%C3%B6rderung> accessed 10 August 2018.

1675 Cf. Wernsmann, 786. As Wernsmann claimed, tax relief mechanisms should be simple and easy to understand, in order to reach their objective, i.e. influencing taxable persons' behaviour. See R Wernsmann, *Verhaltenslenkung in einem rationalen Steuersystem* (Mohr Siebeck, Heidelberg 2005) 140.

1676 Kirchhof, Söhn and Mellinghof.

level of benefits under the *gesetzlichen Rentenversicherung*, or affected in economic sense due to the entry into force of these three acts. It follows from this that the *Riester-Rente* is aimed at supplementing the *gesetzlichen Rentenversicherung* as a retirement provision in saving for an old-age income. In accordance with the underlying objective of the *Rieser-Rente*, – i.e. compensating the increasingly diminishing level of care of the *gesetzlichen Rentenversicherung* – persons eligible for the deduction of contributions as *Sonderausgaben*, are mandatory insured domestic persons in the *gesetzlichen Rentenversicherung* or recipients of domestic salaries in accordance with the Federal Salary Act or Landes Salary Act.[1677] The reference to the obligatory insurance under the *gesetzlichen Rentenversicherung* illustrates the interaction between tax legislation and social security law.[1678]

Regarding the aforementioned eligibility criteria, most taxable persons will be eligible to the deduction of special expenses. Furthermore, these persons are entitled to the so-called *Altersvorsorgezulage*[1679], even if they fulfil the eligibility conditions merely during a part of the calendar year.[1680] It is therefore sufficient when the taxable person is obligatory insured for the *gesetzlichen Rentenversicherung* during one day. A migrant worker, living and working in Germany, who receives a domestic income, is therefore eligible for the *Zulagen* and *Sonderausgabenabzug* of the *Riester*-contributions.[1681]

Noteworthy from a cross-border perspective is that persons insured mandatory under a foreign statutory pension scheme (i.e. social security pension) shall be set equal, under conditions, to persons insured mandatory under the domestic *gesetzlichen Rentenversicherung*, or *Alterssicherung der Landwirte* for the application of §10a EStG (*Sonderausgaben*).[1682] However, for this equation, some conditions need to be fulfilled. The foreign mandatory insurance needs to be comparable to the mandatory insurance under

1677 § 10a, para 1, sentence 1 EStG. Often significantly affected by the retrenchment of the benefits under the *gesetzlichen Rentenversicherung* as well, are spouses, in particular in cases of single earners, or spouses in marginal employments, and, hence, not mandatory insured under the *gesetzlichen Rentenversicherung*. Indirectly, the spouse is deprived from his surviving dependants provision under the *gesetzlichen Rentenversicherung*. Therefore, § 79, sentence 2 EStG, under certain conditions, provides an indirect eligibility for this spouse. It seems that this does not apply to unmarried life partners. This indirect eligibility entitles the spouse to the *Sonderausgabenabzug* (§ 10a EStG) and *Altersvorsorgezulage* (§ 84 and § 85 EStG). See also F Welker, *Das Altersvermögensgesetz und seine konsequenzen für die betriebliche Altersversorgung: arbeits-, steuer- und aufsichtsrechtliche Perspektiven* (Deutscher Universitäts-Verlag, Wiesbaden 2005), 54 ff. and M Myßen and others, *Handbuch Zulagenförderung: steuerlich begünstigte Altersvorsorge* (C.F. Müller, Heidelberg 2006).

1678 For an elaboration on compulsorily insured persons for the *gesetzlichen Rentenversicherung*, See Welker, 49 ff.

1679 Translated freely as 'pension-savings allowance'.

1680 § 10a, para 1, in conjunction with § 79, sentence 1 EStG. Cf. Myßen and others.

1681 Pursuant to § 10a, para 1, sentence 1 EStG.

1682 § 10a, para 6 EStG.

the *gesetzlichen Rentenversicherung.*[1683] In addition, the mandatory insurance needs to be established prior to 1 January 2010.[1684]

However, if the person entitled to the allowance (*Zulage*) relocates his residence or habitual abode outside the Member States of the European Union and the States to which the Agreement on the European Economic Area (EEA Agreement) applies, or if, notwithstanding a residence or habitual abode in one of these States, the person entitled to the allowance is considered to be resident outside the territory of these States under a double taxation convention with a third State, and either there is no allowance entitlement or the contract is in the disbursement phase, then § 93 and § 94 shall apply.[1685] Pursuant to the latter two provisions, the allowances must be repaid. Upon request of the person entitled to the allowance, this repayment may be deferred until the commencement of the pay-out phase.[1686] If the former recipient of the allowance transfers his or her exclusive residence or habitual abode to a Member State of the European Union or a state to which the Agreement on the European Economic Area (EEA Agreement) applies, or the person formerly entitled to the allowance is entitled to it again, the amount to be repaid and the deferral interest already accrued shall be waived by the central body.[1687]

Alternatively, some taxable persons are excluded of the beneficiary group of the *Sonderausgabenabzug*, such as persons mandatorily insured under the *berufsständischen Versorgungswerke* (e.g. attorneys at law or doctors), persons insured voluntarily under the *gesetzlichen Rentenversicherung*, self-employed to the extent they are not compulsorily insured, or marginal employed without compulsory insurance under the *gesetzlichen Rentenversicherung.*[1688] These persons are ineligible since they have not been affected by the retrenchment of the *gesetzlichen Rentenversicherung*, or affected in economic sense due to the entry into force of the *Versorgungsänderungsgesetz.* Contrarily, including these persons in the beneficiary group would be at odds with the consideration underlying the fiscal facilitation of *Riester*-contributions, i.e. compensating the pension gaps as a consequence of the implementation of the *Altersvermögensgesetz, Altersvermögensergänzungsgesetz* or *Versorgungsänderungsgesetz 2001.*

1683 § 10a, para 6, sentence 1, nr 1 EStG.

1684 § 10a, para 6, sentence 1, nr 2 EStG.

1685 See § 95, para 1, sentence 1, nr 1 and 2 EStG.

1686 Pursuant to § 95, para 2 EStG.

1687 Pursuant to § 95, para 3 EStG. See also BMF, *Steuerliche Förderung der privaten Altersvorsorge IV C 3 - S 2015/17/10001:005* (21 December 2017) para 239.

1688 Welker, 53 and Birk and Wernsmann, 257.

Until 8 April 2010, the eligibility for the *Sonderausgabenabzug* of *Riester*-contributions had been made conditional upon unlimited tax liability.[1689] This would mean that a cross-border worker, working in Germany, but having his residence abroad, would not be eligible for the *Sonderausgabenabzug* of *Riester*-contributions, and the related *Zulagen*. The CJEU ruled that the concerning provisions denied cross-border workers and their spouses the right to the allowances, unless they were fully liable to tax in that Member State, and considered this requirement in breach of the European freedoms of movement.[1690] This forced the German legislator to revise the eligibility criteria for the fiscal facilitation of the *Riester-Rente*. Therefore, the circle of eligible person has been extended to mandatory insured domestic persons in the *gesetzlichen Rentenversicherung* or recipients of domestic salaries in accordance with the Federal Salary Act or Landes Salary Act.[1691] A migrant worker, living and working in Germany, who receives a domestic income, is therefore eligible for the *Zulagen* and *Sonderausgabenabzug* of the *Riester*-contributions.[1692] Furthermore, a cross-border worker receiving a domestic income is eligible, as well in cases where he is insured mandatory under the statutory pension scheme of his residence state, provided that the foreign mandatory insurance is comparable to the mandatory insurance under the *gesetzlichen Rentenversicherung* and if this compulsory membership was established before January 1, 2010.[1693] Thus, if the compulsory membership in the foreign statutory insurance scheme has been established after January 1, 2010, the cross-border worker shall be denied these tax allowances. Hence, the Commission sent Germany a letter of formal notice – pursuant to art. 258 TFEU – on 19 May 2022, requesting it to amend its tax legislation on voluntary pension savings contracts, i.e. Riester-Rente.[1694] The disputed German legislation seems to constitute a restriction on the free movement of workers.

1689 This condition has been repealed pursuant to the entry into force of Gesetz zur Umsetzung steuerlicher EU-Vorgaben sowie zur Änderung steuerlicher Vorschriften (EUStVUG).

1690 *Commission vs. Germany* para 69.

1691 Revised pursuant to Gesetz zur Umsetzung steuerlicher EU-Vorgaben sowie zur Änderung steuerlicher Vorschriften (EUStVUG).

1692 Pursuant to § 10a, para 1, sentence 1 EStG.

1693 § 10a, para 6 EStG.

1694 European Commission, 'Provisions on Riester-Rente (voluntary pension) contracts concluded after 01/01/2010 allegedly breaching the free movement of workers Art. 45 TFEU by Germany (INFR(2022)4014)' 19 May 2022) <https://ec.europa.eu/atwork/applying-eu-law/infringements proceedings/infringement_decisions/index.cfm?lang_code=EN&typeOfSearch=false&active_only=0&noncom=0&r_dossier=INFR%282022%294014&decision_date_from=&decision_date_to=&title=&submit=Search> accessed 5 August 2022.

Eligible Retirement Provisions

Pursuant to §10a EStG, merely particular retirement provisions are eligible for *Sonderausgabenabzug.*[1695] These conditions to be met are laid down in the *Altersvorsorgeverträge-Zertifizierungsgesetz.*[1696] Firstly, the retirement provision must provide for a lifelong, and gender independent retirement provision, which, in principle, may not be paid prior the reaching the age of 62.[1697] This retirement age of 62 applies only to pension arrangements concluded after 31 December 2011. Regarding pension arrangements concluded prior to 1 January 2012, a retirement age of 60 applies.[1698] The other conditions remain unaltered. Furthermore, the provider must guarantee that at the start of the pay-out phase, at least the paid pension contributions are available, and these will be used for the disbursement of the benefits.[1699] Also regarding the pay-out options, particular conditions must be met. The pension arrangement must ensure monthly payments for the benefit of the contracting party, in principle, either in the form of a lifelong annuity, or in the form of instalment payments as part of a pay-out schedule with an ensuing partial annuity[1700] at the latest at the age of 85.[1701] Otherwise, the concluded retirement contract may guarantee a lifelong reduction of the monthly users fee for a cooperative housing, occupied by the contracting party or a temporarily limited reduction followed by a partial annuity at the latest at the age of 85.[1702] Furthermore, the benefits ought to be maintained or increased during the entire pay-out phase. As an alternative to the monthly payments, up to 30% of the capital – available at the start of the pay-out phase[1703] – may be disbursed outside the monthly payments.[1704] Lastly, the retirement arrangement shall grant the beneficiary, until the beginning of the pay-out phase, the entitlement to suspend the retirement arrangement, terminate the arrangement and transfer the capital accrued to another retirement arrangement in his name, or, the payment of the capital accrued for the use of the capital for the *Wohn-Riester*, pursuant to §92a EStG.[1705]

1695 Pursuant to §10a in conjunction with § 80 and § 82 EStG.

1696 § 1, para 1 AltZertG. For an elaborate discussion of these conditions, See Hügelschäffer and others, and Kirchhof, Söhn and Mellinghof.

1697 § 1, para 1, nr 2 AltZertG and BMF, *Steuerliche Förderung der betrieblichen Altersversorgung IV C 5 - S 2333/17/10002* para 68. This includes the recently introduced *reine Beitragszusage*, laid down in §§21 ff. BetrAVG, see ibid. para 68.

1698 Pursuant to the transitory provision, laid down in § 14, para 2 EStG.

1699 § 1, para 1, nr 3 AltZertG.

1700 I.e. *Teilkapitalverrentung.*

1701 § 1, para 1, under 4, sub a AltZertG.

1702 § 1, para 1, under 4, sub b AltZertG.

1703 The capital of up to 30% of the available capital from the contract must be withdrawn at the beginning of the pay-out phase, see BMF, *Steuerliche Förderung der privaten Altersvorsorge IV C 3 - S 2015/17/10001:005* para 210.

1704 § 1, para 1, under 4, sub a AltZertG. This capital payment will be taxed pursuant to § 22, nr 5 EStG.

1705 § 1, para 1, under 10 AltZertG.

Providers of Facilitated Riester-provisions

Further conditions have been made with respect to the providers of fiscally facilitated retirement provision as well.[1706] The *Altersvorsorgeverträge-Zertifizierungsgesetz* stipulates the conditions the providers must fulfil.[1707] The most important eligible institutions are domestic life insurance companies[1708], credit institutions[1709] and investment companies[1710].[1711] These certificates, under the *Altersvorsorgeverträge-Zertifizierungsgesetz*, are issued by the *Bundeszentralamt für Steuern*.[1712] The aforementioned institutions may, under certain conditions, also be domiciled in another member state of the European Economic Area, while their eligibility is continued.[1713] It should be noted that this certification only concerns the eligibility for facilitation of the retirement arrangement in accordance with the legal regulations, and does not cover the assessment of profitability or advantageousness of the pension arrangement.[1714]

Allowances and Facilitated Contributions

If the aforementioned conditions are met, the *Riester-Rente* will be subject to fiscal facilitation. Subject to fiscal facilitation shall be, contributions and capital repayments[1715], which the entitled person[1716] pays until the commencement of the pay-out phase, for the benefits of a retirement arrangement in his name, certified in accordance with § 5 AltZertG.[1717] This precise extent of the fiscal facilitation depends on the purpose of the individual allowance, the minimum contribution and the basic allowance.[1718] Firstly, each person directly or indirectly eligible to an allowance, shall, upon request[1719], receive a basic allowance (i.e. *Grundzulage*) for his pension contributions paid in the past contribution

1706 Laid down in *Altersvorsorgeverträge-Zertifizierungsgesetz*.

1707 Pursuant to § 1, para 2 AltZertG.

1708 I.e. *Lebensversicherungsunternehmen*, that must be authorised pursuant to the *Versicherungsaufsichtsgesetz* (VAG).

1709 I.e. *Kreditinstitute*, that must be authorised to operate the deposit business pursuant to § 1, para 1, sentence 2, n. 1 *Kreditwesengesetz* (KWG).

1710 I.e. *Kapitalanlagegesellschaften*.

1711 § 1, para 2 AltZertG.

1712 Pursuant to § 3, para 1 AltZertG. Translated freely as 'Federal Central Tax Office'.

1713 § 1, para 2, nr 2 AltZertG.

1714 See § 5 AltZertG. Cf. Birk and Wernsmann, 258.

1715 The deductibility of capital repayments has been included in § 82, para 1, sentence 1 EStG, pursuant to article 1, nr 6, lit a Gesetz zur verbesserten Einbeziehung der selbstgenutzten Wohnimmobilie in die geförderte Altersvorsorge (Eigenheimrentengesetz – EigRentG).

1716 The entitled persons are stipulated in § 79 EStG.

1717 § 82, para 1 EStG.

1718 Cf. Birk and Wernsmann, 258.

1719 The person entitled to the allowances must submit the application to the provider of his retirement arrangement in accordance with the officially prescribed form, prior to the end of the second calendar year following the contribution year. The further formal requirements regarding the request are laid down in § 89 EStG.

year.[1720] The entitlement to this allowance arises at the end of the calendar year in which the pension contributions have been paid.[1721] Depending on the pension contributions paid, an allowance is paid consisting of a basic allowance (i.e. *Grundzulage* ex. § 84) and a child allowance (*Kinderzulage* ex. § 185).[1722] Since 2018, the basic allowance will be €175 on an annual basis.[1723] This allowance will be increased once by €200, if the entitled persons – referred to in § 79, sentence 1 EStG – has not reached the age of 25 at the beginning of the contribution year, i.e. the so-called career starter bonus.[1724] In addition to the basis allowance, the entitled person will receive a child allowance of €185 annually, for each child for whom he will receive *Kindergeld*[1725].[1726] This child allowance shall be increased to €300, if the child was born after 31 December 2007.[1727] For instance, a person with two children, paying contributions to a *Riester-Rente* for 20 years, receives state allowances amounting to €15,500, which provides a considerable financial buffer at retirement, and, in turn, increasing the disposable income available after retirement.[1728] It should be stressed that to ensure full fiscal facilitation, the allowance must, at all times, be requested.[1729] Over time, the height of the allowances has changed significantly.[1730]

1720 BMF, *Steuerliche Förderung der privaten Altersvorsorge IV C 3 - S 2015/17/10001:005* para 46.

1721 § 88 EStG.

1722 Pursuant to § 83 EStG.

1723 This amount has been raised in order to stimulate the *Riester-Rente*, pursuant to Gesetz zur Stärkung der betrieblichen Altersversorgung und zur Änderung anderer Gesetze (Betriebsrentenstärkungsgesetz). See also BMF, *Steuerliche Förderung der privaten Altersvorsorge IV C 3 - S 2015/17/10001:005* para 46. Regarding the entitlement to this allowance of direct and indirect entitlements of spouses, See Birk and Wernsmann, 259.

1724 Pursuant to § 84, sentence 2 EStG. This constitutes the so-called *Berufseinsteiger-Bonus*, aimed at *encouraging* the conclusion of a *Riester*-provision at the earliest possible stage. A separate request is not required for this increase, see BMF, *Steuerliche Förderung der privaten Altersvorsorge IV C 3 - S 2015/17/10001:005* para 47.

1725 Translated freely as 'child benefits'.

1726 § 85, para 1, sentence 1 EStG.

1727 § 85, para 2, sentence 1 EStG.

1728 Bundesministerium der Finanzen, 'Riester-Rente wird noch attraktiver: Änderungen durch das Betriebsrentenstärkungsgesetz auch bei der privaten Altersvorsorge' 2017) <https://www.bundesfinanzministerium.de/Content/DE/Standardartikel/Themen/Steuern/Weitere_Steuerthemen/Altersvorsorge/2017-08-21-Riester-Rente-wird-noch-attraktiver.html> accessed 31 July 2018.

1729 BMF, *Steuerliche Förderung der privaten Altersvorsorge IV C 3 - S 2015/17/10001:005* para 104.

1730 This overview is derived partly from Welker, 71 ff. and Rürup and Myßen, 221.

Grundzulage		Kinderzulage	
2002-2003	€38	2002-2003	€46
2004-2005	€76	2004-2005	€92
2006-2007	€114	2006-2007	€138
Since 2008	€154	Since 2008	€185
Since 2018	€175		

In order to be fully entitled to the allowances, the taxable person must pay a minimum contribution to the *Riester-Rente*.[1731] This requirement intends to guarantee that the statutory allowances constitute a facilitation of the individual old-age provision, rather than a substitute of the *gesetzlichen Rentenversicherung*.[1732] If the entitled person does not pay the minimum contribution amount, the allowance will be reduced.[1733] The amount of the minimum contribution level initially depends on the obtained contributory income.[1734] The minimum contribution level is then annually set on 4% of the obtained contributory income[1735], during the calendar year preceding the current calendar year, however, not exceeding the maximum amount of €2,100 annually.[1736] This maximum amount includes both the *Riester*-contributions, as well as the *Zulagen*, and has changed considerably over the years.

Year	Maximum amount
2002-2003	€525
2004-2005	€1,050
2006-2007	€1,575
Since 2008	€2,100

Subsequently, this amount is reduced by the allowances, granted pursuant to § 84 and § 85 EStG.[1737] The remaining amount constitutes the required *Mindesteigenbeitrag*. Furthermore, the threshold amount (*Sockelbetrag*) – since 2005 €60 annually – must be taken into

1731 § 10a, para 1, sentence 1 EStG.

1732 Risthaus. See also Birk and Wernsmann, 259 and Wernsmann, 'Die steuerliche Förderung der zusätzlichen kapitalgedeckten Altersvorsorge' 790.

1733 § 86, para 1, sentence 1 EStG.

1734 § 86, para 1, sentence 2, nr 1, 2, 3 and 4 EStG. For an elaboration on the *Beitragspflichtige Einnahmen*, See BMF, *Steuerliche Förderung der privaten Altersvorsorge IV C 3 - S 2015/17/10001:005* para 71 ff.

1735 In this context, the term *beitragspflichtige Einnahmen* (i.e. contributory income) refers to that proportion of the earned income that does not exceed the applicable *Beitragsbemessungsgrenze* (i.e. contribution assessment limit), see ibid. para 71.

1736 § 86, para 1, sentence 2 EStG in conjunction with § 10a, para 1, sentence 1 EStG.

1737 § 86, para 1, sentence 2 EStG.

account.[1738] If the calculated *Mindesteigenbeitrag* is less that €60, the *Sockelbetrag* of €60 must be paid as minimum contribution.[1739] Further, if less than the *Mindesteigenbeitrag* and *Sockelbetrag* has been paid to the retirement arrangement, the allowances will be reduced accordingly.[1740] This reduction is determined by the ratio of the pension contributions to the *Mindesteigenbeitrag*. However, it is to be noted, that also contributions exceeding this amount *Mindesteigenbeitrag*, still qualify as pension contributions, eligible for tax relief.[1741]

However, if the pension agreement provides for a contractual limitation to a fixed maximum amount (e.g. the amount pursuant to § 10a EStG or the *Mindesteigenbeitrag* under § 86 EStG plus the entitlement to an allowance), payments in excess of this amount are considered amounts not owed under civil law, in respect of which the investor is entitled to a refund from the provider. These amounts do not generally constitute pension contributions within the meaning of § 82, para 1 EStG.[1742] The *Berufseinsteiger-Bonus*[1743] will also be included in this reduction for which there is no possibility of catching up in following contribution years.[1744] If the taxable person paid more contributions than the *Mindesteigenbetrag*, this has no fiscal consequences.[1745]

The calculated allowances will be directly remitted to his retirement provision.[1746] These raise the contributions for the pension provision and, in effect, the future benefits. The amount of *Mindesteigenbeitrag*, has been subject to considerable change as well. In previous years, this amount of minimum contribution was differentiated on the basis of the question whether, and to what extent a child allowance had been granted.[1747]

1738 § 86, para 1, sentence 4 EStG.

1739 § 86, para 1, sentence 5 EStG.

1740 § 86, para 1, sentence 6 EStG. For several elaborate examples on calculating the *Mindesteigenbeitrag* and *Sockelbetrag* is refer to BMF, *Steuerliche Förderung der privaten Altersvorsorge IV C 3 - S 2015/17/10001:005* para 67 ff.

1741 Ibid. para 43.

1742 Ibid. para 44.

1743 Pursuant to § 84, sentence 2 EStG.

1744 BMF, *Steuerliche Förderung der privaten Altersvorsorge IV C 3 - S 2015/17/10001:005* para 47.

1745 § 10a, para 1, sentence 1 EStG.

1746 Cf. Myßen and others, and Förster and Rechtenwald.

1747 Welker, 74.

Year	*Mindesteigenbeitrag*
2002-2004	€45 for allowance beneficiaries not receiving a *Kinderzulage*
	€38 for allowance beneficiaries receiving the *Kinderzulage* for 1 child
	€30 for allowance beneficiaries receiving the *Kinderzulage* for 2 or more children
Since 2005	€60 for all allowance beneficiaries, irrespective of entitlements to *Kinderzulage*[*]

[*] § 86, para 1, sentence 4 EStG.

In addition to the aforementioned allowances, the fiscal facilitation of the *Riester-Rente* offers the possibility for taxable persons – who fall under the group of beneficiary persons – to deduct their pension contributions, paid during the assessment period, as *Sonderausgaben*.[1748] In calculating the amount of *Sonderausgaben*, the taxable persons' allowances (*Grundzulage* and *Kinderzulage*) are to be incorporated.[1749]

Most Favourable Tax Treatment

The fiscal facilitation of *Sonderausgabenabzug* shall merely apply, if this is more advantageous for the taxable person than the entitlement to the allowances, i.e. the so-called *Günstigerprüfung*.[1750] In the course of the income tax assessment, the German tax authorities assess *ex officio* – based on the information provided by the taxable person – whether the *Sonderausgabenabzug* is more advantageous to the taxable person with regard to the rendered contributions for the pension provision.[1751] If this is indeed proven to be the case, the reduction of income tax due to the *Sonderausgabenabzug*, will be directly remitted to the taxable person, contrary to the state allowance which will be credited to the *Riester*-provision.[1752] In all other cases, the *Sonderausgabenabzug* shall be withdrawn.[1753] If it is proven that the *Sonderausgabenabzug* is more advantageous to the taxable person,

1748 § 10a, para 1, sentence 1 EStG. See BMF, *Steuerliche Förderung der privaten Altersvorsorge IV C 3 - S 2015/17/10001:005* para 93.

1749 Ibid. para 93. The amount of pension contributions paid by the taxable person must be proven by means of a dataset, provided by the pension provider. Ibid. para 94. For this purpose, the taxable person must inform the pension provider in writing, that he will transmit the pension contributions that will be taken into account in the respective contribution year, to the ZfA (*Zentralen Zulagenstelle für Altersvermögen*, as part of the *Deutschen Rentenversicherung Bund*), stating the *steuerlichen Identifikationsnummer* (i.e. tax identification number pursuant to §139b AO). See for further practical matters ibid. para 98.

1750 Translated freely as ‚most favourable tax treatment'.§ 10a, para 2, sentence 1 EStG and ibid. para 101.

1751 § 10a, para 2, sentence 3 EStG and ibid. para 101. Cf. Förster and Rechtenwald, 170.

1752 § 10a, para 2, sentence 1 in conjunction with § 2, para 6, sentence 2 EStG and BMF, *Steuerliche Förderung der privaten Altersvorsorge IV C 3 - S 2015/17/10001:005* para 104. This amount will be determined separately, pursuant to § 10a, para 4, sentence EStG.

1753 § 10a, para 2, sentence 2 EStG.

the German tax authorities will determine the tax reduction in excess of the entitlement to the allowances separately.[1754] This ensures the precise allocation of the fiscal facilitation to the pension contributions, which is crucial for the tax treatment during the pay-out phase, since merely benefits arising from untaxed income will be subject to tax.[1755]

Furthermore, the assessment of most favourable tax treatment illustrates the strong synergy between *Sonderausgabenabzug* and *Zulagen*. The *Zulage* may, on the one side, be considered an advance payment on the *Sonderausgabenabzug*, and, on the others side, in particular in cases where the taxable person with a low or median income has multiple children, as a facilitation beyond the fiscal facilitation.[1756] This method of determining the most favourable tax treatment (i.e. *Günstigerprüfung*) intends to avoid a double fiscal facilitation of the *Riester-Rente*.[1757] In addition, in cases where it does not lead to the application of *Sonderausgabenabzug*, it intends to guarantee that the *Riester*-contributions arise from untaxed income (i.e. *Zulagen*), which income exemption underlies the principle of deferred taxation.

Altersvorsorge-Eigenheimbetrag: 'Wohn-Riester'

Since the implementation of the *Riester-Rente*, the provision has been criticised in that it hinders the acquisition of owner-occupied dwellings. Schönemann e.a. claim, that living rent-free in an owner-occupied dwelling as a form of retirement provision, remedies the 'pension gap' to the same extent as a monetary supplementary retirement provision would do.[1758]

As a result of the entry into force of the *Eigenheimrentengesetz*[1759], the German legislator increased the flexibility of the payment method of the *Riester*-provision. The *Wohn-Riester* replaced the *Zwischenentnahmemodell* since 2008.[1760] The latter was met with criticism in literature, as the accrued capital could be used only limitedly and not as 'real' equity capital.[1761] Under this facility, the taxable person could withdraw an amount between

1754 § 10a, para 4, sentence 1 EStG.

1755 Birk and Wernsmann, 260.

1756 Cf. Rürup and Myßen, 222.

1757 BMF, *Steuerliche Förderung der privaten Altersvorsorge IV C 3 - S 2015/17/10001:005*, nr. 104. Risthaus, Cf. and Birk and Wernsmann, 260.

1758 K Schönemann, M Dietrich and D Kiesewetter, 'Verbessert das Eigenheimrentenmodell die Integration der eigengenutzten Immobilie in die Altersvorsorge?' 2 StuW 107.

1759 Gesetz zur verbesserten Einbeziehung der selbstgenutzten Wohnimmobilie in die geförderte Altersvorsorge (Eigenheimrentengesetz – EigRentG).

1760 Translated freely as 'interim withdrawal model'. For an elaborate discussion of the model, see Welker, 82 ff.

1761 Schönemann, Dietrich and Kiesewetter.

€10,000 and €50,000 from his *Riester*-provision, prior to the beginning of the pay-out phase, in order to acquire or build an owner-occupied dwelling.[1762]

Under the current so-called *Wohn-Riester*, the taxable person may, prior to the beginning of the pay-out phase, extract a certain amount out of the *Riester*-arrangement, in order to use this capital for the financing of an owner-occupied dwelling.[1763] This illustrates the consideration of the German legislator on the concept of pension, i.e. to some extent, an owner-occupied dwelling may serve the pension objective of maintaining the standard of living after retirement. Since the extracted capital has been fiscally facilitated under § 10a EStG, this, in principle, would be considered the misuse of this fiscal facilitation, and the fiscal facilitation would have to be repaid. However, if the conditions, as laid down in §92a and §92b EStG are met, the extraction of capital from the pension provision will be allowed for fiscal purposes. For instance, the extracted capital must be used for the acquisition or the fabrication of an owner-occupied dwelling, or the repayment of a loan taken out for this purpose, provided that the loan is at least €3,000.[1764] The procedural provisions must be complied with.[1765]

Prior to 8 April 2010, this facility was limited to owner-occupied dwellings situated in Germany. The CJEU ruled that by denying cross-border workers the right to use the subsidised capital for the acquisition or construction of an owner-occupied dwelling unless it is situated in Germany, Germany breached the European freedoms of movement.[1766] This forced the German legislator to revise the concerning provision, and to extend the scope of fiscal facilitation to owner-occupied dwellings, situated in a Member State of the European Union or a State to which the Agreement on the European Economic Area (EEA agreement) is applicable.[1767] Furthermore, this owner-occupied dwelling must constitute the main residence, or the centre of interest of the taxable person.[1768] It is to be noted that these two locations will coincides in most cases. The fiscal facilitation of the *Riester-Rente* over the years, is summarised in the table below.

1762 § 92a EStG (repealed wording). See also Welker, 82.

1763 The so-called *Altersvorsorge-Eigenheimbetrag*, pursuant to §92a EStG. See also BMF, *Steuerliche Förderung der privaten Altersvorsorge IV C 3 - S 2015/17/10001:005* para 167 ff. For a critical analysis of the *Eigenheimrentengesetz*, See Schönemann, Dietrich and Kiesewetter.

1764 § 92a, para 1, sentence 1, nr 1 EStG.

1765 These procedural rules are laid down in § 92b EStG.

1766 *Commission vs. Germany*.

1767 Article 1, nr 10, lit. a Gesetz zur Umsetzung steuerlicher EU-Vorgaben sowie zur Änderung steuerlicher Vorschriften (EUStVUG). See also T Paintner and J Melchior, 'Das Gesetz zur Umsetzung steuerlicher EU-Vorgaben sowie zur Änderung steuerlicher Vorschriften im Überblick' 13 DStR 625.

1768 § 92a, para 1, sentence 5 EStG.

Table 7.1 Development of Fiscal Faciliation of Riester-Rente

	2002/03	2004	2005	2006/07	Since 2008	Since 2018
Maximum	€525	€1,050	€1,050	€1,575	€2,100	€2,100
Grundzulage	€38	€76	€76	€114	€154	€175
Kinderzulage per child	€46	€92	€92	€138	€185	€185
Mindesteigenbetrag	1% minus	2% minus	2% minus	3% minus allowances	4% minus allowances	4% minus allowances
Maximum allowances	€525	€1,050	€1,050 minus	€1,575 minus allowances	€2,100 minus allowances	€2,100 minus allowances
Sockelbetrag						
0 children	€45	€45	€60	€60	€60	€60
1 child	€38	€38	€60	€60	€60	€60
2 or more children	€30	€30	€60	€60	€60	€60

7.4.1.A.II Taxation of benefits during the pay-out phase

Since its introduction, the *Riester-Rente* has been subject to deferred taxation. The disbursed benefits will be taxed as *Sonstige Einkünfte* (other income), similarly to the benefits of the *Direktversicherung, Pensionskasse* and *Pensionsfonds.*[1769] In addition, to the extent that no additional expenses are deducted, an additional *Pauschbetrag* of €102 may be deducted from the tax assessment basis.[1770]

The principle of deferred taxation of the *Riester-Rente*, comprises that although the contributions may be deductible as *Sonderausgaben* during the accrual phase, the benefits – including the reflux of hitherto untaxed capital and the interest included in it – shall be fully liable to taxation.[1771] The tax treatment of benefits arising from the *Riester-Rente* is, however, subject to differentiation, in the sense that the extent to which the benefits shall be subject to deferred taxation depends on the extent to which the contributions have been fiscally facilitated.[1772] The benefits disbursed will be fully subject to taxation, if the contributions paid to the provision have been fully subject to fiscal facilitation during the

1769 Pursuant to § 22, nr 5 EStG, which states *„Sonstige Einkünfte sind Leistungen aus Altersvorsorgeverträgen…"*.

1770 Pursuant to § 9a, para 3 EStG, which states *‚Für Werbungskosten sind bei der Ermittlung der Einkünfte die folgenden Pauschbeträge abzuziehen, wenn nicht höhere Werbungskosten nachgewiesen werden: von den Einnahmen im Sinne des § 22 Nummer 5: ein Pauschbetrag von insgesamt 102 Euro.*

1771 Cf. Wernsmann, 'Die steuerliche Förderung der zusätzlichen kapitalgedeckten Altersvorsorge' 791.

1772 Cf. Birk and Wernsmann, 263 and Wernsmann, 'Die steuerliche Förderung der zusätzlichen kapitalgedeckten Altersvorsorge' 791.

accrual phase, or arise from the provided statutory allowances (i.e. *Zulagen*[1773]), to the extent they do not exceed the maximum amount of §10a EStG.[1774] The facilitated contributions comprise, at least, the granted allowances and the provided *Sockelbeträge*.[1775] For instance, a taxable person has, for more than 25 years, paid exactly the maximum amount of fiscally facilitated contributions, including the allowances.[1776] As of reaching 65 years, he receives a monthly *Riester*-benefit of €500 on a monthly basis. In this case, the yearly retirement benefit shall be fully subject to deferred taxation.[1777]

In cases where the taxable person during the accrual phase, has paid fiscally facilitated as well as non-facilitated contributions to the *Riester*-provision, the tax treatment of the benefits paid out during the pay-out phase shall be differentiated.[1778] This is the case when, for instance, a *Riester*-provision has not been fiscally facilitated during the accrual phase, since not all conditions for facilitation were met, but contributions still have been paid.[1779] Furthermore, the tax treatment shall be differentiated when the taxable person has paid contributions exceeding the maximum amount, for instance as laid down in § 10a EStG. The taxable proportion of the benefits shall be determined by dividing the sum of interest-bearing non-exempted/non-facilitated contributions, by the sum of the actual interest-bearing contributions paid to the date of first pay-out of the benefits.[1780] Subsequently, the fiscally facilitated proportion of the benefits shall be fully subject to deferred taxation.[1781]

1773 Which have been accrued pursuant to section XI EStG. See also BMF, *Steuerliche Förderung der privaten Altersvorsorge IV C 3 - S 2015/17/10001:005* para 131.

1774 § 22, nr 5, sentence 1 and 2 EStG and ibid. para 137. Contributions for which the maximum amount of § 10a EStG has been exceeded, shall not be considered facilitated contributions. Neither do contributions for which the taxable person has not received any allowances or did not receive the *Sonderausgabenabzug*, see ibid. para 134. In addition, income and capital appreciations attributable to unduly paid, and subsequently reclaimed allowances, shall be treated as non-facilitated retirement capital, ibid. para 135.

1775 Ibid. para 131. *Sockelbeträge* within the meaning of § 86, para 1, sentence 4 EStG.

1776 Ibid. para 138.

1777 Pursuant to § 22, nr 5, sentence 1 EStG.

1778 BMF, *Steuerliche Förderung der privaten Altersvorsorge IV C 3 - S 2015/17/10001:005* para 139.

1779 Ibid. para 141. The differentiation ratio has been laid down in BMF, *Steuerliche Förderung der privaten Altersvorsorge und betrieblichen Altersversorgung; Aufteilung von Leistungen bei der nachgelagerten Besteuerung nach § 22 Nr. 5 EStG IV C 3 - S 2257 b - 47/04*, taking into account the changes laid down in BMF, *Steuerliche Förderung der betrieblichen Altersversorgung; Aufteilung von Leistungen bei der nachgelagerten Besteuerung nach § 22 Nummer 5 EStG IV C 3 - S 2257 b/11/10003*.

1780 BMF, *Steuerliche Förderung der privaten Altersvorsorge und betrieblichen Altersversorgung; Aufteilung von Leistungen bei der nachgelagerten Besteuerung nach § 22 Nr. 5 EStG IV C 3 - S 2257 b - 47/04* para 2.2. If this differentiation method, based on the paid contributions, leads to obvious inaccurate results, the pension institution shall, on request of the beneficiary, differentiate the taxable benefits on the basis of actuarial principles, see BMF, *Steuerliche Förderung der betrieblichen Altersversorgung; Aufteilung von Leistungen bei der nachgelagerten Besteuerung nach § 22 Nummer 5 EStG IV C 3 - S 2257 b/11/10003*.

1781 Pursuant to § 22, nr 5, sentence 1 EStG. See also BMF, *Steuerliche Förderung der privaten Altersvorsorge IV C 3 - S 2015/17/10001:005* para 140.

Contrarily, if the contributions were not fully subject to fiscal facilitation, the reflux of capital – which in this case already has been subject to taxation – included in the benefits, may not be fully subject to taxation. Alternatively, if the maximum amount of *Sonderausgaben* (€2,100[1782]) has been exceeded during the accrual phase, the benefits arising from this part of the accrued non-facilitated capital shall not be subject to taxation during the pay-out phase.[1783] Otherwise, the benefits would be subject to double taxation.[1784] This potential double taxation of benefits is avoided by taxing the benefits against the *Ertragsanteil.*[1785] This holds true as well with respect to benefits which are fully attributable to non-facilitated contributions.[1786] For the entire duration of the pay-out phase, the taxable income (i.e. *Ertrag*) shall be set at the difference between the annual amount of retirement benefits and the amount resulting from the equal distribution of the net present value of the retirement provision over the foreseen duration of it.[1787] This *Ertragsanteilbesteuerung* is principally distinctive for individual pension provisions, which cannot be qualified as *Basisversorgung.*

Example: *suppose that the contributions to the Riester-Rente have not been subject to fiscal facilitation during the accrual phase, the benefits shall be taxed against the Ertragsanteil during the pay-out phase. If the taxable person is aged 67 years at the beginning of the pay-out phase, the taxable Ertragsanteil is 17%. If for instance, €200 of the benefits arose from non-facilitated pension capital, only €34 of this amount will be added to the tax basis of the taxable person.*

In cases where the *Riester-Rente* is disbursed as a capital lump sum (also in the pay-out phase), this will – from a fiscal perspective – be considered as 'improper use' of this retirement provision. The tax facilities granted will therefore in principle be reclaimed.[1788]

1782 § 10a, para 1, sentence 1 EStG.

1783 § 22, nr 5, sentence 2 EStG.

1784 Cf. Wernsmann, 'Die steuerliche Förderung der zusätzlichen kapitalgedeckten Altersvorsorge' 791.

1785 § 22, nr 1, sentence 3, under bb and § 22, nr 5, sentence 2, under b and c in conjunction with § 22, nr 5, sentence 2 BMF, *Steuerliche Förderung der privaten Altersvorsorge IV C 3 - S 2015/17/10001:005* para 144 ff. With respect to *Ertragsanteilbesteuerung*, also see Herrmann, Heuer and Raupach.

1786 BMF, *Steuerliche Förderung der privaten Altersvorsorge IV C 3 - S 2015/17/10001:005* para 148.

1787 § 22, nr 1, sentence 3, under bb, sentence 3 EStG.

1788 Pursuant to § 93, para 1 in conjuction with § 95 EStG. §93, para 1 states: *„Wird gefördertes Altersvorsorgevermögen nicht unter den in § 1 Absatz 1 Satz 1 Nummer 4 und 10 Buchstabe c des Altersvorsorgeverträge-Zertifizierungsgesetzes oder § 1 Absatz 1 Satz 1 Nummer 4, 5 und 10 Buchstabe c des Altersvorsorgeverträge-Zertifizierungsgesetzes in der bis zum 31. Dezember 2004 geltenden Fassung genannten Voraussetzungen an den Zulageberechtigten ausgezahlt (schädliche Verwendung), sind die auf das ausgezahlte geförderte Altersvorsorgevermögen entfallenden Zulagen und die nach § 10a Absatz 4 gesondert festgestellten Beträge (Rückzahlungsbetrag) zurückzuzahlen."*

This constitutes a so-called *Rückzahlungsverpflichtung*.[1789] As Scholz points out, the aforementioned violation of the required pay-out as annuity leads to a stricter fiscal sanction as may be the case for pension contributions exempted from tax pursuant to § 3, nr 63 EStG.[1790]

The synergy between the extent to which the *Riester-Rente* will be used for retirement saving and the fiscal facilitation follows from the fiscal consequences of the abuse of the fiscal facilitation during the accrual phase. In cases where the fiscally facilitated *Riester*-provision is not paid out under the terms of the *Altersvorsorgeverträge-Zertifizierungsgesetzes*[1791], the contributions, facilitated under the *Sonderausgabenabzug*, and the statutory allowances must be repaid.[1792] In cases where only a part of the fiscally facilitated retirement capital has been misused, the facilitated contributions and allowances will be reclaimed proportionally. Principally, a pay-out of the retirement provision, following the death of the beneficiary, is considered misuse.[1793] In these situations, the repayment obligation will be lifted, if certain conditions are met.[1794] For instance, if the accrued pension capital will be paid out in the form of a survivor's pension to the spouse, life partner or children for whom the taxable person is entitled to *Kindergeld*.

By means of this provision, the German legislator intends to ensure that the fiscally facilitated retirement provision will actually be used for providing an income after retirement. It could even be argued that the German fiscal legislator strives to foster pension adequacy by means of this fiscal policy of disincentive. The legislator wants to foster and maintain participants' pension adequacy by facilitating the accrual of pensions that ultimately result in the disbursement of lifelong annuities and, on the contrary, reclaim granted tax facilities in cases of lump sum pay-outs, since lump sums may hamper people's pension adequacy.

7.4.1.B Rürup-Rente

7.4.1.B.I Tax Relief during the Accrual Phase

The *Rürup-Rente*, or *Basisrente*, was implemented pursuant to the *Alterseinkünftegesetz*.[1795] This form of retirement provision is particularly interesting for the self-employed not

1789 Translated freely as 'repayment obligation'. Exceptions on this *Rückzahlungsverpflichtung* are formulated in § 93, para 1, under a, b, c and d EStG.

1790 Cf. Scholz, 77 (footnote 421).

1791 More precisely, § 1, para 1, sentence 1, nr 4 AltZertG.

1792 § 93, para 1, sentence 1 EStG.

1793 § 93, para 1, sentence 2 EStG.

1794 These are stipulated in § 93, para 1, sentence 4, under a, b, c, d EStG.

1795 Gesetz zur Neuordnung der einkommensteuerrechtlichen Behandlung von Altersvorsorgeaufwendungen und Altersbezügen (Alterseinkünftegesetz – AltEinkG).

entitled to a form of occupational pension, neither the *Riester-Rente*. Although, this type of pension scheme is not subject to the certification requirements as set out in § 1, para 1 *AltZertG*, it must meet similar requirements laid down in § 10, para 1, nr 2, letter b EStG.

The *Rürup-rente* is also characterised by an even stronger focus on securing an adequate pension income, even stronger than under the *Riester-Rente*, as the entitlements may neither be heritable, transferable, lendable, saleable nor capitalisable.[1796] This underpins that the *Rürup-Rente* should be allocated to the first *Schicht* as a basic pension provision, rather than an occupational pension provision under the second *Schicht*. Furthermore, these conditions guarantee the comparability of the *Rürup-Rente*, as *Basisrente*, with the *gesetzlichen Rentenversicherung*, which forms the underlying principle of the fiscal facilitation of the *Rürup-Rente* under the *Sonderausgabenabzug* ex. § 10 EStG.[1797]

Eligible Contributions and Persons

Besides contributions to the statutory retirement provisions, contributions to individual retirement provisions are deductible as *Sonderausgaben*. The *Rürup-Rente* is qualified as one of these provisions. This expansion of the first *Schicht* was in fact already proposed by the *Sachverständigenkommission*.[1798] In addition, this expansion was considered desirable from a legal perspective, since taxable persons, not entitled to any statutory retirement scheme, would have had no further opportunities to accrue a fiscally facilitated basic pension provision.[1799] Therefore, the broadening of the fiscal facilitation of the first *Schicht*, may also be considered desirable from the social political perspective, i.e. fostering people's pension adequacy by broadening the retirement provision. It may however be questioned whether the allocation of the *Rürup-Rente* is adequate from a fiscal perspective. As Rürup and Myβen assert, from a fiscal perspective the legal basis of a retirement provision may be considered irrelevant.[1800] Decisive is whether the entitlements objectively serve the old-age provision. The fiscal facilitation of the provision is aligned with this objective.

The contributions paid to a *Rürup-Rente* are, however, partially fiscally deductible as *Sonderausgaben*.[1801] In the context of statutory pensions, the *Rürup-Rente* is qualified as a funded retirement provision. The group of eligible persons for this fiscal facilitation is not

1796 Pursuant to § 10, para 1, nr 2, under bb and sentence 2 EStG. These conditions were already stipulated by Abschlussbericht der Sachverständigenkommission zur Neuordnung der steuerrechtlichen Behandlung von Altersvorsorgeaufwendungen und Altersbezügen (BMF-Schriftenreihe) 4.

1797 Cf. Herrmann, Heuer and Raupach.

1798 Abschlussbericht der Sachverständigenkommission zur Neuordnung der steuerrechtlichen Behandlung von Altersvorsorgeaufwendungen und Altersbezügen (BMF-Schriftenreihe).

1799 Kirchhof, Söhn and Mellinghof, and Rürup and Myßen, 197.

1800 Rürup and Myßen, 197.

1801 § 10, para 1, nr 2, under b EStG.

limited, contrary to the eligible persons for the *Riester-Rente*. It is merely required that the contributions ought to be paid by the taxable person. In accordance with the fundamental principle of *Sonderausgabenabzug*[1802], solely the person who is economically affected by the expenses, and who is subject to unlimited tax liability, is entitled to this deduction of these contributions as *Sonderausgaben*.[1803]

Most Favourable Tax Treatment

Between 2005 and 2019, the German tax authorities assessed *ex officio* whether the amount of pension contributions, to be qualified as *Sonderausgaben* is higher for the taxpayer under the legislation in force until 31 December 2004 or under the new legislation (i.e. *Günstigerprüfung*). This most favourable tax treatment intends to avoid a disadvantageous fiscal treatment, due to the implementation of the new legal regime regarding *Sonderausgaben* since 1 January 2005.[1804] In the tax assessment of the taxable person, the highest amount, as a result of the assessment of the most favourable tax treatment, of *Sonderausgaben* will be taken into account.[1805] Besides, in the assessment of most favourable tax treatment, merely the contributions shall be taken into account, which are eligible for deductibility pursuant to the new legislation.[1806] This interaction of old and new legislation under the *Günstigerprüfung*, requires the application of both versions of provisions under the EStG. The underlying method of assessing the most favourable tax treatment is complex, though result-oriented, in the sense that deprivations of tax treatment would be avoided. The latter is desirable, since retirement saving is a long-term savings process in which the legal framework should not be revised to the detriment of the taxable persons.[1807]

Eligible Retirement Provisions and Providers

Not all forms of funded retirement provisions are fiscally facilitated. On the contrary, the retirement provision must fulfil certain conditions in order to be eligible for *Sonderausgabenabzug*.[1808] The retirement provision may only provide the payment of a monthly life-annuity – related to the life of beneficiary – and the benefits may not be paid

1802 Translated freely as 'special expenses deduction'.

1803 Birk and Wernsmann, 254-255 and cited literature.

1804 Cf. Rürup and Myßen, 207.

1805 § 10, para 4a EStG.

1806 See Rürup and Myßen, 208-210 for an example on the calculation of the *Günstigerprüfung*, under legislation in force in 2008, and the so-called phasing out-effect until 31 December 2005 (i.e. *Verpuffungseffekt*) which the legislator has resolved retrospectively in the article 1 Jahressteuergesetz 2007 (JStG 2007).

1807 Cf. Rürup and Myßen, 214. In literature, some alternatives for this method of *Günstigerprüfung* have been discussed, see ibid. 215 and A Risthaus, 'JStG 2007: Günstigerprüfung innerhalb der Günstigerprüfung für Rürup-Renten-beiträge' DB 2773.

1808 These criteria are laid down in § 10, para 1, nr 2, under b EStG.

to the beneficiary prior to reaching the age of 62[1809], although the pension institution and the taxable person may agree on combining up to twelve monthly payments into one disbursement.[1810] The age of 62 is, herewith, brought in line with the retirement age of the *gesetzlichen Rentenversicherung*. Deviating forms of payment are not allowed, such as a payment schedule or a partial lump-sum pay-out allowed under the *Riester-Rente*.[1811] The German legislator has, however, refrained from stipulating that the benefits, stemming from the life annuity, must remain stable. Fluctuations in the benefits paid out from the life annuity, would not lead to the conclusion that the retirement provision does not qualify under the EStG any longer.[1812] However, a structural decrease of the benefits would be not allowed, since the objective of basic pension provision could be called into question.[1813] Otherwise, the *Rürup-Rente* is fiscally treated similarly to the *gesetzlichen Rentenversicherung*, and should for this reason, serve the needs of a basic secure retirement provision.

Besides this, the provision may cover supplementary coverage of occupational disability, reduced earnings capacity, or a survivors' pension. Additionally, the pension entitlements must not be heritable, transferable, lendable, saleable not capitalisable.[1814] In addition to the aforementioned forms of payment, any further entitlements to disbursements are not permitted.[1815] These strict conditions intend to ensure the comparability between the *Rürup-Rente* and the *gesetzlichen Rentenversicherung*. The fiscally permitted pension providers are legally defined as well, i.e. foreign or domestic life insurance companies, banks, investments companies, or a *Direktversicherung, Pensionskasse* or *Pensionsfonds*.[1816] The implementation of § 80, pursuant to the *Jahressteuergesetz* 2007[1817], led to a standardisation of the fiscally allowed providers. With this, the German legislator approves all providers of occupational pensions as providers of statutory pension provisions. Most interesting in a cross-border context is the insurer which has its seat or management

1809 With regard to retirement provisions, concluded after 31 December 2011, a pay-out prior to reaching the age of 62, is not allowed. With respect to provisions, concluded prior to 1 January 2012, the age of 60 still applies. See article 10 RV-Altersgrenzenanpassungsgesetz.

1810 Pursuant to § 10, para 1, nr 2, sentence 3 EStG. Also laid down in BMF, *Einkommensteuerrechtliche Behandlung von Vorsorgeaufwendungen IV C 3 - S 2221/16/10001:004* para 16.

1811 Pursuant to § 1, para 1, nr 4 AltZertG.

1812 More precise, § 10, para 1, nr 2, under b EStG. Cf. Goverts and Knoll, and Rürup and Myßen, 199.

1813 Kirchhof, Söhn and Mellinghof, and Rürup and Myßen, 199.

1814 Pursuant to § 10, para 1, nr 2, sentence 2 EStG. For a short elaboration on each of these conditions, See BMF, *Einkommensteuerrechtliche Behandlung von Vorsorgeaufwendungen IV C 3 - S 2221/16/10001:004* paras 16-34.

1815 Pursuant to § 10, para 1, nr 2, sentence 5 EStG.

1816 § 80 EStG in conjunction with § 1, para 2 AltzertG and § 10, para 2, nr 2 EStG respectively.

1817 Jahressteuergesetz 2007 (JStG 2007).

positioned in an EU Member State or a signatory state to the Agreement on the European Economic Area allowed operating the insurance business domestically.[1818]

The Fiscal Facilitation of Rürup-contributions

There is a dichotomy in the fiscal facilitation of contributions paid to the *Rürup-Rente* as well. This comprises the fact that the contributions will merely be considered *Sonderausgaben* if the term of the insurance contract begins after 31 December 2004, i.e. the entry into force of the *Alterseinkünftegesetz*.[1819] Furthermore, the principle of deferred taxation is laid down in a particular condition regarding the *Sonderausgabenabzug*. The deductible pension contributions may not be directly related to tax-exempt income.[1820] For instance, contributions directly related to tax-free earned income (i.e. *Arbeitslohn*) cannot be deducted as *Sonderausgaben*.[1821] This does, however, not hold true if earned income does not lead to an inflow of earned income, though liable for contributions.[1822] For instance, the earned income converted under *Entgeltumwandlung* for the benefit of a *Direktzusage*. In this respect, the *Bechtel*-case is crucial. The CJEU ruled in the *Bechtel* case that the prohibition of the deduction of *Sonderausgaben* regulated in § 10 EStG, due to the exemption of the underlying wages pursuant to the applicable tax treaty, violates the freedom of movement of workers.[1823] In this case, the interested person – Mrs. Bechtel – resided in Germany, and worked as a civil servant for the French tax authorities. Mrs. Bechtel was denied the deduction of French pension contributions from her income tax basis of assessment in Germany. These contributions were deducted from her wages in France, in contrast to comparable contributions paid to the social security fund of Germany. Furthermore, under the tax treaty concluded between the two Member States, the wages may not be taxed in Germany, and merely increase the tax rate to be applied to other income (i.e. exemption method with reservation as to progressive rates of taxation[1824]). This constituted a breach of article 45 TFEU. In response to this judgment, and in anticipation to a revision of the legal provision, the German Federal Ministry of Finance, issued a policy document, with regards to the *Sonderausgabenabzug* for social security contributions of employees, working abroad and residing in Germany. The

1818 Pursuant to § 10, para 2, nr 2 EStG.

1819 BMF, *Einkommensteuerrechtliche Behandlung von Vorsorgeaufwendungen IV C 3 - S 2221/16/10001:004* para 35. See also Rürup and Myßen, 198, Kirchhof, Söhn and Mellinghof, and Hügelschäffer and others.

1820 Pursuant to § 10, para 2, nr 1 EStG.

1821 BMF, *Einkommensteuerrechtliche Behandlung von Vorsorgeaufwendungen IV C 3 - S 2221/16/10001:004* where reference is made to BFH, BStBl II 18 April 2012. 2012.

1822 BMF, *Einkommensteuerrechtliche Behandlung von Vorsorgeaufwendungen IV C 3 - S 2221/16/10001:004* para 199.

1823 C-20/16 *Bechtel* ECLI:EU:C:2017:488 (CJEU).

1824 In Germany, this reservation as to progressive rates of taxation is referred to as *Progressionsvorbehalt*.

Federal German cabinet adopted the government draft and started the legislative procedure.

Pursuant to the proposed legislation, § 10 EStG will be revised, stipulating that employees, working abroad and residing in Germany are, under certain conditions, eligible for the *Sonderausgabenabzug*. The first condition stipulates that the contributions must have a direct link to income from employment, from a Member State of the European Union or a state, which is a signatory to the Agreement on the European Economic Area.[1825] Secondly, these income elements are exempted from tax domestically, by virtue of a double taxation convention. Lastly, the state of employment, does not allow any fiscal recognition of pension contributions in the course of the taxation of these income elements. This enhancement of the tax treatment of cross-border workers can be illustrated by the following example. By virtue of the revised text, a German resident, working in the Netherlands, may deduct Dutch social security contributions as *Sonderausgaben*, when the contributions have a direct link to income from employment, earned in the Netherlands, and these elements of income have been exempted from tax in Germany by virtue of the tax treaty while the Netherlands does not allow the deduction of these contributions.

Whether the pension contributions fulfils these criteria, shall be examined by the taxable persons themselves, since the *Rürup-Rente* is not certified, contrary to the public certification of the *Riester-Rente* pursuant to the *Altersvorsorgeverträge-Zertifizierungsgesetz*.[1826]

The amount of pension contributions deductible as *Sonderausgaben* shall be calculated as follows. Firstly, the pension contributions paid by the employee shall be determined. As follows from legislative text[1827], these contributions must be paid by the employee, assuming personal identity between the contributor, the insured person and the beneficiary.[1828] Furthermore, this personal identity leads to the conclusion that the accrued entitlements guarantee the taxable person a retirement provision. In the cases of spouses, assessed collectively for income tax[1829], the deduction of *Sonderausgaben* is not depended

1825 Article 2, nr. 3 Entwurf eines Gesetzes zur Vermeidung von Umsatzsteuerausfällen beim Handel mit Waren im Internet und zur Änderung weiterer steuerlicher Vorschriften (Jahressteuergezet 2018).

1826 Birk and Wernsmann, 255.

1827 § 10, para 1, nr 2, under b EStG stipulates: "Beiträge des Steuerpflichtigen zum Aufbau einer eigenen kapitalgedeckten Altersversorgung".

1828 This may, however, lead to interpretative difficulties, when this is applied to occupational retirement provisions. In these provisions, the employer is policyholder, and the employee is the insurance beneficiary, see Rürup and Myßen, 198.

1829 Pursuant to § 26b EStG.

on whether the husband or wife has paid the contributions.[1830] Secondly, in addition to these contributions, the tax-free employer's portion to *the gesetzlichen Rentenversicherung*[1831] and the tax-free employer's subsidy equal to this, shall be added.[1832] The deduction of contributions to the *Rürup-Rente* as *Sonderausgaben* is, however, subject to a maximum.[1833] This maximum amount is based on the maximum contribution to the *knappschaftlichen Rentenversicherung (West)*, rounded up to a full amount in Euros (2023: €107,400)[1834]. For spouses and life partners who file their tax returns jointly, this maximum amount shall be doubled, irrespective of who has paid the facilitated contributions.[1835] Moreover, the maximum amount is reduced for particular categories of persons.[1836] The amount of pension contributions exceeding these respective maxima shall not be deductible as *Sonderausgaben*. What further should be taken into account in calculating the amount of contributions to the *Rürup-Rente*, deductible as *Sonderausgaben*, is the gradual transition to deferred taxation. The amount as calculated above, is, therefore, only partially deductible. However, as of 2023, 100% of the contributions may be deducted.[1837] Thereafter, this amount shall be reduced with the tax-free employer's portion to *the gesetzlichen Rentenversicherung*[1838] and the tax-free employer's subsidy equal to this.[1839] This reduction guarantees equal tax relief opportunities for all taxable persons.[1840] After multiplying the amount of pension contributions with the deductibility ratio, the remaining amount shall be reduced with the tax-free employers' contributions to the *gesetzlichen Rentenversicherung* and tax-free allowances treated as such, pursuant to § 3, nr 62 EStG.[1841] To this extent, the

1830 Laid down in R. 10.1 EStR. These *Einkommensteuer-Richtlinien* – which do not qualify as formal tax legislation – comprise instructions to the tax authorities, intended to simplify the administration, take into account BFH-judgments and legislative changes in the administrative tax practice, and to ensure the equal treatment of taxable persons.

1831 § 3, nr 62 EStG.

1832 § 10, para 1, nr 2, sentence 6 EStG.

1833 § 10, para 3, sentence 1 and 2 EStG.

1834 § 4, para 1, nr 2 Verordnung über maßgebende Rechengrößen der Sozialversicherung für 2023 (Sozialversicherungs-Rechengrößenverordnung 2023).

1835 § 10, para 3, sentence 2 EStG.

1836 § 10, para 3, sentence 3.

1837 § 10, para 3, sentence 4 and 6 EStG. As of 2023, 100% of the contributions will be deductible: *"Der Prozentsatz in Satz 4 erhöht sich in den folgenden Kalenderjahren bis zum Kalenderjahr 2022 um je 2 Prozentpunkte je Kalenderjahr; ab dem Kalenderjahr 2023 beträgt er 100 Prozent."*

1838 § 3, nr 63 EStG.

1839 § 10, para 3, sentence 5 EStG and BMF, *Einkommensteuerrechtliche Behandlung von Vorsorgeaufwendungen IV C 3 - S 2221/16/10001:004* para 73.

1840 Cf. Wernsmann, 'Die steuerliche Förderung der zusätzlichen kapitalgedeckten Altersvorsorge' 793 and cited literature.

1841 § 10, para 3, sentence 5 EStG.

taxable person already has had the opportunity to accrue a retirement provision out of untaxed income. The amount remaining thereafter shall be deductible as *Sonderausgaben.*[1842]

This results in the following hypothetical example (2023).

Deductible *Sonderausgaben* Pursuant to § 10 EStG			
Employee's contribution to *Ges. RenVer.*	€ 3,500		
Employers' contribution to *Ges. RenVer.*	€ 3,500	+	
Contribution to *Rürup-Rente*	€ 1,000	+	
Sum contributions *Basisversorgung*	€ 8,000		
Maximum amount	€ 107,400		
Deductibility ratio			100%
Deductible amount	(100% of € 8,000)	=	€ 8,000
Minus: tax-free employers' contribution to GRV		-/-	€ 3,500
Deductible contributions *Basisversorgung* as *Sonderausgaben*			€ 4,500

7.4.1.B.II *Taxation of Benefits during the Pay-Out Phase*

Benefits arising from the *Rürup-Rente*, which have been fiscally facilitated under the *Sonderausgabenabzug*[1843], will be taxed as other income.[1844] The proportion of the benefits subject to the deferred taxation, is determined on the basis of the so-called *Besteuerungsanteil*[1845]. This taxable proportion shall be gradually raised. Until 2005, the taxable proportion is 50%, after which the proportion shall be raised by 2% per year until 2020, and hereafter with 1% per year.[1846] As of 2040, the paid out retirement benefits shall be fully subject to deferred taxation. The assessment basis for the taxable proportion is formed by the annual amount of pension benefits.[1847] The taxable proportion is based on the annual amount of these pension benefits paid out, which shall then be multiplied with the percentage of the taxable proportion.[1848] This percentage is determined in the first year

1842 § 10, para 3, sentence 5 EStG. For numerous examples regarding the calculation of the amount, deductible as *Sonderausgabe*, See BMF, *Einkommensteuerrechtliche Behandlung von Vorsorgeaufwendungen IV C 3 - S 2221/16/10001:004* paras 75-79. See also BMF, *Gesetz zur Neuordnung der einkommensteuerrechtlichen Behandlung von Altersvorsorgeaufwendungen und Altersbezügen – Alterseinkünftegesetz (AltEinkG) IV C 3-S 2255 - 51/05* (24 February 2005) para 36.

1843 Pursuant to § 10, para 1, nr 2, under b EStG.

1844 Pursuant to §2, para 1, sentence 1, nr 7 EStG in conjunction with § 22, nr 1, sentence 3, under aa EStG.

1845 Translated freely as 'taxable proportion'. See also BMF, *Steuerliche Förderung der privaten Altersvorsorge IV C 3 - S 2015/17/10001:005* para 144.

1846 The percentages of this taxable proportion are laid down in § 22, nr 1, sentence 3, table under aa EStG.

1847 § 22, nr 1, sentence 3, under aa, sentence 2 EStG.

1848 § 22, nr 1, sentence 3, under aa, sentence 3 EStG.

of benefits pay-out, and then fixed for the remainder of the pay-out phase.[1849] The difference between the annual amount of pension benefits and the taxable proportion of the pension benefits constitutes the tax-free amount of pension.[1850] By way of derogation from this if the annual amount of the pension benefits changes, the tax-free proportion of the benefits shall be adjusted in proportion to the change in the annual pension amount to the annual pension amount used to determine the tax-exempt part of the pension.[1851] Regular adjustments to the annual amount of pension, however, do not lead to a recalculation and will be disregarded for the recalculation and shall be fully liable to taxation.[1852] The information necessary to calculate these amounts, shall be provided by the provider of the *Rürup-Rente*, who will transmit this information to the *Deutsche Rentenversicherung Bund*.[1853]

The *Rürup* pension differs from private pension insurance and the *Riester-Rente* in that there is no lump-sum option, i.e. the entitlements cannot be paid out in the form of a lump-sum settlement. A disadvantage is certainly that the claims outside the narrow subscription right are not inheritable, cannot be used as collateral, cannot be sold or pledged.[1854]

7.4.1.C Lebensversicherungen and Other Private Pension Insurances

7.4.1.C.I Fiscal Facilitation during The Accrual Phase

It should be stressed that the term *Lebensversicherung* (i.e. life insurance) is broad, covering numerous varieties of life insurances, such as a pure term life insurance[1855], retirement insurances with or without lump-sum option[1856] or pure endowment insurances[1857].[1858] The outcome of the life insurances, i.e. the retirement benefits, may differ from each other considerably. In order to be eligible for tax relief, these *Renten- and Lebensversicherungen* must fulfil the requirements for pension arrangements, set out by § 1, para 1 AltZertG,

1849 § 22, nr 1, sentence 3, under aa, sentence 5 EStG.

1850 § 22, nr 1, sentence 3, under aa, sentence 4 EStG.

1851 § 22, nr 1, sentence 3, under aa, sentence 6 EStG.

1852 § 22, nr 1, sentence 3, under aa, sentence 7 EStG.

1853 By means of the so-called *Rentenbezugsmitteilungen*. § 22a, para 1, sentence 1 in conjunction with § 81 EStG. These data must be submitted in accordance with the rules of interpretation of the tax authorities as laid down in BMF, *Rentenbezugsmitteilungsverfahren nach § 22a EStG IV C 3 - S 2257-c/10/10005:003* (7 December 2011).

1854 Cf. H Keller, *Praxishandbuch Finanzwissen: Steuern - Altersvorsorge - Rechtsfragen* (Springer Gabler, Wiesbaden 2013) 66.

1855 I.e. *reine Risikolebensversicherung*.

1856 I.e. *Rentenversicherungen mit und ohne Kapitalwahlrecht*.

1857 I.e. *reine Kapitalversicherungen*.

1858 Birk and Wernsmann, 261.

except when it concerns a term life insurance, merely providing a death benefit. The requirement laid down in this provision have been discussed in a preceding section, and will not be reiterated at this point.

The fiscal facilitation of life insurances, and related individual retirement provisions, is subject to a dichotomy, because life insurances concluded prior to 2005, are subject to the so-called *Lebensversicherungsprivileg*[1859].[1860] Therefore, the aforementioned dichotomy allows a clear distinction in the fiscal facilitation of *Lebensversicherungen*, i.e. life insurance contracts concluded prior to 1 January 2005 (i.e. *Altverträge*), or contracts concluded after 31 December 2004 (*Neuverträge*).[1861] As mentioned above, the old contracts – concluded prior to 1 January 2005 and to which an insurance premium was paid until 31 December 2004[1862] – are subject to the *Lebensversicherungsprivileg.* This prerogative comprises that contributions to life insurances, are deductible as *Sonderausgaben.*[1863] This applied to *Risikoversicherungen* (risk insurance policies which only provide a benefit in the event of death), *Rentenversicherungen ohne Kapitalwahlrecht* (annuity insurances without capital option), *Rentenversicherungen mit Kapitalwahlrecht* (annuity insurances with capital option), and *Kapitalversicherungen mit Sparanteil* (endowment insurance with savings component).[1864] The amount of deductible contributions is, however, subject to a maximum of €2,800 per year.[1865] With respect to contributions or benefits of new contracts – concluded after 31 December 2004[1866] – the fiscal facilitation has been phased out gradually. For instance, contributions to pure endowment insurances (i.e. *reine Kapitallebensversicherungen*) are no longer deductible as *Sonderausgaben.*[1867] Contributions to other forms of individual retirement provisions, concluded after 31 December 2004 – are no longer eligible for fiscal facilitation, unless they meet the conditions of the *Rürup-Rente* or *Riester-Rente.*

1859 Translated freely as 'life insurance prerogative'.

1860 Birk and Wernsmann, 261.

1861 Cf. Eckerle, 359-365. See also Wellisch and others, 167.

1862 See §10, para 1, nr 3a EStG. An insurance premium is paid until 31 December 2004 if, in accordance with § 11 paragraph 2 EStG, the premium is attributable to a calendar year prior to 2005. See BMF, *Einkommensteuerrechtliche Behandlung von Vorsorgeaufwendungen IV C 3 - S 2221/16/10001:004* para 123.

1863 §10, para 1, nr 3a EStG which provides "*Beitrage zu Versicherungen im Sinne des § 10 Absatz 1 Nummer 2 Buchstabe b Doppelbuchstabe bb bis dd in der am 31. Dezember 2004 geltenden Fassung, wenn die Laufzeit dieser Versicherungen vor dem 1. Januar 2005 begonnen hat und ein Versicherungsbeitrag bis zum 31. Dezember 2004 entrichtet wurde; § 10 Absatz 1 Nummer 2 Satz 2 bis 6 und Absatz 2 Satz 2 in der am 31. Dezember 2004 geltenden Fassung ist in diesen Fällen weiter anzuwenden*".

1864 See also BMF, *Einkommensteuerrechtliche Behandlung von Vorsorgeaufwendungen IV C 3 - S 2221/16/10001:004* para 122.

1865 § 10, para 4, sentence 1 EStG.

1866 Or which were concluded prior to this date, but to which contributions were paid after this date.

1867 Birk and Wernsmann, 261.

7.4.1.C.II Taxation of Benefits during the Pay-Out Phase

With respect to benefits arising from life insurances, concluded prior to 2004, merely the interest from the savings proportion of the life insurances were subject to taxation.[1868] This interest was, however, exempted from taxation when these were offset with contributions, or when these interests were paid out 12 years after the conclusion of the insurance contract. In principle, the pension capital could be accrued tax-free[1869], and during the accrual phase, the reflux of capital as well as the interest thereon, could be exempted from tax.[1870] Contrarily, in cases where the capital would have been disbursed in the form of annuities, the benefits would be taxed in accordance with the *Ertragsanteilbesteuerung.*[1871] For the so-called old contracts concluded prior to 1 January 2005 (i.e. *Altverträge*[1872]), § 20, para. 1, nr 6 EStG (in the version in force until 2004), still applies.[1873] If the life insurance is paid out in the form of an annuity, merely the *Ertragsanteil*[1874], shall be subject to taxation.

As a result of the entry into force of the *Alterseinkünftegesetz*, the tax treatment of capital payments from life insurances has changed.[1875] After the revision of the tax treatment, capital benefits arising from so-called new contracts (*Neuverträge*[1876]) shall be fully subject to *Ertragsanteilbesteuerung.*[1877] The difference between the paid out lump sum, and the contributions paid to the insurance contract, shall be fully subject to taxation. The tax base will be lowered to 50% of the difference between lump sum and the sum of the contributions paid, if the pay-out takes places after the age of 60 of the taxable person, and twelve years after the conclusion of the life insurance contract.[1878] Both conditions ought to be fulfilled.[1879] This reduction of the tax liability intends to relieve the elderly, and, to encounter the progression-increasing effect of the accumulation.[1880]

1868 Pursuant to § 20, para 1, nr 6, sentence 2 EStG (repealed wording). Ibid. 263.

1869 To the extent the maximum amount, as laid down in § 10, para 3 EStG (repealed wording), had not been exceeded.

1870 Birk and Wernsmann, 261.

1871 § 22, nr 1, sentence 3, under a EStG (repealed wording).

1872 The term *Altverträge* includes insurance contracts, concluded prior to 1 January 2005 and to which at least one contribution has been paid.

1873 § 52, para 28, sentence 5 EStG. See also Eckerle, 370 and Birk and Wernsmann, 263.

1874 Comprising the difference between the paid out insurance benefits and the sum of the contributions paid to it. The *Ertragsanteil* shall reflect the interest income, stemming from the accrued capital during the pay-out phase.

1875 Cf. Eckerle, 371.

1876 The term *Neuverträge* includes insurance contracts, concluded after 31 December 2004 or to which contributions have been paid after that date.

1877 § 20, para 1, nr 6, sentence 1 EStG.

1878 § 20, para 1, nr 6, sentence 2 EStG.

1879 See the table inserted in Eckerle, 374.

1880 Birk and Wernsmann, 264 and cited literature.

Other forms of individual retirement provisions, concluded after 31 December 2004 – which do not meet the conditions of the *Rürup-Rente* nor the *Riester-Rente* – shall be subject to *Ertragsanteilbesteuerung*, which requires taxation during the accrual phase, since the contributions are paid out of taxed income.[1881] During the pay-out phase, merely the interest on the capital shall be taxable, contrary to the reflux of capital.[1882] The taxation pursuant to the *Ertragsanteil* is independent of the conclusion date of the contract, i.e. whether it concerns an *Altvertrag* or *Neuvertrag*.[1883]

7.5 Tax Treatment of German Personal Retirement Provisions in Cross-border Cases

As has been addressed in section 7.5, the globalisation of the economy and the related increase in the mobility of workers implies that the taxation of pensions must not solely be considered from a purely national perspective, but also account must be taken of cross-border aspects. In the section below the tax treatment of German personal pensions in cross-border cases will be discussed, both during the accrual phase as well as in the pay-out phase. As regards the accrual phase, the analysis focuses on whether tax advantages are granted, while; as regards the pay-out phase it is considered how, and to what extent, (foreign and domestic) pension benefits are subjected to tax. If, however, the pension entitlements were partly accrued in Germany (a German pension) and partly in the Netherlands (a Dutch pension), the (cross-border) fiscal consequences need to be identified per pension separately (by source of the retirement income). These situations will not be dealt with in the section below, but this section's content, combined with section 7.3, allows for the (fiscal) assessment of such (dispersed) mixed-pension cases.

The allocation of the taxing rights pursuant to a tax treaty, is taken into account as a proviso/prerequisite for the exercise of taxing rights pursuant to domestic (Dutch) tax legislation. These distribution rules will be discussed in chapter 9. The normative framework pertaining to the tax treatment of cross-border pensions, enshrined in EU law, will be discussed in chapter 8.

If the German taxable person, for instance a migrant worker who resided and worked in Germany, decides to leave Germany and emigrates to the Netherlands, this leads to fiscal consequences with respect to the German personal pensions. In particular, these

1881 § 22, nr 1, sentence 3, under bb EStG.

1882 Birk and Wernsmann criticised this outcome, but assume an inciting function, aimed at encouraging people to conclude a supplementary retirement provision, see Birk and Wernsmann, 264.

1883 Cf. Eckerle, 378.

consequences can be considered significant because of the deferred taxation of pensions in Germany, since the principle of deferred taxation stipulates that the fiscally deductible pension contributions paid out of untaxed income during the accrual phase, give rise to benefits paid out during the pay-out phase, which shall be subject to taxation.[1884] This can be referred to as the internal coherence of the national tax system. Since the former German taxable person is no longer unlimitedly subject to taxation in Germany, the German tax authorities would seek to guarantee that the future benefits, paid out during the accrual phase abroad, will be subject to taxation.

7.5.1 *Migrant Worker*

7.5.1.A Outbound

In the outbound migration situation, the employee is resident in the national territory of Germany (partly) during the accrual phase and lives abroad (the Netherlands) during the pay-out phase. The tax treatment of contributions and the granting of tax relief, during the accrual phase, is hence akin to the tax treatment of a domestic situation, i.e. there is no cross-border situation. There is no nexus with Dutch income tax, levied during the accrual phase. I therefore refer to the section 7.4.1.

However, during the pay-out phase, the person concerned resides in the Netherlands. It depends on the allocation of taxing rights enshrined in the applicable tax treaty where the person is liable to tax for the German private pension benefits. If the tax treaty allocates the taxing right to the Netherlands as residence state (pursuant to art. 17, para 1 of the applicable tax treaty) it is up to that state to subject the German private pension benefits to tax. For this I refer to section 7.3.1.B. The migrant worker concerned will be fully liable to tax in the Netherlands (as a resident).[1885] Annuity payments arising from a foreign provision of which the object and purport corresponds to a Dutch life annuity – within the meaning of art. 3.124 ff. Wet IB 2001 – shall also be taxable.[1886] However, if and insofar as it can be assumed with regard to this foreign scheme that the premiums paid have not been deducted from the income during the period abroad, this does not constitute a taxable periodical benefit (but to that extent shall be taxable as income arising from saving

1884 Cf. R Wernsmann and A Nippert, 'Altersbesteuerung beim Wegzug und Europäisches Gemeinschaftsrecht' FR 1123, In BVerfG, the *Bundesverfassungsgericht* ruled that the taxing right is postponed/deferred.

1885 Pursuant to art. 2.1, para 1, sub a Wet IB 2001.

1886 Pursuant to art. 3.100, para 1, sub c Wet IB 2001. It should be noted that this provision applies to residents of the Netherlands (domestic taxpayers) where, in accordance with international views, the world income is included in the tax. This world income also includes payments from abroad.

and investment in BOX 3).[1887] Hence, insofar as the premiums paid abroad have been deducted from taxable income or have otherwise led to a tax reduction, the benefits from the right shall be included in the Dutch income tax. In doing so, a good level of coherence is achieved between the actual tax treatment of the personal pension scheme abroad and that in the Netherlands. However, if Germany (pursuant to art. 17, para 2) is attributed the taxing rights, a distinction needs to be drawn between the different types of private pension vehicles. However, as the person concerned nor resides in Germany, nor has his habitual abode in Germany, during the pay-out phase he may be subject to limited tax liability pursuant to § 1, para 4 EStG, provided that he receives domestic income within the meaning of § 49 EStG. The principal condition for including these elements of income in the limited tax liability is a domestic source of income, which applies to benefits arising from *Lebensversicherungen, Rürup-Rente,* as well as *Riester-Rente.*[1888]

Lebensversicherungen

With regard to benefits arising from *Lebensversicherungen,* concluded prior to 2004, merely the interest from the savings proportion of the life insurances are subject to taxation.[1889] For these so-called old contracts concluded prior to 1 January 2005 (i.e. *Altverträge*[1890]), § 20, para. 1, nr 6 EStG (in the version in force until 2004), still applies.[1891] If the life insurance is paid out in the form of an annuity, merely the *Ertragsanteil*[1892], shall be subject to taxation.

After the entry into force of the *Alterseinkünftegesetz,* the tax treatment of capital payments from *Lebensversicherungen* has changed.[1893] Other forms of individual retirement provisions, concluded after 31 December 2004 – which do not meet the conditions of the *Rürup-Rente* nor the *Riester-Rente* – shall be subject to *Ertragsanteilbesteuerung,* which

1887 Because foreign provisions can involve widely divergent products, and because it will often be unclear to the Dutch tax authorities how the provision is treated for tax purposes abroad, it was decided to place the burden of proof as to whether or not tax relief has been received on the taxpayer. After all, the taxpayer is in the best position to provide information about his/her actual situation. Possibilities to meet this burden of proof are a reference to foreign tax legislation (for instance if the annuity does not meet the conditions for deduction of premiums applicable there), and the submission of a statement by the foreign tax authorities or the insurer or of relevant tax assessments, see Kamerstukken II, *26 727, nr. 7 (Belastingherziening 2001)* 475.

1888 Pursuant to § 49, para 1, under 7 (*Lebensversicherungen* and *Rürup-Rente*) or 10 (*Riester-Rente*) EStG.

1889 Pursuant to § 20, para 1, nr 6, sentence 2 EStG (repealed wording). Birk and Wernsmann, 263.

1890 The term *Altverträge* includes insurance contracts, concluded prior to 1 January 2005 and to which at least one contribution has been paid.

1891 § 52, para 28, sentence 5 EStG. See also Eckerle, 370 and Birk and Wernsmann, 263.

1892 Comprising the difference between the paid-out insurance benefits and the sum of the contributions paid to it. The *Ertragsanteil* shall reflect the interest income, stemming from the accrued capital during the pay-out phase.

1893 Cf. Eckerle, 371.

requires taxation during the accrual phase, since the contributions are paid out of taxed income.[1894] During the pay-out phase, merely the interest on the capital shall be taxable, contrary to the reflux of capital.[1895] The taxation pursuant to the *Ertragsanteil* is independent of the conclusion date of the contract.[1896]

Rürup-Rente

Benefits arising from the *Rürup-Rente*, which have been fiscally facilitated under the *Sonderausgabenabzug*[1897], will be taxed as other income, similar to benefits arising from the *gesetzlichen Rentenversicherung*.[1898] The proportion of the benefits subject to the deferred taxation, is determined on the basis of the so-called *Besteuerungsanteil*[1899]. This taxable proportion shall be gradually raised. Until 2005, the taxable proportion is 50%, after which the proportion shall be raised by 2% per year until 2020, and hereafter with 1% per year (2023: 83%).[1900] As of 2040, the paid out retirement benefits shall be fully subject to deferred taxation.

Riester-Rente

The *Riester-Rente* is subject to deferred taxation, in that the disbursed benefits will be taxed as *Sonstige Einkünfte* (other income), similarly to the benefits of the *Direktversicherung*, *Pensionskasse* and *Pensionsfonds*.[1901] In addition, to the extent that no additional expenses are deducted, an additional *Pauschbetrag* of €102 may be deducted from the tax assessment basis.[1902] The tax treatment of benefits arising from the *Riester-Rente* is, however, subject to differentiation, in the sense that the extent to which the benefits shall be subject to deferred taxation depends on the extent to which the contributions have been fiscally facilitated.[1903] The benefits disbursed will be fully subject to taxation, if the contributions paid to the provision have been fully subject to fiscal facilitation during the accrual phase, or arise from the provided statutory allowances (i.e. *Zulagen*[1904]), to the extent they do not exceed

1894 § 22, nr 1, sentence 3, under bb EStG.

1895 Birk and Wernsmann criticised this outcome, but assume an inciting function, aimed at encouraging people to conclude a supplementary retirement provision, see Birk and Wernsmann, 264.

1896 Cf. Eckerle, 378.

1897 Pursuant to § 10, para 1, nr 2, under b EStG.

1898 Pursuant to §2, para 1, sentence 1, nr 7 in conjunction with § 22, nr 1, sentence 3, under aa EStG.

1899 Translated freely as 'taxable proportion'. See also BMF, *Steuerliche Förderung der privaten Altersvorsorge IV C 3 - S 2015/17/10001:005* para 144.

1900 The percentages of this taxable proportion are laid down in § 22, nr 1, sentence 3, table under aa EStG.

1901 Pursuant to § 22, nr 5 EstG.

1902 Pursuant to § 9a, para 3 EstG.

1903 Cf. Birk and Wernsmann, 263 and Wernsmann, 791.

1904 Which have been accrued pursuant to section XI EStG. See also BMF, para 131.

the maximum amount of §10a EStG.[1905] In cases where the taxable person during the accrual phase, has paid fiscally facilitated as well as non-facilitated contributions to the *Riester*-provision, the tax treatment of the benefits paid out during the pay-out phase shall be differentiated.[1906] Furthermore, the tax treatment shall be differentiated when the taxable person has paid contributions exceeding the maximum amount, for instance as laid down in § 10a EStG. Benefits arising from non-facilitated contributions are taxed against the *Ertragsanteil*.[1907]

Riester-Rente: Exit Tax in Non-EU Cases

Since the *Riester-Rente* was subject to unlimited tax liability until 15 April 2010, the paid allowances to the *Riester-Rente*, and the facilitated contributions had to be repaid, even when the person entitled to the allowances decided to relocate his residence and habitual residence to another EU Member State.[1908] This provision was applicable to all situations in which the unlimited tax liability of the taxable person ended due to the abandonment of the residence or habitual residence in Germany.[1909] This exit tax was met with considerable criticism, since this exit tax was considered incompatible with EU law, notably the European rights of free movement.[1910]

The CJEU held that this reimbursement obligation of the allowances and *Sonderausgabenabzug*, infringed the freedom of workers and the freedom of citizens.[1911] Moreover, the provisions at issue – § 93 to § 95 EStG – indirectly discriminated migrant

1905 § 22, nr 5, sentence 1 and 2 EStG and ibid., para 137. Contributions for which the maximum amount of § 10a EStG has been exceeded, shall not be considered facilitated contributions. Neither do contributions for which the taxable person has not received any allowances or did not receive the *Sonderausgabenabzug*, see ibid., para 134. In addition, income and capital appreciations attributable to unduly paid, and subsequently reclaimed allowances, shall be treated as non-facilitated retirement capital, see ibid., para 135.

1906 Ibid., para 139.

1907 § 22, nr 1, sentence 3, under bb and § 22, nr 5, sentence 2, under b and c in conjunction with § 22, nr 5, sentence 2. With respect to *Ertragsanteilbesteuerung*, also see C Herrmann, G Heuer and A Raupach, *Einkommensteuer- und Körperschaftsteuergesetz: EStG KStG* (Dr. Otto Schmidt, Köln Aktualisierung 2018).

1908 § 95, para 1, sentence 1 EStG (repealed wording). This provision has been amended pursuant to article 1 of Gesetz zur Umsetzung steuerlicher EU-Vorgaben sowie zur Änderung steuerlicher Vorschriften (EUStVUG). See also Quinten M. and Sona B., 'Die Grenze der Riester-Förderung bei einem Wohnsitz im Ausland' 2 RVaktuell 44.

1909 See for instance F Welker, *Das Altersvermögensgesetz und seine konsequenzen für die betriebliche Altersversorgung: arbeits-, steuer- und aufsichtsrechtliche Perspektiven* (Deutscher Universitäts-Verlag, Wiesbaden 2005) 85-86.

1910 See Richter, 285., Wernsmann and Nippert, and D Birk and R Wernsmann, 'Die Besteuerung der Aufwendungen für die Altersvorsorge und der Alterseinkommen' in B Rürup and F Ruland (eds.), *Alterssicherung und Besteuerung* (Gabler, Wiesbaden 2008) 266-268.

1911 Pursuant to article 18 EC Treaty. C 269/07 *Commission vs. Germany* ECLI:EU:C:2009:527 (CJEU). This had already been recognized by Wellisch and others, 50.

workers.[1912] Following this judgment, the underlying provision was revoked, in order to bring the national tax legislation in line with European law.[1913] § 95, para 1 now sets out that the reimbursement obligation applies in cases where the taxable person, entitled to the allowance, has moved his residence or habitual abode outside the Member States of the European Union and the States to which the Agreement on the European Economic Area (EEA Agreement) applies, or if the person concerned, notwithstanding a residence or habitual abode in one of these States, is considered to be resident outside the territory of these States under a tax treaty with a third State.[1914]

In these non-EU cases, the German tax administration considers this as misuse of the fiscal facilitation granted during the accrual phase.[1915] The facilitated contributions and provided allowances must be repaid. On request, the repayment may be deferred to the beginning of the pay-out phase.[1916] This deferment may, however, be extended if the repayment amount is repaid with at least 15% of the benefits.[1917] The deferral of the repayment is terminated, when the provision will not be paid to the beneficiary in accordance with the conditions of the *Altersvorsorgeverträge-Zertifizierungsgesetzes*, such as a lifelong annuity.[1918] This illustrates the synergy between the conditions underlying fiscal facilitation in the EStG and the conditions for retirement provisions as laid down in the AltZertG. The repayment amount and the already incurred interest on the deferred amount will be remitted, when the former taxable person living abroad, decides to relocate his exclusive resident or habitual residence to a EU Member State or a State to which the Agreement on the European Economic Area (EEA agreement) is applicable.[1919]

7.5.1.B Inbound

In the inbound migration situation, the employee is resident in the national territory of the Netherlands (partly) during the accrual phase and lives abroad (Germany) during the pay-out phase. The tax treatment of contributions and the granting of tax relief, during the accrual phase, is hence akin to the tax treatment of a domestic situation, i.e. there is no

1912 *Commission vs. Germany* para 104.

1913 Pursuant to Gesetz zur Umsetzung steuerlicher EU-Vorgaben sowie zur Änderung steuerlicher Vorschriften (EUStVUG).

1914 This repayment obligation is based on the idea that the pension-savings allowance constitutes a social benefit which is intended to compensate for the reductions in benefits in the relevant pension-savings systems made by the domestic legislature.

1915 § 93, para 1, sentence 1 in conjunction with § 95 EStG.

1916 § 95, para 2, sentence 1 EStG. The request of deferment is to be submitted to the *Deutsche Rentenversicherung Bund*, via the pension provider, see § 95, para 2, sentence 4 in conjunction with § 81 EStG.

1917 § 95, para 2, sentence 2 EStG.

1918 § 95, para 2, sentence 3 EStG refers to § 1, para 1, sentence 1, nr 4 AltZertG.

1919 § 95, para 3, nr 1 EStG.

cross-border situation. For this I refer to section 6.3. There is no nexus with German income tax, levied during the accrual phase.

It depends on the allocation of taxing rights enshrined in the applicable tax treaty where the person is liable to tax for the foreign private pension benefits. If the taxing right is allocated to Germany as a residence state (pursuant to art. 17, para 1 of the applicable tax treaty), the benefits arising from the foreign private pension scheme will be subject to German income tax, where will be fully liable to tax.[1920]

Foreign (Dutch) Private Pension Benefits Qualified as Lebensversicherungen
Lifelong pension benefits arising from foreign private pension schemes qualified as *Lebensversicherungen*, not meeting the preconditions set with regard to *Rürup- or Riester-Rente*, shall be subject to *Ertragsanteilbesteuerung* pursuant to § 22, nr 1, sentence 3, under bb EStG.[1921] The extent to which the benefits shall be subject to taxation does not depend on the extent to which the contributions have been fiscally facilitated, either domestically or abroad. Furthermore, the taxation pursuant to the *Ertragsanteil* is independent of the conclusion date of the contract, i.e. whether it concerns an *Altvertrag* or *Neuvertrag*.[1922]

Foreign Private Pension Benefits Qualified as Rürup-Rente
Benefits arising from foreign private pension schemes qualified as *Rürup-Rente*, will be taxed as other income, pursuant to § 22, nr 1, sentence 3, under aa EStG, provided that the contributions have been subject to deduction as *Sonderausgaben*[1923]. The proportion of the benefits subject to the deferred taxation, is determined on the basis of the so-called *Besteuerungsanteil* (2023: 83%).[1924] This applies to benefits paid by domestic and foreign pension institutions.[1925] However, with regard to benefits emerging from foreign private pension schemes it needs to be ascertained to what extent the contributions paid into the foreign scheme have been subject to *Sonderausgaben*-deduction in Germany. As far as this is proven to be not the case, which seems likely, the benefits emerging from the private pension scheme are subject to taxation against the *Ertragsanteil*, pursuant to § 22, nr 1, sentence 3, under bb EStG.[1926]

1920 Pursuant to § 1, para 1 EStG.
1921 See also Eckerle, 378.
1922 Cf. Ibid. 378.
1923 Pursuant to § 10, para 1, nr 2, letter b EStG.
1924 The percentages of this taxable proportion are laid down in § 22, nr 1, sentence 3, table under aa EStG.
1925 BMF, *Einkommensteuerrechtliche Behandlung von Vorsorgeaufwendungen und Altersbezügen IV C 3 - S 2221/12/10010:004 - IV C 5 - S 2345/08/0001* para 190.
1926 See for instance Wellisch and others, 176.

Foreign Private Pension Benefits Qualified as Riester-Rente
The benefits will be taxed as *Sonstige Einkünfte*, pursuant to § 22, nr 5 EStG. In addition, an additional *Pauschbetrag* of €102 (2023) may be deducted from the tax assessment basis, pursuant to § 9a, para 3 EstG. The tax treatment of benefits arising from the *Riester-Rente* is, however, subject to differentiation, in the sense that the extent to which the benefits shall be subject to deferred taxation depends on the extent to which the contributions have been fiscally facilitated. The benefits disbursed will be fully subject to taxation, if the contributions paid to the provision have been fully subject to fiscal facilitation during the accrual phase, or arise from the provided statutory allowances (i.e. *Zulagen*), to the extent they do not exceed the maximum amount of §10a EStG. In cases where the taxable person during the accrual phase, has paid fiscally facilitated as well as non-facilitated contributions to the *Riester*-provision, the tax treatment of the benefits paid out during the pay-out phase shall be differentiated. Benefits arising from non-facilitated contributions are taxed against the *Ertragsanteil*, pursuant § 22, nr 1, sentence 3, under bb and § 22, nr 5, sentence 2, under a EStG.

7.5.2 *Cross-border Worker*

As a cross-border worker, the mobile citizen works in one State, while residing in another (neighbouring) Member State, to which they commonly return every day or at least once a week. The working state is thus different from the residence state. As no allocation rules exist as regards private pensions (similar to Regulation 883/2004 applicable to statutory pension schemes, i.e. rules stipulating where the cross-border worker participates in a pension scheme), it needs to be determined where the person concerned does actually participate in a private pension scheme. As addressed in Chapter 4 of this research, when it comes to personal pensions (third pillar), both in the Netherlands as well as in Germany, these pension schemes do not have its basis in the performance of work (like occupational pensions) but characteristics such as freedom, personal responsibility and flexibility prevail prevail. The cross-border worker may, hence, choose to either continue his participation, and thus contribution, to a pension scheme in Germany, or may become a participant of the private pension scheme in the Netherlands.

7.5.2.A **Outbound**

In this situation, where Germany is the residence state, the cross-border worker may remain a participant in a German private pension scheme, while working abroad, or become a participant in a private pension scheme in the Netherlands. However, remaining in the residence state-pension scheme seems more desirable in view of possible costs incurred and a possible loss of pension rights in case of the transfer of rights/capital.

Continuance of Participating in German Private Pension Scheme
Provided that, pursuant to the applicable tax treaty (art. 14, para 1), the taxing right pertaining to the remuneration is allocated to the Netherlands (working state), and if the person is treated as fully liable to tax in that state (for instance, as he receives at least 90% of his taxable income in the other state), it is a matter for that state to determine to what extent it allows the contributions paid to the German private pension scheme to be taken into account in the calculation of the domestic tax assessment base. For this I refer to section 6.4.1.B.I. However, if the prevailing tax treaty allocates the taxing right to Germany (pursuant to art. 14, para 1 or 2 of the applicable tax treaty), it may subject the person to unlimited tax liability (pursuant to § 1, para 1, sentence 1 EStG), and the tax treatment of the contributions is akin to a domestic situation, see section 7.4.

As the person resides in Germany during the pay-out phase, the taxation of pension benefits paid out is akin to a domestic situation, provided that Germany – where he will be fully liable to tax – is allocated the taxing right pursuant to the applicable tax treaty (pursuant to art. 17, para 1 of the applicable tax treaty). See section 7.4. In this case, the residence state coincides with the pension's source state. If the taxing right is assigned (pursuant to art. 17, para 2 of the treaty) to the Netherlands as source state, German personal pension benefits will be subject to Dutch income tax. For this, I refer to section 7.3.1.B. Annuity payments arising from a foreign provision of which the object and purport corresponds to a Dutch life annuity – within the meaning of art. 3.124 ff. Wet IB 2001 – shall be taxable.[1927] Insofar as the premiums paid abroad have been deducted from taxable income or have otherwise led to a tax reduction, the benefits from the right shall be included in the Dutch income tax. In doing so, a sound level of coherence is achieved between the actual tax treatment of the personal pension scheme abroad and that in the Netherlands.

However, as regards the eligibility of this outbound cross-border worker as regards the tax relief for the *Riester-Rente*, some observations must be made. Since in order to be eligible for the *Zulagen* or *Sonderausgabenabzug*, the person concerned must have fulfilled the personal requirement (i.e. eligible persons) at least part of the contribution year (i.e. the assessment period).[1928] Persons eligible are mandatory insured domestic persons in the *gesetzlichen Rentenversicherung* or recipients of domestic salaries in accordance with the Federal Salary Act (*Bundesbesoldungsgesetz*) or Landes Salary Act

1927 Pursuant to art. 3.100, para 1, sub c Wet IB 2001. It should be noted that this provision applies to residents of the Netherlands (domestic taxpayers) where, in accordance with international views, the world income is included in the tax. This world income also includes payments from abroad.

1928 BMF, *Steuerliche Förderung der privaten Altersvorsorge (21 December 2017)* (2017) para 1.

(*Landesbesoldungsgesetz*).[1929] In particular the former (mandatory insurance) is the most important for the purpose of the present study. However, in this situation, where the other state is the working state, the cross-border worker is insured, and thus obliged to pay contributions, to the foreign statutory pension scheme.[1930] He will hence, in principle, not be entitled to *Zulagen* or *Sonderausgabenabzug* as regards the *Riester-Rente*. Noteworthy from a cross-border perspective is that pursuant to the amendment by the *Gesetz zur Umsetzung steuerlicher EU-Vorgaben sowie zur Änderung steuerlicher Vorschriften*[1931], as of 1 January 2010, persons insured under a foreign pension scheme shall no longer be set equal to persons insured mandatory under the domestic pension scheme for the application of § 10a, para 1 EStG.[1932] This restriction seems justified since the German legislator has not intervened in these foreign pension systems to reduce benefits. However, for cases prior to 1 January 2010, §10a, para 6 EStG provides for a system for the preservation of acquired rights (*Bestandsschutzregelung*). Pursuant to §10a, para 6, sentence 1 EStG, persons compulsory insured under a foreign statutory pension scheme, are also considered eligible persons under two conditions.[1933] Firstly, this mandatory membership must be comparable with compulsory membership of either the *gesetzlichen Rentenversicherung* or the *Alterssicherung der Landwirte*. Secondly, this compulsory membership must be established prior to 1 January 2010. It is difficult to see that it has not been further elucidated, by instance by setting certain principles or standards of comparability, under what circumstances a foreign statutory pension scheme is considered comparable to the *gesetzlichen Rentenversicherung* or the *Alterssicherung der Landwirte*. This would have ameliorated the foreseeability of (the application of) legislation and government action (i.e. tax authorities).[1934] If these conditions have been met, the person compulsory insured under a foreign statutory pension scheme, is also eligible for the *Zulagen* or *Sonderausgabenabzug*.

1929 § 10a, para 1, sentence 1 EStG. See also ibid. para 4. The persons (not) entitled have been enumerated in BMF, *Steuerliche Förderung der privaten Altersvorsorge (21 December 2017)* (2017), appendix 1.

1930 Pursuant to Article 11, para 3, sub a Regulation 883/2004.

1931 Gesetz zur Umsetzung steuerlicher EU-Vorgaben sowie zur Änderung steuerlicher Vorschriften (EUStVUG).

1932 BMF, para 18.

1933 Ibid. para 19. This paragraph has been implemented pursuant to Gesetz zur Anpassung des nationalen Steuerrechts an den Beitritt Kroatiens zur EU und zur Änderung weiterer steuerlicher Vorschriften (StRAnpG). § 10a, par 6 EStG, sentence 2 EStG will not be discussed any further as this concerns the particular situations of civil servants, judges, professional soldiers and temporary soldiers on leave without pay.

1934 For the purposes of applying § 10a, par 6 EStG, the pension systems of some international organisations are to be regarded as a pension scheme comparable to the *gesetzlichen Rentenversicherung* or the *Alterssicherung der Landwirte*, such as the pension schemes of the European Commission, the European Central Bank, the NATO, the OECD, or the UN. See ibid. paras 22 and 23. It does not become evident from this enumeration which elements or characteristics of pension schemes are considered decisive, or even are taken into consideration, in the assessment of comparability.

Furthermore, it is to be stressed that §10a, para 6 EStG applies to the extent that the persons concerned are subject to unlimited income tax liability or are treated as subject to unlimited income tax liability for the contribution year in accordance with § 1, paragraph 3 EStG.[1935] If compulsory membership in this foreign statutory pension insurance scheme ends or is interrupted for more than one contribution year, the protection of continued existence under § 10a, paragraph 6 EStG is terminated. The German legislator thus relies on the connecting factor relating to mandatory insurance (to the German statutory pension scheme), and the tax status of the persons concerned. The foregoing implies that outbound cross-border workers subject to (or treated as) unlimited tax liability in Germany, who are compulsory insured under a foreign statutory pension scheme, comparable to compulsory insurance in the *gesetzlichen Rentenversicherung* or the *Alterssicherung der Landwirte*, are only entitled to an allowance for *Riester*-contracts concluded before 1 January 2010.[1936] If the aforementioned unlimited tax liability of a person ends by abandoning his or her domestic residence or habitual abode and the person is not treated as being liable to unlimited tax liability pursuant to § 1, para 3, the provision concerning improper use shall apply, pursuant to which the allowances must be repaid.[1937]

Participating in Foreign Private Pension Scheme

If the cross-border worker, resident in Germany, decides to participate in a Dutch private pension scheme, the tax treatment of these Dutch pension contributions must be assessed. If the art. 14, para 1 of the treaty allocates the taxing right pertaining to the remuneration to the the Netherlands, it is a matter for that state to decide to what extent it subjects the contributions paid into a domestic private pension scheme by a non-resident taxpayer to tax (relief). See section 7.2.

However, if the applicable tax treaty allocates the taxing right pertaining to the remuneration to Germany (pursuant to art. 14, para 1 of the applicable tax treaty), and the person concerned is fully liable to tax in Germany (pursuant to § 1, para 1, sentence 1 EStG), these type of workers may continue to pay their pension contributions into the

1935 § 79, sentence 3 EStG.

1936 BMF, para 20. The conclusion of the agreement is decisive in this regard, in that an agreement concluded after December 31, 2009 shall not be taken into account for the examination of the requirements of § 10a, para 6 of the EStG, even if pension plan assets are transferred from an agreement concluded before January 1, 2010. For the application of § 10a (XI) EStG, merely pension contributions in favour of a contract concluded before 1 January 2010 are taken into account. In the case of spouses or life partners of whom only one spouse/life partner is directly entitled to an allowance, the other spouse/life partner is also (indirectly) entitled to a bonus, under certain conditions. See ibid. paras 26-29.

1937 § 10a, para 6, sentence 4 EStG. The provision concerning improper use are §§ 93 and 94 which shall apply *mutatis mutandis*; § 95, para. 2 and 3 and § 99, para. 1 in the version in force on 31 December 2008.

Dutch pension schemes. The *Bundesfinanzhof* holds that comparability of retirement pensions can be assumed in cases where the foreign pension benefits correspond in its core content to the common and typical features of the domestic benefit.[1938] As regards the tax treatment of these foreign private schemes, it must be determined through a comparative legal qualification of the foreign pension scheme, to what extent these foreign schemes are eligible for tax relief. However, practical guidelines as to when a foreign private pension scheme qualifies as either a German *Lebensversicherung, Rürup-Rente* or *Riester-Rente* are not provided by the German legislature, nor the German tax authorities. Setting certain principles or standards of comparability would have ameliorated the foreseeability of (the application of) legislation and government action (i.e. tax authorities). This is also relevant for the cases of an inbound migrant worker receiving pension benefits from a foreign private pension scheme, an outbound posted worker participating in the host state's private pension plan during the period of posting, or if an outbound cross-border worker participates in a foreign pension plan. Below, it is assumed that the foreign private pension scheme is eligible for tax relief in Germany.[1939]

Foreign Private Pension Scheme Qualified as Lebensversicherung

The term *Lebensversicherung* (i.e. life insurance) may cover numerous varieties of life insurances, such as a pure term life insurance[1940], retirement insurances with or without lump-sum option[1941] or pure endowment insurances[1942].[1943] With respect to contributions or benefits of new contracts – concluded after 31 December 2004[1944] – the fiscal facilitation has been phased out gradually. Hence, contributions to other forms of individual retirement provisions, concluded after 31 December 2004 – are no longer eligible for fiscal facilitation, unless they meet the conditions of the *Rürup-Rente* or *Riester-Rente*.

1938 See for instance X R 37/08 BStBl. II 2011 (628) (BFH) in which the Court held: "*Bei der Anwendung des deutschen Steuerrechts ist stets eine rechtsvergleichende Qualifizierung der ausländischen Einkünfte nach deutschem Recht vorzunehmen. Vergleichbarkeit von Altersrenten ist dann anzunehmen, wenn die ausländische Leistung in ihrem Kerngehalt den gemeinsamen und typischen Merkmalen der inländischen Leistung entspricht, d.h. nach Motivation und Funktion gleichwertig ist. Da eine völlige Identität kaum denkbar ist, muss sich diese Beurteilung notwendigerweise auf bestimmte Eigenschaften beider Leistungsarten beschränken und andere als unwesentlich für den Vergleich ausscheiden. Maßgebliche Gesichtspunkte sind die Essentialia der nationalen Norm, also deren Funktion und Struktur nach nationalem Verständnis.*"

1939 Similar as Wellisch and others, 168, 176.

1940 I.e. *reine Risikolebensversicherung.*

1941 I.e. *Rentenversicherungen mit und ohne Kapitalwahlrecht.*

1942 I.e. *reine Kapitalversicherungen.*

1943 D Birk and R Wernsmann, 'Die Besteuerung der Aufwendungen für die Altersvorsorge und der Alterseinkommen' in B Rürup and F Ruland (eds.), *Alterssicherung und Besteuerung* (Gabler, Wiesbaden 2008) 261.

1944 Or which were concluded prior to this date, but to which contributions were paid after this date.

As has been set forth above, merely contributions paid into *Altverträge* are eligible for deduction as *Sonderausgaben*.[1945] The deductibility of the contributions to the so-called *Altverträge* to foreign insurance is permitted, subject to various conditions.[1946] Firstly, the contributions may not have a direct economic connection with tax-free income.[1947] Notwithstanding this condition, contributions shall be taken in so far as three conditions have been met.[1948] These conditions have been implemented in response to the CJEU's ruling in the *Bechtel* case.[1949] Firstly, the contributions must have a direct economic link with income from employment in a Member State of the European Union or a State party to the Agreement on the European Economic Area. The contributions may thus be related to foreign income from employment. Secondly, this income is tax-exempt in Germany pursuant to an applicable tax treaty. Lastly, the state of employment does not allow to take these pension contributions into account in the taxation of this income.

Next to this requirement of not having a direct economic connection with tax-free income, some preconditions have been set as regards the institution to which these contributions are paid.[1950] As regards insurance undertakings, it must have its registered office or its management in a Member State of the European Union or in a Contracting State to the Agreement on the European Economic Area and must be permitted to conduct insurance business in Germany, or have been granted a licence to conduct business in Germany.[1951] As regards insurance undertakings within a EU Member State or a signatory state to the Agreement on the European Economic Area, it can regularly be assumed that their licence applies to the territory of all member states and signatory states – and thus to business operations in Germany.[1952]

During the pay-out phase, the person will reside in Germany and will be liable to German tax[1953], and receive foreign personal pension benefits qualified as *Lebensversicherung*. Under the condition that the applicable tax treaty allocates the taxing right to Germany (pursuant to art. 17, para 1), this situation has been addressed as regards the situation of an inbound migrant worker receiving foreign private pension benefits. I therefore refer to

1945 See §10, para 1, nr 3a EStG.

1946 Enshrined in §10, para 1, nr 3a in conjunction with § 10, para 2 EStG.

1947 § 10, para 2, sentence 1, nr 1 EStG. However, this same provision provides an exception to this rule.

1948 § 10, para 2, sentence 1, nr 1, letter a, b and c EStG.

1949 Implemented through Gesetz zur Vermeidung von Umsatzsteuerausfällen beim Handel mit Waren im Internet und zur Änderung weiterer steuerlicher Vorschriften (UStIntG).

1950 § 10, para 2, sentence 1, nr 2 EStG.

1951 § 10, para 2, sentence 1, nr 2, letter a, double letter aa and bb EStG.

1952 BMF, para 95. The following link can be used to ascertain which companies have a permit, have been notified or maintain a representative office in Germany: https://portal.mvp.bafin.de/database/InstInfo/.

1953 Pursuant to § 1, para 1, sentence 1 EStG.

section 7.5.1.B. However, if the applicable tax treaty allocates the taxing right to the Netherlands (pursuant to art. 17, para 2), these Dutch benefits will be taxable under Dutch income tax. For this I refer to section 7.2.1.

Foreign Private Pension Scheme Qualified as Riester-Rente

If the eligibility criteria conditions are met, the foreign scheme will be subject to fiscal facilitation consisting of, firstly, a basic allowance (i.e. *Grundzulage*) for pension contributions paid in the past contribution year.[1954] Depending on the pension contributions paid, an allowance is paid consisting of a basic allowance (i.e. *Grundzulage* ex. § 84) and a child allowance (*Kinderzulage* ex. § 85).[1955] The calculated allowances will be directly remitted to his retirement provision.[1956] In addition to the aforementioned allowances, the fiscal facilitation of the *Riester-Rente* offers the possibility for taxable persons – who fall under the group of beneficiary persons – to deduct their pension contributions, paid during the assessment period, as *Sonderausgaben*, pursuant to § 10a, para 1, sentence 1 EStG.[1957] The fiscal facilitation of *Sonderausgabenabzug* shall merely apply, if this is more advantageous for the taxable person than the entitlement to the allowances, i.e. the so-called *Günstigerprüfung*.[1958]

During the pay-out phase, the person will reside in Germany and will be liable to German tax[1959], and receive foreign pension benefits qualified as *Riester-Rente*. Under the condition that the applicable tax treaty allocates the taxing right to Germany (pursuant to art. 17, para 1), this situation has been addressed as regards the situation of an inbound migrant worker receiving foreign pension benefits. I therefore refer to section 7.5.1.B. However, if the applicable tax treaty allocates the taxing right to the Netherlands (pursuant to art. 17, para 2), these Dutch benefits will be taxable under Dutch income tax. For this I refer to section 7.2.1.

Foreign Private Pension Scheme Qualified as Rürup-Rente

Under certain conditions, the contributions paid to a *Rürup-Rente* are partially fiscally deductible as *Sonderausgaben*, pursuant to § 10, para 1, nr 2, under b EStG. These conditions have already been discussed in the section dealing with the tax treatment of the

1954 BMF, BStBl I 21 December 2017. 2018, para 46.

1955 Pursuant to § 83 EStG.

1956 Cf. M Myßen and others, *Handbuch Zulagenförderung: steuerlich begünstigte Altersvorsorge* (C.F. Müller, Heidelberg 2006) and W Förster and S Rechtenwald, 'Die betriebliche und private Altersvorsorge' in F Ruland and B Rürup (eds.), *Alterssicherung und Besteuerung* (Gabler, Wiesbaden 2008).

1957 See BMF, para 93.

1958 Translated freely as ‚most favourable tax treatment'. See § 10a, para 2, sentence 1 EStG and ibid., para 101.

1959 Pursuant to § 1, para 1, sentence 1 EStG.

Rürup-Rente. There is a dichotomy in the fiscal facilitation of contributions paid to the *Rürup-Rente* as well, i.e. contributions will merely be considered *Sonderausgaben* if the term of the insurance contract begins after 31 December 2004, i.e. the entry into force of the *Alterseinkünftegesetz.*[1960]

As has been set forth above as regards contributions paid into a foreign pension scheme qualified as a *Lebensversicherung*, certain conditions apply if contributions are paid abroad, in order to be eligible for deduction of the contributions as *Sonderausgaben.*[1961] The foreign insurance undertaking must have its registered office or its management in a Member State of the European Union or in a Contracting State to the Agreement on the European Economic Area and must be permitted to conduct insurance business in Germany, or have been granted a licence to conduct business in Germany.[1962] Pension contributions into a *Rürup-Rente* are solely taken into account if the contributions are made in favour of a contract which is certified in accordance with § 5a AltZertG.[1963] If these contributions have been met, the contributions paid by the outbound cross-border worker to the foreign scheme, qualified as a *Rürup-Rente* are deductible as *Sonderausgaben.* As of 2023, 100% of these contributions may be deducted.[1964] Thereafter, this amount shall be reduced with the tax-free employer's portion to the *gesetzlichen Rentenversicherung*[1965] and the tax-free employer's subsidy equal to this.[1966]

During the pay-out phase, the person will reside in Germany and will be liable to German tax[1967], and receive foreign pension benefits qualified as *Rürup-Rente.* Under the condition that the applicable tax treaty allocates the taxing right to Germany (pursuant to art. 17, para 1), this situation has been addressed as regards the situation of an inbound migrant worker receiving foreign pension benefits. I therefore refer to section 7.5.1.B. However, if the applicable tax treaty allocates the taxing right to the Netherlands (pursuant to art. 17, para 2), these Dutch benefits will be taxable under Dutch income tax. For this I refer to section 7.2.1.

1960 BMF, para 35. See also Rürup and Myßen, 198; P Kirchhof, H Söhn and R Mellinghof, *Einkommensteuergesetz: Kommentar zum EStG* (C.F. Müller, Heidelberg 2018) and H Hügelschäffer and others, *Handbuch Alterssicherung* (C.F. Müller, Heidelberg 2006).

1961 § 10, para 2, sentence 1, nr 2 EStG.

1962 § 10, para 2, sentence 1 nr 2, letter a, double letter aa and bb EStG.

1963 § 10, para 2, sentence 2 EStG.

1964 § 10, para 3, sentence 4 and 6 EStG. As of 2025, 100% of the contributions will be deductible, see the table in ibid., para 73.

1965 § 3, nr 63 EStG.

1966 § 10, para 3, sentence 5 EStG and BMF, para 74.

1967 Pursuant to § 1, para 1, sentence 1 EStG.

7.5.2.B Inbound

In this situation, the cross-border worker is a resident of the Netherlands, while he works in Germany, returning to the Netherlands at least once a week. He may opt to remain a participant in the Dutch private pension scheme, while working in Germany, or become a participant in a German private pension scheme. Both cases will be dealt with below.

Continuance of Participating in Foreign Private Pension Scheme

Provided that, pursuant to the applicable tax treaty (art. 14, para 1 or 2), the taxing right pertaining to the remuneration is allocated to the Netherlands (residence state), and if the person is fully liable to tax in that state, it is a matter for that state to determine to what extent it allows the contributions paid to Dutch private pension scheme to be taken into account in the calculation of the domestic tax assessment base, see section 7.2.1.

However, if the prevailing tax treaty allocates the taxing right to Germany (pursuant to art. 14, para 1), this situation is, as regards the tax treatment of contributions and benefits, similar to an outbound cross-border worker participating in a foreign private pension scheme. However, contrary to the outbound situation, an essential difference lies in the fact that in the present inbound situation, the person concerned is not fully liable to tax in Germany as he is a resident of the Netherlands. However, upon request, he may be treated as fully liable to tax in Germany,[1968] to the extent that he receives domestic income within the meaning of § 49 EStG. This applies solely if the income, received during the entire calendar year, is subject to German income tax for at least 90%, or the income not being subjected to German income tax, does not exceed the exemption threshold (*Grundfreibetrag; 2023: €10,908*) of § 32a, para 1, sentence 2, nr 1 EStG.[1969] If that proves to be the case, the tax treatment of contributions and benefits is akin to the situation discussed under the preceding (outbound) section (section 7.5.2.A), where the cross-border worker contributed to a foreign private pension scheme.

During retirement, the inbound cross-border worker will reside in the Netherlands where he will be fully liable to tax. If the applicable tax treaty allocates the taxing right to the Netherlands (pursuant to art. 17, para 1), these Dutch pension benefits will be fully subject to income tax, see section 7.2.1.B. However, if the applicable tax treaty allocates the taxing right to Germany (pursuant to art. 17, para 2), these Dutch benefits will be taxable under German income tax, see section 7.5.1.B.

1968 Pursuant to § 1, para 3 EStG.
1969 Pursuant to § 1, para 3§, sentence 2 EStG.

Participating in German Private Pension Scheme

If the cross-border worker, resident in the Netherlands, decides to participate in a German private pension scheme, the tax treatment of these domestic pension schemes must be assessed. If the applicable tax treaty allocates the taxing right pertaining to the remuneration/pension to the Netherlands (pursuant to art. 14, para 1), the tax treatment of the German pension contributions and benefits is a matter for that state, where the person concerned shall be subject to unlimited tax liability. For this I refer to section 6.4.1.B.I. However, if the taxing right pertaining to the remuneration/pension is attributed to Germany (pursuant to art. 14, para 1), and the person concerned is treated as fully liable to tax in Germany (pursuant to § 1, para 3 EStG), these type of workers are subject to a tax treatment akin to a domestic worker, notwithstanding that he resides abroad. For the tax treatment of the contributions I therefore refer to section 7.4.

However, as the person concerned will reside in the Netherlands during retirement, he will receive pension benefits emerging from German private pension schemes. Germany will not withhold any withholding tax upon pay-out of these benefits abroad. If the applicable tax treaty appoints the Netherlands as the competent state to tax (pursuant to art. 17, para 1), this is a matter for that State, see section 7.3.1.B. However, if the applicable tax treaty allocates the taxing right on the German personal pension to Germany (pursuant to art. 17, para 2), the person concerned can merely come within the scope of German income tax as a limited taxable person pursuant to § 1, para 4 EStG, as he nor resides, nor has his habitual abode in German, in so far as he receives domestic income within the meaning of § 49 EStG. The principal condition for including these elements of income in the limited tax liability is a domestic source of income, which applies to benefits arising from *Lebensversicherungen, Rürup-Rente*, as well as *Riester-Rente.*[1970] The taxable proportion of these types of benefits depends on whether these benefits are derived from contributions which were subject to tax relief in the Germany.[1971]

7.5.3 *Posted Worker*

7.5.3.A **Outbound**

In the outbound posting case, a German employee is sent to the Netherlands during the accrual phase, i.e. the German parent company posts its German employee to a subsidiary

1970 Pursuant to § 49, para 1, under 7 (*Lebensversicherungen* and *Rürup-Rente*) or 10 (*Riester-Rente*) EStG.

1971 As regards this tax relief, § 49, para 1, under 7 (*Lebensversicherungen* and *Rürup-Rente*) or 10 (*Riester-Rente*) EStG refer to § 10, para 1, nr. 2 EStG (*Sonderausgaben*).

located in the Netherlands. Posting is temporary in nature.[1972] It is therefore assumed, and this is characteristic for the case of posting, that the employee concerned will continue to participate, and contribute, to a German personal pension scheme as the sending state.

According to the applicable treaty provision (pursuant to art. 14, para 2), during the period of posting, Germany (residence state) is allocated the taxing rights as regards the remuneration. In such as case, the tax treatment of the pension contributions is akin to a domestic German situation, see section 6.6. However, as holds true with regard to outbound cross-border workers, as discussed in section 7.5.2.A, an observation must be made with regard to the eligibility of an outbound posted worker as regards the *Zulagen* and *Sonderausgaben* applicable to the *Riester-Rente*. As a general rule, this posted worker remains insured for social security in Germany, being the sending state.[1973] He will thus be compulsorily insured in the domestic *gesetzlichen Rentenversicherung* and eligibility follows directly from § 10a, paragraph 1, section 1, half-sentence 1 EStG (i.e. recipient of domestic income).[1974] The same holds true with regard to civil servants who have been assigned to work for a public institution outside Germany in the official or public interest and who remain in their previous domestic pension scheme.[1975]

Provided that, pursuant to art. 14, para 1 of the applicable tax treaty, the taxing right pertaining to the remuneration is allocated to the working state (the Netherlands), and if the person is fully liable to tax in that state (for instance, as he receives at least 90% of his taxable income in the other state), it is a matter for the Netherlands to determine to what extent it allows the contributions paid to the German personal pension scheme to be taken into account in the calculation of the domestic tax assessment base. As regards the tax relief of contributions (e.g. tax exemption or tax deduction) paid into the German personal pension scheme during the posting period, pursuant to the Dutch tax legislation, it must be determined to what extent these foreign paid contributions are eligible for tax relief in the Netherlands, see section 6.4.1.B.I. Dutch policy as regards the 'fiscal recognition' of contributions paid into foreign personal schemes has been laid down in a decree.[1976] The foreign personal pension scheme can – under certain conditions – be continued by means of premium payments. In order to be eligible for the deduction of the premiums paid, the foreign insurance company must meet the conditions set by the

1972 For instance, article 12, para 1 Regulation on the coordination of social security systems 883/2004 provides that a posted worker remains insured for social security in the 'sending state', provided that the anticipated duration of such work does not exceed 24 months and that he/she is not sent to replace another posted person.
1973 Pursuant to article 12, para 1 ibid.
1974 BMF, para 11.
1975 Ibid. para 12.
1976 Staatssecretaris van Financiën, section 4.9.

Minister of Finance.[1977] If these conditions are met, the contributions paid into the German foreign personal pension scheme, shall be deductible for Dutch income tax purposes.

After the limited time of posting abroad, the worker will return to Germany. If the taxing right is allocated to Germany as residence and/or source state (for instance pursuant to article 17, para 1 treaty Netherlands-Germany), the German personal pension benefits paid out are subject to German income tax. During retirement, he will be fully liable in Germany.[1978] The tax treatment of the pension benefits is then akin to a domestic situation as the residence state and pension state coincide, see section 7.4. Hence, the taxing right cannot be assigned to the Netherlands as this is nor the residence, nor the source state. Benefits emerging from *Lebensversicherungen*, concluded after 31 December 2004 – which do not meet the conditions of the *Rürup-Rente* nor the *Riester-Rente* – shall be subject to *Ertragsanteilbesteuerung*, pursuant to § 22, nr 1, sentence 3, letter a, double letter bb EStG, irrespective of the extent to which the benefits emerge from – in Germany – fiscally facilitated contributions. Benefits arising from *Rürup-Rente*, will be taxed against the *Besteuerungsanteil* (2023: 83%)[1979], in so far as these benefits emerge from – in Germany – facilitated contributions, but taxed against the *Ertragsanteil*[1980] in so far as these benefits were derived from non-facilitated contributions.[1981] This applies to benefits paid by domestic and foreign pension institutions.[1982] Benefits arising from a *Riester-Rente* will be fully subject to taxation, if the contributions paid to the provision have been fully subject to fiscal facilitation in Germany during the accrual phase, or arise from the provided statutory allowances (i.e. *Zulagen*), to the extent they do not exceed the maximum amount of §10a EStG.[1983] Benefits arising from non-facilitated contributions are taxed against the *Ertragsanteil*.[1984] Whether contributions paid into German personal pension scheme were

1977 Pursuant to art. 3.126, para 1, under c Wet IB 2001.

1978 Pursuant to § 1, para 1, sentence 1 EStG.

1979 Pursuant to § 22, nr 1, sentence 3, letter a, double letter aa EStG.

1980 Pursuant to § 22, nr 1, sentence 3, letter a, double letter bb EStG,

1981 Under international tax law, the tax relief, granted during the accrual phase in Germany, is considered a sufficient genuine link which allows Germany to subject the arising benefits to domestic tax. Ibid. 794 and C Richter, *Die Besteuerung grenzüberschreitender Altersversorgung in der EU* (Rechtsordnung und Steuerwesen, Dr. Otto Schmidt, Köln 2010) 352 ff. and 373.

1982 BMF, *Einkommensteuerrechtliche Behandlung von Vorsorgeaufwendungen und Altersbezügen IV C 3 - S 2221/12/10010:004 - IV C 5 - S 2345/08/0001* para 190.

1983 § 22, nr 5, sentence 1 and 2 EStG. Contributions for which the maximum amount of § 10a EStG has been exceeded, shall not be considered facilitated contributions. Neither do contributions for which the taxable person has not received any allowances or did not receive the *Sonderausgabenabzug*. In addition, income and capital appreciations attributable to unduly paid, and subsequently reclaimed allowances, shall be treated as non-facilitated retirement capital.

1984 § 22, nr 5, sentence, letter a in conjunction with § 22, nr 1, sentence 3, under bb EStG. With respect to *Ertragsanteilbesteuerung*, also see C Herrmann, G Heuer and A Raupach, *Einkommensteuer- und Körperschaftsteuergesetz: EStG KStG* (Dr. Otto Schmidt, Köln Aktualisierung 2018).

facilitated under foreign tax legislation during the posted period in the Netherlands is thus relevant. Hence, benefits arising from non-facilitated contributions – paid during the posted period abroad – shall be taxed against the *Ertragsanteil*, rather than the *Besteuerungsanteil*.

7.5.3.B Inbound

As part of the inbound posting case, a Dutch employee is sent abroad during the accrual phase, i.e. the Dutch parent company posts its Dutch employee to a subsidiary located in Germany. It is therefore assumed, that the employee concerned will continue to participate, and contribute, to the Dutch personal pension scheme in the sending state. The peculiarity of posting is that although the retirement benefits are based on contributions paid and (possibly) fiscally facilitated abroad (pursuant to German tax law), the paying institution is located in the state of residence of the recipient, i.e. a domestic pension institution (the Netherlands).

According to the applicable treaty provision (pursuant to art. 14, para 2), during the period of posting, the Netherlands (residence state) is allocated the taxing rights as regards the remuneration. In such as case, the tax treatment of the pension contributions is akin to a domestic Dutch situation, see section 6.3. Provided that, pursuant to art. 14, para 1 of the applicable tax treaty, the taxing right pertaining to the remuneration is allocated to the working state (Germany), and if the person is fully liable to tax in that state (for instance, as he receives at least 90% of his taxable income in the other state), it is a matter for Germany to determine to what extent it allows the contributions paid to the Dutch personal pension scheme to be taken into account in the calculation of the domestic tax assessment base. This has been discussed in more detail in section 7.5.2.A. As has been pointed out above, it must be determined through a comparative legal qualification of the foreign pension scheme, to what extent these foreign schemes are eligible for tax relief in Germany.[1985] However, unfortunately, guidelines (e.g. issued by the German Ministry of Finance, nor the German tax authorities) as to when a foreign private pension scheme qualifies as either a German *Lebensversicherung, Rürup-Rente* or *Riester-Rente* are lacking. Nevertheless, this assessment plays an instrumental role in determining how pension benefits emerging from a foreign scheme shall be subject to tax pursuant to German domestic tax legislation.

After the limited time of posting abroad, the worker will return to the Netherlands. If the taxing right is allocated to the Netherlands as residence and/or source state (for instance pursuant to article 17, para 1 treaty Netherlands-Germany), the Dutch personal pension

1985 See for instance X R 37/08 BStBl. II 2011 (628) (BFH).

benefits paid out are subject to Dutch income tax. During retirement, he will be fully liable in the Netherlands.[1986] The tax treatment of the pension benefits is then akin to a domestic situation as the residence state and pension state coincide, see section 7.2.1. Hence, the taxing right cannot be assigned to Germany as this is nor the residence, nor the source state. The main rule is that annuity payments, except for the payments arising from the net annuity, shall be fully taxable as periodic payments (against a progressive income tax rate) with the person who receives them, irrespective of whether the paid contributions have been deducted.[1987] Until 1 January 2009, the criterion was whether the premiums had been deducted as expenditure for income provision. Hence, the extent to which the Dutch contributions paid abroad during the posting period were subject to tax relief in Germany, is irrelevant in the tax treatment of the pension benefits pursuant to Dutch national tax law.

7.6 Comparative Findings Through the Lens of the Evaluation Framework

Where in the sections above the (tax treatment of) (cross-border) personal pensions – in both the Netherlands and Germany – have been mapped out, the section below evaluates these findings along the (legal) lines of this research's evaluation framework (similarity/comparability; inter-level coherence; inter-system consistency; foreseeability/unpredictability). It is a sliding scale where all variations between fit and unfit can be observed.

As this chapter explored the (tax treatment of) personal pensions, emphasis will be put on the principle of similarity/comparability, since this chapter seeks to explore to what extent the regulatory framework governing the (tax treatment of) personal pensions in both countries are fit for the provision of effective pension information. This principle is marked by the division of power between the European Union and the Member States; the responsibility for the design of a national pension system lies with the Member States, and

1986 Pursuant to art. 2.1, para 1, under a Wet IB 2001.

1987 Pursuant to art. 3.100, para 1, sub b Wet IB 2001. Cf. Dietvorst, 'Lijfrenten' 558. The main rule that annuity payments are taxed regardless of whether the premiums have been deducted, led to the issue of box splitting after the introduction of the Wet IB 2001. See ibid. 556 ff. If premiums are not or not fully deducted, the corresponding (part of the) value shall be taxed in box 3. Strictly speaking, the insurance policy will have to be divided into a box 1 and a box 3 part during the accumulation phase. To take into account the non-deducted premiums, a limited balance method was introduced in 2009, see art. 3.107a Wet B 2001. Insofar as the taxpayer has demonstrated that premiums paid were not deducted in whole or in part, no tax will be due on the benefits. The amount per year of non-deducted premiums that has not been taken into account shall not exceed €2,269.

the European Union falls short of competence to intervene in the Member States' pension systems. What is more, the principle of foreseeability will be tested. Moreover, as this chapter did involve – to a little extent – the role of international tax law as such (this will be discussed in more detail in chapter 9 of this research) the principle of inter-level coherence is also evaluated. Hence, it does concern the scrutiny of coherence with higher-level regulations, and with treaty or other international obligations. Lastly, as the chapter above addressed the application of national regulatory (tax) frameworks, leading to potential (in)compatible outcomes for a specific cross-border situation, the principle of inter-system consistency shall be evaluated. This chapter meets this research second (sub) objective of a legal comparative study in which the legal frameworks in the Netherlands and Germany, as well as on a European and international level, shall be mapped out. Building on this, the 'fitness' of the legal frameworks at the national, European and international level shall be assessed, focusing in particular on any deficiencies that have a potential (distorting) effect on the provision of effective information.

7.6.1 *Similarity/Comparability*

The sections below compare the (tax treatment of) personal pensions in Germany and the Netherlands, and evaluates it in view of the principle of similarity/comparability. Exploring similarity between systems involves a comparison of certain features. The assessment of similarity constitutes a feature-matching process, i.e. it measures the degree to which two objects – the legal character – match each other. Similarity is tantamount to a measurement of common features. A higher degree of similarity helps to ensure the effectiveness of information in terms of the four principles. For instance, the higher the degree of similarity, the easier it is to uphold the information's correctness, trustworthiness, and personal relevance. After all, with a higher degree of similarity, there is less need to observe any underlying structural differences. Moreover, a higher degree of similarity leads to a higher comparability of the different regulatory frameworks/legal constructs, avoiding comparing the incomparable.

7.6.1.A Differences

Comparing (the tax treatment of) Dutch and German personal pensions, the following differences can be observed:

- Under Dutch fiscal legislation, the central definition of life annuities – eligible for tax relief – has been laid down in one central provision (art. 1.7 Wet IB 2001). In Germany, these fiscal eligibility definitions are dispersed over various legal provisions enshrined in the EStG, see section 7.4. What is more, the national (Dutch/German) definitions of 'life annuities' differ considerably.

- The method of 'communicating vessels' between contribution deductions in the third pillar and pension accrual (i.e., pension deficit) in the second pillar renders the Dutch third pillar unique in fiscal terms.[1988] When determining any pension deficit, a foreign occupational pension plan shall also be taken into account.[1989] Under the *jaarruimte*-system, the amount of the annuity premium deduction depends on the pension accrual in the second pillar. Merely those taxable persons who fall short of pension accrual in the second pillar (*pensioentekort*), are entitled to deduction of annuity premiums in the third pillar. Thus, any alterations change in the first and second pillars will affect the fiscal framework of the third pillar. This type of tax treatment pertaining to annuities is unique in Europe.[1990] This linkage does not exist, for example, in the German third pillar system, see section 7.4.1. This emphasizes the role of the Dutch third pillar as a compensatory pillar, i.e. only those who have a need for supplementary retirement provision in the third pillar are eligible for deduction of annuity premiums for fiscal purposes.
- In Germany, fiscal conditions as regard the fiscal facilitation of some personal pension schemes relate to the taxable person's situation/capacity. For instance, in accordance with the underlying objective of the *Rieser-Rente (*not *Rürup-Rente*), – i.e. compensating the increasingly diminishing level of care of the *gesetzlichen Rentenversicherung* – persons eligible for the deduction of contributions as *Sonderausgaben*, must be mandatory insured domestic persons in the *gesetzlichen Rentenversicherung* or recipients of domestic salaries in accordance with the Federal Salary Act or Landes Salary Act.[1991] The reference to the obligatory insurance under the *gesetzlichen Rentenversicherung* illustrates the interaction between tax legislation and social security law.[1992] The group of eligible persons under the *Rürup-Rente* for fiscal facilitation is not limited, contrary to the eligible persons for the *Riester-Rente*. Such linkage with the taxable person does not exist in Dutch fiscal legislation – where it is rather aligned with the eligible life annuities and permitted providers – i.e. every

1988 Cf. Ibid. section 12.3.

1989 Kamerstukken II, *26 727, 3 (Wet Inkomstenbelasting 2001 (Belastingherziening 2001))* (1998/99) 76.

1990 Cf. Dietvorst, 'Lijfrenten' section 12.1.

1991 § 10a, para 1, sentence 1 EStG. Often significantly affected by the retrenchment of the benefits under the *gesetzlichen Rentenversicherung* as well, are spouses, in particular in cases of single earners, or spouses in marginal employments, and, hence, not mandatory insured under the *gesetzlichen Rentenversicherung*. Indirectly, the spouse is deprived from his surviving dependants provision under the *gesetzlichen Rentenversicherung*. Therefore, § 79, sentence 2 EStG, under certain conditions, provides an indirect eligibility for this spouse. It seems that this does not apply to unmarried life partners. This indirect eligibility entitles the spouse to the *Sonderausgabenabzug* (§ 10a EStG) and *Altersvorsorgezulage* (§ 84 and § 85 EStG). See also Welker, 54 ff. and Myßen and others.

1992 For an elaboration on compulsorily insured persons for the *gesetzlichen Rentenversicherung*, See Welker, 49 ff.

taxable person is entitled to an annuity premium deduction each year, see section 7.2.1.A.

- The *Rürup-Rente* is fiscally treated similarly to the *gesetzlichen Rentenversicherung*, and should for this reason, serve the needs of a basic secure retirement provision. Such resemblance with taxation under the first pillar is not discernible in the Netherlands.
- Under the Dutch third pillar, the second pillar pension shall be taken into account when calculating the fiscal leeway (*jaarruimte*) for the premium deduction, see section 7.2.1.A. Such linkage with pension accrual does not exist under German fiscal legislation. Every taxable person is entitled to an annuity premium deduction each year, whereby the amount of deduction is determined by the income received in the previous year, and by the increase in value of his pension entitlements in the second pillar in the previous year.[1993] Furthermore, there must be a so-called 'pension deficit' in the second pillar pension scheme, in the previous calendar year, calculated by means of the accrual of pension in the second pillar in that previous year.
- Contrary to Germany, the Dutch legislator has abandoned the EET system and switched to the TEE system for *nettolijfrenten*.[1994] The net annuity is linked to the capping limit for pensions and annuities of €128,810 (2023) – pursuant to art. 18ga Wet LB 1964 – introduced on the same date and seeks to be a voluntary third pillar provision for the income exceeding this limit.[1995] As contributions paid into these net life annuities are not deductible for tax purposes, these are paid out of the person's net income. Since the premiums are not deductible, the benefits can be paid out untaxed in due course.[1996] In Germany, such net life annuity scheme does not exist. This reflects that expressing the fiscal treatment of pensions in terms of TEE/EET is limited in terms of generally-applicable use as it insufficiently incorporates cross-border situations and, what is more, insufficiently gives expression to the extent to what fiscal facilitation is granted during the accrual phase, and foreign pension benefits are actually subject to tax in the pay-out phase.
- What is more, Germany – contrary to the Netherlands – applies the TEE principle to other forms of individual retirement provisions, concluded after 31 December 2004 –

1993 This increase in value of the occupational pension entitlements in the previous years is expressed in terms of the factor 'A'. This factor A is the value of the pension entitlements attributable to the preceding year (t-1) in so far as the increase is due to an increase in the pension entitlements. It should be noted that the method of calculating the factor A is no more than a rough approximation. The State Secretary indicated for different types of pension schemes how the factor A should be calculated, see Staatssecretaris van Financiën.

1994 Pursuant to Wet van 2 juni 2014 tot wijziging van de Wet inkomstenbelasting 2001, de Wet op de loonbelasting 1964, de Pensioenwet, de Wet verplichte beroepspensioenregeling en de Invoerings- en aanpassingswet Pensioenwet in verband met de aanpassing van het fiscale kader voor oudedagsvoorzieningen (Wet verlaging maximumopbouw- en premiepercentages pensioen en maximering pensioengevend inkomen).

1995 Ibid.

1996 See art. 3.100, para 3 Wet IB 2001.

which do not meet the conditions of the *Rürup-Rente* nor the *Riester-Rente*. These shall be subject to *Ertragsanteilbesteuerung*, which requires taxation during the accrual phase, since the contributions are paid out of taxed income.[1997] During the pay-out phase, merely the interest on the capital shall be taxable, contrary to the reflux of capital.[1998] The taxation pursuant to the *Ertragsanteil* is independent of the conclusion date of the contract, i.e. whether it concerns an *Altvertrag* or *Neuvertrag*.[1999]

- As a result of the entry into force of the *Eigenheimrentengesetz*[2000], the German legislator increased the flexibility of the payment method of the *Riester*-provision. The *Wohn-Riester* replaced the *Zwischenentnahmemodell* since 2008.[2001] Under this facility, the taxable person could withdraw an amount between €10,000 and €50,000 from his *Riester*-provision, prior to the beginning of the pay-out phase, in order to acquire or build an owner-occupied dwelling.[2002] Under the current so-called *Wohn-Riester*, the taxable person may, prior to the beginning of the pay-out phase, extract a certain amount out of the *Riester*-arrangement, in order to use this capital for the financing of an owner-occupied dwelling.[2003] This illustrates the consideration of the German legislator on the concept of pension, i.e. to some extent, an owner-occupied dwelling may serve the pension objective of maintaining the standard of living after retirement. Such a provision – incorporating an owner-occupied dwelling in the (fiscal) concept of retirement income – is unknown in the Netherlands.
- Under the Germany system, benefits emerging from *Lebensversicherungen*, concluded after 31 December 2004 – which do not meet the conditions of the *Rürup-Rente* nor the *Riester-Rente* – shall be subject to *Ertragsanteilbesteuerung*, irrespective of the extent to which the benefits emerge from – in Germany – fiscally facilitated contributions.[2004] Benefits arising from *Rürup-Rente*, will be taxed against the *Besteuerungsanteil* (2023: 83%)[2005], in so far as these benefits emerge from – in Germany – facilitated contributions, but taxed against the *Ertragsanteil*[2006] in so far as

1997 § 22, nr 1, sentence 3, under bb EStG.

1998 Birk and Wernsmann criticised this outcome, but assume an inciting function, aimed at encouraging people to conclude a supplementary retirement provision, see Birk and Wernsmann, 264.

1999 Cf. Eckerle, 378.

2000 Gesetz zur verbesserten Einbeziehung der selbstgenutzten Wohnimmobilie in die geförderte Altersvorsorge (Eigenheimrentengesetz – EigRentG).

2001 Translated freely as 'interim withdrawal model'. For an elaborate discussion of the model, see Welker, 82 ff.

2002 § 92a EStG (repealed wording). See also ibid. 82.

2003 The so-called *Altersvorsorge-Eigenheimbetrag*, pursuant to §92a EStG. See also BMF, *Steuerliche Förderung der privaten Altersvorsorge IV C 3 - S 2015/17/10001:005* para 167 ff. For a critical analysis of the *Eigenheimrentengesetz*, See Schönemann, Dietrich and Kiesewetter.

2004 Pursuant to § 22, nr 1, sentence 3, letter a, double letter bb EStG.

2005 Pursuant to § 22, nr 1, sentence 3, letter a, double letter aa EStG.

2006 Pursuant to § 22, nr 1, sentence 3, letter a, double letter bb EStG.

these benefits were derived from non-facilitated contributions.[2007] This applies to benefits paid by domestic and foreign pension institutions.[2008] Benefits arising from a *Riester-Rente* will be fully subject to taxation, if the contributions paid to the provision have been fully subject to fiscal facilitation in Germany during the accrual phase, or arise from the provided statutory allowances (i.e. *Zulagen*), to the extent they do not exceed the maximum amount of §10a EStG.[2009] Benefits arising from non-facilitated contributions are taxed against the *Ertragsanteil*.[2010] On the contrary, in the Netherlands, the main rule stipulates that annuity payments, except for the payments arising from the net annuity, shall be fully taxable as periodic payments (against a progressive income tax rate) with the person who receives them, irrespective of whether the benefits arise from contributions which have been deducted.[2011] Until 1 January 2009, the criterion was whether the premiums had been deducted as expenditure for income provision, however, this approach has been abandoned.

- The amount of pension contributions deductible as *Sonderausgaben* is calculated as follows. Firstly, the pension contributions paid by the employee shall be determined. Secondly, in addition to these contributions, the tax-free employer's portion to *the gesetzlichen Rentenversicherung*[2012] and the tax-free employer's subsidy equal to this, shall be added.[2013] The deduction of contributions to the *Rürup-Rente* as *Sonderausgaben*

2007 Under international tax law, the tax relief, granted during the accrual phase in Germany, is considered a sufficient genuine link which allows Germany to subject the arising benefits to domestic tax. Ibid. 794 and C Richter, *Die Besteuerung grenzüberschreitender Altersversorgung in der EU* (Rechtsordnung und Steuerwesen, Dr. Otto Schmidt, Köln 2010) 352 ff. and 373.

2008 BMF, *Einkommensteuerrechtliche Behandlung von Vorsorgeaufwendungen und Altersbezügen IV C 3 - S 2221/12/10010:004 - IV C 5 - S 2345/08/0001* para 190.

2009 § 22, nr 5, sentence 1 and 2 EStG. Contributions for which the maximum amount of § 10a EStG has been exceeded, shall not be considered facilitated contributions. Neither do contributions for which the taxable person has not received any allowances or did not receive the *Sonderausgabenabzug*. In addition, income and capital appreciations attributable to unduly paid, and subsequently reclaimed allowances, shall be treated as non-facilitated retirement capital.

2010 § 22, nr 5, sentence, letter a in conjunction with § 22, nr 1, sentence 3, under bb EStG. With respect to *Ertragsanteilbesteuerung*, also see C Herrmann, G Heuer and A Raupach, *Einkommensteuer- und Körperschaftsteuergesetz: EStG KStG* (Dr. Otto Schmidt, Köln Aktualisierung 2018).

2011 Pursuant to art. 3.100, para 1, sub b Wet IB 2001. Cf. Dietvorst, 'Lijfrenten' 558. The main rule that annuity payments are taxed regardless of whether the premiums have been deducted, led to the issue of box splitting after the introduction of the Wet IB 2001. See ibid. 556 ff. If premiums are not or not fully deducted, the corresponding (part of the) value shall be taxed in box 3. Strictly speaking, the policy will have to be divided into a box 1 and a box 3 part during the accumulation phase. To take into account the non-deducted premiums, a limited balance method was introduced in 2009, see art. 3.107a Wet B 2001. Insofar as the taxpayer has demonstrated that premiums paid were not deducted in whole or in part, no tax will be due on the benefits. The amount per year of non-deducted premiums that has not been taken into account shall not exceed €2,269.

2012 § 3, nr 62 EStG.

2013 § 10, para 1, nr 2, sentence 6 EStG.

is, however, subject to a maximum.[2014] What further should be taken into account in calculating the amount of contributions to the *Rürup-Rente*, deductible as *Sonderausgaben*, is the gradual transition to deferred taxation. The amount as calculated above, is, therefore, only partially deductible. As of 2023, 100% of the contributions may be deducted.[2015] Thereafter, this amount shall be reduced with the tax-free employer's portion to *the gesetzlichen Rentenversicherung*[2016] and the tax-free employer's subsidy equal to this.[2017] This reduction guarantees equal tax relief opportunities for all taxable persons.[2018] After multiplying the amount of pension contributions with the deductibility ratio, the remaining amount, shall be reduced with the tax-free employers' contributions to the *gesetzlichen Rentenversicherung* and tax-free allowances treated as such, pursuant to § 3, nr 62 EStG.[2019] To this extent, the taxable person already has had the opportunity to accrue a retirement provision out of untaxed income. The amount remaining thereafter shall be deductible as *Sonderausgaben*.[2020] For this I refer to section 7.4.1.B.I. This computation of deductible contributions is significantly different from the calculation of the Dutch *jaarruimte*, although in both methods of calculation the (tax-free) accrual in the 1st/2nd pillar shall be incorporated. Contrary to the Netherlands, in calculating *Sonderausgaben* tax-free employer's portion to *the gesetzlichen Rentenversicherung* shall be taken into account (where in the Netherlands solely the employee's contributions are taken into account), and a gradual transition to deferred taxation is discernible. As of 2023, 100% of the contributions may be deducted.[2021]

- What is more, pursuant to Germany tax legislation, an additional flat-rate amount of €102 (2023) may be deducted as well from the tax assessment basis.[2022] In the Netherlands, such a flat-rate deduction does not exist; merely the employee's contributions shall be deductible for tax purposes.

2014 § 10, para 3, sentence 1 and 2 EStG.

2015 § 10, para 3, sentence 4 and 6 EStG.

2016 § 3, nr 63 EStG.

2017 § 10, para 3, sentence 5 EStG and BMF, *Einkommensteuerrechtliche Behandlung von Vorsorgeaufwendungen IV C 3 - S 2221/16/10001:004* para 74.

2018 Cf. Wernsmann, 'Die steuerliche Förderung der zusätzlichen kapitalgedeckten Altersvorsorge' 793 and cited literature..

2019 § 10, para 3, sentence 5 EStG.

2020 § 10, para 3, sentence 5 EStG. For numerous examples regarding the calculation of the amount, deductible as *Sonderausgabe*, See BMF, *Einkommensteuerrechtliche Behandlung von Vorsorgeaufwendungen IV C 3 - S 2221/16/10001:004* paras 75-79.

2021 § 10, para 3, sentence 4 and 6 EStG. As of 2025, 100% of the contributions will be deductible, see the table in ibid. para 73.

2022 Pursuant to § 9a, para 3 EStG, which states ‚*Für Werbungskosten sind bei der Ermittlung der Einkünfte die folgenden Pauschbeträge abzuziehen, wenn nicht höhere Werbungskosten nachgewiesen werden: von den Einnahmen im Sinne des § 22 Nummer 5: ein Pauschbetrag von insgesamt 102 Euro.*

- Under the German *Riester-Rente*, next to the deduction of *Sonderausgaben*, most taxable persons are entitled to the so-called *Altersvorsorgezulage*[2023], even if they fulfil the eligibility conditions merely during a part of the calendar year.[2024] The calculated allowances will be directly remitted to his retirement provision.[2025] These raise the contributions for the pension provision and, in effect, the future benefits, see section 7.4.1.A.I. In the Netherlands, such a system of *Zulage* does not exist.
- In order to be fully entitled to the allowances, the taxable person must pay a minimum contribution to the *Riester-Rente*.[2026] This requirement intends to guarantee that the statutory allowances constitute a facilitation of the individual old-age provision, rather than a substitute of the *gesetzlichen Rentenversicherung*.[2027] The remaining amount constitutes the required *Mindesteigenbeitrag*. Furthermore, the threshold amount (*Sockelbetrag*) – since 2005 €60 annually – must be taken into account.[2028] If the calculated *Mindesteigenbeitrag* is less that €60, the *Sockelbetrag* of €60 must be paid as minimum contribution.[2029] These types of minimum contributions – in terms of *Mindesteigenbeitrag* and *Sockelbetrag* – do not exist in the Netherlands. However, under the Dutch Wet IB 2001, premiums for annuities may be taken into account up to an aggregate amount not exceeding 13.3% (2023) of the premium base, whereby the premium base is capped at €128,810 (2023), minus an amount of €13,646 (2023), i.e. the so-called *AOW-franchise*.[2030] Hence, the calculation of deductible contributions deviates significantly between the two states.
- Under none of the German private pension schemes, the tax relief provided during the period of residence in Germany, is reclaimed upon migration to another State. Most recently, the repayment obligation pursuant to § 93-95 EStG pertaining to *Sonderausgaben*-deduction and allowances granted for the benefit of *Riester-Renten* in the event of relocating the place of residence to another EU Member State has been abolished, in response to the CJEU's ruling.[2031] However, as addressed in section 7.3.1.A,

2023 Translated freely as 'pension-savings allowance'.

2024 § 10a, para 1, in conjunction with § 79, sentence 1 EStG. Cf. Myßen and others.

2025 Cf. Ibid.and Förster and Rechtenwald.

2026 § 10a, para 1, sentence 1 EStG.

2027 Risthaus, 'Steuerliche Fördermöglichkeiten für eine zusätzliche private Altersvorsorge nach dem Altersvermögensgesetz (AVmG)'. See also Birk and Wernsmann, 259 and Wernsmann, 'Die steuerliche Förderung der zusätzlichen kapitalgedeckten Altersvorsorge' 790.

2028 § 86, para 1, sentence 4 EStG.

2029 § 86, para 1, sentence 5 EStG.

2030 Pursuant to art. 3.127, par. 1 Wet IB 2001. The premium base consists of the combined amount in the previous calendar year of the profit from business; the taxable wages; the taxable result from other work; the taxable periodic benefits and benefits in kind, see art. 3.127, par. 3 Wet IB 2001. In order to bring the premium deduction for annuities in line with the *Witteveen* framework for occupational pensions, the maximum premium deduction was reduced to 13.3% over a maximum premium base of €128,810 (2023) as of January 1, 2015. See Dietvorst, 'Lijfrenten' section 12.3.

2031 *Commission vs. Germany.*

in order to ensure that annuity contracts are settled in a regular manner and to maintain the tax claim, a regulation has been included in the Dutch Wet IB 2001. Pursuant to Dutch national legislation as it stands, upon emigration, a protective tax assessment shall be issued, pursuant to Dutch national tax legislation.[2032] In addition, revisionary interest (*revisierente*) will be included in the protective tax assessment.[2033] For the amount included in the protective tax assessment imposed, deferral of payment shall be granted for a period of ten years.[2034] In the event that no irregularities occur – for example a lump-sum payment – during the period of deferral, the protective tax assessment shall be waived after ten years.[2035] If such an irregularity does occur within ten years, the insurer of that entitlement shall be liable, up to a maximum of the entitlements' fair value, for the tax due in respect thereof by the person entitled thereto, as well as for the corresponding revision interest due.[2036] The tenability of these protective tax assessments – imposed upon emigration – has moved many authors to reach for their pen.[2037] For this, I refer to section 7.3.1.A.

- As addressed in section 6.4.1.B.I, the Dutch State Secretary has sets cumulative conditions with respect to the 'fiscal recognition' of foreign personal pension scheme, and the corresponding deductibility of (foreign) contributions. In Germany, such standards have not (yet) been laid down in a *BMF-schreiben* or any other policy document.

7.6.1.B Similarities

Comparing (the tax treatment of) Dutch and German personal pensions, the following similarities have been observed:

- In the Netherlands, as well as in Germany the term personal pensions is broad, covering numerous varieties of pension scheme. In the Germany it ranges from *Riester-Rente,* and *Rürup-Rente* to *Lebensversicherungen* (*Alterverträge* and *Neuverträge*); in the Netherlands from *oudedagslijfrente, lijfrentespaarrekening, lijfrentebeleggingsrecht*, and *nettolijfrente*. Yet, the outcome of each these schemes, i.e. the retirement benefits, may differ from each other considerably.
- In both states, personal pensions are mainly regulated by fiscal legislation, stipulating the criteria regarding their fiscal facilitation. A characteristic of the third pillar pension

2032 Pursuant to article 2.8, para 2 in conjunction with art. 3.136, para 1 and 2 Wet IB 2001.
2033 Pursuant to article 30i, para 1, under a in conjunction with para 2 Algemene Wet inzake Rijksbelastingen (AWR).
2034 Pursuant to art. 25, para 5 Invorderingswet 1990 (Tax Collection Act 1990).
2035 Pursuant to art. 26, para 2 Invorderingswet 1990.
2036 Pursuant to article 44b, para 1 Invorderingswet 1990.
2037 See, for instance, Pötgens; Pötgens and Kappelle; Kavelaars, 'Conserverende aanslagen en verdragen (1)'; Kavelaars, 'Conserverende aanslagen en verdragen (2)'; Pötgens,

is that it does not have its basis in the performance of work, as is the case with occupational pensions, and are voluntary.[2038] However, it does form a supplement to the first, and second pillar Dutch/German pensions. Each income provision that cannot fulfil the conditions for the qualification of first or second pillar pension, is categorised as third pillar pension. The insurance under these pension provisions may vary heavily.

- In the Netherlands, as well as in Germany, the relation between fiscal facilitation and saving for retirement exhibit a strong synergy; the more it is ensured that the capital accumulation will be employed for the use of retirement provision, the more the contributions to the accumulation of capital are fiscally facilitated, see section 7.2.1.A and 7.4.1.[2039]
- Under the third pillar in both states, an interaction between the third and first pillar has been revealed. As dealt with in section 7.4.1.A.I, the *Riester-Rente* is aimed at supplementing the *gesetzlichen Rentenversicherung* as a retirement provision in saving for an old-age income. In the Netherlands, (deductible) premiums for annuities are lowered by the so-called *AOW-franchise*, see section 7.2.1.A.[2040] The reference to statutory pensions illustrates the interaction between tax legislation and social security law (apart from their potentially deviating purpose).
- In principle, under Dutch tax law, old-age annuity terms must be lifelong.[2041] In Germany, pursuant to §10a EStG, merely particular retirement provisions are eligible for *Sonderausgabenabzug*.[2042] These conditions to be met are laid down in the *Altersvorsorgeverträge-Zertifizierungsgesetz*.[2043] One of the conditions stipulates that the retirement provision must provide for a lifelong retirement provision as well.[2044]
- In both the Netherlands, as well as in Germany, fiscal (eligibility) conditions pertain predominantly to the personal pension schemes/insurance products, and providers of fiscally facilitated retirement provision as well.[2045] The aforementioned institutions

2038 Dietvorst, *De drie pijlers van toekomstvoorzieningen en belastingen* 65.

2039 Rürup and Myßen, 193.

2040 Pursuant to art. 3.127, par. 1 Wet IB 2001. The premium base consists of the combined amount in the previous calendar year of the profit from business; the taxable wages; the taxable result from other work; the taxable periodic benefits and benefits in kind, see art. 3.127, par. 3 Wet IB 2001. In order to bring the premium deduction for annuities in line with the *Witteveen* framework for occupational pensions, the maximum premium deduction was reduced to 13.3% over a maximum premium base of €128,810 (2023) as of January 1, 2015. See Dietvorst, 'Lijfrenten' section 12.3.

2041 Art. 3.125, para 1, sub a Wet IB 2001.

2042 Pursuant to §10a in conjunction with § 80 and § 82 EStG.

2043 § 1, para 1 AltZertG. For an elaborate discussion of these conditions, See Hügelschäffer and others, and Kirchhof, Söhn and Mellinghof.

2044 § 1, para 1, nr 2 AltZertG and BMF, *Steuerliche Förderung der betrieblichen Altersversorgung IV C 5 - S 2333/17/10002* para 68. This includes the recently introduced *reine Beitragszusage*, laid down in §§21 ff. BetrAVG, see ibid. para 68.

2045 Laid down in *Altersvorsorgeverträge-Zertifizierungsgesetz*.

may, under certain conditions, also be domiciled in another member state of the European Economic Area, while their eligibility is continued.

As has been addressed in the beginning of this section, exploring similarity between systems involves a comparison of certain features, where similarity is tantamount to a measurement of common features. A higher degree of similarity helps to ensure the effectiveness of information in terms of the four principles. For instance, the higher the degree of similarity, the easier it is to uphold the information's correctness, trustworthiness, and personal relevance. After all, with a higher degree of similarity, there is less need to observe any underlying structural differences. However, as follows from the above enumeration, the legal comparison revealed more differences than similarities between the Dutch and German regulatory frameworks. In terms of 'fitness' it can thus be concluded that these structural differences hamper the provision of effective information provision, in terms of similarity/comparability.

7.6.2 Foreseeability

One cannot simply rely on the maintenance of the law in force.[2046] Applicable legislation is designed in view of particular political, economic, societal phenomena. These phenomena tend to change over time, and accordingly, legislation is adapted to the new situation. This also applies to the Dutch and German legislation under scrutiny in this chapter. It is therefore that conveying information on future amounts of retirement income usually involves a certain level of risk as regards continuously changing legislation. Put it differently, predictability is a structure, and information lies where unpredictable change occurs. Along the line of foreseeability, the following conclusions can be drawn:

- As addressed in section 6.4.1.B.I, the Dutch State Secretary has set cumulative conditions with respect to the 'fiscal recognition' of foreign personal pension scheme, and the corresponding deductibility of (foreign) contributions. First, the professional provider or executor must be subject to government supervision that is comparable to that under the *Wet op het financieel toezicht*. Second, it must be a continuation of an annuity, the scope of which corresponds to a Dutch income provision as referred to in Section 3.7 of the Wet IB 2001. It has not been further enunciated which foreign life annuities correspond to an income provision within the meaning of section 3.7 Wet IB 2001, leaving ample room for unforeseeable (application of tax law), and ambiguity surrounding the 'fiscal recognition' of foreign personal pension schemes. In the light

2046 Popelier, 1078.

of foreseeability of the application of tax legislation, generally-applicable, and more meaningful criteria would be helpful in this regard.

- The *Bundesfinanzhof* holds that comparability of retirement pensions can be assumed in cases where the foreign pension benefits correspond in its core content to the common and typical features of the domestic benefit.[2047] As regards the tax treatment of these foreign private schemes, it must be determined through a comparative legal qualification of the foreign pension scheme, to what extent these foreign schemes are eligible for tax relief. However, practical guidelines as to when a foreign private pension scheme qualifies as either a German *Lebensversicherung, Rürup-Rente* or *Riester-Rente* are not provided by the German legislature, nor the German tax authorities. Setting certain principles or standards of comparability would have ameliorated the foreseeability of (the application of) legislation and government action (i.e. tax authorities).
- As dealt with in section 7.5.2.A, for cases prior to 1 January 2010, §10a, para 6 EStG provides for a system for the preservation of acquired rights (*Bestandsschutzregelung*). Pursuant to §10a, para 6, sentence 1 EStG, persons compulsory insured under a foreign statutory pension scheme, are also considered eligible persons under two conditions.[2048] Firstly, this mandatory membership must be comparable with compulsory membership of either the *gesetzlichen Rentenversicherung* or the *Alterssicherung der Landwirte*. Secondly, this compulsory membership must be established prior to 1 January 2010. If these conditions have been met, the person compulsory insured under a foreign statutory pension scheme, is also eligible for the *Zulagen* or *Sonderausgabenabzug*. It is difficult to see that it has not been further elucidated, for instance by setting certain principles or standards of comparability, under what circumstances a foreign statutory pension scheme is considered comparable to the *gesetzlichen Rentenversicherung* or

2047 See for instance X R 37/08 BStBl. II 2011 (628) (BFH) in which the Court held: "*Bei der Anwendung des deutschen Steuerrechts ist stets eine rechtsvergleichende Qualifizierung der ausländischen Einkünfte nach deutschem Recht vorzunehmen. Vergleichbarkeit von Altersrenten ist dann anzunehmen, wenn die ausländische Leistung in ihrem Kerngehalt den gemeinsamen und typischen Merkmalen der inländischen Leistung entspricht, d.h. nach Motivation und Funktion gleichwertig ist. Da eine völlige Identität kaum denkbar ist, muss sich diese Beurteilung notwendigerweise auf bestimmte Eigenschaften beider Leistungsarten beschränken und andere als unwesentlich für den Vergleich ausscheiden. Maßgebliche Gesichtspunkte sind die Essentialia der nationalen Norm, also deren Funktion und Struktur nach nationalem Verständnis.*".

2048 Ibid. para 19. This paragraph has been implemented pursuant to Gesetz zur Anpassung des nationalen Steuerrechts an den Beitritt Kroatiens zur EU und zur Änderung weiterer steuerlicher Vorschriften (StRAnpG). § 10a, par 6 EStG, sentence 2 EStG will not be discussed any further as this concerns the particular situations of civil servants, judges, professional soldiers and temporary soldiers on leave without pay.

the *Alterssicherung der Landwirte*. This would have ameliorated the foreseeability of (the application of) legislation and government action (i.e. tax authorities).[2049]

- As addressed in section 7.3.1.B, annuity payments arising from a foreign provision of which the object and purport corresponds to a Dutch life annuity – within the meaning of art. 3.124 ff. Wet IB 2001 – shall also be taxable.[2050] However, if and insofar as it can be assumed with regard to this foreign scheme that the premiums paid have not been deducted from the income during the period abroad, this does not constitute a taxable periodical benefit (but to that extent shall be taxable as income arising from saving and investment in BOX 3).[2051] Hence, insofar as the premiums paid abroad have been deducted from taxable income or have otherwise led to a tax reduction, the benefits from the right shall be included in the Dutch income tax. In doing so, a sound level of linkage is achieved between the actual tax treatment of the personal pension scheme abroad, and that in the Netherlands. It concerns foreign personal pension provisions that correspond in their scope to annuities that serve to compensate a pension shortfall (within the meaning of art. 3.124, para 1, under a Wet IB 2001). For this to apply, it is not required that a foreign provision corresponds exactly to such a Dutch income provision; it is sufficient that the scope thereof corresponds to an income provision. This implies that the foreign provision must aim to be a provision for old age.[2052] Which foreign personal pension schemes exactly fall under the scope of article 3.101, first paragraph, section c, will have to be clarified in case law and (possible) policy. Setting certain principles or standards of 'corresponding' would have ameliorated the foreseeability of (the application of) legislation and government action (i.e. tax authorities).

2049 For the purposes of applying § 10a, par 6 EStG, the pension systems of some international organisations are to be regarded as a pension scheme comparable to the *gesetzlichen Rentenversicherung* or the *Alterssicherung der Landwirte*, such as the pension schemes of the European Commission, the European Central Bank, the NATO, the OECD, or the UN. See ibid. paras 22 and 23. It does not become evident from this enumeration which elements or characteristics of pension schemes are considered decisive, or even are taken into consideration, in the assessment of comparability.

2050 Pursuant to art. 3.100, para 1, sub c Wet IB 2001. It should be noted that this provision applies to residents of the Netherlands (domestic taxpayers) where, in accordance with international views, the world income is included in the tax. This world income also includes payments from abroad.

2051 Because foreign provisions can involve widely divergent products, and because it will often be unclear to the Dutch tax authorities how the provision is treated for tax purposes abroad, it was decided to place the burden of proof as to whether or not tax relief has been received on the taxpayer. After all, the taxpayer is in the best position to provide information about his/her actual situation. Possibilities to meet this burden of proof are a reference to foreign tax legislation (for instance if the annuity does not meet the conditions for deduction of premiums applicable there), and the submission of a statement by the foreign tax authorities or the insurer or of relevant tax assessments, see Kamerstukken II, *26 727, nr. 7 (Belastingherziening 2001)* 475.

2052 Kamerstukken II, *26 727, nr. 3 (Belastingherziening 2001)* 141. In this context, one can think of provisions such as the Individual Retirement Account (IRA).

7.6.3 Inter-level Coherence

In order to prevent discrepancies in information provision, different fields of multi-level law need to be aligned with each other, i.e. national (Netherlands and Germany); European, and international.[2053] For the purpose and context of the present research, 'coherence' is termed as 'the situation in which all the levels of the regulatory frameworks are logical and consistent, achieving a harmonious connection of these parts, so that the whole 'hangs together'.[2054] This underlines the relevance of certain properties of regulatory frameworks, and its consequences, for information provision, and corresponding implications. A challenge for the provision of effective cross-border pension information is the diversity – and poor coordination – of differentiates pension vehicles, and taxes.[2055] From this point of view, in order to uphold the information's effectiveness, it requires a certain degree of coherence among these levels of legislation. At lower levels, this may involve systematic scrutiny of coherence with higher-level regulations and with treaty or other international obligations, which will be dealt with in chapters 8 and 9 of this research. A higher degree of coherence also helps to ensure the effectiveness of information in terms of the four principles, in that more coherence between low and higher levels of legislation aids ensuring the information's effectiveness. For instance, in a more coherent (logically and consistent ordered) multi-level legal systems, it is far easier to uphold the information's correctness and trustworthiness, as in such a system, there is less susceptibility to error.

Along the lines of this principle, the chapter above revealed the following findings:

– As dealt with in section 7.5.1.A, the *Riester-Rente* was subject to unlimited tax liability until 15 April 2010, and the paid allowances to the *Riester-Rente* and facilitated contributions had to be repaid, even when the person entitled to the allowances decided to relocate his residence and habitual residence to another EU Member State.[2056] This provision was applicable to all situations in which the unlimited tax liability of the taxable person ended due to the abandonment of the residence or habitual residence in Germany.[2057] This exit tax was met with considerable criticism, since this exit tax was considered incompatible with EU law, notably the European

2053 See also OECD, 'Recommendation of the Council of the OECD on Regulatory Policy and Governance' 14.

2054 Oxford Dictionaries.

2055 In the same vein: Sunstein, 'Informing consumers through smart disclosure' 5.

2056 § 95, para 1, sentence 1 EStG (repealed wording). This provision has been amended pursuant to article 1 of Gesetz zur Umsetzung steuerlicher EU-Vorgaben sowie zur Änderung steuerlicher Vorschriften (EUStVUG). See also Quinten M. and Sona B.

2057 See for instance F Welker, *Das Altersvermögensgesetz und seine konsequenzen für die betriebliche Altersversorgung: arbeits-, steuer- und aufsichtsrechtliche Perspektiven* (Deutscher Universitäts-Verlag, Wiesbaden 2005) 85-86.

rights of free movement.[2058] The CJEU held that this reimbursement obligation of the allowances and *Sonderausgabenabzug*, infringed the freedom of workers and the freedom of citizens.[2059] Moreover, the provisions at issue – § 93 to § 95 EStG – indirectly discriminated migrant workers.[2060] Following this judgment, the underlying provision was revoked, in order to bring the national tax legislation in line with European law.[2061] § 95, para 1 now sets out that the reimbursement obligation applies in cases where the taxable person, entitled to the allowance, has moved his residence or habitual abode outside the Member States of the European Union and the States to which the Agreement on the European Economic Area (EEA Agreement) applies, or if the person concerned, notwithstanding a residence or habitual abode in one of these States, is considered to be resident outside the territory of these States under a tax treaty with a third State.[2062] By doing so, by bringing national legislation in conformity with EU law, Germany has established a higher level of inter-level coherence.

- In light of the foregoing, the following should be pointed out. Until 8 April 2010, the eligibility for the *Sonderausgabenabzug* of *Riester*-contributions had been made conditional upon unlimited tax liability.[2063] This would mean that a cross-border worker, working in Germany, but having his residence abroad, would not be eligible for the *Sonderausgabenabzug* of *Riester*-contributions, and the related *Zulagen*. The CJEU ruled that the concerning provisions denied cross-border workers and their spouses the right to the allowances, unless they were fully liable to tax in that Member State, and considered this requirement in breach of the European freedoms of movement.[2064] This forced the German legislator to revise the eligibility criteria for the fiscal facilitation of the *Riester-Rente*. Therefore, the circle of eligible person has been extended to mandatory insured domestic persons in the *gesetzlichen Rentenversicherung* or recipients of domestic salaries in accordance with the Federal Salary Act or Landes Salary Act.[2065] A migrant worker, living and working in Germany, who receives a

2058 See Richter, 285., Wernsmann and Nippert, and D Birk and R Wernsmann, 'Die Besteuerung der Aufwendungen für die Altersvorsorge und der Alterseinkommen' in B Rürup and F Ruland (eds.), *Alterssicherung und Besteuerung* (Gabler, Wiesbaden 2008) 266-268.

2059 Pursuant to article 18 EC Treaty. C 269/07 *Commission vs. Germany* ECLI:EU:C:2009:527 (CJEU). This had already been recognized by Wellisch and others, 50.

2060 *Commission vs. Germany* para 104.

2061 Pursuant to Gesetz zur Umsetzung steuerlicher EU-Vorgaben sowie zur Änderung steuerlicher Vorschriften (EUStVUG).

2062 This repayment obligation is based on the idea that the pension-savings allowance constitutes a social benefit which is intended to compensate for the reductions in benefits in the relevant pension-savings systems made by the domestic legislature.

2063 This condition has been repealed pursuant to the entry into force of Gesetz zur Umsetzung steuerlicher EU-Vorgaben sowie zur Änderung steuerlicher Vorschriften (EUStVUG).

2064 *Commission vs. Germany* para 69.

2065 Revised pursuant to Gesetz zur Umsetzung steuerlicher EU-Vorgaben sowie zur Änderung steuerlicher Vorschriften (EUStVUG).

domestic income, is therefore eligible for the *Zulagen* and *Sonderausgabenabzug* of the *Riester*-contributions.[2066] Furthermore, a cross-border worker receiving a domestic income is eligible, as well in cases where he is insured mandatory under the statutory pension scheme of his residence state, provided that the foreign mandatory insurance is comparable to the mandatory insurance under the *gesetzlichen Rentenversicherung*.[2067] By doing so, by bringing national legislation in conformity with EU law, Germany has established a higher level of inter-level coherence.

- As addressed in section 7.4.1.A.I, prior to 8 April 2010, the facility of *Altersvorsorge-Eigenheimbetrag: 'Wohn-Riester'* was limited to owner-occupied dwellings situated in Germany. The CJEU ruled that by denying cross-border workers the right to use the subsidised capital for the acquisition or construction of an owner-occupied dwelling unless it is situated in Germany, Germany breached the European freedoms of movement.[2068] This forced the German legislator to revise the concerning provision, and to extend the scope of fiscal facilitation to owner-occupied dwellings, situated in a Member State of the European Union or a State to which the Agreement on the European Economic Area (EEA agreement) is applicable.[2069] By doing so, by bringing national legislation in conformity with EU law, Germany has established a higher level of inter-level coherence.
- As dealt with in section 7.4.1.B.I as regards contributions to the *Rürup-Rente*, the CJEU ruled in the *Bechtel* case that the prohibition of the deduction of *Sonderausgaben* regulated in § 10 EStG, due to the exemption of the underlying wages pursuant to the applicable tax treaty, violates the freedom of movement of workers.[2070] In response to this judgment, and in anticipation to a revision of the legal provision, the German Federal Ministry of Finance, issued a policy document, with regards to the *Sonderausgabenabzug* for social security contributions of employees, working abroad and residing in Germany. The Federal German cabinet adopted the government draft and started the legislative procedure. Pursuant to the proposed legislation, § 10 EStG will be revised, stipulating that employees, working abroad and residing in Germany are, under certain conditions, eligible for the *Sonderausgabenabzug*. By virtue of the revised text, a German resident, working in the Netherlands, may deduct Dutch social security contributions as *Sonderausgaben*, when the contributions have a direct link to income from employment, earned in the Netherlands, and these elements of income have been exempted from tax in Germany by virtue of the tax treaty while the

2066 Pursuant to § 10a, para 1, sentence 1 EStG.

2067 § 10a, para 6 EStG.

2068 *Commission vs. Germany*.

2069 Article 1, nr 10, lit. a Gesetz zur Umsetzung steuerlicher EU-Vorgaben sowie zur Änderung steuerlicher Vorschriften (EUStVUG). See also Paintner and Melchior.

2070 *Bechtel*.

Netherlands does not allow the deduction of these contributions. By doing so, by bringing national legislation in conformity with EU law, Germany has established a higher level of inter-level coherence.

– In her 'compartmentalisation-case' (of 14 July 2017) the Dutch Supreme Court found that in cases where the applicable tax treaty allocated the taxing right on pension and annuity benefits to the residence state, the application of the protective tax assessment needs to be compartmentalized. Hence, not all paid premiums may be taken into account when determining the protective assessment, because, according to the Supreme Court, there is no legal framework for taking negative expenditure into account. With respect to annuities, the inclusion in the protective assessment of negative emigration-related expenditure relating to an annuity claim does not conflict with the good faith to be observed in the interpretation and application of the Treaty, in so far as the expenditure in question was made in the period from 1 January 1992 to 1 January 2001 or in the period after 15 July 2009.[2071] The court held that annuity premiums paid under the operation of the legislation in force at that time cannot be considered to be of a conditional nature, see section 7.3.1.A. The Dutch Wet IB 2001 has been adapted accordingly.[2072] By doing so, by bringing national legislation in conformity with the good faith to be observed in the interpretation and application of the Treaty, the Netherlands has established a higher level of inter-level coherence.

7.6.4 *Inter-system Consistency*

In order to prevent discrepancies in information provision, national (Netherlands and Germany) levels of legislation, need to be consistent by themselves. Legal systems consist of, *inter alia*, a set of rules. In general, legislators would prefer that legislation in a particular legal system were consistent. Not only on a domestic level, but in particular where several national legal systems converge as in this research; on Dutch/German level. This requires a certain form of inter-system consistency. For the purposes of this research 'consistency' is termed as `the quality, state, or fact of being consistent; agreement, harmony, compatibility'.[2073] Consistency, in this context, refers to – while applying national regulatory frameworks – not leading to incompatible outcomes for a specific case. Two distinct types of inconsistency may be discerned: treating a person inconsistently over time, and inconsistency between individuals.[2074] It is not uncommon that rules in two legal systems

2071 17/01256, ECLI:NL:HR:2017:1324 (2017) (HR). This concerned the application of art. 3.136, para 2 Wet IB 2001.

2072 As of 1 January 2019, this has been regulated by art. 10a.19 Wet IB 2001.

2073 Oxford Dictionaries.

2074 Steyn, 22.

attach incompatible consequences to a same case. Two or more rules are in actual conflict when they actually apply to one and the same case, and attach incompatible consequences to this case. In terms of inconsistent treatment over time the following should be stressed.

- When cross-border situations are considered, the transition toward downstream taxation in Germany under the *Alterseinkünftegesetz* has thus proved to be appropriate to the extent that the regulation in Germany corresponds to the taxation concept in force in other countries, significantly reducing the extent of positive or negative conflicts of qualification in cross-border situations.[2075] In most countries, including the Netherlands, pension schemes do not give rise to taxation during the accrual period. In Germany, only the *Ertragsanteil* is taxed during the pay-out phase. The coexistence of front-loaded taxation abroad – during the accrual phase – and back-loaded taxation in Germany – during the pay-out phase – leads to intertemporal under-taxation. From the taxpayer's point of view, this leads to the fact that the migration to Germany is thus accompanied with less tax relief compared to remaining abroad.

Along the line of inter-system consistency between individuals, the following conclusions can be drawn:

- The method of 'communicating vessels' between contribution deductions in the third pillar and pension accrual (i.e., pension deficit) in the second pillar renders the Dutch third pillar unique in fiscal terms.[2076] Under the *jaarruimte*-system, the amount of the annuity premium deduction depends on the pension accrual in the second pillar. Merely those taxable persons who fall short of pension accrual in the second pillar (*pensioentekort*), are entitled to deduction of annuity premiums in the third pillar. When determining any pension deficit, a foreign occupational pension plan shall also be taken into account.[2077] By taking into account the accrual in foreign occupational pension plans, these Dutch provisions reflect an 'isolated approach', taking into account any previous or subsequent tax treatment in another (member) state.
- As revealed in section 7.3.1, in the case of a Dutch migrant outbound worker, and if the taxing right is allocated to the Netherlands as a source state (for instance pursuant to article 17, para 2 treaty Netherlands-Germany) Dutch personal pension benefits shall be liable to tax as 'taxable periodical payments and benefits in kind in so far as the premiums paid for them have been taken into account as expenditure for income provisions', and constitute domestic income.[2078] Thus, this taxable proportion of the benefits depends on whether these benefits are derived from contributions which were

2075 Cf. Scheffler and Kölbl, 24.
2076 Cf. Dietvorst, 'Lijfrenten' section 12.3.
2077 Kamerstukken II, *26 727, 3 (Wet Inkomstenbelasting 2001 (Belastingherziening 2001))* 76.
2078 Pursuant to article 7.2, para 2, under d Wet IB 2001. The surrender of periodic income benefits is also covered by this provision.

subject to tax relief in the Netherlands. In the case, of a migrant inbound worker, and if the taxing right is allocated to Germany as a source state, the German pension benefits paid out are subject to German income tax, akin to a domestic situation, see section 7.4. However, as the person concerned nor resides in Germany, nor has his habitual abode in Germany, during the pay-out phase he may be subject to limited tax liability pursuant to § 1, para 4 EStG, provided that he receives domestic income within the meaning of § 49 EStG. The principal condition for including these elements of income in the limited tax liability is a domestic source of income, which applies to benefits arising from *Lebensversicherungen, Rürup-Rente*, as well as *Riester-Rente.*[2079] The taxable proportion of these types of benefits depends on whether these benefits are derived from contributions which were subject to tax relief in Germany.[2080] This reflects that those Dutch, and German, provisions of national tax laws governing the taxation of retirement income, are applied on the basis of an 'isolated approach', without taking into account any previous or subsequent tax treatment in another (member) state.

- Under Dutch tax law, the main rule is that annuity payments, except for the payments arising from the net annuity, shall be fully taxable as periodic payments (against a progressive income tax rate) with the person who receives them, irrespective of whether the paid contributions have been deducted.[2081] Until 1 January 2009, the criterion was whether the premiums had been deducted as expenditure for income provision. Hence, the extent to which the Dutch contributions paid abroad during the posting period were subject to tax relief in Germany, is irrelevant in the tax treatment of the pension benefits pursuant to Dutch national tax law, see the (outbound) poster worker dealt with in section 6.4.1.C.I. However, in the case of an inbound migrant worker (section 7.3.1.B) and outbound cross-border worker (section 6.4.1.B.I), no isolated approach has been taken by the Netherlands. In these cases, annuity payments arising from a foreign provision of which the object and purport corresponds to a Dutch life annuity – within the meaning of art. 3.124 ff. Wet IB 2001 – shall also be

2079 Pursuant to § 49, para 1, under 7 (*Lebensversicherungen* and *Rürup-Rente*) or 10 (*Riester-Rente*) EStG.

2080 As regards this tax relief, § 49, para 1, under 7 (*Lebensversicherungen* and *Rürup-Rente*) or 10 (*Riester-Rente*) EStG refer to § 10, para 1, nr. 2 EStG (*Sonderausgaben*).

2081 Pursuant to art. 3.100, para 1, sub b Wet IB 2001. Cf. Dietvorst, 'Lijfrenten' 558. The main rule that annuity payments are taxed regardless of whether the premiums have been deducted, led to the issue of box splitting after the introduction of the Wet IB 2001. See ibid. 556 ff. If premiums are not or not fully deducted, the corresponding (part of the) value shall be taxed in box 3. Strictly speaking, the policy will have to be divided into a box 1 and a box 3 part during the accumulation phase. To take into account the non-deducted premiums, a limited balance method was introduced in 2009, see art. 3.107a Wet B 2001. Insofar as the taxpayer has demonstrated that premiums paid were not deducted in whole or in part, no tax will be due on the benefits. The amount per year of non-deducted premiums that has not been taken into account shall not exceed €2,269.

taxable.[2082] However, if and insofar as it can be assumed with regard to this foreign scheme that the premiums paid have not been deducted from the income during the period abroad, this does not constitute a taxable periodical benefit (but to that extent shall be taxable as income arising from saving and investment in BOX 3).[2083] Hence, insofar as the premiums paid abroad have been deducted from taxable income or have otherwise led to a tax reduction, the benefits from the right shall be included in the Dutch income tax. In doing so, a sound level of linkage is achieved between the actual tax treatment of the personal pension scheme abroad and that in the Netherlands. Thus, where an outbound posted worker is fully taxed, irrespective of whether the paid contributions have been deducted (abroad), an inbound migrant worker and outbound cross-border worker are taxed to the extent that the premiums paid have been deducted from the income during the period abroad.

- Under the Germany EStG, benefits arising from non-facilitated (foreign) contributions are taxed against the *Ertragsanteil.*[2084] Whether contributions paid into German occupational pension scheme were facilitated under foreign tax legislation during the posted period is thus irrelevant. Hence, benefits arising from non-facilitated contributions – paid during the period abroad – shall be taxed against the *Ertragsanteil*, rather than the *Besteuerungsanteil.* This reflects those German provisions of national tax laws governing the taxation of retirement income, are applied on the basis of an 'isolated approach', without taking into account any previous or subsequent tax treatment in another (member) state. Germany does not adhere the principle of intertemporal correspondence (between facilitation during accrual phase and taxation of benefits during pay-out phase) in cross-border situations, as much as it does in domestic situations.

2082 Pursuant to art. 3.100, para 1, sub c Wet IB 2001. It should be noted that this provision applies to residents of the Netherlands (domestic taxpayers) where, in accordance with international views, the world income is included in the tax. This world income also includes payments from abroad.

2083 Because foreign provisions can involve widely divergent products, and because it will often be unclear to the Dutch tax authorities how the provision is treated for tax purposes abroad, it was decided to place the burden of proof as to whether or not tax relief has been received on the taxpayer. After all, the taxpayer is in the best position to provide information about his/her actual situation. Possibilities to meet this burden of proof are a reference to foreign tax legislation (for instance if the annuity does not meet the conditions for deduction of premiums applicable there), and the submission of a statement by the foreign tax authorities or the insurer or of relevant tax assessments, see Kamerstukken II, *26 727, nr. 7 (Belastingherziening 2001)* 475.

2084 § 22, nr 5, sentence, letter a in conjunction with § 22, nr 1, sentence 3, under bb EStG. With respect to *Ertragsanteilbesteuerung*, also see C Herrmann, G Heuer and A Raupach, *Einkommensteuer- und Körperschaftsteuergesetz: EStG KStG* (Dr. Otto Schmidt, Köln Aktualisierung 2018).

7.7 Interim Conclusion

As has been addressed thoroughly in chapter 1 of this research, the two-dimensional notion of effective pension information articulates that the information's behavioural purpose seeks to inform mobile individuals on an aggregated level about how much pension they can expect, in order to be able to assess the adequacy of their dispersed pension, covering all their forms of pension in each of the (former) working/residence states. The aforementioned behavioural purpose contains the terms 'aggregated' (i.e. assembled at an overall/higher level) and the phrase 'covering all their forms of pension in each of the (former) working/residence states'. However, mobile individuals – who avail(ed) themselves of their European freedoms of movement – see themselves confronted with a wide range of diverging 'pensions', i.e. pension vehicles, schemes, retirement products of all sorts, arising from occupational pension systems in each of the different (former) working states, and/or residence states. This requires putting together dispersed, and deviating, elements of future retirement income, arising in each of these states. This amounts to observing, and 'translating' the intersections between different multi-level legal systems (national, EU and international/bilateral) and the interaction of poorly coordinated legal domains (pension and tax law) – which can all be interwoven in a personal mobile situation – into effective pension information. This was taken as a given and this chapter mapped out the personal pension systems in both the Netherlands, as well as Germany. Moreover, it revolved around the tax treatment of these personal schemes in both the accrual and pay-out phase, in both domestic, and in particular in cross-border situations.

The comparative findings were presented in section 4.5, along the lines of this research's evaluation framework. This comparison revealed a considerable number of differences when it comes to Dutch and German personal pensions, and their tax treatment in cross-border situations. These structural differences should be observed when providing effective cross-border pension information. Also, along the principle of foreseeability of (the application of) legislation several findings were revealed. With respect to inter-system consistency, the findings exhibit a number of situations where applying national regulatory frameworks leads to incompatible outcomes for a specific case, in particular with regard to inconsistency of the tax treatment of pensions of mobile individuals. What is more, it was also found that provisions of national tax laws governing the taxation of retirement income, are applied on the basis of an 'isolated approach', without taking into account any previous or subsequent tax treatment in another (member) state. Lastly, evaluating the regulatory frameworks through the lens of inter-level coherence revealed findings when it comes to the coherence among these levels of legislation, involving systematic scrutiny of coherence with higher-level regulations and with treaty or other international obligations.

In this vein, this chapter meets this research second (sub)objective of a legal comparative study in which the legal frameworks in the Netherlands and Germany shall be mapped out, and evaluated along the lines of this research's evaluation framework.

8 The Regulatory Framework Governing the Tax Treatment of Cross-border Pensions on European Level Through the Lens of Effective Pension Information

8.1 Introduction

Where in the preceding chapters (4-7) the construct, legal character, vesting methods, pension schemes and tax treatment of statutory, occupational, and personal pensions - in the Netherlands and Germany - have been mapped out, this chapter analyses the European regulatory framework. Working and saving for pension across international border implies dealing with multiple pension and tax systems. It is inevitable that EU citizens contributing or working across borders will have to contend with two or more sets of tax rules that differ considerably.[2085] This means that in cross-border situations, both norms derived from international tax law, as well as EU-law norms may apply concomitantly. The emphasis of the analysis in the chapter is put on the mobile citizen, saving for his retirement through either a statutory, occupational or personal pension provision. Although the taxation of pension on the level of social security institutions, pension providers, funds, insurers or institutions might affect the tax treatment of mobile workers' pension, and their personal retirement savings position, this will remain out of scope since this requires a different focus of analysis, also with regard to the applicable regulatory mechanisms.

Moreover, in cross-border situations mobile individuals - who avail(ed) themselves of their European freedoms of movement - see themselves confronted with a wide range of diverging 'pensions', i.e. pension vehicles, schemes, retirement products of all sorts, arising from pension systems in each of the different (former) working states, and/or residence states. Providing, on an aggregated level, mobile individuals information about how much pension they can expect - covering all their forms of pension in each of the (former) working/residence states - requires a complex process of incorporating all types of

2085 European Commission, 'Commission Staff Working Document accompanying Commission Communication 'Removing cross-border tax obstacles for EU citizens" (2010) [SEC(2010) 1576 final].

diverging pension vehicles, schemes, products of all sorts in each of the different (former) working states, and/or residence states. This requires a process of converging these deviating systems, while upholding the information's effectiveness. Putting this dispersed puzzle together also poses considerable challenges in terms of information provision. This amounts to observing, and 'translating' the intersections between different multi-level legal systems (national, EU and international/bilateral) and the interaction of poorly coordinated legal domains (pension and tax law) – which can all be interwoven in a personal mobile situation – into effective pension information. Hitherto, no attention has been paid neither any research has been conducted on the differentiated tax treatment of the fragmented pension rights in each of the (former) working states, and the effect thereof on the ambition to present effective pension information.

This chapter explores how the taxation of cross-border pensions is affected by EU law, i.e. exploring how EU law might alter the tax treatment of the relevant cross-border pension, as primary and secondary EU law emanate a normative effect in this regard.[2086] Rather than putting focus on the precise impact of certain individual cases, rulings and/or communications, this chapter offers an analysis from a bird's eye view of the overly complex system of EU law in the domain of the taxation of cross-border pensions. In addition, it will be explored to what extent the regulatory instruments employed in the domain of European law, as they stand, are apt for the provision of effective pension information, in the light of the principles set in chapter 2 of this research (understandability, technical (legal) correctness, personal relevance, trustworthiness). Given the division of competences as laid down in the European treaties, and, correspondingly, the (legislative) instruments – and their properties – employed in the field of EU law (positive and negative integration) emphasis will be put on the extent to which they aid in establishing inter-level coherence, and inter-system consistency. For instance, as the CJEU held in the *Van Gend & Loos*-case, community law, independently of the legislation of Member States, not only imposes obligations on individuals but is also intended to confer upon them rights which become part of their legal heritage.[2087] It thus constitutes a sovereign field of law *sui generis*, as part of the multi-level legal systems. Hence, it will not be compared to other fields of EU law in terms of similarities, and differences. This chapter answers the sub-research questions of how the taxation of cross-border pensions is governed by European law, and to what extent there is room for improvement, along the lines of the assessment framework drawn up in chapter 2.

2086 See also paragraph I, under 1 of the Protocol to the tax treaty concluded between the Netherlands and Germany. This provision stipulates that it is understood that the law of the European Union takes precedence over the provisions of the Convention. On the interaction between EU law and international tax law see Wattel, Marres and Vermeulen, part I.

2087 26-62 *Van Gend & Loos* ECLI:EU:C:1963:1 (CJEU).

8.2 EUROPEAN (TAX) LAW PERTAINING TO CROSS-BORDER PENSIONS

It should be pointed out at the outset, that there is no specific European legislation on the taxation of retirement provisions, nor a European-wide accepted model for the taxation of pensions. The taxation of pensions in the different European Member States, has not been harmonised not coordinated, at least not through a 'hard law-approach'. However, the taxation of (mainly occupational) pensions in cross-border cases, have been brought closer to each other via a so-called 'soft law-approach'. The instruments, and interventions used under this 'soft law-approach', will be elucidated in more detail below.

8.2.1 Acquis Communautaire

Certain parts of the *acquis communautaire*[2088] will be considered in this chapter. This vast body of legislation encapsulates treaties (TEU and TFEU), protocols, secondary legislation, international agreements, case law and development of legal principles by the CJEU etc. The sources of European EU law can be categorized in primary and secondary law.[2089] Primary EU law finds its origin directly in the Member States, being the founding treaties, i.e. the two main treaties of equal standing; the TEU and TFEU[2090]. Over the course of years, the scope of the treaties has expanded considerably, although not all fields are subject to the same level of integration and EU control. The special nature of these treaties is embedded in the concept of direct applicability. This means that (on the accession of a member state to the Union) all of the treaty provisions automatically become part of the generally binding domestic law of the Member State, which is not only applicable to the member states, but also to the citizens of that state. This form of law is commonly referred to as 'self-executing law'. This implies that the provisions of these laws have legal validity once the treaty has been ratified, without any further action required by that member state, i.e. to include or transform the treaty into the domestic legal order. The CJEU has held consistently a *monist* view, in ruling that provisions of the EU treaties may be invoked

2088 This term is commonly used to refer to the whole body of EU law that has been built up over the years thus far, written and unwritten, in force at that time. see N Foster, *Foster on EU Law* (3rd edn Oxford University Press, Oxford 2011) 110. It means 'what has been achieved by the Union', see also Wattel, Marres and Vermeulen, 15.

2089 A Schrauwen, 'Sources of EU law for integration in taxation' in D Weber (ed.), *Traditional and Alternative Routes to European Tax Integration* (IBFD, Amsterdam 2010) 15 and ECCM Kemmeren, 'Sources of EU law for European tax integration: Well-known and alternative legal instruments' in D Weber (ed.), *Traditional and alternative routes to European Tax Integration* (IBFD, Amsterdam 2010) 29. See for an extensive discussion on the relation between primary and secondary in the sphere of direct tax law G Kofler, 'Das Verhältnis zwischen primären und sekundärem Unionsrecht im direkten Steuerrecht' in M Lang and C Weinzierl (eds.), *Europäisches Steuerrecht (Festschrift Rödler)* (Linde Verlag, Wien 2010) 434 ff.

2090 Foster, 111. The Lisbon Treaty renamed it to its current name.

directly by European nationals (i.e. having 'direct effect') irrespective of the legal traditions of the Member States, i.e. EU law is also the legal concern of individuals and not only the member states.[2091]

The aforementioned treaties (TEU and TFEU) merely provide broad guidelines for striving to achieve certain (commonly) agreed aims and objectives. The implementation thereof is a matter, for the most part, of secondary EU legislation, or, failing that, of the CJEU, which will rule on the interpretation of a certain treaty provision, for instance the term 'worker'.[2092] However, it must be stressed that these two main treaties, and the related amendments, do not constitute the entirety of primary EU law. Primary law contains treaties which amended the aforementioned treaties, such as the treaties of Amsterdam, Nice, Lisbon, and the accession treaties with new EU Member States, and these treaties are supplemented with, what has expanded to a complex and vast range of protocols.[2093] These protocols provide interpretative guidance on the text of the treaty provisions and are commonly used to lay down regulations of more technical matters. Furthermore, a list of member states' declarations complement the two treaties, making uniliteral declaration on a particular matter.[2094] The protocols and declarations will not be discussed in further detail hereinafter.

Contrarily to primary EU law, acts enacted by EU institutions are categorized as secondary EU law. This form of EU law is derived from and based on primary EU law, in that it can only come into existence if a legal basis in the found treaties authorized the EU legislation to adopt such law.[2095] This can take the form of, *inter alia*, regulations, directives, decisions, recommendations and opinions.[2096] This is not an exhaustive enumeration since there are

2091 *Van Gend & Loos.*

2092 See Foster, 112.

2093 Article 51 TEU sets out that Protocols to the Treaties form an integral part thereof. It remains unclear what this means precisely, but is commonly considered that protocols are a lesser, but no less binding, version of an international treaty. See ibid. 112. In the EU legal order, these protocols have treaty status, although the value thereof has not been put under scrutiny before the CJEU.

2094 Akin to the protocols, they may alter the perception of the meaning or application of treaty provision, but have, contrary to the protocols, no explicit treaty status and are very uncertain in EU law. However, pursuant to the Lisbon Treaty, the Charter of Fundamental Rights was appended to the treaties in the form of a declaration stipulating that the Charter does have legal binding force. However, this Charter, albeit not included in the TEU or TFEU, has the same legal value as the founding treaties, and thus is of primary EU law, see Article 6(1) first subparagraph TEU. See more extensively on this matter AG Toth, 'The legal status of the declarations annexed to the Single European Act' 23 Common Market Law Review.

2095 Wattel, Marres and Vermeulen, 15.

2096 See Article 288, para 1 TFEU: "*To exercise the Union's competences, the institutions shall adopt regulations, directives, decisions, recommendations and opinions. A regulation shall have general application. It shall be binding in its entirety and directly applicable in all Member States. A directive shall be binding, as to the result to be achieved, upon each Member State to which it is addressed, but shall leave to the national authorities the choice of form and methods. A decision shall be binding in its entirety. A decision which specifies those to*

many other forms of acts that EU institutions may use to carry out their tasks and competences. The adoption of these acts at EU level, constitutes an important part of so-called 'positive integration' which will be dealt with more extensively below.[2097] This entails the integration of legal orders through agreement on common rules and policies, and the coordination of national policies. It should be noted that in the field of direct taxes, there is little secondary EU law. There are thus little CJEU cases on the implementation of EU legislation. With regard to the tax treatment of cross-border pensions, there is even no secondary legislation.

With regard to the European freedoms of movement, the effect of the European freedom of workers (Article 45 TFEU) and freedom of persons (Article 21 TFEU) on the tax treatment of pensions in cross-border situations will be assessed in particular. The freedom of establishment (Article 49 TFEU)[2098], and freedom of services (Article 56 TFEU) will be considered to the extent appropriate for this assessment, since these European freedoms of movement do not apply to the employed mobile worker on a personal level.[2099] These freedoms rather, in principle, apply to the self-employed persons, pension funds, pension providers, insurers etc. which do not fall in the *ratione personae* of this research.

8.2.2 *EU Law and Abolishing Cross-border Tax Obstacles*

As regards EU law, the body of law discussed in the preceding section, it is to be noted that Article 26, para 1 of the TFEU prescribes that the European Union shall adopt measures with the aim of establishing or ensuring the functioning of the internal market. Such an internal European market, characterised as a national market, requires, *inter alia*, the free movement of goods, services, persons and capital irrespective of national borders[2100], as well as harmonization of national laws insofar as disparities between national laws impede

whom it is addressed shall be binding only on them. Recommendations and opinions shall have no binding force." Article 288 is not exhaustive as regards the legally binding acts that can be enacted by the EU institutions. Other sources of EU law are, for instance, international agreements, treaties and conventions.

2097 Wattel, Marres and Vermeulen, 15.

2098 For instance with regard to *C-480/17 Montag ECLI: EU: C: 2018: 987 (CJEU).*

2099 This research consistently refers to the renumbered Articles.

2100 See Article 26(2) TFEU: *"The internal market shall comprise an area without internal frontiers in which the free movement of goods, persons, services and capital is ensured in accordance with the provisions of the Treaties."*

the functioning of the internal market.[2101] The most apparent tax obstacles in light of the European market are[2102]:

- tax burden on the cross-border relocation of persons (exit taxes);
- substantial differences (disparities[2103]) between national tax laws;
- having to comply with up to 27 different tax administrations and different sets of substantive and procedural tax law';
- differential tax treatment of resident and non-resident taxpayers;
- differential tax treatment of domestic and foreign income;
- differential tax treatment of domestic and foreign pension contributions;
- international juridical double taxation[2104] due to the parallel exercise of taxing rights by source and residence state (e.g. as a result of income characterization mismatches).

Over the course of years, as EU citizens have become more active across borders, it has become apparent that there are several aspects of Member States' tax laws that impede with the Treaty rules. The majority of these obstacles will be discussed below, in the light of the cross-border tax treatment of pensions. It is important to put emphasis on the consequences of these obstacles, as these may considerably affect the proper functioning of the European internal market. For instance, it would impede the rights to freedom of movement of workers if a worker or a person seeking employment, in his state of nationality, to receive treatment less favourable than he would have enjoyed if he had not availed himself of the opportunities offered by the treaty in relation to freedom of movement. Such differences in treatment are likely to deter EU citizens from exercising their rights of free movement, and would, thus, unduly affect their decisions as to, for instance, where to get employed. It should be noted that also excessive administrative burdens may dissuade these citizens from exercising their Treaty Freedoms.[2105]

In order to ensure the proper functioning of the European internal market, a certain degree of integration of Member States' tax systems is required.[2106] This integration may be

2101 See Article 114 TFEU. However, paragraph 2 of this provision states that paragraph 1 shall not apply to fiscal provisions, to those relating to the free movement of persons nor to those relating to the rights and interests of employed persons.

2102 Cf. Wattel, Marres and Vermeulen, 3.

2103 Disparities encompass differences between the (tax) laws and administrative practice of Member States, such as differences in tax rates, connecting factors (residence, source of income) to establish taxing power, or income characterization (deductible or non-deductible), see ibid. 48.

2104 I.e. same tax base and same taxable person.

2105 See for instance C-522/04 *Commission vs. Belgium II* ECLI:EU:C:2007:405 (CJEU).

2106 Cf. Wattel, Marres and Vermeulen, 4.

attained through either 'negative integration'[2107] or 'positive integration'[2108]. Measures adopted in both fields will be discussed elaborately hereinafter. It should be mentioned that positive integration-measures are a more modest contribution to the abolishment of tax obstacles to the international market. However, most of the integration of direct taxes is achieved through negative integration, i.e. CJEU's case-law prohibiting national tax measures contravening EU law. Positive and negative integration may even interact. As long as no positive integration has been established in a given field of law, Member States in principle remain free to regulate as they consider appropriate, except where competence has exclusively been conferred upon the Union. However, as will become evident below, national tax sovereignty has been restricted by the process of negative integration, i.e. although, in the absence of EU legislation, the development of a direct tax system is a prerogative of Member States, they are not allowed to adopt or maintain tax legislation infringing general Treaty rules, such as the principle of non-discrimination.[2109]

8.2.3 *The Role of the CJEU in EU Law*

Since the European treaties largely serve as a framework, they require substantial supplement.[2110] As this may have not been substantiated by secondary legislation in the field of the tax treatment of cross-border pensions, and the Treaties need to interpreted, there is a wide area of activity for the CJEU. In addition, as holds true with regard to all legal systems, legislation cannot possibly cater for all economic and social developments, and legislation has either to be adapted to fit the situation or new rules need to be introduced. However, the Court itself has widened its scope beyond the TEU and TFEU and has developed her own fundamental doctrines and principles, which will be discussed in this chapter.[2111] This now constitutes clearly a persuasive source of a primary EU law-nature, which is binding on the Member States.[2112] The role of the CJEU in creating EU

2107 That is, integration of legal orders through prohibitions of unduly restrictive national tax measures contravening the TFEU, mostly after bringing an infringement procedure before the CJEU.

2108 That is, integration of legislation, coordination and cooperation at EU level through either harmonization of tax laws but, moreover, policy coordination. See, for instance, European Commission, 'The elimination of tax obstacles to the cross-border provision of occupational pensions'.

2109 Wattel, Marres and Vermeulen, 46.

2110 Foster, 119.

2111 For instance the principle of non-discrimination in direct tax matters was recognized in the landmark case of *C-279/93 Schumacker ECLI: EU: C: 1995: 31 (CJEU)*. Foster brings forward three principal Treaty Articles which provide some justification for the CJEU in introducing general principles in the EU legal order: Article 19 TEU, Article 263 and Article 340 TFEU. See Foster, 120.

2112 Wattel, Marres and Vermeulen, 15. As a back-up instrument, Article 280 TFEU provides that the judgments of CJEU shall be enforceable. As Wattel portrayed the role of the CJEU: *"In direct tax cases, the Court is a balancing artist between the interests of the internal market and the 28 separate interests of the Member States*

law, lies, *inter alia*, in assessing to what extent the tax treatment of pensions in cross-border cases under domestic law, is in line with European primary legislation, i.e. the freedoms of movement. In this regard, the question rises to what extent this role entails enhancing coherence among the national pension tax systems? This will be dealt with in section 8.5.

The cases relevant (related to direct taxation on pensions in cross-border cases) and ruled by the CJEU thus far will be discussed. For instance, the *Bachmann*[2113] case is one of the first cases which received considerable attention in the field of the tax-treatment of cross-border pensions.[2114] This case concerned the cross-border deduction (for tax purposes) of life insurance contributions in Belgium. The *Wielocks*[2115] case and the *Safir*[2116] case are recognised as the second generation of cases, considered relevant for the cross-border tax treatment of pensions.[2117] The 'latest' generation of CJEU cases with regard to the cross-border tax treatment of pensions, concern the *Danner* case[2118], *Skandia* case[2119], *Turpeinen* case[2120], *Commission vs. Denmark* case[2121], *Commission vs. Belgium* case[2122] and the *Commission vs. Germany*[2123] case. However, most recently, the CJEU delivered a ruling in the *Kohl*[2124], *Bechtel*[2125] and *Montag*[2126] cases.

8.2.4 Tax Treaties vs. EU (Tax) Law

Pursuant to settled case-law, Member States are free to determine the connecting factors for the allocation of fiscal jurisdiction in tax treaties (e.g. residence, source of income etc.), but this allocation, as discussed in the preceding section, does not allow them to apply

to protect their tax bases, rather than Montesquieu's bouche qui prononce les paroles de la loi (only the mouth that pronounces the words of the law)", see ibid. 47.

2113 *Bachmann.*

2114 C Richter, *Die Besteuerung grenzüberschreitender Altersversorgung in der EU* (Rechtsordnung und Steuerwesen, Dr. Otto Schmidt, Köln 2010) 2.

2115 C-80/94 *Wielockx* ECLI:EU:C:1995:271 (CJEU).

2116 C-118/96 *Safir* ECLI:EU:C:1998:170 (CJEU).

2117 RS Avi-Yonah, 'Back to the Future? The Potential Revival of Territoriality' 10 Bulletin for International Taxation 471, and Richter, 2.

2118 C-133/00 *Danner* ECLI:EU:C:2002:558 (CJEU).

2119 ECLI:EU:C:2003:380 *Skandia* C-422/01 (CJEU).

2120 *Turpeinen.*

2121 C-150/04 *Commission vs. Denmark* ECLI:EU:C:2007:69 (CJEU).

2122 *Commission vs. Belgium II.*

2123 *Commission vs. Germany.*

2124 *Kohll en Kohll-Schlesser.*

2125 *Bechtel.*

2126 *C-480/17 Montag* ECLI:EU:C:2018:987 (CJEU).

measures contrary to the freedoms of movement.[2127] As regards the exercise of the power of taxation allocated by these treaties, the Member States must comply with EU rules.[2128] In the section below, it becomes apparent that EU law is particularly instructive as it has a much broader scope for regulating certain cross-border tax issues, compared to bilateral tax treaties. This broader scope comprises instruments such as positive and negative integration, while using mechanisms such as the Treaty Freedoms and the principle of non-discrimination. Generally, tax treaties suffer from shortcomings as regards the ensuring of equal tax treatment, apart from non-discrimination clauses enshrined in tax treaties.[2129] As regards the latter, these do not regulate all income tax issues arising in cross-border situations.

8.3 Positive Integration: the European Commission's Stance

Contrary to the (fairly harmonized) field of indirect taxation, the primary European Treaties (TEU and TFEU) do not contain provisions stipulating the harmonisation[2130] of direct taxes. Harmonization of taxes is a political highly sensitive topic, since tax sovereignty embodies a fundamental part of national sovereignty. Some ground of competence for harmonizing tax legislation may be read implicitly in Article 115 TFEU, aimed at the establishment or functioning of the internal market.[2131] This is considered one of the most chief bottlenecks in that it requires unanimity voting in the field of direct taxes.[2132] As Wattel portrays it, direct taxation is considered by most Member States as the

2127 See, for instance, *Bechtel para 66.*

2128 C-385/00 *De Groot* ECLI:EU:C:2002:750 (CJEU) para 93 and 94; C-265/04 *Bouanich* ECLI:EU:C:2006:51 (CJEU) para 49 and 50; C-303/12 *Imfeld and Garcet* ECLI:EU:C:2013:822 (CJEU) para 41 and 42.

2129 Such as Article 24 of the Double Tax Convention concluded between the Netherlands and Germany, notable paragraph 6 of this treaty provision regulating the tax treatment of pension contributions paid to foreign pension institutions. See also Article 24 OECD MC. In addition, in the vein of Article 24 on non-discrimination, section XVI, paragraph 1 of the protocol of the treaty concluded between the Netherlands and Germany widens the scope of the German *Ehegattensplitting* in cross-border cases.

2130 It should be stressed that harmonization of enacted written legislation is not akin to the harmonisation of national legal practice, habits and *couleur locale*. Cf. Wattel, Marres and Vermeulen, 7.

2131 G Kofler, 'Ist der Spuk des Europäischen Steuerrechts bald vorbei?' in W Schön and C Heber (eds.), *Grundfragen des Europäischen Steuerrechts* (Springer, Berlin Heidelberg 2015) 3.

2132 Article 115 TFEU: *"Without prejudice to Article 114, the Council shall, acting unanimously in accordance with a special legislative procedure and after consulting the European Parliament and the Economic and Social Committee, issue directives for the approximation of such laws, regulations or administrative provisions of the Member States as directly affect the establishment or functioning of the internal market."* The reference to the ‚Council' is a reference to the Council of the European Union. The Council is the principal decision-making institution within the EU, and, historically, the European Council is, from a legislative perspective, a more powerful institution than the European Parliament. The European Council comprises each of the Member States' Minister depending on the topic under consideration. In a tax context, the council is formed by the national Member States' finance ministers. Summarised, this means that a European Directive cannot be

last 'hardcore' part of their sovereignty within the Union, which implies very little political enthusiasm for positive integration, implying relinquishing political and budgetary sovereignty.[2133] At present, the EU hardly has a tax policy on its own, as taxation plays a limited role as a policy instrument on the EU level. As will become apparent, the European Commission's policy is aimed at aligning national taxes and tax policies in so far as required for the proper functioning of the internal market, abolishing unduly restrictive, discriminatory national taxation.[2134] This EC's policy has been pursued predominantly through the proclamation of the EC's Communications, known as 'soft law'. In these communications, the EC proclaims her perception on certain issues in the field of direct taxes, in order to urge Member States to comply with their obligations under EU law.

The European Commission's position on the tax treatment of cross-border pensions has evolved over the course of years. This Commission's efforts will be dealt with thoroughly below. As the 2001 communication has dealt most extensively with measures of positive integration on the sphere of the tax treatment of cross-border pensions, this document will be touched upon thoroughly. It is remarkably to see, that since then, the Commission has taken no considerable steps in the sphere of positive integration pertaining to the tax treatment of cross-border pensions.

Although over the course of years, the focus of measures devoted to positive integration has shifted to mechanisms aimed at combatting tax evasion and tax fraud, and curbing tax competition between states, the European Commission has taken several steps in order to (better) 'align' the Member States' national tax systems and/or to render these systems (more) compatible with primary and/or secondary European law.[2135] As reiterated in the above, the (level of development of) tax mechanisms and underlying tax policy aimed at promoting supplementary pension schemes, vary greatly across countries. Furthermore, the national tax systems offer different modalities as regards tax benefits, relief, reductions, exemptions, compensation, deferrals and other fiscal advantages[2136]. These tax system's modalities are, commonly, geared to the funding mechanisms and can apply to either the (employer's or employee's) contributions, the scheme's or fund's income (e.g. capital yield from investments) or the benefits paid out to the beneficiary during the pay-out phase.

---

issued on income tax matters without the unanimous agreement of each Member States' finance minister. Cf. *Regeling van de Minister van Sociale Zaken en Werkgelegenheid van 13 april 2018*, 27.

2133 Wattel, Marres and Vermeulen, 5.

2134 Ibid. 8-9.

2135 Cf. Kofler, 'Ist der Spuk des Europäischen Steuerrechts bald vorbei?' 8. For an extensive overview of these initiatives in the sphere of positive integration see ibid. 7.

2136 The CJEU delineates a 'fiscal advantage' as allowing a taxable person to reduce the amount of taxable income and the rate applicable to that income. See, *inter alia*, C-480/17 *Montag* ECLI:EU:C:2018:987 (CJEU) para 23; *Bechtel* para 43 and *Kohll en Kohll-Schlesser* para 39.

Over the course of years, it has become apparent that these national tax systems were subject to a shift; from hardly taking into requirements set by EU law to, gradually, taking into account positive criteria of harmonisation or coordination. These criteria are aimed at mitigating the contradiction of domestic tax rules, which cross-border pensions may suffer from which were domestically orientated, creating obstacles to the development of the single market. These domestic tax systems may be considered to operate consistently in domestic situations, but inconsistencies may emerge in cross-border cases.[2137] For instance, the application of different national tax systems may induce double taxation or double non-taxation. However, in most cases double tax conventions concluded between states offer a solution for these situations, although situations may occur in which the tax treaty may not provide a satisfactory solution.[2138] As will be considered below, developments in the field of positive integration have helped to mitigate the consequences of these situations of inconsistency. For instance, over the course of past years there has been a shift of countries moving more and more towards adopting an EET-system.

It should be pointed out that merely the initiatives aimed at the tax treatment of (cross-border) pensions will be discussed below. Therefore, communications aimed at, for instance, creating a single market for supplementary pensions are out of scope.[2139] This Communication supplemented the proposed Pension Fund Directive by dealing with the tax aspects of cross-border occupational pension provisions.

8.3.1 *EC Communication 1991: Supplementary Social Security Schemes – the Role of Occupational Pension Schemes in the Social Protection of Workers and Their Implications for Freedom of Movement*

When the 1991-communication was issued, supplementary pension vehicles (second and third-pillar) were governed by domestic laws and regulations, apart from statutory pension schemes.[2140] Therefore the situation in this domain was characterized by a lack of harmonization or coordination of national legislation, and international aspects of pensions received little or no attention. Also, the focus of the tax treatment of these pension schemes in cross-border situation was primarily placed on internal situations.

2137 Prats, 13.

2138 If the double tax convention contains a non-discriminatory clause, this may be invoked in cases where it applies.

2139 For instance European Commission, 'Towards a Single Market for supplementary pensions, results of the Green Paper on supplementary pensions in the single market' (1999) [COM(1999) 134 final].

2140 Pursuant to Regulation (EEC) No 1408/71 of the Council of 14 June 1971 on the application of social security schemes to employed persons and their families moving within the Community [1971] L 149/2.

However, as the European Single Market grew more mature, the European institutions' position changed.[2141] In particular the European Commission pointed out that Member States' rules and regulations governing supplementary pension schemes could constitute an obstacle for the development and consolidation of the European Single Market, in particular to the freedom of movement of persons and services. These obstacles may take the form of distortions or discriminatory treatment of cross-border pensions. Hence, the Commission's initiatives were mainly aimed at discovering situations and factors which could lead to obstacles or discriminatory situations, potentially affecting the development of the Single Market.[2142]

In her first communication, released in 1991, the Commission pointed out that the European Community should recognise the principle that each worker should be able to move to a job in another Member State without having to fear any undue loss of rights to future retirement benefits.[2143] The Commission acknowledged that several obstacles to labour mobility are inherent in the regulation of supplementary schemes, some of them caused by the tax treatment of these schemes. In the light of Member States' sovereignty, the Commission noted that the issue how this should be achieved could be left to a very large extent to each Member State or those persons or groups who design and run a supplementary scheme.[2144] In the view of the Commission, progress along these lines would facilitate labour mobility and thereby increase the performance of the labour market and hence the European economy as a whole.

As regards supplementary pension schemes, the Commission rightly stated that these schemes are extremely diverse and a complex issue, involving many different players at different levels, and for this reasons the Community could and should stimulate effort at all levels to remove obstacles to cross-border mobility, i.e. the Community, Member States and social partners.[2145] In achieving this, the Commission would undertake efforts to obtain more and better information on supplementary pension schemes throughout the Community. In this regard, the monitoring of evolutions at the national level and the

2141 Prats, 14.

2142 In this regard, the European Commission regarded Article 51 of the EC Treaty a sufficient basis to take initiatives and to develop secondary EU law.

2143 European Commission, 'Communication from the Commission to the Council – Supplementary Social Security Schemes: the Role of Occupational Pension Schemes in the Social Protection of Workers and their Implications for Freedom of Movement' (1991) [SEC(91) 1332 final] 23.

2144 Section 3.3 of this communication indicated the principal alternatives which were available in order to achieve this goal.

2145 European Commission, 'Communication from the Commission to the Council – Supplementary Social Security Schemes: the Role of Occupational Pension Schemes in the Social Protection of Workers and their Implications for Freedom of Movement' 4, 23.

assessment of the actual or potential impact of various Community measures would be of particular interest.

The Commission observed that a problem which specifically affects international migrant workers is related to taxes.[2146] In this regard, the Commission pointed to the taxation of pension capital transfers. National tax authorities grant tax exemptions for contributions and investment income of the schemes, expecting to levy income tax on the retirement benefits paid out, once the worker has retired. The commission pointed out that in situations where the capital has been transferred abroad, they will not be able to tax these benefits. Consequently, national tax authorities may levy very substantial taxes on transfer values, rendering such transfers far too costly for migrant workers. The commission recognized that in that case, the migrant workers' only option is to maintain their rights in their previous pension fund which may not adequately preserve the real value of the pension rights. Furthermore, as regards short-term migrant workers wishing to remain in the pension scheme of their previous work state, the Commission noted that the tax rules of the country of employment should allow the tax deductibility of contributions paid into a pension scheme established in another country if this scheme enjoys the favourable tax status in its own country.[2147] In this regard, the Commission drew attention to a certain number of infringement procedures against various Member States in order to ensure the tax deductibility of life insurance premiums paid to companies established in another Member State under the same conditions as for premiums paid to a domestic company. Lastly, the commission drew attention to the problem of taxes on transfer values representing pension rights acquired within a previous pension scheme.[2148] The Commission emphasized that whilst taxation cannot be avoided completely by a mobile worker or pensioner, Member states should ensure that migrant workers be not subjected to any form of double taxation.

8.3.2 *EC Green Paper 1997: Supplementary Pensions in the Single Market*

In this Green Paper, the European Commission built on her findings of the 1991 Communication, discussed above.[2149] This paper's aim was to explore, in conjunction with the representatives of Member States, Social Partners and pension funds, how to remove obstacles to cross-border mobility of employed and self-employed persons in the European

2146 Ibid. 19.
2147 Ibid. 20.
2148 Ibid. 22.
2149 European Commission, 'Supplementary pensions in the Single Market: A Green Paper' (1997) [COM(97) 283 final].

Union in the field of supplementary pensions.[2150] The commission pointed out that given the coordination system created for statutory schemes as it stood during the release of the Green Paper, a more flexible approach was required. Chapter 4 of this report discussed obstacles to the free movement of persons relating to supplementary pensions. The Commission found that there remain a number of obstacles to free movement, such as tax difficulties linked to acquiring pension rights in more than one Member State, or the taxation of pension capital transfer abroad.[2151] With respect to removing these tax disadvantages, the Commission holds that Member States could be encouraged to include specific provisions in their bilateral double taxation treaties on the tax treatment to be given to contributions, transfer values and benefits.[2152] Whilst this would allow individual agreements to be adapted to the specific characteristics of the tax systems at issue, the Commission is not in favour of this, as agreeing on these specific provisions in all bilateral treaties would prove to be a lengthy and cumbersome process. The Commission adds that it would also be less transparent than having common rules at Community level, although such rules might be difficult to negotiate. The Commission thus not stated what kind of approach would be preferable, leaving it open for further discussion.

In chapter 5 of the report the Commission elaborates on the importance of taxation of supplementary pensions. The Commission pointed out that the design of pension schemes and the choice between different models of taxation are essentially a matter for Member States.[2153] Therefore, each national government decides which tax environment is most effective, given its circumstances and costs for the State of granting tax relief. The Commission further noted that, as a consequence, national tax rules developed over the course of years have grown extremely complex and specific to each Member State, containing detailed regulation aimed at safeguarding that government income that is foregone to stimulate retirement saving is used solely for that purpose.

As regards the tax treatment of pensions, the Commission considered that the diversity in the national legislation leads to a situation where taxation can be a barrier to the free movement of people and the free movement of services.[2154] The granting of tax relief, as a general rule, depends on the scheme meeting a variety of detailed rules. The Commission notes that, as a consequence, the pension scheme that is approved in one Member State may be very unlikely to meet the fiscal requirements for pension schemes set in another Member State, having the practical effect of deterring contributions to foreign pension

2150 Ibid. 14.
2151 Ibid. 15-16.
2152 Ibid. 17.
2153 Ibid. 18.
2154 Ibid. 18.

schemes. However, it will be discussed in section 0 how these situations are treated under the CJEU's established case-law.

The commission was concerned that any specific tax rules should be consistent with the freedom of movement of persons and of provision of services, both applying to pillar two, as well as pillar three pension vehicles.[2155] Furthermore, with a reference to the *Bachmann* and *Wielockx* cases, the Commission calls into memory, that tax rules that discriminate against policyholders buying policies from a foreign established insurer, run counter to the freedom to provide services, except where the justification ground of maintaining the fiscal coherence of the tax system may be relied on.

As regards the bilateral tax conventions, the Commission pointed out that when it comes to the taxation of occupational pensions, most existing treaties adopt the principle of Article 18 of the OECD Model Treaty in giving the country in which the taxpayer resides the exclusive right to tax pension income from a private employment, preventing the same income from becoming taxed twice.[2156] The Commission further drew attention to some tax treaties between Member States, which specifically cater for pension contributions which a migrant worker may wish to continue to pay to a scheme in his former state of residence, after moving to another state.[2157] As the Commission rightly stated, these provisions essentially provide for a form of mutual recognition of tax-approved foreign pension schemes, extending the tax deductibility in the new state of residence of pension contributions paid to the former state of residence.

The Commission plead for a common approach to resolve the obstacles caused by the unequal extension of tax privileges, taking into account the principle of subsidiarity and proportionality.[2158] She observed that bilateral tax treaties have the considerable advantage that they can be adjusted to the specificities of the tax and pension systems of the two states concerned.[2159] However, it proves to be relatively cumbersome and time consuming to renegotiate all concluded tax treaties. The commission took the position that closer coordination of the tax treatment of cross-border pensions is most suitable but left open for discussion how this coordination could be effected best: through EU law, domestic measures, tax treaties, multilateral measures and so forth. However, she did note that there appears to be particular merit in exploring the concept of mutual recognition of tax-

2155 Ibid. 18.
2156 Ibid. 18-19.
2157 Ibid. 19.
2158 Ibid. 19.
2159 Ibid. 19.

approved schemes, for instance as regards cross-border contributions, in other Member States.

8.3.3 *EC Communication 1999: Towards a Single Market for Supplementary Pensions*

After releasing the Green Paper, the Commission issued another Communication in 1999.[2160] The Commission pointed out that the basic tax problems are identical for both the second pillar and third pillar arrangements, both for practical reasons the first step of staged Community action could tackle the tax treatment of cross-border contributions by migrants workers to second pillar pensions.[2161] The Commission reiterates that the diversity, complexity and specificity of national tax rules that have developed over the years have been identified as major barriers to the free movement of persons and the freedom to provide services in the field of supplementary pensions and life assurance. The problems basically come down to the question how to treat cross-border payments to supplementary pension funds or life insurance companies and the fact that migrant workers are faced with two or more pension and taxation systems which are not necessarily compatible.

The Commission enumerated the following problems resulting from the heterogeneity of tax regimes[2162]:

- As a main obstacle, the tax treatment of supplementary pension contracts and life assurance policies which have been concluded with non-resident institutions is, in many Member States, less favourable than the treatment of policies with resident institutions. As there is no principle of mutual recognition, it is unlikely that a pension scheme approved in one Member State will satisfy the requirements for tax relief which is granted to schemes in another Member State. Hence, if people wish to benefit from tax relief, they are forced to contract national products. As regards foreign established pension and life assurance institutions; they are forced to set up an establishment in each Member State in order to secure the same tax conditions for their product. In the Commission's opinion this runs counter to the freedom of services. In addition, this prevents a worker migrating from one Member State to another from continuing his policy held in his Member State of origin, since the host Member State does not grant the same tax relief.

2160 European Commission, 'Towards a Single Market for Supplementary Pensions: Results of the consultations on the Green Paper on supplementary pensions in the single market' (1999) [COM(l999) 134 final].

2161 Ibid. 30.

2162 Ibid. 31.

- As one of the most serious problems, the Commission considered people moving from a Member State operating an EET-system to a Member State using a TEE-system or vice versa, as this basic mismatch may cause situations of double non-taxation or double taxation. The Commission considered that EET systems are better suited to the EC objectives, and should generally be applied if possible. In addition, this system heeds the effective income principle (which is a requirement arising from the ability-to-pay principle in certain countries[2163]), as no tax is levied on unsure future benefits when a pension is not inherited and the beneficiary may pass away before retirement.
- Furthermore, the Commission observed that pension and life assurance institutions can also face tax obstacles, in particular when investing across borders. In this regard, it appeared that non-resident funds may be treated more detrimental than domestic pension funds in respect of the applicable tax rate. This may become manifest in several ways: not extending the exemption applicable to resident pension funds; not granting the partial exemption, provided that the foreign pension fund or entity does not carry out business through a permanent establishment; not granting the tax deductions and benefits applicable to national investments; or applying withholding taxes in the state of source.[2164]

The Commission also elaborated on how these problems could be overcome.[2165] One of the possible actions was to draw up guideline standards, based on principles and practices which are common to a number of existing bilateral agreements. Alternatively, it could be argued that EU legislation would be the most reasonable solution, aimed at, *inter alia*, the mutual recognition of pension schemes or criteria for the general recognition of genuine old-age schemes for tax purposes. This could either be implemented through, for instance, a multilateral convention or a directive as examples of legally binding measures.

As, at the time of the Communication, there was (and still is) no EU legislation governing the allocation of the right to tax pension income, or the tax treatment of pension capital values, the Commission took the position that a coordinated approach was most suited. In addition, it appeared that there was a general consensus on the need for such a coordinated action on the basis of a step-by-step approach. The Commission formulated several, broadly endorsed, principles which this coordinated approach should build on[2166]:

2163 Cf. Prats, 15.

2164 Prats, 15.

2165 European Commission, 'Towards a Single Market for Supplementary Pensions: Results of the consultations on the Green Paper on supplementary pensions in the single market' 32.

2166 Ibid. 33.

- **No harmonisation:** the purpose is not to seek harmonisation of Member States' taxation systems pertaining to pension and life assurance. The coordinated approach would, rather, adapt to the diversity of Member States' rules.
- **No discrimination:** both the freedom to provide services as well as the free movement of person may not be impeded by unduly restrictive or discriminatory tax treatment of cross-border pensions and life assurance.
- **No revenue shortfall:** the coordinated approach should allow and support Member State to safeguard the tax revenues they are empowered to collect pursuant to their applicable tax legislation. In addition, it should allow for an enforceable and compliance-stimulating system.

The Commission thus sought to draw proposals based on principles that stimulate flexible coordination, respecting the diversity of Member States' tax legislations, do not restrict the fundamental freedoms and preserve tax collection.[2167] The Commission, however, recognized that the obstacles caused by the tax treatment of pension schemes, may have different implications for EU law. In this regard the Commission also pointed out that it is not sufficient to leave the evolution of national tax systems to the interpretative efforts of the CJEU, and called for an enhanced level of action. This action was, on the one hand, aimed at removing tax rules disturbing, discriminating or restricting temporary workers and contributions made in their names, and on the other hand at tax rules restricting the provision of services of supplementary pension schemes, which may imply restrictions on the freedom of establishment and the free movement of capital. As Prats contends, the effects of different fundamental freedoms imply a different reflection of the safeguard mechanisms and the applicable justification criteria for legislation restricting the exercise thereof.[2168]

8.3.4 European Commission 2001: the Elimination of Tax Obstacles to the Cross-border Provision of Occupational Pensions

In 1998, the Council Directive 98/49 entered into force.[2169] However, this Directive merely focused on the elimination of obstacles to cross-border pension mechanisms and the establishment of a common-ground regulation, and did not preclude the application of domestic and international tax rules potentially conflicting with the goals of the European

---

2167 Prats, 15.

2168 Ibid. 16 and cited literature.

2169 Council Directive 98/49/EC of 29 June 1998 on safeguarding the supplementary pension rights of employed and self-employed persons moving within the Community [1998] OJ L 209. The initial proposal contained tax provisions but these were dropped.

internal market.[2170] Hence, the right to a non-discriminatory tax treatment had to be guaranteed through the interpretative action of the CJEU on general EU law principles and the general content of the fundamental freedoms. However, in 2001 the EC released a revised Communication, intended to supplement the proposal for the IORP I-Directive.[2171]

In this communication, of a non-binding nature, the Commission underscored that pensions are an issue of universal concern; for individual citizens who want an adequate provision for their retirement; for employers who seek cost-effective pension provision for their employees; and for governments, who throughout the Union are seeking to maintain adequate pension provision in the face of ageing populations.[2172] Furthermore, it emphasized that the potential benefits of better cross-border pension provision are substantial, as around 5.1 million (2001), and increasing, European citizens aged 15 years and over reside in a Member State other than their Member State of origin. The commission rightly stated that a fully functioning single market for occupational pensions is essential to ensure that citizens are able to exercise their rights to free movement enshrined in the EC Treaty and thus to enhance labour mobility.[2173] In this regard, the elimination of tax-obstacles to the cross-border provision of occupational pensions may contribute to attaining this goal.

The goal of this communication was to seek a coordinated approach adapted to the diversity of Member States' rules rather than attempting to achieve harmonisation, and call for the elimination of unduly restrictive or discriminatory tax rules.[2174] As this communication was aimed at complementing the Pension Fund Directive, its focus was primarily on the second pillar and the pension institutions covered by that proposal.[2175] Nevertheless, much of the points discussed applied similarly to third pillar pensions and life assurance services. For the purpose of this research, the relevance of this communication thus lies in aligning the national tax systems, through diminishing the discriminatory differences between the systems, and to better adapt these systems to rules of primary and secondary European law.

2170 Apart from Article 5 of ibid. which provides: *"Member States shall ensure that, in respect of members of supplementary pension schemes, as well as others holding entitlement under such schemes, supplementary pension schemes make payment in other Member States, net of any taxes and transaction charges which may be applicable, of all benefits due under such schemes."*

2171 Proposal for a Directive of the European Parliament and of the Council on the activities of institutions for occupational retirement provisions of 11 of October 2000 (COM(2000) 507 final).

2172 European Commission, 'The elimination of tax obstacles to the cross-border provision of occupational pensions,' 3.

2173 Ibid. 3.

2174 Ibid. 4.

2175 Ibid. 5.

8.3.4.A The Impact of the Fundamental Freedoms of the (EC) Treaty

Furthermore, the Commission pointed out that many Member states treat foreign pensions and pension contributions less favourable compared to national pension and contributions, e.g. by not extending the tax relief applicable to pension contributions paid to national pension institutions, to contributions paid to pension institutions established in other Member States, or by imposing additional preconditions.[2176] However, since the publishing of the commission's communication the CJEU had delivered a judgement in a broad range of cases, holding that denying pension contributions paid to foreign pension institutions contravenes EU law. The rules arising from the cases will be discussed more thoroughly in section 0. The Commission held that the Treaty obliges Member States to abolish any discriminatory rules.[2177]

The commission distinguished two situations.[2178] Firstly, the case of a person who is a scheme member of a pension institution in a Member State, moving to another Member State and wishing to stay in the same scheme (apart from posted workers[2179]). Secondly, the situation of an employer, or group of employers and representatives of the employees, wishing to make pension arrangements for all employees in different Member States through a pan-European pension institution. These pan-European pension institutions would be located in one Member State and consist of different sections, each section complying separately with the requirements for tax approval and the tax regulations of the State where the member is employed, and its social law. Once retired, the (mobile) worker would obtain benefits from each national section corresponding to the rights acquired under the national rules applying to these separate sections. The Commission observed that this might be possible to implement it without adopting new tax legislation.[2180] In this regard, the practicability can be called into question, as the observation must be made that the implementation of a pan-European pension institution would require amendments of particular domestic provisions, such as to ascertain the source of pension income (i.e. under which section), in order to determine which national tax rules the pension section should comply with.

With a reference to *Safir* and *Bachman* cases the commission observed that it is clear that national restrictions which impede the provision of pensions and life assurance without

2176 Ibid. 7.
2177 Ibid. 8.
2178 Ibid. 8.
2179 Their situation is governed by Enforcement Directive 2014/67 of Posting of Workers Directive 96/71 and Directive 2018/957 amending Directive 96/71.
2180 European Commission, 'The elimination of tax obstacles to the cross-border provision of occupational pensions,' 18.

objective justification are incompatible with Community law.[2181] Furthermore, in the Commission's view no grounds existed which could justify unequal treatment of schemes operated by pension institutions established in other Member States. For instance, it is common ground that the lack of harmonisation of Member States' laws does not prevent the application of the Treaty freedoms.[2182] The Commission's view was that refusing deduction of contributions to foreign schemes by EET or ETT States is disproportionate.[2183] With regard to the latter, I find it not appropriate to classify a whole state as EET or ETT, as within these states there may apply several of these systems, and overlap may occur. For instance, within a same state statutory pension may be subject to tax according to the TEE-system, where occupational may be taxed following the EET-approach. This abbreviation merely provides a (very) rough picture of a Member State's pension tax system.

As regards the fiscal facilitation of pensions, the Commission found it appropriate to distinguish between two basis situations: "sedentary" workers (workers remaining in one Member State) and migrant workers.[2184] In the former case, pension arrangements are newly entered into by a Member State's residents or by persons employed within their territory with pension institutions established in other Member States. The Commission considered that, in this case, Member States are allowed to stipulate that these schemes satisfy conditions applied to similar domestic schemes relating to the nature and level of benefits, retirement age, qualifying beneficiaries, standards or prudential supervision, provided that these conditions are consistent with the Treaties, particularly that they serve legitimate social policy aims, and are not disproportionate in that they unduly restrict the freedom to provide services. In the latter case, pension schemes are already entered into by migrant workers before coming, often temporarily, to the host state. The Commission observed that if in that case a state imposed conditions for tax approval, this would unduly restrict the free movement of workers. In that case, migrant workers would be forced, it they wished to benefit from fiscal advantages in the host State, to join a new scheme, satisfying the tax approval conditions, if it were not possible for the worker to be transferred to another section of the pension institution without terminating the policy. The Commission pointed out that under the equal treatment principle, the host State is normally not obliged to grant more tax deduction than the deduction granted in respect of contributions to domestic pension institutions.

2181 Ibid. 8.

2182 C-270/83 *Avoir Fiscal* ECLI:EU:C:1986:37 (CJEU) para 23.

2183 European Commission, 'The elimination of tax obstacles to the cross-border provision of occupational pensions,' 11.

2184 Ibid. 11.

As regards fiscal supervision as a justification ground the Commission held, referring to the *Bachmann* and *Wielockx* cases, that difficulty of verifying compliance with tax laws in the case of cross-border situations as a justification for different treatment cannot be accepted.[2185] Member States can have recourse to the Mutual Assistence Directive.[2186] The commission, however, points out that it is open to Member States to implement arrangements to ensure the application of their tax laws in the context of cross-border pension provision, in particular by requiring provision of information by pension institutions.

8.3.4.B Rules Arising from the Commission's Considerations

From the foregoing considerations, the following general rules can be inferred[2187]:

- National rules making the deductibility of pension and life assurance contributions conditional on these contributions paid to a domestic pension institution are contrary to the freedoms of movement as laid down in the Treaty.
- Where citizens resident in a Member State join a foreign scheme, the Member State may, in the current state of EU law, require that the scheme meets conditions for tax approval relating to the nature and level of benefits, age of retirement, qualifying beneficiaries and similar proportionate conditions.
- In the case of citizens who already belong to a scheme approved for tax purposes in their home State and then move, often temporarily, to another Member State, the host State cannot refuse to grant tax deduction of contributions paid to the foreign scheme on the ground that the scheme does not meet its conditions for tax approval.
- National tax rules denying equal treatment to pension schemes operated by pension institutions established in other Member States are in breach of the Treaty. Member States must ensure that they grant the same tax deductions for contributions to domestic pension institutions and those established in other Member States. Equal treatment must similarly be granted in relation to any yield tax and in relation to the tax treatment of benefits.

Accordingly, the Commission examined ways in which Member States can take measures to safeguard their revenues, for instance an adequate system of information exchange in the area of pensions. The Commission observed that automatic information exchange is

2185 Ibid. 12.

2186 Council Directive 77/799/EEC of 19 December 1977 concerning mutual assistance by the competent authorities of the Member States in the field of direct taxation [1977] OJ L336/15.

2187 European Commission, 'The elimination of tax obstacles to the cross-border provision of occupational pensions,' 13.

the best means of safeguarding Member States' revenues and promoting the interests of a fully functioning single market in pensions.[2188]

8.3.4.C Dealing with the Diversity of Member States' Tax Arrangements

The Commission considered that the differences between domestic legislation for deductibility of contributions and taxation of benefits may lead to double taxation or non-taxation for migrant workers or persons retiring to another Member State.[2189] For instance, an employee may work in a Member State providing generous relief for contributions and then retire to a Member State which has generous tax arrangements for pension benefits.

The commission further observed that double taxation is, in particular, a problem for cross-border labour mobility and retirement, and arises from the differences in national tax rules and from the treaty practice of Member States, mostly following Article 18 of the OECD Model Tax Convention, imposing residence taxation of pensioners, regardless of whether and where his contributions were deducted.[2190]

As pointed out above and in section 9.2.1, Member States apply different pension taxation systems in terms of whether they tax or exempt contributions, investment income and capital, gains of the pension institution, and benefits. Obviously, a solution for the issues arising from the inconsistent tax treatment of cross-border pensions can either be resolved through amending the tax treatment of the contributions or the pension benefits. In this regard the Commission proclaimed a broader acceptation of the EET-principle, since this would help reduce double taxation and double non-taxation resulting from the differences

2188 Ibid. 15. See for instance Article 1, para 1 Mutual Assistance Directive 77/799 states: "In accordance with the provisions of this Directive the competent authorities of the Member States shall exchange any information that may enable them to effect a correct assessment of taxes on income and on capital." This directive has been repealed by Council Directive 2011/16/EU of 15 February 2011 on administrative cooperation in the field of taxation and repealing Directive 77/799/EEC [2001] OJ L 64. The first paragraph of this latter Directive's preamble points out that the Member States' need for mutual assistance in the field of taxation is growing rapidly in a globalized era. There is a tremendous development of the mobility of taxpayers, of the number of cross-border transactions and of the internationalization of financial instruments, which makes it difficult for Member States to assess taxes due properly. *This increasing difficulty affects the functioning of taxation systems and entails double taxation, which itself incites tax fraud and tax evasion, while the powers of controls remain at national level. It thus jeopardizes the functioning of the internal market.*

2189 European Commission, 'The elimination of tax obstacles to the cross-border provision of occupational pensions,' 18.

2190 However, in Dutch treaty practice the position is taken that source state taxation of pensions should prevail. See Ministerie van Financiën, 'Notitie Fiscaal Verdragsbeleid 2011' (2011) 54. The Netherlands seeks to agree on source state taxation for fiscally facilitated pensions, irrespective of the tax treatment of pension in the (new) state of residence of the pensioner.

in the systems.[2191] Furthermore, aligning Member States' pension tax systems following the EET principle, seems most practical. As a side-effect, providing deferral of tax on pensions incite individuals to save for retirement, and is better able to respond to an ageing population since it reduces tax revenues today in exchange for higher tax revenues at the time when the demographic dependency ratio will be much more unfavourable.

However, the Commission rightly pointed out that a broader acceptance of this EET principle by more Member States would not be a complete solution as even within these EET-systems there are significant differences in the tax treatment.[2192] These differences not only reflect State's individual preferences as regard the design of their tax system but also more fundamental underlying choices or principles pertaining to the structure of their pension system, for instance the relative size of the first and second pillar. Hence, the commission did not intend to propose legislative measures to harmonise the pension tax system but, nevertheless, it encouraged the broader acceptance of the EET-principles as this alignment would help reduce mismatches leading to double (non-)taxation. The Commission thus accepted the co-existence of tax systems, while encouraging broader acceptance of the EET-system, but did not accept the consequence that the tax treatment of domestic and foreign contributions may differ.

As differences between Member States' tax systems will remain in future, the Commission put forward several practical measures to deal with the co-existence of different systems.[2193] For instance, unilaterally provisions to eliminate the double taxation by exempting benefits paid by foreign pension institutions to their residents to the extent that the contributions were not deductible (a kind of balance method). The commission also pointed to eliminating double taxation arising from divergent tax rules on pensions by provisions in double taxation treaties. The commission further pointed to source state taxation in circumstances where there would be uncommonly low taxation in the State of residence.[2194] Furthermore, the functioning of bilateral solutions could be fostered by the introduction of rules to resolve conflicts of interpretation and mechanisms to enable the taxpayer to secure consistent treatment by both authorities concerned.

2191 European Commission, 'The elimination of tax obstacles to the cross-border provision of occupational pensions,' 19.

2192 Ibid. 19.

2193 Ibid. 19.

2194 See for instance Article 18, para 2, under b Double Tax Treaty Netherlands-Portugal which provides an exception to residence taxation where the pension is "not taxed at the generally applicable rate for income derived from dependent personal services, or less than 90% of the gross amount of the pension or similar remuneration ... is taxed".

8.3.5 *EC Communication 2006: Coordinating Member States' Direct Tax Systems in the Internal Market*

In this 2006 communicating the Commission set out her general principles for coordinating tax systems, removing discrimination and double taxation, preventing non-taxation and abuse, reducing compliance costs and simplifying procedures.[2195] It must be noted that as regards the fields of taxes concerned, it did not (at all) address the taxation of cross-border pensions, but the focus lies primary on corporate taxation. The Commission thus appeared to rely on her approach as set out in her 2001 Commission, i.e. supporting the negative integration-approach of the CJEU rather than providing measures of positive integration in the sphere of the tax treatment of cross-border pensions. However, it clarified the Commission's view on the coordination of Member States' direct tax systems. This approach seems unaltered, generally setting out why coordination and cooperation between Member States should be pursued, allowing them to attain their tax policy goals and protect their tax bases, while ensuring elimination of discrimination and double taxation and reducing compliance costs. The Commission thus upholds the same principles as established in the 2001 Communication:

- striving for coordination of tax systems, rather than harmonization;
- adhering the principle of non-discrimination and the Treaty Freedoms; and
- safeguarding the states' tax revenues.

The Commission reiterated that Member States remain largely free to design their direct tax systems so as to meet their domestic policy objectives and requirements.[2196] It is further pointed out that dealing with the interaction of several tax systems poses a challenge for the European internal market, national tax rules developed solely or primarily with the domestic situation in mind may give rise to inconsistent tax treatment when applied in a cross-border context, or discrimination or double taxation and/or additional compliance costs. The Commission points out that this created a disincentive for individuals who wish to work or invest in other Member States. Furthermore, fiscal barriers to cross-border activity remain, as these problems have only been partly addressed through unilateral action by Member States or by means of existing bilateral tax treaties. The Commission

2195 That same day, the Commission issued two Communications in specific areas. The first Communication concerned the area of exit taxes, see European Commission, 'Exit taxation and the need for co-ordination of Member States' tax policies' (2006) [COM(2006) 825 final].

2196 European Commission, 'Coordinating Member States' direct tax systems in the internal market' (2006) [COM(2006)823 final] 3.

notes that hence there remains a need to ensure that unharmonized national tax systems work together properly.[2197]

The Commission also provided the key principles for coherent and coordinated tax treatment: removing discrimination and double taxation, preventing inadvertent non-taxation and abuse, and reducing the compliance costs associated with being subject to more than one tax system.[2198] From the Commission's perspective there is a need for guidance on the principles following from the CJEU's case-law, and how these should be applied to the main areas of direct taxation.[2199] This guidance would further promote greater legal certainty for the benefits of taxpayers, tax authorities and national courts. As a proviso, the Commission stated that this is only a starting point, as it is necessary to find solutions which will guarantee coherent cross-border tax treatment. In some cases, Member States have responded unilaterally by removing domestic tax advantages or by extending requirements for cross-border situations to domestic situations in circumstances where this was not desirable in tax policy terms, from the Commission's point of view. The Commission therefore suggested to set forth a number of initiatives to assist Member States in finding coordinated solutions which will allow them to attain their tax policy objectives, while adhering to the Community law-requirements.

8.3.6 *EC Communication 2010: Removing Cross-border Tax Obstacles for EU Citizens*

In her 2010 communication, the Commission put emphasis on abolishing cross-border tax obstacles of EU citizens as such. She pointed out that 500 million EU citizens derive the right to move to another EU country to live, study, work or retire in other EU countries, from EU law.[2200] In the light of the 'Europe 2020 strategy', promoting smart, sustainable and inclusive growth in the EU, the Commission stated that this strategy entails empowering EU citizens to play a full part in the European single market and giving them the confidence to do so.

2197 Ibid. 4. The Commission pointed out that whereas harmonisation results in the creation of a common body of Community legislation which supersedes national laws, coordination builds on domestic systems to render them compatible with the Treaty and with each other. The aim of coordination is not to replace existing national tax systems by a uniform Community system but to ensure that such national systems can be made to work seamlessly together.

2198 Ibid. 4.

2199 Ibid. 5.

2200 European Commission, 'Removing cross-border tax obstacles for EU citizens' (2010) [COM(2010) 769 final] 2.

The commission rightly acknowledges that the reality is that these EU citizens are confronted with many bottlenecks as regards cross-border activity, and these citizens should be able to benefits in full of their rights to be active across national borders as citizens, workers, pensioners etc. In order to allow these citizens to fully benefits from their granted rights of free movement, actions are required in a range of fields, including taxation.[2201] The Commission rightly stated that tax legislation should not dissuade individuals from benefiting from the internal market.[2202] As EU citizens are increasingly active across borders, such issue grows more and more important.

In this vein, the Communication identified the most pressing cross-border tax issues that these citizens face and outlined possible solutions. These solutions could relate to amendment of Member States' national tax rules to abolish discrimination, the introduction of common EU-wide rules, or closer cooperation between tax administrations across the EU in new areas as well as information and awareness measures. In particular with regard to the intended solutions, as proposed by the Commission, this Communication is interesting in the light of the present research. This Communication sought to explain how the commission could help EU citizens to find solutions to the problems of tax discrimination that they encounter. Hereinafter, I will merely focus on the issues, and proposed solutions, in the sphere of the tax treatment of cross-border pensions.

It appeared that EU citizens' complaints primarily concerned the complexity of foreign tax rules, and issues pertaining to obtaining information on these rules and on rights and obligations under those rules.[2203] These issues were often the consequence of language barriers but also due to a lack of cooperation between countries' tax authorities. It also appeared to be common ground that the information provision by different parts of Member States' tax authorities was contradictory.

The commission also outlined several crucial complaints, of which the relevant ones will be addressed below.[2204] In addition she planned on taking certain actions to address the most important unresolved tax problems, with which EU citizens are confronted in cross-border situations. Firstly, this concerned, above all, difficulties in obtaining allowances,

---

2201 Ibid. 2.

2202 See for instance C 269/07 *Commission vs. Germany* ECLI:EU:C:2009:527 (CJEU) para 109: "*That difference of treatment [domestic provisions requiring beneficiaries to reimburse, on termination of full liability to German tax, the savings-pension bonus received from that State] is likely to discourage workers of German nationality from exercising a professional activity outside Germany.*" See, in the same vein, C-20/16 *Bechtel* ECLI:EU:C:2017:488 (CJEU) para 50.

2203 European Commission, 3.

2204 Ibid. 3.

tax reliefs and deductions from foreign tax authorities, double taxation[2205], and higher progressive tax rates applied to non-residents, by EU citizens who move abroad to work temporarily or permanently or cross borders every day to go to work. To resolve this issue of double taxation, the Commission believed that actions to be taken in a definitive way that go beyond the solutions laid down in tax treaties, for instance binding dispute resolution mechanisms.[2206] Further, EU citizens paying contributions to foreign pension funds are confronted with the non-deductibility of these contributions, the double taxation of pension benefits and tax obstacles to cross-border transfer of pension capital.

In seeking a solution for these issues, for instance through the application of the EU treaty rules, the commission stressed, that it can resolve many problems of discrimination in the tax area but cannot resolve problems such as double taxation due to the coexistence of two tax systems and mismatches between these systems.[2207] However even when national tax rules do not infringe treaty rules, the Commission takes the view that it is not appropriate in a single market that issues such as double taxation, incompatibilities between different tax systems and a lack of access to information on tax legislation should discourage individuals from engaging in cross-border activity. In line with previous communications, the commission stressed that harmonization of all aspects of national tax rules would be neither necessary nor feasible. However, in the commission's view solutions are required that acknowledge the legitimate interest of citizens in the area of free movement, granted by the Treaty Freedoms. This may require that different tax problems may call for different levels of coordination and cooperation between Member States. Hence, the Commission considers measures on EU level important in order to make the Member States' tax systems more compatible, and tackling the tax issues for the benefit of EU citizens.

It is apparent from the above that the commission adheres to the principles of striving for coordination of tax systems, rather than harmonization, and adhering the principle of non-discrimination and the Treaty Freedoms.[2208] As regards the tackling of discrimination in the Member States' tax laws, the commission attaches great importance to this in order

2205 Due to conflicts in tax residence, limitations in the amount of tax credit available under tax treaties etc.

2206 European Commission, 5.

2207 Ibid. 4.

2208 In the same vein as European Commission, 'The elimination of tax obstacles to the cross-border provision of occupational pensions,' (2001) [COM(2001)214 final].

to facilitate citizens in the exercise of their freedoms of movement.[2209] On the commission's part it intends to increase its effort on several measures[2210]:

- ensure greater transparency and information for EU citizens on the outcomes of complaints about Member States' tax laws and infringement actions taken in the tax field (through publishing citizen-friendly information on the Europa website on an annual basis);
- ensure that EU citizens' advice services (Commission's Europe Direct and Your Europe) have at their disposal the information, training and documentation in order to equip them to deal with citizens' complaints pertaining to cross-border tax obstacles and that citizens can more directly get help and advice (information available on the Your Europe website will be provided in a user-friendly format);
- monitor Member States' tax legislation and systematically request Member States to rectify any incompatibilities with EU law within a certain deadline;
- monitor the implementation by EU Member States of the CJEU's rulings in the tax field and ensure that they are implemented also in Member States that were not the subject of the ruling.

It is interesting to see that the commission has put a stronger emphasis on the (better) information provision and transparency for EU citizens as regards taxation in cross-border cases. In an era of ever-increasing complexity of rules and regulations these initiatives are warmly welcomed, intended to enable mobile citizens to ascertain their

2209 As regards instruments available to EU citizens for resolving cross-border tax obstacles and examples of resolved cases of the types of tax rules in Member States that have been found incompatible with the EU Treaties, see European Commission, 'Commission Staff Working Document accompanying Commission Communication 'Removing cross-border tax obstacles for EU citizens'' (2010) [SEC(2010) 1576 final].

2210 European Commission, 'Removing cross-border tax obstacles for EU citizens' 5-9. In addition to these measures, the Commission proposed to establish a dialogue with Member States' tax administrations and stakeholders regarding other solutions to cross-border tax obstacles, EU citizens are confronted with. For instance, establishing central one-stop-shops in tax administrations where mobile workers and investors could not only look for relevant and reliable tax information, but also directly pay taxes and receive all the necessary certificates for their home country's tax authorities. The one-stop-shop consists of *The EU Europe Direct Contact Centre*, *The Europe Direct Information Centres*, the *Your Europe* web portal (which guides users to *Your Europe Advice* and *SOLVIT*) and EURES. See European Commission, 'Commission Staff Working Document accompanying Commission Communication 'Removing cross-border tax obstacles for EU citizens'' 2. The initiative of these central one-stop-shops was announced in European Commission, 'EU Citizenship Report 2010: Dismantling the obstacles to EU citizen's rights' (2010). Secondly, facilitating cross-border tax compliance by striving for greater alignment of tax claim and declaration forms, translating information into other EU official languages and making greater use of information technology. Thirdly, stimulating Member States to adopt special rules for frontier workers and mobile workers that take account of the interaction of tax and social security systems in different Member States. Lastly, promoting better interaction between the different pension taxation regimes so as to encourage worker mobility. The latter ties in with the points set out in European Commission, 'The elimination of tax obstacles to the cross-border provision of occupational pensions.'

legal position as regards cross-border taxes. With regard to the latter two initiatives, the commission not solely relies on the CJEU's negative integration-approach,[2211] but will also, on her own initiative, monitor Member States' tax legislation and systematically request Member States to resolve any incompatibilities with EU law.[2212] Furthermore, the Commission committed herself to monitor the implementation by Member States of the CJEU's judgements in the tax domain and ensure that they are also implemented in states that were not the ruling's subject. The Commission thus strives to extend the scope of the case-by-case judgements, having an *ex-tunc* effect, to (presumably comparable) tax systems. Apparently as a follow-up of her approach enunciated in her 2001 and 2006 Communication, where she supported the negative integration-approach of the CJEU

2211 As advocated in European Commission, 'The elimination of tax obstacles to the cross-border provision of occupational pensions,' and European Commission, 'Coordinating Member States' direct tax systems in the internal market' (2006) [COM(2006)823 final].

2212 The European Commission heeded this promise recently. The European Commission believes that the tax conditions imposed by the Netherlands on international value transfers when employed in another member state violate the freedoms of movement laid down in the TFEU, and, hence, sent the Netherlands a reasoned opinion, see European Commission, 'July infringement package: Commission requests that the Netherlands stop taxing transfers of pension capital by mobile workers' 19 July 2018) <https://ec.europa.eu/commission/presscorner/detail/en/MEMO_18_4486> accessed 8 March 2023 as well as an additional reasoned opinion: European Commission, 'November infringements package: Commission asks the Netherlands to change tax rules amounting to obstacles to the cross-border transfer of pensions' 27 November 2019) <https://ec.europa.eu/commission/presscorner/detail/en/inf_19_6304> accessed 8 March 2023. The Netherlands decided to not heed this call by the EC: see Kamerstukken II, *Brief van de minister van Financiën 21 501-07, nr. 1648* (2019/20) 8. The Commission announced that it is referring the Netherlands to the Court of Justice regarding Dutch security and liability rules surrounding the cross-border transfer of pension capital, see European Commission, 'May infringements package: the Commission refers the Netherlands to the Court for taxing the transfer of pension capital to other Member States, but not domestic transfers' 14 May 2020) <https://ec.europa.eu/commission/presscorner/detail/en/inf_20_859> accessed 8 March 2023 and European Commission, 'Commission decides to refer the Netherlands to the Court for its rules on the cross-border transfer of pension capital and cross-border provision of pensions' 30 October 2020) <https://ec.europa.eu/commission/presscorner/detail/EN/IP_20_1678> accessed 8 March 2023. Following this, the European Commission – as a final step – brought an action against the Netherlands on June 3, 2022, see C-360/22 *European Commission v Kingdom of the Netherlands* (CJEU). The Commission asks the Court to rule that by adopting and maintaining Section 85(1)(b) and Section 87(2)(f) of the Pensions Act, read in conjunction with Section 19b(2) of the Wage Tax Act, the Netherlands has failed to fulfil its obligations under Articles 45, 56 and 63 TFEU and Articles 28, 36 and 40 EEA. At the time of writing – March 2023 – the CJEU has not yet ruled on this case. See for an elaborate discussion on the fiscal conditions – laid down in Dutch tax legislation/regulation – pertaining to international transfer of pension value, as well as the issue with respect the tenability of these conditions under EU law: B Dieleman and P van Straten, 'Individuele internationale waardeoverdracht kan veel beter' 6 PensioenMagazine; D Morales and M Kastelein, 'Europese Commissie zit Nederland op de huid bij grensoverschrijdende waardeoverdracht' ibid; B Dieleman, 'Zijn de Nederlandse fiscale regels voor grensoverschrijdende overdracht van pensioen in strijd met EU-recht?' Ibid; E Lutjens and B Dieleman, 'Grensoverschrijdende waardeoverdracht van pensioen: zijn Nederlandse regels in strijd met EU-recht?' Tijdschrift voor Arbeidsrecht in Context; EAP Schouten, 'Europese Commissie daagt Nederland voor Europese Hof om fiscale eisen grensoverschrijdende waardeoverdracht' PensioenMagazine.

rather than providing measures of positive integration in the sphere of the tax treatment of cross-border pensions, she sets out complementary measures in the 2010 communication.

8.4 Negative Integration: CJEU's Doctrine on Non-discrimination and (In)compatibility with Treaty Freedoms

8.4.1 *Introduction*

EU law is to be applied according the judgments of the Court of Justice of the European Union (CJEU). Next to the European Commission, the CJEU plays a pivotal role in assessing the compatibility of Member States' tax system with requirements under European law, more specifically the freedoms of movement. The CJEU's primary task is interpreting EU law and ensuring its uniform application throughout the EU, putting significant emphasis on the so-called teleological approach, i.e. precedence is given to the objective of the legal provision rather than the actual wording.[2213] This task, and its consequences for national legislation, fits the purpose of this research, i.e. mapping out the legal framework on a European level ('as its stands'), exploring how EU law might alter the tax treatment of the relevant cross-border pension, and it will be explored to what extent the regulatory instruments employed in the domain of European law are apt for the provision of information, in the light of the principles set in chapter 2 of this research (inter-level coherence, inter-system consistency, etc.). For instance, to what extent do they aid in establishing coherence, and consistency? This will be dealt with in the section 8.5.

The CJEU has acknowledged and confirmed several general principles peculiar to the EU legal order. The most fundamental principles are supremacy[2214] and direct effect[2215] of EU law. In the domain of (income) taxes, the principle of non-discrimination (non-residents may, from a tax point of view, not be treated less favourable compared to residents) is of pivotal interest.[2216] It is settled CJEU's case-law that the freedoms of movement prohibit, in any case, all obstacles arising from a difference in treatment by nationality and between domestic situations, on the one hand, and cross-border situations, on the other. This implies that impediments emerging from so-called 'disparities' (differences in national tax legislation) can under EU law, as it stands, in the field of direct taxation, in principle merely be solved through harmonization (Directives) or unification (Regulations). This

2213 Cf. Harris and Oliver, 40.
2214 C-279/93 *Schumacker* ECLI:EU:C:1995:31 (CJEU) para 21.
2215 See *Van Gend & Loos*.
2216 First explicitly acknowledged in the landmark case C-279/93 *Schumacker* ECLI:EU:C:1995:31 (CJEU) and later extending to the domain of pensioners in *Turpeinen*.

can have a potential beneficial effect on the coherence among national tax systems, and their comparability. However, these latter two options appear to be highly unlikely as Member States prove to have a strong preference to retain their fiscal sovereignty.

The pivotal role of the primary-law Treaty Freedoms in the sphere of direct taxes, first became apparent in the *Avoir Fiscal* case in 1986, in which the CJEU expanded the scope of the non-discrimination principle.[2217] The court's ruling in this case overturned the whole conception of international taxation, as the unequal treatment of limited and unlimited taxable persons was considered a cornerstone of international tax law for decades.[2218] Since then, a vast body of CJEU case-law has emerged, acting as a catalyst of overcoming fiscal obstacles to cross-border economic activity in the European Single Market. Whilst the potential impact of Treaty Freedoms was, generally, met with scepticism and criticism[2219], and was underestimated during the early nineteen nighties, the judgment in the landmark *Schumacker*-case[2220], in which the instrumental role of the non-discrimination principle was also extended to natural (taxable) persons, led Member States to overturn this point of view.

During the debates leading up to the adoption of the (European) Constitutional Treaty, it was even suggested to prohibit the CJEU from drawing any tax-related conclusions whatsoever from the Treaty provisions relating to the Treaty Freedoms or to force it to treat Member States' budgetary concerns as overriding reasons in the public interest to justify a restriction.[2221] As it seems, this scepticism and criticism may be the reason why in the last ten years the so-called 'motor of integration' has come to a halt[2222]. It will become apparent below that certain 'generations' are discernible in the CJEU's case-law, in which older generations are not necessarily consistent with younger generations.[2223] This, thus, affects the cohesion of European law pertaining to the cross-border taxation of pensions.

2217 *Avoir Fiscal.*

2218 Cf. Kofler, 'Ist der Spuk des Europäischen Steuerrechts bald vorbei?' 16.

2219 See, *inter alia*, W Vermeend, 'The Court of Justive of the European Communities and direct taxes: 'Est-ce qua la justive est de ce monde?" EC Tax Review; PJ Wattel, 'Red herrings in direct tax cases before the ECJ' 2 Legal Issues of Economic Integration 81, and AC Warren and MJ Graetz, 'Income Tax Discrimination and the Political and Economic Integration of Europe' 115 Yale Law Journal 1186.

2220 *C-279/93 Schumacker ECLI: EU: C: 1995: 31 (CJEU).* The Court later extended the scope of this principle to the domain of pensioners in *Turpeinen.*

2221 M Wathelet, 'Marks & Spencer plc vs. Halsey: Lessons to be drawn' British Tax Review 128, 131.

2222 See for instance M Lang, 'Das EuGH-Urteil in der Rechtssache D. – Gerät der Motor der Steuerharmonisierung ins Stottern' 14 SWI 365, 365 ff. and A Cordewener and E Reimer, 'The future of most-favoured-nation treatment in EC tax law: did the ECJ pull the emergenc brake without real need?' 46 European Taxation 239; Cordewener and Reimer, See also M Lang, 'Direct taxation: is the ECJ heading in a new direction?' Ibid 421, 421 ff.

2223 Cf. PJ Wattel, 'Köbler, CILFIT and Welthgrove: We Can't Go On Meeting Like This' 41 Common Market Law Review 177, 177 ff.

For instance, where the court accepted the justification ground of preserving the fiscal coherence of the tax system in question in the *Bachmann*-case[2224], it narrowed down the scope of this justification ground fairly strictly in the *Wielockx*-case[2225]. In general, this trend is characterized by the curtailment of the economic function of the Treaty Freedoms in favour of national fiscal sovereignty.[2226] Whilst the CJEU, in the early phase of its case-law, could reform the European internal market without any political constraints through its revolutionary judgments, the case-law has increasingly gained political interest, particularly as tax policy issues and significant tax revenues were questioned in the cases more and more.[2227] Moreover, it is to be noted that this instrument of negative integration is not an exhaustive instrument in terms of eliminating fiscal obstacles to the European internal market. Where this instrument cannot be used, the EU must have recourse to the instrument of positive integration, which has already been discussed and its shortcoming have been pinpointed.

The purpose of this section is to set forth the generally applicable rules that follow from this case-law, as part of the 'regulatory framework'. Although the CJEU's case-law generally has an *ex-tunc* effect and the CJEU has adopted a case-by-case approach, generally applicable rules may be inferred from this body of case-law, which may be applied, by analogy, to (presumably comparable) tax systems, and/or situations. In addition, the European Commission committed herself to monitor the implementation by Member States of the CJEU's judgements in the tax domain and ensure that they are also implemented in states that were not the ruling's subject.[2228] These generally applicable rules will be addressed in the section below as they allow for an evaluation in the light of the principles as set out in chapter 2.

8.4.1.A Stages in the Tax Treatment of (Cross-border) Pensions of Particular Interest in the Light of the CJEU's Case-law

As already set forth in section 9.2.1 several stages in the tax treatment of (cross-border) pensions can be discerned. In the light of the CJEU's case-law two situations are of particular interest. Firstly, the tax treatment of contributions paid by, or on behalf of, displaced workers to their previous pension scheme established in their state of origin. Secondly, the tax treatment of contributions paid to a foreign pension scheme by an enterprise and/or worker. It follows from this that domestic rule governing the tax

2224 *Bachmann*.
2225 *Wielockx*.
2226 Kofler, 'Ist der Spuk des Europäischen Steuerrechts bald vorbei?' 20.
2227 Ibid. 18-19.
2228 European Commission, 'Removing cross-border tax obstacles for EU citizens' (2010) [COM(2010) 769 final].

treatment of contributions may affect two treaty freedoms in particular. Firstly, the freedom of movement of workers may be affected by requirements, enshrined in national legislation, of foreign or migrant workers. For instance, a requirement, laid down in national legislation, may force migrant workers to switch pension scheme, leading to additional arrangements and expenses, and dissuading them from exercising their freedom of movement. Secondly, the freedom to provide services may be affected by the detrimental tax treatment of foreign pension schemes. For instance, a national rule may deter mobile individuals from taking out an insurance pension policy with foreign institutions.[2229] The requirements arising from European law with regard to the taxation of pensions in cross-border cases, obviously, depends on how pensions are fiscally treated under domestic legislation in domestic situations, since these European requirements predominantly forbid the adverse tax treatment of pensions in cross-border cases, compared to pensions in solely domestic situations. Below, the settled case law of the CJEU will be set forth and elucidated to the extent considered appropriate for this research's purpose. The cases will be discussed in order of publication.[2230]

8.4.1.B Treaty Freedoms to Be Discussed

Although the *scope ratione personae* of this research concerns mobile citizens, not being self-employed, and hence the focus should primarily be on the freedom of workers and the freedom of persons; the CJEU case-law pertaining to both the freedom of services and the freedom of capital will be discussed as well for the following reasons. Firstly, the (less favourable) tax treatment of, for instance, a pension insurance company, falling under the scope of the freedom of services, may have a (detrimental) effect on the pension situation of the individual citizens, falling under the freedom of workers and/or persons, e.g., additional costs on the part of the pension institution may be passed on to the individual pension saver, through increased premiums or contributions.[2231] Secondly, as observed by the CJEU, the taxable person does not necessarily have to exercise the freedom of movement himself, in order to invoke one of the Treaty freedoms.[2232] For that reason alone, he cannot be assimilated to a purely internal situation. Also, in this regard, the freedom of services and the freedom of capital may play an instrumental role. However, it must be noted in this regard, that the effects of different fundamental freedoms imply different considerations with respect to the safeguard mechanisms and the justification criteria for rules restricting their exercise.[2233]

2229 See for instance *Safir*.

2230 This distinction was also drawn by Avi-Yonah.

2231 Richter, 4. See for instance C-300/90 *Commission vs. Belgium I* ECLI:EU:C:1992:37 (CJEU) para 18.

2232 C-403/03 *Schempp* ECLI:EU:C:2005:446 (CJEU), para 23 and 24.

2233 J Marshall and S Butterworth, 'Pension Reform in the EU: the Unexploded Time Bomb in the Single Market' 37 Common Market Law Review 739, 749 ff.

8.4.2 *First Generation of Cases*

In this section the first generation of CJEU's cases, relevant in view of the direct taxation of pensions in cross-border cases, will be discussed. As already noted, the CJEU's role in creating EU 'law', lies in assessing to what extent the tax treatment of pensions in cross-border cases under domestic law, is in line with European primary legislation, such as the freedoms of movement.

8.4.2.A Bachmann

The *Bachmann*[2234] case is one of the first cases which received considerable attention in the field of the tax-treatment of cross-border pensions.[2235] This case concerned a German national (Mr Bachmann), who originally resided in Germany, but lived and worked in Belgium for the period from 1973 to 1976. Whilst Bachmann wished to continue these insurances while residing in Belgium, Belgian domestic law precluded the deduction of these contributions, since these contributions were not 'paid in Belgium'.[2236] Several justification grounds were brought forward, of which the most important one concerned preserving the cohesion of the Belgian tax system: in cases where no deduction of contributions was allowed, the benefits would be exempt; and contrarily, where contributions were deductible, benefits would be liable to taxation.[2237]

The CJEU ruled that the provision under Belgian domestic law, precluding the deductibility of the (foreign) contributions, constituted a restriction within the meaning of the freedom of movement of workers since the given provision operated to the particular detriment of taxpayers coming to Belgium from another Member State to conduct activities, because they commonly take out insurance in their State of origin.[2238] The CJEU also ruled that the fact that tax levy provisions were not harmonised was not relevant in this regard, since such harmonization cannot constitute a condition precedent to the application of

2234 *Bachmann.*

2235 Richter, 2.

2236 *Bachmann, para 3.*

2237 Ibid., paras 17, 21, 22, 23. With regard to the need to preserve the cohesion of the tax system, the Court held that there exists under the Belgian rules a connection between the deductibility of contributions and the liability to tax of sums payable by the insurers under pension and life assurance contracts, with a reference to *Commission vs. Belgium I.* Furthermore, the CJEU ruled that it follows that in such a tax system the loss of revenue resulting from the deduction of life assurance contributions from total taxable income - which included pensions and insurance payable in the event of death - is offset by the taxation of pensions, annuities or capital sums payable by the insurers. Where such contributions have not been deducted, those sums are exempt from tax (para 22). Lastly, as regards the cohesion-argument, the CJEU observed that the cohesion of such a tax system, the formulation of which is a matter for each Member State, therefore presupposes that, in the event of a State being obliged to allow the deduction of life assurance contributions paid in another Member State, it should be able to tax sums payable by insurers (para 23).

2238 *Bachmann, para 9.*

Article 48 of the Treaty, i.e. Community law does not set any preconditions in this context.[2239] Lastly, the CJEU did consider the argument of the cohesion of a tax system to be a valid justification ground, although the provision in question was not yet in effect in the year in question and, hence, could not be invoked in the given case.[2240] More specifically, the CJEU ruled that it was not possible to ensure the cohesion of such a tax system by means of measures which are less restrictive than those at issue, and that the consequences of any other measure ensuring the recovery by the State concerned of the tax due under its legislation on sums payable by insurers pursuant to the contracts concluded with them, would ultimately be similar to those resulting from the non-deductibility of contributions.[2241] Obviously, the CJEU considered that Belgium did not have the possibility to, eventually, tax the pension benefits because Mr Bachmann was a foreigner and foreigners typically return to their home country after their employment. The disputed Belgian provision was held not in breach of the freedom of movement of workers, since such provisions, in the field of pensions and life assurance, justified the need to ensure the cohesion of the tax system of which they form part.[2242] With this decision, the CJEU introduced for the first time the coherence of the tax system as an overriding reason in the general interest justifying an infringement with the rights of free movement. This conclusion has been the subject of an extensive debate, and criticism among tax scholars, and the scope of this fiscal coherence-justification ground has been limited considerably by the court in the *Wielockx*-case, which will be dealt with below.[2243]

General Rule Arising from *Bachmann*-case:
The freedom of movement of workers and the freedom to provide services preclude domestic tax legislation of a Member State making the deductibility of (foreign) sickness and invalidity insurance contributions, and (foreign) pensions and life assurance contributions conditional on those contributions being paid in that State, that is, precluding contributions paid to a foreign insurer from deduction. However, that condition may be justified by the need to preserve the cohesion of the applicable tax system.

2239 Ibid., para 11.
2240 Ibid., para 27-29.
2241 Ibid., para 27.
2242 Ibid., para 28.
2243 See for instance B Knobbe-Keuk, 'Fundamental Freedoms Enshrined in the EC Treaty by Discriminatory Tax Provisions – Ban and Justification' EC Tax Review 234 ff. This author pointed out that the cohesion of the system in the case at issue was eliminated by the state by signing agreements modifying the consistency between previous deduction and later taxation, when adopting a tax treaty following the OECD Model Convention. In these situations, the state waives the later taxation of income derived from contributions previously exempted or deducted for tax purposes. The CJEU took this criticism into account in its judgment in the *Wielockx*-case.

8.4.2.B Commission vs. Belgium I

In this infringement procedure against Belgium, domestic tax legislation was put under scrutiny.[2244] On the grounds of this domestic legislation, the deductibility from taxable income of supplementary pension or life assurance contributions was made conditional on those contributions being paid – either by the taxpayer himself pursuant to the life assurance contract personally concluded by him or by (the intermediary of) his employer by way of deduction at source from remuneration – to an undertaking established in Belgium or to the Belgian establishment of a foreign insurance undertaking.[2245] The Court held that there is a risk that the domestic legal provision at issue may operate to the particular detriment of those workers who are, as a general rule, nationals of other Member States.

The Belgian government put forward two justification grounds, most importantly the disputed provision was necessary to ensure the cohesion of the tax system at issue.[2246] As regards this justification ground, the CJEU observed that a connection existed under the domestic rules between the deductibility of contributions and the liability to tax of sums payable by insurers pursuant to pension or life assurance contracts.[2247] Under Belgian fiscal law, where contributions had not been deducted for tax purposes, pensions, annuities, capital sums or surrender values payable were exempted from tax. Hence, the loss of revenue following from the deduction of contributions from taxable income was counterbalanced by the taxation of these sums.[2248] The court observed that the cohesion of such a tax system – of which the formulation is a matter for the state itself – presupposes that in the case where that State is obliged to allow the deduction of contributions paid in another Member State, it should be able to tax sums payable.[2249]

After weighing several alternatives, the CJEU concluded that as EU law stood at the time of the main proceedings, it was not possible to ensure the cohesion of such a tax system by means of measures less restrictive than those provided for by the domestic legislation under scrutiny, and that the effects of any other measure ensuring the recovery by the Belgian state of the tax payable pursuant to its legislation on sums would, ultimately, be akin to those effects following from the non-deductibility of contributions.[2250] With respect to the need to preserve the cohesion of the tax systems and the role of double tax

2244 *Commission vs. Belgium I* para 1.
2245 Ibid. para 2-5.
2246 Ibid. para 10.
2247 Ibid. para 14.
2248 Ibid. para 15.
2249 Ibid. para 16.
2250 Ibid. para 17-20.

conventions in this regard, the CJEU acknowledged the existence of these conventions allowing the deduction of contributions paid in a contracting State other than that in which the advantage was granted, and recognizing the power of a single State to subject to tax sums payable by insurers.[2251] In the light of this, the court pointed out that such a solution is possible only by means of such conventions or by the adoption by the European Council of the necessary coordination or harmonization measures. The CJEU concluded that it must be accepted that the contested domestic provisions were justified by the need to safeguard the cohesion of the tax system at issue and, consequently, that they did not infringe the freedom of movement of workers.[2252]

It is to be pointed out that this conclusion is fairly remarkably in the light of the court's judgement in the (later) *Wielock*-case, and should therefore be treated with considerable caution. In the latter case, the CJEU narrowed down the scope of application of this justification ground.[2253] Therefore, fiscal cohesion has not been established in relation to one and the same person by a strict correlation between the deduction of contributions and the taxation of pensions but had been shifted to the level of the reciprocity of the rules applicable in the Contracting States. Up until now, this line of argumentation has consistently been taken by the CJEU.[2254] This aids an approach of cohesion, and a predictable line of reasoning.

General Rule Arising from *Commission vs. Belgium I*-case:
Domestic tax legislation of a Member State making the deductibility from taxable income of supplementary pension or life assurance contributions conditional on those contributions being paid – either by the taxpayer himself pursuant to the life assurance contract personally concluded by him or by (the intermediary of) his employer by way of deduction at source from remuneration – to an undertaking established in Belgium or to the Belgian establishment of a foreign insurance undertaking, does not conflict with the freedom of movement of workers, nor the freedom to provide services as this provision is needed to preserve the cohesion of the national tax system.

2251 Ibid. para 19.
2252 Ibid. para 21.
2253 *Wielockx para 24.*
2254 See, for instance, *Danner* para 36; *De Groot* para 37; *Skandia* para 33; *Commission vs. Denmark* para 72-74.

8.4.3 *Second Generation of Cases*

The *Wielockx*[2255] case and the *Safir*[2256] case are considered the second generation of cases, relevant for the cross-border tax treatment of pensions.[2257] The *Wielockx* case is particularly relevant as regards fiscal coherence as a justification ground, as the CJEU considerably revisited her view on when this coherence may serve as a justification ground, even overturning her judgment in the *Bachmann* and *Commission vs. Belgium I* cases. Fiscal coherence can, therefore, not be put forward as a justification ground in cases where a State waives the right to tax pensions received abroad and, thus, acknowledges that the correlation between pension contributions deducted, and pension benefits taxed is not strict.[2258]

8.4.3.A Wielockx

Mr Wielockx, a Belgian national resident in Belgium, was involved as a partner in a Dutch practice of physical therapists, and received his entire income and was liable to tax there.[2259] Under Dutch domestic tax legislation, resident taxpayers were allowed to deduct contributions to a pension reserve (*oudedagsreserve*) from their taxable income. This reserve established a voluntary pension-reserve tax scheme for self-employed persons. Mr Wielockx, being a non-resident taxpayer, was refused to deduct these contributions to a pension reserve from his taxable income.[2260]

Firstly, the CJEU reiterated, while referring to the *Schumacker*-case[2261], that although direct taxation falls within the competence of the Member States, the latter must nonetheless exercise that competence consistently with Community law and therefore avoid any overt or covert discrimination by reason of nationality.[2262] The court ruled that a non-resident taxpayer, whether employed or self-employed, who receives all or almost all of his income in the State where he works is objectively in the same situation in so far as concerns income tax as a resident of that State who does the same work there, since both are taxed in that State alone and their taxable income is the same.[2263] The CJEU observed that Mr Wielockx, being a non-resident taxpayer who receives all or almost all

2255 *Wielockx*.
2256 *Safir*.
2257 Avi-Yonah, and Richter, 2.
2258 In this regard it can even be argued that the CJEU ruled in correctly in the Bachmann case, Cf. Birk and Wernsmann, 267. See also *Danner*, para 37.
2259 *Wielockx*, para 10.
2260 Ibid., para 2.
2261 C-279/93 *Schumacker* ECLI:EU:C:1995:31 (CJEU), para 21 and 26.
2262 *Wielockx*, para 16.
2263 Ibid., para 20.

of his income in the State where he works (i.e. the Netherlands) but who is not entitled to set up a pension reserve qualifying for deductions under the same tax conditions as a resident taxpayer, suffered discrimination.[2264]

The principle of fiscal cohesion was put forward as a justification ground. Firstly, the principle of fiscal cohesion at the individual level as laid down in the *Bachmann* case, according to which there must be a correlation between the sums deducted from the taxable income and the sums which are subject to tax.[2265] In the present case, the CJEU clearly delineated the scope of the fiscal cohesion principle.[2266] This justification was rejected by the CJEU, since the cohesion of a tax system had shifted to Treaty level, where the taxing rights with respect to pensions was assigned to the residence state, irrespective of the state where the contributions were deducted.[2267] The court considered that fiscal cohesion has therefore not been established in relation to one and the same person by a strict correlation between the deductibility of contributions and the taxation of pensions but shifted to another level, that of the reciprocity of the rules applicable in the Contracting States.[2268] The latter considerations constitute a considerable curtailment of fiscal coherence as a justification ground.[2269] The earlier mentioned *Bachmann* case should therefore be considered with care, with respect to fiscal cohesion as a justification ground. Fiscal cohesion can, therefore, not be put forward as a justification ground in cases where a State foregoes the right to tax pensions received abroad and, thus, acknowledges that the correlation between pension contributions deducted, and pension benefits taxed is not strict.[2270] In short, a state cannot put forward the argument of internal fiscal cohesion

2264 Ibid., para 22.

2265 Ibid., para 23.

2266 European Commission, 'The elimination of tax obstacles to the cross-border provision of occupational pensions,' 9. It may be pointed out that since the *Bachmann* case, the CJEU has not upheld broad and general claims of fiscal cohesion presented by Member States, see: C-294/97 *Eurowings Luftverkehrs AG* ECLI:EU:C:1999:524 (CJEU); *Danner; Skandia*. Furthermore, it can be pointed out that the large majority of Member States' tax treaties, like the treaty concerned in *Wielockx*, apply the principle of residence taxation provided for in Article 18 of the OECD Model Tax Convention. The Court's reasoning in *Wielockx* would therefore apply in such cases. However, some member states take the position in treaty negotiations to introduce source taxation of pension benefits. See Ministerie van Financiën, 54. The Netherlands seeks to agree on a source state taxation on fiscally facilitated accrued pensions, regardless of the tax treatment of pension in the (new) state of residence of the pensioner. However, also in cases of source taxation the refusal of deductibility for contributions paid to pension institutions established in other Member States would be disproportionate as there are less restrictive means of ensuring collection of tax at source by a pension institution established in another Member State.

2267 *Wielockx*, para 24.

2268 Ibid., para 24.

2269 Cf. Birk and Wernsmann, 267.

2270 In this regard it can even be argued that the CJEU ruled incorrectly in the *Bachmann* case, Cf. ibid. 267. See also *Danner*, para 37.

when the internal coherence has been modified by a tax treaty (tax treaty cohesion).[2271] Hence, a Member State should take into account the effect that the tax treaty might have on the fiscal coherence that the particular tax provision creates at a national level.[2272] The CJEU continued its considerations by her observance that since fiscal cohesion is secured by a bilateral convention concluded with another Member State, that principle may not be invoked to justify the refusal of a deduction such as that in issue in the case at hand.[2273] This implies that if under the terms of the tax treaty a Member State allows pension benefits paid to non-residents to be taxed solely in the country of residence, the inability to tax these benefits should not be a justification for denying tax deductibility only when the contributions are paid to a scheme that is established elsewhere in the European Union.

General Rule Arising from *Wielockx*-case:
Domestic tax legislation of a Member State allowing its residents to deduct from their taxable income business profits which they allocate to form a pension reserve but denies that benefit to Community nationals liable to pay tax who, although resident in another Member State, receive all or almost all of their income in the first State, is a discrimination. This discrimination cannot be justified by the fact that the periodic pension payments subsequently drawn out of the pension reserve by the non-resident taxpayer shall not be taxed in the first State but in the State of residence — with which the first State has concluded a double-taxation convention — even if, under the tax system in force in the first State, a strict correspondence between the deductibility of the amounts added to the pension reserve and the liability to tax of the amounts drawn out of it cannot be achieved by generalizing the benefit. Such discrimination is therefore contrary to Article 52 of the Treaty.

8.4.3.B Safir

The *Safir* case concerned the taxation of an inverse life insurance policy, under which contributions were not deductible and benefits were not taxed either. It follows from this case that if a Member State applies such a taxation system, it must do so uniformly for domestic, as well as cross-border contracts. Mrs. Safir, residing in Sweden, disputed the payment of tax on capital life assurance premiums, which she paid in 1995 to Skandia Life Assurance Company Ltd, i.e. a British insurance company operating on the Swedish market and wholly owned by the Swedish company Skandia.[2274] Both in cross-border and

2271 Prats, 18.
2272 European Commission, 'Supplementary pensions in the Single Market: A Green Paper' 18.
2273 *Wielockx*, para 25.
2274 *Safir*, para 2.

domestic situations, premiums for this capital life assurance were not to be deducted from the taxable income while proceeds from policies were not subject to taxation.[2275] However, savings in the form of capital life assurance taken out with companies established outside Sweden were liable to tax pursuant to the specific domestic tax law.[2276] An additional requirement applying to these taxpayers, having taken out a life assurance with a foreign company, was to register themselves and declare the payment of premiums to a central body (*Skattemyndigheten*).[2277]

The domestic legislation put under scrutiny in this case, stipulated that the determination of the tax applicable to insurance premiums is dependent on the assessment by the administration of the tax regime applicable to the insurer not established in Sweden.[2278] The CJEU observed that, as a result, it appeared that such differences of assessment of the tax regime applicable to insurers not established in Sweden are liable to create uncertainty which may dissuade individuals from taking out long-term contracts, such as capital life assurance contracts, with insurers not established in Sweden. The CJEU held that other systems which are more transparent and also capable of filling the fiscal vacuum referred to by the Swedish Government are conceivable, whilst being less restrictive of the freedom to provide services.[2279] In these circumstances, the CJEU concluded that the justifications put forward could not be accepted.[2280] As a result, the CJEU did not need to answer the question whether the domestic legislation in question was incompatible with the freedom of capital.[2281] However, the CJEU did conclude that the freedom of services precluded that application of the domestic legislation in question.[2282]

General Rule Arising from *Safir*-case:
Domestic legislation pursuant to which a policyholder having taken out insurance with a foreign insurer, is treated (fiscally) less favourable than if he had taken out the insurance with a domestic insurer, is incompatible with the freedom to provide services.

2275 Ibid., para 5.
2276 Ibid., para 7.
2277 Ibid., para 10.
2278 Ibid., para 29.
2279 Ibid., para 33.
2280 Ibid., para 34.
2281 Ibid., para 35.
2282 Ibid., para 36.

8.4.4 *Third Generation of Cases*

The 'latest' generation of CJEU cases with regard to the cross-border tax treatment of pensions, concern the *Danner* case[2283], *Skandia* case[2284], *Turpeinen* case[2285], *Commission vs. Denmark* case[2286], *Commission vs. Belgium* case[2287], *Commission vs. Germany* case[2288], and the *Montag* case[2289].

8.4.4.A Danner

The party concerned in this case, Mr Danner, both worked and lived in Germany, where he paid pension insurance contributions to two German insurance institutions, the *Bundesversicherungsanstalt für Angestellte (BfA)*[2290] (part of *gesetzlichen Rentenversicherung*) and *the Berliner Ärzteversorgung* (part of the *berufsständischen Versorgungseinrichtung*).[2291] Subsequently, Mr Danner moved to Finland, and continued the (voluntary) payment of contributions to the aforementioned German pension schemes.[2292]

Pursuant to Finnish legislation, as it stood at the time of the judgement, pension insurance contributions, paid into certain compulsory or statutory schemes were fully deductible for tax purposes, also applying to contributions paid to analogous foreign schemes.[2293] However, contrarily, voluntary pension contributions were deductible under certain conditions and within certain limits, depending on whether contributions are paid to institutions established in Finland or abroad and, in the latter case, when the insurance was taken out.[2294]

Until 1996, when Finland joined the EU, these provisions governing the deductibility of the pension premiums paid, applied without distinction to contributions to either Finnish or foreign insurance institutions.[2295] After joining the EU, Finland amended its domestic legislation, with retroactive effect to 1 January 1996. Pursuant to this adapted legislation,

---

2283 *Danner.*
2284 *Skandia.*
2285 *Turpeinen.*
2286 *Commission vs. Denmark.*
2287 *Commission vs. Belgium II.*
2288 *Commission vs. Germany.*
2289 C-480/17 *Montag* ECLI:EU:C:2018:987 (CJEU).
2290 The BfA was a major pension provider under the German statutory *gesetzlichen Rentenversicherung.* As of 1st October 2005, the BfA was transferred to the *Deutsche Rentenversicherung Bund.*
2291 *Danner,* para 16.
2292 Ibid., para 17.
2293 Ibid., para 3.
2294 Ibid., para 4.
2295 Ibid., para 7.

henceforth, pension contributions for voluntary pension insurance paid to foreign insurance institutions and pension funds were, in principle, no longer deductible for tax purposes.[2296] As an exception, pension contributions were deductible when the pension was granted by a permanent establishment in Finland of the foreign insurance institution, and where the person concerned had moved to Finland from abroad and was not liable to taxation in Finland during the five years preceding that move. In these exceptional cases, contributions were only deductible in the year of move and the three successive years. Furthermore, a transitional provision was introduced.[2297]

The CJEU ruled unequivocally that the national legislation at issue, restricted the freedom to provide services.[2298] Referring to the *Safir* case, the CJEU held that in view of the important role played by the possibility of obtaining tax relief at the time the pension insurance contract is taken out, such legislation is liable to dissuade individuals from taking out voluntary pension insurance with institutions established in a Member State other than Finland, and to dissuade those institutions from offering their services on the Finnish market.[2299]

Several justification grounds were relied on, most importantly, the need to ensure the fiscal cohesion of the Finnish tax system, i.e. the existence of a direct link between deductibility of contributions and the liability to income tax of pension benefits payable.[2300] While referring to the *Bachmann* and *Commission vs. Belgium* cases the CJEU observed that in the case at issue, there was no such direct link between the deductibility of insurance contributions and the taxation of sums payable by insurers, i.e. the Finnish system was not coherent.[2301] Pursuant to Finnish tax legislation, pensions payable by foreign institutions to Finnish residents were taxed, regardless whether the contributions paid to accrue these pensions were, or were not, deducted from the taxable income of the Finnish recipients.[2302] Furthermore, Finland and Germany concluded a double tax convention. With a reference to the *Wielockx* case, the CJEU observed that as a result of double-taxation conventions fiscal cohesion was no longer established in relation to one and the same person by a strict

2296 Ibid., para 8.

2297 Ibid., para 9. For the tax years 1996 and 1997, contributions paid in respect of voluntary pension insurance taken out with foreign institutions before 1 September 1995 continued to be subject to the provisions in force in 1995, subject to a ceiling of FIM 15 000 on the annual deductible amount.

2298 Ibid., para 30.

2299 Ibid., para 31 referring to *Safir*, para 30.

2300 *Danner*, para 33-35.

2301 Ibid., para 36-37.

2302 Since in the case where Mr Danner would have decided to continue to live in Finland, the pensions he would receive from the German institutions, would be subject to German income tax, pursuant to the applicable double tax convention, even though he was not eligible to deduct the contributions paid to those schemes.

correlation between the deductibility of contributions and the taxation of pensions but was shifted to another level, i.e. that of the reciprocity of the rules applicable in the Contracting States.[2303] Hence, the principle of fiscal cohesion may not be invoked to justify the refusal of a deduction such as that at issue.

The CJEU concluded that the freedom to provide services precludes domestic tax legislation restricting or disallowing the deduction of contributions to voluntary pension schemes paid to foreign pension providers, while allowing the deduction of such contributions when they are paid to domestic institutions, provided that this legislation does not at the same time preclude taxation of the pensions paid by the foreign pension providers.[2304] This last proviso with respect to precluding the taxation of benefits paid by foreign pension providers seems a reference to the fiscal coherence of the tax system. This case demonstrates that if a national tax system is inconsistent in itself, the Member State in question cannot plead the need for consistency.[2305]

General Rule Arising from *Danner*-case:
The freedom to provide services precludes domestic tax legislation restricting or disallowing the deduction of contributions to voluntary pension schemes paid to foreign pension providers, while allowing the deduction of such contributions when they are paid to domestic institutions, provided that this legislation does not at the same time preclude taxation of the pensions paid by the foreign pension providers.

8.4.4.B Skandia

In this case, Skandia, a company established in Sweden, took out an occupational pension insurance policy for the benefits of her employee Mr Ramstedt, a Swedish citizen resident in Sweden, with companies established in other Member States (UK, Germany or Denmark).[2306] As regards occupational pension insurance policies taken out by an employer who pays the premiums on behalf of one of his employees, the domestic legislation distinguished between pension insurance and endowment insurance.[2307] To be considered as the former, the pension policy had to, as a rule, be taken out with an insurer established in Sweden.[2308] An insurance policy not taken out with a company established

2303 *Danner*, para 40-41.
2304 Ibid., para 57.
2305 Cf. Wattel, Marres and Vermeulen, 880.
2306 *Skandia*, para 2, 11.
2307 Ibid., para 4.
2308 Ibid., para 5.

in Sweden was, nonetheless, considered a pension insurance under strict conditions.[2309] Life assurances which did not meet these requirements, constituted a so-called endowment insurance.[2310] These two insurance policies were subject to a different tax treatment in terms of deductibility. Premiums paid by the employer to a so-called pension insurance were immediately deductible in calculating his taxable income.[2311] The pension benefits paid out subsequently under this pension insurance were subject to income tax in their entirety in the hands of the retired employee, i.e. the policy's beneficiary. Contrarily, the premiums paid by an employer under a so-called endowment insurance were in principle not deductible from the taxable income but were, nevertheless, deductible when the retirement benefits were actually paid.[2312] Also under this type of insurance the sums received were treated as taxable earned income in the hands of the employee. The disputed disadvantage to the employer in financial terms became thus manifest in the postponement of the right to deduct until the time the pension benefits were actually paid to the employee, Mr Ramstedt.[2313] This disadvantage was liable to dissuade Swedish employers from taking out occupational pension insurance with foreign institutions, as well as to dissuade those institutions from offering their services on the Swedish market.[2314] However, in both situations, the employee who is the beneficiary, was liable to tax at the same time and in the same way. It was not disputed that national legislation such as that at issue in the main proceedings restricted the freedom to provide services.[2315]

Several justification grounds were put forward, amongst which, the fiscal cohesion, i.e. the need to ensure the cohesion of the national tax system in terms of the direct correlation between the deductibility of contributions and the liability to tax on sums payable by insurers. The CJEU rejected this justification ground as there was no connection such as determined in the *Bachmann* case.[2316] The disadvantageous treatment of the employer, in terms of the postponement of deducting the paid contributions, was not compensated in the case at issue. In light of the foregoing, there was no need to assess whether the legislation at issue infringed the free movement of persons and capital.[2317] The CJEU concluded that the freedom of services precludes an insurance policy issued by an insurance company established in another Member State which meets the conditions laid down in national law for occupational pension insurance, apart from the condition that

2309 ibid., para 6.
2310 Ibid., para 7.
2311 Ibid., para 9.
2312 Ibid., para 10.
2313 Ibid. para 28.
2314 Ibid. para 28. See also *Safir*, para 30 and *Danner* para 31.
2315 *Skandia*, para 27.
2316 Ibid. para 34.
2317 Ibid., para 60.

the policy must be issued by an insurance company operating in the national territory, from being treated differently in terms of taxation, with income tax effects which, depending on the circumstances in the individual case, may be less favourable.[2318]

General Rule Arising from *Skandia*-case:
Domestic legislation under which pension benefits, rather than pension premiums, are deductible for tax purposes, solely in the case of an insurance taken out with a non-resident insurer, is contrary to the freedom to provide services.

8.4.4.C Turpeinen

Ms Turpeinen, a retired Finnish national, residing in Spain at the time of the main proceedings, received a retirement pension paid by a Finnish institution, and taxed in Finland.[2319] Her only income comprised a retirement pension paid by a Finnish local government pension insurance, which was, according to the double taxation agreement concluded between Finland and Spain, solely taxable in Finland.[2320] Until 2001, Ms Turpeinen was subject to the tax regime for fully chargeable residents, a regime which covers all of the taxable person's worldwide income.[2321] However, in 2002, the year relevant for the main proceedings, the Finnish Tax Office informed her that henceforth she would be subject to the limited taxation regime, which covered merely income from Finland and applied to Finnish nationals who had not been domiciled in Finland for three years consecutively.[2322] Under this regime her retirement pension was subject to a higher tax rate.[2323] The CJEU considered that persons who have carried out all their occupational activity in the Member State of which they are nationals and who have exercised the right to reside in another Member State only after their retirement, without any intention of working in that State, cannot rely on the freedom of movement of workers.[2324] As a general rule, the CJEU stated that national legislation which places some of its nationals at a

2318 Ibid., para 62.
2319 *Turpeinen* para 2.
2320 Ibid. para 4.
2321 Ibid. para 5.
2322 Ibid. para 6.
2323 Ibid. para 13-14.
2324 Ibid. para 16. The Court has held on many occasions that the provisions of the Treaty relating to freedom of movement for persons are intended to facilitate the pursuit by EU nationals of occupational activities of all kinds throughout the EU, and preclude measures which might place these nationals at a disadvantage when they wish to pursue an economic activity in the territory of another Member State. See C-302/98 *Sehrer* ECLI:EU:C:2000:322 (CJEU) para 37 and ibid. para 32. Provisions of national legislation which preclude or deter a national of a Member State from leaving his country of origin in order to exercise his right to freedom of movement, constitute an obstacle to that freedom even if they apply without regard to the nationality of the workers concerned. See *Turpeinen* para 15; *Sehrer* para 39 and ibid. para 33.

disadvantage simply because they have exercised their freedom to move and to reside in another Member State would give rise to inequality of treatment, contrary to the principles which underpin the status of citizen of the Union, that is, the guarantee of the same treatment in law in the exercise of the citizen's freedom to move.[2325] The CJEU held that the Finnish legislation in question, distinguished between Finnish nationals who continue to reside in Finland and those who had established their residence in another Member State, and treated the latter unfavourably, simply as a result of having exercised their right to freedom of movement.[2326] In this case, non-residents retired persons who reside for three years consecutively in another Member State and receive the same pension benefits as a resident retired person, must bear a higher tax burden compared to these residents.[2327]

The CJEU held that in so far as the retirement pension of Ms Turpeinen constituted all or almost all of her income, non-resident retired persons such as Ms Turpeinen were, objectively speaking, in the same situation as regards income tax as retired persons resident in Finland who receive the same retirement pension.[2328] By this consideration, the CJEU extended the *Schumacker* doctrine[2329] of non-discrimination to the domain of pensioners.

The CJEU concluded, following the Advocate General's opinion, with stating that the freedom of persons precludes national legislation according to which the income tax on a retirement pension, paid by an institution of the Member State concerned, to a person residing in another Member State exceeds in certain cases the tax which would be payable if that person resided in the first Member State, where that pension constitutes all or nearly all of that person's income.[2330]

General Rule Arising from *Turpeinen*-case:
The freedom of persons precludes national legislation pursuant to which the income tax burden on a retirement pension paid to a non-resident taxable person exceeds, in certain cases, the tax which would be payable if that person was a resident taxable person in that Member State, where that pension constitutes all or nearly all of that person's income.

2325 *Turpeinen* para 22. See also *Pusa* para 20 and *D'Hoop* para 34-36.
2326 *Turpeinen* para 24.
2327 Ibid. para 25.
2328 Ibid. para 31.
2329 C-279/93 *Schumacker* ECLI:EU:C:1995:31 (CJEU).
2330 *Turpeinen* para 39.

8.4.4.D Commission vs. Denmark

In this infringement procedure before the Court, the contested Danish domestic tax legislation drew a distinction between life assurance and pension contracts concluded with either pension institutions established in Denmark, or pension institutions established outside Denmark.[2331] As regards the tax treatment of the former, contributions can either be deducted or exempted, whilst payments made pursuant to contracts entered into with the latter, foreign pension institutions, are denied this tax relief.

The CJEU reiterated, referring to the *Safir* case[2332], that the freedom to provide services also precludes the application of any national rules which have the effect of making the provision of services between Member States more difficult than the provision of services purely within in one Member State.[2333] In the case in question, domestic tax legislation required that in order for foreign pension institutions to offer their services on the Danish market with the same tax advantages as those offered by pension institutions established in Denmark, they must have a branch office or a permanent establishment in that Member State.[2334]

In her examination as regards the freedom to provide services the court distinguished two situation in which such a requirement is liable to have a dissuasive effect.[2335] With regard to the free movement of workers, the CJEU observed that salaried workers who have carried on an occupation in a Member State other than Denmark, and who are subsequently employed, or seek employment, in Denmark will normally have concluded their pension and life assurance contracts with insurers established in the first State.[2336] Hence, there is a risk that the contested domestic legislation may work to the particular detriment of these workers who are, generally speaking, nationals of other Member States.[2337] In the light of these considerations, the CJEU held that the grant of a right to deduct or exempt contributions, under the condition that the pension scheme is taken out with a pension institution established in Denmark, is, due to the efforts and costs which it entails, liable to dissuade the insured person from transferring his place of residence to Denmark and, therefore, constitutes an obstacle to the freedom of movement for workers.[2338] For these same reasons, the CJEU took the view that the contested provision also amounted to an

2331 *Commission vs. Denmark,* para 9-22.
2332 *Safir* para 23.
2333 *Commission vs. Denmark* para 38.
2334 Ibid. para 39.
2335 Ibid. para 40.
2336 Ibid. para 41.
2337 Ibid. para 41. The court refers to *Bachmann* para 9 and *Commission vs. Belgium I* para 7.
2338 *Commission vs. Denmark* para 42.

obstacle to the freedom of establishment in Denmark of self-employed workers who are nationals of another Member State, as the denial of tax relief of contributions paid to pension institutions established in other Member States, may dissuade self-employed workers from establishing themselves in Denmark.[2339] Hence, the legislation put under scrutiny amounted to an obstacle to freedom to provide services, freedom of movement for workers and freedom of establishment.

As regards the cohesion of the tax system, the CJEU reiterated that it is established that the need to preserve such cohesion requires the existence of a direct link between a tax advantage and a corresponding disadvantage.[2340] According to the court, the factor liable to affect the cohesion of the Danish tax system is to be found in the fact that the transfer of the residence of the person concerned occurred between the time of payment of contributions to a pension scheme and that of disbursement of the corresponding benefits, and less in the fact that the pension institution is established in another Member State.[2341] The court observed that Denmark had waived its taxing rights on the future pension benefits corresponding to the contributions deducted or exempted, in cases where a Danish resident had, before benefits fall to be paid, transferred his residence to another Member State, at least where it has concluded with the Member State to which the person concerned has transferred his residence a double taxation convention based on the OECD Convention.[2342] Contrarily to the cases *Bachmann* and *Commission vs. Belgium*, where there was a direct link between the deductibility of contributions and the taxation of sums payable by, in the present case no such link was found by the court. Nothing prevented Denmark from exercising its power of taxation over the benefits paid by a pension institution established in another Member State to a taxpayer still resident in Denmark when that payment was made, as a counterbalance to the contributions which it allowed to be deducted or exempted.[2343] The court rejected the cohesion of the tax system as a justification ground for the denial, in general, of granting a tax advantage in respect of contributions paid to a pension institution established in another Member State.[2344]

In the light of the foregoing the CJEU held that by introducing and maintaining in force a system for life assurance and pensions under which tax deductions and tax exemptions for payments are granted only for payments under contracts entered into with pension

2339 Ibid. para 43-44.

2340 Ibid. para 70. The Court refers to *Commission vs. Belgium I* para 14 and C-55/98 *Vestergaard* ECLI:EU:C:1999:533 (CJEU) para 24.

2341 *Commission vs. Denmark* para 71.

2342 Ibid. para 72. Pursuant to which pension benefits are, in principle, liable to tax in the residence state in virtue of Article 18, para 1 OECD Model Tax Convention on Income and on Capital.

2343 *Commission vs. Denmark* para 73.

2344 Ibid. para 74.

institutions established in Denmark, whereas no such tax relief is granted for payments made under contracts entered into with pension institutions established in other Member States, the contested domestic legislation contravenes the freedom to provide services, free movement for workers and freedom of establishment.[2345]

General Rule Arising from *Commission vs. Denmark*-case:
A national tax system whereby payments for life assurance and pensions are tax deductible, or tax exempt, only if made pursuant to contracts entered into with domestic insurers, whereas no such tax relief is granted for payments made under contracts entered into with pension institutions established in other Member States, is incompatible with the freedom to provide services, free movement for workers and freedom of establishment.

8.4.4.E Commission vs. Belgium II

In this infringement procedure against Belgium several elements of Belgian tax legislation regarding the tax treatment of pensions were put under scrutiny. In certain situations, the Belgian income tax provided tax relief by allowing deduction of pension premiums from their taxable income, subject to certain preconditions. However, in these conditions a distinction was drawn between domestic and cross-border situations. This distinction concerned a range of elements.[2346]

In the light of this settled case-law, the court found that making the deductibility of employers' insurance contributions and premiums due in respect of supplementary pension and life assurance subject to the condition that they be paid to an insurance undertaking or welfare fund established in Belgium, the Belgian legislation had the effect of rendering the freedom to provide insurance services from other Member States more difficult than if it were purely within the Kingdom of Belgium.[2347] This applies similarly to making the tax reduction for personal supplementary pension and life assurance contributions in the form of deductions made by the employer from the employees remuneration, or in the form of deductions made by the undertaking from the remuneration of a director who is not under a contract of employment, subject to the condition that the contributions be paid to an insurance undertaking or welfare fund established in Belgium. Both legislative provisions were liable to dissuade individuals from taking out insurance with foreign insurance companies, and, consequently, constituted obstacles to the freedom to provide service. The same conclusion applied in

2345 Ibid. para 77.
2346 See *Commission vs. Belgium II* para 1.
2347 Ibid. para 39.

respect of the provision under which capital or surrender values which were transferred to a pension fund or insurance undertaking established abroad were subject to tax, while no such taxation was imposed for transfers made to a pension fund or to an insurance undertaking established in Belgium.[2348] This provision was liable to further impede the activities of a provider of insurance services established abroad. Finally, this holds similarly true as regards the obligation for an insurance undertaking established in another Member State to appoint a representative in Belgium.[2349] The court found that such a legal obligation, as a result of the costs and constraints which it entailed was liable to dissuade those undertakings from offering their services in Belgium, and, constituted an obstacle to the freedom to provide services. It becomes evident from the above, that also higher administrative/tax compliance burdens on non-residents, compared to residents, may infringe primary EU law.

Under the scope of the freedom of movement the court reviewed the other national measures.[2350] Firstly, making the deduction of employers' insurance contributions and premiums subject to the condition that they be paid to an insurance undertaking or welfare institution established in Belgium. Secondly, making the reduction of tax for personal contributions and premiums subject to the same condition. Thirdly, the taxation of capital or surrender values when they are transferred to a pension fund or insurance institution established abroad. Lastly, the fiction that the payment or allocation of capital, surrender values and savings takes place on the day preceding the transfer of the taxpayer's residence or of the primary location of his assets abroad.

As regards the first point, the court found that the refusal to grant a right to deduct employers' insurance contributions and premiums where they were paid to an insurance undertaking or a welfare institution not established in Belgium, the national legislation had the effect of granting a tax advantage which varied depending on the place in which those contributions and premiums were collected and, consequently, was likely to dissuade employed and self-employed persons from exercising their right to move freely in another Member State.[2351] The same holds true as regards the refusal to grant the tax reduction on personal supplementary pension and life assurance contributions and premiums paid to bodies established in other Member States. It follows that these national measures impair the free movement of employed persons and the freedom of establishment of self-employed persons.[2352] As regards the fiction, the court observed that it sought to allow

2348 Ibid. para 40.
2349 Ibid. para 41.
2350 Ibid. para 61-64.
2351 Ibid. para 66.
2352 Ibid. para 67.

taxation by reason of the crossing of a border by employed or self-employed persons.[2353] The court found that this fiction impaired the freedom of movement of employed persons and the freedom of establishment of self-employed person.[2354] The court pointed out that the same conclusion applied, for the same reasons, as regards the freedom of movement for persons who are not economically active.[2355] As regards the levy of tax on transfer of capital or surrender values where the transfer is made by the pension fund or insurance institution with which the capital or surrender values have been built to another insurance institution established outside Belgium, the court held that this dissuaded employed and self-employed persons from establishing themselves in another Member State by preventing them from forwarding their savings, and consequently it found to impair the freedom of movement of employed persons and the freedom of establishment of self-employed persons.[2356]

General Rules Arising from *Commission vs. Belgium II*-case:

The freedom of movement for workers, freedom of establishment and freedom to provide services preclude national legislation pursuant to which:

- the deductibility of employers' insurance contributions and premiums due in respect of supplementary pension and life assurance are made subject to the condition that they be paid to a domestic insurance undertaking or welfare fund;
- the tax reduction for personal supplementary pension and life assurance contributions in the form of deductions made (withheld) by the employer from the employees' remuneration, or in the form of deductions made by the undertaking from the remuneration of a director who is not under a contract of employment, is made subject to the condition that the contributions be paid to a domestic insurance undertaking or welfare fund;
- the payment or allocation of capital, surrender values and savings paid or allocated to a taxpayer who has previously transferred his residence or the primary location of his assets abroad, are, by fiction, deemed to have taken place on the day preceding that transfer;
- all transfers that are treated similarly as an allocation as referred to under the previous point, lead to the obligation for every insurer to withhold amounts in respect of income tax from capital and surrender/redemption values paid to a non-resident who had been,

2353 Ibid. para 68.

2354 Ibid. para 71.

2355 Ibid. para 72. In this regard the court referred to *De Cuyper* para 39-40. In the *Cuyper* case the court referred to *D'Hoop* para 31 and *Pusa* para 19. It is established that national legislation which places at a disadvantage certain of its nationals simply because they have exercised their freedom to move and to reside in another Member State is a restriction on the freedoms of persons.

2356 *Commission vs. Belgium II* para 73.

at one time or another, resident for tax purposes in Belgium, in so far as those sums have been built up/constituted, entirely or partially, during the period in which the person concerned was a Belgian resident for tax purposes, even though the concluded bilateral tax agreements grant the right to tax such income to another Contracting State;
- tax is levied on transfers of capital or surrender values built up by means of employers' contributions or personal contributions for supplementary retirement benefits, where the transfer is made by the pension fund or insurance institution with which the capital or surrender values have been built up in favour of the beneficiary or persons entitled through him, to another foreign pension fund or insurance institution established, while such a transfer does not constitute a taxable transaction if the capital or surrender values are transferred to a domestic pension fund or insurance institution;
- foreign insurers who have no place of business in the national territory must obtain authorisation, before providing their services in the national territory, for a representative residing in the national territory, who must personally assume, in writing, responsibility towards the State for paying the annual tax on insurance contracts, interest and fines which may be due in respect of contracts relating to risks situated in the national territory.

8.4.4.F Commission vs. Germany

This (infringement) procedure concerned an alleged infringement of the free movement of workers in denying a savings-pension bonus (*Altersvorsorgezulage)* under German domestic law, designed to compensate for the future reduction in the level of the statutory pension. It constituted financial aid designed to encourage the persons concerned to build up a complementary pension throughout their working lives. The bonus was granted principally to salaried workers insured under the statutory pension insurance scheme and was granted independently of the beneficiary's income, its amount depending both on the contributions made under the savings-pension contract and on the number of children for whom the beneficiary received family allowances. However, some impediments as regards this savings vehicle arose in cross-border cases.[2357] It should be stressed at this point that this case does not relate solely to cross-border workers whose income is taxed exclusively in the State of residence, but relates to all cross-border workers. The CJEU observed that the grant of the savings-pension bonus is a social advantage generally granted to workers on the basis of their objective status as workers.[2358]

2357 Paragraphs 79 to 99 EStG were put under scrutiny.

2358 Ibid. The CJEU reiterated that Article 7(2) of Regulation No 1612/68 provides that a worker who is a national of a Member State is to enjoy, in the territory of another Member State, the same social and tax advantages as national workers, and that, according to settled case-law, cross-border may rely on this provision on the same basis as any other worker to whom the Article applies. See ibid.

The CJEU then turned to the question whether the infringement constituted an unduly (indirect[2359]) discrimination. The Court noted that, in the present case, pursuant to Paragraph 79 of the EStG, the grant of the savings-pension bonus was conditional on full liability to German tax.[2360] The cross-border workers, in the present case, whose income was taxed exclusively in their State of residence pursuant to the applicable tax treaty, did not have the possibility of being treated in the same way as fully-liable taxpayers.[2361] The Court observed that in such circumstances, this requirement of being fully liable to tax amounts to a residence requirement, and, consequently, the cross-borders workers at issue who, by definition, have their residence in another Member State, are denied the benefit of the savings-pension bonus.[2362]

Hence, the CJEU ruled that making the grant of the savings-pension bonus subject to a condition amounting to a residence requirement constitutes an infringement of the free movement of workers and Article 7(2) of Regulation No 1612/68.[2363] As a justification ground Germany put forward the coherence of the fiscal system.[2364] The Court rejected this argument rightly since fiscal coherence was ensured on the basis of the tax treaty concluded by Germany with other Member States.[2365] The Court concluded the first complaint by ruling that the national provision making the grant of the savings-pension bonus for cross-border workers and their spouses subject to the condition of full liability for tax, constituted indirect discrimination contrary to the free movement of workers and Article 7(2) of Regulation No 1612/68.

The Court also assessed prohibiting cross-border workers from using the subsidized capital for the acquisition or construction of an owner-occupied dwelling unless it is situated in the Member State of employment (Germany). The court pointed out that while it is certainly true, as Germany submitted, that neither German workers nor cross-border workers may use that capital to acquire or construct a dwelling outside Germany, and the contested provision (§92a EStG) was not specifically directed at non-residents, the fact remained that non-residents are more likely to be interested in purchasing a dwelling

2359 A provision of national law must be regarded as indirectly discriminatory if it is intrinsically liable to affect migrant workers more than national workers and if there is a consequent risk that it will place the former at a particular disadvantage. See ibid.referring to C-57/96 *Meints* ECLI:EU:C:1997:564 (CJEU) para 45 and C-35/97 *Commission vs France* ECLI:EU:C:1998:431 (CJEU) para 38.

2360 Natural persons are fully liable to German tax where, according to Paragraph 1(1) of the EStG, they have their domicile or habitual residence in Germany or, according to Paragraph 1(3) thereof, they make a request to that effect and satisfy the strict conditions laid down in that provision.

2361 Ibid.

2362 Ibid.

2363 Ibid.

2364 Ibid.

2365 Ibid. referring to *Wielockx 25.*

outside Germany than residents.[2366] It follows from this that the contested provision treated cross-border workers less favourable than workers resident in Germany and therefore constituted indirect discrimination on grounds of nationality. The two justification grounds put forward, were rejected by the Court. Concludingly, the Court ruled that denying cross-border workers the right to use the subsidized capital for the acquisition or construction of an owner-occupied dwelling, unless it is situated in Germany, was contrary to the freedom of movement of workers and Article 7(2) of Regulation No 1612/68.[2367]

Lastly, pursuant to domestic legislation, a beneficiary of the bonus who left his domicile or habitual residence in Germany, and who was therefore no longer fully liable to tax, was obliged to reimburse the savings-pension bonuses obtained and, as the case may be, the deductions of *Sonderausgaben (*special expenses*)*.[2368] As regards the position of migrant workers, the Court noted that these type of workers, who are generally non-nationals, are more likely to leave Germany to work and establish their residence in another Member State and thus more likely to cease being fully liable to German tax, and thus more likely to be subject of a disadvantage compared to German workers.[2369] The Court observed that since the contested provisions required beneficiaries to reimburse on termination of full liability to German tax, the savings-pension bonus received from that State, any German worker wishing to avail himself of his right to freedom of movement of workers, and, in particular, his right to establish himself in another Member State, therefore finds himself in a less favourable position than a worker who maintains his residence in Germany and continues to be fully liable to German tax.[2370] This difference in treatment is likely to dissuade German national worker from exercising professional activity outside Germany. The possibility to obtain an interest-free suspension of payment until the beginning of the pay-out phase, which extension is not automatic but at the request of the beneficiary, did not alter this as the rules of reimbursement have a restrictive effect in that they deprive the beneficiary of the enjoyment of a social advantage.[2371] Hence, the reimbursement obligation was liable to impede the freedom of movement for workers. Also with regard to this impediment Germany asserted that it could be justified in the light of the coherence of its tax system. The Court refuted this argument and reiterated that fiscal coherence was

2366 Ibid. In this vein the court referred to C-152/03 *Ritter-Coulais* ECLI:EU:C:2006:123 (CJEU) para 36.

2367 Ibid. In response to this judgment, § 92a, paragraph 1, sentence 5 EStG was amended. It specifies that the dwelling must be situated in a Member State of the European Union or in a State to which the Agreement on the European Economic Area (EEA Agreement) applies.

2368 Ibid.

2369 Ibid.

2370 Ibid.

2371 Ibid. See also C-470/04 *N. vs. Inspecteur* ECLI:EU:C:2006:525 (CJEU), para 36 and C-9/02 *Lasteyrie du Saillant* ECLI:EU:C:2004:138 (CJEU) para 47.

ensured on the basis of tax treaties.[2372] It follows from the foregoing that the CJEU found that the reimbursement obligation on termination of full liability to tax was contrary to the freedom of movement of workers and Article 7(2) of Regulation No 1612/68, and as regards persons who are not economically active, for the same reasons, the freedom of persons.

General Rule Arising from *Commission vs. Germany*-case:
Domestic tax legislation:
- denying cross-border workers and their spouses the right to the savings pension bonus (*Altersvorsorgezulage*), i.e. a social advantage, unless they are fully liable to tax in that Member State;
- denying cross-border workers the right to use the subsidised capital for the acquisition or construction of an owner-occupied dwelling unless it is situated in the national territory;
- requiring the savings-pension bonus to be reimbursed on termination of full liability to tax in that Member State;

are contrary to the freedom of movement of workers and Article 7(2) of Regulation No 1612/68, and as regards the latter point the freedom of persons.[1]

8.4.5 *The Latest Generation of Cases*

Below the latest generation of cases, ruled by the CJEU, will be discussed, i.e. the *Montag, Bechtel* and *Kohll* cases. The common ground of these judgments is the explicit observation whether the persons concerned, being non-resident taxpayers, find themselves in a comparable situation as a resident taxpayer. More emphasis is put on this point, compared to the earlier cases discussed above.

8.4.5.A Kohll

In this case, the Court assessed, in the light of the freedom of movement of persons and workers, a national administrative condition (a tax deduction form) for granting a pensioner's tax credit ('The Pensioners' Tax Credit (PTC)). This tax credit were to be granted by the pension fund or any other body liable for payment of the pension to those pensioners who possessed a deduction form on which the inscription PTC was found. The Luxembourg tax authorities had not granted the pensioners' tax credit as provided for

2372 See also *Wielockx* para 25.

under domestic legislation ('the tax credit'). This tax credit was granted to all taxpayers in receipt of income arising from pensions or annuities, provided that the right to tax the income was attributed to Luxembourg, and who were in possession of a tax deduction form.[2373] The tax credit, constituting a tax advantage, was not granted to taxpayers who were resident in Luxemburg but whose pensions, although taxable in Luxemburg, originated in another State.[2374]

As regards a restriction in the light of the freedom of workers, the Court found that by introducing a differential treatment between taxpayers resident in the national territory, depending on the Member State from which the received retirement pensions, taxable in that state of residence, originate, and by denying the benefit of the tax credit to taxpayers for whom the body liable for payment of the pension is established in another Member State, such national legislation is likely to dissuade workers from seeking or undertaking employment in another Member State.[2375] The legislation at issue therefore entailed a restriction of the freedom of movement of workers.[2376]

In the light of the freedom of persons, the Court held that it is apparent from settled case-law of the Court that a national law which places certain nationals at a disadvantage simply because they have exercised their freedom to move and to reside in another Member State constitutes a restriction on the freedoms of persons.[2377] The Court held that in so far as the tax credit was refused to Luxembourg taxpayers who had exercised their freedom to move and to reside in a Member State other than that of which they were a national and who received, due to their residence in that other Member State, a pension paid by a body liable for payment established in that other Member State, that taxpayer found himself at a disadvantage in comparison to taxpayers who had not exercised their freedom to move and to reside in another Member State.[2378] The legislation was hence likely to deter a taxpayer from exercising that freedom and thus constituted a restriction on the freedoms of persons. Both justification grounds put forward, were dismissed by the Court. As regards the cohesion of the tax system, the Court found no direct link between the tax advantage concerned and the offsetting of that advantage by a particular tax levy.[2379] The freedom of movement of workers and the free movement of persons thus precluded the

2373 *Kohll en Kohll-Schlesser* para 15 and 37.
2374 Ibid. para 39.
2375 Ibid. para 40.
2376 Ibid. para 41.
2377 Ibid. para 42 referring to C-359/13 *Martens* ECLI:EU:C:2015:118 (CJEU) para 25.
2378 *Kohll en Kohll-Schlesser* para 44.
2379 Ibid. para 60-61.

national tax law which restricted the eligibility for the pensioners' tax credit to taxpayers in possession of a tax deduction form.[2380]

General Rule Arising from *Kohll*-case:
The freedom of movement for workers and the freedom of persons precludes national legislation which restricts the eligibility for the pensioners' tax credit (constituting a 'tax advantage') to taxpayers in possession of a tax deduction form, where recipients receiving a pension paid out by a paying institution established in another State, are not issued such a form.

8.4.5.B Bechtel

This case concerned the interpretation of the freedom of movement of workers, pertaining to the inclusion of pension (and health insurance) contributions, paid by Mrs Bechtel in France, in the calculation of their taxable income and the special tax rate to be applied to their taxable income.[2381] Mr and Mrs Bechtel, were married and resided in Germany where they were subject to joint assessment for income tax purposes.[2382] Mr Bechtel received income in respect of his employment as a civil servant with the German civil service, while Mrs Bechtel, a French national, worked as a civil servant for the French tax authority.[2383] In this case, the key question was whether the free movement of workers precludes a national provision under which a taxpayer residing in that Member State (in the present case, Germany) and working for the public administration of another Member State (in the present case, France) may not deduct from the income tax basis of assessment in her Member State of residence the pension contributions deducted from her wages in the Member State of employment, in contrast to comparable contributions paid to the social security fund of her Member State of residence, where, under the tax treaty concluded between the two Member States, the wages must not be taxed in the worker's Member State of residence (Germany) and merely increase the tax rate to be applied to other income.[2384] As regards the applicable treaty freedom, the Court held that Mrs Bechtel comes within the definition of a 'worker' for the purposes of the freedom of movement of workers and her employment in the public administration of a Member State does not have the effect of denying her the rights and protection which that freedom affords her.[2385]

2380 Ibid. para 63.
2381 *Bechtel* para 1 and 2.
2382 Ibid. para 13.
2383 Ibid. para 14.
2384 Ibid. para 26.
2385 Ibid. para 36. The Court pointed out that in that regard, it should be observed at the outset that it is settled case-law that Article 18 TFEU, which lays down a general prohibition of all discrimination on grounds of

The court reiterated that the freedom of movement of workers precludes, *inter alia*, measures which, even if they apply regardless of nationality, are intrinsically liable to affect migrant workers more than national workers and there is a consequent risk that they will place the former at a particular disadvantage.[2386] The domestic tax provision at issue, refused to allow the deduction of the additional pension insurance contributions, while Mrs Bechtel's wages were taken into account for the purposes of determining the special tax rate applicable to the disposable income of Mr and Mrs Bechtel jointly.[2387] This possibility of deduction amounted to a tax advantage.[2388] The condition laid down in domestic legislation by which the expenses must not have a direct economic link with the exempt income, lead to that advantage being refused in situations where a resident taxpayer receives wages in a Member State other than her Member State of residence and where those wages are exempt from taxation in her Member State of residence, whilst being taken into account in the tax rate applicable to the other income of that taxpayer.[2389]

---

nationality, applies independently only to situations governed by EU law for which the TFEU lays down no specific rules of non-discrimination (paragraph 30). Furthermore, in relation to the right of freedom of movement for workers, the principle of non-discrimination was implemented by Article 45 TFEU (paragraph 31) referring to *Gilly* para 38. According to settled case-law, any EU national who, irrespective of his place of residence and his nationality, has exercised the right to freedom of movement for workers and who has been employed in a Member State other than that of residence falls within the scope of Article 45 TFEU (paragraph 32) referring to *De Groot para 76*. As regards the issue whether Mrs Bechtel, who is an employee of the public administration of one Member State, whilst residing in another Member State, comes within the definition of 'worker', for the purposes of Article 45 TFEU, it is important to remember that the legal nature of the employment relationship is of no consequence in regard to the application of Article 45 TFEU and the fact that the worker is employed as a civil servant, or even that the employment relationship is governed by public law rather than by private law, is irrelevant in that respect (paragraph 33). With respect to Article 45(4) TFEU the CJEU observed that it is true that this provision stipulates that the provisions of Article 45(1) to (3) TFEU, which lay down the fundamental principle of the freedom of movement for workers and the abolition of all discrimination based on nationality between workers of the Member States, do not apply to employment in the public service. The CJEU states that however, taking account of the fundamental nature, in the scheme of the Treaty, of the principles of freedom of movement and equality of treatment of workers within the European Union, the exceptions made by that provision cannot have a scope going beyond the aim in view of which that derogation was included. That aim is to allow only Member States the opportunity of restricting admission of foreign nationals to certain positions in the public service, which presume on the part of those occupying them the existence of a special relationship of allegiance to the State and reciprocity of rights and duties which form the foundation of the bond of nationality. Article 45(4) TFEU cannot, conversely, have the effect of disentitling a worker, once admitted into the public service of a Member State, to the application of the provisions contained in Article 45(1) to (3) TFEU (paragraph 34 and 35).

2386 *Bechtel* para 39.

2387 Ibid. para 42.

2388 Ibid. para 43. Since it makes it possible to *reduce the taxable income* and *the rate applicable to that income*. It follows from this that tax deductions come within the definition of tax advantage, while tax credits fall outside this definition, since the latter do not reduce the taxable income, nor affect the tax rate applicable to that income. It should be borne in mind that it refers to tax rate, rather than effective tax rate. See also C-480/17 *Montag* ECLI:EU:C:2018:987 (CJEU) para 23.

2389 *Bechtel* para 44.

As regards the infringement of the free movement of workers, the Court ruled that domestic legislation, such as that at issue, which makes the deduction of expenses subject to the condition that they must not have a direct economic link with exempt income constituted a restriction.[2390] While the Court admitted that it is true that this condition relating to the absence of a direct economic link with the exempt income may be applied not only in cross-border situations, but also in purely domestic situations, it found that the condition may have a greater impact on resident taxpayers receiving wages in a Member State other than that of their residence, which are exempt in their Member State of residence.[2391] Hence, suchlike disadvantageous treatment is liable to dissuade resident workers from seeking, accepting or remaining in employment in a foreign Member State.[2392]

As regards the ground of preserving the cohesion of the national tax system, the Court reiterated that a direct link ought to be established between the tax advantage concerned and the offsetting of that advantage by a particular tax levy, with the direct nature of that link to be examined in the light of the objective pursued by the legislation at issue.[2393] With respect to the domestic legislation at issue, the Court found no direct link between the method of exemption with maintenance of progressivity, by which the State of residence (Germany) forgoes taxing income received in another Member State (France), and the refusal to take into account contributions which have a direct link with the exempt income.[2394] Furthermore, the effectiveness of the progressivity of the income tax in Germany, through the exemption with maintenance of progressivity, was not made conditional on the consideration given to the personal and family circumstances of the taxpayer limited to expenses related to income taxed in that Member State.[2395] Moreover, as Germany agreed that income received in France is only taxed in that Member State, and thus waiving her taxing right, it cannot argue that the disadvantage due to the refusal of deduction is counterbalanced by the fact that it is not taxed in Germany, as such an argument would in fact amount to undermining the allocation of taxing rights as freely agreed in the tax treaty.[2396] The refusal to grant the resident taxpayer the tax advantages arising from the fact that her personal and family circumstances are taken into account in

2390 Ibid. para 51.
2391 Ibid. para 45-48.
2392 Ibid. para 50.
2393 ibid. para 75 referring to, *inter alia, Kohll en Kohll-Schlesser* para 60.
2394 *Bechtel* para 77.
2395 By analogy *De Groot* para 109.
2396 *Bechtel* para 78.

the form of deduction of additional pension and health insurance contributions can, hence, not be justified.[2397]

> **General Rule Arising from *Bechtel*-case:**
> The freedom of movement of workers precludes domestic legislation under which a taxpayer residing in that Member State and working for the public administration of another Member State may not deduct from the income tax basis of assessment in her residence state the pension insurance contributions deducted from her wages in the Member State of employment, in contrast to comparable contributions paid to the social security fund of her Member State of residence, where, under the tax treaty between the two Member States, the wages must not be taxed in the worker's Member State of residence and merely increase the tax rate to be applied to other income (exemption with maintenance of progressivity).

8.4.5.C Montag

In one of the most recent cases in the sphere of the tax treatment of cross-border pensions, the Court assessed the denial for non-residents of the deductibility, as *Sonderausgaben*, of contributions to an occupational pension scheme and to a private pension scheme, in the light of the freedom of establishment. It is of particular interest as the Court applied her doctrine of expenses directly linked to an income-generating activity, while introducing a novelty, i.e. pro-rata parte approach.

The applicant in this case, Mr Montag, a German national, was resident in Belgium where he worked as a lawyer in an international law firm as an equity partner, and held shares in that partnership.[2398] Although he earned most of his income in Germany, Mr Montag

2397 Ibid. para 79. In response to the CJEU's judgment in the *Bechtel* case, the German Ministry of Finance (*Bundesministerium der Finanzen*) issued a *BMF-schreiben*, see BMF, *Sonderausgabenabzug für Sozialversicherungsbeiträge im Ausland tätiger und in Deutschland wohnender Arbeitnehmer; Unionsrechtswidrigkeit des Abzugsverbotes nach § 10 Absatz 2 Satz 1 Nummer 1 ES IV C 3 - S 2221/14/10005:003* (11 December 2017) Pending an amendment of the legislation governing the denial of *Sonderausgaben* for pension expenses in accordance with § 10 paragraph 2 sentence 1 number 1 EStG, the document allowed, under certain conditions, pension contributions paid abroad to be deducted as *Sonderausgaben*. Accordingly, the text of § 10 paragraph 2 sentence 1 number 1 EStG has been revisited. It now stipulates that, irrespective of the issue whether the contributions are directly economically linked to tax-free income, such contributions are deductible provided that: they have a direct economic link with income from employment in a Member State of the European Union or a State party to the Agreement on the European Economic Area; this income is tax-exempt in Germany under a convention for the avoidance of double taxation, and the State of employment does not allow any tax relief of pension contributions as part of the taxation of this income. With this approach, Germany interprets the judgment of the CJEU in the *Bechtel* case in a correct and consistent manner, and does not offer the taxpayer a more generous approach than required by the CJEU.

2398 C-480/17 *Montag* ECLI:EU:C:2018:987 (CJEU) para 8-9.

earned sufficient income, in Belgium, for his personal situation to be taken into account there.[2399] Furthermore, he was registered as 'European lawyer' with the Brussels Bar under the professional title of 'Rechtsanwalt (Cologne) established in Brussels'.[2400] However, in order to practise in that capacity, he was required to be registered with the *Rechtsanwaltkammer Köln* (Cologne Bar Association, Germany)[2401] and, as such, it was compulsory for him to be a member of the *Versorgungswerk der Rechtsanwälte Nordrhein-Westfalen* (The North Rhine-Westphalia Lawyers' Pension Scheme, Germany, 'the lawyers' pension institution'), constituting a pension scheme under the *Berufsständische Versorgung*. Pursuant to German legislation on the *gesetzlichen Rentenversicherung*, employed and self-employed members of an occupational pension scheme are exempt from the obligation of membership of the German statutory pension scheme. This exemption follows if the self-employed person is member, pursuant to a legal obligation, of a so-called *berufsständischen Kammer*. Mr Montag paid pension contributions to the *Versorgungswerk der Rechtsanwälte Nordrhein-Westfalen* of which part were compulsory contributions and part voluntary contributions. Furthermore, he paid contributions into a German private pension scheme.[2402] While being fully-liable to tax in Belgium, the payments to the *Versorgungswerk* were not deductible in Belgium, although mandatory payments to the Belgian statutory social security system were deductible.[2403] The key question in this case was whether the freedom of establishment must be interpreted as precluding legislation of a Member State, under which a non-resident taxable person, subject, in that Member State, to income tax in the framework of limited tax liability, cannot deduct the amount of compulsory and additional contributions paid into an occupational pension scheme or the amount of contributions paid into a private pension scheme, whereas a resident taxable person, subject to income tax in the framework of unlimited tax liability, can deduct such contributions from the income tax basis of assessment to the extent laid down by national law. It thus concerned a differential tax treatment of resident and non-resident taxpayers, as regards the deductibility of pension contributions.

The Court found that as the deduction of pension contributions allows a taxable person to reduce the amount of taxable income, this constitutes a tax advantage, which non-residents subject to limited tax liability is denied.[2404] As this tax treatment of non-residents is less advantageous, it is capable of rendering the establishment of a resident taxable person in

2399 Ibid. para 17.
2400 Ibid. para 10.
2401 Pursuant to recital 12 and Article 3(1) and (2) of Directive 98/5/EC of the European Parliament and of the Council of 16 February 1998 to facilitate practice of the profession of lawyer on a permanent basis in a Member State other than that in which the qualification was obtained [1998] OJ L 77.
2402 C-480/17 *Montag* ECLI:EU:C:2018:987 (CJEU) para 11.
2403 Ibid. para 12.
2404 Ibid. para 23-24.

a foreign Member State less attractive and, accordingly, amounts to a restriction in principle, which is prohibited by the Treaty provisions on the freedom of establishment.[2405] Such a restriction is merely permissible if it relates to situations which are not objectively comparable or if it is justified by an overriding reason in the public interest.[2406]

The CJEU then turned to assessing whether it constituted a comparable situation.[2407] The fact that a Member State does not grant to a non-resident certain tax benefits which it grants to a resident is not, as a rule, discriminatory, given the objective differences between the situations of residents and of non-residents.[2408] The court pointed out that this is different where the non-resident receives no significant income in his residence State and obtains the greater part of his taxable income from an activity performed in the other Member State concerned, and consequently the residence State is not in a position to grant him the benefits that result from taking into account his personal and family circumstances.[2409] In addition, the Court considered that as regards expenses directly linked to an activity which has generated taxable income in a Member State, residents of that State and non-residents are in a comparable situation.[2410] As regards Mr Montag's case, the Court found that, although he earned most of his income in Germany, he had earned sufficient income in Belgium, for his personal and family circumstances to be taken into account there.[2411] Hence, as regards the deduction of pension contributions in Germany, a non-resident and a resident would be in comparable situation only if, irrespective of its characterization under national law as *Sonderausgaben*, the contributions could be treated as expenses directly linked to an activity which had generated taxable income in Germany.[2412]

With respect to the compulsory pension contributions paid to the *Berufsständischen Versorgungswerk*, the CJEU considered that it was compulsory for Mr Montag to be a

2405 Ibid. para 25.

2406 Ibid. para 26 and C-48/13 *Nordea Bank Danmark* ECLI:EU:C:2014:2087 (CJEU) para 23.

2407 The Court observed that it is settled case-law that, in relation to direct taxes, the situations of residents and non-residents within a State are not, as a rule, comparable, since the income received in the territory of a Member State by a non-resident is in most cases only a part of his total income, which is concentrated at his place of residence, and because a non-resident's personal ability to pay tax, determined by reference to his aggregate income and his personal and family circumstances, is easier to assess at the place where his personal and financial interests are centered, which in general is the place where he is habitually resident (paragraph 27).

2408 C-480/17 *Montag* ECLI:EU:C:2018:987 (CJEU) para 28.

2409 Ibid. para 29 referring to C-279/93 *Schumacker* ECLI:EU:C:1995:31 (CJEU) para 36; ECLI:EU:C:2008:566 *Renneberg* C-527/06 (CJEU) para 61 and C-9/14 *Kieback* ECLI:EU:C:2015:406 (CJEU) para 25.

2410 C-480/17 *Montag* ECLI:EU:C:2018:987 (CJEU) para 30 referring to C-450/09 *Schröder* ECLI:EU:C:2011:198 (CJEU) para 40 and C-559/13 *Grünewald* ECLI:EU:C:2015:109 (CJEU) para 29.

2411 C-480/17 *Montag* ECLI:EU:C:2018:987 (CJEU) para 31.

2412 Ibid. para 32 and *Grünewald* para 31.

member of that institution and was required to pay these contributions due to his registration with the Cologne Bar Association.[2413] This registration, in turn, was compulsory in order to be able to practice his profession of *Rechtsanwalt*, both in Germany, and, in accordance with Article 3 of Directive 98/5, in Belgium.[2414] The Court thus found that these compulsory contributions were made because registration with the bar association was necessary in order to practice the activity which generated the taxable income. The contributions must be regarded as having been generated by that activity and therefore as being necessary in order to carry it out.[2415] The Court has consistently held that expenses occasioned by the activity which generated taxable income are directly linked to that activity and are accordingly necessary in order to carry it out.[2416]

The fact that these compulsory pension contributions were directly linked to the income-generating activity, could not be altered by the fact that there was a possibility of being exempted, under certain conditions, from compulsory membership of that institution, which Mr Montag did not seek to do.[2417] The Court considered, firstly, that the fact that Mr Montag should have undertaken given steps in order to avoid the payment of contributions to the pension institution tends rather to show that the activity of a lawyer in question ordinarily generates that type of expense.[2418] Secondly, the fact that he may have been able to prevent these expenses cannot alter the expenses' characterisation, i.e. the existence of a direct link does not mean that an expense must be unavoidable.[2419] Moreover, the existence of a direct link results from the fact that the expense is inextricably linked to the income-generating activity.[2420] In the present case, the pension contributions were inextricably linked to the income-generating activity, as the payment of these contributions was necessary on account of the membership of the bar association, which, in turn, was necessary to perform the income-generating activity.

Furthermore, the court rejected the point that the pension contributions are not principally concerned with practicing as a lawyer in Germany, but with the acquisition of rights for

2413 C-480/17 *Montag* ECLI:EU:C:2018:987 (CJEU) para 35.

2414 Ibid. para 36.

2415 Ibid. para 37.

2416 Ibid. para 33; C-234/01 *Gerritse* ECLI:EU:C:2003:340 (CJEU) para 9 and 27; C-345/04 *Centro Equestre da Lezíria Grande* ECLI:EU:C:2007:96 (CJEU) para 25 and *Grünewald* para 30.

2417 C-480/17 *Montag* ECLI:EU:C:2018:987 (CJEU) para 38-39.

2418 Ibid. para 40.

2419 Ibid. para 41. See also C-346/04 *Conijn* ECLI:EU:C:2006:445 (CJEU) para 22 in which it was held that there was a direct link in respect of costs involved in obtaining tax advice for the purpose of preparing a tax return, since the duty to file such a tax return results from the fact of receiving income in the Member State in question.

2420 C-480/17 *Montag* ECLI:EU:C:2018:987 (CJEU) para 42 referring to *Schröder* para 43 and *Grünewald* para 36.

the purpose of ensuring means of subsistence in old-age, which would prove that they are related to the personal and family circumstances of the taxable person.[2421] The Court held that this does not alter their characterization as expenses which are directly related to the income at issue in so far as, objectively speaking, the expenses are necessary in order to obtain that income.

In light of the above, the Court found that the compulsory contributions were directly linked to the taxable income-generating activity in Germany and in Belgium, and, potentially, in other Member States.[2422] However, in her doctrine of expenses directly linked to an income-generating activity, the Court introduced a novelty, by considering that as regards the compulsory contributions, the situation of a non-resident taxpayer, such as Mr Montag, should be considered comparable to that of a resident taxpayer as regards the share of the contributions paid which corresponds, proportionally, to the share that the taxable income in Germany represents in the total income generated by the activity in question (i.e. 54%).[2423] Under this proportional approach, the comparability of the situation of a non-resident with a resident is therefore limited proportionally.[2424] Concludingly, the difference in treatment cannot legitimately be relied upon in the case of a restriction, in the form of denying the deduction of compulsory pension contributions, in due proportion to the share of the income taxable in Germany.[2425]

As regards the voluntary contributions the Court observed that these were based on a free decision of Mr Montag, to increase his pension entitlement to the level of the maximal amount allowed for contributions.[2426] However, although the expenses arose from the bar association's membership they do not necessarily result from that membership, i.e. they are not necessary in order to practice as a lawyer in Germany or to generate taxable income in Germany.[2427] Hence, a non-resident taxable person, such as Mr Montag was not in a situation comparable to that of a resident taxable person.[2428] The Court pointed out that

2421 C-480/17 *Montag* ECLI:EU:C:2018:987 (CJEU) para 43. The difference with the *Bechtel* case – concerning the refusal to grant a resident taxpayer the advantages arising from his or her personal and family circumstances in the form of deductions of additional pension and health insurance contributions – can be found in the fact that in the *Bechtel* case, the issue of whether expenses in the form of pension contributions are directly linked to the activity which generated the taxable income did not need to be examined, as it was not raised.

2422 Ibid. para 45 and 47.

2423 Ibid. para 49.

2424 Cf. H Niesten and S Kramer, 'Weigering fiscale aftrek verplichte pensioenbijdragen aan niet-inwoners strijdig met EU-recht' – Maandblad BelastingBeschouwingen 371.

2425 C-480/17 *Montag* ECLI:EU:C:2018:987 (CJEU) para 50.

2426 Ibid. para 51.

2427 Ibid. para 52.

2428 Ibid. para 53.

this finding cannot be called into question by the argument that pensions paid by the *Berufsständischen Versorgungswerk* will, in future, be taxable in Germany, as an uncertain link with other future income is not relevant for ascertaining whether such a direct link exists.[2429] Apart from the uncertainty of such future taxation, the court found it suffice to state that the present case concerned the taxation of income generated in Germany by Mr Montag, and that, in order for these expenses to be deductible, they must have a direct link to the income-generating activity (not the future income).

The Court restricted the scope of assessment to the contested domestic tax legislation of the state at issue, i.e. the state of residence. This legislation was found in breach of the freedom to provide services, under the proviso that this same legislation did not preclude the taxation of the pensions paid by foreign pension providers. As regards the justification of the restriction resulting from the denial to deduct compulsory pension contributions paid to the *Berufsständischen Versorgungswerk*, in due proportion to the share of the income taxable in Germany, the Court dismissed all justification grounds put forward.[2430]

As regards these expenses, the Court found that there was no direct link with the activity of practicing as a lawyer which generated the taxable income.[2431] As holds true with regard to the voluntary contributions discussed above, an uncertain link with other income was considered not relevant in determining whether an amount paid into a private pension scheme is directly linked to the income generated in Germany by the activity of Mr Montag.[2432] Thus, as regards these contributions, the situation of a non-resident taxable person, such as Mr Montag, was not comparable to that of a resident taxable person, and accordingly, the difference in treatment of these two situations could legitimately be relied on in this case.[2433]

2429 Ibid. para 54.

2430 Ibid. para 59-62.

2431 Ibid. para 55.

2432 Ibid. para 56.

2433 Ibid. para 57-58. In response to the judgment of the CJEU in the Montag case, and pending a legislative amendment of § 50 EStG, the German Ministry of Finance published a BMF-Schreiben, see BMF, *Sonderausgabenabzug bei beschränkt Steuerpflichtigen für Pflichtbeiträge an berufsständische Versorgungseinrichtungen (§ 10 Absatz 1 Nummer 2 Buchstabe a, § 50 Absatz 1 Satz 3 EStG); EuGH-Urteil vom 6. Dezember 2018, C-480/17, „Montag" IV C 5 - S 2301/19/10004:001* (26 June 2019). In advance of an amendment of § 50, par. 1 EStG, the document establishes an approval for all taxable persons, subject to limited tax liability, who pay mandatory pension contributions into a pension arrangement in the form of a *berufständische Versorgungseinrichting*. In line with the CJEU's judgment in the Montag case, the deduction shall only apply to the proportion of compulsory contributions corresponding to the part of the income taxed in Germany - generated by the professional activity for which authorisation is required - in the total amount of domestic and foreign income, derived from the professional activity practices on the basis of the authorisation. With this concession, the German Ministry interprets the judgment of the CJEU in the Montag case in a correct and consistent manner, and does not offer the taxpayer, subject to limited

General Rules Arising from *Montag*-case:

- The freedom of establishment precludes Member State's legislation under which a non-resident taxable person, subject, in that Member State, to limited tax liability, cannot deduct the amount of compulsory contributions paid into an occupational pension scheme in due proportion to the share of the income taxable in that Member State if directly linked to the activity which generated that income, whereas a resident taxable person, subject to unlimited tax liability, can deduct such contributions to the extent laid down by national law.
- The freedom of establishment does not preclude Member State's legislation under which a non-resident taxable person, subject, in that Member State, to limited tax liability, cannot deduct the amount of additional voluntary contributions paid into an occupational pension scheme or the amount of contributions paid into a private pension scheme, whereas a resident taxable person, subject to unlimited tax liability, can deduct such contributions to the extent laid down by national law.

8.5 Comparative Findings Through the Lens of the Evaluation Framework

Where the sections above explored how the taxation of cross-border pensions is affected by EU law, i.e. exploring how EU law might alter the tax treatment of the relevant cross-border pension, the section below evaluates these findings along the (legal) lines of this research's evaluation framework. It is a sliding scale where all variations between fit and unfit can be observed. Given the division of competences as laid down in the European treaties, and, correspondingly, the (legislative) instruments – and their properties – employed in the field of EU law (positive and negative integration) emphasis will be put on the extent to which they aid in establishing inter-level coherence. This chapter answers the sub-research questions of how the taxation of cross-border pensions is governed by European law, and to what extent there is room for improvement, along the lines of the assessment framework drawn up in chapter 2. Building on this, the 'fitness' of the legal frameworks at the European level shall be assessed, focusing in particular on any deficiencies that have a (distorting) effect on the provision of effective information.

tax liability, a more generous approach than required by the CJEU. Meanwhile, § 50 EStG has already been amended, see para 1a of the provision.

8.5.1 *Inter-level Coherence*

In order to prevent discrepancies in information provision, different fields of multi-level law need to be aligned with each other, i.e. national (Netherlands and Germany); European, and international.[2434] For the purpose and context of the present research, 'coherence' is termed as 'the situation in which all the levels of the regulatory frameworks are logical and consistent, achieving a harmonious connection of these parts, so that the whole 'hangs together'.[2435] This underlines the relevance of certain properties of regulatory frameworks, and its consequences, for information provision, and corresponding implications. A challenge for the provision of effective cross-border pension information is the diversity – and poor coordination – of differentiates pension vehicles, and taxes. From this point of view, in order to uphold the information's effectiveness, it requires a certain degree of coherence among these levels of legislation. At lower levels, this may involve systematic scrutiny of coherence with higher-level regulations and with treaty or other international obligations. A higher degree of coherence also helps to ensure the effectiveness of information in terms of the four principles, in that more coherence between low and higher levels of legislation aids ensuring the information's effectiveness. For instance, in a more coherent (logically and consistent ordered) multi-level legal systems, it is far easier to uphold the information's correctness and trustworthiness, as in such a system, there is less susceptibility to error.

8.5.1.A The Role of the CJEU's Settled-case Law in Achieving Inter-level Coherence

The general rules that follow from each of the CJEU's cases, discussed in section 8.4, have been outlined in the text boxes under each of the judgments. These general rules allow for some concluding remarks as regards the body of settled case-law, as well as the conformity of domestic tax rules with EU law, in terms of inter-level coherence. In addition, these rules serve as a legal framework which must be taken into account when designing tax regulations in conformity with EU law.[2436] Some observations can be made, which will be discussed in further detail below.

8.5.1.A.I *The CJEU's Isolated Approach*

It is evident from the *Wielockx* case that the CJEU does not base its assessment of the tax legislation of one country on the tax treatment of retirement benefits in another country. Under this 'isolated approach', the issue of discrimination is assessed solely on the basis of

2434 See also OECD, 'Recommendation of the Council of the OECD on Regulatory Policy and Governance' 14.
2435 Oxford Dictionaries.
2436 Cf. Wellisch and others, 96.

the rules and regulations of the country at issue.[2437] Whether and how the future country of migration subjects pension benefits to tax is not taken into account when assessing the regulations in the country of departure. This 'isolated approach' follows from the *ex tunc*-effect of the judgements and the case-by-case approach adopted by the CJEU, as already noted in section 8.1, hindering the inter-level coherence. Following this line of reasoning, the subsequent taxation of contributions in the country of departure, solely affecting taxpayers moving away, would be discriminatory, in spite of the fact that the pension benefits would remain tax-free in the country of migration. The CJEU has reaffirmed this isolated approach in the *Danner* case, by ruling that it runs counter to the freedom to provide services, when domestic tax legislation restricts or disallows the deduction of contributions to voluntary pension schemes paid to foreign pension providers, while allowing the deduction of such contributions when they are paid to domestic institutions, provided that this legislation does not at the same time preclude taxation of the pensions paid by the foreign pension providers.[2438] Also in this case, the Court restricted the scope of assessment to the contested domestic tax legislation of the state at issue, i.e. the state or residence. This legislation was found in breach of the freedom to provide services, under the proviso that this same legislation did not preclude the taxation of the pension benefits paid by foreign pension providers.

It is to be noted that the CJEU did not move away, or depart from, this isolated approach in the *Schempp* case.[2439] As part of the issue raised in this case, the CJEU assessed the tax legislation of another Member State (Austria) while German domestic legislation was put under scrutiny. The issue concerned the non-application of the German deduction of *Sonderausgaben* to maintenance payments, which were not subject to tax in Austria. The German deduction was, pursuant to domestic tax legislation, subject to the condition that these maintenance payments should be subject to tax, irrespective of in which state these payments would be taxed. Hence, the tax legislation governing these payments in the other State had to be involved in the assessment. However, unlike the *Sonderausgaben* deduction for maintenance benefits, the tax facilities for pension contributions are not explicitly (nor implicitly) made dependent on the fact that the pension benefits derived from them are taxed in any country when they are received.[2440]

2437 Cf. Ibid. 80.

2438 *Danner*.

2439 *Schempp*. Cf. Wellisch and others, 93-94.

2440 As, for instance, in *Wielockx*.

8.5.1.A.II Equivalent Fiscal Facilitation of Pension Contributions Paid to Either Domestic or Foreign Pension Schemes

Firstly, it becomes evident that if a Member State fiscally facilitates pension contributions paid into domestic pension schemes, it must also, on the same footing, facilitate contributions paid to pension schemes established in other EU countries. Restricting the facilitation to domestic institutions, as well as the requirement for a foreign EU institution to have an establishment in the national territory, runs counter to the freedom to provide services, the free movement of workers, or even the freedom of establishment. These infringements cannot be justified by the need to preserve the coherence of the domestic tax system, where the residence state has waived his taxing right, irrespective of the state where the contributions have been deducted, and the cohesion of a tax system has thus shifted to Treaty level.[2441] The court considered that fiscal cohesion has not therefore been established in relation to one and the same person by a strict correlation between the deductibility of contributions and the taxation of pensions but is shifted to another level, that of the reciprocity of the rules applicable in the Contracting States.

8.5.1.A.III Taxing Fiscally Facilitated Retirement Capital Transferred Abroad

If retirement capital accrued from facilitated contributions is taxable when transferred from a pension institution established in a particular EU state to a pension institution established in another EU state, while the transfer between two institutions established in that EU state does not constitute a taxable transaction, this constitutes an infringement of the Treaty Freedoms.[2442] Such an infringement cannot be justified by the need to preserve the cohesion of the national tax system, as other measures are capable of fulfilling the objective of ensuring payment of that tax that are less prejudicial to the Treaty Freedoms.[2443]

8.5.1.A.IV Taxing Retirement Capital Upon Emigration

If the retirement capital is subject to tax when the taxable person relocates his residence abroad, while the pension capital would not be subject to taxation when the person concerned would remain a resident of the country of departure, this constitutes an infringement of the freedom of persons, the free movement of workers and the freedom of establishment.[2444] Deferral of repayment upon migration to another EU Member State shall be granted automatically, rather than upon request of the taxable person.[2445] The taxable person's leaving a state (emigration) may not be treated adversely compared to a taxable person maintaining his residence in that same state. It is unlikely that this

2441 Ibid., para 24.
2442 *Commission vs. Belgium II.*
2443 By analogy with *Wielockx; Danner* and *Skandia*. Cf.Wellisch and others, 96.
2444 *Commission vs. Belgium II.*
2445 *Lasteyrie du Saillant.*

infringement can be justified by the need to preserve the cohesion of the national tax system, if the state of departure (former residence state) has relinquished his taxing rights by concluding a tax treaty.[2446]

8.5.1.A.V *Taxing Retirement Capital upon Emigration*

The case of migration mirrors the foregoing case of emigration. As holds true with regard to the latter, the case of migration may not be treated less favourably in terms of taxation compared to an internal situation.[2447] Such a detrimental treatment may run counter to the European freedoms of movement. It follows that if a resident's pension benefits, derived from pension contributions paid out of taxed income, are not subject to tax, this also must apply to a 'incoming' pensioner, whose pension contributions have been paid out of income subject to tax in another EU Member State.

8.5.1.A.VI *Restricting the Scope of Tax Advantages to Fully-liable Resident Taxpayers: Comparable Situations?*

The CJEU has repeatedly held that direct taxation does not as such fall within the purview of the Community, but falls under the exclusive competence of the Member States.[2448] However, Member States must exercise their taxing powers consistently with Community law. Furthermore, Member States are free to determine the connecting factors for the allocation of fiscal jurisdiction in tax treaties (e.g. residence), but this allocation does not allow them to apply measures contrary to the freedoms of movement.[2449] In principle, Member States are thus free to connect different fiscal consequences to either limited tax liability or unlimited tax liability.[2450] Thus, the fact that a Member State does not grant to a non-resident certain tax benefits which it grants to a resident is not, as a rule, discriminatory, given the objective differences between the situations of residents and of non-residents.[2451] As a general rule, the CJEU holds that national legislation which places some of its nationals at a disadvantage simply because they have exercised their freedom to move and to reside in another Member State would give rise to inequality of treatment, contrary to the principles which underpin the status of citizen of the Union, that is, the guarantee of the same treatment in law in the exercise of the citizen's freedom to move.[2452]

2446 By analogy with *Wielockx*; *Danner*. Cf.Wellisch and others, 97.

2447 Cf.Wellisch and others, 97.

2448 See C-279/93 *Schumacker* ECLI:EU:C:1995:31 (CJEU) para 21; *Wielockx* para 16; *Safir* para 21; *De Groot* para 75 and *Schempp* para 19.

2449 See, for instance, *Bechtel* para 66.

2450 See *Schröder* and *Grünewald*.

2451 See for instance C-480/17 *Montag* ECLI:EU:C:2018:987 (CJEU) para 28.

2452 *Turpeinen* para 22. See also *Pusa* para 20 *and D'Hoop* para 34-36.

Distinguishing between nationals (fully liable to tax) who continue to reside in the national territory and those who have established their residence in another Member State (limited liable to tax), and treating the latter unfavourably simply as a result of having exercised their right to freedom of movement, constitutes unduly (indirect) discrimination.[2453] A provision of national law must be regarded as indirectly discriminatory if it is intrinsically liable to affect migrant workers more than national workers and if there is a consequent risk that it will place the former at a particular disadvantage.[2454] Making the granting of a tax advantage subject to the condition of full liability for tax, may constitute indirect discrimination contrary to the free movement of workers.

It has become evident, that restricting the fiscal facilitation of pension contributions (e.g. deductibility) to residents, subject to unlimited tax liability, and thus denying non-residents, subject to limited tax liability, this tax advantage, may contravene the Treaty Freedoms.[2455] However, in order to find that the contested legal provision constitutes an unduly discrimination, prohibited under the Treaty Freedoms, the non-resident taxable person must be in a comparable situation as a resident person. However, non-resident taxable person do find themselves in a comparable situations as resident taxable persons, where the non-resident receives no significant income in the State of his residence and obtains the greater part of his taxable income from an activity performed in the other Member State concerned, and consequently the Member State of residence is not in a position to grant him the benefits that result from taking into account his personal and family circumstances.[2456] Moreover, the Court has held, in relation to expenses directly linked to an activity which has generated taxable income in a Member State, that residents of that State and non-residents are in a comparable situation.[2457] However, in the *Montag* case, the CJEU introduced a novelty in her doctrine of expenses directly linked to an income-generating activity, by considering that as regards compulsory pension contributions, the situation of a non-resident taxpayer, should be considered comparable to that of a resident taxpayer as regards the proportion of the contributions paid in that Member State, which corresponds, proportionally, to the proportion that the taxable income in that Member State represents in the total income generated by the activity in question.[2458]

2453 *Turpeinen* para 24.

2454 *Meints* para 45 and *Commission vs France* para 38.

2455 As regards the freedom of establishment: C-480/17 *Montag* ECLI:EU:C:2018:987 (CJEU).

2456 See ibid. para 29 where reference is made to C-279/93 *Schumacker* ECLI:EU:C:1995:31 (CJEU) para 36; ECLI:EU:C:2008:566 *Renneberg* C-527/06 (ECJ) para 61; *Kieback* para 25 and *Grünewald* para 27.

2457 C-480/17 *Montag* ECLI:EU:C:2018:987 (CJEU) para 30 where reference is made to Schröder para 40 and case-law cited and *Grünewald* para 29.

2458 C-480/17 *Montag* ECLI:EU:C:2018:987 (CJEU) para 49.

8.5.1.B The EC's Role in Achieving Inter-level Coherence

The instrument of 'positive integration' takes a central role in achieving inter-level coherence as well. This has extensively been dealt with in section 8.3. In the field of positive integration, the European Commission has taken several steps in order to (better) 'align' the Member States' national tax systems and/or to render these systems (more) compatible with primary and/or secondary European law.[2459] As the 2001 communication has dealt most extensively with measures of positive integration on the sphere of the tax treatment of cross-border pensions, this document will be touched upon thoroughly below. It is remarkably to see that since then, the Commission has taken no considerable steps in the sphere of positive integration pertaining to the tax treatment of cross-border pensions.

In releasing the 2001 Communication, the Commission departed from an earlier approach, issuing a non-binding document, and not seeking to adapt Member States' tax systems by means of a Directive Proposal or Recommendation.[2460] By drawing on an official statement of her position on the issue concerned, the Commission shaped the development of the coordination through a 'soft law-approach', seemingly to overcome Member States' fears of too much integration and the requirement of unanimity. However, the 2001 communication was a significant advance on the Commission's previous work in the domain of the taxation of international (occupational) pensions, as no progress was made on tax issues, i.e. fitting together four tax treatments (contributions, the fund itself, withholding taxes on pension payments, and the taxation of pension benefits).[2461] The globalization of the economy have exacerbated these tax issues.[2462]

The Commission's response in the 2001 Communication was based on the same principles established in prior Communications:

- striving for coordination of tax systems, rather than harmonization;
- adhering the principle of non-discrimination and the Treaty Freedoms; and
- safeguarding the states' tax revenues.

The Commission's approach towards coordinating measures was based on the following actions.

2459 For an extensive overview of these initiatives in the sphere of positive integration see Kofler, 'Ist der Spuk des Europäischen Steuerrechts bald vorbei?' 7.

2460 Prats, 22.

2461 Cf. JF Avery Jones, 'A Framework for Evaluating the Commission's Tax Proposals for Occupational Pensions in the European Union' ibid 27.

2462 Cf. Bobbett and Avery Jones, 9.

Supporting the CJEU on the (Extensive) Interpretation of Non-discrimination Principle and the Treaty Freedoms (i.e. Negative Integration)

In her 2001-Communication, the Commission held up the CJEU's position, and concluded that any discriminatory provision should be eliminated. In doing so, the Commission envisaged to take direct action after reviewing domestic tax rules. This direct action-approach involved three actions: monitoring/ supervising domestic tax measures; ensuring compliance of domestic tax legislation pertaining to pensions with the Treaty Freedoms; and, if necessary, lodging infringement procedures against Member States which impede the exercise of the Treaty Freedoms. The Commission, thus, supported negative integration by the CJEU through infringement procedures, abolishing domestic tax rules that infringe the Treaty Freedoms. At present, there is a range of infringement cases in the sphere of the tax treatment of (cross-border) occupational pensions, see section 8.4.[2463]

Such an approach of more negative integration may have the consequence of leading to different results in different national tax systems, applied in each Member State. Besides applying, for instance, an EET or TEE-system also the level of deductibility of contributions, or degree of taxation of pension benefits varies between Member States. In other words, negative integration does not ensure a (fully) equal treatment of cross-border pensions. Furthermore, it appears that this negative approach may affect countries promoting pension saving through (full) deferred taxation, more directly. Where a Member State operating an EET-system shall be required to extend this favourable tax treatment to contributions to foreign pension schemes as well, a State applying a TEE-system may tax contributions to foreign pension schemes (raising the state's tax revenue), in accordance with EU law. As regards the taxation of retirement income during the pay-out phase, EU law requires that an exemption of pension income will have to be extended to pension income derived from a foreign pension scheme in order to ensure a non-restrictive result, possibly requiring the state of residence to refrain from taking measures to avoid potential double non-taxation.

In endorse Prats' assertion that these consequences are the result of the narrow approach of the compatibility of domestic tax advantages with EU law, prompting Member States to extend domestic tax advantages to comparable cross-border situations.[2464] Furthermore, this approach of negative integration may urge Member States to revisit their tax policies favouring a privileged tax treatment of contributions in order to prevent incompatibility

2463 *Commission vs. Belgium I; Commission vs. Belgium II; Commission vs. Denmark.*

2464 Prats, 23. The CJEU delineates a 'fiscal advantage' as allowing a taxable person to reduce the amount of taxable income and the rate applicable to that income. See, *inter alia*, C-480/17 *Montag* ECLI:EU:C:2018:987 (CJEU) para 23; *Bechtel* para 43 and *Kohll en Kohll-Schlesser* para 39. This term may cover a wide range of tax measures, directly or indirectly, reducing the taxable person's taxable income.

of EU law. Member States may, rather, be inclined to switch to TEE-systems.[2465] Hence, the single (binding) measure of coordination may lead to inconsistencies with the Commission's own tax policy, favouring the broader acceptance of the EET-principle.[2466]

No Explicit (General) Measures of Positive Integration

In her 2001 communication the Commissions refrained from drawing up more general measures of positive integration pertaining to the tax treatment of cross-border pensions. The commission pointed out that it does not envisage proposing legislative measures to harmonise Member States' pension taxation systems.[2467] The commission, rather, would welcome the broader acceptance of the EET-principle, as the alignment of Member States' tax systems would help reduce mismatches, leading to double (non-)taxation. The Commission sees the adoption of the EET-principle as supporting a significant alignment of the Member States' tax systems, both from a theoretical, tax policy and practical point of view.

In doing so, the Commission moves away from her approach in previous reports and Communications, in which she plead for coordinating measures of a general and positive nature, which would help structuring the different national tax systems around a coherent pension scheme that should be assigned binding force. However, the Commission did emphasize that a broader acceptance of the EET-principle among Member States would not provide a complete solution, as even among EET-States significant differences under the second pillar in the levels of deductibility of contributions are discernible.[2468] As Avery Jones asserts, doing nothing would in some situations lead to the correct result (TEE), while following the Commission's approach would, firstly, create a problem in some situations (EEE) and then solve it by subjecting to tax the part of the pension income derived from foreign contributions (resulting in EET) differently compared to the remainder of the pension income derived from domestic contributions, preceding and following the period during which the person was working in the other state (TEE).[2469]

2465 See, for instance, MJGAM Weerepas, 'Taxation of pensions in Europe: a summary of the report of the Committee on International Pensions' 3 EC Tax Review 172 ff.

2466 Prats, 23.

2467 European Commission, 'The elimination of tax obstacles to the cross-border provision of occupational pensions,' 19.

2468 Ibid. 19.

2469 Avery Jones, 29. Avery Jones proposed an alternative approach, in that the tax treatment of the pension should be adapted, leaving the tax treatment of the contributions unaltered. This would have the advantage that states can continue the existing treatment of pension contributions, and change the treatment of pensions only when it is necessary to ensure consistency. Since a state that taxes contributions to a domestic fund will not exempt contributions to a foreign fund there is no difference between the Commission's and the alternative approache where domestic contributions are taxed; the difference arises only where domestic contributions are exempt. The author pointed to the equivalence of EET and TEE, which is important in

This would call for a split tax treatment of the pension. The foregoing implies that the Commission should not have merely stated that a different tax treatment of domestic and foreign contributions constitutes an unlawful discrimination, leaving the tax treatment of pension as such aside. As has become apparent from the above, it is certain that there is no complete solution to the problem allowing both contributions and pension benefits to be treated equally, irrespective of whether they are foreign or domestic.

These encountered differences among the systems in different Member States, also reflect their structure and their relative importance at the pension level. Hence, the Commission refrained from proposing legislative measures to harmonise the national tax systems. One of the arguments brought forward by the Commission underpinning her position, was that completely uniform rules for supplementary pensions will not be easy to achieve while the relative reliance on statutory social security and occupational pension schemes varies significantly from one Member State to another. In the light of the 2001 Communication, I assume that the Commission intended to point out that the reliance on occupational pensions may be higher in some state, and the issue may, hence, be more or less urgent. While the argument seems valid from a content point of view[2470], it is not convincing as regards the relation with the decision not to propose coordinating measures on a more general level. Whilst the replacement rates of occupational pensions may vary between States, this does not diminish the relevance of the tax treatment issues in question.

However, this assertion can hardly be considered of a (general) coordinating nature dealing with issues arising from the application of divergent tax systems in different Member States, let alone of a sufficient coordinating nature. Furthermore, the assertion is not complemented with additional specific measures aimed at underpinning this recommendation, and it is left to the Member States to, whether or not, follow the Commission's approach, notwithstanding that it may lead to situations contravening the Treaty Freedoms. A more coordinated approach would require the structuring of the

evaluating this argument. Avery Jones asserted that if it is accepted that they are equivalent, it must follow that so long as consistency is ensured between the tax treatment of contributions and pensions so that they are either EET or TEE, there is no discrimination even though the treatment of contribution or pension may be different from that used domestically. This proposed alternative approach thus builds on the assumption that one can have different treatment of domestic and foreign contributions or pensions without this being discriminatory. In comparing, and building on the three situations of mobile taxable persons as set out in the introduction of this chapter, and the Commission's and the proposed alternative approach, the author explores any further legislative changes necessary to make the tax treatment consistent with either EET or TEE following an alteration to the tax treatment of (foreign) contributions to make it the same as domestic contributions. However, the desirability of both approaches should be assessed in the light of the actual treatment of cross-border pensions by all EU Member States, in order to determine the frequency with which the tax issues actually arise.

2470 OECD, 'OECD Pensions at a Glance 2017' 108-109.

Member States' deviating tax systems along the lines of a coherence that would adhere to EU law, and Member States' and individual's interests.[2471]

Harmonising vs. Coordination: Beyond a Semantic Discussion

The arguments put forward by the Commission substantiate why she abstained from formulating general measures, aimed at establishing completely uniform, or harmonized rules. The 2001 communication is void of arguments why more general measures of a coordinating measure are lacking. It is assumed that coordination reflects a lower degree of alignment of taxes compared to harmonization.[2472] It, therefore, seems not required to draw up uniform rules in order to support positive integration but; rather; to establish strategies in line with policy objectives and measures devoted to enforce them.[2473] In order to achieve coherent national pension tax systems, from an EU law point of view, and consistent with each other, this would require the development of certain points of agreement in respect of the structure of tax advantages. Further in developing these points, the Commission's principles must be taken into consideration: striving for coordination of tax systems; rather than harmonization, adhering the principle of non-discrimination and the Treaty Freedoms, and safeguarding the states' tax revenues. However, as regards the former, the relevant point in discussion is ascertaining the scope of coordination.[2474] To this end, the Commission must be allowed a certain margin of discretion, given the circumstances and factors potentially having an effect on the outcome.[2475] Yet, it remains difficult to see that the Commission omitted to establish more general measures of coordination rather than the mere assertion that the EET-principle should be adhered to more broadly, since not being able to draw up completely uniform rules does not preclude recommendations of a more general character. The commission could have explored a whole range of other possibilities, provided that it would have been willing to support the positive integration-approach more broadly. For instance, in order to align the national tax systems more with the EET-principle, the proposed measures should have focussed more on the implementation thereof in the tax systems of the Member States concerned,

2471 For instance Prats asserts that the problems arising from the establishment of different approaches to the taxation of occupational pension schemes would require the establishment of general measures that take into account (a) individual equity, in terms of the taxation of individual income, and (b) equity among states, in terms of respecting a correct attribution of income among states and a proper integration of these objectives with the EU law requirements. See Prats, 24.

2472 L Hinnekens, 'The Monti Report: the uphill task of harmonizing direct tax systems of EC Member States' 1 EC Tax Review 31 ff.

2473 Cf. Prats, 24.

2474 Coordination in the sphere of taxes is characterized by a certain level of flexibility, implying both adhering to the subsidiarity principle and the Member States' competence on the one hand and, on the other hand, the establishment in favor of the Commission of a power of decision and initiative, involving both the type of instrument to be used, the scope and content of it. See Hinnekens, 302 ff.

2475 Cf. Prats, 24.

taking account of the deviating specific rules laid down in these Member States' national tax legislation.

It follows from the above, that the 2001 Communication did not consider itself competent to determine generally applicable rules or measures, pertaining to the coordination of the Member States' pension tax systems.[2476] Although the Commission calls for a broader acceptance of the EET-principle – which is easiest for the alignment of Member States' pension tax systems from a practical point of view – the Commission does not point out what should prevail. Although the Commission point of view has been consolidated in well-established CJEU-doctrine[2477], implying that the EU institutions are neither competent to adapt the rules governing the distribution of international taxation rights, nor to coerce (the revisiting of) national tax policy pursuant to Member States' exclusive competence in the sphere of direct taxes. However, in the light of Member States exercising their exclusive competence, reference can be made to art. 94 TFEU providing the legal basis for issuing directives in order to align laws, regulation or administrative provisions of the Member States in so far as they directly affect the establishment of the functioning of the Common Market. However, it seems that the Commission, in taking a more pragmatic approach, was guided by liberalization of the occupational pensions in the European Single Market and, primarily, circumventing the unanimity requirement. The Commission's narrow approach of leaving the development of a coherent (European) approach of the national pension tax systems, and complementing tax policy instruments, to the CJEU's case-by-case interpretation, and to the Member States, lacks decisiveness.

Providing Recommendations of Specific Practical Measures Accompanying This Approach, Aimed at Solving Double (Non-)Taxation in Specific Cases.

Rather than drafting proposals of general coordination measures, the Commission thus, primarily, relied on the CJEU's negative integration accompanied by setting certain specific (unilateral and bilateral) measures aimed at resolving (part of) particular issues relating to double (non-)taxation possible resulting from the divergent tax systems. In doing so, the Commission relied on the practical experience of some (inter)national rules. On the one hand, the unilateral measures were aimed at abolishing double taxation in certain cases, by following some Member States' practice of implementing domestic legal provisions, modifying the EET-principle, in that benefits paid by foreign pension institutions to residents of an EET-state shall be exempted in so far as the contributions

2476 Ibid. 25.

2477 The CJEU has repeatedly held that direct taxation does not as such fall within the purview of the Community, but falls under the exclusive competence of the Member States. See *C-279/93 Schumacker* ECLI:EU:C:1995:31 (CJEU) para 21; *Wielockx* para 16; *Safir* para 21; *De Groot* para 75 and *Schempp* para 19.

were not tax deductible or were taxed in the other state. On the other hand, the Commission proposed a conventional bilateral solution, also aimed at resolving double taxation, by incorporating a specific clause in tax treaties. Such a clause would be aimed at guaranteeing that EET-states will accommodate their tax treatment in cases where a resident of that state receives a pension from the other state, operating a TEE-principle. Pursuant to this treaty clause, pensions (and annuities) arising one Contracting State (source state), paid to a resident of the other State may be taxed in the latter state (residence state), but the residence state shall ensure non-discrimination, by excluding from tax the same amount that would be exempt from tax in the source state if the pensioner were a resident thereof. It would seem more practical for the treaty provision to stipulate that the pension must be exempted on account of the contribution being taxed, instead of referring to what would be the pension's tax treatment in the other state.[2478] In doing, the first state would not have to assess the tax treatment of the pension in the other state, what proves to be fairly cumbersome in practice. However, under both measures proposed, the state operating the EET-system is forced to adapt the national coherence of the tax system, having negative consequences due to the adoption of the TEE-principle by the other state. It seems unlikely that (the increasing number of) states applying the EET-state are willing to do so in the light of reciprocity between states. In fact, and indirectly, TEE-states are thus favoured by the Commission and encouraged to persist do so.

As regards double (non-)taxation, the Commission proposed to include a clause in tax treaties as well, stipulating a conditional source state taxation, rather than residence state taxation (which state applies the TEE-principle). Over the course of the years, however, there has been a shift in treaty (negotiations) on agreeing a (conditional) source state taxation pertaining to pension income. However, it is difficult to see how this (time-consuming) renegotiation of treaties can be considered practical, in that it can be adopted in the short term. The goal of aligning Member States' tax systems more with the EET-principle is thus pursued not only by relying on the CJEU's negative integration, but also by practical specific measures, aimed at resolving double taxation. However, the observation should be made that these measures may be found inconsistent with some of the Commission's objectives, partly due to the Commission's practical approach, leaving aside the theoretical and tax policy side, aimed at achieving coherence at a European level.

In conclusion, *in concreto* the Commission put forward the following specific measures to support the coordination of the pension tax systems:

2478 Cf. Avery Jones, 32. The treaty provision concerned shall be extended to contributions paid to a fund in another state where the taxable person remains in his state of origin.

- supporting the negative integration-approach taken by the CJEU, rather than pursuing positive integration by means of drafting positive rules of secondary EU law, aimed at the integration of the Member States' pension tax systems;
- adopting unilateral (domestic) or bilateral rules, rather than secondary EU law;
- implicitly protecting TEE-systems instead of the EET-principle, notwithstanding that Commission put forward arguments supporting the latter (e.g. more suited to promote occupational pension schemes); and
- protecting the Member States' interests in collecting their tax revenues, without mentioning which principles or criteria apply internal or internationally.

8.6 Interim Conclusion

As has been addressed thoroughly in chapter 1 of this research, the two-dimensional notion of effective pension information articulates that the information's behavioural purpose seeks to inform mobile individuals on an aggregated level about how much pension they can expect, in order to be able to assess the adequacy of their dispersed pension, covering all their forms of pension in each of the (former) working/residence states. The aforementioned behavioural purpose contains the terms 'aggregated' (i.e. assembled at an overall/higher level) and the phrase 'covering all their forms of pension in each of the (former) working/residence states'. However, mobile individuals - who avail(ed) themselves of their European freedoms of movement - see themselves confronted with a wide range of diverging 'pensions', i.e. pension vehicles, schemes, retirement products of all sorts, arising from occupational pension systems in each of the different (former) working states, and/or residence states. This requires putting together dispersed, and deviating, elements of future retirement income, arising in each of these states. This amounts to observing, and 'translating' the intersections between different multi-level legal systems (national, EU and international/bilateral) and the interaction of poorly coordinated legal domains (pension and tax law) - which can all be interwoven in a personal mobile situation - into effective pension information.

Things become more complex as tax sovereignty, i.e. the power to issue tax legislation, lies exclusively with the Member State, pursuant to the European treaties. EU Member States exercise their sovereignty in the sphere of taxes, and it is a matter of these Member States to draw up their tax rules in line with their political preferences. Furthermore, domestic pension arrangements are primarily designed on the basis of domestic policy considerations.[2479] Nevertheless, the domestic tax systems have been increasingly affected

2479 See also paragraph 8 of the OECD commentary on Article 18 OECD MC.

by European law and the CJEU's case-law. In particular as regards the latter, a vast body of settled case-law has emerged, often lacking consistency and marked, as a general rule, by having merely an *ex tunc*-effect[2480] and being too case by case-orientated. As regards the latter, it must be noted that this is peculiar to the procedure of preliminary rulings heard by the CJEU. A more systematic approach to the tracing and testing of possible infringements of EU law in (domestic) direct tax laws would be desirable, although the European Commission has taken a more active role in this.[2481]

This was taken as a given and this chapter explored how the taxation of cross-border pensions is affected by EU law, i.e. exploring how EU law might alter the tax treatment of the relevant cross-border pension, as primary and secondary EU law emanate a normative effect in this regard.[2482] The comparative findings were presented in section 8.5, along the lines of this research's evaluation framework. In this vein, this chapter answered the sub-research questions of how the taxation of cross-border pensions is governed by European law, and to what extent there is room for improvement, along the lines of the assessment framework drawn up in chapter 2.

CJEU's Case-Law as an Instructive Field of EU Law

It is evident from the above that CJEU's case-law considerably affects the taxation of cross-border pensions, i.e. alters the tax treatment of the relevant cross-border pension, along the lines of the Treaty Freedoms and the principle of non-discrimination. This body of settled case-law, adds to complexity of ascertaining the fiscal position of mobile workers. Since the *Avoir Fiscal*-case a vast body of settled case-law has emerged, predominantly having an *ex tunc*-effect[2483] and being case by case-orientated. The general rules inferred from the case-law can be applied, by analogy, to sufficiently comparable legislation.

As regards the compatibility of national tax systems, the CJEU has repeatedly held that although direct taxation falls under the competence of the Member States, that exclusive competence must be exercised in accordance with EU law requirements.[2484] Hence, rules on direct taxation must, therefore, respect the content, scope and requirements of the

2480 See for instance N Wunderlich and L Albath, 'Der Europäische Gerichtshof und die direkten Steuern – Ein Beitrag zum Verhältnis von Gemeinschaftsrecht und national Recht' 93 DStZ 547, 552.

2481 See for instance European Commission, 'Removing cross-border tax obstacles for EU citizens'.

2482 See also paragraph I, under 1 of the Protocol to the tax treaty concluded between the Netherlands and Germany. This provision stipulates that it is understood that the law of the European Union takes precedence over the provisions of the Convention. On the interaction between EU law and international tax law see Wattel, Marres and Vermeulen, part I.

2483 See for instance Wunderlich and Albath, 552.

2484 C-279/93 *Schumacker* ECLI:EU:C:1995:31 (CJEU) para 21; *Wielockx* para 16; *Safir* para 21; *De Groot* para 75 and *Schempp* para 19.

Treaty freedoms as enshrined in the TFEU, implying not only a ban on any (overt or covert) discrimination on the grounds of nationality but also the elimination of any tax measure which may prevent or make less attractive the exercise of these freedoms by EU nationals, unless these are justified on the grounds of an accepted justification ground.[2485]

The CJEU's broad scope of application of the treaty freedoms and the restrictive interpretation of justifications necessitate the redrafting of the territorial scope of tax benefits, advantages and reliefs, compelling Member States to incorporate a European perspective. It is to be noted that European law as such does not compel to change the attributions rules as regards pension income, as laid down in the bilaterally concluded tax treaty, nor does it contain rules as to which state shall or may tax pension income. However, European law may examine whether these rules lead to an unjustified discriminatory or restrictive treatment. In doing so, the CJEU has created an effective instrument against the use of tax policy (given effect through direct taxation) making the movement of workers or the provision of services less attractive.[2486] This instructive doctrine builds on widely-accepted EU principles. The CJEU doctrine implies, in general terms, that domestic tax rules ought to accept:

- an obligation to extend the tax treatment of domestic contributions, on the same footing, to foreign pension schemes, foreign pension funds and pension income derived from foreign pension funds;
- an obligation to abolish unjustified restrictions of inbound or outbound situations having a detrimental effect on cross-border occupational pension schemes. This, hence, affects the tax treatment of pension contributions paid to a foreign pension scheme by – or in name of – a temporary (non-)resident worker;
- the seldom acceptance of justification grounds for restrictive or discriminatory treatment, e.g. preserving the fiscal cohesion of the tax system, the absence of harmonization of Member States' tax legislation, loss of tax revenues, absence of reciprocity and issues in obtaining information.

These general principles have far-reaching consequences for national tax sovereignty, as they limit Member States' freedom to organise their national tax systems in the way they see fit. The guiding principle in the CJEU's settled case-law is that non-resident taxpayers, exercising their internal market freedoms, and to the extent held comparable to resident taxpayers, may not be treated less favourably.[2487] In other words, a Member State may treat

2485 Prats, 16 and F Vanistendael, 'The role of the European Court of Justice as the supreme judge in tax cases' 3 EC Tax Review 104 ff.

2486 Cf. Prats, 20.

2487 As a general rule, the CJEU holds that resident and non-residents are, in principle, not in comparable situations. See, for instance, C-279/93 *Schumacker* ECLI:EU:C:1995:31 (CJEU) para 31. This distinction has

a cross-border situation differently to a domestic situation if this is justified by a difference in the taxpayer's situation. As has become apparent above, even non-discriminatory measures (not distinguishing between non-resident and resident taxpayers) may be incompatible with TFEU Freedoms, as a disadvantageous treatment is liable to discourage resident workers from looking for, accepting or remaining in employment in a Member State other than their Member State of residence.[2488] It could be said, that the emerging body of CJEU's case-law on prohibiting national tax measures making it less attractive to work cross-border, is the largest impact of EU law on national tax legislation.[2489]

The CJEU's cases rarely concern the implementation of devoted EU legislation as there still is no legislation in the field of the taxation of cross-border pensions. In contrary, the cases concern the evaluation of detailed, complex and unharmonized domestic tax legislation and bilateral tax treaties, in the light of EU law principles and TFEU rights of free movement. As Wattel points out, hence, these cases do not so much encompass the interpretation of 'tax' law (since the CJEU is not competent to interpret national law or bilateral tax treaties) as the cases concern more (principles of) 'general EU' law.[2490] This considerable difference in abstraction level of these general principles compared to detailed, complex national tax legislation, and the fact that the CJEU is solely competent to interpret EU law (not domestic and or bilateral tax law), renders negative integration complex and inconsistent. To put it mildly, it does not exactly assist that a third body of law is involved; bilateral tax treaties, largely adopting the principles set out in the OECD MC, and the accompanying Commentaries, and other 'soft law'-instruments (e.g. the

also been recognized in Article 65, para 1, under a FEU, dealing with acceptable limitations on the free movement of capital. The Article states, *inter alia*, that the free movement of capital shall be without prejudice to the right of Member States to apply the relevant provisions of their tax law which distinguish between taxpayer who are not in the same situation with regard to their place of residence. The principle of non-discrimination as laid down in the *Schumacker* case also applies to pensioners earning all or almost all of their income in a state in which they are not resident and, hence, should be treated for tax purposes by that state as if they were residents of that state and have to receive the same deductions and allowances as residents of that State. For such as case, see *Turpeinen* in which the CJEU extended the *Schumacker* doctrine to pensioners. See also PH Schönewille, 'Belastingen en pensioenen in EU-context' in AHH Bollen-Vandenboorn (ed.), *Pensioen en de belangrijkste toekomstvoorzieningen* (Fiscale Geschriften nr 27 SDU, Den Haag 2020) 421.

2488 See, for instance, *Bechtel* para 50.

2489 Cf. Wattel, Marres and Vermeulen, 9.

2490 Ibid. 6.

European Commission's communications)[2491].[2492] It is thus evident that a negative integration-approach has its limitations.[2493] Most importantly, the CJEU can do no more than observe that the TFEU precludes Member States' national legislation infringing the principles as laid down in the TFEU. It can thus not stipulate which measures should replace the contested provision of domestic law. It can thus be characterised as primarily a 'destructive approach', contrary to a 'constructive approach' (i.e. positive integration). Nevertheless, it should be noted that the Court of Justice is increasingly involved in issues in the field which originally had to be solved by harmonization (i.e. in the case of disparities) considering that a disadvantage resulting from a disparity constitutes a barrier to free movement. As a result, negative integration is thus gradually gaining ground.

European Commission's Approach: Towards a More Coherent Approach?

In the Commission's effort to integrate the nationals tax systems more, a certain degree of common ground is discernible. Primarily, the Commission seeks to find a balance between subsidiarity, national states' tax sovereignty and a more coherent approach as regards the tax treatment of cross-border pensions. It could however be said that the Commission has relied too heavily on the case-by-case negative integration-approach, pursued by the CJEU, and lacked decisiveness in this regard. Common elements of her approach are the following:

- **No harmonisation:** the purpose is not to seek harmonisation of Member States' taxation systems pertaining to pension and life assurance. The coordinated approach would, rather, adapt to the diversity of Member States' rules.
- **No discrimination:** both the freedom to provide services as well as the free movement of person may not be impeded by unduly restrictive or discriminatory tax treatment of cross-border pensions and life assurance.

2491 'Soft law' mainly encompasses guidelines and rules of conduct that are not legally binding or enforceable in court. They, rather, support the interpretation and application of enforceable EU law. Some forms of soft law also have relevance for legal persons. However, some forms of soft law are more evident in the system of EU law than others. For instance, the Commission's communications have been held to have a quasi-legal status and, whilst not binding, they are nevertheless influential on the CJEU. However, there is no clear-cut answer as regards the legal validity of these communications. One could say that these communications are in breach of the general principle of legal certainty and democratic legitimacy. Cf. Foster, 131 referring to L Senden, *Soft Law in European Community Law* (Hart, Oxford 2004).

2492 Wattel, Marres and Vermeulen, 47.

2493 See ibid. 47. Firstly, the CJEU cannot strike down every national provision restricting free movement, as it may serve a legitimate purpose of overriding public interest and if so, whether it restricts the Treaty Freedoms no more than necessary to attain that purpose (proportionality). Secondly, the CJEU cannot solve political issues, as it cannot engage in making policy and budgetary choices, which should be left to democratically elected decision-making institutions, for instance decisions on the allocating of taxing rights.

- **No revenue shortfall:** the coordinated approach should allow and support Member States to safeguard the tax revenues they are empowered to collect pursuant to their applicable tax legislation. In addition, it should allow for an enforceable and compliance-stimulating system.

In her 2001 communication the Commission refrained from drawing up more general measures of positive integration pertaining to the tax treatment of cross-border pensions. The commission pointed out that it does not envisage proposing legislative measures to harmonise Member States' pension taxation systems.[2494] The commission, rather, would welcome the broader acceptance of the EET-principle, as the alignment of Member States' tax systems would help reduce mismatches, leading to double (non-)taxation. In doing so, the Commission moved away from her approach in previous reports and Communications, in which she plead for coordinating measures of a general and positive nature, which would help structuring the different national tax systems around a coherent pension scheme that should be assigned binding force.

The 2001 communication is void of arguments why more general measures of a coordinating measure are lacking. It is assumed that coordination reflects a lower degree of alignment of taxes compared to harmonization.[2495] It, therefore, seems not required to draw up uniform rules in order to support positive integration but; rather; to establish strategies in line with policy objectives and measures devoted to enforce them.[2496] In order to achieve coherent national pension tax systems, from an EU law point of view, and consistent with each other, this would require the development of certain points of agreement in respect of the structure of tax advantages.

Further in developing these points, the Commission's principles must be taken into consideration: striving for coordination of tax systems; rather than harmonization, adhering the principle of non-discrimination and the Treaty Freedoms, and safeguarding the states' tax revenues. However, as regards the former the relevant point in discussion is ascertaining the scope of coordination.[2497] To this end, the Commission must be allowed a certain margin of discretion, given the circumstances and factors potentially having an

2494 European Commission, 'The elimination of tax obstacles to the cross-border provision of occupational pensions,' 19.

2495 Hinnekens, 31 ff.

2496 Cf. Prats, 24.

2497 Coordination in the sphere of taxes is characterized by a certain level of flexibility, implying both adhering to the subsidiarity principle and the Member States' competence on the one hand and, on the other hand, the establishment in favor of the Commission of a power of decision and initiative, involving both the type of instrument to be used, the scope and content of it. See Hinnekens, 302 ff.

effect on the outcome.[2498] Yet, it remains difficult to see that the Commission omitted to establish more general measures of coordination rather than the mere assertion that the EET-principle should be adhered to more broadly, since not being able to draw up completely uniform rules does not preclude recommendations of a more general character. The commission could have explored a whole range of other possibilities, provided that it would have been willing to support the positive integration-approach more broadly. For instance, in order to align the national tax systems more with the EET-principle, the proposed measures should have focussed more on the implementation thereof in the tax systems of the Member States concerned, taking account of the deviating specific rules laid down in these Member States' national tax legislation. The Commission's narrow approach of leaving the development of a coherent (European) approach of the national pension tax systems, and complementing tax policy instruments, to the CJEU's case-by-case interpretation, and to the Member States, lacks decisiveness.

The Commission's proposals were driven by the urgency of the situation, the practicality and level of realism thereof. In order to circumvent the unanimity requirement and assuming a lack of competence, the Commission proposed measures of coordination rather than harmonization of the national tax pension systems. However, as Prats contends, these easy and practical solutions do not necessarily correspond to national and international principles and may even give rise to outcomes inconsistent with the Commission's own objectives and EU law.[2499] Furthermore, this approach is surprising since these renegotiations may lead to deviations, discrepancies, specific rules and exceptions, giving rise to inconsistencies in the tax treatment of cross-border pensions. The practical approach would be more upheld if the EU rules would have been proposed stipulating the content for the given tax treaty provisions. The discussion should, hence, not be focussing on whether harmonization or coordination of the tax systems is more adequate, but whether it is necessary to develop measures of secondary EU law (positive or 'soft law') and the content of these measures, taking into consideration the limits imposed by the Member States' exclusive competence, the subsidiarity principle and the unanimity requirement.

In her 2006 Communication, the Commission appeared to rely on her approach as set out in her 2001 Commission, i.e. supporting the negative integration-approach of the CJEU rather than providing measures of positive integration in the sphere of the tax treatment of cross-border pensions. This approach seems unaltered, generally setting out why coordination and cooperation between Member States should be pursued, allowing them

2498 Cf. Prats, 24.
2499 Ibid. 26.

to attain their tax policy goals and protect their tax bases, while ensuring elimination of discrimination and double taxation and reducing compliance costs. The Commission thus upholds the same principles as established in the 2001 Communication.

In line with previous communications, the Commission adhered in her 2010 Communication to the principles of striving for coordination of tax systems, rather than harmonization, and adhered to the principle of non-discrimination and the Treaty Freedoms. In particular, the Commission proposed to monitor Member States' tax legislation and systematically request Member States to rectify any incompatibilities with EU law within a certain deadline, and to monitor the implementation by EU Member States of the CJEU's rulings in the tax field and ensure that they are implemented also in Member States that were not the subject of the ruling. With regard to the latter two initiatives, the Commission not solely relies on the CJEU's negative integration-approach, but will also, on her own initiative, monitor Member States' tax legislation and systematically request Member States to resolve any incompatibilities with EU law. However, she still abstains from formulating more positive measures of a coordinating nature.

Final Remarks

In view of the initiatives on part of the European Commission as set forth above, it is evident that the CJEU's case-law has established a more progressive line of indirect harmonization on the elimination of tax obstacles to the exercise of fundamental freedoms. In the CJEU's case-law as it stands, the court has eliminated a range of domestic tax rules which constitute an unjustified infringement of the Treaty freedoms, or lead to a discriminatory treatment of non-residents.

The extensive interpretation and application of the principle of non-discrimination by the CJEU is, however, met with criticism. The delimitation of tax regimes for supplementary pensions compatible with the Single Market should not just be left to the evolution of CJEU case law and the autonomous reaction of the individual Member States.[2500] Delimitation, in this regard, refers to the requirement of extending the domestic tax treatment of contributions to contributions to foreign pension schemes. Some considerations are of interest in this regard. The CJEU's interpretation of the non-discrimination principle will not have a negative effect on the tax treatment of contributions to supplementary pension schemes in countries operating a TEE-system, since it does not lead to a loss of tax revenue for the state involved. However, as regards countries promoting saving in supplementary schemes through adopting an ETT or EET-system, the CJEU's

2500 Ibid. 21.

approach to non-discrimination may compel these states to extend this tax relief to contributions paid to foreign schemes, causing a loss in tax revenue, while complying with EU requirements. As Prats rightly contends, adopting the CJEU's interpretation of the non-discrimination principle as the primary, if not only, (effective) mechanism of consolidating the Single Market for supplementary pension schemes, may lead to a (tensional) paradox.[2501] While on the one hand, both the European Commission and other European institutions recognize the need to use mechanisms to stimulate the development of supplementary pension schemes to ensure the level of income of European mobile citizens, on the other hand, states that adopted tax mechanisms aimed at the promotion of contributions to these schemes may be hindered by the CJEU's pursuance of the elimination of distortions to the Single Market through its expansive interpretation of the non-discrimination principle. The effect of the requirements arising from the CJEU's interpretation, therefore, should be taken into account in developing policy on the tax treatment of pensions in the Member States.

In light of this research's evaluation framework, I argue that the CJEU's extensive approach is an insufficient instrument in stimulating the further establishment of the European internal market, as other distortions to the proper functioning can hardly be resolved by the court's interpretation of the non-discrimination principle and treaty freedoms, such as disparities or divergences between national tax systems. However, the CJEU is not competent to abolish disparities between national tax legislations.[2502] Mainly due to the absence of secondary EU law on the tax treatment of cross-border pensions, the CJEU is prevented from developing tax principles and specific rules regarding this tax issues. Merely the extensive interpretation of CJEU of both the non-discrimination principle and the fundamental freedoms, as an instrument, is, in itself, not sufficient to support the coherent development of the integration between domestic income tax systems and EU law.[2503] As long as these disparities or divergences among Member States' tax systems are compatible with the non-discrimination principle and the fundamental freedoms, they may, and/or should, persist to exist. However, the convergence and inter-level coherence of these national pension tax systems and the European internal market call for more positive integration at European level.

2501 Ibid. 21.
2502 Wattel, Marres and Vermeulen, 48.
2503 Prats, 21.

9 The Regulatory Frameworks Governing the Tax Treatment of Cross-border Pensions on International level

9.1 Introduction

Where in the preceding chapters (4-8) the construct, legal character, vesting methods, pension schemes and tax treatment of statutory, occupational, and personal pensions – in the Netherlands and Germany – and EU law have been mapped out, this chapter analyses the regulatory framework on an international level. Working and saving for pension across international borders implies dealing with multiple pension and tax systems. It is inevitable that mobile citizens contributing or working across borders will have to contend with two or more sets of tax rules that differ considerably.[2504] Moreover, the confluence of certain tax regimes may, as well, give rise to double (non-)taxation of retirement income. These disparities to the proper functioning of the European internal market can hardly be resolved by the CJEU's interpretation of the non-discrimination principle, as discussed in chapter 8 of this research.[2505] This means that in cross-border situations, both norms derived from international tax law, as well as EU-law norms may apply concomitantly. The emphasis of the analysis in the chapter is put on the mobile citizen, saving for his retirement through either a statutory, occupational or personal pension provision.

Moreover, in cross-border situations mobile individuals – who avail(ed) themselves of their European freedoms of movement – see themselves confronted with a wide range of diverging 'pensions', i.e. pension vehicles, schemes, retirement products of all sorts, arising from pension systems in each of the different (former) working states, and/or residence states. Providing, on an aggregated level, mobile individuals information about how much pension they can expect – covering all their forms of pension in each of the (former) working/residence states – requires a complex process of incorporating all types of

2504 European Commission, 'Commission Staff Working Document accompanying Commission Communication 'Removing cross-border tax obstacles for EU citizens''.

2505 Double taxation may, for instance, occur in the following situation: a worker, resident in State A – which operates an EET-system – is translocated by his employer to state B, applying a TEE-system. As a result, the taxable person may be subject to TET-taxation. While not constituting an unjustified infringement of EU law requirements, the *employer's* contributions to the pension scheme in the state of origin are excluded from tax deduction in state B, leading to a 'disparity'. After returning to his state of origin, and upon retirement, the pension will be subject to double taxation when the pension is paid out.

diverging pension vehicles, schemes, products of all sorts in each of the different (former) working states, and/or residence states. This requires a process of converging these deviating systems, while upholding the information's effectiveness. Putting this dispersed puzzle together also poses considerable challenges in terms of information provision. This amounts to observing, and 'translating' the intersections between different multi-level legal systems (national, EU and international/bilateral) and the interaction of poorly coordinated legal domains (pension and tax law) – which can all be interwoven in a personal mobile situation – into effective pension information. Hitherto, no attention has been paid neither any research has been conducted on the differentiated tax treatment of the fragmented pension rights in each of the (former) working states, and the effect thereof on the ambition to present effective pension information.

This chapter explores how the taxation of cross-border pensions – pursuant to national tax law – is affected by international law, i.e. exploring how international law might alter the tax treatment of the given cross-border pension.[2506] As regards the international level, this chapter will broadly follow the structure of the applicable tax treaty and deals with the different types of relevant treaty provisions successively, shaping the law as it stands. Rather than putting focus on the precise impact of certain individual cases, this chapter offers an analysis from a bird's eye view of the overly complex system of international tax law in the domain of the taxation of cross-border pensions. In addition, it will be explored to what extent the regulatory instruments employed in the domain of international tax law, as they stand, are apt for the provision of effective pension information, in the light of the principles set in chapter 2 of this research. Emphasis will be put on the extent to which they aid in establishing inter-level coherence, and inter-system consistency. This chapter answers the sub-research questions of how the taxation of cross-border pensions is governed by European law, and to what extent there is room for improvement, along the lines of the assessment framework drawn up in chapter 2.

9.2 Models for the Taxation of Pensions on International Level: Non-exhaustive Instruments

As far as the taxation of 'pensions' is concerned, it should be stressed that international tax law does not provide a uniform definition of the concept of pensions. However, there is a certain level of consensus on categorising the different types of pension tax systems. This

2506 See also paragraph I, under 1 of the Protocol to the tax treaty concluded between the Netherlands and Germany. This provision stipulates that it is understood that the law of the European Union takes precedence over the provisions of the Convention. On the interaction between EU law and international tax law see Wattel, Marres and Vermeulen, part I.

categorisation of pension tax systems on an international level (TEE, EET etc.[2507]) merely constitutes a model for the categorization of national tax systems but is not a uniform applied system. Moreover, significant differences in the tax systems persist to exist. From the existence of very different arrangements to provide retirement benefits, cross-border tax issues may arise. Furthermore, where these systems may operate consistently in a domestic situation, inconsistencies may emerge in cross-border situations.[2508] These inconsistencies or mismatches may be a consequence of differences in general tax policy that States have adopted with respect to retirement provisions.[2509] These inconsistencies may occur in three bilateral cases:[2510]

- The person concerned works temporarily in another state, but continues to contribute to a pension fund in the state of origin, to which he will eventually retire;
- The person contributes to a fund in his residence state and eventually retires to another state (i.e. mobile after retirement);
- The person resides, and remains, in one state and contributes to a pension fund in another state.

Also a combination of the second and third situation may arise, where the person concerned contributions to a pension fund established in the other state, and eventually retires in a third state (trilateral situation). Furthermore, combinations of these situations may arise at different points in time throughout the person's working life.

Where in domestic situations, with regard to the tax treatment of pensions, the emphasis is placed on issues such as which basis model of taxation (EET, TEE etc.) is preferable, or how provisions on the tax treatment of pensions relate to provisions in the domain of social security, the focus in cross-border situations (and in this research) is broadened to, for instance,[2511] the distribution of taxing rights on pension benefits as laid down in the applicable tax treaties.

9.2.1 Categorisation of Pension Tax Systems: EET, TEE, ETT, TTE

Despite the considerable different methods of taxation of pensions under each State's domestic legislation, these methods can be categorised by a considerably simplified basic model. This categorisation merely depicts *grosso modo* how pensions are taxed, and are far

2507 The characters of this abbreviation stand for exempt (E), fully taxed (T) or taxed at a reduced rate (R).
2508 Prats, 13.
2509 See also paragraph 9 of the OECD commentary on Article 18 OECD MC.
2510 Cf. Avery Jones, 28.
2511 Cf. Richter, 1.

from watertight and there may even overlap.[2512] Choosing one principle or the other may not be neutral, since it may result in different income tax consequences in transnational situations.[2513] Moreover, the categorisation says nothing about the deductibility of the contributions to foreign pension funds, which issue will be addressed in more detail below.

While there is strong consensus about the tax treatment of mandated schemes (unfunded or funded), consensus is lacking as regards the tax treatment of voluntary schemes, of individual retirement account or employer-sponsored savings arrangements.[2514] Under the former, contributions typically are tax exempt, while benefits are fully taxed; this approach is also adopted for funded pension schemes, where the interest earned is mostly not taxed. However, the level of deductibility of contributions and the taxation of benefits, persists to deviate considerably across Member states.

What is more, Member states may operate more than one system, in particular in an international context. Differences between these systems may lead to detrimental financial consequences, for example, an employee may spend his working career in a TEE State but retire to an EET State, in which case he is likely to be subject to double taxation. In contrary, an employee may work in a state applying the EET-system and retire in a state applying the TEE-system, potentially leading to double non-taxation.[2515] Although, *grosso modo*, the results of a TEE and EET-systems are broadly equivalent, some differences in the tax treatment should be observed in this regard.[2516] In terms of the effective tax burden, the outcomes may be different in practice as, for instance, marginal tax rates will be lower during retirement compared to the phase of an earned income, making an EET-system more favourable.[2517] Furthermore, it should be reiterated that pension contributions might be paid over a period of (around) 40 years during which tax rates and tax systems may vary more than the (mere) difference between work and retirement, i.e. national tax legislation – governing the tax treatment of pensions – may be amended throughout the years.

2512 European Commission, 'The elimination of tax obstacles to the cross-border provision of occupational pensions,' 6.

2513 Prats, 13.

2514 Holzmann and Hinz, 119-120.

2515 As pointed out in *Skandia* para 48.

2516 Cf. Avery Jones, 28.

2517 Cf. ibid. 28. Alternatively, it can be contended that a TEE-system may be more favourable as any better-than-expected yield within the fund is retained entirely by the pensioner, instead of shared with the government in tax as it is in the EET system.

In particular, on the grounds of this model, a distinction is drawn between models in which a pension is taxed in one of the three phases as described below.[2518] The tax treatment of pensions can generally be brown down into three stages: contributions paid by participants into the fund (either taxed – i.e. non-deductible – or exempt); investment/ capital accumulation of contributions held by the fund (taxed or exempt); benefits paid out to the pensioner by the pension fund (taxed or exempt). For instance, under an EET-system contributions are deductible for tax purposes (hence, exempt), investments/capital accumulation is exempt, and eventually pension benefits will be subject to tax. However, to what particular level these pensions are taxed, e.g. to what extent pension contributions shall be deductible for tax purposes, is left open by this categorisation (e.g. EET, TEE, ETT). Furthermore, the fiscal-policy decision for one of these models may vary across the three pillars within one state. For instance, where a state or occupational may be taxed according to the EET-model, a personal (private) pension scheme may be subject to the TEE-model.[2519] In addition, within a pension pillar, the tax treatment (according to one of the models) of a pension scheme may vary compared to a pension scheme attributed to the similar pillar. This proves to be particularly the case in Germany, partly because of the transition from *Vorgelagerte Besteuerung* to *Nachgelagerte Besteuerung*.[2520] With regard to the last phase of taxation, i.e. the decumulation phase, the pension scheme may be subject to differential treatment, depending on in which form the pension benefits are disbursed, i.e. an lifelong annuity or a singly lump-sum.[2521] Therefore, in between these models, numerous mixed models exist, under which the pension contributions are merely partially deductible for tax purposes, and, accordingly, only part of the pension benefits is subject to taxation.[2522] Some states limit the deduction of pension contributions to a certain threshold, which implies that all contributions exceeding this threshold arise from taxed income. In the cases of such mixed model, the letter R is used in order to indicate 'reduced tax'. In particular, this use of these mixed models demonstrates the controversialist, and marginal appropriateness, of these models and labels for system-overarching and uniform use.

2518 See also paragraph 9 of the OECD commentary on Article 18 OECD MC.

2519 Richter, 17.

2520 Ibid. 17. See for an elaborate overview of the differences in the tax treatment of German occupational pensions prior to the implementation of the *Alterseinkünftegesetz*: D Birk, 'Nachgelagerte Besteuerung in der betrieblichen Altersversorgung' Steuer und Wissenschaft 321, 323 and BMF, *Sonderausgabenabzug bei beschränkt Steuerpflichtigen für Pflichtbeiträge an berufsständische Versorgungseinrichtungen (§ 10 Absatz 1 Nummer 2 Buchstabe a, § 50 Absatz 1 Satz 3 EStG); EuGH-Urteil vom 6. Dezember 2018, C-480/17, „Montag" IV C 5 - S 2301/19/10004:001* 442, 449.

2521 Richter, 17; P Johnson, 'The taxation of occupational and pricate pensions in Western Europe' in J Mortenson (ed.), *The future of pensions in the European Community* (Brussel 1992) 10.

2522 See for an elaborate overview: Scheffler and Kölbl. See also H Dürkop, *Alterssicherung in der EG: Eine kritische Bestandsaufnahme der Alterssicherungssysteme für Arbeitnehmer in der Europäischen Gemeinschaft* (Peter Lang, Bern 1992).

Furthermore, in a pure national context, each of these systems has its pros and cons.[2523] Which principle a country will adopt will depend on its politics and the outlook of its fiscal accounts, and any difference in the economic effect of each principle would be of a second order of magnitude. Furthermore, an EET-system is more credible, in that it protects citizens from an inconsistent government that decides to subject pension benefits to tax, while the contributions have not been eligible for deduction. What is more, a tax system adopting the EET-principle best caters for citizen's income experience while adhering more to the ability-to-pay principle, and eliminating distortions on intertemporal consumption and savings decisions. It could be said that, *grosso modo*, under progressive tax system, a TEE-system is likely to provide more tax revenues, while under an EET-system it is likely to provide more incentives for individuals to save for retirement.

Most relevant from the points of view of this research's perspective is that research findings demonstrate that an EET-system contributes more than other systems to an adequate pension system.[2524] As regards cross-border cases, it could be said that the existence of the EET-system is the primary cause of the distribution of taxing rights on cross-border pension benefits. On the contrary, a TEE-system has advantages as well, such as the fact that emigration after retirement in combination with residence taxation does not infringe the tax coherence that may or may not be present.

The internationally accepted model described the taxation of pension be using three letters, in which each of the letters, consecutively, stand for each of the three time spans. Where the pension is subject to tax, this is indicated with the letter T (taxed), while if the pension is exempted from taxation, this is referred by using the letter E (exempt). What is more, a reduced level of taxation is often indicated with a small-letter 't', for instance taxation pursuant to the German *Besteuerungsanteil*. With regard to the tax treatment of contributions paid into the pension vehicle during the accrual phase, the term 'taxed' and 'exempt' may seem rather odd, since the question may rise how a pension contribution, which a pension participant already paid to his pension provider, can be taxed or exempt. It should be pointed out that, in view of pension contributions, where the term 'taxed' refers to the non-deductibility of pension contributions for tax purposes (deducted from the taxable income), the term 'exempt' indicates that the contributions shall be deductible for tax purposes.

2523 For an explanation of these pros and cons of TEE and EET-systems see Holzmann and Hinz, 119-120.

2524 See ibid. 119. The authors contend that an EET system ensures that citizens are stimulated to convert current income into future income and thus ensure an adequate income in the retirement phase.

9.2.1.A Generally Accepted Models

9.2.1.A.I TEE-Models

Under a TEE-model, the pension contributions, paid during the accrual phase, shall be subject to taxation under domestic tax legislation. Either, pension contributions are paid out of taxed income. The taxable person can, hence, not lower his taxable income by deducting these contributions. With regard to the second phase, the yielding investment returns will not be taxed. Lastly, during the decumulation phase, the pension benefits are fully exempt from taxation as well. This rather classical model of taxing pensions 'in front' (rather than 'deferred taxation'), relies on the notion that retirement is merely a particular form of the application of income, and hence the consumption of this taxed income, in the form of the pension benefits, shall thus not be subject to taxation.[2525] The exemption from taxation of the pension benefits is often motivated by a purposely provided compensation.

9.2.1.A.II TTE-Models

As a variation to the former model, under this TTE-model, both the pension contributions paid to the pension scheme, as well as the investment return yielded in the scheme during the accrual phase, are liable to tax. This relies on the notion that the pension that will be paid out eventually, arise not only from the pension contributions paid by the taxable income, but also the investment yield and returns in the intervening period. This does not result in legal double taxation of the same part of income, since in purely domestic situations, under this method it is ensured that pension shall merely be liable to single taxation. It requires certain computation methods and flat-rate calculations to distil the taxable capital yield out of the pension benefits, actually paid to the beneficiary.[2526]

9.2.1.A.III EET-Models

Although Germany gradually moves to deferred taxation with regarding to statutory and occupational pensions, and deferred taxation is (in principle) the standard for Dutch occupational pensions, this cannot be considered a world-wide trend.[2527] Although widespread, and albeit the European Commission proclaimed a broader acceptance of

2525 Cf. Richter, 14; S Dommes, *Pensionen im Recht der Doppelbesteuerungsabkommen* (Schriftenreihe zum Internationalen Steuerrecht, Linde, Wien 2012) 25 and D Birk, *Altersvorsorge und Alterseinkünfte im Einkommensteuerrecht: Verfassungsrechtliche Vorgaben, gesetzliche Regelungen, Neuordnungsmodelle* (Rechtsordnung und Steuerwesen, Schmidt, Köln 1987) 2.

2526 Richter, 14.

2527 Ibid. 16.

this model[2528], there is still a wide variety among states of taxing pensions.[2529] Under this model of deferred taxation, the pension is taxed only upon disbursement. Both pension contributions paid to the scheme, as well as investment yields accrued during the accrual phase are exempt from taxation. The pension contributions may be deducted from the taxable income, exempting them from taxation or are subject to another form of fiscal facilitation.[2530] The notion and motives driving this fiscal facilitation varies per State, i.e. per tax system.[2531] This fiscal facilitation of the contribution paid during the accrual phase, is offset by the full taxation of the paid out pension benefits during the decumulation phase.[2532] Yet, the indication of the model does not clarify how pension benefits are qualified for fiscal purposes (e.g. either as other elements of income or income arising from previous employment).

There is a widespread consensus that this form of deferred taxation is aimed at facilitating saving for retirement. Furthermore, in Member states applying a progressive tax rate to earned (wage) income, deferred taxation is more beneficial to taxable persons, since the taxable income after retirement is, usually, lower compared to the earned income taxed during the active phase, and, thus, resulting in a progression advantage.[2533] Moreover, retirees may be subject to a more beneficial tax treatment.[2534]

2528 European Commission, 'The elimination of tax obstacles to the cross-border provision of occupational pensions'.

2529 See for instance R Taylor, 'Cross-Border Recognition of Occupational Pensions within the EU and beyond' Tax Planning International Review.

2530 For instance in the Netherlands under Article 11, par. 1, under j, nr. 1 Wet LB 1964. In Germany this is effected by the contributions to be deducted as *Werbungskosten*, *Betriebsausgaben* or *Sonderausgaben*. See Dommes, 26.

2531 See for instance BMF, *Sonderausgabenabzug bei beschränkt Steuerpflichtigen für Pflichtbeiträge an berufsständische Versorgungseinrichtungen (§ 10 Absatz 1 Nummer 2 Buchstabe a, § 50 Absatz 1 Satz 3 EStG); EuGH-Urteil vom 6. Dezember 2018, C-480/17, „Montag" IV C 5 - S 2301/19/10004:001.*

2532 Richter, 16 and Dorenkamp, 45 ff.

2533 Richter, 16; Birk, 'Nachgelagerte Besteuerung in der betrieblichen Altersversorgung' 321 ff. and BMF, *Sonderausgabenabzug bei beschränkt Steuerpflichtigen für Pflichtbeiträge an berufsständische Versorgungseinrichtungen (§ 10 Absatz 1 Nummer 2 Buchstabe a, § 50 Absatz 1 Satz 3 EStG); EuGH-Urteil vom 6. Dezember 2018, C-480/17, „Montag" IV C 5 - S 2301/19/10004:001* 133 ff.

2534 For instance, income tax is levied in conjunction with social insurance contributions within the first bracket of the Dutch income tax (pursuant to article 2.10 Wet IB 2001). After reaching the applicable statutory retirement age (*AOW-leeftijd*), retirees are no longer AOW-contributions due. It should be stressed that the income tax rates remain at a similar level, but the total combined rate drops due to, as a pensioner, being no longer AOW-contributions due. Retirees are therefore taxed at a lower rate. However, due to being no longer AOW-contributions due, and a result of the application of article 8.4 Wet IB 2001, the eligible amounts of various tax credits shall be lowered correspondingly, in turn resulting in a partly higher effective tax rate. Furthermore, once having reached the applicable statutory retirement age, taxable persons may, provided that other conditions are met, be eligible to additional tax credits, as laid down in article 8.17, and article 8.18 Wet IB 2001.

9.2.1.A.IV ETT-Models

Although seldom, in States where pension investment yields are subject to tax, in addition to the benefits paid out, this is referred to as 'ETT'. Similar to the ETT-model, it is ensured under this model that the pension is subject to taxation only once. The notion underlying the taxation of the investment yield in the intervening period is similar to those set forth in section 9.2.1.A.II. With regard to the latter two models set forth above, it should be stressed that, from the perspective of the competent state, this holds a liquidity disadvantage as the pension may be taxed only from the time of decumulation of the pension, i.e. pay-out of benefits. In cases where the taxable person decides to leave the facilitating Member State during the accrual phase, this results in a loss of taxing rights, and, eventually, losing taxing revenues. Therefore, Member states, seek to preserve their (future) taxing rights on pension benefits, by imposing a protective tax assessment, albeit that this state may not be allocated the pertinent taxing rights as set out in the underlying tax treaty.

9.3 International Tax Law on Cross-Border Pensions

For the scope of this research, 'international tax law' refers to the regulatory mechanisms as laid down in the applicable bilateral tax treaties. These tax treaties arrange for the allocation of taxing rights on, *inter alia*, pensions. Bilateral tax treaties constitute international agreements under public international law.[2535] The power of a sovereign state to exercise tax jurisdiction is limited by international tax law. Most of the treaty provisions – particularly the allocation provisions – seek to limit the right of a contracting state to include residents of the other contracting state in the tax levy, pursuant to national tax law. In addition, significant differences exist among national tax laws as to the income to be included in the tax. Tax treaties seek to align the application of these mutually different national regimes to some extent through the so-called allocation provisions. Therefore, the evaluation of this chapter – in section 9.4 – will emphasize the principle of inter-level coherence.

Although, in the course of the years, a comprehensive network of bilateral and multilateral tax treaties has developed, merely the bilateral tax treaty concluded between the Netherlands and Germany will be considered, since this relation is the starting point of this research. The treaty between the Netherlands and Germany, has been concluded on 12 April 2012, and entered into force on the 1 December 2016.[2536] As far as considered appropriate, the 'old treaty', which was terminated 1 December 2016, will be dealt with as

2535 See K Vogel, *Klaus Vogel on Double Taxation Conventions* (Kluwer, Deventer 1997), para 28.

2536 Convention between the Kingdom of the Netherlands and the Federal Republic of Germany for the Avoidance of Double Taxation and the Prevention of Fiscal Evasion with respect to Taxes on Income 2012.

well.[2537] Next to the applicable treaty provisions, the protocol to the treaty will be addressed as well, at appropriate points. This protocol, for instance, sets forth the interpretation of the text of certain treaty provisions, e.g. where does a pension arise? The sole difference between treaty and protocol pertains to the substantive meaning of the provisions: those of the protocol are, as a rule, elaborations of certain treaty provisions.[2538] Furthermore, merely the provisions of the treaties allocating taxing rights on pensions (artt. 17 and 18) will be mapped out.

9.3.1 Tax Treaties as International Agreements and Their Purpose

Tax treaties apply to persons investing or engaging in cross-border activities. They allow two or more States under their national tax laws to tax the elements of income. It is to be noted that, for instance contrary to the Regulation 883/2004[2539] in the sphere of social security, tax treaties attribute taxing rights on the basis of elements of income, rather than relying on persons. What is more, contrary to the Regulation 883/2004, under tax treaties an exclusivity principle does not apply, i.e. taxing rights may be either attributed exclusively to the residence state, exclusively to the source state, or the residence, as well as the source state, are attributed a shared taxing right.

In terms of levels of legislation, domestic law forms the background over which other sources of international tax law are overlaid.[2540] It follows from this that the charge to tax is found in state's domestic law. This implies that domestic law lays down when, and in what manner, a domestic charge arises with respect to cross-border pensions, notably identifies so-called 'connecting factors', i.e. relevant factors (most commonly 'source' and 'residence') that bring a transaction within the charge to tax.[2541] As domestic direct tax laws involve the unilateral exercise of sovereignty, they do not coordinate, or integrate, very easily. Hence, bilateral tax treaties are concluded in order to provide for specific integration of two national tax systems.

2537 Avi-Yonah.

2538 Moreover, in term of legal force the treaty and the protocol do not differ, nor in the procedure for amending them. What is more, both the treaty and the protocol are laid down in a formal framework.

2539 Regulation on the coordination of social security systems 883/2004.

2540 See also Harris and Oliver, 15.

2541 At this point it must be stressed that in some jurisdictions, such as Germany, the constitution may have a direct impact on the application of fiscal legislation, contrary to the Netherlands where the constitution virtually has no day-to-day impact. For instance, in countries such as Germany, the constitution may directly refer to taxation or set out general constitutional principles that may affect the imposing of taxes. Furthermore, contrary to the Netherlands, the application of formal (fiscal) legislation may be assessed by the German Constitutional Court (*Bundesverfassungshof*).

Tax treaties constitute a bilateral agreement of international law pertaining to how states agree on the allocating of taxation of cross-border activities. The main purpose of tax treaties is to coordinate the application of domestic tax laws of the contracting states to prevent (judicial[2542]) double (non-) taxation on the basis of reciprocity, and to combat unjustified avoidance of taxation by providing distribution rules[2543], attributing taxing rights.[2544] Tax treaties may also serve to define certain concepts, provide methods for relief of double taxation and provide instruments for the exchange of information. To this end, a tax treaty specifies for each category of income whether the residence state or the source state holds the primary taxing right (the so-called 'allocation rules'; compare the conflict rules in (European) social security law). If this primary taxing right is allocated to the residence state, the source state must refrain from taxation altogether. If, on the other hand, the primary taxing right is attributed to the source state, the state of residence will often still be allowed to include the relevant component in the worldwide income taxed by this state, albeit that the state of residence must prevent effective double taxation of the component attributed to the source state through exemption or credit. Merely to the extent that a state is not prevented by any provision of the tax treaty from taxing a particular item of income, may that state apply its domestic tax rules in full.

With regard to above, it must be noted that tax treaties, in itself, do no create taxing rights, but rather allocate (existing) taxing rights to contracting states, i.e. they are granted 'permissive'. In turn, taxpayers derive their rights from this allocation. These taxing rights can be found in domestic legislation. The allocation of taxing rights pertaining to pension income is, in the applicable tax treaties, commonly based on the principle of residence state taxation, source state taxation or a combination of both. In the division of these taxing rights on pensions, four states may play a role: the pensioner's residence state, the state where the work has been carried out or the state where the employment from which the pension is derived was taxable, the state of establishment of the pension institution, and, lastly, the state where the pension institution has invested.

2542 This form of double taxation occurs when one subject is taxed by several States on the same object (element of income). The common situation is that the taxpayer's State of residence includes its world income in the taxation, while the other State in which a source of income of this taxpayer is located will subject this to taxation as well. In addition to judicial double taxation, economic double taxation may occur. Economic double taxation occurs when more than one subject (person) is actually taxed more than once on the same object (element of income), for instance due to qualification problems.

2543 See for instance preamble to OECD Model Tax Convention on Income and on Capital: "*Intending to conclude a Convention for the elimination of double taxation with respect to taxes on income and on capital without creating opportunities for non-taxation or reduced taxation through tax evasion or avoidance..*".

2544 See paragraph 1-3 Introduction to OECD MC. Dutch treaty policy is also aimed at attempting, where possible, to eliminate economic double taxation. See Ministerie van Financiën, 16.

As the CJEU has consistently held, conventions' purpose is not to ensure that the tax to which the taxpayer is subject in one State is no higher than that to which he or she would be subject in the other state.[2545] Concurrence of taxing rights of different states can lead to double taxation. In addition, tax loopholes, i.e. double non-taxation, may arise, for example due to differences between tax systems of states, e.g. qualification problems. In order to eliminate the (judicial) double taxation that has arisen, the states concerned may, by means of a tax treaty, distribute the taxing rights. This could lead the source state to fully or partly abstain from taxation. Contrarily, the state of residence may forgo his taxing right in whole or in part by granting an object exemption, tax relief or a tax credit.[2546] As regards treaty provision and the distribution of taxing rights, states may agree different ways of distribution per category of income or capital. Moreover, starting positions in treaty negotiations may differ per bilateral relation. For instance, as regards the Netherlands, as a general rule, this state largely follows the distribution rules as set forth in the OECD Model Convention.[2547] However, in the Dutch treaty policy memorandum, more taxing rights are allocated to the source state, compared to the OECD Model Convention. This policy treaty will be discussed further below.

9.3.1.A OECD Model Convention

The OECD and the UN developed treaty models for the distribution of taxing rights. It should be noted that these models are not treaties in itself, but merely a model. Although the OECD MC lacks parliamentary approval and thus in a certain sense legitimacy, it can be asserted that some normative power or 'soft obligation' ensues from the OECD MC. Nevertheless, the OECD MC must be applied unless the Member state has entered original reservations or unless material reasons, such as peculiarities of the domestic law of the Contracting State, weigh against the adoption of the Model, with regard to an individual treaty provision.[2548] It could thus be said that this 'soft law' is akin to a pseudo-legal rule, which must be taken into account and from which one cannot simply deviate without violating obligations under international law.

2545 *Gilly* para 46.

2546 The methods of preventing double taxation by the Netherlands as a state of residence have been set out in the *Besluit voorkoming dubbele belasting 2001* (BvdB 2001) and have been elaborated on in the Staatssecretaris van Financiën, *Syllabus vrijstelling, verrekening, verliescompensatie internationaal belastingrecht* (2004).

2547 Ministerie van Financiën, 22.

2548 K Vogel, *Klaus Vogel on double taxation conventions: a commentary to the OECD-, UN- and US model conventions for the avoidance of double taxation of income and capital: with particular reference to German treaty practice* (Kluwer, Deventer 1991) 34.

Where OECD Model represents the position of developed countries, the latter gives expression to the position of developing countries.[2549] However, these models do not comprehensively regulate a variance of important international tax issues and have not been adopted by countries on a uniform basis. Certain limitations are hence inherent to these models. Moreover, contracting states have the possibility to make reservations and comments on the OECD Model Convention and the related OECD commentaries[2550]. The Dutch government takes the stance that the power of the OECD Model Convention is best maintained if the number of comments and reservations is limited, and, hence, the Netherlands has made little use of this possibility.[2551]

In the interpretation of tax treaties, the OECD MC, as well as the OECD Commentary carry significant weight.[2552] As, *inter alia*, an amendment to the OECD MC could take decades to be reflected in practice, there is a tendency in practice of making substantive amendments by adapting the meaning of the treaty provision by means of amendments to the OECD commentaries.[2553] Furthermore, model tax treaties are built on political compromise, are reactionary, customary and historical in nature.[2554] They originate from existing domestic laws and treaty practice, which still largely dictate the direction of their development. This implies that they suffer from a lack of a certain level of conceptual structure based on principle, and are far from comprehensive. As regards the latter, they only cover those tax issues on which agreement can be reached. However, notwithstanding these limitations, several principles have emerged based on the rules laid down in these model tax treaties.

9.3.1.B Reception of International (Tax) Law: Monist vs. Dualist View

Now that it has become clear what this international field of law comprises, it is to be noted that the extent to which a taxpayer may derive rights from bilateral tax treaties depends on the position each state has taken in relation to the status and reception of these fields of law. It is therefore not self-evident that national legislation is also shaped, and

2549 By the late 1970s it was felt that the conclusion of tax treaties between developed countries and between developed and developing countries should be fostered. The result was the 1980 UN model. This model largely follows the principles adopted in the OECD model, with some exceptions however.

2550 These commentaries have been drafted by the OECD Committee on Fiscal Affairs, largely consisting of tax officials of the OECD member states. Hence, these commentaries have been drafted with the agreement of these member states, apart from any reservations made to it.

2551 Ministerie van Financiën, 23.

2552 Cf. M Lang and F Brugger, 'The role of the OECD Commentary in tax treaty interpretation' 23 Australian Tax Forum 95, 107.

2553 Harris and Oliver, 19.

2554 See JF Avery Jones, L De Broe and M Ellis, 'The Origins of Concepts and Expressions Used in the OECD Model and Their Adoption by States' British Tax Review 695, In this article the authors trace the origin of concepts and expressions used in the OECD MC.

amended, by this extensive body of international and European legislation. For instance, to the extent that the provisions of tax treaties have direct effect – which they almost all do – and set limits to the scope of application of national tax law, national tax rules therefore have no effect. Hence, in treaty situations the first thing to be considered is the national scope of taxation according to national tax laws; subsequently it can be seen to what extent the tax treaty imposes limits on the application of these national tax provisions. It thus may limit the exercise of national tax jurisdiction.

In this vein, a distinction can be drawn between states following a *monist* approach, and states that adopt the *dualist* view.[2555] In the former approach, national law and international law are part of a single system and these fields of law prevail over domestic law. This implies that no further action, or transformation into domestic law, is required in order to confer rights on taxpayers, which can directly rely on and/or invoke the treaty provisions once the treaty has been ratified.[2556] In a way it is thus 'self-executing'. However, this still leaves open the question where on the hierarchy the international law should be placed, and whether it takes priority over all law, i.e. municipal law, ordinary, national law and so forth.[2557] Under a *dualist* view international and national law are considered separate systems existing alongside each other, and (tax) treaties only become part of national law by specific transformation into domestic law. It is left to the member states to determine where the international law is then placed within the national hierarchy of laws. It does not exactly assist in making things less complex that the Netherlands has adopted a *monist* view as regards the legal validity of both international, as well as EU law, and Germany traditionally tends towards the *dualist* approach.[2558] Actually, Germany finds itself in a more pluralist approach, i.e. neither confirm nor denying a monist approach, although it has obvious features tending towards monism. For instance, the German Federal Constitutional Court has shown some tendencies towards dualism.[2559] The differences

2555 See also Foster, 154-155.

2556 In the Netherlands, this has been embedded in article 93 of the constitution providing: *"Provisions of treaties and decisions of organisations governed by international law which, according to their content, are binding on everyone, shall have binding force after they have been published."*

2557 In the Netherlands, this has been embedded in article 94 of the constitution providing: *"Legal provisions in force within the Kingdom shall not apply if such application is incompatible with any mandatory provisions of treaties and of acts of international organisations."*

2558 See Foster, 164-165. In Germany difficulties arose with regard to the relationship between fundamental rights provisions enshrined in the German Constitution and suchlike provisions embedded in the Community and EU legal order.

2559 While Germany, traditionally, adopted the *dualist* approach to the reception of international law, article 25 of the *Grundgesetz* states that general rules of public international law are an integral part of federal law and take precedence over national law. Furthermore, in order to cater particularly for further European integration a new article 23 of the *Grundgesetz* has been added. This Article states that sovereign powers can be transferred to the EU, provided that the transfer has the approval of both the *Bundestag*, as well as the *Bundesrat*. This thus illustrates that under the dualistic view, treaties and national law are mostly on a par

between both approaches may be relevant in the context of the interrelationship between the treaty and provisions of domestic law, for instance how international tax law may affect – the application of – national tax law.

9.3.1.C European Law and Tax Treaties (Policy)

In the light of this chapter's subject, the question emerges whether there are any relevant influences emanating from EU law on tax treaties, as discussed in chapter 8 of this research. On the one hand, the impact of EU law can ensue from policy integration through the implementation of secondary EU law by EU Member states. On the other hand, primary EU law influences tax law, as becomes apparent by the tax-related case law of the CJEU, which has emerged considerably in recent years. However, in the field of cross-border pensions, policy integrations developments that have an effect of treaty policy have remained limited. Secondary EU legislation in the sphere of the tax treatment of cross-border pensions has not been adopted, apparently mainly due to the requirement of unanimity as laid down in article 115 TFEU.

Moreover, as regards the distribution of taxing rights, it is established case-law of the CJEU that, in the absence of measures of unification or harmonisation within the EU, Member states remain competent to define the criteria for allocating their taxing rights in order, inter alia, to avoid double taxation. In this regard, the CJEU has held that a different treatment of nationals of the two contracting parties as a result of the division of taxing rights may constitute discrimination that is not contrary to the freedoms of movement.[2560] The court observed that whether the tax treatment of the taxpayers concerned is favourable or unfavourable is determined not, strictly speaking, by the choice of the connecting factor but by the level of taxation in the competent state, in the absence of any Community harmonisation of scales of direct taxation.[2561]

The CJEU has consistently held that double tax treaties are designed to eliminate or mitigate the detrimental effects on the functioning of the internal market, due to the coexistence of national tax systems.[2562] EU law, as it stands, does not lay down any general criteria for the attribution of areas of competence between the Member states in relation to the elimination of double taxation within the EU, and no uniform or harmonisation

---

in terms of legal force unless national law expressly provides otherwise. See also D Lovric, 'A Constitution Friendly to International Law: Germany and its Volkerrechtsfreundlichkeit' 25 Australian Year Book of International Law 75. With respect to the approach of the *Bundesverfassungsgericht*, see 2 BvM 1/76 *Philippinische Botschaft* (BVerfGE); 1 BvR 624/56 *Kriegsfolgeschäden* (BVerfGE).

2560 *Gilly* para 24 and 30.

2561 Ibid. para 34.

2562 *Kerckhaert/Morres* para 21; *Columbus Container Services* para 44.

measure designed to eliminate double taxation has yet been adopted at EU law level.[2563] The CJEU may not examine the relationship between a national measure, and the provisions of a double tax treaty, since that question does not fall within the scope of EU law.[2564]

Nevertheless, the CJEU has repeatedly held that although direct taxation falls under the competence of the Member states, that exclusive competence must be exercised in accordance with EU law requirements.[2565] In the light of the direct effect of the EU treaty freedoms and the higher ranking of the TFEU in relation to tax treaties, EU law may have an effect on tax treaties. For instance, advantages of a tax treaty to which, according to the provisions of the tax treaty, only residents of the Contracting State are entitled, should, under the same conditions, be extended to non-residents, provided that they are in a comparable situation.

Clear rules on which state may levy taxes provide legal certainty for internationally operating companies and natural persons.[2566] In of view of this, tax treaties contain provisions on administrative cooperation in the sphere of information exchange and assistance by the recovery of taxes.

9.3.2 *National Tax Treaty Policies*

The Netherlands, as well as Germany have set forth their policy pertaining to tax treaties, more specifically their preferences as regards the distribution of taxing rights embedded therein. With these, legally non-binding, policy documents the relevant states give expression to the states' guiding principles they adhere in the realm of treaty negotiations. These documents describe the negotiating stance for ongoing and future treaty negotiations and, what is more, they provide insight as regards what can be expected in new tax treaties in the forthcoming years, i.e. support foreseeability of tax treaties, and their amendments. Against the background of the present research, it is important to further address this as these amendments may have a considerable effect on the future (net) income, and the according information provision.[2567] What is more, amendments to tax treaties in practice often have a much larger financial impact than national law amendments. On top of the

2563 *Kerckhaert/Morres paras 22 and 23.* See also *Columbus Container Services* para 45.

2564 *Columbus Container Services* para 47 and case referred to.

2565 C-279/93 *Schumacker* ECLI:EU:C:1995:31 (CJEU) para 21; *Wielockx* para 16; *Safir* para 21; *De Groot* para 75 and *Schempp* para 19.

2566 Ministerie van Financiën, 14.

2567 In this regard, mention can be made of the quarterly overviews, issued by the Dutch Ministry of Finance, of countries with which treaty negotiations are underway or will be initiated.

changes in, for example, the distribution of taxing rights in the tax treaty, come the different methods of taxation in each of the contracting states, and any adverse effects of these. Overall, this has a significant impact on future net income. This will also become more apparent when the tax treaty, concluded between the Netherlands and German, is dealt with in section 9.3.3. In sum, this section's purpose is to explore to what extent the national tax treaty policies aid in the provision of information, in the light of the principles set in chapter 2, in particular foreseeability.

Regardless of the effect of the OECD Model Convention and United Nations model tax convention, double tax conventions are normally negotiated bilaterally between the contracting states. In these negotiations (future) contracting states often seek to secure agreement on a particular issue. For instance, states are free to agree bilaterally on including either provisions stipulating exclusive residence taxation of pensions, or to adopt (limited) source taxation rights. The conventions are negotiated individually in an intensive negotiation process between contracting states, each pursuing its own particular treaty policy and characterized by its legal tradition and *couleur locale*.[2568] Treaty negotiations are a process of 'give and take', the outcome of which strongly depends on the points to which both sides attach particular importance.[2569] Factors, such as mutual principles, the practical importance of the individual subjects, the economic importance of a treaty relationship and the political desirability of it are observed during treaty negotiations.[2570]

In addition, the circumstance that the potential contracting partner is a neighbouring country plays an instrumental role in treaty negotiations. In such situations, 'tailor-made' treaty provisions may be necessary to prevent differences in the respective national tax regimes – as a part due to geographical proximity – from playing a considerable role in opting for a place of residence or domicile, and taking account of CJEU's case-law. Furthermore, these specific treaty provisions may address issues in the field of cross-border employment, cross-border pensions and/or tax-induced emigration, which may arise between neighbouring countries. This has, for instance, been discussed during the treaty negotiations with Germany. A negotiation result that fits within these frameworks serves the legal certainty desired by taxpayers. By codifying the national tax rights, there is certainty and clarity about the tax treatment in the country of the tax treaty partner and

2568 D Beck, *Qualifikationskonflikte im Internationalen Steuerrecht: Ursachenanalyse, Systematisierung und Lösungskonzepte* (Springer, Wiesbaden 2016) 51.

2569 Cf. Ministerie van Financiën, 15.

2570 Cf. Kamerstukken II, 'Notitie Internationaal fiscaal (verdrags)beleid' (1996/97) 31.

double taxation - if necessary, ultimately through the consultation procedure - will be avoided.[2571]

Normally, at the end of the negotiation process, a number of differences remain that can only be bridged in a total compromise. In those cases, compensation will be sought elsewhere, for example, on points to which great importance is attributed in this nation's treaty tax policy, a concession may sometimes be desirable in order to achieve an end result that, as a whole, contains sufficient positive elements for the contracting state concerned. Therefore, as a result of bilateral treaty negotiations, separate tax treaties may show differences, either in content or in wording.

9.3.2.A Germany's Tax Treaty Policy: Verhandlungsgrundlage

9.3.2.A.I The Verhandlungsgrundlage as a Model for Treaty Negotiations

The German *Verhandlungsgrundlage* (translated as 'negotiation model') for double tax conventions has been issued by the German Ministry of Finance (*Bundesfinanzministerium*) in 2013, prior to which Germany did not have any model convention.[2572] Prior to entering into force, the model was approved by the Finance Committee of the German *Bundestag* and the *Länder*. This parliamentary approval should foster the acceptance, and legitimacy, of the model's content.[2573] However, the model does not preclude individual agreements in the respective agreements and the necessary flexibility in the treaty negotiation process. This will become apparent in the section dealing with the concluded treaty between the Netherlands and Germany.

This model consists of a treaty text, largely following the structure and content of the OECD Model Convection. The model serves as a guiding principle for future treaty negotiations and is aimed at standardising the German treaties. Moreover, it is aimed at increasing legal certainty, and foreseeability for the benefit of the persons subject to the treaty provisions, by using a uniformed wording of the treaty provisions.[2574]

The German Ministry points out that within the framework of the treaty negotiations, a balance must be struck between the competitive interest of the domestic business location,

2571 Ibid. 31.

2572 BMF, *Verhandlungsgrundlage für Doppelbesteuerungsabkommen im Bereich der Steuern vom Einkommen und Vermögen IV B 2 - S 1301/13/10009* (22 August 2013). See also J Lüdicke, 'Anmerkungen zur deutschen Verhandlungsgrundlage für Doppelbesteuerungsabkommen' IStR 26.

2573 J Lüdicke, *Überlegungen zur deutschen DBA-Politik* (Nomos, Baden-Baden 2008) 21.

2574 Cf. Beck, 52 and F Müller-Gatermann, 1032 (1036). 'Aktuelle deutsche Abkommenspolitik' 94 FR 1032, 1032.

the foreign activities of export-orientated German companies and the safeguarding of German taxation interest, all of which are tailored to the specific bilateral economic relations.[2575] As a result of the respective differences in national law and the national treaty policies of contracting states, differences in the form and content of tax treaty provisions continue to remain, depending on the negotiating situation. In view of this, this non-binding document is intended as a guideline for the efficient implementation of the double tax convention's objectives by using, as far as possible, a uniform formulation.[2576] Although the document does not have any legal effect, it does provide guidance as regards the treaty policy pursued by Germany. When necessary, the principles enshrined in this policy document can be amended or supplemented. The guideline follows the OECD Model Convention in form and – largely in – content, although it comprises a few additional provisions embedding statutory developments, in particular pertaining to securing tax revenue by curbing tax avoidance and evasion.

9.3.2.A.II Provisions of the Verhandlungsgrundlage

Although the German negotiation model largely follows the OECD Model Convention, some (deviating) specific points are of interest as regards the tax treatment of cross-border pensions.[2577] Firstly, the provision on employment income (Article 14) stipulates in paragraph 4 that contributions to a pension scheme established and recognized for tax purposes in another state shall, for the purpose of determining the individual's taxable income, benefit from the same tax advantages, under the same conditions and limitations, as contributions made to a pension scheme that is recognized for tax purposes in the employee's residence state, provided that he only became a resident of that state at the start of his employment and contributions had already been made under the same pension scheme.[2578] The deductibility of the pension contributions in the host state does not necessarily have to correspond to a (future) right of taxation in this state, in terms of 'internal coherence' of the national tax system.

Paragraph 5 of that same provision sets out that the term 'pension scheme' means, as far as Germany is concerned, schemes as mentioned under section 1 of *Betriebsrentengesetz*,

2575 Bundesministerium der Finanzen, 'Verhandlungsgrundlage für Doppelbesteuerungsabkommen im Bereich der Steuern vom Einkommen und Vermögen' 2013) <https://www.bundesfinanzministerium.de/Content/DE/Standardartikel/Themen/Steuern/Internationales_Steuerrecht/Allgemeine_Informationen/2013-08-22-Verhandlungsgrundlage-Doppelbesteuerungsabkommen-Steuern-vom-Einkommen-und-Vermoegen.html> accessed 24 March 2020.

2576 Ibid.

2577 See more specifically as regards the deviations Lüdicke, 'Anmerkungen zur deutschen Verhandlungsgrundlage für Doppelbesteuerungsabkommen' 27.

2578 This provision largely corresponds to paragraph 37 of the OECD commentary on article 18 OECD MC. This has also been laid down in article 24, para 6 of the tax treaty Netherland-Germany.

i.e. occupational pensions. As regards the term 'tax benefit' paragraph 6 stipulates that, as German law is concerned, this concerns the exemption of contributions pursuant to § 3, nr. 6 EStG. The latter provision refers to contributions to the schemes of a *Pensionsfonds, Pensionskasse,* or *Direktversicherung.* The *Direktzusage* and *Unterstützungskasse* are, obviously, not mentioned as they are subject to a different form of tax relief. It had already been recognized as a (new) goal of German treaty policy that, in the case of employees working cross-border, the tax deductibility of the pension contributions must be ensured in cases where these contributions are continued to be paid to a pension institution in the country of origin while the employee is working abroad.[2579] In these cases the tax treatment granted to the pension contributions, paid by individuals working outside their home countries, may vary from one country to the other, and are highly dependent on the circumstances of each case.[2580]

In particular worthy of note is the third paragraph of Article 17. This provision, as an exception to the first paragraph, provides that pensions, similar remuneration or annuities may also be taxed in the source state, if they are attributable, in whole or in part, to contributions which were, in that State and for more than 15 years (in total), subject to tax relief.[2581] If both states are entitled to tax, the residence state shall grant a credit for the tax charged in the country of source. As Lüdicke contends, in view of the transition to deferred taxation of pension benefits in Germany, this, from art. 18 OECD MC deviating treaty provision attributing the taxing right to the source state, will increase in relevance for Germany in the coming years.[2582]

With regard to the deferred taxation of pension, particular issues in the domain of cross-border pensions may arise. Firstly, the risk of considerable fragmentation of the taxation of pensions in the case of short-term activities in one State. Secondly, the common enforcement problems which may arise if the pensioner – from the point of view of the former State of employment – who is now resident abroad has paid his pension contribution

2579 Lüdicke, 'Anmerkungen zur deutschen Verhandlungsgrundlage für Doppelbesteuerungsabkommen' 32 and H Krabbe, 'Das neue OECD-Musterabkommen und die deutsche Abkommenspolitik' StbJb 31, 41 ff.

2580 See also paragraph 33 of the OECD commentary on Article 18 OECD MC. For instance, in cases where before starting to work abroad, pension contributions are paid by or for these individuals, these contributions commonly qualify for tax relief in the home country. Upon starting to work abroad, these contributions may, in some cases, continue to qualify for tax relief. In cases where the individual, for instance, remains resident and fully taxable in the home country, pension contributions made to a pension scheme established in the home country will generally continue to qualify for relief there. However, frequently, pension contributions paid in the home country by an individual working abroad do not qualify for tax relief under the domestic laws of either the home country or the host country.

2581 Either by exempting the contributions from the taxable income, deducting them for tax purposes or were allowed some other form of beneficial treatment by the State of source.

2582 Lüdicke, 'Anmerkungen zur deutschen Verhandlungsgrundlage für Doppelbesteuerungsabkommen' 23.

into an old-age provision institution – which is also foreign from the point of view of the former State of employment – possibly in a third State.[2583] Article 17, para 3 attempts to take account of these issues by stipulating that the former State of employment may tax pensions only under certain restrictive conditions, including in particular a 15-year tax-privileged accrual phase.[2584] However, it should be noted that the agreement of these clauses, safeguarding the deferred taxation of pensions, often requires intensive treaty negotiations in cases where the other contracting states also claims a taxing right on retirement income.[2585] The recently concluded tax treaties, such as the treaty Netherlands-Germany, suggest that, by no means, all contracting states will agree, and accordingly take full account, of Germany's negotiating preferences in this regard.

As regards pensions accrued during government service, art. 18, paragraph 2 provides that pensions and other similar remuneration paid by, or out of funds created by, the State, one of its *Länder*, or one of their political subdivisions or local authorities to an individual in respect of services rendered to that State, *Land* or political subdivision or local authority shall be taxable only in that State, except where the individual is a resident, and a national of resident state. In the latter case, the pension will merely be taxable in the resident state.

9.3.2.A.III Article 14, Paragraph 4 Verhandlungsgrundlage and Paragraph 37 of the Commentaries OECD MC: Equality with Co-workers

With a view to the tax treatment of cross-border pensions, Article 14, paragraph 4 of the *Verhandlungsgrundlage* deserves considerable attention. The wording of this provision largely corresponds to paragraph 37 of the commentaries on the OECD MC. Both provisions will be discussed thoroughly below.

This is considered an important provision that should be used more widely, given the number of employees working abroad.[2586] Moreover, individuals working across borders will often seek to continue contributing to a retirement scheme in their country of origin during their absence abroad, since switching pension schemes can result in a loss of pension rights and benefits and practical difficulties may arise from maintaining different pension schemes in different countries.[2587] Furthermore, it is difficult to defend that

2583 Cf. R Portner, 'Steuerrechtliche Aspekte der betrieblichen Altersversorgung bei international mobilen Arbeitnehmern' 44 BB 351, 351.

2584 Lüdicke, 'Anmerkungen zur deutschen Verhandlungsgrundlage für Doppelbesteuerungsabkommen' 33.

2585 Müller-Gatermann, 1036.

2586 Bobbett and Avery Jones, 10.

2587 See also paragraph 32 of the OECD commentary on Article 18 OECD MC.

individuals working side by side (i.e. colleagues) are treated differently for tax purposes, depending on whether their pension scheme was established at home or abroad.[2588]

At this point, a brief word on paragraph 37 of the commentaries is appropriate. Main points of interest are the following:

- The suggested provision covers contributions paid to all types of pension schemes, including individual retirement schemes and social security schemes.[2589] Article 24, paragraph 6 of the Double Tax Convention concluded between the Netherlands and Germany stipulates that for the purposes of this provision, 'pension scheme' includes a pension scheme established under a public social security system. Under the latter provision, no reference is thus made to individual retirement schemes.
- As it is not unusual for individuals to work in a number of different countries in succession, States may extend the suggested provision to funds established in third States by adopting an alternative version of the suggested provision.[2590]
- The tax relief pertaining to the contributions paid to the home country pension scheme under the conditions set out can be given by either the home country (the country where the pension scheme is situated) or by the host country (the country where the economic activities are carried out).[2591]
- The suggested provision applies to non-residents working in the host State, as well as to individuals who attain residence there.[2592]
- The suggested provision is not limited to individuals who are residents of the home State immediately prior to providing services in the host State.[2593]
- The suggested provision imposes no limits on the length of time for which an individual can work in the host State.[2594]

2588 See also paragraph 51 of the OECD commentary on Article 18 OECD MC.

2589 Paragraph 35 of the OECD commentary on Article 18 OECD MC. This paragraph of the commentaries points out that many member countries have entered into bilateral social security 'totalisation agreements' which may help to partially avoid the problem with respect to contributions to social security schemes but these agreements, however, usually do not deal with the tax treatment of cross-border contributions. In the case of an occupational scheme to which both the employer (constituting an employment benefit for the employee) and the employees contribute, the provision covers both these contributions. Furthermore, paragraph 37, para 2, under b refers to a pension scheme as an 'arrangement'. This broad term, is intended to include various forms of pension scheme (social security, occupational or individual retirement schemes), see Paragraph 61 of the OECD commentary on article 18 OECD MC.

2590 Paragraph 38 of the OECD commentary on article 18 OECD MC.

2591 Paragraph 41 of the OECD commentary on Article 18 OECD MC. Paragraph 42 points out that a solution in that the home country would grant tax relief might not be effective, as the individual might have no or little taxable income in that state. Furthermore, practical considerations suggest that it would be preferable that the host would provide the tax relief.

2592 Paragraph 44 of the OECD commentary on Article 18 OECD MC.

2593 Paragraph 46 of the OECD commentary on Article 18 OECD MC.

2594 Paragraph 47 of the OECD commentary on Article 18 OECD MC. It could however be contended that, if an individual works in the host State for sufficiently long, it in effect becomes his home country and the

Furthermore, this extension of the tax relief to pension contributions paid to foreign pension institutions is subject to several preconditions. Firstly, the pension scheme must be accepted by the competent authority of that State (i.e. the host state) as 'generally corresponding' to a pension scheme recognised as such for tax purposes by that State. It has not been further delineated when a pension scheme 'generally corresponds' to a pension scheme recognized in the host state. It is hard to interpret this condition in cases where states have different types of pension schemes, and it would be helpful if the competent authority of each state made general statements about what types of schemes would be accepted as corresponding to the scheme recognized by that State for tax purposes.[2595] Some states have already done so by accepting a broad range of pension schemes, such as social security schemes. As the OECD commentary points out, this first condition does not necessarily ensure the equivalent tax treatment of contributions where an individual was working abroad and of contributions while working in the home country.[2596] This issue arises in cases where the host State's rules for recognizing pension schemes are narrower compared to those of the home state. As a result, the contributions paid to his home country pension scheme could be less favorably treated when he was working in the host country, rather than in the home country. Lastly, it is a matter for the competent authority of the host State to determine whether the home state scheme corresponds to tax recognized schemes in the host State.[2597] Contracting states may seek to specify explicitly to which existing schemes the provision shall apply or to determine how the competent authorities construe the term 'generally corresponding' (how widely interpreted and what tests are imposed). As regards the latter, Germany elucidated her stance on contributions paid to foreign (occupational) pension schemes.[2598] Germany, very briefly, addressed the issue in a *BMF-Schreiben*.[2599]

provision should cease to apply. Hence, some host countries already restrict relief for contributions to foreign pension schemes to cases where the individuals are present on a temporary basis.

2595 Bobbett and Avery Jones, 10.

2596 Paragraph 50 of the OECD commentary on Article 18 OECD MC.

2597 Paragraph 52 of the OECD commentary on Article 18 OECD MC.

2598 BMF, *Steuerliche Förderung der privaten Altersvorsorge und betrieblichen Altersversorgung IV C 3 - S 2015/11/10002/ IV C 5 - S 2333/09/10005* para 314 which has been repealed by BMF, *Steuerliche Förderung der betrieblichen Altersversorgung IV C 5 - S 2333/19/10008:017* para 36.

2599 Critical as regards this approach is Portner, 'Rechtsvergleichende Qualifizierung ausländischer Altersversorgungspläne/-einrichtungen'. The author argues that the decisive factor for the comparability of the foreign pension scheme is that contributions are paid to a legally independent pension institution controlled by the supervisory authority, which provides occupational pension benefits for an employer for the benefit of employees and grants employees their own entitlement to the promised pension benefits. In my opinion, this explanation relies too heavily on the German approach, as laid down in the *Betriebsrentengesetz* and it remains to be seen what is understood under 'granting employees own entitlements'.

As regards paragraph 37 of the Commentaries, it has further been defined, when a pension scheme is 'recognized for tax purposes.' This is true if contributions to the pension scheme concerned would qualify for tax relief in the host State.[2600] Hence, this provision seeks to limit its scope to contributions made to a pension scheme merely if the contributions would qualify for tax relief in that State.[2601] It is pointed out that, in bilateral negotiations, countries may prefer to further delineate the qualifying pension schemes in terms that match the respective domestic laws of the treaty partners.[2602] From a European law perspective, this provision could be considered inadequate since it remains to be seen whether contracting states will agree to the complex German regulatory framework governing the taxation of retirement income, and actually allow the deductibility of contributions paid across borders.[2603]

In short, paragraph 37 ensures that the contributions must be treated for tax purposes in a way which corresponds to the way in which they would be treated if these contributions were paid to a scheme established in the host State, i.e. qualifying for the same tax relief for both the employee and the employer.[2604] This provision does not necessarily ensure equivalent tax treatment of contributions paid when an individual is working abroad compared to contributions paid when he is working in the home country; however, it does ensure an equivalent tax treatment of the contributions of co-workers.[2605] Co-workers would thus be not be treated differently for tax purposes, depending on whether their pension scheme was established at home or abroad.[2606]

9.3.2.B Dutch Tax Treaty Policy: Notitie Fiscaal Verdragsbeleid 2011 and 2020

The Dutch *Notitie Fiscaal Verdragsbeleid* (translated freely as 'Memorandum on Tax Treaty Policy) discusses, more extensively compared to the German *Verhandlungsgrundlage*, the preferences and positions taken by the Netherlands in treaty negotiations. The memorandum was released on 11 February 2011 by the Dutch Ministry of Finance, and has a policy nature.[2607]

2600 Paragraph 37, nr. 2, under b of the OECD commentary on article 18 OECD MC.
2601 Paragraph 64 of the OECD commentary on Article 18 OECD MC.
2602 Paragraph 65 of the OECD commentary on Article 18 OECD MC.
2603 Cf. Lüdicke, 'Anmerkungen zur deutschen Verhandlungsgrundlage für Doppelbesteuerungsabkommen' 32.
2604 Paragraph 55 of the OECD commentary on Article 18 OECD MC.
2605 Paragraph 59 of the OECD commentary on Article 18 OECD MC.
2606 See also paragraph 51 of the OECD commentary on Article 18 OECD MC.
2607 Ministerie van Financiën, 10. See also FPG Pötgens, 'Notitie Fiscaal Verdragsbeleid 2011 en arbeidsinkomsten' 119 TFO.

As regards the Dutch treaty policy, memorandums had already been published in 1987, 1996 and 1998.[2608] Due to worldwide fundamental changes on the political, as well as economic level, these memorandums were largely superseded.[2609] However, the 2011 memorandum had a less technical character than its 1987 and 1998 predecessors and was more policy oriented. However, the position of the Netherlands in treaty policy has shifted from residence state taxation (1987) to source state taxation (2011), for both private pensions as well as public pensions. The 2011 memorandum builds on these previously issued memorandums and the majority of the technical explanations in these memorandums still apply in full.[2610] Hence, the present memorandum solely addresses these technical points where an amendment or development has occurred. This memorandum describes the core objective of Dutch tax treaty policy and the manner in which this core objectives can be implemented. The implementation must fit within a framework of policy principles that take account of changes in economic circumstances, developments in tax policy in the Netherlands as reflected in amendments to national tax laws and international tax developments that are reflected, for example, in amendments to the OECD model treaty.[2611]

The Netherlands also recognized that in treaty negotiations, they will be confronted with a wide variety of tax systems, legal systems, and treaty policy principles.[2612] It is, hence, pointed out that solely, tailor-made proposals can provide a good response to the specific characteristics of such bilateral relations. However, also in this tailor-made approach, the Netherlands strives to conclude tax treaties corresponding, as far as possible, with the OECD Model Convention.[2613] Since the OECD Model Convention serves as a general starting point, in this regard, and the Netherlands strives for gearing the treaty to the specific bilateral relation, a separate Dutch standard treaty was considered no longer suitable.[2614] Therefore, the Netherlands departed from the approach of using a standard

2608 Ministerie van Financiën, 9. See Kamerstukken II, 'Notitie Algemeen fiscaal verdragsbeleid' (1987/88) [20 365]; Kamerstukken II, 'Notitie Internationaal fiscaal (verdrags)beleid' and Kamerstukken II, *Uitgangspunten van het beleid op het terrein van het internationaal fiscaal (verdragen)recht* (1997/98) respectively. For a more extensive discussion of these memorandums see Starink, 117 ff.

2609 These developments are set out in Annexes I, II, III of the memorandum.

2610 Ministerie van Financiën, 13.

2611 Ibid. 14.

2612 Ibid. 9.

2613 Ibid. 9.

2614 Ibid. 10.

treaty[2615], contrary to the German approach of using the *Verhandlungsgrundlage.*[2616] The 2011 memorandum sets forth the main policy principles that shall be uphold during treaty negotiations, and focuses on points where Dutch treaty policy departs from the OECD Model Convention and the memorandums previously issued, which largely retain their value.[2617]

In January 2021, the Dutch State Secretary of Finance reconfirmed that the Netherlands takes the OECD model convention as its starting point in tax treaty negotiations.[2618] Annex 2 to the NFV 2020 contains an article-by-article overview of the Dutch approach and points out in which parts this approach deviates from the OECD Model Convention. This appendix sets out the starting points for treaty negotiations. The Netherlands no longer uses a model treaty, as it did in the past (the 1987 Dutch standard treaty). These model treaties are used to prepare for the negotiations, are constantly amended, contain different options, and change per negotiation. After all, the Dutch commitment differs per negotiation, depending on the position of the country with which it is negotiating. Even though the treaty negotiations are based on model treaty texts, there is no Dutch model treaty that is entirely in line with the NFV 2020.

2615 In 1998 the Dutch State Secretary considered that although a (renewed) *Nederlands Standaardverdrag 1987* (Dutch Standard Treaty 1987) had the advantage of providing a fairly uniform and clear picture of Dutch treaty policy, there was less need to enshrine what there is, but more need to indicate what the Netherlands is striving for. Hence, given the large differences in modalities, the publication of a new standard text was considered less suitable. It was noted that since the relative weight given to a subject may vary from one treaty relationship to another as a result of a multitude of factors, it is virtually impossible to catch Dutch treaty policy and all conceivable margins in a single text for each subject. However, an unequivocal answer about the margins within which the Netherlands will in practice be prepared to accept deviating solutions is not possible, since such margins are highly dependent on the relative weight of each individual subject in the specific bilateral relationship and on the willingness of the potential treaty partner to make any concession on that subject, or to offer compensation elsewhere in the treaty in return. Furthermore, this avoids, as far as possible, the need for Dutch treaty negotiators to explain to such a potential treaty partner why the Netherlands wishes to deviate from the Dutch model treaty in that specific treaty relationship. Lastly, the final result of the negotiations achieved by the Netherlands is therefore always a compromise between the two contracting states and will therefore hardly ever fully correspond to the Dutch standpoint in treaty negotiations. See Kamerstukken II, *Uitgangspunten van het beleid op het terrein van het internationaal fiscaal (verdragen)recht* section 4.2.

2616 Furthermore, the Dutch parliament is only involved in the adoption procedure of a treaty at the final stage of a normally lengthy negotiation process. At that point in time merely two options exist; either full approval to the signed treaty text or abstention from approval. Amendments, as is possible with national legislation, cannot be proposed and initiatives cannot be taken by parliament. Partly as a result of this circumstance, questions of a more policy-related nature were raised in the context of the approval of a number of treaties submitted to the parliament in recent years and concerned lines for the future. It is therefore the intention of this memorandum to outline policy lines for the Dutch commitment to tax treaty negotiations. See Ministerie van Financiën, 13.

2617 Ibid. 10.

2618 Staatssecretaris van Financiën – Fiscaliteit en Belastingdienst, *Beantwoording vragen Notitie Fiscaal Verdragsbeleid 2020* (29 January 2021).

Pensions and Life Annuities: Residence State and/or Source State Taxation
Dutch treaty policy specifies that Dutch national tax legislation assumes that income from employment in the private sector is taxed by the State of employment, i.e. a tax levied by the State where the work is carried out.[2619] This applies to income from current employment, but also to income from previous employment, including pensions. The Netherlands, thus, adheres to the source state-principle. In this regard, pension benefits are considered deferred wages.[2620] This point of view has been (partly) endorsed in literature.[2621] In the treaty policy it is noted that this point of view is reflected in the EET-system, operated by the Netherlands and a similar tax system applies to life annuities.[2622]

Already in the 1998 memorandum, a shift in the Dutch treaty approach became apparent.[2623] The Dutch State Secretary pointed out that in treaty relationships – unlike in 1987 – the Netherlands did not strive for an unabridged residence state taxation for private pensions but, rather, considered that, under certain circumstances, a source state taxation is adequate as a derogation of the residence state-principle. Also in the memorandum '*Belastingen in de 21e eeuw*', more weight was put on the source state's position if that state had fiscally facilitated the pension contributions (thus seeking to preserve, to some extent, internal coherence of the national tax system).

The 2011 memorandum points out that Article 18 of the OECD Model Convention, is based on the attribution of the taxing right to the pensioner's state of residence, as the pensioner benefits from public facilities in his residence state.[2624] Therefore, the 1998 memorandum stipulated that Dutch treaty policy follows the main principle as laid down in Article 18, notwithstanding the tax system enshrined in Dutch tax law, but did define two exceptions.[2625] Firstly, the Netherlands strived to prevent fiscally induced emigration to a state with a favourable tax regiment for surrender values of pensions. Secondly, it sought a (partial or otherwise) source state levy for regular pension benefits if the source state had facilitated the pension accrual for tax purposes, and the state of residence subjects the benefits to a special tax regime.

2619 Ministerie van Financiën, 53.
2620 Ibid. 53.
2621 See for instance I.J.J. Burgers, 'Internationaal verdragsbeleid inzake pensioenen en lijfrenten: quo vado?' WFR 5. This author endorses the position that pension should be treated as deferred wage in discussions on the distribution of taxing rights on cross-border pensions. She argues that, in this regard, a source state levy is more suitable, and arguments underpinning a residence state levy are outdated. See also Starink, chapter 4.
2622 Ministerie van Financiën, 53.
2623 Kamerstukken II, 'Notitie Internationaal fiscaal (verdrags)beleid' 50-51.
2624 Ministerie van Financiën.
2625 Kamerstukken II, 'Notitie Internationaal fiscaal (verdrags)beleid'.

As regards the source state taxation of pension, the Dutch tax treaty policy states that demographic developments, together with the increasingly internationalised labour market, lead to an increase in the number of taxpayers who will receive the pension accrued in the Netherlands after retirement abroad.[2626] Given this, the Dutch position is that this increases the financial importance of the Netherlands as a source state, as pension accrual is facilitated through exemption and deduction of contributions. Furthermore, preferences of fiscally facilitating states are recognized increasingly on an international level.[2627] Apart from the demographic developments (in turn having a budgetary effect), the memorandum sets forth little reasons of principle why, in derogation of article 18 OECD MC (residence state taxation grounded on the consideration that the person benefits from the public facilities in that state) a source state taxation should be pleaded for.[2628] No arguments based on tax theory or policy have been provided; strongly suggesting that the shift in policy is based on budgetary considerations.[2629] The revisited treaty policy and the exceptions involved, have, at least, not rendered the tax system more simple. Kavelaars contends that the Netherlands is going too far in striving for an unlimited source state tax and that a limited source state tax, while applying the credit method in the country of residence, leads to a more balanced result.[2630]

It follows from the above, as a general rule, that the Netherlands in the 2011 memorandum sought to agree a source state levy for fiscally facilitated accrued pensions, both for regular pension benefits as well as for pension surrender values, independent of the tax treatment in the pensioner's (new) state of residence.[2631] In the context of a final compromise, the Netherlands is prepared to, as an alternative, agree with individual treaty partners, on a limited taxing right for the source state, depending on the interaction between the tax

---

2626 Ministerie van Financiën, 54.

2627 Ibid. 54. See Para. 15 ff. Commentary on article 18 Concerning the Taxation of Pensions of Model Tax Convention on Income and on Capital 2017.

2628 Cf. Pötgens.

2629 Cf. Starink, 125-126.

2630 P Kavelaars, 'Arbeidsinkomsten en verdragsbeleid' MBB. He rightly addresses a number of bottlenecks in the new treaty policy. These bottlenecks relate in particular to situations in which the accrual of pension in the source state has not been built up entirely through an EET-system. This occurs if there has been an international pension capital transfer or if the country that applied the EET-system is not the country where the pension provider is established.

2631 Ministerie van Financiën, 54-55. The 2011 memorandum rightly points out that, for this purpose it is also important that experience has been gained with a, whether or not partial, source state levy, whereby the allocation of the right to tax depends partly on the tax treatment of the pension in the pensioner's country of residence and it has been shown that in practice it is not easy to gain insight into the method of taxation in the country of residence in question. In the tax treaty Netherlands-Belgium, the source state taxation of pensions has been made conditional on the pensions' tax treatment in the residence state, see Article 18, para 2 of that treaty. This provision, *inter alia*, set outs that the retirement income shall not be taxed in the Contracting State of which the recipient is a resident at the generally applicable rate of tax on income derived from non-independent occupations, or the gross amount of such income is less than 90 per cent.

systems of the two treaty partners and the likely migration patterns between the states concerned. A limited taxing right, in this regard, refers to levying tax up to a predetermined maximum percentage.[2632] In these cases, pursuant to the Dutch treaty policy, the state of residence, providing the pensioner with access to public facilities, may then, if considered necessary, also subject the pension benefit to tax, taking account of the, pursuant to the treaty, limited amount of tax levied by the source state.[2633]

In May 2020, a revised memorandum was issued.[2634] A new memorandum was needed because the 2011 memorandum was outdated by national and international developments in the field of combating tax evasion, rather than by a focus on pension taxation. Also in the *Notitie Fiscaal Verdragsbeleid 2020*, the Netherlands strives in its tax treaties for an integral source state taxation of tax-facilitated private as well as public pensions, making no distinction between periodic or non-periodic payments (lump sum payments).[2635] The underlying reason for this is the application of the principle of deferred taxation in the Netherlands during the accrual phase, under the assumption that the final payment will be taxed. A similar system applies to annuities (premiums are deductible and payments are taxed). Full source state taxation prevents Dutch taxing rights on pensions accrued in the Netherlands and tax-facilitated after (tax) emigration from being lost. The Netherlands also aims for full source state taxation of benefits paid under the social security legislation of one state to a resident of the other state.

With this, the Netherlands is using an alternative treaty text as described in the OECD commentary. The Netherlands recognizes that this deviates from the exclusive residence state taxation for private pensions and social security benefits as laid down in the OECD model convention, and that on this point the Netherlands is usually the requesting party in treaty negotiations.[2636] The Netherlands recognizes that it will therefore often occur that the Dutch aspiration for an integral source state taxation is not shared by the treaty partner. In those cases, according to the Netherlands, an alternative division of taxation (compromise) can be agreed upon, for example, depending on the bilateral situation, the Netherlands may agree to include only a partial source state levy (e.g. a percentage-limited

2632 Ibid. 55.

2633 Ibid. 55. In drafting such treaty provisions, attention will be paid to aspects of enforceability for the parties concerned, in particular with respect to persons who reside in the Netherlands or the other State only for a short period of time.

2634 Ministerie van Financiën, 'Notitie Fiscaal Verdragsbeleid 2020' (2020).

2635 Ibid. 23-24.

2636 Ibid. 24.

source state tax), in the treaty or to retain the taxing rights on large pensions and on all lump sums.[2637]

9.3.3 *The Double Tax Convention Concluded Between the Netherlands and Germany*

9.3.3.A Introduction

The Double Tax Convention, signed on the 12 April 2012 in Berlin, between the Federal Republic of Germany and the Kingdom of the Netherlands for the Avoidance of Double Taxation and the Prevention of Tax Evasion in the Field of Taxes on Income entered into force on 1 December 2016.[2638] The new tax treaty Netherlands-Germany (2012)[2639] repealed the old bilateral tax treaty (concluded on 16 June 1959 in the Hague[2640]).[2641] As tax treaties are, as a rule, concluded between states having strong economic, financial and political ties, they are also concluded in cases of neighbouring countries, such as the Netherlands and Germany.[2642]

Unlike the Netherlands, in Germany the new tax treaty has been discussed very briefly in parliament.[2643] Partly as a result of the extensive parliamentary debate in the Netherlands, the original intended implementation date of 1 January 2014 was not met. During the debates in Dutch Parliament, attention was regularly drawn to pensioners in Germany

---

2637 Staatssecretaris van Financiën – Fiscaliteit en Belastingdienst, *Antwoorden schriftelijk overleg Notitie Fiscaal Verdragsbeleid* (21 September 2020) 35-36 and 38-39.

2638 Gesetz zu dem Abkommen vom 12. April 2012 zwischen der Bundesrepublik Deutschland und dem Königreich der Niederlande zur Vermeidung der Doppelbesteuerung und zur Verhinderung der Steuerverkürzung auf dem Gebiet der Steuern vom Einkommen and *Verdrag tussen het Koninkrijk der Nederlanden en de Bondsrepubliek Duitsland tot het vermijden van dubbele belasting en het voorkomen van het ontgaan van belasting met betrekking tot belastingen naar het inkomen (met Bijlage, Protocol en Onderlinge Overeenkomst)* (Tractatenblad 2012, nr 123 23 July 2012).

2639 Abkommen Zwischen der Bundesrepublik Deutschland und dem Königreich der Niederlande zur Vermeidung der Doppelbesteuerung und zur Verhinderung der Steuerverkürzung auf dem Gebiet der Steuern Vom Einkommen *BGBl. II* 2012, 1414, 1415; *BStBl. I* 2016, 47, 48 or Verdrag Tussen het Koninkrijk der Nederlanden en de Bondsrepubliek Duitsland tot het Vermijden van Dubbele Belasting en het Voorkomen van het Ontgaan van Belasting met Betrekking tot Belastingen naar het Inkomen, (*Trb.* 2012, 123); *Stb.* 2015, 198.

2640 Agreement between the Kingdom of the Netherlands and the Federal Republic of Germany for the avoidance of double taxation with respect to income and capital and various other taxes, and for the regulation of other fiscal matters, concluded 16 June 1959 and entered into force on 18 September 1960.

2641 To ensure legibility, below the 2012 treaty will be referred to as 'the new treaty', and the 1959 treaty as 'the old treaty'.

2642 See Kamerstukken II, *33 615, nr. 3 (MvT), section I.1* (2013/14). For figures on these economic and financial ties see Statisisches Bundesamt, *Statistisches Jahrbuch: Deutschland und Internationales* (2019) 429 ff.

2643 Entwurf eines Gesetzes zu dem Abkommen vom 12. April 2012 zwischen der Bundesrepublik Deutschland und dem Königreich der Niederlande zur Vermeidung der Doppelbesteuerung und zur Verhinderung der Steuerverkürzung auf dem Gebiet der Steuern vom Einkommen 24 September 2012, nr 17/10752.

with a Dutch pension.[2644] Notwithstanding a so-called general and specific transitional arrangement, intended to mitigate the financial consequences of the new treaty, in particular pensioners in Germany receiving a Dutch pension were financially affected by the amendment of the treaty article on pensions.[2645] This shift in taxing rights may have had an effect on the income position of both Dutch nationals who have moved to Germany after retirement, as well as on the position of German nationals who have worked in the Netherlands as frontier workers in the past and have in the context of their employment relationship built up Dutch pension rights. It may thus have an effect on a Dutch retired employee as well as a German retired employee.

One of the primary grounds for the repeal of the old treaty was that it no longer met the standards as set out by the OECD MC, and was one of the oldest treaties in force concluded by the Netherlands.[2646] Consequently, the treaty no longer reflected the status of the economic ties between the two states.[2647] Besides these common interests of both states in the revision of the old treaty, both states had their own interest during the treaty negotiations. As regards the old treaty, one of the major focus points on the side of the Netherlands was strengthening the (unfavourable) fiscal situation of Dutch resident frontier workers working in Germany.[2648] Drawing on this objective in the treaty negotiations, a compensation scheme and a broader application of the German *Splittingverfahren* for Dutch resident cross-border workers were of vital importance, and efforts were aimed at adopting a scheme to offset higher paid taxes and social security in the other country. Such scheme would ensure the equality of the frontier workers with

2644 Kamerstukken II, *33 615, nr 10 (Motie van de leden Nijboer en Kerstens)*. This was the only motion adopted and concerning the tracing of the consequences of working cross-border for taxation and social security, including pensions. See also Kamerstukken I, *33615 nr. B (Voorlopig verslag van de vaste commissie voor Financiën)*.

2645 The specific transitional scheme focuses specifically on the financial consequences of the amendment to the pension Article, which will be further elaborated on below. See also PHJ Essers, 'Pensionado's in Duitsland met in Nederland opgebouwde pensioenrechten en het nieuwe verdrag Nederland-Duitsland' in B Starink and M Visser (eds.), *Ondernemend met pensioen (Dietvorstbundel)* (Kluwer, Deventer 2015).

2646 Kamerstukken II, *33 615, nr. 3 (MvT), section I.1.*

2647 Entwurf eines Gesetzes zu dem Abkommen vom 12. April 2012 zwischen der Bundesrepublik Deutschland und dem Königreich der Niederlande zur Vermeidung der Doppelbesteuerung und zur Verhinderung der Steuerverkürzung auf dem Gebiet der Steuern vom Einkommen 24 September 2012, nr 17/10752, under A Problem und Ziel.

2648 See Kamerstukken II, *33 615, nr. 3 (MvT), subsection I.4 Grensarbeiders* (2013/14). This paragraph was included in line with the commitments made from the former state secretary for finances de Jager to include explicit considerations on the effects the new tax treaty would have on frontier workers, see for that purpose *Kabinetsstandpunt met betrekking tot de aanbevelingen van de Commissie grensarbeider* (BCPP 2008/2455 9 January 2009). In this regard, reference can be made to Kamerstukken II, *Socialeverzekeringspositie van grensarbeiders* (26834 nr 5 23 February 2001). See also Kamerstukken II, *33 615, nr 10 (Motie van de leden Nijboer en Kerstens)* 1-2 and Kamerstukken II, *25 087, appendix to nr 7* (2010/11), paragraph 2.14.

their colleagues in the working state.[2649] Contrarily, Germany was more concerned about cross-border investment structures and abuse of treaty benefits, for instance through *treaty shopping*[2650].

When the new treaty entered into force, the old treaty ceased to have effect. However, pursuant to Article 33, paragraph 6 of the convention, a transitional regulation had been in effect, allowing any person already entitled to benefits under the old treaty and entitled to higher benefits under the old treaty, compared to the new treaty, to opt to apply the old treaty for one year (during 2017), starting from the entry into force date of the new treaty.[2651]

9.3.3.B Private Pensions: Article 17

9.3.3.B.I Main Rule: Residence State Taxation

As a general rule, and adopting the principles as laid down in the OECD Model Convention, (private) pension[2652] income is taxable only in the state of residence of the recipient of the income, regardless of whether or not this state bears the burden of tax benefits linked to the generation of the income.[2653] This provision stipulates that, subject to the provisions of

2649 Akin to the compensation scheme implemented in the 2001 tax treaty concluded between the Netherlands and Belgium.

2650 In the event of *treaty shopping*, a third country resident obtains access to a treaty benefit through artificial arrangements.

2651 Article 33, paragraph 6 provided: "Notwithstanding paragraphs 2 and 3, if a person would be entitled to higher benefits under the 1959 Convention than under this [2012] Convention, the 1959 Convention shall, at the option of any such person, continue to apply in full in relation to that person for a period of one year from the date on which the provisions of this Convention would be applicable under paragraph 2."

2652 The OECD commentary to article 19 OECD MC points out that the word 'pension', under the ordinary meaning of the word, covers only periodic payments, whilst the term 'other similar remuneration' is broad enough to cover non-periodic payments, see section 5.1 of the OECD commentary on article 19 OECD Model Convention. For instance, a lump-sum payment in lieu of periodic pension payments made to a former State employee after cessation of employment may fall within paragraph 2 of the article. The commentary points out that the issue whether a particular lump-sum payment made in these circumstances is to be considered as other remuneration similar to a pension falling under paragraph 2 or as final remuneration for work performed falling under paragraph 1 is a question of fact which can be resolved in light of the factors presented in paragraph 5 of the Commentary on article 18. However, this paragraph of the Commentary seems deficient to resolve this qualification issue as it (largely) reiterates the first two sentences of paragraph 5.1 of the commentary to article 19 OECD MC.

2653 As laid down in article 17, par. 2 of the treaty. There is no authentic English text of the treaty. However, paragraph XIII of the protocol to the tax treaty sets out that benefits arising from a Dutch *vitaliteitssparen* scheme as part of the *Wet IB 2001*, are taxable only in the Contracting State from which it originates. For the purposes of this Article, the first sentence of paragraph 5 of article 17 shall apply *mutatis mutandis*, as regards the (deemed) source of the benefits. If an employer's payment has unduly been subject to a wage tax deduction, there is the possibility of submitting a refund application, unless the corresponding income from employment has already been subject to an assessment, see BMF, *Steuerliche Behandlung von Alterseinkünften nach Artikel 17 des Abkommens vom 12. April 2012 zwischen der Bundesrepublik*

Article 18, paragraph 2, pensions, and other similar remuneration, derived by a resident of a Contracting State, as well as annuities paid to a resident of a Contracting State, shall be taxable in that state.

The main rule also prescribes that pensions, and other benefits paid under the provisions of a Contracting State's social security scheme (social security pension), paid to a resident of the other Contracting State, shall be taxed in the other State. As a main rule, this provision thus allocates the exclusive taxing right on pension income to the taxable person's residence state[2654] This constitutes a substantial shift compared to the old treaty. The aforementioned change in taxing right was introduced mainly with a view to undoing any unintended advantage from a Dutch point of view, namely the tax facilitation of pension accrual in the Netherlands and the favourable German taxation of foreign pensions.[2655]

Deutschland und dem Königreich der Niederlande zur Vermeidung der Doppelbesteuerung und zur Verhinderung der Steuerverkürzung auf dem Gebiet der Steuern vom Einkommen IV B 3 - S 1301-NDL/15/10002 (24 January 2017) 6-7. Furthermore, income from pension which, in accordance with Article 17 of the treaty, may only be taxed in the Netherlands counts as income not subject to German income tax for the purposes of calculating the income limits for the application for unlimited tax liability in accordance with the second sentence of § 1, para. 3 EStG.

2654 Under the old treaty, article 12, paragraph 1 allocated the taxing right pertaining to private pensions, as a main rule, to the residence state. However, pursuant to article 12, paragraph 2 and 3, under a, the taxing right on statutory pensions was allocated to the source state. For instance, the *AOW* pension benefits of a German-resident pensioner were taxed in the Netherlands. This shift of taxing right from Germany to the Netherland as regards private pensions has had considerable effects on the income position of retired frontier workers. This is mainly due to the favourable treatment of pensions in Germany under the *Ertragsanteilbesteuerung* or *Besteuerungsanteil*, in conjunction with the tax base exemption which was double in the event of partners jointly returning their tax assessment. In many cases, recipients of a Dutch pension amounting to (max.) € 50,000 living in Germany were not due any German income tax. See T Lühn, 'Quellenstaatsbesteuerung von Renten und Ruhegehältern im neuen DBA mit den Niederlanden – Niederländische Begünstigungsregelung ab 2016' 4 IWB. In some cases the tax burden increased with around 895%, see Kamerstukken II, *33 615, nr 8* (2013/14) 27 ff. For numerous calculations on the effects of the shift of taxing right concerning pensions see Kamerstukken II, *33 615, nr 5 (Nota naar aanleiding van het verslag)* (2013/14) 27-30. In 2011 it was found that there is no consistent approach at the *Finanzämter* with regard to the qualification of Dutch occupational pensions. Some *Finanzämter* equate these pensions with *Leistungen aus einer betrieblichen Altersvorsorgung*, as a result of which 58% of them are classified as *Besteuerungsanteil* and some *Finanzämter* classify the pensions as *Leibrente aus einem Altersvorsorgevertrag or aus einer betrieblichen Altersvorsorsorgung*, as a result of which only 18% of them are taxed as *Ertragsanteil.* See B Kloosterman, UP Meyer and D Laruelle, 'Welk buurland is een fiscaal paradijs voor gepensioneerden?' Over de grens.

2655 Kamerstukken II, 16. Under the old tax treaty a pensioner living in Germany and receiving a Dutch statutory and occupational pension, was liable to pay tax in the Netherlands on his statutory pension and in Germany liable to tax on his occupational pension. Under the new treaty, both the statutory pension and the occupational pension are taxable in the Netherlands, provided that the total gross amount exceeds €15,000. This means that the pension will be fully taxed in the Netherlands and the taxpayer can, if he meets the conditions, be regarded as a qualifying foreign taxpayer pursuant to article 7.8 Wet IB 2001. This allows him to be granted the same tax advantages (deductions and tax credits) as a resident of the Netherlands, such as mortgage interest deduction. Under the old treaty, a pensioner residing in the Netherlands had to

This attribution of the exclusive taxing right to the residence state is grounded on several policy and administrative considerations.[2656] One of these grounds is that the recipient's residence state is in a better position, than any other state, to take account of the recipient's overall ability to pay tax, normally being dependent on the taxable person's worldwide income and personal circumstances, in order to apply appropriate tax rates and grant personal allowances concerned.[2657] Furthermore, this exclusive attribution prevents an administrative burden being imposed on the recipient, in terms of having to comply with tax obligations in other states than the residence state. Furthermore, the allocation rule is supported by the idea that, after emigration, the person concerned uses all the public facilities of his new State of residence and, as a resident of that State, must also contribute to the costs thereof.

9.3.3.B.II The Scope of Residence State-taxation: Pensions, Similar Remuneration, Annuities and Social Security Pensions

Commentary on Article 18 of the OECD MC

As regards the scope of Article 18 of the OECD MC the commentaries point out that it does not only cover pensions direct paid to former employees, but also to other beneficiaries (e.g. surviving spouses, companions or children of the employees) and other similar payments, such as annuities, paid in respect of past employment.[2658] This provision of the OECD MC solely applies to payments made in consideration of past employment, hence, for instance, being not applicable to an annuity directly acquired through capital not funded through an employment pension scheme. Furthermore, this exclusive residence taxation applies irrespective of the tax treatment of the pension scheme from which the payment arises, as the provision's text does not refer to 'fiscally facilitated pensions' or a phrase similar to this. Whether payments made to an employee following cessation of his employment fall under the scope of Article 17 will be established by the nature of these payments, taking account of the facts and circumstances in which they are made.[2659] For instance, whilst the ordinary meaning of 'pension' merely covers periodic payments, the phrase 'other similar remuneration' is wide enough to apply to non-periodic payments such as a lump-sum payment.[2660]

---

pay tax in Germany on his German statutory pension and his German occupational pension was subject to tax in the Netherlands. Under the new treaty, both the statutory pension and the occupational pension are taxable in Germany, provided that the total gross amount exceeds the amount of €15,000.

2656 Paragraph 1 of the OECD commentary on article 18 OECD MC.

2657 Paragraph 17 of the OECD commentary on article 18 OECD MC.

2658 Paragraph 3 of the OECD commentary on article 18 OECD MC.

2659 Paragraph 4 of the OECD commentary on article 18 OECD MC.

2660 Paragraph 5 of the OECD commentary on article 18 OECD MC. See also paragraph 6 of the commentary which stipulates that whether a particular payment is to be considered as other remuneration similar to a

As far as the concept 'social security pensions' is concerned, the commentaries provide that this generally refers to a system of mandatory protection that a state establishes in order to provide its population with a minimum level of income or retirement benefits or to mitigate the financial impact of events such as unemployment, employment-related injuries, sickness or death.[2661] It is further noted that a common feature of social security systems is that the level of benefits is determined by the state. The benefits that fall under the scope of this provision, may include retirement pensions available to the general public under a public pension scheme that are made by the state or by public entities constituted to administer the funds to be distributed. This thus applies to the Dutch *AOW*, as well as the German statutory retirement provisions. As social security systems may differ substantially from one state to another, it is important for states to verify and elucidate, during the course of bilateral negotiations, a common understanding of the scope of this provision. Both the Netherlands as well as Germany have done so, which will be looked into further below. It is to be noted that the Netherlands have made an observation to the OECD commentaries on Article 18 OECD MC.[2662]

Pensions Falling under the Scope of Article 17, Paragraph 1 of the Treaty Concluded Between the Netherlands and Germany

At this point, the question rises which Dutch and German pensions, benefits, annuities and other benefits qualify as 'pensions and similar remuneration, annuities and other benefits paid under the provisions of a Contracting State's social security scheme (social security pension)', as provided in Article 17, paragraph 1 of the Treaty. Although an elaborate discussion of the definitions of pension, annuities etc. is beyond the scope of the research, a brief explanation of it is appropriate.

---

pension or as final remuneration for work performed falling under Article 15 is a question of fact, in which the source (e.g. a pension scheme) of the payment is an important factor. Further circumstances that provide guidance are whether a payment is made on or after the cessation of the employment giving rise to the payment, whether the recipient continues working, whether the recipient has reached the normal age of retirement with respect to that particular type of employment, the status of other recipients who qualify for the same type of lump-sum payment and whether the recipient is simultaneously eligible for other pension benefits. However, reimbursement of pension contributions (e.g. after temporary employment) do not fall under "other similar remuneration". In cases where difficulty arise in the taxation of such payments, the Contracting states should solve the matter by recourse to the Mutual Agreement Procedure as laid down in Article 25.

2661 Paragraph 28 of the OECD commentary on article 18 OECD MC.

2662 The Netherlands takes the position that social security payments can in some circumstances fall within Article 15 if they are paid whilst the employment still continues. See paragraph 70 of the OECD commentary on article 18 OECD MC.

Which retirement schemes and benefits specifically fall under the scope of this Article has not been comprehensively enumerated.[2663] However, for the purpose of determining whether the €15,000-threshold has been exceeded, it is pivotal to ascertain which benefits do and don't count for determining this. The Dutch State Secretary for Finance pointed out that, for this purpose, the Netherlands would propose to Germany to agree on an overview of benefits which fall within the scope of Article 17, paragraph 2 of the treaty.[2664] This finally has been agreed on, on 24 March 2021.[2665]

As far as the Netherlands is concerned, the term 'social security pension' includes, *inter alia*, each benefit paid out under the *Algemene Ouderdomswet* (AOW).[2666] It is stressed that some benefits are merely exportable under strict conditions, or not exportable at all.[2667] As regards German social security, this term encompasses each benefit paid by the federal and regional institutions of the *Deutsche Rentenversicherung* and the *Landwirtschaftliche Alterskasse*; any amount paid under a pension scheme for liberal professions (*berufsständische Versorgungseinrichtung*); which is payable periodically at fixed points in time, either during life or during a set or ascertainable period of time, pursuant to an obligation to make the payments, and which must be considered an annuity or similar benefit under section 22, number 1, third sentence of the *Einkommensteuergesetz*.[2668]

As regards the term 'benefits paid under the provisions of a Contracting State's social security scheme' there appears to occur some divergences of interpretation as regards the scope of this term.[2669] More precisely, it concerns the question whether certain German social security benefits fall under the scope of the treaty definition and, thus, fall under Article 17 of the treaty and shall be taken into account when calculating whether a taxable person's pension income exceeds the threshold of €15,000 on a yearly basis. The Dutch State Secretary of Finance pointed out that it is decisive in this regard whether the benefits

2663 Kamerstukken II, (2013/14) 15. The (former) Dutch State Secretary for Finance pointed out that this is not usual to do so under tax treaties.

2664 Ibid. 15.

2665 See De Minister van Buitenlandse Zaken, *Protocol tot wijziging van het Verdrag van 12 april 2012 tussen het Koninkrijk der Nederlanden en de Bondsrepubliek Duitsland tot het vermijden van dubbele belasting en het voorkomen van het ontgaan van belasting met betrekking tot belastingen naar het inkomen zoals gewijzigd door het Protocol van 11 januari 2016* (Tractatenblad 2021, nr 43 7 April 2021). See also De Minister van Buitenlandse Zaken, *Protocol tot wijziging van het Verdrag van 12 april 2012 tussen het Koninkrijk der Nederlanden en de Bondsrepubliek Duitsland tot het vermijden van dubbele belasting en het voorkomen van het ontgaan van belasting met betrekking tot belastingen naar het inkomen zoals gewijzigd door het Protocol van 11 januari 2016* (1 November 2021) 8.

2666 Section XIII, par. 1, under a of the protocol of the Treaty Netherlands-Germany.

2667 Ibid. 15.

2668 Section XIII, par. 1, under b of the protocol of the Treaty Netherlands-Germany.

2669 Staatssecretaris van Financiën, *Rapportage fiscale knelpunten grensarbeiders 2019* (27 September 2019).

are paid out pursuant to the provisions/regulations of the social security system of a Contracting State.[2670] As a result, the qualification of the source state is considered the starting point. Furthermore, he stressed that possible differences in the interpretation are discussed on a regular basis on an administrative level with the German authorities, seeking to solve these issues in an early stage. However, The Dutch State Secretary for Finance stressed that, as far as the Netherlands is concerned, Article 17 of the treaty covers regular *pensioen*, within the meaning of Article 18 *Wet op de loonbelasting 1964* (i.e. occupational pensions), and benefits stemming from so-called *beroepspensioenfondsen* (i.e. occupational pension schemes) and *bedrijfstakpensioenfondsen* (i.e. industry-wide pension funds).[2671]

With regard to the notion of *lijfrenten* (i.e. annuities) in the Netherlands, the treaty[2672] refers to an annuity as mentioned in the Dutch tax legislation, and which benefits shall be included in the taxable income[2673]. This means that the 'conventional annuity insurances' (i.e. contributions paid to an insurance company in order to secure an income after retirement), as well as the less conventional savings account annuities (i.e. *lijfrentespaarrekening*) and investment account annuities (i.e. *lijfrentebeleggingsrechten*) fall under the scope of Article 17 of the treaty.[2674] However, for Germany, the term 'annuities' is delimited more strictly.[2675] For the scope of the treaty, the term refers to a stated sum, payable periodically at stated times during life or during a specified or ascertainable time period, under an obligation to make the payments in return for adequate and full consideration in money or money's worth.

As far as German statutory retirement provisions are concerned, article 17 of the treaty covers the German *Rentenversicherung, landwirtschaftlichten Alterskassen, berufständischen Versorgungseinrichtungen*, and the *Rürup-Rente* and *Riester-Rente*.[2676] From my viewpoint, this categorisation of *Rürup-Rente* and *Riester-Rente* is not entirely consistent with categorisation under German law. Where the *Rürup-Renten* is qualified as first pillar (i.e. statutory pensions) from a '*Schicht*-perspective', it is qualified as third pillar (i.e. personal pensions) from a '*Säulen*-perspective'. As far as the *Riester-Rente* is concerned, this retirement provision is regarded as second pillar from the perspective of the *Dreischichtenmodell*, but considered a third pillar pension from a '*Säulen*-perspective'.

2670 Ibid.
2671 Ibid. 15.
2672 As laid down in article 17, par. 7, under a of the treaty.
2673 More precise: the income from work and home (i.e. *inkomen uit werk en woning (BOX 1)* as stipulated in article 3.1 Wet IB 2001).
2674 Kamerstukken II, 15.
2675 As laid down in article 17, par. 7, under b of the treaty.
2676 Kamerstukken II, 15-16.

With regard to occupational pensions (*Betriebliche Altervorsorge*), the Dutch State Secretary for Finance pointed out that benefits stemming from a *Pensionsfonds, Pensionskasse, Direcktversicherung* fall under the scope of Article 17 as far as they are based on mandatory contributions. At this point as well, it should be pointed out that the occupational schemes of the *Direktzusage* and *Unterstützungskasse* are not mentioned as well, as under these pension schemes beneficiaries are not granted entitlements to the pension benefits. As regard annuities, annuities of private insurance companies fall under the scope of the article as well.[2677]

9.3.3.B.III Non-exclusive Source Taxation of Pensions

In the past years, there has been an ongoing trend to reduce the scope of residence jurisdiction and increase the emphasis on source jurisdiction with regard to the allocation of taxing rights.[2678] In particular, there has been a shift of residence taxation of pension income towards (shared or conditional) source state taxation.

This also holds true as regards the tax treaty concluded between the Netherlands and Germany. By way of derogation of Article 17, paragraph 1 of the convention, paragraph 2 stipulates that in cases where the total gross amount of pension, annuities and social security benefit exceeds the amount of €15,000 per year, the source state is entitled to tax the total amount of benefits received from this country.[2679] If the sum of the total gross amounts (before deduction of taxes and social security contributions) of all pensions, similar remuneration, annuities or social security pensions (within the meaning of paragraph 1 of this article), including benefits of a non-regularly recurring nature (within the meaning of paragraph 3 of this Article), received by a person in a calendar year exceeds the exemption limit of €15,000, such benefits may also be taxed in total by the Contracting

2677 Ibid. 16.

2678 Avi-Yonah, 471 ff.

2679 This threshold will remain unchanged as far as the Dutch government is concerned, see De Minister van Buitenlandse Zaken, 3. The Amending Protocol leaves the €15,000 limit in respect of (social security) pensions untouched, because that limit reduces the administrative burden. Because the treaty assigns the right to tax (social security) pensions and annuities of a combined amount of €15,000 or less per calendar year to the country of residence, residents of the Netherlands receiving a small pension from Germany, for example, only have to file a tax return in the Netherlands. Such administrative burdens do not or only to a very limited extent arise in the case of a source state levy for social security benefits (not being social security pensions), because in cases where such benefits are received there is often already a declaration obligation in the source state in connection with work performed in that state. Furthermore, for (social security) pensions, Germany also taxes them, so the imbalance with respect to social security benefits (not being social security pensions) does not occur with respect to (social security) pensions. Therefore, there is no intention to amend the Treaty on this point. Furthermore, lowering the €15,000 limit would lead to – positive or negative – income consequences for different groups.

State from which they are received.[2680] It is to be noted that this €15,000-threshold refers to the total gross amounts of all types of benefits to which the second paragraph of article 17 applies.[2681]

In the calculation of this threshold, government pensions (article 18 of the treaty) are left aside. This provision thus allows for non-exclusive source taxation and is drafted along the lines of the OECD commentary.[2682] Thus, there is no conditional source state taxation whereby the distribution is made partly dependent on other factors such as whether tax facilitation has taken place in the source state, and the way in which the country of residence levies tax, as in the treaties concluded by the Netherlands with, for example, Belgium and Portugal. The only relevant criterion for source state taxation under the new treaty is therefore the amount of the pension benefits received. As far as Germany is concerned, The Neubrandenburg Tax Office examines whether Germany has a right of taxation under article 17, para 2 or 3 (in conjunction with para 5).[2683] However, with this the Netherlands deviates from the OECD model convention which still assumes a residence state taxation.

It should be noted that the source state's taxing right is not limited to the amount exceeding the threshold of €15,000, nor is it subjected to a limit, usually expressed as a percentage of the payment.[2684] The computation of the total amount of gross pension income, i.e. determining whether the threshold of €15,000 has been exceeded, is based on of the source state's law and regulation.[2685] This limit of €15,000 also ensures that 'small' pensions, annuities and social security benefits are only taxed in the state of residence.[2686] This avoids

2680 With regard to potential disputes concerning the application of source state-taxation, the role of article 17, paragraph 6 of the Treaty should be touched upon as well. This provision stipulates that the competent authorities of the Contracting states shall by mutual agreement settle the mode of application of the second paragraph, i.e. the source state-taxation. They also decide which information should be provided by the resident of the Contracting State for the correct application of the treaty in the other Contracting State (i.e. the source state), primarily to be able to determine whether the condition referred to in the second paragraph (the €15,000-threshold) has been met.

2681 See section XIII, par. 2 of the protocol of the Treaty Netherlands-Germany.

2682 See paragraph 15 of the OECD commentary on article 18 OECD MC.

2683 BMF, *Steuerliche Behandlung von Alterseinkünften nach Artikel 17 des Abkommens vom 12. April 2012 zwischen der Bundesrepublik Deutschland und dem Königreich der Niederlande zur Vermeidung der Doppelbesteuerung und zur Verhinderung der Steuerverkürzung auf dem Gebiet der Steuern vom Einkommen IV B 3 - S 1301-NDL/15/10002* 5-6.

2684 Kamerstukken II, 15. The tax treaty with Belgium was concluded in 2001 contains a €25,000 limit in Article 18, paragraph 2, under b of the treaty, pertaining to the allocation of taxing rights on pensions.

2685 Ibid. 16.

2686 Recently, the Protocol to Amend the Tax Treaty was published. The amendment protocol amends the allocation rules pertaining to social security benefits, while explicitly excluding social security pensions. The reason for negotiating an amending Protocol is the unbalanced outcome of art. 17 of the treaty with respect to a number of specific German short-term social security benefits. This concerns in particular the

that relatively small amounts of pensions, annuities and social security benefits to be received have to be declared by the taxpayer in the source state, leading to an administrative burden. The application of this limit is on an annual basis, as a result of which it can only be determined at the end of the year whether the taxpayer exceeds the limit of €15,000. If it is found that the taxpayer has received less than €15,000 in pension – and the source state has therefore wrongly been allocated the right to tax – this state will refund the tax.[2687]

For instance, in the case of a pensioner resident in Germany receiving an *AOW* pension and an occupational pension jointly exceeding €15,000 per year, the Netherlands is allocated the taxing rights in respect of both pensions and Germany will grant a credit for the tax levied in the Netherlands. This means, *inter alia*, that for pensioners living in Germany with a German and a Dutch pension in part, it depends on the amount of the Dutch pension whether the Netherlands is competent to levy tax on the Dutch pension. The Dutch Tax Authorities are able to establish whether or not a taxpayer exceeds the threshold of €15,000 on the basis of the obligation to provide information pertaining to pensions.[2688]

9.3.3.C Life Annuities

In tax treaties concluded by the Netherlands, the pension provision (article 18) generally applies to annuities and surrender values as well.[2689] This is true as regards the treaty

German *Elterngeld, Krankengeld* and *Mutterschaftsgeld*, but is not limited to these. The right of taxation on wages from employment of frontier workers who live in the Netherlands and work in Germany is in principle granted to the state of employment on the basis of the Treaty. If these frontier workers receive (short-term) social security benefits from Germany and these do not exceed €15,000 in a calendar year (together with certain other benefits, pensions and annuities), the right to tax on these is assigned to the state of residence: the Netherlands. For example, in the case of a social security benefit received by such a cross-border worker in relation with illness, a shift of the taxing right from the state of employment to the state of residence occurs. Many German social security benefits are geared to net wages and remain untaxed in Germany. Because the treaty assigns the taxing right on these benefits to the state of residence in certain cases, the situation may arise that a benefit aligned to net pay in Germany, may be taxed as gross income in the Netherlands. Furthermore, it became clear during the negotiations that (gross) Dutch social security benefits similar to German benefits would be exempted in Germany. Both outcomes were considered unbalanced. The Netherlands and Germany have therefore agreed on an amendment to art. 17 of the treaty, the essence of which is that social security benefits (other than social security pensions) will henceforth be allocated for taxation in all cases to the source state. The amount of the social security benefit (whether or not together with the amounts of certain other benefits) in a calendar year is therefore no longer relevant for this purpose. Merely in the situation where a resident of the Netherlands or Germany receives a combination of a (social security) pension and a social security benefit from the other country, income consequences are conceivable as a result of the amendment. However, it is expected that this will only occur in exceptional cases. See De Minister van Buitenlandse Zaken, 2 ff.

2687 Kamerstukken II, 34.

2688 Ibid. 35.

2689 Ministerie van Financiën, 'Notitie Fiscaal Verdragsbeleid 2011' 57.

concluded between the Netherlands and Germany, more specifically article 17, para 2. What is considered as an annuity for the purposes of the treaty is generally defined in the treaty. The definition of life annuity has been laid down in article 17, para 7 of the treaty. As regards the Netherlands, this term refers to a life annuity as mentioned in Dutch tax law of which the benefits are part of the taxable income in *BOX 1*. What this exactly comprises has been dealt with in the chapter 7. It follows from this definition that the Netherlands seeks to remain firm in preserving the internal coherence of the tax system by merely covering life annuities of which benefits are part of the taxable income, pursuant to Dutch domestic tax legislation. This definition of the concept of life annuities in Dutch tax treaties corresponds to the definition thereof in the *Wet Inkomstenbelasting 2001*, of which the scope until 1 January 2008 was limited to annuities with an insurance character (article 1.7, paragraph 1, letter a Wet IB 2001).[2690] This concerns an entitlement pursuant to a life assurance contract to fixed and equal periodic payments which end no later than in the event of death. An inherent part of the insurance character is that the policyholder pays a premium against which the insurer pays a certain amount to the policyholder or a third party at a certain point in time.

This definition also reflects the main characteristics of the German definition of *Rente* as laid down in article 17, para 7 of the treaty. This demonstrates, once more, that Dutch tax legislation regarding income facilities is continuously subject to changes, in turn, having an effect on the (scope of) the applicable tax treaties. Normally these amendments of legislation can be traced back to shifting positions in national tax policy. As of 1 January 2008, the definition of the concept of annuity in the *Wet IB 2001* has been expanded to annuity savings accounts (*lijfrentespaarrekeningen*) and annuity investment rights (*lijfrentebeleggingsrechten*), i.e. banking annuity variants, without an insurance character (see article 1.7, paragraph 1, letter b, Wet IB 2001).[2691] These annuity forms should also be considered as annuities in the Dutch view for the treaty application, but it is not entirely certain whether this is possible under the current definition of annuities in the pension article in tax treaties.[2692] Such questions about the application of the Convention may also arise in the case of severance payments in the form of so-called *stamrechten*.[2693] Pursuant to Dutch treaty policy, the definition of *lijfrente* in a tax treaty should clarify that benefits derived from these *stamrechten*, in particular, are only covered by the pension article if the benefits are predominantly geared to it, and are intended to meet maintenance needs from the date of termination of employment until retirement

2690 Ibid. 57.
2691 Ibid. 57. See the assimilation with 'regular' life annuities under Article 3.126a Wet IB 2001.
2692 Ibid. 57.
2693 Ibid. 57.

age. All other benefits derived from these *stamrechten* not meeting these requirements, fall under the scope of the treaty provision governing the taxation of income from non-self-employment. In order to avoid as much ambiguity as possible regarding the treaty qualification of *lijfrentespaarrekeningen, lijfrentebeleggingsrechten* and benefits derived from *stamrechten,* the Netherlands strives to define in its tax treaties the term *lijfrente* in accordance with the definition of that term under the *Wet IB 2001* (Income Tax Act 2001), the benefits of which are taxable pursuant to Dutch domestic legislation.[2694] With respect to Germany, the term covers a fixed sum payable periodically at fixed/specific dates, either during life or during a specified or ascertainable period of time, under an obligation to make payments in return for a sufficient and full consideration in cash or money's worth.

9.3.3.D Source of Pension Income: Article 17, para 5

As article 17 of the treaty provides either exclusive residence taxation in paragraph 1 or non-exclusive residence taxation in paragraph 2, this requires determining the state of the source of pensions.[2695] If, in the provision concerned, merely reference is made to a pension 'arising in'; the state of source could be construed as the state in which the fund is established, the State where the relevant work has been performed or the State where deductions have been claimed.[2696] The pension could then consist of different parts, each having a different State of source. Hence, this treaty provision clarifies that a pension or other similar remuneration or annuity shall be deemed to be derived from a Contracting State to the extent that the contributions or payments related to the pension or other similar remuneration or annuity, or the entitlements to such pension or other similar remuneration or annuity, have been eligible for tax relief in that State. It further stipulates that the transfer of a pension or other similar remuneration or annuity from a pension fund or insurance company established in a Contracting State to a pension fund or insurance company established in another State does not restrict in any way the taxing rights of the State mentioned in the preceding sentence. This fiction is subject to the restrictive condition ('insofar') that tax relief was granted in the build-up phase of the respective pensions, similar remuneration and annuities. However, it is to be noted that benefits derived from a social security pension system (within the meaning of article 17, para 1, sentence 2) do not fall under the scope of this provision, as the right of taxation of these benefits are attributed to the state from which these benefits are received, solely pursuant to article 17 paragraphs 1 to 3 of the treaty.

2694 Ibid. 58.

2695 See also paragraph 19 of the OECD commentary on article 18 OECD MC.

2696 Paragraph 19.1 of the OECD commentary on article 18 OECD MC.

Article 17, para 5 of the Convention does not stipulate to what level tax relief had to be granted. Decisive in that regard is therefore that the contributions related to a pension, similar remuneration or a pension in each case were subject to tax facilitation. It appears thus irrelevant whether and to what extent the tax relief actually has had an effect. The restrictive phrase 'to the extent' applies to the retirement income (pension, similar remuneration or annuities), rather than the level of tax facilitation. The provision is based on the consideration that the Contracting State which provides tax relief for the accumulation of the aforementioned old-age income should have a right of taxation when it is paid out. It is irrelevant that the actual payment of such retirement income is made from the State that has facilitated its accumulation for tax purposes. The term 'tax relief', within the meaning of article 17 para. 5 sentence 1, must be interpreted broadly. As regards Germany, this may, for example, consist in the granting of a special expenses deduction (e.g. *Sonderausgabenabzug*), tax exemption for contributions, support in the form of allowances (*Zulagen*) or the profit-reducing formation of pension provisions (*Pensionsrückstellungen*) within the framework of employer taxation to finance a pension commitment in the form of a *Direktzusage*.[2697]

9.3.3.E Government Service: Article 18

Article 18 of the treaty applies to salaries, wages, and other similar remuneration, and pensions, in respect of government service, and (largely) follows the principles as adopted in article 19 OECD MC. Merely the allocation of taxing rights on pensions derived from past employment by a State, are of interest for the present research.

Article 18, para. 2 of the treaty provides that notwithstanding the provisions of the first paragraph, pensions and other similar remunerations paid by, or out of funds created by[2698], a Contracting State, federal state or a political subdivision or a local authority of a Contracting State or federal state, to a natural person in respect of services rendered to that State, federal state or that subdivision or that authority shall be taxed in that State.[2699]

2697 Ibid. 3-4.

2698 Paragraph 5.2 of the OECD commentary on article 19 OECD MC points out that the expression "out of funds created by" in subparagraph a) of paragraph 2 covers the situation where the pension is not paid directly by the State, a political subdivision or a local authority but out of separate funds created by a government body. In addition, the original capital of the fund would not need to be provided by the State, a political subdivision or a local authority. The phrase would cover payments from a privately administered fund established for the government body.

2699 Paragraph 3 of the OECD commentary on article 19 OECD MC sets out that the provisions of the article apply to payments made not only by a State but also by its political subdivisions and local authorities (constituent states, regions, provinces, *départements*, cantons, districts, *arrondissements*, *Kreise*, municipalities, or groups of municipalities, etc.). For an elaborate discussion on which entities qualify as government, State, part of a State, political subdivision or local authority, see Starink, par. 6.3. He also drew

The exclusive taxing rights is thus allocated to the paying State – i.e. the state to which these services have been rendered – which principle can be considered internally accepted.[2700] It is also considered in accordance with the conception of international courtesy, which is at the basis of the article and with the provisions of the Vienna Conventions on Diplomatic and Consular Relations. The rationale behind the allocation of taxing rights to the paying state is that taxing rights on these pensions should be reserved for the state that owes these pensions.

However, as an exception, the taxing rights on these pensions and other similar remunerations are exclusively allocated to the natural person's residence state, provided that the natural person is both a resident, and a national of his residence state. This exception has to be seen against the background that, according to the Vienna Conventions on Diplomatic and Consular Relations, the receiving State is allowed to tax remuneration paid to certain categories of personnel of foreign diplomatic missions and consular posts, who are permanent residents or nationals of that State.[2701] Considering that pensions paid to these retired government officials ought to be fiscally treated similarly as salaries and wages paid during their active time, this exception pertaining to pensions has been incorporated.[2702]

It is to be noted that these allocation rules do not apply if the services are performed in connection with business carried on by a State, or one of its political subdivisions or local authorities, paying the salaries, wages, pensions or other similar remuneration.[2703] If that is true, the ordinary rules apply: article 15 for wages and salaries, article 16 for directors' fees and other similar payments, article 17 for artistes and sportsmen, and article 18 for pensions.

9.3.3.F Allocating Taxing Rights with Respect to a Hybrid Pension: Employee and Civil Servant

Application and practical issues may arise where pensions are paid for combined private and government services.[2704] These issues may arise where a taxable person has been

a flowchart in order to ascertain whether a Dutch pension qualifies as either a private pension or a public pension in international relations, see ibid. 263-264.

2700 Regarding the latter: paragraph 2 of the OECD commentary on article 19 OECD MC.

2701 Section 4 of the OECD commentary on article 19 OECD Model Convention.

2702 Since the condition laid down in subdivision b)(ii) of paragraph 1 of article 19 (the individual did not become a resident of that State solely for the purpose of rendering the services) cannot be valid in relation to a pensioner, the only prerequisite for the receiving State's power to tax the pension is that the pensioner must be one of its own residents and nationals.

2703 Section 6 of the OECD commentary on article 19 OECD Model Convention.

2704 Cf. Section 5.3 of the OECD commentary on article 19 OECD Model Convention.

employed in both the private, as well as the public sector and receives one pension pertaining to both periods of employment. This may either be the case for persons who participated in the same pension scheme throughout their employment or persons whose pension rights were portable. The trend towards more mobility between private and public sector may emphasize the importance of this issue. Further issues may arise when a taxable person has transferred a right to a pension from a public scheme to a private scheme or a transfer in the opposite direction.[2705] It may then be subject to discussion whether article 18 or 19 OECD MC shall apply. However, other States may apportion the pension payment based on the relative source of the pension entitlement so that a proportion of the pension is taxed under article 18 and another part under article 19.[2706] Although apportionment may raise significant administrative difficulties, it may counter possible revenue loss or risk of double non-taxation if the treatment of pensions could be changed by transferring the fund between public and private schemes.[2707]

In cases where a taxable person switches from public to private sector or *vice versa*, it is normally difficult to ascertain exactly which part of the pension should be allocated to which form of employment, taking account of the accrued pension rights, with a view to the applicable treaty provision. By way of derogation from the provisions governing the taxation of private pension income (residence state levy), tax treaties allocate taxing rights on pension income accrued in public-law employment to the state paying out these pensions (i.e. the cash state or government state). However, it is to be noted that in cases where the treaty provision prescribes a general source-state taxation, there is essentially no longer any reason to distinguish pension falling under the scope of either the private pension-provision or the public pension-provision. Below, the policies of both the Netherlands and Germany will be addressed as regards the issue of hybrid pensions.

9.3.3.F.I Dutch Treaty Practice

As regards the division of taxing rights with respect to these hybrid pensions, Dutch treaty practice notes that if the Netherlands cannot achieve its objective of full source state taxation in treaty negotiations, a practical problem arises.[2708] In these cases, the Netherlands seeks to agree on rules of apportion governing the division of taxing rights. Such a provision is based on the so-called *PTT* judgment of the Dutch Supreme Court[2709] and corresponds to section 5.5, second sentence, of the OECD commentary on Article 19

2705 See section 5.4 and 5.5 of the OECD commentary on article 19 OECD Model Convention.
2706 Section 5.5 of the OECD commentary on article 19 OECD Model Convention.
2707 Section 5.6 of the OECD commentary on article 19 OECD Model Convention.
2708 Ministerie van Financiën, 'Notitie Fiscaal Verdragsbeleid 2011' 55.
2709 29 935, ECLI:NL:HR:1994:AA3001 (1994) (HR).

OECD Model Convention.[2710] However, in practice apportionment of pension payment often leads to significant administrative difficulties. Furthermore, Dutch practice has been set out in section 7 of the OECD commentary on Article 19, in which it is pointed out that the Netherlands does not adhere to the interpretation in paragraphs 5.4 and 5.6. Rather, apportionment of pension payments on the base of the relative source of the pension entitlements, private or government employment, is in the Netherlands' view also possible if pension rights are transferred from a public pension scheme to a private scheme.

If a source state levy for pensions has been agreed in an individual treaty, the Netherlands will no longer seek a division between private and public pensions.[2711] However, in cases where, in the context of a final compromise, a (form of) residence state taxation on pensions has been agreed in a treaty, the Netherlands will, in principle, strive to implement a division between private and public pensions, by incorporating a provision stipulating, for these hybrid pensions, which part of the pension is deemed to be a private pension, and which part is considered a public pension.

9.3.3.F.II German Policy: BMF Schreiben 26 October 2021

In this policy document the German Federal Central Tax Office addressed the issue, raised in a mutual agreement procedure with the Netherlands, of whether the paying state-principle should be applied to former state pension funds in the Netherlands.[2712] This concerned pension payments made from a Dutch pension fund to former civil servants, having worked in Dutch public service, and resident in Germany. This pension fund (*Algemeen Burgerlijk Pensionensfonds ABP*) had been transformed from a public-law corporation into a private foundation in the Netherlands in the context of a restructuring of the public-law pension system.

As part of the negotiations on a new tax treaty, both states agreed that the right to tax the pensions of former Dutch civil servants under the *ABP* should be based on the paying state-principle.[2713] The mutual agreement procedures, which concerned exclusively Dutch

2710 This section provides: "*5.5 Where the transfer is made in the opposite direction and the pension rights are transferred from a private scheme to a public scheme, some States tax the whole pension payments under Article 19. Other States, however,* apportion the pension payments *based on the relative source of the pension entitlement so that part is taxed under Article 18 and another part under Article 19. In so doing, some States consider that if one source has provided by far the principal amount of the pension, then the pension should be treated as having been paid exclusively from that source. Nevertheless, it is recognised that apportionment often raises significant administrative difficulties.*"

2711 Ministerie van Financiën, 'Notitie Fiscaal Verdragsbeleid 2011' 56.

2712 BMF, *Deutsch-niederländisches Doppelbesteuerungsabkommen (DBA-NL); Anwendung des Kassenstaatsprinzips auf ehemalige staatliche Pensionsfonds IV B 3-S 1301-NDL/19/10006:004* (26 October 2021).

2713 In the given document reference is made to section XIV of the protocol of the Treaty Netherlands-Germany.

pensions that were accrued within the context of public-law employment relationships, were therefore resolved in the light of the 2012 tax treaty and the taxing right was allocated to the Netherlands in accordance with the paying state-principle. The document further points to the possibility of requesting the taxpayer to complete the form *loonbelasting beschikking LBB20* and submit it to the tax office *belastingdienst buitenland* in Heerlen. Upon receipt of the completed form, this competent tax office will request the pension fund *ABP* to divide the payments of pension benefits into amounts based on public-law employment relationships and amounts based on private-law employment relationships.

9.3.3.F.III Protocol to the 2012 Treaty Netherlands-Germany

As regards the allocation of taxing rights on a mixed private-public pension, paragraph XIV of the Protocol specifies that a pension arising in the Netherlands falls under the scope of Article 18, paragraph 2 to the extent that the entitlement to this pension has been built up in the context of services rendered to a Contracting State or a political subdivision or a local authority thereof (public services), irrespective of by whom this pension is payable.[2714] If the entitlement to a pension was accrued partly in the context of public services, and partly in the context of other employment, the portion of such pension to which article 18, para 2 applies, and the portion to which article 17 applies, shall be determined proportionately on the basis of the number of years during which the entitlement to such pension was accrued respectively in the context of public services, and in the context of other employment, in relation to the total number of years during which the entitlement to such pension was accrued. The application of either article 17 or 18 to mixed pensions (in cross-border cases) is thus determined *pro rata parte.*

Under this approach, the apportion is thus based on the years during which the pension entitlements accrued, rather than that the nature of the institution paying these pensions is decisive. This provision adheres to the so-called *PTT* judgment of the Dutch Supreme Court[2715], corresponds to section 5.5, second sentence, of the OECD commentary on Article 19 OECD Model Convention, and the abovementioned *BMF-schreiben.*[2716]

2714 See also De Minister van Buitenlandse Zaken.

2715 29 935, ECLI:NL:HG:1994:AA3001 (1994) (HR).

2716 This section provides: "*5.5 Where the transfer is made in the opposite direction and the pension rights are transferred from a private scheme to a public scheme, some States tax the whole pension payments under Article 19. Other States, however,* apportion the pension payments *based on the relative source of the pension entitlement so that part is taxed under Article 18 and another part under Article 19. In so doing, some States consider that if one source has provided by far the principal amount of the pension, then the pension should be treated as having been paid exclusively from that source. Nevertheless, it is recognised that apportionment often raises significant administrative difficulties.*"

9.3.3.F.IV Effects of the Act on the Standardisation of the Legal Status of Civil Servants: Neglecting Cross-border Effects

Furthermore, the entry into force of the *Wet normalisering rechtspositie ambtenaren (WNRA)*[2717], has brought about various cross-border consequences in the tax domain. With effect from 1 January 2020, the *Ambtenarenwet 1929*[2718] has been replaced by the *Ambtenarenwet 2017*. As a result of the implementation of this act, the legal status of the majority of civil servants was amended, in that their unilateral appointment pursuant to public law has been replaced by an employment contract governed by private law. Contrarily, some categories of employees were qualified as civil servants.[2719] However, the status of civil servant remains unchanged.[2720]

The effects of standardisation of the legal status of the civil servant can also be observed in the domain of the taxation of pensions pursuant to the applicable treaty article. Depending on how the taxing rights on pension income have been allocated in the given tax treaty, this can lead to a compartmentalisation of the pension. When the treaty article governing the taxation of pension income allocates the taxing rights exclusively to the source state, there is no ground for such a partitioning. However, the protocol to the treaty concluded between the Netherlands and Germany (and Belgium) contains particular provisions as regards the splitting between private and public pensions. The use of the term 'employment relationship pursuant to public law', as a consequence of the implementation of the *WNRA*, gives rise to uncertainty and ambiguity. In order to be able to resolve this, the competent Dutch and German authorities of the Netherlands and Germany have consulted each other.[2721]

Prior to 1 January 2020, the starting point for the application of article 18 of the treaty (pertaining to government functions) in practice, was the prerequisite that it should be an appointment pursuant to public law at a Dutch public-law entity.[2722] However, since the entry into force of the *WNRA* this is no longer considered a sufficiently distinctive criteria, since most civil servants will be employed on the basis of an (private-law) employment contract. Therefore, from the date of the entry into force of the *WNRA*, the applicable treaty article shall be more prevailing as such.[2723] Decisive in this regard is whether an

2717 Translated freely as the Act on the Standardisation of the Legal Status of Civil Servants.

2718 Translated freely as the Civil Servants' Code 1929.

2719 MJGAM Weerepas, 'Grensoverschrijdende gevolgen van Wet normalisering rechtspositie ambtenaren voldoende duidelijk?' Vakblad Grensoverschrijdend Werken.

2720 Staatssecretaris van Financiën, *Rapportage fiscale knelpunten grensarbeiders 2019* (27 September 2019).

2721 Ibid.

2722 Staatssecretaris van Financiën, *Beantwoording vragen n.a.v. toezending afschrift Rapportage fiscale knelpunten grensarbeiders 2019* (17 December 2019).

2723 Ibid.

employment contract with a public-law entity has been concluded.[2724] The application of article 18 (Government service) to pension income, ties in with the treaty article which applied to the earned income on the basis of which the pension was built up.[2725] If article 18 has been applied to that earned income, the pension benefits will, in principle, be liable to tax on the grounds of that same article, provided that all the article's conditions have been met. Contrarily, if article 14 (income from employment) applied to the earned income, then, in principle, article 17 (private pensions) shall be applied to the pension benefits. This turnaround (due to the implementation of the *WNRA*) in establishing the applicable treaty article with respect to pension income, induces compartmentalisation of the pension income for employees who work for a public-law entity on the basis of an employment contract both prior to the implementation date (1 January 2020) as well as after this date. Whether this will actually lead to a division of taxing rights is dependent on the phrasing of the relevant treaty article concerning private pensions, as well as the amount of pension and the tax treatment of the pension benefits paid.

Nevertheless, the amendment protocol to the treaty of 24 March 2021, has clarified the issue set out above, at least to some extent. As regards the application – and split application – of articles 17 or 18 of the treaty, section of XIV of the protocol now adheres to pension accrual in the context of services rendered to a Contracting State or a political subdivision or a local authority thereof (public services), regardless of by whom such pension is payable.[2726] The outdated protocol referred to pension accrual in the context of public law employment, regardless of by whom such pension is paid. Thus, the new protocol no longer ties in with whether the employment relationship is either pursuant to public or private law, but it will be assessed whether there is an employment relationship with a legal entity under public law.[2727]

2724 In this regard it is noted that according to article 19 of the 1963 OECD Draft Convention, the services rendered to the State, political subdivision or local authority had to be rendered "in the discharge of functions of a governmental nature". See section 5 of the OECD commentary on article 19 OECD Model Convention. That expression was deleted in the 1977 Model Convention. Contracting states who are of the view and who feel that such a widening is not desirable may continue to use, and preferably specify, the expression "in the discharge of functions of a governmental nature" in their bilateral conventions. However, this section of the commentary, nor any other provision, does set out what 'of a governmental nature' means.

2725 Staatssecretaris van Financiën, *Beantwoording vragen n.a.v. toezending afschrift Rapportage fiscale knelpunten grensarbeiders 2019.*

2726 See Section XIV of the protocol of the Treaty Netherlands-Germany.

2727 De Minister van Buitenlandse Zaken, 8-9.

9.3.3.G General Transitional Scheme and Specific Transitional Scheme for Pensions under the 2012 Treaty

In particular, the amendment in the allocation of taxing rights over pensions has been a matter of concern during the implementation of the tax treaty. As a result of the shift of taxing rights in the new tax treaty, pensioners living in Germany who have worked as frontier workers in the Netherlands in the past and receive a pension from the Netherlands in excess of €15,000 may be substantially affected in their income position in comparison with the old tax treaty.[2728] In order to alleviate these detrimental income effects, firstly, an unilateral general transitional arrangements had been introduced.[2729] This transitional regime allowed the taxpayer to continue to apply the old tax treaty for the year 2016, without examining whether the person concerned actually enjoys a more favourable tax treatment as a result.[2730] For obvious reasons, this provision has currently lost its effect as of 2021. In view of the aforementioned favourable German tax on Dutch pensions, the pensioner will in most cases have opted for this. In drawing up these transitional arrangements, the Dutch State Secretary of Finance also took a number of factors into account, including the level of tax rates in both countries, the number of pensioners with a Dutch pension income and the ratio between the number of pensioners in both countries.[2731] In view of these factors, Germany and the Netherlands considered the one-year general transitional arrangements laid down in article 33, paragraph 6 of the Treaty to be appropriate.[2732] Furthermore, the Dutch government considered it appropriate to unilaterally introduce an additional specific transitional arrangement, specifically aimed at compensating pensioners resident in Germany, with the specific aim of achieving a more gradual transition, in particular for higher pension incomes, as the new treaty may lead to a higher tax burden especially in these cases.[2733] Contrarily, residents of the Netherlands with a pension, annuity or social security benefit from Germany of less than

2728 This concerns an estimated 5,500 pensioners. Kamerstukken II, *33 615, nr 8* 6.

2729 Pursuant to article 33, paragraph 6 of the Convention. The right of option may be exercised by any person who is entitled to the agreement both under the 2012 treaty and would have been entitled to the agreement under the 1959 treaty. The exercise of the right of option must be declared to the tax authorities at the locally competent tax office.

2730 See also BMF, *Steuerliche Behandlung von Alterseinkünften nach Artikel 17 des Abkommens vom 12. April 2012 zwischen der Bundesrepublik Deutschland und dem Königreich der Niederlande zur Vermeidung der Doppelbesteuerung und zur Verhinderung der Steuerverkürzung auf dem Gebiet der Steuern vom Einkommen IV B 3 - S 1301-NDL/15/10002* 7-8.

2731 Kamerstukken II, *33 615, nr E (Nadere memorie van antwoord)* (2013/14).

2732 Article 2, paragraph 5 of the specific transitional regime regulates confluence with the general transitional regime. If the person liable to tax opted for the general transitional regime for the year 2016, he was not entitled to apply the specific transitional regime for that year.

2733 Kamerstukken II, *33 615, nr E (Nadere memorie van antwoord).*

€15,000 in total did not suffer from an detrimental effect on their income. Hence, no transitional arrangement had been adopted for this group of pensioners.[2734]

In drawing up this unilateral transitional arrangement, the level of tax in Germany compared to the Dutch tax level was also an important factor. This special transitional arrangement was introduced for certain income covered by Article 17, paragraph 2 of the new treaty, for which the taxing right had been allocated to Germany under the old tax treaty.[2735] These items of income were, under certain conditions, taxed at a lower rate during the first six calendar years following the year of entry into force (2016).[2736] The compensation under the special transitional regime was provided through the reduction of the income tax that would be payable under the *Wet IB 2001* as if the special transitional regime would not be applied.[2737] However, several preconditions had to be met in order to be eligible for compensation under the special transitional regime:

- it concerns a pension or other similar remuneration, an annuity or a pension or other benefit paid under the provisions of the social security system of the Netherlands;
- the receiving individual has been a permanent resident of Germany since the date of signature of the Convention on 12 April 2012;
- before the date of entry into force of the Convention (1 January 2016), a payment of an income component mentioned above has been made; (i.e. pensions, annuities, etc. already in payment);
- according to article 17, paragraph 2 of the Convention, the aforementioned element of income may be taxed in the Netherlands, which means that the total gross amount per calendar year of pension or other similar remuneration, annuity or other benefit paid

2734 Kamerstukken II, (table 3 and 4 in the annex).

2735 See Kamerstukken II, *33 615, nr 6 (Nota van wijziging)* (2013/14).

2736 In 2016 and 2017 the total tax burden was capped at 10%; in 2018 at 15%; in 2019 at 20%; in 2020 at 25% and in 2021 at 30%.

2737 The aforementioned reduction is calculated as follows: the total tax payable by a taxpayer in a calendar year shall be reduced by the difference between the part of the total income tax on the income in *BOX 1* according to article 7.2 *Wet IB 2001* of a taxpayer in a calendar year that is proportionally attributable to the elements of income without application of the transitional scheme and the tax payable on these income components calculated according to the lower rates of the specific transitional regime. The proportion of the total tax in *BOX 1* attributable proportionally to the elements of income without application of the transitional regime implies that the amount of the tax due in *BOX 1* is multiplied by the ratio of the relevant elements of income to the total positive income in *BOX 1* in accordance with article 7.2 of the Wet IB 2001. See for an example of this calculation Kamerstukken II, *33 615, nr 6 (Nota van wijziging)*. In this example of calculation Dutch income tax rates of 2016 are used, and tax deductions and tax credits were not taken into consideration. Furthermore, in addition to the pension, annuity or social security benefit, the taxpayer may also have other income components taxable in the Netherlands to which the transitional arrangement does not apply. In that case of a higher income, the tax burden on the pension, annuity or social security benefit will be higher due to the progressive income tax rate. The application of the lower rates of the transitional scheme may then lead to greater compensation, the higher the income.

by virtue of the provisions of the social security system of the Netherlands exceeds the threshold of €15,000;
– the taxing right on this element of income was under the old treaty exclusively allocated to Germany.

These conditions imply that a taxable person who took up residence between 12 April 2012 and 1 January 2016 is not entitled to the application of this special transitional arrangement, or a pensioner residing in Germany with a Dutch pension who emigrated to the Netherlands prior to 1 January 2016 is neither entitled to the transitional arrangement. Nor does the special transitional scheme apply to retired civil servants living in Germany who, in addition to a government pension (article 18 of the treaty), solely receive statutory pension (*AOW*) benefits. The income consequences for these groups will thus not be alleviated. Furthermore, as redemption sums of pensions and annuities fall under the scope of article 17, paragraph 3, these types of benefits do not fall under the specific transitional regime. As the last condition specifies that it should be an element of income over which the exclusive taxing right had been allocated to Germany under the old treaty, social security benefits emerging in the Netherlands do not fall under the scope of the specific transitional regime.

The transitional arrangements are not already applied to the payment of income (pensions, annuities and social security benefits) by the paying agents (pension funds, insurers and Social Insurance Bank, respectively) through withholding, as the reduction to be granted under the transitional regime depends on the amount of any income to which the transitional regime does not apply.[2738] The compensation cannot be obtained by means of a provisional tax assessment, but the taxpayer must file a tax return for the income tax / national insurance contributions.[2739] In practice, this transitional did not appear to have

2738 Ibid.

2739 As regards administrative obligations it can be mentioned that the so-called 'treaty declaration' (application for exemption from wage tax / social security contributions) which had been issued to the pensioner, were not withdrawn immediately after the treaty had entered into force, notably with regard to the possibility of opting to continue to apply the old treaty for 2016 under the general transitional regime. Since the right to tax the pension shifted to the Netherlands, provided that the total gross amount of benefits received exceeded the threshold of €15,000, these declarations ceased to be valid. Furthermore, withdrawal depends on the facts and circumstances of the individual case, such as whether or not the €15,000 requirement is exceeded. The Dutch Tax Authorities has actively contacted pensioners living in Germany with a Dutch pension with the question whether they would like to make use of the aforementioned general transitional arrangement. Subsequently, the Dutch Tax Authorities assessed which treaty declarations should be withdrawn and informed both the taxpayer and the pension providers. The Dutch Tax Authorities committed to inform pensioners residing in Germany receiving a Dutch pension who had received a treaty declaration in connection therewith, by letter about the consequences of the new treaty and the possibility of the one-year transitional arrangement.

much effect for the majority of cases, largely due to the rate structure in the Dutch Wet IB.[2740] Incidentally, a transitional rule for residents of the Netherlands receiving German pensions was not considered necessary, while it is precisely in these situations that the effects can be even more considerable than for residents of Germany.

9.3.4 *The Dutch Nettopensioen Scheme and the Frontier Worker: Double Taxation*

The purpose of this section is to clarify how a national pension vehicle, i.e. the Dutch *nettopensioen*, may (unfavourably) affect the position of a frontier worker under a tax treaty. For a thorough discussion of the *nettopensioen*-scheme I refer to chapter 6 of this research.

It is to be noted that in practice, of the people eligible for using the *nettopensioen*-scheme, only few have actually made use of it.[2741]

It further becomes apparent that treaty negotiations did not sufficiently anticipate the possible negative consequences of the *aftoppingsgrens* introduced unilaterally by the Netherlands.[2742] It also becomes evident that effects of national legislation, which is predominantly drafted through a national lens, on cross-border situations are not sufficiently taken into account when drafting this national legislation. What is more, it reveals that the legislature should be more aware of the impact that new legislation may have on persons availing themselves of the freedoms of movement, i.e. the cross-border consequences should be taken into account when drafting legislation (so-called border impact assessment).[2743]

2740 AHH Bollen-Vandenboorn and others, 'ITEM Grenseffectenrapportage 2016, Dossier 1B: Belastingverdrag Nederland-Duitsland Pensioen' (2016).

2741 See also Minister van Sociale Zaken en Werkgelegenheid, *Evaluatie vrijstelling voor nettopensioen en nettolijfrente*. Research findings demonstrate that of the potential target group of 200 000 people, approximately 35 000 people (approximately 17%) participate in a *nettopensioen* scheme. This mainly concerns *nettopensioen*, while *nettolijfrenten* schemes are hardly used in practice.

2742 Pursuant to Wet van 2 juni 2014 tot wijziging van de Wet inkomstenbelasting 2001, de Wet op de loonbelasting 1964, de Pensioenwet, de Wet verplichte beroepspensioenregeling en de Invoerings- en aanpassingswet Pensioenwet in verband met de aanpassing van het fiscale kader voor oudedagsvoorzieningen (Wet verlaging maximumopbouw- en premiepercentages pensioen en maximering pensioengevend inkomen).

2743 Cf. MJGAM Weerepas, 'Grenswerkers, enige hardnekkige problemen' WFR 5.

This can also take place in the context of the frontier employee participating in a *nettopensioen*.[2744] This concerns the situation of a post-active frontier worker resident in Germany who has worked in the Netherlands and has made use of a *nettopensioen* scheme through his employer. Since the frontier worker already lives abroad, he cannot make use of the tax-free redemption option.[2745] After all, he does not emigrate and must therefore have the *nettopensioen* paid out.

Under the old (1959) tax treaty, Germany would have classified the *nettopensioen* as a pension within the meaning of article 12, para 1 of the 1959 Convention. As a general rule, the right of taxation was allocated to the Member State of residence – Germany in the example. It is unlikely that Germany would respect the distinction between gross pension – to which the reversal rule applied – and net pension.[2746] Nor does the tax treaty concluded, nor the OECD MC, provide instruments to settle these issues. Therefore, Germany would have taxed the benefits from the *nettopensioen* resulting in double taxation as the Netherlands has applied the TEE-principle to this scheme, i.e. not exempted pension entitlements and deducted pension contributions paid.

Under the new treaty, the same problems arise as those dealt with above. Under article 17, para 2 of the treaty, the source state – the Netherlands in the example – may also tax payments from the *nettopensioen*, provided that the total gross amount of the pension to be received exceeds €15,000. However, the Netherlands will not tax these benefits under national law. So far, no double taxation arises. No specific agreements have been made in the new treaty regarding the *nettopensioen* scheme. As a result, Germany will not make any distinction between gross and net pensions under the new treaty either.[2747] Incidentally, the Netherlands will not be granted this right of taxation on an exclusive basis under this withholding tax.

If the Netherlands, as source state, may also levy on the *nettopensioen* of the frontier worker residing in Germany, the credit method shall be applied pursuant to article 22, paragraph 1, letter b, under ee of the treaty in order to avoid double taxation. In doing so, the German tax is offset against the tax due under Dutch tax law. However, as noted above,

2744 Zie voor een uitgebreide uiteenzetting over deze problematiek: A.H.H. Bollen-Vandenboorn, 'De vergeten grensarbeider en zijn nettopensioen', *MBB* 2015/09.

2745 The option is offered in article 5.17e, paragraph 5, under a *Wet IB 2001*.

2746 Cf. Bollen-Vandenboorn. The Dutch State Secretary rightly pointed out that it depends on the tax treatment under domestic law of the new residence state whether the Dutch *nettopensioen* scheme will actually (entirely of partly) be subject to tax, see Kamerstukken II, *32 042, nr 329 (Verslag van een schriftelijk overleg)* (2015/16). He also stated that the number of pensioners receiving a *nettopensioen* is not documented at an aggregated level.

2747 Cf. AHH Bollen-Vandenboorn, 'Belastingverdrag Nederland-Duitsland' 11 MBB paragraph 4.1.

the *nettopensioen* is not taxed in the Netherlands, and on the basis of the credit method, the credit is only granted if tax has actually been levied. Since the *nettopensioen* is not actually taxed, Germany does not grant any credit in respect of the benefits deriving from the *nettopensioen* and therefore double taxation may arise.

9.3.5 *Avoiding Double Taxation under the Tax Treaty and the Per-country Limitation: Double Taxation*

The primary aim of tax treaties is to avoid (judicial) double taxation. If a pensioner, resident in Germany, derives his pension from a Dutch pension scheme and this amounts more than €15,000, the Netherlands will also be entitled to subject this pension to tax as a source state, pursuant to article 17, paragraph 2 of the treaty. This would imply double taxation as both the Netherlands as well as Germany will subject the pension benefits to domestic tax. However, pursuant to article 22, paragraph 1, letter b, under ee of the treaty Germany will grant a tax credit.[2748] This Article sets out that in the case of a resident of Germany, subject to the provisions of German tax law regarding the provision of a credit for foreign tax, the German tax payable in respect of the items of income which may be taxed in the Netherlands in accordance with paragraphs 2 and 3 of article 17 (pensions, annuities and social security benefits) shall be allowed as a credit against the tax payable under Dutch tax law.

This tax credit shall be granted in accordance with German tax law with respect to crediting foreign tax. Article 34c EstG in conjunction with article 68a, paragraph 1 of the EStGV 1955 (*Einkommensteuer-Durchführungsverordnung 1955*) applies in calculating this tax credit.[2749] As Germany taxes the Dutch pensions of pensioners resident in Germany at a low effective rate (due to the application of either the *Besteuerungsanteil* or *Ertragsanteil*), the credit to be granted by Germany in respect of the tax payable in the

2748 See BMF, *Steuerliche Behandlung von Alterseinkünften nach Artikel 17 des Abkommens vom 12. April 2012 zwischen der Bundesrepublik Deutschland und dem Königreich der Niederlande zur Vermeidung der Doppelbesteuerung und zur Verhinderung der Steuerverkürzung auf dem Gebiet der Steuern vom Einkommen IV B 3 - S 1301-NDL/15/10002* 2. This is in accordance with paragraph 15, under c of the OECD commentary on article 18 OECD MC.

2749 This latter provision stipulates: *"Die für die Einkünfte aus einem ausländischen Staat festgesetzte und gezahlte und um einen entstandenen Ermäßigungsanspruch gekürzte ausländische Steuer ist nur bis zur Höhe der deutschen Steuer anzurechnen, die auf die Einkünfte aus diesem ausländischen Staat entfällt. Stammen die Einkünfte aus mehreren ausländischen Staaten, so sind die Höchstbeträge der anrechenbaren ausländischen Steuern für jeden einzelnen ausländischen Staat gesondert zu berechnen."* This provision thus specifies that the foreign tax assessed and paid for income from a foreign state and reduced by any claim for reduction that may have arisen shall only be credited up to the amount of German tax payable on the income from that foreign state. If the income originates from several foreign states, the maximum amounts of the creditable foreign tax must be calculated separately for each individual foreign state.

Netherlands is capped at this small amount of German tax. This increases the total tax burden of pensioners living in Germany and receiving a Dutch pension.

In the reverse case of a resident of the Netherlands receiving a German pension which may be taxed, or are exclusively taxable, in Germany under article 17, paragraph 2, letter b of the Convention – i.e. a total amount in excess of €15,000 – the Netherlands, by virtue of article 22, paragraph 2, letter b of the Convention, exempts these items of income by allowing a reduction in its tax, in conjunction with a reservation as to the progressive rates of taxation. For that purpose, the said items of income shall be deemed to be included in the amount of the items of income which are exempt from Dutch tax under those provisions. This reduction is calculated in accordance with the provisions in Dutch legislation for the avoidance of double taxation.[2750]

9.4 Comparative Findings Through the Lens of the Evaluation Framework

Where in the sections above the (tax treatment of) cross-border pensions under international tax law has been mapped out, the section below evaluates these findings along the (legal) lines of this research's evaluation framework (similarity/comparability; inter-level coherence; inter-system consistency; foreseeability/unpredictability). It is a sliding scale where all variations between fit and unfit can be observed.

As this chapter explored the tax treatment of under international tax law in bilateral situations between the Netherlands and Germany, emphasis will be put on the principle of similarity/comparability, since this chapter seeks to explore to what extent the international regulatory framework governing the tax treatment of pensions is fit for the provision of effective pension information. What is more, the principle of foreseeability will be tested, in terms of how international tax law potentially affects the foreseeability of the tax treatment of pensions in cross-borders cases. Moreover, as this chapter did involve the role of international tax law as such the principle of inter-level coherence is also evaluated. Lastly, as the chapter above addressed the application of regulatory (tax) frameworks, leading to potential (in)compatible outcomes for a specific cross-border situation, the principle of inter-system consistency shall be evaluated as well. This chapter meets this research second (sub)objective of a legal comparative study in which the legal frameworks in the Netherlands and Germany, as well as on a European and international level, shall be mapped out. Building on this, the 'fitness' of the legal frameworks at the national, European

2750 Article 10 Besluit voorkoming dubbele belasting 2001.

and international level shall be assessed, focusing in particular on any deficiencies that have a (distorting) effect on the provision of effective information.

9.4.1 *Similarity/Comparability*

The sections below compare the tax treatment of cross-border pensions - under international tax law - in bilateral cases between Germany and the Netherlands, and evaluates it in view of the principle of similarity/comparability. Exploring similarity between systems involves a comparison of certain features. The assessment of similarity constitutes a feature-matching process, i.e. it measures the degree to which two objects - the legal character - match each other. Similarity is tantamount to a measurement of common features. A higher degree of similarity helps to ensure the effectiveness of information in terms of the four principles. For instance, the higher the degree of similarity, the easier it is to uphold the information's correctness, trustworthiness, and personal relevance. After all, with a higher degree of similarity, there is less need to observe any underlying structural differences. Moreover, a higher degree of similarity leads to a higher comparability of the different regulatory frameworks/legal constructs, avoiding comparing the incomparable.

9.4.1.A Similarities

Building on the preceding sections, the following similarities can be observed:

- Similar to the *Verhandlungsgrundlage*, the *Notitie Fiscaal Verdragsbeleid* leaves ample room for individual agreements agreed on during treaty negotiations, and laid down in the tax treaty, such as transnational schemes. In negotiating with a (potential) treaty partners, the Netherlands attempts to remain as close as possible to internationally customary texts and to the tax treaties already concluded.[2751] In terms of similarity, both the German *Verhandlungsgrundlage*, as well as the Dutch *Notitie Fiscaal Verdragsbeleid* have no legally binding effect. In sum, although the intervention's objective is similar, the manner in which this objective is achieved deviates.
- As dealt with in section 9.3.3.F, both the Netherlands, as well as Germany, allocate taxing rights - pursuant to art. 17 and/or 18 of the treaty - on a mixed private-public pension *pro rata parte*. As part of the negotiations on a new tax treaty, both states agreed that the right to tax the pensions of former Dutch civil servants under the *ABP* should be based on the paying state-principle. If the entitlement to a pension was accrued partly in the context of public services, and partly in the context of other employment, the portion of such pension to which article 18, para 2 applies, and the

2751 Ministerie van Financiën, 'Notitie Fiscaal Verdragsbeleid 2011' 15.

portion to which article 17 applies, shall be determined proportionately on the basis of the number of years during which the entitlement to such pension was accrued respectively in the context of public services, and in the context of other employment, in relation to the total number of years during which the entitlement to such pension was accrued. Under this approach, the apportion is thus based on the years during which the pension entitlements accrued, rather than that the nature of the institution paying these pensions is decisive. This provision adheres to the so-called *PTT* judgment of the Dutch Supreme Court[2752], corresponds to section 5.5, second sentence, of the OECD commentary on article 19 OECD Model Convention, and the abovementioned *BMF-schreiben* of 26 October 2021.

9.4.1.B Differences

Building on the preceding sections, the following similarities can be observed:

- It is not self-evident that national legislation is also shaped, and amended, by this extensive body of international legislation. For instance, to the extent that the provisions of tax treaties have direct effect – which they almost all do – and set limits to the scope of application of national tax law, national tax rules therefore have no effect. In this vein, a distinction can be drawn between states following a *monist* approach, and states that adopt the *dualist* view.[2753] In the former approach, national law and international law are part of a single system and these fields of law prevail over domestic law. This implies that no further action, or transformation into domestic law, is required in order to confer rights on taxpayers, which can directly rely on and/or invoke the treaty provisions once the treaty has been ratified.[2754] In a way it is thus 'self-executing'. However, this still leaves open the question where on the hierarchy the international law should be placed, and whether it takes priority over all law, i.e. municipal law, ordinary, national law and so forth.[2755] Under a *dualist* view international and national law are considered separate systems existing alongside each other, and (tax) treaties only become part of national law by specific transformation into domestic law. It is left to the member states to determine where the international law is then placed within the national hierarchy of laws. Where the Netherlands has adopted a *monist* view as regards the legal validity of both international, as well as EU law,

2752 29 935, ECLI:NL:HR:1994:AA3001 (1994) (HR).

2753 See also Foster, 154-155.

2754 In the Netherlands, this has been embedded in Article 93 of the constitution providing: *"Provisions of treaties and decisions of organisations governed by international law which, according to their content, are binding on everyone, shall have binding force after they have been published."*

2755 In the Netherlands, this has been embedded in Article 94 of the constitution providing: *"Legal provisions in force within the Kingdom shall not apply if such application is incompatible with any mandatory provisions of treaties and of acts of international organisations."*

Germany traditionally tends towards the *dualist* approach.[2756] Actually, Germany finds itself in a more pluralist approach, i.e. neither confirm nor denying a monist approach, although it has obvious features tending towards monism, the German Federal Constitutional Court has shown some tendencies towards dualism.[2757] The differences between both approaches may be relevant in the context of the interrelationship between the treaty and provisions of domestic law, for instance how international tax law may affect – the application of – national tax law.

- As far as Germany is concerned, no policy guidance as regards transitional regimes can be retrieved from the *Verhandlungsgrundlage*. The Netherlands has elaborated on these transitional regimes extensively in the *Notitie Fiscaal Verdragsbeleid*. See section 9.3.3.G.
- In terms of aspirations as regards the tax treatment of pensions, some differences can also be observed. Germany seeks to subject (private) pensions, similar remuneration or annuities to tax in the source state to the extent this pension has been subject to tax relief.[2758] As regards pensions accrued during government service, Germany seeks to subject these pensions in the state where the services were rendered. The Netherlands does no longer draw this distinction between private, and public pensions, in its tax treaty policy. However, the position of the Netherlands in treaty policy has shifted from residence state taxation (1987) to source state taxation (2011), for both private pensions as well as public pensions. No arguments based on tax theory or policy have been provided for this shift; strongly suggesting that this shift in policy is based on budgetary considerations. The revisited treaty policy and the exceptions involved, have, at least, not rendered the tax system simpler.
- With a view to the tax treatment of cross-border pensions, article 14, paragraph 4 of the *Verhandlungsgrundlage* deserves considerable attention. The wording of this provision largely corresponds to paragraph 37 of the commentaries on the OECD MC, and article 24, para 6 of the treaty concluded between the Netherlands, and Germany. This provision on employment income (article 14) stipulates in paragraph 4 that

2756 See Foster, 164-165. In Germany difficulties arose with regard to the relationship between fundamental rights provisions enshrined in the German Constitution and suchlike provisions embedded in the Community and EU legal order.

2757 While Germany, traditionally, adopted the *dualist* approach to the reception of international law, article 25 of the *Grundgesetz* states that general rules of public international law are an integral part of federal law and take precedence over national law. Furthermore, in order to cater particularly for further European integration a new article 23 of the *Grundgesetz* has been added. This Article states that sovereign powers can be transferred to the EU, provided that the transfer has the approval of both the *Bundestag*, as well as the *Bundesrat*. This thus illustrates that under the dualistic view, treaties and national law are mostly on a par in terms of legal force unless national law expressly provides otherwise. See also Lovric. With respect to the approach of the *Bundesverfassungsgericht*, see *Philippinische Botschaft; Kriegsfolgeschäden*.

2758 Either by exempting the contributions from the taxable income, deducting them for tax purposes or were allowed some other form of beneficial treatment by the State of source.

contributions to a pension scheme established and recognized for tax purposes in another state shall, for the purpose of determining the individual's taxable income, benefit from the same tax advantages, under the same conditions and limitations, as contributions made to a pension scheme that is recognized for tax purposes in the employee's residence state, provided that he only became a resident of that state at the start of his employment and contributions had already been made under the same pension scheme.[2759] This provision does not necessarily ensure equivalent tax treatment of contributions paid when an individual is working abroad compared to contributions paid when he is working in the home country; however, it does ensure an equivalent tax treatment of the contributions of co-workers.[2760] Co-workers would thus be not be treated differently for tax purposes, depending on whether their pension scheme was established at home or abroad.[2761] Such a provision has not been laid down in the Dutch *Notitie Fiscaal Verdragsbeleid*. What is more, by doing, so Germany adheres more to the principle of inter-level coherence – paragraph 37 of the commentaries on the OECD MC, and article 24, para 6 of the treaty – compared to the Netherlands.

- With regard to the notion of *lijfrenten* (i.e. annuities) in the Netherlands, the treaty[2762] refers to an annuity as mentioned in the Dutch tax legislation, and which benefits shall be included in the taxable income[2763]. This means that the 'conventional annuity insurances' (i.e. contributions paid to an insurance company in order to secure an income after retirement), as well as the less conventional savings account annuities (i.e. *lijfrentespaarrekening*) and investment account annuities (i.e. *lijfrentebeleggingsrechten*) fall under the scope of Article 17 of the treaty.[2764] However, for Germany, the term 'annuities' refers to a stated sum, payable periodically at stated times during life or during a specified or ascertainable time period, under an obligation to make the payments in return for adequate and full consideration in money or money's worth.[2765] Thus, where the Dutch definition of annuity under the treaty refers to domestic tax legislation, the German definition doesn't, albeit that the latter is hence defined more strictly. It follows from this definition that the Netherlands seeks to remain firm in preserving the internal coherence of the tax system by merely covering life annuities of which benefits are part of the taxable income, pursuant to Dutch domestic tax legislation.

2759 This provision largely corresponds to paragraph 37 of the OECD commentary on Article 18 OECD MC. This has also been laid down in Article 24, para 6 of the tax treaty Netherland-Germany.

2760 Paragraph 59 of the OECD commentary on Article 18 OECD MC.

2761 See also paragraph 51 of the OECD commentary on Article 18 OECD MC.

2762 As laid down in Article 17, par. 7, under a of the treaty.

2763 More precise: the income from work and home (i.e. *inkomen uit werk en woning (BOX 1)* as stipulated in Article 3.1 Wet IB 2001).

2764 Kamerstukken II, 15.

2765 As laid down in Article 17, par. 7, under b of the treaty.

- In particular worthy of note is the third paragraph of article 17 of the German *Verhandlungsgrundlage*. This provision, as an exception to the first paragraph, provides that pensions, similar remuneration or annuities may also be taxed in the source state, if they are attributable, in whole or in part, to contributions which were, in that State and for more than 15 years (in total), subject to tax relief.[2766] Such provision is not existent in the Dutch treaty policy. With regard to the deferred taxation of pension, particular issues in the domain of cross-border pensions may arise. Firstly, the risk of considerable fragmentation of the taxation of pensions in the case of short-term activities in one state. Secondly, the common enforcement problems which may arise if the pensioner - from the point of view of the former state of employment - who is now resident abroad has paid his pension contribution into an old-age provision institution - which is also foreign from the point of view of the former state of employment - possibly in a third State.[2767] Article 17, para 3 attempts to take account of these issues by stipulating that the former state of employment may tax pensions only under certain restrictive conditions, including in particular a 15-year tax-privileged accrual phase.[2768] However, it should be noted that the agreement of these clauses, safeguarding the deferred taxation of pensions, often requires intensive treaty negotiations in cases where the other contracting states also claims a taxing right on retirement income.[2769] The concluded tax treaties, such as the treaty Netherlands-Germany, suggest that, by no means, all contracting states will agree, and accordingly take full account, of Germany's negotiating preferences in this regard.
- Art. 14, paragraph 5 of the German *Verhandlungsgundlage* sets out that the term 'pension scheme' means, as far as Germany is concerned, schemes as mentioned under section 1 of *Betriebsrentengesetz*, i.e. occupational pensions. As regards the term 'tax benefit' paragraph 6 stipulates that, as German law is concerned, this concerns the exemption of contributions pursuant to § 3, nr. 6 EStG. The latter provision refers to contributions to the schemes of a *Pensionsfonds, Pensionskasse*, or *Direktversicherung*. The *Direktzusage* and *Unterstützungskasse* are, obviously, not mentioned as they are subject to a different form of tax relief. Such provision is not existent in the Dutch treaty policy.
- In terms of avoiding double taxation, pursuant to article 22, paragraph 1, letter b, under ee of the treaty Germany shall grant a tax credit.[2770] This article enunciates that

2766 Either by exempting the contributions from the taxable income, deducting them for tax purposes or were allowed some other form of beneficial treatment by the State of source.

2767 Cf. Portner, 'Steuerrechtliche Aspekte der betrieblichen Altersversorgung bei international mobilen Arbeitnehmern' 351.

2768 Lüdicke, 'Anmerkungen zur deutschen Verhandlungsgrundlage für Doppelbesteuerungsabkommen' 33.

2769 Müller-Gatermann, 1036.

2770 See BMF, *Steuerliche Behandlung von Alterseinkünften nach Artikel 17 des Abkommens vom 12. April 2012 zwischen der Bundesrepublik Deutschland und dem Königreich der Niederlande zur Vermeidung der*

> in the case of a resident of Germany, subject to the provisions of German tax law regarding the provision of a credit for foreign tax, the German tax payable in respect of the items of income which may be taxed in the Netherlands in accordance with paragraphs 2 and 3 of article 17 (pensions, annuities and social security benefits) shall be allowed as a credit against the tax payable under Dutch tax law. This tax credit shall be granted in accordance with German tax law with respect to crediting foreign tax. Article 34c EstG in conjunction with article 68a, paragraph 1 of the EStGV 1955 (*Einkommensteuer-Durchführungsverordnung 1955*) applies in calculating this tax credit.[2771] As Germany taxes the Dutch pensions of pensioners resident in Germany at a low effective rate (due to the application of either the *Besteuerungsanteil* or *Ertragsanteil*), the credit to be granted by Germany in respect of the tax payable in the Netherlands is capped at this small amount of German tax. This increases the total tax burden of pensioners living in Germany and receiving a Dutch pension. In the reverse case of a resident of the Netherlands receiving a German pension which may be taxed, or are exclusively taxable, in Germany under article 17, paragraph 2, letter b of the Convention – i.e. a total amount in excess of €15,000 – the Netherlands, by virtue of article 22, paragraph 2, letter b of the Convention, exempts these items of income by allowing a reduction on its tax, in conjunction with a reservation as to the progressive rates of taxation. For that purpose, the said items of income shall be deemed to be included in the amount of the items of income which are exempt from Dutch tax under those provisions. This reduction is calculated in accordance with the provisions in Dutch legislation for the avoidance of double taxation.[2772]

As has been addressed in the beginning of this section, exploring similarity between systems involves a comparison of certain features, where similarity is tantamount to a measurement of common features. A higher degree of similarity helps to ensure the effectiveness of information in terms of the four principles. For instance, the higher the degree of similarity, the easier it is to uphold the information's correctness, trustworthiness,

---

Doppelbesteuerung und zur Verhinderung der Steuerverkürzung auf dem Gebiet der Steuern vom Einkommen IV B 3 - S 1301-NDL/15/10002 2. This is in accordance with paragraph 15, under c of the OECD commentary on article 18 OECD MC.

2771 This latter provision stipulates: *"Die für die Einkünfte aus einem ausländischen Staat festgesetzte und gezahlte und um einen entstandenen Ermäßigungsanspruch gekürzte ausländische Steuer ist nur bis zur Höhe der deutschen Steuer anzurechnen, die auf die Einkünfte aus diesem ausländischen Staat entfällt. Stammen die Einkünfte aus mehreren ausländischen Staaten, so sind die Höchstbeträge der anrechenbaren ausländischen Steuern für jeden einzelnen ausländischen Staat gesondert zu berechnen."* This provision thus specifies that the foreign tax assessed and paid for income from a foreign state and reduced by any claim for reduction that may have arisen shall only be credited up to the amount of German tax payable on the income from that foreign state. If the income originates from several foreign states, the maximum amounts of the creditable foreign tax must be calculated separately for each individual foreign state.

2772 Article 10 Besluit voorkoming dubbele belasting 2001.

and personal relevance. After all, with a higher degree of similarity, there is less need to observe any underlying structural differences. However, as follows from the above enumeration, the legal comparison revealed more differences than similarities in terms of international tax law in the Netherlands, and Germany. In terms of 'fitness' it can thus be concluded that these structural differences hamper the provision of effective information provision, in terms of similarity/comparability.

9.4.2 *Foreseeability*

One cannot simply rely on the maintenance of the law in force.[2773] Applicable legislation is designed in view of particular political, economic, societal phenomena. These phenomena tend to change over time, and accordingly, legislation is adapted to the new situation. This also applies to the legislation under scrutiny in this chapter. It is therefore that conveying information on future amounts of retirement income usually involves a certain level of risk as regards continuously changing legislation. Put it differently, predictability is a structure, and information lies where unpredictable change occurs. Along the line of foreseeability, the following conclusions can be drawn:

- As has become evident in section 9.3.2, non-legally binding tax treaty policy documents/memorandums, enunciate states' guiding principles they adhere to in ongoing and future treaty negotiations and, what is more, they try to provide insight as regards what can expected in new tax treaties in the forthcoming years, i.e. support foreseeability of tax treaties, and their amendments. Against the background of the present research this is important to further address as these amendments may have a considerable effect on the future (net) income, and the according effective pension information provision. However, the role of these policy documents in rendering imminent tax treaty amendments – affecting the (future) net retirement income – more foreseeable, is affected by a range of phenomena. For instance, tax treaty policy follows changes in national laws and regulations. In terms of a comparison, it has become evident that differences exist between the Netherlands, and Germany as regards instruments to articulate their tax treaty policy. The German *Verhandlungsgrundlage* consists of a standard treaty text, largely following the structure and content of the OECD Model Convection, aimed at standardising the German treaties, and increasing foreseeability. Although it is aimed at increasing foreseeability, it does so merely by using a uniformed wording of the treaty provisions.[2774] Contrarily, the Dutch *Notitie Fiscaal Verdragsbeleid* does no longer consist of a standardized treaty

2773 Popelier, 1078.
2774 Cf. Beck, 52 and Müller-Gatermann, 1032.

text, but articulates more extensively compared to the German *Verhandlungsgrundlage*, the preferences and positions taken by the Netherlands in treaty negotiations. A separate Dutch standard treaty was considered no longer suitable, and hence, the Netherlands departed from this approach.[2775] Rather than providing a model as laid down in e.g. the German *Verhandlungsgrundlage*, the Dutch Memorandum deals with considerations as regards the distribution of taxing rights and objectives pursued by the Dutch government in this regard.

– Moreover, although certain aspirations pertaining to the division of taxing rights on retirement income have remained consistent over the course of years, the degree of foreseeability of treaty amendments, and their effect on future net income – created by aforementioned policy documents – is hampered by the fact that expressing these aspirations regarding the distribution of taxing rights does not necessarily mean that these will actually be implemented accordingly in the tax treaty. The final design in the tax treaty is the product of an overall compromise, in which historical, financial, political and economic factors play a greater role than the tax theoretical purity that would correspond best to the principles of tax law.[2776] It can also be observed that in the end result both the interests of both countries, as well as the interests of taxpayers play a role. Moreover, all national tax laws deviate, the implementation of legislation differs and, above all, the wishes of treaty partners differ. For instance, the Netherlands often does not manage to achieve the goal of agreeing on a full source state-taxation on retirement income in relation to emigration countries to which the Netherlands exports many retirement benefits, and which countries export few foreign retirement benefits to residents of the Netherlands. The underlying reason for this appears to be that the other state would not agree on such a full source state-taxation, as it would

2775 In 1998 the Dutch State Secretary considered that although a (renewed) *Nederlands Standaardverdrag 1987* (Dutch Standard Treaty 1987) had the advantage of providing a fairly uniform and clear picture of Dutch treaty policy, there was less need to enshrine what there is, but more need to indicate what the Netherlands is striving for. Hence, given the large differences in modalities, the publication of a new standard text was considered less suitable. It was noted that since the relative weight given to a subject may vary from one treaty relationship to another as a result of a multitude of factors, it is virtually impossible to catch Dutch treaty policy and all conceivable margins in a single text for each subject. However, an unequivocal answer about the margins within which the Netherlands will in practice be prepared to accept deviating solutions is not possible, since such margins are highly dependent on the relative weight of each individual subject in the specific bilateral relationship and on the willingness of the potential treaty partner to make any concession on that subject, or to offer compensation elsewhere in the treaty in return. Furthermore, this avoids, as far as possible, the need for Dutch treaty negotiators to explain to such a potential treaty partner why the Netherlands wishes to deviate from the Dutch model treaty in that specific treaty relationship. Lastly, the final result of the negotiations achieved by the Netherlands is therefore always a compromise between the two contracting states and will therefore hardly ever fully correspond to the Dutch standpoint in treaty negotiations. See Kamerstukken II, *Uitgangspunten van het beleid op het terrein van het internationaal fiscaal (verdragen)recht* section 4.2.

2776 Cf. Starink, 68-69. See also Ministerie van Financiën, 'Notitie Fiscaal Verdragsbeleid 2020' 1.

suffer a considerable financial setback by agreeing on this type of division of taxing rights. It has become evident that – in particular as regards retirement income – tax treaties will not become less complex in future, nor will amendments become more foreseeable. In sum, the foreseeability that the policy documents aim to bring about in theory, is outweighed by the erratic course of treaty negotiations, and the implementation in practice.

- Treaties are negotiated individually in an intensive negotiation process between contracting states, each pursuing its own particular treaty policy and characterized by its legal tradition and *couleur locale*.[2777] Treaty negotiations constitute a process of 'give and take', the outcome of which strongly depends on the points to which both sides attach particular importance.[2778] Factors such as mutual principles, the practical importance of the individual subjects, the economic importance of a treaty relationship and the political desirability of it are observed during treaty negotiations.[2779] The final design in the tax treaty is the product of an overall compromise, in which historical, financial, political and economic factors play a greater role than the tax theoretical purity that would correspond best to the principles of tax law. This renders the eventual design of allocation provisions, enshrined in tax treaties, and their financial consequences fairly unforeseeable. This has been demonstrated in section 9.3.3.
- Furthermore, with regard to the role of transitional agreements in tax treaties concluded by the Netherlands – mitigating the adverse effects of amendments to tax treaties – it is found that the question whether – and to what extent – a transitional arrangement may be desirable varies from case to case, and depends on a number of factors, i.e. effects on actual income, the effects on purchasing power for taxpayers, the number of people involved, the budgetary interests of both countries, the administrative burden, implementation costs associated with a transitional arrangement, and to keep an eye on the relationship with pensioners who have not emigrated or who did not live abroad at the time the pension was accrued. Although these transitional arrangements are often only relevant for a fairly small group of taxable persons, they do often have a relatively substantial financial impact on those concerned. It has been found that – due to these aspects – the conclusion of a transitional agreement is often the result of a political compromise, rendering them less foreseeable. The final arrangement to be included remains a result of a negotiation process and cannot be standardized.[2780] The treaty provision on the division of taxing rights on retirement income will remain a compromise in which the financial interests of both treaty partners play a major role.

2777 Beck, 51.
2778 Cf. Ministerie van Financiën, 'Notitie Fiscaal Verdragsbeleid 2011' 15.
2779 Cf. Kamerstukken II, 'Notitie Internationaal fiscaal (verdrags)beleid' 31.
2780 Ministerie van Financiën, 'Notitie Fiscaal Verdragsbeleid 2020' 24.

Moreover, transitional agreements may take a wide variety of different forms, for example an (integral) source state tax that only applies at a later date. As far as Germany is concerned, no policy guidance as regards transitional regimes can be retrieved from the *Verhandlungsgrundlage.* Overall, these aspects hamper the foreseeability of forthcoming tax treaties amendments, and their likely consequences in terms of net income.

- The Netherlands deviates from the OECD model convention still assuming a residence state taxation (art. 17 of the treaty). As a main rule, this provision thus allocates the exclusive taxing right on pension income to the taxable person's residence state.[2781] Moreover, paragraph 2 of this provision, allows for non-exclusive source taxation and is drafted along the lines of the OECD commentary.[2782] Thus, there is no conditional source state taxation whereby the distribution is made partly dependent on other factors such as whether tax facilitation has taken place in the source state, and the way in which the country of residence levies tax, as in other treaties concluded by the Netherlands with, for example, Belgium and Portugal. The renders the application of this source state-taxation more foreseeable, compared to the conditional source state taxations as laid down in other bilateral tax treaties.

9.4.3 *Inter-level Coherence*

In order to prevent discrepancies in information provision, different fields of multi-level law need to be aligned with each other, i.e. national (Netherlands and Germany); European, and international.[2783] For the purpose and context of the present research, 'coherence' is

2781 Under the old treaty, Article 12, paragraph 1 allocated the taxing right pertaining to private pensions, as a main rule, to the residence state. However, pursuant to Article 12, paragraph 2 and 3, under a, the taxing right on statutory pensions was allocated to the source state. For instance, the *AOW* pension benefits of a German-resident pensioner were taxed in the Netherlands. This shift of taxing right from Germany to the Netherland as regards private pensions has had considerable effects on the income position of retired frontier workers. This is mainly due to the favourable treatment of pensions in Germany under the *Ertragsanteilbesteuerung* or *Besteuerungsanteil*, in conjunction with the tax base exemption which was double in the event of partners jointly returning their tax assessment. In many cases, recipients of a Dutch pension amounting to (max.) €50,000 living in Germany were not due any German income tax. See Lühn. In some cases the tax burden increased with around 895%, see Kamerstukken II, *33 615, nr 8* 27 ff. For numerous calculations on the effects of the shift of taxing right concerning pensions see Kamerstukken II, 27-30. In 2011 it was found that there is no consistent approach at the *Finanzämter* with regard to the qualification of Dutch occupational pensions. Some *Finanzämter* equate these pensions with *Leistungen aus einer betrieblichen Altersvorsorgung*, as a result of which 58% of them are classified as *Besteuerungsanteil* and some *Finanzämter* classify the pensions as *Leibrente aus einem Altersvorsorgevertrag or aus einer betrieblichen Altersvorsorsorgung*, as a result of which only 18% of them are taxed as *Ertragsanteil*. See Kloosterman, Meyer and Laruelle.

2782 See paragraph 15 of the OECD commentary on Article 18 OECD MC.

2783 See also OECD, 'Recommendation of the Council of the OECD on Regulatory Policy and Governance' 14.

termed as 'the situation in which all the levels of the regulatory frameworks are logical and consistent, achieving a harmonious connection of these parts, so that the whole 'hangs together'.[2784] This underlines the relevance of certain properties of regulatory frameworks, and its consequences, for information provision, and corresponding implications. A challenge for the provision of effective cross-border pension information is the diversity - and poorly coordination - of differentiates pension vehicles, and taxes.[2785] From this point of view, in order to uphold the information's effectiveness, it requires a certain degree of coherence among these levels of legislation. At lower levels, this may involve systematic scrutiny of coherence with higher-level regulations and with treaty or other international obligations. A higher degree of coherence also helps to ensure the effectiveness of information in terms of the four principles, in that more coherence between low and higher levels of legislation aids ensuring the information's effectiveness. For instance, in a more coherent (logically and consistent ordered) multi-level legal systems, it is far easier to uphold the information's correctness and trustworthiness, as in such a system, there is less susceptibility to error.

Along the lines of this principle, the chapter above revealed the following findings:
- As regards the extent to which inter-level coherence can be achieved through international tax law, the following fundamental point - as regards treaties' objective and pertinent properties - needs to be stressed. The charge to tax is found in state's domestic law. As domestic direct tax laws involve the unilateral exercise of sovereignty, they do not coordinate, or integrate, very easily. Hence, bilateral tax treaties are concluded in order to provide for specific integration of two national tax systems. Tax treaties constitute a bilateral agreement of international law pertaining to how states agree on the allocating of taxation of cross-border activities. The main purpose of tax treaties is to coordinate the application of domestic tax laws of the contracting states to prevent (judicial) double (non-) taxation on the basis of reciprocity, and to combat unjustified avoidance of taxation by providing distribution rules, attributing taxing rights. With regard to above, it must be noted that tax treaties, in itself, do no create taxing rights, but rather allocate (existing) taxing rights to Contracting states, i.e. they are granted 'permissive'. In terms of achieving inter-level coherence through the coordination of the application of domestic laws, tax treaties can be observed to be of little help, as the charge to tax is found in state's domestic law, which do not coordinate, or integrate, very easily, given their differences, and deviations, as discussed in chapters 4-8 of this research.

2784 Oxford Dictionaries.
2785 In the same vein: Sunstein, 'Informing consumers through smart disclosure' 5.

- Moreover, as regards the distribution of taxing rights, it is established case-law of the CJEU that, in the absence of measures of unification or harmonisation within the EU, Member states remain competent to define the criteria for allocating their taxing rights in order, inter alia, to avoid double taxation. In this regard, the CJEU has held that a different treatment of nationals of the two contracting parties as a result of the division of taxing rights may constitute discrimination that is not contrary to the freedoms of movement.[2786] The court observed that whether the tax treatment of the taxpayers concerned is favourable or unfavourable is determined not, strictly speaking, by the choice of the connecting factor but by the level of taxation in the competent State, in the absence of any Community harmonisation of scales of direct taxation.[2787] The CJEU has consistently held that double tax treaties are designed to eliminate or mitigate the detrimental effects on the functioning of the internal market, due to the coexistence of national tax systems.[2788] What is more, as the CJEU has consistently held, conventions' purpose is not to ensure that the tax to which the taxpayer is subject in one State is no higher than that to which he or she would be subject in the other state.[2789] EU law, as it stands, does not lay down any general criteria for the attribution of areas of competence between the Member states in relation to the elimination of double taxation within the EU, and no uniform or harmonisation measure designed to eliminate double taxation has yet been adopted at EU law level.[2790] The CJEU may not examine the relationship between a national measure, and the provisions of a double tax treaty, since that question does not fall within the scope of EU law.[2791] This confirms that tax treaties can be considered to be of little help, as the charge to tax is found in state's domestic law, which do not coordinate, or integrate, very easily, given their differences, and deviations.
- Although the OECD MC lacks parliamentary approval and thus in a certain sense legitimacy, it can be asserted that some normative power or 'soft obligation' may ensue from the OECD MC as the OECD MC must be applied unless the Member state has entered original reservations or unless material reasons, such as peculiarities of the domestic law of the Contracting State, weigh against the adoption of the Model, with regard to an individual treaty provision.[2792] It could thus be said that this 'soft law' is akin to a pseudo-legal rule, which must be taken into account and from which one

2786 *Gilly* para 24 and 30.

2787 Ibid. para 34.

2788 *Kerckhaert/Morres* para 21; *Columbus Container Services* para 44.

2789 *Gilly* para 46.

2790 *Kerckhaert/Morres* paras 22 and 23. See also *Columbus Container Services* para 45.

2791 *Columbus Container Services para 47 and case referred to.*

2792 Vogel, *Klaus Vogel on double taxation conventions: a commentary to the OECD-, UN- and US model conventions for the avoidance of double taxation of income and capital: with particular reference to German treaty practice* 34.

cannot simply deviate without violating obligations under international law. However, these models do not comprehensively regulate a variance of important international tax issues and have not been adopted by countries on a uniform basis. Certain limitations are hence inherent to these models. Moreover, contracting states have the possibility to make reservations and comments on the OECD Model Convention and the related OECD commentaries[2793]. Although such model conventions do achieve some degree of coordination in the area of international tax law, the actual potential impact is fairly small in terms of inter-level coherence.

– Furthermore, model tax treaties are built on political compromise, are reactionary, customary and historically in nature.[2794] They originate from existing domestic laws and treaty practice, which still largely dictate the direction of their development. This implies that they suffer from a lack of a certain level of conceptual structure based on principle, and are far from comprehensive. As regards the latter, they only cover those tax issues on which agreement can be reached between treaty partners. Yet, it has become apparent that double tax conventions only focus their efforts on the elimination of international double taxation. This role is well demonstrated by the evolution of domestic laws over the past years. Hence, I plea for re-thinking tax principles governing the allocation of taxing rights embedded in (international) tax treaties, where more focus should be put on inter-level coherence.

9.4.4 *Inter-system Consistency*

In order to prevent discrepancies in information provision, different levels of legislation, need to be consistent by themselves. Legal systems consist of, *inter alia*, a set of rules. In general, legislators would prefer that legislation in a particular legal system were consistent. Not only on a domestic level, but in particular where several national legal systems converge as in this research; on a Dutch/German level. This requires a certain form of inter-system consistency. For the purposes of this research 'consistency' is termed as `the quality, state, or fact of being consistent; agreement, harmony, compatibility'.[2795] Consistency, in this context, refers to – while applying national regulatory frameworks – not leading to incompatible outcomes for a specific case. Two distinct types of inconsistency may be discerned: treating a person inconsistently over time, and inconsistency between

2793 These commentaries have been drafted by the OECD Committee on Fiscal Affairs, largely consisting of tax officials of the OECD member states. Hence, these commentaries have been drafted with the agreement of these member states, apart from any reservations made to it.

2794 See Avery Jones, De Broe and Ellis, In this article the authors trace the origin of concepts and expressions used in the OECD MC.

2795 Oxford Dictionaries.

individuals.[2796] It is not uncommon that rules in two legal systems attach incompatible consequences to a same case. Two or more rules are in actual conflict when they actually apply to one and the same case, and attach incompatible consequences to this case. Along the line of inter-system consistency between individuals, the following conclusions can be drawn:

- The tax treatment of the Dutch *nettopensioen*, under tax treaties, reveals that treaty negotiations do not sufficiently anticipate the possible negative consequences of unilateral measures issued by one of the contracting states.[2797] It also becomes evident that effects of national legislation, predominantly drafted through a national lens, on cross-border situations are not sufficiently taken into account when drafting this national legislation. What is more, it shows that the legislature should be more aware of the impact new legislation may have on persons availing themselves of the freedoms of movement, i.e. the cross-border consequences should be taken into account when drafting legislation (so-called border impact assessment).[2798] This can occur in the context of a German frontier employee participating in a *nettopensioen.*[2799] This concerns the situation of a post-active frontier worker resident in Germany who has worked in the Netherlands and has made use of a *nettopensioen* scheme through his employer. Since the frontier worker already lives abroad, he cannot make use of the tax-free redemption option.[2800] After all, he does not emigrate and must therefore have the *nettopensioen* paid out. Under the treaty concluded between the Netherlands and Germany, the same problems arise as those dealt with above. Under article 17, para 2 of the treaty, the source state – the Netherlands in the example – may also tax payments from the *nettopensioen*, provided that the total gross amount of the pension to be received exceeds €15,000. However, the Netherlands will not tax these benefits under national law. So far, no double taxation arises. Yet, no specific agreements have been made in the treaty regarding the *nettopensioen* scheme. As a result, Germany will not make any distinction between gross and net pensions under the new treaty either.[2801] Therefore, Germany would have taxed the benefits from the *nettopensioen* resulting in double taxation as the Netherlands has applied the TEE-principle to this scheme, i.e.

2796 Steyn, 22.

2797 Pursuant to Wet van 2 juni 2014 tot wijziging van de Wet inkomstenbelasting 2001, de Wet op de loonbelasting 1964, de Pensioenwet, de Wet verplichte beroepspensioenregeling en de Invoerings- en aanpassingswet Pensioenwet in verband met de aanpassing van het fiscale kader voor oudedagsvoorzieningen (Wet verlaging maximumopbouw- en premiepercentages pensioen en maximering pensioengevend inkomen).

2798 Cf. Weerepas, 'Grenswerkers, enige hardnekkige problemen' 5.

2799 Zie voor een uitgebreide uiteenzetting over deze problematiek: A.H.H. Bollen-Vandenboorn, 'De vergeten grensarbeider en zijn nettopensioen', *MBB* 2015/09.

2800 The option is offered in article 5.17e, paragraph 5, under a *Wet IB 2001*.

2801 Cf. Bollen-Vandenboorn, 'Belastingverdrag Nederland-Duitsland' paragraph 4.1.

not exempted pension entitlements and deducted pension contributions paid. This exhibits an inconsistent tax treatment between the German frontier worker, participating in a *nettopensioen*, and a Dutch co-worker residing in the Netherlands. Where the former will be confronted with double taxation on the *nettopensioen*, the latter will not. Since the frontier worker already lives abroad, he cannot make use of the tax-free redemption option.[2802] Furthermore, it is difficult to defend that those individuals working side by side (i.e. colleagues) are treated differently for tax purposes, depending on their state of residence.[2803]

9.5 Interim Conclusion

As has been addressed thoroughly in chapter 1 of this research, the two-dimensional notion of effective pension information articulates that the information's behavioural purpose seeks to inform mobile individuals on an aggregated level about how much pension they can expect, in order to be able to assess the adequacy of their dispersed pension, covering all their forms of pension in each of the (former) working/residence states. The aforementioned behavioural purpose contains the terms 'aggregated' (i.e. assembled at an overall/higher level) and the phrase 'covering all their forms of pension in each of the (former) working/residence states'. However, mobile individuals – who avail(ed) themselves of their European freedoms of movement – see themselves confronted with a wide range of diverging 'pensions', i.e. pension vehicles, schemes, retirement products of all sorts, arising from occupational pension systems in each of the different (former) working states, and/or residence states. This requires putting together dispersed, and deviating, elements of future retirement income, arising in each of these states. This amounts to observing, and 'translating' the intersections between different multi-level legal systems (national, EU and international/bilateral) and the interaction of poorly coordinated legal domains (pension and tax law) – which can all be interwoven in a personal mobile situation – into effective pension information. This was taken as a given in this chapter mapping out the regulatory framework on an international level.

Section 9.4 presented the comparative findings along the lines of this research's evaluation framework. This comparison revealed a considerable number of differences when it comes to the role of international tax law in the Netherlands, as well as in Germany. These structural differences should be observed when providing effective cross-border pension information. Also, along the principle of foreseeability of (the application of) legislation

2802 The option is offered in article 5.17e, paragraph 5, under a *Wet IB 2001*.
2803 See also paragraph 51 of the OECD commentary on Article 18 OECD MC.

several findings were revealed. With respect to inter-system consistency, the findings exhibit a number of situations where applying national regulatory frameworks leads to incompatible outcomes for a specific case, in particular with regard to inconsistency of the tax treatment of pensions of mobile individuals. What is more, it was also found that provisions of national tax laws governing the taxation of retirement income, are applied on the basis of an 'isolated approach', without taking into account any previous or subsequent tax treatment in another (member) state. Lastly, evaluating the regulatory frameworks through the lens of inter-level coherence revealed findings when it comes to the coherence among these levels of legislation, involving systematic scrutiny of coherence with higher-level regulations and with treaty or other international obligations. In this vein, this chapter meets this research second (sub)objective of a legal comparative study in which the legal framework on an international level shall be mapped out, and evaluated along the lines of this research's evaluation framework (similarity/comparability, foreseeability, inter-level coherence and inter-system consistency).

10 Reflection, Conclusion and Recommendations: Towards a Further Integration of the Realms of Taxes and Pension Information

10.1 Introduction

This research consisted of nine chapters. Chapter 1 set the scene with several important preliminary matters, such as the grounds for this research, research question, research design, methodology etc. Chapter 2 conceptualised the notion of 'effective information provision', in the light of which the 'fitness' of the regulatory frameworks has been assessed, i.e. the evaluation framework. Chapter 3 revolved around the empirical study conducted as part of this research. Where chapter 2 revolved around the theoretical background – serving as this research's evaluation framework – shaping the notion of 'effective pension information', chapter 3 narrowed down to exploring what effectiveness of information entails when it comes to peoples' question 'what will I get?'. Chapter 4 revolved around the notion of 'pension' in terms of notions, terms and concepts embedded in both the Netherlands, and Germany, as well as several pension classification systems. Chapter 5 discussed the relevant fundamentals of the statutory pension systems in both countries, as well as their tax treatment (in cross-border situations). Along the same lines, chapter 6 looked more closely into occupational pension schemes in both countries. Chapter 7 proceeded by looking into personal pension schemes in the Netherlands and Germany. Chapters 5, 6 and 7 respectively followed the similar structure in considering the relevant rules in domestic law. These chapters form the central base of the comparison, outlining the background material that was relevant in the evaluations. These chapters were structured under two main headings. The first considered the tax treatment of (cross-border) pensions during the accrual phase (i.e. the pension contributions); where the second part proceeded to consider the tax treatment of pension benefits paid out during the pay-out phase. These headings identified a range of tax fundamentals important when projected into the evaluation framework. Where chapter 8 elaborated on the relevant rules on a European level, chapter 9 revolved around the relevant rules on an international level. Each of the descriptive chapters mapping out the regulatory frameworks, concluded by an interim conclusion where, along the principles set out in chapter 2 (evaluation framework) the regulatory frameworks were assessed for their fitness in view of the provision of effective pension information.

This concluding chapter 10 reflects, concludes and elaborates on the evaluation as dealt with in the preceding descriptive chapters, through the lens of the assessment framework as set forth in chapter 2. Through this evaluation, the research's findings have been formulated in the separate chapters. Building on these evaluations, this chapter will provide recommendations on how to cope with, and overcome the problems identified by these findings, and to give impetus to certain developments in the domain of (cross-border) pension information, of which some have already been ongoing. The most important findings, and recommendations have been underlined in the following sections. The common ground of these recommendations is that they envisage a further integration of the realms of taxes, and pension information. Although these conclusions, findings and recommendations bear relevance for other bilateral relations in Europe (other than Germany-the Netherlands), some reservations deserve attention in this respect. As pointed out earlier, there is no Europe-wide taxonomy on mobile EU citizens. Data on intra-EU mobility reveals differences in term of direction (countries of origin and destination), type of occupations, level of education among EU movers, etc. also having effect in the domain of pensions.[2804] Hence, in terms of generalisability of findings and recommendations, account must be taken of these differences when applying this study's findings to other bilateral relations. Moreover, as has been dealt with elaborately in chapters 4-7 of this research, European pension systems are as diverse as the member states themselves. These differences should be borne in mind, as well, when applying this research's findings to other bilateral relations. While taking these differences into consideration, I expect that the majority of this study's findings bear relevance for the Europe-wide socio-economic predicament (i.e. effective cross-border pension information as a first step towards financial resilience in old-age), irrespective of the particular countries concerned.

10.1.1 The Research's Objective and Main Research Question

The general objective of this research was to explore to what extent the regulatory frameworks in the Netherlands and Germany, on a European level, and on an international level, governing the taxation of (cross-border) statutory, occupational and personal pensions, are fit for the provision of effective pension information (net amounts of future pension income) and, and if not so, what legal/non-legal interventions and measures are

2804 See European Commission, 'Annual Report on Intra-EU Labour Mobility 2022'.

needed to ensure, and potentially foster, the effectiveness of the pension information provided. This general research objective is actually threefold and the following sub-objectives can be distinguished. The first goal was to establish a theoretical and conceptual evaluation framework, revolving around the provision of effective pension information. This has been set out in chapter 2 of this research. In particular, the objectives of this chapter were to introduce the reader to the Rational Choice Theory, the science of behavioural economics, explain the idea of the Dual Process Theory, explore the construct of 'social representations' and delineate the notion of 'effectiveness' of information. In doing so, this chapter paved the way for the evaluation of the regulatory frameworks, consisting of psychological and sociological variables, and structural characteristics (for instance, the system's complexity), i.e. adopting a multi-faceted approach. After assembled with the legal (comparative) research part, it provided an integrated account of the shortcomings or inconsistencies of the underlying regulatory frameworks, from an information's perspective. The main research question of this research refers to 'regulatory frameworks' as subject of this research's evaluation. This term covers a multitude of 'government interventions' in the field of law on both a national, as well as on a European and international level, for instance, (national) formal laws, policy decisions (*beleidsbesluiten*), ministerial decrees and memoranda aimed at clarifying the interpretation of given parts of legislation (e.g. *BMF-schreiben*), the CJEU's extensive settled case-law, EC's communications, and bilaterally concluded (international) tax treaties.

As part of creating this evaluation framework – allowing for the assessment of the regulatory frameworks – an experimental (empirical) study has been conducted, which has been addressed elaborately in chapter 3 of this research. Based on this evaluation framework, the legislative instruments in the Netherlands and Germany were assessed for their suitability to provide effective pension information. The second objective was a legal comparative study in which the legal frameworks in the Netherlands and Germany, as well as on a European and international level, were mapped out. This part of the research concerned a mainly descriptive study, which incited to critically assess and value a certain legal phenomenon, i.e. the taxation of pensions in cross-border situations. Chapters 4, 5, 6, 7, 8 and 9 revolved around this second objective. The comparative study allowed for revealing differences and similarities in the tax treatment of pensions in cross-border situations (by laying the tax systems of the two Member states on top of each other) that form a potential hurdle for the provision of effective pension information. In doing so, the comparison constitutes an objective, rather a means. The third objective was the evaluation of the legal frameworks on the basis of the mentioned ('normative') framework as mentioned under the first objective. This has been dealt with in the comparative sections, and interim conclusions, of each of the descriptive chapters (4-9) and will be elaborated on in the sections below. Building on this, the 'fitness' of the legal frameworks at the national, European and international level have been assessed, focusing in particular on any deficiencies that have an (potential detrimental) effect on the provision of effective information. This evaluation incites to formulate points for improvement and recommendations. The results of this evaluation play an instrumental role in this research, since the main research question is of a normative nature.

The main research question of this research encapsulates:

> *To what extent are the regulatory frameworks on a national level in the Netherlands and Germany, on a European level, and on an international level, governing the taxation of (cross-border) statutory, occupational and personal pensions, fit for the provision of effective information and, and if not so, what legal/non-legal interventions and measures are needed to ensure, and potentially foster, the effectiveness of the information provided?*

This research has been conducted from a comparative point of view, regarding the Netherlands and Germany. The national legislation of each of these two Member states has been taken into account to the extent it is considered relevant for the underlying research, as incongruities in the application of this national legislation can lead to cross-border issues. For this purpose, the comparative research design has been employed, apart from the issue whether there is such a thing as 'the' or 'a' comparative design.[2805] I endorse this theorem since the goal of the research determines which method, and the way in which it is conducted, is best suited for carrying out the research.

Moreover, this research's empirical study – chapter 3 – has been conducted through an experimental design, while building on certain behavioural mechanisms explored in the field of 'behavioural economics' and pension information provision. These existing concepts of information provision, and the underlying behavioural mechanisms have been subsumed in a different communication setting, i.e. communicating on the tax treatment of cross-border pensions. The method employed in this research is commonly referred to as RCT[2806]: randomized controlled trial. The survey's participants assigned to the treatment group were confronted with the study's intervention (adjusting the information by showing a net amount of future retirement income, either or not accompanied by a disclaimer, and additional information on the status of the information in the form of an 'important to know-section'). In contrary, the control group were shown a gross amount of future retirement income. This method of randomized experiment

2805 Cf. Leeuw and Schmeets, 115 and cited literature.
2806 This should not be confounded with the abbreviation 'RCT' referring to 'Rational Choice Theory'.

allows exploring whether the 'intervention' has led to any change, i.e. determining the causality between the dependent and independent variable, and that an estimate on the counterfactual can be obtained. This research design is considered the most sound choice to address causal questions ('attribution'), such as questions on the impact of interventions.

Although the foregoing may have given the impression that effective pension information and multi-level legal systems have been treated in this research as two distinct spheres, they have been approached in an integrated manner. This required a methodological-supported translation of the two-dimensional notion of effective cross-border pension information into legal (applicable) concepts, and notions, allowing to intergrate the two abovementioned realms, and enabling to address this research's main research objective, and main research question. This will be discussed in more detail in the following section.

10.1.2 Translating the Two-dimensional Notion of Effectiveness into an Operationalized Paradigm of 'the Law': from Premise to Findings

In chapter 2 of this research, the two-dimensionality of 'effective information' – has been outlined thoroughly, building on the information's behavioural purpose and four principles – largely extracted from Dual Process Theory – which shape the subjective perspective of effective information: understandability, technical (legal) correctness, personal relevance, and trustworthiness. This constituted the embedding of external evaluation criteria, in order to draw conclusions.[2807] This use of external criteria in the assessment framework lead, in turn, to an multidisciplinary nature of the legal research. In doing so, in terms of empirically-gained non-legal insights, this chapter constitutes the framework *generalis*. This is tantamount to this research's first goal, i.e. to establish a theoretical and conceptual evaluation framework, focusing on the provision of effective pension information. Chapter 3 revolved around the empirical study conducted as part of this research, shaping the interdisciplinary perspective of this research. This chapter looked more closely at the notion of 'effective pension information' and, in doing so, serves more as the framework *specialis*. This will be discussed in section 10.1.4 below.

This process of translating/transposing the information's behavioural purpose, and the four principles which delineate the concept of effective pension information into legal (applicable) standards lead to four principles: similarity/comparability, inter-level coherence, inter-system consistency, and foreseeability/predictability. These legal

2807 It can also be referred to as 'assessment by reference on external standard'. See Taekema and Van Klink, 9-10. Tijssen, 74 van Dijck, 22 and Mackor, 79.

standards were used to establish a non-binding framework through which the law's fitness for the provision of effective information provision has been evaluated, i.e. it constituted the 'paradigm' through which the multi-level legal systems are perceived, putting the law in context. This legal lens is better apt for evaluating the fitness of the regulatory frameworks, as it observes certain properties (such as the multi-level property), without accepting it as untestable.

Moreover, it should be noted that not each of these legal principles has been evaluated to the same extent in each of the chapters. The variety in testing against these principles cannot be reduced to certain standard situations. It is much more of a sliding scale where all variations between fit and unfit can be found. This depends on the pertinence with respect to the domain, properties and modalities, of the regulatory frameworks that will be considered. The intensity of this evaluation is partly determined by the purpose of the particular area of legislation (e.g. EU law), but also by its properties and degree of impact (on e.g. national law). For instance, in chapter 4 up to 7 – exploring the national regulatory frameworks – emphasis has been put on the principle of similarity/comparability, since these chapters sought to legally compare the national systems in terms of evaluating their 'fitness'. In addition, in chapters 8 and 9 the principle of inter-level coherence was at the centre of the evaluative findings as this chapter explored the taxation of cross-border pensions governed by European law, and to what extent there is room for improvement in terms of coherence.

Providing, on an aggregated level, mobile individuals information about how much pension they can expect – covering all their forms of pension in each of the (former) working/residence states – requires a complex process of incorporating all types of diverging pension vehicles, schemes, products of all sorts, arising from statutory, occupational and individual pension systems in each of the different (former) working states, and/or residence states. Moreover, it requires observing/applying all relevant domains of fragmented (national) legislation. For instance, it is pivotal that the accrued pension entitlement and the pension to be achieved are calculated in the same way. This requires a process of converging these deviating systems into standardised/uniform information provision, while upholding the information's effectiveness. Putting this dispersed puzzle together also poses considerable challenges in terms of information provision. This amounts to observing, and 'translating' the intersections between different multi-level legal systems (national, EU and international/bilateral) and the interaction of poorly coordinated legal domains (pension and tax law), which can all be interwoven in a personal mobile situation, into effective pension information. In sum, it must be possible to compile the amounts accrued with different pension providers/schemes so that they can be processed in a standardised manner. What is more, this requires a more holistic approach in terms of information provision.

Under this holistic approach, the interwovenness of the two reals of taxes and (effective) pension information manifests itself. For instance, in order to uphold (legal) correctness, combined with understandability, of information, national legal systems together need to be aligned in terms of coherence. In addition, to ensure the information's correctness and – in the long run – trustworthiness regulatory frameworks need to adhere to legislation's foreseeability. This elucidates how the realms of empirically-gained insights from behavioural economics, economic psychology and cognitive psychology, and the realm of multi-level legal systems are related. Although portrayed as two separate spheres (effective pension information and multi-level legal systems respectively), it is my belief that these realms should be integrated better, for the benefits of both spheres. Moreover, this translation into legal (applicable) concepts, and notions, enables to connect the two abovementioned realms, and enabled to address this research's main research objective, and main research question.

Below, the evaluation of the fitness of the regulatory frameworks will be structured around the four legal principles, i.e. similarity/comparability, inter-level coherence, inter-system consistency, and foreseeability/predictability. In doing so, it will be considered what these findings imply in light of the two-dimensional concept of 'effective pension information' (understandability, technical (legal) correctness, personal relevance, and trustworthiness). Building on this, it can be concluded to what extent the regulatory frameworks are fit for effective pension information, and based hereon recommendations will be put forward.

10.1.3 Empirical Results: Practical Insights for Effective Cross-border Pension Information and Expanding Literature

Chapter 3 narrowed down to exploring what effectiveness of information entails when it comes peoples' question 'what will I get?'. In this study I investigated whether adjusting pension information along the ways of providing readers net, or gross amounts of future retirement income, and including a disclaimer, enhances or works to the detriment of the information's ease of comprehension, informativeness and perceived trustworthiness, next to the persons' expected future financial security, and behavioural expectations. Moreover, the study explored the moderating effect of financial literacy, perceived fiscal/pension literacy and self-efficacy in this regard. This study's results offer practical insights for improving the effectiveness of (cross-border) pension information provision. These insights may support in tailoring, and shaping the provision of pension information. In doing so, this study advances retirement research by offering a more profound insight into how net amounts of future retirement income (with disclaimer) are evaluated compared to gross amounts. Moreover, the results demonstrate that adding a disclaimer – pointing out the risks when communicating on net amounts of future retirement income – may have a positive effect on the perceived trustworthiness, rather than a detrimental effect.

The results revealed that exposing participants to a net amount of projected future retirement income has a significantly positive effect on the ease of comprehension, while including a disclaimer does not alter this. This demonstrates that providing a net amount of future retirement income renders the (pension) information more salient, readily available, and easier to understand, since people have encountered a net amount recently or frequently in financial decision-making (e.g. buying a new car, doing groceries). This is further supported by the results of the five open-ended question in the beginning of the survey, where among respondents allocated to the gross-amount text frame, the predominant question pertained to what they would receive as a net amount of future retirement income. This supports this research's hypothesis, drawing on the relativity bias, that people generally want to be provided with a net amount of future retirement income, in order to compare this (easily) to their current net (earned) income, which they employ to finance their current standard of living. Such an easy comparison enables readers to assess the adequacy of their future retirement income, and offers them an action perspective in order to assess whether additional actions, for instance additional pensions savings, are necessary. With respect to the information's perceived trustworthiness, the results revealed that incorporating a disclaimer in information depicting a net amount of future pension income has a statistically significant positive effect on the information's perceived trustworthiness (compared to information depicting a net amount without any disclaimer). In order to ameliorate people's perceived trustworthiness of the information showing a net amount of future pension income, a disclaimer appears to play a pivotal role in this regard, implying that in these cases a disclaimer is an apt intervention. As regards the effect of a disclaimer on expected future financial security, the results made apparent that incorporating a disclaimer in information actually has a statistically significant positive effect on participants' reported expected future financial security. Including a disclaimer seems to induce a certain sense of security. Although the analysis on behavioural expectations did not yield any significant main effect among the three treatment conditions, one of the twelve-point scale was found significant, i.e. the item indicating that he will consult a professional financial advisor. The results revealed that people allocated to the net amount group reported statistically higher behavioural expectations, compared to the respondents allocated to the gross amount-group. It may even be argued that due to the absence of the disclaimer, people show higher behavioural expectations with regard to consulting a professional financial advisor, as they may question the information's credibility, and feel urged to consult a professional. It can be contended that pension-related tasks are more 'salient' than tax-related tasks in retirement planning.[2808] People might also perceive tax-related behavioural expectations as requiring more effort, and might therefore be more reluctant to do so. In addition, the results revealed that including an additional option to read a full-text disclaimer, at a deeper layer of information, appears to be effective, as 92.1% of the respondents allocated to the net amount and disclaimer-group actually made use of this option by clicking the button redirecting them to the full-text disclaimer. This suggests – under the Elaboration Likelihood Model – that incorporating such a possibility invokes a certain motivation among people to think elaborately about the (credibility of the) information under the central route of thinking.

As has been mentioned earlier, conveying a future net amount of future retirement income poses considerable challenges, (legal) risks and tensions in the domain of information provision, for instance, the risk of providing incorrect information due to the legislation's complexity and (un)predictability. In order to mitigate these risks, this study's results provide practical guidance. An instrument to avoid being held liable for providing erroneous information, and making people more aware of the (informative) non-binding status of the information, is including a disclaimer. The results have shown that including a net amount accompanied by a disclaimer has a positive effect on the perceived trustworthiness of the information. Moreover, people exposed to a gross amount reported the highest level of perceived trustworthiness. However, in turn, depicting a gross amount has a negative effect on the perceived ease of comprehension, as aforementioned. This illustrates, part of, the tensions that may arise in pension information provision. Also, in terms of people's expected future financial security, providing a net amount of future retirement income accompanied by a disclaimer, appears to have a positive effect, potentially enhancing the information's effectiveness.

In terms of heterogeneity, fairly little differences have been found when it comes to gender, age, level of income, level of education, and mobility status. In addition, the study examined the moderating role of peoples' financial literacy, perceived fiscal/ pension literacy and self-efficacy. The results revealed virtually no significant effects for these moderators. This suggests that a fairly standardised approach in information provision can be taken when it comes to the form of projections of future retirement income. What is more, it deserves to be noted that although the respondents' primary mobility status did not have a

2808 Tversky, 337. Some research studies observed a common pattern in the sense that the more salient objects, in comparative tasks, occur more often as a response, compared to the less salient object. Factors contributing to the salience of a stimulus include intensity, frequency, familiarity, good form, and informational content.

significant moderating effect between treatment and the dependent variables, the respondents differed considerably as regards their mobility status as such (migrant worker, cross-border worker, posted worker etc.). Although this does not affect information provision as such, it may have more practical implications in terms of legal consequences of this mobility status for ascertaining the tax treatment of cross-border pensions. As demonstrated in chapters 5-9, a person's mobility status plays a pivotal role in ascertaining the applicable rules and regulations in the domain of the tax treatment of (cross-border) pensions. This poses substantial challenges, and tensions, in the domain of information provision, e.g. leading to a high susceptibility in terms of incorrect information. In turn, providing incorrect information may have a potential detrimental effect on the information's (perceived) credibility. Again, including a disclaimer may play a pivotal role in combatting this risk.

Lastly, the study explored the degree of lack of overview, and action perspective among (former) mobile workers as regards their retirement income, and explored the need for a European Pension Tracking Service. The results revealed a considerable lack of insight among mobile citizens into the consequences of their mobility in terms of their pension and its tax treatment, and underlines the growing importance of supporting these mobile citizens in this regard through the provision of cross-border pension information. Further, results indicated that the majority of respondents feel in need of a certain instrument to resolve this lack of insight, and to support them in their retirement, and financial planning, while getting a grasp of the legal consequences of their mobility. In terms of solutions, and interventions needed in the field of cross-border pension information, results revealed that almost 90% of respondents perceive a European Pension Tracking Service, providing a total overview of their pension situation, as helpful in their retirement planning. This supports the call for the development of pension information provision on a European level, aimed at (retired) mobile workers. In order to ensure the proper implementation of certain recommendations, set forth above, it seems most appropriate to harness the momentum of the ongoing development of the European Tracking Service[2809] (hereinafter: ETS) and to catalyse, and give impetus to, the development of a holistic approach on retirement, and financial, planning for mobile individuals, aimed at ensuring their pension adequacy, and herewith reducing the chance of poverty among the retired.[2810] At European level, there appears to be sufficient momentum to turn the tide.

2809 FindYourPension, 'EU project for the pilot phase of a European Tracking Service on Pensions started'.

2810 Addressing gaps in pension adequacy, constituting a significant potential cause of poverty among the elderly, is a response to achieving the Europe 2020 poverty reduction target. See European Commission, 'Green paper: towards adequate, sustainable and safe European pension systems', 3.

10.2 Evaluation and Recommendations along the Lines of the Four Principles

10.2.1 Similarity/Comparability

The information's behavioural purpose stipulates that mobile individuals should be informed on an aggregated level about how much pension they can expect, in order to be able to assess the adequacy of their dispersed pension, covering all their forms of pension in each of the (former) working/residence states. This contains the terms 'aggregated' (i.e. assembled at an overall/higher level) and the phrase 'covering all their forms of pension in each of the (former) working/residence states'. This requires putting together dispersed, and deviating, elements of future retirement income, arising in each of these states. In short, it requires to be able to sum up each of these amount in order to find an answer to the question 'what will I get?'; and 'will this be sufficient?'. Despite the fact that pension systems – and their taxation – in Europe are as diverse as the European Member states themselves, finding a common way of communicating about pensions is not an easy task.

A higher degree of similarity helps to ensure the effectiveness of information in terms of the four principles. For instance, the higher the degree of similarity, the easier it is to uphold the information's correctness, trustworthiness, and personal relevance. After all, with a higher degree of similarity, there is less need to observe any underlying structural differences. Moreover, a higher degree of similarity leads to a higher comparability of the different regulatory frameworks/legal constructs, avoiding comparing the incomparable, and making it less prone to error. Similarity/comparability does not only relate to legal constructs but also to the use of terms, definitions, and concepts. What is more, it has been revealed that existing categorisation systems (e.g. World Bank Model) are of little use in aiding similarity/comparability, but rather take a role in understanding structural differences, once revealed.

Exploring similarity between systems involves a comparison of certain features. The assessment of similarity is described as a feature-matching process, i.e. it measures the degree to which two objects (for instance, the Dutch and German regulatory frameworks) – both considered a set of features – match each other.[2811] Similarity is tantamount to a measurement of common features. The more the systems exhibit common features, the better their comparability. That is, similarity increases with addition of common features and/or deletion of distinctive features.[2812] When it comes to the two systems under

2811 Tversky, 330.
2812 See ibid. 330.

scrutiny, these two regulatory systems have the same objective – i.e. taxing pensions – but have a different shape, historical development, political background, underlying principles, rationales, modalities, and technicalities.[2813] What is more, it has become apparent that tax law is a mix of historical development, compromise and political rhetoric.[2814]

Through the lens of the evaluation framework outlined in chapter 2, the present research revealed impediments in the regulatory frameworks for providing effective pension information. These impediments include, inter alia, fundamental structural differences in the national regulatory frameworks governing the taxation of cross-border pensions.

Each of the descriptive chapters of this research, has been concluded with an interim conclusion pertaining to how the regulatory frameworks stand, and operate in the light of these principles. For the presentation of these comparative findings along the lines of the principle of similarity/comparability, I refer to the comparative-sections of each of the descriptive chapters 4-7. This corresponds to this research's main objective, i.e. explore what impediments for providing effective pension information lie in the regulatory frameworks, governing the taxation of statutory, occupational and personal pensions in cross-border cases between the Netherlands and Germany, and explore what legal/non-legal interventions and measures are needed to ensure, and potentially foster, the effectiveness of the information provided. A brief reflection on these findings will be given below.

As addressed in chapter 4, some terms, notions and concepts may be considered a universal legal concept present in both legal systems at issue, but nevertheless having a different meaning in both systems. While taking this as a guiding principle, chapter 4 reflected on the notions of 'pension' and 'pillar', and explored the legal character of statutory, occupational, and personal pensions in the Netherlands, as well as Germany. The legal

2813 As Danneman argues: "*There is no point in comparing what is identical, and little point in comparing what has nothing in common*". See Dannemann, 384.

2814 In studying the different fields of law pertaining to this research's topic (on national, European and international level) I found these fields reminiscent of Otto Neurath's renowned analogy: "*Es gibt keine tabula rasa. Wie Schiffer sind wir, die ihr Schiff auf offener See umbauen müssen, ohne es jemals in einem Dock zerlegen und aus besten Bestandteilen neu errichten zu können.*" While this analogy applies primarily to the field of epistemology, it also holds similarities with the regulatory frameworks, studied in the present research. As it were, the regulatory frameworks form the ship, in which certain underlying beliefs as regards the system are laid down. These frames cannot be revised with a clean slate (i.e. tabula rasa). In particular in cross-border cases, the consequences hereof become manifest. We cannot abandon everything and start revisiting provision after provision, but revising one provision means adapting another provision, since these provisions are intertwined. It almost seems like "the hierarchical structure of the system is endless, and it is impossible even for insiders to comprehend", see F Kafka, *Het proces* (Atheneum, Amsterdam 2012) 101.

comparison revealed a considerable number of similarities when it comes to the legal character of Dutch and German statutory, occupational, and personal pensions. Moreover, it revealed a range of differences to be observed when providing effective cross-border pension information. What is more, it was found that although there is some consensus to divide pensions into three pillars, a universal agreed definition/classification/taxonomy is still missing. This consensus is missing as on what aspects, elements, modalities of a pension scheme should be prevailing in the classification. Due to this cross-country lack of consensus and consistency, these systems of categorisation merely serve to categorise pension vehicles *grosso modo*, and should be treated with caution when employed in the domain of (cross-border) pension information provision. With regard to the German system, it appeared that the diverging use of the terms *Säule*, and *Schicht* works to the detriment of effective pension information, in terms of the construct 'pension'.

In accordance with the principle of subsidiarity, the (full) responsibility for the organisation of their pension systems, as well as for the decision on the role of each of the three pillars of the retirement system in individual Member states, lies with the Member states. In the descriptive part of this thesis, it has become evident that each of the studied regulatory frameworks has evolved from that country's particular economic, political, social, historical and cultural circumstances. This implies that there is no one-size-fits-all solution for the issues raised in this research but it, rather, requires tailored recommendations.

The comparative findings presented in the comparative-section of chapters 5-9, revealed more differences than similarities when it comes to Dutch and German pensions, and their tax treatment in cross-border situations. Structural differences also take a predominant role in the asymmetric role of pension (pillars) and different cultures. The national tax systems offer different modalities as regards tax benefits, relief, reductions, exemptions, compensation, deferrals and other fiscal advantages[2815]. What is more, structural difference relate to the role of each pension in each state in saving for retirement (and the according tax treatment), the legal cultures, level of discretion left to the tax authorities, responsiveness of legal system to new developments etc. The patchwork of all applicable domestic laws, regulations, decrees, but also European legislation and international legislation, form a dispersed patchwork hampering to 'put the puzzle together'. In order to adhere more to the principle of similarity/comparability, the interdependence of the various national legal fields and jurisdictions should be ensured more. This can be achieved through abandoning an 'isolated approach' and incorporate foreign (tax/pension) legislation in the development of national legislation.

2815 The CJEU delineates a 'fiscal advantage' as allowing a taxable person to reduce the amount of taxable income. See, *inter alia*, C-480/17 *Montag* ECLI:EU:C:2018:987 (CJEU) para 23.

This entails that these structural differences ought to be observed when providing effective cross-border pension information, in particular while upholding the information's (legal) correctness, understandability, personal relevance, and trustworthiness. These obstacles/hindrances are mostly rooted in a lack of coordination between national systems. In terms of 'fitness' it can thus be concluded that these structural differences hamper the provision of effective information provision, in terms of similarity/comparability. The high diversity of pension schemes and the unprecedented high level of complexity of these pension vehicles impairs the comparability of these schemes, and, in turn, the information provided with regard to these schemes. This calls for an improvement and standardization of this information provision. The reasons for this increasing complexity and compaction of rules are manifold:

- The legislation considers it adequate that the scope of application of a certain legal arrangement needs to be expanded or limited and a certain provision needs to be drafted accordingly;
- The codification of (CJEU's) case-law;
- The shift from the budgetary function of tax law to a more instrumental, or guiding[2816], function of tax legislation;[2817]

2816 RAJ Van Gestel and MLM Hertogh, 'Wat is regeldruk? Een verkennende internationale literatuurstudie' (WODC, Den Haag 2006) 29. In view of implementing this 'guiding' legislation, the Dutch legislator assigned more regulatory competences to administrative bodies. See T Koopmans, 'De rol van de wetgever' in HCF Schoordijk (ed.), *Honderd Jaar Rechtsleven* (W.E.J. Tjeenk Willink, Zwolle 1970) 164 and LL Fuller, *The morality of law* (Yale University Press, New Haven-Londen 1969) 80. The guiding objectives are manifold: creating a more attractive environment for businesses, contributing to the transition towards a greener economy, preserving social market economy etc. See European Commission, 'Tax policies in the European Union: 2020 survey' (DG Taxation and Customs Union, European Union, 2020).

2817 Commissie voor de Belastingherziening, 'Graag of niet, Rapport van de Commissie voor de Belastingherziening,' (Den Haag 1991) 16. See also in this regard CM Kleinhuis and E Niemeijer, 'Wet en werkelijkheid. Bevindingen uit evaluaties van wetten' (WODC, Den Haag 2008) 5 and HB Winter, M Herweijer and M Scheltema, *Evaluatie van wetgeving: terugblik en perspectief* (Kluwer, Deventer 1990) 115. Initially, the primary function of legislation was defining the values and standards, generally accepted in society (guarantee function). The law constitutes the legal foundation of government policy, i.e. the constitution of policy, see Koopmans, 161. Furthermore, embedding rules in the law, is intended to provide citizens with certainty as regards the consequences of the events spelled out in those rules. As every citizen is able to read the rules applicable to him/her, they are able to unravel which behaviour the government expects from them, and which government behaviour they may expect themselves. This system of codified rules allows providing certainty to citizens to find out their legal position, in relation to society, but also towards the government. Commonly, tensions may rise between these functions of legislation, see GJ Veerman, 'De wet als zinsbegoochelingstoestel, over de kwaliteit van wetgeving (inaugural speech)' (Universiteit van Maastricht, 2004). Lastly, the aforementioned guarantee function implies that laws may not be incompatible with principle of the rule of law, such as the principle of legal certainty, see Kleinhuis and Niemeijer, 24 and Winter, Herweijer and Scheltema. In particular in the domain of tax law, the 'guiding function' (i.e. fiscal instrumentalism) has become apparent over the course of the years, see JP Boer, *Sturende belastingheffer een monster? Juridische kanttekeningen bij fiscaal instrumentalisme en 'tax nudging'* (Sdu, Den Haag 2013) 7. Fiscal promotion and discouragement arrangements are harnessed to, for instance, stimulate the economy and employment opportunities. See also K Caminada and LGM Stevens,

– the implementation of international and European legislation in domestic legislation.

The overwhelming complexity of the regulatory systems seems mainly due to the fact that there is a lack of an overarching conception, underlying the system.[2818] With respect to the frameworks governing the taxation of cross-border pensions, i.e. national domestic legislation, European legislation and international legislation, each of these fields of law are often treated separately/'in isolation', while they should be regarded in conjunction. What is more, each of these systems have developed in their own manner, without, for instance, a principle requiring to take into account the 'bigger picture'. This is reminiscent of the term 'emergence', i.e. the idea that the whole is being more than the sum of its parts, as characteristics of legal complexity.[2819] Translated to the foregoing, this entails that autonomous components (i.e. national domestic legislation, European legislation and international legislation) interact, from which novel properties emerge.

Regulatory differences, a lack of harmonization or coordination of legislation and complex interactive processes between different legislative instruments and different level of international and/or European law and national law are the most prevalent obstacles to the provision of effective information. These issues of complexity, pluriformity, and fragmentation of legislative instruments partially find their ground in the phenomenon that national pension systems are predominantly based on national policy considerations.[2820] A holistic view on retirement planning (including taxes) is neglected. Policies in the domain of the taxation of pensions are drawn up while not looking at the whole but rather the different parts of which something is built, especially where legislation of a national, European and international level intertwine. In conclusion, the legal toolbox as regards

'Instrumenteel fiscaal beleid: oorzaak en complexiteit en scheefgroei' WFR contending that there is a permanent tension between argument pertaining justice, and argument as regards efficiency. See also RECM Niessen, 'Instrumentalisme en belastingrecht' ibid.

2818 Pertaining to Dutch legislation, see HJ Hofstra, *Eenvoud in de belastingheffing* (De Naamloze Vennotschap, 1947) 141-144.

2819 J Murray, TE Webb and S Wheatley, 'Encountering law's complexity' in J Murray, TE Webb and S Wheatley (eds.), *Complexity Theory and Law: Mapping an Emergent Jurisprudence* (Routledge, London 2018) 12.

2820 Braithwaite even argued for a complete reform of tax legislation and proposed the integration of specific rules into principles, in order to avoid that the prescription of relatively specific acts lead to creative tax compliance, by making the many loopholes in very specific tax legislation. As he puts it, "[a] smorgasbord of rules engenders a cat-and-mouse legal drafting culture…". He argues that a hybrid of rules and principles would provide clear guidance to taxpayers in common situations while mitigating exponential growth in legal complexity, and help to dismantle a tax system that ordinary people cannot comprehend and therefore has low legitimacy. This integration of rules and principles in tax law would, inter alia, entail overarching (holistic) principles that are binding on taxpayers; defining a set of rules to cover the complex area of tax law; the principle is binding with the rules to be used only to assist in applying the given principle; and foster an educative dialogue with judges, company directors and community about the principle in the tax law in the hope that it will develop shared sensibilities on what those principles mean. See V Braithwaite, *Market in vice. Markets in virtue.* (The Federation Press, Leichhardt 2005) 149-150.

the taxation of cross-border pensions – on national, European, and international level – falls short of instruments to mitigate (the consequences of) the lack of coordination/ integration between national legal orders.

The structural differences between the Dutch and German national regulatory frameworks addressed in the comparative-sections of each of the preceding (descriptive) chapters – and revealed through the legal comparison – ought to be incorporated in national law- and policy-making, besides the (financial) consequences of these differences for (former) mobile individuals. What is more, if these differences were not to be taken into account, awareness among policy-makers and other agents/actors in the fields needs to be fostered through information provision, training, and different types of education. By looking across borders, these actors would develop a certain sense of the (tradition of) foreign legal systems. In doing so, they should be able to better understand what mobile persons have to contend with in their (financial) planning, and decision-making.

10.2.2 Inter-level Coherence

In mobile situations, different levels of legislation intertwine. In order to prevent discrepancies in information provision, different fields of multi-level law need to be aligned with each other, i.e. national (Netherlands and Germany); European, and international.[2821] For the purpose and context of the present research, 'coherence' is termed as 'the situation in which all the levels of the regulatory frameworks are logical and consistent, achieving a harmonious connection of these parts, so that the whole 'hangs together'.[2822] This underlines the relevance of certain properties of regulatory frameworks, and its consequences, for information provision, and corresponding implications. A challenge for the provision of effective cross-border pension information is the diversity – and poorly coordination – of differentiates pension vehicles, and taxes.[2823] From this point of view, in order to uphold the information's effectiveness, it requires a certain degree of coherence among these levels of legislation. At lower levels, this may involve systematic scrutiny of coherence with higher-level regulations and with treaty or other international obligations, which has been dealt with in chapters 8 and 9 of this research. A higher degree of coherence also helps to ensure the effectiveness of information in terms of the four principles, in that more coherence between low and higher levels of legislation aids ensuring the information's effectiveness. For instance, in a more coherent (logically and

2821 See also OECD, 'Recommendation of the Council of the OECD on Regulatory Policy and Governance' 14.
2822 Oxford Dictionaries.
2823 In the same vein: Sunstein, 'Informing consumers through smart disclosure' 5.

consistent ordered) multi-level legal systems, it is far easier to uphold the information's correctness and trustworthiness, as in such a system, there is less susceptibility to error.

Evaluating the regulatory frameworks through the lens of inter-level coherence - in the comparative-section of chapters 5-9 – revealed findings when it comes to the coherence among these levels of legislation, involving systematic scrutiny of coherence with higher-level regulations and with treaty or other international obligations. These findings exhibit that national rules and regulations are insufficiently geared up to each other, due to a lack of integration. Interventions to foster this integration lack on an international level and are insufficiently equipped on a European level, i.e. the instruments of positive and negative integration (removing tax obstacles for the European internal market).

In terms of 'fitness' it can thus be concluded that these phenomena of inter-level coherence hamper the provision of effective information provision, as it is more difficult to uphold the information's effectiveness, in terms of understandability, legal correctness, personal relevance, and trustworthiness. In this regard particular attention should be devoted to the interoperability in the multi-level legal system. Interoperability is at the heart of inter-level coherence, and can be harnessed as an instrument to combat fragmentations. Legal interoperability addresses the process of making legal rules cooperate across national jurisdictions, on different subsidiary levels within a single state or between two or more states.[2824]

10.2.2.A Interoperability in a Multi-level Legal System

The interoperability between the different layers of legislation and regulation (national, European, and international level) is, in particular, concerned with the following interwovenness. This has been exhibited, in particular, under the principle of inter-level coherence.

Whether in cross-border cases pension benefits may be taxed under national law depends on the allocation of taxing rights, as laid down in the applicable tax treaty. If the relevant Member State has been assigned a (shared) taxing right, it may (partially) tax the pension income on the basis of national tax law. In cases where a Member State, despite the absence of the allocation of a taxing right on the basis of a tax treaty, subjects pension income to national taxation, there is as a rule a (prohibited) treaty override. Furthermore, it should be noted that once the member state has been assigned the taxing right pursuant to the tax treaty, the way in which this right is exercised – pursuant to national legislation – varies from one member state to another. The interwovenness between national and European

2824 RH Weber, 'Legal Interoperability as a Tool for Combatting Fragmentation' (2014) 6.

tax law concerns the legitimacy of the exercise of national tax rights in cross-border cases in terms of the European internal market without internal borders, in particular achieved through the processes of positive and negative integration. More specifically, this concerns the ability to exercise the European freedoms of movement – guaranteed by the European treaties – without hindrance. The European law principle of non-discrimination prohibits member states from applying their legislation in comparable cases where – in the absence of a justification ground – this is in conflict with the European freedoms of persons, goods, services and capital. In cross-border cases where pension contributions paid to foreign pension institutions are not allowed as a deduction compared to pension contributions paid to domestic pension institutions, European law prohibits the application of the underlying national legislation, provided that the cases are comparable and no justification ground has been accepted. As a corrective mechanism, European law ensures that national tax law is in line with the idea of the European internal market without internal borders. The process of inter-operability has been visualised in figure 10.1.

Figure 10.1 Interoperability in a Multi-layered Legal System

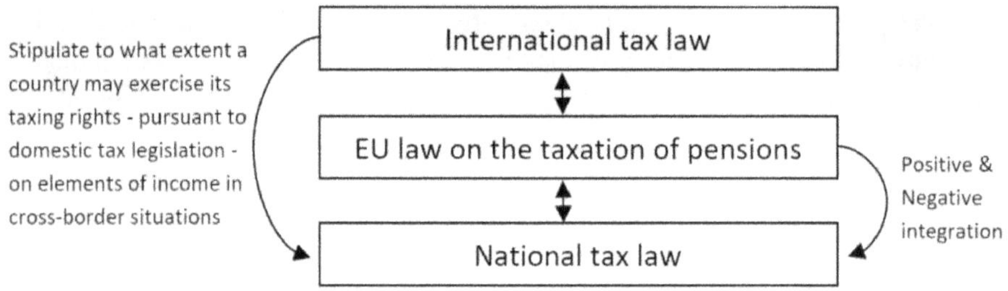

10.2.2.B The EC's role in Achieving Inter-level Coherence

As dealt with extensively in chapter 8, the instrument of 'positive integration' takes a central role in achieving inter-level coherence. In the field of positive integration, the European Commission has taken several steps in order to (better) 'align' the Member states' national tax systems and/or to render these systems (more) compatible with primary and/or secondary European law.[2825] It is remarkably to see, that since the 2001 Communication, the Commission has taken no considerable steps in the sphere of positive integration pertaining to the tax treatment of cross-border pensions.

2825 For an extensive overview of these initiatives in the sphere of positive integration see Kofler, 'Ist der Spuk des Europäischen Steuerrechts bald vorbei?' 7.

In the Commission's effort to integrate the nationals tax systems more, a certain degree of common ground is discernible. Primarily, the Commission seeks to find a balance between subsidiarity, national states' tax sovereignty and a more coherent approach as regards the tax treatment of cross-border pensions. It could however be said that the Commission has relied too heavily on the case-by-case negative integration-approach, pursued by the CJEU, and lacked decisiveness in this regard. Common elements of her approach are the following:

- **No harmonisation:** the purpose is not to seek harmonisation of Member states' taxation systems pertaining to pension and life assurance. The coordinated approach would, rather, adapt to the diversity of Member states' rules.
- **No discrimination:** both the freedom to provide services as well as the free movement of person may not be impeded by unduly restrictive or discriminatory tax treatment of cross-border pensions and life assurance.
- **No revenue shortfall:** the coordinated approach should allow and support Member States to safeguard the tax revenues they are empowered to collect pursuant to their applicable tax legislation. In addition, it should allow for an enforceable and compliance-stimulating system.

In her 2001 communication the Commission refrained from drawing up more general measures of positive integration pertaining to the tax treatment of cross-border pensions. The commission pointed out that it does not envisage proposing legislative measures to harmonise Member states' pension taxation systems.[2826] The commission, rather, would welcome the broader acceptance of the EET-principle, as the alignment of Member states' tax systems would help reduce mismatches, leading to double (non-)taxation. In doing so, the Commission moved away from her approach in previous reports and Communications, in which she plead for coordinating measures of a general and positive nature, which would help structuring the different national tax systems around a coherent pension scheme that should be assigned binding force.

The arguments put forward by the Commission substantiate why she abstained from formulating general measures, aimed at establishing completely uniform, or harmonized rules. The 2001 communication is void of arguments why more general measures of a coordinating measure are lacking. It is assumed that coordination reflects a lower degree of alignment of taxes compared to harmonization.[2827] It, therefore, seems not required to draw up uniform rules in order to support positive integration but; rather; to establish

2826 European Commission, 'The elimination of tax obstacles to the cross-border provision of occupational pensions,' 19.

2827 Hinnekens, 31 ff.

strategies in line with policy objectives and measures devoted to enforce them.[2828] In order to achieve coherent national pension tax systems, from an EU law point of view, and consistent with each other, this would require the development of certain points of agreement in respect of the structure of tax advantages.

Further in developing these points, the Commission's principles must be taken into consideration: striving for coordination of tax systems; rather than harmonization, adhering the principle of non-discrimination and the Treaty Freedoms, and safeguarding the states' tax revenues. However, as regards the former the relevant point in discussion is ascertaining the scope of coordination.[2829] To this end, the Commission must be allowed a certain margin of discretion, given the circumstances and factors potentially having an effect on the outcome.[2830] Yet, it remains difficult to see that the Commission omitted to establish more general measures of coordination rather than the mere assertion that the EET-principle should be adhered to more broadly, since not being able to draw up completely uniform rules does not preclude recommendations of a more general character. The commission could have explored a whole range of other possibilities, provided that it would have been willing to support the positive integration-approach more broadly. For instance, in order to align the national tax systems more with the EET-principle, the proposed measures should have focussed more on the implementation thereof in the tax systems of the Member states concerned, taking account of the deviating specific rules laid down in these Member states' national tax legislation. The Commission's narrow approach of leaving the development of a coherent (European) approach of the national pension tax systems, and complementing tax policy instruments, to the CJEU's case-by-case interpretation, and to the Member states, lacks decisiveness.[2831]

The Commission's proposals were driven by the urgency of the situation, the practicality and level of realism thereof. In order to circumvent the unanimity requirement and assuming a lack of competence, the Commission proposed measures of coordination rather than harmonization of the national tax pension systems. However, as Prats contends, these easy and practical solutions do not necessarily correspond to national and international principles and may even give rise to outcomes inconsistent with the Commission's own objectives and EU law.[2832] Furthermore, this approach is surprising

2828 Cf. Prats, 24.

2829 Coordination in the sphere of taxes is characterized by a certain level of flexibility, implying both adhering to the subsidiarity principle and the Member States' competence on the one hand and, on the other hand, the establishment in favor of the Commission of a power of decision and initiative, involving both the type of instrument to be used, the scope and content of it. See Hinnekens, 302 ff.

2830 Cf. Prats, 24.

2831 For an example of the excrescences of this approach see *Commission vs. Germany*.

2832 Prats, 26.

since these renegotiations may lead to deviations, discrepancies, specific rules and exceptions, giving rise to inconsistencies in the tax treatment of cross-border pensions. The practical approach would be more upheld if the EU rules would have been proposed stipulating the content for the given tax treaty provisions. The discussion should, hence, not be focussing on whether harmonization or coordination of the tax systems is more adequate, but whether it is necessary to develop measures of secondary EU law (positive or 'soft law') and the content of these measures, taking into consideration the limits imposed by the Member states' exclusive competence, the subsidiarity principle and the unanimity requirement.

In her 2006 Communication, the Commission appeared to rely on her approach as set out in her 2001 Commission, i.e. supporting the negative integration-approach of the CJEU rather than providing measures of positive integration in the sphere of the tax treatment of cross-border pensions. This approach seems unaltered, generally setting out why coordination and cooperation between Member states should be pursued, allowing them to attain their tax policy goals and protect their tax bases, while ensuring elimination of discrimination and double taxation and reducing compliance costs. The Commission thus upholds the same principles as established in the 2001 Communication.

In line with previous communications, the Commission adhered in her 2010 Communication to the principles of striving for coordination of tax systems, rather than harmonization, and adhered to the principle of non-discrimination and the Treaty Freedoms. In particular, the Commission proposed to monitor Member states' tax legislation and systematically request Member states to rectify any incompatibilities with EU law within a certain deadline, and to monitor the implementation by EU Member states of the CJEU's rulings in the tax field and ensure that they are implemented also in Member states that were not the subject of the ruling. With regard to the latter two initiatives, the Commission not solely relies on the CJEU's negative integration-approach, but will also, on her own initiative, monitor Member states' tax legislation and systematically request Member states to resolve any incompatibilities with EU law. However, she still abstains from formulating more positive measures of a coordinating nature.

In view of the initiatives on the part of the European Commission as set forth above, it is evident that the CJEU's case-law has established a more progressive line of indirect harmonization on the elimination of tax obstacles to the exercise of fundamental freedoms. In the CJEU's case-law as it stands, the court has eliminated a range of domestic tax rules which constitute an unjustified infringement of the Treaty freedoms, or lead to a discriminatory treatment of non-residents.

The extensive interpretation and application of the principle of non-discrimination by the CJEU is, however, met with criticism. The delimitation of tax regimes for supplementary pensions compatible with the Single Market should not just be left to the evolution of CJEU case law and the autonomous reaction of the individual Member states.[2833] Delimitation, in this regard, refers to the requirement of extending the domestic tax treatment of contributions to contributions to foreign pension schemes. Some considerations are of interest in this regard. The CJEU's interpretation of the non-discrimination principle will not have a negative effect on tax treatment of contributions to supplementary pension schemes in countries operating a TEE-system, since it does not lead to a loss of tax revenue for the state involved. However, as regards countries promoting saving in supplementary schemes through adopting a EET or EET-system, the CJEU's approach to non-discrimination may compel these states to extend this tax relief to contributions paid to foreign schemes, causing a loss in tax revenue, while complying with EU requirements. As Prats rightly contends, adopting the CJEU's interpretation of the non-discrimination principle as the primary, if not only, (effective) mechanism of consolidating the Single Market for supplementary pension schemes, may lead to a (tensional) paradox.[2834] While on one hand, both the European Commission and other European institutions recognize the need to use mechanisms to stimulate the development of supplementary pension schemes to ensure the level of income of European mobile citizens, on the other hand, states that adopted tax mechanisms aimed at the promotion of contributions to these schemes may be hindered by the CJEU's pursuance of the elimination of distortions to the Single Market through its expansive interpretation of the non-discrimination principle. The effect of the requirements arising from the CJEU's interpretation, therefore, should be taken into account in developing policy on the tax treatment of pensions in the Member states.

Against this research's evaluation framework, I argue that the CJEU's extensive approach is an insufficient instrument in stimulating the further establishment of the European internal market, as other distortions to the proper functioning can hardly be resolved by the court's interpretation of the non-discrimination principle and treaty freedoms, such as disparities or divergences between national tax systems. However, the CJEU is not competent to abolish disparities between national tax legislations.[2835] Mainly due to the absence of secondary EU law on the tax treatment of cross-border pensions, the CJEU is prevented from developing tax principles and specific rules regarding this tax issues. Merely the extensive interpretation of CJEU of both the non-discrimination principle and

2833 Ibid. 21.

2834 Ibid. 21.

2835 Wattel, Marres and Vermeulen, 48.

the fundamental freedoms, as an instrument, is, in itself, not sufficient to support the coherent development of the integration between domestic income tax systems and EU law.[2836] As long as these disparities or divergences among Member states' tax systems are compatible with the non-discrimination principle and the fundamental freedoms, they may, and/or should, persist to exist. Moreover, the Commission should move away from her narrow approach of leaving the development of a coherent (European) approach of the national pension tax systems, and complementing tax policy instruments, to the CJEU's case-by-case interpretation, and to the Member states.[2837] She should update the 2001-Communication and urge Member states to abandon the isolated approach, and look across borders in terms of the tax treatment of cross-border pensions. The convergence and inter-level coherence of these national pension tax systems and the European internal market call for more positive integration at European level. It almost seems that the political momentum for the Commission to take appropriate actions in this regard has been seized by other pension-policy initiatives, such as the IORP II-directive and the PEPP-regulation. It is up to the Commission now to pick up the (cross-border) fiscal pension-gauntlet.

When it comes to international tax law, it seems that this regulatory framework is little fit for achieving more inter-level coherence between the different levels of legislation. Tax treaties are built on political compromise, are reactionary, customary and historically in nature.[2838] They originate from existing domestic laws and treaty practice, which still largely dictate the direction of their development. This implies that they suffer from a lack of a certain level of conceptual structure based on principle, and are far from comprehensive. As regards the latter, they only cover those tax issues on which agreement can be reached between treaty partners. Yet, it has become apparent that double tax conventions only focus their efforts on the elimination of international double taxation. This role is well demonstrated by the evolution of domestic laws over the past years.

Besides inter-level coherence between different levels of legislation (international, European, national), there should also be a certain level of inter-system consistency between national legal systems in order to ensure effective (cross-border) pension information. This will be dealt with in the section below.

2836 Prats, 21.

2837 For an example of the excrescences of this approach see *Commission vs. Germany*.

2838 See Avery Jones, De Broe and Ellis, In this article the authors trace the origin of concepts and expressions used in the OECD MC.

10.2.3 *Inter-system Consistency*

In order to prevent discrepancies in information provision, national (Netherlands and Germany) levels of legislation, need to be consistent by themselves. Legal systems consist of, *inter alia*, a set of rules. In general, legislators would prefer that legislation in a particular legal system were consistent. Not only on a domestic level, but in particular where several national legal systems converge as in this research; on Dutch/German level. This requires a certain form of inter-system consistency. For the purposes of this research 'consistency' is termed as `the quality, state, or fact of being consistent; agreement, harmony, compatibility'.[2839] Consistency, in this context, refers to – while applying national regulatory frameworks – not leading to incompatible outcomes for a specific case. This construct of consistency of rules is not only of interest for the development of legal systems, but also of practical interest for the provision of information, building on these legal systems. More specifically, in terms of consistency, rules themselves can constitute a constraint relative to which consistency has to be judged.[2840] In the context of this study, the consistency of rules is assessed against the background of effective information.

It is not uncommon that rules in two legal systems attach incompatible consequences to a same case. For instance, pursuant to Dutch tax law a similar type of occupational pension is subject to deferred taxation, while Germany tax law denies this preferential treatment of this pension, as it holds a deviating perception on what occupational pension schemes comprise, and, hence, shall be eligible for fiscal facilitation. In such cases, the law contains a *prima facie* cross-border rule conflict. Two or more rules are in actual conflict when they actually apply to one and the same case, and attach incompatible consequences to this case.

For instance, in general, it can be observed that both states apply the principle of deferred taxation but the extent to which deviates heavily. It adds to complexity when this is considered from a cross-border perspective. Both states appear – due to fiscal sovereignty – to be reluctant in granting the same (level of) fiscal facilitation to foreign pensions as to domestic pension schemes. They both strictly apply criteria as to the qualification of foreign pension schemes for fiscal purposes. However, these criteria remain fairly vague (for instance in Germany it is termed 'generally corresponding').

The requirement of consistency is not deeply rooted in Dutch, nor German, nor European or international tax legislation. Inconsistency is – generally speaking – one of most

---

2839 Oxford Dictionaries.

2840 Hage, 370.

frequent manifestations of unfairness that a person may encounter.[2841] Where often there are distinctions which justify the difference in treatment, sometimes there is no apparent distinction to be drawn. In this regard, the question rises to what extent – for instance – the CJEU may provide a remedy against the inconsistency of (the application of) legislation, see section 10.2.2.B. Two distinct types of inconsistency may be discerned: treating a person inconsistently over time, and inconsistency between individuals.[2842]

With respect to inter-system consistency, the comparative findings presented in chapter 5-9 exhibit a wide range of situations where applying national regulatory frameworks leads to incompatible outcomes for a specific case, in particular with regard to inconsistency of the tax treatment of pensions of mobile individuals. What is more, it was also found that German provisions of national tax laws governing the taxation of retirement income, are applied on the basis of an 'isolated approach', without taking into account any previous or subsequent tax treatment in another (member) state. For instance, there is no German mandatory legal principle of tax law requiring a direct connection between the taxation of benefits and the deductibility of contributions, provisions of foreign law are not mentioned in the EStG nor does it contain a general rule that a tax benefit, provided pursuant to foreign tax law, shall be treated equally to the application of the EStG's provision.[2843]

In particular Germany should abandon this 'isolated approach', and expand the determination of the tax treatment of pensions – under national tax legislation – by incorporating the tax treatment under foreign tax law in national tax legislation (EStG), i.e. to look across borders. However, noteworthy from this respect is that the Treaty freedoms do not require the Member states to adapt their domestic tax legislation to the fit the tax legislation of other Member states.[2844] In terms of 'fitness' it can thus be concluded that these inter-system inconsistencies hamper the provision of effective information provision, as it is more difficult to uphold the information's effectiveness, in terms of understandability, legal correctness, personal relevance, and trustworthiness.

2841 Steyn, 22.

2842 Ibid. 22.

2843 See also Portner, 'Besteuerung der Auszahlung aus einem U.S.-Altersversorgungsplan – selbst wenn die Beiträge ausschließlich nach U.S.-Steuerrecht gefördert sind und die Summe der eingezahlten Beiträge unter dem Auszahlungsbetrag liegt?' 1177.

2844 *Columbus Container Services.*

10.2.4 *Foreseeability and (Un)predictability*

One cannot simply rely on the maintenance of the law in force.[2845] Applicable legislation is designed in view of particular political, economic, societal phenomena. These phenomena tend to change over time, and accordingly, legislation is adapted to the new situation. This also applies to the Dutch, German, EU and international legislation under scrutiny. It is therefore that conveying information on future amounts of retirement income usually involves a certain level of risk as regards continuously changing legislation. Put it differently, predictability is a structure, and information lies where unpredictable change occurs. What is more, an aspect that seems inherent to tax law is its complexity.[2846] Specific, case and condition-particular, complex rules often lead to uncertainty, especially as regards their application. This uncertainty as regards (the application) of tax law in cross-border cases, originates from various sources, where – as a rule – unpredictability is the outcome of uncertainty. Rules and regulations, surrounded by uncertainty are difficult to predict/foresee. This means unpredictability of legal systems is intertwined with the ability of these systems to adopt to changes with a different background.

First, tax law and regulations are attuned to 'social reality', i.e. it reflects the status quo of society in all its facets. As such, tax law moves with the trends as they are observed in society as a whole, it entails a considerable degree of responsiveness. Second, of a more technical nature, national tax law is responsive to developments in the areas of positive integration, negative integration, and in particular the concept of 'non-discrimination' as interpreted by the CJEU, as discussed in chapter 8. Where national tax legislation is found to be in breach of the non-discrimination principle, Member states are obliged to bring national legislation in line with it, reflecting the concept of the European internal market without internal borders, and ensuring freedom of movement for its citizens.

In addition, tax, as well as pension, legislation is characterized as the outcome of political decision-making, coalition building and compromise. In this respect, reference can be made to the lengthy (article-by-article) parliamentary debate on the Dutch *Wet Toekomst Pensioenen*, which has led to the postponement of the entry into force-date of the legal act. Choices in the tax domain are of a political-administrative nature, and it is often not for the courts to step in. Although political decision-making can be traced back through parliamentary documents, a certain degree of uncertainty is inherent in the system of coalition building and political compromise. As a rule, the final outcome cannot be foreseen *a priori*. This generally falls short of the outcome that is seen as theoretically most

2845 Popelier, 1078.
2846 Cf. Kirchler, *The Economic Psychology of Tax Behaviour* 187.

pure. What is more, long-term decisions incorporate expectations of the future situation (e.g. retirement), as a part of which legal rules and public play an instrumental role.[2847]

When it comes to the foreseeability of (amendments in) tax law, it can be pointed out that in general tax law is less receptive to embedding morality. Generally, people think of taxes as non-normative – not related to behavioural norms – since we opt to subject economically productive behaviour to tax, instead of immoral behaviour. Hence, tax law seems to lack moral legitimacy.[2848] Contrarily, people consider non-tax laws to be, in essence, normative, and evaluate them based on moral imperatives. Non-tax laws – such as civil law or criminal law – embody cultural standards, often mirrored in the law as it stands. As these mandates potentially coincide with generally accepted morality, we consider these laws primarily as stimulating, and upholding, morality.[2849] People thus tend to focus on the moral content of these non-tax laws, and belief that these domains of legislation are more moral and less economically depriving than tax laws. This bias in our perspective of tax and other realms of law is not because we have never considered the inevitable impacts of taxes on (changing) behaviour and of non-tax laws on individuals compared to their economic situation. I endorse Rosenberg's argument that we do not think that way enough and that we tend to fall victim to our (unexamined) assumptions about tax law, which (vastly) over determine the manner in which we both use and perceive taxes/tax law.[2850] As moral imperatives alter at a fairly slower pace, and tax law seems to largely lack moral legitimacy, it seems that tax law is less predictable as it lacks a certain 'compass of stability'. In a sense, moral imperatives ensure a degree of foreseeability. Tax law, rather, adapts to the developments as described above. This degree of tax law's volatility engenders uncertainty, and, hence, unforeseeability.

Moreover, under the current tax systems, mobile person can almost never learn in advance the final consequences of their mobility pertaining to the fiscal treatment of their pension. Hence, mobile persons who have availed themselves of their European freedoms of movement are faced with ambiguous tax consequences and will often be denied certainty about the tax treatment of their retirement provisions, and the effect of their mobility thereon. Only well after time has passed, they will be able to incorporate these fiscal effects in their retirement decision-making. Yet, this is fairly inherent to the qualifications under tax legislation; the tax administration is required to label each element of income (contributions to pension schemes, pension accrual and pension benefits) as either taxable or non-taxable/exempt. On the contrary, in the majority of situations in which taxable

2847 Popelier, 1078; Lamoreux, 510 and Fuß, 66.
2848 Rosenberg, 170.
2849 Cf. Ibid. 171.
2850 Ibid. 170.

person find themselves, and need concrete answers, they have to contend with situations which are inherently shades of grey (arguably/ambiguously either taxable or not). It seems that in situations where taxable persons are in need of concrete answers, such answers are unavailable until after the dispute has unnecessarily erupted.

Each of the descriptive chapters of this research, has been concluded with an interim conclusion pertaining to how the regulatory frameworks stand, and operate in the light of these principles. For the presentation of these comparative findings along the lines of the principle of foreseeability, I refer to the comparative-sections of each of the descriptive chapters 4-7. A brief reflection on these findings will be given below.

In the vein of foreseeability, the authorities' 'Freies Ermessen' can be considered to be at the centre of the principle of (un)foreseeability of (the application of) legislation. The term 'freies Ermessen' refers to authorities' (i.e. Tax administration) competence to act, within certain boundaries, at their own discretion.[2851] This discretionary power is attributed by the legislator, leaving (ample) leeway for decisions, and the implementation of legislation. The decision whether a particular matter is regulated and, if so, to what extent, is thus partially based on the judgement of the given implementing entity. This (regulatory) leeway induces complexity, uncertainty and a lack of foreseeability of rules and regulations, for instance as regards the Dutch and German policy of the 'fiscal recognition' of foreign pension schemes.[2852]

It needs to be stressed that drafting the text and reconstructing legal provisions is, solely, a legislator's task.[2853] The law itself must provide the persons to which the legal provision applies the necessary clarity.[2854] The German BFH further stressed that, in this regard, an explanatory memorandum (*Gesetzesbegründung*) of an incomprehensible provision cannot provide the necessary clarity in such a complex matter.[2855] The foreseeability of

2851 See, for instance, MAC van Elk, "Freies Ermessen' en andere professionele handelingsruimte voor de inspecteur' WFR.

2852 See also *Gillow* 9063/80 (ECHR); C-70/83 *Gerda Kloppenburg v Finanzamt Leer* ECLI:EU:C:1984:71 (CJEU).

2853 See also *Malone* 8691/79 (ECHR) 65.

2854 Critical in this respect: RLG Van den Heuvel, *Duidelijkheid van fiscale wetgeving: een onderzoek naar een nadere invulling van de kwaliteitseis van eenvoud, duidelijkheid en toegankelijkheid voor fiscale wetgeving* (Fiscaal wetenschappelijkse reeks, SDU, Den Haag 2018) 208. He argues that citizens would benefit from an explanation on such a complex legal arrangement, providing clarity as regards the arrangement's application and effects.

2855 *Malone* 63. It remains, however, debatable whether the BFH's consideration goes beyond the interpretation of the legal provision, and the according explanatory memorandum, in question. This particular explanatory memorandum does not shed light on the content of the provision. On the one hand, it mainly deals with the unproblematic cases in which losses have to be fully compensated vertically anyway. On the other hand,

laws and regulations is coming under pressure due to the increasing use of so-called approving policy decisions. Policy decisions are drafted, and applied in practice without the usual democratic safeguards, through parliament, and also without transparent input from implementing organizations, (practitioner) experts and advisors. In the final legislative process to enshrine the approving policy in laws, i.e. codification, there is little or no room for reflection or improvement and weighing various interests involved. Hence, the effect of issuing such policy decisions is often left uncontested in terms of the quality of legislation. Speed to regulation should not be a decisive argument for the use of this policy decisions. Hence, such decisions should therefore be used with restraint in tax matters. In addition, national governments should draw up conditions to which the use of policy decisions should comply.

10.3 Further Recommendations

Although several recommendations have already been put forward in the preceding sections, the following sections put forward a range of recommendations, both in terms of legal, as well as non-legal interventions. This research's objective, and research question, encompasses the exploration of what legal, and non-legal interventions and measures are needed to ensure, and potentially foster, the effectiveness of pension information provided. Legal interventions, and measures, concern tools in the sphere of the regulatory frameworks, for instance the adoption of a different approach by the European Commission in her efforts in the field of positive integration, or adapting national legislation. Non-legal interventions refer to tools in the domain of information provision, for instance, harnessing certain ways of adapting information in order to ensure its effectiveness.

10.3.1 Some Observations Pertaining to Paternalism

Against the background of this research (what legal/non-legal interventions and measures are needed to ensure, and potentially foster, the effectiveness of the information provided), brief mention has to be made of the possible concern that the approaches set forth in the above, may be too paternalistic. From an economics perspective, paternalism can be considered any infringement of consumer sovereignty intended to improve the welfare of

---

it only clarifies that some of the provisions concern the deduction of losses and are therefore placed in a legally incorrect position. In the case of the actually limited loss compensation, the explanation is, at least, subject to interpretation. This implies that the legislative bodies had only a rough idea of the legal arrangement, but ultimately not, as would have been required by the constitution, a clear idea of the standard order to be issued.

boundedly rational individuals.[2856] Paternalism refers to the interventions that are designed to influence choices of individuals for the better, while not infringing individual's freedom of choice (liberal). People are not acting in their best interest if they make "decisions that they would change if they had complete information, unlimited cognitive abilities, and no lack of self-control".[2857] However, a formal definition of, e.g., (in)complete information is missing. An important point to make at this point is that the interventions – within this study – are aimed at providing effective information as described above, rather than guiding people in their choices. Moreover, simplification, to avoid some of the unintended adverse effects of complexity, and the provision of understandable information can, thus, hardly be considered too paternalistic, provided that this information does not steer – through interventions – people unwittingly into a certain direction which is for their better.[2858] If people are prone to making mistakes in their decision-making, a first step is to provide them with information, and armed with the appropriate information enabling them to maximize their utility, i.e. the informed utility approach.

This approach can, rather, be considered a form of 'libertarian paternalism'.[2859] One could think that the term libertarian paternalism is an oxymoron. However, it is considered to be a viable alternative to paternalism, since in numerous cases some organisation or agent must make a choice, for instance adjusting one's retirement planning. It is to be noted that it is a misperception that paternalism always entails coercion. Rather, 'libertarian paternalism' entails an approach that preserves freedom of choice but authorizes institutions to steer people in a certain direction that will promote their (objectively measurable) welfare, for instance by adapting information so that mobile citizens are (better) equipped to assess their pension's adequacy.

10.3.2 Towards a More Citizen-centred Paradigm of Law- and Policy-making

It can be observed that over the years legislation in the field of pension communication has put the perspective of the participant at the heart of the process. However, the preceding chapters illustrate that citizen have not been put sufficiently at the centre of policy, and the subsequent implementation. Rather, legislators, and law- and policymakers, seem to hold firm to a system's reality that is not entirely compatible with the desired

2856 Dhami, 1590.

2857 CR Sunstein and RH Thaler, 'Libertarian paternalism is not an oxymoron' 70 University of Chicago Law Review 1159, 1162.

2858 In the same vein Sunstein, 1410.

2859 See RH Thaler and CR Sunstein, 'Libertarian Paternalism' 93 American Economic Review 175.

citizen's perspective. I'd like to take the stance that citizens should be put more at heart of law- and policy-making, not only on a national level, but in particular on a European and international level.[2860] In particular tax legislation is marked by legal principles, technicalities, detailed legislation, and overwhelming complexity. It remains underexposed that tax legislation also constitutes a domain of heuristics, e.g. individual taxpayers are potentially affected in their attitudes, and subsequent (future) behaviour, by the legislation as its stands. The importance of a citizen-centred policy holds in particular – and even more – with respect to mobile citizens, who find themselves at the intersection of three levels of legislation; international, European, and national. The paradigm of drafting laws and policies is dictated by the paradigm of legal legitimacy. Elements of psychological legitimacy should be more emphasized and incorporated in the process of legislation. Against the background of a variety of cross-border implications it is argued that although the EU may be ascribed legitimacy in terms of legality, this does not ensure psychological legitimacy from the mobile citizen's perspective.

This research's descriptive chapters have demonstrated that the perspective through which the 'law' is drafted in the field of the cross-border taxation of pensions is often lacking the citizen's perspective. Moreover, the relevance of this perspective is often overlooked by policymakers, who rigidly apply a juridical perspective to law-making. This applies to all levels of legislation, i.e. international, European and national. Although the Dutch legislator is becoming increasingly aware of the citizen's perspective, illustrated by incorporating the so-called '*doenvermogen*' in the Dutch IAK (*Integraal afwegingskader voor beleid en regelgeving*), the mobile citizens' perspective remains severely underexposed (i.e. the national perspective of policy-making, ignoring cross-border implications). Moreover, initiatives to incorporate the citizen's perspective by adopting an empirically-informed approach to 'the law' are still lacking. Hence, in drafting and adopting legislation on a national, European and international level the one-sided approach should be abandoned and, rather, adopt a more citizen-centred approach of policy-making.

2860 As regards the Dutch perspective, see Staatssecretaris van Financiën – Toeslagen en Douane, *Aanvullende duiding problemen Belastingdienst* (27 November 2020). The State Secretary recognizes that, in addition to the Tax and Customs Administration's efforts to put citizens and businesses more at the centre, it is also important that signals about the unintended effects of policy and implementation are shared with the policy departments. The sharing of signals from the implementation of policies creates feedback loops that can help make policies more inclusive of citizens and businesses. This commitment offers prospects for favourable developments in this area.

10.3.3 Towards a More Empirically-informed Approach to Law- and Policy-making

10.3.3.A Integrating the Realms of Law-making and Information Provision: Uncharted Territories

When it comes to integrating the reals of law-making and information provision, this is seen as uncharted territories. The realm of information provision and law- and policy-making (in the field of pensions and taxes) appear to be separated spheres, where these should be interconnected vessels. From a bird's eye view, they are reminiscent of 'pillarisation' in the domain of the regulatory frameworks. This not only holds with regard to the national legal orders, but also as regards the European level and/or international tax law. For instance, the CJEU, as well as the European Commission rarely exhibit any awareness of the consequences of their rulings, communications respectively, for other fields such as information provision, going beyond the judicial realm. As regards international tax law pertaining to cross-border pensions, national treaty policies, the OECD Model Convention (and the accompanying commentaries), the tax treaty concluded are void of any signs of taking on board other perspectives than the judicial one. This has – for instance – given rise to an untenable grow of complexity in this domain.

Although this does not alter the fact that these regulatory instruments should be 'correct' from a judicial perspective, in doing so, they fail to incorporate many facets of the 'taxes realm'. The primacy still lies with the legal principles, while incorporating (empirical) insight from other scientific domains may render tax legislation, case-law, and policy more resilient, and consistent (over time). This could be achieved by departing from a theoretical-assumption-approach, and move towards a more empirically-informed-approach, which creates a link between 'the law' and 'the real world'. This can be improved by involving experts in the field of empirical sciences, such as behavioural economics, in the process of policy-making. Also from a scientific viewpoint, the domains of law-making and information provision should be integrated better. I believe that meaningful scientific – and methodological – innovation calls for exploring, and exceeding, disciplinary boundaries, and taking a more holistic approach in our thinking about a multitude of societal problems which we will face.

10.3.3.B Lessons to Be Learned from Initiatives in the Field: 'Best Practices'

In the Dutch process of legislation and policymaking, a trend can be observed towards more empirical-informed processes, i.e. incorporating findings from the domain of behavioural sciences. The Dutch legislator is becoming increasingly aware of the citizen's perspective, illustrated by incorporating the so-called '*doenvermogen*' in the Dutch integrated assessment framework for policies and regulation (*Integraal afwegingskader voor beleid en regelgeving*). The key question of this test is: does the scheme make realistic assumptions about the mental capacity of citizens? However, the mobile citizens' perspective remains severely underexposed (i.e. the national perspective of policy-making, ignoring cross-border implications).

In the following, I will elaborate on this. The importance for this research lies in the fact that this can be seen as a 'best practice', i.e. lessons can be learned – and implemented *mutatis mutandis* – from this for legislative frameworks at the national, European and international level. In particular, at the aggregate level of cross-border cases this deserves further attention, as in these cases these three levels of legislation converge, leading to a higher degree of complexity. It thus deserves attention to create awareness among domestic law- and policymakers about the (often overlooked) cross-border effects of domestic legislation, not only on a domestic level, but also at an international, and European level.[2861]

In recent years, the application of insights from behavioural sciences to Dutch policy has been the focus of attention on a number of occasions.[2862] In the process, the realization has arisen that the perception of humans as conscious, calculating, rational decision-makers is incomplete, inefficient and ineffective, and that assuming a more realistic image of humans makes for more effective and efficient policies. In its report, the Dutch *Wetenschappelijke Raad voor het Regeringsbeleid* (Scientific Council for Government Policy) also noted that the (Dutch) government is increasingly relying on people's ability to cope, while human abilities are limited.[2863] Hence, what citizens can actually do falls short of what the government expects them to do. It is acknowledged that knowledge and intelligence (capacity to think) on its own, are not sufficient to be resilient, but that people must also possess the 'ability to do'. The Dutch government overestimates the financial self-efficacy of her citizens, in particular where two complex domains such as pensions, and taxes, intersect. For many people, rules are too complicated, and not enough consideration is given to people's psychology.[2864] By this, the WRR means the ability to make a plan, to take action, to persevere and to (repeatedly) deal with temptations and setbacks, whereby the conclusion is drawn that many people have only a limited capacity

2861 See for instance OECD, 'Improving the Quality of Laws and Regulations: Economic, Legal, and Managerial Techniques' OECD, 'Recommendation of the Council on Improving the Quality of Government Regulation' and APEC-OECD.

2862 See WL Tiemeijer, CA Thomas and HM Prast, 'De menselijke beslisser: over de psychologie van keuze en gedrag' (WRR-verkenning 22, 2009); WRR, 'Met kennis van gedrag beleid maken' (WRR-rapport nr 92, 2014); WL Tiemeijer, 'Eigen schuld? Een gedragswetenschappelijk perspectief op problematische schulden' (WRR-Verkenning nr 33, 2016).

2863 Wetenschappelijke Raad voor het Regeringsbeleid, 'Weten is nog geen doen: Een realistisch perspectief op redzaamheid' (Den Haag 2017) 19.

2864 See Tiemeijer.

to do so.[2865] This does not only concern 'vulnerable' groups, such as low-literate people, but also people with a good education and a good social position. They too get into situations in which their ability to cope is inadequate, for example when they are not always as alert and well organized as they should be due to the pressure of choice and stress. An important point to highlight in this perspective is that the government considers this report as an encouragement – more so than is currently the case – to take up insights into behavioral knowledge in order to strengthen the effectiveness and legitimacy of government action.[2866]

It is recognized that not only the perspective of implementing organizations is involved, but also the citizen's perspective.[2867] They must not only know the law but also 'be able to' it. It also emphasizes the importance of coherence with other regulatory complexes. In particular this point deserves further attention, as has been elucidated in the previous chapter, i.e. coherence of national, European, and international legislation should be put at the centre of this development. The government wants its policies and the implementation of existing policies always to be based on a realistic citizen perspective, which must become, as it were, a second nature.[2868]

As has been address in chapter 3, indeed, it has been widely acknowledged that people need to be equipped with particular 'skills', for numerous reasons.[2869] These reasons may be found in, for instance, financial (e.g. pension) systems growing more complex, but also, more related to the topic of this research, the growing mobility of workers, and the complexity it entails. What is more, regulatory frameworks, rules and regulations grow more complex in a rapid pace for a wide range of reasons. This may result in a mismatch between skills needed, and skills actually possessed by individuals, i.e. skills mismatches. With a view to these developments, people need certain (financial) skills to cope with these developments, and find out how these developments affect their personal (financial) situation. Self-efficacy is gaining pertinence, as financial literacy, by itself, does not necessarily lead to people's 'empowerment' to cope with certain situations, phenomena, developments etc. Self-efficacy in general is defined as 'judgments of how well one can

2865 Wetenschappelijke Raad voor het Regeringsbeleid, 19 ff.

2866 Minister voor Rechtsbescherming and Minister van Binnenlandse Zaken en Koninkrijksrelaties, *Kabinetsstandpunt op WRR-rapport "Weten is nog geen doen: Een realistisch perspectief op redzaamheid"* (22 January 2018) 2.

2867 Ibid. 3.

2868 Ibid. 9.

2869 See for example A Bandura, 'Self-efficacy: Towards a unifying theory of behavioural change' 84 Psychological Review 191, and Bandura, *Self-efficacy: The exercise of control.*

execute courses of action required to deal with prospective situations'.[2870] These beliefs of self-efficacy are theorized to function as proximal determinants of behaviour.[2871]

The Dutch State Secretary of Finance confirmed that the ability to act will play a structural role in all fiscal legislation and regulations and that, when regulations are being drawn up, an inventory should be made of the extent to which policy alternatives make use of people's limited ability to act.[2872] The methods from the WRR's 'toolbox' will play a structural role in the drafting of Dutch legislation. He also endorses the need to have the fullest possible picture of citizens' capacity to act already when a policy proposal is being drafted, so that this can be taken into account when designing a measure. He also recognizes, however, that feasibility is a complex subject that still requires a great deal of behavioural research and the expertise of civil society organizations is indispensable. The consideration of government-wide capability is currently still under development and not all tools have been elaborated.[2873]

Against the background of the foregoing developments, I argue that the Dutch government is well on its way toward a more empirically informed approach to policy and regulation. The German legislature can draw lessons from this, as developments in this regard appear to be lagging behind. Unfortunately, the approach remains devoid of taking into account the effect of laws and regulations in cross-border cases, i.e., the border effects for mobile workers. This is noteworthy and regrettable since precisely in those situations an appeal to the self-efficacy of these individuals is made, particularly since in these cases multiple complex levels of laws and regulations converge. It is hoped that the effects of laws and regulations in these cross-border cases will also receive more attention and be embedded in legislative programs, while asking questions as, for example, how far does paternalism from the 'government' reach?

In the future, other methods from the WRR's ability to do-toolbox can also be applied to shaping tax policy.[2874] For example, behavioural experts at the Behavioural Network Finance and the Tax Authorities can use field experiments to test how (minor) adjustments in the design and implementation of tax policy improve citizens' ability to do things. Results will be shared via the explanatory memoranda to these future tax bills. The

2870 S Elling and L Lentz, 'Maatwerk in pensioencommunicatie' Design Paper 126 Netspar Industry Paper Series 122 and FD Davis, 'Perceived Usefulness, Perceived Ease of Use, and User Acceptance of Information Technology' 13 MIS Quarterly 321.

2871 Davis, 321.

2872 Staatssecretaris van Financiën, *Doenvermogen in pakket Belastingplan 2021* (16 November 2020) 1.

2873 Ibid. 2. WRR, 'Doenvermogen: Van toets naar tools' (17 September 2020) outlines a number of basic steps for policymakers and legislative lawyers to embed this ability to do in policy design.

2874 Staatssecretaris van Financiën, *Doenvermogen in pakket Belastingplan 2021* 3.

approach to pay more attention to the approach to people also mentions the creation of rule aids, i.e. flowcharts that support the reader to easily find the right authority, rule to be applied and action to be taken in a given situation. This should be implemented with regard to mobile persons.

More attention to behavioral economics and psychological knowledge can contribute to better policy, not only at a national level, but also on a European and international level, for instance as part of the EC's Better Regulations programme.[2875] Behavioural science knowledge therefore deserves a stronger embedding in policy making. In this regard, it is desirable to come to a kind of 'amicus curiae' to support national, European, and international law- and policy-makers in adapting a more empirically-informed approach. As a best practice in this respect, reference can be made to the so-called Behavioural Insights Network NL (BIN NL), which strives to advance the application of behavioral insights within (Dutch) government.[2876] This is a partnership of all ministries for the application of behavioral insights in policy, implementation, supervision and communication, and facilitating the mutual exchange of knowledge and experience. The minister recognizes the added value of the initiatives taken by this network.[2877] Hopefully, this empirical-informed approach will be put at the centre of law- and policy-making on a national, European, and international level, and not turn into a 'check the box'-formality.

10.4 Further Observations and Reservations

10.4.1 *The Notion of 'Pension' (Information) Through the Lens of Social Representations and Their Role in Effective Pension Information*

The construct of 'social representations' has been dealt with in chapter 2 of this research, and allows to put forward certain recommendations, or draw certain reservations, as they play a potentially pivotal role in establishing effective information provision. Related to Dual Processing Theory, if we want to have a profound understanding of how – by certain variables – perceive certain pieces of information, a deeper understanding of how these people try to understand, and make sense, of new concepts is pivotal. Social representations, attitudes and knowledge, may affect how people think about information, and behave (in future).[2878] For instance, people may base their perception and beliefs with respect to

2875 European Commission, 'Better regulation: why and how'.
2876 See BIN NL, <https://www.binnl.nl/default.aspx> accessed 21 June 2021.
2877 Minister voor Rechtsbescherming and Minister van Binnenlandse Zaken en Koninkrijksrelaties, 2.
2878 See for instance the TNS Beliefs Framework: Visser, Kloosterboer and Oosterveld, 12.

pension information on previous experiences, misconceptions and (false) interpretations of the information they were exposed to.[2879] It is hence central that these beliefs and attitudes – which may influence *prima facie* neutral information – are incorporated in pension information provision.[2880] In doing so, this construct helps to explore what non-legal interventions and measures are needed to ensure, and potentially foster, the effectiveness of the pension information provided. In doing so, this allowed to adopt a holistic approach to taxes and pension information provision.

Apart from objective knowledge, people also hold (mental) images about pensions and taxes.[2881] Even people who know little, may hold many images, associations, convictions. These images and representations affect – to a large extent – how people perceive information, what is and is not relevant; what they do or don't believe; how terms are interpreted etc. Thus, how people interpret or appraise information does not only arise from the text itself, but is also strongly influenced by their own associations with and beliefs related to concepts. Taking this insufficiently into account may lead to a discrepancy of what readers think they read and the writer has in mind. This might have an effect on the information's effectiveness as it might steer people away from what the information seeks to achieve.

As Cullis and Lewis rightfully argue, none of these beliefs necessarily have to be 'true' in any 'objective' sense.[2882] However, if the abovementioned actors belief that these notions and beliefs are true (and act accordingly) then reality is constructed, i.e. (social) construction. When people discuss socially-relevant topics (religion, science, environment, economic issues, taxes) they usually exchange lay knowledge, rather than being an expert in the given field. They try to understand and evaluate the issues or phenomena that are unfamiliar but relevant to them. This, in turn, enables social communication and behaviour.[2883] Moscovici termed these concepts in social interaction 'social representations', developing a theory setting forth processes leading from unfamiliar phenomena to familiar concepts.[2884] The primary function of these 'social representations' is to create a

2879 See van Hekken, Hoofs and Bruggen. The results of this study show that many participants base their comments on previous experiences, misconceptions and (sometimes false) interpretations of the information in the text they were exposed to.

2880 Van Hekken, Hoofs and Bruggen point out that a diversified communication strategy, mindful of different beliefs, emotions and attitudes among participants should help to empower citizens to get insight in their financial situation after retirement and to make informed choices, see ibid.

2881 See also Ibid. The results of this study show that many participants base their comments on previous experiences, misconceptions and (sometimes false) interpretations of the information in the text they were exposed to.

2882 Cullis and Lewis, 310.

2883 See for instance Sehity, Kirchler and Muehlbacher.

2884 Moscovici, *La Psychanalyse, son image et son public*; Moscovici, 'The phenomenon of social representations'.

homogeneous and familiar environment for everyday discourse.[2885] Phenomena and contents unknown to people need to be revealed, tried to be understood and be integrated in the field of socially shared and individual knowledge and evaluations. To this end, social representations are made.[2886] When confronted with information, people hold these – already gained – social representations which may affect the way they perceive this information.

As discussed at length in the comparative law chapters 4 through 7, the pension systems (and tax systems) of the Netherlands and Germany differ significantly. Heterogeneity among national legal systems is a universal phenomenon, due to, inter alia, historical developments, adaption to different social developments, economic trends and developments, different political landscapes etc. What is more, as addressed in chapter 4, a universal taxonomy of 'pensions' is missing, and the notion of 'pension' differs per state, and within each of the pension systems. In addition to these national systems – described in chapters 4 to 7 – and the considerable structural differences that exist, the role of each of the pillars also differs considerably with respect to saving for retirement. Apart from actual replacement ratios of each of the pillars in saving for retirement, in Germany, for example, the first and third pillars take a larger role in terms of number of deviating provisions (each having a different envisaged purpose), scope of legislation, degree of detail of legislation, political background of the legislation, while in the Netherlands the role of these pillars (in this vein) is more modest.

Given the national pension systems as they stand – in particular the role of each of the pension pillars when it comes to saving for 'pension'/achieving an adequate pension – it is likely that people differ in their social representation, mental image they may hold when being asked about 'pension', in particular what pillar plays a more central role. Where, for instance, in Germany the first, and third pillar may be more at the centre of this social representation of 'pension', in the Netherlands the second pillar may take a more prominent role. As these representations potentially affect – to a large extent – how people perceive information, what is and is not relevant; what they do or don't believe; how terms are interpreted, this might have an effect on the information's effectiveness as it might steer people away from what the information seeks to achieve. Hence, the role of social representations in the provision of effective cross-border pension information, in particular these deviating representations when it comes to the concept of 'pension', ought to be taken into account by information providers, or law-/policymakers in drafting rules and regulations pertaining to the provision of pension information.

2885 Kirchler, *The Economic Psychology of Tax Behaviour* 29.
2886 See Abric.

10.4.2 Increasing Salience of Taxes (in Information Provision)

As Sunstein rightfully argues, people's attention is generally limited and regulatory objectives are not always served by amending policy or disclosing information, but the relevant policy or information should also be salient.[2887] Moreover, it is often possible to promote regulatory goals by making certain features of a situation more salient to individuals. Although in theory (RCT), it might be expected that there would be no difference whether taxes were to be paid upfront or through withholding from the benefits paid.[2888] However, as has been elucidated in chapter 2, as a potential explanation, research findings suggest that withholding taxes salience/visibility is affected.[2889]

In concreto, in ensuring the effectiveness of information – irrespective of its objective – salience matters considerably. Apart from the issue whether people perceive these taxes as 'costs', these taxes[2890] (*grosso modo*, the difference between gross and net) have a considerable effect, in particular in cross-border situations, where international law, European law, and (several) domestic legal orders intertwine. Nevertheless, they receive little consideration in advance, since they lack salience.[2891] For the majority of mobile citizens, the potential effect of availing themselves of the European freedoms of movement on (the taxation of) their (cross-border) pension, may not be salient at the time of becoming a mobile citizen, even if those effect are considerable. This paradoxical situation refers to the fact that these individuals do not inform themselves about the effect of working cross-border, even when it is clearly in their (financial) interest to do so. Non-legal interventions should be harnessed in this regard, by making the effects of working cross-border more salient, altering people's perceptions, and/or attitudes.

Apart from all other evaluative findings pertaining to the regulatory frameworks in place – such as its complexity, lack of foreseeability and dispersed use of legal instruments – the taxation of cross-border pensions may be considered 'shrouded' to individuals, which may be identified as the source of the lack of attention, leading people to suboptimal decision-

2887 Sunstein, 1405.

2888 See, in a similar vein, R Chetty, A Looney and K Kroft, 'Salience and Taxation: Theory and Evidence' 99 American Economic Review 1145.

2889 See also CR Sahm, MD Shapiro and J Slemrod, 'Check in the Mail or More in the Paycheck: Does the Effectiveness of Fiscal Stimulus Depend on How It Is Delivered?' 4 American Economic Journal: Economic Policy 216. This research demonstrated that a majority of households did not notice the withholding changes, and households who found 'a small but repeated boost to their paychecks' appear to be less likely to use the money for significant purchases.

2890 This also depends on the reference point, potentially affected by policy decisions, and often considered to be the status quo.

2891 See also X Gabaix and D Laibson, 'Shrouded Attributes, Consumer Myopia, and Information Suppression in Competitive Markets' 121 The Quarterly Journal of Economics 505, 511.

making in the domain of finances, and pensions. As the most prevalent question among people is 'what will I get after taxes?' they appear to neglect the effect of the underlying legislation, due to a lack of interest, and attention. The lack of salience is induced by a range of phenomena. For instance, (wage) taxes due on the pension benefits paid out are withheld by the paying institution (not directly visible to the taxpaying individual), pension premiums (deductible under the principle of deferred taxation) are withheld by the employer, the effect of international tax law, and European law on the taxation of cross-border pensions, remains hidden at first glance. Moreover, as regards frequency, taxes withheld are generally salient once a month, and annually when filing the income tax return. Initiatives to increase salience of these taxes, for instance by displaying them in real time, can ensure effectiveness of information (attaining its goal to the better).[2892]

In sum, the lack of salience, and, hence, the absence of people's attention to the taxation of cross-border taxes – which may be shrouded for common individuals – has considerable effect on their income position, and has potential implication for policy-making, especially in the field of information provision.[2893] It may even be argued, that although individuals may possess the relevant knowledge, the effect of the cross-border taxation might not be sufficiently salient to them when embarking on financial decision-making, or consulting relevant pension information, leading them to neglect a particular attribute, while it would be in their financial interest to consider it more closely.

The foregoing suggests that an appropriate instrument to ensure the effectiveness of information is to embrace information disclosure as a regulatory tool, while adopting an empirically-informed approach, appreciating the way people process information.[2894] This empirically-informed approach entails that information disclosure as such may not be sufficient. On the contrary, it is important to consider how information is provided. Information provision should be tailored to *homo sapiens*, not *homo economicus* (the agent in Rational Choice Theory), being sensitive to how people actually process information. Clarity, meaningfulness, and salience play a critical role in this regard.

One of the empirical findings to be harnessed is to increase the salience of the effect of the taxation of cross-border pensions. It can be argued that sensible regulatory policies are

2892 See also WJ Congdon, JR Kling and S Mullainathan, *Policy and Choice: Public Finance through the Lens of Behavioral Economics* (Brookings Institution Press, Washington DC 2011) 113.

2893 Cf. Sunstein, 1355. As regards the traditional logic of Pigouvian taxes – which changes when people are inattentive to certain costs – see H Allcott, S Mullainathan and D Taubinsky, 'Externalizing the Internality' 2011) <http://citeseerx.ist.psu.edu/viewdoc/download?doi=10.1.1.474.4034&rep=rep1&type=pdf> accessed 8 June 2021.

2894 Cf. Sunstein, 1365-1366.

attentive to the importance of salience of taxes in information provision.[2895] Increasing salience can be applied in a wide variety of settings, e.g. smoking prevention, health insurance, taxes, pensions. As has been argued in the above, the relevance and importance holds true with regard to (information with respect to) the taxation of pensions.

The foregoing challenge of increasing salience can be addressed best through the creation of an (open access) Web Portal, as part of the European Tracking Service (FindyourPension).[2896] This does not only address 'salience', but also 'clarity' of information, and the underlying regulatory frameworks. In designing this web portal, and its information content, an empirically informed approach should be adapted. This empirically informed approach ensures responsiveness of 'the system' to how people process information, building on findings in the field of behavioural economics, and cognitive psychology. Designing such a web portal would empower individuals by fostering their attitudes towards, purportedly, overly complex matters, i.e. pension, taxes, legislation etc. comparable to the European Single Digital Gateway (Your Europe).[2897] Moreover, it would enhance their informed decision-making, when it comes to retirement planning.

10.5 Concluding Remarks: in Sum

This concluding chapter 10 reflected, concluded and elaborated on the evaluation as dealt with in the preceding descriptive chapters, through the lens of the assessment framework as set forth in chapter 2. This dissertation sought to answer the main research question to what extent the regulatory frameworks on a national level in the Netherlands and Germany, on a European level, and on an international level, governing the taxation of (cross-border) statutory, occupational and personal pensions, are fit for the provision of effective information and, and if not so, what legal/non-legal interventions and measures are needed to ensure, and potentially foster, the effectiveness of the information provided? Building on these evaluations, this chapter provided recommendations on how to cope with, and overcome the problems identified by these findings, and to give impetus to certain developments in the domain of (cross-border) pension information, of which some have already been ongoing.

2895 Ibid. 1405.

2896 As a 'best practice', reference can be made to Institute for Transnational and Euregional cross border cooperation and Mobility (ITEM), 'Fair Mobility Tool' <https://fairmobilitytool.eu/> accessed 8 June 2021.

2897 As regards the latter see Regulation (EU) 2018/1724 of the European Parliament and of the Council of 2 October 2018 establishing a single digital gateway to provide access to information, to procedures and to assistance and problem-solving services and amending Regulation (EU) No 1024/2012 PE/41/2018/REV/2 OJ L 295, 21.11.2018, 1-38.].

The preceding sections put forward a range of findings and recommendations, both in terms of legal, as well as non-legal interventions. Legal interventions, and measures, concern tools in the sphere of the regulatory frameworks, for instance the adoption of a different approach by the European Commission in her efforts in the field of positive integration, or amending national legislation. Non-legal interventions refer to tools in the domain of information provision, for instance, harnessing certain ways of adapting information in order to ensure its effectiveness. The most important findings, and recommendations have been underlined in the following sections. I am hopeful that the above recommendations will find their way to the relevant stakeholders at the national, European and international legislative and regulatory levels in order to improve the fitness of the regulatory frameworks, so that eventually those who need effective pension information most – i.e. mobile workers – shall be aided in planning for their retirement.

11 Appendix A: Establishing Reliable Amounts of Future Retirement Income

This comprehensive appendix elucidates in detail the data, and methods by means of which the amounts, included in the survey's text frame, have been computed. The empirical study's results have been dealt with elaborately in chapter 3 of this research. This data and methods allow establishing a reliable amount of gross, and net, amount of future retirement income. Below the considerations that played a role in deciding how to establish a reliable amount of future retirement income in the text frame, will be elucidated. Furthermore, in choosing an amount of future retirement income, certain approaches were taken into consideration, which are outlined below as well.

11.1.1 An Equal, Country-Specific or Personal Amount of Predicted Retirement Income

11.1.1.A Equal Amount for All Respondents, Irrespective of Personal Situation

The first option considered was to include an amount, equal for all respondents. The main advantage of this approach is that it is most consistent in the light of finding an unobscured relation between the independent variable, i.e. the intervention in the text (net frame, gross frame and net/disclaimer frame) and the dependent variables, i.e. the information's ease of comprehension, informativeness, trustworthiness, expected future financial security and the person's behavioural expectations. Drawback of this approach is that the amount is independent from a person's working/ living state, personal income and the pension accrual of the pension vehicles he/she is contributing to, and thus, may be far from reality, affecting the participants' responses. However, although the amounts shown to the survey's respondents should be realistic, they merely serve an illustrative purpose, i.e. the study seeks to unravel the effect of net and gross amounts of future retirement income, and not the amount as such. Main contestation against this approach would be the high degree of susceptibility to the high-low pension differential, i.e. high income-respondents will perceive the amount shown as too low, and low-income respondents will perceive the amount as (unrealistically) high. In both cases, the response may be affected by this effect. However, this is mitigated, and controlled for, by the random assignment of all respondents, having a different income, to either the gross amount, net amount, or net amount and disclaimer. Furthermore, since respondents were asked to fill in their income, this allows for exploring this effect.

11.1.1.B Country-specific Amounts

The second option with respect to the amount included in the text frame, was incorporating a country specific-amount, building on country specific data, such as income, (net and gross) pension replacement rates, applicable tax rates etc. Main advantage of this option is that the amounts would prove to be more realistic, and personal relevant. Simultaneously, this would likely prove to be a drawback since the country-specific may have an effect on the relationship between the dependent and independent variable, potentially leading to an obscured relation, as the different amounts may have an, untraceable, effect on the respondents' answers. Moreover, if this approach would have been adopted, the respondent would have been asked to fill in their working country, and/or residence state, potentially scaring people off as this information may be considered too personal. However, to some extent, country specific indicators, such as replacement rates and average earnings are taken into account in the computation of the amounts of future retirement income. This will be addressed in more detail below.

11.1.1.C Amounts Tailored to Personal Situation (Personal Amounts)

The third option would have been to adopt a personal approach, i.e. relating the amount of future retirement income, to be included in the text frame, to the respondent, to the person's approximate personal net income. Under this approach, the level of reality, and personal relevance, of the amount shown, would be highest. Furthermore, this approach would be least prone to the high-low pension differential, i.e. high income-respondents. Predominant drawback of this approach would have been that different amounts apply to different people, elevating the degree of reality of the amount, but still lack full reality since an amount of future income still depends on the personal situation of the respondents, i.e. age of entrance in pension scheme, years of contributions, pensionable income etc. Furthermore, since the approach would require the respondents to fill in their approximate personal monthly net income, and other relevant personal (financial) data, they would most likely become anxious and refuse to (further) fill in the survey. Moreover, the question asking the respondents to record their personal income, would need to include the answering option 'prefer not to say'. Since it seems that people are reluctant to reveal their personal income, it is likely that a considerable number of respondents would reply by ticking the box 'prefer not to say'. This would render the question, at the start of the survey, asking respondents to report their income, redundant.

Weighing the advantages and disadvantages outlined in the above, the equal amount-option was chosen. The amounts referred to in the text frames of the experiment, have been calculated by multiplying the (net or gross) replacement rates, as applicable for Belgium, Germany and the Netherlands, by the average earnings, as established for these three States, which will be elucidated in the next section. The main argument in favor of this approach is that it is most consistent in the light of finding an unobscured relation between the treatment conditions, and the dependent variables. Moreover, the amounts shown to the survey's respondents merely serve an illustrative purpose, and potential adverse effects were mitigated by the random allocation of respondents, and controlling for the effect of their level of income.

11.1.2 Calculating the Amount of Future Pension Income

In the section below I will set forth how I computed the amounts of future retirement income (multiplying the (net or gross) replacement rates by the average earnings), why replacement rates were taken as a starting point, and what assumptions underly these calculations. In addition, underlying heuristics, biases and possible remedies which may occur when using this method of calculation will be discussed.

11.1.2.A Pension Replacement Rates

The amounts referred to in the text frames of the experiment, have been calculated by multiplying the (net or gross) replacement rates, as applicable for Belgium, Germany and the Netherlands, by the average earnings, as established for these three States. It will be elucidated below why the data with regard to these three States have been taken as a starting point for the calculation of the amounts of future pension benefits. To increase the reliability and level of realism of the amounts depicted in the survey's text frame, the amounts of future retirement income have been established on the basis of real replacement rates, rather than fictitious replacement rates.[2898] Replacement rates constitute the most commonly used measure of relative well-being after retirement, are an important indicator of pensions systems, and are used as a key indicator of retirement adequacy.[2899] Gross, and net, pension placement rates, as a measure of pension adequacy, basically, indicate to what extent the predicted retirement income can replace the current income, i.e. the ratio of post-retirement income (e.g. annuities) to pre-retirement income (e.g. earnings). Where the gross replacement rate divides predicted retirement income by current gross earnings, the net replacement rate divides predicted retirement income by current net earnings. Replacement rates were selected for the computation of the future amounts of retirement

2898 These replacement rates have been derived from OECD, 'Pensions Outlook' 2018) <https://read.oecd-ilibrary.org/finance-and-investment/oecd-pensions-outlook-2018_pens_outlook-2018-en#page3> accessed 8 August 2019 and OECD Pensions at a glance 2017, 'Pension replacement rates' 2016) <https://stats.oecd.org/#> accessed 8 August 2019.

2899 Cf. Knoef and others, 57. These replacement rates are used in pension system indicators such as the Melbourne Mercer Global Pension Index.

income, as they are considered as the most reliable proxy for an adequate retirement income.[2900]

Replacement rates were selected for Belgium, Germany and the Netherlands as these are neighboring countries marked by a considerable number of mobile workers, and it was expected that most of this survey's respondents were resident/working in one of these three countries. Moreover, replacement rates in these three countries deviate sufficiently to come to a generally applicable, and realistic, average replacement rate.

11.1.2.B Gross Pension Replacement Rates

The aforementioned gross replacement rate has been defined as the gross pension entitlement, divided by the gross pre-retirement earnings, measuring how effectively pension systems provide a retirement income in order to replace earnings, constituting the main source of income prior to retirement, i.e. the ratio of pensions to individual earnings. It thus provides the level of pension benefits arising from mandatory public and private pension schemes relative to earnings during working career. Data and figures show a considerable cross-country variation in gross replacement rates, with the Netherlands at the top of the range.[2901]

These replacement rates have been calculated for workers with a range of different earnings levels, as provided below: 50%, 100% and 150% of average worker earnings (AW). Since the level of average earnings may vary among the survey's respondents, this range allows a more general analysis of the effects. As discussed above, depending on the level of earnings/income, people's perception on how much income they would need after retirement varies considerably.[2902] It should be stressed that these pension replacement rates have been calculated, merely taken into account mandatory pension schemes.

2900 See OECD, 'OECD Pensions at a Glance 2017'.
2901 Ibid. 100.
2902 Cf. Knoef, 4-5.

Table 11.1 Gross Replacement Rates (Mandatory Pension Schemes)

Gross pension replacement rate (2016)*	50% of average wage	100% of average wage	150% of average wage	Average (unweighted and rounded) of gross replacement rates
BEL	47.7	46.7	36.4	43.6
GER	38.2	38.2	38.2	38.2
NL	98.1	96.9	96.5	97.2
Overall average				59.7

* This has been derived from OECD Pensions at a glance 2017. See also OECD, 'OECD Pensions at a Glance 2017' 101.

It is evident from table 11.1 above that replacement rates vary significantly across the countries and that the Netherlands has comparatively high gross replacement rates, when merely mandatory pension schemes are considered. This may be induced by the relatively high amount of basic pension income, arising from the Dutch statutory pension scheme (*Algemene Ouderdomswet*). When merely mandatory public schemes are included the OECD average for gross replacement rates is 41%. However, when private pension schemes are included, this rises to 53%, and even 59% when voluntary private pension are taken into account as well. When mandatory and voluntary pension schemes are taken into account, the gross replacement rates are as provided in table 11.2.

Table 11.2 Gross Replacement Rates (Mandatory Public Schemes, and Mandatory/ Voluntary Private Pension Schemes)

Gross pension replacement rate*(2016)	50% of average wage	100% of average wage	150% of average wage	Average (unweighted and rounded) of gross replacement rates
BEL	61.8	60.8	47.5	56.7
GER	50.9	50.9	50.9	50.9
NL	98.1	96.9	96.5	97.2
Overall average				68.3

* This has been derived from OECD Pensions at a glance 2017. This data differentiates between male and female. For this research, the mean of the gross replacement rates applicable to male and female has been calculated and adopted as the starting point. With respect to the gross replacement rates in Belgium, Germany, and Netherlands, these were equal for men and women.

Since it may deviate to what extent the survey's respondents save through a (mandatory) public scheme, and/or mandatory private scheme, and/or voluntary private pension scheme, the respondents have been prompted to fill in whether they have adopted multi-pillar retirement savings approach, covering all of their (former) working, and (former) residence states. By this, it can be controlled for to which extent the replacement rate may be unrealistic for the respective respondents. The subject were asked to whether they participate(d) in and/or contribute(d) to either a government-run basic mandatory retirement provision (statutory retirement scheme), and/ or participate(d) in and/or contribute(d), as an employee or civil servant, to a pension fund/provider through his/her employer, or as an independent professional (occupational pension scheme), and/or participate(d) in and/or contribute(d) to a voluntary individual pension product through an insurer or pension provider, outside of his/her employment relationship (personal pension scheme).[2903]

With regard to pension replacement rates, several differences between countries can be observed. Where most countries show higher replacement rates for low-income workers (workers earning half of average worker earnings), compared to replacement rates for average-income workers, in some countries (including Germany), replacement rates are equal for a full career at average and half-average income.[2904] Furthermore, across countries, replacement rates also vary in terms of pre- and post-retirement income. In some countries pensioners receive a significant higher income after retirement compared to their earnings during their working career; in some countries pensioners receive significantly less. Lastly, across countries a difference can be observed in the degree at which gross pension replacement rates fall after reaching the retirement age. These differences are due to the method of indexation of benefits; indexation in line with inflation (replacement rates fall) or indexation in line with wages (replacement rates do not fall).

In some cases, replacement rates provide a ratio of pension benefits to final earnings. However, for the calculation of the replacement rates it is assumed that workers earn a similar percentage of average wage earnings throughout their career. Therefore, a rise in the income distribution, due to an increase in relative earnings level during career, is not taken into account. Hence, final earnings are equalized to lifetime average earnings and recalculated in line with economy-wide earnings growth, resulting in replacement rates as

2903 The answering options were 'yes', 'no', and 'do not know'. Through this last option, it could be explored to what degree the subjects were not 'aware' of the retirement savings provisions, employed by themselves. The level to which respondents adopted this retirement savings approach can also be linked to their current level of income, unravelling to what extent, e.g. higher incomes are more likely to adopt a multi-pillar savings approach, compared to the lower incomes.

2904 OECD, 'OECD Pensions at a Glance 2017' 100.

a ratio of final earnings equal to those as a ratio of lifetime earnings.[2905] This is, however, not the case for people who move up the earnings distribution as they get older, since in these cases their final earnings will be higher than their lifetime average wage. In these cases, total pension benefits are lower, than if they would have spent their whole career at their final wage.

11.1.2.C Net Pension Replacement Rates

Besides the gross replacement rate, the net replacement rate has also been recorded for, among others, Belgium, Germany and the Netherlands.[2906] These rates are listed below. This net replacement rate is calculated by dividing the individual net pension entitlements by the net pre-retirement earnings, taking into account personal income taxes and social security taxes, paid by both workers, as well as pensioners.[2907] Net replacement rates are preferable to gross replacement rates, since the former give a better indication to what extent people are adequately prepared for their retirement.[2908]

Where the aforementioned gross pension replacement rates is a clear indicator of the design of a pension system, i.e. how effectively a pension system provides a retirement income replacing earned income, the net pension replacement rate will be more relevant to individuals since it reflects their disposable income after retirement compared to their individual earned income during their working career.[2909] This allows them to evaluate the adequacy of their retirement income, i.e. will it be sufficient to support their costs of living during retirement. Virtually in all cases, net replacement rates are higher than gross replacement rates. This is primarily due to the preferential tax treatment of retirement income compared to income from employment and, obviously, lower marginal tax rates since income after retirement is generally lower than labor income during employment. Another side effect of the different tax treatment of pension income across the countries, is that the pattern of net replacement rates across countries differs from the pattern of gross replacement rates. For instance, in Belgium, for average earners, the net replacement

2905 Ibid. 100. For gross pension replacement rates which take account of these different earnings profiles, see ibid. 114 ff.

2906 This has been derived from OECD Pensions at a glance 2017. This data differentiates between male and female. For this research, the mean of the replacement rates applicable to male and female has been calculated and adopted as the starting point. With respect to the gross replacement rates in Belgium, Germany, and Netherlands, these were equal for men and women.

2907 The general provisions and the tax treatment of worker (for 2016) were retrieved from the OECD's Taxing Wages report: OECD, 'Taxing Wages' 2019) <https://www.oecd-ilibrary.org/taxation/taxing-wages-2018_tax_wages-2018-en> accessed 6 August 2019. This report provides information on income taxes paid by workers and social security contributions levied on employees and their employers. Guidelines set forth in this report, such as which payments are regarded as taxes, are followed in the Taxing Wages report.

2908 Knoef and others, 76.

2909 OECD, 'OECD Pensions at a Glance 2017' 106.

rate is 20 percentage points higher compared to the gross replacement rate. The net replacement rates depicted in the table below concern replacement rates covering pension benefits merely arising from mandatory public pension schemes.[2910]

Net pension replacement rate*(2016)	50% of average wage	100% of average wage	150% of average wage	Average (unweighted and rounded of) net replacement rates
BEL	62.6	66.1	50.1	59.6
GER	54.7	50.5	49.8	51.7
NL	105.1	100.6	100.2	102
Overall average				**71.1**

* This has been derived from OECD Pensions at a glance 2017. See also OECD, 'OECD Pensions at a Glance 2017' 107. For a graphical overview of gross and net replacement rates (merely including income from mandatory public pension schemes) see OECD, 'Indicators' 2016) <https://data.oecd.org/pension/net-pension-replacement-rates.htm#indicator-chart> accessed 8 August 2019.

Similar as is true as regards the gross replacement rates, net replacement rates rise considerably when pension benefits arising from mandatory, and voluntary, private pension schemes are taken into account. These net pension replacement rates are provided in the table below.

Net pension replacement rate* (2016)	50% of average wage	100% of average wage	150% of average wage	Average (unweighted and rounded of) net replacement rates
BEL	81.3	72.7	60.5	71.5
GER	66.5	65.4	64.6	65.5
NL	105.1	100.6	100.2	102
Overall average				**79.7**

* This has been derived from OECD Pensions at a glance 2017. This data differentiates between male and female. For this research, the mean of the replacement rates applicable to male and female has been calculated and taken as the starting point. With respect to the gross replacement rates in Belgium, Germany, and Netherlands, these were equal for men and women.

Net replacement rates in Germany are comparatively low. When German pensioners miss a basic and minimum pension, this implies that low income-pensioners have to rely on the

2910 These figures have been retrieved from ibid. 109. Pension replacement rates can also be found at OECD Pensions at a glance 2017, but is should be pointed out that these rates merely cover pension benefits stemming from mandatory public and private pension schemes.

old-age safety net, which is comparatively low at 20% of average earnings.[2911] Consequently, low income- and particle career-pensioners may face an inadequate retirement income.

Net replacement rates vary considerably across countries, but also among income categories.[2912] This is mainly induced by the fact that for low earners the effect taxes and contributions on their net replacement rates is less, since they are, relatively, less taxes and contributions due, compared to high earners. Furthermore, low earners are commonly not in the position to make full use of preferential tax treatments for pension income, such as tax allowances, credits etc.[2913] Moreover, net pension replacement rates are measured under the similar assumptions with regard to applicable legislation, length of working career, price inflation, taxes etc. as gross replacement rates have been computed.

Noteworthy is the degree of variation between the countries in the gross and net replacement rates. In particular, the pension replacement rates in the Netherlands are considerably higher, compared to Belgium and Germany, even amounting to a net retirement income replacing 105.1% of the pre-retirement earned income. A possible explanation for the considerable deviations in net replacement rate, could be the variances in the overall tax advantage provided to an average earner, i.e. the present value of taxes saved over a lifetime, expressed as a percentage of the present value of pension contributions.[2914] The overall tax advantage for the Netherlands is 48%, for Germany 21%, and for Belgium just 16%.

11.1.3 Income, Wages and Earnings

As mentioned above, the amounts of future retirement income have been calculated through the replacement rates. Where gross replacement rates divide predicted retirement income by current gross earnings, the net replacement rate divides predicted retirement income by current net earnings. This posed the question which reliable amount, and respective data, could be used to calculate reliable amounts of predicted future pension income. The considerations that were taken into account, are set forth below.

2911 OECD, 'Pensions at a Glance 2017: How does Germany compare?' 2017) <http://www.oecd.org/germany/PAG2017-DEU.pdf> accessed last accessed on 2 August 2019.

2912 See OECD, 'OECD Pensions at a Glance 2017' 106, table 4.8.

2913 Ibid. 106.

2914 OECD, 'Pensions Outlook' 49 which calculations are based on the 2018 tax treatment of the main pension plan in each country.

11.1.3.A Median Disposable (i.e. Net) Equivalized Household Income

The construct of disposable household income[2915] has, deliberately, not been chosen to compute the depicted amount of retirement income, since it comprises certain elements of non-pension wealth. This will be elucidated in more detail below. The concept of 'equivalized household disposable income' refers to the sum of wages and salaries, mixed income, private income from investment and property, net current transfers and social benefits other than social transfers in kind such as old-age pensions, less taxes on income and wealth and social security contributions paid by employees, the self-employed and the unemployed.[2916] This construct is closest to the concept of income generally understood in economics, compared to national income or GDP, mainly to the reallocation of income.[2917] However, it is not the purpose of the present study to measure the income that people have available to buy goods and services, serving as a measure of material living standards. Although data on this construct refers to a median, and is differentiated per income classes, it is not suited for use in the present study. Therefore, the term earnings and income should not be used interchangeably. Moreover, compared to earnings, disposable income includes additional income items that are not pensionable, such as net property income and net current transfers, although it depends on the country's specific legislation which elements of income are taken into account when calculating the accrual of pension entitlements. Including these items in the amount that will be multiplied by the pension replacement rates, leads to a distorted view of income after retirement. Hence, disposable income has not been taken as the basis for the computation of future retirement income.[2918]

11.1.3.B Earnings

For the reasons set forth in the above section, as well as the argument mentioned below, earnings has been taken as the basis for the computation of the amounts of predicted future retirement income. Where gross replacement rates are calculated based on pre-retirement gross earnings, net replacement rates have been calculated drawing on pre-

2915 For data on the (household) disposable income see OECD, 'Household disposable income' 2018 or latest available) <https://data.oecd.org/hha/household-disposable-income.htm#indicator-chart> accessed 6 August 2019 and OECD Statistics, 'Income Distribution and Poverty: by country – INCOME (current prices)' 2019) <https://stats.oecd.org/#> accessed 2 July 2019. For median equivalized net income on an individual basis, see Eurostat, 'Mean and median income by household type – EU-SILC survey' last update: 17 July 2019) <http://appsso.eurostat.ec.europa.eu/nui/submitViewTableAction.do> accessed 7 August 2019.

2916 OECD, 'Household Income and Wealth' <http://www.oecd.org/sdd/03_Household_income_and_wealth.pdf> accessed last accessed on 6 August 2019. See also Eurostat, 'Income and living conditions (ilc): Reference Metadata in Euro SDMX Metadata Structure (ESMS)' <https://ec.europa.eu/eurostat/cache/metadata/en/ilc_esms.htm> accessed 7 August 2019.

2917 OECD, 'Household Income and Wealth'.

2918 Contrarily Knoef and others, and Knoef and others, 77 ff.

retirement net earnings. Unfortunately, adequate data on median earnings is not available.[2919]

Average Annual Gross Earnings

Data on average annual gross wages[2920] have been obtained through OECD Statistics.[2921] This dataset entails data on average annual wages per full-time and full-year equivalent employee, covering all sectors of the economy and all types of dependent employment.[2922] These are calculated by dividing the national-accounts-based total wage bill ('wages and salaries', in the terminology of OECD National Accounts) by the average number of employees in the total economy. This is then multiplied by the ratio of average usual weekly hours per full-time employee to average usually weekly hours for all employees.[2923] The amounts below are expressed as current prices in national currency units.

2919 Although data is available on hourly median earnings, these were not suited for the calculation of predicted retirement income in the present study: Eurostat, 'Median hourly earnings, all employees (excluding apprentices) by age' last update: 9 August 2017) <https://appsso.eurostat.ec.europa.eu/nui/show.do?dataset=earn_ses_pub2a&lang=en> accessed 7 August 2019.

2920 For the context of this study 'earnings' and 'wages' are used interchangeably, since both terms refer to the total wage and salary earnings including basic pay, regular and irregular overtime and bonus payments. Cf. OECD, 'Comparable estimates of average wages per full-time equivalent employee' <http://www.oecd.org/els/emp/AVERAGE_WAGES.pdf> accessed 7 August 2019.

2921 OECD Statistics, 'Average annual wages' <https://stats.oecd.org/Index.aspx?DatasetCode=AV_AN_WAGE> accessed 7 August 2019. These estimates have been based on G Loewenstein, T O'Donoghue and M Rabin, 'Projection bias in predicting future utility' 118 Quarterly Journal of Economics 1209, and OECD Statistics, 'Annual National Accounts Prices and Purchasing Parities Database' <https://stats.oecd.org/Index.aspx?DataSetCode=SNA_TABLE4> accessed 7 August 2019.

2922 OECD, 'Comparable estimates of average wages per full-time equivalent employee'. Rather than the Eurostat structure of earnings survey where earnings were differentiated based on classification of economic activities, see Eurostat, 'Structure of earnings survey: annual earnings' last update: 7 August 2017) <https://ec.europa.eu/eurostat/web/products-datasets/-/earn_ses_annual> accessed last accessed on 7 August 2019.

2923 See also OECD, 'Employment Outlook' 2019) <http://www.oecd.org/employment/outlook/> accessed 7 August 2019 and OECD, 'Employment Database' <http://www.oecd.org/employment/emp/onlineoecdemploymentdatabase.htm> accessed 7 August 2019. This full-time/all employee ratio for usual hours is used due to a lack of corresponding data for paid hours. For more details see OECD, 'Comparable estimates of average wages per full-time equivalent employee'.

Average (rounded) annual gross earnings 2018*	Total population
Belgium	€45,097
Germany	€40,522
Netherlands	€47,422
Overall average	€44,341

* This data has been retrieved from OECD Statistics, 'Average annual wages'. An alternative source for retrieving data on average worker earnings would be the following: OECD Statistics, 'Pensions at a Glance: Average worker earnings' 2017) <https://stats.oecd.org/> accessed 8 August 2019. However, this construct of average worker earnings (AW) was based on an outdated definition of AW (adopted from the second edition of Pensions at a Glance 2007), and most recent data on AW refers to 2016.

However, since these amounts refer to wages in 2018, and the survey has been conducted in 2019, these amounts of average annual gross earnings were adjusted by multiplying them with an assumed price inflation, for all goods, of 2% per year[2924], and an assumed real growth of wage of 1.25% per year, implying a nominal wage growth of 3.275% per year.[2925] These adjusted amounts of annual gross wages were, eventually, used to calculate the depicted amount of future retirement income, by multiplying it with the replacement rate.

Average (rounded) annual gross earnings adjusted for 2019	Total population
Belgium	€46,574
Germany	€41,849
Netherlands	€48,975
Overall average	€45,799

2924 Assuming price inflation to amount to 2% appears realistic and reliable since, based on Eurostat-data, EU-wide price inflation in 2018 was 1.9% (data on 2019 is not available yet), and for Belgium 2.3%, for Germany 1.9%, and for the Netherlands 1.6% (on average 1.93% for these three countries), see Eurostat, 'HICP – inflation rate' last update: 1 August 2019) <https://ec.europa.eu/eurostat/databrowser/view/tec00118/default/table?lang=en> accessed 7 August 2019. This refers to the annual average rate of changes in prices. Consumer Price Inflation (CPI) is measured in this data set as Harmonised Indices of Consumer Prices (HICPs), designed for international comparison of CPI. HICP is, for instance, used by the European Central Bank for monitoring of inflation in the Economic and Monetary Union. Based on the OECD-data, over the first half of 2019 (data available until July), CPI in Belgium was on average 1.94%, for Germany 1.5% (data available until June), and regards the Netherlands 2.6% on average (data available until June). This was measured as 'Consumer Price Indices (CPIs)' comprising all data that was previously referred to as 'Consumer Prices', 'National Consumer Price Indices (CPIs)' and 'Harmonised Indices of Consumer Prices (HICPs) '. These have been chosen as the most relevant prices statistics for which comparable data across countries is available. See OECD Statistics, 'Consumer price indices (CPIs) – Complete database: Consumer prices – Annual inflation' last updated: 7 August 2019) <https://stats.oecd.org/> accessed 7 August 2019.

2925 Consistent with the approach taken by the OECD in calculating the pension indicators, see OECD, 'OECD Pensions at a Glance 2017' 98-99.

Compared to the data retrieved under the structure of earnings survey, conducted by Eurostat[2926], the OECD used in this study has advantages over the former. First, compared to the surveys based on household, labour cost type or structure of earnings, the survey data used is more comprehensive, since it covers all dependent employees (of all ages), from all wages and salary jobs.[2927] Furthermore, it includes full-time, as well as part-time workers at full-time equivalent rate and also part-year workers with a weight corresponding to the proportion of the year that they were taken into account as employees. With regard to earnings, it includes, in principle, undeclared earnings (as part of the 'non-observed economy'), earnings from secondary jobs of workers with two or more jobs, and earnings from mini (part-time) jobs and apprenticeships[2928]. For these reasons, the OECD averages differ from averages provided in Eurostat-statistics, and are likely to give fairly consistent time-series and cross-country comparison of wages.

Average Annual Net Earnings

The data on these annual net earnings has been based on a broadly acknowledged model drawn up by the OECD.[2929] This data set has been used for the following reasons. First, the amounts are country-specific, computed on the basis of country-specific variables. Although differences in income may have a 'distorting' effect on participants' response, this is mitigated by averaging this amount, and by the random allocation of participants. Although the data refers to 2018, the value of net income has been adjusted by multiplying this with consumer price inflation.[2930]

These net earnings are computed from gross earnings by deducting employee's income taxes and social security contributions, and adding family allowances for households with

2926 See for instance Eurostat, 'Structure of earnings survey: annual earnings'.

2927 OECD, 'Comparable estimates of average wages per full-time equivalent employee'.

2928 In some datasets apprentices are excluded from the data. See, for instance, Eurostat, 'Median hourly earnings, all employees (excluding apprentices) by age'. And some datasets leave out companies employing less than 10 employees, see Eurostat, 'Mean annual earnings by sex, economic activity and occupation' last update: 18 May 2018) <https://appsso.eurostat.ec.europa.eu/nui/show.do?dataset=earn_ses14_49&lang=en> accessed 7 August 2019.

2929 Eurostat, 'Net earnings and tax rates: Reference Metadata in Euro SDMX Metadata Structure (ESMS)' <https://ec.europa.eu/eurostat/cache/metadata/en/earn_net_esms.htm> accessed 7 August 2019. The data has been obtained via national sources: for Belgium the DG Strategy (International Affairs and Research) of the Federal Public Service Social Security, regards Germany from Division I b 4 (Income and Wealth Distribution, Social Indicators) of the German Federal Ministry of Labour and Social Affairs, and for the Netherlands the Directorate Social Security of the Ministry of Social Affairs and Employment, see Appendix 'National contact list' of the link above.

2930 Annual earnings (mean) have also been recorded but data collection stopped in 2014, see for instance Eurostat, 'Structure of earnings survey: annual earnings'.

children.[2931] The size and amounts of these elements depend on the individual personal situation. Therefore, a number of different household situations are considered. The figures on annual net earnings have been differentiated with regard to different marital status (single vs. married), number of workers (only in the case of couples), number of dependent children, and level of gross earnings, expressed as a percentage of the gross earnings of an average worker (50%, 67%, 80%, 100%, 125%, 167%).[2932] With regard to the calculation of income taxes and social security contributions, these parameters refer to the beginning of the fiscal year, and, hence, ignoring later changes during the year. With regard to two-earner couples, the level of earnings per partner has been differentiated as well. However, since the survey is taken at individual level, and the provided amounts of predicted future retirement income relate to an individual situation, earnings for couples were left out.

However, similarly to the approach regards the country-specific replacement rates, to obtain one single amount of annual net earnings the average amount covering all these situations has been taken. The average annual net earnings are depicted in the table below.

Average (rounded) annual net earnings 2018*	Total population
Belgium	€29,748
Germany	€30,880
Netherlands	€35,699
Overall average	€32,109

* This data has been retrieved from Eurostat, 'Annual net earnings' last update: 17 July 2019) <https://appsso.eurostat.ec.europa.eu/nui/show.do?dataset=earn_nt_net&lang=en> accessed 7 August 2019.

As follows from these figures, the level of annual net earnings on an individual level are considerably higher in the Netherlands, compared to Belgium and Germany. However, since these amounts refer to earnings in 2018, and the survey has been conducted in 2019, these amount of average annual net earnings were adjusted similarly as the average annual gross wages were brought up to date, i.e. multiplying with nominal wage growth of 3.275% per year.

2931 Eurostat, 'Net earnings and tax rates: Reference Metadata in Euro SDMX Metadata Structure (ESMS)'. Family allowances are referred to as cash transfers paid in respect of dependent children aged between 6 and 11 years. These figures on annual net earnings become available approximately 12 months after the end of the reference period. Therefore, figures referring to 2019 are unfortunately not available yet.

2932 Ibid.

Average (rounded) annual net earnings adjusted for 2019	Total population
Belgium	€30,722
Germany	€31,891
Netherlands	€36,868
Overall average	€33,160

11.1.3.C Non-pension Wealth

As mentioned above, merely retirement income stemming income from statutory, occupational, and third pillar pension provisions have been taken into account in the calculation of a predicted retirement income. Although elements of non-pension wealth contribute substantially to the level of replacement rates[2933], these elements of wealth, such as imputed rental income and net housing wealth, have not been included in the calculation of future retirement benefits for the following reasons.[2934] First and foremost, as discussed in the previous chapters of this thesis, the national notions of 'pension', and to what degree, for instance, 'housing' should be incorporated in retirement saving, although reaching more of consensus, deviates across countries. Furthermore, it is observed that including these elements of wealth in the calculation of gross replacement rates, it increases the replacement rate by about 25%-points for the top quartile of the income classes.[2935] For the bottom quartile of income classes, the increase is less substantial (8%). It can thus be concluded that variation of replacement rates across the income classes is larger when the total pension wealth is taken into account, compared to replacement rates that only incorporate income stemming from statutory and occupational pillar pensions.

In addition, the underlying tax treatment of owner-occupied dwellings (for the purpose of retirement saving) differs considerably between the Member States. For instance, as Knoef et al. note, it is very likely that due to the Dutch fiscal facilitation of home mortgage interest deduction (*hypotheekrenteaftrek*[2936]), people are more inclined to repay their mortgage, having a considerable effect on people's net housing wealth, and, in turn, a positive effect

2933 Knoef et al. found that when merely account is taken of public and occupational pensions, a considerable share of the households (49%) have a gross replacement rate below 70% (which is considered the benchmark), and in cases where the third pillar (i.e. individual pension provisions), private wealth and imputed rental income from net housing are incorporated, the percentage of households having a gross replacement rate below 70%, is just 31%. See Knoef and others, 74.

2934 It has been observed that non-pension wealth contributes substantially to the replacement rates, see ibid. 74, referring, for a comparable analysis in the UK, to R Crawford and C O'Dea, 'The adequacy of wealth of those approaching retirement' (Institute for Fiscal Studies Reports, 2012).

2935 Knoef and others, 75.

2936 Pursuant to artt. 3.1, sub 2, under e in conjunction with art. 3.120 Wet IB 2001.

on net pension replacement rates.[2937] Currently, owner-occupied dwellings are not fiscally facilitated in the Netherlands, as part of retirement saving. Contrarily, in Germany this is to some degree case, since the *Altersvorsorge-Eigenheimbetrag*, as laid down in§ 92a EStG, allows to take out a lump-sum out of a retirement savings account, for the purpose of financing an owner-occupied dwelling.

When imputed rental income or net housing wealth would have been taken into account in the pension replacement rates, not controlling for the differences in tax treatment of housing, this would have had a distorting effect on the eventual replacement rates, i.e. a distorted view of the 'real' pension replacement rates. Furthermore, the data available is void of reliable data on housing wealth, in both Belgium, Germany and the Netherlands. It would have been rather impractical to account for the effect of housing wealth on replacement rates. Although it has been decided to leave out housing as a form of pension wealth, the effect of housing wealth on pension replacement rates, and the underlying effect of the tax treatment of housing, deserves considerable attention in future research.

11.1.4 Computation of the Amounts of Depicted Future Retirement Income

This section discusses how the amounts of future retirement income, depicted in the survey's text frame, have been calculated, while taking into account the considerations set forth above. The amounts have been established by taking an average of a pessimistic, neutral, desirable and optimistic scenario. Furthermore, replacement rates have been averaged for Belgium, Germany, and the Netherlands.

11.1.4.A Scenario-based Approach[2938]

As addressed in section 11.1.6.B, depicting an amount of future retirement income is pivotal in information provision, though surrounded by uncertainties, such as economic growth, inflation, return rates on investments etc. Research findings suggest that people can be unrealistically optimistic about the amount of future pension income, insufficiently taking into account the risks and future costs associated with pensions, since, when evaluating risks, people commonly use heuristics, or mental shortcuts.[2939] To mitigate the adverse effect of this bias/heuristic, the amounts of future retirement income can be

2937 Knoef and others.

2938 Similarly ibid. 69. However, Knoef et al. used an optimistic and pessimistic scenario with regard to the level of indexation of pensions.

2939 Sunstein, 'Empirically Informed Regulation' 1358, C Jolls, 'Behavioral Economic Analysis of Redistributive Legal Rules' Faculty Scholarship Series 1340 and D Kahneman and S Frederick, 'Representativeness revisited: Attribute substitution in intuitive judgment' in T Gilovich, D Griffin and D Kahneman (eds.), *Heuristics and biases: The psychology of intuitive judgment* (Cambridge University Press, New York 2002).

provided in a pessimistic scenario, neutral scenario and optimistic scenario.[2940] However, it should be pointed out that it is not the present study's aim to explore the effect of communicating these amounts based on such a scenario-based approach. Hence, the depicted amounts of gross and net future retirement income will not be provided through a pessimistic, neutral and optimistic scenario. Nevertheless, to incorporate variable elements as regards the computation of future retirement income, such as purchasing power and related risks, an optimistic, neutral, desirable (70%) and pessimistic replacement rate have been used. With regard to the 70% ambition level, it should be pointed out that this is the most recognised, and commonly referred to ambition level in international pension literature.[2941] Yet, it remains questionable whether this is an adequate yardstick for formulating what an adequate pension should amount to, since those with lower income may need more than 70% of their current income after retirement to support their basic needs, compared to those having a higher income.[2942] The possible adverse effect on participants is mitigated by the random assignment of the survey's respondents to each of the three treatments.

Gross Amount Future Retirement Income

These replacement rates have been retrieved from the data on replacement rates as provided in section 11.1.2.B and 11.1.2.C. Furthermore, in selecting these rates, the variance of replacement rates among countries, income categories and the degree of multi-pillar pension saving has been taken into consideration. The latter refers to the extent to which participants save for retirement through either merely mandatory public pension schemes, or mandatory and voluntary pension schemes as well. For the pessimistic scenario, the gross replacement rate has been set on 38%[2943], the neutral scenario on

2940 See, for instance, L van Benthem, N Kortleve and W Otten, 'Betere pensioneringskeuzes met scenariobedragen' 22 Tijdschrift voor Pensioenvraagstukken.

2941 Haveman and others, and Knoef, 4, referring in this regard. This 70%-ambition corresponds to the principle, i.e. ambition level, prescribed by the Dutch legislator's in fiscal legislation until 2014, see Kamerstukken II, 12. As of 1 January 2015 the ambition level, delineating the fiscal facilitation of pension accrual, has been set at a pension income of 75% of the average income, accrued over 40 years, see Kamerstukken II, 8. Kamerstukken II, *Kamerstukken II* 2011/12, 33 110, nr. 1 (Evaluatie informatiebepalingen pensioenwetgeving).

2942 For instance, Knoef et al. found that the median replacement rate amounts to 95% at the lower end of the income distribution, and 34% at the top of the income distribution.

2943 This is the gross pension replacement rate (2016) for Germany for an individual earning 50% of the average wage, merely saving through a mandatory public pension scheme. This has been derived from OECD Pensions at a glance 2017. See also OECD, 'OECD Pensions at a Glance 2017' 101.

47%,[2944] the desirable scenario on 70% as elucidated above, and the optimistic on 98%[2945]. The average of these four scenarios is 63.25%.

When the average gross pension replacement rate of 63.25% is then multiplied with the average (rounded) annual gross wages of €45,799, covering all three countries, this results in an annual predicted future retirement income of (rounded) €28,968. When this is brought down to the eventual amount of future monthly gross retirement income, this is (rounded) €2,414. This is the amount of future gross retirement income per month, depicted in the survey's text frame. Consistent with practice (i.e. the Dutch mijnpensioenoverzicht.nl)[2946] and to avoid the impression among respondents that the amount has been calculated precisely and fully tailored to their personal situation, this amount has been rounded. In addition, an unrounded (precise) number would be at odds with the 'important to know-section', shown in the net amount and disclaimer- text frame, pointing out that the amounts of future retirement income are merely estimates.

Net Amount of Future Retirement Income

The same considerations as apply to the gross replacement rates, apply to the net replacement rates. For the pessimistic scenario, the net replacement rate has been set on 50%[2947], the neutral scenario on 63%,[2948] the desirable scenario on 70%, and the optimistic scenario on 100%[2949]. The average of these four scenarios is 70.75%.

As regards the average net pension replacement rates of 70.75%, the amount of annual predicted future retirement income is (rounded) €23,461, after this has been multiplied with the average (net) annual wages of €33,160. When this is brought down to the eventual

2944 This is the gross pension replacement rate (2016) for Belgium for an individual earning 50% /100% of the average wage, merely saving through a mandatory public pension scheme. This has been derived from OECD Pensions at a glance 2017. See also OECD, 'OECD Pensions at a Glance 2017' 101.

2945 This is the gross pension replacement rate (2016) for the Netherlands for an individual earning 50% /100% /150% of the average wage, saving through a mandatory public pension scheme, and/or a mandatory or voluntary private pension scheme. This has been derived from OECD Pensions at a glance 2017.

2946 As well as certain personal online environments allowing people to check their accumulated pension rights at their specific pension provider (e.g. www.mijnabp.nl).

2947 This is the net pension replacement rate (2016) for Germany for an individual earning 150% of the average wage, merely saving through a mandatory public pension scheme. This has been derived from OECD Pensions at a glance 2017. See also OECD, 'OECD Pensions at a Glance 2017' 107.

2948 This is the net pension replacement rate (2016) for Belgium for an individual earning 50% of the average wage, merely saving through a mandatory public pension scheme. This has been derived from OECD Pensions at a glance 2017. See also OECD, 'OECD Pensions at a Glance 2017' 107.

2949 This is the net pension replacement rate (2016) for the Netherlands for an individual earning 100/150% of the average wage, saving through a mandatory public pension scheme, and/or a mandatory or voluntary private pension scheme. This has been derived from OECD Pensions at a glance 2017. See also OECD, 'OECD Pensions at a Glance 2017' 107.

amount of future monthly net retirement income, this is (rounded) €1,955. This is the amount of future net retirement income per month, depicted in the survey's text frame. For the same reasons as mentioned above, in the section with respect to the gross amounts, this number has been rounded.

Difference Net-Gross Amount

Furthermore, attention should be drawn to (the level of realism of) the relative difference between the monthly net and gross amount of the future retirement income. The differences between gross (€2,414) and net (€ 1,955) predicted pension benefits amounts to (rounded) 20%. This level of tax burden largely corresponds to the average tax treatment of pensions and pensioners in Belgium and Germany, but not with regard to the Netherlands.[2950] Any adverse effect that may be induced by this will be lessened by the random allocation of participants.

Distorting Effects Induced by These Amounts

Since this approach to establishing an amount of predicted future retirement income remains arbitrary, the distorting effects on the participants' response have been mitigated and some survey elements allow for controlling for these effects. Moreover, it should be pointed out that the amounts depicted in the survey's text frame merely serve illustrative purposes. These effects, and the countering measurements, are briefly discussed below.

Since the level of income varies among participants, the replacement rates as such, eventually resulting in either a higher or lower amount of future pension income, may have a distorting effect on the participants' response. Research findings demonstrate that high income-earners report a lower ambition level/perceived replacement rate (needed income after retirement), compared to low income-earners.[2951] The amount depicted in the gross and net frame may, thus, have a distorting effect. However, for the whole of the survey this effect is mitigated through the random allocation of participants to either the gross amount-frame, the net amount-frame, or the net amount-frame including a disclaimer. Moreover, the participants are asked to rate how realistic they perceived the scenario and, more specifically, the amounts as such. This will be controlled for in the analysis. Furthermore, participants were asked to fill in their income. Both instruments allow to control for potential 'distorting effects', induced by the amounts as such.

2950 See OECD Statistics, 'Pensions at a Glance: Tax treatment of pensions and pensioners' 2016) <https://stats.oecd.org/> accessed 9 August 2019. This is expressed as the percentage at the gross replacement rate of average earnings for men.

2951 For instance, Knoef and others.

Furthermore, taking this into account and to increase the level of realism, three scenarios (optimistic, neutral, and pessimistic) have been incorporated.

11.1.5 Assumptions Underlying Replacement Rates

In computing these pension replacement rates; certain economic variables have been taken into account in this study. These assumptions deserve clarification, in order to use the pension replacement rates as comparable indicators, and to avoid comparing incomparable indicators. Since replacement rates are drawn from the OECD Statistics, the assumptions discussed below, correspond virtually entirely to the assumptions used by the OECD to calculate several pension indicators, including the replacement rates. The underlying assumptions are set forth in more detail below.

Legislation and Changes in Legislation

The replacement rates have been computed under the Member State's legislation, that was in force when the rates were calculated (2016).[2952] More recent figures were not available at the time this study was set up (2018), see also section 3.10. It, thus, concerns the situation in the year 2016 and onwards, and changes occurred after 2016 were not included. Therefore, reforms that had been legislated prior to this data were included, provided that sufficient information was available. Alternatively, changes and reforms that already had been legislated and had been phased-in gradually and yearly, were modeled from the year of implementation and onwards.

Working Career

Furthermore, the calculations of the replacement rates assume that a single worker enters the pension system at the age of 20 and retires after having completed a full career. A full career refers to entering the labour market at the age of 20 and continue working until the normal pension age, applicable for this entry age.[2953] This implies, that the length of the working career may vary, since (statutory) retirement ages differ considerable between Member States.[2954] In cases where the retirement age is 62, the working career lasts 42 years, in cases where the retirement age is 65, the working career lasts 45 years. At this point, it should be briefly pointed out that the differences between national retirement ages, in turn, may have significant adverse effects for (former) mobile workers, in the

---

2952 OECD, 'OECD Pensions at a Glance 2017' 98.

2953 Ibid. 98.

2954 Ibid. 92 ff.

domain of pensions, taxes and social security.[2955] Workings careers may be interrupted due to unemployment, full-time education, (informal) care for children, disable and/or elderly relatives etc, for instance, leading to contribution gaps. However, most pension systems comprise mechanisms that can mitigate the adverse effect of interrupted careers, such as pension credits.[2956]

Pension Schemes Covered in Computations

The computation of the replacement rates cover all, both public[2957] and private, mandatory and voluntary pension schemes for private-sector workers.[2958] Drawback of this computation method is that mandatory pension schemes for civil servants, public-sector workers and special professional groups are excluded. In particular for Belgium and Germany this is an adverse effect in the calculation, since in these countries these schemes play a significant role in securing a retirement income. Furthermore, 'quasi-mandatory' schemes[2959], which are particularly important in the Netherlands, are included, under the condition that they cover at least 85% of employees.

Since an increasing number of Member States show a broad coverage of voluntary, occupational pension schemes, especially Germany, playing an increasing role in securing a retirement income, a second set of replacement rates has been calculated including entitlements stemming from these voluntary pension schemes.[2960] Voluntary private pension schemes comprise both voluntary occupational, and voluntary personal pension plans. It is assumed that worker contribute their full career to the voluntary private pension schemes, irrespective of their earnings level. There are, however, exceptions for Belgium and Germany due to a ceiling on pensionable earnings eligible for tax facilitations.

These replacement rates have also been taken into account for the present study, since (quasi-)voluntary pension schemes play a predominant role in the Netherlands, and an

2955 AHH Bollen-Vandenboorn, H Niesten and S Kramer, 'ITEM Cross-Border Impact Assessment: Schemes relating to retirement ages in NL/BE/DE: a multidisciplinary analysis' (available online: https://www.maastrichtuniversity.nl/sites/default/files/dossiers2018/item-cross-border-impact-assessment-2018_dossier3-schemes-retirement-ages-nl-be-de-multidisciplinary-analysis.pdf 2018) 10 ff.

2956 For an elaborate overview of how incomplete careers may affect pension entitlements, see OECD, 'Pensions at a Glance: OECD and G20 Indicators' 2015) <http://www.keepeek.com/Digital-Asset-Management/oecd/social-issues-migration-health/pensions-at-a-glance-2015_pension_glance-2015-en#page1> accessed 10 March 2023, chapter 3 and specifically for childcare and unemployment see Annex 3.A1 at 106 ff.

2957 In this context, the term 'public' refers to pension schemes involving payments of governments or from social security institutions.

2958 OECD, 'OECD Pensions at a Glance 2017' 98.

2959 In this context this refers to schemes with near-universal coverage, see ibid. 98.

2960 Ibid. 103. For the coverage of private pensions plan see ibid. 150 ff.

increasing important role in Germany. In particular for Belgium and Germany, voluntary private pensions are pivotal, since for Belgium the average (for all income categories) replacement rate rises from 43.6% (when merely mandatory schemes are integrated) to 56.7% (when voluntary private pensions are taken into account as well).[2961] The effect of this can be accounted for during the analysis of the survey's results since respondents have been prompted to fill in whether they have adopted multi-pillar retirement savings approach, covering all of their (former) working, and (former) residence states. The subjects were asked to indicate whether:

- they participate(d) in and/or contribute(d) to either a government-run basic mandatory retirement provision (statutory retirement scheme);
- and/ or participate(d) in and/or contribute(d), as an employee or civil servant, to a pension fund/provider through his/her employer, or as an independent professional (occupational pension scheme);
- and/or participate(d) in and/or contribute(d) to a voluntary individual pension product through an insurer or pension provider, outside of his/her employment relationship (personal pension scheme).[2962]

In addition, the computations integrate resource-tested[2963] benefits, for which pensioners may be eligible, as well. With regard to these benefits, the calculations assume that all entitled pensioners fully take out these benefits. Lastly, when calculating the replacement rates, it is assumed that the full retirement income arises from the mandatory pension schemes and voluntary pension schemes.[2964]

Economic Variables

To avoid that pension indicators, including pension replacement rates, are not disturbed by varying economic conditions, certain economic variables are fixed in the calculations. These economic variables focus on elements that may affect the level of pensions, i.e. price inflation, real wage growth, real return on financial assets, discount rate and inflation, and

2961 Ibid. 103, table 4.5.

2962 The answering options were 'yes', 'no', and 'do not know'. Through this last option, it could be explored to what degree the subjects were not 'aware' of the retirement savings provisions, employed by themselves. The level to which respondents adopted this retirement savings approach can also be linked to their current level of income, unravelling to what extent, e.g. higher incomes are more likely to adopt a multi-pillar savings approach, compared to the lower incomes.

2963 Resource-tested refers to benefits which are either means-test, where both assets and income are taken into account, purely income-test or merely pension income. However, where means tests are broader, also taking account of assets, the income test is taken as a given. See OECD, 'OECD Pensions at a Glance 2017' 98.

2964 Ibid. 98.

economic growth.[2965] Accounting for these economic variables, which vary considerable among countries, ensures that differences in pension levels across countries are merely due to differences in pension systems and policies. These variables will be briefly elucidated below.

Price inflation was assumed to be 2% on a yearly basis.[2966] Real growth of wage was fixed at 1.25% per year on average. Adding real growth of wage and price inflation, implies a nominal wage growth of 3.275% per year. With regard to individual earnings, it assumed that these grow in line with the economy-wide average, i.e. it is assumed that the individual remains at the same point in the earnings distribution, receiving the same percentage of average earnings in every year of the working life.[2967] Furthermore, the (real) rate of return on financial assets was assumed to be 3% per year. For the purpose of these calculations, the financial assets related to funded, defined contribution pensions. The defined contribution conversion factor (i.e. computing the pension annuity) applied to the accumulated defined contribution asset, was fixed at 90%.[2968] This factor was the result of administrative charges, fee structures, costs of buying a pension annuity etc. Lastly, the real discount rate was set at 2% per year.

With regard to mortality rates, country-specific projections were retrieved from the United Nationals population database for every year from 2016 to 2080.[2969] It has been decided to move from period based-mortality to cohort based-mortality, since under the latter the increases in the continuing life expectancy after retirement are fully reflected as well. As concerns benefits withdrawal, the calculation of the replacement rates assumes that benefits arising from defined contribution schemes are paid in the form of a price-indexed life annuity at an actuarially fair price, under the assumption of perfect foresights.[2970] This is calculated based on the mortality projections, and taking into account the aforementioned conversion factor. This is not altered by alternative ways of pension benefits withdrawal (e.g. lump sum), since the accumulated capital sum at time of retiring is similar but benefits are spread differently.[2971]

2965 Ibid. 98. See OECD, 'Pensions at a Glance: OECD and G20 Indicators', chapter 4 for a sensitivity analysis of the various economic parameters used in this analysis.

2966 OECD, 'OECD Pensions at a Glance 2017' 98.

2967 Ibid. 99.

2968 Ibid. 99. Although in the last publication the conversion factor was assumed to be 85%, the increase to 90%, and the positive effect hereof on the replacement rate, has been largely offset due to the shift in approach with regard to mortality rates, i.e. from period based mortality to cohort based mortality.

2969 Ibid. 99.

2970 Ibid. 99.

2971 Ibid. 99.

Taxes and Social Contributions

Considerable important, from the perspective of this study, are taxes and social security contributions that are taken into account when calculation the net replacement rates.[2972] As the OECD points out, for numerous reasons, personal income tax plays an important role in old-age support.[2973] Since personal income tax rates are progressive and pension benefits are, usually, lower than earned income, the average tax rate on pension income is generally lower. How pension income is fiscally treated preferentially compared to earned income, differs across countries.[2974] The differences in the taxation of pension benefits under countries' national tax law are taken into account in the computation of the national pension replacement rates.[2975] 'Details' of the rules applied to pensioners under the national tax systems can be retrieved from the online country profiles.[2976] However, these 'details' entail a rather rudimentary description of the tax treatment of pensions under the national tax systems. What is more, with regard to social security contributions the following should be briefly pointed out. Some countries do not levy social security contributions on retirement income at all, some countries levy a lower rate on retirement income, compared to the rate they levy on earned income. The latter is true for Belgium, Germany and the Netherlands.

When calculating the net replacement rates, it was assumed that tax systems and social security contributions remained unchanged in the future.[2977] This is referred to as the 'constant policy assumption'. Although arbitrarily and quite unrealistic, is eases the consistent calculation of the pension replacement rates. This assumption implies that 'value parameters', i.e. tax allowances and contribution ceiling, are adjusted each year

2972 For an exhaustive country-specific overview of the average personal income tax and social security contribution rates on gross labour income, see OECD Statistics, 'Table I.5. Average personal income tax and social security contribution rates on gross labour income' last update: 11 April 2019) <https://stats.oecd.org/Index.aspx?DataSetCode=TABLE_I5> accessed 8 August. For a country-specific overview of all-in average personal income tax rates at average wage by family type, see OECD Statistics, 'Table I.6. All-in average personal income tax rates at average wage by family type' last update: 11 April 2019) <https://stats.oecd.org/Index.aspx?DataSetCode=TABLE_I6> accessed 8 August 2019.

2973 OECD, 'OECD Pensions at a Glance 2017' 104. For a rough overview of the tax treatment of pensions and pensioners per country, see OECD Statistics, 'Pensions at a Glance: Tax treatment of pensions and pensioners'.

2974 Grosso modo, the tax treatment of retirement savings in Germany and the Netherlands is classified as 'EET, and in Belgium as 'TET'. See OECD, 'Pensions Outlook' 45. However, it should be pointed out that when countries offer tax credits on contributions, these are considered taxing contribution, since the tax credit may not fully cover the amount of tax paid on those contributions.

2975 OECD, 'OECD Pensions at a Glance 2017' 105, table 4.6.

2976 Ibid. 106. See OECD, 'Pension at a Glance 2017: Country profiles – Netherlands' 2017) <https://www.oecd.org/els/public-pensions/PAG2017-country-profile-Netherlands.pdf> accessed last accessed on 2 August 2019.

2977 OECD, 'OECD Pensions at a Glance 2017' 99.

consistently with the increase of average worker earnings. Contrarily, 'rate parameters', i.e. personal income tax rates and social security contribution rates, remained unadjusted.

The foregoing illustrates the central phenomenon in this study, i.e. the complexity, inconsistency, and unpredictability of pensions' taxation, particularly with respect to cross-border pensions. Factoring out the effect of this on the net replacement ratio seems almost impractical. To ease the calculation of these ratios, certain assumptions are therefore used which, in turn, abstract from reality in the realm of tax law.

11.1.6 Underlying Heuristics, Biases and Possible Remedies

As mentioned above, the amount of gross and net earnings will be multiplied with the gross, respectively net pension replacement rates in order to establish a reliable amount of monthly predicted retirement income, depicted in the survey's text frame. Although this approach remains rather arbitrary, it is, based on the datasets used, the most reliable way of computing these amounts. What is more, it mitigates the effect of biases on participants' response to the highest possible degree. Moreover, in order to ensure a high level of realism and responding to certain behavioural heuristics and biases participants may be prone to; scenarios of future retirement income have been incorporated in the computation of these final amounts. Hence, these underlying biases and heuristics will be addressed in the section below.

11.1.6.A Projection Bias

When people are exposed to the amounts of predicted retirement income, they may find it difficult to image themselves during retirement, and to envision their preferences during retirement. For instance, they may find it hard to determine whether the amount of predicted future income will be sufficient, in turn, depending on their financial preferences they may have after retirement.[2978] This is referred to as the 'projection bias', which arises when people make predictions about future preferences that are disproportionately influenced by their current tastes, and are commonly not realized in equilibrium.[2979] For instance, when people are asked whether, in one week, they would prefer a salad or French fries, this depends on whether these people are hungry the very moment they were

2978 See, for instance, Knoef, arguing that, due to this projection bias, it is ambiguous to ask people what they expect to be their future expenditures after retirement.

2979 W Eberhardt, W Bruine de Bruin and J Strough, 'Age differences in financial decision making: The benefits of more experience and less negative emotions' 32 Journal of Behavioral Decision Making 1, 1250.

asked.[2980] Further, when individuals shop on an empty stomach, they tend to buy more.[2981] In other words, they project their current preferences onto their future preferences. The reason for this bias lies in the fact that individuals are able to predict the direction of taste/preference changes, but under-appreciate the true magnitude (i.e. absolute value) of the change.[2982]

For the current study, this would imply that participants that currently are financially more vulnerable, overestimate their future financial needs, and would perceive the predicted amount of retirement income as too low, potentially having an adverse effect on their responses. Contrarily, participants who are currently financially more stable would underestimate their financial preferences. For these reasons, a brief notification has been included in the survey, before people were shown the text frames, prompting them to image that they would receive this message (i.e. the text frame) from their pension provider.

11.1.6.B Availability Bias

The expected amount of future pension income is the pivotal element in pension communication.[2983] Through this computed amount of future pension income the participant has an insight in his future financial situation, and is allowed to evaluate his pension adequacy. However, showing a calculated precise amount of future pension is surrounded by uncertainty, since for instance, the value of the pension entitlement and the level of inflation compensation are uncertain factors. Moreover, research findings have demonstrated that, in some domains, people show unrealistic optimism.[2984] For example, many people believe that they are less likely than others to suffer from various, misfortunes, such as diseases, accidents, financial setbacks etc.[2985] This tendency to unrealistic optimism is related to the so-called 'confirmation bias', stating that people give particular weight to information confirming their antecedent beliefs. Given this, this would imply for this experimental study that people can be unrealistically optimistic about the amount of future pension income, insufficiently taking into account the risks and future costs

---

2980 ECLI:NL:GHSHE:2008:BC2720 (Hof 's-Hertogenbosch). See also ECLI:NL:GHAMS:2009:BI6399 (Hof Amsterdam).

2981 ECLI:NL:GHAMS:2011:BU3398 (Hof Amsterdam).

2982 Ibid.and Eberhardt, Bruine de Bruin and Strough, 1251. The latter also argues that this is a plausible explanation of the so-called 'endowment effect'. Furthermore, he argues that due to the 'projection bias', individuals consume too much and, hence, might not save enough. This provides an alternative explanation of savings inadequacy that does not rely on arguments of present-biased preferences, see ibid. 1256.

2983 As recognized by art. 51, par. 11 *Pensioenwet* in conjunction with *Regeling van de Minister van Sociale Zaken en Werkgelegenheid van 13 april 2018*, 6.

2984 Sunstein, 'Empirically Informed Regulation' 1358, Jolls, and Kahneman and Frederick.

2985 Sunstein, 'Empirically Informed Regulation' 1358 and Kahneman and Frederick.

associated with pensions, since, when evaluating risks, people commonly use heuristics, or mental shortcuts.[2986] For example, when evaluating probability, peoples' judgments are often affected by the fact whether a recent event comes readily to their mind, referred to as the 'availability bias'; if an event is cognitively 'available', people tend to overestimate the risk, but if an event is not cognitively available, people tend to underestimate the risk, leading to inaccurate probability judgments of undesirable outcomes.[2987]

These biases and heuristics have been incorporated in pension information provision through the implementation of scenarios, mainly aimed to avoid a too optimistic view of the amount of people's future pension income and, in addition, to provide insights in the risks borne by pension participants.[2988] These more truthful pension information may prevent people from being put on a wrong footing. It has been demonstrated that people have difficulty understanding general risks, since pension participants seem unrealistically optimistic about their future pension income and are averse of risks.[2989] It is therefore argued to personalize, and provide insights into, these pension risks through the use of different scenarios of a depicted future pension income. Through these scenario's pension participants are offered an insight in the purchasing power and risks of their future retirement income. This allows participants to have a more realistic total overview of their pension situation. However, these scenarios will not be used for conduction of the survey, for the following reasons. As has been mentioned before, the amounts depicted in the treatment merely serve illustrative purposes as this research's goal is to focus on the effect of exposing respondents to either a gross amount, or a net amount of future retirement income, while controlling as much as possible for potential adverse effects. Moreover, there is still some discussion on how such variations should be calculated, and shown. From a practical side, the implementation of this approach may be restricted by the availability of country-specific data.

As has been addressed above, the amount of future retirement income, in the net and gross text frame used in the experiment, is calculated by multiplying the average pre-retirement earnings (overall average of Belgium, Germany and the Netherlands), by the gross, or net pension replacement rate. Taking this into account, and to increase the level of realism and to illustrate the purchasing power and the related risks of future pension

2986 Sunstein, 'Empirically Informed Regulation' 1358.

2987 Tversky and Kahneman, 'Availability: A Heuristic for Judging Frequency and Probability' and P Slovic, B Fischhoff and S Lichtenstein, 'Cognitive Processes and Societal Risk Taking' in JS Carroll and JW Payne (eds.), *Cognition and Social Behavior* (Lawrence Erlbaum Associates, Potomac (Maryland) 1976).

2988 Cf.Kamerstukken II, *Wet pensioencommunicatie* 1.

2989 Cf.Sunstein, 'Empirically Informed Regulation'. This is also recognized by the Dutch legislator when drafting the *Wet Pensioencommunicatie* (i.e. Act on Pension Communication): Kamerstukken II, *Wet pensioencommunicatie* 4.

income, four amounts of replacement rates will be used, reflecting an optimistic, neutral, desirable and pessimistic scenario.[2990]

It should be mentioned that pension information provision through these scenarios has been implemented in the Netherlands[2991], and required by law, since it had been demonstrated that pension information appeared to not always have the envisaged effect.[2992] A uniform calculation method to compute this amount has been laid down in secondary regulation (i.e. ministerial decree), to ensure that the future pension is calculated comparably by all pension providers, and participants can sum up the amounts of future pension income.[2993]

2990 As far as pension information provision through the Dutch mijnpensioenregister.nl is concerned, art. 51 of the *Pensioenwet* (Pension Act) stipulates that information concerning the old age pension, shall be depicted on the basis of a pessimistic, expected and optimistic scenario. In addition, art. 46, sub a, under 1 *Pensioenwet* prescribes that the pension provider shall provide the participants, the former participants, the former partner or the retiree, upon request, information on the assumptions made in the depiction of old age pension on the basis of the pessimistic, expected and optimistic scenario.

2991 The different scenarios of predicted future retirement income will be depicted in the Dutch pension tracking service (mijnpensioenoverzicht.nl) as of the 30th of September 2019, allowing participants to have an insight in the real expectation as regards the amount and purchasing power of the future retirement benefits. See Minister van Sociale Zaken en Werkgelegenheid, *Verzamelbrief Pensioenonderwerpen – Vaste commissie voor SZW, PvdA- en CDA-fractie vragen toelichting* (9 July 2019).

2992 Kamerstukken II. Research findings demonstrated that 43% of respondents showed difficulty with understanding the information, see Visser, Kloosterboer and Oosterveld.

2993 *Regeling van de Minister van Sociale Zaken en Werkgelegenheid van 13 april 2018*. Art. 14c of this regulation stipulates that the amount in the expected scenario is based on the 50th percentile of the pension amount for all scenarios, the 95th percentile for the optimistic scenario, and the calculation of the pessimistic scenario is based on the 5th percentile. These calculations of these scenarios are aimed at the future, and the computed amounts reflect the current purchasing power as they are adjusted for future inflation. The calculation method is bases on similar principles, using several thousands of future scenarios, including macro-economic prognoses for key variables for the upcoming decennia, such as life expectancy. These scenario sets are made available each quarter of the year by *De Nederlandsche Bank* (the Dutch Central Bank). A pension provider is then able to calculate to what degree he is able to realise the pension ambition set. When it is found that in a certain scenario a pension provider is not able to grant a supplement on the pensions, while this was incorporated in the ambition, or it is proven that he has to reduce pensions, the effects hereof will be reflected in the depicted pension amounts. Future inflation is also integrated in the computations of these scenarios. See ibid., 6. Also see these reports drawn up by the Dutch Ministry of Social Affairs and Employment: Ministry of Social Affairs and Employment, *Cijfers voor pensioencommunicatie, een uniforme rekenmethodiek voor koopkracht en risico's van pensioen* (13 June 2019) and Ministry of Social Affairs and Employment, *Aanvaardbaarheid en uitvoerbaarheid uniforme rekenmethodiek voor koopkracht en risico's van pensioen* (1 August 2014).

12 APPENDIX B: TEXT OF IMPORTANT TO KNOW-SECTION AND DISCLAIMER

The empirical study's results have been dealt with elaborately in chapter 3 of this research. This appendix addresses how the texts of the important to know-section and the text of the disclaimer have been established, shown to respondents allocated in the net amount and disclaimer-text frame. The text of the important to know-section was shown to respondents immediately, below the sentence stating 'After reaching the applicable retirement age, you will receive a total net pension income of approximately €1,955 per month'. This was followed by a multiple-choice question, querying respondents whether they wanted to see the disclaimer with respect to the amount of future retirement income depicted in the text box. In cases where participants clicked 'yes', then the full text of the disclaimer was shown on the same page. It was recorded whether participants actually had seen the text of disclaimer. Given the possible effects of the text on the participants' response as such and the fact that the formulation of these texts, particularly with regard to the legal consequences, should be done carefully, the formulation will be elucidated in more detail below. Why the texts' formulation needs attention with a view to the legal consequences will be dealt with in more detail below as well.

12.1.1 Drafting the Important to Know-section

The primary objective of this section is to point out that the amounts of future retirement income, shown to the respondents, are merely indications of this future amount, and may differ in future due to a variety of reasons. It has been formulated in this way for the following reasons. Firstly, it is (very) similar to the wording and content of a similar section, depicted in the Dutch mijnpensioenoverzicht.nl (see below). Taking this as a starting point responds to evaluating policy in practice. The first bullet point, referring to new legislation governing taking out (very) small pension benefits, has been left out since it is not relevant for all the respondents of the present study (i.e. merely respondents having pension entitlements accrued through Dutch occupational pension provisions). Furthermore, the hyperlinked reference to the frequently asked questions (*veelgestelde vragen*) has been removed since these are not incorporated in the survey. The phrase referring to 'changes in private or work situation' has deliberately been left open for interpretation, i.e. not including examples of life-events that may affect the future amount of retirement income such as marrying, dismissal, divorce.[2994] Besides that these examples may have a negative effect on people's perception of the text, it does not cover all events that potentially affect the amount of future retirement income, e.g. changes in pensionable earnings, changes in career years, or indexation of pension benefits. As pension systems in Europe deviate considerably, the reasons why an amount of future retirement income may vary, are versatile. In order to avoid a potential confusing effect among the survey's respondents of explicitly enumerating these life-events, it has been decided to leave this open.

12.1.2 *Legal Background of Drafting the Important to Know-section*

While drafting the text of this section the possible legal consequences of providing erroneous amounts of future retirement income have been taken into account. Certain elements of information have been embedded with a view to this legal background. It should, however, be pointed out that these legal consequences pertain to the Dutch applicable law and regulations governing the information provider's liability under civil law for providing erroneous amounts of future retirement income. Analysing how these situations are governed under German and/or Belgian law, is beyond the scope of this study. Besides, irrespective of the potential legal consequences under national law, these elements of the text remain the most important when informing pension participants about future retirement income.

The phrase pointing out that the gross and net amounts of future pension income are estimates, is in line with settled Dutch case-law where courts decide that pointing out that the amounts are estimates may be decisive in establishing whether or not legally enforceable rights may be derived from the amounts of future retirement income, communicated through the pension information (e.g. pension benefit statements).[2995] In principle[2996], the general thrust in Dutch case-law, regarding these cases, is that pension participants cannot derive any rights from this pension information, and are legally not entitled to the

2994 Examples of life-events have been mentioned in a second layer of information at Mijnpensioenoverzicht.nl, 'Veelgestelde vragen' <https://www.mijnpensioenoverzicht.nl/faq> accessed 3 September 2019, under 'Waar moet ik op letten als ik via Mijnpensioenoverzicht.nl mijn pensioengegevens bekijk?'.

2995 See ECLI:NL:GHDHA:2019:76, PJ 2019, 40 (Hof Den Haag); ECLI:NL:GHAMS:2016:3246, PJ 2016, 136 (Hof Amsterdam); ECLI:NL:RBROT:2016:3491, PJ 2015, 138 (Rechtbank Rotterdam); ECLI:NL:RBUTR:2011:BQ3748, PJ 2011, 64 (Rechtbank Utrecht); ECLI:NL:RBROT:2010:BO6473, PJ 2010, 5 (Rechtbank Rotterdam); 18/4786 AW, ECLI:NL:CRVB:2019:2013 2019 (Centrale Raad van Beroep). See also Maatman, 151 ff.

2996 In principle, since under circumstances the legitimate expectation may be created that the information is accurate, to which the participants may derive rights, pursuant to the so-called 'wilsvertrouwensleer' laid down in art. 3:35 BW.

(erroneous) computed amounts of pension provided in the pension information. In cases where, in the relationship between the pension fund and the pension participant, the amount of future pension income has to be computed, the pension agreement concluded between these parties prevails.[2997] In order to elucidate the possible consequences of the amounts' status as estimate, a second phrase has been included, stating that the pension income may be higher or lower than the amounts provided. This renders the status of the amounts being estimates also more recognisable for the readers.

The second bullet point of the section, stating that the amounts have been calculated on the basis of current laws and regulations, and the information provided by the pension provider(s), is incorporated into the text for the following reasons. As such, this is not (yet) one of the circumstances that are taken into consideration by courts when establishing whether pension participants are legally entitled to the amounts, depicted in the pension information. However, it further clarifies why the estimates of future retirement income may differ from the amount of eventual pension income the reader will obtain. The same reasoning holds true with regard to the phrase stating that due to changes in the private and/or work situation, the pension often changes as well, and, hence, readers should check the information annually.

At this point it should also be pointed out that with regard to the elements of the information, there are considerable similarities compared to the information provided in the answers to the frequently asked questions, formulated by the Belgium *mypension.be*.[2998] Although in different wording, it also refers to changes in laws and regulations that may affect the depicted amount of future retirement income. This is also incorporated in the disclaimer used in this study. Furthermore, this Belgian information emphasizes that the information providers are not aware of the precise fiscal situation of the user at the moment of retirement, therefore assuming that he or she is not entitled to any fiscal facilities. It also points out that the calculation of the net amount of future retirement income is based on the current tax rates. Lastly, it stresses that in order to calculate the amount of future retirement income, merely Belgian career years are taken into account. These elements of information have not been included in the important to know-section, since these are too complex to include them in a first (basis) layer of information such as

2997 Interesting in this regard is the disclaimer's text on the website of ABP Pension fund, which explicitly stipulates that the pension arrangement is, besides the information known and provided to the fund, ultimately decisive in establishing the participant's pension entitlements, see ABP, 'Disclaimer' 2019) <https://mijn.abp.nl/disclaimer> accessed 1 October 2019.

2998 Mypension.be, 'Veelgestelde vragen' <https://mypension.onprvp.fgov.be/nl/mypension/Paginas/faq.aspx?category=logging-in> accessed 3 September 2019.

this section.[2999] Moreover, the general thrust that the amounts have been calculated on the basis of legislation currently in force, and that the amounts may vary due to changes in the personal or work situation, have been incorporated in the text.

12.1.3 Drafting the Text of the Disclaimer[3000]

After being shown the amounts of future retirement income and the important to know-section, respondents allocated to the net amount and disclaimer-text frame had the option of reading the full text of the disclaimer. The text of the disclaimer was mainly derived from the disclaimer used in the Dutch mijnpensioenoverzicht.nl. The text of this disclaimer has been adapted and geared to (the objective of) the present study. Below the initial drafting of the disclaimer, used in mijnpensioenoverzicht.nl, is provided.

2999 For instance, the explanation of the methodology and assumptions should not be offered in the first layer of information, since people may put off making decisions when information is unknown or unclear, see EIOPA, 46-47 and cited literature.

3000 It should be stressed that the reliability and (legal) status of the depicted amounts of future retirement are also elucidated in the frequently asked questions (advanced layer of information) on the mijnpensioenoverzicht.nl website: Mijnpensioenoverzicht.nl, under 'Hoe betrouwbaar zijn de gegevens die ik op Mijnpensioenoverzicht.nl zie?'. This information stresses that the gross amounts of future retirement income cannot be considered 'factual' and 'final', and are merely 'indicative', since a lot may change in the mean time, or particular information has not been taken into account while computing these future amounts. Under these frequently asked question, it is also pointed out that the rounded net amounts, provided on mijnpensioenoverzicht.nl, are merely an indication of the predicted pension per month. These amounts are estimated and not factual. Lastly, it is recalled that the net and gross amount of predicted retirement income, provided through mijnpensioenoverzicht.nl, may deviate from the amounts that the pensioner will receive after retiring. Explaining this methodology and assumptions in a second layer of information is consistent with findings in research, see EIOPA, 46-47 and cited literature.

Figure 12.1 Disclaimer Text Derived from mijnpensioenoverzicht.nl.

Disclaimer

1. Deze website is met de grootst mogelijke zorgvuldigheid samengesteld, waarbij de Stichting Pensioenregister streeft naar het geven van correcte en actuele informatie.
2. Op het moment dat u inlogt met uw DigiD, verzamelt de Stichting Pensioenregister aan de hand van uw burgerservicenummer (BSN) de bij de Sociale Verzekeringsbank en de pensioenuitvoerders opgehaalde pensioengegevens.
3. Gezamenlijk zorgen wij dat deze zo juist en volledig mogelijk worden getoond. Wij raden u aan deze gegevens te controleren aan de hand van laatst verstrekte papieren overzicht(en) of bij de Sociale Verzekeringsbank en/of betreffende pensioenuitvoerder(s).
4. De informatie op de website is uitdrukkelijk niet bedoeld als vervanging van de informatie die u ontvangt van de Sociale Verzekeringsbank en/of uw pensioenuitvoerder(s).
5. De op Mijnpensioenoverzicht.nl getoonde bedragen geven een indicatie van uw persoonlijke financiële situatie in de toekomst. Aan de getoonde bedragen kunnen dan ook geen rechten worden ontleend.
6. De Stichting Pensioenregister is niet aansprakelijk voor de schade, van welke aard ook, voortvloeiend uit omstandigheden die niet aan de Stichting toerekenbaar is. Voorbeelden van dergelijke omstandigheden zijn onder meer de volgende gevallen:
    1. schade op grond van het handelen op basis van de getoonde bedragen zonder advies in te winnen;
    2. schade door buitengebruikstelling of storingen in onder meer Mijnpensioenoverzicht.nl, internet of telecommunicatienetwerken;
    3. schade als gevolg van het niet naleven van uw eigen verplichtingen, waaronder het niet naleven van deze gebruiksvoorwaarden.
7. Op de website staan verwijzingen naar websites van derden. Stichting Pensioenregister is niet verantwoordelijk voor de inhoud van deze websites.

Voor de volledige bepalingen t.a.v. privacy, aansprakelijkheid en intellectueel eigendom verwijzen we u naar de Gebruiksvoorwaarden van Mijnpensioenoverzicht.nl.

Below the adapted text of the disclaimer that was used in the survey, is provided.

Disclaimer:[3001]

1. *The information has been prepared with the greatest possible care, whereby the provider strives to provide correct and up-to-date information.*
2. *The information provider ensures that this information is shown as correct and complete as possible. It is recommended that you verify this information through your most recent provided (paper) benefits statement or at the Social Security Office and/or your pension provider(s).*
3. *The information provided is explicitly not intended to replace the information you receive from your Social Security Office and/or your pension provider(s).*
4. *The depicted amount of future retirement income merely provides an indication of your future personal financial satiation. No rights may therefore be derived from these depicted amounts.*[3002]
5. *The information provider shall not be liable for damage, of any kind, arising from circumstances not imputable to the provider. Examples of such circumstance are the following:*
   a. *Damage on grounds of acting on the basis of the amounts shown without seeking advice;*
   b. *damage due to decommissioning or malfunctions in, for instance, the information provision system, internet or telecommunication networks;*
   c. *damage resulting from failure to comply with your own obligations, including failure to comply with these terms of use.*

As mentioned above, the text was derived from mijnpensioenoverzicht.nl and adapted. The elements included in the text above were selected with a view to the elements considered pivotal in settled Dutch case-law pertaining to establishing civil liability for providing erroneous pension information. For instance, the text of point four, pointing out that the depicted amount of future retirement income merely provides an indication, has been considered pivotal in this regard. This will be dealt with in more detail in the next section, addressing the legal background of the text of the disclaimer.

The adoptions of the text related to the following points. First, only the most relevant points, in view of the (in)dependent variables measured in the present study were selected. Second, the organisation/entity responsible for providing the information (e.g. the foundation *Pensioenregister*) was not mentioned, since it is not clear (yet) which organisation will be responsible for providing information on cross-border pensions. For

3001 The text of these bullet points in the disclaimer have been derived, translated and slightly adapted, from points 1, 3, 4, 5 and 6 of the text of the disclaimer used in the Dutch mijnpensioenoverzicht.nl.

3002 See for instance § 5, para 4 *Gesetz Digitale Rentenübersicht.*

the same reason, references to the method of logging into the system or references to third-party websites were left out.

12.1.4 Legal Background of Drafting the Disclaimer

Whilst including a disclaimer may induce ambiguity among readers, it may be considered necessary from the perspective of ensuring that readers understand the status/ informative value of the information. This ambiguity might, in turn, cause the reader to call the information's trustworthiness into question and people might not even use the information in retirement planning.[3003]

The need for ensuring that readers understand the status/ informative value of the information, can be supported as follows. It follows from the case-law referred to in the section 12.1.2, that pension information providers face legal risks when providing information on amounts of future retirement income. Given these legal risks, providers of pension information commonly incorporate a disclaimer in the information, stating that no rights may be derived from the pension information provided. Including such a disclaimer in the pension information, is a fact that is also taken into consideration by the Dutch courts (of appeal) when establishing whether or not pension participants are legally entitled to the computed amounts of pension provided in the pension information, rather than the amounts computed on the basis of the pension arrangement.[3004] In most cases, courts rule that, since the reader was, through the disclaimer's text, informed about the fact that the amounts depicted in the pension information are estimates, no legitimate expectations were created with respect to the amounts of future retirement income. The reader is therefore not legally entitled to the (erroneous) computed amounts of pension depicted in the pension information, but rather to the amounts computed on the basis of the applicable pension arrangement. The perspective adopted in the above is predominantly legal; other factors may play a role as well. It should also be borne in mind that, by their nature, pension benefits are consumptive and that those entitled to them will also have adjusted to a certain spending pattern.[3005] Taking these elements into account, it is a policy

3003 EIOPA, 46-47.

3004 See 2 July 2019). 18/4786 AW, ECLI:NL:CRVB:2019:2013 2019, Centrale Raad van Beroep, (3 February 2009). ECLI:NL:GHAMS:2009:BI6399, Hof Amsterdam, (3 September 2010). ECLI:NL:RBROT:2010:BO6473, PJ 2010, 5, Rechtbank Rotterdam, (6 April 2011). ECLI:NL:RBUTR:2011:BQ3748, PJ 2011, 64, Rechtbank Utrecht, (9 August 2016). ECLI:NL:GHAMS:2016:3246, PJ 2016, 136, Hof Amsterdam, (22 January 2008). ECLI:NL:GHSHE:2008:BC2720, Hof 's-Hertogenbosch, (22 May 2015). ECLI:NL:RBROT:2016:3491, PJ 2015, 138, Rechtbank Rotterdam, (25 October 2011). ECLI:NL:GHAMS:2011:BU3398, Hof Amsterdam, (29 January 2019). ECLI:NL:GHDHA:2019:76, PJ 2019, 40 Hof Den Haag.

3005 Cf. SH Kuiper and MM Koomen, 'Te veel pensioen: terugvorderen, corrigeren? Zes gezichtspunten' PensioenMagazine 35.

question whether, and if so to what extent, it is desirable to confer legally enforceable rights on the recipients of the information pertaining to the future amounts of pension. Moreover, in recent years, the Dutch Financial Services and Markets Authority (AFM) has received an increasing number of signals from pension members about conflicting messages from their pension provider about the amount of their pension.[3006]

The text of the disclaimer underscores the informative nature of the provided information on the amounts of future retirement income. It points out that the information's purpose lies not in conferring any rights on the depicted amount of future retirement income (i.e. a non-binding nature), though rather providing an indication of the future retirement income. This is also a circumstance that is taken into consideration when courts determine whether or not the pension participant is legally entitled to the (erroneous) computed amounts of pension rendered in the pension information.

3006 AFM, 'Jaarverslag 2019' (april 2020) 37.

Bibliography

Literature (Articles, Books, Chapters, Papers, Reports)

J-C Abric, 'A theoretical and experimental approach to the study of social representations in a situation of interaction' in S Moscovici and S Farr (eds.), *Social representations* (Cambridge University Press, Cambridge 1984).

LF Ackert, BK Church and R Deaves, 'Emotion and financial markets' 88 Federal Reserve Bank of Atlanta Economic Review 33.

D Ackley, 'Retirement Benefits Communication Could Use Consumer-Oriented Approach' Pension World.

AFM, 'Jaarverslag 2019' (april 2020).

JR Agnew and LR Szykman, 'Asset Allocation and Information Overload: The Influence of Information Display, Asset Choice, and Investor Experience' 6 Journal of Behavioral Finance 57.

P Ahrend, W Förster and N Rößler, *Steuerrecht der betrieblichen Altersversorgung* (Schmidt, Köln 2017).

W Andreoni, 'Cross-Border Tax Issues of Pensions' 34 Intertax 245.

P Antolín and OM Fuentes Contreras, 'Communicating pension risk to DC scheme members: The Chilean case of a pension risk simulator,' (OECD Working Papers on Finance, Insurance and Private Pensions, no 28, OECD Working party on Private Pensions, 2012).

Aon, 'Survey Financial Pension Planning and Communication' (2020).

M Ap, 'The Future of Financial Advice Reforms: Restorting Public Trust and Confidence in Financial Advisers – an Unfinished Puzzle' 10 Canberra Law Review 188.

APEC-OECD, 'Integrated Checklist on Regulatory Reform: a Policy Instrument for Regulatory Quality, Competition Policy and Market Openness' (2008).

D Ariely and TS Wallsten, 'Seeking Subjective Dominance in Multidimensional Space: An Explanation of the Assymetric Dominance Effect' 63 Organizational Behavior and Human Decision Processes 223.

D Ariely, *Predictably irrational: the hidden forces that shape our decisions* (HarperCollins, New York 2008).

F Attneave, *Applications of information theory to psychology* (Holt, Rinehart and Winston, New York 1959).

Autoriteit Financiële Markten, 'Geef Nederlanders pensioeninzicht: werken aan vertrouwen door dichten van de verwachtingskloof' (2010).

JF Avery Jones, 'A Framework for Evaluating the Commission's Tax Proposals for Occupational Pensions in the European Union' 41 European Taxation.

JF Avery Jones, L De Broe and M Ellis, 'The Origins of Concepts and Expressions Used in the OECD Model and Their Adoption by States' British Tax Review 695.

RS Avi-Yonah, 'Back to the Future? The Potential Revival of Territoriality' 10 Bulletin for International Taxation 471.

S Bagshaw and R Bellomo, 'The need to reform our assessment of evidence from clinical trials: a commentary' 3 Philosophy, Ethics, and Humanities in Medicine 1.

A Bandura, 'Self-efficacy: Towards a unifying theory of behavioural change' 84 Psychological Review 191.

A Bandura, *Self-efficacy: The exercise of control* (New York, Freeman & Co 1997).

W Bank, 'Averting the old age crisis: policies to protect the old and promote growth' (1994).

J Banks and Z Oldfield, 'Understanding pensions: Cognitive function, numerical ability and retirement saving' 28 Fiscal Studies 143.

J Bäßler and R Schwarzer, 'Evaluación de la autoeficacia: Adaptación española de la escala de autoeficacia general [Measuring generalized self-beliefs: A Spanish adaptation of the General Self-Efficacy scale]' 2 Ansiedad y Estrés 1.

D Beck, *Qualifikationskonflikte im Internationalen Steuerrecht: Ursachenanalyse, Systematisierung und Lösungskonzepte* (Springer, Wiesbaden 2016).

J Bell, 'Legal Research and the Distinctiveness of Comparative Law' in M Van Hoecke (ed.), *Methodologies of Legal Research* (Hart Publishing, Oxford 2011).

H Berié and U Fink, 'Europas Sozialmodell – Die europäischen Sozialsysteme im Vergleich: Eine volkswirtschaftliche Analyse' (WISO Institut für Wirtschaft und Soziales GmbH, 2000).

J Binswanger and D Schunk, 'What is an adequate standard of living during retirement?' Journal of Pension Economics and Finance 203.

D Birk and R Wernsmann, 'Die Besteuerung der Aufwendungen für die Altersvorsorge und der Alterseinkommen' in B Rürup and F Ruland (eds.), *Alterssicherung und Besteuerung* (Gabler, Wiesbaden 2008).

D Birk, *Altersvorsorge und Alterseinkünfte im Einkommensteuerrecht: Verfassungsrechtliche Vorgaben, gesetzliche Regelungen, Neuordnungsmodelle* (Rechtsordnung und Steuerwesen, Schmidt, Köln 1987).

D Birk, 'Nachgelagerte Besteuerung in der betrieblichen Altersversorgung' Steuer und Wissenschaft.

LG Block and PA Keller, 'When to accentuate the negative: the effects of perceived efficacy and message framing on intentions to perform a health-related behavior' Journal of Marketing Research 192.

W Blomeyer, K Rolfs and K Otto, *Betriebsrentengesetz: BetrAVG* (C.H. Beck, München 2015).

C Bobbett and JF Avery Jones, 'Treaty Issues related to the Treatment of Cross-Border Pension Contributions and Benefits' 58 Bulletin for International Taxation.

TLJ Bod, *Pensioen en privaatrecht (dissertatie Nijmegen)* (H.D. Tjeenk Willink, Alphen aan den Rijn 1979).

JP Boer, *Sturende belastingheffer een monster? Juridische kanttekeningen bij fiscaal instrumentalisme en 'tax nudging'* (Sdu, Den Haag 2013).

AHH Bollen-Vandenboorn and others, 'ITEM Grenseffectenrapportage 2016, Dossier 1B: Belastingverdrag Nederland-Duitsland Pensioen' (2016).

AHH Bollen-Vandenboorn, 'Belastingverdrag Nederland-Duitsland' 11 MBB.

AHH Bollen-Vandenboorn, 'De vergeten grensarbeider en zijn nettopensioen' 09 MBB.

AHH Bollen-Vandenboorn, *De fiscale aspecten van pensioendeling bij echtscheiding* (Fiscaal Wetenschappelijke Reeks, SDU, Den Haag 2004).

AHH Bollen-Vandenboorn, H Niesten and S Kramer, 'ITEM Cross-Border Impact Assessment: Schemes relating to retirement ages in NL/BE/DE: a multidisciplinary analysis' (available online: https://www.maastrichtuniversity.nl/sites/default/files/dossiers2018/item-cross-border-impact-assessment-2018_dossier3-schemes-retirement-ages-nl-be-de-multidisciplinary-analysis.pdf 2018).

AH Börsch-Supan, 'Zur deutschen Diskussion eines Übergangs vom Umlage- zum Kapitaldeckungsverfahren in der gesetzlichen Rentenversicherung' 55 FinanzArchiv 400.

AH Börsch-Supan, F Heiss and J Winter, *Akzeptanzprobleme bei Rentenreformen: Wie die Bevölkerung überzeugt werden kann* (Deutsches Institut für Altersvorsorge, Köln 2004).

V Braithwaite, *Market in vice. Markets in virtue.* (The Federation Press, Leichhardt 2005).

JD Bransford and MK Johnson, 'Contextual prerequisites for understanding: Some investigations of comprehension and recall' 11 Journal of Verbal Learning and Verbal Behavior 717.

BT Broers, 'Driehoeksverhouding in de Pensioenwet' in AHH Bollen-Vandenboorn (ed.), *Pensioen en de belangrijkste toekomstvoorzieningen* (27 edn Fiscale Geschriften, SDU, Den Haag 2022).

M Browning and A Lusardi, 'Household Saving: Micro Theories and Micro Facts' 34 Journal of Economic Literature 1797.

M Brucks, 'The Effects of Product Class Knowledge on Information Search Behavior' Journal of Consumer Research 1.

R Brügelmann and W Fuest, *Besteuerung der Altersvorsorge und Alterseinkünfte: ein Vergleich verschiedener Formen der gesetzlichen und privaten Alterssicherung* (Beiträge zur Ordnungspolitiek Institut der deutschen Wirtschaft Köln, Deutscher Instituts-Verlag GmbH, Köln 2003).

E Brüggen, 'Tomorrow I will really start with my retirement planning: How to improve retirement decision making' Inaugural speech.

E Brüggen, T Post and K Schmitz, 'Interactivity in online pension planners enhances engagement with retirement planning – but not for everyone' 33 Journal of Services Marketing 488.

I.J.J. Burgers, 'Internationaal verdragsbeleid inzake pensioenen en lijfrenten: quo vado?' WFR.

RE Burnkrant and HR Unnava, 'Self-referencing: A strategy for increasing processing of message content' 15 Personality and Social Psychology Bulletin 628.

JT Cacioppo and RE Petty, 'The Need for Cognition' 42 Journal of Personality and Social Psychology 116.

L Calvert, J Campbell and P Sodini, 'Down or Out: Assessing the Welfare Costs of Household Investment Mistakes' Working Paper, Harvard University.

K Caminada and LGM Stevens, 'Instrumenteel fiscaal beleid: oorzaak en complexiteit en scheefgroei' WFR.

S Chaiken, 'The heuristic model of persuasion' in M Zanna, J Olson and C Herman (eds.), *Social influence: The Ontario Symposium* (Lawrence Erlbaum, Hillsdale 1987).

S Chaiken, 'Heuristic versus systematic information processing and the use of source versus message cues in persuasion' 39 Journal of personality and social psychology 752.

CESifo DICE Report, 'Bismarck versus Beveridge: Social Insurance Systems in Europe' 6 Journal for Institutional Comparisons.

R Chetty, A Looney and K Kroft, 'Salience and Taxation: Theory and Evidence' 99 American Economic Review 1145.

P Clausing, *Oudedagsvoorzieningen – Levensverzekering en Pensioen* (Preadvies voor de Algemene Vergadering van de Broederschap der Candidaat-Notarissen, Nijmegen 1973).

Commissie voor de Belastingherziening, 'Graag of niet, Rapport van de Commissie voor de Belastingherziening,' (Den Haag 1991).

WJ Congdon, JR Kling and S Mullainathan, *Policy and Choice: Public Finance through the Lens of Behavioral Economics* (Brookings Institution Press, Washington DC 2011).

T Cook and D Campbell, *Quasi-Experimentation: Design and Analysis for Field Settings* (Rand McNally, Chicago 1979).

A Cordewener and E Reimer, 'The future of most-favoured-nation treatment in EC tax law: did the ECJ pull the emergenc brake without real need?' 46 European Taxation 291.

JE Cramer, W Förster and F Ruland, *Handbuch Altersversorgung: gesetzliche, betriebliche und private Vorsorge in Deutschland* (Knapp, Frankfurt am Main 1998).

R Crawford and C O'Dea, 'The adequacy of wealth of those approaching retirement' (Institute for Fiscal Studies Reports, 2012).

R Cryer, T Hervey and B Sokhi-Bully, *Research methodologies in EU and International Law* (Hart Publishing, Oxford 2011).

J Cullis and A Lewis, 'Why people pay taxes: From a conventional economic model to a model of social convention' 18 Journal of Economic Psychology 305.

G Dannemann, 'Comparative Law: Study of Similarities or Differences?' in M Reimann and R Zimmermann (eds.), *Oxford Handbook of Comparative Law* (Oxford University Press, Oxford 2006).

A Davidson and RN Kantor, 'On the failure of readability formulas to define readable texts: a case study from adaptations' 17 Reading Research Quarterly 187.

FD Davis, 'Perceived Usefulness, Perceived Ease of Use, and User Acceptance of Information Technology' 13 MIS Quarterly.

L De Broe and R Neyt, 'European Union – Tax treatment of cross-border pensions under the OECD Model and EU law' 63 Bulletin for International Taxation.

PA de Cruz, *Modern Approach to Comparative Law* (Kluwer, Deventer 1993).

RMJM de Greef, *Fiscale pensioenbelemmeringen in de gemeenschappelijke markt* (Fiscale Wetenschappelijke Reeks, SDU, Den Haag 2004).

J De Bresser, M Knoef and L Kools, 'Cutting One's Coat According to One's Cloth: How did the Great Recession affect retirement resources and expenditure goals?' 05/2018-029 Netspar Academic Series.

J De Coninck, 'Behavioural Economics and Legal Research' in M van Hoecke (ed.), *Methodologies of legal research: which kind of method for what kind of discipline?* (Hart Publishing, Oxford 2011).

D De Vaus, *Research Design in Social Research* (Sage, London 2001).

H Deisler, 'Die Alterssicherung der Landwirte' in B Rürup and F Ruland (eds.), *Alterssicherung und Besteuerung* (Gabler, Wiesbaden 2008).

W Devroe, *Rechtsvergelijking in een context van europeanisering en globalisering* (Acco, Leuven 2010).

S Dhami, *The Foundations of Behavioral Economics Analysis* (Oxford University Press, 2016).

B Dieleman and P van Straten, 'Individuele internationale waardeoverdracht kan veel beter' 6 PensioenMagazine.

B Dieleman, 'Zijn de Nederlandse fiscale regels voor grensoverschrijdende overdracht van pensioen in strijd met EU-recht?' PensioenMagazine.

B Dieleman, 'Internationale aspecten van pensioen' in AHH Bollen-Vandenboorn and others (eds.), *Pensioen en de belangrijkste toekomstvoorzieningen* (SDU, Den Haag 2022).

B Dieleman, 'Wet toekomst pensioenen aangenomen: een analyse van de fiscale aspecten' MBB.

GJB Dietvorst, 'Geblokkeerd banksparen: evolutie of revolutie?' WFR.

GJB Dietvorst, 'Geblokkeerd banksparen: het vervolg' WFR.

GJB Dietvorst, 'Lijfrenten' in AHH Bollen-Vandenboorn (ed.), *Pensioen en de belangrijkste toekomstvoorzieningen* (27 edn Fiscale Geschriften, SDU, Den Haag 2022).

GJB Dietvorst, *De drie pijlers van toekomstvoorzieningen en belastingen* (Kluwer, Deventer 1994).

P Dolan, T Peasgood and M White, 'Do We Really Know What Makes Us Happy? A Review of the Economic Literature on the Factors Associated with Subjective Well-Being' 29 Journal of Economic Psychology 94.

M Dolls and others, 'Do retirement savings increase in response to information about retirement and expected pensions?' (CESifo Working Paper 6842, 2018).

S Dommes, *Pensionen im Recht der Doppelbesteuerungsabkommen* (Schriftenreihe zum Internationalen Steuerrecht, Linde, Wien 2012).

DR Donaldson, *Development of a Scale for Measuring Perceptions of Trustworthiness for Digitized Archival Documents* (2015).

DR Donaldson, 'The Digitized Archival Document Trustworthiness Scale' 11 International Journal of Digital Curation 252.

C Dorenkamp, *Nachgelagerte Besteuerung von Einkommen: Besteuerungsaufschub für investierte Reinvermögensmehrungen* (Duncker & Humblot, Berlin 2004).

G Dreher, *Das Alterseinkünftegesetz: Systematische Darstellung und verfassungsrechtliche Zweifelsfragen* (Finanz- und Steuerrecht in Deutschland und Europa, Peter Lang, Frankfurt am Main 2006).

C Dudel and J Schmied, 'Pension adequacy standards: An empirical estimation strategy and results for the United States and Germany' (MPIDR Working Paper WP 2019-003, 2019).

H Dürkop, *Alterssicherung in der EG: Eine kritische Bestandsaufnahme der Alterssicherungssysteme für Arbeitnehmer in der Europäischen Gemeinschaft* (Peter Lang, Bern 1992).

E Eberhardt and others, 'Activating pension plan participants: investment and assurance frames' Design paper 72 Netspar Industry Paper Series.

W Eberhardt, W Bruine de Bruin and J Strough, 'Age differences in financial decision making: The benefits of more experience and less negative emotions' 32 Journal of Behavioral Decision Making 1.

E Eberle, 'The method and role of Comparative law' 8 Washington University Global Studies Law Review 451.

T Eckerle, 'Altersvorsorge und Lebensversicherung' in HJ Feyerabend (ed.), *Besteuerung privater Kapitalanlagen* (C.H. Beck, München 2009).

E Eichenhofer, H Rische and W Schmähl (eds.), *Handbuch der gesetzlichen Rentenversicherung SGB VI* (Luchterhand, Köln 2012).

EIOPA, 'Good practices on information provision for DC schemes: enabling occupational DC scheme members to plan for retirement,' (2013) [EIOPA-BoS-13/010].

EIOPA, 'Technical Advice on the Development of Pension Tracking Systems' (2021) [EIOPA-BoS-21-535].

AB Eisingerich and SJ Bell, 'Perceived Service Quality and Customer Trust: Does Enhancing Customers' Service Knowledge Matter?' 10 Journal of Service Research 256.

S Elling and L Lentz, 'Maatwerk in pensioencommunicatie' Design Paper 126 Netspar Industry Paper Series.

Employee Benefits Research Institute, 'Participant Education: Actions and Outcomes' 169 Issue Brief.

C Engel and others, 'Verhaltenswissenschaftliche Analyse: eine Gebrauchsanweisung für Juristen' in C Engel (ed.), *Recht und Verhalten* (Mohr Siebeck, 2007).

PHJ Essers, 'Pensionado's in Duitsland met in Nederland opgebouwde pensioenrechten en het nieuwe verdrag Nederland-Duitsland' in B Starink and M Visser (eds.), *Ondernemend met pensioen (Dietvorstbundel)* (Kluwer, Deventer 2015).

L Festinger and N Maccoby, 'On resistance to persuasive communications' 68 Journal of Abnormal and Social Psychology 359.

M Fishbein and I Ajzen's, *Belief, attitude, theory and research* (Addison-Wesley, Massachusetts 1975).

LR Flynn and RE Goldsmith, 'A Short, Reliable Measure of Subjective Knowledge' 46 Journal of Business Research 57.

GVG, 'Forderung nach mehr Transparanz in der Altersvorsorge' Pressemitteilung 07/2017.

W Förster and others, *Betriebsrentengesetz: Gesetz zur Verbesserung der betrieblichen Altersversorgung mit zivil-, arbeits- und steuerrechtlichen Vorschriften und Versorgungsausgleich* (Beck'sche Kompakt-Kommentare, C.H. Beck, München 2014).

W Förster and S Rechtenwald, 'Die betriebliche und private Altersvorsorge' in F Ruland and B Rürup (eds.), *Alterssicherung und Besteuerung* (Gabler, Wiesbaden 2008).

N Foster, *Foster on EU Law* (3rd edn Oxford University Press, Oxford 2011).

G Frankenberg, 'Critical Comparisons: Re-thinking Comparative Law' Harvard International Law Journal.

M Friedman, *A Theory of the Consumption Function* (Princeton University Press, New Jersey 1957).

K Friedrich, B Kovac and T Werner, 'Beitragsorientierte Leistungszusage und Beitragszusage mit Mindestleistung – strikt getrennt oder doch eng miteinander verwandt?' BetriebsBerater.

LL Fuller, *The morality of law* (Yale University Press, New Haven-Londen 1969).

E Fuß, 'Der Schutz des Vertrauens auf Rechtskontinuität im deutschen Verfassungsrecht und europäischen Gemeinschaftsrecht' in W Grewe, H Rupp and H Schneider (eds.), *Europäische Gerichtsbarkeit und nationale Verfassungsgerichtsbarkeit* (Nomos, Baden-Baden 1981).

X Gabaix and D Laibson, 'Shrouded Attributes, Consumer Myopia, and Information Suppression in Competitive Markets' 121 The Quarterly Journal of Economics 505.

C Gillion, 'The ILO and Pensions' (ILO: Social Security Department, Geneva 1999).

R Giora, 'On the Informativeness Requirement' 12 Journal of Pragmatics 547.

G Glaser, *Besteuerungszeitpunkte in der Zusatzversorgung: Verfassungsfragen und einkommenssteuersystematische Einordnung* (Verlag Dr. Kovač, Hamburg 2009).

R Gomm, *Social Research Methodology* (Palgrave Macmillan, Houndmills 2008).

O Gough and C Niza, 'Retirement saving choices: review of the literature and policy implications' 4 Journal of Population Ageing 97.

S Goverts and M Knoll, 'Anforderungen an Basisrentenprodukte ("Rürup-Rente") vor dem Hintergrund des BMF-Schreibens vom 24.2.2005' DStR 946.

AG Greenwald, 'Cognitive learning, cognitive responses to persuasion, and attitude change' in

AG Greenwald, TC Brock and TM Ostrom (eds.), *Psychological foundations of attitudes* (Academic Press, New York 1968).

HP Grice, 'Logic and Conversation' in P Cole and J Morgen (eds.), *Syntax and Semantics: Speech Acts* (Academic Press, New York 1957).

J Hage, 'Rule consistency' 19 Law and Philosophy 369.

D Halstead and others, 'The Customer Orientation of Financial Advisers' Financial Literacy and the Limits of Financial Decision-Making 246.

P Hanks, T Hill Long and L Urdang, *Collins English Dictionary* (Collins London 1979).

P Harris and DL Oliver, *International Commercial Tax* (2nd edn Cambridge Tax Law Series, Cambridge University Press, Cambridge 2020).

DJ Hauser, PC Ellwsworth and R Gonzalez, 'Are Manipulation Checks Necessary?' Frontiers in Psychology

R Haveman and others, 'Assessing the Maintenance of Savings Sufficiency over the First Decade of Retirement' 14 International Tax and Public Finance 481.

E Heissmann, *Betriebliche Unterstützungskassen* (Schmidt, Köln 1966).

C Herrmann, G Heuer and A Raupach, *Einkommensteuer- und Körperschaftsteuergesetz: EStG KStG* (Dr. Otto Schmidt, Köln Aktualisierung 2018).

K Heubeck and M Seybold, 'Zur Besteuerung der betrieblichen Altersversorgung nach dem Alterseinkünftegesetz: Übergang vom Drei Säulen- zum Drei-Schichten-Modell nur halbwegs gelungen,' DB 592

L Hinnekens, 'The Monti Report: the uphill task of harmonizing direct tax systems of EC Member States' 1 EC Tax Review.

J Hoewe, 'Manipulation Check' in J Matthes, CS Davis and RF Potter (eds.), *The International Encyclopedia of Communication Research Methods* (Wiley-Blackwell, 2017).

R Höfer, 'Die Neuregelung des Betriebsrentenrechts durch das Altersvermögensgesetz (AVmG)' 21 DB 1145.

JHP Hoffmeyer-Zlotnik and U Warner, 'How to Measure Education in Cross-National Comparison: A Matrix of Education as a New Instrument' (European Conference on Quality in Survey Statistics 2006).

HJ Hofstra, *Eenvoud in de belastingheffing* (De Naamloze Vennotschap, 1947).

R Holzmann and R Hinz, 'Old-Age Income Support in the 21st Century: an International Perspective on Pension Systems and Reform' (The World Bank, Washington D.C. 2005).

HSBC, 'The Future of Retirement. A Balancing Act. Published by HSBC Holdings plc. London' (2015).

J Huber, JW Payne and C Puto, 'Adding Asymmetrically Dominated Alternatives: Violations of Regularity and the Similarity Hypothesis' 9 Journal of Consumer Research 90.

H Hügelschäffer and others, *Handbuch Alterssicherung* (C.F. Müller, Heidelberg 2006).

AA Hung, N Clancy and J Dominitz, 'Investor Knowledge and Experience with Investment Advisers and Broker-Dealers' in OS Mitchell and A Lusardi (eds.), *Financial Literacy: Implications for Retirement Security and the Financial Marketplace* (Oxford University Press, Oxford 2011).

J Husa, 'About the Methodology of Comparative Law – Some Comments Concerning the Wonderland' (Working Paper, Faculty of Law, Maastricht University, 2007).

S Issacharoff, 'The Difficult path from observation to prescription" 77 New York University Law Review.

ILO, 'The ILO Multi-Pillar pension model: Building equitable and sustainable pension systems' <https://www.social-protection.org/gimi/RessourcePDF.action?id=55234>.

MCD Janse and EHM Janssen, 'Werknemerspensioen in de loonsfeer, beroepspensioen en nettopensioen' in AHH Bollen-Vandenboorn (ed.), *Pensioen en de belangrijkste toekomstvoorzieningen* (27 edn Fiscale Geschriften, SDU, Den Haag 2022).

M Jerusalem and R Schwarzer, 'Self-efficacy as a resource factor in stress appraisal processes.' in R Schwarzer (ed.), *Self-efficacy: Thought control of action* (Hemisphere, Washington DC 1992).

D Johnson and K Grayson, 'Cognitive and affective trust in service relationships' 58 Journal of Business Research 500.

P Johnson, 'The taxation of occupational and pricate pensions in Western Europe' in J Mortenson (ed.), *The future of pensions in the European Community* (Brussel 1992).

C Jolls, 'Behavioral Economic Analysis of Redistributive Legal Rules' Faculty Scholarship Series 1340.

M Jung, 'Berufständische Versorgung' in F Ruland and B Rürup (eds.), *Alterssicherung und Besteuerung* (Gabler, Wiesbaden 2008).

E Kades, 'The Laws of Complexity & the Complexity of Laws: The Implications of Computational Complexity Theory for the Law' 49 Rutgers Law Review 403.

J Kaempfe, *Die Systemfunktionen privater Altersvorsorge im Gesamtsystem sozialer Alterssicherung* (Nomos, Baden-Baden 2005).

F Kafka, *Het proces* (Atheneum, Amsterdam 2012).

D Kahneman and A Tversky, 'Prospect theory: An analysis of decision under risk' 47 Econometrica 263.

D Kahneman and S Frederick, 'Representativeness revisited: Attribute substitution in intuitive judgment' in T Gilovich, D Griffin and D Kahneman (eds.), *Heuristics and biases: The psychology of intuitive judgment* (Cambridge University Press, New York 2002).

D Kahneman, *Thinking, fast and slow* (Farrar, Straus and Giroux, New York 2011).

L Kaplow, 'An economic analysis of legal transitions' Harvard Law Review.

PJG Kapteyn and P VerLoren van Themaat, *Introduction to the Law of the European Communities* (3rd33 edn Kluwer Law International, The Hague 1998).

D Katz, 'The functional approach to the study of attitudes' 24 Public Opinion Querterly 163.

P Kavelaars, 'Conserverende aanslagen en verdragen (1)' NTFR-B 7.

P Kavelaars, 'Conserverende aanslagen en verdragen (2)' NTFR-B 13.

P Kavelaars, 'Arbeidsinkomsten en verdragsbeleid' MBB.

C Keinki and others, 'Understandability of Patient Information Booklets for Patients with Cancer' 33 Journal of Cancer Education 517.

H Keller, *Praxishandbuch Finanzwissen: Steuern – Altersvorsorge – Rechtsfragen* (Springer Gabler, Wiesbaden 2013).

ECCM Kemmeren, 'Sources of EU law for European tax integration: Well-known and alternative legal instruments' in D Weber (ed.), *Traditional and alternative routes to European Tax Integration* (IBFD, Amsterdam 2010).

D Kiesewetter and others, *Optimierungsmöglichkeiten bei den bestehenden steuer- und sozialversicherungsrechtlichen Förderregelungen der betrieblichen Altersversorgung* (Würzburg University Press, Würzurg 2016).

P Kirchhof, H Söhn and R Mellinghof, *Einkommensteuergesetz: Kommentar zum EStG* (C.F. Müller, Heidelberg 2018).

E Kirchler, 'Differential representations of taxes: Analysis of free associations and judgments of five employment groups ' 27 Journal of Socio-Economics 117.

E Kirchler, *The Economic Psychology of Tax Behaviour* (Cambridge University Press, New York 2007).

L Klapper and GA Panos, 'Financial literacy and retirement planning: the Russian case' 10 Journal of Pension Economics and Finance 599.

GR Klare, *The Measurement of Readability* (Iowa State University Press, Ames, Iowa 1963).

GR Klare, 'Assessing readability' 10 Reading Research Quarterly 62.

R Klein, 'Die Deckungsmitel der betrieblichen Altersversorgung in 2019' 5 BetrAV 429.

CM Kleinhuis and E Niemeijer, 'Wet en werkelijkheid. Bevindingen uit evaluaties van wetten' (WODC, Den Haag 2008).

B Kloosterman, UP Meyer and D Laruelle, 'Welk buurland is een fiscaal paradijs voor gepensioneerden?' Over de grens

S Kluth and M Gasche, 'Ersatzraten in der Gesetzlichen Rentenversicherung' 235 Jahrbücher für Nationalökonomie und Statistik.

B Knobbe-Keuk, 'Fundamental Freedoms Enshrined in the EC Treaty by Discriminatory Tax Provisions – Ban and Justification' EC Tax Review.

M Knoef and others, 'Measuring retirement savings adequacy: developing a multi-pillar approach in the Netherlands' 15 Journal of Pension Economics and Finance 55.

M Knoef and others, 'De toereikendheid van pensioenopbouw na de crisis en pensioenhervormingen' 68 Netspar Industry Paper Series.

M Knoef, 'Dromen over een goed pensioen: origami en datascience' Inaugural speech.

G Kofler, 'Das Verhältnis zwischen primären und sekundärem Unionsrecht im direkten Steuerrecht' in M Lang and C Weinzierl (eds.), *Europäisches Steuerrecht (Festschrift Rödler)* (Linde Verlag, Wien 2010).

G Kofler, 'Ist der Spuk des Europäischen Steuerrechts bald vorbei?' in W Schön and C Heber (eds.), *Grundfragen des Europäischen Steuerrechts* (Springer, Berlin Heidelberg 2015).

T Koopmans, 'De rol van de wetgever' in HCF Schoordijk (ed.), *Honderd Jaar Rechtsleven* (W.E.J. Tjeenk Willink, Zwolle 1970).

H Krabbe, 'Das neue OECD-Musterabkommen und die deutsche Abkommenspolitik' StbJb 31.

JM Krijnen, M Zeelenberg and SM Breugelmans, 'Decision importance as a cue for deferral' 10 Judgment and Decision Making 407.

SH Kuiper and MM Koomen, 'Te veel pensioen: terugvorderen, corrigeren? Zes gezichtspunten' PensioenMagazine 35.

A Kuyper, *Proeve van pensioenregeling voor werklieden en huns gelijken* (Wormser, Amsterdam 1905).

F Lamoreux, 'The retroactivity of Community acts in the case law of the Court of justice' Common Market Law Review.

M Lang and F Brugger, 'The role of the OECD Commentary in tax treaty interpretation' 23 Australian Tax Forum 95.

M Lang, 'Das EuGH-Urteil in der Rechtssache D. – Gerät der Motor der Steuerharmonisierung ins Stottern' 14 SWI 365.

M Lang, 'Direct taxation: is the ECJ heading in a new direction?' 46 European Taxation 421.

FL Leeuw and H Schmeets, *Empirical Legal Research: A Guidance Book for Lawyers, Legislators and Regulators* (Edward Elgar, Cheltenham 2016).

LR Lentz and HLW Pander Maat, 'Functional analysis for Document Design' 51 Technical Communication 387.

L Lentz, 'Pensioencommunicatie: stel niet het middel maar het doel centraal!' 5 Tijdschrift voor Pensioenvraagstukken.

LR Lentz, ML Nell and HLW Pander Maat, 'Naar een model voor pensioencommunicatie' Netspar Design Paper 1.

High Level Forum on Capital Markets Union, 'A new Vision for Europe's capital markets: Final Report of the High Level Forum on the Capital Markets Union' (2020).

A Lewis, 'Perception of tax rates' 6 British Tax Review 358.

M Ligas, 'Personalizing Services Encounters: The Role of Service Provider Actions in Developing Customer Trust' 25 Services Marketing Quarterly 33.

G Loewenstein, T O'Donoghue and M Rabin, 'Projection bias in predicting future utility' 118 Quarterly Journal of Economics 1209.

C Logan, *Evaluation research in crime and delinquency: a reappraisal* (Journal of Criminal Law, Criminology and Policy Studies, 1972).

D Lovric, 'A Constitution Friendly to International Law: Germany and its Volkerrechtsfreundlichkeit' 25 Australian Year Book of International Law 75.

J Lüdicke, *Überlegungen zur deutschen DBA-Politik* (Nomos, Baden-Baden 2008).

J Lüdicke, 'Anmerkungen zur deutschen Verhandlungsgrundlage für Doppelbesteuerungsabkommen' IStR.

T Lühn, 'Quellenstaatsbesteuerung von Renten und Ruhegehältern im neuen DBA mit den Niederlanden – Niederländische Begünstigungsregelung ab 2016' 4 IWB.

A Lusardi and OS Mitchell, 'Financial Literacy and Planning: Implications for Retirement Wellbeing' Working Paper, Pension Research Council, Wharton School, University of Pennsylvania.

A Lusardi and OS Mitchell, 'Financial Literacy and Retirement Preparedness: Evidence and Implications for Financial Education' Business Economics 35.

A Lusardi and OS Mitchell, 'Financial Literacy around the world: an overview' 10 Journal of Pension Economics and Finance 497.

A Lusardi, 'Information, Expectations, and Savings for Retirement' in H Aaron (ed.), *In Behavioral Dimensions of Retirement Economics* (Brookings Institution Press, Washington DC 1999).

E Lutjens and B Dieleman, 'Grensoverschrijdende waardeoverdracht van pensioen: zijn Nederlandse regels in strijd met EU-recht?' Tijdschrift voor Arbeidsrecht in Context.

E Lutjens, *Asser-serie 7-XI – Pensioen (Bijzondere overeenkomsten)* (Asser-serie, Wolters Kluwer, Deventer 2019).

E Lutjens, *Pensioenvoorziening voor werknemers, juridische beschouwingen voor werknemers* (W.E.J. Tjeenk Willink, Zwolle 1989).

E Lutjens, *De PSW, wetshistorisch overzicht en commentaar* (Kluwer, Deventer 1998).

Quinten M. and Sona B., 'Die Grenze der Riester-Förderung bei einem Wohnsitz im Ausland' 2 RVaktuell 44.

RH Maatman, 'Pensioenfondsen en zorgplichten: uitdijen of indammen?,' in D Busch and others (eds.), *Zorgplicht in de financiële sector* (Serie Onderneming en Recht, Kluwer, Deventer 2020).

OA Mac and others, 'Web-Based Health Information Following the Renewal of the Cervical Screening Program in Australia: Evaluation of Readability, Understandability, and Credibility' 22 Journal of Medical Internet Research.

AR Mackor, 'Legal Doctrine as a Non-Normative Discipline' Recht en Methode.

J Marshall and S Butterworth, 'Pension Reform in the EU: the Unexploded Time Bomb in the Single Market' 37 Common Market Law Review 739.

G Mastrobuoni, 'Do Better-Informed Workers Make Better Retirement Choice? A Test Based on the Social Security Statement' Mimeo, Collegio Carlo Alberto.

MJ Metzger, 'Making sense of credibility on the Web: Models for evaluating online information and recommendations for future research' 58 Journal of the American Society for Information Science and Technology 2078.

C Mihart, 'Impact of Integrated Marketing Communication on Consumer Behaviour: Effects on Consumer Decision – Making Process' 4 International Journal of Marketing Studies 121.

DG Millhouse, 'Best Interest Duties of Financial Advisers – More Law, More Confusion' Enterprise Governance eJournal: Centre for Commercial Law, Bond University.

OS Mitchell and A Lusardi, 'The Outlook for Financial Literacy' in OS Mitchell and A Lusardi (eds.), *Financial Literacy: Implications for Retirement Security and the Financial Marketplace* (Oxford University Press, Oxford 2011).

O Mitchell, 'Worker Knowledge of Pensions Provisions' 6 Journal of Labor Economics 21.

F Modigliani and R Brumberg, 'Utility analysis and the consumption function: An interpretation of cross-section data' in K Kurihara (ed.), *PostKeynesian Economics* (Rutgers University Press, New Brunswick 1954).

D Moore, *Survey of Financial Literacy in Washington State: Knowledge, Behavior, Attitudes, and Experiences* (Social and Economic Sciences Research Center, Washington State University, 2003).

SG Moore, 'Attitude Predictability and Helpfulness in Online Reviews: The Role of Explained Actions and Reactions' 42 Journal of Consumer Research 30.

D Morales and M Kastelein, 'Europese Commissie zit Nederland op de huid bij grensoverschrijdende waardeoverdracht' PensioenMagazine.

JM Morton, 'Qualitative Objectives of Financial Accounting: A Comment on Relevance and Understandability' 12 Journal of Accounting Research 288.

S Moscovici, *La Psychanalyse, son image et son public* (Presse Universitaire de France, Paris 1961).

S Moscovici, 'The phenomenon of social representations' in S Moscovici and G Duveen (eds.), *Social representations: Explorations in social psychoogy* (New York University Press, New York 2001).

F Müller-Gatermann, 1032 (1036). 'Aktuelle deutsche Abkommenspolitik' 94 FR 1032.

J Murray, TE Webb and S Wheatley, 'Encountering law's complexity' in J Murray, TE Webb and

M Myßen and others, *Handbuch Zulagenförderung: steuerlich begünstigte Altersvorsorge* (C.F. Müller, Heidelberg 2006).

RG Netemeyer and others, 'How Am I Doing? Perceived Financial Well-Being, Its Potential Antecedents, and Its Relation to Overall Well-Being' 45 Journal of Consumer Research 68.

RECM Niessen, 'Instrumentalisme en belastingrecht' WFR.

H Niesten and S Kramer, 'Weigering fiscale aftrek verplichte pensioenbijdragen aan niet-inwoners strijdig met EU-recht' – Maandblad BelastingBeschouwingen 371.

M Oderkerk, *De preliminaire fase van het rechtsvergelijkend onderzoek* (Ars Aequi Libri, Nijmegen 1999).

M Oderkerk, 'The Importance of Context: Selecting Legal Systems in Comparative Legal Research' 48 NILR 293.

OECD, 'Improving the Quality of Laws and Regulations: Economic, Legal, and Managerial Techniques' (1994) [OCDE/GD(94)59].

OECD, 'Recommendation of the Council on Improving the Quality of Government Regulation' (1995) [C(95)21/FINAL].

OECD, 'Revised Taxonomy for Pensions Plans, Pension Funds and Pension Entitities' (2002).

OECD, 'Recommendation of the Council of the OECD on Regulatory Policy and Governance' (2012).

OECD, 'OECD Pensions Outlook' (2016).

OECD, 'Pensions at a Glance 2017: OECD and G20 Indicators' (2017) <https://read.oecd-ilibrary.org/social-issues-migration-health/pensions-at-a-glance-2017_pension_glance-2017-en#page3>.

H Oost and A Markenhof, *Een onderzoek voorbereiden* (HB-uitgevers, Baarn 2007).

A Orücü, 'Methodology of comparative law' in J Smits (ed.), *Elgar Encyclopedia of Comparative Law* (Edward Elgar, Cheltenham 2012).

E Örücü, 'Developing Comparative Law' in E Örücü and D Nelken (eds.), *Comparative Law* (Hart Publishing, Oxford 2007).

L Osterloh, K Schmidt and H Weber, *Staat, Wirtschaft, Finanzverfassung.: Festschrift für Peter Selmer zum 70. Geburtstag* (Schriften zum Öffentlichen Recht, Duncker & Humblot, Berlin 2004).

T Paintner and J Melchior, 'Das Gesetz zur Umsetzung steuerlicher EU-Vorgaben sowie zur Änderung steuerlicher Vorschriften im Überblick' 13 DStR 625.

RM Perloff and TC Brock, 'And thinking makes it so: Cognitive responses to persuasion' in ME Roloff and GR Miller (eds.), *Persuasion: New directions in theory and research* (Sage, Beverly Hills (California) 1980).

RE Petty and JT Cacioppo, *Communication and persuasion: Central and peripheral routes to attitude change* (Springer, New York 1986).

RE Petty and JT Cacioppo, 'The Elaboration Likelihood Model of Persuasion' 19 Advances in Experimental Social Psychology 123.

RE Petty and others, 'To think or not to think? Exploring two routes to persuasion' in TC Brock and MC Green (eds.), *Persuasion: Psychological insights and perspectives* (2nd edn Sage Publications, Thousand Oaks 2005).

RE Petty and others, 'To Think or Not to Think: Exploring Two Routes to Persuasion' in TC Brock and MC Green (eds.), *Persuasion: Psychological insights and perspectives* (Sage, Thousand Oaks 2005).

RE Petty and others, 'Historical foundations of the cognitive response approach to attitudes and persuasion' in RE Petty, TM Ostrom and TC Brock (eds.), *Cognitive responses in persuasion* (Lawrence Erlbaum, Hillsdale 1981).

RE Petty, C Haugtvedt and SM Smith, 'Elaboration as a determinant of attitude strength: Creating attitudes that are persistent, resistant and predictive of behavior' in RE Petty and JA Krosnick (eds.), *Attitude strength: Antecendents and consequences* (Lawrence Erlbaum, Mahwah 1995).

W Pintens, *Inleiding tot de rechtsvergelijking* (Universitaire Pers Leuven, Leuven 1998).

B Pokol, *The concept of law: the multi-layered legal system* (Rejtjel Edition, Budapest 2001).

Economic Policy Committee and Social Protection Committee, 'Interim Joint Report on pensions' (2010).

P Popelier, 'Beginselen van behoorlijke wetgeving in de rechtspraak' 1995 Tijdschrift voor Privaatrecht (BE) 1049.

R Portner, 'Rechtsvergleichende Qualifizierung ausländischer Altersversorgungspläne/-einrichtungen' 44 BB 2652

R Portner, 'Steuerrechtliche Aspekte der betrieblichen Altersversorgung bei international mobilen Arbeitnehmern' 44 BB 351.

R Portner, 'Besteuerung der Auszahlung aus einem U.S.-Altersversorgungsplan – selbst wenn die Beiträge ausschließlich nach U.S.-Steuerrecht gefördert sind und die Summe der eingezahlten Beiträge unter dem Auszahlungsbetrag liegt?' 20 BetriebsBerater 1175.

FPG Pötgens and E Kool, 'The Relationship between Tax Treaties and Protective Tax Assessments Issued in Respect of Pensions and Annuities upon Emigration: Pacta sunt servanda and Compartmentalization' 58 European Taxation.

FPG Pötgens and HM Kappelle, 'Over conserverende aanslagen, belastingverdragen en reparatiewetgeving: de geschiedenis lijkt zich te herhalen' WFR.

FPG Pötgens, 'Conserverende aanslag bij emigratie van pensioen- en lijfrentegerechtigde (deels) gesauveerd' 11 NTFR Beschouwingen 19.

FPG Pötgens, 'Conserverende aanslag pensioen (niet) akkoord' NTFR-B.

FPG Pötgens, 'Notitie Fiscaal Verdragsbeleid 2011 en arbeidsinkomsten' 119 TFO.

H Prast and F Teppa, 'The Power of Percentage: Quantitative Framing of Pension Income Communication' 2017 CentER Discussion Paper (Tilburg Center for Economic Research).

H Prast and F Teppa, 'Pensioenperceptie: de non-neutraliteit van kwantitatieve communicatie' 21 TPV.

FAG Prats, 'The Tax Treatment of Cross-Border Pensions from an EC Law Perspective' 41 European Taxation.

H Purton, 'European Welfare States in the 1990's: An Economic Analysis of the Challenges and Efforts at Reform' (CEPS Research Report no. 19, 1996).

JC Reitz, 'How to Do Comparative Law?' 46 American Journal of Comparative Law.

C Richter, *Die Besteuerung grenzüberschreitender Altersversorgung in der EU* (Rechtsordnung und Steuerwesen, Dr. Otto Schmidt, Köln 2010).

C Rickwood and L White, 'Pre-purchase decisionmaking for a complex service: retirement planning' 23 Journal of Services Marketing 145.

SY Rieh, 'Judgment of information quality and cognitive authority in the Web' 53 Journal of the American Society for Information Science and Technology 145.

K Ripken, 58 Baylor L Rev 139,160-63 (2006). 'The Dangers and Drawbacks of the Disclosure Antidote: Toward a More Substantive Approach to Securities Regulation' 58 Baylor Law Review.

A Risthaus, 'Steuerliche Fördermöglichkeiten für eine zusätzliche private Altersvorsorge nach dem Altersvermögensgesetz (AVmG)' 24 DB 1269

A Risthaus, 'JStG 2007: Günstigerprüfung innerhalb der Günstigerprüfung für Rürup-Renten-beiträge' DB 2773.

A Ritchie and others, 'Transforming consumer information' 18 British Actuarial Journal.

W Rombach and C Wirth, *Alterssicherung der Landwirte* (Haufe, Freiburg im breisgau 1995).

JD Rosenberg, 'The Psychology of Taxes: Why They Drive Us Crazy, and How We Can Make Them Sane' 16 Virginia Tax Review.

P Rossi, M Lipsey and H Freeman, *Evaluation: A Systematic Approach* (Sage, San Fransisco 2003).

J Rückert, 'Entstehung und Vorläufer der gesetzlichen Rentenversicherung' in F Ruland (ed.), *Handbuch der gesetzlichen Rentenversicherung: Festschrift aus Anlaß des 100jährigen Bestehens der gesetzlichen Rentenversicherung* (Luchterhand, Neuwied 1990).

F Ruland, 'Die Beambtenversorgung' in F Ruland and B Rürup (eds.), *Alterssicherung und Besteuerung* (Gabler, Wiesbaden 2008).

F Ruland, 'Rentenversicherung' in F Ruland and B Rürup (eds.), *Alterssicherung und Besteuerung* (Gabler, Wiesbaden 2008).

F Ruland, 'Überblick über die Alterssicherung in Deutschland' in B Rürup and F Ruland (eds.), *Alterssicherung und Besteuerung* (Gabler, Wiesbaden 2008).

B Rürup and M Myßen, 'Die steuerlich geförderte private Altersvorsorge' in B Rürup and F Ruland (eds.), *Alterssicherung und Besteuerung* (Gabler, Wiesbaden 2008).

CR Sahm, MD Shapiro and J Slemrod, 'Check in the Mail or More in the Paycheck: Does the Effectiveness of Fiscal Stimulus Depend on How It Is Delivered?' 4 American Economic Journal: Economic Policy 216.

G Samuel, *Epistemology and Method in Law* (Ashgate, Alderhot 2003).

O Sandrock, *Uber Sinn und Methode der zivilistischen Rechtsvergleichung* (Alfred Metzner Verlag, Frankfurt a.M./Berlin 1966).

W Scheffler and S Kölbl, 'Besteuerung der betrieblichen Altersversorgung auf Ebene des Arbeitnehmers im internationalen Kontext' Internationales Steuerrecht.

A Schepanski and T Shearer, 'A prospect theory account of the income tax withholding phenomenon' 63 Organizational Behavior and Human Decision Processes 174.

W Schmähl, 'Steuerliche Behandlung von Altersvorsorge und Alterseinkünften' Wirtschaftsdienst 22.

M Schmitthoff, 'The science of comparative law' Cambridge Law Journal.

G Schmölders, *Das Irrationale in der öffentlichen Finanzwirtschaft* (Suhrkamp, Frankfurt am Main 1960).

G Schmölders, 'Survey research in public finance: A behavioural approach to fiscal theory' 25 Public Finance 300.

L Schobert, *Die reine Beitragszusage: Überlegungen zur Stärkung der arbeitgeberfinanzierten betrieblichen Altersversorgung* (Schriften zum Sozial- und Arbeitsrecht, Duncker & Humblot, Berlin 2017).

J Scholz, A Seshadri and S Khitatrakun, 'Are Americans saving 'optimally' for retirement?' 114 Journal of Political Economy 607.

S Scholz, *Besteuerung der betrieblichen Altersversorgung in Europa* (Deutscher Universitäts-Verlag, Wiesbaden 2006).

K Schönemann, M Dietrich and D Kiesewetter, 'Verbessert das Eigenheimrentenmodell die Integration der eigengenutzten Immobilie in die Altersvorsorge?' 2 StuW 107.

PH Schönewille, 'Belastingen en pensioenen in EU-context' in AHH Bollen-Vandenboorn (ed.), *Pensioen en de belangrijkste toekomstvoorzieningen* (Fiscale Geschriften nr 27 SDU, Den Haag 2020).

EAP Schouten, 'Europese Commissie daagt Nederland voor Europese Hof om fiscale eisen grensoverschrijdende waardeoverdracht' PensioenMagazine.

A Schrauwen, 'Sources of EU law for integration in taxation' in D Weber (ed.), *Traditional and Alternative Routes to European Tax Integration* (IBFD, Amsterdam 2010).

PH Schuck, 'Legal Complexity: Some Causes, Consequences, and Cures' 42 Duke Law Journal 1.

B Schwartz and others, 'Maximizing versus satisfying: Happiness is a matter of choice,' 83 Journal of Personality and Social Psychology 1178.

R Schwarzer and others, 'The assessment of optimistic self-beliefs: Comparison of the German, Spanish, and Chinese versions of the General Self-Efficacy scale' 46 Applied Psychology: An International Review 69.

R Schwarzer and A Born, 'Optimistic self-beliefs: Assessment of general perceived self-efficacy in thirteen cultures' 3 World Psychology 177.

R Schwarzer and M Jerusalem, 'Generalized Self-Efficacy scale' in W J., W S. and J M. (eds.), *Measures in health psychology: A user's portfolio Causal and control beliefs* (NFER-NELSON, Windsor 1995).

R Schwarzer, *Self-efficacy: Thought control of action* (Hemisphere, Washington DC 1992).

C Sedikides, D Ariely and N Olsen, 'Contextual and procedural determinants of partner selection: of assymetric dominance and prominence' 17 Social Cognition.

TE Sehity, E Kirchler and S Muehlbacher, 'Rise and Decline of Social Objects: Ten case studies on the social development of meaning structures' Euro-Workshop (IAREP), Vienna, Austria, 2003.

S Sekita, 'Financial Literacy and Retirement Planning in Japan' 10 Journal of Pension Economics and Finance 637.

F Selnes and SV Troye, 'Buying Expertise, Information Search, and Problem Solving' 10 Journal of Economic Psychology 411.

L Senden, *Soft Law in European Community Law* (Hart, Oxford 2004).

CE Shannon, 'Prediction and entropy of printed English' 30 Bell System Technical Journal 50.

S Shavitt, 'The role of attitude objects in attitude functions' 26 Journal of Experimental Social Psychology 124.

H Shefrin and R Thaler, 'The Behavioral Life-Cycle Hypothesis' 26 Economic Inquiry 609.

L Sherman and others, 'Preventing crime: what works, what doesn't, what's promising?' Washington DC: Nationale Institute of Justice.

SJ Sherman, DM Mackie and DM Driscoll, 'Priming and the differential use of dimensions in evaluation' 16 Personality and Social Psychology Bulletin 405.

SJ Shoemaker, MS Wolf and C Brach, 'Development of the Patient Education Materials Assessment Tool (PEMAT): A new measure of understandability and actionability for print and audiovisual patient information' 96 Patient Education and Counseling 395.

H Siebert, 'The harmonization issue in Europe: Prior agreement or a competitive process?' in H Siebert (ed.), *The completion of the internal market* (Mohr, Tübingen 1990).

MM Siems, 'Legal Originality' 28 Oxford Journal of Legal Studies 147.

HA Simon, 'A behavioral model of rational choice' 69 Quarterly Journal of Economics 99.

HA Simon, 'Theories of decision-making in economics and behavioural science,' 49 The American Economic Review 253.

I Simonson, 'Choice Based on Reasons: The Case of Attraction and Compromise Effects' 16 Journal of Consumer Research 158.

P Slovic, B Fischhoff and S Lichtenstein, 'Cognitive Processes and Societal Risk Taking' in JS Carroll and JW Payne (eds.), *Cognition and Social Behavior* (Lawrence Erlbaum Associates, Potomac (Maryland) 1976).

D Sperber and D Wilson, *Relevance: Communication and Cognition.* (Blackwell's, Oxford 1986).

RA Spreng and RW Olshavsky, 'Exploring the Headwaters of the Prior Knowledge—Search Relationship, in Enhancing Knowledge Development in Marketing' American Marketing Association 220.

G Staats and B Starink, 'De fiscale aspecten van het conceptwetsvoorstel Wet toekomst pensioenen' PensioenMagazine.

B Starink, *Belastingheffing over particulierpensioen en overheidspension in grensoverschrijdende situaties* (Fiscale monografieën, Wolters Kluwer, Deventer 2015).

Y Stevens and L Van Assche, 'The right to retirement pension information' discussion paper Peer Review on pension information.

Y Stevens, 'Pensioenen als instrument van geïndividualiseerd arbeidsmarktbeleid en armoedebeleid' in J Put and Y Stevens (eds.), *Ontwikkelingen van de sociale zekerheid 2011-2016* (Die Keure Brugge 2016).

Y Stevens, *Pensioenen: cyclusboek 2011-2016* (Die Keure, Brugge 2017).

Y Stevens, 'The role of the government in creating or enhancing the access to funded or unfunded pensions in the modern welfare state' in N Da Costa Cabral and N Cunha Rodriques (eds.), *The Future of Pensions Plans in the EU Internal Market* (Springer International Publishing Cham 2019).

Y Stevens, *EU Pension Law* (Elgar European Law, Edward Elgar Publishing, Cheltenham 2022).

LGM Stevens, *Pensioen in de loonsfeer* (FED Fiscale brochures, Deventer 2005).

Y Stevens, 'Communication on pension rights in Europe' Report European colloquium.

K Steyn, 'Consistency – A Principle of Public Law?' 2 Judicial Review 22.

A Strathman and others, 'The consideration of future consequences: Weighing immediate and distant outcomes of behavior' 66 Journal of Personality and Social Psychology 742.

SS Sundar, 'The MAIN model: A heuristic approach to understanding technology effects on credibility' in MJ Metzger and AJ Flanagin (eds.), *Digital media, youth, and credibility* (MIT Press, Cambridge 2008).

CR Sunstein and RH Thaler, 'Libertarian paternalism is not an oxymoron' 70 University of Chicago Law Review 1159.

CR Sunstein, 'Empirically Informed Regulation' 78 The university of Chicago Law Review 1349.

CR Sunstein, 'Informing consumers through smart disclosure' Memorandum for the heads of executive departments and agencies.

CR Sunstein, 'Empirically informed regulation,' 78 The university of Chicago Law Review 1349.

S Taekema and B Van Klink, 'On the Border. Limits and Possibilities of Interdisciplinary Research' in S Taekema and B Van Klink (eds.), *Law and Method* (Mohr Siebeck, Tübingen 2011).

MA Taylor and K Cook, 'Planning and expectations of the retirement experience' 23 Educational Gerontology 273.

SE Taylor, 'The interface of cognitive and social psychology' in JH Harvey (ed.), *Cognition, social behavior, and the environment* (Lawrence Erlbaum, Hillsdale 1981).

R Taylor, 'Cross-Border Recognition of Occupational Pensions within the EU and beyong' Tax Planning International Review.

F Teubner, 'Law and Social Theory: Three Problems' 1 Asian Journal of Law and Society.

RH Thaler and CR Sunstein, 'Libertarian Paternalism' 93 American Economic Review 175.

WL Tiemeijer, 'Eigen schuld? Een gedragswetenschappelijk perspectief op problematische schulden' (WRR-Verkenning nr 33, 2016).

WL Tiemeijer, CA Thomas and HM Prast, 'De menselijke beslisser: over de psychologie van keuze en gedrag' (WRR-verkenning 22, 2009).

A Tiffe and others, 'Ausgestaltung eines Produktinformationsblatts für zertifizierte Altersvorsorge- und Basisrentenverträge' (2012).

HEB Tijssen, *De juridische dissertatie onder de loep: de verantwoording van methodologische keuzes in juridische dissertaties* (Boom Juridische Uitgevers, Den Haag 2009).

AG Toth, 'The legal status of the declarations annexed to the Single European Act' 23 Common Market Law Review.

A Tversky and D Kahneman, 'Judgment under Uncertainty: Heuristics and Biases' 185 Science 1124.

A Tversky and I Simonson, 'Context-Dependent Preferences' 39 Management Science 1179.

A Tversky and D Kahneman, 'Availability: A Heuristic for Judging Frequency and Probability' 5 Cognitive Psychology 207.

A Tversky and D Kahneman, 'The Framing of Decisions and the Psychology of Choice' 211 Science.

A Tversky, 'Features of Similarity' 84 Psychological Review 327.

B Uebelhack, *Betriebliche Altersversorgung: Grundlagen und Praxis* (C.F. Müller, Heidelberg 2017).

M Ulbrich, 'Die Reform der Betriebsrente oder die Befreiung einer Gazelle: Das Betriebsrentenstärkungsgesetz (BRSG) Teil I – Arbeitsrecht' 41 BB.

UNESCO Institute for Statistics, 'International Standard Classification of Education (ISCED)' (2011).

L van Benthem, N Kortleve and W Otten, 'Betere pensioneringskeuzes met scenariobedragen' 22 Tijdschrift voor Pensioenvraagstukken.

HPM Van Bijnen and LMP Jacobs, 'Lijfrentesparen versus lijfrenteverzekering' WFR.

RLG Van den Heuvel, *Duidelijkheid van fiscale wetgeving: een onderzoek naar een nadere invulling van de kwaliteitseis van eenvoud, duidelijkheid en toegankelijkheid voor fiscale wetgeving* (Fiscaal wetenschappelijkse reeks, SDU, Den Haag 2018).

G van Dijck, *Kwaliteit van de juridische annotatie: een empirische studie naar kenmerken en kwaliteitsindicatoren* (Boom Juridische Uitgevers, Den Haag 2011).

JEAM van Dijck, 'Periodieke uitkeringen in de Wet IB' WFR.

MAC van Elk, "Freies Ermessen' en andere professionele handelingsruimte voor de inspecteur' WFR.

RAJ Van Gestel and MLM Hertogh, 'Wat is regeldruk? Een verkennende internationale literatuurstudie' (WODC, Den Haag 2006).

A van Hekken, J Hoofs and EC Bruggen, 'Pension Participants' Attitudes, Beliefs, and Emotional Responses to the New Dutch Pension System' De Economist.

M Van Hoecke, 'Deep Level Comparative Law' in M Van Hoecke (ed.), *Epistemology and Methodology of Comparative Law* (Hart Publishing, Oxford 2004).

MCJ Van Rooij, A Lusardi and RJ Alessie, 'Financial Literacy and Retirement Planning in the Netherlands' 32 Journal of Economic Psychology 593.

F Vanistendael, 'The role of the European Court of Justice as the supreme judge in tax cases' 3 EC Tax Review.

GJ Veerman, 'De wet als zinsbegoochelingstoestel, over de kwaliteit van wetgeving (inaugural speech)' (Universiteit van Maastricht, 2004).

W Vermeend, 'The Court of Justive of the European Communities and direct taxes: 'Est-ce qua la justive est de ce monde?'' EC Tax Review.

J Visser, M Kloosterboer and P Oosterveld, 'Pensioencommunicatie: behoeften en barrières: geïntegreerd rapport van onderzoek onder deelnemers en gepensioneerden' (TNS Nipo, Amsterdam 2012).

MR Visser, 'Verbreding van de digitale snelweg' in B Starink and MR Visser (eds.), *Ondernemend met pensioen: Dietsvorst-bundel* (Wolters Kluwer, Deventer 2015).

K Vogel, *Klaus Vogel on double taxation conventions: a commentary to the OECD-, UN- and US model conventions for the avoidance of double taxation of income and capital: with particular reference to German treaty practice* (Kluwer, Deventer 1991).

K Vogel, *Klaus Vogel on Double Taxation Conventions* (Kluwer, Deventer 1997).

C Von Buddenbrock and HM Kühn, 'Das Sozialpartnermodell – Ablösung bestehender Versorgungssysteme in der bAV durch die reine Beitragszusage' 50 BB 2997.

F Wallau and others, 'Machbarkeitsstudie für eine empirische Analyse von Hemmnissen für die Verbreitung der betrieblichen Altersversorgung in kleinen und mittleren Unternehmen' (Forschungsbericht / Bundesministerium für Arbeit und Soziales, FB444, 2014).

M Warnaar and M Visser, 'Een welvaartsrichtlijn voor pensioen. Wat is een adequaat inkomen? (deel 1)' PensioenMagazine.

M Warnaar and M Visser, 'Een welvaartsrichtlijn voor pensioen. Wat is een adequaat inkomen? (deel 2)' PensioenMagazine.

AC Warren and MJ Graetz, 'Income Tax Discrimination and the Political and Economic Integration of Europe' 115 Yale Law Journal 1186.

PR Warshaw and FD Davis, 'Disentangling Behavioral Intention and Behavioral Expectation' 21 Journal of Experimental Social Psychology 213.

M Wathelet, 'Marks & Spencer plc vs. Halsey: Lessons to be drawn' British Tax Review 128.

PJ Wattel, 'Köbler, CILFIT and Welthgrove: We Can't Go On Meeting Like This' 41 Common Market Law Review 177.

PJ Wattel, 'Red herrings in direct tax cases before the ECJ' 2 Legal Issues of Economic Integration 81.

PJ Wattel, O Marres and H Vermeulen, *European Tax Law* (Kluwer, Deventer 2018).

RH Weber, 'Legal Interoperability as a Tool for Combatting Fragmentation' (2014).

MJGAM Weerepas, 'AOW en Anw' in AHH Bollen-Vandenboorn (ed.), *Pensioen en de belangrijkste toekomstvoorzieningen* (27 edn Fiscale Geschriften, SDU, Den Haag 2022).

MJGAM Weerepas, 'Taxation of pensions in Europe: a summary of the report of the Committee on International Pensions' 3 EC Tax Review.

MJGAM Weerepas, 'Grenswerkers, enige hardnekkige problemen' WFR.

MJGAM Weerepas, 'Grensoverschrijdende gevolgen van Wet normalisering rechtspositie ambtenaren voldoende duidelijk?' Vakblad Grensoverschrijdend Werken.

F Welker, *Das Altersvermögensgesetz und seine konsequenzen für die betriebliche Altersversorgung: arbeits-, steuer- und aufsichtsrechtliche Perspektiven* (Deutscher Universitäts-Verlag, Wiesbaden 2005).

D Wellisch and others, *Besteuerung der Altersvorsorge: ein international Vergleich* (Schriften des Institutes der Ausländisches und Internationales Finanz- und Steuerwesen der Universität Hamburg, Nomos, Baden-Baden 2008).

JM Werbrouck, *Het multidimensionale pensioenbegrip* (Boomjuridisch, Den Haag 2022).

R Wernsmann, *Verhaltenslenkung in einem rationalen Steuersystem* (Mohr Siebeck, Heidelberg 2005).

R Wernsmann, 'Die steuerliche Förderung der zusätzlichen kapitalgedeckten Altersvorsorge' in

Wetenschappelijke Raad voor het Regeringsbeleid, 'Weten is nog geen doen: Een realistisch perspectief op redzaamheid' (Den Haag 2017). Wheatley (eds.), *Complexity Theory and Law: Mapping an Emergent Jurisprudence* (Routledge, London 2018).

P Wilson, *Second-hand knowledge: An inquiry into cognitive authority* (Greenwood Press, Westport, Connecticut 1983).

HB Winter, M Herweijer and M Scheltema, *Evaluatie van wetgeving: terugblik en perspectief* (Kluwer, Deventer 1990).

World Bank, 'The World Bank Pension Conceptual Framework' (World Bank Pension Reform Primer, 2008).

World Bank, 'Adequacy (1) Pension entitlements, replacement rates and pension wealth' (World Bank Pension Indicators and Database, 2012).

WRR, 'Met kennis van gedrag beleid maken' (WRR-rapport nr 92, 2014).

WRR, 'Doenvermogen: Van toets naar tools' (17 September 2020).

N Wunderlich and L Albath, 'Der Europäische Gerichtshof und die direkten Steuern – Ein Beitrag zum Verhältnis von Gemeinschaftsrecht und national Recht' 93 DStZ 547.

YC Xu and Z Chen, 'Relevance judgment: What do information users consider beyond topicality?' 57 Journal of the Association for Information Science and Technology 961.

G Zuccon, 'Understandability Biased Evaluation for Information Retrieval' in N Ferro and others (eds.), *Advances in Information Retrieval: 38th European Conference on IR Research, ECIR 2016* (Springer, Switzerland 2016).

K Zweigert and H Kötz, *Introduction to Comparative Law* (3rd edn Oxford University Press, Oxford 1998).

K Zweigert, 'Zur Methode der Rechtsvergleichung' 13 Studium Generale 193.

Case-law

CJEU & ECHR

26-62 *Van Gend & Loos* ECLI:EU:C:1963:1 (CJEU).
8691/79 [1981] *Malone* (ECHR).
C-70/83 *Gerda Kloppenburg v Finanzamt Leer* ECLI:EU:C:1984:71 (CJEU).
C-270/83 *Avoir Fiscal* ECLI:EU:C:1986:37 (CJEU).
9063/80 [1986] *Gillow* (ECHR).
C-326/85 *Commission vs Netherlands* ECLI:EU:C:1987:547 (CJEU).
C-348/85 *Kingdom of Denmark v Commission* ECLI:EU:C:1987:552 (CJEU).
92 and 93/87 (joined cases) *Commission vs. French Republic/United Kingdom and Northern-Ireland* ECLI:EU:C:1989:77 (CJEU).
C-30/89 *Commission v French Republic* ECLI:EU:C:1990:114 (CJEU).
C-204/90 *Bachmann* ECLI:EU:C:1992:35 (CJEU).
C-300/90 *Commission vs. Belgium I* ECLI:EU:C:1992:37 (CJEU).
C-279/93 *Schumacker* ECLI:EU:C:1995:31 (CJEU).
C-80/94 *Wielockx* ECLI:EU:C:1995:271 (CJEU).
C-57/96 *Meints* ECLI:EU:C:1997:564 (CJEU).
C-35/97 *Commission vs France* ECLI:EU:C:1998:431 (CJEU).
C-336/96 *Gilly* ECLI:EU:C:1998:22 (CJEU).
C-275/96 *Kuusijärvi* ECLI:EU:C:1998:279 (CJEU).
C-118/96 *Safir* ECLI:EU:C:1998:170 (CJEU).
C-294/97 *Eurowings Luftverkehrs AG* ECLI:EU:C:1999:524 (CJEU).
C-55/98 *Vestergaard* ECLI:EU:C:1999:533 (CJEU).
C-302/98 *Sehrer* ECLI:EU:C:2000:322 (CJEU).
C-224/98 *D'Hoop* ECLI:EU:C:2002:432 (CJEU).
C-133/00 *Danner* ECLI:EU:C:2002:558 (CJEU).
C-385/00 *De Groot* ECLI:EU:C:2002:750 (CJEU).

C-234/01 *Gerritse* ECLI:EU:C:2003:340 (CJEU).
C-422/01 *Skandia* ECLI:EU:C:2003:380 (CJEU).
C-9/02 *Lasteyrie du Saillant* ECLI:EU:C:2004:138 (CJEU).
C-224/02 *Pusa* ECLI:EU:C:2004:273 (CJEU).
C-152/03 *Ritter-Coulais* ECLI:EU:C:2006:123 (CJEU).
C-403/03 *Schempp* ECLI:EU:C:2005:446 (CJEU).
C-265/04 *Bouanich* ECLI:EU:C:2006:51 (CJEU).
C-346/04 *Conijn* ECLI:EU:C:2006:445 (CJEU).
C-406/04 *De Cuyper* ECLI:EU:C:2006:491 (CJEU).
C-513/04 *Kerckhaert/Morres* ECLI:EU:C:2006:713 (CJEU).
C-470/04 *N. vs. Inspecteur* ECLI:EU:C:2006:525 (CJEU).
C-520/04 *Turpeinen* ECLI:EU:C:2006:703 (CJEU).
C-345/04 *Centro Equestre da Lezíria Grande* ECLI:EU:C:2007:96 (CJEU).
C-522/04 *Commission vs. Belgium II* ECLI:EU:C:2007:405 (CJEU).
C-150/04 *Commission vs. Denmark* ECLI:EU:C:2007:69 (CJEU).
C-298/05 *Columbus Container Services* ECLI:EU:C:2007:754 (CJEU).
C-527/06 *Renneberg* ECLI:EU:C:2008:566 (CJEU).
C-269/07 *Commission vs. Germany* ECLI:EU:C:2009:527 (CJEU).
C-450/09 *Schröder* ECLI:EU:C:2011:198 (CJEU).
C-303/12 *Imfeld and Garcet* ECLI:EU:C:2013:822 (CJEU).
C-48/13 *Nordea Bank Danmark* ECLI:EU:C:2014:2087 (CJEU).
C-559/13 *Grünewald* ECLI:EU:C:2015:109 (CJEU).
C-9/14 *Kieback* ECLI:EU:C:2015:406 (CJEU).
C-359/13 *Martens* ECLI:EU:C:2015:118 (CJEU).
C-300/15 *Kohll en Kohll-Schlesser* ECLI:EU:C:2016:361 (CJEU).
C-20/16 *Bechtel* ECLI:EU:C:2017:488 (CJEU).
C-480/17 *Montag* ECLI:EU:C:2018:987 (CJEU).
C-360/22 *European Commission v Kingdom of the Netherlands* (CJEU).

Germany

BAG 5 July 1979, 3 AZR 197/78, *NJW* 1980, 79.
BAG 26 June 1990, 3 AZR 641/88, *DB* 1990, 2475.
BAG 16 September 1998, 5 AZR 598/97, *BB* 1999.
BAG 25 January 2000, 3 AZR 769/98, *AP* 38.
BAG 11 December 2001, 3 AZR 512/00, *DB* 2003, 293.
BAG 18 March 2003, 3 AZR 313/02, *BB* 2004, 269.
BAG 7 September 2004, 3 AZR 550/03.

BAG 12 June 2007, 3 AZR 14/06, *DB* 2007, 2722.
BAG 16 March 2010, 3 AZR 594/09, 2010.
BAG 29 September 2010, 3 AZR 107/08.
BFH 18 September 1952, IV 70/49, *BStBl* 1952, 290.
BFH 5 February 1953, IV 41/49 U, *BStBl* 1953, 105.
BFH 26 July 1957, III 161/54 S, *BStBl* III 1957, 314.
BFH 21 December 1982, VIII R 215/78, *BStBl II* 1983, 410 (411).
BFH 30 May 2001, VI R 178/99, *BFH/NV* 2001, 1258.
BFH 12 September 2001, VI R 154/99, *BStBl* 2002, 22.
BFH 6 June 2002, VI R 178/97, *BStBl II* 2003, 34.
BFH 14 September 2004, VI R 148/98, *BStBl II* 2006a, 532.
BFH 20 July 2005, VI R 165/01, *BB* 2005, 1944.
BFH 14 September 2005, VI R 32/04, *BStBl* 2006c, 500.
BFH 1 February 2006, *BStBl II* 2006d, 420.
BFH 15 February 2006, VI R 92/04, *BStBl* 2006b, 528.
BFH 9 August 2006, I R 11/06, *DB* 2006, 2039.
BFH 24 June 2009, X R 57/06 *BStBl* 2009 II S. 1000.
BFH 14 July 2010, X R 37/08 *BStBl* 2011 II S. 628.
BFH 18 April 2012, *BStBl II* 2012, 721.
BFH 26 November 2014, VIII R 39/10 *BStBl* 2016 II S. 665.
BFH 20 September 2016, X R 23/15 *BStBl* 2017 II S. 347.
BGH 7 July 1998, IV ZR 241/97, *BGHZ* 139, 167.
BVerfG 3 December 1969, 1 BvR 624/56, *BVerfGE* 27, 253.
BVerfGE 13 December 1977, 2 BvM 1/76, *BVerfGE* 46, 342.
BVerfG 19 October 1983, 2 BvR 298/81, *DB* 1984, 190.
BVerfG 14 Januar 1987, BvR 1052/79, *DB* 1987, 638.
BVerfG 25 March 2002, 2 BvL 17/99, 105, 73.
BVerfG 29 February 2012, 1 BvR 2378/10, *NZA* 2012, 788.

Netherlands

29 935, ECLI:NL:HR:1994:AA3001 (1994) (HR)
1036566, ECLI:NL:RBROT:2010:BO6473, PJ 2010, 5 (Rechtbank Rotterdam).
ECLI:NL:RBUTR:2011:BQ3748, PJ 2011, 64 (Rechtbank Utrecht).
ECLI:NL:RBROT:2016:3491, PJ 2015, 138 (Rechtbank Rotterdam).
06/00183, ECLI:NL:GHSHE:2007:BB2231 (Gerechtshof 's-Hertogenbosch).
ECLI:NL:GHSHE:2008:BC2720 (Gerechtshof 's-Hertogenbosch).
ECLI:NL:GHAMS:2009:BI6399 (Gerechtshof Amsterdam).

ECLI:NL:GHAMS:2011:BU3398 (Gerechtshof Amsterdam).
ECLI:NL:GHAMS:2015:3978 (Gerechtshof Amsterdam).
ECLI:NL:GHAMS:2016:3246, PJ 2016, 136 (Gerechtshof Amsterdam).
ECLI:NL:GHDHA:2019:76, PJ 2019, 40 (Gerechtshof Den Haag).
18/4786 AW, ECLI:NL:CRVB:2019:2013 2019 (Centrale Raad van Beroep).
19/03758 ECLI:NL:PHR:2020:210 (A-G Niessen).
35 231 ECLI:NL:HR:2001:AD6774 (Hoge Raad).
44 050, ECLI:NL:PHR:2009:BC4725 (Hoge Raad).
43 978, ECLI:NL:PHR:2009:BC5201 (Hoge Raad).
10/00990, ECLI:NL:HR:2011:BN8728 (Hoge Raad).
17/01256, ECLI:NL:HR:2017:1324, BNB 2017/186 (Hoge Raad).
ECLI:NL:HR:2021:518 (Hoge Raad).

Legislation, Legal Acts, Legislative History

Germany

Abschlussbericht der Sachverständigenkommission zur Neuordnung der steuerrechtlichen Behandlung von Altersvorsorgeaufwendungen und Altersbezügen (BMF-Schriftenreihe).

BMAS, 'Neues Sozialpartnermodell Betriebsrente – Mögliche Änderungen im Betriebsrentengesetz' (2015).

BMF, *Steuerliche Förderung der betrieblichen Altersversorgung IV C 5 – S 2333/17/10002* (6 December 2017).

BMF, *Rentenbezugsmitteilungsverfahren nach § 22a EStG IV C 3 – S 2257-c/10/10005:003* (7 December 2011).

BMF, *Anwendung des § 10 Abs. 1 Nr. 2 Buchstabe a EStG i.d.F. des AltEinkG bei Beiträgen an berufsständische Versorgungseinrichtungen IV C 8-S 2221 – 128/06* (7 February 2007).

BMF, *Sonderausgabenabzug für Sozialversicherungsbeiträge im Ausland tätiger und in Deutschland wohnender Arbeitnehmer; Unionsrechtswidrigkeit des Abzugsverbotes nach § 10 Absatz 2 Satz 1 Nummer 1 ES IV C 3 – S 2221/14/10005:003* (11 December 2017).

BMF, *Steuerliche Förderung der privaten Altersvorsorge und betrieblichen Altersversorgung; Aufteilung von Leistungen bei der nachgelagerten Besteuerung nach § 22 Nr. 5 EStG IV C 3 – S 2257 b – 47/04* (11 November 2004).

BMF, *Steuerliche Förderung der betrieblichen Altersversorgung; Aufteilung von Leistungen bei der nachgelagerten Besteuerung nach § 22 Nummer 5 EStG IV C 3 – S 2257 b/11/10003* (14 March 2012).

BMF, *Vorsorgeaufwendungen; Aufteilung eines einheitlichen Sozialversicherungsbeitrags (Globalbeitrag); Anpassung der Aufteilungsmaßstäbe für den Veranlagungszeitraum 2020 IV C 3 - S 2221/09/10013:001* (15 October 2019).

BMF, *Einkommensteuerrechtliche Behandlung von Vorsorgeaufwendungen und Altersbezügen IV C 3 - S 2221/12/10010:004 - IV C 5 - S 2345/08/0001* (19 August 2013).

BMF, *Steuerliche Förderung der betrieblichen Altersversorgung IV C 5 - S 2333/19/10008:017* (21 August 2021).

BMF, *Steuerliche Förderung der privaten Altersvorsorge IV C 3 - S 2015/17/10001:005* (21 December 2017).

BMF, *Verhandlungsgrundlage für Doppelbesteuerungsabkommen im Bereich der Steuern vom Einkommen und Vermögen IV B 2 - S 1301/13/10009* (22 August 2013).

BMF, *Gesetz zur Neuordnung der einkommensteuerrechtlichen Behandlung von Altersvorsorgeaufwendungen und Altersbezügen – Alterseinkünftegesetz (AltEinkG) IV C 3-S 2255 - 51/05* (24 February 2005).

BMF, *Steuerliche Behandlung von Alterseinkünften nach Artikel 17 des Abkommens vom 12. April 2012 zwischen der Bundesrepublik Deutschland und dem Königreich der Niederlande zur Vermeidung der Doppelbesteuerung und zur Verhinderung der Steuerverkürzung auf dem Gebiet der Steuern vom Einkommen IV B 3 – S 1301-NDL/15/10002* (24 January 2017).

BMF, *Steuerliche Förderung der privaten Altersvorsorge und betrieblichen Altersversorgung IV C 3 – S 2015/11/10002/ IV C 5 – S 2333/09/10005* (24 July 2013).

BMF, *Einkommensteuerrechtliche Behandlung von Vorsorgeaufwendungen IV C 3 - S 2221/16/10001:004* (24 May 2017).

BMF, *Sonderausgabenabzug bei beschränkt Steuerpflichtigen für Pflichtbeiträge an berufsständische Versorgungseinrichtungen (§ 10 Absatz 1 Nummer 2 Buchstabe a, § 50 Absatz 1 Satz 3 EStG); EuGH-Urteil vom 6. Dezember 2018, C-480/17, „Montag" IV C 5 - S 2301/19/10004:001* (26 June 2019).

BMF, *Deutsch-niederländisches Doppelbesteuerungsabkommen (DBA-NL); Anwendung des Kassenstaatsprinzips auf ehemalige staatliche Pensionsfonds IV B 3-S 1301-NDL/19/10006:004* (26 October 2021).

BMF, *Steuerliche Förderung der privaten Altersvorsorge und betrieblichen Altersversorgung IV C 3 S 2222/09/10041* (31 March 2010).

Deutsche Rentenversicherung, 'Jahresbericht' (2016) <http://www.deutsche-rentenversicherung.de/Allgemein/de/Navigation/6_Wir_ueber_uns/02_Fakten_und_Zahlen/04_Jahresbericht/jahresbericht_index_node.html>.

Deutsche Rentenversicherung, 'Maßgebliche Rechengrößen und Werte ab 1.1.2023 in der gesetzlichen Rentenversicherung' (2023) <https://www.deutsche-rentenversicherung.de/SharedDocs/Downloads/DE/Statistiken-und-Berichte/statistikpublikationen/aktuelle_daten.html>.

Deutscher Bundestag, *Entwurf eines Gesetzes zur Reform der gesetzlichen Rentenversicherung und zur Förderung eines kapitalgedeckten Altersvorsorgevermögens (Altersvermögensgesetz – AVmG)*, (2000).

Entwurf eines Gesetzes zu dem Abkommen vom 12. April 2012 zwischen der Bundesrepublik Deutschland und dem Königreich der Niederlande zur Vermeidung der Doppelbesteuerung und zur Verhinderung der Steuerverkürzung auf dem Gebiet der Steuern vom Einkommen 24 September 2012, nr 17/10752.

Entwurf eines Gesetzes zur Vermeidung von Umsatzsteuerausfällen beim Handel mit Waren im Internet und zur Änderung weiterer steuerlicher Vorschriften (Jahressteuergezet 2018).

Entwurf eines Siebten Gesetzes zur Änderung des Vierten Buches Sozialgesetzbuch und anderer Gesetze

Entwurf eines Gesetzes zur Verbesserung der Transparenz in der Alterssicherung und der Rehabilitation sowie zur Modernisierung der Sozialversicherungswahlen (Gesetz Digitale Rentenübersicht).

Entwurf eines Gesetzes zur Stärkung der betrieblichen Altersversorgung und zur Änderung anderer Gesetze (Betriebsrentenstärkungsgesetz).

Gesetz zu dem Abkommen vom 12. April 2012 zwischen der Bundesrepublik Deutschland und dem Königreich der Niederlande zur Vermeidung der Doppelbesteuerung und zur Verhinderung der Steuerverkürzung auf dem Gebiet der Steuern vom Einkommen.

Gesetz zur Neuordnung der einkommensteuerrechtlichen Behandlung von Altersvorsorgeaufwendungen und Altersbezügen (Alterseinkünftegesetz – AltEinkG).

Gesetz zur Reform der agrarsozialen Sicherung (Agrarsozialreformgesetz 1995 – ASRG 1995).

Gesetz über die Zertifizierung von Altersvorsorgeund Basisrentenverträgen (AltersvorsorgeverträgeZertifizierungsgesetz – AltZertG).

Gesetz zur Reform der gesetzlichen Rentenversicherung und zur Förderung eines kapitalgedeckten Altersvorsorgevermögens (Altersvermögensgesetz – AVmG).

Gesetz zur verbesserten Einbeziehung der selbstgenutzten Wohnimmobilie in die geförderte Altersvorsorge (Eigenheimrentengesetz – EigRentG).

Gesetz zur Umsetzung steuerlicher EU-Vorgaben sowie zur Änderung steuerlicher Vorschriften (EUStVUG).

Gesetz über die Beaufsichtigung der Versicherungsunternehmen (Versicherungsaufsichtsgesetz – VAG).

Gesetz zur Stärkung der betrieblichen Altersversorgung und zur Änderung anderer Gesetze (Betriebsrentenstärkungsgesetz).

Gesetz zur Neuordnung und Modernisierung des Bundesdienstrechts (Dienstrechtsneuordnungsgesetz – DNeuG).

Gesetz zur Anpassung des nationalen Steuerrechts an den Beitritt Kroatiens zur EU und zur Änderung weiterer steuerlicher Vorschriften (StRAnpG).

Gesetz zur Vermeidung von Umsatzsteuerausfällen beim Handel mit Waren im Internet und zur Änderung weiterer steuerlicher Vorschriften (UStIntG).

Gesetz zur Verbesserung der Transparenz in der Alterssicherung und der Rehabilitation sowie zur Modernisierung der Sozialversicherungswahlen und zur Änderung anderer Gesetze (Gesetz Digitale Rentenübersicht).

Koalitionsvertrag zwischen CDU/CSU/SPD, *Deutschlands Zukunft gestalten* (2013).

Verordnung über maßgebende Rechengrößen der Sozialversicherung für 2023 (Sozialversicherungs-Rechengrößenverordnung 2023).

Koalitionsvertrag zwischen CDU, CSU und SPD, *Ein neuer Aufbruch für Europa, Eine neue Dynamik für Deutschland, Ein neuer Zusammenhalt für unser Land* (2018).

Netherlands

DG Belastingdienst / Concerndirectie Fiscale en Juridische Zaken, *Internationaal belastingrecht. Fiscale kwalificatie buitenlandse socialezekerheidsstelsels DGBD 178296* (26 November 2020).

IAK, *Beantwoording van de 7 vragen uit het Integraal afwegingskader voor beleid en regelgeving (IAK)* (16 December 2020).

Kamerstukken I, *33615 nr. B (Voorlopig verslag van de vaste commissie voor Financiën)* (19 November 2014).

Kamerstukken I, *35 555, nr. 18 (Verslag van de vergadering van 12 januari 2021)* (2020/21).

Kamerstukken I, *35 555, nr. H (Motie van het lid Oomen-Ruijten c.s.)* (2020/21).

Kamerstukken II, *Socialeverzekeringspositie van grensarbeiders* (26834 nr 5 23 February 2001).

Kamerstukken II, *26 727, nr. 3 (Belastingherziening 2001)* (1998/99).

Kamerstukken II, *26 727, nr. 7 (Belastingherziening 2001)* (1999/00).

Kamerstukken II, *25 087, appendix to nr 7* (2010/11).

Kamerstukken II, *33 615, nr 5 (Nota naar aanleiding van het verslag)* (2013/14).

Kamerstukken II, *33 615, nr 6 (Nota van wijziging)* (2013/14).

Kamerstukken II, *33 615, nr 8* (2013/14).

Kamerstukken II, *33 615, nr 10 (Motie van de leden Nijboer en Kerstens)* (2013/14).

Kamerstukken II, *33 615, nr E (Nadere memorie van antwoord)* (2013/14).

Kamerstukken II, *33 615, nr. 3 (MvT), section I.1* (2013/14).

Kamerstukken II, *33 615, nr. 3 (MvT), subsection I.4 Grensarbeiders* (2013/14).

Kamerstukken II, *32 042, nr 329 (Verslag van een schriftelijk overleg)* (2015/16).

Kamerstukken II, *34 414, nr. 6-9 (Voorstel van wet van het lid Klein tot wijziging van de Algemene Ouderdomswet en de Participatiewet in verband met de introductie van de mogelijkheid het AOW-ouderdomspensioen geheel of gedeeltelijk eerder of later te laten ingaan (Wet flexibilisering ingangsdatum AOW))* (2015/16).

Kamerstukken II, *34 414, nr. 55* (2016/17).

Kamerstukken II, *26 727, 3 (Wet Inkomstenbelasting 2001 (Belastingherziening 2001))* (1998/99).

Kamerstukken II, *26 727, nr. 18* (1999/2000).

Kamerstukken II, *Wijziging van de Pensioenwet en de Wet verplichte beroepspensioenregeling in verband met verbetering van de pensioencommunicatie (Wet pensioencommunicatie)* (2013/14).

Kamerstukken II, *Wet tot wijziging van de Algemene Ouderdomswet, de Wet op de loonbelasting 1964, de Wet verhoging AOW- en pensioenrichtleeftijd, de Pensioenwet, de Wet verplichte beroepspensioenregeling en Overige fiscale maatregelen 2013 in verband met de versnelling van de stapsgewijze verhoging van de AOW-leeftijd (Wet versnelling stapsgewijze verhoging AOW-leeftijd)* (2014/15).

Kamerstukken II, *Toekomst pensioenstelsel* (2018/19).

Kamerstukken II, *Brief van de minister van Financiën 21 501-07, nr. 1648* (2019/20).

Kamerstukken II, *Wet toekomst pensioenen* (2019/20).

Kamerstukken II, *Wet van 2 december 2020, houdende wijziging van de Algemene Ouderdomswet en de Wet op de loonbelasting 1964 in verband met de verandering van de koppeling van de AOW- en pensioenrichtleeftijd aan de stijging van de levensverwachting (Wet verandering koppeling AOW-leeftijd), nr. 3 (MvT)* (2019/20).

Kamerstukken II, *35 586, 6 Verslag over het verzoekschrift van de heer C. te M. Betreffende een verzoek om afgifte van een verklaring niet-afgetrokken lijfrentepremies* (2020/21).

Kamerstukken II, *Wijziging van de Pensioenwet, de Wet inkomstenbelasting 2001 en enige andere wetten in verband met herziening van het pensioenstelsel, standaardisering van het nabestaandenpensioen, aanpassing van de fiscale behandeling van pensioen en enige andere wijzigingen ten aanzien van pensioen (Wet toekomst Pensioenen) (Nota naar aanleiding van het verslag) nr. 7* (2021/22).

Kamerstukken II, *Wijziging van de Pensioenwet, de Wet inkomstenbelasting 2001 en enige andere wetten in verband met herziening van het pensioenstelsel, standaardisering van het nabestaandenpensioen, aanpassing van de fiscale behandeling van pensioen en enige andere wijzigingen ten aanzien van pensioen (Wet toekomst pensioenen)* (2021/22).

Kamerstukken II, *Wijziging van de Pensioenwet, de Wet inkomstenbelasting 2001 en enige andere wetten in verband met herziening van het pensioenstelsel, standaardisering van het nabestaandenpensioen, aanpassing van de fiscale behandeling van pensioen en enige andere wijzigingen ten aanzien van pensioen (Wet toekomst pensioenen) (Vierde nota van wijziging) nr. 91* (2022/23).

Kamerstukken II, *Wijziging van de Wet bedrag ineens, RVU en verlofsparen in verband met de herziening van de mogelijkheid tot afkoop in de vorm van een bedrag ineens alsmede tot wijziging van de Wet op de loonbelasting 1964 (Wet herziening bedrag ineens) (Nota naar aanleiding van het verslag)* (2022/23).

Kamerstukken II, 'Notitie Algemeen fiscaal verdragsbeleid' (1987/88) [20 365].

Kamerstukken II, *20 595, 3 (Wet vereenvoudiging tariefstructuur en aftrekposten in de loon- en inkomstenbelasting)* (1989/90).

Kamerstukken II, 'Notitie Internationaal fiscaal (verdrags)beleid' (1996/97).

Kamerstukken II, *Uitgangspunten van het beleid op het terrein van het internationaal fiscaal (verdragen)recht* (1997/98).

Minister van Buitenlandse Zaken, *Protocol tot wijziging van het Verdrag van 12 april 2012 tussen het Koninkrijk der Nederlanden en de Bondsrepubliek Duitsland tot het vermijden van dubbele belasting en het voorkomen van het ontgaan van belasting met betrekking tot belastingen naar het inkomen zoals gewijzigd door het Protocol van 11 januari 2016* (1 November 2021).

Minister van Buitenlandse Zaken, *Protocol tot wijziging van het Verdrag van 12 april 2012 tussen het Koninkrijk der Nederlanden en de Bondsrepubliek Duitsland tot het vermijden van dubbele belasting en het voorkomen van het ontgaan van belasting met betrekking tot belastingen naar het inkomen zoals gewijzigd door het Protocol van 11 januari 2016* (Tractatenblad 2021, nr 43 7 April 2021).

Minister van Sociale Zaken en Werkgelegenheid, *Besluit van 14 januari 2021 tot vaststelling van het tijdstip van inwerkingtreding van de Wet bedrag ineens, RVU en verlofsparen* (21 January 2021).

Minister van Sociale Zaken en Werkgelegenheid, 'Hoofdlijnennotitie uitwerking pensioenakkoord' (22 June 2020).

Minister van Armoedebeleid Participatie en Pensioenen, *Antwoorden op Kamervragen over verlaging van de variabele pensioenuitkeringen* (6 October 2022).

Minister van Economische Zaken en Klimaat, *European Pillar of Social Rights Report 2023 Netherlands: Reporting on the Implementation of the European Pillar of Social Rights Description of main Measures and their Estimated Impact* (24 April 2023).

Minister van Sociale Zaken en Werkgelegenheid, *Evaluatie vrijstelling voor nettopensioen en nettolijfrente* (2 September 2020).

Minister van Sociale Zaken en Werkgelegenheid, *Kamervragen van het lid Omtzigt (CDA) over de hoge marginale druk over een pensioenuitkering ineens en het feit dat het van je geboortedatum afhangt of je soms 20% extra belasting moet betalen over een uitkering ineens* (5 November 2020).

Minister van Sociale Zaken en Werkgelegenheid, *Verzamelbrief Pensioenonderwerpen – Vaste commissie voor SZW, PvdA- en CDA-fractie vragen toelichting* (9 July 2019).

Minister van Sociale Zaken en Werkgelegenheid, *Stand van zaken uitwerking pensioenakkoord* (10 May 2021).

Minister van Sociale Zaken en Werkgelegenheid, *Aanbiedingsbrief evaluatie Wet pensioencommunicatie* (31 January 2020).

Minister voor Armoedebeleid Participatie en Pensioenen, *Volgen voortgang transitieperiode wet toekomst pensioenen* (14 June 2023).

Minister voor Rechtsbescherming and Minister van Binnenlandse Zaken en Koninkrijksrelaties, *Kabinetsstandpunt op WRR-rapport "Weten is nog geen doen: Een realistisch perspectief op redzaamheid"* (22 January 2018).

Ministerie van Sociale Zaken en Werkgelegenheid, 'Rapport Pensioen in duidelijke taal' (Den Haag juni 2012) <available online: https://www.rijksoverheid.nl/documenten/rapporten/2012/06/26/rapport-pensioen-in-duidelijke-taal>.

Ministerie van Financiën, 'Notitie Fiscaal Verdragsbeleid 2011' (2011).

Ministerie van Financiën, 'Notitie Fiscaal Verdragsbeleid 2020' (2020).

Ministerie van Sociale Minister voor Armoedebeleid Participatie en Pensioenen, *Wijziging van de Pensioenwet, de Wet inkomstenbelasting 2001 en enige andere wetten in verband met herziening van het pensioenstelsel, standaardisering van het nabestaandenpensioen, aanpassing van de fiscale behandeling van pensioen en enige andere wijzigingen ten aanzien van pensioen (Wet toekomst pensioenen)* (2022).

Ministerie van Sociale Zaken en Werkgelegenheid, *Consultatieversie wetsvoorstel Wet toekomst pensioenen* (2020).

Staatssecretaris van Financiën, *Besluit Internationaal belastingrecht. Belastingverdragen; uitleg begrip werkgever* (12 January 2010).

Staatssecretaris van Financiën, *Besluit Internationaal belastingrecht. Belastingverdragen; uitleg begrip werkgever nr. DGB2010/267M* (12 January 2010).

Staatssecretaris van Financiën, *Vraag- en antwoordbesluit CRS/FATCA* (13 March 2018).

Staatssecretaris van Financiën, *Verzamelbesluit Lijfrenten nr. 2019-115021* (16 May 2019).

Staatssecretaris van Financiën, *Besluit Loonheffingen, inkomstenbelasting. Pensioenen; beschikbare-premieregelingen en premie- en kapitaalovereenkomsten en nettopensioenregelingen (Staffelbesluit pensioenen) nr. 2019-21333* (20 December 2019).

Staatssecretaris van Financiën, *Loonheffingen. Inkomstenbelasting. Internationale aspecten van pensioenen en stamrechten nr. DGB2015/7010M* (28 October 2015).

Staatssecretaris van Financiën, *Syllabus vrijstelling, verrekening, verliescompensatie internationaal belastingrecht* (2004).

Staatssecretaris van Financiën – Fiscaliteit en Belastingdienst, *Beantwoording vragen Notitie Fiscaal Verdragsbeleid 2020* (29 January 2021).

Staatssecretaris van Financiën – Fiscaliteit en Belastingdienst, *Schriftelijke beantwoording WGO I – Pakket Belastingplan 2023* (20 October 2022).

Staatssecretaris van Financiën – Fiscaliteit en Belastingdienst, *Antwoorden schriftelijk overleg Notitie Fiscaal Verdragsbeleid* (21 September 2020).

Staatssecretaris van Financiën – Toeslagen en Douane, *Aanvullende duiding problemen Belastingdienst* (27 November 2020).

Staatssecretaris van Financiën, *Doenvermogen in pakket Belastingplan 2021* (16 November 2020).

Staatssecretaris van Financiën, *Beantwoording vragen n.a.v. toezending afschrift Rapportage fiscale knelpunten grensarbeiders 2019* (17 December 2019).

Staatssecretaris van Financiën, *Internationaal belastingrecht. Toegelaten buitenlandse aanbieders van pensioenen, lijfrenteverzekeringen, lijfrenterekeningen, lijfrentebeleggingsrechten en arbeidsongeschiktheidsverzekeringen nr. 2022-192641* (21 July 2022).

Staatssecretaris van Financiën, *Buitenlandse sociale verzekeringen. Duitse, Belgische en Luxemburgse sociale zekerheid. Aftrek premie en belastbaarheid uitkeringen nr. DGB 2014/144M* (24 March 2014).

Staatssecretaris van Financiën, *Rapportage fiscale knelpunten grensarbeiders 2019* (27 September 2019).

Staatssecretaris van Sociale Zaken en Werkgelegenheid, *Mededeling van de Staatssecretaris van Sociale Zaken en Werkgelegenheid van 5 november 2021, 2021-0000168058, tot bekendmaking van de pensioengerechtigde leeftijd en de aanvangsleeftijd in 2027* (5 November 2021).

Wet van 8 juli 2009 tot wijziging van enkele belastingwetten (reparatie in verband met arresten van de Hoge Raad inzake pensioen- en lijfrenteaanspraken).

European Union

Convention concerning Migrations in Abusive Conditions and the Promotion of Equality of Opportunity and Treatment of Migrant Workers 1975 (No. 143).

Council Directive 77/799/EEC of 19 December 1977 concerning mutual assistance by the competent authorities of the Member States in the field of direct taxation [1977] OJ L336/15.

Council Directive 98/49/EC of 29 June 1998 on safeguarding the supplementary pension rights of employed and self-employed persons moving within the Community [1998] OJ L 209.

Council Directive 2011/16/EU of 15 February 2011 on administrative cooperation in the field of taxation and repealing Directive 77/799/EEC [2001] OJ L 64.

Decision No A2 of 12 June 2009 concerning the interpretation of Article 12 of Regulation (EC) No 883/2004 of the European Parliament and of the Council on the legislation applicable to posted workers and self-employed workers temporarily working outside the competent State [OJ C 106/5].

Directive (EU) 2016/2341 of the European Parliament and of the Council of 14 December 2016 on the activities and supervision of institutions for occupational retirement provision (IORPs) [2016] OJ L 354.

Directive (EU) 2018/957 of the European Parliament and of the Council of 28 June 2018 amending Directive 96/71/EC concerning the posting of workers in the framework of the provision of services [2018] OJ L 173.

Directive 96/71/EC of the European Parliament and of the Council of 16 December 1996 concerning the posting of workers in the framework of the provision of services [1996] OJ L 18.

Directive 98/5/EC of the European Parliament and of the Council of 16 February 1998 to facilitate practice of the profession of lawyer on a permanent basis in a Member State other than that in which the qualification was obtained [1998] OJ L 77.

Directive 2003/41/EC of the European Parliament and of the Council of 3 June 2003.

Directive 2014/50/EU of the European Parliament and of the Council of 16 April 2014 on minimum requirements for enhancing worker mobility between Member States by improving the acquisition and preservation of supplementary pension rights [2014] OJ L 128.

Directive 2014/67/EU of the European Parliament and of the Council of 15 May 2014 on the enforcement of Directive 96/71/EC concerning the posting of workers in the framework of the provision of services and amending Regulation (EU) No 1024/2012 on administrative cooperation through the Internal Market Information System [2014] OJ L 159.

European Commission, 'Communication from the Commission to the Council – Supplementary Social Security Schemes: the Role of Occupational Pension Schemes in the Social Protection of Workers and their Implications for Freedom of Movement' (1991) [SEC(91) 1332 final].

European Commission, 'Supplementary pensions in the Single Market: A Green Paper' (1997) [COM(97) 283 final].

European Commission, 'Towards a Single Market for supplementary pensions, results of the Green Paper on supplementary pensions in the single market' (1999) [COM(1999) 134 final].

European Commission, 'The elimination of tax obstacles to the cross-border provision of occupational pensions,' (2001) [COM(2001)214 final].

European Commission, 'Coordinating Member States' direct tax systems in the internal market' (2006) [COM(2006)823 final].

European Commission, 'Exit taxation and the need for coordination of Member States' tax policies' (2006) [COM(2006) 825 final].

European Commission, 'Commission Staff Working Document accompanying Commission Communication 'Removing cross-border tax obstacles for EU citizens'' (2010) [SEC(2010) 1576 final].

European Commission, 'Green paper: towards adequate, sustainable and safe European pension systems' (2010) [COM(2010) 365 final].

European Commission, 'Removing cross-border tax obstacles for EU citizens' (2010) [COM(2010) 769 final].

European Commission, 'EU Citizenship Report 2010: Dismantling the obstacles to EU citizen's rights' (2010).

European Commission, 'White paper: an agenda for Adequate, Safe and Sustainable Pensions,' (Brussels 2012).

European Commission, 'Pensioen Adequacy Report 2018: Current and Future Income Adequacy in Old Age in the EU' (Directorate-General for Employement, Social Affairs and Inclusion, 2018).

European Commission, 'A Capital Markets Union for people and businesses-new action plan' (2020).

European Commission, 'Communication from the Commission to the European Parliament, the Council, the European Economic and Social Committee and the Committee of the Regions: a Strong Social Europe for Just Transitions' (2020) [COM/2020/14 final].

European Commission, 'Tax policies in the European Union: 2020 survey' (DG Taxation and Customs Union, European Union, 2020).

European Commission, 'Annual Report on Intra-EU Labour Mobility 2022' (2023).

European Union, 'Joint Practical Guide of the European Parliament, the Council and the Commission for persons involved in the drafting of European Union legislation' (European Union, 2015) on the activities and supervision of institutions for occupational retirement provision [2003] OJ L 235.

Regulation (EEC) No 1408/71 of the Council of 14 June 1971 on the application of social security schemes to employed persons and their families moving within the Community [1971] L 149/2.

Regulation (EC) No. 883/2004 of the European Parliament and of the Council of 29 April 2004 on the coordination of social security systems [2004] OJ L 166.

Regulation (EU) No 492/2011 of the European Parliament and of the Council of 5 April 2011 on freedom of movement for workers within the Union [2011] OJ L 141.

Regulation (EU) 2018/1724 of the European Parliament and of the Council of 2 October 2018 establishing a single digital gateway to provide access to information, to procedures and to assistance and problem-solving services and amending Regulation (EU) No 1024/2012 PE/41/2018/REV/2 OJ L 295, 21.11.2018, 1-38.

Webpages

ABP, 'Disclaimer' 2019) <https://mijn.abp.nl/disclaimer> accessed 1 October 2019.

H Allcott, S Mullainathan and D Taubinsky, 'Externalizing the Internality' 2011) <http://citeseerx.ist.psu.edu/viewdoc/download?doi=10.1.1.474.4034&rep=rep1&type=pdf> accessed 8 June 2021.

BIN NL, '<https://www.binnl.nl/default.aspx> accessed 21 June 2021.

Bundesministerium der Finanzen, 'Verhandlungsgrundlage für Doppelbesteuerungsabkommen im Bereich der Steuern vom Einkommen und Vermögen' 2013) <https://www.bundesfinanzministerium.de/Content/DE/Standardartikel/Themen/Steuern/Internationales_Steuerrecht/Allgemeine_Informationen/2013-08-22-Verhandlungsgrundlage-Doppelbesteuerungsabkommen-Steuern-vom-Einkommen-und-Vermoegen.html> accessed 24 March 2020.

Bundesministerium der Finanzen, 'Riester-Rente wird noch attraktiver: Änderungen durch das Betriebsrentenstärkungsgesetz auch bei der privaten Altersvorsorge' 2017) <https://www.bundesfinanzministerium.de/Content/DE/Standardartikel/Themen/Steuern/Weitere_Steuerthemen/Altersvorsorge/2017-08-21-Riester-Rente-wird-noch-attraktiver.html> accessed 31 July 2018.

Bundesministerium der Finanzen, 'Statistische Auswertungen zur Riester-Förderung' 2018) <https://www.bundesfinanzministerium.de/Content/DE/Standardartikel/Themen/Steuern/Weitere_Steuerthemen/Altersvorsorge/2018-02-07-Statistische-Auswertungen-Riester-Foerderung-2018.html?pk_campaign=Newsletter-02.2018&pk_kwd=07.02.2018_Statistische+Auswertungen+zur+Riester-F%C3%B6rderung> accessed 10 August 2018.

Deutsche Rentenversicherung, 'Entgeltgrenze für Minijobs steigt auf 520 Euro monatlich' 2023) <https://www.deutsche-rentenversicherung.de/DRV/DE/Rente/Allgemeine-Informationen/Wissenswertes-zur-Rente/FAQs/Gesetzesaenderungen/gesetz_mindestlohn_geringf_beschaeftigung/mindestlohn_geringf_beschaeftg.html> accessed 28 February 2023.

DNB, 'Rechtstreekse pensioenregelingen, typen pensioenovereenkomsten' <https://www.dnb.nl/statistieken/data-zoeken/#/details/rechtstreekse-pensioenregelingen-typen-pensioenovereenkomsten/dataset/52c29730-e6d5-44af-b82d-afe561db9a95> accessed 1 March 2022.

EIOPA, 'EIOPA submits its advice on pensions tools to the European Commission' 1 December 2021) <https://www.eiopa.europa.eu/media/news/eiopa-submits-its-advice-pensions-tools-european-commission> accessed 9 December 2021.

European Commission, 'Cross-border workers' <https://ec.europa.eu/taxation_customs/individuals/personal-taxation/crossborder-workers_en> accessed 29 January 2020.

European Commission, 'The European Pillar of Social Rights in 20 principles' <https://ec.europa.eu/commission/priorities/deeper-and-fairer-economic-and-monetary-union/european-pillar-social-rights/european-pillar-social-rights-20-principles_en> accessed 29 January 2020.

European Commission, 'The European Pillar of Social Rights: turning principles into actions' 4 March 2021) <https://ec.europa.eu/commission/presscorner/detail/en/ip_21_820> accessed 5 March 2021.

European Commission, 'May infringements package: the Commission refers the Netherlands to the Court for taxing the transfer of pension capital to other Member States, but not domestic transfers' 14 May 2020) <https://ec.europa.eu/commission/presscorner/detail/en/inf_20_859> accessed 8 March 2023.

European Commission, 'July infringement package: Commission requests that the Netherlands stop taxing transfers of pension capital by mobile workers' 19 July 2018) <https://ec.europa.eu/commission/presscorner/detail/en/MEMO_18_4486> accessed 8 March 2023.

European Commission, 'Provisions on Riester-Rente (voluntary pension) contracts concluded after 01/01/2010 allegedly breaching the free movement of workers Art. 45 TFEU by Germany (INFR(2022)4014)' 19 May 2022) <https://ec.europa.eu/atwork/applying-eu-law/infringements-proceedings/infringement_decisions/index.cfm?lang_code=EN&typeOfSearch=false&active_only=0&noncom=0&r_dossier=INFR%282022%294014&decision_date_from=&decision_date_to=&title=&submit=Search> accessed 5 August 2022.

European Commission, 'November infringements package: Commission asks the Netherlands to change tax rules amounting to obstacles to the cross-border transfer of pensions' 27 November 2019) <https://ec.europa.eu/commission/presscorner/detail/en/inf_19_6304> accessed 8 March 2023.

European Commission, 'Commission decides to refer the Netherlands to the Court for its rules on the cross-border transfer of pension capital and cross-border provision of pensions' 30 October 2020) <https://ec.europa.eu/commission/presscorner/detail/EN/IP_20_1678> accessed 8 March 2023.

European Commission, 'Better regulation: why and how' 2019) <https://ec.europa.eu/info/law/law-making-process/planning-and-proposing-law/better-regulation-why-and-how_en> accessed 29 May 2019.

Eurostat, 'Income and living conditions (ilc): Reference Metadata in Euro SDMX Metadata Structure (ESMS)' <https://ec.europa.eu/eurostat/cache/metadata/en/ilc_esms.htm> accessed 7 August 2019.

Eurostat, 'Net earnings and tax rates: Reference Metadata in Euro SDMX Metadata Structure (ESMS)' <https://ec.europa.eu/eurostat/cache/metadata/en/earn_net_esms.htm> accessed 7 August 2019.

Eurostat, 'HICP – inflation rate' last update: 1 August 2019) <https://ec.europa.eu/eurostat/databrowser/view/tec00118/default/table?lang=en> accessed 7 August 2019.

Eurostat, 'Structure of earnings survey: annual earnings' last update: 7 August 2017) <https://ec.europa.eu/eurostat/web/products-datasets/-/earn_ses_annual> accessed last accessed on 7 August 2019.

Eurostat, 'Median hourly earnings, all employees (excluding apprentices) by age' last update: 9 August 2017) <https://appsso.eurostat.ec.europa.eu/nui/show.do?dataset=earn_ses_pub2a&lang=en> accessed 7 August 2019.

Eurostat, 'Annual net earnings' last update: 17 July 2019) <https://appsso.eurostat.ec.europa.eu/nui/show.do?dataset=earn_nt_net&lang=en> accessed 7 August 2019.

Eurostat, 'Mean and median income by household type – EU-SILC survey' last update: 17 July 2019) <http://appsso.eurostat.ec.europa.eu/nui/submitViewTableAction.do> accessed 7 August 2019.

Eurostat, 'Mean annual earnings by sex, economic activity and occupation' last update: 18 May 2018) <https://appsso.eurostat.ec.europa.eu/nui/show.do?dataset=earn_ses14_49&lang=en> accessed 7 August 2019.

FindYourPension, 'Creating the Pilot ETS: Finding and understanding pensions (Findyourpension 2.0)' <https://www.findyourpension.eu/en/news/creating-the-pilot-ets-finding-and-understanding-p_kgkg61uu.html> accessed 22 June 2021.

FindYourPension, 'EU project for the pilot phase of a European Tracking Service on Pensions started' <https://www.findyourpension.eu/en/ets/about_ets/> accessed 5 April 2022.

FindYourPension, 'Pension Tracker' 2023) <https://www.findyourpension.eu/pension-tracker-coming-soon> accessed 23 February 2023.

GDV, 'Digitale Rentenübersicht startet in öffentliche Testphase' 2023) <https://www.gdv.de/gdv/medien/medieninformationen/digitale-rentenuebersicht-startet-in-oeffentliche-testphase-136924> accessed 10 September 2023.

Grensdata.eu, 'Grenspendel werknemers; nationaliteit, woonland, werkregio (NUTS 3)' <https://opendata.grensdata.eu/portal.html?_la=nl&_catalog=InterReg&tableId=22003NED&_theme=119> accessed 17 December 2020.

Institut für Arbeitsmarkt- und Berufsforschung, 'Tarifbindung nimmt in Deutschland weiter ab' 19 May 2021) <https://www.iab.de/de/informationsservice/presse/presseinformationen/tarifbindungabnahme.aspx> accessed 21 May 2021.

Institute for Transnational and Euregional cross border cooperation and Mobility (ITEM), 'Fair Mobility Tool' <https://fairmobilitytool.eu/> accessed 8 June 2021.

Mijnpensioenoverzicht.nl, 'Veelgestelde vragen' <https://www.mijnpensioenoverzicht.nl/faq> accessed 3 September 2019.

Ministerie van Sociale Zaken en Werkgelegenheid, 'Rapport Pensioen in duidelijke taal' (Den Haag juni 2012) <available online: https://www.rijksoverheid.nl/documenten/

rapporten/2012/ 06/26/rapport-pensioen-in-duidelijke-taal> accessed 3 September 2019.

Mypension.be, 'Veelgestelde vragen' <https://mypension.onprvp.fgov.be/nl/mypension/Paginas/faq.aspx?category=logging-in> accessed 3 September 2019.

NIBUD, 'Pensioenschijf-van-vijf' 2023) <https://www.nibud.nl/tools/pensioenschijf-van-vijf/> accessed 23 February 2023.

OECD, 'Comparable estimates of average wages per full-time equivalent employee' <http://www.oecd.org/els/emp/AVERAGE_WAGES.pdf> accessed 7 August 2019.

OECD, 'Employment Database' <http://www.oecd.org/employment/emp/onlineoecdemploymentdatabase.htm> accessed 7 August 2019.

OECD, 'Household Income and Wealth' 2012) <http://www.oecd.org/sdd/03_Household_income_and_wealth.pdf> accessed last accessed on 6 August 2019.

OECD, 'Pensions at a Glance: OECD and G20 Indicators' 2015) <http://www.keepeek.com/Digital-Asset-Management/oecd/social-issues-migration-health/pensions-at-a-glance-2015_pension_glance-2015-en#page1> accessed 10 March 2023.

OECD, 'Indicators' 2016) <https://data.oecd.org/pension/net-pension-replacement-rates.htm#indicator-chart> accessed 8 August 2019.

OECD, 'Pension at a Glance 2017: Country profiles – Netherlands' 2017) <https://www.oecd.org/els/public-pensions/PAG2017-country-profile-Netherlands.pdf> accessed last accessed on 2 August 2019.

OECD, 'Pensions at a Glance 2017: How does Germany compare?' 2017) <http://www.oecd.org/germany/PAG2017-DEU.pdf> accessed last accessed on 2 August 2019.

OECD, 'Pensions Outlook' 2018) <https://read.oecd-ilibrary.org/finance-and-investment/oecd-pensions-outlook-2018_pens_outlook-2018-en#page3> accessed 8 August 2019.

OECD, 'Household disposable income' 2018 ot latest available) <https://data.oecd.org/hha/household-disposable-income.htm#indicator-chart> accessed 6 August 2019.

OECD, 'Employment Outlook' 2019) <http://www.oecd.org/employment/outlook/> accessed 7 August 2019.

OECD, 'Taxing Wages' 2019) <https://www.oecd-ilibrary.org/taxation/taxing-wages-2018_tax_wages-2018-en> accessed 6 August 2019.

OECD Pensions at a glance 2017, 'Pension replacement rates' 2016) <https://stats.oecd.org/#> accessed 8 August 2019.

OECD Pensions at a glance 2021, 'Assets in retirement savings plans and public pension reserve funds' 2021) <https://www.oecd-ilibrary.org/docserver/d3f11cc6-en.pdf?expires=1692642139&id=id&accname=ocid177396&checksum=9A23AA8939958573C0851CF440B18AC7> accessed 21 August 2023.

OECD Pensions at a glance 2021, 'Gross replacement rates' 2021) <https://www.oecd.org/publications/oecd-pensions-at-a-glance-19991363.htm> accessed 22 February 2022.

OECD Statistics, 'Annual National Accounts Prices and Purchasing Parities Database' <https://stats.oecd.org/Index.aspx?DataSetCode=SNA_TABLE4> accessed 7 August 2019.

OECD Statistics, 'Average annual wages' <https://stats.oecd.org/Index.aspx?DatasetCode=AV_AN_WAGE> accessed 7 August 2019.

OECD Statistics, 'Pensions at a Glance: Tax treatment of pensions and pensioners' 2016) <https://stats.oecd.org/> accessed 9 August 2019.

OECD Statistics, 'Pensions at a Glance: Average worker earnings' 2017) <https://stats.oecd.org/> accessed 8 August 2019.

OECD Statistics, 'Income Distribution and Poverty: by country – INCOME (current prices)' 2019) <https://stats.oecd.org/#> accessed 2 July 2019.

OECD Statistics, 'Table I.5. Average personal income tax and social security contribution rates on gross labour income' last update: 11 April 2019) <https://stats.oecd.org/Index.aspx?DataSetCode=TABLE_I5> accessed 8 August.

OECD Statistics, 'Table I.6. All-in average personal income tax rates at average wage by family type' last update: 11 April 2019) <https://stats.oecd.org/Index.aspx?DataSetCode=TABLE_I6> accessed 8 August 2019.

OECD Statistics, 'Consumer price indices (CPIs) – Complete database: Consumer prices – Annual inflation' last updated: 7 August 2019) <https://stats.oecd.org/> accessed 7 August 2019.

Portal Sozialpolitik, 'Betriebliche Altersversorung sozialversicherungspflichtig Beschäftigter' <http://www.portal-sozialpolitik.de/index.php?page=betriebsrentenstaerkungsgesetz> accessed 18 June 2021.

PSVaG, 'Allgemeines zur Melde- und Beitragspflicht' <https://www.psvag.de/mitglieder-beitrag/allgemeines-zur-melde-und-beitragspflicht.html> accessed 8 March 2022.

Your Europe – European Union, 'National websites on posting' <https://europa.eu/youreurope/citizens/work/work-abroad/posted-workers/index_en.htm#national-websites> accessed 23 January 2020.

Your Europe – European Union, 'Posted workers' <https://europa.eu/youreurope/citizens/work/work-abroad/posted-workers/index_en.htm#national-websites> accessed 23 January 2020.

Maastricht Law Series

The Maastricht Law Series is created in 2018 by Boom juridisch and Eleven International Publishing in association with the Maastricht University Faculty of Law. The Maastricht Law Series publishes books on comparative, European and International law. The series builds upon the tradition of excellence in research at the Maastricht Faculty of Law, its research centers and the Ius Commune Research School. The Maastricht Law Series is a peer reviewed book series that allows researchers an excellent opportunity to showcase their work.

Published in this series:
Volume 1: Reinhard Zimmermann, Does the Law of Succession Reflect Cultural Differences?, ISBN 978-94-6236-856-9
Volume 2: Anna Berlee, Access to personal data in public land registers, ISBN 978-94-6236-841-5
Volume 3: Marcus Meyer, The Position of Dutch Works Councils in Multinational Corporations, ISBN 978-94-6236-848-4
Volume 4: Jaap Hage, Foundations and Building Blocks of Law, ISBN 978-94-6236-860-6
Volume 5: Bastiaan van Zelst, The End of Justice(s)?, ISBN 978-94-6236-881-1
Volume 6: Agustín Parise & Lars van Vliet (eds.), Re- De- Co-dification? New Insights on the Codification of Private Law, ISBN 978-94-6236-900-9
Volume 7: Caroline Rupp, Rafael Ibarra Garza & Bram Akkermans, Property Law Perspectives VI, ISBN 978-94-6236-904-7
Volume 8: Aalt Willem Heringa, Europees Nederlands Staatsrecht, ISBN 978-94-6290-604-4

Volume 9: Symeon C. Symeonides, The "Private" in Private International Law, ISBN 978-94-6236-949-8

Volume 10: Jaap Hage, European Integration: A Theme, ISBN 978-94-6236-981-8

Volume 11: Jan M. Smits, Five Uneasy Pieces. Essays on Law and Evolution, ISBN 978-94-6236-982-5

Volume 12: Hannah Brodersen, Vincent Glerum, & André Klip, The European Arrest Warrant and In Absentia Judgements, ISBN 978-94-6236-985-6

Volume 13: Bram Akkermans & Gijs van Dijck, Sustainability and Private Law, ISBN 978-94-6236-986-3

Volume 14: Antonia Waltermann, David Roef, Jaap Hage & Marko Jelicic, Law, Science, Rationality, ISBN 978-94-6236-989-4

Volume 15: Frans L. Leeuw, Van Legal Realism naar Legal Big Data, ISBN 978-94-6290-781-2

Volume 16: Josua Sitompul, Cross-border Access to Electronic Evidence, ISBN 978-94-6236-133-1

Volume 17: Bram Akkermans & Jill Robbie, Property Law Perspectives VII, ISBN 978-946236-181-2

Volume 18: Bram Akkermans & Anna Berlee, 'Sjef-Sache', ISBN 978-94-6236-197-3

Volume 19: Froukje van den Borne, Luca Cox, Youri Cremers, Daan Groenewoud, Sven Schaghen & Tom Stijns, Het stopzetten van KEI-civiel nader bezien, ISBN 978-94-6290-955-7

Volume 20: Nicholas Mouttotos, The Impact of Europeanization in Cyprus Contract Law and the Spill-Over to Matters of Civil Procedure, ISBN 978-94-6236-206-2

Volume 21: Katja Zimmermann, Facilitating Cross-Border Real Estate Transactions in Europe, ISBN 978-94-6236-220-8

Volume 22: Alexis E. Antoniades, Remedies for human rights violations by the European Union, ISBN 978-94-6236-275-8

Volume 23: André Klip, European Arrest Warrant, ISBN 978-94-6236-284-0

Volume 24: Bram Akkermans, Sustainable Property Law, ISBN 978-94-6236-289-5

Volume 25: Sarah Schoenmaekers & Pauline Melin, The Art of Moving Borders, ISBN 978-94-6236-296-3

Volume 26: Agustín Parise & Olivier Moréteau, Comparative Perspectives on Law and Language, ISBN 978-94-6236-328-1

Volume 27: Renata Barbosa, Vincent Glerum, Hans Kijlstra, André Klip & Christina Peristeridou, Improving the European Arrest Warrant, ISBN 978-94-6236-327-4

Volume 28: Cedric Vanleenhove & Lotte Meurkens, The Recognition and Enforcement of Punitive Damages Judgments Across the Globe, ISBN 978-90-4730-162-2

Volume 29: Jill Robbie, Flore Vavourakis, Víðir Smári, Ivan Allegranti & Aleksa Radonjić, Property Law Perspectives VIII, ISBN 978-90-4730-171-4

Volume 30: Alice Giannini, Criminal Behavior and Accountability of Artificial Intelligence Systems, ISBN 978-90-4730-172-1
Volume 31: Sander Kramer, Effective Cross-Border Pension Information in the Face of Multi-Level Legal Systems, ISBN 978-90-4730-187-5

www.ingramcontent.com/pod-product-compliance
Lightning Source LLC
Chambersburg PA
CBHW082233240926
51846CB00014B/1369
* 9 7 8 9 0 4 7 3 0 1 8 7 5 *